THE EU AND HUMAN RIGHTS

THE
EU AND HUMAN
RIGHTS

edited by

Philip Alston

Professor of International Law, European University Institute,
Florence

with the assistance of

Mara Bustelo and James Heenan
European University Institute

Academy of European Law
European University Institute

OXFORD
UNIVERSITY PRESS

OXFORD

UNIVERSITY PRESS

Great Clarendon Street, Oxford OX2 6DP

Oxford University Press is a department of the University of Oxford
It furthers the University's objective of excellence in research, scholarship,
and education by publishing worldwide in

Oxford New York

Athens Auckland Bangkok Bogotá Buenos Aires Calcutta
Cape Town Chennai Dar es Salaam Delhi Florence Hong Kong Istanbul
Karachi Kuala Lumpur Madrid Melbourne Mexico City Mumbai
Nairobi Paris São Paulo Singapore Taipei Tokyo Toronto Warsaw

and associated companies in Berlin Ibadan

Oxford is a registered trade mark of Oxford University Press
in the UK and in certain other countries

Published in the United States
by Oxford University Press Inc., New York

British Library Cataloguing in Publication Data

Data available

Library of Congress Cataloging in Publication Data
The EU and human rights / edited by Philip Alston, with the assistance
of Mara Bustelo and James Heenan.
p. cm.
Includes bibliographical references (p.).
1. Human rights—European Union countries. I. Alston, Philip.
II. Bustelo, Mara R. III. Heenan, James.
KJE5132.E9 1999 341.4'81'094—dc21 99-28822
ISBN 0–19–829806–4
ISBN 0–19–829809–9 (pbk.)

1 3 5 7 9 10 8 6 4 2

Typeset by Hope Services (Abingdon) Ltd.
Printed in Great Britain
on acid-free paper by
Bookcraft Ltd.,
Midsomer Norton, Somerset

PREFACE

This volume of essays provides the most wide-ranging survey yet to be undertaken of the role of the European Union in relation to human rights. Its contributors analyse the legal, policy, institutional, and philosophical aspects of both the internal and external dimensions of EU activities in relation to a very broad range of issues.

As the EU continues to grow in importance, both as a force in international relations and as an ever more important influence over the lives of those who live within its borders and those living in countries which aspire to membership, its approach to human rights will become increasingly significant. So far, however, its human rights policies are far from comprehensive. In their 'Human Rights Agenda for the European Union for the Year 2000', entitled 'Leading by Example',[1] the *Comité des Sages*, for whom these analyses were originally prepared,[2] characterized the Union's existing policies in this area as having been 'made by and for the Europe of yesterday; they are not sufficient for the Europe of tomorrow. The strong rhetoric of the Union is not matched by the reality.' The *Sages* concluded that 'the Union's present approach to human rights tends to be splintered in many directions, lacks the necessary leadership and profile, and is marginalized in policy-making.' They noted that, despite the very considerable amounts of energy and resources devoted to these issues by the EU, 'the fragmented and hesitant nature of many of its initiatives has left the Union with a vast number of individual policies and programmes but without a real human rights policy as such'.

In many respects, the analyses that are contained in this volume provide a blue-print upon the basis of which the EU can, and indeed should, move to ensure that human rights are accorded a central place in the building of a new European order. Both the Agenda of the *Comité des Sages* and the contributions to this volume resulted from a project designed to contribute to the commemoration of the fiftieth anniversary of the Universal Declaration of Human Rights. The project was funded by the European Commission and was based at the European University Institute in Florence, under the direction of Professor Philip Alston. The project involved a series of consultations with civil society, scholars, experts, Community officials and institutions, members of the European Parliament, non-governmental organizations, and other interested groups and individuals over the course of almost two years. Many individuals contributed to bringing the project to fruition. Mrs Daniela Napoli of DG 1A of the European Commission initiated the discussions which led to this project, and it would not have happened without her strong support. Mr Denis Petit also assisted in relation to the processing of the grant applications to the Commission. The project came to fruition in December 1998 during the first-ever

[1] See Annex to this vol.

[2] The members of the *Comité des Sages* are: Judge Antonio Cassese, Mme Catherine Lalumière, Professor Peter Leuprecht, and Mrs Mary Robinson. They are, of course, not responsible for the contents of this vol. as a whole.

Austrian Presidency of the EU and, from the outset, Ambassador Christian Strohal, of the Austrian Ministry of Foreign Affairs, played a pivotal role in ensuring its success. Ms Ingrid Kircher helped in very many ways, especially in the lead-up to the Vienna conference at which the Agenda was launched in October 1998. Professor Peter Leuprecht was a constant source of inspiration and, as befits a *sage*, wisdom.

In addition the President of the European Parliament kindly agreed to host a conference in Brussels in May 1998 to enable a first reading of the project papers and to obtain crucial inputs from Members of the European Parliament, officials of the Commission, Council, and the two Courts, and from civil society as a whole. Special thanks are due in that regard to Mr Dietmar Nickel, Mr Barry Waters, Ms Ursula Bausch, and Mr Eamonn Noonan of the staff of the Parliament for their generous advice and assistance in this regard. Professor Joseph Weiler made an invaluable contribution to the intellectual design of the project and provided advice and assistance at many critical points along the way.

It should, but apparently does not, go without saying that all of the authors have contributed in their personal capacities and that their views do not necessarily represent those of any of the institutions with which they are associated.

The project was co-ordinated by Ms Mara Bustelo whose expertise, knowledge, efficiency, and tireless efforts were truly indispensable in all its aspects. Following her departure to take up a position at the United Nations, Mr James Heenan proved to be a truly first-rate Project Co-ordinator. At various times important contributions to the project were also made by Mr Mac Darrow, Ms Susan Garvin, Mr Salvatore Zappalá, Mr Simon Bagshaw, and Mr James Turpin, all from the European University Institute. Dr Fabián Pereyra, of the EUI Academy of European Law, made a vital administrative contribution to the project as a whole. Ms Anny Bremner meticulously edited the Agenda, Ms Kate Elliott copy-edited the volume as a whole with great care, and Messrs John Louth and Nigel Sleight from Oxford University Press were helpful and supportive at every turn.

The project as a whole also benefited greatly from the work of a Drafting Group which assisted in the preparation of the draft of the Agenda and made many other substantive contributions. In addition to the three editors of this volume, it consisted of: Madame Catherine Lalumière and Professor Peter Leuprecht from the *Comité des Sages*, Professors Joseph Weiler (Harvard Law School), Gráinne de Búrca (European University Institute), Andrew Clapham (Graduate Institute of International Studies, Geneva), and Bruno de Witte (University of Maastricht), and Mr Michael O'Boyle (secretariat of the European Court of Human Rights).

Throughout the course of the project a particular effort was made to consult with those with an interest or expertise in the issues under consideration. As a result, information, materials, and suggestions were gratefully received from a wide range of sources. In particular, written submissions were received from the following: Professor Carol Harlow, London School of Economics; Dr Gerard Quinn, University College, Galway; Ms Karijn de Jong, European Centre for Development Policy Management, Maastricht; Ms Lotte Leicht, Director of the Brussels Office of Human Rights Watch; Ms Brigitte Ernst, Director, Amnesty International European Office, Brussels; Ms Anita Wuyts, Quaker Council for European Affairs,

Brussels Office; Dr Karin Arts, Institute for Social Studies, The Hague; Professor Peter Brophy and Dr Edward F. Halpin, Centre for Research in Library and Information Management, The Manchester Metropolitan University; Mr Eric Sottas and Mr Ben Schonveld, World Organization against Torture; European Regional Section of the International Lesbian and Gay Association; Dr Lisa Waddington, Institute for Transnational Legal Research, University of Maastricht; Ms Tricia Feeney, Senior Policy Adviser, Oxfam Great Britain; the Commissioner for the Baltic Sea States; Save the Children, European Union Office, Brussels; and Madame Louise Cadoux, a Member of the French *Commission nationale de l'informatique et des libertés*.

Finally, the President of the European University Institute, Patrick Masterson, and many members of the Institute's administrative staff have provided support and assistance without which the project would have been impossible and the present volume would not have seen the light of day.

Florence, March 1999   PHILIP ALSTON

TABLE OF CONTENTS

LIST OF ABBREVIATIONS

AEL	Collected Courses of the Academy of European Law
AFDI	*Annuaire français de droit international*
AJIL	*American Journal of International Law*
ArchVR	Archiv des Völkerrechts
Cambridge LJ	*Cambridge Law Journal*
CDE	Cahiers de droit européen
CIJL	Bulletin of the Centre for the Independence of Judges and Lawyers
CMLRev.	*Common Market Law Review*
Colum. J Trans. L	*Columbia Journal of Transnational Law*
DDC	Documentaçao e Direito Comparado
Duke LJ	*Duke Law Journal*
EJIL	*European Journal of International Law*
ELJ	*European Law Journal*
ELRev.	*European Law Review*
EOR	Equal Opportunities Reports
EPIL	R. Bernhardt et al (eds.), *Encyclopedia of Public International Law*
EPL	*European Public Law*
EuGRZ	Europäische Grundrechte Zeitschrift
EuZW	Europäische Zeitschrift für Wirtschaftsrecht
Fordham Intl. LJ	*Fordham International Law Journal*
GYIL	*German Yearbook of International Law*
Harv. HRJ.	*Harvard Human Rights Journal*
Harv. LRev.	*Harvard Law Review*
HRQ	*Human Rights Quarterly*
ICLQ	*International and Comparative Law Quarterly*
IJEL	*Irish Journal of European Law*
IJRL	*International Journal of Refugee Law*
ILJ	*Industrial Law Journal*
Int. J of Comp. Lab. L and Ind. Rel.	*International Journal of Comparative Labour Law and Industrial Relations*
Int. J Discrim. L	*International Journal of Discrimination Law*
IRJ	*Industrial Relations Journal*
JCMS	*Journal of Common Market Studies*
JLS	*Journal of Law and Society*

JSWL	*Journal of Social Welfare Law*
LIEI	*Legal Issues of European Integration*
LQR	*Law Quarterly Review*
McGill LJ	*McGill Law Journal*
MLR	*Modern Law Review*
NJW	Neue Juristischen Wochenschrift
NQHR	*Netherlands Quarterly of Human Rights*
OJLS	*Oxford Journal of Legal Studies*
Phil. & Pub. Affairs	*Philosophy and Public Affairs*
PL	*Public Law*
RabelsZ	Rabels Zeitschrift für ausländisches und internationales Privatrecht
Rdc	*Recueil des cours* of the Hague Academy of International Law
RDI	*Revue de droit International*
RMUE	*Revue du marché unique européen*
RTDH	*Revue trimestrielle des droits de l'homme*
RUDH	*Revue universelle des droits de l'homme*
SLS	*Social and Legal Studies*
UChic.LR	*University of Chicago Law Review*
UToronto LJ	*University of Toronto Law Journal*
Va. J Intl. L	*Virginia Journal of International Law*
Vand. J Trans. L	*Vanderbilt Journal of Transnational Law*
Yale J Intl. L	*Yale Journal of International Law*
Yale LJ	*Yale Law Journal*
YEL	Yearbook of European Law
ZaöRV	Zeitschrift für ausländisches und internationales Arbeits- und Sozialrecht

NOTES ON THE CONTRIBUTORS

Philip Alston is Professor of International Law at the European University Institute in Florence and Visiting Professor in the Global Law Program at New York University Law School. He chaired the UN Committee on Economic, Social and Cultural Rights for eight years (1991–98) and is currently also Editor of the *European Journal of International Law,* and co-Director of the Academy of European Law. His publications include *The Future of UN Human Rights Treaty Monitoring, Economic and Social Rights: A Bibliography*, and *Peoples' Rights: The State of the Art* (all forthcoming).

Jo Beatrix Aschenbrenner is a research fellow and doctoral candidate at the Institute of International Law at the University of Munich. Specialising in International and European Law, she has studied in Freiburg, Geneva and at the European University Institute in Florence, from where she holds an LL.M. She has also qualified as a junior lawyer in Germany.

Catherine Barnard is a lecturer at the University of Cambridge and a fellow of Trinity College, and formerly held the Jean Monnet Chair in European Integration at the University of Southampton. She specialises in EC law, employment law, and discrimination law. Her publications include *EC Employment Law* (1996) and a study for the UK Department of Employment entitled *The Exercise of Individual Employment Rights in the Member States of the European Community*. She is also a consultant to the European Commission concerning implementation of the Working Time Directive.

Ulf Bernitz is Professor of European Integration Law at Stockholm University and Director of the Stockholm Master of European Law Programme and of the Institute of European Law. He is President of the Swedish Association for European Law and was President of the FIDE (Fédération International de Droit Européen) from 1996 to 1998. He has written extensively on European law, competition law, marketing law, and intellectual property law.

Kieran Bradley is Senior Référéndaire to Advocate General Nial Fennelly at the Court of Justice of the European Communities, Luxembourg. He teaches courses on the law and institutions of the European Union at the Universitat Autònoma de Barcelona and on environmental law at the European Institute for Public Administration, Luxembourg, and occasionally lectures at the Academy for European Law, Trier and the European Centre for Public Affairs, Brussels. He has previously worked at the secretariat of the European Parliament. He has written extensively on the public law of the European Union, including 'Fundamental Rights and European Union: A Selective Overview' (*Polish Yearbook of International Law*, 1994).

Barbara Brandtner is a member of the Legal Service of the Commission of the European Communities, where she is responsible, among others, for human rights and international law aspects in the Communities' external relations. She previously worked in private practice with Cleary, Gottlieb, Steen and Hamilton and for the Legal Department of the Austrian Ministry for Foreign Affairs. Her most recent publication (together with Allan Rosas) is 'Human Rights and the External Relations of the European Community: An Analysis of Doctrine and Practice' (*European Journal of International Law*, 1998).

Mara R. Bustelo is a staff member of the United Nations Office of the High Commissioner for Human Rights, in Geneva, working for the Committee on the Rights of the Child. She has degrees from the Universidad Complutense in Madrid and the Fletcher School of Law and Diplomacy in Boston and was previously Visiting Fellow at the Australian National University's Centre for International and Public Law and Research Fellow at the European University Institute in Florence. She was the Project Coordinator for the project that led to this volume of essays. Her other publications include *Whose New World Order?: What Role for the United Nations* (1991), and, most recently, a study of the UN Committee on the Elimination of Discrimination against Women.

Andrew Clapham is Associate Professor of Public International Law at the Graduate Institute of International Studies in Geneva. He teaches international human rights law and public international law, and has a special interest in European human rights law and the role of the European Union. He was co-editor with Antonio Cassese and Joseph Weiler of the series *European Union—The Human Rights Challenge* (1991). He obtained a doctorate in law from the European University Institute in 1991, and from 1991 to 1997 he was the Representative of Amnesty International at the United Nations in New York, dealing in particular with issues relating to the Security Council, peace keeping, human rights field operations and the High Commissioner for Human Rights. His publications include *Human Rights and the European Union: a Critical Overview* (1991) and *Human Rights and the Private Sphere* (1993).

Bruno de Witte has been Professor of European Law at the University of Maastricht since 1989. He obtained a doctorate in law from the European University Institute in 1985 and was an Assistant Professor at that Institute from 1985 to 1989. His publications relate to the institutional law of the European Union (including the protection of fundamental rights in the EU legal order) and to European and comparative legal developments in the field of culture, language, education and minority protection. He is a member of the editorial board of the Netherlands Yearbook of International Law and the Maastricht Journal of European and Comparative Law.

Emmanuel Decaux is Professor of International Law at the Université Paris X–Nanterre, where he is the co-director of the Centre for International Law (CEDIN). He is Secretary General of the French Society for International Law (SFDI), a member of the French Advisory Commission on Human Rights (CNCDH) and an alternate member of the UN Sub-Commission on Prevention of

Discrimination and Protection of Minorities. His publications cover various topics of international law, including the peaceful settlement of international disputes and the protection of human rights. He was editor, with Louis-Edmond Pettiti and Pierre-Henri Imbert, of *La Convention européenne des droits de l'homme*, (1995). His latest book is the second edition of *Droit international public* (1999).

Pavlos Eleftheriadis is a Lecturer in Law at the London School of Economics and Political Science where he teaches European Union Law and Jurisprudence. His main research interests are in the legal and political theory of European integration and in theories of rights. Having studied in Athens and Cambridge, he was a Visiting Researcher at Harvard Law School in 1993 and 1995 and a Visiting Fellow in comparative and international law at the University of California at Berkeley in the spring of 1998. Before joining LSE he was a Lecturer in Law at Queen Mary and Westfield College, London. His recent publications include: 'The Direct Effect of Community Law: Conceptual Issues' (1996) and 'Begging the Constitutional Question' (1998) both published in the *Journal of Common Market Studies*.

Sybilla Fries is an associate with Covington & Burling in Brussels. She graduated from the University of Munich and also has a law degree from the Sorbonne in Paris. She completed a five month clerkship with Judge Hirsch at the European Court of Justice before spending two years as a visiting researcher at Harvard Law School where she worked with J.H.H. Weiler. She is PhD candidate at the University of Munich and her thesis is on current issues of fundamental rights protection in the European Union.

Giorgio Gaja is Professor of International Law at the University of Florence. He is a member of the Institute of International Law, member of the International Law Commission and the editor-in-chief of the *Rivista di Diritto Internazionale*. He was appointed as an *ad hoc* Judge of the International Court of Justice in 1999 in the case concerning *Legality of the Use of Force (Yugoslavia* v. *Italy)*. He has been a member of a Group of Experts of International Law advising the Legal Service of the Commission of the European Union. His publications cover various subjects of international law, conflict of laws and European Community law. Among his recent writings are a note on Opinion 2/94 by the Court of Justice in the *Common Market Law Review*, a course on the protection of human rights in EC Law for the *Thesaurus Acroasium* and a contribution to the Capotorti Festschrift on the methods of interpretation of the European Convention of Human Rights.

Conor Gearty is Professor of Human Rights Law at King's College London. He is also a barrister at Essex Court Chambers and a member of the Middle Temple. His books on human rights include (edited with A. Tomkins) *Understanding Human Rights* (1996) and *European Civil Liberties and the European Convention on Human Rights: A Comparative Study* (1997). He is also Director of the Civil Liberties Research Unit at King's College London, and has published widely on civil liberties, including (with K. D. Ewing) *Freedom under Thatcher. Civil Liberties in Britain* (1990), and his latest book (again with K. D. Ewing) *The Struggle for Civil Liberties: Political Freedom and the Rule of Law in Britain, 1914–45* (1999). He has advised both the European Union institutions and the Council of Europe on issues relating to human rights and civil liberties. His other academic interest is in terrorism, on which he has also published extensively, most recently *The Future of Terrorism* (1997).

Klaus Günther is Professor of Legal Philosophy, Criminal Law and Criminal Procedure Law at the Johann Wolfgang Goethe Universität, Frankfurt am Main. He obtained a doctorate in law in 1987 and a *habilitation* in legal philosophy, criminal law, criminal procedure law and criminology in 1997. From 1986 to 1990 he was a member of a research group in legal philosophy under the directorate of Jürgen Habermas, and from 1995 to 1996 he was a fellow of the Wissenschaftskolleg in Berlin. His publications include *Der Sinn für Angemessenheit* (1989) (English translation by John Farrell, *The Sense of Appropriateness* (1993)), *Schuld und kommunikative Freiheit* (forthcoming) and articles on legal philosophy, discourse theory of law, and criminal law.

Carol Harlow is Professor of Public Law at the London School of Economics. She teaches public law, specialising in European and English administrative law, and is the joint author with her colleague Richard Rawlings of *Law and Administration* (1984) and *Pressure Through Law* (1992). She also writes widely in periodicals, including the *European Law Journal* and *Modern Law Review*, on whose Editorial Boards she sits. Carol Harlow has a long-term interest in legal services. She served for many years on the Management Committee and as Chair of the Legal Action Group.

James Heenan is a Researcher at the European University Institute in Florence and Project Coordinator of the project 'An EU Human Rights Agenda for the Year 2000', of which this volume forms a part. He previously worked as a lawyer in both private and government practice, specialising in employment law and industrial relations, and is currently completing a research degree on the International Labour Organization and social rights.

Menno Kamminga is Associate Professor of Public International Law at the Erasmus University in Rotterdam. He teaches courses on public international law, human rights law, and international and European environmental law. He is a member of the International Executive Committee of Amnesty International and a former Legal Adviser at the International Secretariat of Amnesty International in London. He is co-rapporteur of the Committee on Human Rights Law and Practice of the International Law Association and a member of the Board of Editors of the *Netherlands International Law Review*. He directs a special research project on multinational corporations and human rights, details of which may be found on its website: www.multinationals.law.eur.nl. He holds a doctorate in international law from Leiden University and is the author of *Inter-State Accountability for Violations of Human Rights* (1992).

Martti Koskenniemi is Professor of International Law at the University of Helsinki. He was previously Counsellor (legal affairs) director of the international law division of the Finnish Ministry for Foreign Affairs (1991–1994) and Counsellor at the Permanent Mission of Finland to the United Nations (1989–1991). A member and legal advisor to Finnish delegations with the United Nations General Assembly since 1981, he has been the representative of Finland at various UN bodies and meetings, and Co-Agent of Finland in the International Court of Justice in the Case Concerning Passage through the Great Belt (1991–92). He is the author of several publications, including *From Apology to Utopia. The Structure of International Legal Argument* (1989).

Stefan Lausegger studied law, Russian and economics in Graz and Málaga, and graduated in law in 1999. He has worked as a research fellow at the European Parliament and the University of Graz.

Charles Leben is Professor of Public International Law and Co-Director of the Institute for Advanced International Studies at the Université Paris II–Panthéon–Assas. He also teaches litigation in European Community law. His areas of interest are general international law, legal theory and international economic law. He is the author of a number of papers in these three fields including publications on counter measures in international law (1982, 1991), international jurisdiction (1989), the legal nature of the European Communities (1991), the principle of equality in law and the theory of judicial interpretation (1992), mining contracts (1980, 1986), and state contracts (1998). He was a member of the French delegation to the Conference on Security and Cooperation in Europe (CSCE) in Malta 1991 for talks on the implementation of a European mechanism for the settlement of disputes.

Hedwig Lokrantz Bernitz is a researcher in European Law at Stockholm University, dealing especially with issues related to European citizenship.

Gregor Noll is a doctoral candidate at the Faculty of Law, University of Lund, Sweden. He is currently finalising his dissertation on access to refugee protection in the European Union, and teaches international refugee law and public international law at undergraduate and graduate level. He has published articles on burden sharing, gender and persecution, readmission agreements, the return of unsuccessful asylum seekers as well as the democratic legitimacy of refugee law.

Manfred Nowak is Professor of Law at the Austrian Federal Academy of Public Administration and Director of the Ludwig Boltzmann Institute of Human Rights at Vienna University. From 1987 to 1989 he was Director of the Netherlands Institute of Human Rights at the University of Utrecht. He is currently an expert member of the UN Working Group on Enforced Disappearances and judge at the Human Rights Chamber for Bosnia and Herzegovina in Sarajevo. From 1994 to 1997 he also served as UN expert on missing persons in the former Yugoslavia. He is member of the International Commission of Jurists and serves on the board of various NGOs active in the field of human rights and development cooperation. He is author of more than 250 publications in the field of constitutional, administrative and international law with particular emphasis on human rights. His books include *Politische Grundrechte* (1988), *UN Covenant on Civil and Political Rights : CCPR* *commentary* (1993), *Europarat und Menschenrechte* (1994) and *World Conference on Human Rights* (1994).

Steve Peers is Senior Lecturer in Law at the University of Essex. He is associated with the University's Human Rights Centre and is the Scheme Director of the LL.M. in European Community Law and Director of the Centre for European Commercial Law. He is the author of *EU Justice and Home Affairs* (1999) as well as over twenty-five articles on the EU's justice and home affairs, external relations and internal market law. He has prepared written and oral evidence for several NGOs on Justice and Home Affairs issues for the House of Lords European Select Committee and is also: a member of the Justice Expert Group on Justice and Home Affairs Law; an assistant editor of *Statewatch European Monitor*; a regular contributor to *Statewatch*; the co-author of a report for the European Parliament on parliamentary scrutiny of Justice and Home Affairs after the Amsterdam Treaty; and the author of a series of forthcoming reports for the Immigration Law Practitioners' Association on the future immigration and asylum law of the European Community.

Miguel Poiares Maduro is Professor of European and International Law at the Universidade Nova de Lisboa. He is also External Professor at the Institute of European Studies of the Universidade Católica Portuguesa and at the Institute of European Studies of Macau. He obtained his doctorate in law at the European University Institute where his thesis was awarded the inaugural Rowe and Maw Prize. In 1997/1998 he was US–EU Fulbright Research Scholar at Harvard Law School. He has also taught in the program for the European Master's Degree in Human Rights and Democratization (Padua) and at the Universidade Autónoma de Lisboa, where he was Director of the European and Economic Studies Centre. He is co-editor with Joseph Weiler of Special Book Review Issue of the *European Law Journal*, and is the author of *We The Court, The European Court of Justice and the European Economic Constitution*, (1998).

Gerard Quinn teaches law at the National University of Ireland (Galway). He has a particular interest in European human rights law and comparative disability law. He was a member of the Irish Government's Commission on the Status of People with Disabilities and is a former Director of Research at the (Irish) Law Reform Commission. He has also worked in DGV of the European Commission on the rights of Europeans with disabilities and continues to advise the Commission on comparative disability law. A barrister-at-law, he holds post graduate degrees in law (LL.M., S.J.D.) from Harvard Law School.

Reinhard Rack is Professor of Constitutional, Administrative and European Law at the Karl-Franzens-Universität Graz, Austria. Since November 1996 he has been the Vice-chairman of the Group of the European People's Party. As a Member of the European Parliament he sits on the Committees for Institutional Affairs, Budgetary Control and Regional Policy as well as on the Delegation for Relations with the United States and the ACP-EU Joint Assembly. In 1994 and 1996 he held a seat in the Austrian National Parliament, and from 1990 to 1994 was Representative of Styria for European Affairs. In 1985 and 1988 he was Guest Professor at the Rutgers

Law School, Camden/New Jersey, USA. His publications concerning human rights include: *A Constitution for Europe* (1995), *The Status of Third Country Nationals in the European Community* (1990), and *Introducing the subject of a Human Rights Reform—the development of the classical notion of human rights at the example of the principle of equality* (1985).

Eibe Riedel holds the chair in German and Comparative Law, European and International Law at the Universität Mannheim. After completing a post-doctoral thesis on 'The Theory of Human Rights Standards in the Area of Economic, Social and Cultural Rights', he was Professor of Public and International Law at the Universities of Marburg and Mainz. Since 1989 he has been the Director of Studies for International and European Law at the Foreign Service Academy of the German Foreign Office, and since 1997 a Member of the United National Committee on Economic, Social and Cultural Rights. His areas of research include human rights, peacekeeping, international protection of the environment, and new technologies and the law.

Allan Rosas is Principal Legal Adviser of the European Commission. He is responsible for external relations, including international trade law, human rights and the bilateral treaty relations of the EU. He is a Doctor of Laws (University of Turku 1977) and was from 1981 to 1996 Armfelt Professor of Law at the Åbo Akademi University (Turku) and from 1985 to 1995 Director of its Institute for Human Rights. He has represented the Finnish Government at a number of international conferences and meetings and acted as an expert for several Finnish Ministries and international organisations, including the UN, UNESCO, OSCE and the Council of Europe. His most recent publications include *The European Union and Human Rights* (1995), *Economic, Social and Cultural Rights: A Textbook* (1995), *The OSCE in the Maintenance of Peace and Security* (1997) and *The New Chemical Weapons Convention: Implementation and Prospects* (1999).

Constanze Schulte is a research fellow at the Institute of International Law at the University of Munich. She studied law in Göttingen, Singapore and Munich, specialising in international and European law. She also engaged in studies and work in the field of international law in The Hague, Florence, Rome, Thessaloniki and Madrid.

Silvana Sciarra is Professor of European Labour and Social Law at the European University Institute and Professor of Labour Law at the University of Florence. She has visited UCLA and Harvard Law Schools as a Harkness Fellow, and was Leverhulme Professor of European Industrial Relations at the University of Warwick. Since 1979, she has been chief editor of the *Giornale di diritto del lavoro e di relazioni industriali* and sits on the boards of other international journals. She is an organiser of the 'Pontignano seminars in comparative labour law', started in 1983 and run by a group of lawyers coming from several European countries, and a Member of the 'Davignon group of experts', reporting on workers' involvement in European companies. She has also been active in other European Commission experts groups. She has published in Italian and foreign journals, especially in the field of labour law and European Law. Her recent publications focus on European Community labour law and on public services and citizenship in European law.

Bruno Simma is Professor of International and European Community law at the University of Munich. He also teaches at the University of Michigan Law School in Ann Arbor. From 1987 to 1996 he was a member of the United Nations Committee on Economic, Social and Cultural Rights. Since 1997 he has been a member of the United Nations International Law Commission. He is co-author (with Alfred Verdross) of *Universelles Völkerrecht. Theorie und Praxis* (Berlin, Duncker & Humblot, 1984). His other books include *The Charter of the United Nations: A Commentary* (1995) and a multi-volume series on the international protection of the environment.

Dean Spielmann holds a *Licence en droit* from the University of Louvain, and a Master of Laws degree from the University of Cambridge. He is a practising lawyer in Luxembourg, a former member of the Conseil de l'Ordre des avocats, a lecturer in criminal law at the Centre Universitaire de Luxembourg and a Member of the Board of the Centre for Human Rights of the University of Louvain. He also teaches as a visiting lecturer in the Law Faculty of the Université Nancy II and for the European Master's Degree in Human Rights and Democratization (Padua). He is Co-editor of *Annales du droit luxembourgeois* and a member of the editorial boards of *Revue trimestrielle des droits de l'homme* and *Bulletin des droits de l'homme*. His publications include monographs and numerous articles concerning, *inter alia*, criminal law and procedure, human rights and administrative law.

Jens Vedsted-Hansen is Professor of Law at the University of Aarhus. He teaches human rights law, refugee law and immigration law, and his research also covers administrative law and social welfare law. He was Associate Professor of Public and International Law at the University of Aarhus from 1984 to 1997. During a sabbatical from 1993 he worked as a senior research fellow at the Danish Centre for Human Rights, and moved to the Law Faculty at the University of Copenhagen as an associate professor in 1997. He served as a member of the Refugee Appeals Board from 1987 to 1994. He is the co-author of a Danish textbook on immigration and refugee law (*Udlændingeret*, 1995), and in 1997 he published a book on residence rights and maintenance (*Opholdsret og forsørgelse,* 1997)). He co-ordinated the legal part of a Nordic research project on temporary protection of refugees from 1995 to 1998, and his most recent publications analyse law and policy issues relating to temporary protection.

Blanca Vila Costa is Professor of Private International Law and Jean Monnet Chair in European Community Law at the Universitat Autónoma de Barcelona (UAB). She also teaches internal market law at the College of Europe, both in Bruges and in Natolin (Warsaw). A Doctor in European Law in 1979, she was Director of the Institut Universitari d'Estudi Europeus (1990–93), and Director of the Masters Degree Course in Advanced European Law Studies (1986–94 and 1997–99) at the UAB. She was also a Legal Expert at the Legal Service of the European Commission in Brussels from 1994 to 1997. Author and Co-editor of *Lecciones de derecho comu-*

nitario europeo (1994). She has been visiting professor in Strasbourg, Toulouse and Aix en Provence, among other institutions. Her principal fields of research are European Economic law, women's law studies and European law, and European migration law, in which she leads a long-term research project for the Spanish Education Ministry.

J.H.H. Weiler is Manley Hudson Professor of Law and Jean Monnet Chair at Harvard University. He also serves as Co-Director of the Academy of European Law at the European University Institute, Florence, Italy. He is a faculty member at the College of Europe in Bruges, Belgium and an Honorary Professor at University College, London University and at the University of Copenhagen. He served as a Member of the Committee of Jurists of the Institutional Affairs Committee of the European Parliament co-drafting the European Parliament's Declaration of Human Rights and Freedoms and Parliament's input to the Maastricht Inter-Governmental Conference. He was a member of the *Groupe des Sages* advising the Commission of the European Union on the 1996/97 Amsterdam Treaty. He is a WTO Panel Member. His most recent book is *The Constitution of Europe: Do the New Clothes have an Emperor?* (1999).

Martin Will is a Senior Research Fellow in Comparative Public, International and European law at the Universität Mannheim. He holds an LL.M. from Cambridge University and has submitted a doctoral thesis in public international law at the University of Mannheim. He also practises as an attorney in Frankfurt-am-Main.

A

Introduction

1

An 'Ever Closer Union' in Need of a Human Rights Policy: The European Union and Human Rights

PHILIP ALSTON AND J. H. H. WEILER*

I. INTRODUCTION

A. Fifty Years of the Universal Declaration

The twentieth century's most important proclamation of human rights, the Universal Declaration of Human Rights, was adopted by the United Nations General Assembly on 10 December 1948.[1] It provided not only the inspiration but also the basis for the drafting of the European Convention on Human Rights, which was adopted less than two years later.[2] Between them, the two instruments enabled the work of building a European community to proceed without a separate human rights foundation.

To mark the beginning of the fiftieth anniversary year of the Universal Declaration, the European Council, meeting in Luxembourg in December 1997, appealed to all states to step up their efforts in the field of human rights by:

—acceding to international instruments to which they are not yet party . . .;
—ensuring more stringent implementation of those instruments;
—strengthening the role of civil society in promoting and protecting human rights;
—promoting activities on the ground and developing technical assistance in the area of human rights;
—strengthening in particular training and education programmes concerning human rights.[3]

---

* This analysis is adapted from a report prepared for the *Comité des Sages* which was responsible for 'Leading by Example: A Human Rights Agenda for the European Union for the Year 2000'. The agenda was made public in Oct. 1998 and is reprinted in Annex 1 of the present volume. The Committee consisted of Judge Antonio Cassese, Mme Catherine Lalumière, Professor Peter Leuprecht, and Mrs Mary Robinson. The authors are deeply indebted to the members of a drafting group which discussed both the outline and many of the details of this report. In addition to the authors it was composed of Ms Mara Bustelo, Mr James Heenan, Mme Catherine Lalumière, Mr Michael O'Boyle, and Professors Andrew Clapham, Gráinne de Búrca, Bruno de Witte, and Peter Leuprecht. They are not, however, responsible for the content of this analysis.
[1] GA Res. 217A (III), 10 Dec. 1948.
[2] G. Cohen-Jonathan, *La Convention européenne des droits de l'homme* (1989), 11.
[3] Conclusions of the European Council meeting in Luxembourg, Dec. 1997, Annex 3 with the title

Although seemingly directed at third States, it goes without saying that such a programme applies as much, if not more, to the European Union and its Member States. This chapter seeks to identify the consequences which should follow from an effort to apply that programme and its underlying assumptions to the activities of the Union.

B. *The Scope and Emphases of the Analysis*

A considerable number of the specific recommendations made in this chapter have previously been made by others. In particular, the European Parliament has long called, and continues to call, for major reforms, some of which follow lines similar to those proposed here.[4] The European Commission has advocated a great many innovations, starting with its unsuccessful 1979 proposal for Community accession to the European Convention on Human Rights, and continuing until today. In a detailed examination of the Union's external human rights policy, the Economic and Social Committee concluded that internal and external policies need to be closely linked, and it endorsed an extensive range of recommendations.[5] In addition, a number of expert groups focusing on specialized issues have reached similar conclusions about the need for human rights reforms.[6] Finally, an earlier set of proposals emanated from a project undertaken to coincide with the introduction of the single market.[7]

The present analysis, however, goes beyond those earlier prescriptions in a number of respects. Moreover, the situation today has changed fundamentally from that which prevailed even as recently as a couple of years ago. The Union is indeed becoming 'ever closer'. A single market, a single currency, and the imminent prospect of a greatly enlarged Union, all have major human rights implications that can no longer be dealt with in a piecemeal fashion. Rather than focusing on either internal or external policies, this chapter insists that only a unified approach embracing both dimensions of the Union's approach to human rights is viable. Finally, this analysis seeks to present a comprehensive and balanced package of reforms which pays very careful attention to the limits of what might be legally and politically feasible. Accordingly, it spells out in considerable detail the legal and political bases upon which the proposed programme can be implemented.

In the light of these objectives the chapter is especially concerned with institutional matters. This is not because we have a naïve and undiluted faith in the powers of bureaucracy, or because we are unconcerned with the substance of the grand chal-

---

'Declaration by the European Council at the Beginning of the Year of the Fiftieth Anniversary of the Universal Declaration of Human Rights', *Bull. EU* 12–1997, point I.21, para. 6.

[4] See, in particular, Annual Report on Human Rights Throughout the World in 1995–1996 and the Union's Human Rights Policy, (*rapporteur*: Mrs Catherine Lalumière), Doc. A4–0400/96 of 28 Nov. 1996.

[5] Opinion of the Economic and Social Committee on 'The European Union and the External Dimensions of Human Rights Policy, 97/C206/21 of 24 Apr. 1997 [1997] OJ C206/117.

[6] See e.g., the 1996 Final Report by a *Comité des Sages*, chaired by Maria de Lourdes Pintasilgo, entitled *For a Europe of Civic and Social Rights*, and the Report of the High Level Panel on the Free Movement of Persons chaired by Mrs Simone Veil presented to the Commission on 18 Mar. 1997.

[7] '1992—What Are Our Rights?: Agenda for a Human Rights Action Plan', in A. Cassese, A. Clapham, and J. Weiler (eds.), *Human Rights and the European Community* (1991), ii.

lenges that emerge from any close examination of the EU's human rights policy. There are, however, several reasons which seem to warrant the approach which has been adopted.

The first is that the potential scope of an analysis such as this is vast. It would be pretentious as well as unrealistic to purport to provide a comprehensive, let alone a minutely well-informed, critique of every aspect of EU policy in all of the many fields touching upon human rights within the confines of such an analysis. Secondly, the EU is a political and bureaucratic entity in which the starting points for major policy reform or innovation are: (i) a reasonably clear-cut acceptance of the proposed policy orientation on the part of policy-makers at each of the key levels; and (ii) the shaping of policy-making, administrative, and judicial structures which are adequately equipped to pursue the more specialized dimensions of human rights policy in relationship to the different sectoral areas.

Third, and closely related, is the fact that there is little point in going into the finer details of policy until the central issue of principle, that of the Union's competences in relation to many aspects of human rights, is resolved. There is no shortage of compelling and highly detailed analyses, whether prepared by specialists, interest groups, scholars, or activists, which seek to spell out what the Community should do in one area or another of internal policy and which simply take for granted that the necessary legal and constitutional competence exists. For the most part they do so with scant regard to the resistance which that proposition continues to encounter from many quarters. In order to avoid the futility which follows from the neglect of the sometimes tedious and arcane, but nonetheless indispensable, legal dimension, this chapter attaches particular importance to establishing a clear and appropriate foundation for the specific measures proposed.

Fourthly, the promotion and protection of human rights is not a one-time undertaking and neither governments nor bureaucracies can be counted upon to remain consistently, let alone insistently, vigilant. There will always be occasions and issues in relation to which it will seem preferable to sweep human rights under the carpet ('temporarily', of course, and only in the interests of a more profound objective which is itself assumed to be human rights friendly). Thus, one of the principal themes running through all aspects of this chapter is that the relevant structures and institutions must be made more open and responsive to pressures from civil society and other watchdogs to respect human rights. The chapter explores how this theme might be translated into practice by concentrating upon the need for more systematic and reliable information, the need to be able to identify who is institutionally responsible for upholding human rights, the need to be able to hold those in power accountable, the need for a system of checks and balances, and the need for more openness and transparency.

II. THE PARADOX OF THE EU'S HUMAN RIGHTS POLICIES

The human rights policies of the European Union are beset by a paradox.[8] On the one hand, the Union is a staunch defender of human rights in both its internal and external affairs. On the other hand, it lacks a comprehensive or coherent policy at either level and fundamental doubts persist whether the institutions of the Union possess adequate legal competence in relation to a wide range of human rights issues arising within the framework of Community policies.

A. The Positive Side of the Balance Sheet

On the positive side of the balance sheet, a strong commitment to human rights is one of the principal characteristics of the European Union. The Amsterdam Treaty proclaims that 'the Union is founded on the principles of liberty, democracy, respect for human rights and fundamental freedoms and the rule of law'.[9] By the same token, any Member State violating human rights in a 'serious and persistent' way can lose its rights under the Treaty.[10] The European Court of Justice has long required the Community to respect fundamental rights and the European Council has issued several major statements emphasizing the importance of respect for human rights.[11] Similarly, the Community has taken notable initiatives in a wide range of fields from gender equality to racism and xenophobia.

Thus, in diverse ways, the European Union has acknowledged that it has an important role to play in promoting respect for the human rights of its citizens and of

---

[8] The Union's policies have been analysed in considerable detail elsewhere. See generally, M. Dauses, 'The Protection of Fundamental Rights in the Community Legal Order', (1985) 10 *European LR* 398; A. Clapham, *Human Rights and the European Community: A Critical Overview* (1991); K. Lenaerts, 'Fundamental Rights to be Included in a Community Catalogue', (1991) 16 *European LR* 367; J. Coppel and A. O'Neill, 'The European Court of Justice: Taking Human Rights Seriously?' (1992) 12 *Legal Studies* 227; G. de Búrca, 'Fundamental Human Rights and the Reach of EC Law' (1993) 13 *Oxford Journal of Legal Studies* 283; P. Twomey, 'The European Union: Three Pillars without a Human Rights Foundation', in D. O'Keefe and P. Twomey (eds.), *Legal Issues of the Maastricht Treaty* (1994), 121; J.-P. Jacqué, 'Communauté européenne et Convention européenne des droits de l'homme', in L.-E. Pettiti, E. Decaux, and P.-H. Imbert (eds.), *La Convention européenne des droits de l'homme: Commentaire article par article* (1995), 83; J. H. H. Weiler and N. Lockhart, ' "Taking Rights Seriously" Seriously: The European Court and its Fundamental Rights Jurisprudence', (1995) 32 *CMLRev.* 51 and 579; N. Neuwahl and A. Rosas (eds.), *The European Union and Human Rights* (1995); G. Cohen-Jonathan, 'Conclusions générales', in P. Tavernier (ed.), *Quelle Europe pour les droits de l'homme?* (1996), 477; Editorial comment: 'Fundamental Rights and Common European Values' (1996) 33 *CML Rev.* 215; A. Toth, 'The European Union and Human Rights: The Way Forward' (1997) 34 *CML Rev.* 491; M. Colvin and P. Noorlander, 'Human Rights and Accountability after the Treaty of Amsterdam' [1998] *European Human Rights LR* 191; Besselink, 'Entrapped by the Maximum Standard: On Fundamental Rights, Pluralism and Subsidiarity in the European Union' (1998) 35 *CML Rev.* 629. An especially valuable source of information is the regular quarterly reports on the EU and human rights by Johannes van der Klaauw, published in the *Netherlands Quarterly of Human Rights*.

[9] Art.6 TEU. All principal references in this chap. to the TEU (Treaty on European Union) and the EC (Treaty establishing the European Community) are to the consolidated versions which will take effect after the entry into force of the Amsterdam Treaty.

[10] Art. 7 TEU. See M. Nowak, 'Human Rights "Conditionality" in Relation to Entry to, and Full Participation in, the EU', in this vol.

[11] See B. De Witte, 'The Past and Future Role of the European Court of Justice in the Protection of Human Rights', in this vol. below; and Weiler and Lockhart, note 8 above.

all others resident within the Union, and of ensuring that those rights are fully respected. This is so despite the fact that the Member States are, and will remain, the principal guardians of human rights within their own territories.

Equally, the Union is a powerful and uniquely representative actor on the international scene. It has the responsibility, reinforced by the capacity and financial resources, to influence significantly the human rights policies of other States as well as those of international organizations. In recognition of this responsibility it has insisted that States seeking admission to the Union must satisfy strict human rights requirements.[12] Other governments wishing to enter into co-operation agreements with the Union, or to receive aid or benefit from trade preferences, must give an undertaking to respect human rights. If that undertaking is breached, serious consequences can ensue.[13] It has adopted a number of declarations underlining the importance of human rights in its external relations and it has given substance to this approach by funding a wide range of development co-operation initiatives with major human rights components.[14] It has sought to strengthen the capacity of civil society in many countries to protect human rights,[15] has funded election monitoring and human rights monitoring, and has played an active role in support of human rights in multilateral contexts.

B. The Other Side of the Balance Sheet

Nevertheless, despite the frequency of statements underlining the importance of human rights and the existence of a variety of significant individual policy initiatives, the European Union lacks a fully-fledged human rights policy. This is true in relation both to its internal policies and, albeit to a lesser extent, its external policies. Some of these shortcomings are noted below. To date, in relation to its internal human rights situation, the institutions of the Community have succeeded in cobbling together a makeshift policy which has been barely adequate, but by no means sufficient. In the future, this approach will be unsustainable, increasingly ineffective and ultimately self-defeating. In relation to its external policies, the irony is that the Union has, by virtue of its emphasis upon human rights in its relations with other States and its ringing endorsements of the universality and indivisibility of human rights, highlighted the incongruity and indefensibility of combining an active external policy stance with what in some areas comes close to an abdication of internal responsibility. At the end of the day, the Union can only achieve the leadership role to which it aspires through the example it sets to its partners and other States. Leading by example should become the *Leitmotif* of a new European Union human rights policy.

The paradoxical nature of the Union's human rights policies may be illustrated by reference to two events of recent months. The first is the final statement adopted by the European Council at Cardiff in June 1998. Its content reveals the ease with which human rights can be rendered almost invisible in major declarations of EU policy.

---

[12] Art. 49 TEU.

[13] B. Brandtner and A. Rosas, 'Trade Preferences and Human Rights', in this vol.

[14] B. Simma, J. B. Aschenbrenner, and C. Schulte, 'Human Rights Considerations in the Development Co-operation Activities of the EC', in this vol.

[15] E. Decaux, 'Human Rights and Civil Society', in this vol.

The phrase 'human rights' is used once in the space of ninety-seven paragraphs, spread over sixteen pages. In that reference, the Council 'calls on Indonesia to respect human rights' in relation to East Timor. Even the word 'rights' appears only twice in the entire document. The first time it is used to laud President Nelson Mandela 'as an example to champions of civil rights'. The second reference is to the 'single market rights and opportunities' of 'citizens and business'.[16] It is true that the virtual absence of references to human rights stands in contrast to the Council's Declaration at Luxembourg in December 1997 when it marked the beginning of the year of the fiftieth anniversary of the Universal Declaration of Human Rights with a twelve-paragraph Annex.[17] The latter, however, focused almost exclusively on the external relations dimensions of the issue. In any case, human rights should be a consistent and prominent theme in all such declarations.

The second event was a ruling by the European Court of Justice on 12 May 1998,[18] which threw into doubt the legal basis for much of the funding provided by the Commission for human rights- and democracy-related activities. Among the results of the judgment are the freezing of a very considerable number of projects, the urgent need to consider draft regulations concerning the EU's external human rights policies, and increased awareness of the entirely unsatisfactory legal basis for many of the activities needed to monitor and promote respect for human rights within the Union.

The time has come, therefore, for the Union to meet its responsibilities and to develop a comprehensive, coherent, balanced, and forward-looking human rights policy. This chapter amplifies the considerations which such a policy should take into account.

C. Internal and External Policies as Two Sides of One Coin

Human rights are all too often assumed to be primarily matters arising in a country's external relations rather than its internal affairs. The project from which this chapter has resulted began with a strong focus on the role of human rights within the external relations of the European Union. It quickly became apparent, however, that the internal and external dimensions of human rights policy can never be satisfactorily kept in separate compartments. They are, in fact, two sides of the same coin.

In the case of the Union, there are several additional reasons why a concern with external policy also necessitates a careful consideration of the internal policy dimensions. First, the development and implementation of an effective external human rights policy can only be undertaken in the context of appropriate internal institutional arrangements. Secondly, in an era when universality and indivisibility are the touchstones of human rights, an external policy which is not underpinned by a comparably comprehensive and authentic internal policy can have no hope of being taken seriously. Thirdly, as the next millennium approaches, a credible human rights policy must assiduously avoid unilateralism and double standards, and that can only

---

[16] Conclusions of the European Council meeting in Cardiff, June 1998, para. 93, *Bull. EU*, 6–1998, at 7–21.
[17] Note 3 above.
[18] Judgment C–106/96, *United Kingdom* v. *Commission* [1998] ECR I–2729.

be done by ensuring reciprocity and consistency. Finally, the reality is that a Union which is not prepared to embrace a strong human rights policy for itself is highly unlikely to develop a fully-fledged external policy and apply it with energy or consistency. As long as human rights remain a suspect preoccupation within, their status without will remain tenuous.

This analysis thus makes no fundamental distinction between the internal and external dimensions of the Union's human rights policy. To use a metaphor, it is clear that both must be cut from a single cloth. By the same token, it is perhaps prudent to acknowledge from the outset that this approach will not easily gain acceptance. There is an unfortunate, although perhaps inevitable, element of schizophrenia that afflicts the Union between its internal and external policies or, to put it differently, between its first, second, and third pillars. The result is that very few officials concerned with the EU will be interested in an analysis of this type as a whole. Instead, those concerned with external relations will focus solely on its implications in that domain, while their internal counterparts will adopt an equally narrow approach. Meaningful action will thus require that the governments of Member States see beyond the narrow and compartmentalized concerns of different bureaucratic and political actors and embrace a vision which recognizes the true place that human rights must come to occupy in the new Europe.

III. THE CURRENT SITUATION

A. How Adequate is the EU's Existing Approach to Human Rights?

The Treaty of Amsterdam marked a significant step forward when it affirmed that the Union 'shall respect fundamental rights, as guaranteed by the European Convention [on Human Rights] . . . and as they result from the constitutional traditions common to the Member States, as general principles of Community law'.[19] But it still remains for these solemn words to be matched by the same institutional, legislative, and administrative follow-up which characterizes other areas. The failure to take adequate measures is particularly striking since the very same Treaty Article provides that '[t]he Union shall provide itself with the means necessary to attain its objectives and carry through its policies'.[20]

Before examining what needs to be done, it is essential to understand the broader historical context within which these commitments were made in Amsterdam. Until the Treaty of European Union, signed at Maastricht in 1992, neither fundamental rights nor the concept of European citizenship had been recognized in the various Community treaties. Nevertheless, even before Maastricht, the Union did not come to the field of human rights with a blank sheet.

Despite the absence of any reference in the original constituent Treaties to the protection of fundamental human rights, the European Court of Justice began in the late 1960s to affirm that respect for such rights was part of the legal heritage of the

---

[19] Art. 6(2) TEU.   [20] Art. 6(4) TEU.

Community. Measures incompatible with fundamental human rights were deemed to be unacceptable and judicial protection of those rights took root in the Community legal order.[21]

B. Negative and Positive Approaches to the Integration of Human Rights

In essence, this initial step was an example of negative integration. Whereas positive integration requires that affirmative steps be taken to expedite the achievement of specified goals, negative integration confines itself to a prohibition of violations of the principle in question. But in this respect, the starting point was no different from that which was used in relation to foundational developments in other fields of Community life. It is instructive to take as an example the centrepiece of the Community, the creation of a Single Market through the establishment of the four fundamental economic freedoms: free movement of goods, services, capital, and labour. There, too, the first step was the creation of an obligation of non-violation; a ban on measures which would compromise the key principles. And again the Court of Justice played an important role in interpreting these interdictions as legally enforceable duties. It is this approach which scholars have characterized as negative integration.[22]

In these other fields it was not long before it became widely accepted that negative integration was insufficient to attain the agreed goals. It needed to be matched and complemented by positive integration. The result was the adoption of specific policies in the various economic fields designed to ensure that the common marketplace would become more than a series of legal prohibitions. It seemed self-evident that courts alone could not ensure the full attainment of the four fundamental economic freedoms. The political institutions had to play their role too. A wide range of major political initiatives followed.

In stark contrast, the move from negative to positive integration in the field of human rights has been far more problematic. Already in 1977 the political institutions of the Community jointly affirmed their support for the basic legal principle of non-violation contained in the jurisprudence of the Court of Justice.[23] But, in retrospect, it is now clear that what should have been no more than an initial political step has become a powerful presumption that Community political activity in the field of human rights should be largely confined to negative prohibitions rather than positive initiatives. Thus, on the one hand, starting with the Single European Act of 1986, the commitment to respect for fundamental human rights has found an increasingly important place, with ever more ringing rhetoric, in the Treaties. On the other hand, however, attempts in the field of human rights to match the legal prohibition on violation with positive measures and a pro-active human rights policy have met with varying degrees of success, and on some occasions with resistance and hostility, principally from various Member States.

A few examples are sufficient to illustrate this inconsistency. In 1978 the Commission proposed to begin a process which would lead to the European Community's

---

[21] See note 9 above.

[22] J. H. H. Weiler, 'The Transformation of Europe', 100 *Yale LJ* (1991) 2403; and P. Pierson, 'The Path to European Integration: A Historical Institutional Analysis' (1996) 29 *Comparative Political Studies* 123.

[23] Joint Declaration by the European Parliament, the Council, and the Commission [1977] OJ C103/1.

accession to the European Convention on Human Rights.[24] The proposal was important not only for its symbolism, but also for a series of practical reasons. In particular, it would have sent the message that Community measures were subject to the obligations contained in the Convention and that if Community institutions, including the Court of Justice, were not vigilant, there would be a prospect of being found to be in violation by the Court in Strasbourg. The relevant provisions of the European Convention (especially the requirement 'to secure' the relevant rights, as Article 1 puts it) have long been interpreted as imposing both negative and positive obligations. But the proposal to accede was not taken up by the Council and the Member States. Attempts to revive the initiative more than a decade later also failed.[25] The result is that the Treaty rhetoric affirms the normative commitment to the European Convention on Human Rights, but this commitment is not matched by political practice.

There are, nevertheless, some important instances within Community law in which the need for human rights measures to go beyond the principle of non-violation has been understood. An inventory of Community activity in the field of human rights would not be negligible. In some cases such activity derives from specific legal bases to be found in the Treaty, where human rights and the objectives of creating a common or single market happen to coincide, at least in part. Such has been the case, for example, in the area of gender discrimination, where Community policies, though far from perfect, have made important contributions and have afforded a degree of protection going well beyond that which was available at the time within the Member States. But, as important as such examples are, they also serve to highlight the fact that in other areas of social policy there has been far less affirmative human rights policy, and in some cases almost none.

In the external relations field, on the other hand, an early emphasis upon linking human rights to sanctions, such as the suspension of aid or trade preferences, has been definitively replaced by a more pro-active emphasis on promoting the development of democratic institutions, strengthening the rule of law, working through civil society, and both encouraging and funding specific human rights initiatives.

C. Institutional Arrangements

The institutional arrangements made by the Community in order to give effect to human rights policies have generally been inadequate, both in relation to internal and external matters. In the great majority of instances, the task has been left to entities with a very vague human rights mandate, reinforced by little expertise and even less interest. In a few isolated instances, however, and especially in relation to external policies, the Commission has established units with a specific mandate. They include Unit 2 of Directorate A of Directorate General 1A, responsible for human rights and democratization; and Unit 4 of Directorate General VIII responsible for the co-ordination of issues relating to the rule of law, fundamental freedoms, democratization, and institutional support. These isolated units have achieved an

---

[24] Memorandum adopted by the Commission, 4 Apr. 1979, *Bull. EC*, Supp. 2/79.
[25] Commission Communication on Community accession to the European Convention for the Protection of Human Rights and Some of its Protocols', Doc. SEC(90)2087 final (19 Nov. 1990).

enormous amount through the promotion of human rights activities in a wide range of areas.

But the complexity and fragmentation of the current arrangements are well illustrated by the composition of the 'Standing Inter-Departmental Human Rights Co-ordination Group', which sets the general guidelines for funding from the main external relations human rights budget (under chapter B7–70). The group is convened by DG IA and includes representatives from the Secretariat General, Forward Studies Unit, Legal Service, and from Directorates General I, IA, IB, II, V, VIII, X, XI, XII, XIII, XV, XIX, XXII, XXIV, XXIII, and ECHO.[26] Even with respect to external relations alone, the regional breakdown of responsibilities among Commissioners means that five different Commissioners and their respective bureaucracies have central roles to play.

This dispersal serves to highlight the extremely unsatisfactory state of affairs in relation to responsibility for human rights matters within a very large institutional apparatus which boasts all too little specialist human rights expertise in this field. It is important that the key human rights-related Units exist within Directorates General IA and VIII. It is disturbing, however, that institutionally there is little more than that in any concerted sense. The result is that the Community landscape of human rights policies is not without some important positive features, but it is clearly fragmented, deficient in overall coherence, and lacking in institutional leadership.

The recent decision of the European Court of Justice, in which it undercut the legal basis of the financial support given by the Community to a myriad of human rights agencies and activities, is emblematic.[27] It was a perfect display of the consequences of human rights activity without a coherent policy, of _ad hoc_ action rather than the achievement of programmatic goals, of almost intentional constitutional ambiguity towards human rights, of the wilful lack of clarity as regards Community competences and jurisdiction, and the embarrassing realization that in this field the Community has had to act by stealth and questionable constitutional means. In a perverse way the decision has had a positive impact in so far as it has drawn both public and official attention to the fact that the existing approach is in crisis and in need of major reform.

The decision also underscores that the European Court of Justice, no matter how carefully it may be attuned to the need to ensure full respect of fundamental rights within the Community legal order, cannot make up for the absence of the necessary legal and policy commitments on the part of the other institutions.

D. Excessive Reliance upon Judicial Remedies

Overall, human rights policy within the Community continues to rely far too heavily on the premise that equipping individuals to pursue existing Community legal remedies (both at the national level and through the possibility of references to the European Court of Justice) is, for the most part, not merely sufficient but is even an effective mechanism to guarantee that rights will not be violated within the

[26] European Parliament, _Report on Setting Up a Single Co-ordinating Structure within the European Commission Responsible for Human Rights and Democratization (Lenz Report)_, A4–393/97, at 14.
[27] See note 18 above.

Community legal space. We challenge this implicit understanding. Judicial protection at the instance of individuals is an important, even foundational, dimension of an effective human rights regime. But while it is necessary, it is not sufficient. Effective access to justice requires a variety of policies that would empower individuals to vindicate the judicially enforceable rights given to them.[28] Ignorance, lack of resources, ineffective representation, inadequate legal standing and deficient remedies all have the capacity to render judicially enforceable rights illusory.

In our view, therefore, too much faith is placed by the Community in the power of legal prohibitions and judicial enforcement. The gap between the political rhetoric of commitment to human rights and the unwillingness to provide the Union with the means to make that rhetoric a living reality has only served to underscore the inadequacy of the excessively judicially-focused strategy of negative integration in relation to human rights. To pretend at the end of this century that human rights and dignity can be guaranteed to all those, especially the weakest in our society, who need them by simply affirming the principle of respect or even by rendering Community and Union measures which are incompatible with human rights putatively illegal if challenged before Community Courts, is a position which, at best, is overly complacent.

E. An Inadequate Information Base

The inadequacy of the Union's approach to human rights is made possible in part by a knowledge and monitoring gap. The United Nations bodies responsible for supervising States' compliance with their international human rights obligations have consistently emphasized that effective monitoring systems are an indispensable foundation upon which domestic human rights policies must be constructed.[29] While there is a great deal of unsystematic information which suggests lacunae and gaps in the vindication of human rights in the field of application of Community law, no observer can have a comprehensive picture in this regard because there is no agency which is empowered to provide or collect such information in a regular, ongoing, and systematic fashion. As a result, the Community lacks the necessary information base upon which it should make decisions about the identification of legislative and policy priorities and the allocation of administrative and budgetary resources in the field of human rights.

A similar vacuum exists in relation to external relations. The absence of any systematic approach to monitoring and reporting has frequently been remarked upon, whether by the Parliament, the Economic and Social Committee, non-governmental organizations involved in EU matters or outside experts. The consequence is that the various policy-making and review exercises undertaken by the different institutions within the Union are based upon inadequate, uneven, and above all unreviewable data and analysis. The resulting situation is unsatisfactory from the point of view of the institutions themselves, of third countries which should know the basis upon

---

[28] See text accompanying note 107 below.
[29] See P. Alston, 'The Purposes of Reporting', in United Nations, *Manual on Human Rights Reporting* (1997), 19; and A. Bloed *et al.* (eds.), *Monitoring Human Rights in Europe: Comparing International Procedures and Mechanisms* (1993).

which an EU evaluation of their performance has been based, and of civil society whose informed capacity to scrutinize is an indispensable element in a consistent, co-herent, transparent, and well-supported human rights policy.[30] If human rights are to be given their due in the context of the second and third pillars, transparent re-porting, based on objective and systematic monitoring, is essential. The availability of such reports would also have the capacity to increase considerably the effective-ness of the role played by the Parliament.

What is needed are not isolated initiatives—a database here, a new report there—nor even greater transparency; rather, a fundamental rethinking of the entire Union posture in this area is required.

IV. WHY DOES THE EU NEED A NEW HUMAN RIGHTS POLICY?

The call for a new human rights policy derives both from an assessment of the cur-rent internal situation and from the particular historical context in which the Union finds itself. It must be emphasized, however, that the need for such a policy is far greater now than it was, even in the recent past. We discuss elsewhere in this chap-ter[31] the judgment of the European Court of Justice of 12 May 1998, which has high-lighted the disarray of important aspects of existing policies. Other current developments within the Union, in Europe as a whole, and in the world at large also make it imperative for action to be taken now. This is demonstrated by a variety of factors, including those noted below.

A. The Internal Human Rights Situation

The approach adopted in this chapter is not driven primarily by a sense that there are systematic violations of human rights occurring within the Union which remain en-tirely unaddressed. But, by the same token, there clearly are many human rights challenges which persist and to which greater attention must be given. This is clear from a wide range of sources, including various reports by the European Parliament, by the European Commission, and by non-governmental groups such as Amnesty International and Human Rights Watch.[32] We do not intend to replicate that infor-mation or to dwell on the details of the violations that persist. Suffice it to note that they include a resurgence in racist and xenophobic behaviour, a failure fully to live

---

[30] See generally Decaux, note 15 above.   [31] See text accompanying note 18.
[32] e.g. Communication from the Commission: An Action Plan against Racism, Doc. COM(1998)183 final (25 Mar. 1998); European Parliament, Annual Report on Human Rights Throughout the World in 1995–1996 and the Union's Human Rights Policy (*rapporteur*: Mrs C. Lalumière), Doc. A4–0400/96 (28 Nov. 1996); European Parliament, Annual Report on respect for human rights in the European Union in 1994 (*rapporteur*: Mrs L. de Esteban Martin), Doc. A4–0223/96 (1 July 1996); European Parliament, An-nual Report on Respect for Human Rights in the European Union (1996) (*rapporteur*: Mrs A. Pailler), Doc. A4–0034/98 (28 Jan. 1998); *Human Rights Watch World Report 1998* (1998) (citing 'significant blem-ishes on Europe's record in promoting human rights'. *ibid.*, at p. xxv); Amnesty International, *Annual Re-port 1998* (1998).

up to equality norms or to eliminate various types of discrimination, major short-comings in the enjoyment of economic, social, and cultural rights of disadvantaged and vulnerable groups, unsatisfactory treatment of refugees and asylum-seekers, in-humane and degrading treatment of detainees, and so on.[33]

Although (for reasons of Community competences *vis-à-vis* those of the Member States) it is not for the institutions of the Union to take it upon themselves to seek to resolve these problems, it can equally well not stand passively by and chant the mantra of exclusive individual Member State competence while taking no steps to contribute to an improvement of the situation. In short, the Union must have a human rights policy, albeit one that takes appropriate account of the various principles upon which it has been established.

B. The EU's Role in the World

The European Union is a key player in world affairs. It has close to 7 per cent of the world's population and almost as many people as the USA and Japan combined. It accounts for 27 per cent of the world's gross domestic product, almost one-fifth of its trade flows, and well over half of the total official development assistance flows to de-veloping countries. While it is true that these figures are only the aggregate of fifteen different sets of national statistics, the Union's determination to be more than the sum of its parts is reflected in a wide range of treaty commitments, policies, and pro-grammes. Along with the power and influence that these statistics represent comes responsibility. The Union cannot be a credible defender of human rights in multilat-eral fora and in other countries (as it has long sought to be) while insisting that it has no general competence of its own in relation to those same human rights.

Thus, for example, the EU strongly supports UN measures to persuade govern-ments to establish national human rights institutions, but it does not have such an in-stitution itself, nor has it encouraged its own Member States to establish them. To take another current example, the Union adopted, in May 1998, a 'Common Posi-tion on Human Rights, Democratic Principles, the Rule of Law and Good Gover-nance in Africa', which proclaimed its objective of working 'in partnership with African countries to promote respect for human rights' and the other stated object-ives.[34] There is, however, no equivalent policy which commits the EU to work act-ively within Europe in relation to human rights. The need to end this double standard can perhaps best be expressed in biblical language by noting that, if it is to be consistent and have credibility, the EU must do unto itself as it would have others do unto themselves.

In short, as Europe finds itself increasingly playing a major role in world politics, the commitment to human rights, democracy, and the rule of law will acquire not simply a greater urgency but a much more coherent and consistent policy towards other countries.

---

[33] Some of these issues are addressed in more detail below.
[34] Common Position of 25 May 1998 defined by the Council on the basis of Art. J.2. TEU, concerning human rights, democratic principles, the rule of law and good governance in Africa: [1998] OJ CL.158/1.

C. Monetary Union

The Union is poised to realize Economic and Monetary Union. Hesitatingly, but steadily, the matching of Europe's external political presence with its internal economic might is occurring. Already from 1 January 1999 EMU will bring a single currency to some 290 million people. Its economic and political significance to the entire Union cannot be overestimated. But it is no secret that, even among the enthusiasts, expectations have been mingled with anxiety and even fear.[35] In part this is fear of the unknown and anxiety over the need to re-imagine oneself as part of a new economic polity. Inevitably the increased economic freedoms of an economic and monetary union make each individual feel smaller and fear the impact on his or her daily activities, especially since EMU is associated with a monetary discipline which poses a particular challenge to the tradition of human solidarity that has characterized the European approach to social and economic policy. It would be appropriate, precisely at this moment of EMU-propelled monetary rigour, to find equally visible and tangible ways to affirm the European humanist tradition.

There is something terribly wrong with a polity which acts vigorously to realize its economic ambitions, as it clearly should, but which, at the same time, conspicuously neglects its parallel ethical and legal obligations to ensure that those policies result in the fullest possible enjoyment of human rights.

D. Enlargement

Eventual enlargement towards Eastern Europe will create the world's largest trading bloc and zone of economic liberty. At present, five new members look very likely, and in the longer term the number may be as high as thirteen countries. To many, enlargement is a moral imperative. And rightly so. But it will not come without costs— and our concern is not simply or primarily with economic costs. Enlargement inevitably means a further diminution in the sense of importance felt by each individual within the polity. As the Union widens and the machinery of governance grows more complex, the sense of individual alienation, of despair at being able both to influence decision-making and understand its rationale, will correspondingly deepen. 'European citizenship' must not become a beautiful phrase devoid of meaningful tools for individual empowerment. Moreover, the challenges posed by enlargement are not only structural or size-related. With enlargement, the Union will be importing a new set of unresolved minority issues as well as additional human rights challenges, whose solutions will test the strength of many Community policies.

In some respects the Union has looked ahead to this prospect. Articles 6(1) and 49 (*ex* Articles F(1) and O) TEU together provide that only a European State which respects the principles of liberty, democracy, respect for human rights and fundamental freedoms, and the rule of law may apply to become a member of the Union. And, as noted earlier, there is a new procedure for the suspension of the rights of

---

[35] See in general H. Ungerer, *A Concise History of European Monetary Integration: From EPU to EMU* (1997); and L. Tsoukalis, 'Economic and Monetary Union', in H. Wallace and W. Wallace (eds.), *Policy-making in the European Union* (3rd edn., 1996), 279.

Member States in case of a 'serious and persistent breach' of these principles.[36] But such policies and procedures look very strange alongside the Union's continuing insistence that it cannot itself have an overall policy to promote human rights within the Union. Now is the time to act to remedy this deficiency. The motivation of action taken only after the enlargement process has borne fruit will be suspect and a strong policy will be much more difficult to achieve at that late stage.

E. Globalization

The globalization of the world economy, coinciding with the acceleration of measures to consolidate the European advanced market-place, gives rise to a variety of additional human rights-related challenges. Some of these are linked to the diminishing capacity of individual governments to deal adequately with certain problems, either because of the increasingly transnational character of the problem or because of the pressures on governments themselves to 'downsize'.[37] Other challenges arise in relation to the new information technologies which are the engine for much of the thrust towards globalization. Issues of privacy and equal access are the most visible of examples of what a new generation of rights must address.

Likewise, the breakdown of traditional distinctions between trade in goods and services, between information and entertainment, between the commercial and material and the cultural and spiritual highlight the need to rethink the compartmentalized *ad hoc* approach to rights which hitherto has characterized the Union's approach. These developments call for new and innovative thinking and approaches, which in turn will inevitably require a significant component of EU-level implementation. In addition, globalization has been accompanied by significant growth in the importance of non-governmental groups and coalitions whose activities and influence transcend the borders of even strong regional groupings of States.

F. The Third Pillar

As the Community assumes far greater administrative and legislative responsibility in relation to Justice and Home Affairs, the need to assure, at the Community level, the rights of those affected by this new jurisdiction becomes more pressing. As long as responsibility in these areas was kept almost entirely outside the competence of the Community, the absence of a strong human rights policy in relation to those matters was defensible. As co-operation develops and the Community moves towards assuming considerably expanded powers, a parallel human rights policy must be seen as an indispensable counterpart.

G. The Amsterdam Treaty

The Treaty of Amsterdam of 1997 introduced a number of elements which require the development of a new human rights policy:

---

[36] Art. 7 TEU.

[37] See generally P. Alston, 'The Myopia of the Handmaidens: International Lawyers and Globalization' (1997) 8 *EJIL* 435; R. Axtmann (ed.), *Globalization and Europe: Theoretical and Empirical Investigations* (1998); A. Razin and E. Sadka (eds.), *The Economics of Globalization* (1998).

- The Treaty now provides for the first time that the EU is founded on the principles of liberty, democracy, human rights, and the rule of law. It would be odd if this innovation were to have no significant policy implications and were instead to be treated as a mere rhetorical flourish.
- The Treaty requires the Court of Justice, in so far as it has jurisdiction, to apply human rights standards to acts of Community institutions. The fact that these institutions are now subject to judicial scrutiny in a more structured way than was possible before should surely prompt careful reflection on what steps could be taken to ensure not only compliance but the active promotion of respect for human rights.
- Amsterdam significantly expands the Community's powers to take appropriate action to combat a wide range of forms of discrimination. Given the problems that remain to be overcome in this area it is inconceivable that new policies will not be needed. The broader human rights context of any such policies should be clearly recognized.
- The third pillar reforms dealing with police and judicial co-operation in criminal matters require significant accompanying initiatives in the human rights field.
- As also noted above, the Treaty introduces the possibility of suspending the rights of a Member State for human rights breaches. That provision cannot be permitted to remain a dead letter. Consideration must be given now to the procedures which will be followed in such an event.

In summary, although there is just cause for satisfaction with a Europe which is taking formidable steps to realize its aspirations, two hard and discomforting truths must also be faced. First, current policies such as monetary union, enlargement, and ever greater engagement with the global economy pose new threats, and create new challenges, to the European commitment towards the safeguarding of fundamental human rights. Secondly, public opinion is deeply ambivalent towards some of the principal developments within the Union. A cleavage between the increasingly generous verbal affirmation of commitment to human rights without matching the rhetoric with visible, systematic, and comprehensive action will eventually undermine the legitimacy of the European construct. In the pursuit of this grand design that is the European Union it is essential to keep constantly in mind the centrality of the individual—the men and women of whom and for whom ultimately Europe is made.

V. OBJECTIVES OF THE PROPOSED NEW
HUMAN RIGHTS POLICY

The preceding parts of this chapter have briefly assessed the EU's existing approach to human rights and examined some of the factors that underscore the need for a new human rights policy. Before developing specific policy proposals it is instructive to begin by clarifying the objectives that such a policy should be designed to meet.

Without going into the specific details, which are developed later in this analysis, the following should be the principal characteristics of a new policy:

1. Acceptance of the fact that there is a need for a comprehensive and coherent EU human rights policy based on a clarification of the constitutional ambiguity which currently bedevils any discussion of Community action in this field;
2. The development of more consistent linkages between internal and external policies and the promotion of greater interaction and complementarity between the two levels;
3. The establishment of detailed, systematic, and reliable information bases upon which the various actors (including Member States, the Commission, the Council, the European Parliament, and civil society) can construct integrated, calibrated, transparent, and effective policies;
4. The development of a pool of knowledgeable and experienced personnel with the necessary technical and policy-making expertise in human rights, thereby overcoming the current dispersion of human and financial resources, especially within the Commission;
5. The promotion of more effective co-ordination among the many Community actions, programmes, and initiatives already being undertaken in the field of human rights by different Commission services so as to achieve a more coherent whole and so as to prevent duplication in this field;
6. Changing the human rights culture of the Community legislative and administrative apparatus—in the way that has to some extent now been achieved in the field of environmental protection and, more recently, in relation to subsidiarity;
7. The elaboration of policy approaches which bring the human rights dimensions of action under each of the three pillars into closer alignment, while respecting the key differences in terms of Community competence, financing, and decision-making processes;
8. Enabling the European Parliament to play a more effective role in shaping human rights policy through giving it greater and more assured access to reliable information and enhanced opportunities to interact constructively with the Council and Commission;
9. Increasing the accessibility of existing avenues for judicial vindication of human rights both through national courts and through the European Court of Justice, as well as through the development of the new judicial opportunities provided for in the Amsterdam Treaty;

10. The identification of new policy options designed to ensure that the culture and methodology of human rights are able to adapt and respond to the needs of a rapidly changing political and economic environment;
11. Creating opportunities for more sustained consultation with non-governmental organizations, as well as civil society in its broadest sense, in all aspects of EU policy-making and, where feasible, in the implementation of those policies;
12. Strengthening the coherence and unity of external human rights policies through the development of more principled, predictable, and transparent procedures and criteria in relation to aid and its suspension;
13. Ensuring a more effective EU role in influencing, shaping, and acting as a catalyst to achieve, where appropriate, greater respect for human rights among some of the Union's interlocutors and partners, including within multilateral fora;
14. Facilitating a more principled and consistent European policy in response to serious violations of human rights among interlocutors and partners. Such a policy would also relate to third countries which are not covered by the two new proposed Community regulations.
15. Being in the vanguard of efforts to provide effective and more assured flows of humanitarian assistance, combined with an appropriate emphasis upon human rights;
16. Supporting the work of other international institutions, particularly that of the United Nations High Commissioner for Human Rights, the United Nations High Commissioner for Refugees, the Council of Europe, and the OSCE.

VI. TOWARDS A NEW APPROACH

A. Rethinking the Tasks and Institutions

There is no shortage of criticism that has been directed at the existing approach. It has been variously described by its critics as piecemeal, *ad hoc*, inconsistent, incoherent, half-hearted, uncommitted, ambiguous, hypocritical, and so on. Indeed, we use some of these terms ourselves elsewhere in this chapter in relation to specific policies.

Nevertheless, it must be emphasized that the existing policies, in their totality, are *not* misconceived, misguided, or wholly inadequate. In fact, it is *not* necessary for there to be a radical departure from the policies that are currently in place. On the contrary, in many respects existing arrangements provide an appropriate basis upon which to construct the new, much-needed policy.

Stated differently, most of the important pieces of the jigsaw puzzle that are required to make up an EU human rights policy already exist in a recognizable form. What now needs to be done is to put them in their correct places and to provide the glue that is indispensable for holding them together as part of a single picture.

As a prelude to identifying the principal elements for a new policy, it is appropriate first of all to emphasize what the policy is *not* about. Thus, the proposed new policy:

- is not premised on the need to recognize new rights;
- does not depend upon future amendments to the Treaty;
- will not significantly alter the existing institutional balance within the Union;
- does not imply any major realignment in the relationship between the Community and the Member States; and
- is not dependent upon a major increase in available resources.

While some changes of this nature might be desirable at some stage in the future, none of them is essential for the implementation of the principal parts of the package that is proposed below.

B. Moving towards New Institutional Roles

The institutional dimension of the proposed human rights policy is based on the assumption that, if it is to be credible, consistent, and effective, such a policy must engage all Community and Union institutions to the extent of their legislative and executive constitutional roles. By the same token, it is in the exercise of those very roles that human rights deficiencies may often occur. There would be an in-built conflict of interest if both supervisory and executory functions were assigned to the EU institutions. They are designed to be the guarantors of human rights, but they are also potential violators. This is a tension that has to be resolved.

The classic model of assigning exclusive supervisory functions to the European Court of Justice is inadequate in itself. Such a court can be an effective guarantor of human rights once cases are brought before it. But, as mentioned, the underlying theme of this analysis is the need to go beyond the model of reliance upon self-help by affected individuals who must invoke judicial protection. Thus, the supervisory function requires pro-active monitoring designed to detect areas of human rights concerns.

What is needed therefore is an institutional model which rests on the development of three already existing foundations. This model should consist, in essence, of:

1. the establishment of a clear set of executive functions to be exercised by the Commission through the creation or designation of a Directorate General with responsibility for human rights, to be headed by a separate member of the Commission;
2. the development of a monitoring function to be achieved through the creation of a new agency or through a substantial expansion in the scope and power of the existing European Monitoring Centre on Racism and Xenophobia in Vienna;[38] the latter should be transformed into a veritable monitoring agency, with monitoring jurisdiction over all human rights in the field of application of Community law; and

---

[38] See Council Reg. (EC) 1035/97 of 2 June 1997 establishing a European Monitoring Centre on Racism and Xenophobia [1997] OJ L151/1.

3. the development of a specialist human rights unit within the functions already envisaged to be performed by the new High Representative for the Common Foreign and Security Policy.

In addition, as part of such a changed institutional framework, all other institutions of the European Union should be called upon to enhance their human rights functions and sensibilities. In subsequent parts of the chapter we amplify on this basic institutional set up.

It must be emphasized, however, that to a very large extent these proposals are part of a single coherent and integrated package of measures designed to reflect a new human rights policy. The adoption of one or two elements, accompanied by neglect of the others, will not achieve the desired overall result. There is a synergy within the various institutional proposals which is especially important. To take but one example, the Parliament needs to have a Commissioner and a specialized Directorate General as interlocutors and to benefit from a more elaborate and sophisticated common foreign and security policy (CFSP) human rights framework if it is to be able to develop its own role to the extent that we, and the Parliament itself, deem desirable.

VII. LEGAL AND CONSTITUTIONAL ASPECTS OF A NEW POLICY

The first essential element in building a new EU human rights policy is to establish that such a policy lies within the constitutional competence of the Community and that it would not violate important principles such as that of subsidiarity.

A. Competences

The need for a comprehensive human rights policy seems so compelling that it will be very difficult for an outside observer to understand why such a policy has not already been adopted. There are many reasons. Principal among them is the issue of competences.[39] Yet the proposal for a significantly expanded human rights policy would be either naïve or fraudulent if the Community and Union lacked the legal competences to enact it.

The Treaty did not, and still does not, even after the measures introduced in Amsterdam, list human rights among its objectives. Opposition to a human rights policy, to accession to the European Convention on Human Rights, to the drafting of a Community 'Bill of Rights', and to a range of other policy proposals which have failed to gain acceptance over the years can all be explained in large measure by a concern that the Community lacks any significant constitutional competence to deal with all but a very circumscribed range of human rights matters. Underlying this concern is a fear that allowing the Community to move beyond a policy of not vio-

[39] See generally J. H. H. Weiler and S. Fries, 'The Competences of the EU in Human Rights', in this vol.

lating human rights would lead it to encroach on areas which are outside its jurisdiction and should be reserved to the Member States. Those who hold this view would argue that the potential reach of human rights policies is almost unlimited. And it is true that human rights do directly affect all activities of public authorities and, depending on their definition, also touch upon many areas of social activities of individuals. The fear is that empowering the Community in the field of human rights would be an invitation to a wholesale destruction of the jurisdictional boundaries between the Community and its Member States. It would be ironic if a proposed new policy, whilst motivated by the desire to vindicate fully the values represented by human rights, trampled over the equally important democratic and constitutional principles of limited governance and attributed powers.

The issue of competences is of particular importance in this context, not only because of the extent to which it has underpinned the resistance to an EU human rights policy on the part of some States, but perhaps more importantly because it has been the preferred excuse invoked by those who do not want such a policy for very different reasons. Those reasons range from a simplistic belief that the Union can and should confine itself to a narrow range of economic aspects of integration to a more general sense that human rights just get in the way of efforts to build a strong and wealthy new Europe. Whatever the motivation, it is essential to put the issue of competences into perspective so that the debate over the real issues can move ahead.

1. Rejecting Extreme Positions Earlier debates about a human rights policy for the Community seemed to oscillate between two, equally untenable, poles. There were those, including in some contexts the Commission, who seemed to believe that the commitment to ensure respect for human rights gave the Community a plenary jurisdiction in this area. Certainly, many suggestions by non-governmental groups have tended to reflect such an assumption and to dismiss arguments to the contrary as being driven by anachronistic concerns to protect state sovereignty. The opposite extreme would suggest that human rights are matters which are almost by definition reserved exclusively for action by the Member States. In this vein, the Council, whilst acknowledging a certain competence in the field of international co-operation and development, has consistently held that a general Community human rights policy, especially one impinging on action by and in the Member States, was outside the legislative jurisdiction of the Community.

In fact, both of these extreme positions are wrong. Neither the Community nor the Union has a plenary human rights jurisdiction in the way that Member States have. However, it is clear that, within carefully delineated boundaries, the Community and the Union do enjoy the necessary jurisdiction to enact a comprehensive and meaningful policy.

2. Human Rights as Cross-cutting Concerns It is instructive, by way of analogy, to consider some of the areas in which the Community has assumed exclusive competences, such as major aspects of the Common Commercial Policy, of the Common Agricultural Policy (which often implicate rights to property), or of the Single Market concerning the free movement of labour. It seems self-evident that in those areas it is only the Community which could reasonably be considered to be the custodian of human rights—in the same way that the Member States are custodians of human rights in the vast areas of state jurisdiction, like criminal law, which are largely outside Community jurisdiction.

It is true that Europe has evolved what is probably the most sophisticated system of judicial protection of human rights, involving both the domestic constitutional orders of the Member States and the European Convention system. Each of these has its unique characteristics that must be preserved and allowed to play its rightful role. But there are also aspects of European Community activity which are not subject to effective human rights control at these levels. Given the consistent expansion of Community responsibilities, it becomes all the more imperative that they be accompanied by necessary measures, at the Community level, to ensure the protection of human rights.

But human rights principles, which impinge upon such a wide and vitally important array of policies at all levels, cannot simplistically and definitively be slotted into a single pigeonhole. Instead, they must be considered to cut across all levels of national and transnational governance and regulation, and each level must be enabled to play its appropriate part. This includes, on the one hand, the United Nations and the Council of Europe with their array of human rights treaties and other instruments and, on the other hand, NGOs, other groups, and individuals, and of course everything that comes in between.

A useful analogy in the context of Community law is the issue of privacy and data protection. This is a classic cross-cutting issue with multiple dimensions which do not fall easily within either the exclusive competence of the Community or that of the Member States. That ambiguity, however, did not prevent the Amsterdam Treaty from providing that all Community institutions would be bound by the relevant privacy principles; nor did it stop it from setting up 'an independent supervisory body' to monitor compliance.[40]

The Community should aim to create what might be termed a 'Common Human Rights Area', in which interlocking and overlapping levels of protection interact synergistically with each other.

B. The Legal Bases for a Human Rights Policy

It sometimes seems to be thought that the reasoning used by the European Court of Justice in its *Opinion 2/94* on Community accession to the European Convention on Human Rights[41] not only prevents such accession in the absence of a specific Treaty amendment, but also makes it virtually impossible to develop a general human rights policy unless it too is specifically authorized by a Treaty amendment. In our view, however, a Treaty amendment is not required in order to provide a legal basis, or legal bases, for the human rights policy we envisage. Such a policy would be perfectly consistent with the jurisprudence of the Court, including its *Opinion 2/94*. At no point in that Opinion did the Court suggest that the protection of human rights was not an objective of the Community, nor did it say that the Community lacked com-

---

[40] Art. 286 EC.   [41] [1996] ECR I–1759.

petence to legislate in the field of human rights. Because of the centrality of this issue, it seems necessary to devote particular and detailed attention to it.[42]

1. Complying with the Interpretations of the European Court of Justice In its jurisprudence, the Court has articulated three critical constitutional principles which inform this field. The first affirms that 'respect for human rights is a condition of the lawfulness of Community acts'. The second affirms that it is the positive duty of the institutions 'to ensure the observance of fundamental rights'. In other words, they are obligated not simply to refrain from violating them, but to ensure that they are observed within the respective constitutional roles played by each institution. Finally, the human rights jurisdiction of the Community extends only 'in the field of Community law'.[43]

A Community Human Rights Policy must, therefore, not extend beyond the field of Community law. That boundary, like many other legal boundaries, is not always razor sharp. There are likely to be some hard cases. But that does mean that the vast areas of Member State action which fall outside the reach of Community law will be beyond the writ of a Community human rights policy. By contrast, all those areas which are regulated by the Community or come within the reach of Community law can and should also be subject to its human rights policy.

Especially since the entry into force of the Single European Act, the question of the legal basis for Community legislation has become critical, given the different political consequences of varying legal bases in terms of voting procedures and the role accorded to the European Parliament. What legal basis, then, could and should be used by the political institutions when exercising their duty to ensure the observance of fundamental rights in the field of Community law?

2. The Specific Treaty Provisions There are several potential legal bases, although attention is given below to only the most salient.

The first is that governing action in a specific field. For example, the Community 'legislative branch' (the Commission, the Council, and the Parliament) could, and in our view should, attach to any legislation it passes a 'human rights clause' dealing with matters such as transparency, the availability of information to interested parties, the possibilities open to those affected to launch an appeal, the availability of legal aid, and the like. This would be consistent with the commitment in Article 1 (*ex* Article A) of the EU Treaty to take decisions 'as openly as possible' and of new Article 255 of the EC Treaty providing for enhanced public access to Community documents. There are few areas of Community activity which cannot, negatively and positively, affect the fundamental rights of individuals and groups. In this way, the Community would consistently and routinely be affirming that it considers its legislative action to conform with its human rights undertakings and would make it possible for those who believe otherwise to take appropriate action.

In some fields, unchallenged Community competences which underpin legislation also coincide with a classic fundamental right—such as the right to freedom of

---

[42] For an excellent analysis of the Opinion see G. Gaja, 'Opinion 2/94' (1996) 33 *CML Rev.* 973.

[43] For an analysis of this jurisprudence see J. H. H. Weiler, 'Fundamental Rights and Fundamental Boundaries: On Standards and Values in the Protection of Human Rights', in Neuwahl and Rosas, note 8 above, at 51.

movement, access to employment, and Article 141 (*ex* Article 119) of the EC Treaty
(EC) establishing the principle that men and women have the right to receive equal
pay for equal work and for work of equal value. In other fields, the importance of
fundamental rights is specifically mentioned—such as in relation to the provisions
dealing with co-operation and development.[44] Similarly, under Article 13 (*ex*
Article 6a) EC as introduced by the Amsterdam Treaty, 'the Council, acting unanimously on a proposal from the Commission and after consulting the European Parliament, may take appropriate action to combat discrimination based on sex, racial
or ethnic origin, religion or belief, disability, age or sexual orientation'. Indeed, such
measures were taken even prior to the enactment of that Article, on the basis of existing non-discrimination provisions, such as in the case of the Broadcasting Directive. Article 13 is especially significant since the right to non-discrimination and the
duties that flow from that right are at the core of a great number of other human
rights and thus provide a broad foundation upon which to build a human rights
policy.

An appropriately broad human rights policy cannot, however, be constructed entirely on the basis of individual provisions of this type. As is the case in a great many
areas of Community activity, certain measures would have to cut across several
fields, in the sense that they have implications for a broad range of horizontal and institutional matters. In relation to these, a prudent usage of Article 308 (*ex* Article
235) would be permissible.

Because this provision was a central focus of *Opinion 2/94* of the European Court
of Justice it is necessary in this context to explore whether our conclusion is compatible with the view expressed by the Court. In its Opinion the Court noted that:

> No Treaty provision confers on the Community institutions any general power to enact
> rules on human rights . . .[45]

This then led the Court to ask whether, in the absence of such express or implied
powers, Article 308 (*ex* Article 235) could provide the necessary legal basis. It
defined the function of the Article thus:

> Article 235 [new Article 308] is designed to fill the gap where no specific provisions of the
> Treaty confer on the Community institutions express or implied powers to act, if such
> powers appear none the less to be necessary to enable the Community to carry out its
> functions with a view to attaining one of the objectives laid down by the Treaty.[46]

In considering whether that Article could then be used as a basis upon which to
proceed with Community accession to the European Convention on Human Rights,
the Court concluded in the following terms:

> That provision, being an integral part of an institutional system based on the principle of
> conferred powers, cannot serve as a basis for widening the scope of Community powers
> beyond the general framework created by the provisions of the Treaty as a whole and, in
> particular, by those that define the tasks and the activities of the Community. On any
> view, Article 235 [new Article 308] cannot be used as a basis for the adoption of provi-

---

[44] Art. 177 EC.   [45] [1996] ECR I–1759, recital 27.   [46] *Ibid.*, recital 29.

sions whose effect would, in substance, be to amend the Treaty without following the procedure which it provides for that purpose.[47]

What then are the implications of this reasoning for the proposal that the Community should adopt a human rights policy which relies, by no means exclusively but at least in part, on Article 308? In our view it is clear that such a policy would be in conformity with the Court's reasoning provided that it:

- does not entail the entry of the Community into a distinct international institutional system;
- does not modify the material content of human rights within the Community legal order; and
- does not have fundamental institutional implications.

In other words, a Community human rights policy which respects the current institutional balance and which scrupulously remains within the field of Community law could be based, in part, on Article 308 EC. The approach suggested in this chapter meets these criteria.

C. Subsidiarity

Finally, a word about the important principle of subsidiarity, which requires that decisions should always be taken at the level closest to the citizen at which they can be taken effectively, thus creating a presumption in favour of action at the level of the Member States except where exclusive Community competence has already been granted.[48]

It seems sometimes to be assumed that the application of this principle requires that responsibility for matters dealing with human rights should remain at the national level. But this is a false assumption which actually undermines the objectives of the principle. Subsidiarity is not a one-way street.[49] Consistently with the principle, Community-level action is warranted if the objective in question cannot adequately be achieved by Member State action alone, and if the scale or effects of the proposed measures favour Community action. Clearly where the measures in question are taken by the Community within the field of Community law it makes no sense to argue that individual Member States are best placed to ensure not only that those measures do not violate human rights but that they do whatever they can to promote respect for them. Moreover, the guidelines contained in the Protocol on subsidiarity attached to the Amsterdam Treaty correctly emphasize that Community action might be necessitated by various factors, including the transnational dimensions of an issue and the existence of treaty obligations.

Thus a Community human rights policy is not only consistent with the principle of subsidiarity, but is in some measure a necessity required by that principle.

---

[47] *Ibid.*, recital 30.

[48] G. de Búrca, 'The Principle of Subsidiarity and the Court of Justice as an Institutional Actor' (1998) 36 *Journal of Common Market Studies* 1; and K. van Kersbergen and B. Verbeek, 'The Politics of Subsidiarity in the European Union' (1994) 32 *Journal of Common Market Studies* 215.

[49] See G. Strozzi, 'Le Principe de subsidiarité dans la perspective de l'intégration européenne: une énigme et beaucoup d'attentes', (1994) 30 *Revue trimestrielle de droit européen* 373.

VIII. THE CONTEXT OF EUROPEAN UNION HUMAN RIGHTS POLICY

A. The Relationship of EU Policy to the Broader Human Rights Setting

An EU human rights policy can be neither conceived nor executed without full account being taken of the broader human rights context in which the Community finds itself. This includes the normative foundations upon which the international and European human rights systems have been constructed, as well as the institutional framework which European States have played a key role in establishing in order to ensure that effect is given to the obligations that they and other States have assumed. But while the European Council, as noted earlier, has long appealed to all States to accede to the principal international instruments to which they are not yet party and to ensure 'more stringent implementation of those instruments', the fact remains that not all EU Member States have ratified even the six core United Nations instruments.[50] Two (Belgium and Ireland) have yet to ratify the Convention against Torture; another (Ireland) is not a party to the Convention on the Elimination of All Forms of Racial Discrimination; three (Belgium, France, and the United Kingdom) have not ratified the Second Optional Protocol (aiming at the abolition of the death penalty) to the International Covenant on Civil and Political Rights (ICCPR); and one (the United Kingdom) has not yet accepted the individual complaints procedure under the (first) Optional Protocol to the ICCPR. The Council's call for 'stringent implementation' also raises the issue of reporting and the desirability of EU States, leading by example. Yet one EU state (Greece) has yet to submit its initial report under one of the UN Covenants which it ratified more than thirteen years ago.[51]

Similarly, although the fifteen Member States of the EU have all been long-term participants in, and very active proponents of, the human rights system established by the Council of Europe, there remain significant and unfortunate gaps in the ratification record of EU States.[52] Thus, for example:

- Protocol No. 4 of 1963, which prohibits imprisonment for breach of contract, guarantees freedom of movement and residence, and bans collective expulsions, has not been ratified by Spain or the United Kingdom;
- Protocol No. 6 of 1983, abolishing the death penalty, has not been ratified by Belgium, Denmark, or the United Kingdom;
- Protocol No. 7 of 1984, dealing with rights of lawfully resident aliens, and rights arising in criminal proceedings, has yet to be ratified by Belgium, Germany, Ireland, the Netherlands, Portugal, Spain, and the United Kingdom.

---

[50] Those instruments are reprinted in United Nations, *A Compilation of International Instruments* (2 vols., 1994). The information concerning UN instruments was derived from the treaty body database of the Office of the UN High Commissioner for Human Rights, on 9 Sept. 1998.

[51] UN Doc. E/1998/22, Annex 1, at 100.

[52] The information concerning Council of Europe instruments was taken from the Council of Europe's website on 9 Sept. 1998. The instruments referred to are reprinted in United Nations, *A Compilation of International Instruments* (1997), vol. II.

While the European Social Charter of 1961 has been ratified by all EU Member States, the various attempts to update it both substantively and procedurally have garnered a lukewarm reception. In particular:

- the Additional Protocol extending the rights recognized has yet to be ratified by Austria, Belgium, France, Germany, Ireland, Luxembourg, Portugal, Spain, and the United Kingdom;
- the Protocol aimed at improving the supervisory machinery has not been ratified by Belgium, Denmark, Germany, Luxembourg, Spain, or the United Kingdom.
- the Additional Protocol providing for a complaints mechanism has been ratified by only five (Finland, Greece, Italy, Portugal, and Sweden) of the fifteen EU States.

The two minority rights treaties adopted by the Council of Europe have also attracted relatively little commitment from within the EU:

- the European Charter for Regional or Minority Languages has been ratified by only two EU States (Finland and the Netherlands);
- the Framework Convention for the Protection of National Minorities has yet to be ratified by eight EU States (only Austria, Denmark, Finland, Germany, Italy, Spain, and the United Kingdom have ratified).

This incomplete record of the EU States sits rather uncomfortably beside the fact that the record of ratification of these treaties by those States which aspire to EU membership has been the subject of careful scrutiny in the context of discussions over the basis for potential membership. It would seem difficult for the Union, either as a matter of fairness or logical consistency, to be imposing requirements on applicant States to meet a level of Community *acquis* which has yet to be fully met by existing Member States.

It might be argued in response to this analysis that the existing level of diversity in relation to the acceptance of international and regional standards is unproblematic and simply honours the principle of subsidiarity by permitting each Member State to decide such matters for itself. But while comprehensive uniformity cannot, and should not, be required in relation to every single international human rights standard, there are powerful reasons for concluding that there must be a common core of shared standards. These should include, as a minimum, the six basic UN treaties and each of the principal Council of Europe treaties, along with their respective protocols. To the extent that this minimum level of uniformity is not achieved, the EU maintains uneven internal levels of human rights commitments and protections, jeopardizes the principles of universality and indivisibility to which it has long paid lip-service, and weakens its own credibility as a human rights proponent especially in relation to its external relations. As noted above, EU leadership is best achieved by example, rather than by urging other States to do what the EU itself has not been willing to achieve.

Indeed, it is curious to be paying homage to the fiftieth anniversary of the Universal Declaration of Human Rights and to be urging other States to mark the occasion by acceding to the principal international instruments, without at the same time embarking upon a major effort to bring the EU's own record up to an optimal level.

Two human rights treaties are specifically referred to in the various EU and EC treaties. They are the European Convention on Human Rights and the European Social Charter. They constitute an important part of the overall context to which we now turn.

B. The EU and the European Convention on Human Rights

The relationship between the Community and the European Convention on Human Rights calls for special comment in the present context. As noted above, the Treaty of Amsterdam commits the Union to 'respect fundamental rights, as guaranteed by the European Convention'. The Convention has also acquired particular significance because of the extent to which it has been cited in the case law of the Court of Justice. The latter has also tended to interpret its provisions in line with the approach adopted by the European Court of Human Rights. The result is that the Convention has played a fundamental role not simply in providing a mechanism for protection but also in underscoring the European commitment to human rights and in emphasizing that such commitment, if taken seriously, involves important concessions which States must make to classical notions of national sovereignty. The European Convention system has become more than a legal safety net. It is now a part of the cultural self-definition of European civilization.

It is for this reason that we return to the long-standing issue of Community accession to the Convention. The reasoning of the European Court of Justice, which concluded that the Treaty would have to be amended to allow Community accession, is unpersuasive. For example, acceptance of the jurisdiction of the European Court of Human Rights, to which the European Court of Justice implicitly seemed to object, cannot reasonably be considered to be of such great constitutional significance as to require a Treaty amendment when the Court was prepared to endorse without demur the Community's acceptance of the dispute-resolution mechanisms of the World Trade Organization. It is true, however, that the Court's Opinion has rendered these matters temporarily moot, and that this is no longer a battle that can be fought on these terms.

Equally disappointing was the reluctance of Member States to take action to include the required amendment called for by the Court as part of the new Treaty of Amsterdam. It appears to be highly anomalous, indeed unacceptable, that whilst membership of the Convention system is, appropriately, a prerequisite of accession to the Union, the Union itself—or at least the Community—remains outside that system. The negative symbolism is self-evident. From a pragmatic point of view, the most troubling aspect is not the persistent, even if less than acute, lacunae in the judicial protection of human rights within the Community legal order. After all, the European Court of Justice does look to the substantive obligations of the European Convention and, as already noted, has more recently begun to pay considerable attention to the jurisprudence of the Strasbourg organs.

As the Council of Europe grows, as the European Convention on Human Rights adapts and absorbs new Member States and new legal traditions and understandings, it is regrettable that there will be no explicit Community voice within the European Convention on Human Rights. Such a voice would have enabled the sensibilities and experiences of the Community to form an integral part of the evolving jurisprudence and extra-juridical activity of the European Convention system. This, almost as much as any other reason, requires that accession to the European Convention on Human Rights remain a live objective. For that reason, the issue should be revisited at the next intergovernmental conference to amend the Treaty.

The setback as regards the European Convention on Human Rights should not prevent other similar activity. The Community could accede, without amending the Treaties, to the European Social Charter, to the Convention of the Council of Europe on Data Protection, and to the Vienna Convention on Human Rights and Application of Biology and Medicine, to give but three examples.

By the same token, taking account of the spirit of subsidiarity, the Community as such does not need to be a member of all human rights treaty regimes. It could, nevertheless, still play an important role in encouraging its Member States to adhere to the various instruments noted above as well as, for example, the Council of Europe's Framework Convention for the Protection of National Minorities and to the core human rights conventions of the International Labour Organization.

C. *The Role of Economic and Social Rights in EU Policies*

The principle of the indivisibility of human rights is a keystone of EU policy. This means that economic, social, and cultural rights should be accorded as much importance as civil and political rights. This principle not only reflects the doctrine embodied in both the Universal Declaration of Human Rights and the Council of Europe's human rights regime but also the consensus on the importance of the European social model. However, the Union's rhetorical commitment has hardly been matched by its practice.[53] This is true in both the internal and external dimensions of EU policy.

1. Social Rights within the Community   In terms of the Community itself, the revisions to the social rights provisions of the Amsterdam Treaty fell considerably short of the proposals made by a range of expert groups, as well as in the report of the *Comité des Sages*, chaired by Maria de Lourdes Pintasilgo.[54] In addition, there is a strong tendency in the great majority of Community documents to focus on 'social policy', designed to promote 'social protection' or overcome 'social exclusion', rather than to focus on 'social rights'.[55] A recent Commission proposal to 'individualize' social rights could assist in this regard, although the human rights dimension should remain central in any such approach.[56]

[53] See S. Sciarra, 'From Strasbourg to Amsterdam: Prospects for the Convergence of European Social Rights Policy', in this vol.; and M. Poiares, 'We Still Have not Found what We Have Been Looking For: The Balance between Economic Freedom and Social Rights in the EU', in this vol.

[54] See note 6 above.

[55] e.g. 'Social Action Programme 1998–2000, Commission Communication', Doc. COM(98)259 of 29 Apr. 1998.

[56] 'The individualisation of rights would aim to halt the practice of taking account of personal links when ensuring social protection of an individual. It would contribute to bringing social protection in line with legislation governing employment contracts, which considers workers as individuals. More

The Treaty of Amsterdam refers in non-restrictive terms to 'respect for human rights and fundamental freedoms', and the preamble to the Single European Act refers to 'the fundamental rights recognized in . . . the European Social Charter'. On this basis, and because the Court of Justice has long referred to 'the constitutional traditions common to the Member States' in identifying applicable human rights standards, one would expect to find a range of references to economic and social rights. In fact, there have been remarkably few such references.

In relation to the Community's internal social policy, note should be taken of the importance of:

- recognizing the right to organize;
- promoting accession by the Community to the European Social Charter;
- encouraging more consistent reference in the judgments of the European Court of Justice to the jurisprudence of the Council of Europe's Committee of Independent Experts on the European Social Charter;
- encouraging all Member States to ratify ILO Convention No. 111; and
- improving the standing rules of the European Court, as suggested below, in relation to social rights issues.[57]

A Group of Experts on Fundamental Social Rights is expected to report by the end of 1998 as a follow-up on the Pintasilgo Report.[58] Very careful attention should be given to their recommendations with a view to strengthening social rights within Europe.

2. Social Rights in External Relations   In terms of the role of social rights in the Union's external relations, two examples of the inadequate attention accorded to them must suffice. The first concerns the criteria for future accession to the Union. In Agenda 2000 the Commission made reference to the compliance of applicant States with the European Social Charter and the UN Covenant on Economic, Social, and Cultural Rights, although minimal attention was actually devoted to the relevant rights.[59]

The second, and perhaps more surprising, example concerns the EU's extensive development co-operation activities. In its landmark resolution of 28 November 1991 on human rights, democracy, and development, the European Council listed a range of positive measures to be taken, but only one was potentially of direct relevance to social rights: 'ensuring equal opportunities for all'. This is an imprecise and flexible concept, but it is often considered to be compatible with policies which accord a very low priority to social rights. Even if interpreted in a more positive sense, it seems to fall far short of a commitment to promoting realization of the inherent social rights of all human beings as a full component of a broader human rights policy.

---

generally, individualisation is in line with the general trend towards a greater autonomy of the individual'. See 'Modernising and Improving Social Protection in the European Union, Communication from the Commission' (1998), http://europa.eu.int/comm/dg05/jobs/forum98/en/texts/socprot.html, sec. 2.4.

[57] See text accompanying note 107 below.

[58] See 'Groupe d'experts en matière de droits fondamentaux', European Commission DG V, Doc. V/D/2/MJC D(97), 12 Sept. 1998.

[59] Commission of the European Communities, *Agenda 2000*, COM(97)2000 final, 2 vols.

A similar concern applies to the Commission's 1998 policy statement in the context of the Lomé Convention, which, from a social rights perspective, speaks only of the goal of 'promoting pluralist civil society in a context of sustainable social and human development'.[60] This broad language is not followed up by reference to any specific social rights-related policies. This is consistent with the fact that the chapter B7–70 budget line is largely confined to activities relating to civil and political rights, despite the fact that economic and social rights are of vital importance to the well-being of many of the stated priority target groups, including women, children, minorities, and indigenous peoples. Funding for projects relating to economic and social rights must be sought under other budget lines.

There are two problems with this approach. One is that investment in social development has been accorded a low priority in most EU aid,[61] even though increased attention is now being given to health and education. The other is that there remains a very significant difference between general social-sector funding and support for economic and social rights as human rights. The time has come for the Union to end its neglect of these rights and to develop and fund a specific programme for the promotion of economic, social, and cultural rights. The funding of initiatives in this field is particularly important. At present these rights are trapped in a vicious circle which leads some governments to argue that neither their conceptual foundations nor the practical measures for their implementation are as yet sufficiently developed to warrant the adoption of specific measures. This approach only reinforces their continuing neglect and overlooks the extent to which the deeper understanding achieved in relation to civil and political rights has in part been possible precisely because of such funding.

Consistently with this approach, it is time for the Union to move beyond the old 'social clause' debate by exploring new approaches.[62] That debate sought to link respect for certain human rights with participation in trade agreements and preference schemes.[63] The Commission has indicated that it will present a Communication in 1998 on the development of the external dimension of European social policy. The adoption by the ILO in June 1998 of the Declaration on Fundamental Principles and

[60] Communication from the Commission to the Council and the European Parliament entitled 'Democratization, the Rule of Law, Respect for Human Rights and Good Governance: The Challenges of the Partnership between the European Union and the ACP States', Doc. COM(1998)146 final, 12 Mar. 1998, para. 2.

[61] Allocations to the social sector accounted for only 10.5% of project aid between 1990–5: ADE final report, *Evaluation of EU Aid to ACP Countries managed by the Commission, Phase I* (July 1997), 20.

[62] See European Parliament, *Summary Record of Presentations made at the Public Hearing on the Human Rights Clause in Trade Agreements* (1996). For a critique of the motivation underlying much of the agitation for a social clause see P. Alston, 'Labour Rights Provisions in U.S. Trade Law: "Aggressive Unilateralism"?', in L. Compa and S. Diamond (eds.), *Human Rights, Labor Rights, and International Trade* (1996), 71. In relation to the more positive, incentive-based approach recently adopted by the EU see Brandtner and Rosas, note 13 above.

[63] e.g. in a 1996 Resolution the Parliament called on 'the Commission to ensure, as part of the activities that it carries out as the European Union's representative at the World Trade Organization, that minimum humanitarian clauses are defined to determine the legality of trade transactions, particularly with regard to work imposed on children, prisoners or other disadvantaged sections of the population': Resolution on human rights throughout the world in 1995–6 and the Union's human rights policy, 12 Dec. 1996, [1997] OJ C20, 94, para. 68.

Rights at Work[64] provides an important opportunity for concerted EU support to its development co-operation partners designed to promote the relevant rights (freedom of association and collective bargaining, elimination of forced labour, abolition of child labour, and elimination of discrimination in respect of employment and occupation). These standards have not received sufficient priority in EU co-operation activities. Moreover, three EU States have yet to ratify the core ILO human rights Convention No. 111 dealing with the latter issue. In general, the proposed Communication should also seek to elaborate a more sustained emphasis on economic and social rights than has so far been the case.

The existing human rights clauses in EU agreements provide an ideal basis upon which to pursue a more systematic approach to economic and social rights,[65] and to promote the rights which have been the prime focus of the 'social clause' debate and are now reflected in the new ILO Declaration.

This Communication, along with other Community projects and policies dealing with social rights in external relations, should:

- reflect consistent use of the terminology of human rights;
- rely as far as possible upon the internationally recognized standards for social rights, including those of the United Nations, the ILO, and the Council of Europe;
- target specific rights-based objectives as priorities; and
- promote the acceptance of the human rights principles of monitoring and accountability.

IX. THE COMMISSION

A. The Commission's Role, especially in the Field of External Relations

In relation to a very large number of countries, the Commission has played a vital, constructive, and often innovative role in supporting human rights and democracy initiatives, providing funds for election support and observation, and ensuring humanitarian assistance. Its budget is one indicator of its particular significance in terms of human rights and democracy. The 'European initiative for democracy and the protection of human rights' (chapter B7–70 of the Community budget) began in 1994 with a budget of 59.1 million euros. It has since almost doubled and some 97.4 million euros were available for grants in 1998. Salaries for EU officials are not included in this amount. By way of comparison, the regular UN budget funding for the Office of the UN High Commissioner for Human Rights, much of which is devoted to salaries, is currently less than one-quarter of this amount (at around US$22 million).[66]

---

[64] ILO Declaration on Fundamental Principles and Rights at Work and its Follow-up, adopted by the International Labour Conference at its Eighty-sixth Session, Geneva, 18 June 1998.

[65] See E. Riedel and M. Will, 'Human Rights Clauses in External Agreements of the European Communities', in this vol.

[66] J. van der Klaauw, 'European Union' (1997) 15 *Netherlands Quarterly of Human Rights* 204, at 208.

The role, impact, and effectiveness of the Commission's activities would be considerably enhanced if measures were taken to address the three major problems which we believe impede the work of the Commission in the human rights area. They are: its legal basis; its internal fragmentation; and its lack of staff, expertise, and bureaucratic 'clout'.[67]

The legal basis: chapter B7–70, the principal human rights budget line, was one of those most heavily affected by the ruling of the Court of Justice of 12 May 1998[68] and the subsequent large-scale freeze on many disbursements and new initiatives.[69] The inadequacy of acknowledged Community competences in this area had already been highlighted by the debates around a draft regulation proposed by the Commission in December 1997, well before the Court's judgment.[70] Those debates have since gathered speed and urgency and have focused on two draft regulations presented by the Council in July 1998. As one report to the Parliament put it, the uncertainty illustrates the fact that the TEU 'does not provide a clear legal basis for comprehensive action by the Union in the promotion of democracy, the rule of law and human rights other than the one upon which the CFSP is based', and that second-pillar basis is inappropriate in a number of respects for this purpose.[71] We deal below with what we consider to be the principal shortcomings in the proposed Council response.

Internal fragmentation: as noted earlier,[72] the problem of administrative fragmentation is illustrated by the fact that the 'Standing Inter-Departmental Human Rights Co-ordination Group' consists of nineteen different entities from within the Commission. In the view of the Parliament, the Commission's strategy for using its funds is lacking and the responsibility unduly divided. It considers the Co-ordination Group to be 'a mirror image of the fragmentation of responsibilities'.[73] There is no doubt that outsiders wishing to understand where and how Commission policy is being developed and implemented will be utterly defeated by existing arrangements. Even more troubling, however, is that insiders themselves, including the representatives of Member States, Members of Parliament, and EU officials, are not much better off. The lack of co-ordination is thus associated with inefficiency, fragmented policy responses, unclear lines of responsibility, an inability to develop necessary expertise, the marginalization of Parliament, and a general lack of transparency.

Lack of staff, expertise and bureaucratic 'clout': the fragmentation of responsibility means that none of the bureaucratic entities responsible for human rights policy is large enough to develop the range of staff and the level of expertise required to contribute to the development of the 'consistent, transparent, efficient, credible and conspicuous' human rights policy to which the Union aspires. This is compounded

---

[67] This analysis draws on Simma, Aschenbrenner, and Schulte, note 14 above.
[68] Note 18 above.
[69] J. van der Klaauw, 'European Union' (1998) 16 *Netherlands Quarterly of Human Rights* 378.
[70] Van der Klaauw, note 66 above, at 208.
[71] 'Working Document on the proposal for a Council regulation (EC) on the development and consolidation of democracy and the rule of law and respect for human rights and fundamental freedoms', *rapporteur*: Mr Galeote Quecedo, COM(97)0357 of 12 Feb. 1998.
[72] See note 26 above.
[73] Resolution on setting up a single co-ordinating structure within the European Commission responsible for human rights and democratization, preamble paras. R and S, 19 Dec. 1997, Doc. A4–0393/97 [1998] OJ C14/403.

by the lack of clear responsibility within the Commission. In formal terms the position is that the President of the Commission is responsible for the overall promotion of a human rights policy, while another Commissioner (currently Mr Van den Broek) is responsible for the horizontal and thematic issues relating to human rights. In practice, however, a range of Commissioners deal with human rights issues. These issues not only cut across thematic portfolios, such as development, social issues, humanitarian affairs, migration, foreign policy, and commercial policy, but also arise in relation to particular regions for which different Commissioners have responsibility. The result is that no individual Commissioner and no senior EU bureaucrat can be identified as the visible face of human rights, either within the Commission or viewed from outside. While perfect consistency and co-ordination will never be attainable, the existing scope for letting many different human rights policies bloom within the Commission is greatly excessive. As one informed observer has accurately concluded, 'the current system . . . simply does not work'.[74]

B. Development Co-operation, Trade, and Related Policies

The EU, especially since around 1990, has done much to ensure the inclusion of human rights provisions in a wide range of its external relations activities affecting aid, trade, and other forms of co-operation.[75] They include: the development co-operation arrangements under the Lomé IV Convention; a variety of other co-operation programmes relating to third countries, including TACIS, PHARE, MEDA, and the Bosnia and Herzegovina Regulations; trade agreements with third countries and in relation to the operation of the EC's Generalized System of Preferences (GSP); and humanitarian assistance policies.[76]

It is appropriate that these policies should place an emphasis upon the principles of universality, indivisibility, and interdependence, reliance upon international standards, a recognition of the need to work with and through multilateral organizations, an insistence upon the centrality of human rights in international relations, a commitment to dialogue with partners, and a preparedness to balance pro-active policies designed to encourage respect for human rights with reactive policies designed to respond to human rights violations, including through sanctions as a last resort.

In recent years there has been a very strong emphasis upon concerns closely related to human rights, such as democratization, the rule of law, and good governance.[77] While it is essential that human rights issues be addressed within their

[74] Gijs M. de Vries, 'Human Rights and the Foreign Policy of the European Union', unpublished paper, Apr. 1998.

[75] See generally K. Tomaševski, *Between Sanctions and Elections: Aid Donors and Their Human Rights Performance* (1997), chap. 3; K. Arts and J. Byron, 'The Mid-term Review of the Lomé IV Convention: Heralding the Future?' (1997) 18 *Third World Quarterly* 73; and K. Arts, 'Principles of Cooperation for Development in ACP/EC Relations', in: E. Denters and N. Schrijver (eds.), *Reflections on International Law from the Low Countries in Honour of Paul de Waart* (1998), 86.

[76] Simma, Aschenbrenner, and Schulte, note 14 above.

[77] See, e.g., the Communication from the Commission to the Council and the European Parliament entitled 'Democratization, the rule of law, respect for human rights and good governance: the challenges of the partnership between the European Union and the ACP States', Doc. COM(1998)146 final, 12 Mar.1998.

broader context, it is also important that the distinctive and authentic human rights component of such policies be ensured. In the Commission's overall external relations policies, specific human rights standards and initiatives seem to have enjoyed an excessively low profile to date in the general context of efforts to promote democracy and the rule of law. While programmes such as PHARE and TACIS have some human rights components to which attention can be drawn in order to deflect criticism, these elements are far smaller than they should be and often seem to be little more than incidental.[78]

In fact, a recent evaluation study undertaken for the Commission recommended that the PHARE and TACIS labels be dropped in favour of a renamed 'EU Democracy Programme'.[79] In some respects, this recommendation highlights a much larger problem. The EU's insistence upon separate programmes for different areas reflects several entirely legitimate considerations, including the distinct legal bases invoked, the specific historical origins of the various initiatives, and the different bureaucratic and political considerations which are at work in support of specific programmes. At a deeper level, however, the preference for maintaining an alphabet soup of diverse and odd-sounding programmes may well be due to a deep-seated reluctance to accept that a democracy programme in its fullness should be undertaken by the EU. In this respect, it might be seen as another manifestation of the reluctance to embrace human rights and related issues as an authentic dimension of the Union.

There are four issues that should be given more prominence in the future development of the Union's policies in these areas.

1. Economic and Social Rights   The first concerns the negligible role accorded to economic and social rights. As noted earlier, despite a strong commitment in principle to these rights, EU co-operation policies have generally tended to neglect them. In the present context two aspects warrant attention. The first is that the financial and related crises dominating the situation in many Eastern European, Asian, and Latin American States make it all the more imperative that a greater emphasis be placed upon these rights, both for their own sake and because of their vital role in reinforcing efforts towards democracy and respect for civil and political rights. The second is that many of the policies already pursued by the Commission could be adapted relatively easily in order to reflect a better balance. To give but one example, the Commission could earmark specific funds for countries wanting to develop the role of national human rights institutions in promoting respect for these rights through more effective monitoring at the domestic level.

2. Transparency and Accountability   The second issue is the achievement of a greater degree of transparency and accountability. Given the amounts of money involved, the considerable potential impact of the projects and the hopes that they represent from a human rights viewpoint, it is essential that the Commission's human rights activities be reasonably transparent. At present, official policy statements and formal reports are readily available, as are some evaluation and financial reports.

[78] See European Commission, *The European Union's Phare and Tacis Democracy Programme: Compendium of Ad-hoc Projects 1993–1997* (1998).

[79] See 'Evaluation of the Phare and Tacis Democracy Programme—1992–1997', Section 6.1, http://eu ropa.eu.int/comm/dg1a/evaluation/ptdp.

Overall, however, the situation is unsatisfactory and makes a careful external evaluation of the effectiveness of the policies virtually impossible. For example, access to country strategy papers and to the national indicative programmes is highly restricted, despite their importance in ensuring that human rights are taken adequately into account in policy-making.

Similarly, very few evaluations have been performed in relation to human rights projects and those that are undertaken do not have any significant human rights dimension.[80] Moreover, the information available on the relevant Commission websites provides few insights into these issues beyond official statements of policy. Similar concerns have been expressed by the Parliament.[81] The Commission should address this issue specifically in the context of a detailed statement designed to improve the transparency of the co-operation process. In addition, it should prepare and publish an annual report providing an overview of the main human rights initiatives reflected in its co-operation activities and an evaluation of their effectiveness.

It is especially important in the context of co-operation programmes aiming to promote human rights that adequate possibilities exist to ensure the Union's accountability in cases in which it is alleged that EU development policies have had a significantly adverse impact or have failed to respect human rights. In theory, various avenues of redress already exist. In principle, the Parliament's Development and Co-operation Committee is able to express concerns and to question Commission officials, but in practice it is ill-equipped to pursue most such concerns effectively. Similarly, EU citizens and others resident or based in a Member State may petition the Parliament, but this is a time-consuming procedure, one which is not available to residents of third States. Another avenue is the Ombudsman, who can receive complaints of maladministration, but that Office has yet to show whether it can be effective in relation to cases of this type. The Court of Auditors is not well placed to pursue individual cases, and for the most part does not. Finally, while a complaint for breach of contractual liability can be brought before the Court of Justice,[82] such a remedy is never going to be very accessible in practice to those complaining of the impact of EU development policies. It has therefore been suggested that the Union should establish an Inspection Panel along the lines of that which has existed for some years within the World Bank.[83] The Commission should consult broadly to assess the most appropriate form which such an initiative within the EU should take.

3. Human Rights Clauses   The third issue concerns the various types of human rights clauses that are now included in over fifty Community agreements.[84] It is entirely appropriate for such clauses to become a standard feature of all such agree-

---

[80] Since it began operations in Jan. 1997, the Evaluation Unit within DC1A has undertaken or begun some 40 evaluations. Of these only one was available on-line by mid-Sept. 1998, and it contains no significant treatment of human rights issues *per se*. See *ibid*.

[81] Resolution on setting up a single co-ordinating structure within the European Commission responsible for human rights and democratization, para. 19, 19 Dec. 1997, Doc. A4–0393/97 [1998] OJ C14/403.

[82] Art. 288 TEC.

[83] See I. Shihata, *The World Bank Inspection Panel* (1994); and P. Feeney, *Accountable Aid: Local Participation in Major Projects* (1998).

[84] Brandtner and Rosas, note 13 above.

ments. The Union should resist measures, whether by developed or developing countries, to exclude such provisions in future agreements. The principal value of these clauses is to ensure that the human rights dimensions of an issue are taken into account whenever relevant. No particular importance should thus be attached to the fact that no such clause has yet been formally invoked as the basis for suspending or otherwise not carrying out trade preference or aid arrangements. This has not prevented a range of other measures from being undertaken in order to enhance respect for human rights with various countries covered by such agreements.[85]

Several innovations are needed, however, in order to improve the operation of these clauses:

- the system of annual country reports, recommended below,[86] should be put in place. These would facilitate a more consistent, coherent, and transparent application of the clauses;
- criteria to be used in applying the clauses should be drawn up. They should go beyond those already identified by the Commission,[87] and should reflect an appropriate balance between the concern for consistency and the need for flexibility; and
- the Community should establish procedural rules to be followed for the suspension and termination of external agreements, and the powers of the Commission in this respect should be clarified.

4. Human Rights Training   If EU officials are to do everything possible not only to make EU co-operation policies consistent with respect for human rights but also actively to promote their realization, they need to have a full understanding of the relevant standards and procedures and of their potential implications in the context of a wide range of development policy situations. Given the complex and increasingly technical nature of these standards and the need to avoid arbitrary or subjective interpretations, systematic training is an essential component of an effective EU policy in this area. Such training is not currently provided on any systematic basis; the Commission should initiate an appropriate programme of this type.

C. The Commission after Amsterdam

Quite apart from the shortcomings that characterize the existing role of the Commission, the entry into force of the Amsterdam Treaty will bring a variety of new demands which would be sufficient in themselves to require a thorough rethinking of the Commission's human rights activity. Apart from the expanded general Community mandate in relation to human rights, discrimination, and related issues, to which the Commission will have to respond, there are three other significant aspects.

The first is that the new arrangements in relation to the common foreign and security policy, which are dealt with below in relation to the Council,[88] will provide not only the opportunity, but also a clear need, for the Commission to work more closely with the Council, through the Troika as well as more generally. The Commission will

---

[85] Riedel and Will, note 65 above.   [86] See text preceding note 97 below.
[87] Doc. COM(1998)146 final, 12 Mar. 1998, Part III, para. 14.
[88] See text accompanying note 103 below.

also need to develop a more systematic input to the work of Council Committees such as COHOM (the Committee on Human Rights).

The second is the Treaty's provision for the suspension of Member States' rights in response to a 'serious and persistent breach' of the 'principles of liberty, democracy, respect for human rights and fundamental freedoms, and the rule of law'.[89] The Commission is empowered to propose that the Council meet to make such a determination. In order to do so it will need to have developed a methodology and guidelines for dealing with such cases, and it will need to be in a position to provide the Council with a detailed analysis of its reasons for concern. This will require the development of the necessary capacity as soon as possible, rather than leaving the provision as a virtual dead-letter to be resuscitated only after a crisis has erupted. For this purpose, the Commission, in consultation with the Council and Parliament, should undertake a study of the procedures to be applied in considering whether to suspend the rights of a Member State for a serious and persistent breach of human rights.

Thirdly, the Amsterdam Treaty formalizes the fact that the acts of the Council, Commission, and Parliament are reviewable by the European Court of Justice in cases in which violations of human rights are alleged. In order to minimize the uses of this procedure in relation to its own work the Commission will need to scrutinize draft legislation and a wide range of other proposed measures to ensure its conformity with the applicable human rights standards as defined in Article 6(2) (*ex* Article F(2)) TEU.

D. Proposed Reforms: A Commissioner and a Directorate General

For all of these reasons, both practical and symbolic, it is essential that human rights become the subject of a central and separate portfolio within the Commission. This raises the question whether the Commissioner for Human Rights should have other responsibilities. On the one hand, the adding of other portfolios may make organizational sense, given that important aspects of human rights policy overlap with responsibilities in fields such as social policy, immigration, and asylum, citizens' rights, humanitarian assistance, and the like. Moreover, status and authority within the Commission sometimes seem to be linked to the number of staff and the size of the budget of a portfolio. On the other hand, there seems to be a significant risk that combining human rights with one or more other portfolios would make the former a subsidiary concern and create possible or actual conflicts of interest on the part of the Commissioner. This would be especially the case if the Commission moved to bring external relations under the responsibility of a Vice-President, as suggested in a Declaration agreed by Member States at Amsterdam, and if that new post were also expected to take the lead on human rights.

It is therefore proposed that a separate Commissioner for Human Rights be appointed within the Commission. It would be best if no major additional portfolio responsibilities were linked thereto; if that is considered to be impossible for general administrative reasons, the only linkage that would seem to be compatible would be

---

[89] Art. 7 TEU.

with humanitarian affairs and the European Community Humanitarian Office (ECHO). In order to facilitate a strong role in policy co-ordination and the mainstreaming of human rights, consideration should also be given to according the status of Vice-President to that Commissioner.

Some observers will inevitably seek to reject this proposal on the grounds that there are already too many Commissioners and, perhaps even more problematically, too many Directorates General. As a result, there are strong pressures towards reducing the existing twenty-six Directorates General down to some ten to fifteen. But the need for administrative streamlining is a poor justification for dismissing the need to remedy a major shortcoming in the Commission's make-up.

The Directorate General which would be responsible to the Commissioner would have three principal functions and responsibilities:

1. In its 'mainstreaming' function it will bear the principal horizontal co-ordinating responsibility within the Commission to ensure that in all their legislative and administrative activities the various Commission services give the necessary attention to human rights concerns. This is a *co-ordinating* responsibility since we do not envisage the Directorate General for Human Rights having an exclusive internal monopoly in this field. On the contrary, we are concerned to enhance human rights sensibility throughout the Commission. This will happen only through regular, streamlined interaction between the various specialized services and the one service (the Directorate General) which has specialist expertise in human rights.
2. The Directorate General will also be the principal interlocutor and recipient of the reports or surveys presented by the Vienna Monitoring Agency. These reports will be the basis for Commission action designed to deal with specific problems highlighted by the Monitoring Agency, in so far as Community-level action is appropriate. Similarly, the Directorate General could undertake or co-ordinate an evaluation function in relation to the human rights components of the development co-operation and other external relations activities of the Commission.
3. Finally, and possibly most importantly, the Directorate for Human Rights will be responsible for developing policies and initiatives designed to make the protection of existing human rights more effective in the long run. This will be done through: contacts and co-ordination with Member States; support for, and consultation with, non-governmental organizations in the field of human rights; legislation attentive to the changing demands required to ensure respect for human rights, contacts, and co-operation with similarly situated bodies at the international and national levels; and, critically, co-operation and consultation within the other parts of the Commission and its specific services.

All three functions will operate synergistically. What is envisaged is a period of strategic thinking and planning in each and every one of the myriad operational services of the Commission, throughout the Secretariat and all its Directorates General. Each Directorate and/or Division should prepare, in consultation with the

Directorate General for Human Rights, an analysis of those areas of responsibility which are 'human rights sensitive'—either in the sense that the Commission or the Community itself may, unwittingly, be an accomplice to abuse or that within the relevant sphere of responsibility the Commission or Community could enhance the respect for fundamental human rights. Following such a period of internal assessment, each service would draw up a plan, setting out the steps and means required to further the objective of enhanced respect for human rights. Once again, this would be done in co-operation with the accumulated expertise of the Directorate for Human Rights. Eventually, a new matrix of action will emerge across the area of activity of the Community. In some cases, action will be required across the board; in others, it will be tailored to the functional and operational specificities of each service.

The means of action will range from educational programmes, measures promoted through citizen and resident information and advice bureaux, and the proposing of strategic legislation and enforcement measures where merited through the support and funding of public and semi-public groups and NGOs operating wholly or partly within the sphere of application of Community law.

The Directorate General for Human Rights will have special responsibility in the field of European Citizenship, some of the details of which are dealt with below.[90]

X. THE EUROPEAN PARLIAMENT

Since at least the late 1970s, the European Parliament has played a very important role in promoting human rights as an integral component of EU policies in both the internal and external domains. It has done so in a variety of ways, including through annual reports on different issues, debates, and resolutions, withholding of its assent to external agreements in cases where serious human rights problems persist, insistence upon increased funding for human rights and democratization programmes, sending of election monitors and parliamentary delegations, and regular calls upon the Commission and the Council to adopt more human rights-friendly policies.[91]

In considering the ways in which Parliament's contribution might be further enhanced in the future, three issues stand out. The first concerns the internal institutional allocation of responsibilities for dealing with human rights-related matters. At present, there are two separate forums which have all too little interaction. They are the Committee on Civil Liberties and Internal Affairs Committee and the Sub-Committee on Human Rights of the Committee on Foreign Affairs, Security, and Defence Policy.[92] The Parliament itself has acknowledged the need for its own 'bodies dealing with human rights and democracy issues to be more effectively co-ordinated'.[93] The existing arrangement, born of various internal accommodations,

---

[90] See text accompanying note 112 below.

[91] For an excellent overview of Parliament's role see P. Craig and G. de Búrca, *EU Law: Text, Cases, and Materials* (2nd edn., 1998), 66. See also de Vries, note 74 above.

[92] M. Westlake, *A Modern Guide to the European Parliament* (1994), 209.

[93] Resolution on setting up a single co-ordinating structure within the European Commission responsible for human rights and democratization, para. 15, 19 Dec. 1997, Doc. A4–0393/97 [1998] OJ C14/403.

reflects and even reinforces the split between the internal and external dimensions of human rights policy which we argue is counter-productive and ultimately incompatible with the quest for a coherent EU policy.

The second issue concerns standards. The Parliament continues to entertain a debate over the normative content of human rights which, on some occasions, has led to a virtual stalemate, especially in relation to the scope and status of social rights. This is essentially an anachronistic debate which, in almost all other contexts, has long since been settled. All EU Member States are parties to the European Social Charter and the International Covenant on Economic, Social, and Cultural Rights. Moreover, a significant range of social rights find explicit recognition in the EU and EC Treaties.

The third and most important issue concerns the relationship between the Parliament on the one hand and the Council and the Commission on the other.[94] Neither has proved to be a consistent or reliable interlocutor on human rights matters. In the case of the Council, Parliament has long been highly critical of the Council's annual memorandum describing the human rights activities of the Council and the Member States in the framework of CSFP on the grounds that it is lacking in detail and is submitted on an irregular and unpredictable schedule. Similarly, reports that are drawn up within the CFSP framework and deal with the human rights situation in third countries are not routinely made available to Parliament. In the case of the Commission, the relationship is also based on inadequate information flows and a degree of uncertainty as to the type of information which Parliament is entitled to seek from the Commission. For several years now the Parliament has sought to spell out the structure that Commission reports should follow and the types of information it would like to receive. Much of this relates to analysis as well as raw data. The response has been limited.

This situation has helped to create and perpetuate something of a vicious circle. The Council and Commission seem unwilling to involve the Parliament in various aspects of human rights policy-making, although the latter has been able to use its budgetary and other limited forms of authority to good effect in certain areas. The Parliament, for its part, is perceived by many observers to have acted too often in ways that might reflect an expectation that it will not be taken very seriously. It is thus sometimes unable to resist the temptation to endorse positions which are lacking in nuance, are not necessarily consistent over time or from one case to another, and in the case of external policy issues are not readily reconcilable with the EU's own internal policies. Its frequent use of 'urgency procedures' in relation to specific situations has also drawn considerable criticism, including from within its own ranks.[95] These shortcomings are, in turn, taken by the Council and the Commission as a confirmation of the appropriateness of their own relatively unforthcoming attitudes.

It is time for this vicious circle to be broken. Although the Parliament was disappointed in terms of many of the reforms that it had hoped to achieve in the Amsterdam Treaty, its powers have nevertheless been steadily augmented. Amsterdam contains a number of innovations which will enhance the role of the Parliament in

---

[94] See Craig and de Búrca, note 91 above, at 70–3.   [95] De Vries, note 74 above, at 14.

human rights matters. They include: the change from co-operation to co-decision as the basis for decision-making in relation to a number of important issues (such as discrimination on grounds of nationality, the right of establishment for foreign nationals, equal opportunities and equal treatment, consumer protection, and data protection); the requirement of consultation in relation to issues of discrimination on all of the prohibited grounds, except for nationality;[96] the role of the Parliament in any procedure under Article 7 (*ex* Article F.1) of the TEU to suspend the rights of a Member State for a 'serious and persistent breach' of human rights; and the inclusion within the Community budget of operational expenditure under the third pillar, which has been classified as non-compulsory expenditure, thus increasing Parliament's role. Parliament itself can make effective use of these opportunities in order to shape a stronger human rights policy.

In addition, many of the proposals contained in the present report would, if adopted, make a very big difference to the capacity of Parliament to exercise a sustained, informed, and responsible role both in exercising oversight and acting as a catalyst in this area. The member of the Commission responsible for human rights would, in the normal course of affairs, appear before the Parliamentary hearings. In its enhanced constitutional role in relation to the appointment of the President and Members of the Commission, Parliament has an important role in ensuring that human rights are given significant weight. Parliament could attach importance to both the competence and the human rights commitment of the designated Commissioner.

Parliament will also play an important supervisory role in overseeing the Commission and the Monitoring Agency, as well as in terms of development of policy, budget, and execution. To the extent that the new human rights policy involves legislation, Parliament will play its role as provided in the Treaties. The monitoring proposals reflected in this report would transform the Parliament's capacity to analyse, to formulate precise and focused recommendations, and to evaluate action taken in response to its own opinions. This applies in particular to the proposed *Annual Report on Human Rights in the World*, the annual report on human rights within the EU to be produced by the Human Rights Monitoring Agency, and the more detailed, regular, and analytical reports to be submitted by the Commission and the Council in relation to their respective areas of responsibility. All of these reports would enable the Parliament to overcome the information gap from which its deliberations currently suffer, would help it to structure its work in a more systematic fashion, would make it easier to identify genuine priorities and to accord less prominence to the hobby-horses sometimes championed by individual MEPs.

Similarly, the access to justice sensibility that informs much of this chapter must also extend to activities under parliamentary auspices, such as the Petitions Committee[97] and the Ombudsman.[98] The function of both extends beyond human rights

[96] Art. 13 TEC.

[97] See generally E. Marias, 'The Right to Petition the European Parliament after Maastricht' (1994) 19 *European LR* 169; E. Marias, 'Mechanisms of Protection of Union Citizens' Rights' in A. Rosas and E. Antola (eds.), *A Citizens' Europe: In Search of a New Order* (1995), 207; Astéris Pliakos, 'Les conditions d'exercice du droit de petition' (1993) 29 *Cahiers de droit européen* 317.

[98] On the current activities of the Ombudsman see J. Söderman, 'A Thousand and One Complaints:

but also overlaps in some considerable measure. It is our impression that neither is especially well known beyond narrow circles and their visibility could and should be enhanced.

Several other recommendations also emerge from this analysis:

1. Parliament should consider moving towards a single integrated Committee structure for dealing with both the internal and external dimensions of human rights policy.
2. The indivisibility of the two sets of human rights should be acknowledged by the Parliament in a way which puts an end to the sterile debates over what is in fact a non-issue.
3. An effort should be made to reinforce the specialist human rights expertise available to the secretariat of the Parliament.
4. There should be greater interaction between the European Parliament and the human rights committees which exist in many of the national parliaments, both within the Community and outside. A more effective relationship with the former would reinforce the impact of Parliament's own work and provide it with a better sense of national policies and concerns.
5. Parliament should develop more systematic, open, and transparent means by which the knowledge and views of non-governmental groups can be taken into account in its work.
6. Parliament should encourage the Commission to undertake a study of the procedures that could be used in considering whether to suspend the rights of a Member State for a serious and persistent breach of the principles contained in Article 6(1) (*ex* Article F(1)) TEU, which include human rights.
7. Parliament should develop a more systematic means of monitoring the implementation of its various policy recommendations by the bodies to which they are directed, and seek to reduce the repetitiveness of the content of its resolutions.

XI. THE ROLE OF THE COUNCIL, ESPECIALLY IN THE FIELD OF EXTERNAL RELATIONS

The Council has always had a central role in relation to human rights issues, particularly because of the limited competences of the Community, the sensitivity of human rights for both the foreign and domestic policies of Member States, and the cross-cutting nature of the issues.[99] The Council's role is, however, of particular importance at the present time for two reasons. The first is because of the implications for human rights of certain provisions in the Amsterdam Treaty designed to

The European Ombudsman *en Route*' (1997) 3 *European Public Law* 351; and K. Heede, 'Enhancing the Accountability of Community Institutions and Bodies: The Role of the European Ombudsman', (1997) 3 *European Public Law* 587.

[99] On the role of the Council in general see M. Westlake, *The Council of the European Union* (1995).

strengthen the framework for the Common Foreign and Security Policy (pillar two). The second reason is that the Court of Justice ruling of 12 May 1998[100] on competences has compelled a re-examination of the grounds upon which the Union operates in relation to the different areas of human rights.

In addition, the Council is uniquely placed to contribute to the co-ordination of human rights concerns among the three pillars which, in the view of most observers, has been clearly inadequate to date. Equally, if the call for a better matching of internal and external human rights policies is to be answered, it will be the Council, both at the level of the European Council and in the specialist settings, that will need to play a leading role. To date, however, the Council has been seen rather as the principal stumbling block in the quest to develop a better integrated and more consistent EU human rights policy.

As in all areas of EU policy-making, the Council performs a variety of tasks in the human rights field. It has a co-ordinating role in relation to some aspects of Member State policies, it assists in the formulation of EU policy, and it has a central co-ordinating and representational role in many external relations settings and especially within the context of multilateral organizations. The objectives which it might thus be expected to pursue in relation to human rights can perhaps best be gauged by reference to the formulation included in the two draft regulations sent to the European Parliament in August 1998. They are designed to establish the legal bases which permit the financing and administering of Community action to enhance human rights, democracy, and the rule of law.

Because of the importance of the proposed approach, it is necessary to quote *in extenso* from the relevant text. Thus, in part, each of the draft regulations provides that:

> . . . consistent with the European Union's foreign policy as a whole, the European Community shall provide technical and financial aid for operations aimed at:
> 1. promoting and defending the human rights and fundamental freedoms proclaimed in the Universal Declaration of Human Rights and the other international instruments concerning the development and consolidation of democracy and the rule of law, in particular:
>
> > (a) the promotion and protection of civil and political rights;
> > (b) the promotion and protection of economic, social, and cultural rights;
> > (c) the promotion and protection of the human rights of those discriminated against, or suffering from poverty or disadvantage, which will contribute to reduction of poverty and social exclusion;
> > (d) support for minorities, ethnic groups, and indigenous peoples;
> > (e) supporting local, national, regional, or international institutions, including NGOs, involved in the protection or defence of human rights;
> > (f) support for rehabilitation centres for torture victims and for organizations offering concrete help to victims of human rights abuses or help to improve conditions in places where people are deprived of their liberty in order to prevent torture or ill-treatment;
> > (g) support for education, training, and consciousness-raising in the area of human rights;

[100] Note 18 above.

(h) supporting action to monitor human rights, including the training of observers;

(i) the promotion of equality of opportunity and non-discriminatory practices, including measures to combat racism and xenophobia;

(j) promoting and protecting the fundamental freedoms mentioned in the International Covenant on Civil and Political Rights, in particular the freedom of opinion, expression and conscience, and the right to use one's own language;

2. supporting the processes of democratization, in particular:

(a) promoting and strengthening the rule of law, in particular upholding the independence of the judiciary and strengthening it, and support for a humane prison system; support for constitutional and legislative reform;

(b) promoting the separation of powers, particularly the independence of the judiciary and the legislature from the executive, and support for institutional reforms;

(c) promotion of pluralism both at political level and at the level of civil society by strengthening the institutions needed to maintain the pluralist nature of that society, including non-governmental organizations (NGOs), and by promoting independent and responsible media and supporting a free press and respect for the rights of freedom of association and assembly;

(d) promoting good governance, particularly by supporting administrative accountability and the prevention and combating of corruption;

(e) promoting the participation of the people in the decision-making process at national, regional, and local level, in particular by promoting the equal participation of men and women in civil society, in economic life, and in politics;

(f) support for electoral processes, in particular by supporting independent electoral commissions, granting material, technical and legal assistance in preparing for elections, including electoral censuses, taking measures to promote the participation of specific groups, particularly women, in the electoral process, and by training observers;

(g) supporting national efforts to separate civilian and military functions, training civilian and military personnel and raising their awareness of human rights;

3. support for measures to promote the respect for human rights and democratization by preventing conflict and dealing with its consequences, in close collaboration with the relevant competent bodies, in particular:

(a) supporting capacity-building, including the establishment of local early warning systems;

(b) supporting measures aimed at balancing opportunities and at bridging existing dividing lines among different identity groups;

(c) supporting measures facilitating the peaceful conciliation of group interests, including support to confidence-building measures relating to human rights and democratization, in order to prevent conflict and to restore civil peace;

(d) promoting international humanitarian law and its observance by all parties to a conflict;

(e) supporting international, regional, or local organizations, including the NGOs, involved in preventing, resolving, and dealing with the consequences of conflict, including support for establishing *ad hoc* international criminal tribunals and setting up a permanent international criminal court, together with measures to rehabilitate and re-integrate the victims of human rights violations.[101]

---

[101] See the '[Draft] Council Regulation (EC) laying down the requirements for the implementation of development co-operation which contribute to the general objective of developing and consolidating

This list seems, at first glance, to be appropriately detailed and comprehensive. Upon closer scrutiny, however, several of its features are rather striking. The first is the remarkable lack of balance reflected in a policy which is so wide-ranging in relation to two sets of third States (those with development co-operation agreements with the EU and those, mainly in Central and Eastern Europe, subject to other specific EU programmes) but which is then not matched by an appropriately comprehensive human rights policy in the field of external relations more generally. The fact that many countries in the world do not fit within the framework of the proposed regulations does not mean that the Union should not address relevant human right issues in those countries.

The second feature, as underlined earlier, is the absence of an equivalent set of Community policies and programmes as an internal counterpart to such an impressive external set of goals and commitments. In other words, whilst the two proposals demonstrate the Union's enthusiasm for supporting human rights and democracy in third countries, there is surprisingly little sensibility to these very issues as regards the Community activity itself. The third feature is the extent to which a variety of very specific civil and political rights policy objectives are identified, whereas economic and social rights objectives are stated in a notably vague and general fashion.

Nevertheless, these objectives provide an excellent illustration of the types of goals which should be considered to be every bit as relevant to second pillar or CFSP activities, as to first pillar co-operation arrangements. Naturally, the constitutional bases for various actions would be different, as would the respective roles played by Member States, Union, and Community. But, as far as possible, the policies pursued at each level could seek to reinforce those at the other levels.

A. The Relationship between the Council and the Commission and Parliament

The two draft regulations referred to above have important implications in terms of this relationship. Without needing to challenge the objectives, the means, or the balance of institutional responsibilities reflected therein, there are several aspects of the proposals which warrant attention.

First, when the Commission carries out the tasks entrusted to it under the draft regulations, it will be necessary for the lead role to be taken by the Directorate General responsible for Human Rights and the new Human Rights Commissioner, albeit of course in co-operation with the various Commission services responsible for development co-operation and for other relations with third countries in the framework of Community co-operation policy. It makes no sense further to entrench the fragmentation of overall human rights responsibility among different Commission services, nor does it make sense to promote an unnecessary gap between the internal and external dimensions.

democracy and the rule of law and to that of respecting human rights and fundamental freedoms'; and its companion '[Draft] Council Regulation (EC) Laying down the requirements for the implementation of community operations, other than those of development co-operation which, within the framework of community co-operation policy, contribute to the general objective of developing and consolidating democracy and the rule of law and to that of respecting human rights and fundamental freedoms in third countries', both of 1 July 1998.

Secondly, the democratic accountability of the Community's proposed action is weak. The European Parliament will, effectively, only be able to exercise control through the budgetary procedure but is excluded from substantive scrutiny and dialogue. In contrast, the 'Human Rights and Democracy Committee', proposed to be set up under Article 12 of both regulations, will perform a powerful oversight role. Yet it will be composed of Member State representatives, even if it is to be chaired by the Commission. The role of the European Parliament must be strengthened and made commensurate to that of the Member States or, in effect, the Council. As envisaged in the present draft, the Committee lacks precisely the democratic accountability which it will be supposed to promote in third countries.

Thirdly, the programmes to be undertaken under the proposed regulations involve the distribution of large sums of money (estimated by the Council at 400 million euros over five years, but likely to be greater) which will be administered either directly by, or on behalf of, the Community by a variety of public, semi-public, or private agencies. Neither under the proposed regulations, nor under the standing procedures for the Ombudsman, are there provisions for individual complaint and/or investigation of the manner in which these funds are spent, or policies are administered, by or on behalf of the Community. It is an area which is susceptible to abuse and misuse. In accordance with the general rule-of-law principle established within the Community, appropriate safeguards should be implemented. The Ombudsman, or a surrogate for the Ombudsman (such as the Inspection Panel suggested above[102]) should be established to receive and investigate such complaints and, where necessary, to take further necessary action.

B. Proposed Reforms in Relation to the Council's Human Rights Role

It will, of course, be for the European Council to take the lead in adopting the initiative for a fully-fledged human rights policy for the Union. And, to the extent that the internal dimension of the human rights policy involves legislation, the Council will play its normal constitutional role in the legislative process, both at primary level and through comitology. The critical role of the Council will, however, be in the external dimension of the human rights policy.[103]

The Union has a key role to play in enhancing human rights in all aspects of its common foreign and security policy and not only in relation to democratization, the rule of law, and good governance in narrowly defined areas of the world. There is, after all, no material, geographical, or political limitation on the reach of the Union under the second pillar. Thus, human rights should become an important, regular, and systematic dimension of the Union's foreign posture under pillar two.

[102] See text accompanying note 83 above.

[103] For a detailed analysis see A. Clapham, 'Where is the EU's Human Rights Common Foreign Policy, and How is it Manifested in Multilateral Fora?', in this vol. Also M. Fouwels, 'The European Union's Common Foreign and Security Policy and Human Rights' (1997) 15 *Netherlands Quarterly of Human Rights* 291; J. Packer, 'Reflections on the Development of a Common and Comprehensive Foreign Policy of the European Union', in *Contemporary International Law Issues: New Forms, New Applications*, Proceedings of the Fourth Hague Joint Conference [of the American Society of International Law and the Nederlandse Vereniging voor Internationaal Recht] held in The Hague, The Netherlands, 2–5 July 1997, 231; and N. Winn, 'The Proof of the Pudding is in the Eating: The EU Joint Action as an Effective Foreign Policy Instrument?' (1997) 13 *International Relations* 19.

Until now, little attention seems to have been given to developing the Council's capacity to make human rights a significant part of its activities.[104] The secretariat of the Council is not currently well-equipped to perform human rights functions. While the Council's Committee on Human Rights (COHOM) plays an important role, it deserves a more focused and better co-ordinated secretariat interlocutor with which to work.

The Amsterdam Treaty creates the new post of CFSP (Common Foreign and Security Policy) High Representative (to be filled by the Council Secretary General). This post has already been popularly dubbed 'Mr or Monsieur Pesc', based on the French acronym for CFSP which is PESC. There will also be a new form of CFSP 'troika' consisting of the Council President, the CFSP High Representative and the Commission. We believe that within the framework of the 'Mr PESC' function under pillar two, a special Human Rights Office should be established. This Office should work in close co-ordination with the Commission's new Human Rights Directorate General, while preserving the constitutional demarcations between pillar one and pillar two. An appropriately modified version of the more robust Community policies should guide CFSP.

Two objections to this proposal can be anticipated. They are that the Council Office will duplicate some of the work that the new Commission structure is supposed to perform and that its creation will only exacerbate the policy disagreements that characterize so much of the Commission–Council relationship. The effect will be to paralyse, or at least further complicate, overall EU human rights policy. These are valid concerns but they underestimate the extent to which the Commission and the Council do, and should, perform rather separate functions under their respective pillar one and pillar two responsibilities. The proposal is also predicated upon the hope that greater expertise and more systematic information, on both sides, will help to align the different policy perspectives.

As already noted, there is no constitutional bar for the Union's foreign policy to pursue policies which would have as their objective and would be aimed at promoting and defending the human rights and fundamental freedoms proclaimed in the Universal Declaration of Human Rights and the other international instruments concerning human rights, the development and consolidation of democracy, and the rule of law in third countries, even outside specific Community policies. The existing Community model should provide guidance to the type of activities to be pursued under pillar two. It warrants emphasizing the fact that this pillar does not contain any constitutional limitations to consensual action in this area.

The specific polices proposed in relation to the Council revolve around monitoring, co-operation, responding to violations, and general policy promotion.

Monitoring: under the auspices of the Commission, which would draw upon its 129 'delegations' in third countries, and in co-operation with 'Mr PESC', an annual report should be prepared giving an overview and details of the state of human rights in

---

[104] The Council's own accounting of its human rights-related activities is reflected in the Annual Memorandum to the European Parliament on this subject. These are reproduced in the relevant issues of the *EPC* (*European Political Co-operation*), *Documentation Bulletin* and its successor *European Foreign Policy Bulletin* on-line at <http://www.iue.it/EFPB/Welcome.html>.

the world from a European Union perspective. Part of this Report would cover those States coming within the EU's co-operation framework—and the main raw material would be generated by the Commission and its delegations. Reports for other countries would draw primarily upon information generated by the Office of Human Rights of CFSP using all resources available to it. It is acknowledged, however, that the precise modalities for drawing up the annual report would clearly need to be the subject of considerable discussion and negotiation among the institutions concerned. It would thus be foolhardy to seek to prescribe them in any detail in this context.

It is sometimes suggested that such reporting, long called for by others, should focus only on countries with which the EU has a specific relationship. But this would make little sense in terms of the resulting coverage and would require many invidious decisions as to which countries to cover and which to overlook. The resulting patchwork would be seen as discriminatory and incomplete.

The very publication of this report—the idea of which, it can safely be anticipated, will be contested by many in the national foreign policy establishments—should be a constant and stable feature of the Union's foreign policy posture. Third countries will simply know that their human rights record will be one element in their relationship with the Union and that it will not be an *ad hoc*, subjective, or avoidable dimension of the relationship.

As noted above,[105] the Parliament has consistently criticized the annual memorandum presented to it by the Council on the grounds that it is both inadequate and greatly delayed. The new report which we propose would be sent annually to the European Parliament and would provide it with an ideal basis upon which to play a constructive and informed role in relation to its long-standing human rights concerns.

Cooperation: over time, the CFSP should adopt and put in place the same types of pro-active programmes which are already a feature of the Community's co-operation and development co-operation frameworks. These would involve support for public and private organizations involved in the enhancement of respect for human rights. Such initiatives could be characterized as common action and be subject to all pillar two management, budgetary, and decisional procedures. They would be designed to give the CFSP the necessary flexibility to provide positive forms of assistance to reinforce its other policy orientations. Perhaps the best example is the possibility for the Council to offer funding and expertise to assist governments in third States to establish national human rights commissions. This is a high-priority objective of the UN human rights programme and has been strongly supported by the EU in that context. Again, however, it is somewhat anomalous that national commissions have not been set up within most EU countries.[106]

---

[105] See text accompanying note 94 above.

[106] There is, of course, a wide range of institutions within different EU countries which perform various, and in some cases most, of the functions undertaken by a fully fledged national human rights commission. It is beyond the scope of this chap. to review those arrangements, but it is revealing that the 'Good Friday' agreement of 10 Apr. 1998 relating to Northern Ireland provides that human rights commissions will be established in both Ireland and Northern Ireland and commits the British government to consider bringing together various existing functions into a 'unified Commission'. But, as has been argued elsewhere, even that proposal falls significantly short of constituting a national human rights commission, *per se*, for Britain. See S. Spencer and I. Bynoe, *A Human Rights Commission: The Options for Britain and Northern Ireland* (1998).

Responding to violations: the Union cannot remain indifferent to large-scale violations of human rights. While acknowledging the particular difficulties faced by the
EU in relation to especially complex and controversial cases, we believe it is essential
for the EU to continue to strive to ensure an appropriate balance between the positive and negative dimensions of its policies. Whilst we do not agree with those who
advocate the automatic application of economic or other forms of sanctions in certain circumstances, and while we consider that the impact of any proposed sanctions
upon human rights must always be taken fully into account, it is clear that sanctions
should not be excluded from the range of policy options available to the Union.
Their appropriate form and duration will inevitably differ from case to case, but
there will be instances in which there is no other reasonable response.

There are two developments which could assist greatly in enabling a tailored and
more effective EU response to violations. The first is the better integration of human
rights considerations into defence and security policy as well as economic and commercial policies. The second is the development of the expertise and routine consideration of human rights which would result from the creation of the proposed
Human Rights Office.

General policy promotion and representational policies: the EU has a particularly
important representational role, especially *vis-à-vis* other international organizations, in the context of which greater attention should be paid to human rights. These
issues are increasingly prominent on the agenda of the UN Security Council and
should be made so in relation to those of the World Bank and the International
Monetary Fund, to name but two important forums. The EU should take a more
pro-active role, both through its individual Member States and collectively, to promote the incorporation of human rights concerns into the mainstream activities undertaken within such settings.

XII. THE EUROPEAN COURT OF JUSTICE AND
ACCESS TO JUDICIAL REMEDIES

The European Court of Justice deserves immense credit for pioneering the protection of fundamental human rights within the legal order of the Community when the
Treaties themselves were silent on this matter. It has been the Court that has put in
place the fundamental principles of respect for human rights which underlie all subsequent developments. It is worth noting that, in the context of individual rights, the
Court, historically, developed a special 'user-friendly' approach to access. This contrasted with the approach taken in other areas in which individual reliance on Community measures to vindicate rights—whether *vis-à-vis* Community institutions or
Member States—is linked to the doctrine of direct effect which requires clear, precise, and unconditional measures.

In the field of human rights, however, the Court has always permitted individual
challenges to the legality of measures on the grounds of an alleged violation of
human rights, even though these, by definition, could not always be considered clear

and precise in the absence of a written Community 'bill of rights' or formal accession to the European Convention. The value and importance of this approach should be underlined. The Court has not only made the material provisions of the European Convention *de facto* binding on the Community, but has also commenced in recent time to rely more extensively on the jurisprudence of the Strasbourg organs. This development is to be strongly welcomed.

There is, however, one area where the judicial protection of individuals within the legal order of the Community and as concerns rights within the field of application of Community law is unsatisfactory, and the remedy to this inadequacy lies in the hands of the Court.

Individual and group standing to challenge Community measures directly before the Court(s) through the means of Article 230 (*ex* Article 173) EC is, and has been, extremely restrictive. The conditions created by the Court of Justice to satisfy the Treaty requirements of being 'individually and directly concerned' are such that individual plaintiffs or groups representing individuals are for the most part shut out from direct challenges before the European Court.[107] This situation is particularly grave when the challenges in question concern alleged violations of human rights by Community institutions or by Member States operating on behalf of the Community.

The Court has indicated in its jurisprudence (such as in the *Greenpeace Case*[108]) that individuals may always seek a remedy before national courts which may, or in prescribed circumstances must, make a reference to the European Court of Justice under Article 234 (*ex* Article 177). But the expansion and complexity of Community governance has demonstrated that the complementarity of Articles 230 and 234 (*ex* Articles 173 and 177) is no longer assured. The rules of standing before national courts may defeat meritorious plaintiffs without the case ever reaching the European Court of Justice. Likewise, there is no guarantee that national courts will always make a preliminary reference.

As a result, the issue of access to justice in the field of human rights requires review both by the Court itself and by the Community legislator. Specifically, consideration should be given to the following measures:

1. The Court should revisit its jurisprudence on Article 230 (*ex* Article 173) with a view to facilitating the standing of individuals and public interest groups alleging the violation of fundamental human rights. Articles 6 and 13 of the European Convention on Human Rights should guide such jurisprudence. Specifically, access to the ECJ should always be available where no other guaranteed judicial route is available before national courts or where national courts have refused to make a reference.

2. The Court should also revisit its jurisprudence and, if necessary, request a revision of its Statute, in order to facilitate intervention by recognized public interest groups. The current automatic right of intervention of Member

---

[107] C. Harlow, 'Access to Justice as a Human Right. The European Convention and the European Union', in this vol.

[108] Case C–321/95 *Stichting Greenpeace Council (Greenpeace International)* v. *Commission*, 2 Apr. 1998.

States must be balanced by a right of intervention by other public groups which may better inform the Court of sensitive societal concerns in the field of human rights

3. Within the sphere of application of Community law, rules of standing before national courts should be amended to allow recognized non-governmental organizations to initiate cases. The Community has already pioneered such a scheme in the field of consumer protection and the same principle should be extended to human rights more generally.

4. Access to justice is often defeated by lack of the resources required to bring meritorious cases or test cases even where procedurally such action would be possible. The Directorate General for Human Rights should be authorized to oversee an adequate legal aid scheme to facilitate the funding of meritorious cases in the field of human rights. Since such cases might be directed at the Commission itself, independent intermediaries must also be found to oversee the allocation of such funding without, however, having their hands tied by conflict of interest.

There is reason to be concerned by the dangers caused by refusal of national courts to make references in the field of human rights on the basis of Article 234, especially when the issue concerns an alleged violation by a Member State within the sphere of application of Community law. At present, the only remedy available to the individual is to lodge a complaint with the Commission in the hope that it will take the matter up through negotiation, and eventually by commencing proceedings under Article 226 (*ex* Article 169). This is an unsatisfactory situation, both practically and symbolically. In meritorious cases individuals should have access to courts without the sanction of those they may be complaining about.

In effect, there should be recognition in the procedural field of the same principle which animated the Court substantively in its *Francovich* jurisprudence. In relation to matters which concern a Community violation, it has already been proposed that the European Court of Justice should revisit its jurisprudence relating to Article 230 (*ex* Article 173). But this would not help *vis-à-vis* Member States.

What is needed is a Treaty amendment to Article 227 (*ex* Article 170) which would allow in such cases for recognized public interest groups to bring an action before the European Court of Justice—although only after the Commission itself declines to do so. The merit of this proposal lies not only in enhancing the judicial protection of human rights within the Community legal order, but also in preventing Member States having to defend before the European Court of Human Rights measures adopted on behalf of the Community without the latter having the right to defend itself.

XIII. THE EUROPEAN HUMAN RIGHTS MONITORING AGENCY

Monitoring is an indispensable element in any human rights strategy. Systematic, reliable, and focused information is the starting point for a clear understanding of the nature, extent, and location of the problems which exist and for the identification of possible solutions. It is also a necessary element in any strategy to garner the support of civil society and the community at large for measures to promote and protect the human rights of vulnerable groups. The transnational dimension of many human rights challenges, combined with the need to facilitate co-ordinated responses within the Union, demand that a general monitoring function be performed by the Community. The principal need is to produce an annual survey of human rights within the EU which would be factual, objective, and designed to facilitate informed policy-making. But it must be emphasized that Community-level monitoring is separate from policy-making, policy implementation, and enforcement. Those functions would not be entrusted to the agency.

Indeed there is no assumption that any form of Community-level action need necessarily follow from the results of the monitoring process. In egregious cases and where a matter is within Community competence, the Community would be expected, and even required, to react to the reports provided to it by the Monitoring Agency. But it will often be the case that the specific measures to be taken either will fall outside the fields of competence of the Community, or would, in any event, be more effectively taken at the national level. Thus, in various ways, we consider that the principle of subsidiarity is again fully compatible with the proposed policy initiative.

It is proposed either that a separate monitoring agency be created or that the jurisdiction of the Vienna Monitoring Centre on Racism and Xenophobia should be enhanced so as to make it into a fully-fledged agency with monitoring responsibility over all human rights in the field of Community law. The latter proposal is put forward because it seems likely to be more politically palatable and less administratively challenging than the creation of an entirely new agency. That option should, however, be pursued if it is more acceptable to Member States. The remainder of this analysis focuses on the Vienna option.

The same logic which justified the establishment of the Vienna Centre, the same legal basis which underpins that initiative, and the same manner of functioning all apply equally to the proposed expanded agency. For those reasons it is highly instructive to review some of the principal elements cited in the Preamble to the Regulation setting up the current Centre:

> (1) Whereas the Community must respect fundamental rights in formulating and applying its policies and the legal acts which it adopts; whereas, in particular, compliance with human rights constitutes a condition of the legality of Community acts;

This first paragraph restates, in an admirably succinct manner, much of the approach that is called for earlier in this chapter.

(2) Whereas the collection and analysis of objective, reliable and comparable information on the phenomena of racism, xenophobia and anti-Semitism are therefore necessary at Community level to provide full information to the Community on those phenomena so as to enable the Community to meet its obligation to respect fundamental rights and to enable it to take account of them in formulating and applying whatever policies and acts it adopts in its sphere of competence;

The importance of monitoring is thus acknowledged, although it is not apparent that the phenomena mentioned are fundamentally different in nature from many of the broader human rights concerns with which our present chapter is also concerned.

(14) Whereas in order to carry out this task of collecting and analysing information on racism, xenophobia and anti-Semitism as well and as independently as possible and in order to maintain close links with the Council of Europe, it is necessary to establish an autonomous body, the European Centre on Racism and Xenophobia (Centre), at Community level with its own legal personality;

. . .

(20) Whereas, in order to enhance Co-operation and avoid overlap or duplication of work, the tasks assigned to the Centre pre-suppose close links with the Council of Europe, which has considerable experience in this field, as well as Co-operation with other organizations in the Member States and international organizations which are competent in the fields related to the phenomena of racism and xenophobia;

. . .

(23) Whereas the Centre must enjoy maximum autonomy in the performance of its tasks;

These three paragraphs underscore the importance of independence which is a necessary element in any effective and authentic human rights institution, while at the same time noting the need for close collaboration with other relevant human rights bodies—especially, in this instance, the Council of Europe.

(15) Whereas the phenomena of racism, xenophobia and anti-Semitism involve many complex, closely interwoven aspects which are difficult to separate; whereas, as a result, the Centre must be given the overall task of collecting and analysing information concerning several of the Community's spheres of activity; whereas the Centre's task will concentrate on areas in which sound knowledge of those problems is particularly necessary for the Community in its activities;

The analysis reflected in this paragraph is particularly apposite to the broader human rights focus since it highlights the impossibility of artificially separating those issues which fall directly within the Community's competence and those which do not. But rather than drawing the conclusion that the Community should thus have no role, it draws the far more logical and acceptable conclusion that, while all relevant information must be collected, particular emphasis must be given to matters which are of relevance to the Community.

(16) Whereas racism and xenophobia are phenomena which manifest themselves at all levels within the Community: local, regional, national and Community, and therefore the information which is collected and analysed at Community level can also be useful to the Member States' authorities in formulating and applying measures at local, regional and national level in their own spheres of competence;

. . .

(17) Whereas therefore the Centre will make the results of its work available to both the Community and the Member States;

These paragraphs reinforce the earlier one by noting that there is no question of excluding any particular levels within society from the remit of the Centre and emphasizing, as we also do, that action at the level of the Community itself will often be unnecessary. This, in turn, in no way limits the role of the Community in making the relevant information available to other levels of government to facilitate their policy-making endeavours.

(18) Whereas, in the Member States, there are numerous outstanding organizations which study racism and xenophobia;
(19) Whereas the co-ordination of research and the creation of a network of organizations will enhance the usefulness and effectiveness of such work;

These paragraphs recognize the essential role of non-governmental organizations in this field and foreshadow a strong co-operative and networking approach between them and the Centre.

The rationale offered by these preambular paragraphs for establishing a European Monitoring Centre on Racism and Xenophobia is entirely compelling.[109] What is not compelling, from a broader perspective, is to limit the focus of such a centre exclusively to racism and xenophobia. Both constitutionally and pragmatically the same rationale that has been developed in relation to those issues can and should be extended to the entire area of human rights coming within the field of application of Community law. The same complexity, the same need for multi-level action, and the same need for autonomy and independent legal personality all apply equally to the broader focus on human rights with which this chapter is concerned. This is reinforced by the new commitments in the Treaty of Amsterdam to respect human rights and to combat all forms of discrimination. In terms of the legal basis for such an initiative, there would appear to be no doubt that it is sufficient.[110]

The European Council should thus make a statement confirming its overall commitment to ensuring effective action to promote respect for human rights by recognizing that a monitoring mechanism is not only a desirable, but also an essential, Community contribution. Accordingly, the objectives of the existing Centre should be expanded and adapted to enable it to perform the necessary tasks.

The new Vienna Human Rights Monitoring Agency should be given a set of objectives which would closely follow those that apply in the case of the existing Centre. In order to give a clear sense of what is involved, the following model is proposed:

1. The prime objective of the Vienna Agency shall be to provide the Community and its Member States reliable and comparable data at European level on respect for human rights in the Community in order to help them when they

[109] See C. A. Gearty, 'The Internal and External "Other" in the Union Legal Order: Racism, Religious Intolerance and Xenophobia in Europe' in this vol.
[110] As Prof. Gaja notes: '*Opinion 2/94* does not appear to imply that the Treaty [would need to] be amended in order to establish within the European Community a monitoring system concerning the respect of human rights by Community institutions and by Member States within the scope of Community law': Gaja, 'New Instruments and Institutions for Enhancing the Protection of Human Rights in Europe?', in this vol.

take measures or formulate courses of action within their respective spheres of competence.

2. The Agency will study the various aspects of human rights and their abuses and examine examples of good practice in dealing with such abuses. To these ends, in order to accomplish its tasks, the Agency shall:

   a. collect, record and analyse information and data, including data resulting from scientific research communicated to it by research centres, Member States, Community institutions, international organizations, and non-governmental organizations;

   b. build up co-operation among the suppliers of information and develop a policy for concerted use of their databases in order to foster, where appropriate at the request of the European Parliament, the Council, or the Commission, wide distribution of their information;

   c. carry out scientific research and surveys, preparatory studies, and feasibility studies, where appropriate, at the request of the European Parliament, the Council, or the Commission. In doing so, the Centre shall take account of already existing studies and other activities (conferences, seminars, ongoing research, publications) in order to avoid duplication and guarantee the best possible use of resources. It shall also organize meetings of experts and, whenever necessary, set up *ad hoc* working parties;

   d. set up documentation resources open to the public, encourage the promotion of information activities, and stimulate scientific research;

   e. formulate conclusions and opinions for the Community and its Member States;

   f. develop methods to improve the comparability, objectivity, and reliability of data at Community level by establishing indicators and criteria that will improve the consistency of information;

   g. publish an annual report on the situation of human rights within the sphere of application of Community law, highlighting examples of good practice, as well as on the Centre's own activities;

   h. establish and co-ordinate a European Human Rights Information Network consisting of the Centre's own units, which shall co-operate with national university research centres, non-governmental organizations, and specialist centres set up by organizations in the Member States or international organizations;

   i. facilitate and encourage the organization of regular round table discussions or meetings of other existing standing advisory bodies within the Member States, with the participation of the social partners, research centres, and representatives of competent public authorities and other persons or bodies involved in dealing with human rights.

In a similar manner, the organizational arrangements, management structure, and budgetary accountability of the new Agency could also be adapted from those of the existing Centre. The most important function of the Monitoring Agency would be the preparation of an annual survey of human rights within the EU. This survey would be forwarded to the Commission and the Parliament for consideration, as well as to the Member States for information.

Finally, it should again be made clear what is not envisaged in calling for the establishment of such a Monitoring Agency. It will not be a policy-making body. It will not be responsible for implementing any human rights policies. It will have no enforcement powers. And it will not address itself solely to the institutions of the Community. Indeed its keys partners will be Member States and the broader network of social partners, research centres, public authorities, and groups with expertise in the human rights field.

XIV. SELECTED ISSUES

Most of this chapter has been devoted to consideration of the procedural and institutional reforms or innovations which would be required in order to sustain and drive a more coherent, comprehensive, and effective human rights policy on the part of the EU. The principal exception concerns certain aspects of external policy which have been considered in greater depth. In the section that follows, brief consideration is given to some of the key concerns that have arisen in the course of the broader examination of EU policy in relation to a few selected issues of concern. It must be emphasized, however, that this listing is highly selective and does not necessarily reflect the overall importance of the issues selected or the lesser importance of issues not dealt with here, such as racism and xenophobia, which are clearly of particular importance in the current climate. In relation to those and many other issues, the reader is advised to consult the specialist studies that have been drawn up and are published elsewhere.[111] Moreover, even those studies are by no means comprehensive and many areas of importance remain to be dealt with in other contexts.

A. European Citizenship

Currently, the limited number of rights mentioned in the citizenship chapter (Part Two of the EC Treaty) are not sufficient to meet the gravity of the concept of European citizenship.[112] We focus here on just two dimensions of that issue—freedom of movement and transparency.

1. Free Movement Free movement is among the most visible privileges which are attached to European citizenship. The implementation of this right is still far from complete. In order to promote awareness of existing rights, the current piecemeal legislation on free movement and accompanying rights should be replaced by a common framework on the 'legal status of European citizens and their families', in which

---

[111] See the other chaps. in this vol.

[112] See generally S. O'Leary, 'The Relationship between Community Citizenship and the Protection of Fundamental Rights in Community Law' (1995) 32 *CML Rev.* 519; P. Neussl, 'European Citizenship and Human Rights: An Interactive European Concept' (1997) 24 *Legal Issues of European Integration* 47; and M. La Torre (ed.), *European Citizenship: An Institutional Challenge* (1998).

differentiation between 'privileged' (economically active) and 'non-privileged' European citizens should be kept to a minimum. Further, the institutions of the Union should complete the measures proposed by the Commission on 1 July 1998 in response to the March 1997 'Report of the High Level Panel on Free Movement of People', chaired by Simone Veil, and continue to examine other measures in response to the more than eighty recommendations made by the Panel.

2. Transparency   Transparency affects the quality of citizens as political beings. Without effective transparency, political responsibility, political control, and the true exercise of political rights and duties are all inhibited or impaired. In order to achieve the necessary degree of transparency, the Community's enhanced freedom of information policy, reflected in Article 255 EC, is not sufficient in itself. This aspect is developed further below.[113]

B. Equality and Non-discrimination

The Community's commitment to the principle of non-discrimination and the promotion of equality is longstanding and increasingly deep-rooted. The principle of equality is a fundamental principle of Community law, which binds not only the Community in all of its activities but also the Member States in relation to all of their activities which fall within the scope of Community law. The inclusion of Article 13 in the EC Treaty following Amsterdam, which provides for measures 'to combat discrimination based on sex, racial or ethnic origin, religion or belief, disability, age or sexual orientation', provides the occasion for sustained reflection on the most effective means by which to achieve its objectives. In the longer term, consideration should be given to the reinforcement of this provision through the addition of a general equal treatment provision in Article 3 EC which would go beyond gender to cover all of the prohibited grounds of discrimination.

In the medium term, consideration should be given to the adoption of a directive covering non-discrimination and equal treatment in relation to all of the grounds mentioned in Article 13 (*ex* Article 6a). Such a directive could be based on Articles 13 and 137 (*ex* Articles 6a and 118) (working conditions) and, if necessary, Article 308 (*ex* Article 235) EC.[114] The aim would be to mirror the provisions of the existing Directive 76/207 on gender, but with additional provisions designed to ban harassment in the workplace along with the provision of an accompanying right to an effective remedy, and to require employers to monitor the composition of the workforce in terms of gender, race, and disability to establish a workplace equal opportunities policy.

In seeking to mainstream these policies, the Commission Directorate General with responsibility for human rights could either supplement or replace the existing inter-service groups dealing with issues such as disability and race.

In relation to *sex equality*, consideration should also be given to adoption by the Community of the Council of Europe's notion of 'parity democracy' in relation to the fair representation of women in the workplace and to the adoption of provisions

---

[113] See text accompanying note 127 below.
[114] See generally C. Barnard, 'Gender Equality in the EU: A Balance Sheet', in this vol.

to make the equal pay principle effective, especially after the Amsterdam Treaty's amendment to Article 141 (*ex* Article 119).

Discrimination based on sexual orientation continues to be widespread and should be more systematically addressed through a Commission action plan and the development of a draft directive on equal treatment.[115]

Protection of the *rights of members of minority groups* should also become a more prominent focus of the Union's policies, both internally and externally.

EU policy towards *persons with disabilities* should reflect a human rights-based approach which aims to eliminate barriers to full participation and equal opportunities within society. In this respect, the move away from an approach which aims to eliminate discrimination towards an active approach which promotes measures to support participation and equal opportunities is especially important. This is also one of the areas in which appropriate policies must be pursued within mainstream policy-making across a very wide range of issues and not simply confined to those areas of direct and obvious concern to persons with disabilities.[116]

C. Immigration and Asylum

1. Asylum-seekers The treatment of asylum-seekers is a key component of human rights policy. Yet it has been a matter of particular political controversy within the Member States of the Union and an issue in relation to which accepted international human rights standards, which are clearly binding on the EU, appear to be most at risk.[117] Recent reports have concluded that EU countries: apply widely differing interpretations in implementing common asylum measures, have adopted very different approaches to third-country cases, provide inadequate safeguards to protect the obligation to ensure *non-refoulement*, have applied different interpretations of who constitutes a refugee, and have not always complied with common EU rules.[118] Counter-measures such as that to establish 'cities of refuge' for persecuted writers are important, but much more needs to be done.[119]

Efforts to co-ordinate national asylum policies within the EU have been under way since 1990 and the entry into force of the Dublin Convention on determining the Member State of the European Union responsible for deciding an asylum application entered into force in September 1997. Once the Amsterdam Treaty comes into effect, Article 63 (*ex* Article 73k) EC gives the Community five years within which to adopt a detailed set of measures on asylum. In implementing this mandate it is

---

[115] See International Lesbian and Gay Association—Europe, *Equality for Lesbians and Gay Men: A Relevant Issue in the Civil and Social Dialogue* (1998); and the 'nine point Community Action Plan', which was proposed in 1993 but has not subsequently been given much attention. See A. Clapham and J. H. H. Weiler, 'A Call for a Nine Point Community Action Plan to Combat Discrimination against Lesbians and Gay Men', in K. Waaldijk and A. Clapham (eds.), *Homosexuality: A European Community Issue* (1993), 395.

[116] See generally G. Quinn, 'The Human Rights of People with Disabilities under EU Law', in this vol.

[117] P. Rudge, 'Challenges to Refugee Protection in the 21st Century. Reconciling State Interests with International Responsibilities: Asylum in North America and Western Europe' (1998) 10 *International Journal of Refugee Law* 7.

[118] e.g. S. Peers, *Mind the Gap!: Ineffective Member State Implementation of European Union Asylum Measures* (1998).

[119] See Council of Europe, *La Charte des villes réfuges: Un réseau contre l'intolérance, pour la protection des écrivains menacés et persécutés* (1997).

essential that full account be taken of the human rights provisions of the Treaty and that the exercise is not governed solely by considerations of migration management. In order to give effect to its obligations to provide protection, rather than yield to short-sighted pressures to promote exclusion, the EU should seek to ensure that the following key elements inform a communitarized asylum policy which should be implemented in national systems.

There should be a coherent and comprehensive policy, encompassing all key elements of the asylum system, to be implemented by the Member States. It should include fair procedures, based on common standards which are in full conformity with the provisions of the 1951 Geneva Convention relating to the Status of Refugees and its 1967 Protocol, including in relation to the granting of asylum in situations of persecution by non-state agents.[120] The next step should be to seek to adopt common regimes designed to provide temporary protection in situations involving large-scale influxes. In addition, a burden-sharing system should be developed in response to the imbalance in numbers of asylum-seekers hosted by different Member States, and similar policies in relation to reception facilities and other matters should be promoted.

In implementing the provisions of the Dublin Convention, procedures are needed which respect the interest of the asylum-seeker, including border/admissibility procedures which allow the asylum-seeker to have his or her claim individually assessed on its merits by competent bodies (if necessary in third States). Policies should also be developed to deal with the many persons who cannot immediately be sent back to their country of origin and whose situation therefore needs to be regularized, at least temporarily. Finally, more attention needs to be given to measures to integrate refugees within the EU so that they are able to enjoy the full range of human rights accorded to others resident within the Union.

The general commitment to respect for human rights of Article 6 (*ex* Article F) TEU is completed, here, by a specific reference to the Geneva Convention of 1951 and the Protocol of 1967 in Article 63(1) (*ex* Article 73k(1)) EC. The institutions of the EU (and the European Court of Justice under its new powers in this field) should be encouraged to give the utmost importance to this reference. In future 'minimum standards' to be adopted under Article 63(1), the Member States should be expressly instructed to respect the standards of the Refugee Convention and of the European Convention on Human Rights (including the relevant case law of the Strasbourg Court on Articles 6 and 8 of the European Convention on Human Rights in the context of immigration).

2. Third-country Nationals   Once admitted to the territory of the EU, third-country nationals constitute an especially sensitive category of concern in human rights terms because of their particular vulnerability. Two specific measures already proposed by the Commission should be adopted. The first is the proposal for a convention—or possibly a directive under Article 63 EC as revised by the Amsterdam Treaty—on rules for the admission of third-country nationals. This not only deals

---

[120] G. Noll and J. Vedsted-Hansen, 'Non-Communitarians: Refugees and Asylum Policies', in this vol.

with admission but also includes a right to seek employment in other Member States. The second is a Commission proposal for amending the Social Security Regulation 1408/71 so as to extend the benefit of its rules to third-country nationals. In any event, such an extension may well be unavoidable as a result of the European Court of Human Rights judgment in the *Gaygusuz* case.[121]

More generally, beyond those two initiatives, progress should be made towards equal treatment of third-country nationals and European citizens—building on the jurisprudence of the European Court of Justice as regards third-country nationals covered by a Community agreement. The fragmented nature of those rights may be an argument to extend them (a) to fields other than just conditions of employment and social security; and (b) to nationals of countries beyond those covered by specific agreements.

D. Children

Issues relating to the well-being of children remain quintessentially within the competence of the Member States. Nevertheless, the increasing importance attached to the concept of children's rights and the major role attributed by the international community to the Convention on the Rights of the Child of 1989 (ratified not only by every EU Member State but by every country in the world except for Somalia and the United States), serve to underline the desirability of a greater EU sensibility in this area. Two dimensions warrant particular consideration. The first is to explore the potential to develop pilot projects and other initiatives designed to promote children's rights within the context of EU development co-operation activities. The second is for the Commission to ensure that all legislation it drafts is fully compatible with the requirements of the Convention.[122]

E. Transnational Corporations and Other Non-state Entities

The impact of private actors on the enjoyment of human rights is growing rapidly in a global economy. Privatization, deregulation, and the diminishing regulatory capacities of national governments have all contributed to enhancing the importance of corporations and other private entities in terms of human rights. However, existing arrangements for monitoring compliance with human rights standards are ill-equipped to respond to these developments. In response to growing corporate awareness and increasing consumer pressure, there has been a significant expansion in the number of voluntary codes of conduct and the like which have been adopted within different business sectors. In principle, these developments are to be welcomed, but they are insufficient. They are not necessarily based squarely on international standards, their monitoring is uneven, they are mostly overseen by the corporations themselves, and they remain entirely optional.[123]

---

[121] European Court of Human Rights, *Gaygusuz* v. *Austria*, judgment of 16 Sept. 1996, Reports of Judgments and Decisions 1996–IV.

[122] See Save the Children, *Towards an EU Human Rights Agenda for Children* (1998).

[123] M. Kamminga, 'Holding Multinational Corporations Accountable for Human Rights Abuses: A Challenge for the European Community', in this vol.

　The EU needs to take the lead in exploring what further options exist in this regard. In 1977 the Council adopted a Code of Conduct for businesses operating in South Africa[124] and in May 1998 it adopted an EU Code of Conduct on Arms Exports.[125] While there are significant differences in the scope and approach of these Codes, it is difficult to accept as the last word a recent statement by the Commission to the effect that existing Community law makes it impossible to develop a code of conduct to oblige EU-based companies operating in third countries to observe human rights norms.[126] The Commission should evaluate existing voluntary codes of conduct and prepare a study on the ways in which an official EU code of conduct for corporations could be formulated, promoted, and monitored. To the extent that changes in Community law will be required, these should be clearly identified.

F. New Information and Communications Technologies

As noted above in relation to citizenship, citizens need to be effectively informed, directly and through the media and other appropriate sources of information. Otherwise, the average citizen is unlikely to have a very clear idea of the types of information to which he or she might be entitled to seek access by invoking the freedom of information principle. The need for better information to raise people's awareness of their rights was highlighted in the recommendations made in the Veil Report. The permanent Dialogue with Citizens and Business, launched by the Commission, is relevant in this regard, as is the Euro-Jus system for providing informal legal advice at the national level in relation to the application of Community law. But more sustained measures are needed.

　The High-Level Expert Group established by the Commission to analyse the social aspects of the information society recognized this fact in its 1997 final policy report. It called upon the EU to implement a democracy project designed to 'step up the interaction between politicians and citizens and increase the latter's participation in the political debate and decision-making' and to 'improve our understanding and the transparency of the democratic process in both national and EU institutions'.[127] Such recommendations are all too easily misread as calling for technological fixes when in fact the principal context in which they should be pursued is one based clearly on respect for human rights.

　The Directorate General responsible for human rights could thus play a central role in developing and implementing an active horizontal policy of transparency and general democracy enhancement in the information society. This should include the creation for each Directorate General and for the Commission as a whole of a stan-

---

　[124] Code of Conduct for companies from the EC with subsidiaries, branches, or representation in South Africa as revised by the Ministers for Foreign Affairs of the ten countries of the European Community and Spain and Portugal, 1977, revised in 1985, reprinted in Clapham, note 8 above, at 155. For an assessment see M. Holland, *The European Community and South Africa: European Political Co-operation Under Strain* (1988), 74.

　[125] Council of the European Union, 2097th meeting, Brussels, 25 May 1998, Press Release 8687/98 (Presse 162), at 16.

　[126] Letter of 14 Nov. 1997 to the Chairman of the European Parliament's Committee on Foreign Affairs, Security and Defence Policy.

　[127] *Building the European Information Society For Us All: Final Policy Report of the High-Level Expert Group* (1997), at 61.

dard of transparency to be effectuated through creative use of the Internet and of all other media forms.

Three other issues are important in this respect.[128] One is the need to tackle and effectively regulate the misuse of the new information technologies, while maintaining a balance which adequately protects the right to freedom of expression and freedom to impart and receive information. This applies especially in relation to the debate over encryption. In this respect, the standards recognized fifty years ago in the Universal Declaration of Human Rights remain entirely valid, but the policies through which they can be upheld need to be constantly updated. As a key player in the field, the EU has a particular responsibility to ensure that sight is never lost of the human rights dimension of this issue. The second is the importance of seeking to make the benefits of the new technologies more accessible to individuals and human rights groups in developing countries. Existing disparities in access are dramatic and should be explicitly addressed in EU development co-operation policies. The third is the need to assist efforts to make human rights information more accessible, better structured, and better managed so as to reduce problems of information overload and to seek to maximize the beneficial use which human rights groups can make of these technologies. Again, the EU, and especially the Commission, have the resources, competence and responsibility to fund and facilitate efforts in this regard.

G. The Third Pillar

Under the Amsterdam Treaty, the third pillar has been significantly restructured. Freedom of movement, immigration, and related issues have been moved to the first pillar, and what remains is a focus on 'police and judicial co-operation in criminal matters'. The addition of trafficking in persons, offences against children, and illicit arms trafficking to existing concerns such as drugs, terrorism, and organized crime gives an indication of the principal areas of concern. While the objective stated in Title VI is to 'provide citizens with a high level of safety within an area of freedom, security and justice', no specific mention is made of achieving these objectives within a framework which fully respects the human rights of all, including non-citizens. Proposals to subject activities taken within this framework, including the activities of an expanded Europol (European Police Office), to review by the European Court of Justice were not accepted by Member States at Amsterdam.

This development leaves a wide area of expanding EU co-operation within which human rights guarantees are, to say the least, neither strong nor visible. The Union must as a matter of urgency explore the means by which the operation of Europol and similar semi-independent agencies (such as the Committee set up under the Customs Information Convention) can be effectively monitored with respect to their human rights performance. Access to the Court should also be assured in relation to any future schemes of police and judicial co-operation.[129]

---

[128] This analysis draws in particular on P. Brophy and E. F. Halpin, 'Information Technology and Human Rights: A Briefing Paper', July 1998; and E. Sottas and B. Schonveld, 'The Beguiling Song of Technology: A European Vision on Technology and Human Rights', June 1998.

[129] For a detailed analysis see S. Peers, 'Human Rights in the Context of the Third Pillar', in this vol.

XV. CONCLUSION

The many recommendations that emerge from this analysis are addressed to virtually every actor within the EU structure. Some are narrow and uncontroversial, while others are extensive and potentially far-reaching. Nevertheless, few of them are startling, wholly original, or highly innovative. The explanation is both simple and compelling. The principal shortcoming of the EU's human rights policy is not a lack of novelty or grand gestures. It is a consistent reluctance to come to grips with some basic home truths about the indivisibility of internal and external human rights policy, the need for a clear and unambiguous commitment at all levels, and the need for effective political and bureaucratic structures to give effect to those commitments. The various components of the recipe for achieving these objectives have been evident for a number of years. Until these indispensable building blocks are put into place by the Member States and the institutions of the Union there will be little point in creating grand new designs for their own sake.

B

Some Philosophical Dimensions of Human Rights Policies within Europe

2

Is there a European Approach to Human Rights?

CHARLES LEBEN

". . . inalienable political rights of all men by virtue of birth would have appeared to all ages [before the 18th century in Europe] a contradiction in terms.

H. Arendt, *On Revolution,* Penguin, 1963, 1965, p. 45.

I. INTRODUCTION

At first sight the question takes us by surprise, so closely linked in our minds are
human rights with the universal, and not the particular. Certain quotations concerning the universal dimension of human rights spring to mind immediately: '[a]ll
men are born equally free and independent' (Virginia Declaration of Rights, June
1776); or 'all men are created equal, . . . they are endowed by their Creator with certain unalienable Rights' (Declaration of Independence of the United States of
America, July 1776), '[m]en are born free and equal in rights', and this is a 'sacred
and inalienable right' (France, 1789).[1] And all those texts reach their apogee, as it
were, in Article 1 of the *Universal* Declaration of Human Rights: '*[a]ll human beings
are born free and equal in dignity and rights*'[2] and this time, moreover, the
man/human being ambiguity is swept aside.

At the second United Nations Conference on Human Rights in Vienna in June
1993, when several third-world countries were leading an attack on what they regarded as the western values expressed in the 1948 Declaration, the Programme of
Action finally adopted on 25 June reaffirmed in its first paragraph that 'the universal
nature of these rights and freedoms is beyond question', and in paragraph 5 that '[a]ll
human rights are universal, indivisible and interdependent and interrelated', that 'it

---

[1] For the complete text of these various declarations of human rights, see S. Rials, *La Déclaration des
droits de l'homme et du citoyen* (1988). On a topic close to that under discussion here, see R.-J. Dupuy, 'Les
droits de l'homme, valeur européenne ou valeur universelle?', *Communication de l'Académie des sciences
morales et politiques*, 18 Dec. 1989, at 414–28.

[2] Universal Declaration of Human Rights, adopted by GA Res. 217 A (III) (1948). In United Nations,
A Compilation of International Instruments (1994), i, Part 1, 1.

is the duty of States, regardless of their political, economic and cultural systems, to promote and protect all human rights and fundamental freedoms', even though the text also states that it is essential to bear in mind 'the significance of national and regional particularities and various historical, cultural and religious backgrounds'.[3]

In the same spirit, the Secretary General of the United Nations wrote in a message marking the inauguration of the year commemorating the fiftieth anniversary of that Declaration that '[h]uman rights are the foundation of human existence and co-existence. Universal, indivisible and interdependent, they are what defines our humanity. They embody the principles which are the sacred cornerstone of human dignity.' And the Secretary General went on: '[h]uman rights derive their strength from their universality, thanks to which no frontier, barrier or enemy can stand in their path.'[4]

On reflection, however, and without the slightest intention of challenging the aspiration to universality which is characteristic of human rights philosophy, the question asked does raise certain doubts: is not the historical basis of all the declarations cited above to be found in the intellectual development of Europe? Are not all those declarations the heirs of European Enlightenment, from Locke to Rousseau and Kant? So it is very natural that, in the context of relations between countries of the old world, Article 49 (*ex* Article O) of the Treaty on European Union, as amended by the Treaty of Amsterdam of 2 October 1997, makes the admission of any new European State to the Union subject to the condition that it 'respects the principles set out in Article 6 (*ex* Article F(1))'.

Article 6(1) states that '[t]he Union is founded on the principles of liberty, democracy, respect for human rights and fundamental freedoms, and the rule of law, principles which are common to the Member States'.[5]

The Treaty on European Union does not, however, merely require its own members to respect those fundamental freedoms. As we shall see, the Union is going to extend and organize systematically a policy of encouraging and defending democracy, human rights, and fundamental freedoms, and the rule of law which the European Economic Community initiated when it introduced into the Lomé III (1985) and Lomé IV Conventions provisions concerning respect for human dignity and human rights.

We are no longer, therefore, dealing with principles which only the members of the European 'club' are supposed to respect, but with principles which are projected onto the relations of this 'club' with any other non-member country since they are considered to be universally valid. And the same applies, with differences of detail, to the policy of defending human rights conducted at international level by the

[3] *Vienna Declaration and Programme of Action*, A/CONF.157/24 (1993). On the Vienna Conference see P. Tavernier, 'L'O.N.U. et l'affirmation de l'universalité des droits de l'homme' (1997) 31 *RTDH*, 379, and M. Delmas-Marty, *Pour un droit commun* (1994), 266–71.

[4] Message of 10 Dec. 1997, reproduced in *Bulletin de l'Association française pour les Nations Unies*, No 27 (Dec. 1997), at 33.

[5] Wachsmann, 'Les droits de l'homme [dans le traité d'Amsterdam]' (1997) 4 *RTDE*, 883, at 894 ff. The text of the Treaty of Amsterdam, and also the consolidated versions of the TEU and the EC Treaty, are reproduced in the same issue of the *RTDE*, at 929–1102.

United States, principally since the Carter presidency.[6] As a result, the question raised, which has perhaps been understood and approached at the outset as a question on Europe as such, *applies to the west* as a whole. We are dealing with a Europe whose intellectual development in the sphere of human rights has taken place in the United States and Australia, and even Latin America. In the circumstances, the question before us concerns the (real or illusory) universal nature of human rights as they have appeared and developed in Europe and the west.

This brings us to a twofold extension of the question: extension of the European Union to Europe in general (or at least western Europe), and then extension of Europe to the western world. Such extension is essential, because how, in the general considerations of the Academy of European Law, can we ignore the charge of ethnocentrism, even of neo-colonialism, levied by certain authors and certain countries against the European/western concept of human rights?

However, the question can just as easily be understood in a more restrictive sense: is there a specifically European approach within those western countries which all claim European descent? An approach which is specifically European by comparison with that of, for example, America? But here too it should be made clear what we mean by 'a European approach'. It would be neither desirable nor even feasible to confine it to the practice of the European Union. It is clear that the European Convention on Human Rights must be taken into account, given in particular the great influence it has on the decisions of the Court of Justice of the European Communities and the reference to the Rome Convention in Article F(2) of the Maastricht Treaty, confirmed by the Treaty of Amsterdam.[7] It seems, however, equally imperative to take into consideration the constitutional provisions of the European States and the mechanisms therein for the protection of human rights, and also the decisions reached by national courts, in so far as certain specifically European features may be identified in this field.[8]

---

[6] See O. Schachter, 'Les aspects juridiques de la politique américaine des droits de l'homme' [1977] *AFDI* 53–74. In a speech given to the General Assembly of the United Nations, President Carter declared that 'no member of the United Nations can claim that ill treatment of its citizens is its affair alone. Nor can any member avoid its responsibility where cases of torture or unjustified loss of liberty in any region of the world are concerned.' This policy has been criticized on numerous occasions because of unilateral measures taken by the USA in cases of serious violations of human rights. But the principle that 'every State has an interest in the protection of human rights' and may adopt 'diplomatic, economic and other measures authorized by international law' in respect of the State responsible for those violations was accepted by the Institut de droit international at its session in Santiago de Compostela. See (1990) 63(II) *AIDI* 338. And see C. Rucz, 'Les mesures unilatérales de protection des droits de l'homme devant l'Institut de droit international' (1992) *AFDI* 579.

[7] See Wachsmann, note 5 above, at 883–902.

[8] Accordingly, it has become possible, in connection with the growing convergence between the decisions of European constitutional courts and those of the courts in Strasbourg and Luxembourg, to speak of progress towards a 'European constitutional law'. See the special edition devoted to this topic in (1995) 7 *RUDH*. See also M. de Salvia, 'L'élaboration d'un "ius commune" des droits de l'homme et des libertés fondamentales dans la perspective de l'unité européenne: l'œuvre accomplie par la Commission et la Cour européennes des droits de l'homme', in F. Matscher and H. Petzold (eds.), *Protection des droits de l'homme: la dimension européenne. Mélanges en honneur de Gérard J. Wiarda* (1988), 555–63. See also Delmas-Marty, note 3 above, at 223–53.

II. *THE WEST AND THE REST*: EUROPE AND THE QUESTION OF THE UNIVERSALITY OF HUMAN RIGHTS

The expression 'the west and the rest' is borrowed from an article by Kishore Mahbubani (former Singapore Assistant Secretary of State for Foreign Affairs[9]). It expresses the revolt of certain Asian or Islamic countries against what they consider to be a manifestation of the old European/western imperialism in respect of the rest of the world, demonstrating once again an arrogant disregard for any tradition or culture other than those of Europe.

That Europe in this instance stands for the west, because it is from Europe that the west was born, can plainly be seen in this extract published in *le Monde* of 15 March 1989 by Mohammed Akoun, Professor of the History of Islamic Thought at the Sorbonne, at the time of the polemic arising out of Ayatollah Khomeini's *fatwa* condemning the writer, Salman Rushdie, to death. It shows that the author, in formulating his criticisms, speaks indiscriminately of Europe and the west. In particular, addressing the intellectuals who had come to Rushdie's defence, he wrote:

> You cannot expect all cultures to follow the path traced for two centuries by France and Europe! To take that line would mean requiring other cultures to lock themselves into '*the one western model*' of historical development, intellectual and artistic achievement. It would mean a repetition of the colonial ideology which legitimized the subjugation of other peoples and cultures by the export of a *civilization created in Europe.* . . Western thought shows that it is incapable of development outside the *historical models set up in Europe and backed up by the technological West.*

A little further on, the author adds:

> The perception of human rights in a western philosophy reduced to nothing more than bare positivist and historicist rationalism increases the misunderstanding with Islam, which conceives of these human rights in the wider context of God's law.[10]

In that text, as in others which could be quoted from the mouths of persons with political authority in Asian countries, there is both a challenge to what is seen as the ethnocentric short-sightedness of Europe/the west[11] and an implied declaration that there can be other approaches, other models of human rights, which are the product of other cultures and which take account of the specific fundamental features of those cultures (or civilizations). European/western consciousness encounters a serious problem here as to the legitimacy of promoting and extending a model of human rights which it knows full well is the product of its own history.

---

[9] Kishore Mahbubani, 'The Dangers of Decadence. What the Rest can Teach the West' (1993) 72 *Foreign Affairs* 10–14. The article appeared in response to a study by Samuel Huntingdon, 'The Clash of Civilizations?' (1993) 72 *Foreign Affairs* 22–49. It will be noted that, like Saudi Arabia, Singapore had not by 1995 ratified any convention on human rights involving an international review body. On the challenge which is sometimes called 'Asianism' in human rights, see the comments of M. Bettati, *Le droit d'ingèrence. Mutation de l'ordre international* (1996), 31–4.

[10] Quoted by P. Wachsmann, *Les droits de l'homme* (1995), 43, emphasis added.

[11] A very striking symbol of the 'European-Western' coupling in the field of human rights is to be found in the pairing of René Cassin and Eleanor Roosevelt, the principal draftsman of the Universal Declaration and the chairwoman of the drafting committee.

A. The European Model of Human Rights: A Concrete Universal

Notwithstanding the protestations of R. Cassin, who announced in his lecture at The Hague that the Universal Declaration, 'not being subject to any particular doctrine not that of natural and absolute rights, nor the individualism of the 18th century, nor Marxist dialectic, is imbued with what is common to all these doctrines, namely the affirmation of the unity of the human family',[12] it is not difficult to show, as has been done on many occasions, how the invention of human rights, which was to lead to the publication of the Universal Declaration, is linked to the political, religious, and philosophical history of Europe and even of certain European countries. The appearance of a form of the State in which traditional political relations, favouring political authority over subjects, are turned on their heads thenceforth to favour the protection of citizens against the power of the rulers marks the passage to a new era. This new era, the earliest origins of which are to be found in the combining of the Graeco-Roman philosophical tradition with the Judeo-Christian religious tradition, was heralded by the philosophy of the Enlightenment, itself anticipated by the 'Glorious English Revolution' of 1689, and was to be proclaimed most solemnly in the declarations of independence of the colonies, and then the United States of America, and also in the Declaration of the Rights of Man and the Citizen of 1789.

In the new European/western State, protection of human rights is based on an individualist vision of society, defending the paramountcy of human beings as persons, which is considered the cardinal value, all of which finds expression in the creation of, first, a liberal and then a democratic State in the service of its citizens. As Bobbio has written in one of his many texts on this subject, the change in the eighteenth century from perceiving society as something organic to perceiving it in contractual terms constitutes a genuine 'Copernican revolution' in political thought, 'since, the relationship between the individual and society being overthrown, society is no longer a fact of nature existing whatever individuals intend, but rather an artificial body created by individuals in their image and pattern, in order to satisfy their interests and needs and for the broadest exercise of their rights'.[13]

This revolution took place at a specific moment in history and in specific places. When, for example, the subject of human rights was no longer merely dealt with in philosophical works such as Locke's second 'Treatise of Government' (1690),[14] but became a declaration of faith justifying rebellion against tyranny and the creation of

---

[12] R. Cassin, 'La Déclaration universelle et la mise en œuvre des droits de l'homme', (1951) 79(II) *RdC* 290. It will be recalled that the first para. of the preamble to the Declaration states: '[w]hereas recognition of the inherent dignity and of the equal and inalienable rights of all members of the human family is the foundation of freedom, justice and peace in the world'. The Universal Declaration was adopted by 48 votes for, none against, but with eight abstentions (Byelorussia, Czechoslovakia, Poland, Saudi Arabia, the Ukraine, South Africa, USSR, and Yugoslavia). Two States were absent—Honduras and Yemen. According to the delegate from the USSR, the rights set forth could only be a matter for 'formal democracy', and the result would necessarily be to encourage interference in the internal affairs of States. The Saudi Arabian representative justified his abstention more specifically on the ground that he could not accept Art. 16 (the right to marry without any limitation due to race, nationality or religion) or Art. 18, which sets out the freedom to change religion. See St. Rials, note 1 above, at 285–7.

[13] N. Bobbio, *Libéralisme et démocratie* (1985), at 20–1.

[14] J. Locke, *Two Treatises of Government* (1997). Of the many quotations which could be selected from the second treatise ('Essay on the origin, limits and true ends of civil government', at 137 ff), I offer this:

an independent political body. Thus, in the declaration of the rights of the State of
Virginia (June 1776), a short introduction states: '[d]eclaration of the rights which
must belong to us, now and for posterity, and which must be regarded as the foundation and basis of government', and then announces in Article 1: '[a]ll men are born
equal and independent: they have certain essential and natural rights of which they
can by no contract deprive their posterity: such as the right to life and liberty, with
the means to acquire and possess property, to pursue and attain happiness and
safety'.[15]

In his commentary on this declaration, Bobbio writes: 'we must acknowledge that
at that moment a new form of political regime was born, by which I mean something
radically "unprecedented", a form of political regime which is neither merely the rule
of law as opposed to that of men, a form of government earlier praised by Aristotle,
but which is at the same time the rule of men and of law, of men who make laws and
of laws which find their limits in existing rights which those same laws may not infringe: in a word, the liberal State which leads, by internal development and without
loss of continuity, to the democratic State.'[16]

The unprecedented phenomenon which appeared at that time and which was to be
given further backing by the events of 1789 in France was, as Hannah Arendt writes
in the sentence which serves as epigraph to our text, 'inalienable rights for all, by
virtue of their birth . . .' or, as Fichte radically expresses it, '[t]he opportunity [for
anyone at all] to acquire rights'.[17] Those rights are first, in what is subsequently recognized as the liberal tradition of human rights, those maintained by the individual
against any power liable to infringe those 'natural' rights: power of the State, of the
Church, of economic might, even of science and technology.[18]

'[t]o exercise absolute and arbitrary power, to govern without *established and permanent laws*, is absolutely incompatible with the objects of society and government, institutions to which men would not
submit, abandoning their natural liberty, unless it were in order to preserve their life, liberty or fortune
and, thanks to *rules expressly defining* law and property, to obtain peace and rest' (para. 137 of the Essay,
at 214).

[15] Text in Rials, note 1 above, at 495.   [16] N. Bobbio, *L'età dei diritti* (1992), 260.
[17] The exact quotation is '[t]his alone constitutes the true right of man which falls to him as a man:
[namely] the possibility of acquiring rights': J. Fichte, *Fondement du droit naturel* (1984), Annex II, §22,
394. This does not mean that the sudden appearance of a human rights ideology between the 17th and
18th centuries happened *ex nihilo*. I argue to the contrary (see text to note 30 below) that this sudden appearance was the culmination of a long history which began on the one hand with religious consciousness
and the declaration in Genesis that man, every man and every woman (at the time of his creation Adam is
both) is created in the image of God, and on the other hand with philosophical awareness and the Greek
heritage. This history continues with the first, then the second, scolasticism, to issue forth in the 17th century in the school of the law of nature and peoples. Statements can therefore be found in the past, and not
only that of the West, which can be translated into the language of human rights. That does not in any way
lessen the unprecedentedness of human rights philosophy as it took shape in Europe and America in the
18th century.
[18] See, e.g., the Universal Declaration on the Human Genome and Human Rights, adopted unanimously by the General Conference of UNESCO on 11 Nov. 1997. Art. 1 declares that the human genome
is the heritage of humanity, and Art. 2(1)(a) states that '[e]veryone has a right to respect for their dignity
and for their rights regardless of their genetic characteristics'. Similarly, in the Council of Europe Convention for the Protection of Human Rights and Human Dignity with regard to the Application of Biology and Medicine, Art. 1 provides that: '[t]he Parties to this Convention shall protect human beings in
their dignity and identity and shall guarantee every person, without discrimination, respect for his integrity and his other rights and freedoms with regard to the applications of medicine'. In a different field,
but one not far removed, the objective of French Law of 29 July 1994, introduced into the Civil Code at
Arts. 16 to 16–9, is to ensure that the human body is respected. Art. 16 states: '[t]he law shall guarantee the

Side by side with this liberal tradition, however, and first appearing in the early texts of the French Revolution, we see the assertion of what are later to be called 'social rights',[19] an expression of the socialist tradition of human rights which came to supplement the liberal tradition in Europe.[20] Thus, the first French Constitution of 3 September 1791 states in the first Title headed 'Fundamental Provisions Guaranteed by the Constitution' that '[a] general system of *public assistance* shall be established and organized, to bring up abandoned children, comfort the poor when they are sick, and provide work for the able-bodied poor who have been unable to find any'. And the following paragraph further states: 'Public Education shall be established and organized, common to all citizens, free as regards the elements of education indispensable for all men'. These 'second-generation' rights are again asserted, with more force and style, in the Montagnard Constitution of 24 June 1793, which includes them in its new Declaration of the Rights of Man and the Citizen. Article 21 declares: '[p]ublic assistance is a sacred duty. Society owes its unhappy citizens the means of subsistence, whether by finding them work or by ensuring that those who are unable to work have sufficient to live on.' Article 22 adds: '[e]ducation is a requirement for all. Society must with all its power promote the progress of public reason, and put education within the reach of all citizens.'

These two great categories of rights, which are still intertwined in the Universal Declaration of 1948 (Articles 22 to 28), were later to form the subject-matter of two separate treaties: the International Covenant on Civil and Political Rights (ICCPR) and the International Covenant on Economic, Social and Cultural Rights (ICESCR).[21] It is, however, clear how far a large part of their content is already present in the great founding texts of the American and French revolutions. Does this deep-rootedness in history mean that doubt is cast on the universal character of the European/western doctrine of human rights or, conversely, that this doctrine represents the only possible path which all the civilizations of the world must necessarily follow? It seems to me that the answer to both questions must be 'No'.[22]

primacy of the person, prohibit any injury to its dignity and ensure that human beings are respected from the moment their life begins'. Art. 16–1 continues: '[e]veryone shall be entitled to have his body treated with respect. The human body shall be inviolable. The human body, its parts and products may not be the subject of any right of property.'

[19] On the opposition between 'freedoms' and 'social rights', see J. Rivero, *Les libertés publiques*, Vol. 1, *Les droits de l'homme* (1997), 97–101; L. Ferry and A. Renaut, 'Droits-libertés et droits-créances' (1985) 2 *Droits* 75–84.

[20] Bobbio, note 16 above, at 262, considers that there are three main currents in European political tradition which have ended up by converging on the question of human rights: liberalism, socialism, and social Christianity.

[21] International Covenants on, Economic, Social and Cultural Rights, and Civil and Political Rights, adopted by GA Res. 2200 A (XXI) (1966), in *International Instruments*, note 2 above, at 8 and 20.

[22] On the question of the universality of human rights, see the collection of articles in the first issue of the *RUDH* (1989), 1–34, with contributions from Badinter, Bedjaoui, Cassese, Imbert, and Kodjo. See also *L'Universalité du droit international des droits de l'homme dans un monde pluraliste*, symposium organized by the Council of Europe (1990); J. D'hommeaux, 'De l'universalité du droit international des droits de l'homme: du *pactum ferendum* au *pactum latum*' [1989] *AFDI* 399–423. Also recommended is the short but excellent analysis by Wachsmann, note 10 above, at 35–49; see also Y. Madiot, *Considérations sur les droits et devoirs de l'homme* (1998), 23–109 (for a natural law and yet evolutionist approach to human rights), and Delmas-Marty, note 3 above, at 254–81; in English see C. Cerna, 'Universality of Human Rights and Cultural Diversity: Implementation of Human Rights in Different Socio-Cultural Contexts' (1994) 16 *HRQ* 740; M. Perry, 'Are Human Rights Universal? The Relativist Challenge and Related Matters' (1997) 19 *HRQ* 461. See also the comments of Bettati, note 9 above, at 31–4.

As Professor P.H. Imbert (Director of Human Rights at the Council of Europe) has so perfectly expressed it, 'for anybody, humanity is accessible only through his own particular culture. In this there is *a priori* no contradiction with the requirement of the universality of human rights'.[23] This is the idea which I myself have tried to express by using the Hegelian concept of 'the concrete universal'.[24] Even so, though, the path taken by the particular culture still actually has to lead man to universality.

B. It is Possible to Conceive of the Universal and Human Rights Starting from Other Traditions

In support of this argument, three points must be developed: (1) contrary to the large-hearted declarations, of the Secretary-General of the United Nations or of the Conference of Vienna of 1993, quoted above, it is not all acknowledged human rights, even within Europe/the west, that have universal scope; (2) in theory it is possible to follow paths to the universal other than those followed by Europe. However, those paths necessarily cross those of Europe/the West at some point; (3) the fact that the idea of the universal first saw light in a certain society at a certain time in certain circumstances in no way detracts from the truth of that idea as universal. It does not descend from some heavenly abstraction, but is the result of the labours of men engaged in their time, its ideology and problems. The universal necessarily emerges from the particular and concrete, just as human freedom is the freedom which each person achieves in his own particular situation.

1. The Universal and the Particular in Human Rights   Human rights as expressed in Europe or the United States do not spring in in their entirety from the universal, that is to say from principles that may be expressed in universal terms. There are accidents of history on both sides of the Ocean and as between European countries themselves. To give just one example, few Europeans would be willing to accept Article II of the American Bill of Rights (1789–91) which states that 'the right of the people to keep and bear Arms, shall not be infringed'. Similarly, speaking of the European Convention of Human Rights, Michel de Salvia points out that: '[t]he rights enshrined in the Convention are those of a man defined by his triple identity: national identity; European identity, and universal identity . . . There is, therefore, room beside a *ius commune* for a *ius proprium* of fundamental rights particular to each State'.[25]

If, then, these particular features exist within the western arena itself, it is in no way inconceivable that a non-western society, from the starting-point of its own history and its own civilization, may formulate human rights which in part belong to the category of rights which we may call universal, but in part arise out of the partic-

---

[23] P.H. Imbert, 'L'apparente simplicité des droits de l'homme, réflexions sur les différents aspects de l'universalité des droits de l'homme' (1989) 1 *RUDH*, 24.

[24] The concept of the concrete universal is developed in *The Science of Logic* which is, beyond a doubt, one of the most difficult works in the history of philosophy. I do not claim to use it in a sense entirely in conformity with Hegelian philosophy. I simply mean that there is no such thing as a universal value arrived at by pure abstraction, irrespective of actual social and doctrinal history. This use of the concept of the concrete universal seems to me to be an approximation of Hegel's highly complex arguments. For an initial approach, see S. Auroux (ed.), *Les notions philosophiques* (1990), ii, 2679, 'Universel concret'.

[25] De Salvia, note 8 above, at 556.

ular features of the society and region in which that society is located. There is no contradiction to be found in the juxtaposition of a European convention of human rights with an American convention or an African charter.[26]

Nevertheless, while it is unarguable that there exists a *ius proprium* of human rights, it is equally unarguable that there exists a universal *ius commune*. This finds expression where both the universal and the regional conventions on human rights set out, in comparable terms, the rights called sacrosanct from which no derogation is permitted. For an example, see Article 15(2) of the European Convention which classes in this category: the right to life (save lawful acts of war), the prohibition of torture and of inhuman and degrading treatment or punishment, the prohibition of slavery and servitude, the principle of the legality of punishment. But the double jeopardy rule in Protocol 7 to the European Convention and the provisions set out in the ICCPR (ratified by all the European States parties to the Rome Convention), which allow no derogations, as well as those corresponding to the case envisaged by Article 15(2) of the Rome Convention (Article 11 prohibits imprisonment for debt, Article 16 enshrines the right to recognition of legal personality, Article 18 enshrines the right to freedom of thought, conscience and religion) must also be taken into consideration.[27]

These are what is known as the nucleus of human rights, which hold good everywhere for everyone and which could, from the point of view of international law, be considered to form part at least of customary international law and, perhaps, even of a *ius cogens* for humanity.[28] Nevertheless, it must be acknowledged that there exists, beyond the first layer of rights, including those mentioned above, a second, and even third or fourth layer which are not unanimously agreed upon, or are at least very differently interpreted: the right of peoples to self-determination, permanent sovereignty over natural resources, the right to development, the right to a healthy environment and so on.[29]

2. The European Universal in its Relations with Other Civilizations   It seems to me to be beyond doubt that the path toward the universal may be found in any civilization. The crux, however, is to discover how, in a given culture, it is possible to progress towards this conception of the universal. As regards European history, it has been

---

[26] On these texts, see F. Sudre, *Droit international et européen des droits de l'homme* (1997), 98–105. It is, however, noteworthy that the author has reservations about the Universal Islamic Declaration of Human Rights (at 106–8) because of the priority given to the principles of *Sharia* law over all binding rules of international law.

[27] *Ibid.*, at 152–6; G. Cohen-Jonathan, *Aspects européens des droits fondamentaux* (1996), 92; Wachsmann, note 10 above, at 55–62; Henkin considers that the rights listed in the first 21 Arts. of the Universal Declaration are rights 'to be enjoyed by all human beings universally', in 'General Course on Public International Law' (1989) 216 (IV) *RdC* 230.

[28] For a discussion of this question, see J.F. Flauss, 'La protection des droits de l'homme et les sources du droit international', in *La protection des droits de l'homme et l'évolution du droit international*, S.F.D.I. conference, Strasbourg, 29–31 May 1997, (forthcoming) 28 ff (typed report). See also what Delmas-Marthy calls 'elemental humanity', note 3 above, at 271–81. To understand that this elemental humanity concerns every human being, it is sufficient, as Mario Bettati has frequently remarked, to put oneself on the side of the victims: one would search in vain for any difference between a man tortured in Europe and one tortured elsewhere in the world, or between a woman raped in Europe and one raped elsewhere in the world, or between a child enslaved in Europe and one enslaved elsewhere in the world.

[29] Compare the lists given in the special edition of the *RUDH*, No. 1–2 (1989), by Badinter, at 3, Bedjaoui, at 9; Cassese, at 17–18, and Imbert, at 25.

remarked that it was the fusion over centuries of the Graeco-Roman philosophical tradition and the Judeo-Christian religious tradition that produced this result.[30] It is not *a priori* inconceivable that the same movement might occur independently in another civilization. In practice, nevertheless, we find that it is when other world civilizations were brought into contact with European/western culture, a contact which in general they did not desire, that they were induced to undertake that labour of self-examination which is the beginning of the journey towards the universal, and towards the ability to conceive of the rights of every human being.

Sometimes this meeting of civilizations occurred peaceably, as for instance when the Greek philosophical tradition was absorbed by the philosophers of the Islamic world such as Al Farabi, ibn Bajja, ibn Sina (Avicenna) and ibn Rochd (Averroes), who were themselves to fertilize Jewish and Christian thought in the twelfth to fourteenth centuries. The joining of intellectual positions which then took place meant that everyone, from the starting-point of his own religious tradition and his grasp of Greek philosophy, could reach out beyond his own particular circumstances to a mode of expressing thoughts comprehensible and meaningful to all.[31] At that time, obviously, the problems were not of human rights, but rather of theological and metaphysical matters. None the less, what was taking shape was a form of universalism. This encounter was short-lived, in particular because philosophical thought was rejected by an Islam turning in on itself.

The circumstances were quite different when, in the nineteenth and twentieth centuries, Islam, like every Asian and African culture, met Europe. Most often, this meant an involuntary and forced encounter with a West which perceived itself as a part of history, and thought in terms of rationalism and recognition of the value of the individual. This meeting necessarily produced adverse effects on traditional societies which, in their turn, found themselves pitched headlong into history, however hard they resisted. And entering history initially leads to the devaluation of tradition, as we can see in the history even of Europe, and in that of the peoples touched by European culture.

The world becomes disenchanted, to use Max Weber's well-known expression; the old values are challenged and sifted by western rationality.[32] The result may be a reflex withdrawal and the expulsion of the carriers of western 'contamination'. This was the case, for example, when Japan shut itself off in the seventeenth century from the European presence. It is also the case where, from approximately the thirteenth century onward, Islamic philosophical thought was repressed or where, in our days,

---

[30] For a historical summary of the formation of the theory of human rights, see H. Lauterpacht, *International Law and Human Rights* (1950), 73–141. In that work, the great British jurist adopts an undeservedly severe position *vis-à-vis* the Universal Declaration of Human Rights. In particular, he criticizes the omission of any action whereby individuals can enforce those rights against States: 'there are, in these matters, no rights of the individual except as a counterpart and a product of the duties of the State. There are no rights unless accompanied by remedies' (at 420–1). But it is for the two Covenants to provide *remedies*, even if they may still be regarded as insufficient. For a historical study of all these declarations of rights, reference may also be made to Chr. Faure, *Ce que déclarer des droits veut dire: histoires* (1997).

[31] Without entertaining any naïve belief in some Edenic Andalucia, it is interesting to read, *Le colloque de Cordoue. Ibn Rochd, Maimonide, Saint Thomas ou la filiation entre foi et raison* (1994).

[32] For a study of Max Weber based entirely on the idea of 'modernity as disenchantment', see P. Bouretz, *Les promesses du monde. Philosophie de Max Weber* (1996).

western values are rejected in the name of a return to the most intolerant traditional values to be found in various corners of the world.

It may, nevertheless, be thought that contamination by the 'ethnocentric' (European) idea of universality[33] is incurable, given the very action of those peoples and civilizations in turning the claim of the universal back on its inventors. For what is the basis for denouncing colonialism, racism or under-development, if it is not the morality of universality?[34] But this cannot long remain a weapon to be used only externally. Sooner or later, this weapon will be seized by individuals who will then turn it against their own authorities.

As noted, for example, by the philosopher and Sinologist, François Jullien, in an interview published in *le Monde* of 19 September 1997: '[m]ost often we waver between a naïve universalism (as if the concept of law had always existed everywhere) and a lazy relativism (as though human rights were not valid for the Chinese, whereas experience shows us that ever since they discovered that concept, they have found it harder and harder to do without it)'. In other words, today the process whereby societies join the stream of history and begin to protect individuals and their rights is under way throughout the entire world. This does not, however, mean that the roads to be travelled by each culture in that process must in every respect resemble those travelled in the west, as alleged by Akoun in the text quoted above. It is clear that for deeply 'holistic' societies, to adopt an expression used by Louis Dumont, in which the relationship between the community and individuals is different from that in Europe (Dumont was thinking particularly of India), the paths will be different.[35]

Those differences cannot, however, serve as camouflage for regimes which quite simply deny all human rights (see the supposedly socialist conception of human rights argued in 1936 by Vichinsky, the Moscow public prosecutor of evil memory, and the representative of the USSR to the UN at the time of the Universal Declaration in 1948). Nor can they be used to classify as illegitimate any criticism of one Asian regime or another under the pretext of cultural differences. It is an essential feature of every political system which truly cares for human rights that it accepts it

---

[33] See E. Weil, 'Du droit naturel', in *Essais et conferences* (1970), i, 191.

[34] Dupuy remarks that the European social and cultural system 'has . . . disseminated throughout every continent, as Europe itself spread by means of colonialism and imperialism, the values of argument. Thus, French school teachers taught the peoples overseas a political philosophy which they were to use against the colonial power'; note 1 above, at 423.

[35] Dumont opposes individualism to the holism of traditional societies. He writes that in those societies 'the emphasis is placed on society as a whole, as collective man; the ideal is defined through the organization of society for the purposes of its own ends (and not those of individual happiness); order and hierarchy are paramount, each individual must contribute in his station to the social order and justice consists of adapting social functions to suit society as a whole', in *Homo hierarchicus. Le système des castes et ses implications* (1966), 23. For another example of the integration of the individual in society, see J. Matringe, *Tradition et modernité dans la charte africaine des droits de l'homme* (1996). It is noteworthy that Rawls, in his essay *Le droit des gens* (1996), maintains that the most fundamental rights, which in his view are 'the right to life and security, to personal property, and the elements of the rule of law and also the right to a certain [*sic*] freedom of conscience and association, together with the right to emigrate' (at 75), can equally well be accepted by traditions which conceive of the individual 'not, in the first place, as citizens possessing citizens' rights, but rather principally as members of groups: communities, associations or corporations'. For him the human rights referred to above can be protected 'in a well-ordered hierarchical State . . .'. This hierarchical State cannot but remind us of Dumont's description of holistic societies. On Marxist holism, see note 56 below.

must live under the critical gaze of its own citizens and of the rest of the world, however uncomfortable such a situation may be.[36]

If those conditions are satisfied, there is no contradiction in positing the existence of 'concrete universals' other than those of Europe/the west, any more than there is a contradiction in demonstrating that within that block there are differences, sometimes far-reaching ones, as to the definition of some of the most fundamental rights of human beings.[37] This argument has been objected to because of its optimism that all great civilizations can make their own way towards the universal. Some of them, perhaps, bar such a path. And this claim refers, pretty often, to Islam. Undoubtedly there are those amongst us who place their stake on the richness of the great cultures which can all, in our opinion, draw on their traditions for the resources which will enable them to chart their passage to the universal in human rights and democracy.

We are not alone in this sentiment. In a recent interview in *le Monde*, Salman Rushdie, who knows better than anyone what fundamentalism and fanaticism mean, responded with the following question to a question put to him: '[d]oes Islam necessarily give rise to that (i.e. religious fanaticism and fundamentalism)? Is it possible to imagine an Islam corrected and amended, an Islam, in short, compatible with human rights?' To which the writer gave a positive reply, on the basis partly of his own experience of Islam in India 'which, because it was a minority religion, had nothing to do with the State and remained a matter of conscience' and partly on the basis of the existence in the twelfth century of a rationalist tendency which 'destroy[ed] the bases of fundamentalism and confer[red] legitimacy on debate as to interpretation, commentary, democracy in a way'. He adds 'these trends have of course always been those of a minority. But at least they have existed! A precious lesson . . . in politics as well as in theology'.[38]

But who can say how much more time will be needed before those civilizations join Europe/the west in recognizing the universal values of the fundamental rights of human beings? Not too long, I should say, in the light of history. First of all, it is noteworthy that a number of countries belonging to non-European cultures have here and now ratified the two United Nations Covenants. This at the least goes to

---

[36] For an insight into the reasoning of a politician from the Asian continent with regard to human rights, see Bilhari Kausikan (South-East Asia Director in the Singapore Ministry of Foreign Affairs), 'Asia's Different Standard', *Foreign Policy* (Fall 1993) 24–41, and the reply given by Aryeh Neier, former director of Human Rights Watch, 'Asia's Unacceptable Standard', *ibid.*, at 42–51. It is interesting to note Kausikan's remark that '[f]or the first time since the Universal Declaration was adopted in 1948, countries not steeped in the Judeo-Christian and natural law traditions are in the first rank' (at 32). Although he does not deny the nucleus of human rights, the author denounces the overly individualistic view of human rights in the west and suspects the west of targeting the cultural characteristics which gave a lead to the economic success of the countries of South-East Asia. For a discussion of the challenge to cultural relativism, see also note 22 above. In the *International Herald Tribune* of 10 Apr. 1998 may be found an article by one of the correspondents of *The Times* in Hong Kong, denouncing the hypocrisy of invoking 'Asian values': J. Mirsky, 'What are "Asian Values"? A Justification for Repression'. See also Bettati, note 9 above, at 31–4.

[37] The reader may be referred to the special edition of the review *Esprit*, 'L'universel au risque du culturalisme' (Dec. 1992), for the quest for a universalism that, without yielding to total relativism, still takes into consideration what in the cultural experience of each of us is unique and empowering for all humankind. See, in particular, the articles 'Les deux universalismes', by M. Walzer, at 102 ff and P. Hassner, 'Vers un universalisme pluriel?', at 114 ff.

[38] *Le Monde*, 10 June 1998, at 13.

show that the values promoted therein are not rejected at first sight as completely pernicious.[39] The observance of those rights, in everyday practice, by some of these countries is perhaps less than satisfactory, to use a euphemism. The power of principles may, however, compel recognition over the course of years, as we saw with the Helsinki Final Act.[40] The fact that in 1975 the USSR and the popular democracies accepted the third package of human rights gave rise to committees for the verification of compliance with those rights which were intended to exert pressure on their governments to abide by the principles they had themselves proclaimed.[41]

3. The Universal and the Eternal: the Birth of Universal Human Rights in and Through History   The criticisms most frequently directed at the philosophy of human rights derive from the facts that the concept is of such recent provenance that the catalogue of rights has been significantly altered over time (Locke, for example, would probably not have subscribed to several of the articles of the Universal Declaration), and that there has always been disagreement on the scope of that catalogue (as indeed there is at the end of the twentieth century). How can it be maintained, in those circumstances, that those rights existed before the law proper which they act to limit? Or, in other words, how can it be envisaged that human rights constitute a universal and eternal superior law?

In actual fact, from our point of view, it is unnecessary to posit a genuine natural law 'over and above' positive law. Thus, to quote the Declaration of 1789, while liberty is one of the natural and inalienable rights of man (Article 2), the limits of the enjoyment of that liberty may be determined only by law (Article 4).[42]

Yet those human rights are said to change over periods of time, and there were times when slavery was 'natural', just as the use of torture was in criminal trials in the Middle Ages and even later. And undoubtedly it would be possible to demonstrate that each of the most fundamental rights of our time had been unknown or denied at one time or another in the past or in one country or another (for example, the practice of 'exposing' babies in Rome[43]). This argument will worry only those with a

[39] On 31 Dec. 1995 the United Nations Covenant on Civil and Political Rights was ratified by 132 States and the Covenant on Economic, Social and Cultural Rights by 133.

[40] Helsinki Final Act, adopted at the Conference on Security and Co-operation in Europe, Helsinki, 1 Aug. 1975, reprinted in (1975) 14 *ILM* 1292.

[41] The Declaration on the Principles Governing the Mutual Relations of the Participating States, the famous Decalogue states that: '[t]he participating States shall respect human rights and fundamental freedoms, including freedom of thought, conscience, religion or conviction. They shall promote and encourage the effective exercise of freedoms and civil, political, economic, social and cultural rights and others which all arise out of the dignity inherent in human beings and which are essential to their free and complete blossoming/development'. See E. Decaux, *Que sais-je? La Conférence sur la sécurité et la coopération en Europe (CSCE)* (1992), 90. People were to take seriously the rights thus proclaimed and contribute to the political and ideological upheavals of the 1990s in all the countries of the Soviet bloc.

[42] In his introduction to No. 2 of the review *Droits* devoted to human rights, St Rials notes clearly the 'change of natural into positive law' marked by the Declaration of 1789. So, while Art. 2 proclaims the 'natural and inalienable rights of man', most of the other Arts. 'charge the legislature with the task of establishing the bounds within which those rights are to be exercised': 'Généalogie des droits de l'homme' (1985) 2 *Droits*, 11.

[43] P. Girard, *Manuel élémentaire de droit romain* (1978), at 131. The *pater familias* can expose children, 'that is to say, abandon them, if he does not want to be responsible for them, as he can abandon slaves, animals, inanimate objects'. The author notes that 'the custom of exposing children is common to Romans, Greeks, Germans and Hindus'. Exposure is not directly an act of infanticide, but death is its highly probable result.

naïve natural law vision of a sempiternal unchanging law. Or possibly, those who cling to the views of the seventeenth and eighteenth century philosophers (Hobbes, Spinoza, Rousseau) who believed that human rights sprang from the rights possessed by an individual marooned in nature.[44]

Nevertheless, Man is a political animal conceivable only in civil society and not in some imaginary state of nature. For societies emerging from subjection to a non-historical tradition and entering history, the idea of universality, and thus of rights valid not just for the citizens of such and such a city but for all human beings, arises from the development of the city. Values are a product of history and their universal application is discovered by those who, in their awareness of their historical position, are seeking rules which may, as the philosopher Eric Weil says, 'be acknowledged *meaningful by all who ponder the question of universal meaning*' (emphasis added).[45] Even so, people must still ask this crucial question, and it is here that the meeting with Europe/the West is crucial, in so far as that is the first culture to have taken its part in history and to have begun the search for universal meaning.[46]

Consequently it is the gradual development of human consciousness which makes it possible to imagine that some rights may be of recent origin and yet express values which are potentially universal. Slavery, torture, the indiscriminate massacre of whole populations have not always been abominations. They have become so recently, and universally, and quite rightly those who do not accept that could be considered to be barbarians. As the philosopher, R. Misrahi, puts it, 'the individual [who holds the rights] is simultaneously a universal foundation and a slow historical discovery'.[47]

The progress of conscience also makes it possible to understand that even if the American declarations that followed Independence and the Declaration of the Rights of Man and the Citizen applied, in their authors' minds, to only part of humankind, the male white part, the seeds of universalism which they contained were, much later but necessarily, to blossom in a (truly) universal Declaration of the rights of every human being.

---

[44] E. Weil, 'Du droit naturel' in *Essais et Conférences* (1970), 194.

[45] *Ibid.*, at 187. See G. Vedel, 'Les droits de l'homme: quels droits? quel homme?' in M. Bettati (ed.), *Humanité et droit international. Melanges Rene-Jean Dupuy* (1991), 349–62, who shows how 'human rights are an intangible but not an immutable inheritance' (at 354) and that 'it is possible to envisage at one and the same time that human rights are everlasting and that they evolve' (at 355).

[46] See the overly catastrophistic tenor of the article by the author of *The Clash of Civilizations and the Remaking of World Order*, S. Huntingdon, 'The West, Unique, not Universal' (1996) 75 *Foreign Affairs* 28.

[47] R. Misrahi, *Qu'est-ce que l'éthique?* (1997), 239. See also Madiot who, after demonstrating that human nature 'develops gradually, throughout the progress of history', writes: '[a] right becomes natural when it is possible to consider, at a given moment of historical progress, that it . . . has acquired such a value that to challenge it is now impossible. That value is conferred on it by the broadest recognition under internal laws (constitutions and statutes) and under international conventions or by a claim to which no reasoned argument is opposed. It is the setting up of a ratchet mechanism to prevent any backward movement (though plainly it cannot prevent attacks on such a right)': note 22 above, at 32–4.

III. EUROPE AND THE WEST: THE EUROPEAN (PROPERLY SPEAKING) DIMENSION OF HUMAN RIGHTS

If I am now to reflect on the specifically European approach to human rights within western countries, it seems to me that I must give a historical perspective on the way in which European countries have tackled this question. If we can consider, as we saw in the first part, that Europe is the birthplace of the theory of human rights, we cannot overlook the fact that this theory remained long disregarded in its homeland. It is only very recently, since 1945 and even since 1970, that protection of human rights has become an essential element in the legal systems of western European countries and in the relations between those countries and non-European countries. Knowing what obstacles Europe has had to overcome will make us better able to evaluate the difficulties encountered by non-European nations in setting up a system for the protection of human rights.

A. Birth, Disappearance, and Rebirth of Human Rights in Europe

In her essay on *Les droits de l'homme et le droit naturel*, Blandine Barret-Kriegel stressed the fact that the fruits of the 1789 Declaration of Rights were belated, in comparison with the rights proclaimed in the American Bill of Rights of 1789–91.[48] There will be a time and a place to qualify that statement (see below pp. 85–6). However, the fact remains that it is only since 1945 that the philosophy of human rights and its translation into law have known their present success.

1. The Enforced Hibernation of the Philosophy of Human Rights in Europe There was in fact a very slow 'dissemination' of the 1789 Declaration in France and Europe, principally in the face of criticism from three points of view: conservative, positivist-Utilitarian, and Marxist.[49] We have no space in which to dwell on conservative criticism of human rights, such as that of Burke or Joseph de Maistre (even though those two authors start from different premises), since it forms part of a more general rejection of the achievements of the French Revolution.[50] I must, however, observe that the philosophical trends which adopted those achievements in whole or in part, and the modern development of political societies, contribute to the eclipse of a general theory of human rights.

---

[48] B. Barret-Kriegel, *Les droits de l'homme et le droit naturel* (1989), 19 ff. For an overview of how the protection of rights developed in the United States, see L. Henkin, 'Les droits européens dans la constitution américaine' [1993] *RIDC* 429–38.

[49] See G. Peces-Barba Martinez, *Curso de derechos fundamentales. Teoria general* (1995), 69–98.

[50] Just as radically, Villey pours scorn on the whole Modernist legal tradition from the 17th century onward which, disregarding the Aristotelian and Thomist definition of law, invented the delusion of individualism, false equality and in addition a whole multitude of pseudo human rights good for nothing but gulling the credulous. It is not surprising that Villey, a Catholic writer in the Thomist tradition, finishes his diatribe against human rights by joining in a Marxist critique in *La Question Juive*, and even pretends to support the logic of the Marquis de Sade, in *Français encore un effort si vous voulez être Républicains*, which demanded, in the name of the rights of man, the freedom to indulge all passions, including incest, adultery and other amusements. See M. Villey, *Le droit et les droits de l'homme* (1990), 152 (for the reference to Marx) and 'Correspondance' in the special edition of the review *Droits*, No. 2 (1985), 44, for the reference to Sade.

Such a consequence resulted, first of all, from the rejection in the nineteenth century of the doctrine of natural law which had given rise to the declarations of rights. It is true that the Declaration of the Rights of Man and the Citizen carried in both its actual title and its contents the seeds of future progress. While 'men are born free and equal in rights' (Article 1) and 'the aim of every political association is the preservation of the natural and inalienable rights of man' (Article 2), it is for the law to establish the limits to every man's liberty (Article 4) and to establish all the safeguards for the rights set out in Articles 4 to 17. And since the law 'is the expression of the general will' (Article 6), it can do no wrong. Only a seditionmonger putting his own selfish interests above the general interest would rise up against the law in the name of pre-existing rights.[51]

Starting from those premises, there was to arise in France and, no doubt, in other European countries, the system known as *l'Etat légal*, i.e. the State governed by the rule of law in which individuals are protected against abuses of power and infringements of their rights and freedoms attributable to acts of the Executive but not against those committed by the Legislature itself. The very idea would have seemed laughable to a man in the third French Republic, even though on numerous occasions one group or another would denounce the adoption of 'unjust' laws running counter to the rights of man. Parliamentary sovereignty, together with the dominant ideology of legal positivism, could conceive of and organize nothing beyond the defence of 'public liberties', as defined by statute and within the limits laid down by those statutes. While the 1789 Declaration still retained its prestige, it was of little effect in legal terms, except perhaps in the *Conseil d'Etat's* working out of the theory of the general principles of law.[52]

A similar result, but from different philosophical bases, was to follow in England from the Utilitarian philosophy of Bentham, and this too for a long period took on all the characteristics of a dominant philosophy.[53] On the question of natural and inalienable rights, Bentham never gave an inch: as soon as American independence was declared in 1776, he expressed his decided opinion that such a doctrine was contradictory, unintelligible, and dangerous. Even after he was convinced of the advantages of democratic government, he continued to argue that a right which had not been created in and by a system of positive law was a contradiction in terms, as if one should speak of cold that is hot or of resplendent darkness (from which we may see that Bentham had no feeling for poetry).[54] In the end, the result to which Utilitarianism was leading was not so far removed, on this point of human rights, from positivism and the Continental theory of a centralized system of law. The corrections

---

[51] On the inevitable absorption of the features of natural law in the 1789 Declaration by positive law, see P. Wachsmann, 'Naturalisme et volontarisme dans la Déclaration des droits de l'homme de 1789' (1985) 2 *Droits*, 13–22.

[52] See B. Janneau, *Les principes généraux du droit dans la jurisprudence administrative* (1954); R. Odent, *Contentieux administratif* (1970–1), 166: 'confining ourselves to the present position of the Conseil d'état on this point, it would seem that most of the principles enshrined in the 1789 Declaration of the Rights of Man and the Citizen . . . must be considered to be general principles of law. . .'.

[53] See H. L. A. Hart, 'Utilitarianism and Natural Rights', in *Essays in Jurisprudence and Philosophy* (1983), 181–97.

[54] *Ibid.*, at 185.

which John Stuart Mill wished to make to his teacher's ideas apparently met with no success.[55]

With regard to the third critique, the most famous and undoubtedly the most influential is that put forward in 1843 by Marx in his study *On the Jewish Question*, which is highly debatable in several respects. In it, he denounces not only the 1789 but also the 1793 Declaration as the manifestation of bourgeois egoism hiding behind an ideology falsely claimed to be universal.[56] That is the source of all the diatribes launched by regimes declaring themselves to be Marxist (or Leninist) against formal bourgeois freedoms as opposed to real human rights to which only socialist States give effect. History would reveal the bloody tragedy spawned by that philosophy, so lending a prophetic note to the first sentence of the 1789 Declaration: 'whereas the sole causes of public misfortune and the corruption of governments are ignorance of or disregard or contempt for the rights of man'.[57]

I must, however, add here that it was not only in Europe that human rights sank out of sight after their solemn announcement in the eighteenth century and their enforced hibernation in the nineteenth century until the middle of the twentieth century. We find a similar phenomenon, albeit with differences of detail, in the United States as well. In that country, it was only very slowly that the wealth of possibilities contained in the declarations of independence and the first ten amendments to the Constitution in 1791 became reality.

The chief distinction, in terms of human rights, between the United States and the old continent lies in the recognition by the Supreme Court in *Marbury v. Madison*[58] that it was open to every judge to ascertain whether any given text, even a law voted by Congress, was compatible with superior law. From then on, the rights of Man, as

[55] See H. L. A. Hart, 'Natural Rights: Bentham and John Stuart Mill', in *Essays on Bentham, Jurisprudence and Political Theory* (1982), 79–104.

[56] Marx writes, for example: 'Let us state first of all that "rights of man", as distinct from "citizens' rights", are nothing but the rights of a member of bourgeois society, that is to say, of selfish man, of man isolated from his fellow man and from his community': *La question juive* (1968), 37, and more generally at 34–5. Even in this piece of Marx's juvenilia we can perceive his proposed 'holistic' conception of socialist human rights: those rights should not divide a man from his community. This is repeated with the greatest precision in the doctrine of the 20th century socialist bloc countries in which, as Dupuy points out, 'man is . . . taken as integrated within his group', and all freedoms are subordinate to the construction of the new society, note 1 above, at 420. On the Marxist critiques of human rights, see L. Ferry and A. Renaut, *Philosophie politique* (1985), iii, 124–9, and Peces-Barba Martinez, note 49 above, at 95–8. It is noteworthy that the virulent opposition of an author such as Althusser, who so deeply influenced the 1960s generation in France, to even the Marxist 'ideology' of human rights contributed to setting back until after the 1970s any recognition of the value of the battle for human rights, so far as a part of the French intelligentsia was concerned. See Althusser, *Pour Marx* (1963), 227–58.

[57] Other important authors have contributed to the systematic devaluation of the doctrine of human rights in Europe: thus Nietzsche writes: '[w]e who acknowledge no fatherland . . . We preserve nothing; no return to the past; we are not "liberals", we do not labour for "progress", we do not have to block our ears so as not to hear the sirens of the future in the market-place singing the tune of "equal rights", the song of "free society" and "no more masters and slaves" none of which we find attractive': *The Joyful Wisdom* (1950), §377, at 11–12. Further on in this text, Nietzsche makes an appeal for danger, adventure, war and the reintroduction of a new slavery 'if necessary'. While we may not impute vile thoughts to Nietzsche, it is clear that the author of 'Beyond Good and Evil', who exerted considerable influence on European thought, was hardly a militant supporter of the rights of 'every human being', to put it mildly, and some of his writings lay themselves open to loathsome interpretations. For a study of other authors, see Ferry and Renaut, note 56 above, at 109–29, and Peces-Barba Martinez, note 49 above, at 69–98 ('*Las negaciones totales del concepto [de derechos humanos]*').

[58] 5 US 137 (1803).

set forth in the amendments to the constitution, were an integral part of the law proper and their breach could be penalized by any court and, at last instance, by the Supreme Court. While I cannot undertake an examination of the case law of the Supreme Court concerning human rights, I shall nevertheless mention these facts with which we are all familiar: when the introduction to the 1787 Constitution speaks of 'promoting the common weal and ensuring the benefits of freedom for ourselves and our descendants', they naturally mean the welfare and freedom of men and, even more specifically, of white men.[59] In other words, the slavery existing in much of the Federation was not affected by that pronouncement any more than by the words of the Declaration of Independence which proclaim that '[we] hold these truths to be self-evident, that all men are created equal, that they are endowed by their Creator with certain unalienable rights, that among these are Life, Liberty and the pursuit of Happiness'.

That irreconcilable contradiction between the theory and the reality of slavery was to lead to the war of secession. The war did not, however, put an end to the problem since, in its judgment in *Plessey* v. *Ferguson*,[60] the Supreme Court granted the Southern States recognition of the constitutionality of their segregationalist laws (equal but separate).[61] It was not until the 1954 judgment in *Brown* v. *Board of Education of Topeka*,[62] that a Supreme Court, presided over by Earl Warren, engaged in a systematic policy of defending *civil rights*. So, finally, as in Europe, though for different reasons, it is only in the second half of the twentieth century that we can see the potential of the theory of human rights being fully realized.[63]

2. Barbarity in Europe and the Renewal of the Philosophy and Positive Law of Human Rights   It is true that concern for human rights had not disappeared from people's consciences, as demonstrated by the (belated) abolition of slavery in France (1848) and in other countries, leading up to the international conventions of 1890 and 1926. Similarly, after 1918, under the ægis of the League of Nations or the International Labour Organization (ILO), various conventions were adopted concerning the prohibition of traffic in women and children, the protection of decent working conditions or the protection of minorities.[64]

[59] It was not until 1808 that the Constitution gave Congress the right to forbid traffic in slaves: see Henkin, note 48 above, at 433. We may also recall the Dred Scott case in which in 1857 the Supreme Court declared that a black slave was a citizen neither of the United States nor of his state of origin and that he had no capacity to bring legal actions: *Dred Scott* v. *Stanford*, 60 US 393 (1857).

[60] 163 US 539 (1896).

[61] The historian H. C. Allen notes: '[a]t the beginning of the 20th century the position of blacks was scarcely better than, and sometimes even as bad as at the time of the Black Codes . . . the 14th and 15th amendments remained a dead letter in the South'. Even before the 1896 judgment, another judgment of the Supreme Court, given on 15 Oct. 1883, cited in *Civil Rights Cases* (109 US 3 (1893)), had essentially deprived the 14th and 15th amendments of any effect in combating discriminatory practices. See *Les Etats-Unis* (1967), i, 220; D. Borstin, *Histoire des Américains* (1991), 1493–5.

[62] 347 US 483 (1954).

[63] On the dismantling of discriminatory legislation after *Brown*, see Borstin, *ibid.*, at 1507–10. On the question of 'affirmative action' and the judgment of the Supreme Court of July 1978, *Allan Bakke* v. *Regents of the University of California*, 438 US 407 (1978) and J. Belz, 'Equal Protection and Affirmative Action', in D. J. Bodenhammer and J.W. Ely Jr., *The Bill of Rights in Modern America. After 200 Years* (1993), 155–73.

[64] For a general view of the international conventions adopted before and after 1945, see F. Capotorti, 'Human Rights: The Hard Road Towards Universality', in R. St. MacDonald and D. Johnston, *The Structure and Process of International Law* (1983), 977–1000.

It was, however, the fall of part of Europe (countries of outstanding culture) into the barbarity of Nazism and Fascism, which were based on the absolute and total denial of the doctrine of human rights, which brought about a complete change in European thinking on this subject.[65] I shall not dwell in this chapter on the pivotal role played by the Rome Convention of 1950, or on the dissemination of the principles of that convention and of the case law of the Court at Strasbourg throughout the legal orders both of the individual States and of the European Union.[66]

I would merely point out that one of the principal changes brought about in Europe after 1945 was due to the adoption by most States (with the notable exception of the United Kingdom) of the Kelsenian system of review of the constitutionality of laws (also called 'the European model' as opposed to the American model).[67] As a result of this, European countries changed their systems from an '*Etat légal*'[68] to an '*Etat de droit*',[69] in which the Legislature itself can be sanctioned by a constitutional court for failure to observe the constitutional laws including (and above all) those safeguarding human rights. In France, as is well known, the Conseil Constitutionnel was to incorporate the 1789 Declaration into the corpus of constitutional law, respect for which it enforces, thus as a Supreme Charter of human rights giving that text its full effect for the first time.[70]

B. Certain Features of the European Concept of Human Rights

1. Sources of European Jus Commune   If I am to attempt to distinguish the specific features of the European conception of human rights, I must begin by identifying the sources likely to provide a list of the rights which are common to Europe, as opposed to the *jus proprium* of one State or another (for example, the extension of the protection of the right to life to the embryo in Ireland). It is clear that the first of these sources is the European Convention on Human Rights, which was specifically intended by its authors to be an instrument in the unification of Europe in the realm of the maintenance and further realization of human rights and fundamental

---

[65] See the beginning of the press conference given by Cassin on 8 July 1947: '[t]he last war was essentially the "Human Rights" War, inflicted on peoples by those who espoused a monstrous racist doctrine, and waged simultaneously against man and the community of men, with unprecedented systematic cruelty'. The full text of the speech is given in Faure, note 30 above, at 297–301.

[66] See G. Cohen-Jonathan, *La convention européenne des droits de l'homme* (1989); and by the same author, *Aspects européens des droits fondamentaux* (1996). See also F. Sudre (ed.), *Le droit français et la convention européenne des droits de l'homme* (1994); L. Sermet, *L'incidence de la convention européenne des droits de l'homme sur le contentieux administratif français* (1996); J.-P. Jacqué, 'Communauté européenne et convention européenne des droits de l'homme', in *L'Europe et le droit. Mélanges en hommage a Jean Boulouis* (1991), 325–40.

[67] See Kelsen, 'Le contrôle de la constitutionnalité des lois. Une étude comparative des Constitutions autrichienne et américaine' (1990) 1 *RFDC*, 17–30.

[68] Translator's note: that is to say, a State in which individuals and the executive are subject to the rule of law, but the legislature is sovereign and acts with impunity.

[69] Translator's note: or '*Rechtsstaat*', a civil law system in which all persons and all organs of government are answerable to the law.

[70] See the decisions on freedom of association (16 July 1971), automatic taxation (27 Dec. 1973) and nationalization laws (16 Jan. and 11 Feb. 1982), in L. Favoreu and L. Philip, *Les grandes décisions du Conseil constitutionnel* (1991), 237 ff, 269 ff, and 470 ff.

freedoms.[71] I scarcely need stress the importance of that treaty and the protocols supplementing it, or refer to the role played by the European Court of Human Rights in Strasbourg, especially since 1974. It has become of even greater importance with the accession of several Central and Eastern European countries to the Rome Convention, although it is still too early to tell whether this is actually an opportunity to extend the protection of human rights to the entire continent of Europe or rather a watering-down of the Convention, owing to the fact that the eastern and western States are so heterogenous.[72]

In any event, the European Convention, which was intended by its authors to be the first embodiment in actual law of the Universal Declaration, established a system for monitoring compliance with its provisions that is to this day unequalled, either at the regional level (although some interesting progress is to be found in the American convention on human rights signed on 22 November 1969[73]), or at the universal. It may be considered *a prime characteristic of the European approach* that, in certain conditions which I need not specify, it affords persons claiming to have had their rights infringed by the States which are parties to the Convention an effective individual right of action before the international courts with the power of review. In the end, a judgment given by a court and possessing binding authority can rule that such a right has been infringed and may possibly afford the plaintiff just satisfaction.[74]

The search for a European conception of human rights cannot, however, be confined solely to consideration of the Rome Convention. We must take into account the way in which the matter of human rights has been raised within the European Community, both because the law in Luxembourg and the law in Strasbourg significantly influence one another[75] and because it is the Community, in its international relations, which applies pressure to non-member countries to make them undertake to observe certain fundamental rights.

Turning to the first point, that is the development within the Community, through the case law of the Court of Justice of the European Communities, of a policy of defending human rights which, as we know, had no legal basis in the original treaties, we find that the Court has had recourse to two methods to achieve its ends. First, it has elevated *the constitutional traditions common to the Member States* concerning the protection of fundamental rights to the Community level by transforming them

---

[71] See the third recital in the preamble to the Convention of Rome: '[c]onsidering that the aim of the Council of Europe is the achievement of greater unity between its Members and that one of the methods by which that aim is to be pursued is the maintenance and further realization of human rights and fundamental freedoms'.

[72] The workload of the Strasbourg Court remained modest until 1973 (17 judgments delivered between 1959 and 1973, as against 448 between 1974 and 1993). See Cohen-Jonathan, note 65 above, at 233, and Faure, note 30 above, at 226 ff, who also lists the Central and Eastern European States which have signed the Convention, with the date of ratification for those which have already done so. As at 29 Feb. 1996, those which had both signed and ratified were: Bulgaria, Hungary, Lithuania, Poland, Romania, Russia, Slovakia, and Slovenia. Those which had signed but not yet ratified were: Estonia, Macedonia, Moldavia, and Ukraine.

[73] See F. Sudre, *Droit international des droits de l'homme* (1997), 98–101.

[74] See Art. 50 ECHR and Cohen-Jonathan, note 65 above, at 212–16.

[75] These cross-influences have been further strengthened by the Amsterdam Treaty, since certain of the provisions of the TEU are henceforth subject to review by the ECJ, to the extent that some authors have even spoken of the 'perverse effect of the complex Amsterdam construction'. See Wachsmann, note 5 above, at 893.

into general principles of Community law.[76] The classic formulation of this policy may be found in, *inter alia,* the judgment in *Wachauf,* in which the Court stated:

> The Court has consistently held, in particular in its judgment of 13 December 1979 in Case 44/79, *Hauer* v. *Land Rheinland-Pfalz* [1979] ECR 3727, that fundamental rights form an integral part of the general principles of the law, the observance of which is ensured by the Court. In safeguarding those rights, the Court has to look to the constitutional traditions common to the Member States, so that measures which are incompatible with the fundamental rights recognized by the constitutions of those States may not find acceptance in the Community.[77]

On the other hand, in seeking relevant general principles, the Court of Justice also turns to the European Convention on Human Rights, which has been ratified by all the Member States and consequently 'is of particular significance'.[78] Thus, as the Court declared in *Rutili,*[79] with regard to the powers of the immigration authorities and the reservation relating to public policy, '[the] limitations placed on the powers of Member States in respect of control of aliens are a specific manifestation of the more general principle, enshrined in Articles 8, 9, 10 and 11 of the Convention for the Protection of Human Rights and Fundamental Freedoms'.

Finally, Article 6(2) (*ex* Article F(2)) of the consolidated version of the Treaty on European Union repeats and confirms the Court's two sources of inspiration, declaring that: '[t]he Union shall respect fundamental rights, as guaranteed by the European Convention for the Protection of Human Rights and Fundamental Freedoms, signed in Rome on 4 November 1950 and as they result from the constitutional traditions common to the Member States, as general principles of Community law'.[80]

The second point of interest concerns the provisions relating to human rights which must be respected by the Member States of the Union and those which the Community seeks to include in its development co-operation agreements and its economic and co-operation agreements with non-member countries.[81]

As we have already seen, respect for the principles set out in Article 6 (*ex* Article F(1)—the principles of liberty, democracy, respect for human rights and fundamental freedoms, and the rule of law) is henceforth an express condition for the accession of new Member States to the Union. It is therefore a condition to be satisfied not merely at the time of accession but also permanently, since the Council,

---

[76] This, however, does pose some awkward problems for national constitutional courts. See *Protection constitutionnelle et protection internationale des droits de l'homme. Concurrence ou complémentarité?,* IXth Conference of European Constitutional Courts, Paris, May 1993, Vol. 2. See also J.-P. Puissochet, 'La Cour de justice et les principes généraux de droit', in Congres des avocats européens, *La protection juridictionnelle des droits dans le systeme communautaire* (1997), 1–19.

[77] Case 5/88, *Wachauf* v. *Germany* [1989] ECR 2609.

[78] See Joined Cases 46/87 and 227/88 *Hoechst* v. *Commission* [1989] ECR 2919. On that whole question, see J.-P. Jacqué , 'La Constitution de la Communauté européenne' [1995] *RUDH* 407 and 'Communauté européenne et convention européenne des droits de l'homme', note 65 above, at 327 ff.

[79] Case 36/75, *Rutili* [1975] ECR 1219.

[80] For this whole question, see Wachsmann, note 5 above, at 883–903, who emphasizes the fact that 'human rights have thoroughly permeated the Community legal system' (at 897).

[81] See the Luxembourg European Council's Declaration on Human Rights, June 1991 *Bull. EC* 6–1991, at Annex V, 17; *Commission Communication on the inclusion of respect for democratic principles and human rights in agreements between the Community and third countries,* COM(95)216 final.

meeting in the composition of the Heads of State or Government, 'may determine the existence of a serious and persistent breach by a Member State of principles mentioned in Article 6(1)' (Article 7 (*ex* Article F.1)). In that case, 'the Council, acting by a qualified majority, may decide to suspend certain of the rights deriving from the application of this Treaty to the Member State in question'.

These provisions are, it has been observed, similar to those laid down by the Council of Europe. Membership of the Council of Europe is open to a State only if it 'accepts the principles of the rule of law and of the enjoyment by all persons within its jurisdiction of human rights and fundamental freedoms' (Article 3 of the Statute of the Council of Europe, as referred to in Article 5). Moreover, 'a Member State of the Council of Europe which has seriously violated Article 3 of the Statute may be suspended from its rights of representation and requested by the Committee of Ministers to withdraw from the Council'.[82]

Returning to the European Community, the Treaty on European Union does not merely call on its own members to respect those fundamental rights, it makes that respect one of the conditions of both its policy of economic co-operation with non-member countries and of its common foreign and security policy.

As regards co-operation policy, in the second half of the 1980s the Community began to introduce clauses on respect for human rights into its agreements with non-member countries and, in particular, in the Lomé Conventions, notwithstanding the great reluctance of its ACP partners. Thus, a common declaration concerning Article 4, annexed to the text of Lomé III, stated that human dignity is an 'inalienable right and constitutes an essential objective in the achievement of the legitimate aspirations of individuals and of peoples'. There is an even greater emphasis in the Fourth Lomé Convention (1989) which calls respect for human rights 'a basic factor of real development'.

Article 5 then states that: '[r]espect for human rights, democratic principles and the rule of law, which underpins relations between the ACP States and the Community and all provisions of the Convention, and governs the domestic and international policies of the Contracting Parties, shall constitute an essential element of this Convention'. And since this concerns an essential element of the convention, Article 366bis declares, pursuant to the ordinary law of treaties (Article 60 of the Vienna Convention), that where there is failure to fulfil those obligations and refusal to consult, 'the Party which invoked the failure to fulfil an obligation may take appropriate steps, including, where necessary, the partial or full suspension of application of this Convention to the party concerned'.[83]

Subsequently the Community went on to make systematic reference to respect for human rights, first in its association agreements with Central European countries (1991 to 1992), and then in other economic co-operation agreements. The Treaty on the European Community confirms that policy, stating in Article 177 (*ex* Article

[82] The procedure under Art. 8 of the Statute of the Council of Europe has only once been set in motion, against Greece under the Colonels. See Wachsmann, note 5 above, at 894–7.
[83] For the text of the Fourth Lomé Convention, see [1991] OJ L229/3, and the Agreement amending the fourth ACP–EC Convention of Lomé signed in Mauritius on 4 Nov. 1995 ([1998] OJ L156/3), and also *Le Courrier-A.C.P.*, No. 120 (Mar.–Apr. 1990). See also J. Kranz, 'Lomé, le dialogue et l'homme' (1998) *RTDE* 451.

130U) that 'Community policy in this area [the sphere of development co-operation] shall contribute to the general objective of developing and consolidating democracy and the rule of law, and to that of respecting human rights and fundamental freedoms'.

Furthermore, in a communication of May 1995, the Commission analysed the various wordings of those 'democracy and human rights' clauses in previous agreements, and proposed that henceforth association agreements and economic and co-operation agreements should contain a standard provision as follows:

(a) in the provisions of the agreement:
a clause stipulating that 'the relations between the Community and the countries concerned and all the provisions of the agreement in question are based upon respect for the democratic principles and human rights which govern domestic and international policy both in the Community and in the country concerned and which constitutes an essential element of the agreement'.

(b) in the preamble
references in general to respect for human rights and democratic values; references to universal and/or local instruments common to the two parties; in specific cases, an express suspension clause or a general non-performance clause may also be proposed.[84]

It can therefore be seen that, just as a Member State which seriously and persistently breaches its human rights obligations may have its rights suspended, so a State bound by an economic agreement with the Community (Lomé Convention, association agreements, etc.) may be penalized, by means of suspension of the Treaty, for breach of those undertakings relating to human rights and democracy 'which constitute an essential element of the agreement'.[85]

I must add that, apart from development co-operation, Article J.1 of the Maastricht Treaty, now Article 11 of the consolidated version of the Treaty on European Union, states that it is one of the objectives of (in this case) the Union's common foreign and security policy 'to develop and consolidate democracy and the rule of law, and respect for human rights and fundamental freedoms' (fifth paragraph of Article 11(1)).

---

[84] See COM(95)216 final.
[85] For a general consideration of this question and a distinctly critical assessment of this type of clause, see J. Verhoeven, 'La Communauté européenne et la sanction internationale de la démocratie et des droits de l'homme' [1997] *AFDI* 799–809. The author concludes his study with the following remarks: '[u]nder the misleading guise of reciprocity, the Community is creating powers for itself the exercise of which could be particularly wrongful since no provision is made for recourse to some arbitrator or third party in the case of dispute as to the lawfulness of the "appropriate steps" taken in response to the alleged breach of "democratic principles". To be troubled by this is not to disregard the fundamental importance attaching to certain rules, or to doubt the good intentions of the Community. On the contrary, the use of wrongful means to the end of respecting democracy is prohibited by democracy itself'. What I find dubious is the equal application of the same rules to all States in the same situation with regard to human rights and respect for democracy. Some lines of La Fontaine spring to mind: '*selon que vous serez puissants ou mis rables*', etc. (depending on whether you are mighty or wretched).

IV. EUROPEAN *JUS COMMUNE* AND
UNIVERSAL *JUS COMMUNE*

I have above contrasted the *jus proprium* of one State with the *jus commune* of Europe. I must now mention the relations which, in this sphere of human rights, connect the individual, the local and the universal, concentrating my argument on the European situation but it being understood that other examples would be equally valid. [86]

The legal provisions adopted by European States concerning human rights may be divided into two parts. One set of provisions expresses the *jus proprium* of each State, which is not to be found at Community level. I have already cited the constitutional protection of the embryo in Ireland; we may also think of the various methods by which religious freedom is taken into consideration, depending on whether it is a secular country such as France, or a country such as the United Kingdom etc. The other set gives expression to values which are common to the countries of Europe and therefore falls within the ambit of European *jus commune*. I would point out here that one of the means used by the Court of Justice in Luxembourg to elucidate that common law is to extract it from the constitutional traditions common to the Member States (see the text p. 88 above).

However, European *jus commune* itself may be divided into two: on the one hand, provisions specific to Europe (for example those deriving from the secular character of the State itself, even if it is not secular on the French model), and, on the other, provisions forming part of a universal *jus commune*. The clearest illustration of this is the European Convention of Human Rights which is intended to represent the transposition into positive law of 'a common standard of achievement for all peoples' heralded by the Universal Declaration of 1948.

Thus each level, whether State, regional, or universal, contains an element of *jus proprium* characteristic of its level, and an element of *jus commune* from the upper level. So when considering the question of the European approach to human rights, we have to distinguish the part of European law which is the expression at European level of universal rights from the part which is specific to Europe and constitutes its *jus proprium*.

(a) If we now inquire what this universal *jus commune* of Europe, and more particularly the European Union, may consist of, we will first encounter those provisions for the protection of human rights and fundamental freedoms with which Europe requires non-member countries to comply (see the text p. 91 above). Indeed, it is inconceivable that Europe should demand compliance with its *jus proprium* in the narrow sense; rather it is the *jus universale* contained in the *jus proprium* which must be observed.

In this regard it will be observed that the Community does not call for respect only for human rights and fundamental freedoms but for a wider whole which also includes respect for democracy and the rule of law. By implication, this means that

---

[86] See N. Valticos, 'Nations, états, régions et communauté universelle: niveaux et étapes de la protection des droits de l'homme', in *Mélanges René-Jean Dupuy*, note 45 above, at 339–48.

protection of human rights can be guaranteed only under constitutional arrangements similar in kind to those of the Member States of the Union, since the Union 'is founded on the principles of liberty, democracy, respect for human rights and fundamental freedoms, and the rule of law, principles which are common to the Member States' (Article 6(1) of the Treaty of Union, *ex* Article F(1)).

The ultimate, ambitious aim of Community foreign policy is therefore to promote the European constitutional model, which alone is considered capable of guaranteeing genuine protection of human rights and fundamental freedoms. It might appear that such an intention is unconscionable and justifies the vituperation of those in the Third World who denounce the neo-colonialism of European (and American) human rights policy. However, I must observe that the links between democracy/rule of law/human rights and fundamental freedoms are not or are no longer a special feature of European *jus proprium*. Thus, in the Vienna Declaration and Action Programme, Article 8 states:

> Democracy, development and respect for human rights and fundamental freedoms are interdependent and mutually reinforcing. Democracy is based on the freely expressed will of the people to determine their own political, economic, social and cultural systems and on their full participation in all aspects of their lives.

Article 9 goes on to state that '[t]he World Conference on Human Rights reaffirms that least advanced countries committed to the process of democratization and economic reforms . . . should be supported by the international community'.

There is a reference to the rule of law in the ninth recital in the preamble, which emphasizes the need to 'promote and encourage respect for human rights and fundamental freedoms for all . . . and also democracy, justice, equality, *the rule of law*, pluralism etc'.[87]

We can see, therefore, that the triad of human rights/democracy/rule of law, which is not to be found either in the Universal Declaration (but see Article 21(3) on the will of the people as the basis of the authority of government) or in the Covenants, makes an appearance at international level, without any doubt on account of the actions of European States (but also of the countries of North America[88]). Furthermore, this 'activism' has only been made possible by the collapse of the Soviet bloc and the peculiar conception of democracy promulgated by that bloc. This is clear to see in the documents adopted by the Conference on Security and Co-operation in Europe after 1989, such as the Copenhagen Document of 29 June 1990 or the Charter of

---

[87] It will however be observed that at a recent regional summit meeting in Entebbe, in which Eritrea, Ethiopia, Kenya, Tanzania, Congo-Kinshasa, Rwanda, Zimbabwe, and the Organization of African Unity took part, the participants signed the 'Entebbe Declaration', in which they undertook to 'pursue a dialogue on the democratic process, recognizing that there is no defined/definite model of democratic institutions'. President Clinton, who had been invited to that regional summit meeting, also declared that 'there is no one model for the functioning of a democracy', *le Monde*, 1 Apr. 1998.

[88] For American policy in the Carter era, see note 6 above. President Clinton has in part adopted a policy of international action in favour of democracy and human rights (with the same gaps as European policy, especially *vis-à-vis* the People's Republic of China). At the regional summit meeting of African countries in Entebbe on 31 Mar. 1998, the 'Entebbe Declaration', note 87 above, invites the participating States to work towards democracy, liberalization of the economy and respect for human rights, so as to avoid the recurrence of genocide in that area after Rwanda. As regards democracy, the States undertake to 'continue a dialogue on the democratic process, recognizing that there is no definitive model for democratic institutions'. See *le Monde*, 1 Apr. 1998.

Paris for a New Europe, of 21 November 1990, both of which also refer to the triad of 'human rights, democracy and the rule of law'.[89]

It may therefore be considered that what was once only one of the requirements of the European concept of human rights is at present being transformed into a universal concept. This does not, however, imply that third countries are aligning themselves completely on the European model, as we can see if we subject the distinctive features of that model to closer scrutiny.

Jacqué felt impelled to describe the characteristics of what was to be a kind of 'Constitution of the European Community'; that is to say, the introduction by the European institutions (legislative bodies and the Court of Justice of the European Communities through its decisions) of a body of provisions concerning the fundamental values of the Union, its structural principles, and the principles governing the relations between the Community and the Member States.[90]

Among the sources used by Jacqué to establish the fundamental values of the European constitution, he cites the document on European identity adopted by the Conference of Heads of State and of Government in Copenhagen on 14 December 1973. According to that document, the Heads of State and Government there present:

> Desiring to ensure that the legal, political and moral values to which they are attached are respected, and anxious to conserve the rich variety of their national cultures, sharing the same conception of life, based on the desire to build a society conceived and created in the service of men, . . . intend to safeguard the principles of representative democracy, the rule of law and social justice, the aim of economic progress and respect for human rights, which are the fundamental constituents of a European identity'.[91]

Jacqué goes on to show that the case law of the Court of Justice confirms the five fundamental values set out in that text which form a sort of European constitution, namely: (a) respect for the principle according to which the Community legal order constitutes a 'Community governed by the rule of law'; (b) respect for fundamental rights; (c) the democratic principle; (d) the protection of social justice; and (e) the protection of cultural pluralism.[92]

It is striking how closely that list matches the list of provisions inserted in the Community's economic agreements. The 'Community governed by the rule of law' corresponds to 'the rule of law', and respect for fundamental rights and democracy (representative democracy according to the text of 1973) is to be found in both lists. On the other hand, there is no missionary zeal at the international level to propagate the protection of social justice and cultural pluralism, which rightfully belongs to the domain of the Constitution of Europe. It may well be thought that views on the last two points differ so much that in this sphere there may be a European *jus proprium* which does not, at least for the time being, lend itself to a process of universalization.

(b) If we turn now to this European *jus proprium* (which is at the same time the *jus commune* of the European States) and compare it with the *jus proprium* of the United States (in order to compare two bodies of legislation of equivalent importance), our

---

[89] See Decaux, note 41 above, at 94–6; Sudre, note 26 above, at 97–8.
[90] Jacqué, note 78 above, at 397–423.   [91] *Ibid.*, at 406.   [92] *Ibid.*, at 406–12.

starting point may specifically be the greater attention paid in Europe to social matters. It is true that (western) Europe shares with the United States the conviction
that, between freedom and equality, priority must be given to the principle as formulated by Rawls in his *Theory of Justice*, positing in the first place that '[e]ach person is to have an equal right to the most extensive total system of equal basic liberties
compatible with a similar system of liberty for all'.[93]

Europe, however, which bears the stamp of social democracy, and France in any
event (but Germany too, with its own vision of a social market economy), places
greater emphasis than do the United States on the need for the State to take action to
implement second-generation human rights, the celebrated 'social rights'. America,
by contrast, is characterized by deep suspicion of State intervention. Hannah Arendt
previously contrasted the American 'political revolution' with the French 'social
revolution'. Habermas, explaining the different sources of inspiration for 1776 and
1789, writes: '[t]hen [1776], it was a matter of giving free rein to the spontaneous
forces of self-governance in keeping with natural law, whereas now [1789] the objective is to impose, in the teeth of a depraved society and corrupted human nature, a coherent whole based on natural law'.[94] Notwithstanding the effects of 'globalization',
those two consciousnesses remain on either side of the Atlantic. Furthermore, it is
noteworthy that Rawls' second principle (the principle of difference and equality of
opportunity) is closer to social-democratic philosophy than to Reaganite
liberalism.

A second feature of the European approach seems to me to be the awareness, arising out of the tragic history of the 1930s and 1940s, of the need actively to defend
human rights against the enemies of humanity. This raises an important question of
substance formulated during the French Revolution by Saint Just: what freedom
must the enemies of freedom be allowed? Confronting that question, the United
States display great liberalism (the almost supreme right to free speech), which finds
expression in the first reservation included in the ratification (in June 1992) of the
International Covenant on Civil and Political Rights, which states: 'Article 20 [pro-
hibiting war propaganda and any appeal to racial or religious hatred] shall neither
authorize nor require the United States to adopt laws or other measures liable to restrict the freedom of speech and association protected by the Constitution and the
laws of the United States'.

Europe, on the other hand, adopts a much more restrictive position arising from
its historical experience. This is expressed in Article 17 of the European Convention:
'[n]othing in this Convention may be interpreted as implying for any State, group or
person any right to engage in any activity or perform any act aimed at the destruction of any of the rights or freedoms set forth herein or at their limitation to a greater

---

[93] J. Rawls, *A Theory of Justice* (1987). Rawls gives a list of the most important basic freedoms: 'political liberty (the right to vote and to be eligible for public office) together with freedom of speech and assembly; liberty of conscience and freedom of thought; freedom of the person [which includes] freedom
from arbitrary arrest and seizure as defined by the concept of the rule of law. These liberties are all required to be equal by the first principle.'

[94] J. Habermas, *Théorie et pratique* (1975), i, 129.

extent than is provided for in the Convention'. That is also the tenor of the provisions of the German Basic Law on the protection of the Constitution.[95]

The Europe/United States comparison can be taken further, following the American reservations made to the ratification of the International Covenant on Civil and Political Rights. Under the second reservation, 'the United States reserve the right, subject to the limitations imposed by their constitution, to pronounce the death penalty against any person (other than a pregnant woman) duly found guilty under the laws in force or future laws permitting the imposition of the death penalty, including its imposition for crimes committed by persons aged less than 18'. We know that, by contrast, the countries of Europe have not merely acceded to the Sixth Protocol to the European Convention, abolishing the death penalty in peace-time, but have also made abolition a condition of membership of the Council of Europe. It will astonish no one that this American reservation raised objections from several European States, such as Denmark, Finland, Norway, and Sweden. The same countries have also objected to American reservations concerning the 'cruel, inhuman or degrading treatment or punishment' which are to be interpreted in accordance with the amendments to the American constitution.

Objections have also been raised to some of the declarations of interpretation made by the United States, particularly the first, in which that country considers that exceptions to the prohibition on distinctions based on race, colour, sex, language, religion, or political opinion etc. are 'permissible where they are at least reasonably connected to a legitimate objective of public interest'. This interpretation, considered by some to be in fact a reservation, is of course used to take account of *affirmative action* policy. More generally, however, it demonstrates the tendency in the United States to think of society in terms of groups which may lawfully receive special treatment, subject to the review of the Supreme Court, if their situation is particular. This applies as much to minorities, whether ethnic, sexual, or linguistic, as it does to the status of women or elderly persons, etc. In general, the consensus in Europe is to refuse any classification of citizens, which explains the unease experienced by several European States (including France) faced with any text concerning the protection of minorities—except of course minorities in other countries.[96]

The contrast between European and American attitudes to policies for minorities leads me to qualify the claim set out above, concerning European countries' greater sensibility to social questions. We may well consider that certain actions undertaken,

---

[95] Art. 18 of the Basic Law of 23 May 1949: '[a]ny person who abuses the freedom of expression of opinions . . . in order to challenge the liberal and democratic constitutional order shall lose those fundamental rights. That loss, and its extent, shall be declared by the Federal Constitutional Court'. See S. Rials and D. Baranger, *Que Sais-je? Textes constitutionnels étrangers* (1995), 50.

[96] The Conciliation Committee of the European Conference for Peace in Yugoslavia considered that 'respect for the fundamental rights of human beings and the rights of peoples and minorities' was part of the 'overriding rules of general international law which . . . are imperative for all parties to the succession (i.e., former Yugoslavia)'. See [1992] *RGDIP* 264–6. However, as regards this matter within Western European countries, we note the adoption of a European Charter on regional or minority languages ([1993] *RGDIP* 411) and of a framework convention of the Council of Europe for the protection of national minorities, of 10 Nov. 1994. See Sudre, note 26 above, at 158–63. See also the decision of the European Court of Human Rights in the *Belgian Linguistics Case (No 2)*, ECHR (1968) Series A, No. 6, Cohen-Jonathan, note 66 above, at 518–20.

and undertaken in an authoritarian manner, in the United States, in order to break the vicious circle of poverty and of communities trapped in the margins of society, such as bussing or affirmative action, would be hard to imagine in Europe, or at least in France. When I say this, I am not unaware of the contradictions and perverse effects to which those practices give rise.

V. CONCLUSION

In the end, is there a European approach to human rights? Without a doubt. European practice is distinguished simultaneously by the pioneering role played by Europe in this sphere, which it continues to play, the fairly homogenous nature of European countries, and the close relations of those countries within the European Union and the Council of Europe, to which might be added, with regard to the countries of Eastern Europe, the Organization for Security and Co-operation in Europe, in the expectation that some of those States will in the end join the Union.

In comparison with protective systems with characteristically 'holistic' features, that stress personal duties as well as rights, such as the African Charter or, to a lesser extent, the American Declaration of Human Rights and Duties, the European approach has preserved the stamp of eighteenth-century revolutionary individualism. But unlike its counterpart which struck independent root on the other side of the Atlantic in the same period, Europe, with variations according to country, has never rejected continued action by the State, that is to say the government; while government is admittedly the body against which rights have to be protected, it is also the representative of the will of the people and as such must guarantee that rights and fundamental freedoms are in fact protected.

Beside the technical details concerning one subject-area or another, this protection is intended to defend the dignity of a human being, and thus of humanity itself, a term which is a good expression of the twofold dimension of this value: the *human* in man but also *humankind* which must, still and for ever, be protected from the scourges of tyranny and oppression which, to quote the Preamble to the Universal Declaration, 'have resulted in barbarous acts which have outraged the conscience of mankind'. What is most outrageous, however, is that 50 years after the Declaration the 'barbarous acts' and 'untold sorrow' spoken of by the Charter of the United Nations belong, not to our world's vanished past, but to its unhappy present.

3

The Effect of Rights on Political Culture

MARTTI KOSKENNIEMI

I wish to make two arguments. First, while the rhetoric of human rights has historically had a positive and liberating effect on societies, once rights become institutionalized as a central part of political and administrative culture, they lose their transformative effect and are petrified into a legalistic paradigm that marginalizes values or interests that resist translation into rights-language. In this way, the liberal principle of the 'priority of the right over the good'[1] results in a colonization of political culture by a technocratic language that leaves no room for the articulation or realization of conceptions of the good.

Secondly, I will argue that rights-rhetoric is not as powerful as it claims to be. It does not hold a coherent set of normative demands that could be resorted to in the administration of society. To the contrary, despite its claim for value-neutrality, rights-rhetoric is constantly reduced to conflicting and contested arguments about the political good. The identification, meaning, and applicability of rights are dependent on contextual assessments of 'proportionality' or administrative 'balancing' through which priorities are set among conflicting conceptions of political value and scarce resources are distributed between contending social groups. Inasmuch as such decision-making procedures define what 'rights' are, they cannot themselves be controlled by rights. To this extent, the 'priority of the right over the good' proves an impossible demand, and insisting upon it will leave political discretion unchecked. The problem lies in how to move from an uncritical postulation of legal rights into a political culture in which delegated authority would be actively controlled by a condition of civic public-mindedness in the community at large.

Let me stress what I do *not* claim. I do not hold the Benthamite view that rights talk is 'nonsense upon stilts'. I do not think that rights have absolutely no value or that they encapsulate a bourgeois ideology in contrast to some deeper truth. In a thoughtful contribution to this volume Klaus Günther argues that rights have significance inasmuch as they open political culture to experiences of injustice and fear, and provide a voice through which the pain of torture, for example, can be articulated and listened to and the social practice of torture condemned and perhaps eradicated. I have no quarrel with that. Günther concedes, however, that rights sometimes degenerate into 'human rights talk' that aims at a legitimation of the

---

[1] J. Rawls, *A Theory of Justice* (1973), 31.

status quo. But while he thinks this is a marginal problem, I shall argue that it is the central focus of human rights in Europe today: the banal administrative recourse to rights language in order to buttress one's political priorities. The experience of pain and injustice are again on the margins—as part of history, or embedded in Europe's geographical fringes (former Yugoslavia)—while the anxious question must be: might such banalization at some point do away with the ability of human rights language to convey any sense of pain and injustice? The strength of Günther's argument lies in its being made at a philosophical level. I shall counter it by drawing on the practice of European institutions in order to highlight the mundane experience of rights constantly deferring to political priorities.

The usefulness of rights lies in their acting as 'intermediate stage' principles around which some communal values and individual interests can be organized. As the German and Italian Constitutional Courts, in a series of well-known cases in the late 1960s, challenged the supremacy of European Community (EC) law over the fundamental rights provisions included in the constitutions of those Member States this was precisely so as to distinguish and emphasize national core values, the overriding of which by a European-wide community policy seemed inadmissible. But rights often remain insufficiently normative to ground a sense of community and insufficiently concrete to be policy-orienting. The majority of United Nations (UN) Member States, for instance, have no difficulty in subscribing to most of the annual resolutions of the UN Commission of Human Rights and the Third Committee of the General Assembly without this indicating that we are any nearer to a world federation than, say, fifty years ago.

Finally, a political culture that officially insists that rights are foundational ('inalienable', 'basic'), but in practice constantly finds that they are not, becomes a culture of bad faith. A gap is established between political language and normative faith that encourages a strategic attitude as the proper political frame of mind as well as an ironic distance to politics by the general population. Human rights are erected as a façade for what has become, on the one hand, a technical administration of things and, on the other, a struggle for power and jurisdiction between different organs entrusted with policy-making tasks.[2] So, while rights-rhetoric does form an important and occasionally valuable aspect of political life, it covers only a part of it and, if allowed to colonize the whole, will have a detrimental effect on the concept of politics.

I

Rights are grounded in a profound mistrust of conceptions of the good society. Such conceptions are assumed to bring forth conflicts of subjective value and of political passion that cannot be settled by reason. The liberal Enlightenment aimed at con-

---

[2] This is precisely the criticism made against the European Court's development of its fundamental rights doctrine in countermove to the critiques by the German and Italian supreme courts in the influential article by J. Coppell and A. O'Neill, 'The European Court of Justice: Taking Rights Seriously?' (1992) 29 *Common Market Law Review* 669–92.

structing a political order that would no longer be dominated by such passion, conducive as it was to civil war (Hobbes) and tyranny (Locke, Mill). It was assumed that '[t]he health of the political realm is maintained by conscientious objection to the political'.[3]

In the public realm, the mechanism for attaining this was the separation of legislation and administration (adjudication) by reference to the subjective/rational scheme. Where legislation was the proper field of value and power (of subjectivity), those elements needed to be purged from administration. How administration was to be constrained by what is rational and non-subjective has been conceptualized in different ways and has engendered a series of losses of faith.

For early liberals, constraint was initially received from an autonomous *'reason'* (naturalism) that delimited the sphere of individual freedom as against the social order in a universally homogenous way, and provided apolitical principles that constrained those in administrative positions without relying on anybody's political preferences. As faith in the self-evidence of reason started to seem doubtful, constraint was sought from legal rules and *textual form* (positivism). Rules and texts, however, soon seemed unable to take account of life's 'real necessities' and appeared vulnerable to interminable interpretative controversy. Loss of faith in formalism was followed by calls for recourse to the social ends ('utility', effectiveness) that were assumed to lie behind rules, and 'balancing' of the conflicting interests of social groups and classes (realism).

The use of *rights* in the political discourse of liberal societies in the 1960s and 1970s should be seen as a further move in liberalism's efforts to constrain politics, now against the realist emphasis on social utility and interest-balancing that seemed just a camouflage for making (contested) policy-decisions by those in administrative positions. Ronald Dworkin's famous thesis of rights as 'trumps' is directed precisely at limiting administrative discretion by recourse to realist 'policies'.[4] Contrary to 'policy', rights were assumed to be unpolitical in that they were *universal* (i.e. independent of time and place; unamenable to political controversy) and *'factoid'* (i.e. self-evidently 'there'—'fact-like'—with compelling consequences—unlike the consequences of a statement such as 'do good').[5]

Rights arguments detach the interests of individual right-holders or groups of right-holders from political subjectivity and 'restate the interests of the group as characteristics of all people'.[6] In this way, they may seem to avoid partaking of the political subjectivity that 'raw' interests possess.[7] Claims of right can be recast as claims of an objective reason, reflected in the fact that rights 'straddle' between legal positivity and naturalism. To demonstrate their independence from the political passions of the day, rights appear as ahistorical and universal. Yet, to disclose their

---

[3] M. Wight, 'Western Values in International Relations', in H. Butterfield and M. Wight, *Diplomatic Investigations; Essays in the Theory of International Politics* (1966), 122.

[4] 'Individual rights are political trumps held by individuals. Individuals have rights when, for some reason, a collective goal is not a sufficient justification for denying them what they wish': R. Dworkin, *Taking Rights Seriously* (1977) p. xi.

[5] Cf. D. Kennedy, *A Critique of Adjudication (fin de siècle)* (1997), 305–6.   [6] *Ibid.*, at 307.

[7] Because there is no essential conception of a right, it seems difficult to object to the common practice in Western societies whereby beneficiaries of a policy dress their interests in the fulfilment of that policy in terms of their 'human rights'.

concrete (and democratic) content, they are translated into positive constitutions (fundamental rights) and other legal enactments. Hence the extraordinary rhetorical power of rights: on the one hand, they are 'outside' the political community in the sense that the legislator's task is merely to declare their presence in positive law, not to create them. On the other hand, they are also 'inside' the community by being fixed in constitutions and other positive legal enactments and thus amenable to objective confirmation.

Yet this duality creates an ambivalence: the more we insist on the ability of rights to impose an external standard for the community, the more it starts to resemble theology, and the more difficulty we have in aligning it with the ideal of popular sovereignty with which, as Jürgen Habermas has shown, rights have emerged.[8] To fall back on constitutional or other positive law standards, again, questions the universalism with which rights are associated and focuses on the procedural aspects of the constant struggle about where to draw the line between community interests and individual rights.

II

Social morality cannot, however, be translated exhaustively into rights language. Such language is based on an ideal of individual autonomy that perceives social conflict in terms of interpersonal relationship: for every right, there is a correlative duty; and for every duty, there exists a correlative right.[9] However, in existing societies, many people are confronted with normative demands that cannot be reduced into right-duty relationships. Religions, for instance, typically impose duties on people without the assumption that somebody is in possession of a correlative right. Nor can aspirations for virtue or personal excellence plausibly be translated into rights-language.[10] If a morality seeks to regulate a person's private behaviour, a right-duty relationship can only be constructed by the tenuous fiction of envisaging the holder of the right and the duty to reside in the same person.[11] The priority of the right over the good leaves little room for political value: citizenship is reduced to private reliance on right. Civic virtue, public-mindedness and political participation be-

---

[8] J. Habermas, 'Human Rights and Popular Sovereignty. The Liberal and Republican Versions' (1994) 7 *Ratio Juris* 2–6.

[9] On individual autonomy as the social ideal informing rights, cf. C. Nino, 'Introduction', in C. Nino (ed.), *Rights* (The International Library of Essays in Law & Legal Theory: Schools; 8 1992), pp. xxvi–xxvii. The correlativity of rights and duties (or powers/liabilities, immunities/disabilities, claims/no-rights, etc.) is a familiar theme of analytic jurisprudence. Although one may, from a conceptual point of view, question the necessity of such correlativity, the point is that rights seem socially effective (and, as such, 'real') often only inasmuch as they are reflected in somebody's (legally enforcible) duties.

[10] Cf. J. Raz, *The Morality of Freedom* (1986), 196–7.

[11] The argument may of course be made that there is no reason for the law to regulate private behaviour. This, however, is not a value-neutral view, but one that builds upon the kind of individualistic premises that characterize one distinct type of liberal theory, and the question remains as to the criteria whereby what is 'private' is delimited.

come a profession that seems indissociable from the advancement of private interests, an object of contempt and a source of popular cynicism.[12]

More generally, the notion of some things as intrinsically praiseworthy cannot find a place in rights-language. And yet, there are a number of contexts in which the very identity of a community depends on a conception of non-instrumental, intrinsic value. Nationalism provides one example. Typical claims of justice embedded in controversy about nationhood envision nations—or a particular nation—as an uninstrumental good, worthy of more than the human lives that inhabit it. Because they are not reducible to claims of rights by individuals, liberal theory tends to think of religion or nationalism as fundamentally irrational.[13] Hence, as Nathaniel Berman has argued, international efforts to find a compromise in nationalist conflicts, such as those involving Jerusalem, have failed. The passions of the parties, of the Arabs and the Israelis, cannot find their way into any of the proposed 'rational' schemes for the city's administration. The antagonists do not see themselves as rational right-claimants in the way liberal theory assumes in order to work.[14] Or think about indigenous societies that construct their sense of identity by a special relationship to land. Members of such societies may have duties to the land that has traditionally belonged to the community; yet no one thinks of himself or herself as an individual right-holder. A legal system that can conceptualize a lien with land only in terms of property and contract (and thus through a basic relationship between the right of the property-owner and the duties of others) cannot articulate the normative reality of such a community. Or think about the solidarity of friendship: there may be a duty between friends to compensate the loss of something even if nobody has committed a wrong. Such duty is independent of the existence of any right in anyone; yet, in terms of friendship, it makes perfect sense to say that the loss ought to be compensated by a person who was involved in bringing it about and has the resources to do so.

In a similar way, and famously, the relationship between the employer and the wage-labourer, or the sexual relations between man and woman, can only with a loss of meaning be described in rights language, for which the focus is on the terms of the contract concluded between two fully rational and autonomous individuals, assumed to trade their rights from a decontextualized negotiating position. The quality of the overall relationship, the purposes for which the work or the sexual act was carried out, or the contract's effects on third parties (e.g. within the family) cannot find articulation. Of course, late modern law includes a plethora of informal considerations that are taken account of in the assessment of such relationships. But these considerations reflect substantive ideals about the labour market and the quality of family life that override and delimit what can justifiably be concluded by reference to rights. Only through them does it becomes possible to assess whether or not the literal terms of the contract should be honoured. The deformalization of contract law by notions of reasonableness, good faith, and public order presumes the presence of

---

[12] Cf. C. Mouffe, *The Return of the Political* (1993), 82–8.

[13] In the manner of, e.g., E. Kedourie, *Nationalism* (1960).

[14] N. Berman, 'Legalizing Jerusalem or, of Law, Fantasy and Faith' (1996) 45 *The Catholic University of America Law Review* 823–35.

a perspective of the good society from which the rights established by the contract may be evaluated.[15]

The power and the weakness of rights is that they focus on the need to protect the individual against oppression and injustice by the community or the State, as explained usefully in Klaus Günther's contribution to this volume. Although 'rights-talk' has of course spread beyond individual rights to characterize various kinds of economic, social, and cultural objectives as well as different collective goods (right to peace, right to the environment), the latter differ from the former in the all-important sense in which they are understood to be ('merely') programmatory; setting guidelines to legislators and policy objectives to governments instead of creating legally enforceable claims (or powers, immunities) for any person or group of persons.[16] To the extent that such rights may be thought to create legally enforceable claims, they too portray social conflict as *ultimately* having to do with the rights of individuals.[17] In such a case, the relevant social goods worthy of protection are reduced to private interests: I have a right inasmuch as somebody else has a duty not to violate my (legally protected) interest (i.e. right). Since Marx, such a view has been criticized as a formalist, 'alienating' vehicle for the perpetuation of the liberal-capitalist society. The projection of society as merely so many individuals behaving and forming their conceptions of justice from behind a 'veil of ignorance' of their particular character, abilities, desires, and histories is, as later communitarians have insisted, an ideological fiction, examining social normativity 'not by investigation of human beings as we find them in the world, with their diverse histories and communities, but by an abstract concept of the person that has been voided of any definite cultural identity or specific historical inheritance'.[18]

For our purposes, the relevance of this critique lies in the fact that an abstract personhood and the conception of individual rights that goes with it cannot address the sense of injustice that arises, for example, from structural (economic/social) causation or from the sense of belonging to an oppressed minority. But also in many other contexts, posing the normative issue in terms of individual rights fails to grasp its social meaning. To take an example from Joseph Raz: I may own a painting by Van Gogh. Nonetheless, I may have a duty not to destroy it even if nobody has a correlative right. The value of art, in this case, cannot be expressed in rights language—just as little as, for instance, the value of a clean environment in a conflict concerning the carrying out of a contract for a large industrial project.[19]

---

[15] For the (Weberian) argument about the destructive effects to liberal legalism of such deformalization cf. R. M. Unger, *Law in Modern Society. Towards a Criticism of Social Theory* (1977), 192–200.

[16] It may be conjectured that economic and social rights entered political language as a (left) counter-move to invest (left) social objectives with the same kind of dignity or *prima facie* absoluteness that 'bourgeois' objectives in the field of civil and political rights had managed to attain by recourse to rights rhetoric.

[17] This is implied in scholarly discussion about the enforceability of such rights. Cf. M. Scheinin, 'Economic and Social Rights as Legal Rights', in A. Eide, C. Krause, and A. Rosas, *Economic, Social and Cultural Rights* (1995), 41–62. Likewise, Bercusson, 'Fundamental Social and Economic Rights in the European Community', in A. Cassese, A. Clapham, and J. Weiler, *Human Rights and the European Community: Methods of Protection* (1991), 200–1.

[18] J. Gray, *Enlightenment's Wake. Politics and Culture at the Close of the Modern Age* (1995), 2.

[19] Raz, note 10 above, at 212–13.

III

Yet rights are not foundational but depend on collective goods that are evaluated independently from the rights through which we look at them. Freedom of speech is dependent on and intended to support the collective good of the system of political decision-making and public information that prevails in society. The protection of the freedom of contract presumes the existence of, and is constantly limited by, the conditions of the market. Rights protect personal autonomy but 'autonomy is possible only if various collective goods are available'.[20] In a society that offers no choices, autonomy is meaningless. The extent of the availability of such collective goods again is a pure issue of political value; of struggle and compromise between alternative views about what a good society would be like.

That rights refer back to contested notions of the political good is reaffirmed daily in the public decision-processes in which rights-discourse is being waged. A famous example is the *Handyside* case, in which the European Court of Human Rights discussed the margin of appreciation available to national authorities in the field of free speech. The Court affirmed the national authorities' competence to set limits to free speech (in a matter of publications that might offend the sensibilities of the reading public) inasmuch as there did not seem to exist 'a uniform European conception of morals'.[21] The importance of such affirmation is not so much in who the Court saw as the relevant decision-maker, the national or the international judge (though the fact that its focus was on *jurisdiction* is not irrelevant for the argument of this article), but that it expressly spelled out the fact that freedom of speech was a matter of moral assessment, itself independent from the conflicting rights (of free speech and privacy) to which it set a determined boundary.

The insufficiency of rights-rhetoric becomes evident as we try to seek justification or limits to rights. Here a curious paradox emerges. To the extent that rights are assumed as foundational (and this was the argument behind the view of rights as 'trumps') there can exist no perspective from which to justify (or examine/criticize) them. Any justification would relegate the right to a secondary position, as an instrumentality for the reason that justifies it. If the reason is not present, or not valid, then the right is not valid, or applicable, either. Thus, recourse to rights remains an irrationalist strand in liberal theory—or perhaps a bad faith irrationalism ('well, we know we cannot really defend them'). For rights are constantly examined, limited, and criticized from the perspective of alternative notions of the good. This is evident particularly as we examine the problems of field constitution, the relationship between rights and exceptions to them, conflicts between and the indeterminacy of rights.

---

[20] *Ibid.*, at 247. See J. Finnis, *Natural Law and Natural Rights* (1980), 210–18. Likewise, Mouffe, note 12 above, at 30–2; and M. Tushnet, 'An Essay on Rights' (1984) 62 *Texas Law Review* 1364–71.

[21] *Handyside* v. *United Kingdom*, ECHR (1976), Series A, No. 24, 22; *Müller and others* v. *Switzerland*, ECHR (1988), Series A, No. 133, 22.

A. Field Constitution

Whether or not a conflict is seen as a rights problem and what rights may seem relevant depends on the language we use to structure the normative field in focus. Examining the question whether the concept of fair trial included the right to legal counsel, Judge Fitzmaurice put his finger on the relevant problem:

> Both parties may, within their own frames of reference, be able to present a self-consistent and valid argument, but since these frames of reference are different, neither argument can, as such, override the other. There is no solution to the problem unless the correct—or rather acceptable—frame of reference can first be determined; but since matters of acceptability depend on approach, feeling, attitude, or even policy, rather than correct legal or logical argument, there is scarcely a solution along these lines either.[22]

In other words, the choice of the relevant language ('frame of reference')—whether the normative field is seen in terms of 'human rights' or, for example, 'economic development' or 'national security'—reflects upon a prior political decision independent of the language finally chosen, often having to do with which authority should have the competence to deal with a matter.

A good example of field constitution is provided by the development of a fundamental rights jurisprudence by the European Court of Justice. As is well known, after a period of reluctance in applying human rights,[23] the Court changed its attitude in response to the challenge by the German and Italian Constitutional Courts and asserted its jurisdiction to examine the compatibility of Community instruments with fundamental rights as inspired by Member States' constitutions (*Stauder, Nold, Hauer*[24]). Thereafter, such power of review was extended also to (some) Member State legislation in the field of Community law (*Rutili, Wachauf, Grogan*[25]). As a result of the Court's wish to reassert its jurisdiction as against that of (some) Member States, to borrow a phrase from Ian Ward, '[a]ll sorts of things are bandied around as potential fundamental or human rights',[26] including various political rights (freedom of information), administrative and procedural rights, and rights in the area of social law.[27] The Court has in a particularly striking way also reconstituted the field of economic activity in terms of human rights: '[i]t should be borne in mind that the principles of free movement of goods and freedom of competition, together with freedom of trade as a fundamental right, are general principles of Community law of which the Court ensures observance'.[28]

[22] *Golder* v. *United Kingdom*, ECHR (1975), Series A, No. 18, dissenting opinion of Fitzmaurice, at para. 23.

[23] Cf. Case 1/58, *Stork* v. *High Authority* [1959] ECR 17.

[24] Case 29/69, *Stauder* v. *City of Ulm* [1969] ECR 419; Case 4/73, *Nold KG* v. *Commission* [1974] ECR 491; Case 44/79, *Hauer* v. *Land Rheinland-Pfalz* [1979] ECR 3727.

[25] Case 36/75, *Rutili* v. *Minister for the Interior* [1975] ECR 1219; Case 5/88, *Wachauf* v. *Germany* [1989] ECR 2609; Case 159/90, *Society for the Protection of the Unborn Child* v. *Grogan* [1991] ECR 4685.

[26] I. Ward, *The Margins of European Law* (1996), 142.

[27] Cf. G. de Búrca, 'The Language of Rights and European Integration', in J. Shaw and G. More, *New Legal Dynamics of European Union* (1995), 30–9 and B. de Witte, 'The Past and Future Role of the European Court of Justice in the Protection of Human Rights', in this vol.

[28] Case 240/83, *Procureur de la République* v. *Association de défense des brûleurs d'huiles usagées* [1985] ECR 531, at 548.

While the Court has redescribed entitlement to property and land as well as the confidentiality of business information in fundamental rights language,[29] no such language has been used to describe problems relative to immigration or asylum, racial discrimination, minorities or environmental protection. Such selectivity is of course not dictated by any 'essential' nature of those problems. It is a matter of (political) preference: which interests, which visions of the good merit being characterized as 'rights' and thus afforded the corresponding level of protection, and which do not? What moves are needed to ensure jurisdiction and control?[30]

In its advisory opinion on the *Legality of the Threat or Use of Nuclear Weapons*, the International Court of Justice reconstituted that field in the language of human rights, protection of the environment, humanitarian law, and national self-defence. The decisive concerns, it seems, came for the field of national security that led to the Court's unprecedented *non liquet*.[31] One is left wondering whether that would have been the result had the Court restricted itself to characterizing the use of nuclear weapons in human rights terms (particularly by reference to Article 6 of the 1966 UN Covenant on Civil and Political Rights[32]). The point here is that the choice of the relevant legal field—human rights/environmental law/humanitarian law/self-defence—was crucial for the outcome of the decision, but that this choice, unarticulated though it seemed, could only follow from an external preference about which kinds of concerns are most significant in relation to nuclear weapons.[33]

B. Rights are Conflictual

In every important social conflict, it is possible to describe the claims of both sides as claims for (the honouring of) rights. One typical generic form of rights-conflict is that between right-as-freedom and right-to-security. If, for example, the State's authority to intervene for the prohibition of rape in marriage is conceptualized in terms of a 'right to privacy', then the husband's right to (sexual) freedom is privileged against the wife's right to security. Such a conflict cannot be resolved by mere rights-talk. The boundaries of freedom and security cannot be drawn from any intrinsic or essential meaning of the relevant 'rights'. On the contrary, the debate over where such boundaries should lie reflects back on culturally conditioned ways of thinking about family relationships and the function of the State.

Justification for the imposition of constraint in a morally agnostic society may often seem to lie in the need to limit freedom by the freedoms of others. If your use of your freedom creates harm for me, such use is prohibited. But the formal principle of

---

[29] Cf. Case 44/79, *Hauer* v. *Land Rheinland-Pfalz* [1979] ECR 3744–50. Cf. also Case 168/91, *Konstantinidis* v. *Stadt Altensteig, Standesamt and Landesamt Calw, Ordnungsamt* [1993] ECR I–1191 in which the general principles of Community law were restricted to apply only in the economic field.

[30] As Weiler puts it, the Court's language is that of human rights while the deep-structure is that of supremacy, in 'Methods of Protection: Towards Second and Third Generation of Protection', in Cassese, Clapham, and Weiler, note 17 above, at 580–1.

[31] *Legality of the Threat or Use of Nuclear Weapons (Advisory Opinion of 8 July 1996)* (1996) 35 ILM 809.

[32] International Covenant on Civil and Political Rights, adopted by GA Res. 2200 A (XXI) (1966), in United Nations, *A Compilation of International Instruments* (1994), i, part 1, 20.

[33] Cf. M. Koskenniemi, 'Faith, Identity and the Killing of the Innocent. International Lawyers and Nuclear Weapons' (1997) 10 *Leiden Journal of International Law* 137–62.

preventing 'harm to others' merely shifts focus to the concept of 'harm' and fails to indicate which of the competing conceptions of 'harm' should be preferred.[34] Think of the problem of public intervention in rape in marriage again. Here 'harm' for the woman is constituted by the husband's physical aggression, while the 'harm' the husband will suffer follows from the outside intervention on his sexual liberty that he had purchased in the act of marriage. The politically and culturally conditioned character of the notion of 'harm' is perhaps easiest to see in the classic debates about matters of sexual morality. For while most liberals would today feel that homosexual acts between consenting adults should not be taken to 'harm' society,[35] the practice of prostitution or pornography might seem degrading and, as such, harmful for women at large.

But this is just one aspect of the right to freedom/right to security conflict. Embedded in the former in most cases is the ideology of *laissez-faire*, while embedded in the latter is a communal ethic of responsibility, and the dilemma is that 'any effort to keep the state out of our personal lives will leave us subject to private domination'.[36]

It does not follow, however, that rights conflicts could be solved simply once we have decided whether to prefer individualism or altruism; neither is an unmitigated good. Individualism is the Dr Jekyll for the egoism of Mr Hyde. Communal ethic grounds also suffocating, totalitarian practices. But if there is no general recipe for the solution of rights conflicts, no single vision of the good life that rights would express, then everything hinges on the appreciation of the context, on the act of *ad hoc* balancing, that is to say, on the kind of politics for the articulation of which rights leave no room.

European human rights organs repeatedly deal with conflicts involving an individual's right to privacy and the right of other individuals to security that the State has been tasked to guarantee. Are prison authorities, for instance, authorized to censor prisoners' letters? Again, the matter turns on policy, or 'striking a balance between the legitimate interests of public order and security and that of the rehabilitation of prisoners'.[37]

But, obviously, there are no technical means of calculating the relative weights of the two kinds of interests. Any 'balancing' will involve broad cultural and political assumptions about whether the good society should prefer the values of public order or those of rehabilitation. It is hard to think of a more openly politico-cultural divide than that. In the *Grogan* case involving the prohibition of dissemination of information on abortion in Ireland, the Advocate-General of the European Court perceived a conflict that required 'balancing two fundamental rights, on the one hand the right

---

[34] This is of course John Stuart Mill's famous doctrine: '[t]he only purpose for which power can rightfully be exercised over any member of a civilized community, against his will, is to prevent harm to others': J.S. Mill, *On Liberty* (1859/1974), 68. For the point that 'harm' cannot be defined in a morally neutral way, cf. N. MacCormick, 'Against Moral Disestablishment', in N. MacCormick, *Legal Right and Social Democracy: Essays in Legal and Political Philosophy* (1982), 28–30.

[35] On the classic debate between Hart and Lord Devlin on the Wolfenden Report on abolishing the criminality of homosexual practices, cf. H.L.A. Hart, *Law, Liberty and Morality* (1963) and P. Devlin, *The Enforcement of Morals* (1959).

[36] F. Olsen, 'Liberal Rights and Critical Legal Theory', in C. Joerges and D.M. Trubek, *Critical Legal Thought: An American–German Debate* (1989), 251.

[37] *Silver and others* v. *United Kingdom*, ECHR (1987) Series B No. 51, 75–6, (1983) Series A, No. 61.

to life as defined and declared to be applicable to unborn life by a Member State, and on the other the freedom of expression'. This was to be dealt with by reference to the Strasbourg Court's criteria of whether any restriction had a legitimate aim and was necessary in a democratic society, criteria which were 'analogous to the principle of proportionality used in Community Law'.[38] Summarizing the task, he concluded: 'the correct justification under general principles of Community law is public policy and/or public morality, because the rule at issue here is justified by an ethical value-judgement which is regarded in the Member State concerned as forming part of the bases of the legal system'.[39]

Alternatively, think of environmental policies. The rights of the upstream industrial user of a common watercourse may conflict with the right of the downstream user to clean water. Neither right enjoys an absolute preference. Any balancing will have to invoke the values of either economic prosperity or clean environment without any expectation that the attained outcome would manifest some sort of an inherent or non-political equilibrium between them.

Another rights conflict is that between formal equality and substantive equality; or equality of opportunity and equality of result. For the women's movement, it has sometimes seemed important to argue from the right to equality (equality of voting rights, for instance), while in other cases the fact that formal neutrality may advance male interests has seemed to compel arguing in favour of (reverse) discrimination. From the perspective of a universalizing rights-rhetoric, this appears as incoherence; while from the perspective of political struggles, incoherence translates into a political necessity.

The resolution of rights-conflicts (and every social conflict is amenable to a description as such) presumes a place 'beyond' rights, a place that allows the limitation of the scope of the claimed rights and their subordination to 'some pattern, or range of patterns, of human character, conduct and interaction in community, and the need to choose such specification of rights as tends to favour that pattern, or range of patterns. In other words, we need some conception of human good, of individual flourishing, in a form (or range of forms) of common life that fosters rather than hinders such flourishing.'[40]

What this pattern might be in Community law was famously stated by the European Court in *Wachauf* as follows:

> The fundamental rights recognized by the Court are not absolute, however, but must be considered in relation to their social function. Consequently, restrictions may be imposed on the exercise of these rights, in particular in the context of a common organization of the market, provided that these restrictions in fact correspond to objectives of general interest pursued by the Community and do not constitute, with regard to the aim pursued, a disproportionate and intolerable interference impairing the very substance of those rights.[41]

---

[38] Case 159/90, *Society for the Protection of the Unborn Child* v. *Grogan* [1991] ECR I–4685. Opinion of the AG at para. 34.

[39] *Ibid.*, at para. 35.   [40] J. Finnis, *Natural Law and Natural Rights* (1980), 219–20.

[41] Case 5/88, *Wauchauf* [1989] ECR 2639. Likewise in Case 44/94, *The Queen* v. *Ministry of Agriculture, Fisheries and Food, ex parte National Federation of Fishermen's Organisations and Others, Federation of*

The point here is not, of course, that the Court's statement should be seen as a mistaken or cynical position about rights but that recourse to the language of 'functions', 'objectives', 'general interest' and 'proportionality' which seems so far removed from our intuitive association of rights with an absoluteness, or 'trumping character', against social policies, is simply unavoidable. A right is, often, a policy and must be weighed as such against other policies. Here there is no question of Klaus Günther's memories of pain and injustice that would seek articulation. The European Court's judicial everyday is the banal exercise of coping with conflicts of (most commonly economic) interests, and allocating scarce resources. The fact that those interests are dressed in rights language does not change this pattern, but it does obscure the political nature of the task.

C. Rights Always Come with Exceptions and it is a Matter of Policy to which One Resort is Made

One example concerns the historical vicissitudes of the right of free speech in the United States, in which that right is always conditioned by the balancing test of the First Amendment and the 'clear and present danger' standard. One of the limitations has been to allow free speech only in places that are 'public forums', excluding for instance leafleting in shopping-centres and prohibiting the posting of signs on city-owned buildings in a way that reflects deeply ingrained political assumptions of American culture.[42]

Within the European system, the relations between rights and the power to derogate from them is in principle conditioned by the criterion of what may be 'necessary in a democratic society'. As Susan Marks has recently shown, this is a criterion that is heavily contextualized in the political self-understanding of post-war Western societies.[43] There is nothing a-historical (or unpolitical) in the conclusion, for instance, that if a person loses his opportunity to work because of the disclosure by public authorities of secret information on him, it still remains the case that 'having regard to the area of discretion which must be left to the State in respect of the defence of the national security . . . [the interference was] . . . "necessary in a democratic society in the interests of national security" '.[44]

The neat scheme of right/derogation that is embedded in the European Convention on Human Rights is constantly undermined by the experience that there is no unpolitical rule or standard that would set out when to apply the right and when the derogation. Why would letter-opening and wire-tapping, with limited judicial con-

---

Highlands and Islands Fishermen and Others, [1995] ECR 3115; Case 22/94, *Irish Farmers Association and Others* v. *Minister for Agriculture, Food and Forestry, Ireland, and the Attorney General* [1997] ECR 1809. As the Court stated in *Nold*: 'if rights of ownership are protected by the constitutional laws of all Member States . . . the rights thereby guaranteed, far from constituting unfettered prerogatives, must be viewed in the light of the social function of the property and activities protected thereunder': Case 4/73, *Nold* [1974] ECR 491.

   [42] Cf. D. Kairys, 'Freedom of Speech', in D. Kairys (ed.), *The Politics of Law. A Progressive Critique* (Revised ed., 1990), 262–3.

   [43] Cf. S. Marks, 'The European Convention of Human Rights and its "Democratic Society" ', (1995) LXVI *BYIL* 209–38. For an extension of the same point to recent international legal debate see S. Marks, 'The End of History? Reflections on Some International Legal Theses' (1997) 8 *EJIL* 449–77.

   [44] *Leander* case, ECHR (1987), Series A, No. 116, 18, 26–7.

trol, be 'necessary in a democratic society'? To answer such questions the Commission and the Court have developed a balancing practice that uses abstract notions such as 'reasonable', 'proportionate', 'public order', and 'morals' to justify reference either to the right or to the exception.[45] In this way, the scope of rights becomes conditioned by policy choices that seem justifiable only by reference to alternative conceptions of the good society.

The European Court of Justice has been quite express in this respect. Already its early human rights jurisprudence was based on the assumption that a fundamental right was subject to restrictions inasmuch as 'the restrictions . . . correspond to objectives of general interest pursued by the Community or whether, with regard to the aim pursued, they constitute a disproportionate and intolerable interference with the rights'.[46] It is now 'settled case-law that fundamental rights . . . are not absolute and their exercise may be subject to restrictions justified by objectives of general interest pursued by the Community'.[47] Such restrictions may even follow from 'proportionality'—a utilitarian test, if there ever was one.[48] It matters little if the Court holds the valid test to be that of 'disproportionate' or 'intolerable' effect. The point is that all such language indicates that the characterization of social objectives in terms of the 'rights' of their beneficiaries adds little to the administrative pattern of dealing with them. This involves a political give-and-take and *ad hoc* decision-making in which no memory of pain or injustice is being articulated.

D. Rights are Formulated in Indeterminate Language

It is a truism that the linguistic openness of rights discourse leads to policy being determinative of particular interpretive outcomes. Discussing the concept of 'degrading' treatment, the European Court of Human Rights came to a conclusion that seems practically self-evident, namely that '[t]he assessment is, in the nature of things, relative: it depends on all the circumstances of the case and, in particular, on the nature and context of the punishment itself and the manner and method of its execution'.[49]

But indeterminacy exists far beyond such simple semantic openness. It is hard to imagine a standard that would seem more straight-forward than the right to life under Article 2 of the European Convention on Human Rights (ECHR). Yet even its application is revealed as a weighing standard. Does the right to life also include abortion? The European Commission's practice has been summarized as follows: 'even if one assumes that Article 2 protects the unborn life, the rights and interests involved have been weighed against each other in a reasonable way'.[50]

---

[45] For one discussion and critique, cf. P. Van Dijk and G.V. Van Hoof, *Theory and Practice of the European Convention on Human Rights* (1990), 604.

[46] Case 44/79, *Hauer* [1979] ECR 3747.   [47] Case 84/95, *Bosphorus* [1996] ECR 3953.

[48] In *Internationale Handelsgesellschaft*, for instance, the Court concluded that the system of deposits imposed on cornflour exporters did not violate fundamental human rights because '[t]he costs involved in the deposit do not constitute an amount disproportionate to the total value of the goods in question'. Case 11/70, *Internationale Handelsgesellschaft* [1970] ECR 1136.

[49] *Tyrer* case, ECHR (1978), Series A, No. 26, 15.

[50] Van Dijk and Van Hoof, note 45 above, at 220.

The same concerns the ending of life: 'the value of the life to be protected can and must be weighed against other rights of the person in question'.[51]

The normative limit of the right to life is established through an act of balancing with a view, supposedly, of attaining an aggregate good. It may seem hard to think of a context in which utilitarian approaches seem more out of place than this. None the less, it seems equally clear that the right to life cannot be taken as an absolute standard but involves a prohibition against the arbitrary taking of lives, while what is 'arbitrary' depends on the context.[52]

Again, such assessment involves precisely the kind of discretion that the concept of rights (as 'trumps') was intended to do away with, including balancing between requirements of State security and individual interests.[53] The Strasbourg Court's much-criticized doctrine of the margin of appreciation, 'at the heart of virtually all major cases that come before the Court',[54] is from this perspective nothing more than a healthy admission that there is always interpretative indeterminacy in the construction of particular rights-claims and that often it is local courts, and not Strasbourg organs, that are most competent to police the matter. The main point is that rights not only determine and limit policies, but that policies are needed to give meaning, applicability, and limits to rights.

In a recent piece, Philip Alston has reviewed similar arguments I have made elsewhere as a 'standard post-modernist critique', noting that it is 'unduly focused on conceptions of rights as "trumps" '.[55] What he suggests is that human rights 'can provide a meaningful basis for social order without being rigid, absolute or forever enduring', and that they are:

> capable of partly transcending the institutions that gave birth to them, and those very same institutions (or their successors) which seek to exercise responsibility for their elaboration and interpretation.[56]

For Alston, the above critique works with a straw-man conception of human rights, a conception that is impossibly rigid, and as such does not really exist anywhere. Of course rights are flexible and dependent on evaluation and process, but they are also partly reflective (and creative) of a political consensus without having to assume that they involve a banalization of rights that would do away with 'their capacity to mobilize, to inspire and to exhort'.[57]

I am uncertain about the force of these arguments. I agree that in practice rights are downgraded from their status as 'trumps' to the level of soft policies in favour of

---

[51] Van Dijk and Van Hoof, note 45 above, at 220–1. On the proportionality standard in this context see *ibid.*, at 222–3.

[52] Cf. the discussion of the International Court of Justice of the right to life in Art. 6 of the International Covenant on Civil and Political Rights and of genocide in the *Legality of the Threat or Use of Nuclear Weapons*, note 31 above, at paras. 24–26: 'after having taken due account of the circumstances of the specific case', at para. 26.

[53] Van Dijk and Van Hoof, note 45 above, at 232.

[54] R. St J. Macdonald, 'The Margin of Appreciation in the Jurisprudence of the European Court of Human Rights', in *International Law at the Time of Its Codification: Studies in Honour of Roberto Ago* (1987), 208.

[55] P. Alston, 'Introduction', in P. Alston (ed.), *Human Rights Law* (The International Library of Essays in Law and Legal Theory, Areas 27, 1996), pp. xvi–xvii.

[56] *Ibid.*   [57] *Ibid.*, at p. xv.

this or that social objective. Like any other policies, they may or may not reflect a consensus of opinion within some part of the population, and being acknowledged as such may also help to mobilize political forces. Indeed, that they are often a policy is the gist of the argument of this chapter.

However, the point I want to make is that although this is true of a large number of those social goods that we tend today to call 'rights', none of us would wish that to be true of a certain limited number of 'core rights', namely those that we most commonly associate with the adjectives 'inalienable' or 'fundamental', and that are capable of articulating Klaus Günther's memories of fear and injustice. But in order to uphold *that* distinction we must, I think, fall back on a naturalist (or 'mythical') conception of basic rights whose special character depends on their not being subject to the kinds of legal-technical arguments and proof that justify—and make vulnerable—'ordinary' rights as policies. The right of property, for instance, is as strong or weak as the economic or social justification that its exercise has in a particular case. It may be assessed and, if necessary, overridden by alternative political preferences. The right to be free from torture operates differently. Its validity is not relative to the force of any justification that we can provide for it, but is intrinsic in a manner that cannot be articulated through the forms of legal-technical argument.

We seem to have good reason to distinguish between two types of rights: those that are an effect of politics and those that constrain it. But upholding the distinction creates two difficulties. First, it seems difficult to defend special rights (memories of fear and injustice) on the basis of their intrinsic value, irrespectively of any arguments we can produce to support them—which means that they must be accepted outside rational convention; as part of our self-definition, as part of our identity as members of our communities; perhaps as taboo. Secondly, identifying the distinction compels an acceptance that *other* rights are no different from policies, in the sense that whether and to what extent they are applicable must be determined by reference to the kinds of 'balancing', 'proportionality', and other kinds of utilitarian considerations that are a commonplace of bureaucratic practice. The problem is that the rights of the former group seem too strong to be defensible within a democratic order, while the rights of the latter group seem too weak to constitute an effective constraint on policy. Indeed, they are indistinguishable from policy.

IV

Rights discourse sometimes appears as an offshoot of inflexible (and, as such, Utopian) legalism: '[t]o make a political issue that is deeply morally contested a matter of basic rights is to make it non-negotiable, since rights . . . are unconditional entitlements, not susceptible to moderation. Because they are peremptory in this way, rights do not allow divisive issues to be settled by legislative [or adjudicative] compromise: they permit only unconditional victory or surrender.'[58]

[58] Gray, note 18 above, at 22.

The absoluteness of rights discourse is not, however, an accidental property in it, but follows from its justification within liberal theory, its purpose to create a set of un-political normative demands intended to 'trump' legislative policies or administrative discretion. The very point of rights as a special type of normative entitlement lies in their absoluteness, their uncontextual validity, and immediate applicability. Under-stood in such a way, rights discourse has three broad cultural effects on politics.

One is the entrenchment of the idea of politics as already constrained by a non-political vision of the good society, understood as the sum total of individual rights that exist in a co-terminous relationship to each other. This is the core sense of liberal naturalism, the view that rights 'exist' outside political society and are then brought inside through legislation. Politics are thereby reduced to the declaration of truths already established elsewhere and the realization of a society already in virtual exis-tence. As politics lose their creative, 'imaginative' character, they are transformed from their core sense as human *vita activa* into an exercise of technical competence by experts.[59] Exit from the tragedy of incompatible and contested goods is bought at the expense of the bureaucratization of politics into balancing or the search of ag-gregate utility—paradoxically precisely the outcome that rights discourse originally sought to combat.

But inasmuch as rights are not naturally given, but, as I have argued above, the re-sult of the application of policies, then an offshoot is that politics become the politics of procedure, a struggle for the power to define, for jurisdiction: the question is not so much whether a weighing of interests has to take place, but rather which author-ity in the final analysis is empowered to do the weighing.

This aspect highlights the priority of process to substance in rights discourse. And for those immersed in that discourse the natural cultural preference is that 'only the Strasbourg organs are competent to conduct the weighing of interests involved in the Convention'.[60]

Secondly, rights are inescapably individualist. For even as they necessitate refer-ence to social values and communal goods, rights always occupy the perspective of the single individual, slightly removed from those values and interests herself. For rights discourse, the individual is a separable, unitary entity that has values or inter-ests, and thus rights, only as external attributes to itself but whose identity is not formed by them.[61] Yet it is not clear if a distinction can be made between the self and the values and interests it carries. But the rhetoric of rights fails to articulate the re-ality where our individual selves are (also) products of the contexts in which we live, of the values and interests of our communities. Besides, often our selves are torn be-tween competing values and interests, and no unitary standpoint beyond them can be found. Thinking of politics in terms of rights is unable to reach the process in which the interests of individuals (and their 'individuality') are formed, omitting the question whether having such interests is good in the first place, and failing to dis-criminate between interests that conflict but which we feel equally strongly about.

[59] For this argument at greater length, cf. M. Koskenniemi, 'The Wonderful Artificiality of States' (1994) *ASIL Proceedings* 22–9.
[60] Van Dijk and Van Hoof, note 45 above, at 601.
[61] Cf. generally M. Sandel, *Liberalism and the Limits of Justice* (1983).

Moreover, rights individualism loses a creative conception of the political, reducing citizenship to passive reliance on rights and political decision-making to an oscillation between (individual) ethics and economics. No idea of civic virtue or political participation can be sustained through insistence on the priority of the right over the good, and, inasmuch as such ideas occasionally emerge, they find no resonance in a right-based political culture.[62]

A third general consequence of the proliferation of rights-rhetoric everywhere in administration is the inauguration of what could be called a *political culture of bad faith*. For liberal agnosticism, a conception of natural rights, situated outside political society, remains ultimately an unjustifiable, even mythical, assumption that cannot be brought within the conventions of liberal political debate as they would thereby lose their fundamental character. For seeking to justify rights makes those rights vulnerable to the objections that can be directed against the justifying reasons: should people have a right to free speech because that produces the largest aggregate utility, is in accordance with human nature, or corresponds to popular will? Each explanation condenses a contested theory about the political good. As providing such explanations will infect rights with the weaknesses that attach to those theories, they can no longer be used to overrule conflicts over them and their point is lost. Hence, paradoxically, rights seem effective only if they can be accepted by unquestioning faith—a faith the absence of which provided the very reason for having recourse to them. If the critique of rights (as 'political') is correct, then the beneficiality of rights would seem to presuppose that the critique is not known![63]

But no such unthinking faith in rights can be taken for granted. Everyone knows that politics are not 'really' about translating natural rights into positive law; that at issue are struggle and compromise, power and ideology, and not derivations from transparent and automatically knowable normative demands. Nor can the critiques of formalism and realism be undone. Everyone knows that administration and adjudication have to do with discretion, and that, however much such discretion is dressed in the technical language of rights and 'balancing', the outcomes reflect broad cultural and political preferences that have nothing inalienable about them.

So, how does one deal with loss of faith? One response is simply to give up rights. But this would be an unwarranted conclusion inasmuch as there does not exist any other language either, in which political conflict would already have been solved. Another, and the more common response is to continue rights talk without actually believing in the a-political or foundational nature of rights: '[d]o not mind that you cannot really defend your rights. If they effectively produce the political outcomes you wished to produce, just continue. Remember, no one else is in possession of a stronger or more convincing political language and if your justifications cannot withstand internal criticisms that are familiar from 200 years of liberal rhetoric, neither can theirs.' To succeed, however, such a strategy may require not disclosing your own loss of faith. For this might 'jeopardize the idea that human rights are fundamental and universally applicable which is a fiction Europe at least should try to adhere to'.[64]

---

[62] Cf. Mouffe, note 12 above, at 32–8 and 139–41.   [63] Tushnet, note 20 above, at 1386.
[64] E. Steyger, *Europe and Its Members. A Constitutional Approach* (1995), 49.

In this way, you may be compelled—in order to advance the cultural politics of a 'Europe'—to choose a purely strategic attitude towards rights. Even as you know that rights defer to policy, you cannot disclose this, as you would then seem to undermine what others (mistakenly) believe one of your most beneficial gifts to humanity (a non-political and universal rights rhetoric). It is hard to think of such an attitude as a beneficial basis from which to engage other cultures or to inaugurate a transcultural sphere of politics.

The question would then not be so much which rights we have, or should have, but what it takes to develop politics in which deviating conceptions of the good—whether or not expressed in rights language—can be debated and realized without having to assume that they are taken seriously only if they can lay claim to an a-political absoluteness that is connoted by rights as trumps.

4

The Legacies of Injustice and Fear: A European Approach to Human Rights and their Effects on Political Culture

KLAUS GÜNTHER

I. EUROPEAN HUMAN RIGHTS AND THE POLITICAL CULTURE OF A COLLECTIVE MEMORY OF INJUSTICE AND FEAR

To ask for a European approach to human rights is ambivalent. If the question is whether the genesis, nature, and scope of human rights are essentially European, one runs immediately into the endless debate about universalism versus particularism of human rights. Obviously, the question does not aim at a European approach to human rights as the expression of a particular historical culture which should be extended to all different cultures of the world. Instead of this, the question seems to aim at a specific European contribution to human rights which are already considered to be valid for all human beings, as is declared in the Universal Declaration of Human Rights.[1]

To ask the question in this way of course does not mean that one could avoid the problem of cultural relativism. Every European approach and every European contribution to human rights has to keep in mind that the idea of universal human rights is in itself a particular European idea and that it has a long history of misreading, selective interpretation, and wrong application. The idea of universal human rights, as well as the history of its selective realization, is therefore deeply rooted in European history and culture. To say that *all* human beings are created equal and that *every* human being is provided by nature with inalienable rights presupposes something that is common to all human beings as human beings. It is still the language of the Christian religion. The idea that all human beings are equal was interpreted by the Christians on the basis of a belief in a God who is the creator of human beings, and who has created them according to his own image. This reading of universality already included particularity, because it referred primarily to those human beings who believed in the Christian God, and it excluded all those who did not. After

---

[1] Universal Declaration of Human Rights, adopted by GA Res. 217 A (III) 1948. In United Nations, *A Compilation of International Instruments* (1994) i, part 1, 1.

secularization, these presuppositions were often interpreted in a specific way which led to an exclusion of certain human beings who lacked certain features from the realm of human rights. For example, if reason was considered as the fundamental common feature of human beings, and women were regarded as human beings who lacked the full capacity of reason, then it seemed to be only natural to exclude women, at least in part, from the protection of human rights.[2] And if the common feature of all human beings was interpreted according to the standards of the western, European-American 'civilization', then it seemed to follow that members of other cultures lack certain capabilities and competences which were considered as necessary for a human being to be a bearer of human rights. Thus, it was the experience of the people who were colonized by European States that made the experience that universalism can turn into cultural, economical, and political hegemony. The consequences are often dramatic. Human rights, interpreted and treated in this way, give a licence to draw a distinction between human beings who are under the protection of human rights and beings who are considered as not being completely human, and who therefore have no rights at all. Furthermore, it seems to be that this licence also gives a right to discriminate, expropriate, chase, imprison, torture, rape, and kill those dehumanized men, women, and children. The violation of human rights does not begin with their explicit negation and rejection, but with their implicit neutralization—at first with perceiving a human being as somebody who does not in all respects belong to the community of human beings, and secondly with the right to treat them as something which does not deserve the protection of human rights.

'We', living in the rather secure milieu of Western Europe, have no reason at all to feel superior not merely with regard to our own history. How difficult it can be here and now to avoid exclusionary distinctions based on dehumanizing images of human beings becomes clear for 'us', if we look at our attitudes towards those human beings who—according to 'our' point of view—are or behave as if they were barbaric, who are considered as perpetrators of human rights, or who allegedly 'abuse' human rights for their own private interests. Foreigners or asylum seekers from poor countries belong to this category, or certain criminals—not to mention the asylum seeker *as* a criminal. When we look at a television or newspaper report about a man who sexually abused and killed a child, or when we listen to politicians describing a wealthy drug dealer, or a Mafia boss, then we can sometimes observe how human beings are presented as non-members of the community of human beings. The implicit question which follows is: should these people have human rights? Let us imagine the extreme case of an *enemy* of human rights. Are human beings who command, organize, or execute genocide really human beings who deserve to be protected by human rights; for example, by a fair trial and a kind of punishment which respects Protocol No. 6 of the European Convention on Human Rights (ECHR) (Abolition of the Death Penalty)? On a low level of self-observation we can easily discover in our own imagination at least some categories of human beings which provoke a reaction of dehumanization already in our perception. Before we argue

---

    [2] For such an interpretation of Art. 1 of the Universal Declaration and its critique see C. Bretherton, 'Universal Human Rights', in C. Bretherton and G. Ponton (eds.), *Global Politics* (1996) (quoted from the German translation in U. Beck (ed.), *Perspektiven der Weltgesellschaft* (1998), 263).

about the legitimacy of a claim which is raised by a foreigner who refers to his or her human rights, we should carefully look at our perception and imagination of the other.

Even the more subtle versions of universalism cannot completely avoid a dehumanizing misreading. The attempt to look for and to accept differences, to create new human rights for members of minorities and for the protection of different cultural identities, is still in danger of simply extending the European reading of human rights. This is true as long as the differences are marked, described, and considered from the point of view of our own identity. The interest in differences does not naturally turn into equal concern and respect for the Other. As the example of 'Orientalism' has demonstrated, an interest in the Exotic Other can satisfy needs of our own cultural identity.[3] As the contemporary debates about the academic field of Area Studies (like Chinese or Indian studies) demonstrate, one can never be sure that the interest in differences does not serve some strategic interests in self-maintenance—as long as the other is not regarded as someone with whom one has to enter in a dialogue among equals.[4]

II. SIMPLE AND COMPLEX UNIVERSALISM

In order to deal with these problems, one could, as Richard Rorty suggests, reject any kind of 'foundational' thinking and justification of human rights, and turn to 'sentimentality'.[5] This means to tell stories about people suffering from pain, humiliation, and injustice, like 'Uncle Tom's Cabin', in order to convince others of the value of human rights. Instead of this, I would like to pursue the idea of entering into a dialogue with the other instead of describing and marking differences from one's own point of view. To distinguish these two approaches more adequately, I suggest distinguishing between two kinds of universalism: simple or Archimedian versus complex universalism. Simple universalism is abstract, epistemic, and essentialist. It presupposes general common features of human beings which can be observed and recognized and which are considered as pre-given. It uses them as a criterion for exclusion and inclusion; it applies them like a litmus paper in chemistry in order to distinguish between acid and base. It has some similarities with Michael Walzer's critical concept of 'covering law universalism', which consists in a simple extension of one culture's law to other cultures.[6] Complex universalism is not epistemic, i.e. based on pretended knowledge of properties which can be observed or ascribed. Complex universalism goes a step further. It makes the step from difference to dialogue, and therefore it refers to human beings who are speaking and acting—to their performance of voice and agency. If one takes this step seriously, it forces us to make

---

[3] E. Said, *Orientalism. Western Conceptions of the Orient* (2nd edn., 1995).
[4] R. Heilbrunn, 'The News From Everywhere' [1996] *Lingua Franca* 49–56.
[5] R. Rorty, 'Human Rights, Rationality, and Sentimentality', in S. Shute and S. Hurley (eds.), *On Human Rights* (1993), 111–34.
[6] M. Walzer, 'Two Kinds of Universalism', Tanner Lectures on Human Values (German translation: 'Zwei Arten des Universalismus' (1990) 7 *Babylon* 10.

an important shift in the discourse on human rights. What is at stake is not this or that particular human right, its content, and its claim to universal validity and recognition. Instead, complex universalism focuses on the question whether human rights can be traced back and linked with the voice and agency of individuals. The context and procedure of the formation of human rights become more important than a particular human right. This kind of universalism is procedural and deliberative. The procedural element consists in the inclusion of every single individual who raises his or her voice. What will in the end be recognized as a human right does then not depend on certain properties of the person, but on the procedure of common will-formation, in which every human being is equally included. Of course, a complex universalism which starts with human beings who have a voice and who can say 'yes' or 'no' will also include more or less severe conflicts about what should be regarded as a human right that is universally valid. But what matters here is that the conflict is not considered and treated as an obstacle to will-formation, but as an enabling condition or a medium. Conflict and dissent presuppose and provoke good reasons, by which every opponent could be convinced—provided that common will-formation by arguing about reasons is regarded as an alternative to violence. This is the deliberative element of complex universalism. To look for convincing arguments in order to overcome a dissent also includes the procedural element that every single participant in the conflict has to be recognized as an equal human being who has a 'right to voice' and who has a right to participate in a procedure which consists of an exchange and critique of reasons.

The kind of difference which is important here is not the one which I discover, when I compare myself to the Other, but the difference which I realize when the Other says 'no', the difference of *dissent*. It forces us to de-centre our own point of view. But this is, of course, not enough. Neither 'we' nor 'they' speak with one voice only. It is one of the peculiar and irritating features of the current debate on cultural relativism that 'we' do not look carefully enough with whom we are talking when we are confronted with cultural differences in the human rights discourse. As long as we listen to dictators only, who defend the priority of communal values over individual rights, or with members of other cultures whose representative role has an unclear legitimation, we can never be sure that we still do not continue to deal with an artificial and wrong image of the Other.[7] This is also true with ourselves. We can never be sure whether our dominating contemporary reading of human rights is not the reading of the privileged classes who are the winners of the social, political, economic, and cultural struggles in our own countries. Therefore, the procedure has to be really inclusive, particularly with regard to those who lack the capability and the courage to raise their voices.

Of course, even a complex universalism of this kind does not easily escape the danger of turning into a simple universalism. This would be the case if one linked the capability of having a voice and saying 'no' again with certain features which can or

---

[7] How difficult it can be not to ignore a 'voice' which dissents from our own ideas is demonstrated by the case of clitoridectomy in Africa by K. Engle, 'Female Subjects of Public International Law: Human Rights and the Exotic Other Female', in D. Danielsen and K. Engle (eds.), *After Identity: A Reader in Law and Culture* (1995), 210–28.

cannot be ascribed to human beings. This becomes obvious in the case of human beings who are not able to speak or who do not want to speak, or those who have lost
the courage to raise their voices. The property of having a voice was used as a criterion for inclusion or exclusion in the same way as the property of having reason. A
difficult case is also that of the vicarious voice, someone speaking on behalf of someone else who has no voice or who is not able to raise his or her voice. Contemporarily we are facing these problems in the cases of abortion and euthanasia: is the foetus
a human being with a 'voice' which should be respected? Is someone who has irre-
versibly lost consciousness someone with a 'voice'?

In order to avoid these dangers, I shall argue for complex universalism in a rather
complex way. 'Voice' is a feature which is self-attributive. It can be attributed to
someone by a third person, but the person to whom it is attributed also has to make
use of it. He or she has to realize that he or she has a voice, and that it is his or her own
voice. As a consequence, 'voice' is strictly individual, it is impossible to substitute
one's own voice with the voice of somebody else. The voice of a person cannot be represented or generalized. On the other hand, 'voice' also implies an inter-subjective
relationship. It requires a third person who listens and who answers. Although it is
also possible to speak to oneself alone, this kind of making use of one's voice is not
the prominent one. Listening and answering require at least a minimum of mutual
recognition, of taking the voice of the other seriously. Obviously, this does not go
without saying. It is the first step to recognition—before I take a position to the
claim, which is raised by a speaker with his or her assertion, and before I react to
what he or she has said, I have to recognize him or her as a competent speaker at all,
as a person who has something to say, and who says it, among others, to me. Since I
do not listen naturally, it can be a kind of obligation only. But where does this obligation come from, how is it justified, and why should I accept it? The obligation must
be derived from principles which require that each individual shall be regarded as an
end in itself.

These principles are explained and justified by different traditions of philosophy
and moral theory, which are deeply rooted in European history. They provide arguments for the claim of human rights to be universally valid. One tradition refers to
rationality as the most important element of social relationships. Rationality
means—among other things—arguing with objections raised against a proposition,
giving and testing reasons, and determining one's own position and intention according to the best reasons available. If we violate the principle of mutual recognition, we violate the idea of rationality, we behave irrationally. The other tradition
refers to the emotional need of human beings to avoid pain and suffering. Every
human being's need to avoid pain and suffering, and to maximize his or her pleasure,
shall be recognized equally. According to these traditions, it is rational to recognize
each individual's voice, and to be recognized is a necessary condition for each individual to express his or her interest in the avoidance of pain and suffering. The first
tradition respects the autonomy of every individual, the second the basic need of
every individual to avoid pain and suffering. Obviously, these two traditions are
traditions, i.e. they express a cultural self-understanding of the people in Western
Europe and North America. But this is not the whole story. Permanently arguing

against objections of ethnocentrism, the philosophical approaches, which are rooted in these traditions, meanwhile have reached a high degree of complexity.[8] The procedural and deliberative approach, which I have presented in outline above, is one example. Although it is of course still possible to detect some hidden ethnocentric (and other exclusionary) premises of the argument, the advantage of this position consists in its capability of being open to those objections—critical self-correction is part of the claim to universalism.

But a problem remains even if one admits that the philosophical foundation of the mutual obligation to recognize each other's voice and to listen to each other as a prerequisite of human rights is sound, and—with the proviso of further corrections— convincing for every human being, at least in the long run. It does not explain why selective misreading of universal human rights occurs again and again. Furthermore, the philosophical foundation does not help to avoid the experience of those people who are confronted with abstract ideas only, without being able to link them to their own experience. Often, it is not their voice which is represented by human rights. Complex universalism remains too simplistic when it refers only to those human beings who already have a voice, who are articulate, and who claim that others must listen to their voice, and to whom others are always already listening. They are able to use human rights for the promotion of their interests. Human rights are then in danger of being transformed into human rights rhetoric, as it is described in Martti Koskenniemi's chapter.[9] This is the other side of the history of misreading and selective application: the more human rights become an unproblematic part of daily political and legal practice, the more they operate with silent exclusions, ignoring suffering, needs, and interests as long as they do not fit with the scope of their application.

It seems to be that the problem is not so much the philosophical foundation of the universalism of human rights, but its insufficient degree of complexity. This is more a matter of the meaning and understanding of human rights. Struggles and debates about human rights refer to claims to universalism and their foundation in moral and legal principles only on the surface—in fact, what are at stake are often questions like this: which interest shall be recognized as a matter of human rights, who shall have the power to raise a claim to human rights—e. g. should pornography be considered as a violation of women's integrity, and how should the conflict with the right to freedom of expression be solved?[10] Are those interests legitimately excluded from the scope of application of human rights? In order to deal with these questions, it seems to be necessary to start with the experience of those human beings who were or are excluded. This means considering the struggle on exclusion as a central part of the meaning of human rights. The step from content to procedure has already led us to the contexts and conditions under which a claim to a human right or a claim that a human right shall be recognized is raised. The procedural element of complex universalism referred to each human being's voice and the obligation to listen. The

[8] See, as a contemporary example of a comprehensive approach to human rights which very convincingly ties together the two traditions, C.S. Nino, *The Ethics of Human Rights* (1991).
[9] M. Koskenniemi, 'The Effects of Human Rights on Political Culture', in this vol.
[10] See C. MacKinnon, *Only Words* (1993).

experience of exclusion then consists in the exclusion of one's voice, in the experience of ignorance with regard to one's claims and needs. This is the case not only when someone raises his or her voice and nobody listens, but already and most severely when someone does not raise his or her voice at all, because he or she lost the courage to do so, or because she considers her situation as fate which has to be endured in of silent suffering.

The discourse on human rights then refers to experiences of this kind. What happens there is a long and complicated process, which begins with negative experiences like pain, suffering, and fear. These experiences lead to a loss of voice, to silent suffering, because nobody listens to the persons who try to report their suffering. Human rights discourse is a process by which these negative experiences are overcome. First, pain, suffering, and fear have to be considered as injustice and not as fate or, in the worst case, as the victim's fault. The situation of the excluded victim has to be rejected with the claim of injustice. This claim entails a whole pattern of concepts and practices which are linked to each other: The concept of a person, his or her intention, and his or her capacity of control, which allow for the attribution of responsibility for the pain and suffering of the victim. When the human rights discourse has reached this level, the discourse on the justification and acceptability of the victim's claim can begin. But it already requires that the victim's voice is recognized and that the other participants attribute weight to his or her propositions. During the process of human rights discourse, the victim regains his or her voice which she lost after her negative experience. When her claim is accepted as justified and as a valid human right, she has completely regained voice and agency.

If one conceives of human rights discourse in this way, a supplementary meaning has to be added to the meaning of human rights. Human rights have to be considered and understood as the result of a process of the loss and recovery of voice with regard to negative experiences like pain, fear, and suffering. Because 'voice' is self-attributing, this process is always one for the individual who is concerned, who regains her own voice and standing in her relationship to the other members of the community of human beings. By the same process these other members change their attitude towards the negative experience of the victim, when they recognize it as a matter of injustice instead of a matter of fate or the victim's own fault. One could describe it as a learning process by negative experiences. Then, in any case in which a human being raises a claim to a human right which is already established and generally accepted, he or she refers to the collective memory of negative experiences which initiated the learning process that resulted in the particular human right to which he or she is appealing. And, by raising such a claim, or even by raising a claim to the participants of a human rights discourse that something, which hitherto was considered merely as fate or as the victim's own fault, shall be considered as an injustice or as the victim's own fault—by raising a claim that a rejection of a negative experience shall be accepted as a human right—in all these cases, the human being has to be recognized as a performative person, who has a voice and who takes a position with regard to her negative experience in relation to others, who has standing in the eyes of the others. This is the additional meaning of human rights and human rights discourse in the theory of complex universalism. Compared to usual definitions of the concept of human rights, as they are for example suggested by Carlos Nino, this addition does not change these definitions. According to Nino,[11] human rights refer to:

(i)   the opportunity for the holder of the right to perform or not to perform certain actions;

(ii) the exclusion of actions of third parties which involve some harm to the holder of the right (either they deprive him of something or do him some injury); or requirements on third parties which involve a benefit for the holder of the right;

(iii) the enjoyment of some good or the avoidance of some evil.

What is characterized here as harm and injury, good and evil, and even as an opportunity to perform an action, can be traced back to negative experiences which are overcome by the recognition of human rights. In addition, it is important to emphasize a fourth element: a human right refers to the performative capacity of a person who can raise her voice in order to raise a claim.[12]

III. A EUROPEAN APPROACH: SUFFICIENT SENSITIVITY TO NEGATIVE EXPERIENCES

This complex way of explaining complex universalism in opposition to simple universalism leads us back to the question at the beginning—what could be a European contribution to human rights which does not fall prey to the selective applications, misreadings, and exclusions which characterize the European history of human rights? The only answer which is available with regard to the requirements of complex universalism is: Europe has to take its own history of exclusionary interpretation and practice of human rights seriously. A European approach to human rights has to make *an argument* out of the European history of human rights. What matters is not the foundation of the claim to universalism in moral principles and discourses, but the insufficient sensitivity to negative experiences of human beings under the regime of well established and sufficiently justified human rights. Complex universalism of human rights has to be sensitive to the voices of those human beings who suffer from pain and humiliation, who live with fear, and who reject it as injustice. It makes a difference if we talk to those members of a different culture who are in power or to those who are imprisoned, tortured, disadvantaged, or discriminated. Consequently, we have to deal with our own conception of human rights with the same attitude. We should listen to the stories of those who are excluded from the exercise and the advantage of human rights in our own cultures, to their experiences of pain, humiliation, fear, and injustice. A community becomes able to discover what is

---

[11]   Nino, note 8 above, at 30.

[12]   Cf. *ibid.*, at 27ff, where he criticizes the attempt to define rights as claims. Nino refers to the implication that rights as claims entail duties by third parties—which is not true in any case of human rights. Here, I would emphasize the activist meaning of rights as claims, as is suggested by Feinberg (see below, text accompanying note 35), so that Nino's critique does not apply to this aspect of the equation of rights as claims.

wrong with its own one-sided, exclusive reading of human rights if it begins to trace its own conception of human rights back to its own negative experiences. If we consider our European conception of human rights as the result of a long process of negative experiences, then we become more interested in talking to the dissidents and victims among the members of other cultures than to the officials or to the members of a majority. Of course, this approach cannot mean that any subjective experience of injustice leads to human rights. But it links the core meaning of human rights to something like a negative universality. It is the universality of recognition of those who suffer now or in the past from deliberate infliction of pain, humiliation, and fear, and who have reason to reject it as injustice. Nobody who suffers now or in the past from these experiences shall be excluded from raising his or her voice, and everybody must listen. The advantage of such a conceptual framework is that it allows for the consideration of a European approach to human rights which keeps in mind its historical and cultural dependency on negative experiences without any exclusionary consequences. It makes us sensitive to our own past and, at the same time, makes us sensitive to the negative experiences of others. It is because of this consciousness that Europe can affirmatively speak of a European approach to human rights.

Europe's history is a history of suppression, violence, war, and of the annihilation of human beings and groups of human beings.[13] In the beginning, it is the experience of unequal and arbitrary treatment by the political power of people who are imprisoned indefinitely and without any legal reason. The right to be free from arbitrary and unjustified imprisonment could be considered the *original* basic right.[14] It started with Article 39 of the Magna Carta. Later, arbitrary imprisonment became a major problem again, when it became part of the general unequal treatment of people by reason of their faith. As a consequence, this right was extended in the Petition of Rights in 1628, and reconfirmed in the Habeas Corpus Act in 1679. At the same time, the right to freedom of conscience and of religious faith was sought as a reaction against religious discrimination by the State. Then, it was the experience of suppression and unequal treatment of people by reason of their birth. Among other negative experiences, it led to the Declaration of Independence and the *Déclaration des Droits de l'Homme* in 1789. The fatal consequences of social, economic, and gender inequality are further experiences of the nineteenth and twentieth centuries. Unequal treatment, suppression and murder of human beings because of their ethnicity or 'race', is another example of the violation of human rights in this century. The most terrible violation of human rights took place in Germany, in the middle of Western Europe: the Holocaust. The Universal Declaration of Human Rights of 1948 is a reaction to this atrocity. At the end of this century, one can observe a change of attitude towards European history. We realize that the European history of human rights is written in blood. And it goes on. The violation of human rights in

---

[13] Many of the thoughts which are set out in this chap. were elaborated together with Cornelia Vismann in Berlin, in particular during my stay at the *Wissenschaftskolleg* in Berlin in 1995–6. See C. Vismann, 'Das Recht erklären. Zur gegenwärtigen Verfassung der Menschenrechte' (1996) 29 *Kritische Justiz* 321–35. All flaws in the argument and lack of clarity are my responsibility.

[14] For the characterization of the right against arbitrary imprisonment as the original basic right ('*Ur-Grundrecht*') see M. Kriele, *Einführung in die Staatslehre* (1990), 151–6.

civil wars is also a contemporary European experience. It seems to require a major change in the conception of human rights. From the Magna Carta to the Universal Declaration, the State—be it the State of the medieval or absolutistic monarch or the modern nation State—was at once the protector and the violator of human rights, the State was the addressee. Today, injustice and fear are experienced not merely as a result of the arbitrary use of state power, but also of the abuse of private power or the power of para-state organizations, like the war lords in former Yugoslavia or in some regions of Africa.

This brief and cursory European history of human rights has already led several authors to the conclusion that human rights have to do with negative historical experiences and collective traumata.[15] They are embedded in a *memory of injustice and fear*. Of course, this memory is not explicitly incorporated in the text of human rights. But it forms an important, perhaps even the most important, part of the *political culture* in which these rights are accepted and criticized, given, claimed, interpreted, applied, and enforced. If you want to know what is meant by 'human dignity' or 'equal concern and respect' for every human being, you can either look at various kinds of legal definitions, at a huge record of legal cases, or you can think of the German Gestapo torturing a political opponent or the Holocaust of the European Jews. Human beings differ in wealth, gender, ethnicity, and other properties, but what they all have in common is the experience of pain and humiliation.[16] It is this experience which gives us a feeling of belonging together, even if we are different.

It is difficult to draw a concrete political consequence from this link between human rights and the memory of injustice and fear. At the end of this century, when we look back at European history and begin to interpret it within the framework of human rights, then the focus shifts from political and social history, from the national history of different European countries, to the history of injustice and fear *within* these different countries, and *between* them—and to the individuals who had to suffer from violations of their rights or those who were responsible for their violation. A consequence would be to discover this history of injustice and fear as a common European history, and to maintain and to keep its memory, to discover that it is a memory that *is shared* by all people in Europe. The articulation, shaping, and reconstruction of this memory are, and can only be, a collective work in progress, a project that will never end. It has to be undertaken by the people themselves, as a part of their collective self-understanding and identity. But it is also a matter of education, of historical research, and of public reasoning and deliberation. As a consequence, the rights of freedom of information and expression have to be defended. It seems that we still have not uncovered all cases of violations, that there are still a lot of experiences of injustice and fear which are not made public and are not part of the collective memory. A perhaps surprising concrete consequence may be

[15] E. Denninger, *Menschenrechte und Grundgesetz* (1994), 89; S. Brugger, 'Stufen der Begründung der Menschenrechte' [1992] *Der Staat* 19–38; E. Riedel, 'Menschenrechte der dritten Dimension' [1989] *EuGRZ* 10.
[16] Rorty, note 5 above.

the following: a human right to access to the archives of the State and its institutions. The archives have to be opened to the public, and they may never be closed!

IV. WHAT FOLLOWS FROM THE POLITICAL CULTURE OF THE MEMORY OF INJUSTICE AND FEAR FOR THE INTERPRETATION OF HUMAN RIGHTS?

Embedded in the political culture of a memory of injustice and fear, the European concept of human rights has a hidden or supplementary meaning, which forms a part of every single human right. From a historical point of view, it becomes obvious that human rights are the result of a certain kind of interpretation of the experience of injustice and fear, from which he or she suffers by reason of the overwhelming social power, in most of the historical cases, of the State. A human right is the *rejection* of a concrete historical experience of injustice and fear, caused by actions of the State. By referring to a human right, a person *articulates* his or her suffering from an offence or a harm, and he or she claims that everybody is obliged *to listen* to the individual report of this experience. The declaration of a human right represents this experience, rejects it, and gives a conceptual framework to the interpretation of new experiences of injustice and fear, caused by actions of the State, in the future. This is the *performative* meaning of human rights. Its importance is obvious, for example, at the 'Truth Commissions' in South Africa (although this is not a European example). As a consequence, 'human rights' can never be completely and comprehensively declared. They depend on a concrete historical experience, and they come into being as a performative practice of human beings, which can never be completely transformed into positive law. Any convention or declaration of human rights can be 'amended', if new experiences of injustice and fear are articulated, and if human beings begin to 'talk' publicly about their experience. In the following, I shall give a more detailed reconstruction of the meaning of human rights.

A. The Experience of Pain and Humiliation and its Effects: The Loss of Voice and Control

The core of the experience is suffering from pain. Among the different kinds of pain it is the pain of being tortured and bodily violated which is most obvious. This example already includes what is presupposed in the following: that it is the State or another overwhelming social power which causes pain by infliction of torture. Of course, the feeling of pain is not necessarily connected with violation of the body. It can be painful to be captured and isolated against one's own will by armed forces or by people who act under the command of the State, without knowing why, where, and how long for. Correspondingly, people suffer from pain who lose their wives, husbands, children, relatives, and friends through the intentional force of state agents. These experiences are often accompanied by another experience, which can also be suffered without bodily violation. This is the experience of humiliation and degradation. Being raped does not merely cause pain because of the violation of the body, but also the humiliation of being disregarded and of not being treated as an equal human being but as something minor, as a thing, as something that could and should be thrown away. This can reach the highest degree if one loses the sense of the value of one's own life, if one gives up oneself, wishes to be not alive any more, because one cannot bear it any longer.[17]

Some common features of the different grades and experiences of pain, suffering, and humiliation consist of the effects which they have for the subjects who suffer from pain and humiliation. The first and direct effect results from the mere presence of physical pain, another effect from the possibility and the anticipation of its repetition. Against a single action of torture you can react with a scream. When the presence of pain becomes overwhelmingly intense, you lose your voice, you are reduced to your body, and to pre-linguistic forms of expression like screaming.[18] When torture is not just a singular event, but when it—as usual—continues, or when the torturers say that they will come back in ten minutes, an hour, the next morning, or sometime later without your knowing exactly when, and when you begin to imagine that it might happen again—then you will react with *fear* of repetition. When you are in a situation which makes it impossible for you to avoid the repetition, because you are imprisoned, because you cannot or will not leave the country, or because resistance to the regime of torturers is hopeless, then the fear will become a part of your self, it will capture your mind, your plans, your actions, your social relations—your life. And even if things change so that you are safe and certain that torture will not happen again, there remains a higher or lower degree of fear that will throw its shadow on your life. In many cases, when the fear is overwhelming, the victim becomes mute. Often, the loss of voice which is already the effect of the shocking experience of intense pain inflicted by torture is definite; you are unable to regain speech. The forward-looking fear of repetition increases the victim's quietness and passivity. Alone with his or her awful experience and with the fear that it might happen again, the victim not only keeps quiet, but he or she behaves very cautiously in general. It is better to say nothing. It is better not to ask someone for something. It is better not to trust other people. It is better not do something which involves a small risk. In general, reality seems to be something which just happens to the victim; he or she has the impression or the certainty of having *no control* at all—no control over his or her body, no control over his or her social relations, even no control over things. The victim becomes helpless.[19] Of course, we never have complete control over the world outside or even over ourselves, and we obviously ought not to have it. But the victim loses more; he or she loses—gradually—his or her fundamental feeling of agency, of

[17] Torture is often analysed and rejected from the point of view of men as victims. But a special kind of torture refers to women only, as is demonstrated by Bretherton, note 2 above, at 269ff.

[18] See the very comprehensive description and analysis of the effects of torture by E. Scarry, *The Body in Pain* (1985), 27ff, especially at 49: '[t]he goal of the torturer is to make the one, the body, emphatically and crushingly *present* by destroying it, and to make the other, the voice, *absent* by destroying it. It is in part this combination that makes torture, like any experience of great physiscal pain, mimetic of death; for in death the body is emphatically present while that more elusive part represented by the voice is so alarmingly absent that heavens are created to explain its whereabouts.'

[19] See the classical study of M.E.P. Seligman, *Helplessness: On Depression, Development, and Death* (1974).

being able to change something by his or her own intentional action. It does not matter what he or she does—things will happen anyway, and he or she will not change the way in which things happen. This is already true for the initial experience of pain during torture, when the victim realizes that he or she cannot prevent the torturer's tools from intruding into his or her body, or when his or her body collapses. The victim loses his or her *voice* and the fundamental security of having a certain degree of *control* over him- or herself and his or her social and natural environment. This is the silencing and chilling effect of an experience of pain and humiliation and of the fear of its repetition. In an ironic way, it transfers agency from the victim to the State and its representatives—the power of the State becomes overwhelming, because it has monopolized agency and voice.

Of course, experiences of pain and humiliation are radically subjective and cannot in themselves be generalized. There are also different kinds of pain and humiliation with different kinds of causes and different reactive consequences, like, for example, illness or traumata caused by natural events such as an earthquake. Apart from the fact that there is also no simple connection between physical pain and verbal communication, pain itself is inexpressible. It essentially resists language and objectification in language.[20] From pain itself follows everything. It would be too simplistic to draw a direct line from the experience of pain to the idea of human rights. Human cultures have different schemes of interpretation and forms of communication for the expression of pain.[21] This becomes more obvious in the case of humiliation. In order to interpret a violation as a case of humiliation, a whole pattern of social creations and constructions is necessary, like generalized expectations, rules, collective and individual identities, concepts of agency. What is and what counts as a case of humiliation is defined and interpreted within this pattern as well as the expected, obligatory, and appropriate ways of reaction like, for example, shame or revenge. These patterns also make possible descriptions, representations, and interpretations of the victim's experience which deny its meaning as a humiliation, which turn its expression in a different direction. The gap between pain and language is even deeper than between humiliation and language. There is no description of pain which does not make use of analogies. Therefore, the social and normative patterns of description and interpretation are much more alien to the experience of pain than to that of humiliation, of which they form a constitutive part. As a consequence, the danger of intentional or unintentional misdescription and misinterpretation of pain is much higher.[22] Language as a medium of the expression of pain is

[20] Scarry, note 18 above.

[21] For different attitudes towards pain and different consequences for the idea of human rights see T. Assad, 'On Torture, or Cruel, Inhuman and Degrading Treatment', in R.A. Wilson (ed.), *Human Rights, Culture and Context* (1997), 111–33. Below I will be concerned with infliction of pain against the will of the victim only. I am conscious of the fact that this description of this kind of case already presupposes an interpretive scheme ('against one's own will') which is in itself problematic, at least from a culturalist's point of view.

[22] This is not only true just for authoritarian regimes which try to misrepresent the suffering of their subjects, but also for many kinds of commercial and professional images of suffering in modern societies. See A. Kleinman and J. Kleinman, 'The Appeal of Experience; the Dismay of Images: Cultural Appropriations of Suffering in Our Times', in A. Kleinman *et al.* (eds.), *Social Suffering* (1997), 1–23. E.g., the commercialization of images of victims which become an important part of the 'infotainment on the nightly news' (at 1) or 'the aestheticization of child sexual abuse' (at 11).

highly ambivalent. Language can be used to 'unmake' the experience of pain; for example, in the case of torture by representing it as a sign of the presence of power. When the state monopolizes the voice, it can talk about the pain which is deliberately inflicted on the victim, can 'justify' it or 'explain' why it is necessary. The creative capacities of the human condition and imagination are necessary in order to find more adequate ways of description and interpretation which do not simply wipe out the experience of a body in pain. It is, of course, impossible to detect the one and only authentic expression of an experience. But it is possible to distinguish between different kinds of expression and media of representation according to the degree with which they allow the victim's voice to make itself explicit. Elaine Scarry distinguishes different 'arenas in which physical pain begins to enter language'.[23] There is the individual who tries to find expressions and sentences besides the mere scream, or other persons who vicariously try to describe pain on behalf of the person who suffers. Another arena is the different kinds of medical discourses.[24] A third one is art as a medium for the description and expression of pain. At last, Scarry refers to the letters and annual reports of Amnesty International about the victims of torture and to transcripts of personal injury trials as records of 'the passage of pain into speech'.[25]

As Scarry points out, communicative arenas for the passage of pain into speech, like the Amnesty letters or the personal injury trial, have additional goals and functions. They provoke or are intended to provoke certain reactions of other people, because of the report of pain. They should protest and intervene or take some legal, political, or even violent remedies in order to stop the infliction of pain. On the other hand, these records are often based on the reports of the victim. The victim has to tell his or her story, which becomes a part of the record. By this step, the victim begins to regain his or her voice, and his or her voice is strengthened by the voices of others who communicate the report. Obviously, these arenas also presuppose and make use of interpretive schemes, expectations, social rules, and cultural patterns.[26] But within these patterns, human beings try to make use of their creativity with the intention of overcoming the experience of pain without denying, misinterpreting, misrepresenting it, without giving a distorted report of their experience as does the State which justifies torture. Even if one admits that there is no pure and authentic description of pain, because every verbal description unavoidably makes use of analogies and metaphors, these arenas differ from others in which distorted reports are used to justify torturers, to legitimize the system of state power which organizes the deliberate infliction of pain. The difference lies in the focus on the recovery of the victim's voice in the presence of his or her memory of pain, and—by further steps—in the recovery of agency and control.

[23] Scarry, note 18 above, at 10.
[24] Medical discourse is of course—as is any discourse on pain and suffering—interrelated with cultural representations of suffering and with social and economic factors: see A. Kleinman, *Writing at the Margin: Discourse Between Anthropology and Medicine* (1996).
[25] Scarry, note 18 above, at 9. For the 'action files' of Amnesty International see *Amnesty International Report 1998* (German edn., at 63–6). For the role of NGOs for the passage from experiences of pain and humiliation to human rights discourse see E. Decaux, 'The Role of Civil Society', in this vol.
[26] For a contemporary account of the different discourses on and cultural representations of suffering see Kleinman *et al.*, note 22 above, at p. xxvi, 'Introduction': 'we have gone beyond the point where the subject of suffering can be examined as a single theme or a uniform experience'.

B. The Distinction between Misfortune and Injustice

If one tries to reconstruct the way in which the victim regains his or her voice and control, one could tell a meaningful story about the emergence of a sense of injustice. First of all, pain is not regarded as something that just happened because it had to happen. The pain does not result from a disease or from an accident, and it is not beyond the reach of human intervention, like an earthquake. It is not like the pain which one suffers from toothache or from a stone which falls on one's feet, and not even from another person who unintenionally, by accident, steps on one's feet. Among the causes of pain are other human beings, who acted deliberately, with knowledge of the consequences, and who inflicted pain intentionally.[27] This is obvious in the example of torture. The infliction of pain by torture implies human beings who are acting deliberately, who intentionally act in certain ways, or make use of instruments *because of* their property of producing pain. The anonymous and indefinite power of the State becomes present in the deliberate and intentional actions of its torturers who are acting under its command. The first fundamental distinction which is implied in the interpretive scheme is the distinction between *nature and fate* on the one hand and *meaningful human actions* on the other.

Several other concepts are included in this fundamental distinction. If the causes of pain are attributed to meaningful human actions, a concept of the person is presupposed according to which he or she can build his or her own aims and intentions, and can control his or her actions according to an intention, who has a voice and agency or control of him- or herself, and of the world outside. In general, a person in a normal psychic state who is not coerced by anybody else is regarded as being able to *avoid* an intentional action; for example, an intentional infliction of pain. Despite all the conflicts about the appropriate interpretation of the meaning of an action, despite all the explanations, justifications, and excuses which are offered by torturers or by government officials, according to which the 'strong interrogation' was 'unfortunately unavoidable', and despite all the hierarchies among those who give orders and those who execute them, there are at least some persons who have voice and control, and who, consequently, could have avoided the torture. Because certain kinds of pain, like those inflicted by torture, can be interpreted as effects of avoidable, meaningful human actions, it is possible to take a position on this action, to say 'yes' or 'no' to it. One can *reject* the intention to inflict pain, and one can claim that the corresponding action *should* be avoided. By this step, a human being begins to regain his or her voice. He or she does not quietly accept a fate, but is able to say 'no' to the things which happened to him or her. To reject an intention like the infliction of pain by torture and to claim that its execution can and shall be avoided means that it is *unjust* to do it. If the action is avoidable, it can be rejected and imputed to

---

[27] This distinction between suffering caused by 'nature' and by intentional human action is of course not *a priori*. Furthermore, the causes of illness and the kind of treatment are linked with social arrangements and structures which are again dependent on intentional human actions and omissions; e.g. the difference between poor and rich or the distribution and organisation of health care. See A. Young, 'Suffering and the Origins of Traumatic Memory', and P. Farmer, 'On Suffering and Structural Violence: A View from Below', both in Kleinman *et al.*, note 22 above, at 245–84.

the torturers and those members of the government who gave the command, and they can be regarded and treated as *responsible* for an act of injustice.

This kind of rejection, which includes a judgement about the injustice of the act done and an attribution of responsibility to the actor, entails a specific meaning for the victim. It means that the infliction of pain was neither a matter of nature and fate nor *the victim's fault*. To consider damage as the result of one's own fault is also a reason to keep quiet—because, for example, one feels ashamed of one's own inability to anticipate and to avoid dangerous situations. As long as the victim interprets her situation as her own fault, she will have no reason to raise her voice and to say 'no'. In the best case, she will look for some strategy for avoiding the risk that bad things happen again. She will be unable to regain her voice unless she stops feeling responsible for the pain she suffers from and attributes responsibility to those who acted intentionally and who could have avoided their intentional action, i.e. the commanders and their executioners. The fundamental distinction between nature, fate, and meaningful human action can be extended to the distinction between *misfortune and injustice*.[28] The victim not only regains his or her voice by saying 'no' to the things that happened to him or her, but is now also able to *address* him- or herself to someone who is responsible for the things which happened, and to others who should accept the claim of injustice.

The concept of injustice is related to expectations and norms as well as to rules of imputation of unjust actions to persons who are held responsible for them. The distinction between misfortune and injustice is neither pre-given nor invariable. What is considered as something that just happens, for which nobody is responsible and which has to be borne by the victim him- or herself, depends on human ability to intervene in the world and, most of all, on the social interpretations of the world. A prominent example of the first requirement is genetic engineering. As long as the genes of an individual human being were simply inherited by his or her parents and, therefore, so to speak, given by nature without any opportunity of changing them, his or her genetic equipment with all its consequences for his or her life was nothing more than fate, misfortune, or luck. Nobody could be held responsible for his or her genetic equipment. To the extent that it is now and will in future be possible to alter genes by genetic engineering, the genetic equipment becomes a matter of intentional human intervention, of justice and injustice, and of responsibility. A prominent example of the second requirement is poverty. Is it the result of wrong decisions by the individual, i.e. the victim's fault, or is it the fate of an anonymous market—or is it something that could be prevented by political decisions, legal rules, and social institutions? The answer to this question depends not only on human ability to intervene in the world, but also on the social interpretations of individual achievement, of the interdependence between individuals and society.

No matter how the question ought to be answered, the assertion that something is unjust and that someone is responsible for it changes the communicative arena. It is at least possible to argue about the borderline between misfortune and injustice. If it is in general possible to react to meaningful social actions by taking a position and

---

[28] For the distinction between misfortune and injustice see J. N. Shklar, *Faces of Injustice* (1990), chap. 3 (German edn. 1997, 67ff.).

saying 'yes' or 'no' to them, then it is also possible to put social arrangements, social structures, institutions, laws, rules, and conventions, as far as they are constituted by and consist of meaningful human actions, into question and under the *demand of justification*. It at least makes sense to claim that negative discrimination and social exclusion by reason of gender, race, religion, or other human properties are not a misfortune and not the victim's own fault, but injustice. This is, of course, the result of a long history full of conflicts and obstacles. It is part of European history that some people began at some time not to take social exclusion by reason of birth as given by nature or by God, but demanded that any such exclusion be justified. In this regard, gender or race makes no difference to the critique of social exclusion.

The demand for justification is of course ambivalent. It is possible to justify negative discrimination and social exclusion. It is even possible to have a law that justifies all actions of the State which are done with the aim of exclusion, expropriation, exploitation, or even the annihilation of minorities. It is possible to have a law that justifies torture or the killing of a citizen who illegally crosses the border in order to leave the country. The claim that such actions are unjust and the demand of justification could easily be answered by saying that there is a law that justifies them. As a consequence, the assertion of injustice and the demand of justification have to be extended to the justifications which are offered for such atrocities.

Needless to say people differ very much one from another in what they believe to be an injustice. On the one hand, the experience and interpretation of injustice are radically subjective, on the other hand, in particular in pluralistic societies with a certain degree of cultural relativism, there are different convictions about what is just, about the primary rules, according to which one could identify an action as a matter of injustice.[29] Together with the ambiguity of primary rules and norms, which can also be used to justify torture and to legitimize an oppressive system of power, the distinction between injustice and misfortune and the demand of justification have to be extended to the rules and norms themselves. What matters is the recognition of every individual as an equal participant in the political process which leads to a decision on primary legal rules. To regain (or to preserve) voice and control does also mean that one has the power and the ability to criticize and to amend the rules of justice. This is the most important effect of human rights on political culture.

Whether or not a negative experience will be considered as an injustice, with its consequent rejection according to a valid human right, depends of course on the universal principles according to which a judgement on such an experience is made. This could be, for example, a principle of role-exchange.[30] A negative experience is an injustice, if everybody who takes the perspective of the victim rejects her experience as an injustice. There are similar principles, like the categorical imperative, utilitarian principles or the procedure suggested by discourse ethics, which comes close to the idea of taking each human being's voice seriously.[31] But these principles can be

---

[29] For a very sensitive description of the experience of being a victim of injustice, see: *ibid.* (German edn., at 52).

[30] I am grateful to Robert Alexy for urging me to make this point clear.

[31] See, e.g., C.S. Nino and R. Alexy, 'Diskurstheorie und Menschenrechte', in R. Alexy, *Recht, Vernunft, Diskurs* (1995), 127–64; J. Habermas, *Between Facts and Norms* (German edn. *Faktizität und Geltung* (1993), chap. 3).

applied to a negative experience only *after* it is already considered as a discourse on justice and injustice and not as fate or the victim's own fault. These principles cannot substitute the requirement of an increasing and sufficient sensitivity to negative experiences and their potential meaning as a matter of injustice.

V. THE EFFECTS OF HUMAN RIGHTS ON POLITICAL CULTURE

The idea of human rights emerges from the rejection of pain and humiliation, caused by the state or by an overwhelming social power, as an injustice. But the reconstruction of human rights as resulting from negative experiences like suffering from pain and humiliation focuses on other aspects too. What matters here is not so much the propositional content of a human right and its justification, but the way in which a victim regains voice and control facing a negative experience like pain and humiliation inflicted by the state. One step is the interpretive scheme, according to which suffering from pain is not misfortune—to which one can only adapt—and not the victim's own fault. It allows the victim to insist on his or her experience and to reject all misinterpretations and pseudo-justifications or excuses for the infliction of pain or for degrading treatment. But this is of course not the whole story. The victim would not be able to regain voice and control if nobody listened to his or her report of a negative experience, if nobody cared about it, or if everybody denied that it is really a negative experience, or, finally, if everybody considered it as a misfortune or as the victim's own fault. Whereas the latter reactions presuppose that the opponent has at least listened, although he or she denies what the victim claimed, the former reactions consist of mere ignorance. The victim becomes marginalized, because his or her voice is considered as having no meaning or simply as disturbing. What is necessary here—and this seems to be the decisive move—is that the victim is taken seriously, that others listen to his or her voice. Listening here implies of course more than the behaviour of a Nazi or Stalinist judge in a show trial. It means, first of all, that the story of the victim *counts*, that it has considerable *weight* with regard to the question whether his or her painful and humiliating treatment is an injustice.[32]

When this move of recognition of the victim's voice is extended to all human beings, something like the idea of human dignity is established. One cannot deny that the history which led to the principle that human beings have to recognize each other as persons who have a voice which counts and has weight is a long and complicated one, which is full of hindrances and obstacles.[33] In addition, 'voice' has also to be understood metaphorically, because this concept has also to be applied to those who

---

[32] Often, the victim's voice obtains weight indirectly, as is demonstrated by the examples of widows and relatives in Argentina or Guatemala, who do not stop searching for their husbands and kin who were killed during the time of dictatorship, and publicly asking questions about their fate.

[33] Contemporary examples of the difficulties of establishing a public forum for the expression of experiences of pain and humiliation are the cases of rape and sexual abuse during the civil war in former Yugoslavia. See K. MacKinnon, 'Crimes of War, Crimes of Peace', in Shute and Hurley, note 5 above, at 83–110.

are mute or to future generations. With these additions in mind, one could say that the claim which is raised by a victim who gives a report on his or her experience of pain and humiliation is that nobody shall be excluded from the realm of human beings who take each other seriously by listening to each other and by each attributing weight to what the other says. The victim is now regarded by others and understands him- or herself as somebody who has preferences and intentions, who has agency and control, and who can raise claims and demand justifications. From now on, it is impossible to treat him or her as a mere object of one's own interests only, and he or she sees him- or herself with different eyes.

It is by this step that the idea of equal human rights comes into being. But instead of focusing on the propositional content of the right—for example, Article 5 of the Universal Declaration of Human Rights—I have tried to look at the process in which a victim of injustice regains voice and control. The idea of human rights is something like an *abbreviation* of this process by which the victim overcomes a negative experience of pain or humiliation with their consequences of muteness, passivity, and helplessness. The propositional content of a human right depends on the kind of social practice which is experienced as painful and humiliating, like torture, arbitrary imprisonment, exclusion from basic social goods. In the background of these rights are always individuals who suffer, who have fear, who raise their voices, who claim that others shall listen to their report of their negative experience, and who demand justification and reject the justifications for the kind of social practice which produces these negative experiences. This reconstruction is even more true in those cases where individuals claim to have human rights which are still not recognized and established. Here, the individual is not able to claim a right which already contains a symbolic abbreviation of the past ways out of the shadows of pain and humiliation, but he or she has to go on the long path of recognition of his or her experience of injustice.

Joel Feinberg has explained the concept of rights with regard to their activist and performative role and meaning. Looking for a distinctive feature of a right, which distinguishes rights from other entitlements, he discovers the internal link between certain rights and *claims*.[34] Claim-rights are the strongest kind of rights, because they entail corresponding duties of others. The possibility of claiming links an abstract and general right to the concrete situation of a person who raises a claim to have this right. For every right there is a right to claim in appropriate circumstances that one has that right. To claim a right is like asserting something to others with the claim that it shall be accepted. 'To claim that one has a right . . . is to *assert* in such a manner as to demand or insist that what is asserted be recognized.'[35] Feinberg pays particular attention to this activist meaning of claiming, because it is the feature of the concept of a right which is important for the social identity and the self-understanding of the person who raises a claim to a right. 'Why is the right to demand recognition of one's rights so important? The reason, I think, is that if one

[34] In the tradition of Roman civil law, the relationship (and difference) between rights and claims was at first introduced by Winscheid in the nineteenth century.

[35] J. Feinberg, 'Duties, Rights, and Claims', in J. Feinberg, *Rights, Justice, and the Bounds of Liberty* (1980), 141.

begged, pleaded, or prayed for recognition merely, at best one would receive a kind of beneficent treatment easily confused with the acknowledgement of rights, but in fact altogether foreign and deadly to it.'[36] This explains why and how rights are the medium in which the victim becomes able to regain voice and control in the presence of pain and humiliation.

In his reconstruction of *the activity of claiming* as the salient feature of rights, Feinberg distinguishes two different meanings of 'claiming' with regard to rights. It makes sense to say that a person is 'making a legal claim to' a right as well as to say that a person is 'claiming that' he or she has a right. The first meaning of claiming refers to rights which one already has, for example, those given by a legal system which already entails abstract individual rights which can be claimed by a person in a concrete case if he or she is qualified (by the appropriate circumstances) to make this claim. A more definite case is the claim to a title which follows from a person's right that is already recognized and (legally) confirmed. These are the usual ways in which a right becomes the right of a person in a concrete situation, in which it becomes something like a 'real' right that is exercised by the person who has it, with real legal consequences. For this reason, Feinberg attributes to the activity of claiming a performative meaning: '[l]egally speaking, making claim to can itself make things happen. This sense of "claiming", then, might well be called "the performative sense". The legal power to claim (performatively) one's right or the things to which one has a right seems to be essential to the very notion of a right.'[37]

On the other hand, a person can claim that he or she has a right, although and because he or she does not have it, because, for example, it is not presupposed by the rules of a legal system. Here, it is the content that matters. Feinberg calls this kind of activity 'propositional claiming'. Whereas a claim to a right can be raised by the person who has this right only, the claim that one has a right can also be raised by others. As a German citizen, I can (currently) raise *the claim that* foreigners should have a voting right in parliamentary elections, and if it were the case that a legal rule existed which provided foreigners with such a right, then only a foreigner could *make a claim to* his or her voting right. As Feinberg points out, the former content-oriented kind of claiming has social consequences too, but they are different from the legal consequences of the exercise of a right: '[t]o claim that one has rights is to make an assertion that one has them, and to make it in such a manner as to demand or insist that they be recognized'.[38] This kind of claiming does not differ from the general claim to recognition and acceptance, which is raised for the propositional content of every sincere assertion, like the truth claim which is raised for the assertion that '[i]t is raining here and now'. With this kind of claim, a speaker addresses him- or herself to a hearer, he or she enters into a communicative space: 'part of the point of propositional claiming is to *make sure* people listen'.[39] If this interpretation is correct, one could say that propositional claiming also entails performative claiming. To claim *that* I have a right then has the performative meaning that I am willing to enter into

---

[36] J. Feinberg, 'Duties, Rights, and Claims', in J. Feinberg, *Rights, Justice, and the Bounds of Liberty* (1980), 141.

[37] J. Feinberg, 'The Nature and Value of Rights', in Feinberg, note 35 above, at 150.

[38] *Ibid.*   [39] *Ibid.*

the communicative space where I want to be taken seriously, where my voice has a weight, where others listen to me and argue about my claim by demanding and giving justifications. In a constitutional democracy, this communicative space is called the *public sphere*.

Feinberg's interpretation of the activity of claiming is relevant for the reconstruction of the idea of human rights which I am suggesting here. In the case of human rights, the claim to a human right is as important as the claim that one has a human right. Performative claiming prevents the victim from losing voice and control with regard to a concrete situation in which she suffers pain or humiliation. He or she can claim a right which she already has. 'Having rights, of course, makes claiming possible; but it is claiming that gives rights their special moral significance.'[40] The moral significance of the performative claiming to a right consists exactly in the ability to regain one's voice.

> Having rights enables us to 'stand up like men', to look others in the eye, and to feel in some fundamental way the equal of everyone. To think of oneself as the holder of rights is not to be unduly but properly proud, to have that minimal self-respect that is necessary to be worthy of the love and esteem for others. Indeed, respect for persons (this is an intriguing idea) may simply be respect for their rights, so that there cannot be the one without the other; and what is called 'human dignity' may simply be the recognizable capacity to assert claims.[41]

Of course, it happens quite often that the victim has a right, but that she is prevented from making a claim to it. Propositional claiming is much more difficult, but is has a similar effect for the proponent of a human right as performative claiming—exactly because of its additional performative meaning. The proponent of a new human right at least makes claim to a right to enter into the public sphere, to be taken seriously in his or her report of pain and humiliation. Thus, the proponent of a (new) human right always makes a claim to the right to human dignity, apart from the claim that he or she shall have a human right with a new propositional content, for example, the right to development.

If a person makes a claim to a right or is claiming that he or she has a right, then it does not go without saying that the person already has or obtains the right. It all depends on a third aspect of claiming. According to Feinberg, a claim has to be justified or *valid*.[42] This is obvious in the case of performative claiming, because a person can make a valid claim to a right only if the right is presupposed by the legal system and if he or she is able to demonstrate and to prove that the appropriate circumstances are given and that the conditions are met under which the claim to the right is valid. To make a claim to a right then means that one has a *prima facie* case of a right. Propositional claiming is, again, more difficult, because there is (still) no right. Feinberg takes the example of 'manifesto writers' who identify needs and argue for their recognition as human rights. It is intriguing, according to Feinberg, that these proponents speak of these rights as already given. By this, they try to suggest that the needs they identified are already valid claims to rights. But it is only an effective

---

[40] *Ibid.*, at 151.
[41] *Ibid.* The text was published in 1979, but I think what is meant here can easily be extended to women.
[42] *Ibid.*, at 152.

rhetorical tool to urge the world community to recognize certain needs as valid claims to rights, and 'a powerful way of expressing the conviction that they ought to be recognized by states here and now as potential rights and consequently as determinants of present aspirations and guides to present policies'.[43]

Again, one can interpret this effect as the performative meaning of claiming *that* one has a right. In addition, this case demonstrates how the proposal of a (new) human right can become in itself a case of performative claiming. The so-called manifesto writers argue as if there already were an existing right to which one could make a *prima facie* claim, because they refer to a 'higher law', for example, to natural law, which already entails a right which should be recognized and confirmed by a system of positive law. From their point of view, the 'new' right turns out to be an 'old' one. In this case, propositional claiming not only has the additional performative meaning of entering into the public sphere and claiming for an audience which listens, but it is also always linked to performative claiming in the strong sense, as far as it refers to a 'higher law' which already entails the kind of rights to which the claim is made.

By this step, the manifesto writer does more than merely express himself in a powerful way and make use of effective rhetorical skills, as Feinberg seems to suggest. By referring to 'higher law', she gives a reason for the claim that people should have certain rights, which shall justify the claim to recognition. At the same time, she traces her authority, her right to a voice, back to such a 'higher law', which gives her the legal power to make a claim to the right. It is of course difficult to say what is meant by 'higher law', particularly if one addresses the world community which consists of a plurality of different cultures with different opinions about 'higher law'. The appeal to 'natural law' was a historical European approach to justifying the claim to rights which were not recognized by the State and a majority of people in a community as something which is already given by nature, so that nobody could ever deny or abolish them. This appeal also provided the proponents with power and authority in order to justify their licence to speak against a power which denied this right. The members of the *Assemblée Nationale* in 1789 could legitimize themselves as authors of the Declaration of the Rights of Man only by referring to an 'incontestable and irresistible authority'.[44] In a similar way, the authors of the American Declaration of Independence acted in the name of 'the laws of nature and in the name of God'.[45] As Gauchet, Derrida, and several other authors have pointed out, this is a case of self-authorization on the one hand and authorization in the name of some higher law and authority on the other *at the same time*. The authors of the declarations could derive their authority only from themselves—but by empowering themselves, they have put themselves under a higher authority or a higher law, which bound them from the moment in which they received their power. Although 'natural law' or 'God' are no longer appropriate references, every contemporary claim *that* a human right, which is not recognized yet, *should* be recognized, traces its performative power back to some 'higher law'. There is something like a performative circle between claiming a

[43] J. Feinberg, 'The Nature and Value of Rights', in Feinberg, note 35 above, at 153.
[44] M. Gauchet, 'Menschenrechte', in F. Furet and M. Ozouf (eds.), *Kritisches Wörterbuch der Französischen Revolution*, (1996), ii, 1189.
[45] J. Derrida, 'Nietzsches Otobiographie oder Politik des Eigennamens' [1980] *Fugen* 67.

human right and claiming to have a human right. The political debate in the public sphere about the claim *to have* a right is already bound by human rights—although it is the political process which creates these rights. This is the interplay between self-rule and self-authorization on the one hand, and law rule and authorization by prior law on the other, which is already established in constitutional democracies and which has to be extended to human rights legislation.[46]

A consequence of this *performative* nature of human rights is that they are dependent on citizens, who are not only able, but also willing, to make use of their rights, to participate in the performative practice. To become 'rights in action', and not merely 'book rights', they have to be used. The willingness to make use of rights can be threatened by different political, social, economic, cultural, and individual obstacles. The experience of such threats is also a specific European experience. The effectiveness of human rights also, but not only, depends on public conventions and judicial institutions for the enforcement of these rights. It is also necessary that people see themselves as holders of these rights, that they see themselves as citizens conscious of a community of human rights. This is a matter of political culture. People have to be empowered and enfranchised to raise their claims. As long as I am poor, belong to a minority which is publicly despised and systematically disadvantaged, which is excluded from communication, I lack the courage to use my rights—even if am a holder of those rights. Here one can observe a kind of interplay between political culture and human rights. Rights to social welfare and education, rights to individual liberty, and rights to political participation have, apart from their specific meaning, the general meaning of encouraging people to consider and to treat themselves as well as each other as conscious subjects of human rights, as equal members of a legal community, which is constituted by the subjects of human rights, and which exists only as long as they make use of their rights. As a consequence, human rights have to be defended and strengthened not merely because they are human rights, but also because they have an effect on the European political culture which enables its citizens to make use of their rights and to develop the identity of equal members of a community of human rights.

To sum up, one could say that the performative meaning of human rights is most important for the status and self-understanding of the human being who articulates his or her negative experience of injustice and fear. If somebody refers to human rights when he or she articulates his or her experience of injustice and fear, he or she claims to have a *voice*. As an interpreter of his or her experience, he or she becomes the author of the human rights which he or she claims to have. Of course, a mere expression of injustice is not enough for the recognition of a violated right. The claim of the performative practice of human rights that everybody has *to listen to* the

---

[46] This loop between law and politics is recognized even by opposing political philosophies: see J. Derrida, *The Force of Law* (German edn. *Gesetzeskraft* (1991), 58), and Habermas, note 31 above, at chap. 3. For a 'joint interpretation' of Derrida's and Habermas' account see A. Wellmer, 'Menschenrechte und Demokratie', in G. Lohmann and S. Gosepath (eds.), *Philosophie der Menschenrechte* (forthcoming, 1998). For a reconstruction of this loop in constitutional democracies see F. Michelman, 'Can Constitutional Democrats be Legal Positivists? Or Why Constitutionalism?' (1996) 3 *Constellations* 293ff; O. Gerstenberg, *Deliberative Demokratie. Zur Rekonstruktion des Zirkels von Rechtsstaat und rechtserzeugender Politik* (1997).

report of an individual experience entails the claim that everybody can put him- or herself in the shoes of the victim. This explains why human rights are always rooted in an individual and *particular* historical experience, but at the same time are declared to be rights which claim to *universal* recognition. Together with the claim that everybody can put him- or herself in the shoes of the victim, the person refrains from asserting a concrete identity: he or she becomes the abstract identity of a bearer of rights, and claims to be recognized as such a person.

VI. CONTEMPORARY PROBLEMS: FROM PUBLIC TO PRIVATE POWER

The European approach to human rights, which consists in a complex universalism with a sufficient degree of sensitivity to negative experiences of human beings, faces at least two problems, which could even become a serious objection, because they are linked together by current developments and changes in the political culture and the institutions of human rights. The first problem results from the emphasis on negative experiences, the loss and regaining of the victim's voice, and the memory of injustice and fear as the most salient features of the political culture of human rights. Human rights are considered by this approach from *the victim's point of view*. The second problem results from my primary concern in explaining complex universalism as a particular European contribution to human rights. Hitherto, my primary concern has been experiences of pain and humiliation, which were caused by *the State and its representatives*. But contemporarily, many, perhaps most, of the negative experiences of pain and humiliation which can be legitimately rejected as cases of injustice and serious violations of human rights are not committed by a State and its representatives, but by powerful social groups or by para-state organizations: war lords operating in civil wars who deprive people from basic resources of food and who order or tolerate torture, rape, and genocide, as in some regions of Africa, in former Yugoslavia, or in Algeria; militant fundamentalist groups who deny basic rights to women, as in Afghanistan. Often, powerful economic organizations, like big oil companies, work together with repressive regimes in order to deny claims of aborigines to their land from which they are expropriated.[47] This is the problem of violations of human rights by private organizations.

The emphasis on the victim's perspective can be dangerous for two reasons. First, it tends to exclude, paradoxically, the victim for a second time. As long as the victim is labelled and treated as a victim, and as long as the victim labels him- or herself, he or she is kept and captured in a passive role. This becomes more obvious when the victim's claim to human rights also aims at its potential consequences: the attribution of responsibility to the perpetrators. Then, the claim to human rights is linked with a relationship between victim and perpetrator. Charles Taylor has observed that a 'discourse of accusation' which prevails in public discourse can easily become

[47] For a more detailled account of the role of corporations and non-state actors see M. Kamminga, 'Regulating Corporations and Other Non-State Actors: The EU Role', in this vol.

'sterile', as sometimes happens in societies which have to deal with a past of state terrorism.[48] As a consequence, those groups which are obsessed by their role as victim
remain within the realm of the community, but do not participate actively in it.[49]
This kind of exclusion and self-exclusion has to be avoided by a practice of complex
universalism. The focus on negative experiences and the memory of injustice and
fear will not keep human beings in the passive role of victim. Instead, the performative meaning of the claim to human rights has to be extended to the role of the victim.
The claim to human rights refers to the status of an equal participant in the discourse
of human rights. The role of the victim is only part of the memory of injustice and
fear to which anyone appeals who raises a claim to human rights.

The other reason why the emphasis on the victim's perspective could be dangerous
to complex universalism has to do with the second problem. From the victim's perspective, it makes no difference if he or she is tortured or raped by the agents of the
State, by an ordinary citizen committing a crime, or by armed forces under the command of a war lord. Complex universalism of human rights, as is suggested here,
blurs the distinction between crimes which consist in a violation of criminal laws that
are given by the legislator of a particular State and human rights violations. The advantage of this position is that it allows one to deal with all violations of human
rights which are not committed by the State but by powerful social groups or para-
state organizations. The disadvantages are the change in the role of the State, which
is required as a consequence, and the exclusionary consequences for the perpetrators.

The State was the traditional addressee of human rights. Its role was, although
ambivalent, clearly defined. The State was considered as the pre-eminent protector
of human rights as well as the pre-eminant violator. The experience of violation
came first—this is why all approaches to human rights try to demonstrate how and
why human rights are above the State and a legally constituted society, and why
human rights are primarily negative rights, directed against unjustified interference
by the State. The idea that the State is also protector of human rights emerged together with the experience that human rights can also be jeopardized by overwhelming social power, for example, by an unequal distribution of primary goods which
are necessary for a decent life. As soon as the negative experience of economic inequality was declared as unjust (i.e. as not pre-given by nature, fate, or as the fault of
the disadvantaged and poor), people raised their voices and made a claim to social
rights. Their institutionalization depended on a kind of power which was able to re-
distribute goods—the welfare state. Human rights of the second and third generation resort 'to state as the guarantor of human rights'.[50]

Meanwhile, private power became stronger and stronger. It increased the danger
of violations of individual rights which cannot be overcome by tort law or criminal
law. The division of labour between human rights, directed against the State, and internal laws, which included individual rights protected by tort law and criminal law,
begins to fade. The State becomes more and more the vehicle for protection of the

---

[48] C. Taylor, 'Demokratie und Ausgrenzung' (1997) 14 *Transit* 95. [49] *Ibid.*
[50] B. de Sousa Santos, 'Toward a Multicultural Conception of Human Rights' (1997) 18 *Zeitschrift für
Rechtssoziologie* 2.

people against pain and humiliation inflicted by private power. This is the problem of third party-applicability of human rights,[51] or their horizontal effectiveness in the relationships between citizens. Human rights as constitutional basic rights are interpreted as rights which entail 'duties of protection'[52] (*'Schutzpflichten'*) which are addressed to the State, which has to act in order to protect the citizens by, for example, enforcing strong criminal laws and providing an effective criminal justice system. The contemporary public debate about the enforcement of criminal law and the effectiveness of the criminal justice system, which takes place in many European countries today with regard, for example, to sexual abuse of children or organized crime, often takes the victim's perspective in order to raise a claim against the State to better protection against criminal offences.

A further step is already taken in those cases where the nation State is too weak to cope with severe violations of human rights or where the State is itself the perpetrator. The suggestion of establishing an international court of criminal justice transposes the idea of a 'duty to protection against violations of human rights' from the level of the relationship between State and citizens to the level of international relations between States, powerful social groups, and individuals—individuals as potential victims and bearers of human rights.

A consequence of this development is that the State and civil society, or even supranational organizations and individual human beings, begin to merge at least to the extent that the victim's perspective and civil society or the global society are identical. The State is no longer seen as the sole violator of human rights—although human rights in particular emerged from negative experiences with the State's power to punish. Arbitrary imprisonment was, as already said, the first right, the *'Ur-Grundrecht'*. In Europe today, many people have fewer negative experiences and less fear with regard to the punishing State than with regard to crime. But if the victim's perspective prevails, then the danger of dehumanization emerges again; this time with regard to the perpetrator. When the distinction between civil society and State is blurred by the idea that human rights generally entail a 'duty to protect' people from becoming victims of human rights violations, then the human rights of the (potential) perpetrator become important too. What is necessary, then, is a balance between the human rights of the potential victims of human rights violations and the human rights of the potential perpetrators. The emphasis on the victim's perspective may not mean that the perpetrator has no human rights at all—otherwise, the perpetrator him- or herself will become a victim, who can legitimately reject his or her negative experience (for example, torture by the police or cruel punishment) as a matter of injustice and as a violation of human rights.

---

[51] W. Kälin, 'Menschenrechtsverträge als Gewährleistung einer objektiven Ordnung', in W. Kälin *et al.* (eds.), *Aktuelle Probleme des Menschenrechtsschutzes* (*Current Problems of Human Rights Protection*) (1994), 9–48, especially 32.

[52] Denninger, note 15 above, at 23ff and 33.

VII. CONCLUSION: THE THREAT OF 'HUMAN RIGHTS TALK'

As Martti Kosekenniemi has demonstrated in his chapter,[53] the institutionalization of human rights and daily human rights practice cannot ensure that human rights do not degenerate into mere talk. Such degeneration is facilitated by the abuse of human rights for other purposes, economic or political, or the ideological use of human rights for the legitimation of a *status quo*. This provokes the criticism that human rights are no more than ideology, rhetorical tools, which can be used for the purpose of stopping political struggle over the ordering of social affairs. This kind of criticism of human rights talk is as old as the idea of human rights itself. The classical topics were already named by Burke, Mill, and Marx. In general, the criticism is that human rights contain an individualistic bias, that they ignore the complexity of social relationships and individual needs, that they destroy collective identities, and that they insert artificial boundaries and barriers into politics, which is particularly dangerous when democratic self-legislation is at stake.[54]

Koskenniemi's critique of human rights talk can be interpreted as another argument for complex universalism of human rights. Rights rhetoric can be criticized from within the idea of human rights, when it is traced back to negative experiences of injustice and fear, as it is suggested here. It relates human rights to those who are affected, whose voice is not or only insufficiently represented in human rights discourse and practice, and whose experiences are excluded from human rights discourse. This is the reason complex universalism suggests making a shift from particular human rights and their contents to the procedures, in which each human being has a right to a voice and to express his or her negative experiences as a matter of injustice. Only if human rights have the additional meaning of a claim to recognition of being an equal participant in these discourses, the division between politics and an empty and ritualized human rights talk can be avoided. Rights depend on politics, and they entrench politics at the same time. While human rights should be given in a democratic political process only, they also shape this process by presupposing and requiring that each participant shall be recognized a person with a right to a voice, with a right to express his or her negative experiences and to claim that these experiences are a matter of injustice. Democratic politics give rights—and at the same time, rights shape and organize the democratic process. This is why the circular relationship between rights and politics, as mentioned above, is necessary.

The dangerous development, described by Koskenniemi, cannot be halted by simply substituting rights by politics, but only by accelerating the interaction between rights and politics. This could happen if we conceived of human rights as a memory of injustice and fear, which is linked with experiences of individuals who lost and regained their voices with regard to negative experiences such as suffering from the intentional infliction of pain and humiliation. It would make us more sensitive to the silent exclusions of our daily human rights practice. Keeping the long history of

---

[53] Koskenniemi, note 9 above.

[54] See the following essays: Edmund Burke's *Reflections on the Revolution in France*, Jeremy Bentham's *Anarchical Fallacies*, and Karl Marx's *On the Jewish Question*, in J. Waldron (ed.), *'Nonsense Upon Stilts'—Bentham, Burke and Marx on the Rights of Man* (1987).

exclusionary readings and selective applications of human rights in mind, this could be the message of a European approach to human rights: to encourage people to re-capture their human rights by regaining their voices with regard to experiences of pain and humiliation. When we begin to conceive of human rights as the legacy of in-justice and fear, it could happen that the universalism of human rights turns out no longer to be a problem.

C

The Human Rights Context within which the European Union Functions

5

A Human Rights Policy for the European Community and Union: The Question of Competences

J. H. H. WEILER AND SYBILLA C. FRIES

I. PROLOGUE—DON'T DO WHAT I DO, DO WHAT I TELL YOU TO DO

The question of Community competences in the field of human rights came back into sharp focus with the publication of the Proposal for a Council Regulation (EC) on the development and consolidation of democracy and the rule of law and respect for human rights and fundamental freedoms, submitted by the Commission on 24 July 1997.[1] It was followed, in October of that same year, by an Opinion of the Legal Service of the Council on this proposal, a restricted document which, however, was widely leaked and circulated.[2] The exchange is by now obsolete. First, the Commission and Council reached a cosy, *don't ask don't tell*, compromise reflected in an amended set of Commission proposals.[3] The Commission would get the sizeable funds it required to spread the good word of human rights; so long as the Commission formally accepted a legal regime which would expunge any official reference to a Community human rights policy relating to any activity in and by the Member States, the Council would not ask how exactly the Commission was spending the money and turn a blind eye even to funding instances which egregiously contravened that very policy.

The apple cart was famously overturned by the subsequent decision of the Court outlawing expenditures without firm legislative authorization.[4] It should be emphasized, however, that this decision, contrary to the impression given in its immediate wake, eschewed the principal issue of competences. What exercised the plaintiffs and the Court were the respective institutional competences of Commission and Council. The case was based on the implicit assumption that, had only the Council given its legislative approval, all contested expenditures would be *intra vires*. Also implicit in the decision was the notion that, were the contested expenditures

---

[1] [1997] OJ C282/14, COM(97)357 final– 97/0191(SYN).

[2] Brussels, 16 Oct. 1997; 11402/97 LIMITE; JUR 347; DEVGEN 72; COHOM 2; PESC 184.

[3] Commission proposals of 1 July 1998, DEVGEN 43 and 44. See 'Working Document on the Proposal for a Council Regulation (EC) on the Development and Consolidation of Democracy and the Rule of Law and Respect for Human Rights and Fundamental Freedoms': *rapporteur*, Mr Galeote Quecedo, COM(97)357, 12 Feb. 1998.

[4] Case C–106/96, *United Kingdom* v. *Commission*, judgment of 12 May 1998.

truly to fall in the 'non significant' pilot and exploratory category, they would be equally legitimate. The practical effect of the decision was not to limit the competences of the Community, but to limit somewhat the autonomy of the Commission and to strengthen that of the Council. The expenditures in that case concerned actions which were, arguably, firmly within the socio-economic aspects of the Single Market. They did not concern specifically the more controversial dimensions of human rights expenditures by the Commission.

Until recent years the debate about Community human rights competences mostly turned on the reach of the judicial writ of the European Court of Justice especially to certain classes of Member State acts[5] and to that trusty perennial accession to the ECHR, which has been with us at least since 1978. With the publication of the 1997 and 1998 Commission proposals, the discussion shifts firmly from Court to political institutions.

On its face this seems to be a simple morality tale. The Commission, champion of human rights, proposes and the Council (Legal Service) seeks to place niggardly restrictions and constraints. The burden of the Council position turns on the following legal propositions. The Council first repeats the Court's affirmation in *Opinion 2/94*[6] that:

> No treaty provision confers on the Community institutions any general power to enact rules on human rights or to conclude international conventions in this field.

Following what it believes is the burden of *Opinion 2/94* the Council comes to the conclusion that Article 308 (*ex* Article 235) also could not be used to enact rules on human rights.

As regards the use of Article179 (*ex* Article 130w) which refers to the objectives set out in Article 177 (*ex* Article 130u), the Council, purporting to follow the decision of the Court in *Portugal* v. *Council*[7] argues that Article 179 cannot be a legal basis for measures the main object and purpose of which is democratization and human rights rather than co-operation development.[8]

The Council (Legal Service) then concludes that Articles 179 and 308 may only be used to support human rights and democratization measures which are part of, and

---

[5] See, e.g. D. Binder, 'The European Court of Justice and the Protection of Fundamental Rights in the European Community: New Developments and Future Possibilities in Expanding Fundamental Rights Review to Member State Action', *4/95 Harvard Jean Monnet Working Paper Series*, available at: http://www.law.harvard.edu/Programs/JeanMonnet/ and sources cited therein.

[6] *Opinion 2/94* [1996] ECR I–1759.

[7] Case C–268/94, *Portuguese Republic* v. *EU Council* [1996] ECR I–6207.

[8] We accept that this is a plausible reading of *Portugal* v. *Council* by the Legal Service. What may be questioned is the decision of the Court to read Art. 130u(2) (now Art. 177(2)) as necessarily an ancillary provision to a more generic co-operation development policy and not allow an autonomous Community measure or Community agreement (*ex* Art. 130y (now Art. 181)) to be directed entirely at democracy, rule of law and human rights. Why, one may ask, would the provisions of Art. 130u(1) (now Art. 177(1)) alone appropriately describe a co-operation development measure but Art. 130u(2) not? Art. 130u(1) provides: 'Community policy in the sphere of development cooperation . . . shall foster: the sustainable economic and social development of the developing countries, and more particularly the most disadvantaged among them; the smooth and gradual integration of the developing countries into the world economy; the campaign against poverty in the developing countries'. Art. 130u(2) provides: 'Community policy in this area shall contribute to the general objective of developing and consolidating democracy and the rule of law, and to that of respecting human rights and fundamental freedoms'. Why Art. 130u(1) should be privileged over Art. 130u(2) is not altogether clear.

ancillary to, general co-operation development instruments. It also would allow, following existing practice,[9] the use of Article 308 as a basis for human rights and democratization measures in instruments of co-operation in relation to countries which are not, strictly speaking, developing countries, citing such famous programmes as Phare, Tacis, and Meda, provided that, where necessary, the enabling regulations are suitably amended.

Even then not all measures envisaged by the Commission proposal were to be allowed. According to the Council any measure outside a specific co-operation programme could only be based on Article 13 (*ex* Article J.3) TEU, which does not require a Commission proposal.[10] This, of course, would split the operation and transfer some of the power away from the Commission services promoting the proposed regulation. The Council Legal Service even went so far as to suggest that the whole proposal could be put under Article 13 TEU. Of course, this would only apply to external human rights action for, as noted, the Council is emphatic that:

> in any case, no measure in this area could be directed towards actions promoting the observance of human rights and democratic principles by and in the Member States.

We believe that, as this legal tale unfolds, there are no clear saints and villains. All Institutions seem to be playing a corporatist game, intent on promoting and preserving their own prerogatives under the guise of concern for human rights. They all seem to be giving a new meaning to the term '*chutzpah*' by preaching to others what they do not practise themselves—following faithfully the officers' maxim: don't do what I do, do what I tell you to do. In this they seem to be taking their cue from the Community as a whole, which is extremely apt to preach democracy to others when it, itself, continues to suffer from serious democratic deficiencies and to insist that all newcomers adhere to the ECHR when it, itself, refuses to do the same.

The Court has—laudably—found no difficulty over the years in asserting a comprehensive basis for the judicial protection of human rights covering the entire field of Community law, including, where appropriate, Member State acts. However the proposed accession to the ECHR would, in the Court's eyes, in a passage in *Opinion 2/94* noted for its opaqueness and cryptic nature as well as its self-serving nature:

> entail a substantial change in the present Community system for the protection of human rights in that it would entail the entry of the Community into a distinct international institutional system as well as integration of all the provisions of the Convention into the Community legal order.

Such a modification of the system for the protection of human rights in the Community, with equally fundamental institutional implications for the Community and for the Member States, would be of constitutional significance and would therefore be such as to go beyond the scope of Article 308. It could be brought about only by way of Treaty amendment.

---

[9] See the excellent A. Rosas and B. Brandtner, 'Human Rights and the External Relations of the European Community' [1998] *EJIL* (forthcoming) for chapter and verse.

[10] See Art. 18 (*ex* Art. J.8(3)) EU. Compared to the Commission's right to initiative in the EC Treaty this not only means that the Council can act without a proposal, but also that, if there is one, the voting requirements of Art. 250(1) (*ex* 189a(1)) EC do not apply.

Of course, given the political reality and voting requirements of Treaty amendment, this decision meant the end to accession.[11]

We are left to wonder why accession to the Convention would be of constitutional significance greater than, say, membership of the new WTO with its new dispute resolution procedures, or of adherence by Member States most of which did not require a constitutional amendment to join the ECHR. Likewise, the alleged need to integrate all the provisions of the Convention which seems to trouble the Court, seems to us a colossal red herring. After all, some form of mixed agreement could be explored if the Court's concern stemmed from a fear that the Community would not be in a position to fulfil all provisions of the ECHR and, in any event, how could this be a concern without seeing the negotiated accession instruments? Clearly some provisions of the ECHR would have to be modified to permit EC membership.

The suspicion is, therefore, despite strenuous denials by certain members of the Court, that it was the 'institutional implications' that caused most trouble and that principal among these was the institutional implication which would submit the Court of Justice, like its constitutional brethren in the Member States, to scrutiny by the Strasbourg Court. There is, indeed, no small measure of *chutzpah* in a Court which has endless creative resources when it comes to interpretations which consolidate the legal order over which it presides, but discovers the virtues of hermeneutic prudence when its own position may be over-shadowed, or where the vaunted European order itself may be seen to be subjected to a higher law judicially enforced by others.

Be that as it may, we will argue contrary to the Council Legal Service, that it is possible to read *Opinion 2/94* as permitting a Community human rights policy, provided that certain conditions are maintained.

The position of the Council, as reflected in the opinion of its Legal Service, has no less *chutzpah* than the Court. This is evident when you consider that the same Council (and the same Legal Service) which, in relation to a human rights policy, gravely state that:

> the observance and promotion of human rights as such are not included among the Community's actions or tasks as specifically listed in article 2 and 3 of the EC Treaty.

had just approved a common position, and subsequently a directive, on tobacco advertising—a measure masquerading as harmonizing obstacles to free movement in the internal market, but in fact conceived and conspicuously explained in its earlier life as having a principal public health objective (and thus requiring as its principal legal basis Article 152 (*ex* Article 129) which inconveniently precludes legislation).[12]

---

[11] Accession has been opposed by various Member States, mostly the UK, but also by other countries such as Portugal, Ireland, and France at different times. Still, this opposition was always carefully couched as stemming from a constitutional concern regarding competences—a position which could have been undermined had the Court opened the way at least to exploring accession without amending the Treaties.

[12] See Common Position of the Council of 12 Feb. in respect of an amended proposal for a Council Dir. on the approximation of Member States' laws, regs., and administrative provisions on advertising for tobacco products: COM(92)196 final—SYN 194 (submitted by the Commission pursuant to Art. 149(3) (now repealed) of the EEC Treaty on 30 Apr. 1991) [1991] OJ C167/3. Even in the European Parliament which has been very sympathetic to the social objectives of the proposed legislation the measure barely passed the scrutiny of the Legal Affairs Committee. The vote was 15–13: *Europe*, 1 Feb. 1992, at 10. In plenary session the measure was passed by 150–123–12 as regards the final resolution. 158–141–8

It is curious to note the shifting sensibility to an objective analysis of object and purpose of legislation as a condition for establishing legal basis.

Nonetheless, we do not disagree with the Council analysis of the limits of Article 177 (*ex* Article 130u)—we just marvel at the elasticity with which it uses the underlying methodology depending on the outcome it desires. We do by contrast strongly disagree with their overall conclusion that there is no legal basis for a Community human rights policy which would affect human rights within and by the Member States. We shall argue that, so long as such a policy is in the field of Community law, what is sauce for the judicial goose is also sauce for the legislative gander.

Finally the Commission. It is not our purpose or task in this essay to analyse or critique the Commission proposal. And giving money to worthy NGOs ('partners') is always a good thing—though the proposal would allow handouts to all manner of public bodies, including governments and 'private sector operators'. The Commission proposal in many respects is, however, a disappointing and ugly document which, at its worst, mocks the very values which it purports to promote. Pragmatically, most, if not all, of what the Commission proposed to support financially in the proposal had already been funded in recent years under various budget items, most of which are to be found in chapter B–7 (External Actions).[13] Several of these budget items did not have any Council regulation as a legal basis. Instead Article 11 (*ex* Article J.1) TEU and Article 177 are quoted alongside Council and Parliament resolutions on human rights and democracy.[14] In truth, the Commission proposal was not a new beginning, but an attempt to consolidate the hodge-podge of the past into a 'basic regulation' in the sense of Chapter IV, Point 3(c), of the 1982 Joint Declaration on various measures to improve the budgetary procedure[15] so as to provide continuity instead of a year-to-year decision and greater flexibility as regards amounts, since without a basic regulation budget items, according to the Joint Declaration, cannot go beyond a 'significant' amount,[16] as well, of course, as freeing their hands even further concerning who will enjoy Commission largesse.

---

as regards the Commission proposal as amended by the Parliament. The question of competence and legal basis was one of the central planks of the opposition to the measure.

[13] Thus, e.g., in subchap. B7–7, under the heading 'European Initiative for Democracy and the Protection of Human Rights', which was introduced in 1994, the Community, under various titles, supports NGOs in democratization and human rights activities throughout the world, funds rehabilitation centres for torture victims and organizations offering help to victims of human rights abuses, spends money on the Hague and Rwanda war tribunals, and offers subsidies to certain activities of organizations pursuing human rights objectives. Not in chap. B7 of the budget would be fundings to NGOs which work on the establishment of an international criminal court (Art. 2(2) of the proposal) which are to be found in Part A 304 1 (administrative appropriations/Community subsidies) or support for migrants (B3–4110 in B3 Training, youth, culture, audiovisual media, information, and other social operations).

[14] Council Resolution of 28 Nov. 1991 on human rights and democracy in the developing countries and follow-up Resolution of 18 Nov. 1992; EP Resolution of 14 May 1992 on a European Initiative for Democracy; EP Resolution of 13 July 1993 on human rights, democracy, and development.

[15] [1982] OJ C194/1.

[16] Needless to say, it is highly contested what a 'significant' amount would be. The Council locates it somewhere between 2 and 5 million ECU. See S. Strasser, *The Finances of Europe* (1997), 139ff. On the other hand: '*[w]o kein Kläger, da kein Richter*'. Although many of the abovementioned items offer 'significantly' more money than that, the Council does not seem to want to take the other institutions to Court for spending money on such good causes as human rights.

In its 1995 memorandum on human rights policy,[17] the Commission had stated that, for the various financial instruments promoting respect for human rights to be used to best advantage:

> they must be flexible to ensure their compatibility with the specific objectives pursued and guarantee in particular the availability of financial resources at a minimum of notice in case of urgent operations, and be adjustable to the specific requirements of human rights issues;
> they must complement each other (technical assistance, development cooperation funds, specific 'human rights' headings, etc.) so as to avoid duplication and ensure continuity of the desired impact;
> amounts must be made available as an incentive and granted in respect of progress achieved by way of reward, particularly in such areas as institutional reform, establishing the rule of law and democratization;
> there must be transparency of information relating to the various sources of funding and their use.[18]

The Commission may be right about all of this. But in this field, too, the Commission has relied on its constitutional right to expend insignificant sums of money on pilot projects and exploratory action designed to enable it to exercise its proposal role in the legislative procedure.[19] Even a cursory examination of Commission activity in this field raises doubts whether many of its activities would truly fall within the definition of 'insignificant', 'pilot', or 'exploratory' and did not fall into a scheme against which the Court warned about, namely 'to circumvent application of the principle that a basic act must first be adopted'.[20] And even as regards those items which did come under the legal definition of Commission authorized autonomous action or were authorized in some manner by the Council, we would respectfully submit that many could not be considered as coming within the field of application of Community law, however widely defined.[21]

The document borrows canonical language:

> of developing and consolidating democracy and the rule of law, and to that of respecting human rights and fundamental freedoms.

In the legal order, respect for the jurisdictional limits of the Community is an important dimension of the rule of law and of democracy. A Community and Union which transgress such limits not only breach an important constitutional principle but also contribute to a continuous aggregation of power in the centre compromising an important aspect of democracy.

It is difficult to read the proposal as drafted, with its loose language, such as Article 2(d) which would apparently allow unrestricted support to operations:

> supporting local, national, regional or international institutions involved in the protection or promotion of human rights

---

[17] 'The European Union and the external dimension of human rights policy: from Rome to Maastricht and beyond': Communication from the Commission to the Council and the European Parliament, COM(95)567 final.

[18] *Bull. EU Suppl. 1995.* See also the homepage of DG IA at http://www.europa.eu.int.

[19] Case 106/96, *UK* v. *Commission* [1998] ECR I–2729, para. 29.   [20] *Ibid.*, para. 36.

[21] See some of the examples in note 24 below.

as if the Commission really believes that the Community and Union truly have no limits on such activities or that, because of the important aims, others will be shamed into not contesting the proposals.

This may well have been the case in the past. Under title B7–7040 ('subsidies for certain activities of organizations pursuing human rights objectives'), you find funding for operations both inside and outside the Community.[22] Thus, the European Human Rights Foundation, an NGO that was founded in 1980 on the Commission's initiative,[23] through its European Human Rights Fund hands out subsidies from this budget line (which is 7 milllion ECU total) to support other NGOs, 55 per cent of which are Western European, with 15 per cent of activities targeted in Western Europe.[24]

The words 'rule of law' appear again and again, but nowhere will you find material restrictions limiting such support to those fields in which the Community may act appropriately. Respect for constitutional divisions of powers in the federal structures that have been set up in many of the countries to which this instrument is aimed would be part of the rule of law that one tried to instill and encourage. What an exquisite irony that it is done by an instrument which shows no sensitivity to that very issue.

The same is true of another word which appears, again and again, in the Commission proposal: democracy. But are the democratic controls which the Commission proposes for itself in this field adequate?

An Advisory Committee of Member State nominated mandarins? An annual report to the European Parliament with a *summary of activities* but no continuous Parliamentary oversight? The notoriously non-transparent and undifferentiated (all-or-nothing) controls through the budgetary procedure? The conspicuous absence of transparency as regards financial order of magnitude envisaged?

There are two other elements which cannot but strike the reader of this proposal: the almost exclusive reliance on financial handouts to others as the method of vindicating the objectives of the proposal and, more egregiously, the total absence of any notion that the Community and Union themselves (and their institutions) might

[22] See description of this budget item in 'Digest of Community Resources Available for Financing the Activities of NGOs and Other Governmental and/or Decentralized Bodies Representing Civil Society in the Fields of Development Co-operation and Humanitarian Aid', VIII/207/97EN, at 78 (document is on the homepage of DG IA, see note18 above).

[23] EHRF claims to be independent from the EU. On the other hand it moved to Brussels in 1991 to be closer to the Commission. It works very closely with the Commission, carries out various research projects on human rights issues relevant to EU policy and helps the Commission manage Phare and Tacis.

[24] See e.g. European Human Rights Foundation , 'The First Fifteen Years', Report 1995, at 16ff:
—seed grants: to Britain and Ireland Human Rights Project or to Prisoners Legal Services Foundation;
—reports and studies on sectarianism in Northern Ireland, gypsies in Europe, child labour in Portugal, bans on political activity in Scotland, procedures of inquest in the UK;
—general grants to 'Article 19' (UK), to the British Institute on Human Rights, the Committee of Concerned Forensic Scientists (Denmark), Index on Censorship (UK), the International Lesbian and Gay Association (Belgium), JUSTICE (UK), Parity Foundation (Netherlands),
—legal aid and legal services to costs of the ECHR *Cabales* case (discriminatory immigration laws in the UK), costs of the ECHR *Wilden* case (Swedish child care), specialized legal service for women in the UK, legal aid for prisoners in England and Wales, legal advice for prisoners in the UK, advice centre on European and international human rights laws in the UK, legal proceedings in Greece to obtain recognition of the right to conscientious objection. See generally Case C–106/96, *United Kingdom* v. *Commission*, judgment of 12 May 1998.

have room for improving the situation of their own human rights record, other than through support of other bodies which typically deal with Member State abuses and not with the Community as such.

Some of the NGOs—especially those operating in third countries—can sigh with relief, since the legal opinion of the Council provides the way through skilful amendment and word-smithery here and there to make the necessary pay-outs. But one cannot but lament this document as a poor substitute for a fully fledged human rights policy which the Commission could have and should have presented. Such a policy—*Leading by Example*—has now been proposed.[25] Maybe the invitation of Article 13 (*ex* Article 6a) TEC will provide an incentive for the Commission and Council to take that proposal seriously—to lead by example.

What we propose to do is to explain our contention that a legal basis for a comprehensive human rights policy of the Community does exist on the basis of the current Treaty and jurisprudence.

II. TOWARDS A GENERAL PRINCIPLE OF HUMAN RIGHTS COMPETENCES

What, then, are the competences of the Community in the field of human rights? It is, of course, possible to try and formulate an overarching statement of positive Community law defining such competences. Such an exercise could, we believe, be of some utility in establishing some general principles and ways of thinking about the issue. But it is not enough. The proverbial 'no vehicles in the park' gives us a general orientation as to what may and may not be allowed in the park, but will not answer specifically the question whether skateboards or perambulators are allowed in.

Thus, one would have, in due course, to apply these principles to any comprehensive human rights policy which may be proposed.

For decades the European Court of Justice has held, in slightly differing formulae, that 'respect for human rights is a condition of the lawfulness of Community acts'.[26] The source and material definition of such rights has likewise become canonical: Community human rights are rooted in, and derive from, 'the constitutional traditions common to the Member States and from the guidelines supplied by international treaties for the protection of human rights on which the Member States have collaborated or of which they are signatories'.[27] These fundamental rights form 'an integral part of the general principles of [Community] law' and their autonomy from their national source has been regularly emphasized: 'the question of a possible infringement of fundamental rights by a measure of the Community institutions can only be judged in the light of Community law itself'.[28]

---

[25] See Academy of European Law, *Leading by Example: A Human Rights Agenda for the European Union for the Year 2000—Agenda of the Comité des Sages and Final Project Report* (1998), available at http://www.iue.it/AEL/.

[26] Recently, *Opinion 2/94* [1996] ECR I–1759, para. 34.

[27] *Ibid.*, at para. 33.

[28] Case 44/79, *Hauer* v. *Land Rheinland-Pfalz* [1979] ECR 3727, paras. 14 and 15.

Somewhat less noticed in this field is a classical move which is one of the hermeneutic hallmarks of the Court: the move from norms to institutional duty, from substance to procedure, from *ius* to *remedium*. We are mostly familiar with this move in the constitutional area which defines the relationship between the Community legal order and that of the Member States. Norm-oriented doctrines such as direct effect or supremacy are regularly, and without fuss, turned into institutional duties on Member State courts. The high tide of this move in that area is the *Francovich*[29] jurisprudence. Another remarkable example of the Court's norm-duty jurisprudence is its decision which found France in violation of its obligations under the Treaty for failure to prevent the obstruction of the free movement of goods by private individuals.[30]

In *Commission* v. *France* the Court, *inter alia*, held:

> The fact that a Member State abstains from taking action or, as the case may be, fails to adopt adequate measures to prevent obstacles to the free movement of goods that are created, in particular, by actions by private individuals on its territory aimed at products originating in other Member States is just as likely to obstruct intra-Community trade as a positive act.
>
> Article 30 [now Article 28] therfore requires the Member States not merely themselves to abstain from adopting measures or engaging in conduct liable to constitute an obstacle to trade but also, when read with Article 5 [now Article 10] of the Treaty, to take all necessary and appropirate measures to ensure that that fundamental freedom is respected on their territory.
>
> ...
>
> It should be added, by virtue of the combined provisions of Articles 38 to 46 [now Articles 32 to 38] and Article 7(7) [now repealed] of the EC Treaty, the foregoing considerations apply also to Council regulations on the common organization of the markets...[31]

We are, of course, aware of the difference between the fundamental freedom when it concerns free movement and the fundamental freedom of human rights. The former is an object of the Treaty in the sense of Article 3; the latter, in say, Article 7 (*ex* Article F(2)) is a duty of the Union as a whole which, under Amsterdam, will become justiciable. But even if we take a minimalist view, the transverse notion of human rights means that in any measure adopted by the Community following its Article 3-type objectives, respect for human rights is mandated. And in this respect, at least, abstaining from taking action is, as the Court reasons in *Commission* v. *France*, just as likely to cause an obstruction to fundamental human rights as would a positive violative act.

Thus, in *T. Port* v. *Bundesanstalt für Landwirtschaft und Ernährung*[32] the Court addressed various aspects of the duty of the Community legislator to act in the context of the transition from a national regime to a Community common organization which require certain transitional measures and where the possibility of an Article 232 (*ex* Article 175) action exists.

---

[29] Joined Cases 6 and 9/90, *Francovich and Bonifaci* v. *Italy* [1991] ECR I–5357.
[30] Case C–265/95, *Commission* v. *France*, judgment of 9 Dec. 1997.
[31] *Ibid.*, at paras. 31, 32, 36.   [32] Case 68/95, [1996] ECR 6065.

The Court's words are suggestive:

Those transitional measures must address difficulties encountered after establishment of the common organization of the market . . . [Recital 36]

. . .

When assessing whether transitional measures are necessary, the Commission has broad discretion . . . As the Court held in its order in Case 280/93R *Germany* v. *Council* . . . the Commission, or the Council . . . are, however, obliged to take action if the difficulties associated with the transition from national arrangements to the common organization of the market so require. [Recital 38]

It is for the Court of Justice to review the lawfulness of the Community Institutions' action or failure to act. [Recital 39]

The *Community Institutions are required to act in particular when the transition to the common organization of the market infringes certain traders' fundamental rights protected by Community law, such as the right to property and the right to pursue a professional or trade activity.* [Recital 40, emphasis added].

It seems that the Court is moving beyond the prohibition on measures which, in and of themselves, violate human rights, and is setting up a positive duty to take measures to ensure that certain rights should not be compromised.

We submit that such legislative competence is inherent in each and every field of legislative competence of the Community.

Put differently, in the first instance, from the negative prohibition on obstacles to free movement was derived a positive institutional duty (the contours and reach of which should not be exaggerated) effectively to ensure such freedom, and from the second instance of the common organization was established a duty to act so as to ensure that human rights are respected even when, arguably, the Community measure itself does not create a violation.

The Court has made a similar move in the area of human rights: In *Cinéthèque* (and elsewhere) it expressed the normative statement about human rights (respect for human rights as a condition for lawfulness) as an institutional, nay, Institutional duty: 'it is the duty of this Court to ensure the observance of fundamental rights in the field of Community law'.[33] In *ERT* it imposed, somewhat controversially, a similar duty on Member State courts as regards a certain class of Member State acts.

Cinéthèque is important because it belongs to the pre-Single European Act (SEA) and pre-TEU era, namely to an era in which fundamental human rights were not explicitly mentioned or even alluded to in the Treaties—the Constitutional Charter of the Community. This absence did not prevent the Court from articulating the norm—human rights as part of Community general principles of law, nor of a redefinition[34] of its institutional role, right, and duty to ensure that human rights are not violated. This duty which the Court imposed on itself did not relate to an explicit objective laid down in the Treaty, but was, it is presumed, considered necessary to

---

[33] Joined Cases 60 and 61/84, *Cinéthèque SA* v. *Fédération Nationale des Cinémas Français* [1985] ECR 2605, para. 26.

[34] Cf Case 1/58, *Stork* [1958–9] ECR 41: '[s]imilarly, under Article 31 the Court is only required to ensure that in the interpretation and application of the Treaty, and of rules laid down for implementation thereof, the law is observed. It is not normally required to rule on provisions of national law. Consequently, the High Authority is not empowered to examine a ground of complaint which maintains that, when it adopted its decision, it infringed principles of German constitutional law . . .'.

enable the Community to carry out its functions. Respect for and protection of human rights were, thus, conceived as an integral, inherent, transverse principle forming part of all objectives, functions, and powers of the Community. Otherwise, whence came the jurisdiction of the Court to ensure, in the entire field of Community law, the observance of fundamental rights?

In articulating a general principle of Community competences in the field of human rights it seems to us as following from the Court's overall jurisprudence to suggest that it is not only the Court, as one of the institutions of the Community, that has a duty to ensure the observance of fundamental rights in the field of Community law, but that such a duty rests, inherently, on all Institutions of the Community exercising their competences *within the field of Community law*. Why would such a duty fall on the Court, in some instances on Member State courts, in some instances on the executive or legislative agencies of the Member States but not on the political Institutions of the Community—primarily Commission, Council, and Parliament?

Of course the political Institutions enjoy wide discretion in exercising their powers to attain the functions of the Community. Thus, their duty to ensure the observance of human rights within the field of Community law could not, under normal circumstances, be the subject of, say, an Article 232 (*ex* Article 175) action.[35] But equally, should Commission, Council, and Parliament decide to discharge their inherent duty to ensure the observance of fundamental rights in the field of Community law by legislating to do just that, and provided such legislation did not stray from the field of Community law, it is hard to see on what ground their overall competences could be challenged. Would the Commission and Council not, for example, have the competences simply to codify what the Court has done in its jurisprudence so that its jurisprudence can have a greater impact on all public authorities?[36]

We now have to address as a matter of principle two issues: what would or could be the content of legislative and administrative action by the political institutions in this field; and what could be the legal basis of such action?

The first question we will answer briefly since it is dealt with extensively elsewhere.[37] If we are to take seriously the notion of ensuring respect for human rights, long gone are the days in which the mere provision of formal judicial remedies would be considered a sufficient and effective guarantee. The great movement in the 1970s and 1980s of access-to-justice has taught us that formal rights are often just that; that making rights effective often requires positive action, such as the provision of legal services, the dissemination of information, the education of people about their rights, the provision of new forms of legal actions such as the class action, and a whole variety of procedural, financial, and institutional measures. Justice without 'access' is justice denied. To take human rights seriously would require broad action by the political institutions.

What would be the specific legal basis on which such action may be contemplated?

In particular since the entry into force of the SEA, the question of the legal basis for Community legislation has become critical, given the different political

[35] Cf Case 22/70, *Commission* v. *Council* (*ERTA*) and Case 8/73, *Hauptzollamt Bremerhaven* v. *Massey-Ferguson* [1973] ECR 897.
[36] But cf *Vedder in Europarecht 1996*, at 309ff.   [37] See Chap. 1 above.

consequences of differing legal bases in terms of voting procedures and involvement of the European Parliament. What legal basis, then, could and should be used by the political institutions when exercising their duty to ensure the observance of fundamental rights in the field of Community law?

There seem to be three categories of legal basis. The first is the legal basis governing action in a specific field. The Community 'legislative branch' (Commission, Council, Parliament) could (and arguably should) attach to any legislation it passes 'human rights' concerning, say, transparency, information to interested parties, right to appeal, legal aid, and the like. There are few areas of Community activity which cannot, negatively or positively, affect the fundamental rights of individuals and groups. It cannot be stated often enough: the simple fact that individuals have, under certain circumstances, the right to challenge Community acts before the Court or through Article 234(b) (*ex* Article 177(b)) is not in many circumstances in and of itself sufficient to ensure the observance of fundamental human rights.

In some fields, the Community legislation coincides with a classic fundamental right, such as Article 141 (*ex* Article 119) EC. Even here one notes the interplay between norm and affirmative duty.[38]

In other fields concern for fundamental rights is specifically mentioned—such as co-operation and development (Article 177 (*ex* Article 130u) EC), and, under Amsterdam, Article 13 (*ex* Article 6(a)).[39] This is significant since the duty and right of non-discrimination and equality are at the core of all other human rights and can provide a broad platform for a human right policy.

The second legal basis would be a broader use of Article 95 (*ex* Article 100a). Member State measures designed to protect fundamental human rights could constitute an obstacle to one of the fundamental freedoms. Subject, perhaps, to the principle of subsidiarity,[40] there could be a Community harmonization measure designed to protect fundamental human rights in the field of application of Community law, just as there is a Community harmonization measure designed to protect the physical life or safety of individuals in this field of free movement.

It may, however, be considered necessary, to enable the Community to carry out its functions with a view to attaining one of the objectives laid down by the Treaty, to have a measure which is not directly connected to any specific policy or is not a legitimate harmonization measure. Imagine the aforementioned notion of codifying the Court's jurisprudence in the interest of transparency and efficiency. Imagine the setting up of information bureaux to advise Community citizens of their rights, including their human rights, under the Treaty. Imagine the creation of a mechanism to monitor and report on the status within the field of Community law of those very

[38] Art. 119(1) (now Art. 141(1)): '[e]ach Member State shall ensure that the principle of equal pay for male and female workers for equal work or work of equal value is applied'.
[39] Art. 6a (now Art. 13): 'without prejudice to the other provisions of the Treaty and within the limits of the powers conferred by it upon the Community, the Council, acting unanimously on a proposal from the Commission . . . may take appropriate action to combat discrimination based on sex, racial or ethnic origin, religion or belief, disability, age or sexual orientation'.
[40] The Commission view is that Art. 100a (now Art. 95) is an exclusive competence and, thus, may be understood as not subject to subsidiarity: see Commission Document SEK(92)1990. We can only accept this view if it means that after Art. 95 legislation, the field is pre-empted. Surely, before exercising its Art. 95 jurisdiction, the subsidiarity considerations should apply.

human rights the observance of which it is the duty of the Court, and other institutions, to ensure, such as the annual report on human rights in the European Union presented by the Internal Affairs and Civil Liberties Committee of the European Parliament.

Surely ensuring such observance would be enhanced by, and in some cases depend on, such monitoring. And surely some institutional arrangement would be necessary for such monitoring to be effective. But what would be the legal basis? And if, more audaciously, the Commission wished to bring under one *chapeau* all threads of the Community's human rights activities within the field of Community law? What if the Community wanted to have a general policy and institutional set-up designed, in an integral and co-ordinated way, to ensure the protection of human rights within the field of Community law?

As the Court in *Opinion 2/94* reminds us in paragraph 27:

> No Treaty provision confers on the Community institutions any general power to enact rules on human rights . . .

We have already argued that where there is a specific legislative competence, one can imply a competence to enact provisions designed to ensure that in the specific field human rights are respected. But what if there is not even an implied power? Again the Court in *Opinion 2/94*, paragraph 28, provides guidance:

> In the absence of express or implied powers for this purpose, it is necessary to consider whether Article 235 [now Article 308] of the Treaty may constitute a legal basis . . .

In paragraph 29 of *Opinion 2/94* the Court defines the function of Article 308 (*ex* Article 235) as follows:

> Article 235 [now Article 308] is designed to fill the gap where no specific provisions of the Treaty confer on the Community institutions express or implied powers to act, if such powers appear none the less to be necessary to enable the Community to carry out its functions with a view to attaining one of the objectives laid down by the Treaty.

The Court added in paragraph 30:

> That provision, being an integral part of an institutional system based on the principle of conferred powers, cannot serve as a basis for widening the scope of Community powers beyond the general framework created by the provisions of the Treaty as a whole and, in particular, by those that define the tasks and the activities of the Community. On any view, Article 235 [now Article 308] cannot be used as a basis for the adoption of provisions whose effect would, in substance, be to amend the Treaty without following the procedure which it provides for that purpose.

In the *Opinion* the Court had to decide about accession to the ECHR. It reached a negative conclusion. But its reasoning should be read strictly. In paragraphs 34 and 35 the Court came to the following conclusions:

> Accession to the Convention would, however, entail a substantial change in the present Community system for the protection of human rights in that it would entail the entry of the Community into a distinct international institutional system as well as integration of all the provisions of the Convention into the Community legal order.

Such a modification of the system for the protection of human rights in the Community, with equally fundamental institutional implications for the Community and for the Member States, would be of constitutional significance and would therefore be such as to go beyond the scope of Article 235 [now Article 308]. It could be brought about only by way of Treaty amendment.

What, then, does a strict reading yield? We think it is more than permissible to conclude that the Court would have allowed, and in the light of its earlier jurisprudence on Article 235 (now Article 308)[41] would have had to allow, reliance on Article 235 in the field of human rights, if the measure in question:

- did not entail a substantial change in the present Community system for the protection of human rights;
- did not entail the entry of the Community into a distinct international institutional system;
- did not modify the material content of human rights within the Community legal order;[42]
- did not have fundamental institutional implications (especially to the hallowed position of the Court);

and more generally

- would not and could not be considered of 'constitutional significance'.

Put differently, a Community human rights policy which respected the current institutional balance, which avoided formal accession to the ECHR, which left intact the definition of the material contents of rights and their Community autonomy and which, critically, scrupulously remained within the field of Community law, would not and could not be considered of 'constitutional significance' in the sense used by the Court in *Opinion 2/94*, and, thus, could be based, where necessary (i.e. where other provisions did not exist[43]) on Article 308 (*ex* Article 235) EC.

How then should one define the field of Community law for the purposes of human rights jurisdiction?

One possible definition would equate human rights legislative competence to judicial supervisory competence. With one possible exception, in all those areas and within the domain in which the Court regards itself entitled to pronounce on the lawfulness of measures—Community and Member State—the political institutions may exercise their legislative and administrative competences.

The equation between the Court and the legislator can go only so far. The Court's human rights primary jurisdiction addresses Community acts which, additionally, may be subject to competences jurisdiction. A Community act may not violate human rights and may, additionally, not transgress the legislative limits of the Community. None the less, the inseparability of human rights concern from all aspects of

---

[41] See e.g. Case 242/87, *Commission* v. *Council (Erasmus)* [1989] ECR 1425.

[42] This is our current formula for attending to the Court's (misconceived) concern about integration of all the provisions of the Convention into the Community legal order.

[43] See e.g. Case 45/86, *Commission* v. *Council (Tariff Preferences)* [1987] ECR 1493.

public policy must mean that 'the field of Community law' must include a large area of Community regulatory competence.

It seems to us, thus, uncontrovertible that the political institutions may adopt measures of human rights in all those fields which are controlled materially by Community law, either under exclusive or concurrent jurisdiction, and in which the object of the human rights legislation would be either Community institutions or complementary to Community laws and policies. If Community law controls, say, the conditions of access of migrant workers to the labour market in the Community, then in those fields human rights enhancement action would be permitted.

This does not mean, to continue with this example, that all those life situations where one can find migrant workers would or could be subject to Community human rights legislation. What of the example of an intra-Community migrant worker condemned to have his arm chopped off as punishment for stealing a loaf of bread?[44] Would such a Member State act be justiciable before the Court? The Court's answer seems to have been no. It would not, any more than would an alleged violation by other aspects of the penal code, the law of contracts, or delicts, or property in any of the Member States in which a migrant happened to live or work. Provided the migrant was not discriminated against, provided the occurrence did not happen in an area already governed by Community law—such as conditions of permanence—the jurisdiction of the Court would be barred and, by extension, so would any human rights jurisdiction by the political institutions. To hold otherwise, i.e. to hold that the Community had jurisdiction in any situation involving a migrant worker, would give the Community practically limitless jurisdiction.[45]

The Court has extended the exercise of its human rights jurisdiction to Member State measures in two types of situation: (a) the agency situation—when the Member State is acting for and/or on behalf of the Community and implementing a Community policy (*Klensch*[46] and *Wachauf*[47]); and (b) when the State relies on a derogation to fundamental market freedoms (*ERT*[48]) and most recently developed in *Bauer*.[49]

The rationale for agency review is simple and, in our eyes, compelling. All of us often fall into the trap of thinking of the Community as an entity wholly distinct from the Member States. But of course, like some well-known theological concepts, the Community is, in some senses, its Member States; in other senses separate from them. This, as 2,000 years of Christian theology attest, can at times be hard to grasp. But in one area of Community life it is easy. In the EC system of governance, to an extent far greater than any federal state, the Member States often act as, indeed are, the executive branch of the Community. When, to give an example, a British

---

[44] Cf Jacobs AG in Case C–168/91, *Konstandinidis* v. *Stadt Altensteig, Standesamt and Landesamt Calw, Ordnungsamt* [1993] ECR I–1191; see generally Binder, note 5 above.

[45] See Case 299/95, *Kremzow* v. *Austria* [1997] ECR 2629, especially La Pergola AG, para. 7 and Judgment, paras. 15–18.

[46] Joined Cases 201 and 202/85, *Klensch* v. *Secrétaire d'Etat à l'Agriculture et à la Viticulture* [1986] ECR 3477.

[47] Case 5/88, *Wachauf* v. *Germany* [1989] ECR 2609.

[48] Case C–260/89, *ERT* v. *DEP* [1991] ECR I–2925.

[49] Case 368/95, *Vereinigte Familiapress Zeitungsverlags- und Vertriebs GmbH* v. *Heinrich Bauer Verlag* [1997] ECR 3689.

customs official collects a Community-imposed tariff from an importer of non-Community goods, he or she is organically part of the British customs service, but is functionally wearing a Community hat. If the Court's human rights jurisdiction covers, as it clearly does, not merely the formal legislative Community normative source, but its *mise-en-œuvre*, is it not really self-evident, as Advocate-General Jacobs puts it in *Wachauf*, even on a narrow construction of the Court's human rights jurisdiction, that it should review these 'Member State' measures for violation of human rights. In this case the very nomenclature which distinguished Member State and Community acts fails to capture the reality of Community governance and the Community legal order. Not to review these acts would be legally inconsistent with the consistent human rights jurisprudence and, from the human rights policy perspective, arbitrary: if the Commission is responsible for the *mise-en-œuvre*, review will take place, but if it is a Member State, it will not?

It appears to us that the political institutions should also have human rights competence in this area, even if it means that they would be directly imposing human rights obligations in and by the Member States. On what grounds could one fault the Community legislator if in its enabling legislation under the *Klensch* or *Wachauf* situations it explicitly, rather than implicitly, instructed the Member States in question on their human rights obligations in administering milk quotas?

More problematic is the *ERT* line of jurisprudence. This would be the exception to our principle of equation between Court jurisdiction and institutional competence.

Let us first review the jurisprudence of the Court and draw the judicial jurisdictional line and rationale. The development in *ERT*, foreshadowed by the Opinion of the Advocate General in *Grogan*[50] is more delicate.

The Treaty enjoins Member State measures which interfere with the fundamental free movement provisions of the Treaty. This injunction applies to any Member State measure, regardless of its source. The mere fact that the interference may emanate from a constitutional norm is, in and of itself, irrelevant. Likewise, the fact that the constitutional measures may be an expression of a deeply held national societal value is, in and of itself, irrelevant. If, say, a Member State, even under widespread popular conviction and support, were to adopt a constitutional amendment which, 'in the interest of preserving national identity and the inalienable fundamental rights of our citizens', prohibited an undertaking from employing foreigners, including Community nationals, ahead of Member State citizens or from purchasing foreign goods ahead of national products, such a constitutional provision would be in violation of Community law.

Community law itself defines two situations which may exculpate such a national measure from the Treaty injunction. First, the national measure itself must be considered as constituting an illegal interference with market freedom. The Treaty is very vague on this, and the Court has developed a rich case law in this regard. Not every measure which on its face seems to interfere will necessarily be construed as a violation of one of the market freedoms. Secondly, even a national measure which on its face constitutes a violation of the interdiction may, under Community law, be

---

[50] Case C–151/90, *SPUC* v. *Grogan* [1991] ECR I–4685.

exculpated if it can be shown to fall under derogation clauses to be found in the Treaty. Article 30 (*ex* Article 36), for example, speaks of measures 'justified' on grounds of public morality, health etc.

The crucial point is that defining what constitutes a violation of the basic market freedoms is, substantively and jurisdictionally, a matter of Community law and for the Court to decide, as is the exculpatory regime. Substantively the Court will interpret the language of the Treaty—often opaquely: what, for example, does (or should) 'justified' mean? or 'public order' etc.? Jurisdictionally, the Court (in tandem with national jurisdictions) will supervise that the Member States are in fact fulfilling their obligations under the Treaty.

One way of explaining the 'extension' of human rights jurisdiction to Member State measures in the *ERT* situation is simple enough. Once a Member State measure is found to be in violation of the market freedoms, *but for* the derogation it would be illegal. The scope of the derogation and the conditions for its employment are all 'creatures' of Community law, Treaty- and judge-made. Now it could be argued in opposition, and we would not consider this a specious argument, that one should look at the derogations as defining the limit of Community law reach. We are not persuaded. Even from a formalist perspective, the very structure of, say, Articles 28–30 (*ex* Articles 30–36) indicates the acceptance by the Member States that the legality or otherwise of a measure constituting a *prima facie* violation of the prohibition on measures having an effect equivalent to quantitative restrictions becomes a matter for Community law. From a policy perspective it could hardly be otherwise. Imagine the state of the common market if each Member State could determine by reference to its own laws and values, without any reference to Community law, what was or was not covered by the prohibition and its derogation. Surely how wide or narrow the derogation is should be controlled by Community law. The concomitant consequence of this is that once it is found that a Member State measure contravenes the market freedom interdictions such as Article 28 (*ex* Article 30), even if it is exculpated by a derogation clause in the Treaty, the Community's legislative competence is triggered and it may become susceptible to harmonization.

Let us illustrate this by taking the most telling instance: the rule of reason doctrine developed principally in *Cassis de Dijon*,[51] of which *Cinéthèque* is an example. Here the Court has carved out new circumstances, not explicitly mentioned in the Treaty derogation clause, which would allow the Member States to adopt measures which otherwise would be a violation of Article 28 (*ex* Article 30). I do not recall any protest by Member States complaining about the Court's rather audacious construction of Articles 28–30 (*ex* Article 30–36) in this regard. But, obviously the Member States are not given a free hand. The Court will have to be persuaded that the Member State measures seeking to benefit from the rule of reason are, for example, as a matter of Community law, in the general interest and of sufficient importance to override the interest in the free movement of goods, that they are proportionate to the objective pursued, that they are adopted in good faith, and are not a disguised restriction on trade. So the ability of the Member States to move within the derogations to the free

---

[51] Case 120/78, *Cassis de Dijon* [1979] ECR 649.

movement provisions is subject to a series of limitations, some explicitly to be found in the Treaty, others the result of judicial construction of the Treaty.

In construing the various Community-law limitations on the Member States' ability to derogate from the Treaty and in administering these limitations in cases that come before it, should the Court insist on all these other limitations and yet adopt a 'hands off' attitude towards violation of human rights? Is it so revolutionary to insist that when the Member States avail themselves of a Community law-created derogation they also respect fundamental human rights, deriving from the constitutional traditions of the Member States, even if the European Community construction of this or that right differs from its construction in this or that Member State? After all, *but for* the judicially constructed rule of reason in *Cassis*, France would not be able to justify at all its video-cassette policy designed to protect French cinematographic culture. To respect the Community notion of human rights in this scenario appears to us wholly consistent with the earlier case law and the policy behind it.

It could be argued that in supervising the derogation the Court should not enter into the policy merits of the Member State measure other than to check that it is proportionate and not a disguised restriction on trade. Human Rights review, on this reading, is an interference with the merits. Again, we are not persuaded. First it must be understood that the doctrine of proportionality also involves a Community-imposed value choice by the Court on a Member State. Each time the Court says, for example, that a label informing the consumer will serve a policy adequately compared to an outright prohibition, it is clear that at least some consumers will, despite the label, be misled. There are ample studies to demonstrate the limited effectiveness of labels. Thus, in the most banal proportionality test 'lurks' a judicial decision by the ECJ on the level of risk society may be permitted to take with its consumers.

Secondly, even if human rights review may be more intrusive in some cases than in others, it need not always interfere with the actual merits of the policy pursued and could still leave considerable latitude to the States to pursue their own devices. Provided they do not violate human rights, the Court will not interfere with the content of the policy. Admittedly this may sometimes thwart their wills, but that, after all, would also be the case under the ECHR. That on some occasions it might give teeth to the European Convention in those countries which have, decades later, still not incorporated it into national law must, we assume, be welcomed by those who profess to take rights seriously.

One conclusion from this analysis is that the standard of review in this situation should not be the normal Community standard, but the standard that would be applied by the ECHR.[52] Unlike the *Wachauf* situation where the Member State is

---

[52] President Due and Judge Gulman introduce a note of caution into this debate which we fully share: '[n]ot surprisingly, when laying down the necessary criteria for the definition of the area of application of Community fundamental rights in the national legal orders, there is one essential requirement which the Court will have to fulfill, i.e. the need to give a convincing explanation, based on the specific requirements of the Community legal order, why it is necessary, for national authorities to respect the same fundamental rights as those respected by the Community institutions. In cases concerning the relationship between Community law and national law and, in particular, where delicate problems of fundamental rights are at stake, the authority of the Court depends on its ability to convince': O. Due and C. Gulman, 'Community Fundamental Rights as Part of National Law', in C. Gulman (ed.), *Scritti in Onore di F. G. Mancini* (1998), 422. We cannot judge if the rationale we have provided is convincing. But we respectfully disagree with

merely the agent of the Community and the Member State measure is in truth a Community measure, here we are dealing with a Member State measure in application of a Member State policy. The interest of the Court and the Community should be to prevent a violation of core human rights, but to allow beyond that maximum leeway to national policy.

For the same reason we do not believe that the Community would have legislative competences in this area other than in a situation, discussed above, where the Member State human rights measure itself constituted an obstacle to free movement and could, thus, be subject to an Article 95 (*ex* Article 100a) harmonization measure.

III. EPILOGUE

How then do these considerations affect a would-be Community human rights policy?

1. Though the Council Legal Service seems to have drawn the correct implications from *Portugal* v. *Council*, one may question, as we have, the reasoning of the Court. If an agreement *ex* Article 181 (*ex* Article 130y) or a programme *ex* Article 179 (*ex* Article 130m) would be legitimate instruments of co-operation development if fostering—exclusively—the objectives referred to in Article 177(1) (*ex* Article 130u) there is no clear reason to exclude agreements or programmes which would, exclusively, contribute to the objectives mentioned in Article 177(2).

2. Even absent such an interpretation the Community may adopt a general human rights policy the purpose of which would be to ensure that, in the field of Community law, the fundamental human rights recognized by the Court are effectively ensured. Given the transverse nature of human rights, such a policy may have as its legal basis the entire gamut of legislative competence with, where appropriate, Article 308 (*ex* Article 235). Such a programme should be scrupulous in restricting its operation, including contributions to 'operators' and 'partners', to those whose activities fall within the field of Community law.

the learned judges on one point: in *ERT*-type review, we do not believe that the ECJ should hold the Member States to the same rights as Community institutions but only to the ECHR standard which may differ. In *Bauer* the Court affirmed its doctrine of *ERT* explicitly as regards mandatory requirements. Significantly, it then made exclusive reference to the ECHR (Art. 10) and not to Community standards as such. Also significant was its reference to a judgment of the European Court of Human Rights—as if shoring up the legitimacy of its jurisprudence by reminding the national courts and national authorities that it is holding them only to a standard that they have already accepted: paras. 24–6 of the judgment.

6

Human Rights and the Third Pillar

STEVE PEERS*

I. INTRODUCTION

Is the 'free movement' of prosecutions and investigations compatible with the protection of human rights? This is the fundamental question underlying co-operation in the field of Justice and Home Affairs (JHA) in the European Union (EU). It can be answered by analysing first the potential role of the European Court of Justice (ECJ) in ensuring human rights protection in the third pillar, and then by critically examining the practice of the Council of the EU.

II. THIRD PILLAR INSTITUTIONAL STRUCTURE

The Amsterdam Treaty has transformed the approach to JHA co-operation in the European Union. Such co-operation, initially agreed informally, outside the scope of the Community institutions, was formalized by the Maastricht Treaty on European Union (TEU), placed at first largely in the intergovernmental Title VI of that Treaty.[1] Pre-Maastricht JHA co-operation was arranged through various working groups reporting to immigration or interior ministers, ultimately through a 'Co-ordinators Group' of senior national interior ministry officials. The ministers adopted either conventions or soft-law measures such as resolutions or recommendations. Maastricht formalized this structure, providing that the meetings of immigration or interior ministers would now be meetings of the 'Council', allowing for adoption of joint actions or joint positions in addition to conventions.[2] The Commission was now allowed shared competence with the Member States to make proposals in most aspects of JHA co-operation,[3] and the European Parliament was

---

* My thanks go to SEMDoc for copies of some of the Council documents discussed in this chap.

[1] For an overview and analysis of all substantive and institutional aspects of JHA co-operation see S. Peers, *Justice and Home Affairs in the EU* (1999), and literature cited therein.

[2] The Council has also adopted a number of 'soft-law' conclusions, recommendations, and resolutions despite the absence of any reference to such measures. On the legal nature of JHA acts, see Meyrins, 'Intergovernmentalism and Supranationality: Two Stereotypes for a Complex Reality' (1997) 22 *EL Rev.* 221.

[3] Except for police co-operation, criminal judicial co-operation, and customs co-operation (Art. K.3(2)).

entitled to be informed of discussions and consulted on the 'principal aspects' of co-operation.[4] The ECJ was only awarded the *possibility* of jurisdiction over interpretation and application of Conventions.[5] However, this jurisdiction was awarded in eight of ten third-pillar conventions agreed in the five years following the entry into force of Maastricht,[6] and in particular in six out of the eight conventions that address criminal, policing, and customs matters.[7]

Provision for human rights protection was made twice.[8] First, the well-known Article F(2) in the EU Treaty asserted that 'the Union shall respect fundamental rights', as guaranteed by the European Convention on Human Rights (ECHR), and the 'consititutional principles common to the Member States' as 'general principles of Community law'. Despite the reference to the *Union* and the position of Article F(2) in Title I of the EU Treaty, setting out 'Common Provisions' governing all three pillars of the Union, the reference to 'Community law' suggested that the provision might not have been intended to govern the third pillar. However, there was a more specific second reference in the core of the third pillar provisions: Article K.2(1) stated that the matters referred to in Article K.1 (now Article 29) (the subjects of JHA co-operation) 'shall be dealt with in compliance with' the ECHR and the 1951 Geneva Convention relating to the Status of Refugees,[9] and 'having regard to' Member States' protection of persons persecuted on political grounds. While there is no reference to either other international human rights treaties agreed by the Member States *or* national constitutional principles, the standard of review ('shall be dealt with *in compliance with*') is stronger than the principle stated in Article F(2). However, the ECJ was given no power to interpret either of these provisions directly, because it was confined by Article L (now Article 46) of the EU Treaty to jurisdiction over first-pillar measures, the final provisions of the EU Treaty (Articles L–S—now Articles 46–53) and, at the Council's discretion, third-pillar conventions.

The Amsterdam Treaty renames the JHA, now referring instead to the creation of '[a]n Area of Freedom, Security and Justice'. It also moves a chunk of the content of Title VI TEU[10] to a newly-created Title IV of Part 3 of the European Community

---

[4] Art. K.6.   [5] Art. K.2(3)(c).

[6] This excludes the conventions on accession of the new Member States to the Brussels and Rome civil co-operation Conventions and relevant protocols ([1997] OJ C15). Including these, 10 of 12 post-Maastricht third-pillar conventions award jurisdiction to the ECJ.

[7] Conventions on Europol ([1995] OJ C316/1); the Customs Information System (CIS) ([1995] OJ C316/33); Protection of Financial Interests (PIF) ([1995] OJ C316/48; see First Protocol at [1996] OJ C313/1 and Second Protocol at [1997] OJ C221/11); corruption ([1997] OJ C195/1); Naples II ([1998] OJ C24/1); and driving disqualification ([1998] OJ C216/1); ECJ Protocols to the Europol ([1996] OJ C299/1), CIS ([1997] OJ C151/15) and PIF ([1997] OJ C151/1) Conventions. The exceptions to ECJ jurisdiction are the Conventions on consented and disputed extradition (respectively [1995] OJ C78/1 and [1996] OJ C313/11) and the Protocol on privileges and immunities attached to the Europol Convention ([1997] OJ C221/1).

[8] On human rights and the ECJ in the Maastricht-era third pillar, see, among others, P. Twomey, 'The European Union: Three Pillars Without a Human Rights Foundation?' in D. O'Keeffe and P. Twomey (eds.), *Legal Issues of the Maastricht Treaty* (1994) and D. O'Keeffe, 'Recasting the Third Pillar' (1995) 32 *CML Rev.* 908–11.

[9] Convention relating to the Status of Refugees, adopted on 28 July 1951 by the UN Conference of Plenipotentiaries on the Status of Refugees and Stateless Persons convened under GA Res. 429 (V) (1950), hereinafter 1951 Refugee Convention. In United Nations, *A Compilation of International Instruments* (1994), i, Part 2, 638.

[10] Immigration, asylum, and civil co-operation.

(EC) Treaty, restructures the instruments available for addressing the subject-matter remaining in Title VI,[11] and alters the role of the EU institutions. In particular, the new Treaty grants the Commission shared competence with the Member States to make proposals on the criminal, police, and customs matters remaining in the third pillar;[12] requires the Council to consult the European Parliament on every proposed measure except proposed common positions;[13] creates new instruments (framework decisions and decisions) in place of joint actions and joint positions;[14] integrates the Schengen Convention and measures implementing it (the 'Schengen *acquis*') into EC and EU law;[15] and awards the ECJ wider jurisdiction than in the 1993 TEU. Under Article 35 (*ex* Article K.7) EU, the Court now has jurisdiction to give preliminary rulings on the interpretation and validity of framework decisions and decisions, the interpretation of conventions, and the interpretation and validity of measures implementing them.[16] However, this applies only where a Member State has accepted the ECJ's jurisdiction, and Member States may choose to allow final courts only to refer.[17] The Court is now also able to settle disputes between Member States on the interpretation or application of all third-pillar measures except common positions and between the Commission and the Member States on the interpretation or application of third-pillar conventions,[18] and also now has jurisdiction over direct annulment actions brought by the Commission or any Member States against framework decisions or decisions on grounds identical to those set out in Article 173 (now Article 230) EC.[19] The preliminary rulings and dispute settlement jurisdiction are similar to the jurisdiction previously agreed for most third-pillar criminal, customs, and police conventions.

Article F(2) is renumbered Article 6(2), but is otherwise unchanged. A new Article 6(1) EU provides that '[t]he Union is founded on the principles of liberty, democracy, respect for human rights and fundamental freedoms, and the rule of law, principles which are common to the Member States'. However, there is no longer a human rights reference specific to the third pillar, with Article K.2(1) deleted and not replaced.[20] The formal justiciability of these provisions has been altered, with Article 46 EU (formerly Article L) now providing that the Court can interpret the 'provisions of Title VI, under the conditions provided for by Article 35' (paragraph (b)) and 'Article 6(2) [EU] with regard to action of the institutions, insofar as the Court has jurisdiction under the Treaties establishing the European Communities and under this Treaty' (paragraph (d)). There is no reference to interpreting Article 6(1).

---

[11] Criminal judicial co-operation and co-operation on policing, including criminal law aspects of customs.
[12] Art. 34(2).   [13] Art. 39.   [14] Art. 34(2).
[15] See Prot. on Schengen attached to the EC and EU Treaties.   [16] Art. 35(1).
[17] Art. 35(2) and (3). At time of writing, Germany, Austria, Belgium, Greece, and Luxembourg had stated they would allow all courts to refer, and the Netherlands had indicated that it would make a declaration awarding the ECJ competence but had not indicated whether it would permit all courts or just the final ones to refer ([1997] OJ C340/308).
[18] Art. 35(7).   [19] Art. 35(6).
[20] The Geneva Convention on refugees is now mentioned in the first pillar provisions (see Art. 63 EC).

Because the Court had jurisdiction only over third-pillar conventions until the entry into force of the Amsterdam Treaty, and because the first post-Maastricht third-pillar convention had only just entered into force at time of writing,[21] there is no ECJ case law yet on the application of any third-pillar rule, still less the role of human rights in the third pillar. The only third-pillar-related case law concerns access to documents[22] and the boundaries between the first and third pillars.[23] So it is obviously premature to ask whether the Court takes 'human rights seriously' in these spheres. What we can ask is how judicial protection for human rights principles will work as the Court develops its jurisdiction and whether, in its third-pillar practice, the *Council* has been taking rights seriously.

III. FRAMEWORK FOR JUDICIAL PROTECTION OF HUMAN RIGHTS IN THE THIRD PILLAR

The sources of human rights in the *first* pillar are, as principles established by the Court of Justice, common national constitutional principles and international treaties upon which the Member States have collaborated, particularly the ECHR. The ECJ has jurisdiction to give a ruling on these principles to ensure that they are observed in the interpretation of Community law, national measures implementing or administering EC law, and national measures derogating from Community law rights, or to rule Community acts invalid if they breach the principles.[24] Article F(2) of the EU Treaty appeared to narrow these sources, declining to mention international human rights treaties other than the ECHR or the Protocols to the ECHR, and could have been interpreted to restrict the Court's jurisdiction, by means of Article L EU, which restricted the Court from interpreting the 'common provisions' of the EU Treaty. But the Court did not resile post-Maastricht from applying the full extent of its established jurisdiction, including the 'offensive jurisdiction' over national implementation and national derogations.[25] The Court, with the Court of First Instance, even slipped a few 'cheeky' references to Article F(2) into its judgments, despite its inability to interpret the clause outright.[26] The Court has also repeatedly reiterated post-Maastricht that international human rights treaties other

---

[21] The Europol Convention, on 1 Oct. 1998. However, the Convention is not operational yet, because some implementing measures have not been agreed and the Prot. on privileges and immunities has not been fully ratified. In any case, many Member States still have to ratify the Prot. on preliminary references to the ECJ.

[22] Case T–194/94, *Carvel and Guardian* v. *Council* [1995] ECR II–2765 and Case T–174/95, *Svenska Journalistforbundet* v. *Council* (CFI judgment of 17 June 1998, not yet reported).

[23] Case C–268/94, *Portugal* v. *Council* [1996] ECR I–6177 and Case C–170/96, *Commission* v. *Council* [1998] ECR I–2763.

[24] See De Witte's contribution in this vol.

[25] For examples, see respectively Case C–13/94, *P* v. *S* [1996] ECR I–2143 and Case C–368/95 *Familiapress* [1997] ECR I–3689. Jacobs AG's Opinion in Case C–84/95, *Bosphorus* [1996] ECR I–3953, describes Art. F(2) as confirming the previous jurisprudence, not limiting the Court's jurisdiction.

[26] *Opinion 2/94* [1996] ECR I–1759; Case T–10/93, *A* v. *Commission* [1994] ECR II–179; Joined Cases T–213/95 & T–18/96, *SCK and FNK* v. *Commission* [1997] ECR II–1739.

than the ECHR still inform the general principles of human rights law,[27] and has specifically interepreted one such treaty recently.[28]

Are the sources of and jurisdiction over human rights law in the the third pillar the same? While the pre-Amsterdam Article K.2 EU, as noted above, restricted the sources of third-pillar human rights law to the ECHR, the Geneva Convention and national rules on the politically persecuted, the lack of a post-Amsterdam replacement for this clause means that Article 6(2) EU is the only *written* source of third-pillar human rights rules. The contradictory structure of the clause, suggesting that the entire Union is bound by a general principle of *Community* law, has been exacerbated by the new Article 46(d) EU, giving the Court jurisdiction to apply Article 6(2) EU to the third pillar as well as the first. Since the amendments to the Treaty are clearly an attempt to authorize the Court's jurisdiction over human rights principles in the first and third pillars, it is submitted that the reference to 'Community law' in Article 6(2) is vestigial, and that the Article should be read as referring to *Union* law.

This could potentially lead to a temporal problem in application of the Court's third-pillar human rights jurisdiction; it could be argued that when interpreting the six or seven pre-Amsterdam customs, police, and criminal law third-pillar conventions over which it has jurisdiction,[29] the Court should either apply *no* human rights principles at all (because it was not formally able to interpret Articles F(2) or K.2(1) EU) or it should apply only Article K.2 (thus absenting any consideration of national human rights principles) because it was *lex specialis* and the application of Article F(2) to the EU Treaty was uncertain. Both interpretations should be rejected, for several reasons. First, it is submitted that the Court should adopt a consistent principle of interpretation[30] that the principles of interpretation governing pre-Amsterdam third-pillar measures must be the same as those governing post-Amsterdam third-pillar measures as far as possible, because of the continued existence of many pre-Amsterdam measures and their integration with post-Amsterdam measures.[31] Secondly, the place of Article F(2) in the common provisions of the EU Treaty indicated a clear intent to extend human rights principles to all aspects of EU co-operation, despite the reference to *Community* law; Article 46(d) EU should therefore be interpreted as *confirming* the scope of Article F(2)/6(2) EU, rather than enlarging it.

Thirdly, it would not be outrageous for the Court to interpret a third-pillar convention in the light of Article F(2) even if that Convention had been agreed before

---

[27] *Opinion 2/94*; *A* v. *Commission* and *SCK and FNK* v. *Commission*, note 26 above; Case C–299/95, *Kremzov* [1997] ECR I–2629; Case C–309/96, *Annibaldi* [1997] ECR I–7493; and Case C–249/96, *Grant* [1998] ECR I–621.

[28] The ICCPR (*ibid.*). See also the Opinion in *Bosphorus* (note 25 above) applying the First Prot. to the ECHR.

[29] In addition to the 6 conventions agreed at the time of writing (note 7 above), the Council agreed a short Protocol to the CIS Convention in late 1998 ([1999] OJ–C91/1), and it seemed likely that the Council would agree a convention on mutual criminal assistance in mid-1999.

[30] The term 'principle of interpretation' is used here to refer to approaches the Court uses to analysing texts; it is a more restricted concept than the 'general principles of Community law' which also bind Community authorities, national authorities, and national courts.

[31] For an analysis of every aspect of the Court's JHA jurisdiction after Amsterdam, see S. Peers, 'Who's Judging the Watchmen? The Judicial System of the Area of Freedom, Security, and Justice' (forthcoming).

the Court was formally able to interpret Article F(2). While it would be inappropriate for the Court to assert jurisdiction to interpret Article F(2) *independently* of any acts over which it has jurisdiction, interpreting a justiciable measure *in the light of* Article F(2) is another matter. The Court has long exercised 'ancillary' (or 'indirect') jurisdiction of that sort.[32] Acknowledging such an interpretive principle would, in the circumstances, be far less judicially activist than the initial creation of Community human rights principles out of thin air. Indeed, if the ECJ refused to recognize its jurisdiction over the human rights principles governing pre-Amsterdam third-pillar acts, and that such principles have wide sources, there might be greater rebellion from national courts than if it did not.

Fourthly, it is submitted that there is a general interpretive principle of 'wide jurisdiction' for the ECJ, with the effect that the Court's jurisdiction can usually only be restricted or ousted by express, unambiguous wording.[33] No such wording prevents the use of Article F(2) as an interpretive principle applying to pre-Amsterdam acts. Fifthly, it is clear from the regular references to Articles F(2) and K.2(1) EU in secondary third-pillar acts adopted by the Council[34] that the principles in those clauses were meant to apply to the interpretation of third-pillar acts. Finally, in the alternative, even if the Court does not automatically have the jurisdiction to apply Articles F(2) and K.2(1) to the interpretation of all pre-Amsterdam EU Conventions, it must surely have the jurisdiction to apply the clauses to those conventions which mention them.

While, as pointed out above, Article K.2(1) did appear to have a greater impact than Article F(2) because it pointed more clearly to the invalidity of third-pillar acts if they did not conform to human rights principles, this distinction is irrelevant because the Court had no jurisdiction over annulment of third-pillar acts pre-Amsterdam and it will have no jurisdiction over annulment of conventions post-Amsterdam.

Two important related questions are the sources of human rights rules in the Schengen *acquis* and the scope of the Court's jurisdiction over them. The Protocol on the Schengen *acquis* attached to the EC and EU Treaties provides that, once the Council allocates the Schengen *acquis* to the first and third pillars,[35] '[w]ith regard to such provisions and decisions and in accordance with that determination, the Court of Justice of the European Communities shall exercise the powers conferred upon it by the relevant applicable provisions of the Treaties'.[36] It is assumed that even if the Council fails to agree the allocation Decision, the ECJ has jurisdiction over the Schengen *acquis*, which will be located in the third pillar in default of adoption of an allocation Decision.[37] However, the Schengen Convention made no reference to the ECHR or to national constitutional principles, although it did contain several other human rights rules:

[32] For more detailed analysis of the 'ancillary' (or 'indirect') jurisdiction principle, see *ibid.*
[33] For more detailed analysis of the 'wide jurisdiction' principle, see Peers, note 31 above.
[34] See sect. IV below for more detail.
[35] The Council had not yet agreed this allocation Decision at time of writing. For a draft, see House of Lords Select Committee on the European Communities, *Incorporating the Schengen Acquis into the European Union* (31st Report, 1997–8), App. 3.
[36] Prot. 2, Art. 2(1).
[37] See argument in Peers, note 31 above.

(a) it applied 'subject to' the Geneva Convention on refugees and its New York Protocol;[38]

(b) it required its parties to 'undertake . . . to implement a level of protection for personal data which complies with the principles' of Recommendation R (87) 15 of the Council of Europe Committee of Ministers, when transmitting personal data pursuant to its police co-operation provisions;[39]

(c) it required parties to 'adopt the national provisions required to achieve a level of protection at least equal to that resulting from' the 1981 Council of Europe data protection Convention, when processing any data transmitted pursuant to the Convention automatically;[40]

(d) more specifically, it obliged parties to 'make the national arrangements necessary' to achieve the same goal when transmitting data pursuant to the provisions on the Schengen Information System (SIS) and further provided that such arrangements should ensure that transmission was 'in compliance with' Recommendation R (87) 15;[41]

(e) finally, it required the joint supervisory authority established to oversee the application of the SIS to carry out its tasks 'in accordance with' the 1981 Council of Europe Convention and 'taking into account' the 1987 Recommendation.[42]

To what extent do the additional human rights principles guaranteed by Article 6(2) EU apply to the Schengen *acquis*? It is submitted that they apply fully. The Schengen Convention does not rule out the application of such principles and the Schengen States were not legally able, in agreeing the Convention, to escape either from their national constitutions or their international human rights obligations. The authority for the Court to 'exercise the powers conferred upon it' when ruling on Schengen *acquis* cases does not exclude any aspect of its powers, and should not be taken to exclude its jurisdiction over human rights matters without any wording to that effect. Nor is there any wording in the EC or EU Treaties which would block the Court from applying the human rights principles to the Schengen *acquis* if the entire *acquis* is allocated to the third pillar in default of a proper allocation—assuming that the Court has jurisdiction over the *acquis* in default of an allocation Decision.

Some may have doubts about applying the human rights principles if the Court finds that it has jurisdiction to rule over Schengen *acquis* cases where the dispute arose before the integration of Schengen into the EC/EU legal system,[43] but here it is submitted again that if the temporal scope of the Court's jurisdiction extends to such

---

[38] Art. 135, Schengen Convention; see also Art. 28, in which the Contracting Parties 'hereby reaffirm' their obligations under these treaties. However, a draft Council Decision defining the Schengen *acquis* for allocation omits these clauses (see App. 3, *Incorporating the Schengen Acquis*, note 35 above), on the ground that the Bonn Protocol to the Schengen Convention has made all the asylum provisions of the latter redundant in light of the entry into force of the Dublin Convention ([1997] OJ C254/1).

[39] Art. 129(1), Schengen Convention, referring to Title III, Chap. 1 of the Convention (Arts. 39–47).

[40] Art. 126(1), Schengen Convention, but this principle does not apply to all data transmitted under the Convention: see Art. 126(4). In fact, all Member States have now ratified the 1981 Council of Europe Convention.

[41] Art. 117(1), Schengen Convention. 　　　　[42] Art. 115(1), Schengen Convention.

[43] On this temporal scope issue, see Peers, note 31 above, arguing that the Court has jurisdiction over such cases.

disputes, EU human rights principles must extend also, because there is nothing in the EC or EU Treaty to suggest that the Court can ever exercise any of its jurisdiction without applying human rights principles.

The next question is whether the sources of third-pillar human rights principles extend beyond the ECHR and the principles common to national constitutions, to include the Protocols to the ECHR and other international human rights treaties upon which Member States have collaborated. While Article 6(2) EU does not mention any additional sources, there is nothing to exclude their application in an appropriate case and, as noted above, Advocate-General Jacobs has already assumed that the First Protocol to the ECHR still forms part of the general principles of Community law, even given restrictions of the Maastricht-era Article F(2).[44] In the alternative, third-pillar measures must be interpreted in the light of such additional sources, at least where the relevant measure refers to such sources.[45]

The next, and crucially important issue, is the scope of the Court's third-pillar human rights jurisdiction. It seems beyond doubt that it extends to 'defensive jurisdiction', requiring the application of the human rights principles to the validity and interpretation of third-pillar acts. The application of the human rights principles to validity stems from the combined effect of Articles 46(b) and (d), 6(2) and 34(6) EU, the last of which establishes that grounds for review in a direct action include 'infringement of this Treaty or of any rule of law relating to its application'.[46] General principles of Community law, including human rights, have always formed part of the rules of law referred to in Article 173 (now Article 230) EC, which Article 34(6) EU copies, an effect confirmed by Article 6(2) EU and which the Court can interpret and apply according to Article 46(b) and (d) EU. Indeed, with the formal justiciability of Article 6(2) EU, it is arguable that a breach of human rights principles is a breach of the EU *Treaty*, not a breach of a rule of law relating to its application.[47]

Will the Court's third-pillar human rights jurisdiction also extend as far as it has previously extended in the first pillar, to include 'offensive jurisdiction' as well? The text of Article 46(d) EU, in referring to 'action of the institutions', could be interpreted to mean that the Court has no such jurisdiction in either the first or the third pillar. But it is submitted that at least national implementation of Community or Union acts must still fall within the Court's jurisdiction, because such implementation is inseparable from interpretation of the acts themselves. The application of human rights principles to national derogations from Community law rights protected in the EC Treaty is problematic in light of Article 46(d) EU; but this type of jurisdiction appears less relevant to the third pillar. The third pillar does not create free movement rights for individuals and firms, and where Member States do derogate from third-pillar provisions intended to protect individual rights (see, in particular, the *non bis in idem* principle discussed below), it is a derogation exercised pursuant to a provision of *an act of the institutions*, not pursuant to the EU Treaty itself. As such,

---

[44] Opinion in *Bosphorus* (note 25 above).   [45] See discussion below for examples.
[46] The ECJ has always appeared to assume in the first pillar that grounds for review in an indirect action are the same as those in a direct action: see T. Hartley, *The Foundations of European Community Law* (4th. edn., 1998), 407–8.
[47] The distinction is irrelevant except for the argument that the sources of human rights principles are wider than those listed in Art. 6(2) EU when they form part of the rules of law.

the Court can apply its human rights jurisdiction to the derogation, because it is still interpreting an act of the EU institutions. While Article 35(5) EU does provide that the Court has 'no jurisdiction to review the validity or proportionality of operations carried out by the police or other law enforcement services of a Member State or the exercise of the responsibilities incumbent upon Member States with regard to the maintenance of law and order and the safeguarding of internal security', this proviso refers only to acts of Member States; it does not prevent the Court from interpreting acts of the Council upon which national implementation and derogations are based. This analysis also conforms to the general principle of interpretation that the first and third pillars should be interpreted in a consistent manner as far as possible.[48]

The final issue is the extent of the jurisdiction of the European Court of Human Rights over the Union's third-pillar acts and Member States' implementation of those acts. Here the finding that an ECHR party is still bound by the ECHR even where it is transposing a Community directive[49] should apply *mutatis mutandis* to the third pillar, where the ratification of the Council's conventions requires acts of the Member States and framework decisions are identical to directives except for their lack of direct effect. Third-pillar decisions, which will not be approximating national legislation, are a different question; while it seems less likely that they will infringe human rights principles, the prospect should not be excluded.[50] It would be awkward for the Strasbourg Court to exercise jurisdiction over such acts; it would first have to decide whether the EU is an international organization, in which case its jurisdiction might be clarified in a pending case,[51] or instead a *congerie* of Member States, in which case it will still be difficult to find that Member States are breaching the ECHR unless there are national adminstrative acts relating to the Council Decision. In any event, Europol is an international organization with legal personality,[52] even if the Union is not, although it is arguable that the Strasbourg Court at least has jurisdiction over Member States' relations with Europol.

IV. COUNCIL PRACTICE

Although a widespread critique of the Council's activity in the third pillar is that it has accomplished little, this critique may be wide of the mark. First, it is questionable whether it is accurate to conclude that the Council has accomplished little, because by its nature much police and customs co-operation will be operational, not normative. Secondly, even if it is true that the Council has accomplished little, this may be no bad thing if third-pillar co-operation is insufficiently developed institutionally to ensure sufficient safeguards for the protection of individual rights.

[48] For a detailed argument in favour of this principle, see Peers, note 31 above. The principle is based on an interpretation of public international law which takes into account the identical parties of the EU and EC Treaties and the 'consistency' principle of Art. 3 EU, more particularly the level of existing and planned integration of first-and third-pillar measures.

[49] *Cantoni* v. *France*, ECHR Reports (Judgments and Decisions) 1997 V–1614.

[50] E.g., it is possible that the Council could adopt a decision to establish an EU-wide database, with any change in national laws either unnecessary or agreed by means of a separate framework decision.

[51] *Whaite et al.* v. *Germany*, pending.   [52] Europol Convention (note 7 above), Art. 26.

An analysis of Council third-pillar human rights practice should begin by assessing the conceptual approach to human rights taken by the Council.[53] Just as the first pillar of the Union aims at furthering the free movement of goods, services, persons, and capital, and the Convention on Jurisdiction and the Enforcement of Judgments in Civil and Commercial Matters 1968[54] (Brussels Convention) and other civil co-operation measures aim at furthering the 'free movement of judgments', the third pillar aims at furthering the 'free movement of prosecutions' and the 'free movement of investigations'. Free movement is furthered by means of both negative legal integration (removing national barriers to the entry or mutual recognition of persons or measures regulated by another Member State's legal system) and positive legal integration (replacing national regulation of internal matters by some level of European-level regulation).[55] There is a hierarchy of positive legal integration measures, starting from 'soft law' and rising through 'minimum standards' to 'complete standards' up to the creation of a European-level agency or pan-European legal structure. Within the first pillar, additional facilitation of free movement beyond that provided for by the EC Treaty is often agreed in a measure, or related measures, which combine positive and negative legal integration—a 'package deal' in which Member States agree to allow further free movement because they have all committed themselves to some form of positive legal integration ensuring that (most frequently) minimum standards are met. A classic example is the Data Protection Directive: since all Member States will be ensuring an acceptable minimum standard of protection for personal data as detailed in the Directive, data can move freely between Member States.[56]

This approach is followed in the third pillar, but the twist is that as a general rule, the Council has declined to adopt any minimum standards of its own because such standards *are provided by international human rights obligations.*[57] So the role of human rights treaties is to serve as a type of positive legal integration justifying the negative legal integration agreed or proposed in several instruments. But it is arguable that the minimum standards in human rights treaties are not high enough to justify the intensive amount of free movement proposed or agreed in the third pillar, and that the very nature of the type of free movement and the rights to be protected make it harder to ensure that the minimum standards are actually being enforced. This thesis will be tested by examining three areas of Council practice: data protection rights; telecommunications interception; and trial rights.[58]

---

[53] For further development of the following analysis, see Peers, note 1 above, chap. 1, and S. Peers, 'Salvation Outside the Church? Theorizing European Legal Integration in light of the Amsterdam Treaty' (forthcoming).

[54] Consolidated text at [1998] OJ C27/1.

[55] It should be noted that negative and positive *legal* integration are not quite the same as negative and positive *political* integration, because the latter focuses on the creation of institutions, but the former focuses on the source of regulation. A dir. providing for mutual recognition of qualifications is an act of the EC institutions, but unless it provides for minimum standards for attaining a qualification in all Member States it is an act of negative legal integration, because in principle it requires Member States to refrain from applying their own law and to accept the prior regulatory competence of another Member State.

[56] Dir. 95/46 [1995] OJ L281/31.

[57] This argument is frequently asserted in the Action Plan on Organized Crime [1997] OJ C251, which sets out a detailed framework for subsequent Council negotiations.

[58] Of course, this is not an exhaustive list of third-pillar human rights issues. On police co-operation, see C. Joubert and H. Bevers, *Schengen Investigated: A Comparative Interpretation of the Schengen*

A. Data Protection Rights

Given the third pillar's emphasis on information exchange, particularly when ensuring the 'free movement of investigations', Council practice is first and foremost concerned with data protection rights, as implemented by specific human rights instruments. Such privacy rights need to be protected, both where information is occasionally exhanged in the framework of a specific investigation and when a database of some sort is etablished.[59]

The first type of privacy protection issue arises from such measures as the Council's Resolution on the exchange of DNA analysis results,[60] sundry measures on public order,[61] and in the draft Convention on mutual assistance in criminal matters.[62] Data protection issues arising from the last Convention will be 'resolved', according to a draft Council declaration, in a Protocol to be negotiated after the parent convention is agreed, although Member States disagree about whether the Protocol will have regard to the 1981 Council of Europe Convention and whether it will extend data protection rules to manual processing of data.[63] The Resolution on DNA analysis aims to lay the groundwork for a future EU-wide database, inviting Member States to establish national databases with standard technology so that information can be exchanged between Member States as the first step toward establishing the database. The national databases must have national rules on personal data 'in accordance with' the 1981 Council of Europe Convention, with Recommendation (87) 15 'taken into consideration'. Future exchange between Member States must merely 'offer sufficient safeguards concerning the security and protection of personal data'.

The Recommendation on hooliganism states that 'Member States should use a common format for police intelligence reports about known or suspected groups of troublemakers', including an 'overall assessment of the potential for disorder' and detailed information on travel plans. Certainly such information should be shared in the interests of preventing violence; but what protection is available for persons wrongly tagged as 'troublemakers'? The Recommendation makes no reference at all to national or international standards on data protection. The subsequent Resolution aims to cnsure that stadium exclusions imposed by civil law in one Member State are mutually recognized by other Member States, but there are no provisions for challenging such mutual recognition. Finally, the joint action insists that Member States provide information on large groups 'which may pose a threat to law and order' which are 'travelling to another Member State in order to participate in events', such as 'sporting events, rock concerts, demonstrations and road-blocking

Provisions on International Police Cooperation in the Light of the European Convention on Human Rights (1996).

[59] This chap. does not examine the data protection rules in the Dublin Convention or the proposed Eurodac Convention, because those measures fall outside the chap.'s scope.

[60] [1997] OJ C193/2.

[61] Recommendation on guidclines for preventing and restraining disorder connected with football matches [1996] OJ C131/1; Resolution on preventing and restraining football hooliganism through the exchange of experience, exclusion from stadiums, and media policy [1997] OJ C193/1; Joint Action on cooperation on law and order and security [1997] OJ L147/1.

[62] Council doc. 8637/98, 19 May 1998 (latest draft available to author).   [63] See *ibid.*, at 3.

protest campaigns'. Again there is no reference to control of the information transmitted and no recognition that such groups are exercising their right to freedom of association.

A slightly more advanced model of data protection can be found in the 'Naples II' Convention on co-operation between customs administrations.[64] This Convention aims to assist free movement of (customs) investigations by setting out rules governing requests for information, surveillance, and enquiries from the investigating Member State to another Member State;[65] obliging Member States to offer 'spontaneous assistance' without previously receiving a request when they believe information exchange or surveillance might assist another Member State's investigations;[66] and allowing the use of cross-border hot pursuit, surveillance, 'controlled deliveries', covert investigations, and joint special investigation teams.[67] When exchanging information, customs administrations must 'respect the relevant provisions of' the 1981 Council of Europe Convention[68] and a further nine principles apply to exchange of data.[69] These principles comprise:

(a) a 'speciality' rule, limiting the use of transferred data to specified institutions for specified purposes (although both are widely defined);
(b) rules on the erasure of inaccurate or wrongly transmitted data;
(c) the 'effective right to correct the data' for the persons concerned;
(d) recording of data transfer;
(e) the obligation to inform the person concerned about use of the data at his or her request (but with a broad public interest exception);
(f) liability under national law for wrongful processing or communication of data;
(g) the obligation to delete the data when no longer necessary for the purposes requested;
(h) equivalent data protection as that provided for national data; and
(i) the requirement to take 'appropriate measures to ensure compliance' with these principles with 'effective controls', which task 'may' be assigned to national supervisory authorities.

More elaborate provisions on privacy protection can be found in the measures establishing the three large Union databases: the CIS, SIS, and Europol. Data exchange under the CIS Convention is 'subject to' the 1981 Council of Europe Convention[70] and any Member State wishing to use the database must 'adopt the national provisions sufficient to achieve a level of protection at least equal to that resulting from' the 1981 Council of Europe data protection Convention (an obligation almost identical to the principles governing Schengen co-operation).[71] CIS data can be used for purposes other than investigations 'tak[ing] into account the relevant principle of Recommendation (87) 15'.[72] Information in the CIS system contrary to

[64] Note 7 above.   [65] Title II (Arts. 8–14).   [66] Title III (Arts. 15–18).
[67] Title IV (Arts. 19–24).
[68] Art. 25(1). The definition of 'processing of personal data' is taken from the 1995 EC Dir. (Art. 25(3)).
[69] Art. 25(2), (a) to (i).   [70] Preamble, CIS Convention, note 7 above.   [71] Art. 13(1) and (2).
[72] Art. 8(1).

the provisions of the 1981 Convention must be corrected or deleted,[73] and the joint supervisory authority set up by the Convention, like the equivalent Schengen authority, must perform its task 'in accordance with' the 1981 Convention taking into account Recommendation (87) 15.[74]

The CIS Convention allows specified types of data to be entered into the CIS system (names, dates and place of birth, nationality, sex, physical characteristics, reason for inclusion of data, suggested action, and a warning code)[75] to assist with investigations, although the first four types of data can only be included if there are 'real indications' that a person has committed, is committing or will commit 'serious contraventions of national laws'.[76] Certain further information gathered during Member States' subsequent investigations can then be entered into the system.[77] Only national customs authorities and other national law enforcement authorities can have access to the system, although the Member States may agree a protocol allowing access to the system by international or regional organizations.[78] In principle, there is a rule of 'speciality' restricting use of CIS data for customs investigation purposes, but Member States may also use the information 'for administrative or other purposes' with the authorization of, and subject to conditions imposed by, the Member State supplying the information.[79] Data obtained from the system can, with the same *caveats*, be supplied to national authorities other than customs administrations, or to non-member States or international or regional organizations, with the only additional proviso that the transmitting Member State must take 'special measures' to ensure the security of the transmission.[80] Inclusion of data is governed by the law of the supplying Member State and use of data by the law of the using Member State.[81] Only the supplying Member State can correct information which it supplied to the system, subject to the obligation to recognize all Member States' court judgments requiring such deletion.[82] As with the Naples II Convention, information should only be kept for limited periods, although there is a more specific obligation here to review the need for holding such information annually.[83]

Personal data protection is subject to more precise rules than under the Naples II Convention. The right of access to information held on a person must be exercised according to the law of the State in which the right is invoked, possibly (depending on the Member State) via a national data protection supervisory authority,[84] although it is possible for a person to 'forum-shop' and ask the supervisory authority of another Member State to check the system.[85] However, access to information

---

[73] Art. 15(3). See also Art. 21(1).   [74] Art. 18(2).   [75] Art. 4.   [76] Art. 5(2).

[77] Art. 6.   [78] Art. 7.   [79] Art. 8(1).

[80] Art. 8(3). There is no reference to any privacy standards that the third parties must uphold as a condition of transmission, although potentially the Member State which initially supplied the information could insist on such standards.

[81] Art. 9.

[82] Art. 11. There is no procedure for then informing other authorities, organizations, and non-member States which have had access to the system or which have been supplied with the information that an error has occurred.

[83] Art. 12(1). Again there is no obligation to inform other recipients of information or system users about the deletion of any information.

[84] Art. 15(1).   [85] Art. 17(2).

may be refused on broad grounds (during surveillance, sighting, and reporting, or if access would impede such acts, or 'in order to protect the rights and freedoms of others').[86] A person may have inaccurate or wrongly included information altered or deleted[87] and has a right of access to courts or administrative authorities to obtain access, correction, or deletion of data or obtain compensation for wrongful acts.[88] The national supervisory authorities shall carry out regular checks on the CIS system to ensure that the Convention's rules on the processing and use of data are observed,[89] while the joint supervisory authority will supervise the protection of individual rights in the operation of the system more generally.[90] Finally, there are detailed rules on security of data.[91]

The principles set out in the CIS Convention are essentially the same as those in the Europol and Schengen Conventions. The Schengen provisions differ substantially in scope, as they cover the inclusion of data in a far greater number of situations and can be accessed by a broader array of national authorities, although there is no provision for the transmission of data to third parties or bodies within the Member States and the only possible administrative use of data relates to the grant of visas and residence permits.[92] Additionally, ther rules on deletion of data are very precise, setting out specified time periods after which certain categories of data have to be deleted.[93]

The Europol Convention allows a much narrower group of persons to access the database, and contains more detailed provisions on checking data, but the information collected and analysed by Europol can be passed on to a large number of third States and bodies after agreements are concluded with them. Four sets of rules governing such agreements were *de facto* agreed even before entry into force of the Convention.[94]

There are common problems with the privacy provisions governing all three types of database. First is the difficulty which individuals face in finding out what information is actually held on them. Without disclosure of such information, there is no way that an individual can know if it is inaccurate and there is little chance of ascertaining whether it was wrongly included in the database. Any subsequent prospect of bringing an action for compensation against a Member State which wrongly supplied or used such information is obviously ephemeral. One can accept that, given the possible use of such information in ongoing investigations, there should be no automatic right of access to the information in all circumstances, a principle upheld by the Strasbourg Human Rights Court.[95] But this is a minimum standard, and there is no recognition in the third-pillar conventions that higher standards can still apply: the minimum standard provided by international treaties is considered sufficient to justify the construction of these huge databases.

---

[86] Art. 15(2).   [87] Art. 15(3).

[88] Art. 15(4). The liability rules (Art. 21(2)) provide that national law on liability applies; either the supplying or using State may be liable; and concurrent liability is possible.

[89] Art. 17(1).   [90] Art. 18.   [91] Arts. 19–20.   [92] Art. 102, Schengen.

[93] *Ibid.*, Arts. 112–13.

[94] For the texts, see House of Lords Select Committee on the European Communities, *Europol: Third Country Rules* (29th Report, 1997–8), App. 3.

[95] *Leander* v. *Sweden*, ECHR (1987), Series A, No. 116, 48.

Nor are there effective administrative law rules governing the application of individual requests for information, such as the right to have a reply within a reasonable or specified time (except under the Europol Convention) and the duty to give reasons for a refusal,[96] although the national law of some Member States likely applies such principles to requests. Each convention provides only for broadly defined reasons for *refusing* requests; no convention sets out or suggests circumstances in which requests for information *must* or *should* in principle be accepted.

Secondly, the powers of the national or joint supervisory authorities in each convention are relatively weak. These authorities have access to the relevant systems but otherwise have little power to assist in individual cases. Where they perform checks on individuals' behalf, such checks are subject to the national law of the Member State to which the request is made. Whether or not the supervisory authority has the right to check the system in detail, or to bring national court action to defend its right of access, will depend on national law. If a supervisory authority informs an individual that data concerning him or her have been entered or processed incorrectly, the information is of little use unless the individual is also given details of what information is included and how it has been misused, otherwise an action for correction, deletion, or liability will be too imprecise to have any hope of success.

Thirdly, the CIS and Europol Conventions create a serious risk that inaccurate information will end up in the hands of other national bodies (in the case of CIS data) or third States or bodies, after which the information cannot be corrected and against which the individual has no guaranteed rights. The CIS Convention lacks any standard rules governing the onward transmission of data except those which the transmitting State, or the State which originally supplied the data, choose to apply. The CIS Convention only obliges Member States to inform the joint supervisory authority of the security measures relating to the transmission of such data,[97] rather than the criteria for transmission or the fact of transmission. There are no 'tracing' provisions to require that the transmitting State specify the source of the data or requirements upon the sender and recipient to record the fact of transmission. So not only does the Convention lack substantive criteria which would apply to limit the scope of onward transmission of data, it lacks any procedural mechanism to ensure that any criteria which are applied are followed or which would enable individuals, national supervisory authorities, or the joint supervisory authority to keep any kind of check on transmission. Perhaps individual Member States have clear legislation governing this topic, but how easily can a person in one Member State wishing to check use of any data compiled on him or her gain access to information on other Member States' procedures?

The Europol rules for agreements with third States also give rise to misgivings. The rules on transmission of information do provide clearly that information cannot be transmitted to third States or bodies unless the latter ensure both that the information is not passed on any further and that only law-enforcement authorities may use the information.[98] This is a huge improvement on the CIS Convention.

---

[96] Indeed there is no right to know *whether* the relevant systems hold information on a person.
[97] Art. 8(3) of the CIS Convention.
[98] See Art. 5 of the rules on transmission of data by Europol, note 94 above.

However, the rules on receipt of information only block Europol from storing information obtained by a third State 'in obvious violation of human rights'.[99] This places no restraint on the onward transmission of such data; although Member States may be in agreement that such data, in light of its problematic source, should only be transmitted in emergencies, there is no provision in the rules placing any such restriction.[100] It is instructive to compare the third-pillar data protection provisions to the EC Data Protection Directive, which does establish minimum standards higher than the 1981 Convention and which sets strict rules on the external transmission of data to third States which do not have sufficiently high standards of their own.

Finally, there is a further institutional limitation in the path of effective supervision and accountability of Europol activity: the Protocol on Privileges and Immunities.[101] Although the immunity of Europol and its employees from suit or from requirements to give testimony can be waived, there is no judicial or other control of the decision whether to grant such a waiver. There are ominous national precedents where police have created a 'wall of silence' when accused of wrongdoing, and to bolster such an inherent inclination with a *fiat* of official immunity risks not only that any future wrongdoing will be hard to uncover or investigate, but also that the *deterrent* effect of liability actions against the police will be lost. It is arguable that the Protocol breaches the ECHR in light of the very recent Strasbourg Court decision in *Osman* v. *UK*, limiting national principles which automatically shield police from liability claims in the conduct of prosecutions.[102]

B. Telecommunications Interception

A vexed issue frequently before the Strasbourg organs is the interception of telecommunications by Member States. While such interception is allowed for the purposes of fighting crime, States' ability to bug telephones is not unlimited.[103] Bugging must have some basis in domestic law and that law must be clear, precise, and accessible, setting out rules on the categories of people whose telephones can be bugged, the offences for which telephones can be bugged, and limits on duration of the bugging and the use and deletion of information obtained by the process. In a recent concurring opinion, Judge Pettiti expressed some despair that ECHR States paid little attention in practice to these principles.[104]

Member States' diligence in applying the obligations of Article 8 ECHR has not been improved by the European Union.[105] A Council resolution on the lawful interception of telecommunications, not published for nearly two years after its adoption, sets out a detailed list of what '[l]aw enforcement agencies' require from network service-providers.[106] Only a brief preambular clause refers to 'observing human rights

---

[99] See Art. 4(4) of the Rules on transmission of data by Europol, note 94 above.
[100] See *ibid.*, Opinion of the Committee, paras. 92 and 93.   [101] Note 7 above.
[102] Judgment of 26 Oct. 1998, not yet published.
[103] See the summary of established principles in the recent Strasbourg judgment in *Valenzuela Contreras* v. *Spain* (judgment of 30 July 1998, not yet published).
[104] Opinion in *Kopp* v. *Switzerland* (judgment of 25 Mar. 1998, not yet published).
[105] At time of writing, the Council had just begun to discuss draft proposals on bugging the Internet.
[106] [1996] OJ C329/1.

and the principles of data protection'. The resolution does not admit to its context: it echoes requirements imposed by the Federal Bureau of Investigation (FBI) in the United States, and a later (unpublished) Memorandum of Understanding signed by all the Member States with the United States and several other countries aims to encourage co-operation among national law enforcement agencies so that requirements for bugging remain sufficiently similar to facilitate information exchange.[107]

The proposed Convention on mutual assistance in criminal matters also contains provisions on bugging telephones, although the details were still partly in dispute at the time of writing.[108] These provisions aim to assist the free movement of investigations by ensuring that a Member State can oblige another Member State to bug the telephone of a person with a terrestrial telephone in that Member State, or oblige a Member State which hosts a satellite telephone ground station to bug the telephones of persons who have satellite telephones which can only be tapped at the ground station for technical reasons. There are no human rights rules proposed to govern the application of these taps except the minimum standards of the ECHR.

It has been alleged that these provisions in the mutual assistance Convention are linked with the Council Resolution and Memorandum of Understanding and aim to facilitate the establishment of a global surveillance system under the co-ordination of the FBI. This has been denied by the United Kingdom government—not that it would confirm such a plan if there were one—but it is at least clear that when implementing requests under the mutual assistance Convention, Member States will likely be applying the common principles of the Resolution, and that the application of the Resolution may well lead to an increase in usable data in the light of its harmonized rules on the requirements of law enforcement agencies.

C. Trial Rights

The draft Convention on mutual assistance on criminal matters may potentially, if agreed in the form of the most recent draft available,[109] have a significant impact on trials with cross-border aspects. First, it should be noted that no draft of the Convention seen by the author has referred to cross-border assistance with tracing defence witnesses or the cross-border involvement of victims in trials. The provisions on evidence-gathering in the Convention presumably apply to cross-border disclosure of prosecution evidence, or evidence that might assist the defence, although it would be preferable to have explicit confirmation of the application of the 'equality of arms' principle of Article 6 ECHR.

Article 9 on cross-border hearings by video conference is particularly problematic in several respects.[110] The rules applying to cross-border hearings of witnesses and

---

[107] See *Statewatch*, July–Oct. 1997.

[108] See Arts. 6–8 of the draft published with the House of Lords Select Committee on the European Communities, *Mutual Assistance in Criminal Matters* (14th Report, 1997–8), App. 3.

[109] Note 62 above.

[110] The negotiators have apparently dropped the plans in earlier drafts to allow hearings by telephone, which had no clear rules for human rights protection and would have presented even greater practical difficulties in ensuring that the rights of the defence were protected (see Art. 12(10) of earlier draft, note 108 above). One can imagine how these judicial 'chatlines' might have been publicized to prosecuting magistrates: '[c]an't get a conviction on your own? Get a conviction on the phone!'

experts[111] require the requested Member State to agree to a request for such a hearing 'provided that the use of the video conference is not contrary to its fundamental principles of law', with the forthcoming explanatory report to explain that this phrase should not be interpreted widely.[112] The planned video conference will result in a mandatory summons to the desired witness or expert.[113] During the hearing, the witness or expert will be joined by a 'judicial authority of the requested Member State', potentially with an interpreter to assist the judicial authority.[114] The forthcoming explanatory report will explain that the requesting State *may* ask that counsel for the witness or expert be allowed to attend and the Convention provides that the requesting Member State may require that the witness have an interpreter,[115] but there is no provision for the *witness* to insist on either right on his or her own behalf. However, the witness will at least have the right to refuse to testify under the law of either the requesting or requested State,[116] although it might be hard to exercise this right without counsel present and the witness and counsel may well be unfamiliar with the conditions applying to that right in the requesting State. A footnote indicates that the subject of refusing to give evidence will be dealt with in a protocol, so it may be that the negotiators will try to weaken this clause later. Requested Member States will be obliged to apply their rules on perjury or refusal to testify when under an obligation.[117] There is no provision addressing the status of evidence given by the witness in subsequent proceedings in the requesting State, or preventing the subsequent use of the witness's evidence against the witness. More importantly, there is no reference whatsoever to the possibility of cross-examination of the witness by counsel in the requesting Member State.[118] Indeed, there is no reference to human rights protection in the provisions on hearing of witnesses and experts.

A remarkable provision follows: the final part of the draft Article 9 allows Member States to hold video conferences involving the *accused*.[119] It should be emphasized that this important provision was not in the draft of the Convention submitted to the European Parliament or the House of Lords Select Committee, and it is not known whether these bodies (or other national parliamentary bodies) are aware of the addition. Member States have the option to use this proviso by bilateral agreement, 'in conformity with their national law and relevant international instruments, including the 1950 European Convention on Human Rights'. The accused would have to give his or her consent to such hearings, and '[r]ules as may be necessary, with a view to the protection of the rights of accused persons, shall be adopted by the Council in a legally binding instrument'. A declaration to the Convention would state that such rules 'shall respect Member States' obligations' under the ECHR, but the forthcoming explanatory report will explain that cross-border hearings would

[111] It is arguable that this clause covers cross-border hearings of defence witnesses, since it does not exclude them, although since the Convention does nothing to facilitate contacting such witnesses it will likely more often be used for the benefit of the prosecution.
[112] Art. 9(2), draft Convention.   [113] Art. 9(4).   [114] Art. 9(5)(a).   [115] Art. 9(5)(d).
[116] Art. 9(5)(e).   [117] Art. 9(8).
[118] Cross-examination is not excluded as such, but it is curious that there is no reference to it. If the Convention is read as preventing cross-examination, usually it will prevent defence counsel from cross-examining prosecution witnesses, although, as suggested in note 111 above, it may sometimes prevent prosecution counsel from cross-examining defence witnesses.
[119] Art. 9(9).

still be allowed even before the Council adopts such rules. So no principles would govern these hearings before that point and there is no guarantee that the accused will be able to rely upon any national laws of the requested or requesting State which are more favourable than the minimum standards of the ECHR.

D. Non bis in idem

It must be admitted that in one area, EU third-pillar measures have contributed to human rights protection rather than diminished it: the support for an international *non bis in idem* principle. The first appearance of this principle was in a Convention agreed by the Community Member States in 1987, but it later became an important part of the Schengen Convention.[120] Anyone 'who has been finally judged' by a Schengen State 'may not be prosecuted' by another Schengen State 'for the same offences provided that, where he is sentenced, the sentence has been served or is currently being served or can no longer be carried out'. A Member State may declare that it will not apply the principle in three circumstances: where the acts related to the foreign judgment took place wholly or partly in its territory (unless they took place partly on the territory of the Member State which has already given judgment); where the acts are an offence against the derogating Member State's 'state security or other equally essential interests'; or where the acts were committed by an official of that Member State in violation of his obligations. A Member State imposing this second penalty must deduct any detention served 'on account of the offences in question' and take account, to the extent that national law permits, of the imposition of other types of sentences. Member States prosecuting an individual but suspecting that he or she has already been sentenced for a related offence in another Member State should contact the other Member State to ask for relevant information, which shall then be 'taken into consideration'. There is no explicit right for the individual to insist upon the application of this principle.

The Schengen rules have been adopted almost word-for-word in PIF and Corruption Conventions,[121] and a recent report on the operation of Schengen indicates that several early cases on the Convention relate to the application of the *non bis in idem* principle.[122] This suggests that *non bis in idem* cases may be among the earliest third-pillar references reaching the Court of Justice. The Court will thus have an early opportunity to show that it 'takes rights seriously' in the third pillar.

It is submitted that the principle must be interpreted broadly and any exceptions should be interpreted narrowly. For example, a settlement with the national authorities, a frequent occurrence in criminal proceedings over fiscal matters, should be classified as a judgment for the purposes of applying the *non bis in idem* rules. The derogation for state security or similar interests should be interpreted very narrowly, following the principles established by the Court in Community free movement cases. Indeed, a further reason for interpreting the *non bis in idem* principle widely is the deterrent effect of a threatened second prosecution on free movement of people: a person facing such a threat may be protected by his or her Member State's refusal to extradite its nationals, but only as long as he or she *does not leave that Member*

---

[120] Arts. 54–58.   [121] Note 7 above.   [122] Sch (98) 0060.

State. Finally, the Court should interpret the *non bis in idem* rule in the light of the standard criminal-justice principle that Member States often do not require a prisoner to remain in detention for the full period of his or her sentence (or, alternatively, national courts sometimes suspend sentences). Thus the period of *sentence* of deprivation of liberty should count as the period 'served' for the purposes of deducting previous periods of deprivation of liberty.

V. CONCLUSIONS

National criminal and policing laws must always strike a familiar difficult balance. Established civil liberties principles require protection for the rights of suspects, but concern for public safety leads Member States to strive for effective investigations and prosecutions. Since many crimes have cross-border aspects, and it is widely believed that the single market's free movement principles lead to more opportunities to commit cross-border crimes, the free movement of prosecutions and investigations has followed gradually in the wake of the furthering of economic freedoms. But the third-pillar types of free movement have relied almost entirely on the application of minimum human rights standards, and particularly those standards (applying to criminal investigations) which are most difficult to enforce. The risk is not only that higher national standards of human rights protection will be compromised but also that even the minimum international standards cannot be guaranteed. *Salus populi suprema lex* is an insufficient reply in a Union 'founded on the principles of liberty, democracy, respect for human rights and fundamental freedoms, and the rule of law'.

7

Access to Justice as a Human Right: The European Convention and the European Union

CAROL HARLOW*

I. ACCESS TO JUSTICE AS A HUMAN RIGHT

A Eurobarometer poll taken in 1997 records that more than 90 per cent of European citizens polled put equality before the law among rights *to be respected at all times*, while more than 80 per cent believed in a right to *legal protection* against discrimination. In sharp contrast, only 66 per cent thought the right to vote should be respected under all circumstances.[1]

This finding is somewhat surprising. Procedural rights of due process in the context of criminal trials and police action are more likely than not to be denigrated by the media, while the legal profession is certainly not used to a position at the head of the popularity stakes. One might then have expected that the principle of equality before the law would seem less fundamental to non-lawyers than those substantive human rights—the right to life, in Article 2 of the European Convention on Human Rights (ECHR), or not to be tortured in Article 3 ECHR, for example—which figure towards the top of the European Convention. Indeed, it might seem natural to categorize the latter as 'first order' rights, demoting procedural rights to the 'second order'. Lawyers would, however, certainly contest this ranking.

Lawyers tend to see substantive rights as founded on procedure, as the pre-trial and detention procedures protected by Article 5 ECHR provide security against breaches of Articles 2 and 3. This is certainly the line taken in the ECHR, probably due to the signatories' recent experience of situations in which rights to fair trial had notably been ignored. Articles 5 and 6 ECHR stress the importance of judicial process: fair trial and access to justice, in the determination of one's 'civil rights and obligations'. To modern eyes it is again surprising to find these procedural rights preferred to the 'dignitary' rights of non-discrimination protected by Article 14. In the ECHR these are essentially 'parasitic' in character, coming into operation only when

---

* My thanks are due to my research assistant, Keith Vincent, without whom this chap. could not have been written.
[1] Eurobarometer OP No. 47 (1997), 1.

another Convention right is in issue. In the American literature of rights it is, however, common to find due process characterized as a 'dignitary' right.[2] Procedural rights, notably the rights of formal equality before the law and of access to a court, are seen as an essential buttress for substantive rights; a celebrated theory of judicial review is indeed wholly based on this premiss.[3] To lawyers, in short, procedural rights are essential, even if not fundamental.

In classical legal theory procedural rights feature as central to the principle of the rule of law,[4] and the link between the rule of law principle and human rights is well established. It is, for example, acknowledged in the constitution of the International Commission of Jurists, which exists to give help to 'peoples to whom the Rule of Law is denied' and advice and encouragement to 'those who are seeking to secure the fundamental liberties of the individual'.

The rule of law was acknowledged in the Preamble to the Treaty of Rome. Subsequently, as the importance of law as an integrating force for the Community became clear, the idea was fleshed out in the jurisprudence of the Court of Justice. The signatories to the Treaty on European Union (TEU) in 1992 confirmed their 'respect for human rights and fundamental freedoms and the rule of law', and it was in this Treaty that, for the first time, specific reference was made to respect for 'fundamental rights, as guaranteed by the European Convention' (*ex* Article F.2 TEU, now Art. 6 TEU). Thus in both the ECHR and EU contexts, access to justice, legal remedy, and the rule of law occupy prominent positions, and the 'political correctness' of this attitude receives confirmation in the Eurobarometer poll cited above. Here then we have sufficient basis for a relatively high place on the rights agenda for the procedural value of access to justice.

It is when we move on to consider what might be comprised in such an agenda that there is less consensus. The content of the access to justice concept has received only nominal consideration in the context of EC law. It must include at the very least the formal right of access to a court, if only because this conception of access to justice is premissed in the rule of law ideal to which the EC Treaty accords such prominence; it has also found express recognition in the jurisprudence of the European Court of Justice. But this is a largely conceptual and formalist vision of equal access, to the law and to limit the idea of access to justice to this formalist meaning would be very restrictive. This point has been recognized by a statement from the European Court of Human Rights that:

> The Convention is intended to guarantee not rights that are theoretical or illusory but rights that are practical and effective. This is particularly so of the right to access to the courts in view of the prominent place held in a democratic society by the right to a fair trial.[5]

---

[2] See especially J. Mashaw, 'Dignitary Process: A Political Psychology of Liberal Democratic Citizenship' (1987) 39 *U Florida L Rev.* 155; J. Mashaw, *Due Process in the Administrative State* (1985); L. Tribe, *American Constitutional Law* (1988), 666.

[3] J. Hart Ely, *Democracy and Distrust: A Theory of Judicial Review* (1980).

[4] Especially in the celebrated version elaborated by A.V. Dicey, *Introduction to the Study of the Law of the Constitution* (1885).

[5] *Airey* v. *Ireland*, ECHR (1979), Series A, No 32; 2 EHRR 305, para. 24.

The concept of access to justice figures prominently also in the jurisprudence governing interest or standing to sue. There has been considerable criticism of the standing rules contained in Articles 230 and 232 (*ex* Articles 173 and 175) EC and the case for change has been made, though unsuccessfully, at the Inter-Governmental Conference before the TEU. The very prominence of the standing issue, however, creates the danger of distortion: that the case for access to justice will be whittled down to a procedural argument for new standing rules. Admittedly, access to the courtroom is an important element in access to justice, which may explain the fact that it has been accorded Treaty recognition in Article 230 (*ex* Article 173) EC. But standing is only a small part of the debate. It would be wrong to let discussion of the rule of law stop short at the level either of principle or of procedure without any consideration of societal inequality.

If access to the courtroom is a human right, then so must access to legal services be. In line with its interest in practical and effective rights, the Court of Human Rights has considered the issue of access to legal services (see section III below); the European Court of Justice (ECJ) has not yet had to pronounce generally on the issue, though questions concerning costs and legal aid have, of course, surfaced. Legal services have been welcomed on to the agenda of the Council of Europe (see section IV below). The Community[6] has only begun to scratch some surfaces.

This omission no doubt stems largely from the fact that Community competence in the area of legal services is peripheral. In the Community, justice is largely administered through the national legal systems, responsible for procedure (see section II B.1 below), while justice and home affairs have not yet been brought properly within the Community competence.[7] In governmental parlance, legal aid tends to be classified as a welfare function or social service, and welfare and social services form an extremely restricted area of Community competence. As we shall see, not only is input into legal services necessarily restricted by questions of competence but also, with the exception of consumer services, it seems peripheral to the core activities of the Community. The doctrine of subsidiarity is also a factor. We must remember the Council's exhortation that the Community should confine its activities to those subjects best undertaken at Community level.[8]

Legal aid is moreover an expensive, open-ended, social service, whose demand-led budgetary needs are hard to forecast and create a steady drain on government funds. To policy-makers, legal aid may seem a second-order need, comparable to the administration costs of a charity, certainly secondary to the right of minimum existence which underlies social assistance; or to the highly prized 'right' to health care which heads the popular list of human rights in the UK; less productive than services such as education or housing, seen as an investment in the future. Legal aid expenditure is

---

[6] To avoid complications over use of the terms EC and EU, the word Community will be used throughout this chap.

[7] The Treaty of Amsterdam inserts a new Title VI, which empowers the European Union to create an 'area of freedom, security and justice' and to develop 'common action . . . in the fields of police and judicial cooperation in criminal matters'. But this is not an area of full EC competence, nor does the ECJ have full jurisdiction: Art. 7, Amsterdam Treaty.

[8] Art. 2 (*ex* Art. B) TEU and Art. 3(b) EC, repeated in the Treaty of Amsterdam. See, for discussion, A. Duff (ed.), *Subsidiarity within the European Union* (1993). And see Intergovernmental agreements on Democracy, Transparency, and Subsidiarity: *Bull. EC* 12–1992.

under pressure in many of the Member States and, indeed, more widely throughout the common law countries which have so far led the field in their provision.[9] This chapter therefore accepts that, in a period of concern over the Community budget, it would be wholly inappropriate to ask for a substantial input of resources. This does not, however, imply that nothing should be done. Part of the defence of the Government of Ireland in the *Airey* case (see the text to note 77 below) concerned the financial implications of generalizing a right to civil legal aid. The Court of Human Rights took notice that 'the further realization of social and economic rights is largely dependent on the situation—notably financial—reigning in the State in question'. This did not deter it from insisting on civil legal aid in the case in point, in practice creating a budget line.[10]

This chapter argues that access to legal services is an important part of a human rights agenda and, further, that this is particularly the case in the Community. The Community legal order has provided a central force in integration and contributed to the core of the constitutional order.[11] Yet, in the absence of a centralized administration, law enforcement is often left to private parties exercising their rights under Community law in national courts.[12] Yet public legal services in many Member States are rudimentary, and where they were formerly good, they are currently, as already remarked, under pressure. Thus this chapter—while it does not argue for a large input of resources—argues that legal services, as the practical dimension of the right of access to the court, should occupy a larger place in Community policy-making.

Again, the chapter does not argue for controversial extensions of competence; indeed this would be perverse in the light of *United Kingdom* v. *Commission*,[13] which brakes the Commission's power to incur significant expenditure or to fund action programmes not authorized by prior adoption of a basic act sanctioning expenditure. A legal basis is essential for any substantial budget line. Nor does the chapter seek to rely on Treaty amendment, unlikely to be forthcoming in the near future. Instead it concentrates on the useful work which can be done within existing competences, adding on to policy initiatives which are already under way and listing incremental improvements and initiatives which might form a useful periphery to a substantive European human rights agenda. Finally, the chapter suggests maximization of resources through co-operation, rather than the customary competition between the two main European policy-making bodies, the European Commission and Council of Europe.

To summarize, the chapter argues that, without added competences or Treaty amendment, without heavy demands on resources, there is much which can be done by the Community to provide better legal services to its citizens.

[9] See R. Smith (ed.), *A Strategy for Justice, Publicly Funded Legal Services in the 1990s* (1992). In the UK, the situation has worsened since the publication of this research.

[10] *Airey* v. *Ireland*, note 5 above.

[11] See J.H.H. Weiler, 'Journey to an Unknown Destination: A Retrospective and Prospective of the European Court of Justice in the Arena of Political Integration' (1993) 31 *J Common Mkt. Stud.* 417.

[12] The Commission possesses important law-enforcement functions under Art. 226 (*ex* Art. 169) EC but in practice these are limited to monitoring incorporation of EC law into national law.

[13] Case C–106/96, *UK* v. *Commission*, 12 May 1998.

II. ACCESS TO JUSTICE AND THE COURTS OF THE EUROPEAN UNION

A. Right of Access to the Court

The ECJ has so far adopted a limited view of access to justice. The starting point has been a classical and largely formalist interpretation of the rule of law with emphasis on formal 'equality before the law', a central aspect, as already noted, of the rule of law principle. There is a clear link too between the priority accorded by the ECJ to the rule of law ideal and the doctrine of 'direct effect', according to which rights in EC law are enforceable through actions brought by private parties in the courts of the Member States.[14] Thus the ECJ has concentrated on the enforcement, interpretation, and determination of rights through *access to the court*.

The right of access to justice receives implicit recognition inside the doctrine of direct effect; indeed, it is fair to describe direct effect as premised on a right of access to justice. The seminal case of *Van Gend en Loos*[15] operated to confer upon individuals under EC law 'rights which become part of their legal heritage'. From then on, legal enforcement by 'individuals' became a central feature of the Court's integration strategy.[16] A division of competence was established between the EC and national legal systems, according to which the ECJ ruled definitively on the principles of EC law (which after *Van Gend* were paramount in all areas of EC competence), while national legal systems provided the machinery for the enforcement of rights under EC law. Questions of procedural law, including the rules on standing, were properly left to national law.[17] Latterly, this division of labour has broken down. The ECJ has on the one hand increased its pressure for the removal from national legal systems of procedural rules inhibiting the enforcement of rights under EC law;[18] and on the other has insisted on the creation of remedies in national law where none were previously in existence.[19] It is significant for the argumentation of this chapter that these developments are usually justified in terms of the principle of equal access to justice through the Community.

In the crucial case of *Marguerite Johnston*,[20] the applicant sought to challenge a policy not to issue arms to female police officers as incompatible with Article 119 (now Article 141) EC and the directives made thereunder, which guarantees equality of the sexes in employment. Article 6 of Council Directive 76/207 acknowledged the right of access to justice, requiring that persons aggrieved should be able 'to pursue

---

[14] See E. Szyszczak, 'Making Europe More Relevant to its Citizens' (1996) 21 *EL Rev.* 351.

[15] Case 26/62, *Van Gend en Loos* v. *Nederlandse Administratie der Belastingen* [1963] ECR 1.

[16] P.P. Craig, 'Once Upon a Time in the West: Direct Effect and the Federalisation of EEC Law' (1992) 12 *OJLS* 453.

[17] Case 33/76, *Rewe-Zentralfinanz eG and Rewe-Zentral AG* v. *Landwirtschaftskammer für das Saarland* [1976] ECR 1989.

[18] See Cases C–312/93, *Peterbroeck* [1995] ECR I–4599 and C–430, 431/93, *Van Schindelen* [1995] ECR I–4705.

[19] Joined Cases 6, 9/90, *Francovich and Bonafaci* v. *Italy*, [1991] ECR I–5357; Joined Cases C–46/93 and C–48/93, *Brasserie du Pêcheur SA* v. *Germany* and *R* v. *Transport Secretary ex p. Factortame (No 3)* [1996] ECR I–1029. And see J. Steiner, 'From Direct Effects to Francovich: Shifting Means of Enforcement of Community Law' (1993) 18 *EL Rev.* 3.

[20] Case 222/84, *Johnston* v. *Chief Constable of the Royal Ulster Constabulary* [1986] ECR 1651.

their claims by judicial process'. A public-interest defence was raised in a Northern Ireland employment tribunal through the procedural device of a ministerial certificate of public interest deemed in terms of national legislation to be conclusive and binding on the tribunal.

Questioned on the compatibility of this certificate with EC law, the ECJ ruled that:

> the principle of effective judicial control . . . does not allow a certificate issued by a national authority . . . to be treated as conclusive evidence so as to exclude the exercise of any power of review by the courts.

This decision was based on the terms of a specific directive. By the time that *Heylens*[21] fell to be decided, confidence had grown. The ECJ granted specific recognition to the right of access, ruling that:

> the existence of a remedy of a judicial nature against any decision refusing the benefit of that right is essential in order to secure for the individual effective protection of that right.

B. Procedural Access

1. Standing to Sue: Articles 230 and 232 (ex Articles 173 and 175) EC   In a paper assessing the contribution of legal process to the protection of human rights in the EU, a major non-governmental organization (NGO) recently remarked:

> In the view of many experts, the desire to protect human rights under the Treaty should be only part of a broader concern for effective judicial review across the whole field of Community law, *and the most pressing need is for an enlarged standing for individuals before the ECJ under Article 173 of the EC Treaty.* [22]

This assessment should, I think, be questioned.

Briefly, the relevant Treaty provisions allow for the ECJ to 'review the legality' of various types of 'act' of the EC institutions (Article 230 EC) or to challenge infringements of the Treaty (including failures to act) by the Member States (Articles 226, 227, 232 (*ex* Articles 169, 170, 175) EC). The ECJ may also give preliminary rulings on the interpretation of the Treaty or the validity and interpretation of Community acts after a preliminary reference from a court of a Member State (Article 234 (*ex* Article 177) EC). The Articles provide for only two types of standing. The first is privileged standing for the institutions (Commission and Council and, to a limited extent, the Parliament and Bank) and Member States. The second is standing for 'any natural or legal person', limited under Article 230 to proceedings against a decision which is either addressed, or 'is of direct and individual concern', to the challenger.

In the context of human rights, the standing provisions can be criticized on three main grounds.

First, the privileged institutional standing may seem inappropriate, in that it places the State—classically the defendant in human rights proceedings—in a position of ad-

---

[21] Case 222/86, *UNECTEF* v. *Heylens* [1987] ECR 4097. The case concerned equivalence of qualifications for football trainers and turned on the failure of the French authorities to provide a reasoned decision.
[22] JUSTICE, *Judging the European Union: Judicial Accountability and Human Rights* (1996), 12 (emphasis added). JUSTICE is the British arm of the International Commission of Jurists.

vantage, augmented by the absolute right of Member States and the institutions to intervene in proceedings between third parties before the Court (EC Statute, Article 37). No parallel right is available for private parties or NGOs, who may intervene only when directly affected. (This difficulty is dealt with more fully in section II below.) While these privileges undoubtedly reflect international law origins, they could be seen as wider than the privileges of signatory States to the ECHR.[23]

A further disparity is introduced by the differential rights accorded by Article 230(1) EC, which authorizes the review of 'acts', a term wide enough to include general legislative and regulatory acts; and the restrictive wording of Article 230(4) EC, which limits individual applicants to challenging 'decisions', narrowly construed by the Court to exclude general regulatory measures. This restriction is more stringent than that usually found in national systems of administrative law, which normally allow citizens to challenge the validity of regulation, though not always of statute law. In the context of human rights, this creates imbalance: challenge to regulation is in the hands of the privileged parties, while legislation, a frequent ground of challenge in ECHR proceedings, is out of reach of individuals.

Secondly, it is generally considered that the double test of 'direct' and 'individual' concern imposed by Article 230 EC for individual standing is too restrictive and that the rules are out of line with more generous rules of standing currently in use in national legal systems. While this is broadly true, it is worth remembering that the standing test of Article 230 is not necessarily narrower than that of the ECHR, where individual petition is confined to the '*victim* of a violation', a term construed by the Commission and Court of Human Rights to mean someone 'directly affected'. The difference may lie in the attitude of the two jurisdictions. Thus leading commentators, while noting that the ECHR does not 'provide for actions in the form of an *actio populari*', also describe:

> the elasticity of the notion of victim in the Commission's case-law as well as the uncertain and shifting boundaries between those directly affected by a particular measure and those remotely affected. [24]

Thus in the celebrated affair of *Open Door and Dublin Well Woman* v. *Ireland*,[25] women of child-bearing age were accepted as potential victims of an injunction barring abortion information in Ireland. This must be very close to an *actio popularis*.

In contrast, the ECJ has on numerous occasions confirmed its own restrictive jurisprudence on individual standing, though things may be changing.[26] The difficulty

---

[23] In addition to 'state party' proceedings, States had significant privileges in the Council of Ministers in deciding remedies, abolished by the new Prot. 11.

[24] D. J. Harris, M. O'Boyle, and C. Warbrick, *Law of the European Convention on Human Rights* (1995), 633.

[25] *Open Door and Well Woman* v. *Ireland* (1984) 38 D&R 74. Compare Case C–159/90, *SPUC* v. *Grogan* [1991] ECR I–4685.

[26] A. Albors-Llorens, *Private Parties in European Community Law: Challenging Community Measures* (1996), in an exhaustive study of individual standing, concludes (at 223) that the ECJ is making a 'continuing effort to soften the severity of the *locus standi* conditions imposed by Article 173(2) EC'. The author points to the more generous attitude in anti-dumping cases, citing Case C–152/88, *Sofrimport* [1990] ECR I–2477 and Case C–309/89, *Codorniu* v. *Council* [1994] ECR I–1853. Albors-Llorens predicts (at 228) that the CFI will be 'willing to follow the liberal trend inaugurated by the ECJ', citing the competition Cases T–3/93, T–2/93, *Société Anonyme et Participation Ouvrière Cie Nationale Air France* v. *Commission* [1994] ECR II–121 and Case T–435/93, *Aspec* v. *Commission*, 27 Apr. 1995.

has been compounded by a tendency to fuse two tests of Article 230 EC, which calls (i) for a 'decision' and (ii) for 'direct' and 'individual' concern. A 'decision' has been defined as an act which is individual in character, while an act applicable to groups generally is likely to be construed as regulatory, hence unreviewable. The requirement of 'individual' concern, on the other hand, tends to preclude review by members of a group. Once again the case law is inconsistent. For a leading commentator,[27] 'it is hard to avoid feeling that the Court decides first whether it wants the application to be admissible and then applies whichever test will produce the desired result'.

It must be said that it is common for case law on standing to be confused and even downright contradictory. Much depends on the objectives of judicial review in a particular legal system, which may be both various and variable.[28] The explanation generally advanced by the commentators[29] for the restrictive attitude of the ECJ is that it uses standing as a rationing device to keep its case-load down to manageable numbers—a perfectly legitimate objective and one of the main functions of standing rules. Thus, while discouraging direct actions, the policy of the ECJ has been to encourage preliminary references under Article 177 (now Article 234) EC, where standing is governed by the practice of the national court making the reference.[30] In some cases, where national law recognizes associational standing, allows an *actio popularis* or public interest action, or uses a 'sufficient interest' test for individual standing, this rule has had the effect of softening the Court's restrictive standing rules. On the other hand, it has had the effect of drawing attention to the disparity of national standing requirements, provoking demands for harmonization.

The third ground for criticism of ECJ standing rules lies in the absence of any specific associational standing for NGOs, which must generally bring themselves within the test for individual standing.[31] There is an important difference here between the EC Treaty and the ECHR, in that the former discourages 'group' action, while Article 25 ECHR specifically authorizes petition by a 'non-governmental organization or group of individuals'. This has undoubtedly acted as a stimulant to NGOs. In human rights litigation, in which NGOs have traditionally played a major role, lack of associational standing is a significant obstacle.

Assuming reform to be desirable, the obvious avenue is the 'enlarged standing for *individuals*' advocated in the JUSTICE report cited at note 22 above. Such an enlargement entails no fundamental change to the existing dual model of privileged and 'individual' standing, in which group and representational access by NGOs is

[27] T. C. Hartley, *The Foundations of European Community Law* (1994), 368. The leading case is Case 25/62, *Plaumann* [1963] ECR 95.
[28] See P. Cane, 'The Function of Standing Rules in Administrative Law' [1980] *PL* 303, and 'Standing up for the Public' [1995] *PL* 276; C. Sunstein, 'Standing and the Privatisation of Public Law' (1988) 88 *Colum. L Rev.* 1432 and 'Interest Groups in American Public Law' (1985) 38 *Stanford L Rev.* 29.
[29] H. Rasmussen, 'Why is Article 173 Interpreted against Plaintiffs?' (1980) 5 *EL Rev.* 114. See also N. Neuwahl, 'Article 173 Paragraph 4 EC: Past, Present and Possible Future' (1996) 21 *EL Rev.* 17. For an alternative approach, see T. Kennedy, 'First Steps Towards a European Certiorari?' (1993) 18 *EL Rev.* 121, noting Case C–343/90, *Lourenco Dias* v. *Director da Alfandega do Porto*, 16 July 1992. For criticism, see de Witte's contribution to this vol.
[30] Case 158/80, *Rewe-Handelsgesellschaft Nord mbH and another* v. *Hauptzollamt Kiel* [1981] ECR 1805 (The Butterbuying Cruises Case).
[31] C. Harlow, 'Towards a Theory of Access for the European Court of Justice' (1992) 12 *YEL* 213.

premised on that of individuals. It could be presented as an enlargement to human rights in the EU solely in terms of conformity to the principle of equality before the law.

Research studies indicate, however, that the docket of the ECJ is at present largely dominated by corporate and commercial entities,[32] an imbalance due less to rules of standing than to the limited competences of the EU. Litigation seems to bear a marked relationship to trade patterns and follows Community policy-making in being predominantly concerned with trade and commerce—company law, free movement of goods, taxation, and competition.[33] On the one hand, litigants in the Community courts must generally show themselves to be economic actors, a status increasingly reserved in modern society for corporate entities; on the other:

> large corporations doing business throughout Europe have strong incentives to support completion of the common market, and have consistently pursued this goal through litigation in which the ECJ was encouraged to assess the validity of national measures through frequent preliminary rulings.[34]

This point has been endorsed by the Commission, concerned over the protection of environmental interests:

> Access to justice is, in general, sufficiently ensured if economic interests are at stake. Enforcement of litigation designed to create the framework for prosperous business, for instance in the industrial, commercial or agricultural sector, is likely to be encouraged by economic operators with sufficient resources to fight for enforcement.[35]

There are areas (such as social security) where litigation is likely to be personal, though not necessarily individual. Again, though often collective in character and supported by unions, pressure groups, or statutory bodies, litigation on gender equality referred to the ECJ under Article 141 (*ex* Article 119) EC has contributed largely to the inventory of cases brought by individuals. The coming of the Social Charter may add to this litigation. The partial incorporation of third-pillar matters after Amsterdam may stimulate litigation in the fields of immigration, asylum, and eventually policing and criminal justice—the central core of human rights litigation in other jurisdictions. After Amsterdam a firmer commitment to human rights is incorporated in the Treaties, while the EU institutions are charged by Article F2 TEU to respect human rights and the ECHR. In time this might change the face of judicial

---

[32] C. Harding, 'Who Goes to Court in Europe? An Analysis of Litigation against the European Community' (1992) 17 *EL Rev.* 105 and, for Art. 288 (*ex* Art. 215) EC cases, F. Fines, *Etude de la Responsabilité extra-contractuelle de la Communauté* (1990).

[33] N. Brown and T. Kennedy, *The Court of Justice of the European Communities* (1994), 416–17. Later figures recorded by A. Stone Sweet and T. Brunell, *The European Court and the National Courts: A Statistical Analysis of Preliminary References, 1961–95*, Harvard Jean Monnet WP 14/97 (1997), Table 3, show that principal subject areas for Art. 234 (*ex* Art. 177) references are agriculture (12.5%); free movement of goods (14.9%); tax (8.5%) and competition (8.2%). In all except social security cases (10%), which have declined steadily since 1961, social provisions (8.8%), and free movement of workers (3.2%), commercial entities are likely to dominate. Figures cited are for 1991–5 but the pattern is relatively consistent.

[34] J. Golub, *Modelling Judicial Dialogue in the European Community: The Quantative Basis of Preliminary References to the ECJ*, EUI Working Paper, RSC No. 96/58. See also W. Mattli and A.-M. Slaughter, *Constructing the European Community Legal System from the Ground Up: The Role of Individual Litigants and National Courts*, EUI Working Paper, RSC No. 96/56, at 14–15.

[35] Communication from the Commission, *Implementing Community Environmental Law* (1996), COM(96)500, at para. 36.

review under Articles 230 and 232 EC. At present, however, opportunities for rights litigation by natural persons in the Community courts seem likely to remain limited, and corporate and commercial litigation is likely to remain the pattern for the foreseeable future.

Nor is the ECJ likely to wish to move boldly into a field already so heavily occupied as that of human rights. Such a move would inevitably increase the potential for conflict with Strasbourg[36] and national constitutional courts.[37] Although we may see increased reference to the ECHR in the jurisprudence of the ECJ, it is unlikely that it will move far from the cautious stance adopted in *SPUC* v. *Grogan*.[38] Asked whether abortion services fell within the freedom to supply services protected by Article 49 (*ex* Article 59) EC, the ECJ ruled that they did, though in the instant case an Irish restriction on access to information about such services outside Ireland did not, since the information was distributed by Irish nationals. But the Court went on to sidestep the issue of freedom of expression and to receive and impart information under Article 10(1) ECHR, for which it was harshly criticized by many commentators.[39] But the ECJ sharply distinguished its function from that of the national court:

> where national legislation falls within the field of application of Community law the Court, when requested to give a preliminary ruling, must provide the national court with all the elements of interpretation which are necessary in order to enable it to assess the compatibility of that legislation with the fundamental rights—as laid down in particular in the European Convention on Human Rights—the observance of which the Court ensures. However, the Court has no such jurisdiction with regard to national legislation lying outside the scope of Community law.

Other cases do make reference to and seek to integrate the ECHR. For example, in a recent decision concerning access to correspondence between the Commission and national courts mentioned in a Commission *Report on Competition Policy*, Article 6 ECHR is mentioned, though this is used by the Court of First Instance to deduce a public interest privilege for the Commission:[40]

> The right of every person to a fair hearing by an independent tribunal means, *inter alia*, that both national and Community courts must be free to apply their own rules of procedure concerning the powers of the judge, the conduct of proceedings in general and the confidentiality of the documents in particular.

This case was a commercial case brought by an individual, but 'in his capacity as a lawyer and member of a firm which deals with cases raising questions of competition at Community level'.

[36] Note 72 below.

[37] A.-M. Slaughter, A. Stone Sweet, and J. Weiler, *The European Courts and National Courts: Doctrine and Jurisprudence* (1998).

[38] Case C–159/90, note 25 above. Contrast Case C–368/95, *Bauer* [1997] ECR I–3689, cited by de Witte in his contribution to this vol.

[39] S. O'Leary, 'The Court of Justice as a Reluctant Constitutional Adjudicator: An Examination of the Abortion Information Case' (1992) 17 *EL Rev*. 138; J. Coppel and A. O'Neill, 'The European Court of Justice: Taking Rights Seriously' (1992) 12 *Legal Studies* 227; D. Phelan, 'Right to Life of the Unborn v. Promotion of trade and Services: The European Court of Justice and the Normative Shaping of the European Union' (1992) 55 *MLR* 670; C. Forder, 'Abortion: A Constitutional Problem in European Perspective' (1994) 1 *Maast.J Eur. & Comp.L* 56.

[40] Case T–83/96, *Gerard van der Waal* v. *Commission*, 19 Mar. 1998.

To enlarge individual standing would almost certainly stimulate a further flow of corporate and commercial litigation, increasing the advantages corporate actors already possess in the Brussels lobbying system.[41] Evidence is beginning to emerge of sophisticated litigation strategies run by commercial groups and lobbies.[42] There is a real danger that, if corporate actors were seen to be regularly invoking the ECHR to support commercial claims or procure procedural protections, there would be a whiplash effect on public opinion.

Alternative models of access might therefore prove more effective in promoting human rights litigation in the Community courts. A simple change would be to come into line with Article 25 ECHR and specifically authorize actions by a 'non-governmental organization or group of individuals'. This would need to be coupled with a minor Treaty change to Article 230(4) EC, allowing group challenges to 'acts', including legislative acts, instead of 'decisions'. But arguing for an enhanced programme of citizens' rights, the Euro Citizen Action Service (ECAS) has proposed [43] a more wide-ranging group privilege of legal action to defend rights guaranteed by the Treaty. In addition to individual rights of action, a case could 'also be introduced by associations established anywhere in the Union, provided they can demonstrate a legitimate interest'. Caution may be necessary here; such a right could unleash a flood of unexpected test cases throughout the courts of the Community.

2. Intervention: EC Statute, Articles 20 and 37   For all but the privileged parties, the present rules restrict third-party intervention in litigation before the Court to very limited circumstances. An intervener who is not a party must show a sufficient interest in the result of the case; moreover the intervener is not free to introduce a wide range of material and argument but 'can only support or request the rejection of the case already made by one of the parties with the authority of his presence in court and the ingenuity of the arguments he puts forward'.[44] In respect of references under Article 234 (*ex* Article 177) EC, intervention will be governed by the national rules, since only the privileged parties plus parties to the proceedings *before the referring court* may intervene. In practice, rights of intervention are regularly granted to trade associations, trade unions in staff cases, and other interest groups, but always subject to the proviso that an interest can be shown, usually framed in terms of repercussions on members' rights. Public-interest interventions by NGOs of the type which have become so familiar in human rights litigation[45] are unusual, being almost precluded by the stringency of the rules.

The difficulty that public-interest groups have with these rules is illustrated by the experience of BEUC, the European umbrella for consumer groups. In the *Ford*

---

[41] J. Greenwood (ed.), *European Casebook on Business Alliances* (1995) and *Representing Interests in the European Union* (1997), 101–32.

[42] R. Rawlings, 'The Euro-Law Game: Some Deductions from a Saga' (1993) 20 *JLS* 309; Mattli and Slaughter, note 34 above, at 10–12.

[43] ECAS, 'Giving Substance to Citizens' Europe in a Revised Treaty', available at: www/en/com/dg04/igc-home/instdoc/ngo/ecas.htm.

[44] K. Lasok, *The European Court of Justice: Practice and Procedure* (1994), 168. Chap. 5 provides a good account, with reference to the relevant jurisprudence. See also EC Statute, Arts. 20 and 37, with Rules of Procedure of the ECJ, 123.

[45] Harris *et al.*, note 24 above, at 668–71.

case[46] on anti-competitive practices, BEUC based a successful intervention on the procedural point that the proceedings had originated in complaints made to the Commission by BEUC and the English Consumers Association, which gave them an interest in the outcome—a narrow ground. In a later case[47] involving anti-dumping proceedings by the Commission, where BEUC had asked to be heard and submit written observations and later sought access to Commission documentation, BEUC's claim to standing was explicitly based on the argument that consumer interests could best be expressed by a representative body, the alternative of membership of consumer groups, whose members would be directly affected, being both 'unreasonable and unpracticable'. The ECJ held the action admissible on the ground that the Commission letter amounted to a 'decision' by which BEUC was 'directly affected', but went on to deny access to the documentation. The Court also made an enigmatic reference to the fact that BEUC 'might eventually be allowed to intervene' if legal proceedings between the primary parties were to transpire.

The gap left by the present rules is highlighted by a series of cases in which animal welfare was a central issue, though never central to the legal argument. This is an area in which policy disagreement between Member States has hampered progress towards uniform higher standards,[48] a cause of public disorder in the UK. In *Hedley Lomas*,[49] the UK Ministry of Agriculture and Fisheries (MAFF) had forbidden the export of live cattle to Spanish abbatoirs, seeking to justify its action in terms of the public interest exception in Article 30 (*ex* Article 36) EC, on the plea that the facilities fell below the standards required by EC law. The exporters demanded compensation. Addressing state liability, Advocate-General Leger focused narrowly on issues of integration and Member States' loyalty to the Community. There was no informed discussion of animal welfare issues. This set the tone of the judgment, in which the ECJ ruled against MAFF on the grounds (i) that enforcement powers were normally vested in the Commission and (ii) that MAFF had no real evidence of contravention by the Spanish abbatoir.

Two further cases in the UK courts involving the export of live farm stock concerned the interference with the free movement of goods occasioned by closure of ports and airports to quell demonstrations.[50] In the first, not referred to the ECJ, an intervention was accepted from Compassion in World Farming. The same group subsequently proceeded against MAFF in respect of its failure to prohibit export of calves for rearing by the 'veal crate system', in a case[51] referred to the ECJ on the question of the potential validity of a ban in terms of Article 36 (now Article 30) EC. The ECJ ruled that a ban on export of live veal cattle fell outside the terms of Article 36 once the EC had regulated the area with a valid directive (EC 91/629).

---

[46] Cases 228, 229/82, *Ford* v. *Commission* [1984] ECR 1129.

[47] Case C–170/89, *Bureau Européen des Unions des Consommateurs (BEUC)* v. *Commission* [1992] CMLR 820.

[48] On the animal welfare movement in Europe, see M. Radford, 'Animal Passions, Animal Welfare and European Policy Making' in P. Craig and C. Harlow, *Lawmaking in the European Union* (1998).

[49] Case C–5/94 *R* v. *Ministry of Agriculture and Fisheries, ex parte Hedley Lomas (Ireland) Ltd* [1996] ECR I–2553.

[50] *R* v. *Coventry City Council, ex parte Phoenix Aviation* [1995] 3 All ER 37; *R* v. *Chief Constable of Sussex, ex parte International Trader's Ferry Ltd* [1997] 3 WLR 132.

[51] Case C–196, *R* v. *MAFF, ex parte Compassion in World Farming and RSPCA*, 19 Mar. 1998.

The failure in these various judgments to treat issues of animal welfare seriously clearly justifies the intervention of the NGOs to inform courts. The series exemplifies the use of courts for campaigning purposes[52] by an NGO using techniques familiar in the field of human rights. This parallel has recently been completed by the inclusion in the Treaty of Amsterdam of an exhortatory Protocol on improved protection and respect for the welfare of animals in formulating the Community's agriculture, transport, internal market, and research policies. At national level, the NGO found no difficulty in obtaining standing and intervention rights. These bought it indirect entry to the ECJ through an Article 177 (now Article 234) reference. Had the group sought to raise a similar issue through, or intervene in, Article 173 (now Article 230) proceedings against the Commission, the doors of the Court would probably have been barred against it. Arguably, there is a need for a 'public interest action' in the Community courts if human rights points are to be appropriately represented.

3. The Public Interest Action Standing and intervention rights for public interest bodies are found in various forms in many national legal systems. In general, however, the ECJ has shown itself conspicuously unwelcoming to the public interest action. Two celebrated exceptions involve actions in national courts; Article 234 (*ex* Article 177) EC, not 230 (*ex* 173). In these cases[53] it was suggested that environmental quality standards might create directly effective rights for individuals:

> whenever the exceeding of the limit values could endanger human health, the persons concerned must be in a position to rely on mandatory requirements in order to be able to assert their rights.

But this amounts to creating an *actio popularis* in national courts, a form of standing unknown in Germany, where environmental associations have struggled to obtain nominal standing rights.[54] This must be an unwarranted extension of EC law.

By way of contrast, in *Stichting Greenpeace*,[55] Greenpeace and its national branches were involved in fighting the construction of two power stations in the Canary Islands, partly financed by the Community Regional Development Fund. In the course of the campaign they sought to access Commission documentation and, on refusal, applied to the court. Challenged on admissibility, Greenpeace argued that its standing should be determined 'in the light of criteria other than those already laid down in the case-law': in other words, an argument for a public interest action based on the practice in the Member States was advanced. Both the Court of First Instance and, on appeal, the ECJ rejected the argument, refusing out-of-hand to expand the restrictive jurisprudence of Article 173(4). This is a distinctly old-fashioned approach.

---

[52] On the use of litigation by animal welfare groups, see C. Harlow and R. Rawlings, *Pressure Through Law* (1992) 217–222.

[53] Case C–361/88, *Commission* v. *Germany* [1991] ECR I–2567, and Case C–59/89, *Commission* v. *Germany* [1991] ECR I-2607. This leads J. Hans, 'Legal Protection in European Environmental Law: An Overview' in H. Somsen (ed.), *Protecting the European Environment: Enforcing EC Environmental Law* (1996), 81, to conclude that the ECJ has endorsed the public-interest action.

[54] T. Ormond, ' "Access to Justice" for Environmental NGOs in the European Union', in S. Deimann and B. Dyssli (eds.), *Environmental Rights, Law, Litigation and Access to Justice* (1995).

[55] Case T–585/93, *Greenpeace and Others* v. *Commission* [1995] ECR II–2205 and on appeal (4 July 98).

One way to move forward would be to 'level up' through harmonization of standing provisions, widening access to the ECJ via Article 234 (*ex* Article 177). This undoubtedly involves too great an interference with the autonomy of national legal orders. More hopeful would be to build on the practice of including in EC legislation provisions on enforcement: for example, the fact that environmental actions are typically fought by collective action has been recognized in EC law by a mention of group standing in relevant environmental directives,[56] and national legislation contains precedents for vesting similar rights in consumer groups. At national level, group standing has been awarded to official and semi-autonomous entities; the English Commission for Racial Equality and Equal Opportunities Commission (EOC), for example, possess such powers which the EOC has used with some success to enforce the provisions of Article 141 (*ex* Article 119) EC on gender equality.[57] An equivalent right to fund and support or bring test cases or intervene in its own name in cases involving racism or xenophobia could be bestowed on the Vienna Monitoring Centre on Racism and Xenophobia. Any extension of the jurisdiction of the Monitoring Centre into the field of general human rights would, of course, bring with it an extension of these powers.

Alternatively, a formal right of 'access to justice' throughout the EU for 'common interest groups, which have as their object the protection of nature and the environment' has been proposed to the Commission.[58] The same approach is currently being explored by the Commission in consumer affairs. Thus Article 11 of Directive 97/7/EC on distance selling[59] contains provisions for public bodies and 'consumer organizations having a legitimate interest in protecting consumers' to take action before national courts and administrative bodies. Again, Directive 98/27/EC on injunctions for the protection of consumers' interests is concerned with 'public interest' or representative actions and not class or membership actions;[60] it concentrates on collective interests, defined as 'interests which do not include the cumulation of interests of individuals who have been harmed by an infringement'. The directive is not coercive. It sets out two options, one wider than the other, to which national legal systems should conform:

> *Whereas* one option should consist in requiring one or more independent public bodies, specifically responsible for the protection of the collective interests of consumers, to exercise the rights of action set out in this Directive; *whereas* another option should provide for the exercise of those rights by organizations whose purpose is to protect the collective interests of consumers, in accordance with criteria laid down by national law;

The Directive also requires Member States to permit any 'qualified entity', meaning a 'body or organization which, being properly constituted according to the law of a

---

[56] Launched by the Amended Proposal for a Council Dir. on civil liability for damage caused by waste [1991] OJ C192/4.

[57] Harlow and Rawlings, note 52 above, at 282–7.

[58] The proposed draft dir. is reprinted in Ormond, note 54 above. The national situations are also outlined there. A similar solution is advocated in E. Rehbinder, '*Locus Standi*, Community Law and the Case for Harmonization' in Somsen, note 53 above, at 156.

[59] Proposal for a dir. on protection of consumers in respect of contracts negotiated at a distance (distance selling), COM(92)11 final: agreed, [1997] OJ L144/1.

[60] For the distinction see Harlow, note 31 above, at 241–2.

Member State, has a legitimate interest in securing that the provisions [of the Directive] are complied with', to litigate. A list of qualified entities is to be compiled by the Commission. Statutory standing and intervention rights could certainly be the shape of things to come.

Wider, but probably more satisfactory to NGOs because it does not depend on approval of 'qualified entities' by the authorities, would be the creation of a specific public interest action in the Community courts. This solution is neater because it allows for the important questions of interventions and costs to be swept up into one package, tailored to deal with the pattern of NGO litigation as it is emerging.[61] The distinctive public interest action currently taking shape in England[62] provides a pattern. It involves special standing for a representative body or group wherever (i) a case raises important points on the use of public power by a public body and (ii) the court considers that it is in the public interest for the applicant to make the application. The body must be representative in the sense of possessing special expertise, or representing a section of the public likely to be affected by a challenged decision or possessing a statutory role in the matter; criteria similar to, though less restrictive than, those evolving in the ECJ.[63]

Admittedly, this approach raises problems of cost, delay, and inconvenience to parties, but these can be met. Intervention can, for example, be strictly limited, perhaps to a single, written brief to form part of the court file. Costs fall on the intervener, who classically must be in a position to bear them.[64] This need not, however, mean that the public interest goes unrepresented for want of resources. A prime advantage of openly acknowledging the public-interest action is precisely that it enables a sum to be set aside and ring-fenced in the legal aid budget for public interest litigation.

III. THE ECHR AND ACCESS TO JUSTICE

Turning to the wider area of access to legal services, it is not surprising to find the European Court of Human Rights making the running. Judicial redress receives specific mention as a protected right. Article 6 ECHR generally deals with access to justice[65] and Article 6(1) provides that:

[61] On which see generally Harlow and Rawlings, note 52 above, especially chap. 6. For a costs order in public interest litigation, see *R* v. *Lord Chancellor, ex parte Child Poverty Action Group* [1998] 2 All ER 755.

[62] C. Harlow and R. Rawlings, *Law and Administration* (1997), 548–52. And see Law Commission, *Administrative Law: Judicial Review and Statutory Appeals*, Law Com. No. 226 (1994), 41–4; Justice/Public Law Project, *A Matter of Public Interest: Reforming the Law and Practice on Interventions in Public Interest Cases* (1996).

[63] See *R.* v. *Inspector of Pollution, ex parte Greenpeace* [1994] 1 WLR 570. And see P. Lasok, note 44 above, at 156, 160; Case 15/63, *Lassalle* v. *European Parliament* [1964] ECR 1; Case 155/79, *AM & S Europe Ltd.* v. *Commission* [1982] ECR 1575.

[64] For the ECJ, see Lasok, note 44 above, at 157; Cases 41, 43–48, 50, 111, 113–4/73, *Générale Sucrière SA* v. *Commission* [1973] ECR 1465.

[65] Note that, while all present Member States have ratified the Convention, not all the prots. have been ratified. Prot. No.7, unratified by 7 Member States and dealing with lawfully present aliens and matters ancillary to criminal proceedings, is especially relevant to the subject matter of this chap.

In the determination of his civil rights and obligations or of any criminal charge against
him, everyone is entitled to a fair and public hearing within a reasonable time by an independent and impartial tribunal established by law.

The Court has said that there is no justification for interpreting Article 6(1) restrictively,[66] and it has certainly taken its own advice to heart.

Court of Human Rights jurisprudence has already begun to have an impact on the
administrative law of Europe. Expansive interpretation of the phrase 'civil rights
and obligations' in Article 6(1) has had the effect of reconstituting administrative
justice as a human right,[67] applicable throughout European systems of administrative law. The early case of *König* v. *Germany*[68] involved a licence to operate a clinic—
a classic public law operation. For purposes of Article 6(1), however, withdrawal of
the licence was said to involve the determination of a civil right. *Feldbrugge* v.
Netherlands[69] involved the withdrawal of sickness benefit after a finding of fitness to
work. This was the first case in which social security payments were held to entail a
civil right because 'of the predominance of features of private law'. The significance
of the case lies in the finding that the documentary procedure used by the Appeals
Board, based on a medical case-file, violated Article 6(1) because it did not allow for
'proper participation' by the applicant. These decisions are important because of
their cost implications both for national administrations and for the Community.
The Commission has a wide, indirect regulatory competence, for example, in agricultural grants, food safety, state aids, or structural grants. It has direct administrative responsibility in competition matters. These are areas which dominate the docket
of the Community courts.[70]

Differences of opinion over the applicability of Article 6(1) in proceedings
classified as administrative rather than penal have been known to bring Luxembourg into conflict with Strasbourg. Amongst the most celebrated achievements of
the ECJ is its contribution to the development of principles of administrative justice.[71] At the same time, it has been criticized for giving the Commission too much
procedural latitude. This has brought it up against the Court of Human Rights,
whose mandate in criminal proceedings has created a preference for trial-type, adversarial procedures.[72] With the continuing diffusion of Article 6(1) jurisprudence
through administrative law systems, a serious problem could arise. If Commission
practice and the attitude of the ECJ were to diverge too far from that of the Court of
Human Rights, a conflict of authority would arise which could only be settled if the
ECJ and Commission were to come into line with the Court of Human Rights. Does

[66] *Moreira de Azeredo* v. *Portugal*, ECHR (1990) Series A, No. 189 (1990) 13 EHRR 74.
[67] Bradley, 'Administrative Justice: A Developing Human Right?' (1995) 1 *EPL* 347.
[68] *König* v. *Germany*, ECHR (1978), Series A, No. 27.
[69] *Feldbrugge* v. *Netherlands*, ECHR (1986), Series A, No. 99.   [70] Note 32 above.
[71] Schwarze, 'Developing Principles of European Administrative Law' (1993) *PL* 229.
[72] Cases 47/87 and 227/88, *Hoechst* [1989] ECR 2859; Case 85/87, *Dow Benelux* v. *Commission* [1989]
ECR 3137; Case 374/87, *Dow Chemicals Iberia* v. *Commission*; Cases 87–99/87, [1989] ECR 3165; Case
374/87, *Orkem* v. *Commission* [1989] ECR 3283 discussed by Spielmann in his contribution to this vol.
Compare *Funke* v. *France* (1993) 15 EHRR 297, noted with similar jurisprudence from the Court of
Human Rights by A. Sherlock at (1993) 18 *EL Rev.* 465. And see now Cases T–213/95 and 18/96, *Stichting Certificatie Kraanverhuurbedrif (SCK) and Federatie van Nederlandse Kraanverhuurbedrijven (FNK)*
v. *Commission*, 22 Oct. 1997.

the wording of the new Article 6 TEU (*ex* Article F.2 TEU) (above) suggest that they should?

On the other hand, the insistence of the Court of Human Rights on the trial-type model brings its own problems in the form of assaults on tested systems of administrative justice.[73] This can be resolved only by a greater understanding of the needs of administrative justice and a more inventive attitude to dispute resolution,[74] a point picked up later in the chapter.

Article 6(3)(c) ECHR introduces a right to legal services and legal aid. The Article guarantees to someone charged with a criminal offence the opportunity:

> to defend himself in person or through legal assistance of his own choosing or, if he has not sufficient means to pay for legal assistance, to be given it free when the interests of justice so require.

Developed as the so-called 'equality of arms' rule, this provision has meant that legal representation may sometimes be mandatory. Thus in *Boner* v. *UK*[75] it was held that both representation and legal aid were essential to appeal against a conviction where the sentence was eight years' imprisonment and the court possessed a considerable margin of discretion in deciding the appeal. Legal aid must be positively proffered to vulnerable groups, such as minors or the mentally impaired.

The 'equality of arms' principle embodied in Article 6(3)(c) has been applied (though sparingly) to civil cases as a development of the provisions of Article 6(1) ECHR. The first step was to confirm the right of access to the court, the second to pin to it an ancillary right of access to legal advice. In *Golder*,[76] the applicant was a prisoner, who successfully complained that censorship of his correspondence in prison impeded his right to initiate civil proceedings against the prison authorities and claimed the right of uncensored correspondence with his solicitor.

A further step was taken in *Airey* v. *Ireland*,[77] undoubtedly the most significant case on the necessity for legal aid in civil proceedings. The applicant wished to petition for judicial separation in the Irish High Court but was unable to afford a lawyer. The Court of Human Rights rejected the argument that the applicant in fact enjoyed access to the court, albeit unassisted. In line with the ECHR commitment to 'practical and effective' rights, the test was whether the applicant would be able to 'present her case properly and satisfactorily', with the Court of Human Rights applying the equality of arms test and stressing the adversarial requirement:

> It seems certain to the Court that the applicant would be at a disadvantage if her husband were represented by a lawyer and she were not. Quite apart from this eventuality, it is not

---

[73] e.g., English habeas corpus and judicial review procedure: *Weeks* v. *UK* (1988) 10 EHRR 293; appeal in Dutch administrative law, *Benthem* v. *Netherlands*, ECHR (1986), Series A No. 97 (1987) 8 EHRR 1; and appeal to the Swedish Supreme Administrative Court, *Spörrong & Lonnröth* v. *Sweden* (1983), 5 EHRR 35. In all cases objection was grounded in the absence of provision for appeal on the merits, not necessarily a sound objection.

[74] R. Abraham, 'Les principes généraux de la protection juridictionnelle administrative en Europe: L'influence des jurisprudences européennes' (1997) 9 *EPLR* 577; C. Glasser and C. Harlow, 'Legal Service and the Alternatives: The LSE Tradition' in R. Rawlings (ed.), *Law, Society and Economy* (1996), 334–5; Harlow and Rawlings, note 62 above, at chap. 12.

[75] *Boner* v. *UK*, ECHR (1994), Series A, No. 300–B.

[76] *Golder*, ECHR (1975), Series A, No. 18.

[77] *Airey*, note 5 above, noted by C. Thornberry (1980) 29 *ICLQ* 250.

realistic, in the Court's opinion, to suppose that, in litigation of this nature, the applicant could effectively conduct her own case, despite the assistance which, as was stressed by the government, the judge affords to parties acting in person. [78]

This decision is the more remarkable when we learn that no legal aid was available in any form of civil proceedings in Ireland at this date. Yet the cost of obtaining judicial separation as estimated by the Irish government was relatively high: between £500–700 in uncontested, and £800–£1,200 in contested proceedings. The judgment was therefore likely to have a considerable 'ripple effect' even if applied solely to the matrimonial field.[79]

The *Airey* case draws attention to the 'inequality of arms' which may exist in practice between litigants in the various Member States. At the date of the *Airey* judgment, for example, an extensive judicare system, applicable to advice and representation in criminal and civil proceedings, had been in operation in the neighbouring UK since 1945.[80] It is on national legal orders that primary responsibility falls to ensure conformity with the ECHR; inequality of access to legal aid, advice, and services is thus a problem for national governments. In the Community, justice remains a matter for 'common action', even after Amsterdam, and 'judicial co-operation' and 'framework decisions' specified to be without direct effect (Article 29 (*ex* Article K1) TEU, Articles 27 and 29 (*ex* Article 29 and 34) Treaty of Amsterdam). This is a point to which we shall return.

IV. LEGAL AID AND THE COUNCIL OF EUROPE

The origins of the Council of Europe's legal services policy go back to the heady period of world-wide enthusiasm for access to justice, when Cappelletti's mammoth research programmes were under way at the European University Institute.[81] Access to justice was a main theme of the Ninth Conference of European Ministers of Justice held in Vienna in May 1974. A Council of Europe Committee on Legal Co-operation was established to study 'the economic and other obstacles to civil proceedings'. Studies were conducted of Member States' legal aid systems and the results of a questionnaire were later published. Following a pattern observable at national level, a committee of experts set up in 1974 gave its main attention to legal aid and advice, publishing a number of resolutions aimed at establishing minimum standards and co-ordination; in 1980, however, attention turned to the simplification of civil justice procedure.[82]

---

[78] 2 EHRR 314–5.
[79] *Ibid.*, at 310. The Irish government expressed its intention of introducing legal aid in family law matters by the end of 1979.
[80] Outlined in R. Smith, *Justice: Redressing the Balance* (1997), chap. 1. And see B. Abel-Smith and R. Stevens, *Lawyers and the Courts* (1967).
[81] M. Cappelletti and B. Garth (eds.), *Access to Justice* (1978), 3 vols. See also M. Cappelletti *et al.*, *Toward Equal Justice: A Comparative Study of Legal Aid in Modern Societies* (1975).
[82] Recommendation R (81) 7 on measures facilitating access to justice (adopted 14 May 1981), reprinted in Council of Europe, *The Administration and You* (1996), 375.

Under the terms of the initial resolution,[83] a Member State must grant to nationals of other Member States, as well as to habitual residents, the same treatment in matters of legal aid as accorded to their own nationals.

A later resolution on the protection of physical and legal persons in the face of administrative authorities[84] requires that a person concerned 'may be assisted or represented in the administrative procedure'. It does not, however, deal with legal aid—perhaps as well, since legal aid in administrative proceedings is frequently hard to come by. This is left to a later resolution,[85] the Preamble to which moves into the modern era by insisting that:

> facilitating the provision of legal aid should no longer be regarded as a charity to indigent persons but as an obligation of the community as a whole.

An annex to the resolution contains a series of important principles governing legal aid, stated to be applicable 'before any court determining civil, commercial, administrative, social or fiscal matters'. The Preamble recommends governments to take 'all measures which they consider necessary with a view to the progressive implementation of the[se] principles'. The legal aid principle was carried into Eastern Europe by the Demosthenes (1989) and Themis (1993) programmes, designed to assist in establishment of the rule of law in ex-Communist societies. The latter counselled a necessity for state-funded legal aid services.

A final recommendation[86] acknowledges the need for alternative dispute resolution (ADR), referring to the escalating case-load as liable to interfere with everyone's right to a hearing within a reasonable time under Article 6(1) ECHR. It invites governments to encourage conciliation, mediation, and friendly settlement of disputes 'either outside the judicial system, or before or during judicial proceedings'. It also recommends arbitration, and the provision of extrajudicial machinery for small claims and other specified areas of law. Here we have the standard components of an ADR programme which reflects world-wide interest in ADR, as governments take fright at the growing legal aid bill, the escalating number of complaints about and to government and its agencies, backlogs and delay in courts, and the cost of litigation.[87]

---

[83] Resolution (76) 5 on legal aid in civil, commercial, and administrative matters (adopted by the Committee of Ministers, 18 Feb. 1976), in Council of Europe, note 82 above, at 332.

[84] Resolution (77) 31 on the protection of the individual in relation to the acts of administrative authorities (adopted 28 Sept. 1977), note 82 above, at 336, 344.

[85] Resolution (78) 8 on legal aid and advice (adopted 2 Mar. 1978), note 82 above, at 346. This may be the work of a committee recorded in the previous Resolution (note 82 above, at 344) as already engaged in a comprehensive examination of legal aid.

[86] Recommendation R(86) 12 concerning measures to prevent and reduce the excessive workload in the courts (adopted 16 Sept. 1986), note 82 above, at 418.

[87] See R. Abel (ed.), *The Politics of Informal Justice: The American Experience* (1982); *Dispute Resolution: Civil Justice and Its Alternatives*, *MLR* Special Issue (1993) 56 *MLR* 277–470 and R. Smith (ed.), *Achieving Civil Justice, Appropriate Dispute Resolution for the 1990s* (1996). For the UK, see also Lord Woolf, *Access to Justice, Report to the Lord Chancellor on the civil justice system in England and Wales* (1996). The interim report is reviewed in a comparative context in R. Cranston and A. Zuckerman (eds.), *The Woolf Report Reviewed* (1995).

V. AN AGENDA FOR ACCESS TO JUSTICE

In devising a Community agenda for access to justice, it is best to build on what is already happening. Work is most advanced in consumer policy, probably because in this area the Community competence is undisputed. As early as 1993, a Green Paper was published on the settlement of consumer disputes in the single market.[88] The second action plan[89] listed access to justice, and especially minor consumer disputes, as an area in which the 'Europe of the consumer' had yet to be realized. A contemporaneous article from BEUC[90] described cross-border consumer transactions as 'a legal quagmire'. Noting the small number of cross-border disputes pursued by consumers, the writer catalogued the many good reasons not to pursue such cases. One problem was the patchy provision for collective action, typically restricted to action on behalf of domestic consumers. Another obstacle was the difficulty of obtaining free legal advice or aid, when the national schemes applied only to domestic litigation. BEUC asked (i) for harmonization of national consumer law and (ii) Community action to facilitate cross-border complaints.

An action plan on consumer access to justice and the settlement of consumer disputes[91] containing an initiative for the promotion of 'extra-juristic procedures' followed. The strategy of the resulting directives is to use consumers to police consumer law, partly through public-interest actions in national courts.[92] But a novel and interesting facet of the directives is the concern with settlement. Thus Directive 98/27/EC on injunctions for the protection of consumers' interests[93] allows Member States to provide for litigation to be started only after the party has made an attempt at settlement with the defendant with or without the help of a 'qualified entity' or consumer group listed by the Member State. This provision seems to give consumer groups the dual role of representing the collective consumer interest and mediating individual disputes, a combination usually considered unsatisfactory.

The progression of this programme suggests an interesting parallel with developments in the public sector. Throughout Europe, there has been in recent years a real determination to open up public services and make them more responsive to their 'customers'. Alongside sophisticated systems of judicial review, a 'bottom up' complaints culture has been developed as an essential component of the Citizen's Charter movement.[94] The original UK Charter was intended to raise the standards of delivery of public services and to empower the citizen when the service delivered was sub-standard. An effective complaints system was a management tool, allowing the public to tell organizations how they matched up to the standards they set themselves. This is very like the Commission strategy for consumer enforcement of EC

[88] COM(93)576 final.
[89] Second Action Plan, 1993–5, 'Placing the single market at the service of consumers', COM(93)378 final.
[90] M. Goyens, 'Cross-Border Disputes: A Legal Quagmire' (1993) 3 *Consumer Policy Rev.* 92.
[91] COM(96)13 final: *Bull. EU* 1/2–1996, at 1.3.218.   [92] See text to note 60 above.
[93] Art. 5 of Dir. 98/27/EC on injunctions for the protection of consumers' interests: Commission proposal COM(95)712 final.
[94] *The Citizen's Charter, Raising the Standard* (1991). For the parallel with the private sector see C. Adamson, 'Complaints Handling: Benefits and Best Practice' (1991) 1 *Consumer Policy Rev.* 196.

consumer law. The complaints procedures outlined by the Citizen's Charter Unit (playing the role of the Commission in standard-setting through the UK public service) went on to specify that complaints systems should be:[95] easily accessible and well-publicized; simple to understand and use; speedy, responsive, and communicative; fair, with a full and impartial investigation; and effective in the sense of providing appropriate redress. A majority of complaints should be settled internally. Only intractable complaints should move on to an external complaints system such as an ombudsman, alternatively to the judicial level. Here again the interest in appropriate dispute resolution parallels that of the Commission.[96]

The Commission's interest in ADR extends into environmental matters, where it currently has under consideration the need to establish minimum criteria for procedures to handle environmental complaints. New, user-friendly complaints mechanisms are clearly seen as an alternative to courts, of which the Commission remarks:

> [E]ven apart from questions of access, there are inherent problems within legal systems, including eg. costs and delays, which can make it unhelpful as a means for individuals to enforce Community environmental law: litigation should be the solution of last resort. A non-judicial complaint investigation procedure could have the advantage of avoiding these inherent problems: it could contribute to a quick and low cost settlement of an issue more accessible to the citizen without any need for legal assistance.[97]

Suggested procedural Guidelines might cover:[98]

> the power to receive complaints (eg. both from individuals and from non-governmental organizations) regarding the procedures for administrative decisions affecting the environment, to request information from administrative bodies in response to such complaints, and to issue recommendations (which would be persuasive rather than of a legally binding nature).

Yet the Commission draws back from the logical deduction, concluding that it would not be necessary:

> for such a mechanism to rule on questions of substance, which are more appropriately considered either by administrative bodies or the courts, according to the administrative and legal systems within the Member States.

This is the downside of the creeping growth of Article 6(1) ECHR jurisprudence and the parallel jurisprudence of the ECJ on access to the court. It is in fact very hard today to exclude judicial remedy, and this hampers the development of alternatives. Appropriate boundary lines need to be developed.

This chapter forms part of a human rights project, to which consumer rights are clearly peripheral, even if environmental law is beginning to be included within the fold. Yet outside the area of consumer justice (where consumer interests do not receive recognition as human rights) and enforcement of environmental law, the role of the Community is arguably limited. So is there a place for legal services in a human

---

[95] Citizen's Charter Unit, *Effective Complaints Systems: Principles and Checklist* (1993); *If Things Go Wrong...*, Discussion Papers 1–5 (1994); *Putting Things Right* (1995); *Good Practice Guide* (1995).

[96] Options are discussed in Harlow and Rawlings, note 62 above, at chap. 12 and later chaps.

[97] Communication from the Commission, *Implementing Community Environmental Law*: COM(96)500, para. 31.

[98] *Ibid.*, at para. 33.

rights agenda for the Community? The comparative success of the gender equality programme in the Community (Article 141 (*ex* Article 119) EC) suggests that there is. Statutory bodies at national level have played their part in supplying information and supporting a test case strategy in the ECJ; at Community level, the Commission has helped with networking and feedback into national legal systems.[99] A new Treaty commitment made at Amsterdam[100] empowers the Commission and Council to 'take appropriate action' to combat discrimination based on racial and ethnic origin, religion or belief—a traditional human rights formulation. Who can doubt that a strategy based on legal action would be appropriate here?

An extended role for the Community in promoting legal services thus seems unavoidable. As already indicated, the Council of Europe has so far made the running. Its concern with human rights is more direct. It started earlier. Its programme is more coherent and more advanced than work in the Community, divided perforce between Commission Directorates. The preamble to the initial resolution of the Council of Europe's Committee of Ministers reads like a blueprint for a legal services agenda in the Community and falls well within the Treaty competences:[101]

> Considering that with a view to eliminating economic obstacles to legal proceedings and permitting persons in an economically weak position more easily to exercise their rights in member states, it is expedient to secure equality of treatment in granting legal aid to nationals of member states of the Council of Europe and to those aliens for whom equality of treatment appears to be most justified . . .

The principles set out in Council of Europe resolutions are general in character and respect the subsidiarity principle. A 'minimum standards' approach has been adopted, leaving modalities to be decided by the national authorities within their budgets and in the context of the different legal systems. Given the huge disparities in funds and standards, this is wise.

BEUC's strictures with respect to legal aid and advice have so far been met in the Community by publication of a handbook.[102] A study is also under way to encourage removal of obstacles to cross-border legal aid,[103] in practice likely to benefit those involved in consumer or commercial disputes. In common with former studies,[104] this chronicles divergent schemes for legal aid at national level. Criteria for eligibility differ. Not all systems cover cross-border applications or third party nationals. Methods of delivery range from *pro bono* action by the legal profession, through public legal services and law centres, to legal insurance. Not only legal services but information about them are difficult to access. These barriers are difficult to dismantle when responsibility for legal services is split in three or more ways, between the Council of Europe, the Community, Member States, and often regional bodies, such as the German *Länder*.

---

[99] C. Docksey, 'The European Community and the Promotion of Equality' in C. McCrudden (ed.), *Women Employment and European Equality Law* (1987).

[100] Art. 13, Amsterdam Treaty.   [101] Resolution (76) 5, note 83 above.

[102] D. Walters, *Guide to Legal Aid and Advice in the European Economic Area* (1996).

[103] A. Wood, Jean Monnet Chair in European Legal Studies, Univ. of Angers, 'Access to Legal Aid in the Member States of the European Economic Area: Problems and Tentative Solutions' (unpublished conference paper). The initiative is that of the Justice and Home Affairs Unit of the Commission.

[104] Notably that of Cappelletti and Garth, note 81 above.

The Commission action plan for 1996–8 acknowledged the limited action taken to inform and educate consumers: 'since consumers' ability to "self protect" is fundamentally linked to knowledge, it is indeed imperative to endeavour to improve this aspect considerably'. This objective is transferable to human rights and should be linked with developments in the citizenship programme. At least since Maastricht, the need to make the Union more transparent and bring it closer to its citizens has been acknowledged.[105] By and large the EU institutions have responded to the challenge of information technology and are using it to make their work more transparent, and this is represented also in the work of a high-level expert group.[106] All the material so far cited is, for example, available on the Internet in the Community languages, as is the current jurisprudence from the Community courts. Interactive programmes, allowing citizen participation in Commission initiatives, are also being developed.[107] This type of information is helpful to NGOs and advisers but it does not yet reach out to individuals.

The provision of legal services is heavily information-based, yet the introduction of technology to facilitate consumer access is in its infancy. Experiments are under way with telephone advice services. Electronic kiosks are coming into use in some North American courts. These guide litigants through the process of completing forms necessary for small claims, where litigants are typically not legally aided.[108] An international legal services network (www.ilsn.org) has been set up to exchange information on legal services. Underfunded, this is at an experimental stage, needing funding, experiment, and extension. There is as yet no European umbrella organization for legal services and no European legal network. Proactive measures are essential for the dissemination of information about EC law, and Commission support for development in this sphere falls clearly within its mandate. This will be enhanced when the Treaty of Amsterdam is ratified, making provision for specified measures in the field of co-operation in certain matters of civil justice.[109]

In one area more than any other, legal services are essential. Among the most important obligations binding Member States is that enshrined in the 1951 Geneva Convention relating to the Status of Refugees not to return a refugee to a country where he or she would be in danger.[110] Although the ECHR does not specifically guarantee rights of asylum, it has been held that the extradition of a non-national to face a real risk of torture or inhuman treatment contravenes Article 3 ECHR.[111]

---

[105] TEU Declaration No. 17 on the right of access to information; Intergovernmental agreements on Democracy, Transparency and Subsidiarity: *Bull. EC* 12–1992.

[106] *Building the European Information Society For Us All: Final Report of the High-Level Expert Group* (1997) discussed in Agenda of the *Comité des Sages* and Final Project Report. In Academy of European Law, *Leading by Example: A Human Rights Agenda for the European Union for the Year 2000* (1998), 103.

[107] As, e.g., the ECAS proposals cited at note 43 above.

[108] R. Smith (ed.), *Shaping the Future: New Directions in Legal Services* (1995), 82; and *Achieving Civil Justice: Appropriate Dispute Resolution for the 1990s* (1996), 38–42.

[109] New Title III, Arts. 57 and 65 (*ex* Arts. 73c and m).

[110] Art. 33, Convention relating to the Status of Refugees, adopted on 28 July 1951 by the UN Conference of Plenipotentiaries on the Status of Refugees and Stateless Persons convened under GA Res. 429 (V) (1950). In United Nations, *A Compilation of International Instruments* (1994), i, Part 2, 638.

[111] *Soering* v. *UK*, ECHR (1989), Series A, No. 161; *Cruz Varas* v. *Sweden*, ECHR (1991), Series A, No. 201; and *Vilrajah* v. *UK*, ECHR (1991), Series A, No. 215, suggest that the circumstances in which the right can successfully be claimed will be very exceptional.

Chahal v. *UK*[112] takes this jurisprudence into the procedural area. Here the Court of Human Rights found breaches of Articles 5(4) (remedy to challenge legality of detention) and 13 (right to an effective remedy) when a panel of advisers to which the matter had been referred by a Minister declined to operate a trial-type procedure, did not permit legal representation, gave no reasons for its decisions, and consequently could not be fully reviewed by a court. Procedural *lacunae* have become more visible with the entry of the Community into the field of immigration and asylum.

Common migration policies have been on the Community agenda since the Single European Act of 1986 stipulated free movement of persons within its borders.[113] The Schengen Agreement initiated common internal borders in 1985 and has since been extended.[114] Schengen provided for common provisions on visas, common immigration rules, and border control procedures. Co-operation was extended by the Dublin Convention,[115] which removed the right of asylum-seekers to apply for asylum in more than one signatory State. Other resolutions deal with manifestly unfounded asylum applications and safe third countries. There was little control over policy-making in an area where the ECJ lacked jurisdiction.[116] A new Treaty Title inserted at Amsterdam helps by taking immigration, asylum, and border controls into the Community proper and extends the jurisdiction of the ECJ to such matters.[117] A protocol annexed to the TEU integrates the Schengen *acquis* into the Community.

In 1995, a Council Resolution set out to provide minimum guarantees for asylum applications and to establish procedural rules. It guarantees a right of appeal and provides for asylum procedure to have legislative force in each Member State. Further, it sets out procedural guarantees, including access to an interpreter and legal adviser; the right to a written decision; an adequate time to appeal; and a right to remain pending appeal other than in cases involving a 'safe third country'. Yet a study made for NGOs in 1998 of implementation of the third-pillar requirements on visas and asylum procedures[118] reveals enormous divergence in national procedures. Appeal, which lies at the heart of effective procedural protection for asylum-seekers, is not always available. It may sometimes be lodged only from outside the country, in-

---

[112] See also *R* v. *Secretary of State for the Home Department, ex parte Chahal* [1995] 1 All ER 658.

[113] See for an extended account S. Collinson, *Migration, Visa and Asylum Policies in Europe* (1995); E. Guild, *The Developing Immigration and Asylum Policies of the European Union* (1996).

[114] See Convention Applying the Schengen Agreement of 14 June 1985 between the Governments of the States of the Benelux Economic Union, the Federal Republic of Germany and the French Republic on the Gradual Abolition of Checks at their Common Borders, Schengen, 19 June 1990. Reprinted in H. Meijers *et al.*, *Schengen: Internalisation of Central Chapters of the Law on Aliens, Refugees, Privacy, Security and Police* (1992), 177.

[115] Convention Determining the State Responsible for Examining Applications for Asylum Lodged in One of the Member States of the Community, Dublin, 15 June 1990. Entered into force 1 Sept. 1997 [1997] OJ C254/1.

[116] E. Guild, 'The Constitutional Consequences of Lawmaking in the Third Pillar of the European Union' in Craig and Harlow, note 48 above.

[117] Art. 68 (*ex* Art. 73p), Amsterdam Treaty extends Art. 234 (*ex* Art. 177) procedure but the reference may only be made by a final court.

[118] S. Peers, *Mind the Gap! Ineffective Member State Implementation of European Union Asylum Measures* (1998).

creasing difficulties with access to information and legal aid and services. The author
concluded that:

> important aspects of procedural protection have not been harmonized effectively by the
> minimum guarantees resolution. Some Member States do not provide for translation of
> the rejection reasons given to the applicant. Most do not have an effective system for in-
> forming a third state that the asylum seeker's application has not been examined as to
> substance, leaving a risk that the third state will then itself reject the admissibility of the
> asylum-seeker's claim without a substantive examination. More importantly, there are
> substantial divergences on the core issues of procedural protection. Member States fall
> into three camps on the treatment of asylum-seekers who make an appeal against an ini-
> tial negative decision, including those states that will not provide any suspensory effect
> of 'safe third country' and/or manifestly unfounded appeals; those states which allow for
> limited possibility of requesting such suspensory effect; and those which allow auto-
> matic suspensory effect. There are also huge divergences in treatment of asylum-seekers
> at the border. In several cases, the ability to make an application at the border is not
> available in practice, a clear breach of one of the most important guarantees in the reso-
> lution. [119]

Cross-border problems also arise. Dutch observers note, for example, that entry
to the Netherlands after Schengen has grown harder, as migrants have to conform to
Dutch rules and those of other Schengen States. Refusal of an entry visa might now
be based on a French exclusion order registered on the common database, which
would have to be contested in France. The French court might interpret the Schengen admissions criteria differently from a Dutch court, but there is as yet no common
court to which individuals can appeal; even after Amsterdam, Article 234 (*ex* Article
177) reference will be restricted. Yet a comparative study covering four of the EU
countries found much disparity[120] in access to legal aid and advice. Legal aid was frequently not available and registration of advisors was exceptional.

The significance of access to justice, in the sense both of access to an independent
court and of access to legal advice and help in circumstances like these is fairly obvious, and the manifest deficiencies point to the need for immediate co-ordination.
Harmonization of appeal procedures, together with improvement in the standard of
immigration advice, is imperative. Immigration problems should become a priority
area for legal services.

VI. CONCLUSIONS

This chapter has tried to identify a place for access to justice in a human rights
agenda. This involves establishing new priorities. As with environmental issues, an
'access to justice' audit and legal aid impact assessment should accompany all new
policy-making. This assessment could act as a basis for new proposals for legislation.

---

[119] *Ibid.*, at 16–17.
[120] Unpublished study carried out for the Lord Chancellor's Department by JUSTICE, Dec. 1997,
covering the regulation of immigration advice and assistance in Australia, Canada, The Netherlands,
Denmark, Germany, and Austria.

The need for such an initiative is highlighted by the draft regulations sent to the Parliament in August 1998 which deal with the legal base for Community action in the sphere of human rights.[121] These justify Community action in:

> (a) promoting and strengthening the rule of law, in particular upholding the independence of the judiciary and strengthening it, and support for a humane prison system; support for constitutional and legislative reform;
> (b) promoting the separation of powers, particularly the independence of the judiciary.

This text is notable on the one hand for its allusion to a classical conception of the rule of law principle; centuries of European political philosophy are implicit in these paragraphs. On the other hand, it is notable for what is not said. How is the rule of law to be strengthened and promoted without access to legal services? This point is sufficiently important to have been spelt out.

The English Legal Action Group has recently set out principles for legal services which, as adapted below, could serve as a starting point for promotion of a·Community policy for legal services:

> —Access to justice is a constitutional right
> —The goal is not only procedural but substantive justice
> —People have need for legal assistance in respect of civil, criminal and sometimes administrative law
> —Access to justice requires policies which include education and information
> —Programmes for legal services must take account of realistic levels of resources but these should be seen as limiting policies rather than as defining them
> —The full potential of technological advances must be harnessed

As I have argued, legal services are especially important to persons charged with criminal offences (Article 5 ECHR) and to immigrants, who risk deportation to countries where they may suffer cruel and inhuman treatment. Throughout the Schengen area, a right of access for asylum-seekers to legal advice should be established. Using the technique of minimum harmonization, a threshold of legal advice and representation to which national immigration and asylum procedures must conform should be specified. Minimum standards for immigration advisory services should also be established and consideration given to accreditation. A network of immigration NGOs is already in being, and some funding has been made available to them by the Commission for research and policy-making. Funding should be made available to NGOs and impartial observers for the specific purpose of monitoring implementation of asylum procedures, including the quality and availability of advice.

Funding for group representation in public-interest actions should also be assured. A limited fund could be set aside and administered by the ECJ as part of the tiny legal aid budget for such cases.[122] It might be possible for a minimum standard provision for the same purposes in Member States to be agreed.

---

[121] These paras. are cited and further discussed in the Agenda of the *Comité des Sages* and Final Project Report, note 106 above, at 76–80.

[122] The present legal aid budget is indeed tiny, the 1998 appropriation amounting to 20,000 ECUS: EC Budget [1998] OJ L44/1.

This implies the creation of a 'public-interest action' in the ECJ and Court of First Instance permitting associational representation in cases where an issue of public interest—the invalidity of general legislation or of a decision where no individual interest is affected—arises. A study of standing in national legal systems should be undertaken, with a view to (i) encouraging voluntary measures of harmonization and (ii) drafting guidelines for minimum standards. Statutory standing, at least to environmental and consumer groups, is another alternative. Intervention rights for NGOs in the ECJ should be developed and formalized in rules or guidance. These changes could be of particular importance in human rights cases, which in other jurisdictions are classically litigated by NGOs. Programmes on procedural law should ideally be undertaken under the ægis of the ECJ in collaboration with national courts. In such a framework, a working party to examine the practice of Member States and make recommendations would be useful.

Work is also needed on forms of dispute resolution appropriate for use within the Community. The spread of the Citizens' Charter movement provides a prototype for complaints handling, while the European Ombudsman, whose office itself represents a form of ADR widely accepted through the Member States, could also play an important part in developing access to appropriate justice for individual citizens. This could be part of the Community's citizenship initiatives.

Again as part of citizenship initiatives, the Commission's Legal Service should play an increased role in information and education about access to justice throughout the Union. As has been done in other areas, notably with women's, consumers', and environmental networks, the Commission should encourage the setting up of appropriate legal services networks. It should help them with information technology to disseminate information. A legal services network on the internet; video programmes sited in national courts; and 'lawyer to lawyer' campaigns could all form part of the programme. The Commission could also play a role in co-ordinating national policies on legal aid, as it is starting to do in cross-border litigation and consumer disputes. Research should not be forgotten. The full extent of problems with access to legal aid and services is under-researched and itself hard to access.

This agenda is not over-ambitious. Only the question of extended access to the Community courts and the creation of a general public-interest action would require Treaty amendment, and even this could be avoided if the nomination of qualified entities in Community legislation were adopted. Much of the work in the area of legal services is already under way, as part of one or another existing initiative. The way forward is simply through incremental generalization. Council of Europe prototypes can also provide a model.

The only new and costly initiatives on this agenda involve racism and migration. Surely humanity demands that in this area legal services are taken seriously?

8

Gender Equality in the EU: A Balance Sheet

CATHERINE BARNARD[1]

> ... the principle which regulates the existing social relations between the two sexes—the legal subordination of one sex to the other—is wrong in itself, and now one of the chief hindrances to human improvement; and that it ought to be replaced by a principle of perfect equality, admitting no power or privilege on one side, nor disability on the other.
>
> J.S. Mill, *The Subjection of Women* (1869).

The realization of sex equality has been the central and most highly developed pillar of the European Community's fragile social policy. For the Commission, equal opportunities is the 'legal framework reflecting social policy at European level [which] has been a catalyst for change in the Member States'.[2] The importance of equal opportunities to the Community is underlined in the Commission's vision of a 'European social model'. This is based around the 'values of democracy and individual rights, free collective bargaining, the market economy, equality of opportunity for all and social welfare and solidarity'.[3] Equal opportunities also appears as one of the four pillars around which the employment guidelines, intended to co-ordinate Member States' employment policies from 1998,[4] are structured.

While there is general agreement that equal opportunities is a 'good thing' this is also where the consensus ends. For many years the debate about sex equality has focused on the sameness/difference argument. Should women aspire to being the same as men, and enjoy the same rights (the symmetrical approach)? Or should women campaign to have their differences from men recognized in law (the asymmetrical approach)?[5] Either way 'law', enforced through individual rights, is seen as the way to resolve the difficulties. However, some feminists see a liberal rights-based approach as a vehicle for entrenching the real inequalities which women face and that

---

[1] I am grateful to T. Hervey, K. Paradine and the participants in the Brussels conference, May 1998.

[2] White Paper on Social Policy, COM(94)333, at 41.   [3] *Ibid.*

[4] Presidency Conclusions: Extraordinary European Council Meeting on Employment Luxembourg, 20 and 21 Nov. 1997. Available at: http://europa.eu.int/en/comm/dgos/elm/summit/en/papers/concl.htm.

[5] As Mackinnon argues: '[u]nder the sameness standard, women are measured according to our correspondence with man, our equality judged by our proximity to his measure. Under the difference standard, we are measured by our lack of correspondence with him, our womanhood judged by our distance from his measure. Gender neutrality is thus simply the male standard, and the special protection rule is simply the female standard, but do not be deceived: masculinity or maleness, is the referent for both': C. Mackinnon, *Feminism Unmodified: Discourses on Life and Law* (1987), 34. Cf. C. Gilligan, *In A Different Voice: Psychological Theory and Women's Development* (1982).

it does more harm than good in practice.[6] Further, they argue that law is a masculine construct and serves to reinforce male power, and that the legal instruments that protect women have been developed primarily by men in a male-oriented world.[7] Others are more pragmatic and see law as a useful, albeit limited, vehicle for attaining social goals and that a rights discourse offers a significant vocabulary in which to formulate political and social grievances.[8] They argue that it is important that law be reinterpreted to include a female perspective on the law.[9] This is the approach that will be adopted in this chapter: law, if construed imaginatively and accompanied by supporting flanking policies, can accommodate some of the concerns of women. Further, the emphasis of this piece will be on creating legally enforceable and effective rights. It therefore fits squarely within the civil rights orientation of this project.

This chapter will focus on the employment dimension of sex equality but not social security. It will adopt the following structure. Part I will briefly describe the Community and international legislation governing sex equality and will examine the principle of equality underpinning these rules. Part II will then consider the way in which the operation of the existing sex equality laws can be improved. This, in turn, will be divided into three sections: legal measures necessary to eliminate discriminatory employment practices; measures to remove barriers to effective labour market participation; and fair participation in work.[10] Finally, in part III some broader issues will be raised and some conclusions drawn.

I. LAW AND POLICY OF SEX EQUALITY

A. The EC and International Sources of Law

1. Sex Equality in the EC Context   Article 141 (*ex* Article 119) of the amended EC Treaty establishes the principle that men and women should receive equal pay for equal work and for work of equal value.[11] Article 119 on equal pay for equal work was introduced into the Treaty of Rome largely to serve an economic purpose: to 'correct or eliminate the effect of specific distortions which advantage or disadvantage certain branches of activity'.[12] France insisted on the inclusion of the provision in the Treaty since it feared that its worker protection legislation, including its laws

---

[6] C. Mackinnon, *Towards Feminist Theory of State*, discussed in I. Ward, 'Beyond Sex Equality: The Limits of Sex Equality Law in the New Europe', in T. Hervey and D. O'Keeffe (eds.), *Sex Equality Law in the European Union* (1996).

[7] R. Cook, 'Women's International Human Rights Law: The Way Forward' (1993) 15 *HRQ* 232.

[8] *Ibid.*, at 238.   [9] See D. Rhode, *Justice and Gender* (1989), 318.

[10] See the division drawn in K. Ewing (ed.), *Working Life: A New Perspective on Labour Law* (1996).

[11] See further E. Ellis, *Sex Equality Law* (1998); S. Prechal and N. Burrows, *Gender Discrimination Law of the EC* (1990); C. Barnard, *EC Employment Law* (1996), chap. 4; A. Dashwood and S. O'Leary (eds.), *The Principle of Equal Treatment in EC Law* (1997); C. McCrudden (ed.), *Women, Employment and European Equality Law* (1990).

[12] The Spaak Report, at 61 (author's translation). Comité Intergouvernemental créé par la conférence de Messine, Rapport des Chefs de Délégations aux Ministères des Affaires Etrangères of 21 Apr. 1956. The Committee, comprising the heads of delegations, was established at the Messina conference in June 1955 under the chairmanship of M. Paul Henri Spaak, then Belgian foreign minister.

on equal pay, would put it at a competitive disadvantage in the common market, due to the additional costs borne by French industry.[13] Given the emphasis at that early stage on the creation of a European *Economic* Community, it comes as little surprise that there was no reference to the social and moral justification for sex equality. Yet, within twenty years the Community had adopted other directives on equality, and the Court of Justice had started to recognize that the principle of equality was a fundamental right[14] which served a social as well as an economic function.[15] As the Court said in *Defrenne (No 3)* 'respect for fundamental personal human rights is one of the general principles of Community law . . . there can be no doubt that the elimination of discrimination based on sex forms part of those fundamental rights'.[16]

It is, however, striking that arguments that principles of equality interfere with freedom of contract and disrupt any economic benefits which might be derived from operating a discriminatory pay policy did not predominate, when either the Treaty was drafted or secondary legislation was adopted. In the United States, by contrast, such arguments have attracted considerable attention. Posner has argued that sex discrimination laws, if successful in meeting their goals, diminish social welfare; that the laws are ineffective in meeting their goals, and that to the extent that the laws have been successful in meeting their goals, the laws have actually harmed their intended beneficiaries.[17] His views naturally have their critics. For example, Donohue argues that discrimination laws can promote efficiency by more rapidly eliminating discriminators, by inducing potential productivity, and by reducing the inefficiencies associated with statistical discrimination.[18] Hepple is also critical of the 'fashionable economic model of society', where markets are sets of unplanned spontaneous exchanges which reward individual efforts and abilities, and so are bound to generate unequal incomes.[19] He argues that this perspective leads to the

[13] See O. Kahn-Freund, 'Labour Law and Social Security', in E. Stein and T. Nicholson (eds.), *American Enterprise in the European Common Market: A Legal Profile* (1960), 300, discussed in C. Barnard, 'The Economic Objectives of Article 119', in Hervey and O'Keeffe, note 6 above. See also the influence of ILO Convention No. 100: C. Hoskyns, *Integrating Gender* (1996), chap. 4.

[14] See, e.g., Case 149/77, *Defrenne* v. *Sabena (No 3)* [1978] ECR 1365, 1378; Case 152/84, *Marshall* v. *Southampton and South West Hampshire Area Health Authority (Teaching) (No 1)* [1986] ECR 723, at para. 36; Case 151/84, *Roberts* v. *Tate & Lyle Industries* [1986] ECR 703, at para. 35 and Case C–132/92, *Roberts* v. *Birds Eye Walls Ltd* [1993] ECR I–5579, at para. 17; Case C–408/92, *Smith* v. *Avdel Systems*, [1994] ECR I–4435 para. 25 and Case C–13/94 *P* v *S* [1996] ECR I–2143; and C. Docksey, 'The Principle of Equality between Men and Women as a Fundamental Right Under Community Law' (1991) 20 *ILJ* 258.

[15] This ambivalence can be seen most clearly when the Court famously observed in its landmark judgment in Case 43/75, *Defrenne (No 2)* [1976] ECR 455: 'Article 119 pursues a double aim. *First*, . . . the aim of Article 119 is to avoid a situation in which undertakings established in states which have actually implemented the principle of equal pay suffer a competitive disadvantage in intra-Community competition as compared with undertakings established in states which have not yet eliminated discrimination against women workers as regards pay. *Second*, this provision forms part of the social objectives of the Community, which is not merely an economic union, but is at the same time intended, by common action to ensure social progress and seek the constant improvement of living and working conditions of their peoples . . . This double aim, which is at once economic and social, shows that the principle of equal pay forms part of the foundations of the Community' (emphasis added).

[16] Case 149/77, [1978] ECR 1378.

[17] A. Posner, 'An Economic Analysis of Sex Discrimination Laws' (1989) 56 *UChic.LR* 1311.

[18] J. Donohue, 'Prohibiting Sex Discrimination in the Workplace: An Economic Perspective' (1989) 56 *UChic.LR* 1337.

[19] B. Hepple, 'The Principle of Equal Treatment in Article 119 EC and the Possibilities for Reform', in Dashwood and O'Leary, note 11 above, at 141.

conclusion that the woman seeking part-time work loses the opportunity of being paid at the same rate as a man doing full-time work because of her preference and taste for looking after children. In this model the woman is assumed to be a calculating person able freely to choose her economic relations. Her preferences, such as caring for her children, are valued only in the process of exchange. Her right, as a human being, to equal treatment and respect is not seen as a social value in itself. However, as Hepple points out, the economic model does not correspond to the real world in which individuals do not have a free choice, precisely because of differences in wealth, social class, gender, and race.

A more liberal view recognizes that equal opportunities are acceptable so long as they do not interfere significantly with the operation of the single market. Elements of this perspective can be found in the Court of Justice's case law. For example, it has allowed indirect discrimination to be justified by objective factors, which have included market forces arguments,[20] and it has imposed temporal limitations on the retrospectivity of judgments.[21] What these groups have yet to realize is that equality can be seen as an input into growth of the Member States. Equal opportunities practices can be used to attract and retain the most efficient staff. The role of the EC is to create a floor of rights in which equal opportunities can be realized. As the Commission's White Paper on social policy recognized, the 'adaptability and creativity of women is a strength which should be harnessed to the drive for growth and competitiveness in the EU'.[22]

These tensions concerning the role and function of equality rights have been seen in the development of EC legislation on equality. This has meant that progress has, by no means, been linear. The Social Programme following the Paris Communiqué in 1972 aspired to create a 'situation in which equality between men and women obtains in the labour market throughout the Community, through the improvement of economic and psychological conditions, and of the social and educational infrastructure'. Three important directives were passed as a result:

- Directive 75/117/EEC on equal pay for male and female workers, enshrining the principle of 'equal pay for equal work' laid down in Article 119 of the EEC Treaty, and introducing the concept of 'equal pay for work of equal value', now supplemented by two codes of practice intended to give practical advice on measures to ensure the effective implementation of equal pay;[23]
- Directive 76/207 on equal treatment with regard to access to employment, vocational training, promotion, and working conditions, aimed at eliminating all discrimination, both direct and indirect, in the world of work and providing an opportunity for positive measures;
- Directive 79/7 on the progressive implementation of equal treatment with regard to statutory social security schemes.

[20] Case C–127/92, *Enderby* v. *Frenchay Heath Authority* [1993] ECR I–5535. At para. 26 the Court said: '[t]he state of the employment market, which may lead an employer to increase the pay of a particular job in order to attract candidates, may constitute an objectively justified ground'.

[21] See, e.g., Case C–262/88, *Barber* v. *Guardian Royal Exchange Assurance Group* [1990] ECR I–1889; Case C–109/91, *Ten Oever* v. *Stichting Bedrijfspensioenfonds voor het Glazenwassers- en Schoonmaakbedrijf* [1993] ECR I–4879.

[22] COM(94)333, at 41.   [23] COM(94)6; COM(96)336 final.

Subsequently, there followed three Action Programmes targeted specifically at equal opportunities for men and women.[24] In the 1980s, at a time of stagnation in Community social policy, two specific directives were adopted on equality:

- Directive 86/378/EEC on implementation of equal treatment in occupational schemes of social security. The Directive was amended by Directive 96/97/EC in the light of the *Barber*[25] judgment;
- Directive 86/613/EEC on equal treatment for men and women carrying out a self-employed activity, including agricultural activity.

The 1989 Social Action Programme[26], implementing the Community Social Charter 1989, led to the enactment, on the basis of Article 138 (*ex* Article 118a of the EC Treaty, of a Directive on pregnancy:

- Directive 92/85/EC improving the health and safety of workers who are pregnant or have recently given birth

The Social Policy Agreement (SPA) annexed to the Treaty on European Union (the Maastricht Treaty), from which the UK secured an opt-out, led to the enactment of two further measures:

- Directive 96/34/EC on reconciling family and working life (parental leave). This was the first Directive which used the new procedure provided for by the SPA, allowing the social partners to negotiate a framework agreement which was then extended to all workers by a directive.
- Directive 97/80/EC on the burden of proof in cases of discrimination based on sex. Under the terms of this Directive, the onus is on defendants accused of discrimination at work to prove that the principle of equal treatment has not been violated.

A change of government in the UK has meant that these two measures are to be readopted under Article 94 (*ex* Article 100) EC and will apply to the UK. Finally, the social partners were also consulted with regard to combating sexual harassment at work. UNICE, the European employers' association, pulled out of this in September 1997.

A variety of soft-law measures have also been adopted. The most recent ones relate to the integration of equal opportunities into the Structural Funds,[27] balanced participation by men and women in decision-making,[28] and equal participation by women in an employment intensive growth strategy in the EU.[29] Although these texts are not legally binding they may form part of the 'softening up process' paving the way for the Commission's preferred course of action should a 'policy window' open up.[30]

[24] Action Programme 1982–5 [1982] OJ C186/3, *Bull. EC* 5–1982, point 2.1.48 and *Bull. EC* 7/8–1982, point 2.1.67; Equal Opportunities for Women Medium-term Community Programme 1986–90, *Bull. EC Suppl.* 3/86 and *Bull. EC* 6–1986, point 2.1.116; Third medium-term Action Programme, COM(90)449 final.

[25] Case 262/88, *Barber* [1990] ECR I–1889.   [26] COM(89)568.   [27] [1994] OJ C231/1.

[28] [1995] OJ C168/3 and Council Recommendation 96/694/EC [1996] OJ L319/11.

[29] [1994] OJ C368/2.

[30] L. Cram, *Policy Making in the EU: Conceptual Lenses and the Integration Process* (1997).

The Treaty of Amsterdam, agreed in June 1997, explicitly introduces equality be-tween men and women as one of the tasks (Article 2) and activities (Article 3) to be undertaken by the Community. A new article, Article 13 (*ex* Article 6a) states that the Council, acting unanimously on a proposal from the Commission, may take ac-tion to combat any form of discrimination, including that based on sex.[31] Elsewhere, Article 119 on equal pay has been amended significantly and renumbered (Article 141). Article 141(1) extends the definition of equal pay for equal work by reference to 'or work of equal value'.[32] The new Article 141(3) has finally provided an express legal basis for the Council to adopt measures, in accordance with the Article 251 (*ex* Article 189b) co-decision procedure, 'to ensure the application of the principle of equal opportunities and equal treatment of men and women in matters of employ-ment and occupation, including the principle of equal pay for equal work or work of equal value'. The absence of an express legal basis to date has meant that two of the important equality directives, Directive 75/117 on equal pay and Directive 76/207 on equal treatment, had to be adopted on general legal bases, Article 94 (*ex* Article 100) and Article 308 (*ex* Article 235) respectively, both requiring a unanimous vote in Council and only simple consultation with the European Parliament. Finally, the new paragraph 4 allows Member States to adopt or maintain positive-action meas-ures for the underrepresented sex in respect of professional careers (see the text to note 86 below).

More generally, institutional support for the realization of equality has long been provided at EU level: there are special committees concerned with women's issues in the European Parliament, including the Women's Rights Committee, and an Equal Opportunities Unit within DGV of the European Commission, assisted by nine Net-works of Experts,[33] and an Advisory Committee on Equal Opportunities for men and women.[34] In addition, the Equal Opportunities Working Party of Members of the Commission examines and monitors the integration of the gender dimension into all relevant policies and programmes. At its instigation, the Commission adopted, on 21 February 1996, a Communication on incorporating equal opportu-nities for women and men into all Community policies and activities.[35]

Further, the Commission has made efforts to promote specific measures aimed at improving the situation of women in practice, particularly with regard to employ-ment, through successive multi-annual action programmes designed and imple-mented in partnership with the Member States. The fourth medium-term Community action programme (1996–2000) aims to incorporate equal opportunit-

[31] The new Art. 13, adopted by the Amsterdam Treaty, will allow the Council to extend the protection of the non-discrimination principle to 'sex, racial or ethnic origin, religion or belief, disability, age or sex-ual orientation'.
[32] See the proposals made in A. Dashwood, *Reviewing Maastricht: Issues for the 1996 IGC* (1996), es-pecially at 297. Art. 1 of Dir. 75/117/EEC already makes provision for this, and as the Court pointed out in Case 96/80, *Jenkins* v. *Kingsgate Clothing Ltd* [1981] ECR 911, Art. 1 'is principally designed to facilit-ate the practical application of the principle of equal pay outlined in Article 119 of the Treaty [and] in no way alters the content or scope of that principle as defined in the Treaty'.
[33] On a more independent basis the Centre for Research on Women (CREW) has been established, as has the European Network of Women (ENOW) and the Women's Lobby. See further E. Szyszczak, 'L'Espace Sociale Européenne, Reality, Dreams or Nightmare' (1990) 33 *GYIL* 298.
[34] Established by Commission Dec. 82/43/EEC [1982] OJ L20/35.					[35] COM(96)67.

ies into the process of defining and implementing the relevant policies at Community, national, and regional levels (mainstreaming). Finally, on 12 February 1997, the Commission adopted its first annual report on equal opportunities for women and men in the European Union (1996).[36] This reviews progress with regard to equality at Member State and Union level and represents an instrument for monitoring equal opportunities policies.

2. The International Environment The developments at Community level have been occurring alongside, but with surprisingly little reference to, the developments at international level. Although ILO Convention 100 on equal pay had some influence on the inclusion of Article 119 in the EC Treaty,[37] generally the systems have developed separately. There is, a strong commitment to equality in many international instruments:[38]

- The UN Charter states the determination of the peoples of the UN to reaffirm faith 'in the equal rights of men and women'. Article 1(3) sets out the organization's purpose of promoting respect for human rights 'for all without distinction as to race, sex, language, or religion'.[39]
- Article 2 of the Universal Declaration of Human Rights (UDHR) says that 'everyone' is entitled to the rights declared 'without distinction of any kind, such as race, colour, sex, language, religion, political or other opinion, national or social origin, property, birth or other status'.[40] Article 7 recognizes that '[a]ll are equal before the law and are entitled without any discrimination to equal protection of the law. All are entitled to equal protection against any discrimination in violation of this Declaration and against any incitement to such discrimination.'
- By Article 2 of the International Covenant of Civil and Political Rights[41] (ICCPR) States undertake to ensure to all within their territory the rights recognized in the Covenant 'without distinction of any kind'. The list of prohibited distinctions is identical to that in the UDHR. Under Article 3, States further undertake to "ensure the equal right of men and women" to enjoyment of all rights set forth in the Covenant'. Article 26 provides '[a]ll persons are equal before the law and are entitled without any discrimination to the equal protection of the law. In this respect the law shall prohibit any discrimination and guarantee to all persons equal and effective protection against discrimination on any ground such as race, colour, sex, language, religion,

---

[36] Luxembourg, Office for Publications of the European Community, 1997. A second report was issued in 1997.

[37] Hoskyns, note 13 above. ILO Convention No. 100, Equal Renumeration, in ILO, *International Labour Conventions and Recommendations 1919–1991* (1992), ii, 529.

[38] See generally H. Steiner and P. Alston, *International Human Rights in Context. Law, Politics and Morals: Text and Materials* (1996), Part E, chap. 13, 'Women's Rights'.

[39] Art. 55(c) is to the same effect.

[40] Art. 16 provides that men and women are entitled to equal rights as to marriage, during marriage, and on its dissolution: Universal Declaration of Human Rights, adopted by GA Res. 217 A (III) (1948), in United Nations, *A Compilation of International Instruments* (1994), Vol. 1, First Part, 1.

[41] International Covenant on Civil and Political Rights, adopted by GA Res. 2200 A (XXI) (1966), in *International Instruments*, note 40 above, at 20.

political or other opinion, national or social origin, property, birth or status.'
Similar provisions appear in the International Covenant on Economic, Social
and Cultural Rights[42] (ICESCR).

*   Perhaps, most importantly, the Convention on the Elimination of Discrimin-
    ation Against Women (CEDAW) was agreed in 1979. This is a powerful
    international instrument with its own Committee.[43] It imposes obligations on
    states to eliminate discrimination against women in all fields, but in particu-
    lar in the political, social, economic, and cultural fields, including education,
    employment, and health.
*   The International Labour Organization has agreed conventions on equal re-
    muneration No 100 (1951), and on discrimination in employment and occu-
    pation No 111 (1958), and a recommendation on the same subject, and a
    convention on equality of treatment in social security (1962).[44]
*   Finally, the European Convention on Human Rights provides in Article 14
    that '[t]he enjoyment of the rights and freedoms set forth in this Convention
    shall be secured without discrimination on any ground such as sex, race,
    colour, language, religion, political or other opinion, national or social ori-
    gin, association with a national minority, property, birth or other status'.[45]
    Article 4(3) of the 1961 Social Charter provides for the right of men and
    women to equal pay for work of equal value and Article 8 requires protection
    for employed women during maternity leave and while they are nursing. Art-
    icle 20 of the 1996 Social Charter provides for the right to equal opportunities
    and equal treatment in matters of employment and occupation without dis-
    crimination on the grounds of sex. It says '[w]ith a view to ensuring the effec-
    tive exercise of the right to equal opportunities and equal treatment in matters
    of employment and occupation without discrimination on the grounds of sex,
    the Parties undertake to recognise that right and to take appropriate mea-
    sures to ensure or promote its application in the following fields: (a) access to
    employment, protection against dismissal and occupational reintegration;
    (b) vocational guidance, training, retraining and rehabilitation; (c) terms of
    employment and working conditions, including remuneration; (d) career
    development, including promotion'.

While these international instruments will inform the discussion that follows, in
many places EC law goes further and provides more detail. It may well be that comparative law provides greater insights for reform of EC law than international law.

[42] International Covenant on Economic, Social and Cultural Rights, adopted by GA Res. 2200 A
(XXI) (1966), in *International Instruments*, note 40 above, at 8.
[43] A. Byrnes, 'The "Other" Human Rights Treaty Body: The Work of the Committee on the Elimination of Discrimination against Women' (1989) 14 *Yale J Int'l L* 1. The older body, the UN Commission
on the Status of Women, has primary responsibility for monitoring and encouraging implementation of
international law on women's rights. Convention on the Elimination of All Forms of Discrimination
Against Women, adopted by GA Res. 34/180 (1979), in *International Instruments*, note 40 above, at 150.
[44] See ILO, note 37 above.
[45] See generally D. J. Harris, M. O'Boyle, and C. Warbrick, *Law of the European Convention on Human
Rights* (1995), chap. 15.

B. What is Meant by Equality?

1. The Definition of Equality   It is clear, both from the EC and the international in-struments, that equality has a central role to play in a civic society. But what is meant by the principle of equality?[46] The principle of equality cannot stand alone: it needs an answer to the question 'equal to what?' Aristotle had an answer. He said that '[e]quality in morals means this: things that are alike should be treated alike'. This is often described as the principle of formal equality or the similarly situated test. Aris-totle continued 'while things that are unalike should be treated unalike in proportion to their unalikeness';[47] '[e]quality and justice are synonymous: to be just is to be equal, to be unjust is to be unequal'.[48] But who is alike? The very nature of human beings is that they are all unique—and different.[49] It cannot mean treating everyone in an identical manner—the young, the old, the sick, the healthy. It is a moral judge-ment on who is alike. This leads Westen to conclude that the concept of equality is tautological. He says equality 'tells us to treat like people alike; but when we ask who "like people" are, we are told they are "people who should be treated alike". Equal-ity is an empty vessel with no substantive moral content of its own. Without moral standards, equality remains meaningless, a formula that has nothing to say about how we should act'.[50]

Since equality provides no internal guidance on the relevance of particular char-acteristics of individuals or groups, the principle of non-discrimination helps to fill this vacuum. At Community level this can be seen in Article 141 (*ex* Article 119) which provides for '[e]qual pay without discrimination on the grounds of sex'.[51] Art-icle 2(1) of Directive 76/207 says that the 'principle of equal treatment' means 'there shall be no discrimination whatsoever on grounds of sex either directly or indirectly by reference in particular to marital or family status'. A similar approach can be found in Article 26 of the ICCPR. As we have seen, this has a general equality clause defined in terms of non-discrimination. It is the legislature which has defined the principle of non-discrimination, prohibiting both direct and indirect discrimination. Further, it is the legislature, and not the court, which has taken the policy decision and identified which people should be treated alike or, using the American terminol-ogy, it has decided which classifications are suspect. In the Community context it has decided that women should be treated like men (and married people like

---

[46] This section draws heavily on C. Barnard, 'The Principle of Equality in the Community Context: *P, Grant, Kalanke* and *Marschall*: Four Uneasy Bedfellows?' (1998) 57 *Cambridge L.J.* 352.

[47] Aristotle, *Ethica Nicomachea* V.3.1131a–1131b (W. Ross, trans., 1925), cited in P. Westen, 'The Empty Idea of Equality' (1982) 95 *Harv. L. Rev.* 543.

[48] Aristotle, *Ethica Eudemia* VII.9.1241b (W. Ross, ed., 1925), cited in Westen, note 47 above, at 543.

[49] Hobbes recognized and addressed this point in *Leviathan*. In the section entitled 'Men by nature are equal', he said '[n]ature hath made man so equal, in the faculties of body and mind; so that though there be found one man sometimes manifestly stronger in body, or of quicker mind than another; yet when all is reckoned together, the difference between man, and man, is not so considerable, as that one man can claim thereupon claim to himself any benefit, to which another may not pretend, as well as he'.

[50] Westen, note 47 above, at 547.

[51] Art. 1 of Dir. 75/117 explains that the principle of equal pay outlined in Art. 119 means 'the elimin-ation of all discrimination on grounds of sex'.

non-married people), and now the Court of Justice has added that transsexuals should be treated like a person of the sex they had belonged to previously.[52]

2. Formal versus Substantive Equality   In the context of sex discrimination, the formal equality model requires women to be treated like men. The choice of a (male) comparator can be problematic. Are men and women really similarly situated? Can and should women aspire to a male life pattern?[53] Many women are not in a position to compete as equals since their domestic and caring responsibilities preclude this. This means that they often take time out to fulfil these roles and/or seek part-time work which suits their domestic responsibilities, since inadequate and often expensive childcare facilities limit their flexibility. Consequently the limited, formal notion of equality adopted by the law can assist only the minority who are able to conform to the male stereotype, but cannot reach or correct underlying structural impediments.[54] As Fredman puts it, this formal equality model reinforces the liberal ideas of 'the primacy of the neutrality of law, the rights of the individual as individual, and the freedom of the market'.[55] Further, she argues, equal treatment of individuals who are not socially equal perpetuates inequalities.[56] This has prompted calls for a more substantive notion of equality, one aimed at achieving equality of outcome or results.[57] This demands not merely that persons should be judged on individual merit, but that the real situation of many women which may place them in a weaker position on the market should be addressed.[58] This marks a shift away from the individual to the group, looking at the way in which individuals' opportunities are determined by their social and historical status.

This suggests a more positive role for the principle of equality which goes beyond the Aristotelian notion of formal equality and aims instead at equality as a societal goal. This might involve some form of positive action,[59] or even positive discrimination,[60] to achieve equality in the longer term. However, from the Aristotelian perspective any form of positive discrimination faces the accusation that it itself is discriminatory, this time against the dominant group (men) and therefore contravenes the principle of equality, and is therefore impermissible.

In order to resolve this paradox, some have called for a reconceptualization of the principle of equality. Lacey, for example, argues that the problem with the discrimination model is that the legislation is framed in terms of difference rather than disad-

---

[52] Case C–13/94, *P* v. *S and Cornwall County Council* [1996] ECR I–2143.

[53] See further Mackinnon, note 5 above, at 32–45, and 'Reflections on Sex Equality under Law' (1991) 100 *Yale LJ* 1281; on the British Sex Discrimination Act see N. Lacey, 'Legislation against Sex Discrimination—Questions from a Feminist Perspective' (1987) 14 *Journal of Law and Society* 411.

[54] S. Fredman, 'European Community Discrimination Law' (1992) 21 *ILJ* 121.

[55] S. Fredman, *Women and the Law* (1997), 383.   [56] *Ibid.*, at 596.

[57] In Case C–136/95, *CNAVTS* v. *Thibault* [1998] ELR I–2011 the Court claimed that the result pursued by the Dir. was substantive, not formal, equality (para. 26). This suggests a narrower concept of substantive equality than the one advocated in this chap.

[58] H. Fenwick and T. Hervey, 'Sex Equality in the Single Market: New Directions for the European Court of Justice' (1995) 32 *CML Rev.* 445.

[59] Positive action allows for a variety of measures ranging from encouragement to apply for positions where women are underrepresented and vocational training, to, more substantively, reorganizing working life and greater provision for childcare.

[60] Positive discrimination goes further and allows for the imposition of quotas or goals for the underrepresented sex.

vantage: it constructs the problem to be tackled as sex discrimination rather than as discrimination against and disadvantage to women and certain ethnic groups.[61] She argues that this not only seriously misrepresents the social problems to which the legislation purports to respond but it also means that any kind of protective or remedial measure addressing disadvantage is suspect. Mackinnon reaches a similar conclusion.[62] She argues that to be 'similarly situated', a test which relies on and produces counter-hierarchical comparisons as the essence of equality reasoning, cannot remain the threshold for access to equality guarantees. If inequality is concrete, no man is ever in the same position as a woman is, because he is not in it as a woman. She therefore concludes:

> If the point of equality law is to end group-based dominance and subordination, rather than to recognise sameness or accommodate difference, a greater priority is placed rectifying the legal inequality of groups that are historically unequal in society, and less solicitude is accorded to pure legal artefacts or reversals of social fortune.

Fiss makes the point more explicitly, arguing:

> that the anti-discrimination principle embodies a very limited conception of equality, one that is highly individualistic and confined to assessing the rationality of means. I also want to outline another mediating principle—the group disadvantaging principle—one that has a good, if not better claim to represent the idea of equality, one that takes fuller account of social reality, and one that more clearly focuses the issues that must be decided in equal protection cases.[63]

The Canadian model offers some interesting insights in this respect. Section 15(1) of the 1982 Canadian Charter provides: 'every individual is equal before and under the law and has the right to the equal protection and benefit of the law without discrimination and, in particular, without discrimination based on race, national or ethnic origin, colour, religion, sex, age, or mental or physical disability'. Further, section 15(2) says that section 15(1) does not preclude any law, program, or activity that has as its object 'the amelioration of conditions of *disadvantaged* individuals, or groups' (emphasis added), including those disadvantaged for one of the enumerated grounds. Section 1 preserves as constitutional any reasonable limits on Charter rights which are 'prescribed by law' and which can be 'demonstrably justified in a free and democratic society'.

These equality provisions were interpreted by the Supreme Court in Canada in two seminal decisions, *Andrews* v. *British Columbia*[64] and *Turpin* v. *The Queen*.[65] In *Andrews*, a case concerning discrimination on the grounds of nationality, McIntyre

---

[61] N. Lacey, 'From Individual to Group?', in B. Hepple and E. Szyszczak, *Discrimination: The Limits of the Law* (1992), 104.

[62] Mackinnon, note 53 above, at 1325.

[63] O. Fiss, 'Groups and the Equal Protection Clause', in M. Cohen, T. Nagel, and T. Scanlon (eds.), *Equality and Preferential Treatment* (1977), 85.

[64] [1989] 1 SCR 143. See M. Gold, 'Comment: *Andrews v. Law Society of British Columbia*' (1989) 34 *McGill LJ* 1063.

[65] [1989] 1 SCR 1296. Subsequent developments have been less positive: see, e.g., D. Beatty, 'The Canadian Conception of Equality' (1996) 46 *U. Toronto LJ* 349; D. Lepotsky, 'The Canadian Judicial Approach to Equality Rights: Freedom Ride or Roller Coaster?' (1992) 55 *Law and Contemporary Problems* 167; D. Beatty, 'The Canadian Charter of Rights: Lessons and Laments' (1997) 60 *MLR* 490; T. Ison, 'A Constitutional Bill of Rights—The Canadian Experience' (1997) 60 *MLR* 500.

J rejected the Aristotelian 'similarly situated test' as 'seriously deficient',[66] since, if applied literally it could be used to justify the Nuremberg laws of Adolf Hitler and the separate but equal doctrine of *Plessey* v. *Ferguson.*[67] Instead, the Court favoured an approach to discrimination based on disadvantage rather than difference.[68] McIntyre J said:

> [D]iscrimination may be described as a distinction, whether intentional or not but based on grounds relating to the personal characteristics of the individual or group, which has the effect of imposing burdens, obligations or disadvantages on such individual or group not imposed upon others, or which withholds or limits access to opportunities, benefits, and advantages available to other members of society.[69]

This view was endorsed in *Turpin* where Wilson J added '[a] finding of discrimination will, I think, in most but not all cases, necessarily entail a search for disadvantage that exists apart from and independent of the particular legal distinction being challenged'. This approach is consistent with the objective spelt out in the CEDAW Convention. Article 3 provides that States Parties shall take in all fields 'all appropriate measures, including legislation, to ensure the full development and advancement of women, for the purpose of guaranteeing them the exercise and enjoyment of human rights and fundamental freedoms on a basis of equality with men'.

3. The EC Model of Equality: Equal Opportunities   If legislative approaches to sex equality range from formal equality at one end of the spectrum to a disadvantage-based substantive approach to equality at the other end, the EC 'equal opportunities model' lies somewhere in between. This is based on the idea that true equality cannot be achieved if individuals begin the race from different starting points.[70] The aim is therefore to equalize the starting points through a combination of formal and substantive equality measures. While focusing on the importance of the individual, it does recognize that sex-based policies may be used as a transitional remedial measure to address structural discrimination. Therefore, Article 2(4) is included in Directive 76/207. This provides that the Directive shall be 'without prejudice to measures which promote *equal opportunity* for men and women, in particular by removing existing inequalities which affect women's opportunities'.

However, despite the existence of Article 2(4) and the recognition that Community law outlaws both direct *and* (unintentional) indirect discrimination,[71] the concept of formal rather than substantive equality has wielded considerable influence in

---

[66] LEAF, an organization set up to litigate for women's equality using the Charter guarantees, was granted intervenor status in *Andrews* which allowed it to put forward Canadian women's proposals for a new interpretation of equality. See G. More, 'Equal Treatment of the Sexes in European Community Law: What does 'Equal' Mean?' (1993) 1 *Feminist Legal Studies* 45 citing S. Razack, *Canadian Feminism and the Law* (1991).

[67] 163 US 537 (1886).

[68] C. Lynn Smith, 'Adding a Third Dimension: The Canadian Approach to Constitutional Equality Guarantees' (1992) 55 *Law and Contemporary Problems* 211.

[69] *Andrews*, note 64 above, at 174. Judge McIntyre also said that not every legal distinction between groups would breach the equality guarantee. The words 'without discrimination' in s.15(1) were interpreted as forming a kind of 'qualifier built into s.15 itself and limit[ing] those distinctions which are forbidden by the section to those which involve prejudice or disadvantage'.

[70] Fredman, note 55 above, at 384.

[71] Case 170/84, *Bilka-Kaufhaus* v. *Weber von Hartz* [1986] ECR 1607 (see further note 120 below).

the Court's interpretation of Community legislation. For example, in *Hofman* v. *Barmer Ersatzkasse*[72] the Court made clear that Directive 76/207 was not 'designed to settle questions concerning the organisation of the family or to alter the division of responsibility between parents'. In *Bilka-Kaufhaus* the Court recognized that the exclusion of part-time workers from a company pension scheme which affected substantially more men than women was indirectly discriminatory and needed to be justified by an objective criterion unrelated to sex. However, it stopped short of imposing a positive requirement on companies to organize their occupational pension schemes in such a way as to accommodate the needs of their employees. Further, in *Helmig*[73] the Court ruled that there was no discrimination when part-timers, who were predominantly women, did not receive overtime rates for hours worked over their normal contractual hours but less than the full-time hours. As the Court said, a part-time employee whose contractual working hours are eighteen receives, if he works nineteen hours, the same contractual overall pay as a full-time employee who works nineteen hours. This decision disregarded the concept of indirect discrimination (it is harder for women to work full time hours than men) and so this meant that the Court did not need to look at the question of objective justification. As Rubinstein said, if the function of overtime premia is to discourage employers from requiring overtime because of its social consequences, it is certainly arguable that a demand to work one hour's overtime is likely to be more disruptive in terms of arrangements for part-timers than full-timers.[74] These decisions serve to highlight the fact that, while the Court will require non-discrimination in the world of work, it is reluctant to look at the effects of its decisions in the domestic sphere. The creation of an artificial distinction between the world of work and the family further prejudices the many women who are not 'well assimilated' to the male norm and denies them *de facto* equality.[75] This approach perpetuates, in Mackinnon's words, the male experience of the world, since it allows male power and male interests to be concealed within apparently universal and objective standards.[76]

Perhaps the high point of the formal equality approach to Community law can be found in *Kalanke*.[77] *Kalanke* concerned the Bremen law on positive discrimination[78] which, in the case of a tie-break situation, gave priority to an equally-qualified woman over a man if women were underrepresented.[79] Relying on this provision the state of Bremen promoted Ms Glißman to the post of section manager in the parks department. Mr Kalanke argued that he had been discriminated against on the grounds of sex, contrary to Article 2(1) of the Equal Treatment Directive; Bremen relied on Article 2(4). The Court explained that Article 2(4) did permit national

[72] Case 184/83, [1984] ECR 3047. See T. Hervey and J. Shaw, 'Women, Work and Care: Women's Dual Role and Double Burden in EC Sex Equality Law' (1998) 8 *Journal of European Social Policy* 43.
[73] Case C–399/92, [1994] ECR I–5727.   [74] [1995] IRLR 183.
[75] See H. Cullen, 'The Subsidiary Woman' (1994) 16 *JSWL* 408.
[76] Mackinnon, note 5 above, at 244.
[77] Case C–450/93, *Kalanke* v. *Freie Hansestadt Bremen* [1995] ECR I–3051.
[78] For some lively discussion on the positive discrimination debate, see the essays by D. Kennedy and R. Delgado in J. Donohue III (ed.), *Foundations of Employment Discrimination Law* (1997).
[79] Underrepresentation exists where women 'do not make up at least half the staff in the individual pay, remuneration and salary brackets in the relevant personnel group within a department'.

measures relating to access to employment, including promotion, which give a specific advantage to women with a view to improving their ability to compete on the labour market and to pursue their career on an equal footing with men (paragraph 19).[80] However, measures which at the decision stage depart from the principle of individual merit contravene Article 2(4): the Court said that national rules which guarantee women *absolute and unconditional priority* for appointment or promotion go beyond promoting equal opportunities and overstep the limits of the exception in Article 2(4) of the Directive.[81] Consequently, the Bremen system 'substitutes for equality of opportunity as envisaged in Article 2(4) the result which is only to be arrived at by providing such equality of opportunity'.

Advocate General Tesauro's opinion offered a similarly individualistic perspective. He said: '[g]iving equal opportunities can only mean putting people in a position to attain equal results and hence restoring conditions of equality between members of the two sexes as regards starting points'. This means removing existing barriers to achieving such a result. He then reasoned that since the man and woman in *Kalanke* had equivalent qualifications, this implied that the two candidates have had and continue to have equal opportunities: 'they are therefore on an equal footing at the starting block'. Consequently, by favouring the woman, this created a position of equality of results which exceeded the scope of Article 2(4). He said:

> In the final analysis, must each individual's right not to be discriminated against on grounds of sex—which the Court itself has held is a fundamental right the observance of which it ensures—yield to the rights of the disadvantaged group, in this case women, in order to compensate for the discrimination suffered by that group in the past?

Put this way the answer was, inevitably, no. He said that positive discrimination brought about a quantitative increase in female employment, but it also most affected the principle of equality as between individuals. He concluded:

> I am convinced that women do not merit the attainment of numerical—and hence only formal—equality—moreover at the cost of an incontestable violation of a fundamental value of every civil society: equal rights, equal treatment for all. Formal numerical equality is an objective which may salve some consciences, but it will remain illusory and devoid of all substance unless it goes together with measures which are genuinely destined to achieve equality. . . . [W]hat is necessary above all is a substantial change in the economic, social and cultural model which is at the root of the inequalities.

The judgment was much criticized for its excessive reliance on the formal, non-discrimination model, its focus on the individual, its failure to show any sensitivity towards the position of women,[82] and the absence of any attempt to weigh up any policy arguments. In *Marschall*[83] the Court made some attempt to address these criticisms. Mr Marschall, a teacher, applied for promotion. The district authority informed him, however, that it intended to appoint a female candidate on the basis of

---

[80] Referring to the preamble to the recommendation on positive action (84/635/EEC [1984] OJ L331/34).

[81] At para. 22 (emphasis added).

[82] See, e.g., D. Schiek, 'Positive Action in Community Law' (1996) 25 *ILJ* 239; S. Prechal, 'Case Note' (1996) 33 *CML Rev.* 1245; and Fredman, note 55 above, at 392.

[83] Case C–409/95, *Marschall* v. *Land Nordrhein-Westfalen* [1997] ECR I–6363.

the state law which provided for priority to an equally-qualified woman where women are underrepresented. However, unlike *Kalanke,*[84] the state law contained a saving clause: priority was given to the woman '*unless reasons specific to an individual [male] candidate* tilt the balance in his favour' (emphasis added).

Advocate General Jacobs thought that the saving clause did not alter the discriminatory nature of the rule in general. He agreed with Advocate General Tesauro in *Kalanke* that the measures permitted by Article 2(4) were those designed to remove the obstacles preventing women from pursuing the same results on equal terms. He said Article 2(4) did not permit measures designed 'to confer the results on them [women] directly, or, in any event, to grant them priority in attaining those results *simply because they are women*'. He said that the reasoning in *Kalanke* suggested that the rule in *Marschall* was also unlawful: if an absolute rule giving preference to women on the ground of sex was unlawful, then a conditional rule which gave preference to men on the basis of admittedly discriminatory criteria must *a fortiori* be unlawful.

The Court of Justice disagreed. While recognizing that a rule which automatically gave priority to women when they were equally qualified to men involved discrimination on grounds of sex, it distinguished *Marshall* from *Kalanke* on the ground that in *Marschall* the state law contained a saving clause. It said that this national rule was compatible with Article 2(4) because:

> ... even where male and female candidates are equally qualified, male candidates tend to be promoted in preference to female candidates particularly because of prejudices and stereotypes concerning the role and capacities of women in working life and the fear, for example, that women will interrupt their careers more frequently, that owing to household and family duties they will be less flexible in their working hours, or that they will be absent from work more frequently because of pregnancy, childbirth and breastfeeding.[85]
>
> For these reasons, the mere fact that a male candidate and a female candidate are equally qualified does not mean that they have the same chances [paragraphs 29–30].

It therefore concluded that a state law with a saving clause might fall within the scope of Article 2(4) 'if such a rule may counteract the prejudicial effects on female candidates of the attitudes and behaviour described above and thus reduce actual instances of inequality which may exist in the real world'. The Court then added a proviso. The state rule did not breach Article 2(4) provided that 'in each individual case the rule provides for male candidates who are equally as qualified as the female candidates a *guarantee* that the candidatures will be the subject of an *objective assessment* which will take account of *all criteria specific to the individual candidates* and will override the priority accorded to female candidates where one or more of those criteria tilts

---

[84] The Bremen law at issue in *Kalanke* did not contain a saving clause. The Federal Labour Court, however, read exceptions into the Bremen law in accordance with the Grundgesetz. While this was mentioned to the ECJ (see para. 9), the questions referred to the ECJ made no reference to these exceptions. It therefore seems that the Court answered the question in *Kalanke* on the basis of the absence of such a clause.

[85] See also the views of the Federal Labour Court when the *Kalanke* case returned to it (Nr 226), Urteil vom 5 Mar. 1996—1 AZR 590/92 (A). It said that it was impossible to distinguish between opportunity and result, especially in the case of engagement and promotion, because the selection itself was influenced by circumstances, expectations, and prejudices that typically diminish the chances of women.

the balance in favour of the male candidate. In this respect it should be remembered that those criteria must not be such as to discriminate against the female candidates' (paragraph 33, emphasis added).

Paragraphs 29–30 of *Marschall* contain the first true recognition by the Court of Justice that equality law is about disadvantage and not just difference. This is an important step forward. It shows imagination on the Court's part to think in true sex equality terms.[86] The new Article 141(4) introduced by the Amsterdam Treaty, amending Article 6(3) of the Social Policy Agreement, may have provided some guidance in this respect. This provides: '[w]ith a view to ensuring *full equality in practice between men and women* in working life, the principle of equal treatment shall not prevent any Member State from maintaining or adopting measures providing for specific advantage, in order to make it easier for the underrepresented sex to pursue a vocational activity or to prevent or compensate for disadvantages in their professional careers' (emphasis added).

However, the Court continues to conceptualize positive action measures as *prima facie* directly discriminatory, although justifiable in accordance with one of the exceptions set out in the Equal Treatment Directive.[87] A truly radical remodelling of 'equality' in EC law would be to define positive action measures as promoting equality in *themselves*[88] and to reconceptualize 'discrimination' to include 'substantive equality'. Article 4 of the CEDAW Convention adopts this approach. It provides that adoption by States Parties of 'temporary measures aimed at accelerating *de facto* equality between men and women shall not be considered discrimination as defined in the present Convention, but shall in no way entail as a consequence the maintenance of unequal or separate standards'. It goes on to provide that 'these measures shall be discontinued when the objectives of equality and equal treatment have been achieved'.

There are signs that the greater sensitivity shown by the Court to the position of women in *Marschall* may have marked a turning point. This can be seen in the recent decision in *Hill*.[89] The case concerned discrimination arising from a job-sharing scheme. The Court, having established that the measure was indirectly discriminatory, looked to the question of objective justification (paragraph 34). At paragraph

---

[86] See Mackinnon, note 53 above, at 1327: '[g]iven the pervasiveness of inequality, imagination is the faculty required to think in sex equality terms'.

[87] C. Barnard and T. Hervey, 'Softening the Approach to Quotas: Positive Action after *Marschall*' (1998) 20 *JSWFL* 333.

[88] The German Constitutional Court had been moving in this direction. The concept of sex equality found in Art. 3, paras. 2 and 3 of the Grundgesetz has been interpreted by the Federal Constitutional Court as not being confined to the principle of formal equality but as also including substantive equality. This can be seen in its decisions on pension ages (28 Jan. 1997, BVerfG (E) 74, 163), night work for women (22 Jan. 1992, BVerfG (E) 85, 191), mothers' pensions (7 June 1992, BVerfG (E) 87,1), discriminatory non-employment of a female metal worker (11 Nov. 1993, BVerfG (E) 89, 279), and on local fire brigades where women were held unfit for service (24 Jan. 1995, BVerfG (E) 92, 91). The objective can justify positive action provided that there are no other suitable measures to achieve substantive equality and that positive action is narrowly tailored in order not to unduly impair the interests of men. See J. Shaw, 'Positive Action for Women in Germany: The Use of Legally Binding Quota Systems', in Hepple and Szysczak, note 61 above; Schiek, note 82 above, at 242. The second question referred in *Kalanke* raised the issue of whether Arts. 1(1) and 2(1) of the Dir. embody substantive equality. The Court did not answer this question.

[89] Case C–243/95, *Hill* v. *Revenue Commissioners* ECR I–3739 [1998].

41 it said that almost all job-sharers were women, most of whom chose that option 'in order to be able to combine work and family responsibilities which invariably involve caring for children'. The Court then added:

> Community policy in this area is to encourage and, if possible, adapt working conditions to family responsibilities. Protection of women within family life and in the course of their professional activities is, in the same way as for men, a principle which is widely regarded as being the natural corollary of the equality between men and women, and which is recognised by Community law [paragraph 42].[90]

For the purposes of this project we are not advocating the wholesale rejection of the Community non-discrimination model—far from it. As Mackinnon points out, '[i]n one's zeal to make deeper change, it should not be overlooked that actually having the best that any group currently has . . . would be a big improvement for most of us.'[91] That being said, we do advocate a more substantive approach to equality and a reconceptualization of the principle of discrimination to include concepts of disadvantage. Although the Court has shown some signs of following this route, a legislative amendment could help provide the political and textual basis for this rectification.[92] One way forward would be to include a positive right to equal treatment which is defined in terms of eliminating disadvantage. This would become a standard in the light of which all other provisions are interpreted.

4. Equality and Levelling Up and Down   Liberals expect that the realization of equality necessarily equates with improvement. In *Defrenne (No 2)*[93] the Court accepted this. It is said that in view of the connection between Article 119 (now Article 141) and the harmonization of working conditions while the improvement is being maintained,[94] it was not possible to comply with Article 119 in other ways than by raising the lowest salaries.[95] This will not always be the case: as Fredman points out, if there is no background requirement of distributive justice, formal equality is satisfied whether the two parties are treated equally well or equally badly.[96] This can be seen in *Smith* v. *Avdel*[97] where the Court permitted the levelling down of the entitlement so that women received their pension at 65, the age at which the men had received it, rather than 60, as they had previously. A privilege enjoyed by women has been removed in the name of equality. On occasion the benefit has been removed from both parties.

The Canadian Supreme Court has taken a rather different perspective. In *Andrews* McIntyre J said: 'a bad law will not be saved merely because it operates equally upon those to whom it has application'. In *Schachter*[98] the Supreme Court indicated that in certain circumstances it would be prepared to read the excluded group into

---

[90] See also Case C–1/95, *Gerster* v. *Freistaat Bayern*, [1997] ECR I–5253 at para. 38.
[91] See Mackinnon, note 53 above, at 1326.   [92] See *ibid.*, at 1325.
[93] Case 43/75, [1976] ECR 455.
[94] See Art. 117 (new Art. 136) and Case 126/86, *Zaera* [1987] ECR 3697.
[95] Case 43/75, [1976] ECR 455. See also Case C–102/88, *Ruzius Wilbrink* [1989] ECR I–4311 where the Court stated that part-timers are entitled to have the same system applied to them as other workers in proportion to their working hours, and the application of this in the case of collective agreements—Case 33/89, *Kowalska* [1990] ECR I–2591.
[96] Fredman, note 55 above, at 350.   [97] Case C–408/92, [1994] ECR I–4435.
[98] *Schachter* v. *Canada* [1992] 2 SCR 679.

the legislation to ensure they received the benefit, although on the facts it was not prepared to do this. Instead, it declared the discriminatory provision invalid but suspended the declaration to allow the legislative body to weigh up all the relevant factors in amending the legislation to meet the Constitutional requirements.

The argument is sometimes made that if all parts of the pay package are to be equalized then levelling up could lead to a continued ratcheting up of pay by comparators which would eventually lead to the ruin of employers. While this may be true, levelling up would force employers to reconsider their pay structures and remove elements of discrimination. We therefore recommend that any principle of equality must be combined with a statement that the removal of a particular benefit contravenes the principle and that there is an assumption of levelling up of conditions.

C. Equality as a Free-standing Fundamental Right

The right to sex equality in the Community context is derived from Article 119 (now Article 141) and the Directives. The more 'general principle of equality'[99] recognized by the Court applies only to limit the acts of the *Community* institutions[100] and not as a free-standing, directly effective basis for legal action by individuals against the Member States and private parties in the national courts.[101] In this context, for the principle of equality to apply there must be some other Community law 'for the principle to bite on', such as Article 119 or one of the Directives.[102] Nevertheless, the Court has not been slow to draw on the rhetoric of equality as a fundamental right to give a broad interpretation to the principle of non-discrimination. This can be seen in *P* v. *S and Cornwall County Council*[103] where the Court of Justice said that 'the Directive is simply the expression, in the relevant field, of the principle of equality, which is one of the fundamental principles of Community law'.[104] The Court then reasoned that since the right not to be discriminated against on grounds of sex is one of the fundamental human rights whose observance the Court has a duty to ensure, the scope of the Directive could not be confined simply to discrimination based on the fact that a person is of one sex or another.[105] It then said that in view of the purpose and the nature of the rights which it seeks to safeguard, the scope of the Directive applies to discrimination arising from the gender reassignment of the person concerned, since 'such discrimination is based, essentially if not exclusively, on the

[99] See also Joined Cases 117/76, *Albert Ruckdeschel and another* v. *HZA Hamburg-St.Annen* and 16/77 *Diamalt AG* v. *HZA Itzehoe* [1977] ECR 1753: 'equality which is one of the fundamental principles of Community Law'.

[100] This point was confirmed in Case C–249/96, *Lisa Jacqueline Grant* v. *South-West Trains Ltd* [1998] ECR I–621, at para. 45.

[101] Although non-discrimination can be invoked in the national court to challenge the validity of a *Community* measure—Case C–27/95, *Woodspring* v. *Bakers of Nailsea*, [1997] ECR I–1847.

[102] Ellis, note 11 above, Chap. 3. See Case 149/77, *Defrenne (No. 3)* [1978] ECR 1365.

[103] Case C–13/94, [1996] ECR I–2143.

[104] See also the AG's Opinion at para. 22: '[t]he Directive is nothing if not an expression of a general principle and a fundamental right . . . Respect for fundamental rights is one of the general principles of Community law, the observance of which the Court has a duty to ensure.'

[105] Paras. 18–19. The Court reached this conclusion even though Tesauro AG pointed out that it was indisputable that the *wording* of the principle of equal treatment laid down by the Dir. referred to the traditional man/woman dichotomy.

sex of the person concerned'.[106] Such ideas did not permeate *Grant* v. *South West Trains (SWT)*, where the Court was not prepared to use the fundamental rights argument to extend the protection of the principle of non-discrimination to gays and lesbians.[107]

However, Advocate General Tesauro in *P* and Advocate General Elmer in *Grant* might have been wishing for a more fundamental re-evaluation, pushing the Court to rule that equality is a free-standing, fundamental right enforceable against the Member States, like the equal protection of laws found in the Fourteenth Amendment of the US Constitution, and even against 'private' employers. Advocate General Tesauro said that 'the prohibition of discrimination on grounds of sex is an aspect of the principle of equality, a principle which requires no account to be taken of discriminatory factors, principally sex, race, language and religion' (paragraph 19). In a similar vein Advocate General Elmer said:

> There is nothing in either the EU Treaty or the EC Treaty to indicate that the rights and duties which result from the EC Treaty, including the right not to be discriminated against on the basis of gender, should not apply to homosexuals, to the handicapped, to persons of a particular ethnic origin or to persons holding particular religious views. Equality before the law is a fundamental principle in every community governed by the rule of law and accordingly in the Community as well.

As the Court tacitly noted in *Grant* matters such as discrimination on the grounds of race, ethnic origin, religion, age, sexual orientation, and disability currently fall outside Community competence. A Treaty amendment would be required to address this.[108] Article 13, introduced by the Treaty of Amsterdam,[109] has, as the Court noted in *Grant*, at least provided a legal basis for the Community to enact measures in this field.

Should the Community have a free-standing, directly effective equality clause? The Commission's *Comité des Sages*[110] argued that if the Union wishes to become 'an original political entity, it must have a clear statement of the citizenship it is offering its members. Inclusion of civic and social rights in the Treaties would help to nurture that citizenship and prevent Europe from being perceived as a bureaucracy assembled by technocratic elites far removed from daily concerns'.[111] It said that these rights should include equality before the law, and the ban on any form of discrimination. It also said that equality between men and women should have full and immediate effect. Such a clause would have the advantage of reorienting the

[106] Paras. 20–21.
[107] Compare the decision of the Canadian Supreme Court in *Egan* v. *Canada* [1995] 2 SCR 513 and *Vriend* v. *Alberta*, judgment of 2 Apr. 1998 where the Canadian Sup. Ct. included sexual orientation as an analagous ground under s.15(1) of the Charter. See R. Wintemute, 'Discrimination Against Same Sex Couples: Sections 15(1) and 1 of the Charter: *Egan* v. *Canada*' (1995) 74 *Canadian Bar Review* 682.
[108] *Opinion 2/94* [1994] ECR I–1759, at para. 33. [109] See note 31 above.
[110] European Commission, DGV, *For a Europe of Civic and Social Rights*, Report by the *Comité des Sages* chaired by Maria de Lourdes Pintasilgo, Brussels, Oct. 1995–Feb. 1996.
[111] The responses of the European Parliament, ECOSOC, and the ETUC to the Commission's Green Paper on Social Policy also called for 'the establishment of the fundamental social rights of citizens as a constitutional element of the European Union'—COM(94)333, at 69. The *Molitor Report* (COM (95) 288 final, at 39) on legislative and administrative simplification called for the adoption of a Bill of Rights. See also G. Kenner, 'Citizenship and Fundamental Rights: Reshaping the Social Model', in G. Kenner (ed.), *Trends in European Social Policy: Essays in Memory of Malcolm Mead* (1995), especially 78–84.

principle of equality from an economic tool to achieve a level playing field to a principle of human rights.

If the Community were to have such a clause this raises the question whether it should adopt the American equal protection of laws approach or the Canadian/ICCPR model. The US model is the more flexible, but such an open-textured provision also gives business interests the opportunity to challenge legislative decisions on the grounds of infringement of a principle of equality. Further, the Fourteenth Amendment places considerable power in the hands of the court to decide what are the suspect classifications and the level of protection they deserve. This has led the US Supreme Court to make distinctions between levels of scrutiny to be given to sex and race cases. Discrimination against some categories of persons (notably on grounds of race) in state law is classified as 'suspect'; to justify the law that state must show a 'compelling governmental interest' and that the measure is 'narrowly tailored' to meet the specific state practice (a strict proportionality test). This test applies both to *invidious* classifications based on race (i.e. classifications which negatively affect racial minorities) and now, according to the majority (five to four) of the Supreme Court in *Adarand Constructors* v. *Pena*,[112] to *benign* (federal) action designed to improve the position of the minority group. However, legislation which discriminates on grounds of sex is subject to a lower 'intermediate' (in between 'suspect' and 'non-suspect') level of scrutiny, requiring demonstration that the discrimination 'serves an important governmental objective and has a fair and substantial relationship to the object of the legislation'.[113] Other grounds of discrimination are subject only to a rational basis review.[114]

The interpretation of the new Constitution in South Africa has benefited from the US and Canadian experience. Section 9 provides:

> (1) Everyone is equal before the law and has the right to equal protection and benefit of the law.
>
> (2) Equality includes the full and equal enjoyment of all rights and freedoms. To promote the achievement of equality, legislative and other measures designed to protect or advance persons, or categories of persons, disadvantaged by unfair discrimination may be taken.
>
> (3) The state may not unfairly discriminate directly or indirectly against anyone on one or more grounds, including race, gender, sex, pregnancy, marital status, ethnic or social origin, colour, sexual orientation, age, disability, religion, conscience, belief, culture, language and birth.
>
> (4) No person may unfairly discriminate directly or indirectly against anyone on one or more grounds in terms of subsection (3). National legislation must be enacted to prevent or prohibit unfair discrimination.
>
> (5) Discrimination on one or more of the grounds listed in subsection (3) is unfair unless it is established that the discrimination is fair.

The provisions of the interim Constitution were very similar and their application was considered in *Harksen* v. *Lane*.[115] The Supreme Court (Goldstone J) proposed a four-stage approach:

---

[112] 515 US 200 (1995).

[113] *Reed* v. *Reed*, 401 US 71, 92 S Ct. 251, 30 L Ed. 2d 225 (1971); *Kahn* v. *Shevin*, 416 US 351, 94 S Ct. 1734, 40 L Ed. 2d 189 (1974).   [114] See generally G. Stone *et al.*, *Constitutional Law* (1996), chap. 5.

[115] Case CCT 9/97, 1997 (11) BCLR 1489. The Court relied heavily on the analysis in *Prinsloo*, 1997 (3) SA 1012 (CC); 1997 (6) BCLR 759 (CC).

(a) Does the provision differentiate between people or categories of people? If so, does the differentiation bear a rational connection to a legitimate government purpose? If it does not then there is a violation of section 8(1). Even if it does bear a rational connection, it might nevertheless amount to discrimination.

(b) Does the differentiation amount to unfair discrimination? This requires a two stage analysis:

(b)(i) Firstly, does the differentiation amount to 'discrimination'? If it is on a specified ground, then discrimination will have been established. If it is not on a specified ground, then whether or not there is discrimination will depend upon whether, objectively, the ground is based on attributes and characteristics which have the potential to impair the fundamental human dignity of persons as human beings or to affect them adversely in a comparably serious manner.

(b)(ii) If the differentiation amounts to 'discrimination', does it amount to 'unfair discrimination'? If it has been found to have been on a specified ground, then unfairness will be presumed. If on an unspecified ground, unfairness will have to be established by the complainant. The test of unfairness focuses primarily on the impact of the discrimination on the complainant and others in his or her situation.

If, at the end of this stage of the enquiry, the differentiation is found not to be unfair, then there will be no violation of section 8(2).

(c) If the discrimination is found to be unfair then a determination will have to be made as to whether the provision can be justified under the limitations clause (section 33 of the interim Constitution).

Once again, it is striking that the Supreme Court's analysis focuses on 'the construction of patterns of disadvantage such as has occurred only too visibly in our history'.[116] In the earlier case of *Hugo*[117] the Court had said:

> [41] The prohibition on unfair discrimination in the interim Constitution seeks not only to avoid discrimination against people who are members of disadvantaged groups. It seeks more than that. At the heart of the prohibition of unfair discrimination lies a recognition that the purpose of our new constitutional and democratic order is the establishment of a society in which all human beings will be accorded equal dignity and respect regardless of their membership of particular groups. The achievement of such a society in the context of our deeply inegalitarian past will not be easy, but that that is the goal of the Constitution should not be forgotten or overlooked.
>
> . . .
>
> [43] To determine whether that impact was unfair it is necessary to look not only at the group who has been disadvantaged but at the nature of the power in terms of which the discrimination was effected and, also at the nature of the interests which have been affected by the discrimination.

As a result, the adoption of the Canadian/ICCPR/South African model is recommended which provides for equality combined with a non-exhaustive list of prohibited grounds of discrimination embedded with concepts of disadvantage. This list could be extended in cases of analogous grounds where, as in Canada, a 'discrete and insular' minority is affected. Factors taken into account by the Canadian courts in determining whether the category is analogous include whether the ground has been recognized by existing human rights statutes or other anti-discrimination laws, whether the country is under an international obligation to eliminate a certain type

---

[116] Para. 49. [117] 1997 (6) BCLR 708 (CC).

of discrimination and whether the ground is analogous in the sense that it involves either an intimate, immutable physical attribute or a fundamental personal choice, akin to one's religion, which is constitutionally immunized from state intrusion.[118] In South Africa the Court said in *Harksen* that the analogous or unspecified grounds are those which have 'the potential to impair the fundamental dignity of persons as human beings, or to affect them adversely in a comparably serious manner'.[119] This approach would keep any free-standing equality clause sharply focused on protecting those disadvantaged groups which it was intended to serve, keeping out economic and business distinction cases which have preoccupied US courts. It would also strike a balance between leaving manageable breathing room for legislative activity and for judicial recognition of additional groups requiring equality rights protection, as experience accumulates. However, any interpretation of such a clause, and any secondary legislation adopted under any non-discrimination clause, must take into account the differences between the protected groups, as well as the similarities.

We therefore recommend that a free-standing principle of equality should be adopted along the lines of the Canadian/South African model.

II. REFORM OF THE LAW

In this section I shall examine how the specific provisions of EC sex discrimination law can be reformed. First, I will examine how the law can be better amended to ensure the elimination of discriminatory employment practices, focusing on certain key areas. Secondly, I shall look at methods to remove barriers to encourage effective labour market participation. Finally, I shall look at fair participation at work. Together these will be known as the 'equality package'. This section should be read subject to the general principles outlined above.

A. Elimination of Discriminatory Employment Practices

1. A Common Regime   As we have seen, there are two regimes regulating equality issues: that related to pay and that related to equal treatment. With the ever wider definition of pay [119a], the division of responsibilities is less clear than first intended. There are anomalous differences between the two regimes. For example:

- Article 119 (now Article 141), a Treaty provision, has both vertical and horizontal direct effect.[120] The Equal Treatment Directive, if not correctly implemented, has only vertical direct effect;[121]

---

[118] See Lepofsky, note 65 above.

[119] Para. 46. However, as L'Heureux-Dubé J acknowledged in *Egan* v. *Canada* above note 107 '[d]ignity [is] a notoriously elusive concept . . . it is clear that [it] cannot, by itself, bear the weight of s.15's task on its shoulders. It needs precision and elaboration.'

[119a] See text to notes 204–21 below.

[120] In Case 43/75, *Defrenne (No 2)* [1976] ECR 455 and Case 129/79, *Macarthys* v. *Smith* [1980] ECR 1275 the Court suggested that Art. 119 was not directly effective in the context of 'indirect or disguised

- Article 119 contains no express derogations; Directive 76/207 provides three express derogations;
- Article 119 concerns discrimination on the grounds of sex; Directive 76/207 concerns discrimination on the grounds of sex and on the grounds of marital and family status.

We therefore recommend that these provisions should form part of one, accessible code which contains and harmonizes the provisions of Directives 75/117 and 76/207, and Article 119 should be replaced by a Constitutional right to equality (outlined above) which identifies non-discrimination on the grounds of sex, *inter alia*, as a fundamental right.

2. Forms of Discrimination   Both Article 119 (now Article 141) and Directive 76/207 require the elimination of *direct* and *indirect* discrimination on the grounds of sex.[122] Direct or 'overt' discrimination involves one sex being treated differently and usually less favourably than the other: in the context of equal pay it may mean that the woman is receiving less pay than the man on the grounds of her sex. The motive or intention to discriminate is not a necessary element of direct discrimination: it is enough that the effect of the measure is discriminatory.[123]

By contrast, indirect discrimination arises when the application of a gender-neutral criterion or practice[124] in fact disadvantages a much higher percentage of women than men, unless that difference can be justified by objective factors unrelated to any discrimination on the grounds of sex.[125] As the Burden of Proof Directive says:

> Indirect discrimination exists where an apparently neutral provision, criterion or practice disadvantages a substantially higher proportion of the members of one sex, unless

discrimination, the identification of which . . . implies comparative studies of entire branches of industry and therefore requires, as a prerequisite, the elaboration by the Community and national legislative bodies of criteria of assessment' (para. 15). Yet in Case 170/84, *Bilka-Kaufhaus* [1986] ECR 1607, the Court recognized that indirectly discriminatory measures contravened Art. 119 unless they could be objectively justified, and that individuals could rely on Art. 119 to secure the elimination of this discrimination. It now seems that although the Court continues to pay lipservice to the potential limitation on the direct effect of Art. 119 (see, e.g., Case C–262/88, *Barber* [1990] ECR I–1889, at para. 37) the limitation is, in reality, redundant, for the Court has found Art. 119 to be directly effective in areas involving great complexity, including occupational pensions and survivors' benefits (*Barber*, above, and Case 109/91, *Ten Oever* [1993] ECR I–4879 respectively).

[121] Case 152/84, *Marshall (No 1)* [1986] ECR 723. This means that an individual may, after the expiry of the period prescribed for implementation, rely on a clear and unambiguous provision of a Dir. directly against the Member State in default (Case 148/78, *Pubblico Ministero* v. *Ratti* [1979] ECR 1629 and Case 8/81, *Becker* v. *Finanzamt Münster-Innenstadt* [1982] ECR 53). The traditional justification for this is that Member States may not take advantage of their own failure to comply with Community law to deny rights to individuals. The same argument does not apply to private individuals who are defendants; as the Court explained in *Marshall (No 1)* (above), since the binding nature of a dir. exists only in relation to 'each Member State to which it is addressed . . . it follows that a Directive may not of itself impose obligations on an individual and that a provision of a Directive may not be relied upon as such against such a person'. Consequently, clear and unambiguous provisions of an unimplemented or incorrectly implemented dir. cannot have horizontal direct effect.

[122] Art. 119 which can be identified 'solely with the aid of the criteria based on equal work and equal pay': Case 43/75, *Defrenne (No 2)* [1976] ECR 455.

[123] Case 69/80, *Worringham and Humphreys* v. *Lloyd's Bank* [1981] ECR 767, and Ellis, note 11 above, Chap. 2.

[124] Case 170/84, *Bilka-Kaufhaus* [1986] ECR 1607; Case C–127/92, *Enderby* [1993] ECR I–5535.

[125] Case 171/88, *Rinner-Kühn* [1989] ECR 2743.

that provision, criterion or practice is appropriate and necessary and can be justified by objective factors unrelated to sex.[126]

The notion of indirect discrimination is designed to target those measures which are discriminatory in *effect*. At first the Court of Justice had some difficulty in appreciating the full ambit of indirect discrimination. In *Jenkins* v. *Kingsgate*,[127] a case concerning part-time workers receiving a lower hourly rate than full-time workers, the Court looked at the employer's intention[128] to see whether discrimination had occurred. Now it seems that the Court has recognized that Article 119 applies to both intentional indirect discrimination,[129] where the employer deliberately uses indirectly discriminatory conduct to disguise a discriminatory intent, and unintentional indirect discrimination,[130] where the employer does not intend to discriminate but the effects of any policy are discriminatory. The culpability of the employer should be reflected in the remedy.

Indirect discrimination is one area where Community law has taken on the notion of disadvantage. In particular, it has been a useful tool to address less favourable treatment of part-time workers on the ground that considerably fewer men than women work part-time.[131] Unless the differential treatment can be objectively justified the part-time workers are entitled to have the same scheme applied to them as that applied to other workers, on a basis proportional to their working time.[132] It is important that the prohibition of unintentional discrimination be retained. This makes Community law far more potent than the US equal protection clause.[133] The concept of indirect discrimination is, however, far easier to state than to apply in practice. What is the appropriate pool of comparators? What is meant by 'disadvantages a substantially higher proportion of the members of one sex'? These issues are extremely complex and have led to divergent views on the part of the national courts[134] and a reference to the European Court of Justice in *R* v. *Secretary of State for Employment, ex parte Seymour-Smith*.[135] Constructive guidance should be given.

Should the distinction between direct and indirect discrimination continue? In *Birds Eye Walls*[136] the Advocate General said that direct and indirect discrimination

---

[126] Art. 2(2).   [127] Case 96/80, [1981] ECR 911.   [128] Para. 14.

[129] Case 96/80, *Jenkins* v. *Kingsgate* [1981] ECR 911, at para. 14. The employer, who had previously paid men and women at different rates, changed his system so that he paid part-timers, the majority of whom were women, less than full-timers. There was a concern that the employer had replaced a directly discriminatory system by an intentionally indirectly discriminatory system.

[130] See, e.g., Case 170/84, *Bilka-Kaufhaus* [1986] ECR 1607, and Case 171/88, *Rinner-Kühn* [1989] ECR 2743.

[131] See, e.g., Case 96/80, *Jenkins* v. *Kingsgate* [1981] ECR 911; Case 170/84, *Bilka-Kaufhaus* [1986] ECR 1607; Case 171/88, *Rinner-Kühn* [1989] ECR 2743; Case 33/89, *Kowalska* [1990] ECR I–2591; Case C–360/90, *Bötel* [1992] IRLR 423; Case C–184/89, *Nimz* [1991] ECR I–29; Case C–1/95, *Gerster*, [1997] ECR I–5253; and Case C–100/95, *Kording* v. *Senator für Finanz* [1997] ECR I–5289.

[132] Case C–102/88, *Ruzius Wilbrink* v. *Bestuur van de Bedrijfsvereniging voor Overheidsdiensten* [1989] ECR 4311.

[133] *Washington* v. *Davis*, 426 US 229 (1976).

[134] See, e.g., *R.* v. *Secretary of State for Education, ex parte Schaffter* [1987] IRLR 53; *Staffordshire County Council* v. *Black* [1995] IRLR 234; *London Underground* v. *Edwards (No 2)* [1997] IRLR 157 (EAT and CA).

[135] [1997] IRLR 315. The Court delivered its decision after this manuscript was completed in Case C–167/97, [1999] 1 RLR 253 and discussed by Barnard and Hepple 'Indirect Discrimination: interpreting *Seymour-Smith*' [1999] CLJ forthcoming.

[136] Case C–132/92, [1993] ECR I–5579.

could not always be distinguished with clarity.[137] Further, in *Enderby*[138] the Court did not bother to make a distinction between direct and indirect discrimination. It merely said that the fact that rates of pay of two jobs of equal value, one carried out almost exclusively by women and the other predominantly by men, were different, led to the requirement that the employer show that the difference is based on object- ively justified factors unrelated to any discrimination based on sex. Despite these problems, the distinction between direct and indirect discrimination should remain, so that the framework of the legislation remains intact. This would help to defeat any moves to allow employers to justify directly discriminatory conduct (see the text to note 238 below).

The newly revised text should contain an express definition of the terms direct and indirect discrimination which should remain separate concepts. Guidance should also be provided on determining the appropriate pool of comparators for indirect discrimination and how the principle of disadvantage could be developed.

3. Defences and Justifications

(a) Objective Justification and Indirect Discrimination

There is no defence to a claim of *direct* discrimination unless an express derogation is provided. While the Equal Treatment Directives contain such derogations[139] there are, as we have seen, no equivalents in the field of pay. In the case of *indirect* dis- crimination, by contrast, the discriminatory conduct may be objectively justified on grounds other than sex.[140] In *Bilka-Kaufhaus*[141] the Court laid down a three-stage test for justification for the national court to apply: the measures chosen must 'cor- respond to a real need on the part of the undertaking, are appropriate with a view to achieving the objectives pursued and are necessary to that end'. This loosely equates to the American intermediate scrutiny test. Objective justifications may take ac- count of economic factors relating to the needs and objectives of the undertaking.[142] This may include permitting the employer to pay full-timers more than part-timers in order to encourage full-time work,[143] and paying certain jobs more in order to at- tract candidates when the market indicates that such workers are in short supply.[144] The economic arguments do not, however, permit justifications on the ground that avoidance of discrimination would involve increased costs.[145] Generalizations

---

[137] E.g., while *Birds Eye Walls* looked like a case of direct discrimination, if emphasis were laid on the fact that the employer calculates the bridging pension in the same way but the result of such calculation is that for 5 years women receive a lower bridging pension, this constitutes indirect discrimination.

[138] Case C–127/92, [1993] ECR I–5535.

[139] Art. 2(2), (3), and (4) of Dir. 76/207; Art. 7(1) of Dir. 79/7.

[140] Case 96/80, *Jenkins* v. *Kingsgate* [1981] ECR 911, at para. 114. See T. Hervey, 'Justification of In- direct Sex Discrimination in Employment: European Community Law and United Kingdom Law Com- pared' (1991) 40 *ICLQ* 807 and *Justifications for Sex Discrimination in Employment* (1992), chap. 8.

[141] Case 170/84, [1986] ECR 1607, at para. 36.

[142] Case 96/80, *Jenkins* v. *Kingsgate* [1981] ECR 911.

[143] Bilka-Kaufhaus argued that the employment of full-time workers entailed lower ancillary costs and permitted the use of staff throughout opening hours. In general, it said, part-time workers refuse to work in the late afternoons and on Saturdays.

[144] Case C–127/92, *Enderby* [1993] ECR I–5535. If the national court can determine precisely what proportion of the increase in pay is attributable to market forces, it must necessarily accept that the pay differential is objectively justified to the extent of that proportion.

[145] Case C–243/95, *Hill*, [1998] ECR I–3739, at para. 40.

about certain categories of workers—such as the belief that part-time workers are not as integrated in, or as dependent upon, the undertaking employing them as full-time workers—do not constitute objectively justified grounds.[146] In the past generalizations about length of service have constituted objectively justified grounds on the basis that there is a special link between length of service and acquisition of a certain level of knowledge or experience,[147] but the Court has now modified its view on this. In *Nimz*[148] the Court said that although experience goes hand in hand with length of service, and experience enables the worker in principle to improve performance of the tasks allotted to him, the objectivity of such a criterion depends on all the circumstances in each individual case, and in particular on the relationship between the nature of the work performed and the experience gained from the performance of that work on completion of a certain number of working hours. This approach has also been adopted by the Court in the more recent cases of *Gerster* and *Kording*.[149] Finally, separate collective bargaining does not constitute objective justification. In *Enderby*[150] the Court also ruled that the fact that rates of pay of two jobs of equal value, one carried out almost exclusively by women and the other predominantly by men, were arrived at by collective bargaining was not sufficient objective justification for the difference in pay between the two jobs. The Court reached this conclusion despite the fact that the collective bargaining was carried out by the same parties, and, taken separately, the collective agreements had in themselves no discriminatory effect.

In the context of indirectly discriminatory *legislation* the Court has formulated a similar test to that in *Bilka* for objective justification. In *Rinner-Kühn*[151] the Court ruled that in the case of indirectly discriminatory legislation the Member State could justify such legislation provided that it could show that the means chosen met a necessary aim of its social policy and that the legislation was suitable for attaining that aim. More recently, however, the Court has shown signs of diluting this test of justification in the context of social security in the cases of *Nolte*[152] and *Megner and Scheffel*.[153] The cases concerned German social security law under which individuals working less than fifteen hours per week and whose income did not exceed one seventh of the monthly reference wage[154] were termed 'minor' or 'marginal' part-time workers. Since these workers were also not subject to the statutory old-age insurance scheme covering invalidity and sickness benefit, they did not have to pay contributions. They were also exempt from paying contributions for unemployment benefit.

Although the legislation affected considerably more women than men, the German government argued that the exclusion of persons in minor employment corresponded to a structural principle of the German social security scheme, and that there was a social demand for minor employment which it was determined to foster within

[146] Case 171/88, *Rinner-Kühn* [1989] ECR 2743.   [147] Case 109/88, *Danfoss* [1989] ECR 3199.
[148] Case C–184/89, *Nimz* [1991] ECR I–297, at para. 14.   [149] See above note 131.
[150] Case C–127/92, [1993] ECR I–5535.   [151] Case 171/88, [1989] ECR 2743.
[152] Case C–317/93, *Nolte* v. *Landesversicherungsanstalt Hannover* [1996] ECR I–4625.
[153] Case C–444/93, *Megner and Scheffel* v. *Innungskrankenkasse Vorderpfalz* [1996] ECR I–4741.
[154] The average monthly salary of persons insured under the statutory old-age insurance scheme during the previous calendar year.

the structural framework of the social security system by excluding minor employment from compulsory insurance. The German government also argued that if it subjected marginal workers to compulsory insurance the jobs lost would not be replaced by full or part-time employment subject to compulsory insurance but that there would be an increase in unlawful employment (black employment) and an increase of circumventing devices (for instance false self-employment). At paragraph 24 the Court cited *De Weerd*[155] and repeated the standard test for objective justification. It then said that social policy is a matter for the Member States, which can choose the measures capable of achieving the aim of their social and employment policy. They therefore have a broad margin of discretion. It then concluded at paragraph 30:

> It should be noted that the social and employment policy aim relied on by the German government is objectively unrelated to any discrimination on the grounds of sex and that, in exercising its competence, the national legislature was *reasonably entitled* to consider that the legislation in question was necessary in order to achieve that aim.

The Court reached similar conclusions in *Laperre*[156] and *Van Damme*.[157] The test of 'reasonableness' applied here is significantly weaker than the more rigorous test envisaged by *Rinner-Kühn* and the subsequent cases. Using the US terminology this marks a shift from an intermediate standard of scrutiny to a rational basis review. It is also striking that the Court of Justice itself decided in *Megner and Scheffel* that 'the legislation in question was necessary to achieve a social policy aim unrelated to any discrimination on the grounds of sex',[158] even though in *Lewark* the Court said that drawing such conclusions was a task for the national court. Further, the Court reached this conclusion without citing any evidence, or considering whether the social policy aim in question could be achieved by other means.[159] Finally, although the Court has insisted that mere budgetary considerations may not constitute a justification,[160] it seems that almost any other social-policy reason (provided it meets the proportionality test) will justify indirect discrimination in state social security schemes.[161]

(b) Objective Justification and Direct Discrimination

As we have seen, the Court seems to have recognized that *direct* discrimination cannot be objectively justified[162] except by reference to any derogations expressly provided by the legislation. The absence of any such derogations from Article 119 (now

[155] Case C–343/92, *De Weerd* [1994] ECR I–571.
[156] Case C–8/94, *Laperre* v. *Bestuurcommissie beroepszaken in de provincie Zuid-Holland* [1996] ECR I–273.
[157] Case C–280/94, *Van Damme* [1996] ECR I–179.
[158] It decided similarly in Case C–317/93, *Nolte* [1996] ECR I–4625 and Case C–8/94, *Laperre* [1996] ECR I–273.
[159] The ECJ's approach contrasts unfavourably with the decision of the British House of Lords in *R.* v. *Secretary of State for Employment, ex parte EOC* [1994] IRLR 176 that the Secretary of State had failed to show that discriminatory service thresholds could be objectively justified.
[160] Case C–343/92, *De Weerd* [1994] ECR I–571.
[161] Case C–280/94, *Van Damme* [1996] ECR I–179, and Case C–8/94, *Laperre* [1996] ECR I–273.
[162] Case 262/88, *Barber* [1990] ECR I–1889, at para. 32 and Case C–177/88, *Dekker* [1990] ECR I–3941, at para. 12.

141) has created problems. This has prompted the Commission in *Birds Eye Walls*[163]
to suggest that direct discrimination could be objectively justified 'since the very concept of discrimination, whether direct or indirect, involves a difference in treatment
which is unjustified'. In the same case the Advocate General suggested that the Court
has not stated that direct discrimination can never be justified by objective factors,[164] making it arbitrary to permit the possibility of justifying a clear inequality of
treatment dependent on whether that inequality is direct or indirect. However in
Grant v. *South West Trains* Advocate General Elmer reasserted the orthodox position and said 'direct discrimination cannot be justified by reference to objective circumstances'.[165]

Although the Court did not expressly rule on this point in *Birds Eye Walls* it
did contemplate in *Smith* v. *Avdel Systems*[166] the possibility of taking objective
justification into account in the context of not applying the equality principle to pension benefits payable immediately post the *Barber* judgment.[167] Similarly in *Webb*[168]
the Court ruled in the context of the Equal Treatment Directive that the termination
of a contract for an indefinite period on grounds of the woman's pregnancy, which
constitutes direct discrimination *'cannot be justified* by the fact that she is prevented,
on a purely temporary basis, from performing the work for which she has been engaged' (emphasis added). By implication this does suggest that termination of a
fixed-term contract on the grounds of pregnancy might be justified. This situation
could perhaps be more satisfactorily dealt with through an express derogation. If it
is recognized that direct discrimination on the grounds of sex is unacceptable then
any derogations to such a fundamental principle must be democratically agreed and
then narrowly construed. The availability of 'objective justification' would run directly counter to such jurisprudence and would seriously undermine discrimination
law as it now stands.

(c) Genuine Occupational Qualifications
As we have seen, the only express derogations can be found in the Equal Treatment
Directive: first, where the sex of the worker constitutes a determining factor (Article
2(2)); secondly, where women need to be protected, particularly as regards pregnancy and maternity (Article 2(3)); and thirdly, where the state has implemented
'positive action' programmes (Article 2(4)).[169] Under English law such express exceptions are known as Genuine Occupational Qualifications (GOQs); under US law
they are referred to as Bona Fide Occupational Qualifications (BFOQs). These exceptions, being a derogation from an individual right laid down in the Directive, are
interpreted strictly, have to be regularly reviewed,[170] and are subject to the principle
of proportionality.[171] Furthermore, this list of exceptions is exhaustive: as the

[163] Case C–132/92, [1993] ECR I–5579.
[164] See, e.g., Case C–217/91, *Spain* v. *Commission* [1993] ECR I–3923, at para. 37: '[t]he principle of
equal treatment viewed as a general principle of Community law requires that similar situations shall not
be treated differently and that different situations shall not be treated in the same manner unless such differentiation is objectively justified'.
[165] Para. 38.
[166] Case C–408/92, [1994] ECR I–4435.
[167] Paras. 30 and 31.
[168] Case C–32/93, *Webb* [1994] ECR I–3567.
[169] See Part I, B, 3 above.
[170] See also Arts. 3(2)(c), 5(2)(c), 9(1) and (2).
[171] Case 222/84, *Johnston* v. *RUC* [1986] ECR 1651, at para. 36.

United Kingdom discovered in *Johnston* v. *RUC*,[172] the Court is not prepared to subject the principle of equal treatment to, for example, any general reservation as regards measures taken on the grounds of public safety. However, within the framework of the Directive Member States have the choice whether to take advantage of the derogation,[173] and they retain a reasonable margin of discretion as to the social measures which they adopt and the detailed arrangements for their implementation.

The scope of these GOQs has been fleshed out by the Court. As far as Article 2(2) is concerned, the Court has accepted that certain kinds of employment in private households might fall within its scope.[174] However, it has ruled that a general exclusion of the application of the principle of equal treatment to employment in a private household or in undertakings with no more than five employees goes beyond the objective which may lawfully be pursued under Article 2(2).[175] On the other hand, the Court had found that it was lawful to limit men's access to the post of midwife in view of the 'personal sensitivities' which may play 'an important role in relations between midwife and patient'.[176] Similar reasoning can explain the Court's acceptance that it was lawful to reserve posts primarily for men in male prisons and for women in female prisons.[177] Further, the Court accepted in *Johnston*[178] that certain policing activities in Northern Ireland may be such that the sex of the police officers constitutes a determining factor. In that case the Chief Constable of the Royal Ulster Constabulary (RUC) decided not to renew the contract of Mrs Johnston and other women and not to give them training in the handling of firearms. The Court of Justice accepted unquestioningly that the justification for this policy related to the special conditions under which the police had to work in Northern Ireland. It seemed to accept that if women were armed they might become a more frequent target for assassination, and that their firearms could fall into the hands of their assailants, which would conflict with the idea of an unarmed police force.

Article 2(3) permits a derogation from the principle of equal treatment to protect women 'particularly as regards pregnancy and maternity'. In *Johnston*[179] the Court made clear that this provision was intended 'to protect a woman's biological condition and the special relationship which exists between a woman and her child', a view supported by the decision in *Hofman* v. *Barmer Ersatzkasse*.[180] In that case the father took unpaid paternity leave to look after his new-born child while the mother, having completed the initial obligatory period of maternity leave, returned to work. The father's claim for the state maternity allowance, which was payable to mothers, was refused. The European Court of Justice accepted that Article 2(3) permitted Member States to introduce provisions which were designed to protect both 'a woman's biological condition during pregnancy and thereafter until such time as her physiological and mental functions have returned to normal after childbirth' and 'to protect the special relationship between a woman and her child over the period

---

[172] *Ibid.*   [173] Case 248/83, *Commission* v. *Germany* [1985] ECR 1459.
[174] Case 165/82, *Commission* v. *UK* [1983] ECR 3431.
[175] *Ibid.* Contrast this with Case C–189/91, *Kirshammer-Hack* v. *Sidal* [1993] ECR I–6185.
[176] Case 165/82, *Commission* v. *UK* [1983] ECR 3431.
[177] Case 318/86, *Commission* v. *France* [1989] 3 CMLR 663.
[178] Case 222/84, *Johnston* v. *RUC* [1986] ECR 1651.   [179] *Ibid.*
[180] Case 184/83, *Hofman* v. *Barmer Ersatzkasse* [1984] ECR 3047

which follows between pregnancy and childbirth, by preventing that relationship from being disturbed by the multiple burdens which would result from the simultaneous pursuit of employment'.[181] However, while Article 2(3) can be used to justify special protection of women where their condition requires it, the derogation cannot be used to justify a total exclusion of women from an occupation, such as the police force, because public opinion demands that women be given greater protection than men when the risks faced are not specific to women.[182] Similarly, the Court held in *Stoeckel*[183] that women cannot be excluded from nightwork where, with the exception of pregnancy and its aftermath,[184] the risks relating to nightwork are common to men and women.[185]

The risk with these GOQs is that they serve to reinforce prejudicial assumptions about sex: that women are fit for certain roles, that their 'biological condition' marks them out in some way, and that they are more vulnerable as a result. It could therefore be argued that the Article 2(2) exception should be removed altogether. A test based on suitability or merit is likely to produce the desired result in appropriate cases.

We therefore recommend that:

- A clear distinction between direct and indirect discrimination should be maintained.
- It should be expressly stated that direct discrimination can never be objectively justified.
- The objective justification test should be tightened up so that the employer must show that the means correspond to an essential need on the part of an

---

[181] Both requirements need not be present: in Case 163/82, *Commission* v. *Italy* [1983] ECR 3273, the Court found that an Italian law which gave a woman but not her husband the entitlement to the equivalent of maternity leave when they adopted a child under 6 years old was justified 'by the legitimate concern to assimilate as far as possible the conditions of entry of the child into the adoptive family to those of the arrival of a new born child in the family during the very delicate initial period'. Although Art. 2(3) was not cited, the thinking is very similar to the requirement of safeguarding the 'special relationship' between mother and child.

[182] Case 222/84, *Johnston* v. *RUC* [1986] ECR 1651. The Commission discussed the implications of the *Johnston* decision in its Communication on Protective Legislation for Women (COM(87)105 final; Council Conclusions of 26 May 1987 on Protective Legislation for Women in the Member States of the European Community ([1987] OJ C178/04)). It examined all national protective provisions, in particular in the light of Arts. 3(2)(c) and 5(2)(c) of the Equal Treatment Dir. which require Member States to revise all protective legislation which is no longer justified. It found that 'a mosaic of extremely varied and highly specific regulations exist, the reasons for which are not clearly defined' and concluded that protective legislation which does not relate to pregnancy or maternity should be made to apply equally to both sexes or be repealed.

[183] Case C–345/89, *Stoeckel* [1991] ECR I–4047. See also Case C–13/93, *ONEM* v. *Minne* [1994] ECR I–371 where the Court held that discriminatory derogations from the prohibition of nightwork contravened Art. 5 of Dir. 76/207/EEC.

[184] Case C–421/92, *Habermann-Beltermann* [1994] ECR I–1657, at para. 18; and Art. 7 of Dir. 92/85 [1992] OJ L348/1, on pregnant workers.

[185] However, in Case C–158/91, *Levy* [1993] ECR I–4287, the Court recognized that while Art. 5 of Dir. 76/207 requires national legislation prohibiting nightwork by women to be set aside, this rule does not apply in cases where the national provision was introduced by virtue of an agreement concluded with a non-member country before the entry into force of the EEC Treaty. The French law at issue, Art. L 213–1 of the French *Code du travail* preventing women from working at night, was based on ILO Convention No 89. None of the 15 Member States is now party to the Convention. A new, non-discriminatory Convention has now been passed (No. 171) which the ILO hopes all Member States will ratify: Art. 234(1) EEC/EC. See also *Minne* [1994] ECR I–371. See EIRR 219, Apr. 1992.

undertaking, that the means are narrowly tailored to that objective, and that there is no non-discriminatory alternative way of achieving that objective.[186] The decisions in *Megner and Scheffel* and *Nolte* should be reversed.

- The GOQs should be re-examined and the abolition of Article 2(2), at least, should be considered.
- The principle of positive action in Article 2(4) should remain since it constitutes an essential element in fair participation (see below). The terms of Article 141(4) (*ex* 119) EC and Article 2(4) should be harmonized. Further, positive action should be reconceptualized to reflect the need to rectify disadvantage, following the South African model,[187] and as a component part of the steps taken to achieve equality, following Article 4 of the CEDAW Convention.

4. Comparator   Article 119 (now 141) provides that 'men and women should receive equal pay for equal work'. This suggests that there must always be a comparator of the opposite sex,[188] usually chosen by the applicant.[189] The choice of the comparator can be crucial. In *Grant,* the applicant, a lesbian, was denied benefits for her female partner. She claimed, *inter alia*, direct discrimination on the grounds of sex since her (heterosexual) male colleague received these benefits for his female partner. The Court, however, chose a homosexual male as the comparator. Ms Grant lost her case since both (homosexual) men and women were being treated equally, albeit equally badly. Had the Court chosen a heterosexual male comparator, as she had argued, there would have been discrimination on the grounds of sex. In *P* v. *S*, by contrast, the case concerning the dismissal of a transsexual on the grounds of his sex change, the comparator selected was a person of the sex to which P was deemed to have belonged prior to the gender reassignment. Discrimination was found. As the Advocate General recognized, had the Court chosen a female to male transsexual, as the UK government had argued, the result might have been different.

It seems the comparator must be a real, identifiable person and not a 'hypothetical worker'.[190] This prevents a woman from arguing that she was the victim of discrimination because if she had been a man she would have received a higher salary. The Court excluded such claims on the ground that it would necessitate comparative studies of entire branches of industry which would require further Community legislation. While hypothetical comparators present considerable problems of proof, this requirement potentially limits the effectiveness of the quality legislation in sectors predominated by women. Under UK law hypothetical comparators are allowed in the context of the Sex Discrimination Act 1975 but not under the Equal Pay Act 1970.

---

[186] See note 10 above.   [187] See Part I, B, 3.

[188] This ensures that Art. 119 cannot be used to outlaw pay discrimination against gays, lesbians, and transsexuals.

[189] This is the British rule: *Ainsworth* v. *Glass Tubes & Components Ltd* [1977] IRLR 74.

[190] Case 129/79, *Macarthys* v. *Smith* [1980] ECR 1275. This argument was based on the distinction the Court had drawn between direct and indirect discrimination. If the comparator were to be a hypothetical male this would be classed as indirect, disguised discrimination which would require comparative studies of entire industries. At that stage Art. 119 was only directly effective in respect of direct discrimination. Since the law has now changed this approach may require reassessment. See also Case C–200/91, *Coloroll* [1994] ECR I–4389.

This problem is exacerbated by the additional requirement, thought to be derived from *Defrenne (No 2)* that the comparator must be employed in the same establishment or service as the applicant. This requirement prevents a woman from making comparisons with colleagues in other establishments belonging to the same employer or with comparators working for different employers. It also prevents female workers, in a sector predominated by women, relying on Article 141 (*ex* 119) to make cross-industry comparisons.[191] However, in *Defrenne (No 2)* the Court actually said that the principle of equal pay applies '*even more* in cases where men and women receive unequal pay for equal work carried out in the same establishment or service, whether public or private'[192] (emphasis added). Consequently the Advocate General in *Commission* v. *Denmark*[193] has expressed doubts about the validity of the single workplace rule which might defeat the purpose of the principle of equal pay.[194]

The Court has also stressed that the woman and her comparator must be in 'identical situations',[195] albeit that they do not have to work contemporaneously.[196] This requirement has been used in *Birds Eye Walls* v. *Roberts*[197] to frustrate the requirement of equality. In that case the employer paid a man a bridging pension between the age of 60 and 65 but paid Mrs Roberts a reduced bridging pension because she received a state pension at the age of 60 which her male comparator did not. The Court ruled that no discrimination occurred since the 'difference as regards the objective premise, which necessarily entails that the amount of the bridging pension is not the same for men and women, cannot be considered discriminatory'.

The principal drawback with the requirement of a comparator in the context of sex equality is that, as we have seen, it takes the male as the norm and assumes that a woman is like a man and should be placed in the same position as a man. In some contexts, notably pregnancy, this makes no sense. Comparisons adopted by some courts between a pregnant woman and a sick man are artificial, inaccurate, and misleading. This point was recognized in both *Dekker* and *Webb*. In *Dekker*[198] a woman was refused a job on the ground that she was pregnant; another woman was appointed and there were no male candidates. Nevertheless, the Court found that discrimination had occurred. It reasoned that since employment can only be refused because of pregnancy to a woman, such a refusal constituted discrimination on the grounds of sex. In *Webb*[199] the Court confirmed that 'there can be no question of comparing the situation of a [pregnant] woman . . . with that of a man similarly incapable for medical or other reason'. It has therefore been argued that a male comparator is not needed when a woman has clearly been disadvantaged by the use

---

[191] In these circumstances it may be possible to argue that no comparator is required. See Case C–177/88, *Dekker* [1990] ECR I–3941 and the text attached to note 198 below.

[192] Case 43/75, *Defrenne (No 2)* [1976] ECR 455, at para. 22.

[193] In Case 143/83, *Commission* v. *Denmark* [1985] ECR 427.   [194] COM(94)6 final

[195] Case C–132/92, *Birds Eye Walls* [1993] ECR I–5579. Unfortunately the Court did not explain how closely identical the man's and woman's situations had to be. If it adopted a vigorous approach to this requirement it could significantly undermine the effectiveness of the equal pay principle.

[196] Case 129/79, *Macarthys* v. *Smith* [1980] ECR 1275.

[197] Case C–132/92, *Birds Eye Walls* [1993] ECR I–5579. See also Case C–342/93, *Gillespie* [1996] ECR I–475.

[198] Case C–177/88, [1990] ECR I–3941.   [199] Case C–32/93, [1994] ECR I–3567, at para. 24.

of a sex-specific criterion, in other words by a condition which could never hurt a man (the asymmetrical approach), whereas a comparison must be carried out where discrimination can only be established on the basis of the different treatment accorded to men (the symmetrical approach).[200]

We therefore recommend that more use should be made of asymmetrical comparisons where appropriate. Sexual harassment is one such area (see section 6 below). Further, reference to hypothetical comparators should be used in the context of both pay and equal treatment. In highly sex-segregated sectors, applicants should be able to compare themselves to workers in other sectors.

5. Pay   Although the principle of equal pay has been enshrined in the EC Treaty since 1957, women still earn, on average, only 75 per cent of the pay of men.[201] Eurostat has recently conducted some research into the hourly earnings of women in four countries. It found that Sweden is the country which comes nearest of the four to equal remuneration for men and women; the average earnings for women are 84 per cent of those for men, compared with 73 per cent in Spain and France and 64 per cent in the UK (Table 1).

Eurostat found that in three of these Member States the female managers were the worst remunerated occupational group in comparison with their male counterparts. In the fourth Member State, the UK, they actually come off even worse, receiving only two-thirds of male earnings, but women employed in craft and related trades in the UK earn an even smaller percentage of male earnings. Women in the lower-paid non-manual occupations (clerks and service workers, shop and market sales workers) come nearest to male earnings in the same occupations.

The research also discovered that there is a noticeable trend which is remarkably consistent in all four countries, that the older the age-group of women is considered, the further it falls short of the average earnings of their male contemporaries. Similarly the most highly-qualified women, those with third-level education, though they receive more pay than women with lower qualifications, actually earn a smaller percentage of male earnings.

However, Eurostat found that even when women's earnings are recalculated to remove structural effects (educational qualifications, occupation, and industry) women's earnings come closer to men's, but there still remains an hourly earnings difference between a man and a woman with a comparable educational background in the same occupation and industry, of 13 per cent in Sweden, 22 per cent in Spain, 23 per cent in France, and almost 25 per cent in the UK. The pay gap is due to a variety of factors. First, women are segregated both in terms of occupation and establishment. Predominantly female occupations attract consistently lower rates of pay than men. This is particularly the case where women work part-time, as the facts of *Enderby* highlight. In that case the majority of the speech therapists were women working part-time while the majority of pharmacists were men working full time. Speech therapists earned up to 60 per cent less than pharmacists. Secondly, even where men and women do the same kind of work in the same organizations women

---

[200]   K. Banks, 'Equal Opportunities for Women and Men', *Social Europe* 3/91, 65.
[201]   This experience is not confined to Europe, see P. Sloane and H. Jain, 'Use of Equal Opportunities Legislation and Earnings Differentials: A Comparative Study' (1990) 21 *IRJ* 221.

Table 1. Hourly earnings of women as a percentage of those of men:[202] full-time and part-time workers, excluding bonuses and overtime

	E	F	S	UK
OCCUPATION				
Managers	69.7	70.2	80.1	65.8
Professions	77.4	78.9	87.7	82.9
Technicians & associate professionals	82.7	86.1	84.6	68.9
Clerks	76.4	92.5	95.5	89.8
Service & sales workers	79.1	70.5	96.2	80.7
Craft & related trades workers	70.6	67.0	88.7	61.3
Plant & machine operators	73.5	76.3	92.0	74.5
Elementary occupations	83.9	76.2	87.4	73.6
ECONOMIC ACTIVITY				
Mining & quarrying	66.7	57.9	78.8	75.3
Manufacturing	69.7	72.1	85.2	66.3
Electricity, gas & water supply	82.6	72.1	77.5	76.1
Construction	94.8	93.0	78.2	74.5
Total Industry	*73.6*	*74.1*	*84.3*	*67.4*
Wholesale & retail trade; repair of motor vehicles	70.7	61.0	84.3	62.4
Hotels & restaurants	79.4	61.1	79.7	75.7
Transport, storage and communication	85.9	92.4	93.6	82.3
Financial intermediation	75.5	63.1	64.2	51.4
Real estate, renting & business activities	69.4	68.5	76.4	62.8
Total Services	*71.1*	*70.6*	*82.1*	*62.6*
AGE				
Less than 20 years	92.9	98.0	90.7	91.0
Between 20 and 24 years	86.6	94.1	94.5	82.6
Between 25 and 29 years	86.5	88.4	88.4	79.7
Between 30 and 44 years	77.8	77.1	86.1	63.1
Between 45 and 54 years	74.4	69.3	79.8	53.6
55 years and more	70.6	64.5	77.4	58.1
EDUCATION				
Less than upper secondary level	73.8	73.8	87.3	70.9
Upper secondary level	74.2	78.7	82.1	70.8
Third level (university orotherwise)	64.9	66.5	80.4	68.4
TOTAL	*72.7*	*72.9*	*84.0*	*64.4*
After discounting main structural effects (occupation, economic activity, education)	*78.2*	*76.6*	*86.8*	*75.4*

Source: Eurostat, *Statistics in Focus, Population and Social Conditions, How Evenly are Earnings Distributed?* (No. 15, 1997), 7.

[202] Because of the differences which have already been noted in the patterns of full-time and part-time work of men and women, and in overtime work, a comparison of male and female earnings is best carried out on the basis of hourly rates, excluding bonuses and overtime payments.

tend to attract lower pay because they are concentrated in lower paying specialisms, they occupy lower-status jobs and the method of remuneration impacts differently on men and women (by, for example, rewarding seniority or flexibility). Further, women's skills are often undervalued. The proposals in this section are based around the idea of 'pay equity' or fair pay for all. One important step in this direction would be an adequate minimum wage which would go some way towards addressing the problem of extremely poor wages earned by many women. At Community level this is problematic since 'pay' is expressly excluded from the Community's competence.

The importance of combating discrimination on the grounds of sex has been highlighted by recent research conducted by the Equal Opportunities Commission, Northern Ireland (EOC(NI)). They argue that in the absence of discrimination women's earnings would rise by 14 per cent and the gender pay gap would fall from 23 per cent to 7 per cent. The biggest increase would be experienced by single women relative to married men, where, in the absence of discrimination (defined as men and women with the same labour market characteristics receiving the same pay), single women's pay would rise by almost 40 per cent.[203]

(a) Definition of Pay

How has the Union responded to these problems? First, by defining 'pay' broadly it has ensured equality for women in respect of a wide range of benefits. 'Pay' refers to the ordinary basic minimum wage or salary, which would include pay received as piece rates or time rates, 'and any other consideration, whether in cash or in kind, which the worker receives directly or indirectly in respect of his employment from his employer'. The Court has added further glosses to this definition. It has said that pay can be 'immediate or future' provided that the worker receives it, albeit indirectly,[204] in respect of his employment from his employer.[205] The legal nature of the facilities is not important—they can be granted under a contract of employment, as a result of legislative[206] provisions or made *ex gratia*[207] by the employer[208]—provided that they are granted in respect of employment.[209] Sick pay,[210] redundancy payments, be they statutory or contractual,[211] or resulting from voluntary or compulsory

---

[203] *Gender and the Earnings Gap: Unequal Treatment or Unequal Workers?*, considered in (1997) 73 *EOR* 4.

[204] Since Art. 119 also applies to money received indirectly from an employer, it would cover occupational pensions paid out of a trust fund, administered by trustees who are technically independent of the employer—see *Barber* [1990] ECR I–1889.

[205] Case 80/70, *Defrenne (No 1)* [1971] ECR 445; Case 12/81, *Garland* v. *British Rail Engineering* [1982] ECR 359.

[206] See Case 43/75, *Defrenne (No 2)* [1976] ECR 455, at para. 40 and Case C–262/88, *Barber* [1990] ECR I–1889.

[207] *Ex gratia* payments are 'advantages which an employer grants to workers although he is not required to do so by contract'—Case C–262/88, *Barber* [1990] ECR I–1889, at para. 19 and Case 12/81, *Garland* [1982] ECR 359.

[208] Case C–360/90, *Arbeiterwohlfahrt der Stadt Berlin e V* v. *Bötel* [1992] ECR I–3589.

[209] Contrast the position with additional voluntary contributions which are not granted in respect of employment—Case C–200/91, *Coloroll* [1994] ECR I–4389.

[210] Case 171/88, *Rinner-Kühn* [1989] ECR 2743.

[211] Case C–262/88, *Barber* [1990] ECR I–1889.

redundancy,[212] occupational pensions,[213] survivors' benefits,[214] bridging pensions,[215] additional statutory redundancy payments,[216] special bonus payments made by the employer[217] and a severance grant payable on the termination of an employment relationship[218] also constitute pay within the meaning of Article 119 (now 141). Similarly, compensation in the form of paid leave or overtime pay for participation in training courses given by an employer to Staff Committee members[219] and rules governing the automatic reclassification to a higher salary grade can constitute pay.[220] The only legislative provisions which do not constitute pay are those based on statutory social security schemes which are not paid by reason of the existence of the employment relationship,[221] to which Directive 79/7 on equal treatment in social security, and not Article 119 (now 141), applies.

(b) Equal Value

The version of Article 141 (*ex* 119) amended by the Amsterdam Treaty now recognizes that Article 119 applies to equal pay for equal work and for work of equal value, thereby amending the Treaty in line with Article 1 of Directive 75/117 and the decision in *Jenkins* v. *Kingsgate*.[222] Assessing equal value is a difficult and subjective task. A job classification or job evaluation scheme,[223] while not obligatory,[224] offers

---

[212] Case C–262/88, *Barber* [1990] ECR I–1889, concerned *compulsory* redundancy. Case 19/81, *Burton* [1982] ECR 555 concerned voluntary redundancy where the Court suggested that Dir. 76/207 did not apply to discriminatory age conditions. The Court seems, *sotto voce*, to have overruled this decision (see Curtin (1990) 27 *CML Rev.* 482) and it seems likely that Art. 119 would apply to both.

[213] Case 170/84, *Bilka-Kaufhaus* [1986] ECR 1607 (supplementary pensions); Case C–262/88, *Barber* [1990] ECR I–1889 (contracted-out pensions).

[214] Case C–109/91, *Ten Oever* [1993] ECR I–4879.

[215] Case C–132/92, *Birds Eye Walls* [1993] ECR I–5579.

[216] Case C–173/91, *Commission* v. *Belgium* [1993] ECR I–673.

[217] Case 58/81, *Commission* v. *Luxembourg* [1982] ECR 2175 where a special 'head of household' allowance was deemed to be pay. Individual pay supplements to basic pay (Case 109/88, *Danfoss* [1989] ECR 1399) and increments based on seniority (Case 184/89, *Nimz* [1991] ECR 322) are considered to be pay. So, presumably, would shift premia, overtime, and all forms of merit and performance pay constitute 'pay' within Art. 119 (COM(94)6 final).

[218] Case C–33/89, *Kowalska* [1990] ECR I–2591. Such payments are deemed to be deferred pay.

[219] Case C–360/90, *Arbeiterwohlfahrt der Stadt Berlin e V* v. *Bötel* [1992] ECR I–3589.

[220] Case C–184/89, *Nimz* [1991] ECR I–297.

[221] Case 80/70, *Defrenne (No 1)* [1971] ECR 445. In Case C–7/93, *Bestuur van het Algemeen Burgerlijk Pensioenfonds* v. *Beune* [1994] ECR I–4471 the Court sought to clarify the criteria necessary to identify state social security schemes. It ruled that a pension scheme directly governed by statute is a strong indication that the benefits provided by the scheme are social security benefits. It then added that Art. 119 does not embrace social security schemes or benefits such as retirement pensions directly governed by statute, which apply to general categories of employees where no element of collective bargaining is involved. Finally, the Court recognized that although these schemes are funded by the contributions of workers, employers, and possibly the public authorities, the funding is determined not so much by the employment relationship between the employer and the worker as by considerations of social policy.

[222] Case 96/80, [1981] ECR 911. See also Case 69/80, *Worringham and Humphreys* v. *Lloyd's Bank* [1981] ECR 767, at para. 21; Case C–262/88, *Barber* [1990] ECR I–1889.

[223] Job classification is a non-analytical process used to categorize jobs. Job evaluation, used in the UK and Ireland, is a more analytical approach to assess the relative demands of a job. The analytical approach involves breaking jobs down into their component elements for the process of comparison, whereas the non-analytical approach considers the relative worth of the job based on a whole job comparison. While analytical schemes are more objective, the whole process is still subject to judgements made by evaluators which reflect their own background, experience and attitudes—COM(94)6 final.

[224] Case 61/81, *Commission* v. *UK* [1982] ECR 2601.

one method of determining whether a man and woman's work is of equal value. This is recognized by Article 1(2) of Directive 75/117 which provides that:

> Where a job classification system is used for determining pay, it must be based on the same criteria for both men and women and so drawn up so as to exclude any discrimination on the grounds of sex.

The contents of a job classification system were discussed in *Rummler* v. *Dato-Druck*,[225] a case concerning the value to be attached to a criteria of strength. The Court said that the nature of the work to be done must be considered objectively and not by taking account of the subjective characteristics of the individual concerned. It did not explain what was meant by objective strength. It added that when calculating the amount of physical exertion needed, a criterion based solely on the values of one sex, for example the average strength of a woman, brought with it the threat of discrimination, for it might result in work requiring use of greater physical strength being paid in the same way as work requiring less physical strength. Secondly, the Court accepted that even though a strength criterion might generally favour male employees, the classification system was not discriminatory on this ground alone. Instead, it said that the scheme must be considered overall and, in order for it to accord with the principles of the Directive, it had to be designed so that, if the nature of the work permitted, 'it includes as "work to which equal value is attributed" work in which other criteria are taken into account for which female employees may show particular aptitude'. This case reveals the problem with the concept of 'value'. It runs a high risk of being reimbued with the stereotypes currently associated with men's and women's work.

(c) Proportionate Pay

If, as a result of a job evaluation study or an enquiry into work of equal value, it is discovered that the woman's work is 75 per cent of the value of the man's but that she is only being paid 50 per cent of what he earns, there is, at present, no facility under EC law for the woman's work to be rewarded the proportionate increase. She will receive the same amount as her male comparator only if the work is *equal*. Article 141 (*ex* 119) does, however, cover the situation where the woman is doing work of greater value than the man, is being paid less than the man, and wishes to be paid the same as the man. This was the situation in *Murphy* v. *Bord Telecomm Eireann*.[226] The Court said that since the principle of equal pay forbids women engaged in work of equal value to that of men from being paid less than men on the grounds of sex, *a fortiori* it prohibits a difference in pay where the woman is engaged in work of higher value. To adopt a contrary interpretation would be 'tantamount to rendering the principle of equal pay ineffective and nugatory', for an employer could circumvent the principle by assigning additional duties to women who could then be paid a lower wage.

Given the subjective nature of calculating work of equal value, the unlikelihood of two jobs being precisely equal in value, and the expense involved in making a claim, it is unlikely that women will make use of the equal pay provisions. Indeed, in the

---

[225] Case 237/85, [1986] ECR 2101.   [226] Case 157/86, [1988] ECR 673.

UK equal value claims have dropped to the their lowest level since 1984 when the equal value law came into operation: barely 100 applications were made. If the possibility of proportionate pay existed, this would represent a valuable incentive for women to bring proceedings. Further, it would represent a major step forward in addressing the general undervaluation of women's work.

(d) Pay Equity

Some relatively minor amendments to the provisions on equal pay, as outlined above, would make them more effective.[227] However, a more radical approach could be adopted. The Ontario Pay Equity Act provides a model. This legislation starts from the premise that women are underpaid and that their underpayment is the result of discrimination. The Act declared that its purpose was to 'redress systematic discrimination in compensation for work performed by employees in female job classes'. The general scheme laid down by the Pay Equity Act is as follows:

- Employers are obliged to examine their pay structures for evidence of discrimination—predominantly male and predominantly female jobs have to be assessed to determine their relative values, and predominantly female jobs 'matched' where possible, to predominantly male jobs having comparable value.
- Employers (with exceptions) have to draw up 'pay equity plans' which detail how jobs have been compared, which male and female jobs have been determined to be of comparable value, and what is to be done about pay discrepancies between them.
- 'Pay equity adjustments' have to begin to be paid in line with deadlines which depend on the size and nature (public/private sector) of the employer, and have to continue to be paid until all matched male and female job classes have reached parity.

While this Act has not enjoyed the success some hoped, it provides some inspiration for a model that could be adapted in the Community context. We recommend:

- that there be a Treaty amendment or a Directive which contains a clear definition of the term 'pay' in the light of the Court of Justice's case law. Further, given the trend towards a very broad interpretation of the term 'pay' it could now be argued that Article 141 (*ex* 119) requires both access to and the amount of all benefits to be non-discriminatory.
- that legislation be introduced as a matter of urgency to allow for proportionate pay.
- Following the Ontario model a duty should be imposed on employers to examine their pay structures for pay equity. Further, the Community should contemplate the possibility of allowing collective agreements to be referred to national equality agencies or the equivalent to ensure that they are consistent with the idea of pay equity as identified above. The social partners should also have the power to amend or adjust the agreement to advance pay equity.

---

[227] This section is taken from A. McColgan, *Just Wages for Women* (1997), chap. 7.

6. Sexual Harassment The problems of sexual harassment have already been identified to a limited extent through soft law measures: a Council Resolution, a Commission Recommendation,[228] and a Code of Conduct. The definition of sexual harassment is useful:

> conduct of a sexual nature, or other conduct based on sex affecting the dignity of women and men at work, including conduct of superiors and colleagues.

This conduct is deemed to constitute an intolerable violation of the dignity of workers or trainees and is unacceptable if:

(a) such conduct is unwanted, unreasonable and offensive to the recipient;

(b) a person's rejection of or submission to such conduct on the part of employers or workers (including superiors or colleagues) is used explicitly or implicitly as a basis for a decision which affects that person's access to vocational training, access to employment, promotion, salary or any other employment decisions; and/or

(c) such conduct creates an intimidating, hostile or humiliating work environment for the recipient.[229]

Thus, the definition of what constitutes sexual harassment is subjective, not objective: account is taken of the effect of the conduct upon the particular individual concerned rather than examining the effect of equivalent conduct on a 'reasonable person'. The motive of the perpetrator is largely irrelevant. The Code suggests that the conduct may take the form of physical conduct of a sexual nature, ranging from unnecessary touching to assault, verbal conduct of a sexual nature, including unwelcome sexual advances, suggestive remarks and innuendoes, non-verbal conduct of a sexual nature, including the display of pornographic or sexually explicit pictures, leering, whistling or making sexually suggestive gestures, and sex-based conduct, such as sex-based comments about appearance or dress. The essence of the definition is that the conduct is unwanted by the recipient: in the words of the Code, 'sexual attention becomes sexual harassment *if it is persisted in once it has been made clear that it is regarded by the recipient as offensive*, although one incident of harassment may constitute sexual harassment if sufficiently serious' (emphasis added).[230] The definition of sexual harassment also distinguishes between conduct which damages the employee's working environment ('hostile work environment',[231] using US terminology (Article 1(c))) and conduct which is used as a basis for employment decisions affecting the victim (Article 1(b)). In either case the woman can be said to enjoy less favourable working conditions than her male employees. This invokes the language of Article 5 of the Equal Treatment Directive.

---

[228] Commission recommendation of 27 Nov. 1991 on the protection and dignity of men and women at work: 92/131/EEC [1992] OJ L49/1.

[229] Art. 1 of the Council's Resolution on the Dignity of Women and Men at Work [1990] OJ C157/3. For further definitions see the American EEOC's Guidelines on Sexual Harassment, 1980, 29 CFR, s.1604. 11(f) and the discussion in Ellis, note 11 above, at 214ff.

[230] See, in the British context, *Bracebridge Engineering* v. *Darby* [1990] IRLR 3 where the EAT accepted that a single serious sexual assault constituted unlawful sexual discrimination.

[231] In *Meritor Savings Bank* v. *Vinson*, 477 US 57, 65, the US Sup. Ct. distinguished between hostile work environment and *quid pro quo* claims. Both are cognizable under Title VII though a hostile environment claim requires harassment that is severe or perverse. In *Burlington Industries* v. *Ellerth*, 26 June 1998, the Sup. Ct. doubted the utility of these terms, and it is not proposed to adopt this distinction here.

Legal effect is given to the prohibition of sexual harassment through Directive 76/207. The Council Resolution and the Commission Recommendation make clear that sexual harassment '*may* be, in certain circumstances, contrary to the principle of equal treatment within the meaning of Articles 3, 4 and 5 of Council Directive 76/207/EEC'. This is the approach adopted in the United Kingdom and Ireland where there has been judicial acceptance that sexual harassment may constitute unlawful discrimination:[232] usually the victim of the sexual harassment would not have been harassed or treated in that way had she been a man. She is thus a victim of discrimination. The link with the Equal Treatment Directive imposes certain constraints on the development of a framework which would successfully eliminate all forms of sexual harassment. It imposes the requirement, first, that there should be a comparator who is more favourably treated; and secondly, that the comparator and the victim should be of opposite sexes. Therefore, those who work in a single-sex environment who find, for example, the display by their colleagues of pornographic photographs offensive, are left without a remedy. Similarly, those who discover that their comparators would be treated equally badly are also unable to claim that they are the victims of discrimination.[233] A principle of equality based on notions of disadvantage might help here (see discussion at page 224ff). Furthermore, those who face harassment as a result of their sexual orientation, a situation envisaged by the Code of Conduct,[234] are unable to bring their claims within the confines of the Directive after the decision in *Grant*.[235] Neither the Equal Treatment Directive nor the Council Resolution on Dignity of Women and Men at work, despite its title, provides a general legally enforceable right to dignity in the workplace nor any legal protection against a hostile work environment.

Employers also stand to suffer from this rather unnatural link between sexual harassment and the Equal Treatment Directive. Faced by a claim of direct discrimination they may find themselves vicariously and strictly liable. Unless the Court introduces the possibility that direct discrimination can be objectively justified, the employer can only resort to the defences contained in the Equal Treatment Directive which cover very limited situations and, being derogations, are narrowly construed. Consequently, employers who have fully implemented the Code of Conduct but are

---

[232] See respectively *Strathclyde Regional Council* v. *Poricelli* [1986] IRLR 134 and *A Worker* v. *A Garage Proprietor*, Labour Court, 1985.

[233] See in the British context *Stewart* v. *Cleveland Guest (Engineering) Ltd* [1994] IRLR 440, where the Industrial Tribunal accepted that the display by male employees of pictures of nude women was detrimental to the applicant, but no discrimination had occurred because a hypothetical man might also have complained, so that the applicant had not shown that she had been treated less favourably.

[234] See discussion of para. 3. 3 of the Code of Conduct. On the question whether less favourable treatment on the ground of homosexuality may constitute direct discrimination, see A. Byre, 'Equality and Non-Discrimination', in A. Clapham and K. Waaldijk (eds.), *Homosexuality: A European Community Issue: Essays on Lesbian and Gay Rights in European Law and Policy* (1993). She suggests that the refusal to hire gay men may be directly discriminatory because it involves gender-based assumptions that homosexual men are unreliable, which do not take an individual's suitability for a job into account. These assumptions may not apply to female applicants. See also the European Parliament's Resolution on Equal Rights for homosexuals and lesbians in the EC [1994] OJ C61/40.

[235] The US Sup. Ct. recently decided in *Oncale*, 523 U.S. 75; 118 S.Ct. 998, that same-sex sexual harassment was actionable as sex discrimination under Title VII.

still faced with a claim of sex discrimination will not be able to raise a defence that they took all reasonably practicable steps to prevent the harassment.[236]

We therefore propose the introduction of a separate provision at Community level, distinct from the Equal Treatment Directive, protecting workers against harassment and a hostile working environment. This could be negotiated by the social partners and extended by a Directive, or adopted directly by the members. The definition of harassment should be based on the existing Community legislation. Further, the employer should be placed under a positive duty to create and maintain an environment free from harassment as far as reasonably practicable. This duty would include the establishment and publication of fair and effective procedures for dealing with complaints of harassment, as well as the institution of informal counselling and advice. These procedures might be negotiated by the equal opportunities forum.[237] If this is not possible then the asymmetrical approach to non-discrimination should be adopted. The British Employment Appeal Tribunal has started to follow this approach. In *British Telecommunications* v. *Williams*[238] the Court ruled that because the conduct which constitutes sexual harassment is itself gender-specific, there is no necessity to look for a male comparator, and it would be no defence to a complaint for sexual harassment that a person of the other sex would have been treated similarly.

7. Burden of Proof The Court has ruled that in principle the burden of proving the existence of sex discrimination lies with the complainant.[239] It has, however, recognized that adjustments to national rules on the burden of proof may be necessary to ensure the effective implementation of the principle of equality. In *Danfoss*[240] the Court demonstrated its commitment to ensuring that pay structures and systems of recruitment are transparent. In that case the employers' pay structure provided the same basic wage to all employees but paid additional individual supplements on the basis of mobility, training and seniority. This resulted in the average wage paid to men being 6.86 per cent higher than that paid to women. This system so lacked transparency that female employees could only establish differences between their pay and that received by men by reference to average pay. Consequently, the Court concluded that the applicants would be deprived of any effective means of enforcing the principle of equal pay before the national courts if the effect of producing such evidence was not to impose upon employers the burden of proving that their pay practices were not in fact discriminatory. Therefore, once the female employees have established a *prima facie* case of discrimination the legal, rather than the evidential, burden of proof shifts to the employer to rebut this presumption. Similarly in *Enderby* the Court concluded that if the pay of speech therapists was significantly

---

[236] Cf. s.41 of the British Sex Discrimination Act 1975; employers are liable for 'anything done by a person in the course of his employment . . . whether or not it was done with the employer's knowledge or approval' subject to the defence that the employer 'took such steps as were reasonably practicable to prevent the employee from doing that act'.

[237] See the text following note 320 below.   [238] [1997] IRLR 668.

[239] Case C–127/92, *Enderby* [1994] ECR I–5535.

[240] Case 109/88, *Danfoss* [1989] ECR I–3199. See further Case 318/86, *Commission* v. *France* [1988] ECR 3559; Case 248/83, *Commission* v. *Germany* [1985] ECR 1459; Case C–127/92, *Enderby* [1994] ECR I–5535.

lower than that of pharmacists, and the speech therapists were almost exclusively women while the pharmacists were predominantly men, there was a *prima facie* case of discrimination, at least where the two jobs were of equal value and the statistics describing the situation were valid. As a result it was for the employers to show that there were objective reasons for the difference in pay and for the national court to assess whether it could take those statistics into account and to assess whether they covered enough individuals, whether they illustrated purely fortuitous or short-term phenomena, and whether in general they appeared to be significant.[241]

Against this background Directive 97/80 on the burden of proof was introduced. This is due to be implemented by 1 January 2001. Article 4 provides that Member States shall take such measures as are necessary, in accordance with their national judicial systems, to ensure that:

> when persons who consider themselves wronged because the principle of equal treatment has not been applied to them establish, before a court or other competent authority, facts from which it may be presumed that there has been direct or indirect discrimination, it shall be for the respondent to prove that there has been no breach of the principle of equal treatment.

8. Remedies   It is a long-established principle of Community law that under the duty of co-operation laid down in Article 10 (*ex* Article 5) TEC the Member States must ensure the legal protection which individuals derive from the direct effect of Community law. In the absence of Community rules governing a matter, it is for the domestic legal system of each Member State to designate the courts having jurisdiction and to lay down detailed procedural rules governing actions for safeguarding rights for individuals (the principle of procedural autonomy). However, such rules must not be less favourable than those governing similar domestic actions (the principle of non-discrimination), nor render virtually impossible or excessively difficult the exercise of rights conferred by Community law (the principle of effective judicial protection).[242]

The question of the adequacy of national remedies has already been extensively considered in the context of the Equal Treatment Directive. Article 6 of Directive 76/207 requires Member States to introduce into their national legal systems such measures as are necessary to enable all persons who consider themselves wronged by the failure to apply to them the principle of equal treatment to pursue their claims by judicial process.[243] Article 6 does not prescribe a specific sanction, leaving Member States free to choose between different solutions.

The Court has, however, circumscribed the Member States' discretion. First, Member States cannot exclude judicial control altogether.[244] Secondly, the Court

---

[241] See also Case C–400/93, *Royal Copenhagen A/S (Specialarbejderforbundet i Danmark* v. *Dansk Industrie* [1995] ECR I–1275.

[242] See, e.g., Case 33/76, *Rewe-Zentralfinanz eG* v. *Landwirtschaftskammer für das Saarland* [1976] ECR 1989, at para. 5; and see C. Kakouris, 'Do the Member States Possess Judicial Procedural Autonomy?' (1997) 34 *CML Rev.* 1389; W. van Gerven, 'Bridging the Gap between Community and National Laws: Towards the Principle of Homogeneity in the Field of Legal Remedies?' (1995) 32 *CML Rev.* 679.

[243] Art. 6 of the Equal Pay Dir. 75/117/EEC requires Member States to ensure that the principle of equal pay is applied, and that effective means are available to ensure that the principle is observed. In addition, Art. 2 of the Dir. requires Member States to allow those who consider themselves wronged by the failure to apply the principle of equal pay to pursue their claims by judicial process.

[244] Case 222/84, *Johnston* v. *RUC* [1986] ECR 1651.

has insisted that any sanction provided for by the national system must be such as to 'guarantee real and effective judicial protection . . . it must also have a real deterrent effect on the employer'.[245] Therefore, if the Member State chooses to penalize the discrimination by the award of compensation that compensation must be adequate in relation to the damage sustained.[246] In both *Von Colson* and *Harz*,[247] the compensation was limited to a purely nominal amount—the reimbursement of the travelling expenses incurred. The Court considered that this would not satisfy the requirements of Article 6.[248] Similarly, the Court held in *Marshall (No 2)*[249] that the imposition of an upper limit on the amount of compensation received and the exclusion of an award of interest do not constitute proper implementation of Article 6. It reasoned that such limits restrict the amount of compensation '*a priori* to a level which is not necessarily consistent with the requirement of ensuring real equality of opportunity through adequate reparation for the loss and damage sustained as a result of discriminatory dismissal'.[250] However, in *Sutton*[251] the Court of Justice said that while in *Marshall (No 2)*, a case concerning a discriminatory dismissal, full compensation for the loss and damage sustained could not leave out of account factors such as the effluxion of time, *Sutton* concerned the right to receive interest on amounts payable by way of social security benefits. Those amounts were not compensatory in nature and in no way constitute reparation for loss or damage sustained. Therefore, the Court said that its reasoning in *Marshall (No 2)* could not be applied and Article 6 of Directive 79/7 merely required that the Member States adopt the measures necessary to enable all persons who consider themselves to have been wronged by discrimination to establish the unlawfulness of such discrimination and to obtain the benefits to which they would have been entitled in the absence of discrimination. The payment of interest on arrears of benefits could not be regarded as an essential component of the right. However, in *Magorrian*,[252] a case concerning national time limits, the Court was more lenient. It considered, in effect, that a British law which provided that no award of arrears of pay could be made relating to a period earlier than two years before the date on which the proceedings were instituted rendered any action by individuals relying on Community law impossible in practice, and therefore contravened Community law.

[245] Case 14/83, *Von Colson* [1984] ECR 1891, at para. 23.

[246] *Ibid.*, at para. 23; Case C–271/91, *Marshall (No 2)* [1993] ECR I–4367, at para. 26; C. McCrudden, 'The Effectiveness of European Equality Law: National Mechanisms for Enforcing Gender Equality Law in the Light of European Requirements' (1993) 13 *OJLS* 320. See also B. Fitzpatrick, 'Towards Strategic Litigation? Innovations in Sex Equality Litigation Procedures in the Member States of the European Community' (1992) 8 *Int. J of Comp. Lab. L and Ind. Rel.* 8.

[247] Case 79/83, *Harz* [1984] ECR 1921. See, further B. Fitzpatrick, 'The Effectiveness of Equality Law Remedies: European Community Law Perspective', in Hepple and Szyszczak, note 61 above.

[248] See further D. Curtin, 'Effective Sanctions and the Equal Treatment Directive: The *Von Colson* and *Harz* Cases' (1985) 22 *CML Rev.* 505. See subsequently Case C 180/95, *Nils Draehmpaehl* v. *Urania Immobilienservice OHG* [1997] ECR I–2195 (noted (1997) 34 *CML Rev.* 1259).

[249] Case C–271/91, [1993] ECR I–4367.

[250] English law now complies with the *Marshall (No 2)* decision as a result of SI 1993/2798, The Sex Discrimination and Equal Pay (Remedies) Regs. 1993.

[251] Case C–66/95, *The Queen* v. *Secretary of State for Social Security, ex parte Eunice Sutton* [1997] ECR I–2163.

[252] Case C–246/96, *Mary Teresa Magorrian and Irene Pratricia Cunningham* v. *Eastern Health and Social Services Board and Department of Health and Social Services* [1998] ECR I–7153.

While the Court has made important strides in ensuring that remedies are effective, the actions brought are dependent upon the initiative of the individual. There is
much concern that this is a significant deterrent to many from bringing proceedings.
It is widely recognized that some form of class action would offer significant advantages.[253] First, it would offer support to those bringing proceedings. Secondly, it
would indicate that the problem is not individual but more structural. Thirdly, it
would have a greater impact than a single award. The problem, as we have seen, is
that procedural matters are generally considered to be issues of domestic law and
that Community competence in this field is somewhat uncertain. However, the Community could encourage national courts to allow for greater use of class actions in
this field.

Remedies could also be used to achieve more fully the goals of affirmative action
programmes expressly authorized by Article 2(4) of Directive 76/207 and the new
Article 141(4) of the Treaty. The decision of the Supreme Court of Canada in *Action
travail des Femmes* v. *Canadian National Railway*[254] shows the way. The Court upheld the order of a human rights tribunal directing the railway to implement a special programme for the recruitment of women into blue-collar jobs. The tribunal
found that the complainants were the victims of discrimination resulting from long-
standing recruitment practices at CNR which had placed undue reliance on strength
tests and other physical requirements. The tribunal ordered the company to hire
women for one in every four blue-collar jobs until such time as their representation
levels matched their availability in the workforce. It also ordered the railway to report four times a year on its progress. Giving his reasons, Dickson CJ explained that:

> When confronted with such a case of 'systematic discrimination', it may be that the type
> of order issued by the tribunal is the only means by which the purposes of the Canadian
> Human Rights Act can be met. In any program of employment equity, there simply can-
> not be a radical dissociation of 'remedy' and 'prevention'. Indeed there is no prevention
> without some form of remedy. [255]

We therefore recommend:

- The remedies provision should be more explicit. It should say that any national sanction must be such as to 'guarantee real and effective judicial protection . . . it must also have a real deterrent effect on the employer'.
- The decision in *Sutton* should be reversed.
- While the national systems may impose temporal limitations for bringing
  claims, they cannot impose limits on the possibility of backdating benefits.
- Legislation should be introduced making it possible to order more pro-active
  remedies. This might involve a programme of affirmative action, a legally
  binding direction as to future conduct, or a general finding of discrimination.
- Member States should also be encouraged to provide for class actions for individuals bringing proceedings.

---

[253] See, further, B. Hepple, 'Equality and Discrimination', in P. Davies *et al.*, *European Community
Labour Law: Principles and Perspectives* (1996), 254–5.
[254] [1987] SCR 1114.   [255] At 1141–2.

9. Institutional Reform   The institutional steps already taken to achieve equality have already been outlined. Much more can be done. In this section we select two key reforms, an equality agency or equality 'ombudsman' and gender auditing.

(a) Equality Agency/Equality 'Ombudsman'

The Community institutions themselves have failed to deliver equality. Only five Commissioners out of twenty in the Santer Commission are women. As Charlesworth *et al.*[256] observe of the international law field, women are excluded from all major decision making institutions on global policies and guidelines, despite the often disparate impact of those decisions on women. The silence and invisibility of women also characterize those bodies with special functions regarding the creation and progressive development of international law—and in our context—European Union law. There has never been a female judge at the European Court of Justice and only one female Advocate General. This would also suggest that there is an important role for training of judges.[257]

If the Community is genuinely committed to the achievement of equality, first between the sexes and, perhaps later, on other grounds, it should consider setting up a specific equality agency or, perhaps, an equality 'ombudsman' along the lines of the successful European ombudsman, following the Scandinavian model.[258] If an agency, it must be based in Brussels with a budget and staff sufficient to deliver the tasks set. The mandate of this agency could be engaged in fact-finding, to receive complaints, investigate them and try to negotiate a settlement without the matter having to go to court. Further, it should also be consulted on all legislative proposals, as part of the gender auditing process, be able to draw up codes of practice and make legislative proposals to the Commission. Further, the Member States could be required to report annually or biennially on the realization of equality in their countries. The experience of countries reporting to CEDAW has been good, with one country reporting that the task of preparing the report has been a 'positive exercise in thought, analysis and self-appraisal'.[259] Finally, any such organization must maintain contacts with grass roots organizations which have more direct experience of the situation in the Member States. In this way it could act as a bridge between such organizations, the States and the Union.

The management board could be comprised of representatives of official national equality agencies, NGOs, trade unions, and employers' organizations, providing them with an opportunity to share their experiences. In addition, representatives of the main Community institutions need to be on the board and it would be accountable to the Commission and European Parliament.

There are many risks with such a proposal. First and foremost, experience with agencies of this kind has not always been happy. In the UK, the two principal equality agencies, the CRE and the EOC, have been consistently underfunded,

[256] Charlesworth, C. Chinkin, and S. Wright, 'Feminist Approaches to International Law' (1991) 85 *AJIL* 621.

[257] See L. Clark, 'Liberalism and the Living Tree: Women, Equality, and the Charter' (1990) 28 *Alberta Law Review* 384.

[258] See A. Ryel, 'The Nordic Model of Gender Equality Law', in Hervey and O'Keeffe, note 13 above.

[259] Initial Report of Guatemala submitted to the CEDAW Committee, CEDAW/C/Gua/1–2, 2 Apr. 1991, cited in Steiner and Alston, note 38 above, at 888.

suffered from judicial review of their activities,[260] and accused of inactivity.[261] Secondly, there is a risk that establishing an agency of this kind equates in some minds with the realization of equality and that no further governmental initiatives are required. Thirdly, there is a concern about ghettoization: that sex equality is a marginal 'women's matter' of no interest to the mainstream. Fourthly, control over the institution's purse strings is by those very Member States whose activities the agency is supposed to control. This might make it hesitant and circumspect in its criticism.[262] Despite these serious difficulties, there is a role both practical and symbolic for a body such as an equality agency, and we suggest that it be established.

(b) Gender Auditing

Beveridge and Nott suggest that if women are to achieve substantive, as opposed to purely formal, equality there has to be some way of predicting the potential impact of policy-making and decision-making on women.[263] They therefore suggest the introduction of gender auditing—a procedure intended to demonstrate whether women would benefit to the same degree as men from a particular policy and, if not, whether steps can be taken to address this. They point out that this does not mean that if a particular policy can be shown to prejudice women, but not men, it cannot be acted on; rather, they argue, in these circumstances compensatory measures for women might be appropriate. They suggest that models for auditing already exist in the Community and the Member States: Directive 85/337/EEC on environmental impact assessment; Council resolution on administrative simplification for enterprises, especially SMEs, which invited the Commission to prepare impact assessments on all proposals which might give rise to substantial impacts on SMEs;[264] and Policy Action and Fair Treatment (PAFT) in Northern Ireland requiring government departments and agencies in Northern Ireland to consider how any new policy affects certain groups in society (people of different religious beliefs or political opinions, men and women, people of different ethnic groups and people of different sexual orientation). Gender audits following these models could form an important part of mainstreaming equal opportunities issues into the Community system.[265]

We therefore recommend:

- A Community Equality Agency or Equality ombudsman be established.
- The Community consider introducing the requirement of a gender audit in respect of its own proposed legislation and require Member States to engage in a gender audit in respect of all major pieces of domestic legislation.

[260] G. Appleby and E. Ellis, 'Formal Investigations: The Commission for Racial Equality and the Equal Opportunities Commission as Law Enforcement Agencies' [1984] *PL* 236.

[261] See the discussions in C. Barnard, 'A European Litigation Strategy: The Case of the Equal Opportunities Commission', in J. Shaw and G. Moore (eds.), *New Dynamics of European Integration* (1996); E. Meehan, 'Priorities of the EOC' (1983) 54 *Political Quarterly* 69; V. Sacks, 'The EOC—Ten Years On' (1986) 43 *MLR* 560. The experience has not differed greatly in Canada: see J. Hucker, 'Anti-Discrimination Laws in Canada: Human Rights Commissions and the Search for Equality' (1997) 19 *HRQ* 547.

[262] See Byrnes, note 43 above, on this aspect of the CEDAW committee's work.

[263] F. Beveridge and S. Nott, 'Gender Auditing—Making the Community Work for Women', in O'Keeffe and Hervey, note 13 above.   [264] [1992] OJ C331/3.

[265] On the importance of mainstreaming, see A. Gallagher, 'Ending the Marginalization: Strategies for Incorporating Women into the United Nations Human Rights System' (1997) 19 *HRQ* 283.

B. *Removal of Effective Barriers to Labour Market Participation*

With women taking primary responsibility for childcare in most Western societies, their flexibility to participate fully in work is limited. Since the first equality action programme the Commission has recognized that full equality of opportunity can only be achieved by taking measures which will 'enable men and women to reconcile their occupational and family obligations'.[266] As a result, any strategy designed to remove barriers relating to female participation must address the following factors. First, pregnant women must be provided with adequate protection. The Directive on Pregnant Workers makes an important contribution in this respect. Secondly, consideration must be given to maternity and paternity leave. The Directive on parental leave negotiated by the social partners marks a significant step forward; and thirdly, specific provision needs to be made for childcare. The adoption of a Council recommendation on child-care represents one step in this direction.[267] This aspect of 'the equality package' is particularly important in respect of those countries from central and eastern Europe wishing to join the Union. The transition to market economies has been borne disproportionately by women. Job retraining has been focused primarily on men. At the same time the free or subsidized childcare facilities which enabled women to work outside the home under the socialist regimes are disappearing, rendering it increasingly difficult for women to participate in the formal economy. Further, governments have followed policies of encouraging women to leave paid employment and 'return home' as a means of dealing with high levels of unemployment.[268]

1. Pregnancy   As we have seen, the similarly situated model of sex discrimination legislation breaks down in the context of pregnancy. The Court of Justice has recognized this and has shown imagination in addressing the problem of dismissal or refusal to appoint a woman on the grounds of her pregnancy.[269] In the first case, *Dekker* v. *VJV Centrum*,[270] the employer decided not to appoint the applicant, who was pregnant, even though she was considered the best person for the job, on the ground that the employer's insurers refused to cover the costs of her maternity leave. Despite the fact that all the other candidates for the job were women, the Court of Justice ruled that as employment can only be refused because of pregnancy to a woman, refusal to appoint a woman on the grounds of her pregnancy constitutes direct discrimination on the grounds of sex, contrary to Articles 2(1) and 3(1) of the Equal Treatment Directive. Unlike the English courts, the European Court refused to undertake the tortuous exercise of finding a male comparator 'suffering from an equivalent problem'.[271] Instead, it struck at the heart of the problem: since only

---

[266] Third para. of point 16 of the Social Charter of 1989.

[267] Council Recommendation 92/241/EEC [1992] OJ L123/16.

[268] B. Einhorn, *Cinderella goes to Market: Citizenship, Gender and Women's Movements in East Central Europe* (1993), cited in Steiner and Alston, note 38 above, 896.

[269] See, further, J. Vegter and S. Prechal, *Report of the Network of Experts on the Implementation of the Equality Directives on Indirect Discrimination and Discrimination on Grounds of Pregnancy and Maternity*, V/6008/93–EN. Also, see G. More, 'Reflections on Pregnancy Discrimination under European Community Law' (1992) 14 *JSWL* 48.

[270] Case C–177/88, [1990] ECR I–3941.

[271] See, e.g., the approach of the English CA in *Webb* v. *EMO Air Cargo* [1992] 1 CMLR 793. The ECJ in Case C–32/93, *Webb*, said 'pregnancy is not in any way comparable with a pathological condition'.

women can become pregnant, less favourable treatment on the grounds of pregnancy automatically constitutes direct discrimination. Therefore, in the context of pregnancy it adopted an asymmetrical model of equality, a model focusing on the employment disadvantages suffered by pregnant women rather than their different treatment from men.

While *Dekker* concerned the refusal to appoint a woman on the grounds of her pregnancy, in *Hertz* [272] the Court ruled that the *dismissal* of a female worker on account of pregnancy also constitutes direct discrimination on the grounds of sex contrary to Articles 1(1), 2(1), and 5(1) of the Equal Treatment Directive. [273] The Court also adopted this approach in the more difficult case of *Webb* v. *EMO Air Cargo Limited.* [274] Ms Webb was appointed by EMO Air Cargo Ltd initially to replace another employee, Mrs Stewart, who was about to go on maternity leave, but then to continue working on Mrs Stewart's return. Shortly after starting work Ms Webb announced that she too was pregnant. When she was dismissed on the grounds, according to her employer, not of pregnancy but her unavailability to work, she claimed that she had been discriminated against on the grounds of sex. Emphasizing the fact that Ms Webb was not employed on a fixed-term contract the Court ruled that 'dismissal of a pregnant woman *recruited for an indefinite period* cannot be justified on grounds relating to her inability to fulfil a fundamental condition of her employment contract'(emphasis added). It therefore concluded that 'the dismissal of an employee who is recruited for an unlimited term with a view, initially, to replacing another employee during the latter's maternity leave' and 'who cannot do so because she is pregnant' was contrary to Articles 2(1) and 5(1) of the Directive. *Thibault* [275] concerned the situation of a woman in employment. In that case the Court said that the principle of non-discrimination requires that a woman who continues to be bound to her employer by a contract of employment during maternity leave should not be deprived of the benefit of working conditions which apply to both men and women.

However, the European Court has not provided women suffering from the problems of pregnancy or childbirth with absolute protection. This can be seen in two lines of case law, one concerning sickness and the other concerning pay. In *Hertz* [276] the plaintiff suffered from a complicated pregnancy, causing her to take a lot of sick leave. When the maternity leave came to an end she returned to work, but shortly afterwards had to take a further 100 days' sick leave due to an illness resulting from her pregnancy. The Court distinguished between two situations: first, the period of maternity leave, and secondly, the period after the maternity leave. During the first period the Court said a woman is protected against dismissal due to absence; during the second period the Court saw no reason to distinguish an illness attributable to pregnancy or confinement from any other illness. It reasoned that although certain disorders are specific to one or other sex, the only question is whether a woman is dis-

---

[272] Case C–179/88, *Hertz* [1990] ECR I–3979.
[273] This view was confirmed in Case C–421/92, *Habermann-Beltermann* [1994] ECR I–1657. See also Art. 10 of Dir. 92/85/EC, note 183 above.
[274] Case C–32/93, [1994] ECR I–3567.
[275] Case C–136/95 [1998] ECR I–2011.			[276] Case C–179/88, [1990] ECR I–3979.

missed on account of absence due to illness in the same circumstances as a man. If this is so then there is no direct or indirect discrimination on the grounds of sex. The Court reaffirmed this ruling in *Larsson*.[277] It said that the Directive does not preclude dismissals which are the result of absences due to an illness attributable to pregnancy or confinement even where that illness arose during pregnancy and continued during and after maternity leave. While these decisions can be justified by reference to practical necessity, by avoiding giving women *de facto* a permanent right to employment, they cannot be defended in terms of logic: if the dismissal of a female worker on account of pregnancy constitutes direct discrimination, the dismissal of a woman on account of a pregnancy-related illness from which only women can suffer should also automatically constitute direct discrimination. However, recently the Court in *Brown* v. *Rentokil*[278] qualified the decision in *Larsson*. It said that where a woman is absent owing to illness resulting from pregnancy or childbirth, and that illness arose during pregnancy and persisted during and after maternity leave, her absence not only during maternity leave but also during the period extending from the start of her pregnancy to the start of her maternity leave cannot be taken into account for computation of the period justifying her dismissal under national law. This answer was not affected by the fact that a contractual term permitted the employer to dismiss employees of either sex after a stipulated number of weeks of continuous absence. On the other hand, as the Court said in *Hertz*, a woman's absence after maternity leave may be taken into account under the same conditions as a man's absence due to incapacity for work caused by illness resulting from that pregnancy.

The issue of pay during maternity leave was considered in *Gillespie*.[279] In that case the plaintiffs, who were on maternity leave, had their pay reduced during their maternity leave and did not receive the benefit of the backdated pay rise. While accepting that maternity benefit constitutes pay within the meaning of Article 119 (now 141), the Court said that 'discrimination involves the application of different rules to comparable situations or the application of the same rule to different situations'.[280] The Court then argued that since this case concerned women taking maternity leave provided for by the national legislation they were in a special position requiring them to be afforded special protection. This situation was not comparable either with that of a man or with a woman actually at work. Consequently, it would seem that pregnant women who are still working must be treated in the same way as their colleagues who are at work and, as a result of the decisions in *Hertz* and *Dekker*, any less favourable treatment automatically constitutes direct discrimination. However, once a woman goes on maternity leave she is in a 'special position', and it is no longer possible to compare her with a person in work since they are in different situations. In respect of payment during maternity leave, the Court said that neither Article 119 (now 141) nor Article 1 of Directive 75/117 required that women should continue to receive full pay during maternity leave, nor did those provisions lay down any specific criteria for determining the amount of benefit to be paid to them during that period. The Court did add, however, that the amount payable could not be so low as

---

[277] Case C–400/95, [1997] ECR I–2757. [278] Case C–394/96, judgment of 30 June 1998.
[279] Case C–342/93, *Gillespie* v. *Northern Health and Social Services Board* [1996] ECR I–475.
[280] See note 194 above.

to undermine the purpose of the maternity leave, namely the protection of women before and after giving birth. In order to assess the adequacy of the amount payable, the national court must take into account not only the length of the maternity leave but also the other forms of social protection afforded by the national law in the case of justified absence from work. On the facts of the case there was nothing to suggest that the amount of benefit granted was such as to undermine the objective of protecting maternity leave. On the other hand, the Court said that a woman on maternity leave should receive a pay rise awarded before or during that period. To deny her such an increase would discriminate against her purely in her capacity as a worker since, had she not been pregnant, she would have received the pay rise.

The Court has accepted that differential treatment on the grounds of pregnancy may be lawful if the employer's actions are caught within the derogation contained in Article 2(3) of Directive 76/207 (protection of women, particularly on the grounds of pregnancy and maternity). In *Habermann-Beltermann*[281] the Court held that prohibition on night-time work by pregnant women was 'unquestionably compatible with Article 2(3)'. However, since the prohibition on night-time work by pregnant women takes effect only for a limited period in relation to the total length of an indefinite contract 'the termination of a contract without a fixed term on account of the woman's pregnancy . . . cannot be justified on the ground that a statutory prohibition, imposed because of pregnancy, temporarily prevents the employee from performing night-work'.[282]

Further special treatment can be given to pregnant women as a result of Directive 92/85/EC[283] designed to protect pregnant workers and workers who have recently given birth or who are breast feeding.[284] The Directive is intended to provide *minimum* requirements for encouraging improvements,[285] especially in the working environment, to protect the health and safety of pregnant workers. The Directive provides three pillars of employment protection which, with one exception, exist from the first day of employment. First, pregnant workers are entitled to time off, without loss of pay, in order to attend ante-natal examinations, if such examinations have to take place within working hours.[286] Secondly, they are entitled to a continuous period of at least fourteen weeks' maternity leave, of which at least two weeks must be allocated before and/or after confinement.[287] During this period the pregnant workers' rights connected with the contract of employment, with the exception of pay, must be maintained.[288] The maintenance of pay or an adequate

---

[281] Case C–421/92, [1994] ECR I–1657.   [282] See also Art. 7 of Dir. 92/85, note 183 above.

[283] Council Dir. 92/85/EEC, note 184 above, on the introduction of measures to encourage improvements in the safety and health at work of pregnant workers who have recently given birth or are breast feeding (10th individual Dir. within the meaning of Art. 16(1) of Dir. 89/391/EEC). The Dir. was based on Art. 118a (new Art. 138). See, further, V. Cromack, 'The EC Pregnancy Directive Principle or Pragmatism' (1993) 15 *JSWL* 261.

[284] These 3 terms are defined by reference to national law and practice and are dependent on the worker informing her employer of her condition (Art. 2). The term pregnant worker will be used to apply to the 3 situations unless otherwise stated.

[285] Art. 1(3) provides that the Dir. may not have the effect of reducing the level of protection afforded to pregnant workers.

[286] Art. 9. This Art. naturally only applies to pregnant workers.   [287] Art. 8(1) and (2).

[288] Art. 11(2)(a). See Case C–342/93 *Gillespie* [1996] ECR I–475 at note 279 above.

allowance[289] must also be ensured, but Member States may make entitlement to pay conditional upon the worker fulfilling the conditions of eligibility for such benefits laid down by national legislation.[290] Thirdly, pregnant workers cannot be dismissed during the period from the beginning of their pregnancy to the end of their maternity leave, save in exceptional cases not connected with their condition, which are permitted under national law or practice.[291] Employers must provide pregnant workers who are dismissed within this period with duly substantiated written grounds for dismissal.[292] Finally, the Member State must provide a remedy for pregnant workers who are dismissed.[293] The Directive also provides more specific rights to protect the health and safety of the pregnant worker.

We therefore recommend:

- While the Court of Justice's view that discrimination on the grounds of pregnancy *per se* constitutes direct discrimination is an imaginative departure from the symmetrical model of discrimination, for the sake of clarity an amendment to the Pregnant Workers Directive should be made, stating that it is unlawful (a) to refuse to appoint or to promote or offer training opportunities on the grounds of her pregnancy; or (b) to terminate the employment of a woman at any time on the grounds of her pregnancy, including pregnancy-related illnesses for so long as they remain after the birth of the child; or (c) to subject her to any other detriment on the grounds of her pregnancy, except as permitted by the health and safety legislation.[294]
- Provision should also be made for adequate remuneration throughout maternity leave and full pay for at least the early part of it, and the benefit of all accrued rights during the period of maternity leave and that no loss be suffered on her return.

2. Maternity and Paternity Leave; Parental and Family Leave   The first collective agreement concluded by the social partners under the Social Policy Agreement of the Maastricht Treaty was the Framework Agreement on Parental Leave,[295] which lays down minimum requirements designed to facilitate the reconciliation of parental and professional responsibilities for working parents.[296] It provides all workers, both men and women, who have an employment contract or an employment relationship[297] with a non-transferable right to parental leave.[298]

The collective agreement envisages two main rights. First, the agreement entitles men and women workers to parental leave on the birth or adoption of a child to

---

[289] Art. 11(2)(b). An allowance is adequate (Art. 11(3)) if it guarantees income at least equivalent to that which the worker concerned would receive in the event of a break in her activities on grounds connected with her state of health, subject to any ceiling laid down by national legislation—in other words sick pay. However, a statement of the Council and the Commission added to the Dir. ([1992] OJ L348/8) states that the reference to the state of health is not 'intended in any way to imply that pregnancy and childbirth equate with sickness'. The link with such allowance is intended to serve as a concrete fixed reference in all Member States for the determination of the minimum amount of maternity allowance.

[290] These conditions may not, however, provide for periods of previous employment in excess of 12 months immediately prior to the presumed date of confinement: Art. 11(2)(b) and (4).

[291] Art. 10(1).   [292] Art. 10(2).   [293] Art. 10(3).   [294] See further note 10 above.

[295] The draft agreement was concluded on 6 Nov. 1995 by ETUC, CEEP, and UNICE and formally agreed on 14 Dec. 1995. See COM(96)26 final.

[296] Cl. 1(1).   [297] Cl. 1(2).   [298] Cl. 2(2).

enable them to take care of that child, for at least three months, until a given age up to 8 years, to be defined by the Member States or the Social Partners.[299] In order to ensure that workers can exercise their right to parental leave, they must be protected against dismissal on the grounds of applying for or taking parental leave in accordance with national legislation, collective agreements, or practice.[300] At the end of the parental leave workers have the right to return to the same job, or, if that is not possible, to an equivalent or similar job consistent with their employment contract or employment relationship.[301] In addition, rights acquired by the worker or in the process of being acquired on the date on which parental leave starts must be maintained as they stand until the end of the parental leave. These rights, including any changes arising from national law, agreements, or practice, will apply.[302] Secondly, the agreement provides that workers are entitled to time off on the grounds of *force majeure* for urgent family reasons in cases of sickness or accident, making the immediate presence of the worker indispensable.[303] Member States and/or social partners may specify 'the conditions of access and modalities of application of this clause'.

Indeed, a large number of issues are left to be resolved by the Member State and/or social partners. In respect of parental leave, the Member States and/or the social partners may decide whether parental leave is granted on a full-time or part-time basis, in a fragmented way or in the form of a time credit system, whether entitlement to parental leave be subject to a period of work qualification and/or length of service qualification (which cannot exceed one year), whether to adjust conditions for access and modalities of application of parental leave to the special circumstances of adoption and whether notice periods be given by the worker to the employer specifying the beginning or the end of the parental leave.[304] In addition, the Member States and the social partners can define the circumstances in which the employer is allowed to postpone the granting of parental leave for justifiable reasons relating to the operation of the undertaking[305] and authorize that special arrangements be made for small undertakings.[306] Member States and the social partners must define the status of the employment contract or employment relationship for the period of the parental leave.[307] All matters relating to social security in relation to the agreement are left to be determined by the Member States according to national law.[308] Throughout the document, no reference is made to issues such as income during leave.

As we have seen, the rights provided here are minima and Member States can maintain or introduce more favourable provisions than those set out in the Agreement.[309] Indeed, the implementation of the provisions of the collective agreement 'shall not constitute valid grounds for reducing the general level of protection afforded to workers in the field of this agreement'. However, 'this does not prejudice the right of the Member States and/or social partners to develop different legislative, regulatory or contractual provisions, in the light of changing circumstances (includ-

---

[299] Cl. 2(1).   [300] Cl. 2(4).   [301] Cl. 2(5).   [302] Cl. 2(6).   [303] Cl. 3(1).
[304] Art. 2(3)(a)–(d).
[305] E.g., where the work is of a seasonal nature, where a replacement cannot be found within the notice period, where a significant proportion of the workforce applies for parental leave at the same time, where a specific function is of strategic importance.
[306] Cl. 2(3)(e)–(f).   [307] Cl. 2(7).   [308] Cl. 2(8).   [309] Cl. 3(1).

ing the introduction of non-transferability), as long as the minimum requirements provided for in this agreement are complied with'.

Insufficient time has elapsed in which to assess the effectiveness of the agreement which was implemented by directive. Nevertheless, experience from the Nordic countries, where parental leave already exists, indicates that it is usually the woman who takes the parental leave. This needs to be addressed to encourage recognition of joint parental responsibility. We therefore recommend that:

- In order to ensure that fathers participate in the early care of their child a father should be entitled to (at least four weeks') paternity leave on full pay. Women on maternity leave should receive the same amount for the same duration.
- As far as family leave is concerned, both parents should be given ten days per year.
- In order to ensure that fathers take equal responsibility, the leave should be non-transferable.

3. Childcare   Despite increasing numbers of women entering the labour force there has not been a correlative decrease in women's share of family responsibilities. As a result there is a particular need to ensure properly resourced and supervised child-care facilities for working parents, including pre- and after-school care, and vacation care. Recognizing the importance of this for the integration of women into work, the Commission adopted a non-legally binding recommendation on childcare. This provides that Member States, possibly in co-operation with national, regional, or local authorities, management and labour, other relevant organizations and private individuals should take and encourage initiatives in four areas:

1. The provision of childcare services while parents:
   —are working
   —are following a course of education or training in order to obtain employment

   or

   —are seeking a job or a course of education or training in order to obtain employment;
2. Special leave for employed parents with responsibility for the care and upbringing of children;[310]
3. Adaptation of the environment, structure, and organization of work to make them responsive to the needs of workers with children;[311]
4. The sharing of occupational, family, and upbringing responsibilities arising from the care of children between women and men. This includes, according to Article 6, encouraging increased participation by men in order to achieve a more equal sharing of parental responsibilities.

---

[310] These special leave initiatives apply to both men and women. They are intended to combine some flexibility as to how leave may be taken (Art. 4).

[311] This includes action, in particular within the framework of a collective agreement, to create an environment which takes into account the needs of all working parents with childcare responsibilities, ensure that due recognition is given to persons engaged in childcare services and the social value of their work; and promote action, especially in the public sector, which can serve as an example in developing initiatives in this area (Art. 5).

Childcare services, defined as any type of childcare, whether public or private, individual or collective, should be affordable, flexible, and diverse. They should combine reliable care, from the point of view of health and safety, with a general upbringing and a pedagogical approach. Furthermore, they should be available in all areas and regions of the Member States, and be accessible to parents and children, including children with special needs.[312] Although the Recommendation is not legally binding it has a symbolic value in demonstrating the European Community's commitment to childcare, and Member States are obliged to inform the Commission of the measures taken to give effect to the Recommendation.[313] That being said, a more pro-active approach is necessary which involves imposing duties on states to provide childcare.

We therefore propose that local authorities should have the duty to provide subsidized places for day-care for children in their areas. The funding should be shared between parents, employers, and the general community.

4. Flexible Working Hours   Paid time off work clearly helps parents when their children are young or when they are sick, but flexible working time is also important.[314] A duty to accommodate (see the text to note 331 below) might help parents to request flexibility in their working hours. If workers (primarily women) choose to work part-time, either due to inadequate childcare or so that they can spend time with their children, they need adequate protection. The legal device of indirect discrimination (see the text to note 124 above) has provided some assistance, but employers can always justify, for objective reasons, the difference in treatment between part-time and full-time employees.

The principle of non-discrimination between part-time and full-time workers has been included in Directive 97/81/EC on part-time work[315] but, as with the Court of Justice's case law, combined with the possibility of justifying differences in treatment. The Directive also provides that:

> As far as possible, employers should give consideration to:
> (a) requests by workers to transfer from full-time to part-time work that becomes available at the establishment and vice versa . . .
> (c) the provision of timely information on the availability of part-time and full-time positions in the establishment . . .
> (d) measures to facilitate access to part-time work at all levels of the enterprise . . .

While this provision may well give some assistance to working parents, the weak language draws the teeth of the provision. We therefore recommend:

- There should be an obligation imposed on employers to allow workers to transfer from full-time to part-time work unless there are compelling reasons why this is not possible.

[312] Art. 3.

[313] The Commission intends to follow up the Childcare Recommendation by assessing the implementation of the Recommendation and establishing baseline data on childcare infrastructure and services in the Member States—COM(94)333, at 43; 92/241/EEC [1992] OJ L123. See also, 'Work and Childcare: Implementing the Council Recommendation on Childcare—A Guide to Good Practice', *Social Europe—Supplement* 5/96.

[314] See, generally, K. Schiewe, 'The Gender Dimension in German Labour Law: Time Revisited', in Y. Kravaritou (ed.), *The Sex of Labour Law in Europe* (1996), 53–87.

[315] Cl. 4.

- Protection should also be given to others who find themselves in a vulnerable position in the workplace, such as those on fixed term contracts and those working as temps (*travail intérimaire*).

5. Training The importance of training for women cannot be underestimated. In its resolution on the reintegration and late integration of women into working life[316] vocational training was considered a central pillar in achieving this objective, a theme also picked up in, among others, the Council Resolution on the quality and attractiveness of vocational education and training.[317] Table 2 indicates the level of activity rates for men and women at different ages and highlights the consistently lower levels of activity for women.

However, reference to the importance of training is insufficient. What is needed in this field is gender-sensitive macro- and micro-economic and active labour market policies, as well as gender-balanced training policies, with emphasis on addressing the obstacles to women's education, training, and skill diversification and flexibility linked to the emerging skill needs in the changing labour market and changes in technology.[318] We therefore recommend that:

- Continued emphasis needs to be placed on training specially designed to accommodate women's interests.
- This needs to be combined with adequate funds to pay for any necessary childcare.

C. Fair Participation

So far we have considered two strategies necessary to promote equal opportunities: on the one hand an anti-discrimination strategy and on the other removing barriers to effective equality of opportunity. A third strategy focuses on fair participation[319] at work, a strategy recognized to some extent by the Fair Employment (Northern Ireland) Act 1989, which provides for fair participation by the two dominant religious communities in Northern Ireland, and the 1986 Employment Equity Act in Canada. We have already looked at affirmative action, which has an important role to play in fair participation. In this section we shall first examine workplace monitoring and fair participation; secondly, the duty to accommodate; thirdly, contract compliance; and fourthly, representation of sexes.

1. Workplace Monitoring, Fair Participation In Northern Ireland the Fair Employment (Northern Ireland) Act 1989[320] has as its main aim the promotion of 'fair participation in employment',[321] a term which is not defined in the statute but, as Fredman notes, is openly result-oriented.[322] The Act prescribes that employers must

---

[316] [1988] OJ C333/01.   [317] [1994] OJ C374/01.

[318] See, E. Date-Bah, 'Appropriate Policy for Gender Equality in Employment: Insights from the ILO Interdepartmental Project on Equality for Women in Employment' (1996) 2 *Int. J Discrim. L* 7. See also Council Resolution of 15 Dec. 1997 on the 1998 Employment Guidelines OJ 1998 C30/1.

[319] This section draws on *Working Life*, note 10 above, at 170–2.

[320] See C. McCrudden, 'Affirmative Action and Fair Participation: Interpreting the Fair Employment Act 1989' (1992) 21 *ILJ* 170. See also J. Knox and J. O'Hara, 'Fair Employment Legislation in Northern Ireland' in Hepple and Szyszczak, note 61 above, and Part VII of the Northern Ireland Act 1998.

[321] Ss.31(1), 32(5), 36(1)(c) of the Fair Employment Act 1989.

[322] Fredman, note 55 above, at 588.

Table 2. Activity rates by age, educational level, and sex—1995

	25–39 years						40–59 years					
	ISCED 5–7		ISCED 3		ISCED 0–2		ISCED 5–7		ISCED 3		ISCED 0–2	
	M	F	M	F	M	F	M	F	M	F	M	F
B	96.4	90.1	96.2	81.6	90.9	61.7	93.4	74.1	87.5	75.8	72.5	35.9
DK	95.6	89.6	94.3	81.5	86.7	64.9	93.9	91.4	88.5	78.9	80.4	63.8
D	96.7	84.4	91.1	74.8	91.3	56.4	93.6	83.8	87.4	68.8	80.4	51.7
GR	95.5	85.8	96.0	62.9	95.6	48.7	89.7	71.8	87.1	39.0	88.9	40.1
E	93.2	84.2	93.1	70.4	93.1	53.8	94.8	81.3	93.2	61.7	85.7	34.3
F	95.4	87.1	97.2	82.5	94.0	66.5	95.6	83.5	89.8	74.7	81.6	61.6
IRL	96.1	84.8	95.7	68.9	90.0	44.8	94.7	71.3	91.6	43.9	81.2	30.0
I	92.0	84.1	87.8	69.8	91.1	47.4	95.9	83.3	90.2	61.0	77.1	31.5
L	95.3	72.8	93.3	60.1	94.3	53.0	95.2	66.7	88.8	40.3	78.9	35.3
NL	94.8	87.3	95.8	70.7	82.8	52.0	93.2	76.9	86.4	54.8	72.8	37.7
A	94.7	92.5	94.2	78.9	92.0	70.3	97.0	81.9	86.6	62.6	81.6	53.4
P	98.0	95.6	90.3	79.4	94.7	75.6	95.0	90.5	91.1	75.2	86.5	58.3
S	93.7	90.4	92.9	87.4	94.5	75.6	97.8	97.0	97.6	95.8	95.5	89.3
FIN	95.0	85.3	89.6	78.6	86.9	68.4	91.9	91.1	82.8	81.4	73.4	73.5
UK	96.9	87.0	95.3	76.7	91.4	63.2	93.8	84.5	89.4	77.6	81.8	65.0

Level of Education Obtained

The different categories of education ISCED (International Standard Classification of Education) have been grouped into three different levels:

—level ISCED 0–2 covers people who have received education up to and including the middle of secondary school, corresponding usually to the minimum school-leaving age;

—level ISCED 3 covers people who have continued their education beyond the minimum school-leaving age to a level corresponding usually to the end of secondary school;

—level ISCED 5–7 covers people who have received some recognized form of higher education and obtained the appropriate qualification

Source: Eurostat, Statistics in Focus: Population and Social Conditions (1997/1).

register with the Fair Employment Commission and then monitor the composition of their workforce.[323] Public employers must also monitor applications for employment[324] followed by periodic reviews to ascertain whether members of each community are enjoying fair participation in employment in the employer's concern.[325] Where it appears to an employer that members of a particular community are not enjoying fair participation, the employer must determine what, if any, affirmative action would be reasonable and appropriate.[326] In Canada the 1986 Employment Equity Act required all federally-regulated employers with more than 100 employees to file an annual report on the representation levels in their workforce of each of the so-called designated groups—women, aboriginal peoples, visible minorities, and the disabled—and their distribution by occupational category and salary range.[327] A similar breakdown was also to be provided on the number of employees hired, promoted, and terminated.[328] In addition, employers were required to prepare annual plans indicating how they intended to achieve employment equity.[329] Given problems with the operation of the Act, a new Act was passed in 1995 which applied to both the public and private sectors. It empowered the Canadian Human Rights Commission to undertake compliance audits of employers and where necessary to direct an employer to establish short-term hiring goals.[330]

We therefore recommend that:

- The Union should introduce the goal of fair participation combined with a duty to monitor at least the gender composition of the workforce. Where an employer fails to do this, this constitutes a *prima facie* case of discrimination in relation to any worker who thereby suffers a disadvantage. If, as a result of this monitoring, there appears to be a significant underrepresentaton of one sex remedial affirmative action needs to be considered, as the Canadian railways case suggested.[331]

- Employers should be under a duty to conduct their employment decisions with regard to the duty to provide fair participation. Specifically, employers could be required by legislation to create in each workplace (possibly over a certain size, at least initially) an equal opportunities forum where equal opportunities could be discussed with employee representatives and/or trade union members. Legislation could also prescribe that such a forum be under a duty to develop and implement an equal opportunities policy for the workplace; that employers consult the forum over equal opportunities issues; and that they jointly develop an equal opportunities plan. There would also be an obligation on employers to disclose and discuss the outcome of annual workplace monitoring to the forum and to discuss with the forum any significant changes in the composition of the workforce in the year to come to ensure that principles of equal opportunities are not jeopardized. Where disputes arose

---

[323] S.27 FEA. The duty is confined to employers employing more than 10 employees and all public employers (ss.23 and 25).

[324] This also applies to private employers with a staff of over 250. [325] S.31(1) FEA.

[326] S.31(2)(3) FEA. [327] S.6(1). [328] S.6(1)(d).

[329] S.5(1). See generally J. Hucker, 'Moving Towards the Ellusive Goal of Equality: Reflections on Canada's System of Human Rights Enforcement' (1995) 25 *Cambrian L. Rev.* 33.

[330] Ss.22–26. See Hucker, note 329 above. [331] See note 254 above.

the forum would have the power to refer matters to the national Equal Opportunities Commission or to the Community Equal Opportunities Agency or 'Ombudsman'.
- It is also recommended that equal opportunities officers be appointed in each workplace to whom initial complaints can be made.

2. Duty to Accommodate   In Canada the Supreme Court has read into discrimination legislation the duty to accommodate the special needs of racial, religious, and other minorities, where their full and equal participation in employment is impeded by neutral requirements with discriminatory effects, and where accommodation would not impose undue hardship on the party imposing the unintentionally discriminatory barrier.[332] In *Alberta Human Rights Commission* v. *Central Alberta Dairy Pool*[333] the Supreme Court of Canada affirmed that in order to meet this duty the employer may have to accept some inconvenience, expense, or operational disruption. The case involved a complaint made to the Alberta Human Rights Commission by an individual who asked that he would not have to work on days which conflicted with his Sabbath. The employers refused to accede to this request. In the case Wilson J enumerated a non-exhaustive list of factors relevant in deciding whether undue hardship had been established:

> financial cost, disruption of a collective agreement, problems of morale of other employees, interchangeability of the workforce and facilities. The size of the employer's operation may influence the assessment of whether a given financial cost is undue or the ease with which the workforce and facilities can be adapted to the circumstances. Where safety is at issue both the magnitude of the risk and the identity of those who bear it are relevant considerations.[334]

She added that if the employer could cope with an employee's being away sick or away on vacation on Mondays, it could surely accommodate a similarly isolated absence of an employee due to religious obligation.

Such a duty to accommodate could usefully assist women who might want to transfer from full-time to part-time work for reasons of child care or the care of elderly relatives. It might help those who wish to rearrange their working hours for similar reasons. We therefore recommend that a legislative duty to accommodate be included in Community legislation.

3. Contract Compliance   Given the obligation, at both national and EC level, on the public sector to put work out to tender, the principle of contract compliance could be adopted far more extensively than currently. Once a notion of fair participation is incorporated into the legislation, it would be possible to make compliance with the duty to ensure fair participation a condition for the award of public sector contracts.

We therefore recommend that the EC Public Procurement Directives should be amended to require public authorities to include an obligation on contractors to have complied with the duty of fair participation.

4. Representation of the Sexes on Official Bodies   Gender equality in employment should lead to balanced representation of women in the higher levels of enterprises

[332] *Simpson-Sears* [1985] 2 SCR 547–50.
[333] *Alberta Human Rights Commission* v. *Central Alberta Dairy Pool* [1990] 2 SCR 489.   [334] At 521.

where policies are formulated. Yet women continue to be significantly underrepresented in managerial and higher administrative positions, even in organizations dominated by women. The ILO estimates that, on the basis of current trends, it will take at least 500 years for equal representation of women to be achieved.[335] The Court of Justice has taken certain steps to ensure that at least part-time women are represented on works councils and other similar bodies. In *Bötel*[336] the Court ruled that German legislation providing that both part-time and full-time workers be compensated up to the limit of their respective normal working hours disadvantaged part-time workers, and thus indirectly discriminated against women, breached Article 119 (now 141) unless it could be objectively justified. *Lewark*[337] concerned much the same point but this time the Court gave a broad hint that any discrimination could be objectively justified.

On the political scene, the level of female participation is demonstrated by Tables 3 and 4 below. As the Council of Europe puts it, 'true democracy should not ignore half of the citizens of Europe in decision making processes. ... Parity democracy can only be achieved through partnership between women and men'.[338]

The Council issued a resolution,[339] and then a Recommendation on Balanced Participation[340] which requires, *inter alia,* that balanced participation be promoted

Table 3. Women's participation in political decision-making

Country	Date Women Won the Right to Vote	Most Recent Election to Lower Chamber	% Women in Lower Chamber	% Women in Upper Chamber
Belgium	1948	1995	11	24
Denmark	1915	1994	33	—
Germany	1919	1994	26	19
Greece	1952	1993	6	—
Spain	1931	1993	23	13
France	1944	1993/1995	6	6
Ireland	1922	1992	13	13
Italy	1945	1994	14	8
Luxembourg	1918	1994	17	—
Netherlands	1919	1994/1995	31	23
Austria	1919	1995	25	25
Portugal	1974	1995	12	—
Finland	1906	1995	34	—
Sweden	1919	1994	40	—
United Kingdom	1928	1992	9	7

Source: M.Leijner, *How to Create a Gender Balance in Political Decision-Making* (1996) 10.

[335] Cited in Date-Bah, note 318 above, at 15.

[336] Case C–360/90, *Arbeiterwohlfahrt der Stadt Berlin* v. *Bötel* [1992] ECR I–3589.

[337] Case C–457/93, *Kuratorium für Dialyse* v. *Lewark* [1996] ECR I–243. See also Case C–278/93, *Freers* v. *Deutsche Bundespost* [1996] ECR I–1165. See generally C. Cockburn, *In the Way of Women: Men's Resistance to Sex Equality in Organizations* (1991).

[338] Congress of Local and Regional Authorities: Declaration on Women and Politics', Press Release 123(97).

[339] Council resolution [1995] OJ C168/3.

[340] Council recommendation 96/694/EC [1996] OJ L319/11.

Table 4. Women's participation in European cabinets, European Parliament, regions, and local councils (percentages)

Country	Date of Formation of Government	Government	European Parliament	Regional Parliament	Local Parliament
Belgium	1995	12	32	18	20
Denmark	1994	35	44	31	28
Germany	1994	16	36	29	22
Greece	1995	4	16	#	4
Spain	1994	18	33	19	#
France	1995	13	30	12	21
Ireland	1995	19	27	—	14
Italy	1994	8	13	11	22
Luxembourg	1995	25	33	—	10
Netherlands	1994	35	32	—	22
Austria	1996	29	33	20	#
Portugal	1995	9	8	9*	11
Finland	1995	39	63	—	30
Sweden	1994	50	45	48	41
United Kingdom	1992	7	18	—	#

\# no data available
— no regional government
* only the autonomous regions of Azores and Madeira have regional parliaments and governments

Source: M. Leijner, *How to Create a Gender Balance in Political Decision-Making* (1996), 11.

at all levels in government bodies and committees, on commissions and working parties at national and Community levels; and that a coherent set of measures be developed for encouraging equal opportunities in the public sector. In Norway a measure has been adopted requiring both men and women to be represented on all official bodies, councils, and committees.[341] When a public body appoints or elects a committee with four members or more, each sex must be represented by at least 40 per cent of its members. Exceptions may be granted only where special circumstances render the requirements evidently unreasonable.

The Recommendation also provides that the private sector should be encouraged to increase the presence of women at all levels of decision-making, notably by the adoption of, or within the framework of, equality plans and positive action programmes. As we have already seen, positive action has a lot to offer in this field. One way forward would be for a 'roll-over' programme of positive action to be adopted. This requires that the number of women at the second level in the hierarchy should reflect the percentage of women at the first level. Women should be promoted until this percentage is attained. The same approach is adopted at level three in the hierarchy and so on. We recommend that the goal of balanced participation should be imposed as a duty on employers. A more vigorous programme of positive action should be pursued with this aim in mind.

[341] See note 258 above.

III. BEYOND LEGISLATION

The law can provide a floor to prevent the most obvious manifestations of discriminatory behaviour.[342] An improved version of the law, taking on board the suggestions outlined in Part II, would make the law a more effective tool.[343] Ward, however, argues that '[t]inkering around with Article 119, or the handful of equal treatment Directives is not going to make much difference to the situation of the overwhelming number of women in Europe today'.[344] Such a strategy, he says, is limited, since it ignores the vast majority of women who are excluded from the ideology of the right because they are marginalized from the free market (see Annex). Women who are outside the workplace are powerless since, as we have seen, the Community has consistently refused to interfere in the private sphere. This criticism is valid. Community law does primarily deal with the 'included' rather than the excluded. It is therefore important that there be adequate social protection and social security measures to reconcile reproductive and productive activities.[345] Therefore, perhaps the most beneficial policy that the Union can pursue is to ensure growth and prosperity. Evidence from various countries indicates that austerity is a female responsibility: men tend to maintain their social and personal expenditures, while women are expected to make ends meet with fewer resources, by working longer hours within and outside the home.[346]

At the same time, the position of those in work cannot be ignored. As Clark observes, the primary job of government in relation to the elimination of sex inequality includes the provision of positive rights to ensure not only women's equal opportunities of access to the public sphere, but their substantive equality in both the public and private sphere through the mechanism of enforced employment equity programmes.[347] This requires a supportive legislative framework and enforcement mechanism. Legal rights have an important role to play in shaping social behaviour and providing a vehicle for individual complaints.[348] Further, policies have been suggested to ease the transition from excluded to included for those who want to participate.

At times, the Court has also attempted to recognize the social as well as the economic dimension of the equality provisions. The introduction of the concept of 'citizenship of the Union' by the Maastricht Treaty might eventually help in this process of reorientation. If social citizenship is a key component of citizenship then equality clearly has a central role to play. As Date-Bah concludes:

> the promotion of gender equality is an integral part of not only human rights but also democracy . . . Gender equality in opportunity and treatment also contributes to economic efficiency and sustainable development since it permits the harnessing of the diverse skills of the different population groups to enhance, for example, an enterprise's productivity and, indeed, the survival of the larger society.

[342] Sloan and Jain, note 201 above.
[343] L. Dickens, 'Anti-discrimination Legislation: Exploring and Explaining the Impact on Women's Employment', in W. McCarthy, *Legal Intervention in Industrial Relations: Gains and Losses*, (1992).
[344] Ward, note 6 above, at 376.   [345] Date-Bah, note 318 above, at 7.
[346] B. Sadasivam, 'The Impact of Structural Adjustment on Women: A Governance and Human Rights Agenda' (1997) 19 *HRQ* 630.   [347] Clark, note 257 above, at 391.
[348] See R. Cotterell, *The Sociology of Law: An Introduction* (1992); N. Bamforth, *Sexuality, Morals and Justice: A Theory of Lesbian and Gay Rights Law* (1997), chap. 8.

ANNEX

Table 5. Labour force survey 1997—males

	EU-15	B	DK	D	EL	E
Total Population—1000	179096	4966	2590	39246	4932	18967
Population older than 15 years						
—1000	146480	4039	2120	32759	4135	15791
—% of total population	81.8	81.3				
Active population						
—1000	96488	2450	1529	22228	2600	9838
—Activity rate (15–64 years)—%	77.5	72.2	85.2	79.3	76.9	75.1
Total Employment						
—1000	87206	2277	1460	20159	2439	8231
—Employment rate (15–64 years) %	69.9	67.1	81.3	71.8	71.9	62.7
—Full-time—%	94.2	96.7	87.9	95.8	97.4	96.8
—Part-time—%	5.8	3.3	12.1	4.2	2.6	3.2
In agriculture—%	5.6	3.0	5.5	3.2	17.9	9.5
In industry—%	39.2	37.4	36.0	46.5	27.7	38.7
In services—%	55.1	59.6	58.6	50.3	54.3	51.8
Employees						
—1000	69809	1851	1280	17537	1296	6122
—% of total employment	80.1	81.3	87.6	87.0	53.2	74.4
Contract of limited duration—%	11.5	4.6	10.6	11.5	10.2	32.4
Contract of unlimited duration—%	88.5	95.4	89.4	88.5	89.8	67.6
Usual hours worked per week						
—employees working full-time	41.3	38.9	39.3	40.4	41.5	41.1
—employees working part-time	19.0	22.1	13.5	16.0	23.3	19.0
Unemployment						
—1000	9283	174	69	2069	162	1607
—Unemployment rate—%	9.6	7.1	4.5	9.3	6.2	16.3
Unemployment by duration (%):						
—less than 6 months	34.3	23.4	55.5	34.1	30.9	34.3
—6 to 11 months	18.2	17.2	18.3	18.8	23.4	19.9
—12 months and more	47.5	59.4	26.2	47.1	45.8	45.8
Unemployed (%):						
—seeking first job	17.9	20.3	7.5	5.6	40.2	18.0
—seeking part-time job	4.3	1.5	10.2	3.1	3.0	1.5
—with an attained educational level < than upper secondary	48.9	56.6	24.4	23.2	45.3	71.1
Total of non-actives						
—1000	49992	1589	591	10531	1534	5954
—In education—%	25.3	26.9	16.7	23.1	25.5	30.8

F	IRL	I	L	NL	A	P	FIN	S	UK
27496	1797	27466	206	7618	3818	4671	2481	4368	28476
21846	1362	22974	167	6158	3104	3936	1987	3522	22580
	83.6	81.0		80.8	81.3	84.3	80.1	80.6	79.3
13834	933	14188	108	4404	2145	2642	1309	2299	15980
75.2	76.0	72.2	75.7	81.4	80.0	76.7	75.8	78.6	83.1
12301	838	12810	106	4214	2036	2489	1116	2047	14685
66.8	68.0	65.0	74.3	77.9	75.9	71.9	64.5	69.8	76.3
34.5	94.6	96.7	99.0	83.0	96.0	94.3	92.4	90.7	91.2
5.5	5.4	3.3	1.0	17.0	4.0	5.7	7.6	9.3	8.8
5.7	15.6	6.9	3.0	4.6	6.2	11.7	10.0	4.7	2.5
36.3	35.8	37.5	33.3	32.1	41.2	39.8	39.6	38.2	38.0
58.0	48.5	55.6	63.7	63.3	52.5	48.5	50.5	57.1	59.5
10398	604	8763	95	3633	1745	1756	884	1710	12135
34.5	72.0	68.4	90.1	86.2	85.7	70.5	79.2	83.5	82.6
12.1	7.1	7.3	1.8	8.8	7.3	11.7	15.3	10.1	6.5
87.9	92.9	92.7	98.2	91.2	92.7	88.3	84.7	89.9	93.5
40.5	41.6	39.7	14.3	39.3	40.2	42.3	39.8	40.1	45.8
22.4	19.2	28.3	25.7	19.4	22.2	27.2	17.3	18.9	16.9
1533	95	1378	2	190	108	153	193	252	1295
11.1	10.2	9.7	1.8	4.3	5.1	5.8	14.8	11.0	8.1
41.1	22.1	18.8	34.2	23.4	57.9	35.2	51.0	45.3	39.8
20.9	14.6	14.7	33.2	26.7	13.2	11.4	16.6	19.1	15.3
38.0	63.3	66.5	32.7	49.9	28.9	53.4	32.3	35.6	44.9
10.2	15.5	49.5	25.1	26.7	5.9	16.1	24.7	4.9	12.3
3.8	3.4	3.5	2.0	29.9	6.2	0.9	5.1	4.4	8.0
46.8	77.0	63.4	65.5	41.0	28.1	80.4	34.5	30.4	52.8
8012	429	8786	59	1754	959	1294	678	1222	6599
28.6	38.4	27.4	26.4	19.8	22.5	31.0	24.5	28.6	17.0

Source: Eurostat, *Statistics in Focus, Population and Social Conditions, Labour Force Survey Principal Results 1997* (1998), 5.

Table 6. Labour force survey 1997—females

	EU-15	B	DK	D	EL	E
Total Population—1000	188416	5188	2646	41321	5334	19943
Population older than 15 years						
—1000	157413	4304	2201	35145	4588	16951
—% of total population	83.5	83.0	83.2	85.1	86.0	85.0
Active population						
—1000	71724	1765	1299	16934	1611	6299
—Activity rate (15–64 years)—%	57.6	52.9	74.2	61.8	46.0	46.7
Total Employment						
—1000	62865	1561	1215	15141	1415	4475
—Employment rate (15–64 years)—%	50.4	46.7	69.4	55.2	39.1	33.5
—Full-time—%	66.7	68.6	65.6	64.9	91.9	82.6
—Part-time—%	32.3	31.4	34.4	35.1	8.1	17.4
In agriculture—%	4.0	2.1	1.7	2.6	23.1	6.1
In industry—%	15.9	13.2	14.5	18.9	13.4	13.6
In services—%	80.1	84.7	83.8	78.5	63.5	80.2
Employees						
—1000	54837	1326	1143	13911	815	3517
—% of total employment	87.2	84.9	94.1	91.9	57.6	78.6
Contract of limited duration—%	13.0	8.6	11.6	11.9	11.9	35.7
Contract of unlimited duration—%	87.0	91.4	88.4	88.1	88.1	64.3
Usual hours worked per week						
—employees working full-time	39.0	37.2	37.6	39.4	39.0	39.6
—employees working part-time	19.8					
Unemployment						
—1000	8860	204	84	1794	246	1753
—Unemployment rate—%	12.4	11.5	6.4	10.6	14.8	28.1
Unemployment by duration (%):						
—less than 6 months	30.6	22.2	53.3	28.6	18.6	24.5
—6 to 11 months	18.7	16.3	18.8	17.8	19.2	18.2
—12 months and more	50.7	61.5	27.9	53.6	62.2	57.3
Unemployed (%):						
—seeking first job	23.5	23.0	4.9	5.8	53.5	27.7
—seeking part-time job	21.3	14.7	16.5	23.2	5.8	7.0
—with an attained educational level < than upper secondary	45.9	49.7	32.2	24.3	41.6	59.1
Total of non-actives						
—1000	85689	2539	902	18210	2927	10722
—In education—%	15.8	16.8	16.0	13.1	14.3	19.1

F	IRL	I	L	NL	A	P	FIN	S	UK
29322	1808	29182	210	7717	4089	5177	2632	4469	29379
23901	1396	24949	172	6321	3407	4449	2159	3666	23805
81.5	77.2	85.5	82.0	81.9	83.3	85.9	82.0	82.0	81.0
11526	596	8671	66	3201	1660	2199	1184	2070	12664
61.0	49.8	43.6	47.1	61.3	61.8	60.3	69.8	74.1	66.9
9856	535	7222	63	2972	1572	2034	1005	1870	11927
52.1	44.7	36.2	45.4	56.9	58.5	55.5	59.2	66.8	63.0
69.1	76.8	86.3	79.8	32.4	71.0	85.0	84.4	60.1	55.2
30.9	23.2	13.7	20.2	67.6	29.0	15.0	15.6	39.9	44.8
3.4	3.5	5.9	1.2	2.4	7.7	15.2	5.3	1.7	1.1
14.5	17.2	21.4	6.6	9.4	14.6	20.3	13.9	11.7	13.2
82.2	79.3	72.7	92.1	88.3	77.6	64.5	80.8	86.6	85.7
8898	484	5554	58	2663	1363	1483	909	1746	10966
90.3	90.5	76.9	92.0	89.6	86.7	72.9	90.4	93.4	91.9
14.2	12.1	9.7	2.7	14.9	8.4	12.6	18.9	13.9	8.3
85.8	87.9	90.3	97.3	85.1	91.6	87.4	81.1	86.1	91.7
38.6	37.9	36.2	37.8	38.8	39.8	39.1	38.2	40.0	40.8
		22.2	19.4	18.8	22.4	20.3	21.8	24.9	18.3
1670	61	1449	2	229	88	165	180	200	736
14.5	10.2	16.7	3.6	7.1	5.3	7.5	15.2	9.7	5.8
38.5	33.4	17.5	42.7	16.6	45.5	31.5	52.8	45.7	54.7
20.5	19.7	16.2	21.3	34.9	26.1	10.9	20.2	21.8	17.5
41.0	46.9	66.2	36.0	48.5	28.4	57.7	27.0	32.5	27.8
12.8	18.8	56.6	31.0	20.3	10.1	20.1	22.6	7.0	16.2
22.1	33.7	22.1	23.8	78.6	38.1	2.7	11.5	19.3	41.9
45.9	53.9	53.9	80.2	44.4	40.0	79.0	30.9	26.5	55.0
12357	800	16278	106	3120	1747	2249	975	1596	11142
20.2	21.5	16.0	13.8	13.1	13.1	19.6	19.2	22.6	10.6

Source: Eurostat, *Statistics in Focus, Population and Social Conditions, Labour Force Survey Principal Results 1997* (1998) 5

9

The Human Rights of People with Disabilities under EU Law

GERARD QUINN

INTRODUCTION

There is a definable rights-based perspective to disability. This perspective, which has its origins in the civil rights movements of the 1960s, is working a revolution both at the level of ideas and also in the way established institutions and practices are coming under sustained pressure for change. Put simply, it amounts to the assertion that people are not problems, they have rights. From the rights perspective the main problem lies in the lack of space made for human difference in society and not in the difference presented by disability itself.

The rights-based perspective is fortified in the way international human rights law is being interpreted and applied. This is so whether the rights in question are civil or political on the one hand or economic, social, and cultural on the other. Inevitably, this revolution is now lapping against the shores of EU law and calls into question the capacity and willingness of the Union to respond accordingly.

The general status of people with disabilities across the Union is a genuine cause for concern. According to official estimates some thirty-seven million European citizens have some form of disability or other. This figure will be greatly inflated with the advent of enlargement. Though the nature and severity of disability vary greatly there is one common denominator. The well-attested experience of Europeans with disabilities is one of needlessly low levels of educational attainment, persistently high levels of under-employment, inadequate access to transport, as well as daily occurrences of small but cumulatively significant acts of discrimination.[1] The result is

* This chap. is dedicated to Mr Hywel C. Jones who retired in 1998 as Deputy Director General of DG V of the European Commission and who has given a lifetime of service to the building of a common European home for all. Special thanks are due to Dr Lisa Waddington, Leo Flynn, Michael O'Neill, Dr Arthur O'Reilly, and Rachel Hurst for useful comments on an earlier draft. All errors are mine alone.

[1] For representative statements of these experiences see European Parliament Committee on Petitions, *Report on the Rights of Disabled People (Rapporteur Mary Banotti MEP)*, 21 Nov. 1996, Doc. PE 218.897/fin. (report was based on actual petitions); HELIOS II European Disability Forum, *Report on Violence and Discrimination against Disabled People*, which was issued in 1996 in response to Resolution B3–580/93 of the European Parliament on the upsurge of violence against handicapped people; P. Jones and J. Pullen, *Inside We Are All Equal: A Social Policy Survey of Deaf People in the European Community* (1989).

endemic social and economic exclusion, poverty, and needless dependence on welfare. People with disabilities have been famously described as Europe's 'invisible citizens'. Lacking an effective and visible presence in the mainstream and being subjected to unfavorable coverage in the media, simply reinforces the perception that people with disabilities lack ability or have no right to be there.[2] This in turn leads to a self-perpetuating cycle of exclusion.

Asserting that the status of people with disabilities is problematic from a human rights perspective is one thing. Making the extra assertion that this problem is one that can be and should be addressed at the level of the Union is quite another. It is only when a problem registers as such at the level of the Union that Union-inspired solutions can be crafted. The main question posed by this chapter is in what way does the status of Europeans with disabilities engage the legal responsibility of the Union? Does EU treaty law have the capacity to become amenable to the just claims being made in the name of the rights-based revolution in the disability field? The answers to these questions are both difficult and evolving and are to be found by exploring three related issues:

- the extent to which the growing human rights dimension to the Union can make a difference for people with disabilities;
- the sensitivity or otherwise of the process of internal market regulation to the different needs of people with disabilities; and
- the extent to which changes in European social policy—and indeed the European social model generally—can help advance the rights-based perspective.

In assessing whether EU law adequately respects the rights of people with disabilities it is important to realize that the Treaty of Amsterdam represents but the latest stepping stone in the construction of Europe. It moves the process of absorbing the rights-based perspective on disability into the corpus of EU law forward to some degree. It provides fairly limited tools but, as usual, much will depend on whether the new tools are used creatively by the Institutions, and especially by the Commission, since it retains the exclusive right to propose legislation. However, the ultimate vision is still imperfectly secured, even after Amsterdam, and much remains to be done and will be outlined in detail later.

Though this chapter focuses on the rights-based perspective to disability under EU law it touches on a much broader theme—one that is directly related to the need for a new human rights agenda in the next stage of European construction. In general terms, the human rights agenda associated with post-War Europe had to do with protecting people against the power of the State. Freedom was predominantly viewed in terms of shelter or seclusion from public power. That agenda was successful. The new evolving human rights agenda has much more to do with the empowerment of people to assume active lives and to participate in all aspects of the life of the polity—whether it be in the economic sphere, in civil society, in cultural life, or in the social sphere. For ease of exposition this may be referred to as 'public freedom' as against 'private freedom'. In truth, this is not really a new idea. The highest form of

---

[2] See, e.g., C. Barnes, *Disabling Imagery and the Media: An Exploration of the Principles for Media Representation of Disabled People* (1992).

freedom to the ancient Greeks involved the right to enter and participate in all aspects of the life of the community.[3]

The theme of 'public freedom' is powerfully present in the way the Union is reshaping its own policies, whether they be on the areas of social protection, equal opportunity, employment, or non-discrimination. It sits well with the notion of a People's Europe. The shift to public freedom means that there will be—or ought to be—as much emphasis placed on the liberating potential of human rights as well as on their more familiar protective role. Furthermore, the idea of public freedom is forcing a greater awareness that market mechanisms can be harnessed to achieve social ends in a way that underpins, and not undermines, market rationality. There is a corresponding shift away from protection against market forces to an emphasis on securing appropriate levels of active participation and insertion into the market. This has long been associated with American economic and social policy and is beginning to take hold in Europe. It may be explained in part as a response to the increasing globalization of the economy. It is chiefly responsible for the considerable state of flux that exists at present within the so-called European Social Model. What is slowly emerging is a refreshed European Social Model—one that imbibes the traditional American focus on participation without sacrificing the traditional European value of social solidarity.

However, the move toward public freedom has its limits as well as possibilities. There is a danger that at some point the emphasis on active measures may translate into a denial of essential social supports. This raises acute dilemmas generally for policy-makers but especially in the field of disability, where reliance on formal measures alone is seldom enough. There are legitimate fears that the process of change, though largely welcome, might entail the erosion of essential social supports. But the overall shift does seem to be occurring and looks fairly irresistible.

On balance this shift from protection to participation is worthwhile. We have inherited processes across Europe that exclude those who are significantly different, and that consign them to the margins of the social and economic mainstream. Our societies seem to be constructed on concentric circles of graduated exclusion. In large measure this process is unconscious. It is not therefore a case of apportioning blame. The fact that the process is unconscious, and therefore has the appearance of naturalness and inevitability, makes it all the harder to reveal the implicit exclusion, much less reform it.

The reality, however, is that human difference, specifically the human difference of disability, has become (or remained) a ground for exclusion and not a cause for celebration and inclusion. This is first and foremost a moral issue and implicates profound questions relating to human rights. For the right to participate and assume an active and productive role in society is nothing if not assured to all on equal terms and with parity of esteem. But it is also an economic issue, and one that therefore goes to the rationality of the internal market since the process of exclusion is profoundly irrational, unproductive, and unsustainable.

This chapter is divided into five parts.

[3] On the historical ideal of public freedom see E. Barker, *The Political Thought of Plato and Aristotle* (1959).

Part I looks at the nature and significance of the shift to the rights-based perspective on disability. As will be seen, public freedom and the associated notion of equal opportunity is now the dominant framework of reference in the disability field. The key to overcoming indirect discrimination in the context of disability is the obligation to engage in 'reasonable accommodation'—in short to accommodate the difference in as much as that is practicable as well as feasible. In this Part we shall also assesses the authority or legal grounding of this perspective under international and regional human rights law. This is essential background to a clear appreciation of the possibilities as well as the limitations of recent developments under the Amsterdam Treaty.

Part II assesses the relative invisibility of people with disabilities under EU law prior to the Treaty of Amsterdam and its adverse effects. It does so under the closely related headings of human rights, internal market regulation, and social policy.

Part III traces the genesis and nature of the arguments made by many bodies including especially the European disability NGO movement (or rainbow of movements) for changes to be made to the Treaties to make the rights-perspective a reality under EU law. The most crucial demand of all was for a broadening of the main anti-discrimination provision of the TEC, Article 12 (*ex* Article 6), to mention specifically disability and to require measures ('reasonable accommodation') to tackle indirect discrimination. Although the Commission had shifted its ground quite significantly in the run-up to Amsterdam, the final—indeed the only—say on treaty revision rested with the Member States through the Intergovernmental Conference which lasted from March 1996 until June 1997 (spanning the Italian, Irish, and Dutch Presidencies respectively).

Part IV evaluates the changes made by the Treaty of Amsterdam in the context of disability and again under the three related headings of human rights, internal market regulation, and social policy. As will be seen, the new human rights provisions, although welcome, remain relatively weak vehicles with which to transpose a thoroughgoing rights-based perspective on disability into EU law. The new anti-discrimination provision (Article 13, *ex* Article 6a) is symbolically very important since disability is mentioned for the first time in the Treaties. However, its overall utility is in some considerable doubt, at least in the short term and for a variety of reasons to be explored later. The argument for making the power of the Community as it pertains to the internal market sensitive to the rights-based claims of people with disabilities made much headway at Amsterdam but ended up as a Declaration attached to Article 95 (ex Article 100a). Despite appearances, this may well turn out to have been the most significant treaty change of all. Lastly the addition of the social chapter, and especially the new employment chapter, into the body of the Treaties could prove highly beneficial depending on how sensitively they are used. However, as mentioned, a major defeat was suffered when the draft provisions on social exclusion were amended at the last moment deliberately to exclude any mention of persons with disabilities. This effectively forces recourse to Article 235 as a basis for the adoption of a social action programme in the field of disability.

Part V looks to the future. It looks to the potential in the Treaty of Amsterdam. It looks beyond Amsterdam to ensure that the rights-based perspective becomes much more explicitly embedded in the evolving Treaty law of the Union. The changes made by the Treaty of Amsterdam in the areas of human rights, non-discrimination, internal market regulation, and social policy are steps in the right direction, but much more needs to be done. Some general strands are then drawn together and conclusions drawn about the future of public freedom in the Union.

PART I: THE HUMAN RIGHTS PERSPECTIVE ON DISABILITY

The rights-based perspective on disability is new and not widely appreciated. Contrary to the way the popular mind interprets it, it does not translate into automatic claims for greater resources or largesse (at least not directly). Put simply, it translates into a claim for public freedom and the right to participate in all facets of life on genuinely equal terms with everyone. To assess whether this perspective is reflected under EU law or whether there is any possibility for a better 'fit' between it and EU law it is necessary to explain the move to the rights-based paradigm and its significance in the field of disability.

A. Disability as a Problem of the Person

The traditional approach to disability was to view it as a problem of the person.[4] Language is revealing in this regard. The very term 'disabled person' gives rise to the impression—or reinforces an impression deeply embedded in culture—that the entirety of the human personality is negated by disability. In other words, disability was not generally viewed as one facet of a person but as something that invaded that person and spoiled the entirety of his/her personhood. To paraphrase Blackstone, upon being labeled disabled a person suffers a form of civil death, and the story of human rights is a story of the slow but steady return to the person of the full *indicia* of personhood.

The traditional view was reflected, for example, in the fact that most legal systems allowed for one crude distinction between full legal capacity and utter incapacity.[5] Little allowance was made for the possibility of different kinds of capacity (or different levels of capacity) or for the positive role to be played by independent advocates who can act and speak on behalf of the person. One result of the slow but sure application of rights-talk to this sphere is that it is creating space for more finely-tuned judgements to be made on capacity on the basis of fact and not mere supposition.[6]

Two significant policy implications arose from the traditional approach. The general policy response was either:

---

[4] See generally M. Oliver, *The Politics of Disablement* (1990).

[5] See Report of the Committee on Petitions, European Parliament, on the rights of the mentally handicapped, Doc A3–0231/92/Annex II.

[6] See e.g., *Mental Incapacity*, Law Commission (England & Wales) Report No. 231. The Council of Europe is currently preparing a draft Recommendation on the legal protection of incapacitated adults and the Hague Conference on Private International Law is currently working on a draft convention dealing with conflicts of law in the same field.

(1) to try to bridge the gap between the norm and the deviation by attempting to eliminate the disability or rehabilitate the person to the greatest extent possible given the state of medical science, or

(2) to accept the gap as given and to endeavour to compensate for it through relatively generous welfare supports and payments.

The first policy focus on rehabilitation is criticized by many people with disabilities as evincing a lack of respect for difference (in which one may legitimately have pride). The second policy focus on compensation is criticized by many as amounting to an acceptance that those who cannot be made to emulate the norm have no place in society, and so the only question is to compensate them for the loss in a way that meets their basic needs. Implicit in this is an acceptance that society has no moral responsibility to accommodate difference—only to compensate for the lack of public freedom or the right to participate. In reality, however, the real objection to these two policy responses was not so much that they were not justifiable in their own right, since they clearly are. Rather, the real cause of concern was that they were unaccompanied by any thoroughgoing sense of the moral responsibility of society to remove arbitrary barriers in the way of participation. In short, the two traditional policy responses were viewed as pale substitutes for active efforts to make space in society for human difference and to forge pathways into the mainstream.

The narrow range of policy options traditionally pursued was reflected in the kinds of government ministries that typically had authority over disability policy—generally the 'caring' ministries of Health and Welfare. Disability was not seen as a civil rights issue and, unlike in the USA, is still not dealt with by civil rights or justice ministries in the majority of Member States. Nor was disability mainstreamed into the other policy ministries with responsibility for education, training, employment, and transport, etc. Provision for disability in these fields was conceptualized as 'special' and therefore separate—an arrangement that predictably tends to perpetuate the cycle of exclusion. The traditional state of affairs was said to correspond to the 'welfare model' or 'medical model' of disability'.

Throughout the 1970s and 1980s the rehabilitation/welfare perspective was increasingly viewed as being part of the problem. This is not to deny the critical importance of rehabilitation and welfare. Instead, it is to emphasize that these policy goals are not ends in themselves and must be harnessed more closely to the achievement of higher and person-centered ends such as the human rights of the individual.

Disabilities are conventionally defined in medical science on a three point scale established by the World Heath Organization in 1980 ranging from impairment, disability, and handicap (International Classification of Impairments, Disabilities, and Handicaps—ICIDH[7]), which is part of the WHO family of classifications. *Impairment* refers to the physical or mental loss or abnormality which may take many forms. *Disability* refers more properly to the reduction in the range of functions considered normal for a human being as a result of the impairment. *Handicap* refers to the social and other disadvantages experienced by such persons which compound

---

[7] World Health Organization, *International Classification of Impairments, Disability and Handicap* (ICIDH), which can be found at http://www.who.int/whosis/icidh.htm.

the impairment and disability. Handicap refers essentially to the social or economic impediments that magnify the effect of an impairment (usually exclusionary in effect, if not by design). Strictly speaking, medical science is founded on high ethical principles concerned with the dignity and integrity of the person. However, given the way in which the ICIDH was expressed, together with popular perceptions of the medical establishment as an agent of control rather than liberation, it is not surprising that many international NGOs saw in it a reflection of an attitude they felt had imprisoned and not liberated. For one thing the ICIDH gives rise to the impression that disability subsumes the person. For another, it is insufficiently sensitive to the barriers placed in the way of the person. The handicap dimension is tacked on only at the end and through the use of language felt to be hurtful. It is therefore no surprise to learn that the ICIDH—which is undergoing a process of review within the WHO—has come under strong attack from the international NGOs.[8] Largely because of the advent of the rights-based approach the current revised draft version replaces the term 'handicap' with 'participation', which looks much more closely at the barriers placed in the way of the person by society.[9]

Situating the problem of disability in the person (as the original ICIDH appeared to do) tends, of course, to reinforce a self-fulfilling prophesy of exclusion and low levels of participation.[10] When the person sees himself as the problem he internalizes an externality: namely the particular perspective and value (or lack of value) society takes on disability. Not unnaturally, spoilt identity and a wasting of human talent can and do result.[11]

B. Towards the Rights-based Perspective—Disability as a Social Construct

The first building block toward a rights-based perspective on disability entails viewing disability in a radically different light. Much modern thinking in the field focuses not on the impairment as such, nor indeed on the limitation of the normal range of human functions. Rather, the focus is placed on how society (consciously or otherwise) compounds the impairment by constructing social and economic processes that fail adequately to take account of the disability in question. In other words, the focus is now being placed on how society disables by failing to provide equal opportunities for participation[12].

The idea that disability is (or can be viewed as) a 'social construct' is central to an understanding of the rights-based approach in this field[13]. It can be rendered in two different ways. First, it may be said that disability, like any condition, is not inherent but is defined *in relation* to some idealized norm. In this case the norm is

---

[8] See e.g., M. Oliver, *Redefining Disability: A Challenge to Research*, 5 Research, Policy & Planning, at 9.

[9] *International Classification of Impairments, Disabilities and Participation: Beta-1 Draft for Field Trials* (1997).

[10] See e.g., D. Nelkin and L. Tancredi, *Dangerous Diagnosis—The Social Power of Biological Information* (1989).

[11] See J. Read and S. Barker, *Not Just Sticks and Stones: A Survey of the Stigma, Taboos and Discrimination Experienced by People with Mental Health Problems* (1996).

[12] See D. Stone, *The Disabled State* (1984).

[13] See C. Liachowitz, *Disability as a Social Construct: Legislative Roots* (1988).

able-bodiedness which can be reduced to a medical image of normal species-type functioning.[14] From this perspective the important question is not whether there is a deviation from a norm but why the core norm was selected as core in the first place, by whom, and for what reasons. It follows that society *creates* or *constructs* disability (with an associated label) by implicitly accepting some idealized norm as given and by measuring deviation therefrom.

What converts an otherwise harmless academic insight into a powerful lever for change is the realization that the core norm is used not merely to differentiate between people but also to construct the life world. In reality, and largely for the sake of convenience, societies everywhere tend to create and define pathways into public space by reference to a controlling norm. The terms of entry and participation depend on compliance with the selected norm. It follows that deviation from the norm not merely *marks* the person apart but *keeps* the person apart since, by definition, such persons cannot gain access to common space which was deliberately constructed in a way that ignores their difference. Such space is 'common' only to those who conform and cannot be said to be 'public', since a large percentage of the public is implicitly excluded. Those who do not conform tend to become and remain invisible—marginalized outsiders. This is seldom done consciously or explicitly in culture, which explains the appearance of the inevitability or naturalness of the exclusion—but it is done. Furthermore, lacking 'presence' in common space simply serves to reinforce the prejudice that people who differ in a major way have no right to be present, which sets in train a vicious cycle of exclusion.

C. A Revolution in Ideas: The Move to the Rights-based Approach to Disability

Building public space around a norm is perhaps convenient. But it is fundamentally unethical as well as irrational from an economic point of view. Labeling disability as a social construct whose meaning is defined by others and in relation to an arbitrary norm is interesting, but does not develop our understanding of the field unless one adopts a vantage point with which to analyse it, judge it, and prescribe a meaningful programme of change. The human rights perspective provides that critical vantage point.

It is necessary to distinguish between three different variants to the rights-based perspective to disability.[15]

First of all, human rights violations can cause disability. Torture, the use of children as soldiers, and indiscriminate maiming through landmines come readily to mind. It must also be borne in mind that violations of economic, social, and cultural rights can also cause disability. For example, malnutrition, avoidable industrial accidents, a failure to intervene early enough in the education process to correct the effects of a predictable onset of disability, and inadequate provision of health care can also cause, or at least contribute, to disability. Structural or distributive injustice—

---

[14] On the relationship of health status to species-type functioning see N. Daniels, 'Health Care Needs and Distributive Justice' (1983) 12 *Phil. & Publ. Affairs* 146.

[15] See generally L. Despouy, *Human Rights and Disabled Persons, Special Rapporteur of the Sub-Commission on Prevention of Discrimination and Protection of Minorities*, United Nations Human Rights Studies Series No 6, (1993).

whether within States or as between States—is also an invisible but powerful determinant of the incidence of disability.

Secondly, it is possible to evaluate the status of persons with disabilities by taking each human right individually as a benchmark. Indeed, many of the early moves toward reform took this shape. One might therefore unpack the full catalogue of human rights and measure compliance in the field of disability. The mental health field is the chief example. In a sense this was an easy field, since the traditional right of civil liberty was implicated, and its application in this sector raised issues that were familiar to human rights lawyers and obviously required reform. The field only became muddy when the claims for enhanced due process protections against civil commitment laws began to be transformed into claims for affirmative rights to treatment once incarcerated.[16] Yet, although correct in its own right, this particularistic approach fails to capture the full power of the rights-based revolution in the disability field.

Thirdly, one might view the human rights mission as greater than the sum of its various parts. Human rights are fundamentally corrosive of conventional world-views and established ways of doing things. True, they protect the person against power but they also question and inject an ethic of rational justification into political and legal arrangements. Put positively, they can inspire programmes (not necessarily redistributive in the classic sense) to create pathways for the marginalized back into public space. In truth, there can be few better examples of the subversiveness of the rights perspective in action than in the area of disability.

From this perspective the core right implicated is equality. The right to equality—in its plenitude—addresses the rationality or otherwise of various overt and more subtle forms of exclusion. The fact that this exclusion is (to a degree) unwitting does not take away from the force of the argument. It is the equality perspective that gives added meaning to the infringement of other rights such as liberty, the right to health care, the right to education, and the right to work. For it is not so much these rights that are at stake in isolation but the securing of equal effective enjoyment of these rights to people with disabilities.

D. The Equal Opportunity Model and Disability—Forging Pathways into Public Space

Identifying equality as the controlling benchmark moves analysis forward and places a premium on finding optimal policy solutions to achieve it. Quite obviously, the solution pivots on constructing and implementing an effective equality strategy—one that reverses the effects of exclusion and that sets the terms of entry and participation into all areas of public space on a genuinely equal footing. This, of course, implicates a much deeper debate about equality and, in crude terms, forces a choice between three general renderings of equality; (1) formal or juridical equality, (2) equal opportunity, or (3) equality of results.

---

[16] See e.g., G. Quinn, 'Civil Commitment and the Right to Treatment under the European Convention on Human Rights' (1992) 5 *Harv. HRJ* 1.

1. Formal Equality—Direct Discrimination   The first rendition is quite familiar and entails an outright prohibition against direct discrimination. The general norm receives only partial expression in the text of the TEC (Articles 12 and 141, *ex* Articles 6 and 119). The main limitation of the first rendition as applied in the context of disability is quite simple. Juridical equality aims to avert the gaze of a would-be discriminator away from the subject of discrimination. It requires ignorance of a characteristic deemed arbitrary from a moral point of view.

Disability is different, in that to achieve equality the would-be discriminator is asked to do something which appears quite contradictory. On the one hand he is required to ignore the difference of disability when making certain decisions, such as who to admit to a restaurant and, on the other, to take the human difference of disability into account by taking all reasonable steps to overcome obstacles and render the right of access genuinely equal to all.

This difference causes a policy dilemma of sorts.[17] To take the difference into account means doing justice to the difference but at the possible price of perpetuating stereotypes about the nature of the difference. To ignore the difference means avoiding perpetuating stereotypes but at the price of failing to do justice to the reality of the difference. Clearly, disability taxes the notion of formal equality to breaking point.

2. Equal Opportunity—Indirect Discrimination and 'Reasonable Accommodation'
The equal opportunity rendering of equality entails a conscious effort at identifying and removing barriers to inclusion. Given our inheritance, this means designing a coherent programme to undo existing obstacles. Its component parts can be parsed quite logically.

First, the notionally equal right to participate means relatively little unless all *preparatory processes* for participation are made available on genuinely equal terms for all, including people with disabilities. Such processes embrace, in the main, open (i.e. integrated or inclusive) education and training.

Secondly, *access barriers* need to be progressively removed and a positive plan put in place to ensure that all pathways remain open and readily usable. The usual barriers include transportation and all aspects of the built environment. Communications barriers also inhibit full and equal access. Additionally, public attitudes and the portrayal of difference by the media might also be conceptualized as a barrier.

Thirdly, it is seldom enough to prepare the person for participation or to clear pathways into common space. It also proves necessary to tackle discrimination within public space. That means that the relevant anti-discrimination law needs to reach private actors—including private employers—since most people lead most of their lives in spheres controlled or mostly controlled by market forces.

The first two elements of the equal opportunity model are programmatic in character. Equality norms in constitutions or treaties do not generally require such programmes, but can at least support and permit them and control the use of power where indirect discrimination might otherwise occur. The third element—non-discrimination law—is familiar but assumes a radically different form in the context

---

[17] M. Minow, *Making all the Difference: Inclusion, Exclusion and American Law* (1990).

of disability. In essence, it requires due account to be taken of indirect discrimination whereby unequals are treated as if they were equal. The notion of 'reasonable accommodation' is the key to tackling indirect discrimination. In essence it requires due notice to be taken of material difference and reasonable efforts to be made to accommodate the difference in order to avoid indirect discrimination.

Reasonable accommodation is *the* core demand of most disability NGOs. As a term it was in fact contrived by the US judiciary in the 1970s on a realization that to apply notions of formal equality strictly would not only prove counterproductive but also bring the law—and more importantly the idea of seeking justice through the law—into disrepute.[18] Reasonable accommodation is now widely used in advanced anti-discrimination law in the field of disability worldwide[19].

Importantly, reasonable accommodation is distinguishable from positive discrimination or affirmative action in that it does not aim to create an artificial opportunity where none might otherwise exist.[20] Rather it serves to open up pathways to opportunities hitherto foreclosed. While it can peacefully coexist with positive discrimination or affirmative action, it does point to policy options of a different order.

3. Equality of Results   The last major rendition of equality is more robust and substantive—equality of results. It characteristically involves an assertion of the equal moral self-worth of all human beings and a corresponding claim on the resources of society to meet basic as well as disability-specific needs. Curiously, this variant of equality has not played a prominent part in the contemporary debate concerning disability.

In sum, the equal opportunity model is now the dominant approach to disability from within the rights-based perspective. It displaces the person as the locus of the 'problem', and instead locates the main problem in the way social and economic structures are designed.[21] It is attractive in this context for a variety of reasons.

First, it is not tainted by association with either state welfare or paternalism. On the contrary, it holds out the post-modern allure of empowerment and participation. It promises independence both from the actions of other private parties and also from the suffocating embrace of the traditional welfare State.

Secondly, it fits with (or at least is not visibly hostile towards) the market as the dominant mechanism for allocating scarce resources in our societies. It is designed to underpin and not undermine market rationality and might with some ease be defended as a productive factor in an advanced economy.[22] The reasons for this are

---

[18] For a recent review of the effectiveness of the US legislation see National Council on Disability, *Achieving Independence: The Challenge for the 21st Century—A Decade of Progress in Disability Policy Setting an Agenda for the Future* (1996).

[19] On British legislation see B. Doyle, *Disability Discrimination Law: Law and Practice* (1996). For comparative perspective see G. Quinn, C. Kimber, and M. McDonagh, *Disability Discrimination Law in the United States, Canada and Australia* (1993).

[20] See A. Hendricks, 'The Concepts of Non-Discrimination and Reasonable Accommodation', in 1995 Report of the European Day of the Disabled, *Disabled Persons' Status in the European Treaties—Invisible Citizens* (1995), 53 at 58.

[21] See generally G. Hales (ed.), *Beyond Disability—Towards an Enabling Society* (1996); and J. Swain, V. Finkelstein, S. French, and M. Oliver (eds.), *Disabling Barriers—Enabling Environments* (1993).

[22] See e.g., cost-benefit analysis of the US administration in adopting regs. under Title I of the Americans with Disabilities Act (1990); (1991) 56 Federal Register 8578.

straightforward. Opening up the preparatory processes (education, training) for future economic participation to all persons on the basis of ability cannot but have pronounced effects in terms of the preparedness of people to assume productive roles in society. It expands the labour pool. Breaking down access barriers cannot but ensure that the labour market achieves a better fit between supply and demand. Making the workplace adaptable to the requirements of people with disabilities similarly ensures a better market fit. Raising levels of employment entails less dependence on treasury-funded welfare, higher tax receipts, more disposable income that leads to higher levels of economic activity, and more independence. Ensuring that market standards for goods and services are sufficiently sensitive to the needs of persons with disabilities is good business sense. In a sense, equal opportunity programmes meet market failure in a way that cannot be done by markets on their own.

Thirdly, the *form* (as distinct from the content) of the main legal tool—anti-discrimination law—used to achieve equal opportunity is familiar to and compatible with market dynamics. Such law is generally defended as a way of making markets more rational, and therefore more efficient. It has long been noted that market theory depends for its rationality in part on equality, since any market that screens 10 per cent of the population cannot be said to be rational, much less fair.

It must be said, however, that the equal opportunity model has marked limitations. This is not so surprising since such constructs are as much defined by what they react against and strive to get away from (dependence) than what they are for (independence). The most obvious limitation of the model has to do with the limits of market logic. Such logic gives out in the case of those who, for one reason or another, lack full capacity to participate in (or contribute to) all or most aspects of collective life. Of course, what counts as a 'contribution' to collective life is contested ground. It could certainly be argued that in a People's Europe economic participation is but one facet to participation, and that other forms of participation generate as much social value and should be regarded as such. For the moment, however, economic contribution seems to be the only contribution genuinely valued in our societies. That may change, however, as new forms of work emerge into the next century.

Another—but related—limitation has to do with the flimsy foundation for substantive socio-economic rights from within the equal opportunity model. Equal opportunity assumes some bedrock of socio-economic provision. But the provision of such supports is predicated on a presumption of a capacity to participate and contribute. Socio-economic supports are designed only to prepare people for participation. This can provide a rationale for a health care right, but only up to a point. The equal opportunity model is also on weak ground when it comes to supporting socio-economic provision for those who lack capacity or sufficient capacity to contribute. The fact that one is impelled to package substantive socio-economic claims into the market-friendly lexicon of equal opportunity speaks volumes about the powerful undertow of market logic on rights claims. It is plain that such supports are vital for people with disabilities who have different and often ongoing needs above and beyond the needs of the average person. Hence, in order to ground substantive rights one needs to fall back on a theory of equality of results which, in the present market-oriented climate, has limited power. The adroit use of pressure politics might achieve the same result, but there is no guarantee unless the different groups coalesce and translate numbers into votes.

Whichever element of the equal opportunity model is accentuated it will inevitably entail costs. A traditional redistributive programme would, of course, spread the costs throughout society. The interesting feature of much anti-discrimination law in the context of disability is that private actors are also affixed with at least some of the direct costs through the notion of 'reasonable accommodation', with due allowance being made for targeted tax breaks and technical assistance. Private actors have, however, a natural tendency to see only costs and not benefits. However, many cost-benefit studies show that the costs are generally small and are in fact a net benefit to private actors.[23] One problem is that at some point the imposition of these costs might be held by the courts to offend against the right to property, as in fact happened recently in Ireland.[24] In other words, equality eventually bumps up against the prerogatives of property. It is interesting to note in passing how the US system, which is dedicated to the market, nevertheless makes considerable space for equal opportunity programmes despite the competing claims of property.

E. The Equal Opportunity Model Gains International Authority

The rights-based perspective on disability generally and the equal opportunity model in particular were slow in gaining ground under international law and policy in the field of disability. However, from the mid-1970s onwards, they have manifested themselves at the United Nations level in four ways: (1) at the level of ideas, especially as reflected in the various non-binding declarations and resolutions of the General Assembly and in UN sponsored studies,[25] (2) in the way the general human rights treaties are being interpreted, (3) in the drafting of thematic human rights treaties, and (4) in the ongoing work and work programmes of the various specialized agencies.

The early work done at the UN level became hugely significant in a European context. Most of the disability NGOs took their moral inspiration in agitating for change at Amsterdam from various UN initiatives. A host of resolutions were passed by the General Assembly throughout the 1970s and 1980s on the rights of persons with disabilities.[26] This initial flurry of activity culminated in 1982 when the

---

[23] See e.g., President's committee on Employment of People with Disabilities, *Jobs Accommodation Network Report* (1996). This report found that 50% of accommodations cost between US$1–500. Only 3% were found to cost US$5.000.

[24] This was in fact held to be the case with respect to very mild proposals by the Irish Parliament and struck down by the Sup. Ct. on the grounds of property: *Re: Article 26 and the Employment Equality Bill, 1997*, judgment of the Sup. Ct., May 1997.

[25] See e.g., E-I.A. Daes, *Principles, Guidelines and Guarantees for the Protection of Persons Detained on Grounds of Mental ill Health or Suffering from Mental Disorder* (1986). Perhaps the most influential of all the studies was the final report of the special *rapporteur* (Leandro Despouy) on the Sub-Commission on Prevention of Discrimination and the Protection of Minorities, *Human Rights and Disability*, E/CN.4/Sub. 2/1991.

[26] See e.g., GA Res. 2856 (XXVI) (1971), Declaration on the Rights of Mentally Retarded Persons and GA Res. 3447 (XXX) (1975), Declaration on the Rights of Disabled Persons. For commentary and full texts of the early documentation see M.R. Saulle, *Disabled Persons and International Organisations* (1982). For more contemporary analysis, as well as full texts of recent documentation, see T. Degener and Y. Koster-Dreese (eds.), *Human Rights and Disabled Persons* (1995).

General Assembly proclaimed the *World Programme of Action Concerning Disabled Persons*[27] (WPA). The first two parts of the WPA reflected the traditional policy themes of prevention and rehabilitation. The third theme—and the novelty in the programme—looked *forwards* and embraced the theme of equalization of opportunities which was stated to mean:

> the process through which the general system of society, such as the physical and cultural environment, housing and transportation, social and health services, educational and work opportunities, cultural and social life, including sports and recreational facilities are made accessible to all.[28]

The WPA ushered in the International Decade of the Disabled (1983–92) which at least helped to raise consciousness of the issue. The Global Meeting of experts which took place in 1987 to review the implementation of the WPA actually recommended the preparation of a thematic convention dealing with the rights of persons with disabilities. Drafts were prepared by Italy and Sweden but, as no consensus existed on the matter, ECOSOC recommended the drafting of a special resolution.[29]

The Vienna Declaration and World Programme of Action further reinforced the relevance of the rights-based approach to disability and joined ECOSOC in calling for the adoption of a special resolution by the General Assembly. Importantly the Vienna Declaration stated that:

> The place of disabled persons is everywhere. Persons with disabilities should be guaranteed equal opportunity through the elimination of all socially determined barriers, be they physical, financial, social or psychological, which exclude or restrict full participation in society.[30]

Also of background significance in the Declaration and Programme of Action adopted by the World Summit for Social Development held in Copenhagen in 1995[31]. Among other things, it urged governments to:

> work towards the equalization of opportunities so that people with disabilities can contribute to and benefit from full participation in society. Policies regarding people with disabilities should focus on their abilities rather than their disabilities and should ensure their dignity as citizens.[32]

The General Assembly duly adopted a new resolution—the *UN Standard Rules on the Equalization of Opportunities for People with Disabilities*[33] (SRE). By now—and in the short space of ten years—the accent was squarely and exclusively on equal opportunity. Part I of the rules deals with certain preconditions for equal opportunity. Part II deal with target areas for equal participation. Part III deals with implementation measures, and Part IV sets up a monitoring process. The monitoring process involves a special *rapporteur*—currently Bengt Lindqvist of Sweden. Despite the fact

[27] GA Res. 37/52 (1982). [28] World Programme of Action, para. 12.

[29] Before dealing with the follow-through to the WPA the General Assembly adopted a major resolution of significance in the mental health field—*Principles for the Protection of Persons with Mental Illness and the Improvement of Mental Health Care*—adopted by GA Res. 46/119 (1991).

[30] Vienna Declaration and World Programme of Action, A/CONF.157/23 (1993), para. 64.

[31] See A/CONF.166/9 (1995). [32] *Ibid.*, at para. 75 (k).

[33] GA Res. 48/96 (1993). For comment see B. Lindqvist, 'Standard Rules in the Disability Field—A United Nations Instrument', in Degener & Koster Dreese, note 26 above, at 63.

that these rules have no binding force in law they have become quite authoritative worldwide and were in fact adopted as a benchmark by the European Commission in 1996 (see Part III below).

Although neither the International Covenant on Civil and Political Rights (ICCPR) nor that on Economic, Social, and Cultural Rights (ICESCR) mentions disability they are currently being interpreted in a way that strongly supports the rights-based perspective on disability. General Commentary No. 19 to the ICCPR which deals with the right to equality (Article 25) states that:

> The enjoyment of rights and freedoms on an equal footing . . . does not mean identical treatment in every instance . . . the principle of equality sometimes requires States parties to take affirmative action in order to diminish or eliminate conditions which cause or help to perpetuate discrimination prohibited by the Covenant.[34]

Likewise the Committee on Economic, Social, and Cultural Rights adopted a landmark General Comment on disability and the rights secured under the convenant in 1994.[35] The accent on this commentary was placed on utilizing economic and social supports as levers with which to forge pathways into the mainstream.

Many of the thematic conventions either have explicit provisions on disability or are being interpreted in light of the needs of persons with disabilities. Article 23 of the Rights of the Child Convention specifically requires that a child with a disability should enjoy a full and decent life in conditions which ensure dignity and promote self-reliance and his/her active participation in the community.[36] General Commentary No 18(x) under the UN Convention on the Elimination of All Forms of Discrimination Against Women requires that States parties should separately include information on the status of women with disabilities in their periodic reports.

In keeping with this sea-change the various UN specialized agencies have also been very active in promoting the equal opportunity perspective on disability in the past few years.[37]

Closer to home, the Council of Europe has had a long history of involvement in the general disability field through the inter-governmental activities it sponsors. It

---

[34] A/45/40 (1990), at paras. 8–10. See generally A. Hendricks, 'The Significance of Equality and Non-Discrimination for the Protection of the Rights and Dignity of the Disabled Person', in Degener and Koster-Dreese, note 26 above, at 40.

[35] See General Comment No. 5 (1994). See generally P. Alston, 'Disability and the International Covenant on Economic, Social and Cultural Rights', in Degener and Koster-Dreese, note 26 above, at 94.

[36] See T. Hammerberg, 'The Rights of Disabled Children—The U.N. Covenant on the Rights of the Child', in Degener and Kosetr-Dreese, note 26 above, at 147.

[37] Many of the specialized agencies have a natural interest in the field given their own areas of responsibility. The WHO Regional Office for Europe issued a report in 1992 entitled *Better Opportunities for Disabled People*, Eur/ICP/RHB 016 Rev. 1 (1992). The International Labour Organization keeps a close watch on the employment situation confronting people with disabilities and has concluded a number of conventions on the subject, including Convention No. 159, Convention Concerning Vocational Rehabilitation and Employment (Disabled Persons) 1983: in ILO, *International Labour Conventions and Recommendations 1919–1991* (1992), ii, 1278. The ILO was one of the co-sponsors in 1994 (with UNESCO and the WHO) of a position paper on *Community Based Rehabilitation for and With People with Disabilities*. UNESCO issued a major declaration in 1981 (the Sundberg Declaration) on education and disability. It issued a more general declaration in 1990 entitled the *World Declaration on Education for All: Meeting Basic Learning Needs*, Art. 3(5) of which focuses on the education rights of persons with disabilities. See also UNESCO, *Salamanca Statement: Final Report World Conference on Special Needs Education: Access and Quality* (1994).

adopted the equal opportunity model in 1992 in Recommendation R(92)6, *A Coherent Policy for the Rehabilitation of Disabled People*. Despite its title this Recommendation deals mainly with equality of opportunity. A Committee on Rehabilitation and Integration of People with Disabilities meets under the ægis of the Council's Partial Agreement in the Social and Health Field. Recently an important working group has been formed under that Committee to evaluate legislation on the topic of discrimination against persons with disabilities.

Unfortunately, the relevant provision of the European Convention on Human Rights (ECHR) dealing with non-discrimination (Article 14) is quite narrowly drawn and has not so far availed applicants with a disability. Several test cases have begun to arrive in Strasbourg and have thus far been firmly rebuffed. One application involved the question of access to private beaches in Italy.[38] The applicant claimed that a failure on the part of the Italian authorities to provide equal effective access (which coincidentally violated Italian law) amounted to a failure to respect private life as protected under Article 8 of the Convention, considered alone or in conjunction with Article 14. The Commission concluded by twenty votes to ten that there had been no violation of Article 8 and unanimously that no separate issue arose under Article 14 in conjunction with Article 8. Clearly, and unlike its UN counterparts, the Commission does not interpret the phrase 'any other status' under Article 14 to include persons with disabilities.

Two other cases involved allegations of a failure to respect an equal effective right of access to education on behalf of disabled children under Article 2 of the First Protocol (*SP* v. *United Kingdom, Cohen* v. *United Kingdom*).[39] The main question in *SP* was whether a failure to provide an assessment of special education for a dyslexic child contributed to a record of poor educational attainment and subsequent social problems, including suicidal tendencies. If so, then did this failure amount to a violation of Article 2 of the Protocol? The child had been frequently moved from various schools by his mother in an effort to obtain appropriate educational facilities. The application was unanimously declared inadmissible. The Commission reasoned that the child had not been excluded from school as such. It afforded a wide margin of appreciation in how resources could be allocated. On the facts the public authorities in question were not faulted since the first independent report did not support the claim for an assessment. Perversely, the result in this case might be interpreted to place the blame on the child's mother for having tried in vain to find an appropriate educational environment. The commentary on this case in the *European Human Rights Law Review* is quite revealing. The reviewer states:

> In this case the applicant clearly had access to schools and the Commission was not prepared to consider whether the teaching he received was such that he could be said to have received no *effective* education. The Commission is clearly anxious to prevent its hearings becoming an alternative forum for allegations of educational negligence.[40]

---

[38] *Maurizio Botta* v. *Italy* (App. No. 21439/93). For a summary of the decision on the merits see European Commission of Human Rights, *Information Note No. 138* (13 Dec. 1996), 6.
[39] *SP* v. *United Kingdom*, App. No 28915/95, decision of Commission, 17 Jan. 1997; *Cohen* v. *United Kingdom*, App. No 25959/94, decision of Commission, 28 Feb. 1996.
[40] (1997) EHRLR 289.

It is possible to view the case as airing mere allegations of educational neglect. However, it is equally possible to view the case as raising questions of first principle regarding the interaction of the right to education with the right to non-discrimination. The right to education is itself of little utility if rendered in purely formal terms. What really matters is the right to equal effective access to education. This application shows that the Commission was simply neither alive to, nor genuinely sympathetic towards, the essence of the claim being brought forward on behalf of children who are different.

The *Cohen* application involved a child with special educational needs who was earmarked by local authorities to be admitted to a certain school. The parents preferred another school which was further away and which would require free public transport. Ordinarily, the choice of the parents would be respected under British law, but in this instance, since a statement of special educational needs was made, the determination of the local authorities took precedence. The parents alleged that the real reason for the determination was the fact that the transport would cost extra. They alleged violations of Article 2 of the First Protocol, Article 14, and Article 13. Interestingly, the British government had entered a reservation to Article 2 of the First Protocol along the lines that the obligations created thereby would be accepted only 'in so far as is compatible with the provisions of efficient instruction and training, and the avoidance of any unreasonable public expenditure'. In a roundabout way this seems to concede that Article 2 is capable of being interpreted robustly to give rise to substantive claims on State resources. The effect (and indeed validity) of the reservation was not in issue, since the Commission ruled the application inadmissible in any event. The Commission held that Article 2 of the First Protocol:

> cannot be used to derive a right to free transport to the school of one's choice where an alternative is available which would [also] involve free transport and which has not been shown in conflict with the parent's convictions.[41]

If no realistic or effective alternative were available different considerations might conceivably enter the equation. The Commission also rejected an argument based on Article 14 which was to the effect that the precedence afforded local authorities under the special needs legislation which inverted the normal practice differentiated irrationally between two sets of parents. However, the Commission found that 'no relevant difference in treatment has been shown to exist which could constitute discrimination against the applicant in the enjoyment of his Convention rights'.[42]

Article 14 of the Convention has of course been the focus of much argument for reform over the years. It appears that an additional protocol may be prepared which will significantly expand the target groups included under a newer and somewhat broader non-discrimination norm. So far it appears that disability is not included in any of the options being prepared.[43] This narrow approach apparently adopted so far to the reform of Article 14 seems at odds with positive developments on disability taking place within the Council of Europe.

---

[41] EHRR, Commission Supplement, CD104, 104, para. 1.   [42] *Ibid.*, at para. 2.
[43] See generally J. Lathouwers, *Council of Europe: The Plans for an Additional Protocol on Non-Discrimination to the ECHR*, paper delivered at an international conference on non-discrimination law in Utrecht, Netherlands, 25 June, 1998.

The Council of Europe's Social Charter of 1961 did contain some provisions of relevance in the context of disability. Principle 15, which applies to all contracting parties, stated that:

> Disabled persons have the right to vocational training, rehabilitation and resettlement, whatever the nature and origin of their disability.

This principle was further amplified by Article 15 of the Charter which was, unfortunately, merely optional for the contracting parties. The undertakings created by Article 15 (for those contracting States that voluntarily undertook to be bound by it) placed an accent on specialized institutions for training and sheltered employment. In other words the relevant provisions were still based largely on a rehabilitation/compensation model.

However, the Revised Social Charter of 1996 fully absorbs the movement to a rights-based perspective. The new principle 15 is squarely in the rights-based approach and reads:

> Disabled persons have the right to independence, social integration and participation into the life of the community.

The revised Article 15, which, unfortunately, is still optional for contracting States, is more detailed and in the same philosophy. The Revised Charter has not yet come into operation. Significantly, a new Optional Protocol which was opened for signature in May 1996 creates the possibility for international NGOs who have consultative status with the Council of Europe to lodge collective complaints. The main pan-European NGO umbrella, the European Disability Forum, is at present considering applying for consultative status, and will thereby be enabled to lodge such complaints if, of course, the Optional Protocol becomes operative with respect to the country in question. Its usefulness will be substantially diminished if contracting States do not ratify the Revised Charter or if they ratify but fail to indicate an intention to be bound by the revised Article 15.

In sum, it can be seen that the rights-based perspective on disability gained increasing authority under international and regional law from about the 1970s onwards. This culminated in the UN Standard Rules of 1993. The Council of Europe has reflected this shift in its own policy documents. However, the one major shortcoming was the narrowness with which Article 14 of the ECHR was drafted and interpreted.

PART II: INVISIBLE CITIZENS—THE STATUS OF EUROPEANS WITH DISABILITIES UNDER EU TREATY LAW BEFORE AMSTERDAM

The preceding part of this chapter set out the rights-based perspective on disability and explored the extent to which that perspective is gaining ground in the way international or regional human rights treaties are being drafted and interpreted. The question of the status of people with disabilities under European Union law has only recently begun to attract sustained attention.[44] This is partly due to the fact that the bulk of responsibility rests with the Member States, and will indeed continue to do so even after the Treaty of Amsterdam. It is also due to the fact that the founding Treaties did not mention disability. This had pronounced implications since the Treaties transferring power to the Community were silent on how that power was to be used as it affected or potentially affected the lives of thirty-seven million European citizens. Set out below is a detailed consideration of the invisibility of disability under the Treaties prior to Amsterdam and its effects. This is prelude to a proper understanding of the arguments made for changes in the Treaties.

A. EU Human Rights—Limited Utility in the Field of Disability

As stated at the outset, the Union does not have an enforceable Bill of Rights and presently lacks competence to accede to the European Convention on Human Rights[45]—deficient as it is in the area of disability.

The human rights provisions might be divided into

(1) fundamental rights of all persons under general principles of Community law and as reflected in Article F(2) TEU (now Article 6 of the Treaty of Amsterdam);
(2) EU citizens' rights including Article 6 (now Article 12) (non-discrimination on the basis of nationality); and
(3) fundamental social rights.

Social rights are looked at separately below. The Court of Justice developed the notion of general principles of Community law and treated human rights as an integral part of those principles. Such rights could be used as an interpretive guide to the Treaties, as a guide in the exercise of powers, or as criteria for the legality of Community acts. They were inspired by the constitutional traditions of the Member States and applied within the framework of the structure and objectives of the TEC.[46] International human rights treaties on which the Member States had collaborated or of which they were signatories could also be taken as a guideline. This included the European Convention on Human Rights.[47] Significantly, equality—or, more accurately, the right against non-discrimination—was expressly held by the court to be one such right. Advocate General Elmar recently opined that this principle inured to the benefit of people with disabilities.[48] His opinion was not, however, followed by the Court, partly because it was seen as pre-empting the new

---

[44] For a recent review of the current status of people with disabilities within the Member States' legal systems see S.M. Machado and R. De Lorenzo, *European Disability Law* (1997).

[45] *Opinion 2/94, Accession by the Community to the European Convention for the Protection of Human Rights and Fundamental Freedoms* [1996] ECR I–1759. For analysis see S. O'Leary, 'Accession by the European Community to the European Convention on Human Rights (1996) 1 EHLR 326.

[46] Case 11/70, *Internationale Handelsgesellschaft mbH* v. *Einfuhr- und Vorratsstelle für Getreide und Futtermittel* [1970] ECR 1125.

[47] Case 44/79, *Hauer* v. *Land Rheinland-Pfalz* [1979] ECR 3727.

[48] Case C–249/96, *Jacqueline Lisa Grant* v. *South West Trains Ltd.* [1998] ECR I–621.

anti-discrimination provisions of the Amsterdam Treaty.[49] It remains to be seen whether the new Article 13 on non-discrimination (see Part IV below) might embolden the Court to expand its conception of non-discrimination within the general principles of Community law accordingly.

The reference to human rights in the preamble to the Single European Act and the formulation contained in Article F(2) of the TEU (now Article 6 of the Treaty of Amsterdam) did no more than to formalize the reality under European Court of Justice case law dealing with general principles of Community law. One problem with the Article F(2) formulation was that it referred back to the ECHR which, as seen above, is singularly unavailing in the context of disability. Furthermore, constitutional provisions on equality or non-discrimination in the Member States are, with the notable exception of Germany, silent on disability.[50] Article F(2) was in any event rendered beyond the competence of the European Court of Justice by article L (now Article 46).

Nevertheless, it was always possible to influence the way directives were drafted with reference to general principles of Community law including human rights. A good case in point is the Data Protection Directive of 1995 which carves out an exception for legitimate journalistic activity in explicit deference to Article 10 of the ECHR.[51] The disability lobby was never as strong as the media lobby and, in any event, the rights-based perspective on disability is not strongly rooted either under the ECHR or in the domestic laws of the Member States.

With respect to EU citizens' rights it could fairly be said that Article 6 TEC (now Article 12) was not completely irrelevant in the context of disability. For one thing it was directly effective. In essence it required Member States to treat non-national migrants from fellow Member States in the same way as nationals. If domestic law happened to confer rights on nationals with disabilities or extended the protection of non-discrimination law then the benefits of such legislation could not be withheld from non-nationals with disabilities if resident in the Member State in question. At best, however, this would ground a claim to discrimination on the ground of nationality and not on the ground of disability. However, since many Member States do not grant special rights to persons with disabilities there was little for Article 6 to latch onto. In any event it would only be of benefit to those who migrated from one Member State to another. Such migration by persons with disabilities was never likely to take place in meaningful numbers because of a host of educational, training, transport, and social security barriers. Indeed, the Commission openly acknowledged that achieving the right granted to citizens of the Union under Article 8a (now Article 18) to move freely and take up residence between the territories of the Mem-

---

[49] Judgment of the Court in *Grant, ibid.*, at para. 48.

[50] S. 3(3), cl. 2, of the German Constitution was amended in 1994 to read as follows '[n]obody may be disadvantaged on the grounds of disability'. The wording is deliberate to try to immunize existing programmes of positive discrimination.

[51] Dir. 95/46/EC of the European Parliament and of the Council on the protection of individuals with regard to the processing of personal data and on the free movement of such data. Para. 10 of the preamble and Art. 9 set out the exception to certain parts of the Dir. for the sake of legitimate journalistic activity which is based on Art. 10 ECHR (freedom of expression): [1995] OJ L321/6.

ber States was encountering practical and administrative obstacles in the case of people with disabilities.[52]

Article 199 EC (now Article 268) might similarly avail women with disabilities, but only if similarly situated male workers with disabilities were paid or treated differently. However, if no provision were in fact made for male disabled workers, or if female disabled workers were treated equally unfavourably, then Article 119 had nothing to latch onto. As one commentator concluded:

> Like Article 6 there has to be [under Article 119] an initial level of protection, which is determined exclusively by Member States, before Article 119 can be relied upon.[53]

It was no surprising that reform of Article 6 (now Article 12) became a rallying point for many different social movements.

B. Internal Market and Free Movement—Freedom to Discriminate Against People with Disabilities

The absence of a firm non-discrimination anchor in the Treaties—one that embraced disability and that showed sensitivity to the need to avoid indirect discrimination—was not just symbolic. It had had adverse implications for the way the freedoms associated with the internal market were operationalized. For example, free movement of workers—and all associated rights and supports—was held by the Court of Justice not to include a disabled worker.[54] The worker in question was a German national working in paid employment in the Netherlands. He was paid a wage and had a labour contract. The form of work he was engaged in was preparatory to insertion into the open labour market and is quite common among workers with disabilities. Indeed, some 300,000 Europeans with disabilities work in sheltered or semi-sheltered employment.[55] The Court held that, notwithstanding the outward appearance of the work, it was essentially social in its nature and therefore failed to attract any of the rights associated with the free movement of workers.

Not only was the achievement of free movement for workers with disabilities adversely affected by the absence of an appropriate anti-discrimination clause, but internal market issues were debated as if 10 per cent of the European population simply did not exist. In the absence of a general anti-discrimination clause mandating attention to the needs of persons with disabilities various directives or draft directives dealing with standards in the internal market failed to address the situation pertaining to Europeans with Disabilities. The Teleterminal Directive of 1991, which set standards for teleterminal equipment in order to ensure free movement of goods, failed to take account of the needs of the visually impaired—something that,

---

[52] European Commission, *White paper on European Social Policy—A Way Forward for the Union*, COM(94)333 final.

[53] L. Waddington, 'Disabled people are Invisible in the Treaties—Why the European Treaties should Contain a Non-discrimination Provision', 1995 'Report of the European Day of the Disabled', note 20 above, 9 at 11.

[54] Case 344/87 *Bettray* v. *Staatssecretaris van Justitie* [1989] ECR 1621.

[55] E. Samoy, *Sheltered Employment in the European Community* (1992).

technically speaking, could have been done.[56] The Driver Licence Directive as initially proposed discriminated against deaf drivers.[57] The original draft Directive on Buses and Coaches did not contain any mandatory access provisions for disabled passengers. The last draft Directive is still under protracted negotiation.

Even from a purely economic point of view this makes no sense. Design for all ensures that more economic activity that normal will take place and has multiplier effects for other groups, including the elderly. Any deficiency in design for all means that other economic competitors (mainly the United States) are allowed to dominate many sectors of economic activity without sufficient competition. European enterprise loses out, as well as European consumers. What all the above demonstrates is that it is vitally necessary to factor in the disability perspective at the initial or design stage in the preparation of legislation because it becomes almost impossible later on to adjust an existing draft. This puts the Commission in the spotlight, since it has the exclusive power to propose legislation. The problem was that there was (and still is) nothing in EU law compelling the Commission to factor disability into the overall equation.

Another implication due to the absence of an anchoring provision was that a myriad of European programmes—whether run by the Commission or by the Member States—failed adequately to mainstream the participation of Europeans with disabilities.

C. Fundamental Social Rights and Disability

Social progress and the raising of living conditions might be said to be either a function of economic development or a precondition for it. If the former view is taken then the best form of social policy is economic policy. If the latter view is taken then social policy can be seen as a necessary underpinning to the market, and indeed autonomous from market forces. The former seems to have effectively predominated in the EC until at least the 1980s. Rhetoric aside, the notion of a social dimension to the market was a late arrival on the European scene.

European social policy has always been *sui generis*, in that it relates to the social dimension or preconditions to a particular kind of market—namely a transnational market. It is geared primarily at providing the social preconditions necessary to make that particular market work. While it has always been evident that such preconditions are necessary, it has nearly always been resisted because it is often perceived as an indirect way of reaching into domains that lie properly within the exclusive province of the Member States and as a way of ratcheting upwards the level of social provision available within the Member States. Hard powers in the social field were therefore wanting and Articles 117–122 EEC (now Articles 136–145) gave the Institutions little or no competence to enact legislation unless Article 100 (now 113) or 235 (now 308) was invoked.

This is not to say that the institutions did not pay any interest to the social dimension to the market. Indeed, the first social action programme dated back to 1974.[58]

---

[56] Council Dir. 91/263/EEC [1991] OJ L128/1.
[57] Council Dir. 91/439/EEC [1991] OJ L237/1.   [58] See [1974] OJ C12.

Such a concept was vitally necessary as a legitimizing counterweight to the traditional focus on economic policy and the market. The need to accentuate the social dimension coincided with the drive to complete the market in the 1980s and early 1990s. It is interesting to note in passing that the concept of *l'espace social Européen*[59] was marketed politically by the Commission as being not merely a precondition to the establishment of the internal market and free movement of workers but as a way of ensuring and promoting standards of social protection throughout Europe.

The Single European Act inserted Article 118a TEC (now Article 138), which deals with the health and safety of workers, which created a competence that has been generously interpreted by the European Court of Justice.[60] The drive to develop the social dimension led to the Community Charter of Fundamental Social Rights for Workers of 1989 which was adopted by way of 'solemn declaration.[61] Article 26 of the Charter, the very last substantive provision, stated:

> All disabled persons, whatever the origin and nature of their disability, must be entitled to additional concrete measures aimed at improving the social and professional integration. These measures must concern, in particular according to the capacities of the beneficiaries, vocational training, ergonomics, accessibility, mobility, means of transport and housing.

However, the opportunity to add a social chapter was not grasped by the Member States at Maastricht, and in its place was put an awkward Social Protocol which allowed eleven of the then twelve Member States to use the Institutions of the Union to implement the terms of an attached social agreement. This created the possibility of two social Europes—one based on the text of the TEC and one based on the Protocol/Agreement. The limited number of directives enacted under this arrangement had no direct bearing on persons with disabilities.

In the intervening period between Maastricht and Amsterdam, and despite the sheer invisibility of persons with disabilities in the above Treaty provisions, DG V of the Commission did manage to maintain an active interest in the disability field. The first Community Social Action Programme on disability was commenced in 1983 as the Communities' contribution to the UN World Programme of Action.[62] The legal basis for this programme and successor programmes (HELIOS I 1988–91[63] and HELIOS II 1993–96[64]) rested on a Council decision under Article 235 (now Article 308). The later of these programmes, HELIOS II, came to an end in December 1996.

---

[59] See *Bull. EC* 2–1996, at 12. See, generally, E. Lundberg, 'The Protection of Social Rights in the European Community: Recent Developments', in K. Drzewicki, C. Krause, and A. Rosas (eds.), *Social Rights as Human Rights: A European Challenge* (1994), 169.

[60] See L. Waddington, 'Towards Healthier and More Secure European Social Policy: Case C–84/94 United Kingdom v Council', [1997] *MJ* 4.

[61] Adopted by the Heads of State or Government of the Member States of the European Community meeting at Strasbourg on 9 Dec. 1989.

[62] Community Social Action Programme on the Social Integration of Handicapped People (1983–8), [1981] OJ C 347/1.

[63] The HELIOS I (Second) Community Social Action Programme for Disabled People [1988] OJ L104/38.

[64] The HELIOS II (Third) Community Social Action Programme to Assist Disabled People [1993] OJ L56/30.

Its main achievement was to enhance civil dialogue within the disability NGO community.[65] It allowed common perspectives to emerge and emboldened NGOs to assume a more active part in democratic debates about the future of disability policy, both at the level of the Union and within the Member States. One practical result was the elaboration of a HELIOS II European Guide of Good Practice on areas such as social integration and independent living, educational integration, functional rehabilitation, work, and preparation for employment.[66] It is fair to say that the HELIOS II programme was a catalyst to the awakening of the European NGO community to the significance of EU Treaty law.

Article 308 (*ex* Article 235) does provide a legal basis for social action where the Treaties are clear about objectives but less forthcoming on methods. However, the Achilles heel to Article 308 is that it requires unanimity in the Council. The extension of continuation of various social action programmes was blocked by the Council in the mid-1990s because the requisite unanimity could not be found. Much of the attention in the run up to Amsterdam was on crafting a new legal basis for social action programmes that required only qualified majority voting (QMV) at council, so that the need to have recourse to Article 308 would be diminished. It was likely in 1996 that a proposal from the Commission on a new social action programme in the field of disability would suffer a similar fate to the other blocked programmes. It is relevant to note that the proposal for a fourth poverty programme did not receive support from Council in 1995.[67] Small-scale expenditure in the form of pilot action programmes was however approved by the budgetary authority which, in turn, provoked a court challenge by the United Kingdom (joined by Denmark, Germany, and the Council).[68] The Court recently ruled that these measures did not comprise 'non-significant expenditure' and therefore required a 'basic act' (i.e. formal decision of Council).[69] This decision throws into sharp relief the need for a hard legal basis in the Treaties permitting expenditure in support of civil society to take place. Short of that, the judgment calls for a revised inter-institutional agreement to provide a more flexible meaning for 'non-significant expenditure'.

There were other Community programmes besides HELIOS II of relevance in the field of disability. TIDE, for example, was concerned with the development and application of new technologies with a liberating potential for people with disabilities.[70] Employment-Horizon within the European Social Fund was targeted on

---

[65] For excerpts from Interim Evaluation see COM(96)8 final, For final evaluation see *Evaluation of the Third Community Action Programme to Assist Disabled People (HELIOS II)*, COM(98)15 final. The final evaluation was based on the independent evaluation done by Dione Hills and Elliot Stern of the Tavistock Institute, London.

[66] *HELIOS II European Guide of Good Practice: Towards Equal Opportunities for Disabled People,* (1996).

[67] The text of the proposal for a Poverty 4 programme is contained in COM(93)435 final.

[68] Heading B3–4103 of the general budget of the European Union for the financial year 1995 [1994] OJ L369/1.

[69] Case C–106/96, *UK* v. *Commission*, judgment of the Court, 12 May, 1998.

[70] Technology Initiative for Disabled and Elderly People (TIDE) which was initiated as a pilot project in 1991 and will continue to run until late 1997 as a bridge phase, and then as part of the Fourth Framework Programme in RTD. The latest phase embraces the liberating potential of ICTs: see European Commission DG XIII, *Towards a Programme of Work for Telematics for the Integration of Disabled and Elderly People in the Fourth Framework Programme* (1994).

raising employment levels for people with disabilities.[71] Much of the money available through Horizon was in fact used to fund training centres. One problem was that there was little concerted co-ordination between HELIOS II and these other programmes, with the result that the possibility for developing policy perspectives and optimizing synergies was not as great as it could have been.

The Council retained a sporadic interest in the subject throughout the 1980s and early 1990s. Two Council documents which, as such, had no legal effect, are nonetheless worthy of note. A Council Recommendation was adopted on 24 July 1986 concerning the employment of disabled people in the Community.[72] It urged Member States to 'take all appropriate measures to promote fair opportunities for persons with disabilities in the field of employment and vocational training'. It also set out a guideline framework for positive action. A subsequent Commission study on its effectiveness claimed that the Recommendation had contributed to a review of national policies, had provided a framework of reference, and had encouraged Member States to introduce new measures that were in keeping with the spirit of the Recommendation.[73] Another Resolution was adopted by the Council (and by Ministers of Education meeting within the Council) on 31 May 1990 concerning the integration of children and young people within ordinary systems of education. The Commission had in fact taken an active role in monitoring the move toward integrated education since the early 1980s.[74] It stated essentially that the integration of children with disabilities into mainstream education should be considered as a first option, and that extra resources should be made available. A subsequent Commission study on progress made with regard to the policy of school integration noted some progress, but was hampered in its analysis by the way Member States adopted divergent approaches to the issue.[75] Clearly, no matter how useful, something more than recommendations and resolutions was called for.

In sum, the main human rights weapon in the TEU, Article 6 (now Article 12), was effectively of no avail to people with disabilities. In the absence of a strong anti-discrimination provision, one that explicitly included disability and that reached indirect discrimination, many legislative and policy proposals were allowed through that adversely affected people with disabilities and that further compounded their exclusion. This included particularly legislative proposals dealing with internal market harmonization. Various social action programmes which themselves rested on the rather unstable terrain of Article 308 at least helped to develop NGO confidence to the point that these arrangements could be effectively and articulately challenged.

---

[71] See European Commission, DG V, *Employment-Horizon: Provisional Directory of Projects Working Document—Vol. 1. The Disabled* (1996).

[72] [1986] OJ L225/43. [73] COM(88)746 final, at 120.

[74] See *Working Paper of the Commission Services on the Progress in Implementing the Policy of School Integration of Handicapped People,* SEC(86)1758 and SEC(86)1758/2.

[75] *Report of the Commission on the Progress with Regard to the Implementation of the Policy of School Integration in the Member States (1988–91),* SEC(92)1891 final.

PART III: PRE-AMSTERDAM—THE ARGUMENTS FOR ADDING A DISABILITY PERSPECTIVE TO THE TREATIES

By the mid-1990s it was obvious that drastic changes were required in the Treaties. The argument for expanding the relevant non-discrimination provision (Article 6 TEC, now Article 12) held the key.

The Treaty of Amsterdam took some steps in the right direction but stopped short of the key demands, as will be seen. Fully to understand the changes made by the Amsterdam Treaty in the context of disability and to appreciate what remains to be done it is important to look at the changing attitudes and positions of many of the main stakeholders in the debate.

A. NGO Agitation for Treaty Changes

The HELIOS II programme had an NGO strand called the HELIOS II European Disability Forum. One of its constituent members, Disabled Persons International (DPI), proposed and organized (with the help of an advisory group from the EDF) a *Disabled Persons' Parliament* in the precincts of the European Parliament in Brussels which took place on 3 December 1993. This was the first European Day of People with Disabilities. Significantly, that assembly passed a resolution calling for a general anti-discrimination provision to be added to the TEU. Ever since then, 3 December has been marked throughout Europe as the European Day of the Disabled with support form the European Commission and Parliament.

At each subsequent European Day a special publication has been commissioned. The most influential of these reports was issued in 1995 and was entitled *Disabled Persons' Status in the European Treaties—Invisible Citizens*. It contained a devastating critique of the extent to which the needs of persons with disabilities were ignored and even compounded by Community legislation and policies. It laid the groundwork for the arguments which were to follow for amending the Treaties at the Intergovernmental Conference which began in March 1996, and especially for the introduction of a much broader anti-discrimination clause. It contrasted the situation under EU law quite unfavourably with that obtaining in the United States, Canada, and Australia. This report was widely circulated and had a lasting effect on the Institutions of the Union.

An important follow-through report marking the 1996 European Day of Disabled People[76] was accompanied by a separate and detailed document[77] that evaluated a range of options facing the IGC leading up to the Amsterdam summit. After carefully evaluating—and rejecting—various 'soft' options (which included amending Article F.2 TEU, now Article 6) this document proceeded to lay a clear and convincing case for amending (expanding) the main anti-discrimination provision, Article 6 (now Article 12), to cover disability. Significantly, it contained economic

---

[76] 1996 European Day of the Disabled Report, *Towards the Equalization of Opportunities for Disabled People—Into the Mainstream?* (1996).

[77] 1996 European Day of the Disabled Report, *The Legal and Economic Implications of a Non-discrimination Clause in the Treaty on European Union* (1996).

analysis of the impact of such a provision. Unsurprisingly, this analysis pointed to the gains to be made by such a development. A draft non-discrimination clause was proposed and discrimination was defined, *inter alia*, as the denial of 'reasonable accommodation' to people with disabilities. One of the more significant arguments advanced in the 1996 European Day Report was that an expanded non-discrimination clause would not of itself add to the competencies of the Community. It would merely affect (control) the way existing competencies were used.[78] A saver for positive measures was added to accommodate the reality that some Member States already had such positive measures in place and might be fearful lest an anti-discrimination norm might bring them into question. The group was clearly mindful of the ruling of the Court of Justice in *Kalanke* v. *Bremen*.[79] The 1996 Report, and especially the document dealing with the arguments for and potential effects of a relevant non-discrimination provision, was circulated widely and especially to foreign ministries with responsibilities for the preparation of the IGC.

The independent European Disability Forum (EDF), which was the successor body to the HELIOS II Forum and which is not attached to any Community programme, lobbied the various governments extensively on the need for an expanded anti-discrimination provision in the lead-up to the Amsterdam Summit.

One key to their success was the alliances forged with other social movements through, for example, the Platform of the European Social Policy NGOs. The European Social Forum, of which the Platform is an integral part—opened up a civil dialogue between the Commission and the broad sweep of social movements and was first convened by the Commission in March 1996. It was convened again in June 1998 to review the progress made at Amsterdam.[80] One indicator of the progress made in such a short space is the fact that the more important background papers for the 1998 Forum explicitly treat the situation of persons with disabilities.[81]

The EDF also worked particularly closely with national disability NGOs of the Member States holding the Presidency during the IGC, namely, Italy, Ireland, and the Netherlands, to ensure that the disability issue remained on the agenda. In this they were largely successful.

B. The IGC Reflection Group Reacts Favourably to the Arguments Put Forward by the Disability NGOs

A reflection group was set up by the European Council to prepare for the IGC. It was comprised of representatives of the governments of the Member States, the Commission, and the European Parliament. It met under Carlos Westendorp from July

---

[78] While this argument is correct on its face some Member States may have been fearful that an expanded and directly effective non-discrimination clause would confer enhanced competency to the ECJ.

[79] Case C–450/93, *Kalanke* v. *Bremen*, 17 Oct. 1995.

[80] The Forum has its origins in the Declaration on co-operation with charitable association attached to Art. 117 TEC. The Medium Term Social Action Plan 1995–7 (MSAP) contained a commitment periodically to convene the Forum to discuss, *inter alia*, disability with the widest possible range of interested parties.

[81] See in particular the following background papers prepared for the June 1998 Social Forum: Peter Townsend, *The Future World of Work*, at para. 3.7 and Introductory Paper, *Promoting Participation and Citizenship*. All papers are available at www.europa.eu.int/dg05/jobs/forum98/en/texts.

to December 1995 and proved quite receptive to the arguments being made by the EDF. Its report stated in the general part that:

> Many of us think it important that the Treaty should clearly proclaim such European values as . . . non-discrimination on grounds . . . [of] disability and that it should include . . . a procedure for its enforcement.[82]

In a later section dealing explicitly with non-discrimination a majority of the members of the Westendorp group favoured amending Article 6 TEC (now Article 12) to include a reference to disability.[83] This would have meant giving the expanded Article 6 direct effect. A majority of the group was also in favour of giving special consideration to the situation of persons with disabilities in one of the substantive chapters of the Treaties subject to a more detailed assessment of their economic and legal implications. This was presumably a reference to the argument for an amendment of Article 100a (now Article 95) dealing with the process of setting internal market standards. The group was of the view that some sort of saving clause might be necessary to limit any disproportionate economic consequences.

One member of the Westendorp group was stated in the report to be of the view that any new competencies in such a sensitive area were unnecessary and best dealt with at national level. It is widely believed that the individual concerned represented the then British government.

While the Commission's submission to the reflection group was silent on the issue its submission to the IGC proper was somewhat open-ended on the matter. In its IGC submission the Commission stated under the heading of 'A People's Europe':

> The Conference . . . should also incorporate into the Treaty provisions banning discrimination of any kind—particularly on the basis of sex, thereby extending the provisions on equal pay—and condemning racism and xenophobia.[84]

The emphasis in the text following upon the words 'of any kind' was not intended as a rejection of the arguments of the disabled community, or indeed of those of other groups. Nevertheless, the fact that disability was not specifically mentioned in the Commission's submission served to galvanize the NGO community to campaign even more vigourously to keep the issue on the agenda.

C. The Philosophical Switch from Passive to Active Social Policy—The Commission's Green and White Papers on European Social Policy

Fresh thinking on the part of the Commission in the more general field of social policy also fueled the general momentum in favour of an expanded non-discrimination clause. A Green Paper on European Social Policy was issued by the Commission in November 1993.[85] It signalled a significant shift in ideas in the social field generally, but also as applied to disability. It stated in the section dealing with disability that:

> Social segregation, *even with adequate income maintenance and special provision, is contrary to human dignity* . . . Special facilities . . . are obviously necessary, but they should

---

[82] *Reflection Groups's Report, First Part: A Strategy for Europe* (1995), IV.   [83] *Ibid.*, at 13.
[84] *Commission Opinion—Preparation of an Intergovernmental Conference* (1996), at para. 9.
[85] *Commission Green Paper: European Social Policy—Options for the Union*, COM(93)551 final.

not be an obstacle or an alternative to the principle of 'mainstreaming'—that is to say acceptance of people as full members of society, with opportunities for integrated education, training and employment, and to lead their lives independently.[86]

In short, the accent had turned from protection to public freedom and active participation. The Green Paper asked for submissions on the question whether specific Community legislation should be presented in this field. The ensuing White Paper, which was published in July 1994, was even more explicit. It asserted that:

> as a group, people with disabilities undoubtedly face a wide range of obstacles which prevent them from achieving full economic and social integration. There is therefore a need to build the fundamental right to equal opportunities into Union policies.[87]

For its part the Commission stated in the White Paper that it would endeavour to ensure that the needs of persons with disabilities are adequately taken into account in relevant legislation, programmes, and policies. From the perspective of EU law this was entirely gratuitous. The Commission also undertook to prepare an appropriate EU instrument 'endorsing' the UN Standard Rules which in fact occurred in July 1996 (see section D below).

D. *The Commission and Council Align Themselves Explicitly with the Rights-based Perspective on Disability: Communication and Council Resolution of 1996 on Disability*

The Commission had an opportunity to reflect on its position with respect to disability in 1996. The opportunity arose partly because the Commission had already committed itself in its 1994 White Paper to prepare an instrument 'endorsing' the UN Standard Rules. It also arose because the HELIOS II social action programme was scheduled to come to an end in December 1996. The prospect of securing the necessary unanimity in Council on the basis of Article 235 (now Article 308) for a new programme did not seem promising. The time was right to lay down a new strategy. Although this process of reflection and the eventual adoption of a Communication in July 1996 were wholly unconnected with the IGC process they did serve nevertheless to keep governments and broader public opinion alert to the issues.

The Commission produced its Communication or policy statement on disability in July of 1996: *Equality of Opportunity for People with Disabilities—A New Community Disability Strategy*.[88] For the first time the Commission broke clearly and decisively with policies based on paternalism and adopted the rights-inspired equal opportunity model as the appropriate one. In so doing it aligned itself with the UN Standard Rules. For its part it 'undertook' to mainstream the disability perspective into

- the formulation of policy and legislation;
- the employment strategy initiated at the Essen Summit;

[86] *Ibid.* at 48. Emphasis added.
[87] *Commission White Paper: European Social Policy—A Way Forward for the Union*, COM(94)333 final, at 51.
[88] COM(96)406 final. For the response of the European Parliament see EP Resolution on the Commission's Communication on Equality of Opportunity for People with Disabilities [1997] OJ C132/313.

- its thinking on the Information Society; and
- in the Structural Funds.

With respect to mainstreaming in the formulation of legislation the Commission followed through by significantly strengthening its own internal inter-service consultation process. This action was aimed at trying to ensure that legislative and policy proposals emanating from the different Directorates General that may have an impact in the field of disability are identified early on in the process, with a view to appropriate modification if the need arises. Like the mainstreaming commitment in the White Paper this was not, of course, a legal 'undertaking' since no basis existed in the Treaties for the same. However, given the exclusive right of the Commission to propose legislation and conduct policy analysis, these 'undertakings' were significant. They signaled a sea-change in attitude. The only piece missing in the jigsaw was a legal base on which to propose legislation.

The goal of mainstreaming in the formulation of policy is proceeding. One example is the mainstreaming of the disability perspective into current thinking on the nature and future of the Information Society.[89] Indeed, the New Transatlantic Agenda of 1995, which forms the basis of an agreement between the US administration and the Commission on co-operation, is now being activated in the context of disability and the Information Society.

In frank recognition of the fact that most of the competencies remain with the Member States—and indeed continue to do so after Amsterdam—the Commission proposed to facilitate political dialogue between the Member States on the best way to advance the rights of people with disabilities. To do this it proposed to establish a High Level Group of representatives of Member States on disability, which is a familiar tool used to enable Member States to share experiences. This group has now been established and has been in operation since early 1997. It holds an annual liaison meeting with the EDF.

The Communication also contained a related proposal to establish an observatory or information network on disability policy. Observatories are typically used by the Commission to expand the available knowledge base on any given subject. This is especially important in the area of disability, since the available information is patchy and generally non-comparable. Unfortunately, there has been little movement in establishing such an observatory or network, even though there are many precedents dealing, for example, with social exclusion, family policy, and employment monitoring.[90] This is a major drawback, since a large knowledge gap continues to hamper the rational development of European policy perspectives on disability.

The Commission also proposed to encourage and facilitate the social dialogue process to address the relevant employment issues arising in the context of disability. A healthy sign is that a working group within the social dialogue process has in fact

---

[89] See e.g., *Commission Green Paper: Living and Working in the Information Society—People First*, COM(96)389 final, at paras. 112–113); and COM(97)397 final, at paras. 20–21). See generally A. Hunt and M. Berkowitz, *New Technologies and the Employment of Disabled Persons* (1992).

[90] For a detailed list and description of observatories and networks already in operation in the general social policy field see European Commission, *Community Social Policy—Programmes, Networks and Observatories* (1996).

commenced work on the topic an is currently preparing a compendium of good practice for inclusion of the disabled into the labour market.[91]

Last, but certainly not least, the Commission proposed in its communication to support civil dialogue through its support of disability NGOs throughout Europe and through the EDF. Such actors in civil society are recognized as the agents for change and as legitimate stakeholders in the process of change.

It is important to realize that though this Communication was the product of DG V on Social Affairs it was in fact agreed to across all Directorates General, including those dealing with internal market issues.

Council responded with a sister resolution in December 1996 which was similarly based on the human rights approach.[92] In this resolution the Member States collectively reaffirmed their commitment to the UN Standard Rules of 1993, and indeed to the Council of Europe's Recommendation of 1992. They specifically confirmed their commitment to the principle of equal opportunity in the development of comprehensive policies in the field of disability and to the principle of avoiding or eliminating any form of negative discrimination on the sole ground of disability. The notion of 'avoiding negative discrimination' was intended to immunize measures taken to achieve positive discrimination. The resolution further called on Member States to:

- take into account certain policy orientations including the need to empower people with disabilities;
- the need to mainstream the disability perspective into all relevant sectors of policy formulation, enabling people with disabilities to participate fully in society by removing barriers; and
- to nurture public opinion to be receptive to the abilities of persons with disabilities and toward strategies based on equal opportunities.

By its Resolution the Member States furthermore invited the Commission to:

- take into account, where appropriate and within the provisions of the Treaties, the principles of equal opportunity for people with disabilities;
- to promote the exchange of useful information and experience;
- to submit periodic reports on the basis supplied by the Member States describing progress made and obstacles encountered.

The first 'invitation' is particularly important since it fortifies the 'undertaking' given by the Commission in its communication on mainstream disability.

In sum, between Maastricht and Amsterdam the disability NGOs put forward a rational and convincing series of arguments for changes in the Treaties. A majority on the Westendorp reflection group had reacted favourably to the arguments. The arguments fitted well with the Commission's overall switch from passive to active policies designed to increase participation rates for all in society. The Commission itself had explicitly aligned itself to the rights-based approach, and the Member States

---

[91] See UTUC, UNICE, CEEP, *Social Partners' Contribution to the Employment Summit* (1997), at para. 35.

[92] *Resolution of the Council and of the representatives of the Governments of the Member States meeting within the Council of 20 Dec. 1996 on equality of opportunity for people with disabilities* [1997] OJ C12/1.

through Council reconfirmed their commitment to the UN Standard Rules. Expectations were running high that at last people with disabilities would be treated as equal European citizens. The stage was therefore set for the IGC and the Amsterdam Summit.

PART IV: THE TREATY OF AMSTERDAM—RAISING THE VISIBILITY OF EUROPEANS WITH DISABILITIES

How did the arguments fare at Amsterdam and what remains to be done? The IGC itself was required to take place under the terms of Article N(2) TEU (now Article 48(2)). Two drafts were prepared by the Conference in preparation for the Amsterdam summit. The first was prepared under the Irish Presidency and presented to the Dublin European Council in December 1996 as the General Outline for a Draft Revision of the Treaties (Dublin General Outline).[93] The second draft was styled as a mid-term addendum to the Dublin General Outline and prepared under the Dutch Presidency in March 1997.[94] Significant differences appeared between the two drafts on the subject of disability. The resulting Treaty of Amsterdam amends the TEC, TEU, and related acts.[95]

For ease of exposition I divide the changes proposed by the drafts throughout the Conference as they bear on disability and their varying degrees of success at the Summit between human rights, internal market provisions, and social policy provisions.[96]

A. The New Human Rights Provisions as They Affect Disability

It is useful to distinguish between general human rights provisions and non-discrimination provisions under the general heading of human rights.

1. New General Human Rights Provisions and Disability   No concrete proposal to add a Bill of Rights or to amend the Treaties to enable the Union to accede to the ECHR or any other international human rights treaties was put to the Amsterdam Council, although the Dublin General Outline did refer to the possibility of incorporating a new Article to clarify judicial control of respect for fundamental rights.[97] Instead steps were taken to heighten the profile of the Union as one based more visibly on the principles of human rights as follows.

First, Article 6(1) TEU (*ex* Article F) now states that the Union as such is founded 'on the principles of liberty, democracy, respect for human rights and fundamental

---

[93] Conference of the Representatives of the Governments of the Member States, *The European Union Today and Tomorrow—Adapting the European Union for the Benefit of Its Peoples and Preparing it for the Future—A General Outline for a Draft Revision of the Treaties*, CONF/2500/96 CAB (Dublin General Outline).

[94] CONF/2500/ADD 1 (1996).   [95] The final text is contained in CONF/4005/97 (1997).

[96] See generally B. Tonra, *Amsterdam: What the Treaty Means* (1997); Institute of European Affairs, Conference Papers, *The Legal and Constitutional Implications of the Amsterdam Treaty* (1998). Regarding the specific implications of the Amsterdam Treaty in the context of disability see European Disability Forum, *Guide to the Amsterdam Treaty* (1998).

[97] Dublin General Outline, note 93 above, at 11.

freedoms, and the rule of law'. This is at least symbolically significant, in that it seems to suggest that the Union is based on principle and not (or not just) on the fiat of the will of the Member States.

Secondly, Article 49 TEU (*ex* Article O) states that only those European States which respect the principles set out under Article 6(1) (*ex* Article F) may apply to become members of the Union. In the context of this chapter this places a premium on the question whether the relevant principles themselves are expansive enough to embrace the rights-based approach to disability. In other words, must the benchmarks for entry explicitly refer to the situation of persons with disabilities, and in the overall context of achieving equal opportunity and avoiding indirect discrimination? If the relevant principles are read together with the new Article 13 (see below) then arguably so. In any event the European Parliament will have a large role to play in determining eligibility for membership. The Parliament's disability inter-group is not likely to accept human rights benchmarks for entry that fail adequately to absorb the disability perspective.

Thirdly, Article 6(2) TEU (*ex* Article F(2)) states that the Union 'shall respect fundamental rights, as guaranteed by the European Convention on Human Rights . . . and as they result from the constitutional traditions common to the Member States, as general principles of Community law'. However, the basic problem here is that the ECHR (and indeed most constitutions of the Member States) is not itself sufficiently attuned to the disability perspective. As pointed out before, Advocate General Elmar did indicate in a recent case that the notion of general principles of community law was capable of embracing disability within an expanded conception of non-discrimination. His view was not followed by the Court, but for other reasons.[98] Nevertheless the Court did refer to the fact that the new Article 13 TEU would transform the scene with the clear implication that it might alter the content of general principles. This is a good portent since the new Article 13 refers explicitly to disability in the context of discrimination (see section 2 below).

Fourthly, a new mechanism is provided in a new Article 7 TEU to deal with Member States that persistently and seriously violate the principles set out in Article 6(1). An elaborate (and exclusively political) process is set out according to which the relevant determinations are to be made. The sanction is the suspension of certain rights, including possibly voting rights of the Member States concerned. The political costs involved in invoking Article 7 are formidably high.

It is remotely possible that Article 7 might become relevant in the context of disability if, for example, a Member State commenced and persisted with some form of eugenics programme. That possibility might have been greater if the Parliament were given the right to initiate the process, as was in fact foreseen by the Dutch mid-term addendum. However, such violations might be expected to be handled by other means.

In sum, the new general human rights provisions just mentioned are welcome. While they do not in themselves meaningfully advance the rights-based perspective

---

[98] Opinion of Elmar AG in Case C–249/96 *Lisa Jacqueline Grant* v. *South West Trains Ltd.* [1998] ECR I–621.

on disability within the Union they nonetheless raise the profile of human rights which enables the rights perspective to take gradual hold .

2. The New Non-discrimination Provision—Article 13 The Communities' main non-discrimination provision, Article 6 TEC, was always going to be amended in some way or other because it was seen as a vital building block in developing the notion of a Peoples' Europe. The absence of any mention of race in the non-discrimination provision of the TEC was a standing embarrassment. The only questions were which groups should be specifically mentioned, whether they should be mentioned in the body of the non-discrimination clause so that it could have direct effect or otherwise, and whether the new provision would extend to encompass indirect discrimination.

The Dublin General Outline referred in a general way to the need to 'extend significantly the grounds on which action could be taken by the Community to prohibit discrimination'.[99] It did not in fact propose that the body of Article 6 be amended, which would have had direct effect under Community law. Instead, it proposed that a new Article 6a (now Article 13) should be inserted to the effect that:

> Within the scope of application of this Treaty and without prejudice to any special provisions contained therein, the Council, acting unanimously, on a proposal from the Commission and after consulting the European Parliament, may take appropriate action to prohibit discrimination based on . . . disability.[100]

The suggested Article 6a of the Dublin General Outline included a reference to social origin to embrace the travelling or gypsy community. A reported Dutch Presidency suggestion to drop the reference to disability as well as sexual orientation was not accepted by the Conference.[101] Note the draft Article 6a of the Dublin General Outline referred to action to 'prohibit' discrimination—language that is usually redolent of legislation.

In the result, the old—and directly effective—provision relating to discrimination based on nationality (Article 6) was retained and renumbered as Article 12, and a new non-discrimination provision, Article 13, was added which refers expressly, *inter alia*, to disability. It now reads:

> Without prejudice to the other provisions of this Treaty and within the limits of the powers conferred by it upon the Community, the Council, acting unanimously on a proposal from the Commission and after consulting the European Parliament, may take appropriate action to combat discrimination based on . . . disability . . .

The original words, 'prohibit discrimination' were changed to 'combat discrimination' as if to emphasize that legislative measures were not contemplated. However, it is probable that the term 'appropriate action' includes legislative measures. It is, of course, a major disappointment that the body of Article 12 (*ex* Article 6) was not itself expanded to give direct effect to the norm of non-discrimination in the context of disability. Furthermore, like Article 308 (*ex* Article 235), the new Article 13 is hostage to political forces, in that unanimity is required in Council. The text of

---

[99] Dublin General Outline, note 93 above, at 11.   [100] *Ibid.*, at 15.
[101] See J. Kingston, 'Fundamental Rights and Non-Discrimination in the Treaty of Amsterdam', in Institute of European Affairs, note 96 above. at 53.

Article 13 might be considered deficient in that it does not explicitly refer to indirect discrimination, nor does it state that failure to 'reasonably accommodate' disability amounts to discrimination, which was strongly argued by the EDF. Furthermore, any 'action' adopted under Article 13 must still be taken within the limits of the powers set out under the Treaties.

The Commission has recently stated its intentions with respect to Article 13 in its new *Social Action Programme 1998–2000*. There it stated:

> [The Commission will] present a proposal for legislation to combat racial discrimination once the new Treaty is ratified, *and launch a broad debate on the use of Article 13 including the possibility of a framework programme to combat all forms of discrimination.*[102]

Clearly the problem of racial discrimination is one where the possibility of securing unanimity in Council is at its greatest. The real significance of Article 13 for the moment rests on the implicit concession at the level of principle that discrimination does occur in the context of disability, and that this is capable of being of Community concern. Despite appearances this does mark a major breakthrough. There may be creative ways in which the Commission might invoke Article 13 as moral, political, and perhaps legal support for initiatives under different aspects of the Treaties. In other words, a synergy might develop between Article 13 and other competences. If so, and pending an amendment to make Article 13 directly effective, its main utility might be in helping to put a disability-friendly gloss on other parts of the Treaties. However, the one thing that would have given Article 13 real bite would have been to make it directly effective.

B. The Internal Market and Disability—Declaration to Article 95 (ex Article 100a)

The arguments advanced by the NGOs to amend Article 100a so that the disability perspective could be fully taken on board were acceptable at a political level. The Dublin General Outline contained a comment that suggestions had been made that provision might also be made in the Treaty to take special account of persons with a disability.[103] This echoed the majority view of the Westendorp group. The comment further suggested that reference might be made, for example, to Article 127 (now Article 150, dealing with vocational education) or Article 100a (dealing with internal market harmonization). Implicit in this comment was that consideration should be given to amending the *body* of these two Articles.

However, the change when it came was not to the body of the text of either Article but was instead appended as a Declaration to Article 100a (renumbered as Article 95). The Declaration to Article 95 reads:

> The Conference agrees that, in drawing up measures under Article 100a [now Article 95] of the Treaty establishing the European Community, the Institutions of the Community shall take account of the needs of persons with a disability.

In its essence the Declaration reiterates the 'undertaking' previously outlined by the Commission in its communication of 1996 and the 'invitation' issued by the

---

[102] COM(98)258 final, at 12. Emphasis added.
[103] Dublin General Outline, note 93 above, at 15.

Council to the Commission on mainstreaming in its resolution of 1996 in the particular context of drawing up measures under Article 95. Declarations are not legally binding and internal market directives that ignore the needs of people with disabilities cannot be challenged in the Court of Justice. However, it may be referred to by the Court of Justice in assisting it when interpreting directives.

The Declaration, at least implicitly, concedes a point of principle which is that market rationality is best served by factoring in the needs of people at the outset in drafting measures to harmonize the internal market. Disability is now seen not merely as a soft social policy issue but as an internal market concern.

Of especial interest are the stated intentions of the Commission with respect to this Declaration. It stated in its new *Social Action Programme* that the Commission will:

> pursue the strategy set out in its 1996 Communication on equality of opportunity for people with disabilities and *implement the commitment made in the declaration annexed to the Treaty of Amsterdam to take account of the needs of people with disabilities in measures taken under Article 95 (formerly Article 100a).*[104]

While EU law may not require this it does not seem to place an insurmountable obstacle in its path. The argument for 'disability proofing' would have been helped greatly if the Declaration were appended to the body of the text, and this will no doubt feature as a key demand of disability NGOs in the future.

C. The New Social Policy and Employment Provisions in the Context of Disability

Two issues dominated the debate about social policy provisions before Amsterdam. First, there was the question regarding the status of the Social Protocol and Agreement. The time had come in the eyes of many to make Europe the business of all, by which is really meant that European citizens must be convinced that the European project is not merely about the perfecting of remote and impersonal market mechanisms but that it can have a direct and positive bearing on how people live their lives. A new balance should thereby be struck between economic and social progress. The social dimension, which was always latent, needed to be accentuated, and the best way to do this would be to end the phenomenon of two social Europes—one based on Articles 136–145 (*ex* Articles 117–122) and one based on the Protocol/Agreement.

The Dublin General Outline did not go into any detail on the issue since it was plain that while most of the Member States were in favour of giving social policy a higher profile one Member State (commonly assumed to be the UK) remained adamantly opposed.[105] The issue was therefore wisely left until later in the proceedings of the Conference.

Secondly, there was the argument made in the name of developing a People's Europe to introduce a new chapter or title dealing with employment. Both of these demands were successful at Amsterdam and have varying degrees of relevance in the context of disability.

---

[104] COM(98)259 final, at 12. Emphasis added.
[105] Dublin General Outline, note 93 above, at 46.

1. The New Social Provisions With the advent of a new British government in May 1997 it became clear that there would no longer be any British objection to the effective transposition of the Protocol and Agreement on Social Policy into the body of the EC Treaty, thus creating new competencies for the Community. These new provisions are contained in Chapter I (Articles 136–145) of Title XI TEC (*ex* Title VIII, Articles 117–122). This means that the limited number of measures adopted under the old Protocol/Agreement will now apply to the UK, which was in fact given a two-year period of grace within which to prepare for transposition.

Article 136 amends Article 117 to include Article 1 of the Protocol and makes explicit reference to the fundamental social rights such as those set out in the Council of Europe's Social Charter of 1961 and the Community Charter of 1989. As already seen, both these documents refer in turn to the rights of persons with disabilities. It would have been preferable from a disability point of view to mention the Council of Europe's Revised Social Charter. That was not possible, since the revised version was opened for signature only on 3 May 1996 and is not yet operative. In any event, Article 136 does not in itself create competencies. Nevertheless the reference to the 1961 and 1989 documents may be of some use when interpreting the ambit of competencies created elsewhere under Chapter I.

Article 137 (*ex* Article 118) lies at the heart of Chapter I. Among other things it states that 'the community shall support and complement the activities of the member States in . . . the integration of persons excluded from the labour market without prejudice to Article 150'[106] (Article 137(1)). To this end, Article 137(2) confers specific competence on the Council to adopt directives under certain conditions. Council may enact directives under Article 137 in areas such as health and safety. Subject to certain exceptions set out under sub-section (3), qualified majority voting applies. The Social Dialogue process, which for the first time is to be given an explicit basis in Treaty law, must be consulted before the Commission submits social policy proposals. Within that process management and labour may jointly request the Commission to submit collective agreements to Council for a decision as to implementation. This is quite significant given the interest shown of late by the social partners in the whole area of disability and working life.

The Dublin General Outline considered that the Conference should consider:

> whether certain *improvements* of substance should be made in order to strengthen the effectiveness of the Community's social policy including for example the proposal which has been made to strengthen the Treaty provisions on social exclusion.[107]

No draft text was contained in the Dublin General Outline on this point, but it seems fairly evident that the Outline had in mind the arguments being made for the provision of an explicit legal base for the adoption of social action programmes—one that would be based on qualified majority voting (QMV) in Council and thus avoid the need to have recourse to Article 308 (*ex* Article 253). Indeed, the text developed at the Conference on Article 118 contained an explicit mention of disability (as well as

---

[106] Art. 150 deals with vocational training within Chap. 3 of Title XI (Education, Vocational Training, and Youth).
[107] Dublin General Outline, note 93 above, at 46. Emphasis added.

the elderly) in the context of enabling Council to adopt measures aimed at developing exchanges of information and promoting innovative approaches, etc. The reference to disability did not survive. The relevant part of Article 137 (*ex* Article 118) now reads:

> The Council, acting in accordance [with the procedure under Article 251, *ex* Article 189b] may adopt measures designed to encourage co-operation between the Member States through initiatives aimed at improving knowledge, developing exchanges of information and best practices, promoting innovative approaches and evaluating experiences *in order to combat social* exclusion [emphasis added].

The words 'or in favour of elderly or disabled persons' would have been added at the very end of the passage just quoted if the Conference proposal had survived. There is, in any event, a debate within the disability movement about the appropriateness of the 'social exclusion' model in the context because of its traditional focus on poverty. Much depends on how these terms are used. The Dutch sociologist, Engberson, defines poverty, for example, as:

> the structured exclusion of citizens from social participation, coupled with permanent dependence on the state.[108]

Indeed, the idea of linking disability to social exclusion had previously received strong support from some sections of the business community.[109]

There are two views of the legal significance of the absence of any explicit reference to disability in the relevant part of Article 137. The first view is that since it was deliberately removed the generality of the provision is of no avail in the context of disability. The second view is that the generality of Article 137 is of sufficiently wide ambit to encompass people with disabilities as a constituent group of the socially excluded. It is possible that the Commission will consider proposing such a programme based on Article 137 but such a move would entail considerable risk.

2. The New Employment Provisions   In 1997, for the first time ever and in response to the Commission's communication of 1996, a specific chapter on the employment situation of persons with disabilities was included in the Commission's annual report on employment in the Union.[110] It stated that the average employment rate for people with disabilities runs at 44 per cent, which is about 17 per cent lower than for the rest of the population. It also stated that the proportion of people with disabilities who are (economically) inactive is much greater than the rest of the population. The Commission released a working document on disability and employment in February 1998 (to be developed later into a full communication) outlining and clarifying the nature of the difficult challenges that lie ahead.[111]

---

[108] Quoted in a paper by B. Cantillon, I. Marx, and K. Van den Bosch, *Who are the Socially Excluded: Poverty and the Adequacy of Social Protection in OECD Countries: Trends and Policy Issues* (1996), 3.

[109] See *European Declaration of Business Against Exclusion* (1995).

[110] Report of the Commission, *Employment in Europe: 1997*, COM(97)429 final. On the current state of employment legislation as it affects workers with disabilities throughout the Member States see generally P. Thornton and N. Lunt, *Employment Policies for Disabled People in Eighteen Countries : A Review* (1997). For an outline of EU employment policy as it affects workers with disabilities see L. Waddington, *Disability, Employment and the European Community* (1996).

[111] European Commission DG V, Working Paper, *Raising Employment Levels of People with Disabilities—The Common Challenge* (1998).

The new employment title, Title VIII (Articles 125–130), is also of great potential significance in the field of disability. Until Amsterdam the Community lacked a clear competence in the field since employment was considered an exclusive prerogative of the Member States. The argument for an employment chapter was central to the demands for a People's Europe. As if to accentuate the emphasis now been placed on such concerns the new title was placed immediately after Title VII dealing with economic and monetary policy.

Employment is now a Community concern—of sorts. Article 125 (ex Article 109n) states in part that the Member States and the Community will 'work towards developing a co-ordinated strategy for employment and particularly for promoting a skilled, trained and adaptable workforce'. The Member States are furthermore required to 'regard promoting employment as a matter of common concern and shall co-ordinate their action in this respect within the Council' subject to the provisions of Article 128 (*ex* Article 109q). The Community as such is required to 'contribute to a high level of employment by encouraging co-operation between Member States and by supporting and, if necessary, complementing their action' (Article 127(1)). Furthermore the Community as such is now obliged to take into account the objective of high employment when considering the formulation and implementation of Community policies and activities (Article 127(2)).

The heart of the new employment chapter is contained in Article 128(2) which enables Council (acting on the basis of a proposal from the Commission and on a qualified majority and after consulting certain other institutions and bodies) to adopt employment guidelines which the Member States 'shall take into account in their employment policies'. Each Member State is further obliged to provide the Council and the Commission with an annual report 'on the principal measures taken to implement its employment policy in light of the guidelines'. Specific recommendations may be adopted, if necessary or appropriate, with respect to the policies of any Member State.

Interestingly, since the employment chapter does not give rise to a competence to adopt legislation, the Amsterdam Summit decided to implement the employment provisions immediately and even before ratification of the Treaty, and asked the Luxembourg Presidency to prepare a special European Council on the topic. The draft Guidelines presented by the Commission to the Luxembourg Council which was held in November 1997 did not contain very strong references to disability.[112] A much stronger reference to disability was in fact inserted into the Guidelines by the Luxembourg Council.[113] The Guidelines agreed to at Luxembourg were formally adopted by the Heads of State on 15 December 1997—a fact that lends them extra authority. The four general headings in the guidelines are (I) improving employability, (II) developing entrepreneurship, (III) encouraging adaptability in business and their employees, and (IV) strengthening policies for equal opportunities. The fourth heading (equal opportunity) is explicitly stated to apply to disability. Under the

---

[112] COM(97)497 final. A minor reference to disability was contained at 4 of the communication under the heading of tackling long-term and youth unemployment.
[113] See Council Resolution of 15 Dec. 1997 on the 1998 Employment Guidelines.

sub-heading entitled 'promoting the integration of people with disabilities into working life' the relevant part of heading (IV) reads:

The Member States will:

—give special attention to the problems people with disabilities may encounter in participating in working life.

One problem with this approach has to do with whether the general equal opportunities heading as it touches on disability stands alone, or whether it informs the preceding three headings (employability, etc.). National action plans (NAPs) based on the Guidelines were submitted in early April 1998. Revised draft guidelines will be presented by the Commission in October 1998. All NAPs dealt in detail with disability and equal opportunity. Among the more forward-looking were those of the United Kingdom, Spain, Germany, and Sweden. In a background report analysing the detail of the various NAPS the Commission stated:

All Member States implement a wide range of measures to promote the participation of disabled people in the mainstream labour market. Although it is not uncommon for people with disabilities to be given early access to employment measures for the unemployed, priorities vary considerably from one Member State to another. Measures for people with disabilities include anti-discrimination legislation against disabled people, quota systems, rehabilitation and vocational programmes, wage subsidies, subsidies for the acquisition of technical aids and tools, information and awareness campaigns against prejudices affecting people with disabilities.[114]

The background report also noted that the absence of comparable or even national data made it difficult to identify the various obstacles people with disabilities face in getting a job which, in turn, made the choice of rational policies as well as monitoring of those policies difficult.

In its formal communication on the NAPs the Commission summarized the plans in the context of disability as follows:

Member States are firmly committed to getting more people with disabilities into jobs, and policy actions show interest in mainstreaming the issue into other policies in particular on employability.[115]

Employability looks likely therefore to become a key focus of attention. However, the reference to disability under the general equal opportunities framework is extremely valuable in guiding how employability issues should be looked at. Furthermore, to focus exclusively on employability might unwittingly serve to divert attention away from the need to make adjustments in how enterprises can adapt in order to make space for the skills and abilities brought to the labour market by people with disabilities. The Commission's views on how or whether the guidelines need to be refined in this field are keenly awaited later in 1998.

A new Employment Committee is envisaged by Article 130 (*ex* Article 109s). Its basic task is to monitor and evaluate the employment situation as well as to formu-

---

[114] European Commission, *Background Report, From Guidelines to Action: The National Action Plans for Employment* (1998).

[115] Communication from the Commission, *From Guidelines to Action: The National Action Plans for Employment*, COM(98)316 final, at 11.

late opinions on its own initiative or at the request of the Commission or Council. It is required to consult the social partners in carrying out its mandate.

Also of potential interest is the concept of 'incentive measures' available under the employment chapter (Article 129, ex Article 109r). Such measures will be designed to:

> encourage co-operation between the Member States and to support their actions in the field of employment through initiatives aimed at developing exchanges of information and best practices, providing comparative analysis and advice as well as promoting innovative approaches and evaluating experiences, in particular by recourse to pilot projects.

Since unemployment is one of the biggest scourges facing people with disabilities it would be hard to imagine a better case for such incentive measures. No harmonization measures are possible under this Article.

Of especial interest is the extent to which official thinking in the institutions is now moving toward linking employment policy with the Structural Funds. Objective 3 of the Structural Funds deals, *inter alia*, with combating long-term unemployment and facilitating the integration into working life of people excluded from the labour market. Within the Social Fund the Community initiative, Employment-Horizon, deals specifically with the integration of disabled people into working life. The overall budget for Horizon is ECU 950 million of which the Union provides at least ECU 500 million. The extraordinary Employment Council at Luxembourg expressed the hope and expectation that the forthcoming reform of the Structural Funds will aim to make optimum use of the funds to serve employment needs wherever possible, while respecting the main purpose of the funds, which is to enable regions lagging behind to catch up.[116] This call was echoed in the preambular provisions to the December 1997 Resolution of the Heads of Government or State in which the guidelines were formally adopted. If this is implemented it could convert the Social Fund initiatives into a useful laboratory for the continual evolution of employment policy and the periodic revision of the Guidelines. Article 13 may provide a key inspiration in this endeavour.

In sum, the argument that the principle of non-discrimination should include people with disabilities was accepted at the level of principle but did not find expression where it needed it most—in the directly effective provisions of Article 12 (*ex* Article 6). The argument that the process of setting standards for the internal market should be sensitized to the needs and equal rights of persons with disabilities was accepted at the level of principle but ended up in a non-binding declaration. Important gains were made within social policy that may well prove critically important, and particularly in the employment field. However, social action programmes in favour of people with disabilities will still have to rely in all likelihood on Article 308 (*ex* Article 235).

---

[116] Presidency Conclusions, Extraordinary European Council Meeting on Employment, Luxembourg, 20 and 21 Nov. 1997, issued on 24 Nov 1997; *Bull. EU* 11–1997, at 7.

PART V: CONCLUSIONS—UNFINISHED BUSINESS

What conclusions and recommendations of relevance for a new EU Human Rights Agenda are warranted by the above analysis?

Human Rights as the Appropriate Framework of Reference

The post-War legal architecture for Europe is being slowly transformed. The Union, which always had political ends but which concentrated on economic means, is now returning in a fashion to those political aims and beginning to market itself as being based ever more visibly on human rights, the rule of law, and democracy. The new human rights competences are important, not merely in themselves but also in the way they may potentially impact on the more traditional economic competences.

It is this new phenomenon that makes EU law relevant in the context of disability. Both the rights-based arguments and those based on economic rationality point in the direction of reform in the context of disability. There is a synergy between both sets of arguments. There is also a complementarity between them. Where, for example, a market-based argument fades (as it would for those who lack any capacity to participate) a rights-based argument takes over.

We recommend:

- that the notion of a Europe for all based on inclusion and on a celebration of human difference should be strongly reiterated;
- that the rights-based perspective on disability should be specifically endorsed;
- that the synergy between markets and rights be recognized whilst placing primacy on the rights and dignity of the individual.

A New EU Human Rights Agenda should Emphasize the Positive Role of Rights in Ensuring an Active and Participatory life in the Mainstream

The philosophical shift of the EU from passive to active policy options is supported by human rights. The second conclusion is that the general philosophical shift within the thinking of the institutions away from passive measures of social support toward viewing social policy as a tool with which to leverage increased and increasing levels of active participation and citizenship is one that admirably fits with the needs of most people with disabilities.

We recommend:

- that a new European Human Rights Agenda should accentuate the extent to which rights are tools with which to build active participatory lives and not just protective devices;
- that the movement away from passive to active measures to support participation and equal opportunities (and with it the remodelling of the European Social Model) be specifically endorsed;
- that disability should be systematically mainstreamed into all policy debates of this kind since it represents a classic case where passive maintenance has failed and it stands to benefit greatly from the shift;

- that very careful attention be given to the ongoing and substantive needs of persons with disabilities in an effort to ensure that the movement from the passive to the active mode does not leave people with disabilities even more disadvantaged than hitherto.

There is a Need to Fill the Knowledge Gap and a Role for the Union

The knowledge gap about the nature and extent of the barriers of equal opportunity is a serious barrier to reform. Not only is information sparse within countries, it is often not comparable as between Member States. With respect to the monitoring of the Employment Guidelines the Commission has already indicated its intention to assist in the development of an agreed comparable database as well as agreed indicators of performance.[117] This is a set in the right direction but more is needed.

We recommend:

- that the observatory or information network outlined in the Commission's Communication of 1996 should be set up as a matter of urgency. This body should provide useful, objective, and comparable analysis to assist in the process of reform both within the Member States and at the level of the Union where appropriate;
- that a series of well targeted studies should be commissioned to assess the nature of the barriers and to evaluate the range of solutions available.

The Right of Equality is the Core Benchmark for Reform

Notions about equality and non-discrimination lie at the very heart of the debate about disability and EU law. Unfortunately, while the non-discrimination norm in Article 6 (now Article 12) TEC (which has its roots both in human rights and in the need to ensure market rationality) is very powerful, it suffers from the defect of limited reach. Article 6 was always going to be the focal point in the demands for change on the part of many different social movements. The new Article 13 made a breakthrough at one level, in that it implicitly concedes the reality of discrimination in the context of disability. The war of ideas is over. Yet the process of renewing the Union's main human rights weapon is incomplete. Article 13 is not directly effective. It does not explicitly embrace the reality of indirect discrimination nor make positive space for 'reasonable accommodation'.

There is no saver for affirmative action in the form of quotas for those Member States that wish to adopt the same. Measures adopted under it are still subject to unanimity in Council. A People's Europe calls for much more.

With respect to the existing text of Article 13 it is recommended:

- that the Commission should consult widely before introducing legislative proposals based on Article 13 in the context of disability, and
- that the Commission should prepare the ground politically for legislative initiatives by commissioning cost/benefit analyses on the utility of regulation

---

[117] *Social Action Programme 1998–2000*, COM(98)259 final, at 5.

and by carrying out useful comparative legal analysis of countries where such legislation has been successful.

With respect to the further development of the text of Article 13 it is recommended:

- that the Union should move to the elaboration of a core right to equality— one that should inform the entirety of EU Treaty law;
- that this core right would be directly effective;
- that this core right would include a principle of non-discrimination which would inure to the benefit of many indicative groups including persons with disabilities;
- that indirect discrimination would also be prohibited by the new norm and should be defined in the context of disability to include failure to provide 'reasonable accommodation' to the needs of persons with disabilities;
- that a saver should be inserted for affirmative or positive action including quotas for those Member states that so desire;
- that a section somewhat akin to section 5 of the Fourteenth Amendment to the US Constitution be added to the effect that the Legislature (the Institutions) should have a wide margin of appreciation in legislating for equal opportunities.

Harnessing Market Power: Disability and Internal Market Regulation

The war of ideas with respect to the internal market and disability is also over. The argument that indirect discrimination can occur through the process of setting internal market standards and should therefore be avoided has now been accepted. However, it has only been accepted at a political level. The Declaration attached to Article 95 (*ex* Article 100a) has moral force only, and perhaps some persuasive force in the interpretation of directives in the Court of Justice. It would have been far preferable if the core idea—which is that indirect discrimination should be avoided—were written into Article 95 itself. In other words, the core idea has yet to be accepted at the legal level. Nevertheless, the undertaking by the Commission in its new *Social Action Programme 1998–2000* to 'implement' the declaration is to be greatly welcomed.

With respect to the 'implementation' of the Declaration on Article 95 it is recommended that a proofing mechanism should be adopted which builds on and develops the inter-service consultation process already underway.

With respect to the further development of the Declaration on Article 95 the following is recommended:

- the content of the Declaration should be moved to the body of the text of Article 95;
- Article 3(2) (following the Treaty of Amsterdam) contains an *integration clause* requiring that with respect to all the activities listed in Article 3(1) (activities of the Community) 'the Community shall aim to eliminate inequalities and to promote equality, between men and women'. Similar clauses exist

under Articles 151(4) dealing with culture (*ex* Article 128), 152(1) with respect to health protection (*ex* Article 129), and 153(2) with respect to consumer protection (*ex* Article 129a). It is recommended that a similar clause be included with respect to people with disabilities.

Harnessing Labour Market Power: Employment Policy and Disability

The new employment chapter may prove to be immensely powerful, given that the employment guidelines refer explicitly to the situation of people with disabilities. It is important to remember, however, that this reference in the guidelines is purely gratuitous from the perspective of EU law. It would have been preferable to have a mandatory legal requirement to do so. Again, this would have been strongly implicit if Article 13 had been made directly effective and if it had explicitly embraced the notion of indirect discrimination.

With respect to the development of EU employment policy in the context of disability it is recommended:

- that the reference to disability in the heading of equal opportunities should be preserved in the Employment Guidelines;
- that the equal opportunities heading should be understood to inform and animate the preceding parts of the Guidelines;
- that any employment incentive measures should have a disability application;
- that all debates about the Information Society and employment should specifically include a consideration of the impact on persons with disabilities;
- that the obligation of 'reasonable accommodation' in the context of employment should be fully studied and costed.

New Social Provisions and Disability

The adoption of the social chapter (more accurately the social title) is of potentially great benefit. Many of the legislative proposals that might emerge will affect workers generally, and the Commission should be alert to the need to avoid indirect discrimination against people with disabilities. However, such alertness will be done to the commitment and foresight of the Commission—it is not required even after Amsterdam. The deliberate deletion of any reference to people with disabilities in provisions dealing with social exclusion at a late stage in the Amsterdam summit was a setback, and it is too early yet to say whether it precludes people with disabilities altogether from the social exclusion provisions. It would have been better to remove the doubt by letting the reference stand.

With respect to the existing social provisions it is recommended that any proposals for social legislation should fully take into account the needs of people with disabilities.

With respect to the further development of social provisions at the next IGC it is recommended:

- that the reference to disability in the context of social exclusion (Article 137, *ex* Article 118) be restored;

- that support for civil dialogue be added as a legitimate aim of Community law thus avoiding the difficulties of finding a legal base for the relevant parts of social action programmes.

In sum, the Treaty of Amsterdam marks one more stepping stone toward the creative merger of human rights imperatives with free market logic and the processes that regulate them at the level of the Union. That journey is incomplete and much needs to be done.

The merging of a concern for human rights with the way markets are regulated is the challenge ahead. If human rights—and especially equal opportunity for all regardless of human difference—can be seen as underpinning and not undermining market forces then the way will have been smoothed. As the disability field shows, the claim for a right is not the same as the claim for largesse. It is essentially a claim for equal citizenship, the right to participate, and for public freedom.

10

The Internal and External 'Other' in the Union Legal Order: Racism, Religious Intolerance and Xenophobia in Europe

CONOR A GEARTY*

I. INTRODUCTION

At the centre of the plan for a new European landscape there is to be found a hard seed of hate. Though small, it has been carefully nurtured by the malevolent and has thrived on the past inattention of Europe's master-gardeners. In the excitement of the march to unity, the push for the single currency, and the rejuvenation of our Euro-wide institutions, it has been tempting to ignore its venomous potential and to concentrate instead on the rekindled Renaissance that seems to beckon for the Europe of the New Millennium. This seed of hate is however more than a mere detail or the pedantic obsession of a gardener responsible for only a small part of the whole. It is the evil of racism and its associated negative passions of religious intolerance and general xenophobia.

If left alone, this seed will grow. Its germination will drive its poisonous buds across the whole of Europe, swamping the undergrowth with virulent weeds and threatening fatally to pollute the fragile roots of idealism and co-operation on which the idealists' new Europe must rely to achieve its full flowering. The European project has successfully made unthinkable a war between its partner nations. Now it must make equally incomprehensible the new war on some of its people that a thriving racist movement would gleefully incite. Until this too has been achieved, the lessons of the Second World War will not have been fully and finally learned. 'The defence of human rights and fundamental freedoms, core values of the European integration project, cannot be separated from the rejection of racism. Indeed, the struggle against racism is a constituent element of the European identity.'[1]

Racism is a dangerous enemy because its inefficiency, its irrationality, and its immorality make it so senseless to informed opinion that its power is invariably

---

* The author is grateful to the Civil Liberties Research Unit at King's College, London, for its administrative support on this project. The author is particularly grateful to Ms Clair Milligan of the Unit for her research assistance on the project.

[1] *Communication from the Commission on racism, xenophobia and anti-semitism and proposal for a Council Decision designating 1997 as European Year Against Racism*, COM(95)653 final, at 4.

underestimated. Of course it is a counter-productive irrelevance for any society dedicated to human rights and to an efficient market to wage war on a segment of its citizenry merely on account of the colour of its skin or the nature of its religious belief. It is like declaring war on the left-handed or on people born on Tuesday.[2] Such stupid intolerance messes up the market while also infringing the basic tenets of all our established religions. The rejection of the very idea of human dignity that racism inevitably involves also falls foul not just of this or that provision of this or that human rights treaty but of the whole concept of respect for human rights; the racist never sees a whole person, only the colour he or she happens to be. Despite these truths, academic studies still court controversy by appearing to correlate race and intelligence,[3] the deeply religious Afrikaners managed for decades contentedly to reconcile their racialism with their belief in God, and even the United States, one of the homes to human rights in their modern form, tolerated official racism within its borders for much of the twentieth century. In the western culture the roots of racism are as deep as its moral and rational justification is shallow.

This is truer of Europe than of anywhere else within that culture. The Jews were early victims, punished collectively for their separateness in the homogeneously Christian society that was mediaeval Europe. The re-emergence of this people from its secure ghettos around the start of the nineteenth century led to a beneficial interaction between cultures, but reawakened as well the old forms of hate. At the same time, the increase in travel that facilitated and characterized Europe's age of imperialism led to far greater contact between peoples than had previously been the case. With these exciting changes and opportunities came also fresh forms of racism, rooted in colonial superiority but also now manifesting itself in new branches of scientific study such as in anthropology and natural science. The French writer and diplomat, Joseph-Arthur Comte de Gobineau, published his four-volume *Essay on the Inequality of Human Races* in 1853–5, spelling out 'his racism in awesome detail and . . . based upon the best scholarship then available, as well as upon his own observations made during extensive travels'.[4] Into this heady mix was added, after the revolutionary excitements of 1848, a fresh nationalist ingredient, to give the old racism a new, more aggressive flavour.

The catastrophe of Nazism and of the institutionalized racism of middle twentieth-century Europe was the culmination of these nineteenth-century developments, but the destruction of fascism that followed in 1945 did not extirpate entirely the evil that lay behind the Holocaust and the other terrible crimes against humanity which racist ideology had then inspired. After a generation in relative abeyance, 'the political discourse of racism'[5] has once again forced itself onto Europe's agenda. Since

[2] See J. Waldron, 'Whose Nurembourg Laws' (1998) 20 *London Review of Books* 12. There is a good statement of the market argument against discrimination in D. Curtin and M. Geurts, 'Race Discrimination and the European Union Anno 1996: From Rhetoric to Legal Remedy?' (1996) 14 *NQHR* 155.
[3] Note the recent controversy that surrounded publication of R.J. Herrnstein and C.A. Murray, *The Bell Curve: Intelligence and Class Structure in American Life* (1994).
[4] G.L. Mosse, *Towards the Final Solution. A History of European Racism* (1978), 51. This is a comprehensive work. Also valuable is J. Wrench and J. Solomos (eds.), *Racism and Migration in Western Europe* (1993).
[5] The phrase is from A.G. Hargreaves and J. Leaman (eds.), *Racism, Ethnicity and Politics in Contemporary Europe* (1995), 113. For a good summary of the position up to the mid-1990s, see the editors' 'Racism in Contemporary Western Europe: An Overview' in the same vol. at 3–30.

1984, the National Front Party in France has regularly secured between 10 and 14 per cent of the national vote. The Party now holds the balance of power in a number of localities after recent nation-wide elections gave it even more success. (This was despite the fine of £30,000 imposed on the Party leader, Jean-Marie Le Pen, in December 1997 for having described the Nazi gas chambers as nothing more than a detail in the history of the Second World War.) In Austria Jorg Haider's Freedom Party (FPO) has also been highly effective, while in Italy late in 1993 the granddaughter of Benito Mussolini took 44 per cent of the vote as a Movimento Sociale Italiano (MSI) candidate in Naples. A resurgence in right-wing parties of a racist nature has been evident across most continental European nations in the 1990s.

Inevitably these electoral successes and the revival of racist thinking have translated themselves into violence on the streets. 'Overall, it is estimated that about 16 million of the 320 million residents of the twelve member states of the European Community originate from outside the Community, that is, about 5% of the population'.[6] These people have been subjected to greatly increased levels of racially motivated attacks. German unification has been followed by a sharp increase in racist violence, where the 'racism endemic in many societies has exploded in a public way . . . in the past five years'.[7] In December 1997 the neo-nazi Kay Diesner was sentenced to life imprisonment for the murder of a police officer and the attempted murder of three other people in Germany. In September the same year, three Danish fascists were jailed for sending letter bombs to, among others, a well-known British swimmer married to a black athlete and the UK-based Anti-Fascist Action organization. Earlier that Summer in Madrid a 19-year-old Moroccan was shot in the back as he walked with his girlfriend in the centre of the city, his assailant (a police officer) being heard to ask '[a]re you Moroccan?' moments before the killing. At around the same time, eleven racist skinheads were finally jailed in Portugal for between fourteen and eighteen years for having beaten a young man to death in a racist attack in Lisbon two years before; the eleven had been part of a gang of some fifty skinheads who had rioted in the town, attacking black people with iron bars and baseball bats. Racism has been no respecter of borders, of electoral defeat or of a relatively tranquil culture. Even in the United Kingdom, where racist parties have done far worse in recent elections than many of their European counterparts, there has been a dramatic increase in the reported levels of racist crimes in recent years.[8]

These various attacks have not been isolated acts of criminality. They have thrived not only on the success of Europe's far right political groups but also on the breadth

---

[6] European Commission, *Legal Instruments to Combat Racism and Xenophobia* (1993), 7. There is a good assessment of the composition of the ethnic minority groups across Europe at 7–10. The Commission figure does not include illegal or undocumented aliens. It also appears not to be restricted to persons born outside the Community; see by way of comparison the estimate by JUSTICE that 'there are around four million non-white citizens of member states, three million nomadic people living in the Union, and at least ten million legally resident third country nationals': JUSTICE, *The Union Divided. Race Discrimination and Third Country Nationals in the European Union* (1997), note 2.

[7] Human Rights Watch/Helsinki, *'Germany for Germans'. Xenophobia and Racist Violence in Germany* (1995).

[8] Human Rights Watch/Helsinki, *Racist Violence in the United Kingdom* (1997). Also valuable is S. Virdee, *Racial Violence and Harassment* (1995). And see also The Stephen Lawrence Inquiry. Report of an Inquiry by Sir William Macpherson of Cluny (Cm 4262, the Stationery Office, London, 1999).

of the racist sentiments across Europe into which these parties have been able successfully to tap. In this regard the most recent Eurobarometer opinion poll into racism and xenophobia in Europe, published in December 1997, makes depressing reading.[9] Even making allowances for any doubts we might have about the methodology of such a result, it is surely of great concern that this poll revealed that only one in three of those interviewed across Europe felt able to describe themselves as 'not at all racist'. One in three declared themselves 'a little racist' and as many as one third openly expressed quite or very racist feelings. Nearly one in ten of the interviewees admitted to being 'very racist'. The survey found no significant differences between the answers of men and women, and no predominance of racism in urban over rural areas, despite the lower presence of minorities in the latter. Though there were country-wide variations, only Portugal and Luxembourg reflected a majority of respondents prepared to identify themselves as 'not at all racist'.

The European Union has not been passive in the face of this racist threat; 'the rhetoric of the governing elite is long established and prolific'.[10] The Eurobarometer poll results were presented to the closing conference of the European Year against Racism which had been officially proclaimed by the Member States for 1997[11] and which had been officially launched on 30–31 January at a two-day conference in The Hague. On the first day of that Conference the Dutch Prime Minister and then President-in-Office of the Council, the President of the Commission, and the President of the European Parliament issued a declaration entitled 'Europe Against Racism'. The Parliament has engaged in detailed studies of the problem as long ago as 1985[12] and 1991,[13] has studied and debated it on many occasions,[14] and has passed resolutions drawing attention to the evils of racism (both within and outside the EU) on no fewer than eleven occasions since the start of 1993.[15] Following the Council Joint

[9] European Commission Employment and Social Affairs, *Racism and Xenophobia in Europe*, Eurobarometer Opinion Poll No. 47.1. The details that follow are drawn from the draft final report presented at the closing conference of the European Year Against Racism, held at Luxembourg, 18–19 Dec. 1997.

[10] Curtin and Geurts, note 2 above, at 148.

[11] Resolution of the Council and the Representatives of the Governments of the Member States meeting within the Council of 23rd July 1996 concerning the European Year against Racism (1997) [1996] OJ C237/1.

[12] European Parliament, Committee of Inquiry into the Rise of Fascism and Racism in Europe, *Report on the Findings of the Inquiry (The Evrigenis Report)* (1985).

[13] European Parliament, Committee of Inquiry on Racism and Xenophobia, *Report on the Findings of the Inquiry (The Ford Report)* (1991).

[14] The Committee on Civil Liberties and Internal Affairs of the European Parliament has been particularly active. See the following of the Committee's reports: Report on the Resurgence of Racism and Xenophobia in Europe and the Danger of Right-wing Extremist Violence (*Rapporteur:* Mr Cesare De Piccolo) (1993); Report on the Status of Nationals of Non-member Countries in the European Union (*Rapporteur:* Mrs Djida Tazdait) (1993); Report on the Situation of Gypsies in the Community (*Rapporteur:* Mr Juan de Dios Ramirez Heredia) (1994); Report on the Communication from the Commission on Racism, Xenophobia and Anti-semitism and on the Proposal for a Council Decision designating 1997 as European Year against Racism (*Rapporteur:* Mr Arie Oostlander) (1996); Report on the Proposal for a Council Regulation establishing a European Monitoring Centre for Racism and Xenophobia (*Rapporteur:* Mr Glyn Ford) (1997); and Report Containing a Draft European Recommendation to the Council on Fundamentalism and the Challenge to the European Legal Order (*Rapporteur:* Mr Arie Oostlander) (1997).

[15] EP Resolution of 21 Apr. 1993 on the resurgence of racism and xenophobia in Europe and the danger of right-wing extremist violence [1993] OJ C150/127; EP Resolution of 2 Dec. 1993 on racism and xenophobia [1993] OJ C342/19; EP Resolution of 20 Apr. 1994 on ethnic cleansing [1994] OJ C128/221; EP Resolution of 21 Apr. 1994 on the situation of gypsies in the Community [1994] OJ C128/372; EP

Action of 15 July 1996 concerning action to combat racism and xenophobia,[16] a European Monitoring Centre for Racism and Xenophobia was provided for,[17] to help the European authorities 'to track events and developments and [to] give us a clearer picture of what we are up against'.[18] The Centre was officially established in Vienna on 28 January 1998. In the last two months of 1997, the Council issued two further Declarations, on the fight against racism, xenophobia, and anti-Semitism in the youth field[19] and on respecting diversity and combating racism and xenophobia.[20] At the same time, the EU Consultative Commission on Racism and Xenophobia (the Kahn Commission)[21] adopted a Charter on European political parties for a non-racist society, and a Conference on this and related matters was held in Utrecht at the end of February 1998. Other studies of workplace discrimination have also been conducted at the European level,[22] and the Council has joined with the representatives of Member States' governments meeting within the Council to issue resolutions on the fight against racism and xenophobia in the fields of employment and social affairs[23] and the response of educational systems to these two problems.[24]

The pace of the European anti-racism discourse has therefore escalated sharply in recent years, and the success of the just concluded Year Against Racism has been an additional spur. Such talk cannot root out its enemy by argument, no matter how well-honed, widely supported, or well endowed. As the provisional minute of a January 1998 resolution from the European Parliament gloomily noted, 'despite the many international initiatives against racism and xenophobia launched in recent years . . . some sections of the population continue to hold racist and xenophobic views, views which sometimes even find expression in insults and violent attacks which leave the victims with psychological and physical injuries and permanent disabilities and in some cases even result in their death'.[25] The Parliament is surely right

Resolution of 27 Oct. 1994 on racism and xenophobia [1994] OJ C323/154; EP Resolution of 27 Apr. 1995 on racism, xenophobia and anti-semitism [1995] OJ C126/75; Resolution of 15 June 1995 on a day to commemorate the Holocaust [1995] OJ C166/132; EP Resolution of 13 July 1995 on discrimination against the Roma [1995] OJ C156/249; EP Resolution of 26 Oct. 1995 on racism, xenophobia and anti-semitism [1995] OJ C308/140; EP Resolution of 9 May 1996 on the communication from the Commission on racism, xenophobia and anti-semitism [1996] OJ C152/57; and EP Resolution of 30 Jan. 1997 on racism, xenophobia and anti-semitism and the European Year Against Racism [1997] OJ C55/17.

[16] [1996] OJ L185/5.   [17] Council Reg. 1035/97 [1997] OJ L151/1. See further COM(95)653 final.
[18] Speech by Commissioner Padraig Flynn to the European Trade Union Confederation's Conference, Brussels, 21 Mar. 1997.
[19] Declaration by the Council and the Representatives of the Governments of the Member States, meeting within the Council, of 24 Nov. 1997 [1997] OJ C368/1.
[20] Declaration by the Council and the Representatives of the Governments of the Member States, meeting within the Council, of 16 Dec. 1997 [1998] OJ C1/1.
[21] The establishment of such a Commission was agreed at the Corfu summit meeting of the European Council in June 1994. See *Activities of the Consultative Commission on Racism and Xenophobia—Final Report*, 6906/1/95 RAXEN 24 REV 1 (1995).
[22] See in particular J. Wrench, *European Compendium of Good Practice for the Prevention of Racism at the Workplace* (1997); *Joint Declaration on the Prevention of Racial Discrimination and Xenophobia and Promotion of Equal Treatment at the Workplace* (1995). See generally European Commission, *The European Institutions in the Fight against Racism: Selected Texts* (1997).
[23] Resolution of the Council and the Representatives of the Governments of the Member States, meeting within the Council, of 5 Oct. 1995 [1995] OJ C296/13.
[24] Resolution of the Council and the Representatives of the Governments of the Member States, meeting within the Council, of 23 Oct. 1995 [1995] OJ C312/1.
[25] B4–0108/98: Provisional minute of the Resolution on racism, xenophobia, and anti-semitism and the results of the European Year Against Racism (1997). Apart from the EU initiative, the Resolution

to declare its conviction that 'if they are to have a sustainable positive impact, the wide range of measures launched to combat racism must be continued and further developed now that the European Year Against Racism has ended' and that the Year 'should be seen as a basis for further measures, and not simply as a reminder of a problem'.

The time is right for strong action to supplement the fine words. Inevitably the immediate question is what kind of action? Whilst it is of course true that the origins of racism are many and varied, there are lessons here from the Eurobarometer poll. The survey found that racism was fed by personal insecurity and fear of the future. 'Those who declared they had racist feelings presented common characteristics: many were dissatisfied with their life circumstances and feared losing their jobs; they felt insecure about the future ("the situation will get worse"); and/or had experienced a deterioration of their personal situation.' The pollsters reported that the fear of losing one's job was a bigger factor in determining a racist attitude than the actual fact of being unemployed. If personal insecurity and pessimism about the future are indeed the key factors behind a susceptibility to racist beliefs, then we can understand more easily the growth of such opinions. One of the more alarming of the poll's findings concerned the extent to which such insecurity is now common across Europe: 'nearly half of those interviewed worked in a company that had made at least one person redundant in the past five years. Nearly one third had themselves been unemployed at one stage during the last five years. Over half had friends or family who had been affected by unemployment at one stage during this period.' Here is empirical support for the late Ralph Miliband's trenchant comment that while 'apologists celebrate the virtues and triumphs of capitalism, ominous signs appear of the recrudescence of ethnic and national racism among young men and women bred in hopelessness and disaffection, and whose prospects in life are utterly dismal'.[26]

No single action can be guaranteed to eradicate racism. The disposition towards such negative sentiments is not entirely determined by one's success or failure as a person within one's society. Nevertheless if racism is to be effectively tackled it would seem that the problems of job insecurity and the fear of unemployment will need to be vigorously addressed, as central aspects of the European mission rather than as peripheral, unwanted consequences of success elsewhere.[27] The problem of racism is also inseparable from the institutional health of the EU. The Eurobarometer poll found that:

> [n]early half of those who declared themselves as quite or very racist were dissatisfied with the political working of their country . . . Nearly three out of four of the interviewees (between 70% and 80%) said that 'public services look less and less after the interests of people like me', 'the way government and public bodies work is getting worse',

refers to the United Nations 'International Year of Tolerance' and '[a]ll different, all equal'—the European youth campaign organized by the Council of Europe against racism, xenophobia, anti-semitism, and intolerance.

[26] R. Miliband, *Socialism for a Sceptical Age* (1994), 14.

[27] Cf. Curtin and Geurts, note 2 above, at 150: 'we acknowledge that action against racism and xenophobia will only be effective where it is embedded in a wider range of policies *inter alia* aiming to improve economic conditions which are seen as potentially aggravating factors'.

'corruption amongst politicians is increasing' and that 'the people who run the country are more concerned with themselves than with the good of the country'.

The radical changes on the brink of which the EU now stands must not be allowed to compound the sense of despairing detachment and alienation that too many of our residents already feel towards the organs of their States. The perpetuation both of this cynicism and of the personal insecurity that is already so strongly felt would lead to ever higher levels of moral and political disillusion, on which racialist demagogues would be able to feed in ever increasing numbers.

The long-term answer to racism depends therefore on the extent to which the Europe of the new millennium succeeds for its people as well as for its markets and its business classes. The search for a solution on this macro level is no alibi for inactivity now: direct action must also be taken in the short and medium term. The Treaty of Amsterdam finally opens up a new and legally unchallengeable vista for Community action in this regard. The new Article 6 (*ex* Article F) of the EU Treaty commits the European Union to respect for human rights, fundamental freedoms, and fundamental rights, as guaranteed by the European Convention for the Protection of Human Rights and Fundamental Freedoms and as they result from the constitutional traditions common to the Member States. The first paragraph of the new Article 29 (*ex* Article K.1) lays down as one of the objectives of the new Europe 'the prevention and combating of racism and xenophobia in order to provide citizens with a high level of safety within an area of freedom, security and justice'. By new Article 13 (*ex* Article J.3), 'the Council, acting unanimously on a proposal from the Commission and after consulting the European Parliament, may take appropriate action to combat discrimination based on . . . racial or ethnic origin, religion or belief'.

The Eurobarometer poll brings good news for those wary of tackling the racism that its respondents have so depressingly revealed. Racist Europe is embarrassed by its prejudice and anxious for someone or body to take a lead. No fewer than 77 per cent of those questioned thought designating 1997 as the European Year Against Racism was 'a good decision', and 82 per cent considered that the effort should now be continued on a long-term basis. Even a greater percentage (84 per cent) considered that the 'European Institutions should take a stronger role in the fight against racism'. Paradoxically therefore the racist atmosphere in Europe makes strong action against it less, rather than more, likely to be resisted. In its January 1998 resolution, the European Parliament called on the Commission to propose an action programme setting out 'appropriate measures' whereby various racist actions[28] can be categorized as criminal offences and punished effectively in all the EU Member States. The Parliament also called on the Commission, 'immediately after the entry into force of the Treaty of Amsterdam, to propose "appropriate action" on the basis

---

[28] These were: incitement to racism and xenophobia and to commit racist and xenophobic acts; denial of the Holocaust and crimes against humanity; production, printing, and dissemination of racist, xenophobic, and revisionist material; participation in the activities of groups involved in racist or xenophobic actions or which advocate racist, xenophobic, and revisionist doctrines: provisional minute of the Resolution on racism, xenophobia, and anti-semitism and the results of the European Year Against Racism (1997), para. 3.

of the provisions on non-discrimination set out in the new Article 13 of the EC Treaty, in order to prevent and combat discrimination on the grounds of race, ethnic origin or religion'.[29] In its Communication entitled 'An Action Plan against Racism', dated 25 March 1998, the Commission declared its intention 'to table a proposal for legislation to combat racial discrimination before the end of 1999'.[30]

The question not yet fully answered, and begged once again both by Article 13, by the Parliament's resolution, and by the Commission's Communication is what kind of action in this area can best be regarded as appropriate. Acknowledging the gravity of the mischief is a necessary precondition to the design of effective measures to counteract it. The drive for an effective solution, of the sort suggested by the Parliament, must itself be structured on principled lines. An ill-conceived remedy has the potential merely to compound the problem it seeks to address, either by exacerbating public estrangement or by substituting new perceived injustices in place of older, imagined grievances. The European people want their institutions to tread, but to tread carefully.

The right framework of principle for such sensitive engagement is that provided by the language of human rights. The concept of such basic and inalienable freedoms commands widespread support across Europe. No fewer than 86 per cent of Eurobarometer's respondents opposed 'any discrimination based on a person's race, religion or culture'. Over 80 per cent of interviewees declared their commitment to the principles of 'equality before the law', 'legal protection against discrimination', 'the right to one's own language and culture', and 'religious liberty and freedom of conscience'. Even more uplifting were Eurobarometer's findings that some 75 per cent of those asked welcomed the development of a 'multi-cultural' society, while seven out of ten accepted that people from 'minority groups are being discriminated against in the job market'. These were many of the same respondents who had admitted to having racist views. Whatever misgivings some of us might have about over-reliance on such data, it would seem reasonably clear that if the EU's intervention on racism can be presented as a key part of its human rights mission in Europe, there is every likelihood of a widespread acceptance of its efforts, even on the part of those who see themselves as somewhat racist in outlook and also on the part of those who may have to change their ways if such action is to be fully effective. The nature of the problem of racism, together with proper respect for the principle of subsidiarity mean that there will also be a role here for the nation States, in partnership with which all EU initiatives will need to be effected.

In this chapter, we set the human rights context in which EU action on racism should take place, and we identify the kinds of EU actions that could, consistently with the principle of subsidiarity, most appropriately take place from the human rights perspective. We must first, however, tackle the key question of definition. What is meant by 'racism, religious intolerance and xenophobia'?

---

[29] European Year Against Racism (1997), at para. 4.
[30] COM(98)183 final. See further COM(98)259 of 29 Apr. 1998, 'Social Action Programme', at 12.

II. QUESTIONS OF DEFINITION

The key word is 'racism'. It gives a flavour to the terms that follow it, thereby helping also to define them, and instantly evokes images of the kind of unacceptable conduct towards which any law in this field will necessarily be directed. A modern
dictionary definition describes the noun as meaning '1. hatred, rivalry or bad feeling
between races. 2. belief in the inherent superiority of a particular race or races over
others, usually with the implication of a right to be dominant. 3. discriminatory
treatment based on such a belief'.[31] The problem here becomes immediately apparent. The idea of racism depends on that of 'race', but as Hargreaves and Leaman
have pointed out, the 'division of humankind within a taxonomy of "races", where a
few selected physical characteristics (skin colour, skull shape, etc.) are employed to
distinguish between basic types and are frequently linked to mental characteristics,
has been acknowledged as scientifically bankrupt and thus as part of the problem'.[32]
As one senior British judge put it, 'I apprehend that anthropologists would dispute
how far the word "race" is biologically at all relevant to the species amusingly called
homo sapiens'.[33] The very concept of race can therefore be seen to be a throwback to
the old nineteenth century commitment to scientific racism. Even if the word had an
objective meaning, a racism defined solely by reference to it would in any event have
little connection with the social and economic factors discussed above that largely
explain the virulence of modern racism. In particular it does not capture the element
of heterophobia, or fear of the different, that is the unifying element in our three
phrases, racism, religious intolerance, and xenophobia.[34]

Mindful of these difficulties, modern anti-racism law has tended to surround the
term with broader concepts, so as collectively, if not individually, to encompass the
core mischiefs at which such legislation is aimed. Thus the path-breaking ILO Convention on Discrimination in respect of Employment and Occupation adopted in
1958 referred to discrimination as 'any distinction, exclusion or preference made on
the basis of race, colour, sex, religion, political opinion, national extraction or social
origin'.[35] Seven years later the International Convention on the Elimination of
All Forms of Racial Discrimination[36] extended its remit (in certain circumstances)
to 'any distinction, exclusion, restriction or preference based on race, colour, descent, or national or ethnic origin', and this has been the approach adopted in both
Belgian and Dutch law.[37] French legislation defines racism as any manifestation 'of

---

[31] *Chambers 21st Century Dictionary* (1996), 1143.

[32] Hargreaves and Leaman, note 5 above, at 16, citing R. Miles, *Racism* (1989). See also the Report of
the World Conference to Combat Racism and Racial Discrimination, Geneva, 14–25 Aug. 1978, UN
Doc. A/CONF. 92/40 (1979): '[a]ny doctrine of racial superiority was scientifically false, morally condemnable, socially unjust and dangerous, and had no justification whatsoever'.

[33] *Ealing London Borough Council* v. *Race Relations Board* [1972] AC 342 at 362, *per* Lord Simon of
Glaisdale.

[34] European Commission, note 6 above, at 12.

[35] ILO Convention No. 111, Convention concerning Discrimination in respect of Employment and
Occupation (1958). In United Nations, *A Compilation of International Instruments* (1994), i, Part 1, 96.

[36] International Convention on the Elimination of Racial Discrimination, adopted by GA Res. 2106
A (XXI) (1965). In *ibid.*, at 66.

[37] European Commission, note 6 above, at 12. In 1976, the Dutch Sup. Ct. rejected an argument that
the word 'race' should be defined in biological terms: *ibid.*, at 13.

discrimination, hate or violence in regard to a person or a group of persons by reason of their origin or their belonging or not belonging to a particular ethnic group, nation, race or religion'. The German constitutional guarantee of equality before the law declares *inter alia* that '[n]o one may be disadvantaged or favoured because of his ... race, language, homeland or origin, faith, or religious or political opinions', and it is generally accepted that the term 'race' here must be understood broadly to prevent discrimination against a wide category of potentially oppressed minorities.[38] In the same country's criminal code, 'racial hatred' is defined as hatred against 'a national, racial, religious or ethnically distinct group'.

Leaving aside for a moment the question of what constitutes a religious group, it is noticeable that these various definitions attempt to add ballast to the concept of race by introducing the parallel idea of ethnicity. A Commission of Experts that advised on the introduction of Ireland's Prohibition on Incitement to Hatred Act 1989 considered ethnic origin to be a classification based on cultural traits. The concept of ethnicity also appears in the United Kingdom where the 1976 Race Relations Act defines a racial group as meaning 'a group of persons defined by reference to colour, race, nationality or ethnic or national origins'.[39] The absence of religion from this list has been the stimulus behind a succession of cases in that jurisdiction in which the issue of what constitutes an ethnic group has been closely analysed at the highest judicial levels. This is a jurisprudence of some value, the main points of which could usefully be captured in any EU legislative action in this area. The unhelpfulness of the concept of race means that the notion of ethnicity will be likely to be more heavily relied upon in identifying those towards the protection of whom any such legislation should be directed.

The leading case is *Mandla* v. *Dowell Lee*,[40] in which the issue for decision was whether the Sikhs could be said to be a group defined by reference to their 'ethnic origins'. In the course of arriving at an affirmative answer to this question, Lord Fraser giving a judgment with which his colleagues on the bench in the UK House of Lords (the supreme judicial body) agreed, said this:

> For a group to constitute an ethnic group in the sense of the Act of 1976, it must, in my opinion, regard itself, and be regarded by others, as a distinct community by virtue of certain characteristics. Some of these characteristics are essential; others are not essential but one or more of them will commonly be found and will help to distinguish the group from the surrounding community. The conditions which appear to me to be essential are these: (1) a long shared history, of which the group is conscious as distinguishing it from other groups, and the memory of which it keeps alive; (2) a cultural tradition of its own, including family and social customs and manners, often but not necessarily associated with religious observance. In addition to these two essential characteristics the following characteristics are, in my opinion, relevant; (3) either a common geographical origin, or descent from a small number of common ancestors; (4) a common language, not necessarily peculiar to the group; (5) a common literature peculiar to the group; (6) a common religion different from that of neighbouring groups or from the general community surrounding it; (7) being a minority or being an oppressed or a

---

[38] Art. 3(3). See I. von Munch and P. Kunig, *Grundgesetz* (1992), i, Art. 3, note 97. For a rare case under Art. 3(3) see BVerfG, 14 Feb. 1968, BVerfGE 23, 98.
[39] S. 3(1).   [40] [1983] 2 AC 548.

dominant group within a larger community, for example a conquered people (say, the inhabitants of England shortly after the Norman conquest) and their conquerors might both be ethnic groups.[41]

The value of this framework lies in its expansion of the concept of ethnicity beyond strictly racial or biological classifications, but not as far as a merely cultural or social diversity. The idea 'conveys a flavour of race'[42] but is used 'nowadays in an extended sense to include other characteristics which may be commonly thought of as being associated with common racial origin'.[43]

This discussion is also helpful when we come to consider the concept of 'religious intolerance'. It would seem obviously right to accord the protection of an anti-racist law of the type defined above to the Jewish people and the Rastafarians in Britain,[44] not least because both of these are examples of religions with a powerful ethnic tinge. While the same might be true (though perhaps less obviously) of the established Church in the same country, it would not be the case anywhere with respect to a cult of sun-worshippers, or to a religion which drew its adherents from a wide variety of ethnic sources.[45] In such situations, the concept of religious intolerance must stand or fall apart from ethnicity in a way that is not altogether unproblematic. The difficulty lies in the unnecessary breadth of the concept of religious intolerance, and in the assumption in the phrase that any manifestation of religious intolerance should not be permitted by law.

Let us take first the idea of a religion. 'It would be difficult, if not impossible, to devise a definition of religion which would satisfy the adherents of all the many and various religions which exist, or have existed, in the world.'[46] An attractive solution for the present work is surely to accept a subjective definition of religion and to accord the protection of the law to honestly held religious beliefs.[47] This is where difficulties are encountered with the concept of intolerability. If a wholly subjective approach were to be adopted, the effect of a prohibition on the expression of intolerance towards religion would be to allow any person or group to immunize its views from virulent verbal attack by the simple expedient of cloaking its beliefs in the garb of religion and by then insisting that the law protect it from the intolerant reaction of others that those views might in turn provoke. This protection would extend well beyond the violent attacks from which the law already protects us all. The concept of

[41] *Ibid.*, at 562. See further *Commission for Racial Equality* v. *Dutton* [1989] IRLR 8. An important and influential case in the development of this area of the law was *King-Ansell* v. *Police* [1979] 2 NZLR 531.

[42] *Ibid.*, at 561.

[43] *Ibid.*, at 562. For a recent Swiss case where the race discrimination laws were extended to cover asylum seekers, see Obergericht Solothurn, 25 Nov. 1996 [1997] *Schweizerische Juristenzeitung* 490.

[44] See *Dawkins* v. *Department of the Environment* [1993] IRLR 284.

[45] *Quaere* whether the Catholics would fall to be protected in Great Britain if it could be shown that the members of that Church in the country were disproportionately from one ethnic or cultural group (i.e. the Irish).

[46] *Adelaide Company of Jehovah's Witnesses Inc.* v. *Commonwealth of Australia* (1943) 67 CLR 116 at 123, *per* Latham CJ.

[47] See Art. 1(1) of the UN General Assembly's Declaration on the Elimination of All Forms of Intolerance and of Discrimination Based on Religion or Belief of 25 Nov. 1981: '[e]veryone shall have the right to freedom of thought, conscience and religion. This right shall include freedom to have a religion or whatever belief of his choice, and freedom, either individually or in community with others and in public or private, to manifest his religion or belief in worship, observance, practice and teaching': GA Res. 36/55 (1981): in *International Instruments*, note 35 above, at 122.

'intolerance' also falls well short of the conscious expression of hatred which drives the antagonism to racial minorities discussed above. While such intolerance might well lead to discrimination, the idea of intolerance is itself wider than that of discrimination. The essence of intolerance lies more in the unendurability of an opinion to the listener, and in the active hostility that the unacceptability of those opinions then excites. This notion of intolerance is inevitably bound up with the exercise of power by a dominant force; the *Oxford Companion to Law* defines it as '[t]he unwillingness or refusal to recognize or permit the existence of views other than those held by a dominant group'.[48] Legislating against such strong reactions to religious opinion, in the absence of any outward criminal conduct, act of discrimination, or intentional incitement to hatred, is probably unnecessary and undesirable in principle from a human rights perspective.[49] The better solution would surely be to drop the notion of intolerability from any future legislative lexicon, and to include in any future law action against incitement to religious as well as to racial hatred, and discrimination based on religious beliefs as well as on race, with religion being given a subjective meaning.[50]

It is for reminding the lawmakers in this field that their main concern must be with the damage caused by an 'intense fear or dislike of foreigners or strangers'[51] that the word xenophobia is particularly useful in this area. As the European Commission has noted, however, 'it is not a term that appears in legal instruments',[52] and were it to do so it would either merely duplicate the concepts of racism and religious intolerance or take on such a broad meaning as to threaten many distinctions based on citizenship which are at present widely accepted in both national and international law and which have no relationship with issues of ethnic hatred or religious intolerance. It is true that these laws regulate the status of aliens in the Member States of the European Union, and as such they may indeed be ripe for critical analysis,[53] but the issues involved are so different from those relating to racism and religious intolerance that it is best to keep the two questions apart. Accordingly, for the purpose of dealing with the social mischief with which this chapter is concerned, it is considered

---

[48] D. M. Walker, *The Oxford Companion to Law* (1980), 646.

[49] See *Otto-Preminger-Institut* v. *Austria*, ECHR (1994), Series A, No. 295, (1994) 19 EHRR 34, at para. 47: '[t]hose who choose to exercise the freedom to manifest their religion . . . cannot reasonably expect to be exempt from all criticism. They must tolerate and accept the denial by others of their religious beliefs and even the propagation by others of doctrines hostile to their faith. However, the manner in which religious beliefs and doctrines are opposed or denied is a matter which may engage the responsibility of the State. . . . Indeed, in extreme cases the effect of particular methods of opposing or denying religious beliefs can be such as to inhibit those who hold such beliefs from exercising their freedom to hold and express them.' See also the recent German decision reported at [1995] Neue Justiz 615 (Verfassungsgerichtshof Berlin, 16 Aug. 1995).

[50] Note that the Declaration on the Elimination of All Forms of Intolerance and of Discrimination Based on Religion or Belief, note 47 above, defines 'intolerance and discrimination based on religion or belief' as 'any distinction, exclusion, restriction or preference based on religion or belief and having as its purpose or as its effect nullification or impairment of the recognition, enjoyment or exercise of human rights and fundamental freedoms on an equal basis'. Here the notion of discrimination drives the first part of the definition and that of intolerance the second, purposive part.

[51] *Chambers 21st Century Dictionary* (1996), 1643.

[52] European Commission, note 6 above, at 13.

[53] See in particular the critique by Curtin and Guerts, note 2 above, at 159–67, where the engagement of the EU institutions in the issue is well set out. Also good on the background is JUSTICE, note 6 above, at chap. 4.

that the terms 'racism' and 'religious belief', as defined above, are sufficient to perform the task for which the laws described below will be designed. It goes without saying that it is vital to the success of any EU-wide initiative on racism that it extend to non-EU citizens resident within the boundaries of the EU, by analogy with the EU's developed jurisprudence on sex discrimination. This is quite separate from the question whether, as a separate matter of justice and fairness, such persons are or should be given a status equal to that of Community nationals.[54] It is the author's view that this inequality of status at the core of the EU undermines much of the message intended to be communicated by the commitment to the idea of human rights so publicly revealed at the rhetorical level by so many of the Community's institutions. Whether or not this is in fact the case, it would clearly make an insulting nonsense of any EU action on racism if the primary victims of it were unable to rely on the law's protection.

III. THE CLASH OF HUMAN RIGHTS

To locate the inquiry about the need for legislation on racism in the context of human rights is not automatically to produce a series of findings in line with contemporary moral intuitions. The values traditionally upheld by European legal systems have only recently come to embrace principles of racial equality. The far older commitments to freedom of speech, the protection of property, and the enforcement of contracts remain deeply rooted in our legal soil. They find expression today, on both the national and the international stage, as aspects of our modern code of human rights. There is in this field an inevitable clash of rights between these old and still well-entrenched and widely supported rights and the new commitment to equality and anti-discrimination, which must seek to address the urgent demands of the moment and which, in doing so effectively, must inevitably jostle with the old rights establishment and its deeply-held assumptions and priorities. The unpalatable truth is that racist sentiment has in the past been an unintended beneficiary of liberal democratic society's commitment to free speech, property, and contract.

The most obvious illustration of this truth lies in the realm of free speech. Long protected as a principle of the common law,[55] the right to free speech finds constitutional expression throughout the new legal order that was erected after the Second World War, and is guaranteed in Article 10(1) of the European Convention on Human Rights (ECHR) in even wider terms, as a right enjoyed by '[e]veryone' to 'freedom of expression' which is specifically said to include the 'freedom to hold opinions and to receive and impart information and ideas without interference by

---

[54] Note in this regard the conclusions of JUSTICE, note 6 above, at 23. Under the approach set out in the text, discrimination on grounds of nationality would continue to be permitted as long as such discrimination was not ethnic in substance, under cover of nationality.

[55] At least in the realms of judicial rhetoric and academic scholarship, but as an illustration of how much in fact depended on the nature of such speech: see *Duncan* v. *Jones* [1936] 1 KB 218.

public authority and regardless of frontiers'.[56] Though (for reasons we shall
presently see) never permitted to develop in the extreme form that has been allowed
in the United States,[57] the right to free speech has nevertheless offered a political,
spuriously moral, and occasionally a legal shield for post-war racist talk across the
nation States of the EU. The effect of unregulated speech in various modern media,
particularly the internet, has become an issue of great concern to informed opinion
in recent years.[58] A closely allied right is that of freedom of association, which is
guaranteed in Article 11 ECHR and which provides an additional protection for
those whose inclination it is to share their racist thoughts with associates and members of similarly inclined organizations.

Less obvious, but of more long-term impact on ethnic equality, have been the
rights to property and the enforcement of contracts.[59] It must immediately be remarked that the most degrading way in which the right to property can be exercised
is now universally prohibited by national and international law. Article 4 of the Universal Declaration of Human Rights declares that '[n]o one shall be held in slavery
or servitude; slavery and the slave trade shall be prohibited in all their forms'. In a
similar vein, Article 4 ECHR asserts first that '[n]o one shall be held in slavery or
servitude' and second that '[n]o one shall be required to perform forced or compulsory labour'. Even the common law's commitment to property ownership had drawn
the line at putting its power entirely at the disposal of the slave-owner. As early as
1772, in the famous case of *James Sommersett*,[60] the Lord Chief Justice of England,
Lord Mansfield, had granted habeas corpus to a 'negro . . . confined in irons on
board a ship . . . bound for Jamaica'.[61] The slave trade was 'so odious, that nothing
can be suffered to support it, but positive law'.[62] There being no such law here, the
man had to be freed. A hint of the deeper commercial values that then underpinned
and still dominate our law can however be seen in the following passage:

> Contract for sale of a slave is good here; the sale is a matter to which the law properly and
> readily attaches, and will maintain the price according to the agreement. But here the
> person of the slave himself is immediately the object of enquiry; which makes a very mat-
> erial difference . . . . [The slave owner] advances no claims on contract; he rests his whole
> demand on a right to the negro as slave.[63]

Of course no such contract would be enforceable today. But the solicitude for property and contract rights displayed here finds its contemporary expression as a human
right in Article 17 of the Universal Declaration:

---

[56] Clearly based on Art. 19 of the Universal Declaration of Human Rights: '[e]veryone has the right to
freedom of opinion and expression; this right includes freedom to hold opinions without interference and
to seek, receive and impart information and ideas through any media and regardless of frontiers'. Universal Declaration, adopted by GA Res. 217 A (III) (1948): in *International Instruments*, note 35 above, at
1.

[57] An extreme example offering an illustration of the protection afforded even Nazi groups in the USA
is the well-known case of *Village of Skokie* v. *Nationalist Socialist Party of America* (1978) 373 NE 2d 21.
See further *Collin* v. *Smith* (1978) 578 F 2d 1197.

[58] See *Communication to the European Parliament, the Council, the Economic and Social Committee and
the Committee of the Regions, 'Illegal and Harmful Content on the Internet'*, COM(96)487.

[59] Mention may also conveniently be made at this juncture of the potential of the right to privacy as a
guarantor of racist activity in certain circumstances. The right is now to be found in Art. 8 of the ECHR.

[60] (1772) 20 State Trials 1.   [61] *Ibid.*   [62] *Ibid.*, at 82.   [63] *Ibid.*, at 81.

(1) Everyone has the right to own property alone as well as in association with others.
(2) No one shall be arbitrarily deprived of his property.

The right is manifested explicitly and implicitly in the European Convention. The clearest guarantee is in the first paragraph of Article 1 of the First Protocol:

> Every natural or legal person is entitled to the peaceful enjoyment of his possessions. No one shall be deprived of his possessions except in the public interest and subject to such conditions provided for by law and by the general principles of international law.

Also relevant as a protection are parts of the first sentence of Article 6(1):

> In the determination of his civil rights and obligations . . . everyone is entitled to a fair and public hearing within a reasonable time by an independent and impartial tribunal established by law.

In *Association of General Practitioners* v. *Denmark*, the European Commission of Human Rights accepted that in principle the right to the enforcement of a contract was a possession for the purposes of the First Protocol.[64] The well-known case of *Ringeisen* v. *Austria (No 1)* marked the beginning of an expansive approach to Article 6(1) on the part of the European Court of Human Rights, the effect of which has been to bring property rights within the protection provided by its procedural guarantee:

> For Article 6(1) to be applicable to a case ('*contestation*') it is not necessary that both parties to a proceeding should be private persons, which is the view of the majority of the Commission and of the Government. The wording of Article 6(1) is far wider; the French expression '*contestations sur (des) droits et obligations de caractère civil*' covers all proceedings the result of which is decisive for private rights and obligations. The English text, 'determination of . . . civil rights and obligations', confirms this interpretation.
>
> The character of the legislation which governs how the matter is to be determined (civil, commercial, administrative law etc.) and that of the authority which is invested with jurisdiction in the matter (ordinary court, administrative body, etc.) are therefore of little consequence.[65]

In *Ringeisen* the relevant civil right recognized by the Court was the 'right to have the contract for sale which they had made with him approved'[66] if he fulfilled certain relevant statutory obligations.

The effect of the operation of a system of laws which prioritized these interests in property and contract to the exclusion of other public interests may be seen in a trilogy of illustrative cases drawn from a time when their manifestation in law was untrammelled by modern ideas about racial and religious equality. In *Schlegel* v. *Corcoran*,[67] an Irish court held that a landlord had not acted unreasonably under the relevant legislation in refusing to consent to the transfer of rooms for a dental practice to Nathaniel Gross, whose only disqualifying characteristic was his Jewishness. Delivering judgment at the start of the Second World War, Gavan Duffy J felt able

---

[64] App. No. 12947/87 (1989) 62 D&R 226, 234. See also App. No. 7742/76 *A. B. and Company A.S.* v. *The Federal Republic of Germany* (1978) 14 D&R 146, 168: '[i]t is certainly not excluded that a debt can constitute a possession (French "*biens*") within the meaning of Article 1 of the First Protocol'.

[65] *Ringeisen* v. *Austria (No 1)*, ECHR (1971), Series A, No. 13, 1 EHRR 455, at para. 94.

[66] *Ibid.* [67] [1942] IR 19.

to assert that the practice 'may, under Mr Gross, develop a Jewish complexion, and such an anticipation is not groundless in a locality with a number of Jewish residents'. Anti-Semitism was the product of an 'antagonism between Christian and Jew [which] has its roots in nearly 2,000 years of history and [which] is too prevalent as a habit of mind to be dismissed off-hand'. In *Scala Ballroom (Wolverhampton), Ltd* v. *Ratcliffe*,[68] sixteen years later, the English Court of Appeal considered that a policy of debarring non-whites from a newly opened ballroom 'was a course which they were entitled to adopt in their own business interests'.[69] In 1965, the Chancery Division of the same country's High Court upheld as valid a legacy to the Royal College of Surgeons to fund studentships which were to be available only to British-born subjects who were not of the Jewish or Roman Catholic faiths; the restriction may have been 'undesirable, but it [was] not . . . contrary to public policy'.[70]

These three cases are drawn from States whose legal systems were unaffected by the racially-motivated legal revolution that accompanied the expansion of Nazi power through much of continental Europe. They illustrate the extent to which even the liberal democratic home to which these countries' legal systems returned after the collapse of that power were not places in which ethnic equality was automatically welcomed. Mindful of this, the new codes of human rights that were then established did not merely parrot the ethical priorities of pre-fascist Europe. The new language of human rights in which these earlier interests were now repackaged as 'rights' to speech, property, and contract also contained such guarantees as 'the right to freedom of thought, conscience and religion'.[71] All these rights were in turn explicitly limited so as to allow restriction in the name of other public interests. Thus the right to property in the ECHR, quoted above, is subject to 'the right of a state to enforce such laws as it deems necessary to control the use of property in accordance with the general interest', while the right to expression is qualified by any restriction which is 'prescribed by law and . . . necessary in a democratic society, in the interests of national security, territorial integrity or public safety, for the prevention of disorder or crime, for the protection of health or morals, for the protection of the reputation or rights of others, for preventing the disclosure of information received in confidence, or for maintaining the authority or impartiality of the judiciary'.

More importantly for present purposes, these post-war human rights agreements have implicitly involved a central tenet which has been very well put by the late Paul Sieghart in his classic study, *The Lawful Rights of Mankind*:

> The distinguishing characteristic of all human rights is that they are universal: . . . they 'inhere' in all human beings by virtue of their humanity alone, and they are 'inalienable'. Logically, it must follow that one cannot discriminate between different individuals in respect of their human rights: no special characteristic of any individual entitles him or her to any more or any fewer human rights than anyone else.[72]

---

[68] [1958] 3 All ER 220.   [69] *Ibid.*, at 221, *per* Hodson LJ.
[70] *In re Lysaght* [1966] 1 Ch. 191 at 206, *per* Buckley J. The College refused the gift.
[71] Art. 9 ECHR. See also the General Assembly's Declaration on the Elimination of All Forms of Intolerance and of Discrimination based on Religion or Belief, note 47 above.
[72] P. Sieghart, *The Lawful Rights of Mankind* (1986), 75.

In explicit recognition of this principle, the Charter of the United Nations declares one of its primary purposes to be 'promoting and encouraging respect for human rights and for fundamental freedoms for all without distinction as to race, sex, language, or religion'.[73] Article 2 of the Universal Declaration of Human Rights is in the following emphatic terms: '[e]veryone is entitled to all the rights and freedoms set forth in this Declaration without distinction of any kind, such as race, colour, sex, language, religion, political or other opinion, national or social origin, property, birth or other status'.

The two United Nations Covenants on Human Rights contain similar guarantees[74] and the European Convention version is to be found in Article 14, according to which, '[t]he enjoyment of the rights and freedoms set forth in this Convention shall be secured without discrimination on any ground such as sex, race, colour, language, religion, political or other opinion, national or social origin, association with a national minority, property, birth or other status'.

In keeping with the basic structure of the Convention, the rights secured by it may be deployed only against public authorities and not against private individuals within a State.[75] It needs also to be immediately observed that neither Article 2 of the Universal Declaration nor Article 14 of the European Convention is a guarantee against discrimination as such.[76] Rather the obligation for equal treatment is in respect of the rights asserted elsewhere in each document. Of the substantive right to racial equality or to the avoidance of discrimination on racial grounds there is no immediate sight.[77] In an early decision of the European Commission on Human Rights it was stated that 'discrimination based on race could, in certain circumstances, of itself amount to degrading treatment within the meaning of Article 3 of the Convention',[78] but the breakthrough has not been built on, with a later decision of the Court emphasizing that the impugned discriminatory treatment in issue in that case did not breach Article 3 because it 'did not denote any contempt or lack of respect for the personality of the applicants and . . . was not designed to, and did not, humiliate or

---

[73] Art. 1(3).

[74] See Art. 2(2) of the International Covenant on Economic, Social and Cultural Rights (ICESCR), and Arts. 2(1) and 26 of the International Covenant on Civil and Political Rights (ICCPR), adopted by GA Res. 2200 A (XXI) (1966): in *International Instruments*, note 35 above, at 8 and 20.

[75] But see, *inter alia*, *Young, James and Webster* v. *United Kingdom*, ECHR (1981), Series A, No. 44, (1982) 4 EHRR 38 in which the requirement seems to have been loosely applied by the European Court of Human Rights.

[76] Note however that Art. 26 of the ICCPR has the potential to be a stand-alone provision: '[a]ll persons are equal before the law and are entitled without any discrimination to the equal protection of the law. In this respect, the law shall prohibit any discrimination and guarantee to all persons equal and effective protection against discrimination on any ground such as race, colour, sex, language, religion, political or other opinion, national or social origin, property, birth or other status'. Note also that there has been recent discussion about the possibility of an additional protocol to the ECHR, dealing with the general question of discrimination.

[77] But see Art. 4 of the Fourth Prot. of the Convention which prohibits the collective expulsion of aliens, and Art. 1 of Prot. No. 7 which deals with the due process rights that should be accorded to an alien prior to his or her expulsion. See also the Council of Europe Convention concerning the legal status of migrant workers.

[78] *East African Asians* v. *United Kingdom* (1981) 3 EHRR 76. Art. 3: '[n]o one shall be subjected to torture or to inhuman or degrading treatment or punishment'.

debase'.[79] The 'certain circumstances' in which racial discrimination will breach Article 3 would appear on this test to be few and far between.[80]

A new and innovative flank in the development of a human rights language with which to tackle racial discrimination was opened on 21 December 1965. The International Convention on the Elimination of All Forms of Racial Discrimination which was then agreed,[81] and which came into force on 4 January 1969, was the initiative of the United Nations Commission on Human Rights, and followed the Declaration on the Elimination of All Forms of Racial Discrimination which had been resolved by the General Assembly on 20 November 1963.[82] The Convention reported the conviction of the international community that 'any doctrine of superiority based on racial differentiation [was] scientifically false, morally condemnable, socially unjust and dangerous and that there [was] no justification for racial discrimination, in theory or in practice, anywhere'. Its State parties '[a]larmed by manifestations of racial discrimination still in evidence in some areas of the world' reaffirmed that 'discrimination between human beings on the grounds of race, colour or ethnic origin [was] an obstacle to friendly and peaceful relations among nations and [was] capable of disturbing peace and security among peoples and the harmony of persons living side by side even within one and the same State'.

These admirable sentiments produced an apparently powerful international intervention, with the Convention obligating its States parties 'to pursue by all appropriate means and without delay a policy of eliminating racial discrimination in all its forms and promoting understanding among all races'.[83] The Convention also condemned 'all propaganda and all organizations which are based on ideas or theories of superiority of one race or group of persons of one colour or ethnic origin, or which attempt to justify or promote racial hatred and discrimination in any form', with the States parties undertaking 'to adopt immediate and positive measures designed to eradicate all incitement to, or acts of, such discrimination'.[84] These measures were agreed to include the criminalization of 'all dissemination of ideas based on racial superiority or hatred'[85] and the proscription of racist organizations, 'with due regard to the principles embodied in the Universal Declaration of Human Rights'.[86] The rights which people were entitled to enjoy 'without distinction as to race, colour, or national or ethnic origin' went way beyond the narrow lists of earlier eras to include '[t]he right to inherit', '[t]he rights to work [and] to equal pay for equal work', '[t]he right to housing' and '[t]he right of access to any place or service intended for use by the general public, such as transport, hotels, restaurants, cáfes, theatres and parks'.[87]

[79] *Abdulaziz, Cabales and Balkandali* v. *United Kingdom*, ECHR (1985), Series A, No. 94, (1985) 7 EHRR 471.
[80] App. No. 14818/89, *Hector* v. *United Kingdom*, Apr. 1990.   [81] Note 36 above.
[82] GA Res. 1904 (XVIII). Earlier documents of significance had been the Convention concerning Discrimination in respect of Employment and Occupation adopted by the ILO in 1958 (note 35 above) and the Convention against Discrimination in Education adopted by the United Nations Educational, Scientific and Cultural Organisation in 1960: 429 UNTS 93.
[83] Art. 2(1). The general goal is then developed by reference to five objectives the achievement of which the States Parties are then required to undertake: see Art. 2(1)(a)–(e).
[84] Art. 4.   [85] Art. 4(a).   [86] Art. 4.
[87] The full list is set out in Art. 5.

With the States parties aware of the problems of enforcement that were bound to attach to such an ambitious international statement, this Convention became the first UN instrument of its type to construct a system for the legal protection of the human rights within its remit. It provided for the establishment of a Committee for the Elimination of Racial Discrimination to investigate state complaints of violations by other States and to review state action (or inaction) under the Convention.[88] There was undoubted potential in the framework of scrutiny set out in the Convention, and it has been built upon subsequently in other fields,[89] but from its inception the Committee has 'felt constrained to tread cautiously'.[90] The reporting mechanism has not always functioned as well as might be expected, with one informed commentator remarking that in 'general . . . few members of the Committee appear particularly well briefed, and the questioning is somewhat desultory and lacking in depth'. Even more seriously, the same writer found that the 'Committee has been starved of adequate funds. During the latter part of the 1980s and the early 1990s many sessions were curtailed or canceled due to the failure of some states to contribute toward the expenses of the Committee.'[91]

IV. THE EUROPEAN UNION'S ROLE

If Articles 3 and 14 ECHR had developed a different juristic life, or if the enforcement mechanism in the Convention on the Elimination of All Forms of Racial Discrimination (or indeed in other relevant international law agreements[92]) had been made to work effectively, it might not have been thought so pressing or so urgent for the European Union to articulate a separate voice on the issue of racism. But the weaknesses in these earlier international interventions, allied to the sharp rise in racist violence that has been recently experienced in Europe and to which we have earlier referred, has led to increased pressure on the Union to intervene.[93] This eventually culminated in the proposed changes to the Treaty of European Union and the Treaty establishing the European Communities which were agreed at Amsterdam on 2 October 1997. When in place these amendments will provide the legal basis for

---

[88] See generally Part II of the Convention. Art. 14 also allows for individual communications if the relevant State Party has agreed to the jurisdiction. A Council resolution on the fight against racism and xenophobia adopted in May 1990 recognized that acts inspired by racism would be countered by, *inter alia*, ratification of relevant international instruments and recognition of the right of individual petition in Art. 14 of the Convention: see [1990] OJ C157/1.

[89] See for one such example D. McGoldrick, *The Human Rights Committee. Its Role in the Development of the International Covenant on Civil and Political Rights* (1994).

[90] *Study of the Work of the Committee on the Elimination of Racial Discrimination and Progress Towards the Achievement of the Objectives on the International Convention on the Elimination of all Forms of Racial Discrimination*: A/Conf. 92/8 (1978), para. 194, cited by McCrudden, note 91 below, at 444.

[91] C. McCrudden, 'Racial Discrimination' in C. McCrudden and G. Chambers (eds.), *Individual Rights and the Law in Britain* (1994), 444.

[92] It is not even clear that norms prohibiting racism, discrimination, or xenophobia have become part of customary international law: see European Commission, note 6 above, at 34.

[93] For the extent of that political pressure, see Part I above.

action against racism the existence of which has hitherto been debilitatingly controversial.[94]

The key provisions are three. First, the centrality of the human rights basis for the
whole European enterprise is made more explicit than it has ever been in the past, in
a newly invigorated Article 6 (*ex* Article F) of the Union Treaty:

> 1. The union is founded on the principles of liberty, democracy, respect for human
> rights and fundamental freedoms, and the rule of law, principles which are common to
> the Member States.
> 2. The Union shall respect fundamental rights, as guaranteed by the European Con-
> vention for the Protection of Human Rights and Fundamental Freedoms signed in
> Rome on 4 November 1950 and as they result from the constitutional traditions com-
> mon to the Member States, as general principles of Community law.
> 3. The Union shall respect the national identities of its Member States.
> 4. The Union shall provide itself with the means necessary to attain its objectives and
> carry through its policies.[95]

Secondly, there is the last clause in the opening paragraph of the new Article 29 (*ex*
Article K.1) of the Treaty on European Union:

> Without prejudice to the powers of the European Community, the Union's objective
> shall be to provide citizens with a high level of safety within an area of freedom, security
> and justice by developing common action among the Member States in the fields of po-
> lice and judicial co-operation in criminal matters and by preventing and combating
> racism and xenophobia.[96]

This clause is further supplemented by the commitment that this objective 'shall be
achieved by preventing and combating crime . . . through [*inter alia*] close cooperation between police forces, customs authorities and other competent authorities in
the Member States, both directly and through the European Police Office (Europol),
in accordance with the provisions of Articles K.2 and K.4 [now Articles 30 and 32]'.
These and other provisions for police and judicial co-operation that are set out in the
Amsterdam agreement provide a new and potentially efficient way of dealing with

---

[94] For a rare example of an EC anti-racist law before Amsterdam, see Council Dir. 89/552/EEC on the
co-ordination of certain provisions laid down by law, regulation or administrative action in Member
States concerning the pursuit of television broadcasting activities [1989] OJ L298. Arts. 12 and 22 require,
respectively, the prohibition of racist advertising and of broadcasts containing 'any incitement to hatred
on grounds of race, sex, religion or nationality'.

[95] Also relevant at this level of basic principle are (i) the changes to the seventh recital to the TEU which
inter alia now expresses the determination of the States to 'promote . . . social progress for their peoples
. . . within the context of . . . reinforced cohesion . . . and to implement policies ensuring that advances in
economic integration are accompanied by parallel progress in other fields'; (ii) the new Art. 2 of the TEU,
in which the Union sets itself, *inter alia*, the objective of promoting 'social progress and a high level of employment' and of achieving 'balanced and sustainable development . . . through the strengthening of economic and social cohesion'; (iii) the new Art. 2 of the EC Treaty whereby the Community is assigned the
task of, *inter alia*, promoting within its borders 'a high level of employment and of social protection,
equality between men and women . . . and social cohesion and solidarity among Member States'; (iv) the
Eleventh Declaration, annexed to the Final Act of the Treaty of Amsterdam, on the status of churches
and non-confessional organizations, which is in the following terms: '[t]he European Union respects and
does not prejudice the status under national law of churches and religious associations or communities in
the Member States. The European Union equally respects the status of philosophical and non-confessional organisations.'

[96] Note also the strengthened position of the European Court of Justice in relation to this provision:
Art. 35 (*ex* Art. K.7) of the TEU.

the problem of transnational racism, albeit one that raises well-known concerns about the democratic and political accountability of this part of the fast developing European executive branch.[97]

At the technical legislative level, the vital new provision from the point of view of anti-racism is the third Amsterdam change, which is the provision of a new Article 13 (*ex* Article 6a) in the Treaty establishing the European Community:

> Without prejudice to the other provisions of this Treaty and within the limits of the powers conferred by it upon the Community, the Council, acting unanimously on a proposal from the Commission and after consulting the European Parliament, may take appropriate action to combat discrimination based on sex, racial or ethnic origin, religion or belief, disability, age or sexual orientation.

Though not so wide as the kind of provision for which certain bodies pushed in the run-up to Amsterdam,[98] the Article nevertheless represents a considerable advance on the Community's previous position with regard to discrimination generally and racist and religious discrimination in particular. In contrast with the old Article 6 prohibiting discrimination on grounds of nationality (now recast as Article 12), there is no limitation to 'the scope of application of this Treaty', and this should be enough to prevent the absurdity, already warned against, of any protective EC action under Article 13 being extended only to EU nationals. (This point takes on an added urgency in view of the failure of the Amsterdam Treaty significantly to improve the position of third-country nationals within the EU, at least in the short to medium term.[99]) On the other hand, it would seem clear that the Article is not designed to have any direct effect, and it is quite explicit that the only action that may be taken under it requires the unanimous support of the Council. Though the latter hurdle may be too high for legislation on some of the goals mentioned in the Article, it is unlikely to block for ever action against discrimination based on 'racial or ethnic origin, religion or belief', since this is an area where, as we have seen, European consciousness has already been raised, not least by the dismally high levels of violence to which we earlier drew attention.

In view of this particular background, it is probably right to sever discrimination on racial or ethnic origin, religion, or belief from the rest of Article 13 and to subject it to separate analysis. With respect to any action that might flow from Article 13, two key but preliminary questions need to be addressed. Article 13 is discretionary, not mandatory, so it is necessary at this juncture to revisit in a focused way the question why the European institutions should engage in this field at all. Secondly, if the institutions are to be persuaded to act, the second issue left open by Article 13 is what kind of action would be most 'appropriate' in order to deal with racist and religious discrimination?

[97] See T. Bunyan, *The Europol Convention* (Statewatch Publication, undated).

[98] See in particular Standing Committee of Experts on International Immigration Refugee and Criminal Law (The Meijers Committee), *Proposals for the Amendment of the Treaty on European Union at the IGC in 1996* (1995); and the proposals made by the Kahn Commission's Working Group on Treaty Amendment (Chair: Professor William Duncan) discussed in JUSTICE, note 6 above, at 18. A key early document was Starting Line Group, *The Starting Point: A Proposal for Amendments to the European Community Treaty* (1994).

[99] But see the newly recast Arts. 61–63 (based on what were formerly Arts. 73i, 73j, and 73k) which provide a dynamic whereby the situation of such persons can be improved by legislative action.

Turning first to the need for action, the short answer recalls the racist violence and the electorally successful racial hatred that has escalated across the Union, and the reluctant racism of two-thirds of her citizens, and points therefore to the absolute imperative of some European-wide action. This argument draws strength from the widely-based support across Europe for any such initiative, a support shared—as we noted earlier—even by those inclined to racist feelings. A further impetus for action is provided by the dramatic refocusing of Community principles on *inter alia* human rights and fundamental freedoms which is evident in the new Article 6(1) (*ex* Article F) of the Union Treaty. The value of the breath of this first paragraph lies in the fact that its foundational message is not complicated by an over-reliance conceptually on the ECHR, which, as we have seen, is a valuable though not ideal human rights in-strument in our field of study.[100] Against the backdrop of these general points of principle, it will be immediately appreciated that the more traditional arguments for Community action have greater than usual force. These have been well put in a paper published in 1993 by a leading pressure group in this field:

> (i) In the single market, unjust discrimination will interfere with the free movement of persons and services by preventing persons who suffer it from obtaining jobs, housing or services they seek;
> (ii) Variations between national levels of protection will discourage persons likely to suf-fer discrimination from moving to those States where protection is small or non-existent;
> (iii) Prompt action is required for the proper functioning of the single market: a Com-munity Directive would impose a time-limit on Member States for producing their own legislation, and would lay down a common pattern providing some guarantee to the per-sons likely to suffer unjust discrimination that they would, in any part of European Community territory, have a legal remedy.[101]

It is not possible in a chapter of this length critically to evaluate the state of the law on the control of racism and religious hatred in the various Member States of the EU, and readers are directed to two recent and substantial studies covering the whole field.[102] We should however note the observation of the European Commis-sion that such local laws 'vary considerably in their coverage and strength'.[103] It is important also to recognize that only a handful of the Member States have enacted comprehensive codes against racism and racial discrimination,[104] and that the loose-ness of the engagement of some Member States in this area is likely to be even clearer when the Community expands to the East in the course of the next decade.[105]

---

[100] It is surely the case that the concept of human rights in the first para. of Art. 6 is wider than the specific reference to that Convention in the second.

[101] The Starting Line Group, *The Starting Line: A Proposal for a Draft Council Directive concerning the Elimination of Racial Discrimination* (1993), 3. I have taken the liberty of renumbering the points made in the Group's paper, as its first point duplicated the argument made above on the basis of human rights, but without the references to the Treaty of Amsterdam changes, which would of course not then have been known to the writers.

[102] European Commission, note 6 above. European Commission against Racism and Intolerance (ECRI), *Legal Measures to Combat Racism and Intolerance in the Member States of the Council of Europe: A Report Prepared by the Swiss Institute of Comparative Law, Lausanne* (1996).

[103] European Commission, note 6 above, at 35.   [104] See generally *ibid.*, at chap. 6.

[105] The laws on racism and intolerance in the Czech Republic, Estonia, Hungary, Poland, and Sloven-ia are dealt with in the Council of Europe Lausanne Report, note 102 above, at 69, 95, 189, 315, and 365 respectively. The commentaries reveal a series of legal systems in a variety of predictably rudimentary states on this particular issue.

V. THE NATURE OF THE EU'S INTERVENTION

If Community action is therefore required, the next question that arises is as to what kind of action. There is general agreement that the best way to proceed would be by way of a directive. As is well known, such an approach would allow Europe to state definite goals to be achieved, but then to allow those goals to be flexibly achieved by Member States within a prescribed time-frame. The analogy with the highly successful EU involvement in sex discrimination is an influential precedent in favour of proceeding by way of a directive.[106] Given the sensitivities that accompanied the drafting of Article 13 (with, for example, its careful construction to avoid direct effect), it is moreover unlikely that all the Member States, or even more than a handful of them, would agree to a regulation in this area. Quite apart from these political and precedential considerations, such a directly intrusive institutional engagement as a regulation would in any event be inappropriate from the perspective of principle. It is important that national legislatures are involved in the process of law creation in this area, since it will be by such engagement that the consciousness of the need for anti-racist action will be raised across Europe. The principle of subsidiarity in the newly numbered Article 5 (*ex* Article 3b) of the Treaty establishing the European Community is of direct relevance here:

> In areas which do not fall within its exclusive competence, the Community shall take action, in accordance with the principle of subsidiarity, only if and in so far as the objectives of the proposed action cannot be sufficiently achieved by the Member States and can therefore, by reason of the scale or effects of the proposed action be better achieved by the Community.

Buttressed as it now is by a separate and extensive Protocol agreed at Amsterdam,[107] this principle further supports the argument for an active partnership with the Member States in dealing with racism and religious hatred. In this context it is important to recognize that the concept of ethnic identity, which, as we have seen, is at the core of the meaning of 'race', has a situationality that must never be ignored. One author has put the point particularly effectively: '[o]ne may be Welsh in England, British in Germany, European in Thailand, White in Africa. A person may be Afro-Caribbean by descent but British by upbringing . . . Similarly, a person may be an East African Asian, an Indian, a Sikh or a Ramgarhia.'[108]

The late Sebastian Poulter has remarked that the 'particular features of a group's culture, which are identified as significant by members and outsiders, and precisely where the boundary is drawn with other groups, especially the majority community, often depend upon the context or situation in which an issue arises'.[109] This makes the subject a particularly appropriate one for the operation of the principle of

---

[106] See Curtin and Guerts, note 2 above, at 154, where the comparison with the sex discrimination directive is discussed.

[107] See the Prot. on the Application of the Principles of Subsidiarity and Proportionality annexed to the TEU and to the EC Treaty.

[108] C. Peach, 'Introduction' in C. Peach (ed.), *Ethnicity in the 1991 Census*, (1996), ii, 5, quoted in Poulter, note 109 below, at 7.

[109] S. Poulter, *Ethnicity, Law and Human Rights. The English Experience* (1998), 7.

subsidiarity alongside European supervision, since in principle it will be the national authorities responsible for anti-discrimination law who will be best able to target their energies on the ethnic, cultural and religious groups within their jurisdiction which are most in need of protection, and be best able to resolve the frequently complex question of how to delineate these groups for enforcement purposes.[110]

VI. THE STARTING LINE GROUP'S DRAFT DIRECTIVE

With the ground cleared both as regards the need for Community action and as regards the type of action that is judged most desirable, we need now directly to consider the content of any such legislation. Our perspective remains that of the principled proponent of a human rights framework within which both to view the problem of racism and religious hatred and to propose solutions to it. As we observed earlier, the human rights traffic in this field is not all one way, and it will be important in framing any such legislation to get the balance right, lest in addressing too enthusiastically the problems of racist and religious hatred we trespass in a way that is both significant and counterproductive on other equally cherished human rights commitments, such as to free speech, to privacy, and to property.

In considering the nature of legislation in this area, we are fortunate in being able to build on the work of the Starting Line Group. This is an informal network of non-governmental bodies, semi-official organizations, and independent experts which was formed in 1991 with the aims of 'raising awareness of racial discrimination in the member states of the European Union' and of 'promoting legal measures to combat' that discrimination.[111] In April 1993 the Group published a proposal which it entitled a *Draft Council Directive concerning the Elimination of Racial Discrimination* and it followed this up with *The Starting Point, A Proposal for Amendments to the European Community Treaty*, which it issued in July 1994, after its first intervention had raised predictable questions about Community competence. With the latter issue now having been largely resolved by the Amsterdam amendments, the Group has recently returned to its 1993 initiative and produced a much wider draft of what it now titles a *Draft Council Directive Concerning the Elimination of Racial and Religious Discrimination*.[112] The Group aims with this text 'to produce a model which

[110] An example of the difficulties that can be caused by insensitive ethnic labelling was the provision in the 1991 British census of a single undifferentiated ethnic group, 'white' alongside 8 other ethnic categories. As a result the Irish community in Britain had no option other than to designate itself part of the dominant culture, despite the fact that it has had a long history of extensive ethnic discrimination and many of its members continue to suffer in this way today: see Commission for Racial Equality, *Discrimination and the Irish Community in Britain* (1997).

[111] The quotations are from a briefing paper issued by the Group in Dec. 1996 under the title, 'The Starting Line: Campaign to Eliminate Racial Discrimination'.

[112] Starting Line Group/Commission for Racial Equality (I. Chopin and J. Niessen (eds.)), *Proposals for Legislative Measures to Combat Racism and to Promote Equal Rights in the European Union* (1998). The terms of the proposed directive appear in part II, Starting Line Group, *The New Starting Line: Proposal to the European Parliament, Council and Commission, and to the Member States of the European Community for a Draft Directive Concerning the Elimination of Racial and Religious Discrimination* (1998).

could be a landmark in European efforts to overcome the evils of racism, xenophobia, anti-Semitism and religious intolerance'.[113] Certainly it is the most sophisticated, well researched, and intelligent contribution to our field of study that has yet been concluded, and as such its detailed proposals deserve rigorous examination from the human rights perspective to which we have earlier committed ourselves. We shall now consider the Group's draft, examining first its proposals on racial and religious discrimination and secondly its suggestions on how these new rules can be adequately enforced.

Turning first to the Starting Line Group's proposals on racial and religious discrimination, the key provision in the draft is Article 3:

> Member States shall take the measures necessary to ensure that laws, regulations and administrative provisions and practices relating to the areas listed in Article 1(2) shall conform to the principle of equal treatment defined in that Article.

This is promptly reinforced by Article 4(1)(a), which commits Member States to 'take the necessary measures, in conformity with their legal systems, to prohibit by legal sanction . . . any discrimination of the kind mentioned in Article 2(1) and 2(2) and 2(3) practised by any natural or legal person and group or organization'.

To understand the framework the Group has in mind it therefore becomes necessary to consider in turn Articles 1(2) and 2(2) and (3). Article 1(2) defines the principle of equal treatment as meaning:

> the absence of any discrimination, direct or indirect, based on racial or ethnic origin, or religion and belief, and in particular in the following areas:
> —the exercise of a professional activity, whether salaried or self-employed;
> —access to any job or post, dismissals and other working conditions;
> —social security;
> —health and welfare benefits;
> —education;
> —vocational guidance and vocational training;
> —housing;
> —provision of goods, facilities and services;
> —participation in political, economic, social, cultural, religious life or any other public field.

This principle begs definitional questions about the meaning of discrimination, and about the difference between 'direct' and 'indirect' discrimination, and it is these issues that are then considered in Article 2(1) and (2). As far as the first of these is concerned, 'direct discrimination' exists where, in respect of any of the areas in Article 1(2), a person receives less favourable treatment on grounds of racial or ethnic origin or religion or belief than other persons receive or would receive in any situation where the relevant circumstances of those other persons are the same or not materially different'. The principal purpose of this prohibition on 'direct discrimination' is to prohibit the gross acts of overt racism which can proliferate in countries with no, or only very limited, legal regimes dealing with discrimination. However, the experience of the United Kingdom has been that even in sophisticated legal environments

---

[113] Chopin and Niessen, note 112 above, at 20.

where overt racism has been driven underground, direct discrimination continues to
have a role to play, with the case law having established that such impugned discrimination need not be solely on racial grounds[114] and can occur regardless of
whether the motive for the impugned conduct is itself racist.[115]

In recognition of the fact that some discrimination in 'participation in political,
economic, social, cultural, religious life or any other public field' on the basis of
'religion and belief' would be inevitable even in the fairest of societies, Article 1(5)
provides the following exception:

> (a) This directive shall be without prejudice to the right of member states to exclude
> from its field of application any occupational activities (and where appropriate the train-
> ing leading thereto), and any other activities for which by virtue of their nature or the
> context in which they are carried out the racial or ethnic origin or religion or belief of the
> person is an essential determining factor.
> (b) Member states shall periodically assess any such exclusions in order to decide, in
> the light of social or other developments, whether there is justification for maintaining
> the exclusions concerned. They shall notify the Commission of the results of this assess-
> ment.

Some such caveat is required both to ensure the popular credibility of the Directive
and to get its human rights balance exactly right.

There can be little doubt that this prohibition on direct discrimination is largely
consistent with international human rights standards.[116] The key principle informing
our culture of human rights is respect for human dignity, and explicit discrimination
of the type covered here is an affront to this foundational value, one that is made even
worse by the absence of any redeeming interest which could perhaps at least begin to
explain the infringement.[117] Even in the absence of any international law commitment to anti-discrimination law, therefore, it is improbable, to say the least, that any
regime of human rights would allow the rights to property, privacy, or due process to
be marshalled so as to destroy legislation aimed as explicitly as this at individual dignity and self-empowerment. The existence of the Convention on the Elimination of
All Forms of Racial Discrimination and the other anti-discriminatory measures to
which we have earlier referred simply confirms what was already inherent and apparent in any proper reading of international human rights law.

The same logic supports and underpins the value from the human rights perspective of the further attack on discrimination that the Starting Line Group has
mounted, through their extension of their draft Directive to the concept of 'indirect
discrimination' in Article 2(2). The reasoning behind this idea is that a directive
which merely drives the problem of discrimination underground is not worth the
effort required to secure its enactment. Originating in the United States,[118] and
developed further in the United Kingdom's race relations and sex discrimination

---

[114] See *Owen and Briggs* v. *James* [1982] ICR 618.
[115] *R.* v. *Commission for Racial Equality, ex parte Westminster City Council* [1984] ICR 770, [1985] ICR
827.
[116] But not wholly: see below text at note 132.
[117] Such as, e.g., national security, public safety, or territorial integrity.
[118] See in particular *Griggs* v. *Duke Power Company*, 401 US 424 (1971).

legislation of the mid-1970s,[119] the Starting Group's definition of the term is as follows:

> [I]ndirect discrimination exists where in respect of any of the areas in Article 1(2) an apparently neutral provision, criterion or practice disproportionately disadvantages persons of a particular racial or ethnic origin or religion [and] belief, unless that provision, criterion or practice is appropriate and necessary and can be justified by objective factors unrelated to race, ethnic origin or religion [and] belief.[120]

An understanding of how such a concept would work in practice may be gleaned from the United Kingdom case law where the courts have been concerned with it for over twenty years.

A good illustration of a disproportionate disadvantage flowing to a minority group from an apparently neutral provision is the decision of *Mandla* v. *Dowell Lee*,[121] which we have already encountered in the course of our search for a coherent definition of what is meant by an ethnic group. The impugned regulation in that case was a school rule to the effect that all pupils at the establishment were required to wear the school uniform, and it was on this basis that the head teacher refused a place to a boy from an orthodox Sikh background whose family-supported communal identity would have required him to wear a turban at all times, and specifically (for the purposes of this case) while he was at school. Clearly the proportion of Sikhs disabled by the rule from attending the school was far higher than the proportion of the general population so inhibited, and this was what the House of Lords duly found. To similar effect is *Commission for Racial Equality* v. *Dutton*,[122] where a 'No Travellers' notice on the window of a public house was held disproportionately to impact on the gypsies, which the Court of Appeal found to be an ethnic group engaged in a nomadic way of life which brought them within the prohibition. Interestingly in both cases, it was technically possible for members of each group to comply with the rules by engaging in a manageable physical action, in the first by removing the turban and in the second by rejecting the travelling life and settling down, though neither court held this to be required. The rules in each case were sufficiently prohibitive if they could not be complied with in a way that was consistent with 'the customs and cultural conditions of the racial group'.[123] The jurisprudence of any EU directive on this point would be expected to follow a similar interpretive path.

More problematic is the exemption from the full rigours of the prohibition on indirect discrimination of which certain persons and authorities will be able to avail under the Group's proposal. It is clear that the reconciliation of the various relevant human rights and the trade-off between such rights and other societal interests requires such a balancing to occur. As drafted, the directive would allow such an exemption where the aim of the impugned rule or practice (i) is appropriate *and*

---

[119] The Sex Discrimination Act 1975, s. 1(1)(b) introduced the concept into British law. The relevant provision of the Race Relations Act 1976 is s. 1(1)(b).

[120] Art. 1(3). The second and third square brackets contain suggested amendments to the Group's draft.

[121] *Mandla* v. *Dowell Lee*, note 40 above.

[122] *Commission for Racial Equality* v. *Dutton*, note 41 above.

[123] *Mandla* v. *Dowell Lee*, note 40 above, at 566, *per* Lord Fraser. See also *Price* v. *Civil Service Commission* [1978] ICR 27.

necessary, *and* (ii) can be justified by objective factors unrelated to racial or ethnic origin, or religion [and] belief. By way of comparison, a similar test in British law requires that the impugned treatment be shown to be 'justifiable irrespective of' the discriminatory impact it is said to have on the complainant. The classic illustration of the operation of the exemption is *Panesar* v. *Nestlé Co. Ltd*,[124] where it was held that 'a rule forbidding the wearing of beards in the respondent's chocolate factory was justifiable . . . on hygienic grounds notwithstanding that the proportion of Sikhs who could conscientiously comply with it was considerably smaller than the proportion of non-Sikhs who could comply with it'. The justification there was purely a matter of public health and nothing whatever to do with racial grounds.[125] Applied rigorously in this fashion, it is clear that such an exemption is a vital element in any coherent attack on indirect discrimination.

Draft Article 2(3)(a) provides that the definition of discrimination 'shall include victimisation'. Under draft Article 2(3)(b), '[v]ictimisation occurs where in respect of the areas under Article 2(1) a person or group of persons is subject to any detriment by reason of that person or group of persons being involved in or suspected of being involved in making a complaint or assisting a complaint alleging racial or religious discrimination, provided the allegation was not false and was made in good faith'.

Enforcement of these various prohibitions on discrimination is primarily addressed in Article 4(1) of the Starting Line Group's proposals, and it goes far beyond the subparagraph (a) to which we have already referred. Apart from the requirement to prohibit the direct and indirect forms of discrimination in that paragraph, Member States would also be required by the proposal to prohibit the following by legal sanction:

(i) incitement or pressure to racial or religious discrimination;
(ii) the establishment or operation of any organization which promotes such incitement or pressure together with membership of any such organization and the giving of aid, financial or otherwise to any such organization;
(iii) any act or practice by a public authority or public institution of racial or religious discrimination against persons, groups of persons or institutions;
(iv) the financing, defence or support by any public authority or public institution of racial or religious discrimination by any person, group or organization.

There can be no doubt that the logic that drives this list of state obligations is a laudable one. As was the case with indirect discrimination, the intention of the drafters is to leave no stone unturned in the effort to root out racist and religious discrimination in all its forms. Other aspects of the proposed enforcement of the draft directive are driven by the same objective. '[A]ppropriate bodies', with wide powers of investigation,[126] are to be established in each Member State to oversee the operation of the directive.[127] Not only will those who consider themselves to have been 'the object of discrimination contrary to the principles set out in this Directive' be guaranteed 'recourse to a legal remedy, in accordance with the most effective na-

---

[124] [1980] ICR 144.
[125] This description of the case is drawn from Lord Fraser's judgment in *Mandla*, note 40 above, at 567.
[126] Art. 4(4)(e).　　　　　　　　　　　　　　　　　　　　　　　[127] *Ibid.*

tional procedures',[128] but they will also have the opportunity, if successful in their actions, of securing 'adequate compensation for both pecuniary and non-pecuniary damages', with there being 'no limitations on the ability of the court or other competent authorities . . . to award compensation or such other remedy as is provided for by national law'.[129] Apart from such victims, the draft directive would also allow relevant non-governmental organizations 'to institute or support legal actions in civil, administrative and criminal courts enforcing the rights granted under this Directive'.[130] Under the proposed Article 5, where a complainant establishes facts 'from which [it] may be presumed that there has been direct or indirect discrimination, it shall be for the respondent to prove that no such discrimination has occurred' with the complainant nevertheless retaining the 'benefit from any doubt that may remain'.[131]

Taken together with the breadth of the penal provisions proposed in the draft directive, this is an extensive agenda for intrusive state action, and the question arises whether it is in its entirety 'appropriate action' under Article 13, particularly bearing in mind the deepened commitment to human rights principles declared at Amsterdam and inserted, as we have seen, more explicitly than ever in Article 7 (*ex* Article F.1) of the Union Treaty. The intrusion into rights of due process and privacy that is necessarily involved in such provisions as we have described above would almost certainly pass muster before any tribunal charged with balancing the rights argument in this inherently sensitive area. More problematic is the duty described above to proscribe 'any organizations which promote such incitement or pressure [to racial or religious discrimination] together with membership of those groups or organizations and aid, financial or otherwise, to any such organization'. This is a somewhat draconian interference with freedom of association that may moreover be somewhat counter-productive, at least to the extent that it would drive underground those groups and organizations that at present, being perfectly lawful, are more easily infiltrated by national law-enforcement authorities. Much less controversial from a human rights point of view, and it is suggested more satisfactory in terms of dealing with the mischief at which the directive is directed, would have been a duty to proscribe by law incitement to racial and/or religious hatred.[132]

---

[128] Art. 4(4)(a). The option of conciliation procedures is also to be made available: Art. 4(4)(f).

[129] Art. 4(4)(b). Also relevant here is the proposed Art. 4(4)(c) under which States will be obliged to ensure that 'an effective judicial remedy' is in place to 'enable persons who consider themselves wronged to defend their rights', and this will be required to include 'support in respect of legal costs in accordance with the most favourable provisions of national law'.

[130] Art. 4(4)(d).

[131] As the JUSTICE report, note 6 above, commented, at 15, note 54: '[t]he inclusion of a clause on the burden of proof is guided by experience in the field of sex discrimination, where this is still a contentious issue'.

[132] The most relevant decision under the ECHR is that of *Glimmerveen and Hagenbeek* v. *The Netherlands*, Apps. Nos. 8348/78 and 8406/78 (1980) 18 D&R 187 in which strong domestic controls on racist speech were upheld through the application of Art. 17, which is in the following terms: '[n]othing in this Convention may be interpreted as implying for any state, group or person any right to engage in any activity or perform any act aimed at the destruction of any of the rights and freedoms set forth herein or at their limitation to a greater extent than is provided for in the Convention'. For the supporting view of the Court, see *Jersild* v. *Denmark*, ECHR (1994), Series A, No. 298 (1994) 19 EHRR 1, at para. 35. See also *X* v. *Federal Republic of Germany*, App. No. 9235/81 (1982) 29 D&R 194; *T* v. *Belgium*, App. No. 9777/82 (1983) 34 D&R 158; *Kuhnen* v. *Federal Republic of Germany*, App. No. 12194/86 (1988) 56 D&R 205;

VII. CONCLUSION

In any European-wide engagement in the field of anti-racism it will be important to monitor the discharge by the Member States of the various duties that will inevitably be imposed on them by such a supra-nationalist intervention. Anxieties about local enforcement naturally accompany many European initiatives in all areas, but such concerns are likely to be particularly to the fore here, in view of the sensitivity of the subject matter and the choice of the directive as the most appropriate tool for community action. Anti-racism is an area where talking and promising are very much easier than action, and no State should be offered the temptation of assuming that EU legislation in the field amounts in reality to no more than noisy Community window-dressing on a pressing though insoluble moral issue. Alive to this possibility the Starting Line Group states that:

> Member States shall adopt the laws, regulations and administrative provisions neces-
> sary to comply with this Directive no later than two years after the adoption of the
> Directive. They shall forthwith inform the Commission thereof.[133]

Just as important from this perspective is Article 10(1) of the draft:

> Member States undertake to submit to the Commission a report on all legislative, judi-
> cial, administrative or other measures which they have adopted and which give effect to
> the provisions of this directive to enable the Commission to draw up a report for the
> Council and the [European Parliament]:
>
>> (a) within one year following the expiration of the period of two years provided for
>>   in Article 9(1); and
>> (b) thereafter every two years.

Under draft Article 10(2), '[t]o assist the Commission in drawing up the report for the purposes of paragraph 1, the Commission may request further information from member states and may receive information from non-governmental organizations'. And under Article 10(3), '[i]n drawing up the report for the purposes of paragraph 1, the Commission may make suggestions and general recommendations based on the examination of the reports and information received from member states'.

Furthermore, under draft Article 11(1), '[w]ithin one year after the adoption of this directive, the European Monitoring Centre shall specify standard criteria for an-nual monitoring of the performance by member states of their obligations under this directive'. And under Article 11(2), '[m]ember states shall submit annual monitoring returns based on the specified criteria to the European Monitoring Centre, the first to be submitted within one year after the expiration of the period of two years pro-vided for in Article 9(1)'.

H, W, P. and K. v. *Austria*, App. No. 12774/87 (1989) 62 D&R 216. In none of these cases were any appli-cants able successfully to rely upon the Convention's guarantee of free speech to protect state action against their racist speech. No issue of association under Art. 11 was directly raised in any of them.

[133] Art. 9(1). Under Art. 9(3), 'Member States shall communicate to the Commission the texts of the provisions of national law already adopted or being adopted in the field governed by this Directive'.

It will be recalled that the Centre here referred to was set up in 1997 by the Council of the European Union[134] and has as its 'prime objective' the supply to the Community and its Member States of 'objective, reliable and comparable data at European level on the phenomena of racism, xenophobia and anti-Semitism in order to help them when they take measures or formulate courses of action within their respective spheres of competence'.[135] As presently envisaged, the main focus of the Centre is on study, data collection, and problem analysis. It may be that a Community initiative of the type we have discussed in this chapter would be well served by an accompanying expansion of the remit of the Monitoring Centre, and it should be understood that this would require a further regulatory intervention by the Community organs. It is to be expected, for example, that any draft directive in this field would make provision for concerted action against racism in the fields of education and training, the media, and the public service,[136] and it would seem entirely appropriate that the Centre should be given a galvanizing role in any European-wide strategic engagement of this sort. It is well known that the Council of Europe is already highly active in this field, and the Centre should also be able to co-ordinate directly with the relevant authorities in Strasbourg so as to maximize the drive against racism and minimize the risk of a duplication of energy and resources.[137] This co-ordinating role could be extended upwards to embrace international organizations and downwards to include anti-racism actors engaged at the national level.[138]

If a directive on anti-racism is agreed by the Community, then it would seem appropriate to widen the terms of reference for the Centre so as to make it the primary Community organ in the oversight of the measure's implementation and effectiveness. Clearly this would involve more than a monitoring of events, and as such a change in the Centre's title, legal base, and personnel to reflect its widened remit would probably be desirable. It is suggested that consideration should be given to its re-establishment as the European Centre for Ethnic and Religious Equality. It would be to such a body that Member States would need to report, and the Centre would need to be given an enforcement role, in partnership with the Commission, where Member States were defaulting in their duties. The Centre is currently required to publish annual reports[139] and in its expanded role it could use these as occasions to report on progress and to make suggestions concerning the need for further reform, both nationally and at the Community level, basing if need be its recommendations on a close scrutiny of best practice in the Member States.[140] The Centre would be able also to conduct special studies of such difficult and sensitive

---

[134] Council Reg. 1035/97 [1997] OJ L151/1.   [135] Art. 2(1).

[136] See, e.g., Arts. 4(2) and (3), 8, and 9(2) of the Starting Line Group's draft.

[137] This is a role already contemplated for the Centre: see Art. 3(2) of Reg. 1035/97. The Council of Europe has long been active in the field of combating racism and intolerance, with the European Commission against Racism and Intolerance, established under its ægis, being directly involved in a variety of projects. See its website at: www.ecri.coe.fr.

[138] Art. 7 of Reg. 1035/97 provides a model.   [139] Art. 2(2)(g).

[140] Any dir. in this area would certainly contain a clause like that to be found in Art. 7 of the Starting Line Group's Draft: '[t]he provisions of the present Directive do not affect national legislation or applicable international treaties granting more favourable guarantees against racial [and religious] discrimination'.

issues as that of affirmative action, which has proved very controversial in the field of gender equality. It would also be able to report on the extent to which any future EU equality law in this field was being deployed in a counter-productive way by already dominant cultures and groups, so as further to buttress their position in society, a risk that unfortunately cannot be ignored in legislation so broadly drawn as any directive in this area is likely to be.

In our present context, affirmative action raises the question whether the achievement of substantive equality by a particular ethnic community is judged so greatly to be desired that a sacrifice should be required of an unknown number of as yet unspecified members of the dominant cultural community. How one answers this question depends ultimately on whether one takes a primarily liberal or primarily egalitarian approach to the organization of one's society. This is not an issue that can be appropriately defined as one involving a clash of human rights. The Starting Line Group would leave the issue to the discretion of the Member States: '[t]his Directive shall be without prejudice to national laws, regulations and administrative provisions favouring certain disadvantaged groups with the aim of removing existing inequalities affecting them or promoting effective equality of opportunity between members of society'. [141] It may be that the Commission will want to consider taking a lead on this difficult issue in the context of its proposals for legislation, due before the end of 1999, though a robust stance on affirmative action would probably require Treaty amendment.[142]

Most importantly of all, a Centre of the type proposed here would have as its singular purpose the protection of ethnic and religious minority cultures from discrimination and from the effects of the fomenting of racialist and religious hatred. Its independence from other Community institutions would allow it to assess the performance of the EU as a whole in this field, and would allow it to raise issues about which other EU bodies, more intimately involved in the management of the Union, would naturally be more sensitive. In particular it would be such a Centre that would be able to report on the extent to which the activities of the EU in the economic sphere were adding to or detracting from the drive against communal intolerance. While properly administering its part of the picture, such a Centre would have the skill and the commitment not to forget, and the independence to point out again and again if necessary, that the issues of racism, intolerance, and xenophobia are inextricably intertwined with those of jobs, security, and the quality of the European citizen's life. These are the most vital human rights of all in the battle against an intolerance that seems difficult, if not impossible, wholly to suppress but which shows itself to be particularly venomous when driven to the surface by deep despair.

[141] Art. 1(4) of the Starting Line Group's draft. For the position in the Member States, see European Commission, note 6 above, at 18, 72–4.
[142] See the analagous provision on gender discrimination in the new Art. 119(4) (new Art. 141) proposed by the Treaty of Amsterdam for the EC Treaty.

11

Non-Communitarians: Refugee and Asylum Policies

GREGOR NOLL AND JENS VEDSTED-HANSEN*

I. INTRODUCTION

While the internal dimension of immigration policies has been an integral part of EC co-operation ever since the 1957 Treaty of Rome, immigration policies *vis-à-vis* third-country nationals, and the related issue of asylum, became a serious EC concern only in the mid-1980s. Developing the single market and abandoning internal border controls were seen as conditioned upon the establishment of common control at the external borders. This resulted in the attempts to harmonize immigration policies with respect to non-EC citizens, and asylum policies as well. As it will emerge, there are important disparities in harmonization of the two policy areas.

In this chapter we are going to discuss the human rights implications of the harmonization process. The focus of analysis will first and foremost be on asylum policies and other issues pertaining to refugee protection. Aspects of non-asylum immigration policies might be relevant, in so far as human rights commitments may raise questions relating to the entrance and residence of 'non-communitarians' in Member States; yet this topic goes beyond the scope of our discussion. The interrelatedness between migration control and refugee protection leads us to scrutinize the human rights implications of control policies, with a view to identifying different options for an EU refugee protection strategy in the years to come.

The Treaty of Amsterdam has provided new competencies for the EC institutions, as well as new procedures for their adoption of measures with respect to asylum and immigration. Setting out from this repartition of competencies and the new regulatory measures to be adopted, we are going to discuss those areas of the policy harmonization process which seem most relevant, and probably most challenging, from a human rights perspective. The existing EU asylum *acquis* will therefore be critically analysed, focusing especially on the various categories of persons in need of international protection; the dilemmas raised by the increasing tendencies to prevent the arrivals of refugees and asylum-seekers; questions relating to Member States'

* While this text as a whole should be seen as the result of a co-operative effort, Jens Vedsted-Hansen has focused on sections III, IV. B, IV. D, and IV. E, and Gregor Noll has focused on sections II, IV. A, IV. C, and IV. F.

burdens and responsibilities for examining asylum applications and extending protection, and the procedural safeguards in status determination; standards for the reception of asylum-seekers, including the crucial issue of detention; and the problems relating to return of unsuccessful asylum-seekers.

The possibility exists that the asylum *acquis* will simply be carried over from the third to the first pillar of the EU when adopting new legislative measures. To what extent this will happen obviously depends on political developments rather than legal considerations. In connection with our analysis of the *acquis*, however, an attempt will be made to assess which norms are most likely to persist in a new legal form, and which of them most strongly need to be improved in the future harmonization process, so as to enhance their effectiveness in ensuring compliance with international human rights standards.

In order to frame the analysis of the EU *acquis* and its future after the Amsterdam Treaty, the initial discussion will focus on the regulatory strategies and principles on which the Union may base its development of norms pertaining to asylum and immigration. Here the systemic conflict between migration control and human rights protection is the point of departure, leading to the attempt to identify various strategies for harmonization. The impact of the transfer of competencies to the EC institutions, and of harmonization in the form of binding acts, will then be discussed. We shall come back to these issues in the final section, where they will serve as a basis for our conclusions on policy priorities in this area.

II. REGULATORY STRATEGIES AND THEIR NORMATIVE BASIS

A. Universalism versus Particularism

By its very nature, migration and asylum law is situated in the conflict zone between particularism and universalism. In ultimate questions, participants in this discourse have a choice between two foundational paradigms—one striving for the global realization of human rights and another giving preference to the interests of a certain state population. Provided that resources for the realization of civil, political, economic, social, and cultural rights are scarce, should we opt for a limited level of their protection for an extensive group or for an extensive level of protection for a limited group? Is the vision of a good life most efficiently attained if an elitist *avant-garde* paves the way, or does justice demand that progress is made at the same pace for everybody? Or, finally, how should the resource of state protection be distributed?

Any differences in protection are regulated by means of thresholds. Within the context of state protection, a decisive threshold exists between non-citizens and citizens. This becomes clear in constitutional law as well as international human rights law, both according a more favourable position to state citizens. Another threshold of focal interest severs those within state jurisdiction from those outside it. The latter threshold is usually linked to a person's presence on state territory. Again, international human rights law may serve as an illustration, as its major treaty instruments extend a basic form of protection to all persons in the jurisdiction of States parties.

As a corollary of their territorial supremacy, states are entitled to control the composition of their populations,[1] which means nothing less than delimiting the group to which protection is extended. This prerogative entails a right to control borders understood in a literal and a metaphorical sense—covering physical borders as well as administrative thresholds severing citizens from non-citizens, participants from non-participants, beneficiaries from non-beneficiaries, and tolerated from non-tolerated. The means by which such controls are exercised stretch from naturalization to forcible removal.

These thresholds assist in forming a group of persons separate from the rest of the world population—a *demos*. The variety of decisions on inclusion and exclusion are all predicated on the foundational question of 'who is the *demos*'. The totality of these decisions in a given society forms its answer to that question. To justify such answers, a variety of assumptions on the ultimate link between individual and society are on offer: While some societies base their approach on kinship and descent, others focus on presence and integration. In brief, the *demos* is a formula by means of which a given society specifies the right balance between inclusion and exclusion. In the course of time, it attains a mythical quality, which moves the concrete balance out of the reach of rational discourse.

If identifying the *demos* is already painstaking at the level of the nation State, these difficulties are amplified in a supranational setting. For all that is certain, the project of a European Union can be described as simultaneously extending and limiting protection. Seen from the perspective of the Member States, the Union is about sharing protection with the populations of other Member States. Seen from the outside, the Union appears as a merger of mighty sovereigns promoting protection for its populations at the expense of others. Extending protection means giving up the established link between a preconceived *demos* and inclusion. Limiting protection begs the double question of where to draw the line and how to justify it.

Here, the necessary responsiveness to universality and equality poses specific problems for the intergovernmental particularist professing *d'abord l'Europe*. In the absence of any common 'national identity' predicated on a traditional *demos* concept of mythical force, integration and the ensuing sharing of resources can be justified only by the universality of certain values. If free trade is a common good, it is definitely so for all, not just for Member State populations. In the same way that the particularist argument of 'national interests' loses power within the Union, arguing the exclusion of non-Union interests becomes more difficult. Presently, there is no 'Union identity' capable of competing with the foundational qualities of its national counterpart.[2] In the absence of a mythically delimited *demos*, justification of

---

[1] In its judgments concerning Art. 3 ECHR, the European Court of Human Rights has repeatedly spelt out that States are entitled to control the entry of aliens on their territory. See e.g. *Nsona* v. *The Netherlands*, ECHR (1996) V, No. 22, at para. 92.

[2] Ultimately, the core of the legal regimes spawned within the Union framework is citizenship of a Member State. This becomes particularly clear in the formulation of European Citizenship in Part II of the EC Treaty. From a national perspective, the EU is a regulatory mechanism for the differentiated

exclusion hinges solely on functional arguments: that is, building the European Union is only justifiable as a *first step* in the global realization of freedom, security, and justice. For to be successful, this step needs to be taken in a secure and controlled environment, limiting the amount of outside interference. Thus, the move to an ever closer Union produces its own Orwellian paradoxes: integration is attained by means of exclusion, freedom achieved by means of control. The liberal paradigm behind the dismantling of borders is complemented by a control paradigm erecting new ones.

These paradoxes become particularly visible in the regulation of free movement in the European Union. The abolition of internal borders is bought at the expense of erecting ever higher external borders. Such a trade-off tends to undermine the very ideal of freedom of movement, as its justification hinges precisely on universality. The only defence would be, once more, to display the elitist solution as a first step to the universal implementation of rights.

But, for the time being, the European Union does not make any claims in that direction. On the contrary: while the realization of free movement for Communitarians is the object of a considerable amount of supranational and intergovernmental effort, the question of migration at large is met with a deafening silence and, ultimately, referred back to the single Member States. As long as the Union fails to develop a credible notion of its *demos*, the setting of thresholds remains a technical exercise, predicated on the tools designed for the framework of the nation State and governed solely by an underlegitimized rationale of controlling migration.[3]

In all, the Union's *demos* is controlled, yet undefined. This entails a number of consequences. In the absence of a pre-established balance between universalism and particularism, the latter remains unchecked and tends to colonize the former. In accordance with the present self-interest of Member States, particularism translates into co-ordinating policies of exclusion, while little or no co-ordination is taking place on inclusion. The prevalence of control carries with it a considerable risk of simply externalizing the *demos* problem: Where real or potential asylum-seekers simply do not reach the territories of Member States, or, once there, vanish in illegality, the visibility of inclusion demands fades away. Together with the universalist perspective, human rights considerations risk to disappear in discourse.

B. Migration Control versus Refugee Protection

Since the inception of the Single European Act in 1986 and the elitist co-operation spawned by the Schengen States in 1985, refugee protection has figured mainly as a

treatment of aliens. Citizens from other Member States are generally accorded more favourable treatment than other citizens. Finally, the nation State's division between citizen and non-citizen remains intact.

³ It is highly ironic that Member States enforce a control paradigm even if it rebounds on their own citizens. The so-called Spanish Protocol stipulates that all Member States shall regard each other as safe countries of origin when determining asylum claims from Union citizens. This is unique in so far as the EU consciously places citizens from other Member States in a *less favourable* position than citizens of third States. The Spanish Protocol has been rightly criticized for undermining a non-discriminatory application of the 1951 Convention relating to the Status of Refugees: Protocol on Asylum for Nationals of Member States of the European Union, annexed to the TEU and to the EC Treaty, 6 Oct. 1997, Doc. No. CONF 4007/97, TA/P/en 24.

technical problem within the context of free movement between the Member States. This may entail the—faulty—impression that refugee protection is subordinated to the accumulated sovereignty of the Union's Member States. However, it should be borne in mind that refugee protection is not a problem of migration control.[4] Refugees have lost the protection of their home community, which makes them conceptually different from migrants. Thus, migration control and refugee protection are separate systems pursuing different systemic goals. In order to realize these goals, the input of individual cases is processed in the light of accepted norms to produce outcomes. The systemic goal of migration control is to manage the inflow, presence, and outflow of non-citizens on state territory. In short, it is about the preservation of a particularistic community.

Any reasoning on the systemic goals of refugee protection should look back to the instrument representing the foundation of the international human rights system. In 1948, the General Assembly of the United Nations approved the Universal Declaration of Human Rights,[5] stating in Article 14 that '[e]veryone has the right to seek and to enjoy in other countries asylum from persecution'. Like the other civil, political, economic, social, and cultural rights enshrined in the Universal Declaration, Article 14 must be seen in the light of Article 28:

> Everyone is entitled to a social and international order in which the rights and freedoms set forth in this Declaration can be fully realized.

This provision assigns States to optimize the international order for an accommodation of the exercise of human rights. By the virtue of this Article, the Universal Declaration can be regarded as a starting point for the development of a comprehensive human rights regime. While the 1966 Covenants[6] were designed to safeguard human rights under national jurisdictions, the 1951 Refugee Convention,[7] the Convention relating to the Status of Stateless Persons,[8] and the Agreement relating to Refugee Seamen[9] were conceived as subsidiary means of human rights protection. Broadly speaking, their rationale was to safeguard human rights, when the country of origin had failed to protect individuals under its jurisdiction.

Thus, refugee protection is about the universal safeguarding of a certain level of human rights. It follows that refugee protection is not a sub-system of migration

---

[4] For an analysis of the tension between control and protection in the context of asylum procedures, see J. Vedsted-Hansen, 'Control v. Protection in Asylum Procedures', paper presented at the Technical Symposium on International Migration and Development (1998, forthcoming in the proceedings of the symposium).

[5] Universal Declaration of Human Rights, adopted by GA Res. 217 A (III) (1948). In United Nations, *A Compilation of International Instruments* (1994), i, Part 1, 1.

[6] International Covenant on Economic, Social and Cultural Rights (ICESCR) and the International Covenant on Civil and Political Rights (ICCPR), both adopted by GA Res. 2200 A (XXI) (1966): in *International Instruments*, note 5 above, at 8 and 20.

[7] Convention relating to the Status of Refugees, adopted on 28 July 1951 by the UN Conference of Plenipotentiaries on the Status of Refugees and Stateless Persons convened under GA Res. 429 (V) (1950), hereinafter 1951 Refugee Convention: in *International Instruments*, note 5 above, i, Part 2, at 638. Reference to the 1951 Refugee Convention below covers the Convention as modified by the Prot. relating to the Status of Refugees, 31 Jan. 1967: in *International Instruments*, note 5 above, i, Part 2, at 655.

[8] Convention relating to the Status of Stateless Persons. Adopted on 28 September 1954 by a Conference of Plenipotentiaries convened by ESC Res. 526 A (XVII) (1954). In *International Instruments*, note 5 above, i, Part 2, at 625.

[9] Agreement relating to Refugee Seamen of 23 Nov. 1957: 506 UNTS 125.

control, as both pursue different systemic goals. However, their fields of operation overlap, and they share some norms guiding processes in each system. [10]

We are left with a formidable conflict between the State's prerogative to exclude and the human rights imperative to include. It should be made clear that the resolution in the conflict of rights hinges on our initial assumptions about international law. Do state interests trump individual interests, as international law is ultimately conceived by States and not individuals? Or is the protective content of human rights law, once unleashed, beyond the logic of state interest? In the absence of an arguable right of way for one or the other, all that can be done is to balance both interests.

If the earlier described prevalence of a control paradigm has tipped over the scale in favour of particularism, Article 6 (*ex* Article F) of the Treaty on European Union (TEU) as amended by the Treaty of Amsterdam offers itself as a counterbalance. It provides that the European Union shall respect fundamental rights as general principles of Community law. It follows from Article 2 (*ex* Article B) of the Treaty that the objectives of the Union shall be achieved in accordance with, and are thus subordinated to, the general principles set forth in Article 6.

Human rights, as embraced by the general principles, must therefore guide the adoption of measures under Title IV of the EC Treaty,[11] concerning visas, asylum, immigration and other policies relating to the free movement of persons, as well as other measures establishing the Union as an area of freedom, security, and justice, and related measures taken under Title V of the EU Treaty on a common foreign and security policy. This means nothing less than a reintroduction of the universalist perspective, albeit of considerable abstraction, in the discourse on how to delimit the protective commitments of the Union.

C. The Controlled Market of Deflection

In the system of refugee protection, two main areas of regulation can be discerned. The first is on administering movements; which means all measures impacting on the departure, itinerary, arrival, and allocation of asylum-seekers. Such direct administration of movements attempts to steer the physical presence of the asylum-seeker as well as the administrative responsibility for her. The second is on affording protection, which means all measures impacting on the human rights situation of the asylum-seeker. Both areas are interrelated—inevitably, the standard of protection to be expected in a certain country may be a factor taken into consideration by the asylum-seeker in the choice of destination country. Moreover, as the discourse on temporary protection and mass influx situations shows, the equation can be reversed: in practice, actual or even anticipated movements may also influence standards of protection.

Why would state actors wish to steer the movements of asylum-seekers? The most prominent reason is plainly to avoid becoming a State of destination. Another motivation may be to effect a distribution of asylum-seekers according to a certain

---

[10] Both systems are operated under the rule of law, which implies *inter alia* that they should produce outcomes in a predictable and non-discriminatory fashion.

[11] In this text, references to the EC Treaty as well as the EU Treaty comprise their amendment by the Treaty of Amsterdam unless otherwise indicated.

pattern. When this pattern is intended to bring about an equitable sharing of the protection responsibility, the exercise is referred to as 'burden-sharing'. Within a state grouping such as the European Union, there may be the double goal of deflection and burden-sharing. There is an interest in deflecting[12] at least parts of the movement of real or potential asylum-seekers to the region at large. Within the Union, however, this deflection by single Member States may lead to a burden on other Member States. Thus, in order not to undermine solidarity, measures of deflection must be taken in a concerted fashion. In combination, there is also an interest, at least with the presently most-affected States, in sharing the responsibility for those who manage to arrive in spite of deflective measures. Steering movements thus comprise two typecast relationships—one between the Member States and the individual asylum-seeker, another between the Member States themselves.

In the following sections, it will become clear that Member States have made a major effort in the regulation of movement. Apart from some feeble attempts to define a common policy, the area of protection has been left largely to the discretion of each single Member State. Drawing on another terminology, it could be claimed that the EU resorted to planning economy in steering movements. The dynamics of this economy are creating a thrust for restrictive solutions, which are developed by single Member States in a competitive market environment.

III. THE TREATY OF AMSTERDAM: REPARTITION OF COMPETENCIES AND NEW REGULATORY MEASURES

A. Communitarization of Asylum and Immigration Policies

1. Stages in the Harmonization Process   The scenario following the entry into force of the Treaty of Amsterdam can be better analysed by looking back to pre-EU developments within asylum and immigration. As mentioned, the harmonization process took its beginning in connection with the introduction of the Single European Act of 1986. While the 1984 Fontainebleau European Council had proposed the abolition of police and customs formalities for persons crossing internal borders before mid-1985, it soon became clear that this would take more time to realize. Given the necessity gradually to introduce common policies towards third-country nationals, 1992 was set as a deadline for the adoption of such policies, in accordance with the 'Europe without Frontiers' plan advanced by the President of the Commission.[13]

Similarly, the Commission's 1985 White Paper on the Single Market recognized the necessity of common policies concerning third-country nationals. With a view to dismantling internal border controls in 1992 the Commission would therefore

---

[12] In the present context, deflection means any measure inhibiting any more lasting access to a territory. The concept thus comprises non-arrival policies as well as the mechanism of referral to safe third countries. See text accompanying note 68 below.

[13] *A People's Europe: Bull. EC Suppl.* 7/85, at 8–9.

initiate proposals for directives on immigration, asylum, and refugee status, and visa policies.[14] Some draft directives were actually submitted in 1988, yet they were never adopted. As the work of the *Ad Hoc* Group on Immigration, established within the parallel framework of European Political Co-operation, did not progress sufficiently, various steps towards a more structured harmonization process were taken during the preparations for the revision of the Treaty at the 1991–2 Inter-Governmental Conference.

As is known, the outcome was the adoption of Title VI of the Maastricht EU Treaty, concerning co-operation in Justice and Home Affairs within the Union's so-called third pillar. Under Article K.1 (now Article 29) Member States agreed to consider as issues of common interest, i.e. (1) asylum policies; (2) rules on the passage of persons across the external borders of Member States, and the exercise of control thereon; (3) immigration policy and policies towards third-country nationals as regards their entry and movement, conditions for their residence on the territories of Member States, including family reunification and access to employment, and combating illegal immigration. Measures to be unanimously adopted with a view to harmonization of these policy issues were, according to Article K.3 (now Article 31), 'joint positions', 'joint actions', and conventions.

Before we discuss the experience of third-pillar co-operation, an attempt will be made to categorize the efforts towards harmonization of asylum and immigration policies at the EC/EU level. This may serve as a basis for assessing the legal and political impact of co-operation in Justice and Home Affairs, while at the same time giving an additional overview of developments within an area of third-pillar co-operation which is particularly relevant from a human rights perspective.

2. Three Different Approaches to Harmonization   The harmonization of refugee and asylum policies was perceived to be intrinsically connected to the development of the single market. For analytical purposes, however, this does not give a one-dimensional explanation of the forms of harmonization and the substance of measures taken to that effect. First, it might seem questionable whether the realization of such market structures actually depends on the dismantling of internal border controls. As mentioned, the absence of such controls is exactly what has been invoked as necessitating the reinforcement of external border controls; this in turn was often the reason given for restricting asylum policies.

As regards the latter issue, the point has been correctly made that establishing common external borders does not define the criteria under which these borders may be crossed by third-country nationals; such criteria still have to be established by political decision. Moreover, it is not evident that the functioning of the single market would require total abandonment of control on persons crossing internal borders. Summary forms of control, already known at borders where there is a practical need in that regard, do not seem to be blocking economic exchange between markets across the borders involved. Neither is the exercise of such control incompatible with the symbolic functioning of passport-free travel. In any event, common control of

---

[14] European Commission, *Completing the Internal Market. White Paper from the Commission to the European Council* COM(85)310 final, at 14–16.

external borders does not in itself mean restricted criteria of access, just as it does not lead automatically to repressive enforcement of such criteria. It is therefore hard to avoid contemplating whether EU Member States have taken advantage of the economic integration, making it an institutional pretext for restricting access for refugees in search of protection. In other words, what has been framed as a technical necessity turns out to be rather a political choice.

As posited by a North American observer, EC governments seem to have seized upon the impending termination of immigration controls at intra-Community borders to demand enhanced security at the external frontiers.[15] But does enhanced economic integration have to result in such increased external security measures? The same observer suggests an answer in the negative by concluding as follows with respect to the lessons of the European experience:

> First, that increasing levels of economic integration lead logically towards a policy of generalized freedom of movement within the economic zone, which in turn will require some coordination of strategy regarding external frontiers. Second, that the self-interested drive towards unification presents states with an opportunity to reconceptualize refugee flows as irritants to coordination, and to pursue with impunity generalized policies of deterrence. Third, that the intergovernmental structures requisite to detailed alignment of economic policy can be used in order to shield protectionist lawmaking from scrutiny or review, allowing the human rights mandate of refugee law to be effectively undercut. Finally, and most profoundly, the experience to date shows that the basic commitment to balance domestic self-interest with the human rights of those forced to flee in search of protection is now extraordinarily fragile, even in the very states which crafted the modern international human rights and refugee regimes.[16]

Assuming that there is no link of structural necessity between EC/EU integration and the reinforcement of external border controls, it would seem that control policies are in principle open to modification, according to political priorities allowing for human rights standards to influence the control strategy. With a view to our discussion of the possible impact of the Treaty of Amsterdam in this respect, it is noteworthy that during the past harmonization process quite different approaches have been taken by the EC/EU and Member States to designing asylum and immigration policies *vis-à-vis* third-country nationals. There may be some chronological coincidence of the three approaches described below; yet policy priorities seem to have been changing significantly over time, the emphasis being still more on the third approach.[17]

As a first approach, immigration policies and the inherent control strategies were kept *separate* from issues pertaining to refugee protection. This was the case for the EC Commission's 1991 Communications on the right of asylum and on immigration. In the former document the Commission stated that '[a]lthough both matters are linked and interrelated, they are each governed by *specific policies and rules* which reflect *fundamentally different* principles and preoccupations'.[18] While

---

[15] J. Hathaway, 'Harmonizing for Whom? The Devaluation of Refugee Protection in the Era of European Economic Integration' (1993) 26 *CILJ* 719.   [16] *Ibid.*, at 734–5.

[17] These approaches obviously can be seen as reflecting the systemic conflict discussed at II. B., above.

[18] European Commission, *Communication from the Commission to the Council and the European Parliament on the Right of Asylum*: SEC(91)1857, at para. 2 (emphasis added).

immigration from third countries was seen as primarily an economic phenomenon, the right of asylum was considered first and foremost a right and a humanitarian challenge. Here, the starting point was the 1951 Refugee Convention, 'a fundamental common legal instrument'; from this basis Member States had formulated national laws that remove the possibility of refusing in a discretionary manner to admit an asylum-seeker to their territory. As 'preventing abuse of the right of asylum' and 'harmonization of the formal and substantive right of asylum' were the two aspects of the common EC interest of the right of asylum, full respect for the humanitarian principles embodied in the 1951 Refugee Convention was declared the starting point.[19] In its 1994 Communication, the Commission appears by and large to have maintained this approach, although perhaps slightly adjusting towards the next category.[20]

There may be only a gradual difference from the second approach, rather than one of quality. Despite recognizing the *interrelatedness* of asylum and immigration policies, the measures adopted have not taken account of the practical consequences that flow from the interaction between the two policy areas. As a significant example, the 1991 Draft Convention on the Crossing of the External Borders stated that its provisions should apply 'subject to' the provisions of the 1951 Refugee Convention, in particular Articles 31 and 33.[21] Likewise, the 1990 Schengen Convention obliges Member States to impose penalties on carriers transporting aliens who do not possess the necessary travel documents, 'subject to' the obligations arising out of the accession to the 1951 Refugee Convention.[22] Thus, while compatibility with refugee protection was declared as the principled objective, *no operational measures* were taken to that effect;[23] not less importantly, key provisions of these instruments could hardly be implemented without affecting refugees and asylum-seekers in a manner violating the 1951 Refugee Convention, formally claimed to prevail.

Finally, as the third and most recent approach, immigration control and asylum policies are gradually merging. Having defined the prevention of 'irregular' arrivals as the overall rationale, this seems to be a process in which the control strategy is bound to take over from the exigencies of refugee protection. A striking example of this trend in EU asylum policies will be presented and discussed later in this chapter.[24] At the general policy level, a recent draft strategy paper has revealed some

---

[19] *Ibid.*, at paras. 4–5. See also para. 3: '[s]uch harmonization could not be used as an excuse for reducing the humanitarian commitments they have entered into under the Geneva Convention'.

[20] European Commission, *Communication from the Commission to the Council and the European Parliament on Immigration and Asylum Policies*: COM(94)23 final; see in particular paras. 81, 85, 88, and 105.

[21] Art. 27 of the Draft Convention on the Crossing of the External Borders of the Member States of the EC: SN 2535/91 (WGI 829) (1991).

[22] Art. 26, Convention Applying the Schengen Agreement of 14 June 1985 between the Governments of the States of the Benelux Economic Union, the Federal Republic of Germany, and the French Republic on the Gradual Abolition of Checks at their Common Borders, Schengen, 19 June 1990, reprinted in H. Meijers *et al.*, *Schengen: Internationalisation of Central Chapters of the Law on Aliens, Refugees, Privacy, Security and Police* (1992), 177.

[23] Cf. Hathaway, note 15 above, at 731: '[w]hile the [Draft Convention on the Crossing of External Borders] pays lip service to the legal rights of refugees, it contains no specific exemptions in fact to address the needs of genuine asylum seekers'. See also note 82, at 731–2.

[24] See IV. B. 4., below.

support for this approach.[25] Although both have caused concern about the EU's genuine commitment to human rights principles, a crucial question is to what extent the Treaty of Amsterdam may give such control-determined positions a chance to be substituted by a more significant role for protection norms and values.

3. Deficiencies of the Third-pillar Co-operation Ever since the entry into force of Title VI of the EU Treaty, various forms of criticism have been raised against the functioning of asylum and immigration policies under the Maastricht system. The issues and premises of this criticism appear to be partly divergent, in so far as some discutants have been focusing on substance in the texts adopted, while others were more concerned with organizational issues; redesigning the institutional framework was sometimes seen as the key to solving substantive problems as well. The most important criticism has been addressing the efficiency of the third-pillar co-operation; its impact on the domestic law of Member States; issues of consistency with relevant norms and principles of international law; and problems of democratic and judicial control. While the latter problems will be discussed in the following analysis of the Treaty of Amsterdam, the issues of efficiency and legal impact will be dealt with here.

As an indication of the lack of *efficiency* of harmonization activities under the third pillar, reference has been made to the limited output of instruments, compared to what might have been foreseen under Articles K.1 and K.3 (now Articles 29 and 31) of the EU Treaty. Instead, traditional non-binding instruments such as resolutions and recommendations have been resorted to more or less in the same manner as was practised under the pre-Maastricht inter-governmental co-operation.[26] Reasons for this may be the absence of specification in the Treaty about which legal measures should be taken, on which policy issues, and within which time frame. Furthermore, the fact that decisions require unanimity obviously can explain the lack of (formal) efficiency in the adoption of instruments. The organizational structure of the third pillar of the Union has also been mentioned as part of the explanation for slow movement towards harmonization; a rather complicated decision-making procedure has surrounded the so-called K.4 Committee, yet subsequently modified. This may be due entirely to Member States' reluctance to enter into binding commitments to harmonize asylum policies. Whatever the reason, the outcome does not suggest that the framework invented in Maastricht was the guarantor of fast and efficient harmonization.[27]

As far as the *impact* of harmonization efforts is concerned, the *non-binding* nature of most third-pillar instruments provides much explanation of why they may not have been implemented effectively by Member States. It must be taken into account, though, that the legally binding status of EC/EU instruments is not decisive to the degree of implementation at the domestic level. As an example one could mention

---

[25] 'Note from the Presidency to the K.4 Committee: Strategy Paper on Immigration and Asylum Policy' (9804/98, ASIM 170) (1998).

[26] See generally R. Bank, 'The Emergent EU Policy on Asylum and Refugees: The New Framework Set by the Treaty of Amsterdam: A Landmark or a Standstill?', *Nordic Journal of International Law* (forthcoming, 1999).

[27] *Ibid.*, at 8: 'the creation of the third pillar and the introduction of asylum matters into this framework has been formulated in Art. K.1 TEU as an issue which should serve the purposes and aims of the EU. It can hardly be argued that this can be achieved by inaction.'

the 1992 (pre-Maastricht) London resolutions which apparently have had great impact on 'safe third-country' practices and the utilization of special procedures for 'manifestly unfounded' asylum applications in Member States.[28] In contradistinction, certain elements of the measures adopted under Title VI of the EU Treaty do not seem to be effectively implemented in domestic law.[29] Again, one has to realize that such lack of implementation is not just a result of the legal nature of these instruments. Another explanation can sometimes be found in the drafting process, and the political compromises that were made in order to obtain unanimity.[30]

As a consequence of this state of affairs, it has been suggested that Member States may in reality compose their 'Europe *à la carte*' by returning to the European harmonization argument if they want to change their laws and practices accordingly, but without having to accept the whole menu.[31] While such selective implementation certainly is a possibility inherent in the political and administrative flexibility and the legal nature of third-pillar harmonization under the EU Treaty, it may at the same time serve as an illustration of the problems of accountability and transparency, both in the legislative stages and in the implementation. Behind closed doors, decision-makers may be in a position to invoke domestic legal arguments in the drafting process; subsequently they may implement the EU instruments adopted, or they may not, yet still without transparency and legal or public scrutiny.

4. The Treaty of Amsterdam: Towards Communitarization   While the transfer of asylum and immigration policies from the third pillar to the first pillar of the Union was, in principle, provided for by Article K.9 (now Article 37) of the Maastricht EU Treaty, there never seems to have been any serious effort towards implementing this possibility of legal and institutional reform under the existing Treaty. Again, the lack of action may be seen as a result of the reluctance of Member States to commit themselves more formally to harmonization. Another possible explanation may be that they were well aware of the fact that the transfer of pillars would be on the agenda for the Inter-Governmental Conference stipulated to begin in 1996; this may obviously have been a disincentive for Member States to initiate the complex transfer discussion. Be that as it may, it is now clear that the outcome is a significant transfer of pillars regarding asylum and immigration policies.

As a background to the analysis of the EU asylum *acquis* we shall here briefly outline the impact of the Treaty of Amsterdam in this respect. The development towards communitarization of asylum and immigration policies occurs to varying degrees at different levels, i.e. the legal, the institutional, and the political level.

In a purely legal sense, the transfer of pillars has already taken place in the Treaty of Amsterdam. Under the new Title IV of the EC Treaty, visa, asylum, immigration,

---

[28]   EC Ministers Resolutions of 30 Nov.–1 Dec. 1992 on a Harmonized Approach to Questions Concerning Host Third Countries (SN 4823/92), and on Manifestly Unfounded Applications for Asylum (SN 2836/93, WGI 1505). See also Bank, note 26 above, at 10.

[29]   Cf. S. Peers, *Mind the Gap! Ineffective Member State Implementation of European Union Asylum Measures*, report prepared for the Immigration Law Practitioners' Association and the Refugee Council (1998).

[30]   See at IV. A. 3., mentioning the example of the Joint Position of 4 Mar. 1996 on the harmonized application of the definition of the term 'refugee'.

[31]   Bank, note 26 above, at 10.

and other policies related to the free movement of persons will be subject to the adoption of Community acts, as defined in Article 249 (*ex* Article 189). Thus, policy harmonization concerning asylum and immigration issues is going to take place in the form of traditional EC regulatory measures, binding upon Member States, and to a certain extent even directly applicable at the national level.

The political and institutional elements of communitarization, however, have been only half-heartedly included in the Treaty. During the transitional period of five years following the entry into force of the Treaty of Amsterdam, the adoption of policy measures under Title IV still requires unanimity, except for those decisions on visa requirements and visa uniform format which are already subject to qualified majority voting.[32] By the same token, the remaining measures concerning visa policies shall, after the five-year period, be adopted by the Council in accordance with the procedure under Article 251, i.e. by a qualified majority.[33] Hence, to the extent deficiencies in the Third Pillar co-operation can be attributed to the requirement of unanimous decision-making, there may be little hope for improvement during the first five years after the entry into force of the Amsterdam Treaty. Things may change after the transitional period, in so far as the Council shall then take a decision with a view to moving all or parts of the areas covered by Title IV into the qualified majority voting procedure under Article 251 (*ex* Article 189b).[34] The wording of this provision leaves some uncertainty about the real duration of the transitional period, in particular given that a decision to abandon the unanimity requirement must be taken unanimously. According to a declaration from the Inter-Governmental Conference, however, the future decision-making procedure will have to be revised at the end of the transitional period; thus preparations for the review must be made during this period.[35]

In terms of substance, it is noteworthy that a number of policy measures will have to be adopted within the five years after the entry force of the Treaty of Amsterdam, while others will not. There seems to have been a tendency to give more control-oriented measures priority here. As mentioned, visa policies will automatically be subject to majority voting. A number of other so-called flanking measures directly related to the free movement of persons, with respect to external border controls, asylum, and immigration, will have to be adopted within the transitional period, yet under the unanimity requirement, and thus with some political uncertainty. And importantly, certain measures bearing on refugee protection have expressly been exempted from the five-year time limit, such as the adoption of burden-sharing mechanisms pursuant to Article 63(2)(b) (*ex* Article 73k).[36]

[32] Art. 67(3) (*ex* Art. 73o) EC Treaty; cf. Art. 62(2)(b)(i) and (iii). See also the Maastricht EC Treaty Art. 100C(2) and (3) (now repealed).
[33] Art. 67(4) EC Treaty; cf. Art. 62(2)(b)(ii) and (iv).   [34] Art. 67(2) EC Treaty.
[35] Declaration on Art. 73o of the EC Treaty (Declaration No. 21 annexed to the Final Act of the Inter-Governmental Conference): '[t]he Conference agrees that the Council will examine the elements of the decision referred to in Article 73o(2), second indent, of the Treaty establishing the European Community before the end of the five year period referred to in Article 73o with a view to taking and applying this decision immediately after the end of that period'.
[36] See below at IV. C. 2.

B. Transparency, Accountability, and Judicial Control

As previously mentioned, much of the criticism of third-pillar EU co-operation has been focusing on problems of democratic and judicial control. From both a legal and a political viewpoint there has been concern about the low level of transparency in decision-making in Justice and Home Affairs. Strong tendencies towards secret decision-making under the 1990 Schengen Convention and within the EC co-operation on asylum and immigration policies were not remedied by the 1992 Maastricht Treaty, as the third pillar basically suffered from many of the same deficiencies regarding democratic and judicial control.[37] Thus, the Parliament has a rather marginal role, at best of a consultative nature, subject to the discretionary initiative of the Presidency and the Commission. The Court of Justice is, practically speaking, absent in this part of the Treaty, being given only a potential competence by conventions drawn up under Article K.3(2)(c) (now Article 31).[38]

These features of the third-pillar co-operation have been characterized as incompatible with fundamental principles of democracy and the rule of law. Not only would decisions normally be made in secret, but in certain circumstances the secrecy might even extend to the contents of policy decisions. Leaving aside the issue of democratic accountability of decision-makers at the EU level, it would often be difficult to establish the exact role of individual Member States in connection with the adoption of policy measures. At the domestic level, this would similarly result in non-transparent decisions on the implementation of EU instruments, likely to be much of the reason for the 'Europe *à la carte*' development earlier described.[39] Furthermore, due to the lack of jurisdiction of the Court of Justice, the opportunities for challenging the instruments adopted, as well as their implementation in national law, were equally lacking.

Have the hopes for improvement been met by the Treaty of Amsterdam? To some extent the answer is yes. Yet there are still deficiencies, some of which will not be remediable even after the transitional period of five years. As regards *transparency* and *democratic influence*, the role of the Parliament will gradually be increased, first, because the Council must consult the Parliament when acting on a proposal from the Commission or on the initiative of a Member State. This procedure will already exist during the transitional period, cf. Article 67(1) (*ex* Article 73o). Secondly, the procedure under Title IV may eventually be changed, in whole or in part, to be governed by Article 251 (*ex* Article 189b) providing the Parliament with significant competence. It has to be seen to what extent this could result in effective influence on the substance of decisions, and in which direction the Parliament might then influence the harmonization of asylum and immigration policies. The Parliament has, so far, been less restrictive and more focused on human rights protection than the Council and many Member States. This is obviously not bound to persist; furthermore, it seems uncer-

[37] Cf. D. Curtin and H. Meijers, 'The Principle of Open Government in Schengen and the European Union: Democratic Retrogression?' in H. Meijers *et al.*, *Democracy, Migrants and Police in the European Union. The 1996 IGC and Beyond* (1997), 13–44.
[38] See C. Groenendijk, 'The European Court of Justice and the Third Pillar' in *ibid.*, at 45–59.
[39] Bank, note 26 above, at 10; see above at III. A. 3.

tain whether the Parliament would be able to steer future humanitarian priorities through to the final decision-making process.

Not least importantly, transparency will be enhanced as a result of public access to proposed legislative acts at a much earlier point in time than is the case for the third-pillar co-operation. This improvement of the conditions for democratic debate and openness will already materialize during the transitional period, as the Parliament must be consulted on each proposal, even while having no formalized competence. In the same vein, consultation will be established with the United Nations High Commissioner for Refugees (UNHCR) and other relevant international organizations on matters relating to asylum policy.[40] This should provide for increased, and at least more systematic, dialogue on protection-related issues, contrary to the present situation where the attitudes of the incumbent Presidency seem to have been quite decisive in this respect.

With regard to *judicial control*, however, the solution provided for by the Treaty of Amsterdam is less satisfactory. According to Article 68 (*ex* Article 73p) of the EC Treaty, there will be access to preliminary rulings from the Court of Justice where a question on the interpretation of Title IV or on the validity or interpretation of EC acts based on this Title is raised in a case pending before a court or a tribunal of a Member State against whose decisions there is no judicial remedy under national law. This implies two significant constraints on the role of the Court of Justice in comparison with the general jurisdiction to give preliminary rulings under Article 234 (*ex* Article 177): Firstly, it is only possible to have a preliminary ruling when an asylum or immigration case is pending before a court or a tribunal of *last instance*; under Article 234 lower courts, too, may request the Court of Justice to give a ruling. Secondly, even in the last instance (final court of appeal) access to a preliminary ruling is conditioned upon the court or the tribunal considering that a decision on the question is necessary to enable it to give judgment. This seems to give national courts and tribunals a certain amount of discretion when deciding whether to submit an issue to the Court of Justice; pursuant to Article 234, such discretion can be exercised by the lower courts, while courts and tribunals of final appeal are obliged to bring relevant matters before the Court of Justice.

The fact that judicial control at the EC level is thus contingent upon discretionary decisions at the level of national courts is likely to weaken the effective implementation of harmonization measures under Title IV.[41] It seems evident that the limited access to preliminary rulings within the area of asylum and immigration results from a perceived risk of overburdening the Court, and correspondingly causing delay in cases pending before national courts. Such fear may be well-founded, or it may be exaggerated; it is beyond doubt, though, that the arrangement under Article 68 (*ex* Article 73p) reduces the legal safeguards for individuals. It may also result in the reduced effectiveness of harmonization measures, by domestic courts competent to prevent themselves from being bound by preliminary rulings.

---

[40] See Declaration on Art. 73k of the EC Treaty, Declaration No. 17 annexed to the Final Act of the Inter-Governmental Conference.
[41] Cf. Bank, note 26 above, at 29–31.

Exemptions from judicial control at the EC level will exist where issues of national security can be invoked by a Member State. According to Article 64 (*ex* Article 73l), Title IV shall not affect the exercise of the responsibilities incumbent upon Member States with regard to the maintenance of law and order and the safeguarding of internal security. It may be questioned whether the establishment of such security issues may in itself restrain the competence of the Court of Justice. This appears inconceivable, though, not only because it would render judicial control partly ineffective, but also due to the wording of the Treaty itself. Article 68(2) provides that the Court of Justice shall not have jurisdiction to rule on any measure or decision taken pursuant to Article 62(1) (*ex* Article 73j(1)) relating to the maintenance of law and order and the safeguarding of internal security. The express exemption of specific security-related measures makes it clear that the Court is otherwise competent under such circumstances; at least, this competence allows the Court to review the validity of the security reasons invoked by a Member State under Article 64 (*ex* Article 73l).

It is important to notice that the exemption of the Court's jurisdiction under Article 68(2) relates only to measures with a view to ensuring the absence of controls on persons crossing *internal* borders. Hence, judicial control can be curtailed only to a limited extent due to circumstances affecting the maintenance of law and order or the internal security of a Member State.

IV. AREAS OF POLICY HARMONIZATION; THE EU ASYLUM *ACQUIS*

A. Protection Categories

1. The Acquis *and Protection Categories*   In part II, B., refugee protection was identified as a subsidiary means of human rights protection. Of critical importance is the question who is determined to be a beneficiary of that system. Why is that so? To identify categories of persons entitled to some form of international protection also means to set the parameters for the whole system. By way of example, the legal logic underlying the 1951 Refugee Convention requires that the persons claiming to be its beneficiary are entitled to a determination procedure. The same logic requires that such procedure will be adapted to identify the existence of facts relevant for the Convention's definition. This goes to show that protection categories function as systemic centrepieces, towards which each single part of the system is geared.

How were protection categories emanating from refugee law, human rights law, and domestic law handled within the EU co-operation on Justice and Home Affairs? To be sure, the paramount importance of landmark instruments in the field has been acknowledged by the EU Council, when it made clear that the 1951 Convention as well as the 1967 Protocol are part of the EU *acquis* in the fields of Justice and Home Affairs. Both instruments have been qualified as 'inseparable from the realization of the Union's objectives', and, consequently, States aspiring tor Union membership must accede to them.[42]

The European Convention on Human Rights (ECHR) has been endowed with the same status; accession to it now forms a precondition for candidate States' entry into the Union. Protocols Nos. 4, 6, and 7 to the ECHR also form part of the *acquis*, but merely on a non-obligatory basis.[43] It should be noted, though, that the ECHR and its protocols do not figure under the heading of asylum in the draft list of the *acquis*, but rather under the less specific heading of human rights.

However, recognizing the importance of the named three instruments does not imply that Member States are well on the way to a common system of protection categories. The rationale of harmonized categories is to counter an evolving market mechanism, where States compete to minimize the number of applications they will receive by restricting the categories of beneficiaries. Such competition would be detrimental not only for persons in need of protection, but also for the interest of those Member States whose burden of reception is increased by their more successful competitors.

Therefore, it comes as little surprise that the Commission's 1994 Communication on Asylum and Immigration Policy identifies three subjects of harmonization. The first is the refugee definition, the second relates to 'policies concerning those who cannot be admitted as refugees, but whom Member States would nevertheless not require to return to their country of origin in view of the general prevailing situation in that country', and the third to temporary protection.[44]

But a requirement of harmonization also flows from the operation of the Dublin Convention. As explained below, this instrument denies a claimant the right to choose between different countries of asylum in the EU. From the perspective of the claimant, predictability and equality in treatment require Member States to operate protection categories under international law with identical material scope.[45]

Thus, a successful harmonization of categories needs to fulfill two basic requirements: It has to be all-encompassing and binding. It will not do to harmonize some categories, while leaving others to the free interplay of forces. First and foremost, any legal instrument purporting to create uniform definitions of beneficiaries must be formally binding as such. But the categories posited in it need also be sufficiently concrete and devoid of any deference to national law in order to be effective.

[42] Item note from the Presidency to Coreper, 'Draft list of the "acquis" of the Union and of its Member States in the field of Justice and Home Affairs'. Doc. No. 6437/2/98 REV 3 (20 Mar. 1998) (hereinafter Draft List), para. I. A. b.

[43] *Ibid.*, at para. XII. A. b. and D. Prots. 4, 6, and 7 to the ECHR are considerered as 'instruments which have not all been signed and/or ratified by all Member States, and the Member States are not mutually bound to ratify them, although in the case of some of them there is a political commitment by their Governments to initiate the internal process of ratification. States applying to join the European Union should endeavour to become parties to these Conventions on the same basis as the Member States': *ibid.*, Introduction. Prot. 6 is of special interest in this context, as it contains a provision on the abolishment of the death penalty in Art. 1. See also Final Act of the Treaty of Amsterdam, Declaration on the Abolitition of the Death Penalty, CONF 4007/97, AF/TA/en2.

[44] SEC(91)1857, note 18 above, at 42, paras. 6, 8, and 9.

[45] This was acknowledged in a discussion paper on subsidiary protection prepared by the Danish delegation for the EU Council: note by the Danish delegation to the Migration and Asylum Working Parties, 'Subsidiary Protection', Doc. No. 6746/97 ASIM 52 (17 Mar. 1997), 4.

2. The Scope of Harmonization   Hitherto, the only attempt to come to terms with
the definitional and interpretational disparity between Member States[46] is the 1996
'Joint Position Defined by the Council on the basis of Article K.3 of the Treaty on
European Union on the harmonized application of the definition of the term
"Refugee" in Article 1 of the Geneva Convention of 28 July 1951 relating to the sta-
tus of refugees'.[47] The very existence of the 1996 joint position gives proof of an as-
piration to inhibit this kind of market mechanism in a spirit of solidarity between
Member States, which is perfectly in line with the principle of solidarity laid down in
Article 1 (*ex* Article A) TEU. It is all the more lamentable that this effort has to fail
on purely formal grounds. A mere look at paragraph 3 of the preamble confirms that
Member States were not prepared to revamp their domestic asylum systems for the
sake of harmonization:

> This joint position is adopted within the limits of the constitutional powers of the
> Governments of the Member States; it shall not bind the legislative authorities or affect
> decisions of the judicial authorities of the Member states.

Whatever the mandatory force of a joint position may be, this paragraph clearly indicates the non-binding nature of the definitional efforts enshrined in the instrument.[48] By way of conclusion, neither the requirement of all-encompassing
harmonization nor that of bindingness has been satisfied hitherto. The task of harmonization still remains the responsibility of the informal spiral of restriction described above.[49] But apart from these functional reflections on the all-encompassing
nature of harmonization, it is striking to see that a human rights protection category
is conspicuously absent from the legislative work of the EU Council. This absence
need not imply its non-recognition, as the case law of the European Court of Justice
with relation to Article 3 ECHR generally enjoys acceptance amongst Member
States.[50] It is, however, of concern that the triad of refugee law, human rights law,
and domestic categories is presently reduced to a duality of refugee law and domestic categories by the EU Council. The wording of paragraph 1 of the 1996 joint position is indicative in this regard:

> This document relates to implementation of the criteria as defined in Article 1 of [the
> 1951 Refugee] Convention. It in no way affects the conditions under which a Member
> State may, according to its national law, permit a person to remain in its territory if his
> safety or physical integrity would be endangered if he were to return to his country be-
> cause of circumstances which are not covered by the Geneva Convention but which con-
> stitute a reason for not returning him to his country of origin.

Lamentably, Article 63(1)(c) (*ex* Article 73k) of the EC Treaty seems to perpetuate
this reductive approach to protection categories. It stipulates that, within five

---

[46] On the disparate interpretation of the refugee definition, see generally J.-Y. Carlier *et al.* (eds.), *Who is a Refugee? A Comparative Case Law Study* (1997).

[47] [1996] OJ L63. According to the draft list, this instrument is part of the *acquis*.

[48] Apparently, the cited para. was inserted on the intitative of the British and German delegations. See J. van der Klaauw, 'Refugee Protection in Western Europe: A UNHCR Perspective' in J.-Y. Carlier and D. Vanheule (eds.), *Europe and Refugees: A Challenge?* (1997), 240.

[49] See II. B. above.

[50] Some Member States relate explicitly or implicitly to the ECHR in domestic law. See, e.g., s. 53(4) of the German Aliens Act and Chap. 3, s. 3(1) of the Swedish Aliens Act.

years after the entry into force of the Treaty of Amsterdam, the Council shall adopt:

> (1) measures on asylum, in accordance with the Geneva Convention of 28 July 1951 and the Protocol of 31 January 1967 relating to the status of refugees and other relevant treaties, within the following areas:
>
> . . .
>
> > (c) minimum standards with respect to the qualification of nationals of third countries as refugees.

The wording of this provision must be reasonably understood to cover exclusively a harmonized interpretation of the 1951 Refugee Convention definition, as it expressly refers to the 'qualification . . . as refugees'.

It could be asked, though, whether Article 63(2)(a) should be regarded as an obligation on the Council to posit human rights-based protection categories within the same five-year time-frame. The Council shall adopt:

> (2) measures on refugees and displaced persons within the following areas:
> > (a) minimum standards for giving temporary protection to displaced persons from third countries who cannot return to their country of origin and for persons who otherwise need international protection

A careful reading suggests an affirmative answer, as this provision actually covers two groups for which certain minimum standards shall be devised. One will contain certain displaced persons from third countries, and the other would consist of persons who otherwise need international protection. It should be noted that there is no express reference to the qualification of beneficiaries as in Article 63(1)(c). It could be argued that Article 63(2)(a) would allow for a stipulation of categories by the EU Council without laying down an obligation to do so. Presently, Member States seem to accept this provision as a basis for deliberations on the harmonization of protection based on human rights instruments.[51]

The discourse on temporary protection has indicated that Member States have been reluctant to define categories of beneficiaries of such an order. This reluctance is expressed quite unambiguously in the 'Council Resolution on Burden-Sharing with Regard to Admission and Residence of Displaced Persons on a Temporary Basis of 25 September 1995'.[52] Its personal scope comprises various categories of vulnerable persons 'whom Member States are prepared to admit on a temporary basis under appropriate conditions in the event of armed conflict or civil war, including where such persons have already left their region of origin to go to one of the Member States'.[53] Clearly, these categories must be taken as mere exemplifications without any definite character. The European Commission's proposal for a 'Joint Action on Temporary Protection'[54] uses the same technique of exemplifying rather

---

[51] One could also argue that Art. 63(3)(b), covering measures on illegal immigration, could lend itself as a basis for an express exemption of categories protected from repatriation. This alternative appears, however, somewhat far-fetched.

[52] [1995] OJ C262/1. According to the draft list, this instrument is part of the *acquis*.

[53] *Ibid.*, Art. 1(a).

[54] Amended proposal for a joint action concerning temporary protection of displaced persons (presented by the Commission pursuant to Art. 189a(2) of the EC Treaty): COM(1998)372 final/2.

than defining. Article 1 of this proposal contains a non-exhaustive list of beneficiary groups, at best serving inspirational purposes. Article 3 regulates how a temporary protection regime is initiated in a given situation. A relevant Council decision shall also determine the groups of beneficiaries. This solution may be characterized as an *ad hoc* harmonization of protection categories. While it retains a great margin of discretion for Member States in picking and choosing categories of beneficiaries for a given Temporary Protection regime, Article 3 of the Proposal has the advantage of blocking the spiral of restriction for the period after the launching of the regime.

As a consequence of a Danish initiative within the Council, a questionnaire on protection subsidiary to the 1951 Refugee Convention has been circulated amongst Member States.[55] Moreover, a study on the same subject has been undertaken by the Secretariat of the Council.[56] It is too early yet to predict the outcome of this initiative. For the functional reasons expounded above, the present state of affairs is clearly dissatisfying, as continued divergence between protection categories may result in reception inequalities between Member States as well as protection differences for individuals. It follows that future co-operation needs to widen the scope of harmonization from the refugee definition to other categories and has to be given a binding and concrete form devoid of exceptions.

3. The Substantial Content of the 1996 Joint Position In the preceding sub-section, we addressed the formal aspects of harmonization. Nevertheless, the sole achievement of category harmonization—the 1996 joint position—also has some material implications worthy of reflection. Thus, before adopting a 'measure' under Article 63(1)(c) (*ex* Article 73k), the criticism directed against the content of the 1996 joint position should be contemplated by the Member States. This criticism has been focusing mainly on the issue of the extent to which the 1951 Refugee Convention offers protection to the victims of persecution by third parties.[57]

Generally, the following situations must be kept distant when discussing persecution by third parties:

1. Persecution by state agents.
2. Acquiescence by state agents of persecution carried out by non-state agents.
3. Incapacity of state agents to hinder persecution carried out by non-state agents.

Cases of direct violations under the first and second categories are rather unproblematic in this context, while the third category represents the focal point of the dispute on persecution by third parties. Precisely as in the second category, violations are committed by private actors. But unlike the second category, however, the State

[55] Note from the General Secretariat of the Council to the Migration and Asylum Working Parties, 'Summary of replies concerning the national instruments of protection falling outside the scope of the Geneva Convention—Subsidiary protection': Doc. No. 13667/97 ASIM 267 (6 Jan. 1998).

[56] Note from the General Secretariat of the Council to the Migration and Asylum Working Parties, 'Study on the international instruments relevant to subsidiary protection': Doc. No. 10175/98 ASIM 178 (13 July 1998).

[57] See UNHCR RO Bonn, Press Release, 'UNHCR äussert Bedenken zur europäischen Asylpolitik', 24 Nov. 1995. ECRE, 'Note from the European Council on Refugees and Exiles on the Harmonization of the Interpretation of Article 1 of the 1951 Geneva Convention', June 1995.

is simply unable to offer protection. In extreme cases, inability to control is due to the vanishing of State structures altogether. For the latter situation, the term 'failed State' has been introduced. In times when civil war has become the dominant form of armed conflict, the implications for protection under the 1951 Refugee Convention, in terms of the numbers likely to be involved, can hardly be overestimated.

A comparative analysis commissioned by the Dutch Ministry of Foreign Affairs concludes that for Canada, the UK, Sweden, Italy, and the Dutch District Court (*Arrondissementsrechtbank*) governmental complicity in persecution is not essential, while the opposite is true for Germany, Switzerland, France, and the Dutch Council of State (*Raad van State*).[58]

The 1996 joint position mirrors the difference in interpretation between individual Member States in a very graphic fashion. To start with, paragraph 5.2 of the 1996 joint position states that:

> Persecution by third parties will be considered to fall within the scope of the Geneva Convention where it is based on one of the grounds in Article 1A, is individual in nature and is encouraged or permitted by the authorities. Where the official authorities fail to act, such persecution should give rise to individual examination of each application for refugee status, in accordance with national judicial practice, in the light in particular of whether or not the failure to act was deliberate. The persons concerned may be eligible in any event for appropriate forms of protection under national law.

This wording was the result of a French compromise proposal, mediating between inclusionary and exclusionary positions.[59] It seems to suggest deliberateness in state failure to act as the guiding criterion without entirely clarifying the consequences. One reading would be that such cases are either excluded from protection at large, or at least from protection offered under the 1951 Refugee Convention. Such a reading would point to the argument that the establishment of a guiding criterion is meaningless if free choice between inclusion under and exclusion from the scope of the 1951 Refugee Convention was intended to continue. But it could also be argued that the wording does not expressly inhibit States from including such cases under the scope of the 1951 Refugee Convention. This interpretation would point to the wording, 'in accordance with national judicial practice', in the second sentence and, 'in any event', in the third sentence as indicators of such a discretionary margin. More problematic than this ambiguity, though, is the fact that paragraph 5.2 condones the existence of irreconcilable interpretations of the refugee definition.

However, one Member State felt the need to state that the third category may very well be included under the scope of the 1951 Refugee Convention. In a statement for the Council Minutes, the Swedish delegation said it was:

> of the opinion that persecution by third parties falls within the scope of the 1951 Geneva Convention where it is encouraged or permitted by the authorities. It may also fall within the scope of the Convention in other cases, when the authorities prove unable to offer protection.

---

[58] B. Vermeulen *et al.*, *Persecution by Third Parties* (1998), 34.
[59] For the drafting history of the 1996 joint position, see *ibid.*, at 31–2.

This clear divergence proves a point made earlier, namely the limited harmonization potential of the 1996 joint position. It gives rise to concern, though, that a restrictive position gained entry to the document, while the inclusive position was relegated to a mere interpretatory statement. The least that can be said about the 1996 joint position is that it offers a presumption for the exclusion of cases under the third category.

Ultimately, the dispute on persecution by third parties hinges on the choice between particularism and universalism. The universalist approach focuses on the protective needs of the individual and denies a contingency of extraterritorial protection on state agency. Instead, it seeks to establish a direct legal relationship between the victim of a violation and the State from which extraterritorial protection is sought. The particularist approach relies mainly on an idea of international law as an inter-State phenomenon. Without state agency, there is no attributability of violations to a State. Without attributability, the violation is beyond the protective scope of international refugee law. In the case of failed States, particularists have to accept that the obligation to protect human rights vanishes in a black hole in the universe of state responsibility.

What would be a viable base for trespassing the ambiguity of the 1996 joint position in a future measure under Article 63(1)(c) (*ex* Article 73k)?

First, it has been shown that it is illogical to exclude *persecution* by third parties from the scope of the 1951 Refugee Convention while operating the concept of internal flight to the extent that it relies on the *protection* of third parties.[60] While third-party activities are stated not to have a bearing on the availability of extraterritorial protection in the former case, the opposite is true in the latter. Thus, legal coherence would be promoted if issues of persecution by third parties, 'failed States', civil war, and internal flight alternatives were dealt with in an interrelated manner.

Secondly, normative coherence would also demand that account be taken of the case law of the European Court of Human Rights. The Court has summarized its position by stating that the 'principle' of extraterritorial protection under Article 3 ECHR:

> has so far been applied by the Court in contexts in which the risk to the individual of being subjected to any of the proscribed forms of treatment emanates from intentionally inflicted acts of the public authorities in the receiving country or from those of non-state bodies in that country when the authorities there are unable to afford appropriate protection.[61]

This position has been further expounded elsewhere in the Court's case law.[62]

While the European Court of Human Rights refrained from formulating a theoretical base for its findings, the doctrine of negative and positive obligations fits well as an explicatory framework. By signing human rights instruments, States have taken upon themselves a negative obligation to refrain from violating certain rights, as well as a positive obligation to protect certain rights. This positive obligation includes cases in which third parties act as perpetrators. Clearly, failure to protect may

---

[60] For the drafting history of the 1996 joint position, 14 and 22.
[61] *D* v. *UK*, ECHR Reports 1997–III, No. 37, at para. 49.
[62] *Chahal* v. *UK*, ECHR Reports 1996–V, No. 22; *Ahmed* v. *Austria*, ECHR Reports 1996–VI, No. 26; *HLR* v. *France*, ECHR Reports 1997–III, No. 36.

also represent a human rights violation when intention by the State is lacking. Thus, a particularist and restrictive reading of the 1951 Refugee Convention with regard to the third category would bring it at odds with the underlying structure of human rights law at large.

It should be emphasized that persecution by third parties is not the only issue on which Member States diverge in their interpretation of the 1951 Refugee Convention. By way of example, the question whether gender-related cases of persecution are within the scope of this instrument is far from clear in European practice. The 1996 joint position is silent on the issue, while strong legal arguments militate for the inclusion of such cases on the grounds of political opinion, religion, or membership of a particular social group.[63] A future instrument under Article 63(1)(c) would provide an opportunity to augment coherence in this regard.

4. The Future of Protection Categories in Europe   Given the importance of protection categories as steering parameters for the whole system of protection, how is the latter affected by the current normative and political developments? The preceding analysis has exposed the following problems:

- The harmonization of protection categories lacks bindingness and comprehensiveness.
- As long as the framework of temporary protection contains no protection category in its own right, it is unfit for harmonization purposes.
- No provision is made for a protection category based on norms of human rights law prohibiting *refoulement*.
- Areas of protection properly covered by the 1951 Refugee Convention or human rights instruments such as the ECHR are relegated to national law and the normative grey zone of temporary protection.
- The scope of the protection category contained in the 1951 Refugee Convention is restricted by the exclusion of persecution by third parties which the State is incapable of controlling.

It is not easy to offer a diagnosis based on the variety of symptoms dealt with above. One possible reading would be that Member States' consensus does not go further than a restrictively interpreted 1951 Refugee Convention as the sole mandatory basis for protection, apart from a highly discretionary framework of either national law categories or a harmonized form of temporary protection. To say the least, such a conception would not only stretch the ordinary canons of interpretation with regard to the 1951 Refugee Convention, but also represent a systemic disregard of the protection imperatives enshrined in human rights law.[64]

---

[63] See generally H. Crawley, *Women as Asylum Seekers: A Legal Handbook* (1997); T. Spijkerboer, *Women and Refugee Status* (1994); K. Folkelius and G. Noll, 'Affirmative Exclusion? Sex, Gender, Persecution and the Reformed Swedish Aliens Act' (forthcoming 1999 in *IJRL*).

[64] The move from law to discretion would be exacerbated if Member States permitted themselves to postpone refugee determination under a temporary protection regime. The Commission's Proposal accomodates such decisions of postponement under national law. See its Art. 10(2).

B. Controlling or Preventing Arrival

1. Introductory Remarks on Non-admission and Non-arrival Policies   The commitment to refugee protection is not exclusively a matter of protecting refugees who come within the jurisdiction of European States and request asylum in their territories. Although territorial asylum traditionally is the core feature of protection, and the present refugee regime was premised on the idea of free access to apply for asylum for those who managed to get out of their country of origin, it has become even more evident that protection needs go further than that. For many refugees moving to Europe or other developed regions is simply not an option, due to a variety of circumstances forcing them to remain within their region of origin.

In recent years this reality has been systematically reinforced by the policies of the very same States that were traditionally open to persons in search of protection. An array of mechanisms introduced by EU Member States since the mid-1980s have the effect of blocking access to European asylum procedures. While such policies are normally justified as combating illegal immigration and abuse of the asylum system, they have significantly changed the balance between immigration control and refugee protection. As further analysed below, these policies have undoubtedly been detrimental to the latter.

The existence of protection needs outside the EU territories is a fact that has to be taken into account within the framework of the common foreign and security policy, the objectives of which include the development and consolidation of respect for human rights and fundamental freedoms.[65] Devising mechanisms of extra-territorial protection is all the more called for as the needs partly result from the policies of the EU and its Member States. To the extent that protection problems remain unsolved, and are possibly even increased, by the asylum policies pursued, they ought to be met with compensating foreign policy measures. It is therefore relevant to look at policies and practices having the effect of 'externalizing' the problems of refugee protection.

Some procedural mechanisms can be seen as features of a *non-admission* policy, because they set up restrictive criteria of admissibility to the asylum procedure.[66] These mechanisms may reflect an inadequate balance between control and protection, yet they are still based on the principle that each and every asylum application must be examined on its merits. On the other hand, the policies discussed here are characterized by the *absence* of examination of applications; they operate as barriers for asylum-seekers to access a jurisdiction where they could seek protection and receive it, if necessary. Such policies simply keep asylum-seekers 'from the procedural door',[67] in the sense that they aim to prevent them from having their refugee status determined and their need for protection examined. This phenomenon can therefore be most precisely described as *non-arrival*[68] policies. At worst, they may result in exposing people to the risk of persecution, by blocking their flight from the country of

---

[65] Art. 11(1) (*ex* Art. J.1) EU Treaty.   [66] See IV. D, below.
[67] G.S. Goodwin-Gill, *The Refugee in International Law* (1996), 333.
[68] The notion of *non-entrée* covers largely the same phenomenon: see J.C. Hathaway, 'The Emerging Politics of Non-Entrée' (1992) 91 *Refugees* 40–1.

origin or their onwards movement from unsafe transit countries from which they may be forcibly returned to the home country.

The legal mechanism around which non-admission and non-arrival policies have evolved is the requirement that citizens of certain States must be in possession of a visa to enter EU Member States. While visa policy as such is a traditional and legitimate element of States' control over the entry of foreigners to their territory, the *enforcement* of such requirements is the crucial matter from a human rights perspective. As long as compliance with visa requirements is being monitored by the country of destination, it is a normal feature of sovereign border control aimed at persons within its jurisdiction; this jurisdiction has to be exercised in conformity with international law, and accordingly entails the responsibility of the acting State.

European States have devised methods largely moving the control *away* from their own frontiers, thus apparently absolving themselves of the responsibilities that would otherwise be incurred. As the balance between immigration control and refugee protection is shifting, and control is 'externalized' to take place outside the territory of the State of destination, responsibility under international law may eventually become diffused. The extent to which this objective is actually achieved depends on the specific mechanisms employed by States.[69] Various legal notions have been introduced in this connection, some of which are turning into legal fictions, as will become clear from the following.

The particular role of the EU in this development of externalized immigration control is twofold. Under the harmonized policies visa requirements have been adopted for almost every country whose nationals would statistically have a well-founded claim to refugee status; although Member States might have invented similar policies on their own, the EU harmonization of visa policies implies that Member States are bound to adhere to such measures designed to prevent the arrival of asylum-seekers.[70] Furthermore, the means of control have been harmonized in a way which reinforces the tendencies of externalization. In sum, both the substantive policies and the enforcement measures adopted at the EU level are such that the Union must be considered an important actor in the development of non-arrival policies, and therefore ought to take this into account in designing future asylum *and* foreign policies bearing on refugee protection.

2. Carrier Sanctions   The combination of visa requirements and sanctions on transport carriers for bringing passengers without a valid passport and visa engages carriers in immigration control. This mechanism reduces the costs of control and asylum procedures, and it may as well relieve States of their responsibility for actions taken by private companies. Their document inspection takes place within a framework not formally defined as border control. In reality, however, transport companies act under the instruction of States, under threat of being sanctioned for non-compliance.

---

[69] Cf. Goodwin-Gill, note 67 above, at 141–5 and 252; J.C. Hathaway and J.A. Dent, *Refugee Rights: Report on a Comparative Survey* (1995), 10–17.

[70] Council Reg. 2317/95 determining the third countries whose nationals must be in possession of a visa, adopted in pursuance of Art. 100 C EC Treaty [1995] OJ L234/1; see also Joint Action of 4 Mar. 1996, adopted by the Council on the basis of Art. K. 3 (now Art. 31) of the EU Treaty, on airport transit arrangements [1996] OJ L63/8.

From the nature of the sanctions system it seems to follow that carriers' refusal of embarcation is part of the enforcement of visa policies. Although indirect in terms of organizational setting, this is an expression of state sovereignty, like that carried out at the border of arrival. It is therefore arguable that it implies responsibility for the State engaged, in an essentially similar way to cases of ordinary exercise of jurisdiction. This obviously runs counter to the total absence of human rights considerations and the failure to introduce specific regulations for undocumented passengers in need of protection. Therefore, as concluded by various experts, the effects of carrier sanctions are incompatible with basic norms and principles of international refugee law.[71]

Notwithstanding its legal objectionability, this mechanism of immigration control has become even more widespread since the mid-1980s; perceived as efficient and at the same time invisible, it seems to be so well-established that it is rather unlikely to be discarded by States. Instead, international air transportation standards have been amended so as better to fit with this control strategy.[72] Particularly interesting in the context of EU asylum policies, carrier sanctions have been codified as a compulsory control mechanism under the 1990 Schengen Convention,[73] now in the process of being integrated into EU/EC law in consequence of the Treaty of Amsterdam.[74]

3. Extra-territorial State Jurisdiction   Another version of 'external' control is the practice of some European States of posting immigration officers at their diplomatic missions in countries from which they want to reduce exit movements towards their borders. While these officers' jobs may partly be ordinary administrative activities, there are quite worrying examples of functions with evident human rights implications. Being carried out by official state authorities, such control functions effectively breach the illusion of privatized control so far asserted in relation to carrier sanctions.

Relatively little information has been published about these external (im)migration control activities. However, posted immigration officers have been reported to carry out training of airlines' check-in staff in airports which might serve as exit points for passengers with false documents or no documents at all.[75] This is already tantamount to taking over important elements of the functions from transport companies whose private organization might otherwise be the legitimate basis of delegating control, and thereby also responsibility.

[71] UNHCR, *Transport Carriers and Refugee Protection*, Working Paper for the Tenth Session of the ICAO Facilitation Division, ICAO Doc. FAL/10–WP/123 (1988); H. Meijers, 'Possibilities for Guaranteeing Transport to Refugees' in M. Kjærum (ed.), *The Role of Airline Companies in the Asylum Procedure* (1988), 17; E. Feller, 'Carrier Sanctions and International Law' (1989) 1 *IJRL* 48.
[72] Cf. J. Vedsted-Hansen, 'Amendments to the ICAO Standards on Carriers' Liability in Relation to Immigration Control' in M. Kjærum (ed.), *The Effects of Carrier Sanctions on the Asylum System* (1991), 23.
[73] Art. 26 of the 1990 Schengen Convention obliges States Parties to introduce carrier sanctions.
[74] Prot. to the Amsterdam Treaty, integrating the Schengen *acquis* into the framework of the EU. This is not the first attempt to introduce carrier sanctions as a formal element of EC law; a provision to the same effect was included in Art. 14 of the 1991 Draft Convention on the Crossing of the External Borders of the Member States of the EC (SN 2535/91 (WGI 829) (1991)).
[75] See, e.g., Danish Immigration Service, *Rapport om udlændingeattachéer* (Report on immigration attachés) (1997).

European immigration officers also personally carry out control of travel documents in foreign airports; in doing so, they may co-operate closely with the border police authorities of the exit or transit country in which they are acting. These controls may result in the refusal of transportation of some passengers, in accordance with the terms of reference of the officers in action.[76] Yet there is no indication of the nature of the inter-state police co-operation, nor of possible reservations due to the human rights record of the partner States. Similarly, it is unclear whether protection aspects will be taken into account in order to modify the purely technical control of travel documents, in accordance with human rights norms.

Again, what might already be invented and practised by Member States has now become a part of the EU *acquis*. In 1996 the EU Council adopted a joint position on 'pre-frontier assistance and training assignments', setting up objectives and guidelines for such extra-territorial control activities, such as the following:

> *Whereas* checks carried out on embarkation on to flights to Member States of the European Union are a useful contribution to the aim of combating unauthorized immigration by nationals of third countries, which, pursuant to Article K.1(3)(c) of the Treaty, is regarded as a matter of common interest;
> *Whereas* the posting to airports of departure of Member States' officers who are specialized in such checks, to assist the officers who carry out checks on departure locally on behalf of the local authorities or on behalf of the airlines, is a means of helping to improve those checks, as is also the organizing of training assignments aimed at airline staff;
> . . .
> Article 1 Assistance Assignments
>
> 1. The joint organization of assistance assignments at third-country airports shall be carried out within the Council with full use being made of the possibilities for cooperation offered.
> 2. Assistance assignments shall have as their objective the provision of assistance to officers locally responsible for checks either on behalf of the local authorities or on behalf of the airlines.
> 3. Assistance assignments shall be carried out in agreement with the competent authorities of the third country concerned.
> 4. Assistance assignments may be of varying duration. For this purpose, a list of airports at which joint assignments could be carried out on a temporary or permanent basis shall be drawn up . . .[77]

In the absence of human rights and refugee protection considerations, it cannot be ruled out that these control activities affect people in need of protection, blocking their access to asylum procedures. This may in consequence lead to human rights violations, either in a country of transit where such people may be considered illegal entrants, or in their country of origin; some individuals will be prevented from leaving that country in the first place, others may be returned in spite of the principle of *non-refoulement*, and thereby eventually exposed to risk of persecution.

To the extent that such human rights violations result from the pre-screening of passengers in airports through which they might otherwise arrive at EU borders,

---

[76] *Ibid.*
[77] Joint position of 25 Oct. 1996 defined by the Council on the basis of Art. K.3(2)(a) (now Art. 31) of the TEU, on pre-frontier assistance and training assignments [1996] OJ L281/1.

carried out or assisted by officials of potential destination States, the involvement of
EU States seems sufficiently active to engage their responsibility under international
law. Thus, in contrast to the possible discharge by means of invoking the private nature of the agents of control carried out by transport companies, here States have
abandoned the legal construction of delegated powers and exercise actual jurisdiction. It is consequently beyond doubt that they will be responsible for human rights
violations that may occur following the extra-territorial immigration control. Yet
the co-ordinated EU measures to this effect have apparently failed to take this aspect
into account, by simply (re)defining the exercise as one of 'combating unauthorized
immigration'.

4. Exit Control by Third Countries Replacing Immigration Control   As a kind of ultimate step towards 'externalizing' immigration control, the EU has recently moved
into more direct co-operation with third States in order to have their authorities undertake control functions which would otherwise be carried out upon arrival in EU
States. Thus, immigration control is not only moving out to the extra-territorial
sphere, but furthermore shifting into *exit* control and, according to the same logic,
taken over by the authorities of third countries from which the unwanted persons in
question are supposed to attempt to move on towards EU territory.

This may seem just a gradual development from the 'external' control practices
described above. The formal organization, however, leads to qualitative differences
when enforcement is left with a third State. Compared to posted immigration
officers and 'pre-frontier assistance and training', control measures carried out by
third-country authorities, fully under their terms of reference, are likely to be less
transparent and less susceptible to influence from the EU States on whose behalf
they have been undertaken. Another difference is the measures accompanying delegation of control. While assistance programmes in Central Europe have involved the
reinforcement of border controls, they also aimed at enabling transit countries to improve their refugee protection systems. Indeed, preventing asylum-seekers from
continuing towards the West, and allowing for the return on 'safe third-country'
grounds of those who do so anyway, is an important element of assistance programmes.[78] What distinguishes them from the control delegation here discussed is
the capacity-building effort which was normally an essential part of these programmes.

Similar efforts have not been given high priority in recent initiatives to prevent
people from seeking asylum in EU countries. Following the quite high numbers of
Iraqi asylum-seekers in Western Europe in the past few years, and in particular the
increased numbers arriving in Italy during the winter of 1997–8, the EU Council
adopted an action plan on the 'influx of migrants from Iraq and the neighbouring region'.[79] The language used and actions proposed are particularly remarkable given

---

[78] As an example, the Nordic States' programmes in Estonia, Latvia, and Lithuania, partly driven by
fear that great numbers of asylum-seekers might arrive from transit countries further East via the Baltic
States, could be mentioned. See J. Vedsted-Hansen, 'Immigration and Asylum in Scandinavia: Losing In-
nocence in Europe?' (1996) 7 *Oxford International Review* 24.
[79] EU action plan on the influx of migrants from Iraq and the neighbouring region, adopted by the EU
General Affairs Council, 26–27 Jan. 1998 (5573/98 ASIM 13) (hereinafter EU Action Plan).

the fact that a mass influx had not occurred into any EU country, neither had such a situation been imminent.[80]

In a far-reaching version of the 'externalized' approach to immigration control, the action plan sets up an array of control measures. Some of these will engage the authorities of non-EU States; interestingly, Turkey plays a key role among the third countries.[81] The Union's protective response is relatively modest, being limited to exchange of information, policy review, monitoring of humanitarian needs, and the like.[82] In general, control measures seem far more operational than the few protection-oriented measures included in the action plan.[83] In the section entitled 'combating illegal immigration' it describes a number of measures to be taken by the EU or Member States, among which are the following:

26. The Council to ensure *effective application* of the Joint Position on *pre-frontier* assistance and training assignments in relation to *countries of origin and transit*.

27. Member States . . . to promote joint missions to *specific departure points* to train carriers in the detection of false documents in accordance with the Joint Position on pre-frontier assistance.

. . .

29. Member States to arrange *training and exchanges* between officials of Member States and *third countries concerned* . . .

. . .

32. Member States to *exchange officials* by mutual agreement, both between themselves and with the *third countries concerned*, in order to observe the effectiveness of measures to prevent illegal immigration.

33. Member States to *send experts to the third countries concerned*, by mutual agreement, to advise on the *operation of controls at land and sea frontiers*.

34. Member States with particular experience to share technical knowledge and expertise with other Member States and . . . with the *third countries most heavily affected*.

35. Routine and effective implementation by Member States at national level of *security measures and carrier's liability legislation* against carriers bringing undocumented passengers and passengers with forged documents to the EU . . .[84]

The action plan can be characterized as a strategy for the containment of asylum-seekers in 'third countries concerned', primarily Turkey. Whereas the affected individuals have been termed 'illegal migrants', and their displacement 'illegal immigration', the document does not provide any qualification of these notions as opposed to refugee protection. Although 'migrants from Iraq' may have complex motives to leave that country, they are to a large extent genuine refugees. Hence there is a presumption that they are in need of international protection which they

---

[80] This assessment is in accordance with UNHCR's position; in consultations with EU and Member States UNHCR held the view that, in spite of the increasing numbers and their concentration in a few countries, the number of Iraqi asylum-seekers could not be considered a mass influx.

[81] It is noteworthy that Turkey has made a geographical reservation pursuant to Art. 1 B of the 1951 Refugee Convention, thus having no Convention obligations towards non-European refugees.

[82] EU Action Plan, note 79 above, at paras. 4–6 (on humanitarian aid) and 7–12 (on 'effective application of asylum procedures').

[83] Cf. J. van der Klaauw, 'European Union' (1998) 16 *NQHR* 92–3.

[84] EU Action Plan, note 79 above (emphasis added). More specified proposals for implementing the Action Plan were set out by the Presidency in a note of 29 Jan. 1998 to the third pillar working groups on asylum, EURODAC, Migration, Visa and Europol, and CIREA and CIREFI (5593/98 ASIM 15).

have often not been able to find outside Europe.[85] Processing their cases might rebut this presumption, yet control measures blocking access to asylum procedures do not become more legitimate by redefining asylum-seekers into the non-deserving category 'illegal migrants'.

If this is the overall objective of the action plan, the main 'relevant third country' seems to have understood the message. On a follow-up mission EU representatives met Turkish officials who expressed their interest in increased information, exchange, and technical assistance in tackling 'illegal immigration'. Furthermore:

> [a]s regards asylum issues, the Turkish authorities mentioned their plans to establish reception centres for illegal migrants, but were reluctant to involve UNHCR in the process of screening asylum applicants . . .
>
> The Turkish authorities did not see UNHCR involvement in the reception houses as appropriate, since only illegal immigrants would be held there, nor were they happy to see closer co-operation generally on this issue with UNHCR. They could, however, accept a contribution (most obviously by UNHCR) in screening training provided to Turkish border guards.[86]

The EU involvement in organizing controls operated by third-country authorities provides strong reasons to assume that, if the action plan is implemented, EU States will incur responsibility for this more or less indirect exercise of jurisdiction. Considering the evident (and intended) implications for refugee protection, the disregard of human rights concerns is striking.

Given the extra-territorial framework, the very rationale of this kind of immigration control, it would be inadequate to pretend to mitigate the effects merely through external border-crossing measures as those to be adopted under Article 62(2) (*ex* Article 73j) of the EC Treaty. While certain human rights-based modifications will have to be included in such legislation, refugee policy has manifestly been brought into the arena of foreign relations, beyond the traditional scope of asylum and immigration policies. The logical consequence is therefore to develop future asylum strategies so as to make protection available extra-territorially for those asylum-seekers who are affected by the 'externalized' controls.[87]

C. Sharing the Burden of Responsibility

1. Burden-sharing in the EU?   Under international law, there is no binding norm prescribing the sharing of costs in connection with inequitable reception of persons in need of protection.[88] Burden-sharing must be properly understood as a functional

---

[85] This is confirmed by UNHCR assessments of the status of the persons involved, and certainly also by the practices of national asylum authorities in European countries which would be likely to recognize the need of protection for many Iraqi asylum-seekers, were they to have their cases examined.

[86] Note from the Presidency to the K.4 Committee (6938/1/98 Rev. 1, ASIM 78), 21 Apr. 1998, at paras. 3 and 9. Police authorities also identified the need for 'enhanced co-operation and support from UNHCR to assist in the return of failed asylum seekers' (at para. 6).

[87] This has been recognized in principle, yet with limited protective ambition, in the proposals for implementing the action plan. In the note of 29 Jan. 1998 (5593/98 ASIM 15), the Presidency 'recognizes the clear Second Pillar element to this action point' (referring to point 7 of the action plan).

[88] However, an effort to endow burden sharing with the quality of an obligation under customary law is made in J-P.L. Fonteyne, 'Burden Sharing: An Analysis of the Nature and Function of International Solidarity in Cases of Mass Influx of Refugees' (1983) 8 *AYBI* 175ff. Fonteyne holds that States are

prerequisite for the observation of the norm prohibiting *refoulement,* the preservation of protection capacities, and access to territory of potential host States. However, it is not a *legal* prerequisite for compliance with the norm of *non-refoulement.*

In Western Europe, norms levelling out inequalities in reception, making the onus for single States predictable and thereby maintaining States' willingness to receive those in need, are still lacking to a large extent.[89] This became particularly clear as the Balkan conflict dragged on. The largest populations of protection seekers from Bosnia were found in Western European countries which were either geographically proximate or already hosting immigrant communities from former Yugoslavia. In descending order, *per capita,* Austria, Sweden, Germany, and Switzerland[90] received most of these. In total numbers, Germany alone had accommodated 63 per cent of all Bosnian refugees hosted by EU Member States.[91]

It is of interest to track the relevant normative developments in the EU context. Burden-sharing was declared to be one of the issues to be examined by the Council in 1994 according to the priority work plan for that year. Accordingly, the German presidency presented an ambitious 'Draft Council Resolution on Burden-sharing with Regard to the Admission and Residence of Refugees'[92] in July 1994. However, the draft had difficulty in attracting the necessary support.

During the Spanish presidency, a limited consensus on burden-sharing had finally begun to develop, as the adoption of a 'Council Resolution on Burden-sharing with Regard to Admission and Residence of Displaced Persons on a Temporary Basis' on 25 September 1995 indicated.[93] This instrument is part of the asylum *acquis.*[94] How does the German draft of 1994 compare to the 1995 Resolution?

The most daring feature of the draft was to propose a specific distributive key which 'could be used by Member States'.[95] This key was based on Member States'

—percentage of the total Union population;
—percentage of Union territory; and
—percentage of the Unions' Gross Domestic Product.

obliged to practise burden-sharing by customary law. Perluss and Hartman argue that the international community chose not to mould burden-sharing into an obligatory form, as this would risk weakening rather than strengthening protection, providing front-line States with an excuse for *refoulement* if no assistance from less affected States were to materialise: D. Perluss and J. Hartman, 'Temporary Refuge: Emergence of a Customary Norm' (1986) 26 *Va.J.Int'l L.* 588.

[89] For a full account of the normative and factual developments regarding European burden-sharing in the 1990s, see G. Noll, 'Prisoners' Dilemma in Fortress Europe: On the Prospects for Equitable Burden Sharing in the European Union' (1997) 40 *GYIL* 405. For a global account on the topic, see Secretatiat of the Inter-Governmental Consultations on Asylum, Refugee and Migration Policies in Europe, North America and Australia, *Study on the Concept of Burden-Sharing* (1998).

[90] At the time, Austria and Sweden had not acquired membership of the European Union. Switzerland was not and is not a member of the EU.

[91] Address by Udo Heyder, Federal Ministry of the Interior, *Hohenheimer Tage des Ausländerrechts 1997,* 31 Jan. 1997.

[92] Doc. No. 7773/94 ASIM 124 (hereinafter the draft).

[93] [1995] OJ C262/1 (hereinafter the 1995 Resolution).

[94] Draft List, note 42 above, at para. I. C.

[95] The draft, note 92 above, at para. 7.

Each of these criteria should be given equal weight. The draft featured a table of indicative figures[96] for each Member State which were to be revised every five years by joint agreement. The possibility of departing from these figures by joint agreement was expressly provided for in paragraph 8 of the draft.

The centrepiece of the envisaged redistribution mechanism was contained in paragraph 9: '[w]here the numbers admitted by a Member State exceed its indicative figure under paragraph 8, other Member States which have not yet reached their indicative figure under paragraph 8 will accept persons from the first Member State'.

Accordingly, the draft intended to introduce compulsory resettlement, relying on a distributive key. However, a reduction of reception obligations was envisaged with respect to military expenditure triggered by intervention in the refugee-producing crisis[97] and the Convention refugee population already present in a Member State.[98] In terms of *realpolitik*, the resistance to the draft can be explained by the fact that Germany would have been its first beneficiary, with additional reception responsibilities falling upon all other Member States.

Turning to the 1995 Resolution, it is striking to see that the indicative figures have vanished and the stipulated distributive key is devoid of any precision:[99]

> 4. The Council agrees that the burden in connection with the admission and residence of displaced persons on a temporary basis in a crisis could be shared on a balanced basis in a spirit of solidarity, taking into account the following criteria . . .:
>
> > —the contribution which each Member State is making to prevention or resolution of the crisis, in particular by the supply of military resources in operations and missions ordered by the United Nations Security Council or the Organization for Security and Cooperation in Europe and by the measures taken by each Member State to afford local protection to people under threat or to provide humanitarian assistance,
> > —all economic, social and political factors which may affect the capacity of a Member State to admit an increased number of displaced persons under satisfactory conditions.

In a footnote linked to the first paragraph of this Article, it is said that '[t]hese criteria are norms of reference that may be supplemented by further criteria in the light of specific situations'. This statement reveals the contradiction contained in the present instrument. In the preamble, it is correctly stated that 'situations of great urgency . . .

---

[96] The draft, note 92 above, at para. 7. A look at these figures might help to understand both the German urge and the failing support of other large Member States. In descending percentage order, the figures read as follows: Germany (21.58), France (19.40), Italy (15.83), United Kingdom (14.28), Spain (13.63), Netherlands (3.55), Greece (3.20), Portugal (2.65), Belgium (2.42), Denmark (1.78), Ireland (1.54), Luxembourg (0.12).

[97] Para. 9 of the draft states: 'Member States which are helping, by means of particular foreign and security policy measures in the country of origin of the persons referred to in paragraph 1, to control the refugee situation in the State in question, need not admit the full figure assigned to them under paragraph 8. The resulting shortfall should be covered by the other States in proportion to their indicative figures. Measures of this nature include in particular peace-keeping or peace-making initiatives in the framework of the United Nations, NATO or the Western European Union.'

[98] According to para. 11 of the draft, Convention refugees are set off against the indicative figure in para. 8.

[99] With regard to the vagueness of the given criteria, we omit a detailed discussion of their implications. For a critical analysis, see ECRE, *Comments from the European Council on Refugees and Exiles on the 1995 'Burden Sharing' Resolution and Decision adopted by the Council of the European Union.*

require prompt action and the development beforehand of principles governing the admission of displaced persons'. However, these principles are developed *ex post facto* by the Council. The 'Decision on Alert and Emergency Procedure for Burden-Sharing with Regard to the Admission and Residence of Displaced Persons on a Temporary Basis'[100] operates along the same pattern of tackling a crisis after it has materialized. Consequently, a cautious State would rather block access for refugees than trust in the outcome of this *ad hoc* exercise in the Council.[101]

Nevertheless, the issue of burden-sharing resurfaced in March 1997, when the European Commission launched a proposal on a Joint Action concerning Temporary Protection of Displaced Persons.[102] The European Parliament proposed a number of amendments, but the real obstacles to adoption were some Member States, which were unable to accept a provision on burden-sharing inserted into the proposal. The Commission changed tactics and put forward a new proposal in June 1998. It divided the single draft text of March 1997 into two separate drafts. One joint action would deal with a Union-wide 'Temporary Protection Regime' and contain a number of minimum rights[103] and a mechanism for the common opening up and phasing out of such a regime.[104] Another joint action would be entirely devoted to burden-sharing or, rather, according to the terminology of the Commission, 'solidarity'.[105] With professional optimism, the Commission states that:

[t]he proposed revision must facilitate the adoption of the text by the Council. In so far as the central question resides in possible solidarity measures, the following strategy is suggested:

- on the one hand, to propose a specific text on solidarity, so that this subject does not delay the progress on temporary protection;
- on the other hand, the two texts (temporary protection and solidarity in reception and residence) could only enter into force simultaneously, that is to say on the date of adoption by the Council of each of these two instruments.[106]

However, it cannot be ruled out that the Council condones the Temporary Protection Proposal, while rejecting the Solidarity Proposal.

---

[100] [1996] OJ L63/10. According to the draft list, note 42 above, at para. I. C., this instrument is also part of the *acquis*.

[101] The importance of a detailed and predictable burden-sharing framework seems to have been realized by the authors of the German Draft Resolution. See para. 5 of the draft, note 92 above: '[t]he Council is convinced that if Member States are to be able to react promptly in emergencies, they must first devise an appropriate range of measures for the admission of refugees from war or civil war. Such measures must include prior agreement on principles for distributing refugees. Otherwise there is a risk that, in situations in which prompt action is necessary to avert serious danger to human life, decisions which need to be taken urgently will be delayed by the fact that complicated consultation procedures must first be initiated.'

[102] [1997] OJ C106/13.

[103] European Commission, *Amended Proposal for a Joint Action Concerning Temporary Protection of Displaced Persons (Presented by the Commission Pursuant to Article 189a(2) of the EC Treaty)*: COM(1998)372 final/2 (hereinafter the TP proposal), Arts. 6–9. If the goal of harmonization is to be taken seriously, a deviation from these minimum rights in favour of beneficiaries is improbable.

[104] *Ibid.*, Arts. 3 and 4.

[105] European Commission, *Proposal for a Joint Action Concerning Solidarity in Admission and Residence of Beneficiaries of the Temporary Protection of Displaced Persons (Presented by the Commission Pursuant to Paragraph 2(b) of Article K3 of the EU Treaty)*: COM(1998)372 final/2 (hereinafter Solidarity Proposal).

[106] Communication from Mme Gradin to the Commission, attached to Doc. No. O/98/187, at para. 2.

What exactly is the content of the latter? Primarily, Member States would share the burden by way of a system of financial compensations. First, fixed emergency aid is proposed, limited to the first three months of a crisis and intended to cover accommodation, means of subsistence, and emergency medical assistance.[107] The budgetary support for this item remains to be created. Secondly, reception projects could be financed by using an existing item in the EU budget.[108] This longer-term measure would cover accommodation, social assistance, and education.

While financial burden-sharing is the core of the instrument, a subsidiary provision in Article 5 of the Solidarity Proposal envisages also distributing among different States the burden in terms of those receiving protection. A decision setting up a temporary protection regime 'may also, as a secondary measure, define the rules allowing the beneficiaries of temporary protection to be distributed between Member States, before or on arrival in the territory of Member States'. Lamentably, this is merely a variation on the *ad hoc* mechanism already put in place by the 1995 Resolution. By way of a metaphor, putting trust in this Article means attempting to sign an insurance policy after the occurrence of an accident.

In general terms, a system of financial burden-sharing would be an important step towards the safeguarding of openness *vis-à-vis* persons in need of protection. Such a system will find acceptance only if it moves beyond the present pattern of allocating responsibility and attains the quality of mutual insurance against a certain level of fiscal reception costs. In a long-term perspective, financial burden-sharing could allow for reintroducing liberal elements of choice into protection systems. In an attempt to exploit the integrative potential of family and social networks, Member States could permit claimants to choose a host country in which such a network already exists. The total cost of integration would be diminished, while the relative costs for single States would be redistributed by means of financial burden-sharing. However, the social and political costs of acceptance by and integration into host societies should not be underestimated. As it is difficult to convert the latter into fiscal terms, it is reasonable to assume that some Member States will insist on the development of schemes redistributing persons to be protected.

2. The Dublin Convention: Concentrating the Burden   In their attempts to steer the movements of asylum-seekers, the European Union and its Member States have created a rather elaborate mechanism deflecting movements to the Union's territory. It comprises norms of non-arrival (carrier sanctions, pre-exit immigration controls, technical assistance to third countries' exit control, interdiction and containment of asylum-seekers in third countries) as well as norms of reallocation to safe third countries.

The mechanism of deflection impacts not only on single asylum-seekers, but also on the policies and practices of single Member States. The bottom line of the reallocation criteria in the Dublin Convention is that facilitation of entry and failure to re-

---

[107] Art. 4, Solidarity Proposal, note 105 above; financial statement attached to the Solidarity Proposal.
[108] For 1998, the proposal assumes a need for ECU 3,750,000 for these measures targeted at reception projects: financial statement, *ibid.*

move entails responsibility.[109] Moreover, the criteria disfavour countries with existing populations from countries of origin, as such networks will attract further direct arrivals. Finally, those countries having an external border of the Union will find themselves with a larger proportion of arrivals than countries without such borders. The example of Germany may serve as an illustration for the accumulated effects of the Dublin criteria. Initially, the German government had set high hopes for the Dublin Convention, just to find that its application leaves Germany with a net increase of cases. This increase affects not only applications, but also decisions on accepted requests and actual transfers:

Table 1. The Impact of the Dublin Convention on the Situation of Germany

	Total	Acceptance	Denial
Requests by other States Parties to Germany	7972	5956 (75%)	1109 (13%)
Requests by Germany to other States Parties	2533	752 (30%)	743 (30%)

Strikingly, the percentage of German acceptances in relation to the total number of requests is higher than the average acceptance percentage of all other States Parties. In the same period, 1,417 people were transferred to Germany, while Germany turned over 365 persons to other States party to the Dublin Convention.[110] This goes to show that the Dublin criteria provide for burden-concentration instead of burden-sharing.

Such consequences form a strong incentive for each single Member State to conduct ever more scrupulous and restrictive visa, admission, and border-control policies, as it cannot put its hope in other States sharing the responsibility for arrivals. Coupled with these restrictions on movements, affected States will downgrade protection benefits. The rationale for doing so is, first, to create a disincentive for potential asylum-seekers and, secondly, to stretch resources.

Turning around the logic of these developments, a burden-sharing mechanism is indeed the key to safeguarding refugee protection on the territory of the Member States. If combined with a material harmonization of protection categories and reception standards, it would mitigate competition for deflection as well as for the downgrading of territorial protection. Ideally, such a mechanism should have been launched concurrently with the mechanisms of migration control, so as to inhibit the latter setting the preconditions for the operation of the former.[111] When applying

[109] Convention Determining the State Responsible for Examining Applications for Asylum Lodged in One of the Member States of the Community, Dublin, 15 June 1990 (hereinafter Dublin Convention), Arts. 5–7: entered into force, 1 Sept. 1997 [1997] OJ C254/1. It could be discussed whether the family reunion criterion in Art. 4 represents a disincentive for States to grant Convention status, as this may trigger the responsibility to process applications from family members. However, it would be hard to verify such a hypothesis in practice.

[110] Letter of 18 Aug. 1998 by the Federal Office for the Recognition of Refugees (Bundesamt für die Anerkennung ausländischer Flüchtlinge) on the implementation of the Schengen and Dublin Conventions (on file with the authors). Period: 97–09–01 to 98–07–31.

[111] In this respect, it is of interest to compare the development in the EU with the bilateral developments between Germany and Poland. The EU's Member States put a readmission mechanism in place

Article 6 TEU to the area of asylum, equitable burden sharing imposes itself as a priority measure of decisive importance, irrespective of the exemption of the topic from the time limit set by Article 63 TEC. Sensibly, a viable solution could take into account and compensate for the concentration of claimants in certain countries as a result of the criteria laid down in the 1990 Dublin Convention.

D. Procedures for Admission and Examination of Asylum Applications

1. Allocation of Responsibility   Among the measures on asylum to be adopted under the Treaty of Amsterdam is 'criteria and mechanisms for determining which Member State is responsible for considering an application for asylum submitted by a national of a third country in one of the Member States' (Article 63(1)(a) (*ex* Article 73k) of the EC Treaty). This obviously aims to establish a first-pillar instrument replacing the 1990 Dublin Convention. It is reasonable to expect that there will be some incitement for copying the Convention into a legislative act, most likely a regulation. The recent coming into force of the Dublin Convention and the five-year time limit for the adoption of this measure increase the likelihood that this will be considered the most opportune solution.

However, there are good reasons for taking this opportunity to reconsider the Dublin Convention criteria and procedure for determining responsibility. In that respect there is an additional basis of experience to draw on, as a similar allocation mechanism has been applied under the Schengen Convention since 1995. Experience suggests that certain elements of the Dublin mechanism be adjusted, even while Member States may not want to re-open negotiations on the basic criteria, i.e. the authorization of applicants' entry or presence in the territory,[112] modified by family or cultural links to a certain Member State.[113]

When adopting an instrument under Article 63 (*ex* Article 73k), it will be timely to assess how the latter criteria are being implemented. Due to the *authorization* criteria asylum-seekers will often be transferred to another EU State for reasons totally unrelated to their personal situations. While the transfers' potentially arbitrary effects on access to protection should be resolved by other harmonization measures, personal and cultural sensitivity must be achieved under the provisions regarding links to a specific country. Here, it might be that too many cases depend on discretionary allocation because of insufficient operation of the criteria concerning family members; and it is possible that Member States do not apply the discretionary provisions in the same manner.

without any link to the question of burden-sharing. By contrast, the named bilateral arrangement seized the opportunity by linking readmission with rudimentary forms of burden-sharing. In both cases, the readmission agreements covering return of third-country nationals (a) contained a burden-sharing clause for cases of massive inflows and (b) was coupled to an agreement on financial assistance: Abkommen zwischen der Regierung der Bundesrepublik Deutschland und der Regierung der Republik Polen über die Zusammenarbeit hinsichtlich der Auswirkungen von Wanderungsbewegungen, 7 May 1993, Arts. 6 and 2.

[112] Cf. Dublin Convention, Arts. 5–7; Schengen Convention, Art. 30(1)(a)–(g).
[113] Cf. Dublin Convention, Arts. 4 (close family; mandatory allocation) and 9 (cultural links; discretionary allocation); Schengen Convention, Arts. 35 and 36. Dublin Convention, Art. 3(4), and Schengen Convention, Art. 29(4), may operate in a similar way, yet also on a discretionary basis.

Moreover, the Dublin Convention has not fully secured access to protection, as was intended. At least two deficiencies can be identified, one being the problem of 'safe third countries' which remains unsolved by the Convention. The other protection-related deficiency partly results from the time-consuming procedure under Articles 11–13 for settling the issue of responsibility upon request for transfer to another State; this procedure may in itself be a reason for the lack of efficiency of the Dublin mechanism.[114]

In order to avoid such administrative complications, Member States may prefer to apply special accelerated procedures to rejecting cases on substantive grounds, even if they feel that another State would actually be responsible for examination. This happened under the Schengen Convention, and a similar practice is likely to occur, though arguably not compatible with Article 3(4) of the Dublin Convention.[115] Thus, the first-pillar instrument needs to include provisions to the effect that such *procedure-shifting* does not undermine the procedural safeguards in asylum cases. The phenomenon described here is connected with the issue of procedures for manifestly unfounded applications, both regarding the definition of this category and the permissible level of safeguard-reduction.[116]

Finally, the *burden-sharing* implications of the Dublin criteria for allocation of asylum-seekers, as discussed above, may be pertinent in the process of adopting measures under Article 63. Should experience prove the Dublin Convention to be evidently inequitable, this would be the chance for Member States to make the necessary adjustments. Alternatively, they may take heed of such problems in the burden-sharing measures to be adopted pursuant to Article 63(2)(b).

2. Pre-procedure Return: 'Safe Third Countries' An additional protection problem related to the Dublin Convention is the practice of returning asylum-seekers to 'safe third countries'. Article 3(5) allows for 'safe third country' clauses in domestic law to take precedence over the Convention mechanism. This results in asylum-seekers being returned to non-EU countries without having their application examined by the Member State that would be responsible according to the criteria in Articles 4–9, despite the objective of securing the examination of every application for asylum (cf. Preamble, paragraph 4, and Article 3(1)). Being another *procedure-shifting* mechanism, this significantly affects the Convention's reliability as an instrument securing access to fair and efficient asylum procedures.[117]

It goes beyond the scope of this chapter to analyse the legal basis and implications of the 'safe third country' notion, employed by States to refuse admission to the asylum procedure on the ground that an application should rather be dealt with by another State.[118] As this notion has become part of the EU asylum *acquis*, future

---

[114] For instance, bilateral readmission agreements have been concluded between Denmark and Sweden, and between Denmark and Germany, for the purpose of settling cases in a more expeditious manner than under the Dublin Convention procedure.

[115] Cf. van der Klaauw, note 48 above, at 235–6.   [116] See IV. D. 3, below.

[117] Cf. van der Klaauw, note 48 above, at 236–7.

[118] See generally, R. Marx, *'Non-Refoulement*, Access to Procedures, and Responsibility for Determining Refugee Claims' (1995) 7 *IJRL* 383–405; G. Goodwin-Gill, note 67 above, at 333–44; R. Byrne and A. Shacknove, 'The Safe Country Notion in European Asylum Law' (1996) 9 *Harv. HRJ* 185–228; G. Noll, 'Non-Admission and Return of Protection Seekers in Germany' (1997) 9 *IJRL* 416–452;

legislation is bound to deal with its harmonized application. The measure replacing the Dublin Convention would seem the most appropriate instrument to regulate the issue, assuming that this act under Article 63 (*ex* Article 73k) will still have the objective of securing access to examination for every asylum-seeker. Hence, the main legal concerns raised by the *acquis* concerning 'safe third countries' shall be identified. Not only does the problem of 'safe third country' practices persist under the Dublin Convention, due to the prevalence given to domestic law by Article 3(5), it has indeed been exacerbated by the 1992 London Resolution which provides that Article 3(5) must be applied *in advance* of settling the responsibility issue in accordance with the Dublin criteria.[119] In itself a remarkable combination of a Convention *allowing* domestic law to prevail, and a non-binding text *committing* Member States to utilize this scope of action to the widest extent possible,[120] this regulatory mechanism deserves quite thorough scrutiny; the process of adopting first-pillar measures will be the obvious occasion for doing so.

Experience has shown strong reasons for caution in applying the 'safe third country' notion. Apart from the fundamental problem of ascertaining individuals' safety on the basis of presumptions, more concrete problems have occurred regarding, for example, the procedure followed in deportations *vis-à-vis* the asylum-seeker as well as the third country in question; previous links between the individual and the third country presumed to be responsible for examining the case; and the criteria for establishing that a given country is 'safe' for asylum-seekers and refugees. Not surprisingly, a variety of national 'safe third country' practices have developed, and the 1992 London Resolution has not brought about effective harmonization between Member States in this area.[121]

The Resolution sets unfortunately low standards for so-called 'host third countries', hardly in accordance with the 1951 Refugee Convention and human rights instruments to which Member States have committed themselves. Focusing on negative requirements—such as the *absence* of threats to life or freedom within the meaning of Article 33 of the 1951 Refugee Convention, and the *absence* of exposure to torture or inhuman or degrading treatment—the Resolution fails to take account of the positive obligations under international law that have to be fulfilled by an asylum country to which responsibility may be transferred.[122] Whereas the Resolution modestly refers to 'fundamental requirements', thus not excluding the broader meaning of refugee protection obligations, a binding instrument under Article 63 of the EC Treaty ought to be more carefully drafted in this respect.

N. Lassen and J. Hughes, *Safe Third Country Policies in European Countries* (1997); J. Vedsted-Hansen, 'Non-Admission Policies and the Right to Protection: Refugees' Choice v. States' Exclusion?' in F. Nicholson and P. Twomey (eds.), *Refugee Rights and Realities* (forthcoming, 1999).

[119] EC Ministers Resolution of 30 Nov.–1 Dec. 1992 on a Harmonized Approach to Questions Concerning Host Third Countries (SN 4823/92), paras. 1(a) and (d), and 3(a).

[120] The authors are indebted to K.U. Kjær for pointing out this regulatory particularity.

[121] See description of cases and practices in Lassen and Hughes, note 118 above; Peers, note 29 above, 10–14 and 17–20; and in ECRE, *'Safe Third Countries'. Myths and Realities* (1995).

[122] Cf. EC Ministers Resolution, note 119 above, at para. 2. See also R. Fernhout and H. Meijers, 'Asylum', in P. Boeles *et al.*, *A New Immigration Law for Europe? The 1992 London and 1993 Copenhagen Rules on Immigration* (1993), 17–18; UNHCR, *An Overview of Protection Issues in Western Europe: Legislative Trends and Positions Taken by UNHCR* (1995), 18–20; Goodwin-Gill, note 67 above, at 334 and 338.

3. Special Procedures for Manifestly Unfounded Applications   Pursuant to Article 63(1)(d) (*ex* Article 73k) of the EC Treaty, 'minimum standards on procedures in Member States for granting or withdrawing refugee status' shall be adopted within the transitional period of five years. Again, notwithstanding the temptation to carry over the asylum *acquis* to the coming first-pillar measures, it will be timely to rethink the content and structure of existing instruments. As illustrated below, the texts on procedures are lacking precision in defining key concepts; in addition, they give prevalence to domestic law regarding crucial issues.

There is particular reason for reconsideration of the accelerated procedure that can be operated for 'manifestly unfounded' applications; within this category, the standards set for processing asylum cases at the border are likely to be the most problematic. The relevant instruments are deficient in terms of both definition of the cases undergoing accelerated procedures and the level of safeguards to be retained in such procedures. In general, the harmonization of asylum procedures is incomplete.[123] This may indicate a predilection in Member States for procedural flexibility in the international standards, enabling them to assert that national exceptions or restrictions are compatible with these standards.[124]

The 1992 London 'Resolution on Manifestly Unfounded Applications for Asylum' includes a wide range of vaguely defined cases and situations in this category. An application for asylum shall be regarded as manifestly unfounded if it is clear that it meets none of the substantive criteria under the 1951 Refugee Convention, either because 'there is clearly no substance to the applicant's claim to fear persecution in his own country' or because 'the claim is based on deliberate deception or is an abuse of asylum procedures'.[125] If this may be relatively uncontroversial, the examples of cases within the two subcategories are at risk of creating a presumption that applications are *a priori* 'manifestly unfounded',[126] just as they are far from the definition adopted by the UNHCR Executive Committee.[127]

It is not difficult to imagine that the criteria listed may lead from discretion to arbitrariness in allocating cases to special procedures. Certain of these criteria are not necessarily pertinent to the issues of refugee status and protection need; at least, it may take much more than an accelerated procedure to rebut the presumptions on which the criteria are based.[128] In order to balance fairness against efficiency it would be more appropriate to establish a special procedure for cases likely to result in a *positive* decision; 'manifestly well-founded' applications should be given special treatment, reversing the notion of accelerated procedures already recognized.

---

[123]   See Peers, note 29 above, at 6–17.

[124]   Cf. the 'Europe *à la carte*' metaphor suggested by Bank, note 26 above, at 10. See also A. Terlow and P. Boeles, 'Minimum Guarantees for Asylum Procedures' in Meijers, note 37 above, at 103–4.

[125]   Resolution on Manifestly Unfounded Applications for Asylum, note 28 above, at para. 1(a).

[126]   *Ibid.*, at paras. 6, 7, 9, and 10. Remarkably, the wide definition of cases to undergo accelerated procedures is accompanied by a rather modest description of the procedural safeguards involved: see paras. 2–4.

[127]   See EXCOM Conclusion No. 30 (1983) in which the Executive Committee defined the category of 'manifestly unfounded' asylum applications in an objective and restrictive manner. Available at http://www.unhcr.ch/refworld/unhcr/excom/xconc/excom30.htm.

[128]   Cf. Goodwin-Gill, note 67 above, at 346: '[t]his elision is manifestly inappropriate, begging precisely the question which refugee procedures exist to answer'.

Notwithstanding proposals to this effect,[129] this way of maintaining the balance is not known to have been considered in the EU harmonization process.

As a further cause for concern, some Member States have established accelerated procedures melding examination in *substance* with the formal *admissibility* decision. This was endorsed by the 1995 'Resolution on Minimum Guarantees for Asylum Procedures', irrespective of its expression of the principle that asylum procedures will be applied in full compliance with the 1951 Refugee Convention and other obligations under international law in respect of refugees and human rights.[130] While the asylum-seeker in 'manifestly unfounded' cases may still generally remain in the territory until the final decision,[131] this guarantee has been undermined by leaving the possibility open for Member States to deal with applications in the framework of *border control*. If that is happening, there is no longer any requirement as to the suspensive effect of appeal, and the organizational safeguards relating to the review may be significantly reduced:

> Member States may, inasmuch as a national law so provides, apply special procedures to establish, *prior to the decision on admission*, whether or not the application for asylum is manifestly unfounded. No expulsion measure will be carried out during this procedure.
>
> Where an application for asylum is manifestly unfounded, the asylum seeker may be refused admission. In such cases, the national law of a Member State may permit an *exception to the general principle of the suspensive effect of the appeal* . . . However, it must at least be ensured that the decision on the refusal of admission is taken by a ministry or comparable central authority and that *additional sufficient safeguards* (for example, prior examination by another central authority) ensure the correctness of the decision. Such authorities must be fully qualified in asylum and refugee matters.[132]

Although not a blank exclusion from having an application examined on its merits, this may in effect encourage States to merge substantive determination of the applicant's refugee status with the admissibility decision. Because of the risks inherent in fast decision-making in connection with the exercise of border control, it may consequently lead to a pre-screening of applications which allows access to full examination only for cases *not* considered manifestly unfounded in the summary pre-admission decision.

Combined with the broad and vague definition of 'manifestly unfounded' applications, this implies a possibility that the operation of ordinary asylum procedures will eventually be limited to those applicants who appear *prima facie* eligible for refugee status. Focused on admissibility, and further conditioned on summary assessment of the well-foundedness of applications, the examination mechanism may thus turn into what could be seen as a *proceduralised* approach to the protection issue.

In conclusion, both the 1992 London Resolution and the 1995 Minimum Guarantees Resolution will need to undergo fundamental revision if they are to be part of

---

[129] ECRE, *Fair and Efficient Procedures for Determining Refugee Status* (1990).

[130] EU Council Resolution of 20 June 1995 on Minimum Guarantees for Asylum Procedures [1996] OJ C274/13, at para. 1; cf. para. 2.

[131] *Ibid.*, at para. 19; cf. para. 17. In such cases the ordinary appeal possibility may be derogated from if an independent body, distinct from the examining authority, has already confirmed the decision.

[132] *Ibid.*, para. 24(2) (emphasis added).

the platform for future EC legislation on asylum procedures. If the wording of Article 63 (*ex* Article 73k), requiring 'minimum standards on procedures', is to be taken seriously, then something more than a formally binding instrument is called for. First and foremost, the repeated deference to domestic law must be abandoned, as the measure to be adopted will be setting out *minimum* standards. The necessity for such standards to be in conformity with generally recognized international standards is emphasized by the fact that under the Dublin Convention every single Member State processes asylum applications on behalf of *all* EU States.[133]

E. Reception During Asylum Procedures

Unlike most issues of future harmonization, the minimum standards on the reception of asylum-seekers to be adopted under Article 63(1)(b) (*ex* Article 73k) of the EC Treaty, will not be replacing any specific instrument already in the EU asylum *acquis*. Our analysis must therefore start by welcoming the fact that this question has now been put on the agenda of the harmonization process. One may naturally ask what kind of standards will be adopted, and which level they can be expected to set for the treatment of asylum-seekers during the period when their applications are being processed.

In the absence of common standards, it seems evident that asylum-seekers are largely left to the discretion and goodwill of the Member State which happens to examine their cases. To the extent that there is a choice of country of examination, the actual conditions for asylum-seekers may be one of the criteria for making that choice, even though hardly a key criterion for most applicants. Correspondingly, granting more favourable conditions than the average of States in the sub-region may be perceived by States as a threatening 'magnet effect'. This in turn could lead States to utilize such standards as one parameter in a 'market strategy' of deterring potential asylum-seekers.

As there is in reality still less freedom of choice for asylum-seekers, the present state of affairs has become unsustainable, rendering the basic living conditions of individuals and families dependent on incidental factors. Thus, the identification of one Member State to be responsible for examining an application on behalf of the whole EU should logically lead to the adoption of common standards not only for asylum procedures, but also for the treatment of applicants during the examination period.

Certain problems will arise in the process of adopting harmonized standards for asylum-seekers. Among these we would mention how reception standards should relate to the 1951 Refugee Convention to which reference is made in Article 63(1); under what circumstances are such standards for persons whose applications are under examination bound to take Convention rights into account? Although this is not normally the case, the result may be different under protracted asylum procedures, especially if procedures have been suspended.

---

[133] For that same reason, and given the decisive impact of rules of *evidence* in refugee status determination, the instrument should also attempt to harmonize this aspect of asylum procedures; cf. at IV. A. 4, above.

Thus, the treatment of asylum-seekers should be seen in connection with the minimum standards to be adopted under Article 63(2)(a) for temporary protection to displaced persons. Since the proposed temporary protection standards are premised on the suspension of individual case processing, it has to be clarified when, and to what extent, they should be more favourable than the standards of treatment for ordinary asylum-seekers. In any event, general human rights instruments must frame the drafting of reception standards; being at a minimum level, such standards cannot disregard the provisions of 'other relevant treaties' imposing certain obligations on Member States with respect to civil, social, and economic rights.

A particularly controversial issue to be dealt with by the Article 63 measure is the detention of asylum-seekers. Needless to say, the deprivation of liberty as such must be regulated in accordance with Article 5 ECHR and Articles 9–10 of the International Covenant on Civil and Political Rights (ICCPR). Perhaps more complex, the conditions for detained asylum-seekers will have to be settled as well. Here some guidance can be found in the recent Report from the European Committee for the Prevention of Torture and Inhuman or Degrading Treatment or Punishment (CPT) which includes a section on the standards of treatment for 'immigration detainees', among whom are asylum-seekers and persons refused entry.[134]

From a human rights perspective, it will be interesting to see whether harmonized standards can reverse current trends towards reinforcing deterrent policies by reducing social benefits to asylum-seekers, often combined with procedural restrictions or attempts to prevent individuals from using their procedural rights. In this sense reception standards are not only a logical imperative in the harmonization of asylum policy, but also somehow a litmus test of the commitments to protection in this common policy.

F. Return

1. Background   Typically, the substantial determination of an asylum claim may produce two different outcomes. A claimant is either considered to be in need of protection or she is not. If there is a need for protection recognized by international or national law, the individual claimant will be allowed to stay. As a rule, temporary leave to remain pending the outcome of the determination procedure will be transformed into some form of status—from mere tolerance to full-fledged refugee status. However, if no such need for protection is established in determination procedures, the individual becomes a rejected asylum-seeker:

> The term rejected asylum seekers . . . is understood to mean people who, after due consideration of their claims to asylum in fair procedures, are found not to qualify for refugee status, nor to be in need of international protection and who are not authorized to stay in the country concerned.[135]

---

[134] European Committee for the Prevention of Torture and Inhuman or Degrading Treatment or Punishment, *Seventh General Report* (CPT/Inf. (97) 10) (22 Aug. 1997), at paras. 24–36.

[135] 'Memorandum of Understanding between the United Nations High Commissioner for Refugees (UNHCR) and the International Organization for Migration (IOM)' (May 1997), at para. 29. It should be noted that IOM also uses the term 'unsuccessful asylum seekers', which includes in addition those persons who have chosen not to pursue further an asylum claim once filed.

Regularly, the State in question will ask a rejected asylum-seeker to leave its territory. Ideally, the individual complies with this order voluntarily, the country of origin receives her back, and the *status quo ante* is restored.

Comprehensive repatriation policies build on four considerations, which will be briefly presented in the following.[136] A primary consideration of repatriation policies is to ensure the rejectee's *voluntary compliance* with the obligation to leave the host country. Promotion of voluntary repatriation ranges from simple measures informing on the situation in the country of origin to programmes involving financial assistance. Concerning the latter, States are usually anxious not to create unintended incentives, where return assistance would attract further migrants.[137]

A second consideration for returning States is to devise measures responding to non-compliance with the obligation to leave. Some of these measures are intended to secure the *preconditions of removal*; they serve the identification (i.e. by means of fingerprinting, database checks, or language tests), localization (reporting obligations and detention), documentation (obligations to assist with travel document procurement) and, finally, the actual removal (expulsion orders and escorts).

Disputes on nationality, delays in issuing travel documents, or an outright denial of readmission by countries of origin may also inhibit efficient return practices. Thus, a third consideration of returning States is to ensure the co-operation of the country of origin.

Finally, a fourth consideration is to secure the co-operation of third States in return operations. This may take the form of setting up negotiating cartels to exert pressure on recalcitrant countries of origin. To name another example, repatriating States may also approach potential transit States lying *en route* on the migratory trajectory in order to negotiate agreements on the readmission or at least the transit of third-country nationals.

2. Co-operation on Return within the EU In the EU context, all four categories of repatriation activities have been the subject of continued intergovernmental deliberations. These have resulted in binding, as well as non-binding, norms. On a binding level, the 1990 Dublin Convention contains an obligation for States Parties to readmit a rejected asylum-seeker who has entered the territory of another State Party without being authorized to reside there, provided that it has not expelled the alien.[138] This obligation provides an incentive for a consistent expulsion strategy, as States Parties want to avoid the responsibilities flowing from the obligation to readmit.

Among non-binding instruments, the following have a direct bearing on return:

- Recommendation of 30 November 1992 regarding practices followed by Member States on expulsion;[139]

[136] For a comprehensive overview of the issue of return and a case study on Germany, see G. Noll, 'Unsuccessful Asylum Seekers: The Problem of Return', paper prepared for the Technical Symposium on International Migration and Development (1998, forthcoming in the proceedings of the Symposium).

[137] See the sixth recital in the preamble to the Council Dec. of 26 May 1997, note 150 below: '[w]hereas it should be avoided that such assistance leads to undesired incentive effects'.

[138] Dublin Convention, Art. 10(e). An identical obligation is contained in Chap. VII, Art. 34 of the Schengen Convention. Chap. VII of the Schengen Convention has been replaced by the Dublin Convention upon the entry into force of the latter.

[139] WGI 1266, reprinted in E. Guild and J. Niessen, *The Developing Immigration and Asylum Policies of the European Union* (1996), 219.

- Recommendation of 30 November 1992 regarding transit for the purposes of expulsion;[140]
- Recommendation of 1 June 1993 concerning checks on and expulsion of third-country nationals residing or working without authorization;[141]
- Council Conclusions of 30 November 1994 on the organization and development of the Centre for Information, Discussion and Exchange on the Crossing of Frontiers and Immigration (CIREFI);[142]
- Recommendation of 30 November 1994 concerning the adoption of a standard travel document for the removal/expulsion of third-country foreign nationals;[143]
- Recommendation of 30 November 1994 concerning a specimen bilateral readmission agreement between a Member State of the European Union and a third country;[144]
- Recommendation of 24 July 1995 on the guiding principles to be followed in drawing up protocols on the implementation of readmission agreements;[145]
- Recommendation of 22 December 1995 on harmonizing means of combating illegal immigration and illegal employment and improving the relevant means of control;[146]
- Recommendation of 22 December 1995 of concerted action and co-operation in carrying out expulsion measures;[147]
- Council Conclusions of 4 March 1996 concerning readmission clauses to be inserted in future mixed agreements;[148]
- Decision of 16 December 1996 on monitoring the implementation of instruments adopted by the Council concerning illegal immigration, readmission, the unlawful employment of third-country nationals, and co-operation in the implementation of expulsion orders;[149]
- Council Decision of 26 May 1997 on the exchange of information concerning assistance for the voluntary repatriation of third-country nationals.[150]

All of these instruments belong to the *acquis*.[151]

Regarding the promotion of voluntary repatriation, it is somewhat surprising that the Council did not bother to deal with the most dignified and least costly solution earlier than in 1997.[152] It was decided to collect information on Member States' programmes supporting voluntary return for purposes of comparison and dissemination.[153] This decision stands out alone amongst the earlier multitude of instruments dealing with implementation of return against the will of the individual.

---

[140] WGI 1266, *The Developing Immigration and Asylum Policies of the European Union* (1996), at 239.
[141] WGI 1516, *ibid.*, at 275.   [142] [1996] OJ C274/50.   [143] [1996] OJ C274/18.
[144] [1996] OJ C274/20.   [145] [1996] OJ C274/25.   [146] [1996] OJ C5/1.
[147] [1996] OJ C5/3.   [148] Doc. No. 4272/96 ASIM 6 and 5457/96 ASIM 37.
[149] [1996] OJ L342/5.   [150] [1997] OJ L147/3.
[151] Draft List, note 42 above, at 12–14.
[152] As early as in its 1994 Communication, the Commission had called for an approximation of voluntary repatriation schemes, emphasizing that such schemes are 'cost-effective, when compared with the costs of involuntary repatriation': Commission Communication, note 18 above, 30, at para. 111.
[153] Council Dec. of 26 May 1997, note 150 above.

Regarding the second consideration of securing the preconditions of removal and actually carrying it out, a basic rule is that people found to have failed definitively in an application for asylum and to have no other claim to remain should be expelled, unless there are compelling reasons, normally of a humanitarian nature, for allowing them to remain.[154] Where such a person is, or is likely to be, detained before expulsion, the period of detention should be used to obtain the necessary travel documents for expulsion.[155] Moreover, Member States are recommended to make use of a one-way travel document to facilitate the expulsion of persons lacking the necessary travel documents.[156]

With regard to the co-operation of countries of origin, Member States should implement specific mechanisms to improve the procurement of the necessary documentation from the consular authorities of the third State to which third-country nationals are to be expelled when they lack travel or identity documents.[157] It should also be noted that the Council has recommended Member States to conclude bilateral readmission agreements with third countries affirming the obligation to take back one's own nationals. To guide Member States in this respect, a specimen agreement as well as guidelines for readmission protocols have been drafted by the Council. This specimen contains provisions on readmission of persons proven or validly assumed to be nationals and former nationals.[158] In 1996, the Council took further steps to disseminate readmission obligations covering both nationals and third-country nationals. It laid down that the inclusion of *inter alia*:

- a clause stipulating an obligation to readmit nationals, and
- a clause stipulating an obligation to conclude bilateral agreement on the readmission of third-country nationals with Member States which so request into future mixed agreements between the Member States of the EU and third States shall be considered when adopting the guidelines for their negotiation.[159]

Concerning the co-operation of third States, it should be noted that the whole array of instruments adopted in the field represents an effort under this heading. In addition to the aforementioned norms, Member States are recommended to carry out expulsions, in appropriate instances, as a concerted effort with other Member States.[160] As an example of such co-operation, information exchange on available seats on expulsion flights may be mentioned.

Though not directly related to repatriation, a number of other EU initiatives improve Member States' control capacities. One of the more noteworthy attempts is a Council decision for the establishment of a Union-wide dactylographic database (EURODAC). Such a base would enable Member States to register, store, and

[154] Recommendation of 30 Nov. 1992, note 139 above, at para. 2; Recommendation of 1 June 1993, note 141 above, at para. 1.
[155] Council Recommendation of 22 Dec. 1995, note 147 above, at para. 10.
[156] Recommendation of 30 Nov. 1994, note 143 above. For a critical commentary, see Guild and Niessen, note 139 above, at 388.
[157] Council Recommendation of 22 Dec. 1995, note 147 above, at para. 1.
[158] Specimen Agreement annexed to the Recommendation concerning a specimen bilateral readmission agreement between a Member State of the EU and a third country, note 144 above, at Art. 1, para. 1.
[159] Conclusion of 4 Mar. 1996, note 148 above.   [160] *Ibid.*, at para. 6.

exchange fingerprints of asylum-seekers, thereby impeding double applications under different identities.

Return is also contained in the agenda set by the Treaty of Amsterdam. According to Article 63(3)(b) (*ex* Article 73k) of the EC Treaty, the Council shall adopt measures on 'illegal immigration and illegal residence, including repatriation of illegal residents' within a five-year time limit.[161]

Secondly, the Schengen *acquis* will be applicable for all EU Member States from the day on which the Amsterdam Treaty enters into force.[162] Article 23 of the 1990 Schengen Convention spells out the principle that an alien without permission to stay on the territory of a State Party must leave the common territories without delay. The same provision obliges State Parties to expel such an alien.[163] Moreover, the Schengen Convention comprises a comprehensive information exchange by means of the Schengen Information System (SIS), facilitating, *inter alia*, the identification of aliens illegally staying on the territories of State Parties.[164]

3. A Critical Assessment of the Acquis *Regarding Return*　Throughout recent years, the issue of repatriation has been high on the agenda of asylum countries in the industrialized world. It was held that considerable numbers of rejected asylum-seekers never left the territory of the determining State and that this put the credibility of asylum-systems into question. While it is certainly true that there is a logical nexus between rejection and return, one should be aware that the lack of statistics makes it difficult to assess whether return policies are sufficiently effective in the EU today. While the number of claims as well as recognitions under various categories are known, it remains obscure how many rejected claimants return voluntarily and how many move on to third countries.[165] Consequently, it is extremely hard to estimate how many rejectees actually remain in the territory of the State in which the determination procedure was carried out. Given the absence of reliable data, one should be reluctant to make any definite claim on the legal-political significance of the problem.

It is quite another matter that some Member States devote large political and financial resources to forcible return. The EU co-operation reflects their concerns in the impressive number of instruments related to return. However, important normative *lacunae* remain. Member States have largely failed to address issues related to the rights and interests of rejected asylum-seekers.[166] We will focus below on four areas where major shortcomings exist: voluntary return, detention decisions, condi-

---

[161] Art. 63(3)(b) EC Treaty. Measures adopted under this para. do not prevent Member States from maintaining or introducing national provisions which are compatible with the Treaty of Amsterdam and with international agreements.

[162] 'Protocol integrating the Schengen *acquis* into the framework of the European Union', 2 Oct. 1997.

[163] Schengen Convention, Art. 23, para. 3.　　　　　　　　　[164] *Ibid.*, Art. 38.

[165] This is acknowledged in a recent document prepared by the Austrian Presidency for the K.4 Committee. Note by the Presidency to the K. 4 Committee, 'A Strategy for Migration and Asylum Policies', Doc. No. ASIM 170 (1 July 1998), at para. 72.

[166] This has been observed by the Commission in its 1994 Communication, where it recommended Member States to sign and ratify the International Convention on the Protection of the Rights of All Migrants Workers and Members of their Families, adopted by GA Res. 45/158 (1990): in *International Instruments*, note 5 above, i, Part 2, at 554. This instrument has a bearing on the matter, as it also covers illegal migrant workers. Hitherto, no Member State has followed this suggestion.

tions of detention, and the use of force during removal. Due to space constraints, other areas such as non-discrimination, mass expulsion,[167] and the content of readmission agreements[168] will be omitted.

4. Voluntary Return, In Dubio Mitius, *and Detailed Safeguards* Any observer of the EU co-operation in issues of return will be struck by the predominance of forcible return. It is generally undisputed that voluntary return is more dignified and incurs less financial, as well as political, cost than its forcible counterpart. In Germany, the average cost of an escorted expulsion by air was US$840 in 1995, which should be compared to the price-tag for an assisted voluntary return in co-operation with the International Organization for Migration (IOM) (US$490).[169] This suggests that a first approach to the problem of return should have been to offer incentives in a co-ordinated fashion. Only if such an approach had failed in a statistically determinable manner, would it be reasonable to move on to more intrusive and expensive measures. Instead, Member States were eager to establish co-operation on expulsion from an early stage. Any instrument adopted under Article 63(3)(b) should attempt to correct this by including the maxim *in dubio mitius* for the whole area of return. From a human rights perspective, this cautionary rule implies that a less intrusive measure is chosen in case of doubt.[170] Thus, a preference for voluntary return over forcible removal would be established.

Of course, the tool of voluntary return programmes would be worthy not only of comparison, as suggested in the 1997 Council Conclusions, but also of harmonized minimum standards. Practice hitherto suggests that increased attention must be devoted to the overall impact of repatriation programmes on stability in the country of origin, especially if the number of returnees is substantial. Devising mechanisms for the protection of individuals upon repatriation is another topical issue where a common solution for all Member States may increase both legitimacy and efficiency of repatriation policies.

However, the maxim *in dubio mitius* should apply equally to measures securing the precondition of removal and its implementation. But an abstract maxim alone will not suffice to ensure compliance with the dictates of international human rights law in this field. Experience has shown that there is a considerable risk of human rights violations flowing from non-voluntary return practices. Apart from the non-binding rights engulfing expulsion decisions referred to above, the present *acquis* does not lay down any safeguards for the individuals affected by practices of forcible removal. The risks entailed by such practices should be mitigated by a forthcoming EU instrument on return, setting binding and detailed minimum standards to be observed by all Member States regardless of domestic legislation. Of particular regulatory

---

[167] See further Noll, note 136 above, at chap. D. 2. c.

[168] See Meijers, 'Forced Repatriation: Towards Minimum Guarantees for Repatriation Treaties' in Meijers, note 37 above, at 105–15. A catalogue of minimum requirements to be inserted into readmission treaties can be found at 111. At large, neither the Specimen Readmission Agreement nor the Prot. recommendations adopted by the Council correspond to these requirements.

[169] Oral information provided by an official within the UN system.

[170] Thus, in our particular case, the maxim is used in analogy to penal law. In the context of interpretation of international law, *in dubio mitius* suggests that norms must not be interpreted in such a way as to exceed the intention of the States making them. In the latter case, the beneficiary of a more favourable outcome is the Contracting State, while it would be the individual rejectee in our case.

interest are detention decisions, the conditions of detention, and the use of force during removal.

5. Detention Decisions   Decisions to detain rejected asylum-seekers must conform with Article 5(1)(f) ECHR. This implies not only that such a decision must be based on law and decided in a proper procedure, but also a limitation to a narrowly circumscribed purpose. A rejectee may only be detained when 'action is being taken with a view to deportation'. Detention for purposes other than those enumerated in Article 5(1) ECHR is illegal. Thus, it is important to identify the exact content of the wording in Article 5(1)(f). Trechsel has pointed out that the purpose of this provision is to allow for the implementation of removal.[171] Thus a deprivation of liberty in order to prevent an alien from going into hiding is covered by paragraph (1)(f), as well as the deprivation of liberty inherent in forcible removal itself. Trechsel emphasizes that the serious intention to remove, held by the authority in question, is of decisive importance. If it turns out that actual removal cannot be performed, this does not make past detention illegal. But, by the same token, it would be illegal to continue detention in spite of the fact that removal is rendered impossible.[172]

This entails two conclusions. First, it is illegal to detain a rejected asylum-seeker, who cannot reasonably be presumed to go into hiding. It must be emphasized that such an assessment must be made on a case-by-case basis. Rejection of a claim cannot automatically be equated with a risk of going underground. Accordingly, routinely detaining rejected asylum-seekers does not conform with Article 5(1)(f) ECHR. Secondly, it is illegal to detain a rejected asylum-seeker when removal proceedings have come to a halt. This can be the case if there are legal obstacles to removal (for example, under Article 3 ECHR), or if factual impediments render repatriation impossible (for example, if the home country declines to receive its nationals, or if it is logistically impossible to transport the individual to her country of origin). It should be emphasized that the turning point is not the absolute impossibility of removal, but its improbability within a reasonable time-frame.

In addition, it should be emphasized that detention for the purpose of punishing the rejected asylum-seeker for failing to co-operate is illegal. So is the use of detention merely to deter other aliens from exercising their right to seek asylum.

6. Detention Conditions   The living conditions in detention facilities have been a recurrent source of reproach directed at state practices. Within the EU context, the 1996 *Annual Report of the Committee on Civil Liberties and Internal Affairs of the European Parliament* criticized the 'deplorable conditions' under which asylum-seekers are kept in detention for expulsion purposes.[173] The Parliament has designated the Committee to elaborate a specific report on that issue and to visit detention facilities in that context.[174] Further, the CPT has been noting inadequate state practices with regard to the holding of 'immigration detainees'. This group contains rejected asylum-seekers. The CPT in its seventh *General Report* emphasizes that persons deprived of their liberty for an extended period under aliens legislation should be held in centres specifically designed for that purpose.[175]

[171] S. Trechsel, 'Zwangsmassnahmen im Ausländerrecht' [1994] *Aktuelle Juristische Praxis* 48.
[172] *Ibid.*   [173] EP Doc. A4–0034/98, at para. 26.   [174] *Ibid.*
[175] CPT, note 134 above, at para. 29.

In general terms, detention conditions must correspond to relevant international standards, especially those flowing from Article 3 ECHR and Article 10(1) and (2) of the ICCPR. Reference should also be made to the UN Body of Principles for the Protection of All Persons under any Form of Detention and Imprisonment.[176] In numerous cases, rejected asylum-seekers are not separated from other groups in detention.[177] Thus, the findings in the discourse on detention conditions for asylum-seekers are largely applicable to the detention conditions prevailing for rejected asylum-seekers as well.[178] These normative sources should be expressly incorporated into a forthcoming EU instrument.

7. The Use of Force During Removal   Apart from detention, other activities related to secure and effective removal fall under the ambit of human rights norms. At all stages of expulsion procedures, the alien must never be exposed to torture, inhuman or degrading treatment, or punishment. For the purposes of this text, it is perfectly sufficient to focus on the least intrusive of the measures falling under Article 3 ECHR. Drawing on the case law of the European organs relating to Article 3 ECHR, a refined understanding of the threshold of suffering regarding inhuman measures and the threshold of humiliation regarding degrading measures can be established. In the assessment of suffering or humiliation, it should be asked whether the treatment causing suffering is proportional with regard to legitimate goals the actor (in this case, the repatriating State) seeks to attain. By way of example, one might resort to cases of solitary confinement, where the additional suffering adduced by solitude has been regarded as motivated by the detainee's exceptional dangerousness. In such cases, the interests of the claimant are weighed against the interests of the State. In other words, a particular treatment or punishment is inhuman or degrading when the suffering or humiliation occasioned is disproportionate with regard to the legitimate goals the actor seeks to attain by it.[179]

The use of force in deportation should be seen against this backdrop of purposefulness, severity, and proportionality. Not all use of force is illegal under Article 3 ECHR. But state obligations under this provision are engaged when there is no proportionality between the legitimate goal of migration control and the measures taken to achieve it. Migration control on the whole is not an all-legitimizing goal. It must be recalled that an individual removal contributes to this goal only as a fraction

[176] Body of Principles for the Protection of All Persons under Any Form of Detention or Imprisonment, adopted by GA Res. 43/173 (1988): in *International Instruments*, note 5 above, at 265.

[177] Taking the example of Germany, it has been established that three federal States generally separate rejectees from other groups, while four States do not maintain any separation of categories. See R. Göbel-Zimmermann, 'Die Anordnung und der Vollzug der Abschiebungshaft' and R. Wolf, 'Materielle Voraussetzungen der Abschiebungshaft' in K. Barwig and M. Kohler (eds.), *Unschuldig im Gefängnis? Zur Problematik der Abschiebungshaft* (1997), 25 and 59 respectively.

[178] On detention of asylum-seekers in general, see UNHCR, *Detention of Asylum Seekers in Europe* (1995); J. Hughes and F. Liebaut (eds.), *Detention of Asylum Seekers in Europe: Analysis and Perspectives* (1998).

[179] The Court also takes into account whether alternative means of pursuing that goal exist: '[a] further consideration of relevance is that in the particular instance, the legitimate purpose of extradition could be achieved by another means which would not involve suffering of such exceptional intensity or duration': *Soering v. UK*, ECHR (1989), Series A, No. 161, 111. In that case, the legitimate goal of bringing a person suspected of murder before a court could be attained by trying him in the UK. Thus, the proportionality test is further supplemented by the maxim '*in dubio mitius*'.

of total removals. Thus, the use of handcuffs, sedative medication, and other intrusive measures in removal cases can give rise to serious legal concerns. In each individual case, the suffering and humiliation effected by it must be weighed against the contribution of the individual's removal to migration control. Any future EU instrument on removal should incorporate this proportionality test.

V. CONCLUSIONS : THE FUTURE OF THE *ACQUIS*

As indicated in the foregoing, the decision-making EU bodies may be inclined to take the asylum *acquis* as a starting point when adopting measures under Title IV of the amended EC Treaty. The impact of existing texts may be increased due to the obligation to adopt a number of measures within the five-year transitional period, in combination with the continued requirement of unanimity during this period. Taken together, this might lead to the *en bloc* adoption of third-pillar instruments in the form of EC legislation, a solution which would be unfortunate for several reasons.

First, such a legislative strategy would fail to take account of the regulatory difference between non-binding political texts, as those hitherto predominant within the third-pillar co-operation, and the binding acts stipulated under Title IV of the EC Treaty. Secondly, an unmodified upholding of the normative contents would disregard persuasive criticism that has been articulated towards essential parts of the *acquis*. Thirdly, as a related issue, there is a need for substantive revision of the texts concerning asylum and refugee protection in the light of the embracing of human rights as a guiding principle for the Union's legislative activities. Finally, but not least importantly, constraining the adoption of future measures by reference to the existing *acquis* would fall short of meeting the challenge of comprehensive solutions to the problem of forced displacement; the exigency of this approach has been frequently pointed out in policy debates during recent years, and is now being emphasized by the EU Treaty itself.

In accordance with the general framework for asylum and refugee policies established by the Treaty of Amsterdam, it should be a matter of priority for the EU to devise mechanisms for the protection of refugees outside the Union territory. Such protection mechanisms would be the logical consequence of measures already taken with respect to external border controls and, as a compensating strategy, they would amply reflect the evolving recognition of international obligations to respect basic human rights extra-territorially. Correspondingly, the exercise of control on the external borders of the EU will have to be sensitized towards protection needs of persons forced to leave third countries.

As there will undoubtedly be a continued need for the admission of persons requiring protection to the territories of the EU Member States, mechanisms for the equitable and efficient sharing of the burden and responsibility of protection among Member States should be adopted in order to enhance protection capacities. Such measures could take into account the burden-concentrating effect of the criteria for state responsibility already laid down in the 1990 Dublin Convention.

On the basis of the above principles and considerations of the future harmonization process, we will point out the most significant implications regarding concrete policy measures which are bound to be adopted within the five-year transitional period. Under the Dublin Convention, any Member State is acting on behalf of the whole EU when examining asylum applications. This must necessarily be reflected in the scope of harmonization measures to be adopted under Title IV, both for reasons of effective burden-sharing and management of asylum procedures, and in due regard for principles of the rule of law. Thus, it is indispensable that all categories of persons in need of international protection be included in the future legislation. Not only is the EU bound to do so in order to ensure compliance with human rights obligations, but this is also likely to be the area with the clearest links between formal burden-sharing and substantive harmonization.

In the same vein, EU standards for asylum procedures should ensure that everyone seeking asylum in a Member State will have the application examined in accordance with EU standards, i.e. in the State responsible under the Dublin Convention or parallel conventions that may be concluded in the years to come. When adopting standards for examination, procedural safeguards will have to be enhanced, taking full account of generally recognized guidelines and human rights obligations. In particular, access to the substantive examination of all applications must be ensured, irrespective of the asylum-seeker's formal status, possession of travel documents, etc. Any deference to national laws and practices of Member States should be ruled out, incompatible as this would be with the very objective of setting minimum standards on behalf of the whole Union.

Human rights obligations impact on asylum procedures beyond procedural safeguards. First and foremost, this should be taken into account when adopting minimum standards for the reception of asylum-seekers during procedures. Such standards must be in accordance with international obligations to respect human dignity and, as a matter of increased relevance, the minimum level of treatment must be complied with regardless of the applicant's utilization of legal remedies under domestic law. The same is true for the preparation and implementation of the return of rejected asylum-seekers: detention and forcible removal are particularly sensitive areas, where Member States need to transform general human rights obligations into context-sensitive standards. Most efficient would be to avoid intrusive practices by means of a Union-wide harmonized effort promoting voluntary return programmes.

As regards the contents of harmonization measures, it is of significant importance that the comprehensive definition of protection categories does not result in further restrictions of the application of universal protection instruments. On the contrary, it must be ensured that the harmonized application of the refugee definition fully corresponds with the well-established *acquis* under the 1951 Refugee Convention. Hence, all relevant forms of persecution, regardless of their perpetrator, should be considered to be covered by the definition. Furthermore, the measure should take account of an evolving sensitivity to gender-related forms of persecution, which is properly covered by the 1951 Refugee Convention.

To avoid the colonizing effects of migration control on issues of refugee protection, future control measures should be synchronized with protection measures. No measure of control should be adopted without it being complemented by a measure safeguarding protection and ensuring rights in the area affected by the control measure. Forming such thematic links is nothing less than rebalancing particularism with the universalist content in Article 6 (*ex* Article F) of the EU Treaty.

A great deal of scepticism has been voiced about the *acquis* as it stands today. The entry into force of the Treaty of Amsterdam implies momentous changes within this policy area, as future harmonization will take place in the form of binding acts. This legal and institutional reform could provide the Union with the competencies to enhance refugee protection by means of more comprehensive policy strategies, as well as firmer commitments for Member States to protection-oriented standards. Whereas restrictionism has been implemented without the legal obligations to do so, the binding instruments to be adopted may prove more efficient in terms of implementation of human rights standards in the broad sense at the domestic level. It remains to be seen, though, whether the Treaty of Amsterdam represents a sufficient framework to meet the increasing challenges in this sensitive and controversial policy area.

12

The Quest for a Consistent Set of Rules Governing the Status of non-Community Nationals

BLANCA VILÁ COSTA

I believe that, in order to prove to them our interest, it would suffice to abolish all those measures which, whilst providing no benefit to the State, appear to be marks of contempt . . . By extending to the metics eligibility for tenure of all the reputable offices . . . we will increase their goodwill whilst adding to the strength and eminence of our country. More-over, as we have within our walls numerous unoccupied sites, the State should allow those of them who so request, and who are considered most worthy, to own the land on which they have built: I believe that, in such circumstances, a far greater number of estimable foreigners will be attracted to Athens as a place of residence . . . It seems prob-able that all stateless persons would wish to establish themselves in our city, and so increase its revenues.

Xenophon, *Poroi* (II, 2, 5, 6)[1]

I. INTRODUCTION: SUBJECT-MATTER OF THE PAPER

Why the reference to aliens 'who are not Community nationals'?
Why the proposed change in our methodological approach?

The answer to these questions lies in the fact that, on this level, the way in which the 'great task' facing the Community is portrayed is highly deceptive; that task is presented in an extremely fragmented and confused form (what about, for example, the common principles of legal certainty and administrative co-ordination?), con-cealing, behind disputes over spheres of competence between protagonists seeking to exercise 'controlling powers', a permissive attitude to extremely substantial re-strictions on human rights: the right to dignity, the right to family life, the right to live in reasonably close proximity to one's place of work, the right to privacy, the

---

[1] See P. Gauthier, 'Un commentaire historique des Poroi de Xenophon', cited in M.F. Baslez, *L'étranger dans la Grèce antique* (1984), 140.

right to social protection, and the right to guaranteed security against the adoption of unjustified or unreasonable deportation measures.

The aim of this chapter is therefore to stimulate reflection on the coherence of the Community system, as it currently exists, in the light of the unity and universality of human rights. With that end in view, the topic chosen for discussion is a very pressing one, namely the status within the European Community of aliens who are not Community nationals, given the shortcomings inherent in the concept of 'freedom of movement for persons' within the strict meaning of that term.

It should be pointed out, first, that, like, *a posteriori*, the concepts of subsidiarity and proportionality, the specific powers conferred on the Community are not only 'subject' to constraints necessitating respect for fundamental rights in the exercise of the activities of the Community but must, in addition, be dynamically 'guided' by the need to respect those rights in the achievement of results in all situations which require to be regulated.

Secondly, the diversity of the various national provisions regulating the situation of non-Community nationals in the internal market (as regards entry, residence/ work permits, family reunification, treatment in the workplace, access to social advantages, etc.) necessarily gives rise in the absence of Community action, or as a result of the ambiguous nature of the action already taken, to a great many highly unsatisfactory situations. These reflect, as will be shown by means of various recent examples, a very widespread general tendency.

We are not dealing here with mere *distortions*, involving obstacles to the free movement of persons. The situations which it is proposed to discuss go far beyond the concept of simple *obstacles*; they are real situations, involving violations of fundamental rights within the area of the Community, which extend beyond the ambit of straightforward regulation of the market but which are structurally linked to the reality of that market, and which call for methods of regulation establishing and conferring a real, tangible status on the persons concerned.

As matters presently stand, twelve million nationals of third countries who are legally settled in Europe are living in the shadow of a costly, uncertain and precarious 'legality', generating great fear, at every stage in their daily lives. This affects such matters as the attainment of majority, dismissal from employment, or the termination of a lease. It is proposed very briefly, and on the basis of recent case law, to examine those limitations and then to attempt to draw up a balance sheet.

The arsenal of provisions laid down in international instruments relating to, *inter alia*, the rights of aliens is quite considerable. The range of those instruments includes the Universal Declaration, adopted in 1948 by the General Assembly of the United Nations, Article 13 of which purports to establish, in paragraph (1), that '[e]veryone has the right to freedom of movement and residence within the borders of each State', and, in paragraph (2), that '[e]veryone has the right to leave any country, including his own, and to return to his country'; the International Covenant on Civil and Political Rights of 16 December 1966, Article 13 of which lays down very clearly the guarantees to be respected in the adoption of deportation measures; and the International Convention on the Elimination of all Forms of Racial Discrimination, signed in New York on 7 March 1966, Article 5(1) of which confirms that 'right to freedom of movement'.[2] All of those instruments declare a principle of freedom of movement (entry and departure). This is not, however, an absolute principle, being subject to strict conditions concerning decisions by sovereign States as to the right of entry into their territory and the right to reside there. They also lay down relatively stringent conditions governing the adoption and implementation of measures for the deportation of aliens,[3] but none of those international legal instruments, including the 1950 European Convention on Human Rights, contains any declaration as to the existence of any real right not to be deported.

Closer examination of Article 5(1)(f) of the ECHR (which concerns the right to liberty and security and contains a straightforward reservation regarding the legality of all deportation measures) and, in particular, Article 8 of that Convention (concerning a person's right to respect for his private and family life, his home, and his correspondence), as well as the fourth and seventh protocols thereto, shows that it adopts a head-on approach to the rights of aliens. In tackling the unsatisfactory situations which most frequently arise, and since the right not to be deported is enshrined neither in the wording of the Convention nor in the relevant case law (see, in particular, *Abdulaziz, Cabales and Balkandali* v. *UK*[4]), the task of the European Commission Court of Human Rights has been to ascertain the limits of the compatibility of the deportation measures taken by European States with the obligations assumed by those States by virtue of their ratification of the Convention, whilst not directly challenging State competence in that sphere.

Thus, inasmuch as there is no direct scrutiny of the basic conditions giving rise to a deportation order, those bodies have sought to ensure that the other rights protected by the Convention are respected and are not prejudiced (see *Agee* v. *UK*[5]). Those other rights include the right to life and the right not to suffer torture or inhuman treatment (Articles 2 and 3 apply where deportation is ordered to a country which may carry out the death penalty and the State in question has signed the Protocol, or where torture is practised); they also include, most especially, the right to respect for private and family life enshrined in Article 8 of the Convention, which applies in cases involving the reunification of families, an area in which case law has played a key role in determining the criteria which must be satisfied in order to enable the substance and scope of that right to be correctly interpreted.

---

[2] Universal Declaration of Human Rights, adopted by GA Res. 217 A (III) (1948), in United Nations, *A Compilation of International Instruments* (1994), i, Part 1, 1; International Covenant on Civil and Political Rights (ICCPR), adopted by GA Res. 2200 A (XXI) (1966), in *International Instruments, ibid.*, at 20; International Convention on the Elimination of All Forms of Racial Discrimination, adopted by GA Res. 2106 A (XX) (1965), in *International Instruments, ibid.*, at 66. See also Art. 22(1), International Convention on the Protection of the Rights of All Migrant Workers and Members of their Families (ICMW), adopted by GA Res. 45/158 (1990), in United Nations, *A Compilation of International Instruments* (1994), i, Part 2, 554.

[3] On the guarantees to be respected in any deportation measure, see Art. 13 ICCPR, the terms of which are adopted in Protocol No. 7 to the ECHR; see also Art. 22(1) ICMW, which prohibits collective deportation measures.

[4] *Abdulaziz, Cabales and Balkandali* v. *UK*, ECHR (1985), Series A, No. 94, (1985) 7 EHRR 471.

[5] *Agee* v. *UK*, App. No. 7729/76, D&R (1977).

The decisions in *Berrehab* v. *Netherlands, Moustaquim* v. *Belgium* and *Abdulaziz, Cabales and Balkandali* v. *UK*[6] may be seen as classic examples of the unsatisfactory situations which arise in the context of violations of the fundamental rights recognized by the Convention. The first of those cases concerned a Moroccan married to a Dutch citizen; the Court held that there had been a violation of Article 8 of the Convention, in that a deportation order had been made against him by virtue of his having been refused a residence permit following the couple's divorce and, consequently, following the cessation of existence of the factor underlying the previous grant of the permit. The fact that the couple had been awarded joint custody of their daughter was considered by the Court, which held that the concept of family life enshrined in Article 8 of the Convention meant that, from the moment of a child's birth, there exists between him and his parents a bond amounting to 'family life', even if the parents are not living together. In the case of *Moustaquim*, which concerned the deportation of an alien who had arrived in the country at the age of 22 months and who had remained there for over twenty years, the Court applied the concept of the 'second generation' immigrant; it held that, where a State which is a party to the Convention sends back to his country of nationality a person who has never lived in that country and who is not linked to it by any emotional tie whatever, and, in so doing, seriously disturbs his family life by separating him from all the other family members, that State commits a violation of the Convention. Lastly, in all of the cases at issue in *Abdulaziz, Cabales and Balkandali* v. *UK*, in which the husbands of female workers had been prohibited from joining their wives on the ground that this would have a negative effect on the national labour market, the Court declined to rule that there had been a direct violation of Article 8 of the Convention, holding instead that the manner in which the contested measure had been applied amounted to sex discrimination, on account of the fact that the Moroccan workers concerned were women.

Having regard to the fact that at least 20 per cent of the applications admitted by the Commission on Human Rights are brought by aliens against the States in whose territory they reside, and that, in statistical terms, the States most frequently concerned are the United Kingdom, the Federal Republic of Germany, Switzerland, France, Belgium, and the Netherlands, most of them Member States of the European Union, it may clearly be seen that the action taken by the Community to eliminate the precariousness of the legal position of aliens residing and working within its territory is inexcusably inadequate.

As part of an attempt to portray so diverse and so contradictory a range of national measures, I propose to consider, by way of example, a number of decisions reported in recent Spanish case law. They all date from 1997 and concern deportation measures taken following the non-renewal of residence/work permits. Jurisdiction to review administrative acts (such as refusal of a residence permit, which is closely linked to the grant or renewal of a work permit following the making of an offer of employment or the conclusion of an employment contract) is organized in such a way that, once all possible remedies have been exhausted in the administrative

---

[6] *Berrehab* v. *Netherlands*, ECHR (1989), Series A, No. 138, (1989) 11 EHRR 332; *Moustaquim* v. *Belgium*, ECHR (1991), Series A, No. 19, 20; *Abdulaziz, Cabales and Balkandali* v. *UK*, note 4 above.

sphere, first-instance proceedings (i.e. contentious administrative proceedings) must be brought before the *Tribunal Superior de Justicia* (High Court of Justice) of the autonomous region concerned, whose decision is subject to appeal to the *Tribunal Supremo* (Supreme Court, Third Chamber). The latter forum tends to adopt a very strict and formal approach in its assessment of the cases before it, only very rarely taking into account the factual circumstances constituting the real background against which the competent administrative authority (normally the *Direccion Provincial de Trabajo* (Provincial Labour Office) or the *Direccion Provincial de Migracion* (Provincial Migration Office) of the respective central government Ministries) adopted its decision. Consequently, it very frequently happens that, in cases which have lasted on average for some six to seven years, the *Tribunal Supremo* annuls well-substantiated decisions of the *Tribunales Superiores de Justicia*, which are competent to review the facts of the cases brought before them and which are, as a general rule, reasonably sensitive to the circumstances underlying the dispute, such as the degree of actual integration (previous legal residence, working activities actually carried on, membership of the 'second generation' of immigrants, etc.) of the alien in question in the society in which he is settled.

Thus, in its judgment of 4 November 1997 in the case of *M. Laghrib* v. *State Administration*, the *Tribunal Superior de Justicia* of Catalonia (Chamber for Contentious Matters, Fifth Division) annulled the resolution of the Minister of the Interior (Civil Government) of 23 September 1994 ordering the deportation of, and prohibiting re-entry by, a Moroccan national who had arrived in Spain in 1973, aged 5 years old, with his family. All the other members of his family had acquired Spanish nationality; he resided with his parents and his four brothers and worked legally in the locality, having lived since his arrival in the same town, where the family owned a residential property. Since his arrival as a child, he had completed his basic education and occupational training in the locality; and in 1985, upon attaining his majority, he had obtained his residence permit. His failure punctually to renew that residence permit (on which the validity of his work permit depended) on its expiry led to a series of administrative measures being taken against him, and his position was exacerbated by periods of internment in a psychiatric institution (in 1990, 1991, and 1996), drug addiction, and, finally, a suspended custodial sentence for theft. In the fourth ground of its judgment, the court ruled as follows:

> in considering all these facts and matters, it must be borne in mind that a deportation order may have very serious consequences where it is made against a person who has undoubtedly put down roots, having been legally resident in Spain since 1973, and the members of whose family, who are presumably willing to help him in his difficulties, are of Spanish nationality and legally resident in Spain.

The court held that the deportation order made against him was disproportionate.[7]

The judgment of the *Tribunal Superior de Justicia* of Catalonia (Chamber for Contentious Matters, Second Division) of 18 December 1997 in *Raffik Tuzani* v. *D.G.T. and S.S.* concerned a refusal to renew a contingent work permit issued to a

---

[7] Cited in Y. Madiot, 'Un statut européen de l'étranger dans la jurisprudence de la CEDH', [1992] *Annales de la Fac. de Droit de Poitiers*.

Moroccan worker (which made it impossible for him to obtain a legal residence permit) on the ground that he did 'not have a stable employment record', having merely worked during the period of validity of his first permit in a series of temporary jobs of an intermittent nature (in the hotel and seasonal trades). The worker in question was affiliated to the social security scheme and was, moreover, registered with the national employment office as a person seeking work. In its consideration of the case, the regional *Tribunal Superior de Justicia* took the opportunity to express its very broad acceptance of the evidence put forward by the applicant in support of his claim that the first permit should be renewed, namely: the rationale underlying his seasonal work in the hotel trade (which must not be confused with unstable employment), his affiliation to the social security scheme, and the production by him of a contract of employment covering the period following the submission of his renewal application, all of which matters formed the factual background to the case at issue.[8]

Lastly, the judgment of the same court (Chamber for Contentious Matters, Second Division) of 16 May 1997 in *K. Benmira* v. *DG de Migraciones del Ministerio de Asuntos Sociales* concerned a refusal to issue a work permit, alternatively, a refusal to issue a residence permit (involving, as always, the risk of deportation), to a Moroccan woman who had been legally resident in Spain for over fifteen years. She had entered the country with her Moroccan husband, who had worked legally in Spain and who had died there, and with her son, who was one year old at the time of entry. She had applied for and obtained two work/residence permits, had been engaged in various part-time jobs as an office cleaner and was registered as unemployed with the national employment office. Whilst unemployed, she had for a long time taken advantage of the vocational training courses organized by the European Social Fund. The permit was refused just at the time when 'social integration' assistance of a minimum sum of 40,000 pesetas per month, which she claimed quite openly, had been extended for a further period, thus creating a paradoxical and unsatisfactory situation. The refusal in issue purported to be based on 'non-fulfilment, in the circumstances of the case, of the criteria laid down by law for such renewal', including, in particular, the production of 'proof of current employment in work of an occasional nature and evidence of a desire to obtain regular employment during the ensuing period'. The court took into consideration the fact that Mrs Benmira had openly enrolled for vocational training, regarding this in a positive light; it then proceeded, at length and in well-substantiated detail, to rule that the initial decision should be annulled, basing its conclusion on the need to take into account 'one of the fundamental pillars of the legal order governing the position of non-Spanish nationals in Spain, which involves matters such as the family roots and cultural, social and professional ties' of such persons.[9]

That sensitivity on the part of certain courts would make for extremely positive reading were it not for the fact that the various administrative authorities of the State systematically bring successful appeals against their decisions before the *Tribunal Supremo* (Third Chamber), which is a by-word for leisurely progress (cases take six to seven years to be heard) and inflexible rulings on the legal issues applicable in the

---

[8] Unpublished judgment of the *Tribunal Superior de Justicia* of Catalonia of 4 Nov. 1997.
[9] Unpublished judgment of the *Tribunal Superior de Justicia* of Catalonia of 18 Dec. 1997.

cases in question, generally culminating in annulment of permits 'revived' seven years previously by the regional courts[10] (on refusals to grant work permits, alternatively residence permits, to Norwegian and Moroccan nationals respectively; the permits were subsequently 'revived' by the *Tribunales Superiores de Justicia* of the Canary Islands and of Catalonia, but their refusal has now, once again, been held to be in accordance with the applicable Spanish law).

If unsatisfactory situations are to be avoided in this sphere, there is now, more than ever, a need for Community action leading to the establishment of a set of rules governing the minimum status to be enjoyed by non-Community nationals residing and working on a regular basis in one of the Member States comprising the integrated market which is the European Union. The disparity between the policies, rules, and judicial interpretations applying in the different Member States is incompatible with the principles of legal certainty, coherence, and administrative co-ordination, all of which rank as essential elements of the constitutions of the Member States of the Community. Indeed, to refrain from taking action until such time as the free movement of persons within the Community becomes an issue goes no way towards resolving the question of how to avoid the unsatisfactory situations described above.

To that end, this chapter is based, therefore, in terms of the premises underlying its consideration of the Community system as it currently exists, on two fundamental factors. The first concerns the voluntary absence of a real 'systematic body of rights', formulated in clear and sufficiently precise terms and applying to all aliens who are integrated and gainfully employed within the EU; the need to address that absence subsists *a fortiori* since the conditions attaching to citizenship of the Union are now, more than ever, such as to require clarification of the status of aliens. The second factor concerns the ambiguity surrounding the historical existence, until the Treaty of Amsterdam, of real Community competence in matters of immigration policy (notwithstanding, once again, the existence in theory of freedom of movement for persons). These two concepts lie at the heart of the 'unfinished tasks' facing the Community, and are central to the unsatisfactory situations described above.

Moreover, this chapter does not set out merely to analyse developments arising from work recently carried out (ranging from the activities of the Conference on the Maastricht Treaty to those of the Intergovernmental Conference culminating in the Treaty of Amsterdam, for example); it also seeks to provide an explanation based on the structural 'weaknesses' inherent in the concept of an 'internal market' for persons, rather than the advantages which that concept offers.

In the context of the *factors giving rise to inconsistency* which it is proposed to examine (in Part I), it must be acknowledged that, given the necessarily limited scope of the powers conferred on the Community, and in view of the nature of its decision-making process, characterized as the latter is, despite the frequent exertions of the European Parliament and the Commission in that regard, by considerations of political expediency and efficiency in specific areas based on priorities fixed more or less exclusively by its Member States, the activities of the Community in certain areas

---

[10] *Tribunal Supremo*, 3rd Chamber, 4th Div., 22 Apr. 1997, Rec. 11284/1990 and 29 Apr. 1997, Rec. 7764/1990.

(such as freedom of movement for persons, which has not yet been secured) take the form of, and are dictated by, acts and proposals which have different legal bases and which encompass both Community matters (subject to review by the Court of Justice) such as the policy on visas, covered by Article 100c of the EC Treaty (now repealed), and intergovernmental matters (such as the measures provided for in Article 31 (*ex* Article K.3) of the Treaty on European Union); those matters have hitherto involved both the internal structure of the Union and, in tandem with action taken by certain of its Member States, its external relations (Schengen), as well as *ad hoc* structures. Such limited action, the parameters of which are indistinct and the nature of which is wholly fragmented, gives rise to very serious inconsistencies in terms of respect for human rights and fundamental freedoms, especially inasmuch as it affects, by virtue of the reductionist consequences of a simple 'market approach', such areas as the lives of individuals, their movements, and the scope of the rights enjoyed by them.

What action needs to be taken? Suggested answers to that question will be found in Part II. First, it is necessary to undertake a diagnosis of the results of this 'structural disorder' characterizing the actions of the Union, and to realize that certain priority measures which were initially, and naïvely, thought to be expedient but which are now no longer justifiable, such as the strengthening of controls at external frontiers and the elimination of controls at internal borders, have given rise, in the action which has been taken, to disparities which are intolerable in a Union comprised to a very considerable extent of aliens who are active and, in some cases, socially irreplaceable members of our society, who are legally resident in the Community, and who are waiting for their rights to be defined in some way or other.

An attempt will be made, in putting forward possible remedies, to move away from the realm of purely theoretical logic to that of reality, by advancing proposals for a change of method centred on an integrated, non-fragmentary approach to the phenomena analysed. Those proposals are based on a status-oriented construction, to be applied on the same lines as the approach adopted in creating the concept of citizenship of the Union, of the concepts or categories of concepts relating to nationals of third countries who have become integrated into the life of the Union. The aim is to produce a result which is, at the same time, also consistent with the approach needing to be adopted in agreements with third countries, particularly those from which the persons concerned originate.

II. FACTORS GIVING RISE TO INCONSISTENCY

A. Limited Competence and Fragmentary Methodologies

The European Union and, more particularly from the point of view of the free movement of persons, the European Community possess specifically conferred powers which are necessarily limited. The primary result of this is that, whilst any legal rule, by the fact of specifying and circumscribing within its structure a given situation or

relationship which it is designed to regulate, has the effect, to some extent, of severing and separating such situations from the reality in which they occur in daily life,
the fragmentation of inherently *communautaire* legal concepts gives rise to a double
dismemberment, namely that arising from the fact of forming, like any legal rule, a
vehicle for legislative action which is necessarily limited and, in addition, that of
constituting the subject-matter of the exercise of Community competence and of
consequently being subject to specific restrictions.

Although that twofold constraint has not had the effect of causing a very extensive
acquis communautaire, carefully monitored by the Court of Justice, to come to grief,
it nevertheless places a heavy burden on the legislative task to be fulfilled, since it is,
by definition, in the sphere of freedoms and Community policies relating to individuals that all the lacunae, overlapping characteristics, and limitations of the legal
techniques adopted tend to converge.

There are, in fact, some areas which lend themselves well to the transfer of competence and to management at Community level (such as the internal market in goods
and competition law, to cite a couple of examples). However, the task of defining and
circumscribing the rights of individuals has not proved an easy one: it took thirty-
five years to progress from the concept of a 'national of a Member State carrying on
an economic activity' and to arrive, by means of a precarious extension of the benefit ·
of certain rights to non-workers, at the notion of citizenship of the Union, based on
the grant to all Community nationals of a common nucleus of rights.

Is it in fact possible to speak of the existence of real rights and freedoms for individuals at Community level, whether they are citizens of the Union or not, if those
freedoms are characterized only by the fact of their being effectively exercised on a
transnational basis? Is it possible for us, as individuals, to fall within the scope of
Community law as regards the conditions governing access to the occupations which
we carry on or our family life, while at the same time falling outside that scope (inasmuch as we may choose not to exercise our freedom of movement and may decide to
remain in our country of origin, thereby placing ourselves in a 'purely internal' situation)? Does this not inevitably involve a 'dismemberment' running counter to the
very concept of fundamental rights? Obviously, the foregoing remarks are not in any
way intended—indeed quite the reverse—to belittle the invariably paramount task
of the Court of Justice in consolidating a real *acquis* of rights arising from the exercise of freedom of movement, prime examples of which are to be found in a number
of important recent decisions.[11] However, the interpretational inconsistencies are
relatively marked, as the Commission itself acknowledged not long ago in its proposal of 30 July 1997 (presented pursuant to Article 31 (*ex* Article K.3) of the Treaty
on European Union) for a Council Act establishing the Convention on rules for the
admission of third-country nationals to the Member States:

[11] See the judgment of 12 May 1998 in Case C–85/96, *Martinez Sala* v. *Freistaat Bayern* [1998] ECR
I–2691 (reference for a preliminary ruling) and the extension of the previous case law introduced by the
judgment of 30 April 1998 in Case C–24/97, *Commission* v. *Germany* [1998] ECR I–2133; see also the interesting Opinion of Ruiz-Jarabo AG, delivered on 30 Apr. 1998 in Case C–18/95, *Terhoeve* v. *Inspecteur
van de Belastingdienst* (not yet reported) concerning the social security contributions payable by migrant
workers by comparison with those payable by workers who are nationals of the host country.

Community law governs the admission of third-country nationals who, being members of the families of Union citizens, are admitted on the family reunification principle and exercise the right to freedom of movement. There is consequently a lacuna as regards family reunification in the case of persons not exercising that right. National law covers the situation in some cases, but generally on a restrictive basis (age of children, rights of relatives in the ascending line). As Union citizenship is a single citizenship, the gaps in the current situation should be filled in by a provision for equal treatment of all Union citizens.[12]

Moreover, we are not concerned here with the problems deriving from *interlegality*, that is to say, those which arise when bodies possessing competence in the protection of human rights or fundamental freedoms concern themselves with matters falling within the scope of Community law, nor with the course to be followed in order to promote such protection, which currently forms the subject-matter of the legislative mandate conferred by Article 6 (*ex* Article F) of the Treaty on European Union. That course has been made quite clear by a judicious line of case law, in particular the judgment of 18 June 1991 in *ERT*:

[The Court of Justice] has no power to examine the compatibility with the European Convention on Human Rights of national rules which do not fall within the scope of Community law. On the other hand, where such rules do fall within the scope of Community law, and reference is made to the Court for a preliminary ruling, it must provide all the criteria of interpretation needed by the national court to determine whether those rules are compatible with the fundamental rights the observance of which the Court ensures and which derive in particular from the European Convention on Human Rights.

In particular, where a Member State relies on the combined provisions of Articles 55 and 56 in order to justify rules which are likely to obstruct the exercise of the freedom to provide services, such justification, provided for by Community law, must be interpreted in the light of the general principles of law and in particular of fundamental rights.[13]

By contrast, the very point with which we are here concerned is a problem of *intralegality*, which is clearly structural in origin: if the fundamental rights of individuals either fall within the scope of Community law (as is the case with the nucleus of specific rights conferred on nationals of the Member States, entitling them to receive the same treatment as nationals of other Member States as regards the exercise of freedom of movement by them and by their spouses, even where the latter are not Community nationals), or are affected by the competence conferred on the Community (as is the case with the rights of third-country nationals, who are already affected as regards visas (see Article 100c (now repealed) and the two regulations adopted on the basis of that Article[14]), it necessarily becomes imperative to ensure that the protection of those rights is not jeopardized by the existence of any lacunae

---

[12] COM(97)387 final, at 18, commentary on Art. 25.

[13] See, amongst the academic writings on this issue, the very recent article by G. Rodriguez Iglesias 'El Derecho comunitario y las relaciones entre el TJCE, el TEDH y los Tribunales Constitucionales nacionales' (1997) 1 *Revista de Derecho Comunitario Europeo* 329–76; extract from the ECJ judgment of 18 June 1991 in Case C–260/89, *ERT* v. *DEP* [1991] ECR I–2925.

[14] The regs. in question are Reg. 1683/95 (29 May 1995) laying down a uniform format for visas ([1995] OJ L164/1) and Reg. 2317/95 (25 Sept. 1995) determining the third countries whose nationals must be in possession of visas when crossing the external borders of the Member States ([1995] OJ L234/1).

within, or on the external perimeter of, Community law, and at the same time that they are susceptible of a coherent interpretation.

The following examples serve to illustrate various inconsistencies which still currently exist; they are mentioned by way of reminder of the unsatisfactory situations arising in the area under consideration. Naturally, the chosen starting-point concerns situations which are undoubtedly covered by Community law.

Article 141 (*ex* Article 119) of the EC Treaty, which does not specifically define its precise scope, and which remained, pending the entry into force of the Treaty of Amsterdam, one of the 'first-generation' provisions yet to be updated, lays down the principle of the 'fundamental right' of male and female workers to receive equal pay for equal work. Its wording draws its inspiration from that of the relevant conventions and from the constitutions and evolving legislation of the Member States. That fundamental right, which is structurally linked, in its regulation of the relations in the workplace determining its application, to the obligations incumbent on the Member States, logically covers what may be termed 'purely internal situations', without imposing any requirement regarding objective transnationality or any condition relating to the nationality of those whom it is intended to benefit. However, for reasons connected, in all probability, with the absence of any positive definition of the wide scope of that right as it appears in the law from which it originates, one searches in vain, amongst a compendious body of case law, for a single case brought before the Court of Justice in which the principle of equality has been relied on by a female worker who is not a Community national in the context of an application to the Community judicature for an interpretation of its scope.[15]

Nevertheless, the question arises why it should not be possible to extend that method of promoting a solid nucleus of personal rights far beyond the ambit of any element of transnationality in relations in the workplace, accompanying it where necessary (see the new Article 13 (*ex* Article 6a) of the EC Treaty as inserted by the Treaty of Amsterdam) by changes reflecting the corresponding difference in the concept of the market.

Let us consider a different situation. The sphere in which the Community freedoms laid down by Articles 39, 43, and 49 (*ex* Articles 48, 52, and 59) of the EC Treaty may properly be exercised is clearly a purely transnational one, defined in relation to the exercise of those freedoms on an intra-Community basis by persons on whom they are conferred. It follows that 'purely internal situations' remain outside the scope of Community law, save for the purposes of considering the purely subjective right to exercise those freedoms. The consequence of this is well recognized, namely, the possibility of reverse discrimination between Community nationals, arising from the fact that the positive content of the rights granted, taken as a whole (in particular, the right to equal treatment, without discrimination based on nationality, as regards access to employment, conditions of work and employment, or any other social advantage), cannot be relied on in such cases, being structurally linked to the exercise of freedoms on a transnational basis. This brings us back to the

---

[15] However, a number of important decisions concerning workers from third countries, most of them married to Community nationals, are to be found in the case law relating to judicial review of the application of the staff regs. of officials.

example, cited above, of a Community national married to a third-country national who resides in his/her Member State of origin or who resettles in that Member State after spending a period of time outside the Community, and who does not have the right (save where it is granted by the domestic law of the Member State concerned or, as more frequently happens, by an international agreement with the country from which his/her spouse originates) to family reunification with his/her spouse. Alternatively, the spouse of the Community national concerned may be denied economic rights or employment rights arising from his/her circumstances, as would be the case if Regulation 1612/68[16] and Directive 68/360[17] were applicable. Consequently, the dichotomy between the body of 'fragmentary' rights conferred by Community freedoms (as extended, even with regard to those members of a worker's family who are not Community nationals, by the initial implementing regulations adopted in 1968 and 1971) and the concept of a Union citizenship 'applicable to all' enables lacunae to subsist, giving rise to discrimination between citizens and sometimes imposing severe limitations on the right to live together as a family, particularly in cases where a family member is subjected, often without justification, to measures refusing him entry into the country concerned or forcing him to leave it in consequence of his having been denied a work permit or residence permit.

We must not overlook, however, the momentous interpretation recently applied in the case of *Martinez Sala* to the interrelation between Article 17(2) (*ex* Article 8(2)) of the EC Treaty and Article 12 (*ex* Article 6), which prohibits any form of discrimination on grounds of nationality between Community nationals. In its judgment in that case, the Court of Justice ruled as follows:

> 62. Article 8(2) of the Treaty attaches to the status of citizen of the Union the rights and duties laid down by the Treaty, including the right, laid down in Article 6 of the Treaty, not to suffer discrimination on grounds of nationality within the scope of application *ratione materiae* of the Treaty.
> 63. It follows that a citizen of the European Union, such as the appellant in the main proceedings, lawfully resident in the territory of the host Member State, can rely on Article 6 of the Treaty in all situations which fall within the scope *ratione materiae* of Community law . . .[18]

Does this mean, however, that that provision, which, until the adoption of the concept of the 'free movement of persons', was specifically directed at persons who are 'occupationally active', now also covers 'non-active' persons?[19] Article 18(1) (*ex* Article 8a(1)) of the EC Treaty confers on every citizen of the Union 'the right to move and reside freely within the territory of the Member States, *subject to the limitations and conditions* laid down in this Treaty and by the measures adopted to give it effect'. If it is to be construed as meaning that citizenship of the Union necessarily involves the application, without discrimination, of the rights which *it itself* grants to

---

[16] [1968] OJ Spec.Ed. 475.   [17] [1968] OJ Spec.Ed. 475.

[18] Paras. 62 and 63 of the judgment of 12 May 1998 in Case C–85/96, *Martinez Sala* v. *Freistaat Bayern* [1998] ECR I–2691.

[19] The relevant dirs. are Dir. 90/364/EEC (28 June 1990) on the right of residence ([1990] OJ L180/26), Dir. 90/365/EEC (28 June 1990) on the right of residence for employees and self-employed persons who have ceased their occupational activity ([1990] OJ L180/28) and Dir. 93/96/EEC (29 Oct. 1993) on the right of residence for students ([1993] OJ L317/59).

all, how can the decision in *Martinez Sala* be reconciled with certain forms of discrimination (particularly in relation to the criteria governing access to the right to freedom of movement for persons who are not workers) between Community nationals who continue to 'conform' to the concept of citizenship itself, having regard to the 'conditions' imposed by the 1990 and 1993 directives on students, retired persons, and residents generally?

It may easily be seen, in those cases, that structural implications subsist in the dichotomy between persons who are workers and persons who are not. Thus, the latter must be in a position to prove, like most aliens not covered by legislative provisions in general, (1) that they are covered by (social) insurance in their country of origin and (2) that they possess sufficient financial means to enable them to avoid being a 'social burden' on the economy of the host country. Does that 'rebuttable presumption of non-productivity' not constitute a further trivialization of the very substance of the right to freedom of movement for Community nationals, and at the same time an 'invitation' to all sorts of abuse of the type familiar to the competent authorities responsible for matters concerning foreigners from the various Member States? The dichotomy in this instance arises from the extension of personal rights arising on the creation of the internal market, which was of a purely formal nature only. In other words, it involved a *personal* extension of rights accompanied by a *substantive* reduction of those rights. Consequently, discrimination subsists between citizens of the Union.

B. Plurality of Legal Bases and Excessive Diversity of Authorities Empowered to Take Action

A second *factor giving rise to the inconsistency* inherent in the multifarious restrictions on the fundamental rights of 'aliens' under Community law is to be found in the great diversity, giving rise, in turn, to substantial differences in the applicable legal bases, existing amongst the various authorities empowered to take action in a naturally fragmentary sphere such as that involving issues relating to 'aliens', all of them forming the subject-matter of legislative policies pursued by the Community and by the Member States: entry controls, asylum, immigration, visas, the prevention of clandestine immigration, terrorism, drug trafficking, and co-operation between police forces in those areas. We are a long way here from the models establishing the status of aliens which are to be found in the United Nations Convention of 1990 on the Protection of the Rights of Migrant Workers and Members of their Families or in the provisions of the Council of Europe Convention of 1977 on the Legal Status of Migrant Workers, which focus on the substantive rights of workers (including those working illegally) in the long term.[20]

That diversity, which is so apparent in the European Union, operates both as an external factor (in non-Community dealings, including those of a multilateral nature, between Member States, as evidenced, in particular, by the Schengen Agreements, *ad hoc* working parties on co-operation and the network of bilateral

---

[20] Council of Europe, Convention on the Legal Status of Migrant Workers, of 24 Nov. 1977, in force in the States which have ratified it since 1 May 1983, BOE, No. 145 (16 June 1983).

agreements between Member States and third countries (normally, former colonies)) and as an internal factor (initially brought into practice as a result of the need to 'supplement' the Community rules requiring freedom of movement for persons within the internal market, subsequently given structured form (save as regards policy on visas: see Article 100c (now repealed) of the EC Treaty) within the third pillar under the Treaty on European Union, and now on the point of being partially rectified by the absorption within the Community sphere of matters of asylum and immigration policy and of what is termed the 'Schengen *acquis*'). Those instances of diversity, which, having initially fallen within the ambit of extra-Community affairs (in 1986–93 and 1997), have proceeded to come within the diversified scope of internal matters covered by the European Union (in 1993 and from 1997 onwards[21]), and the essential elements of which have not been eliminated, despite the successive moves to bring about 'rationalization' (aspects of which will be discussed in the text to note 23 below), are bound to increase confusion and legal uncertainty amongst individuals, instead of producing unequivocally successful results in the areas concerned.

In fact, for the purposes of analysing that diversity of authorities (and despite the fact that it has been possible since 1976, with the setting up of the Trevi Group, to speak in practical terms of intergovernmental co-operation between Member States in matters concerning asylum and immigration, as well as the fact that eleven Member States have now ratified the Schengen Agreements of 1985 and the 1990 Convention on the Implementation of the Schengen Agreements[22]), it will be seen that it is the fundamental amendments to the EC Treaty introduced by the Single European Act which, ingenuously and paradoxically, will bring about the decisive methodological step leading to the 'internalization' of certain external factors in the years to come, by establishing the objective of the *internal market* as the parameter for the 'free movement of persons' provided for by Article 18(2) (*ex* Article 8a(2)) of the EC Treaty, with the latter forming an integral part of the former.

Why this incomplete paradox? The reason is that that legislative declaration was enshrined in the Treaty on the assumption that the field of freedom of movement for persons could be transferred to the sphere of Community competence, thus marking the beginning of the open conflict between Community competence (in matters involving movement within the Community) and national competence (in matters of immigration from outside the Community), the result being a trend towards a *de facto* proliferation of the procedures applied within the area corresponding to the territory of the Communities and their Member States—the future area of the Euro-

---

[21] The dates referred to are those of the successive reforms of the Treaties which substantially altered the situation regarding competence in this area.

[22] Convention Applying the Schengen Agreement of 14 June 1985 between the Governments of the States of the Benelux Economic Union, the Federal Republic of Germany and the French Republic on the Gradual Abolition of Checks at their Common Borders, Schengen, 19 June 1990, reprinted in H. Meijers *et al.*, *Schengen: Internalisation of Central Chapters of the Law on Aliens, Refugees, Privacy, Security and Police* (1992), 177. The Trevi Group, composed of the EC ministers for home affairs and comprising working parties and subgroups, had in fact been set up in order to combat terrorism. During the 1980s, work was carried out in the fields of justice and home affairs not only by the *Ad Hoc* Working Party on Immigration but also by the European Committee to Combat Drugs (CELAD), the Groupe Assistance Mutuelle (GAM), empowered to act in the field of customs, and the Schengen operational structure units.

pean Union. Thus, the procedures adopted by the *Ad Hoc* Working Party on Immigration, composed since 1986 of the ministers responsible for such matters, were purely intergovernmental in nature. In 1988 the European Council of Rhodes charged the Intergovernmental Co-ordination Group on Freedom of Movement for Persons with the task of analysing the requisite criteria for the creation of a 'space without internal frontiers' within the meaning of Article 18 (*ex* Article 8a) of the Treaty, whilst proposing measures intended to lead to the elimination of internal controls. A crucial stage was reached in 1989 with the presentation by the Spanish Presidency of the 'Palma Document', offering a working plan for the different fields of co-operation in the fields of justice and home affairs, which sought to circumvent that fragmentation and to apply a degree of rationality to that entire scenario.

Despite everything, the limitations naturally inherent in a course of action which had been developed, in essence, by numerous different authorities along intergovernmental lines necessarily heralded, in 1991, the advent of the Treaty of Maastricht, in which (with the exception of the new Article 62 of the EC Treaty, forming part of the first pillar and governing the sole issue brought within the Community sphere, namely that of a single visa permitting entry into the territory of the Community) all matters not subject to strictly Community procedures were relegated to the third pillar: Title VI consolidates, on paper, all of the 'provisions on co-operation in the fields of justice and home affairs'. That structure was designed to meet the urgent need to integrate the opaque system of existing groups under a single, global umbrella within the Union, by circumventing the dual involvement of numerous different authorities and by co-ordinating their activities. Since November 1993, work in this area has been co-ordinated by the 'K.4' Committee, composed of officials from the Member States, of which the Commission is an associate member. Provision is made in Article 31 (*ex* Article K.3) TEU for the methods to be used and for consultation between the Member States with a view to co-ordinating action throughout the Union. The legal instruments which may be used comprise *joint action*, the adoption of *joint positions*, and the drawing up of *conventions* (see Article 31 (*ex* Article K.3) (2)(a), (b) and (c) TEU).

However, inasmuch as Title VI was itself enacted in response to the multiplicity of authorities involved in the pluralistic regime previously operating (combining, in paragraphs 1 to 9 of Article 29 (*ex* Article K.1), a series of highly diverse matters, including asylum (Article 29(1)), the crossing of frontiers (Article 29(2)) and immigration policy (Article 29(3)), together with the fight against drug addiction (Article 29(4)) and international crime (Article 29(9)), and in so far as its aim of continuing development was to be achieved by means of intergovernmental co-operation, inconsistencies were bound to remain. In fact, its enactment as an integrated whole was forced through only *ratione auctoritatis* by ministers—in particular, the ministers for home affairs—'wearing the same hat', the structural criterion applied being, of necessity, certain minimum rules of intergovernmental relations, the only ones possible in the circumstances.

Let us now examine in greater detail the method employed in the 'dismemberment' of those matters relating to the rights of aliens which are enshrined in the Treaty on European Union. Even though, within the list contained in Article 29 (*ex*

Article K.1) in Title VI of the Maastricht Treaty, the rationalization and order of the operative wording created certain advantages as regards the first three areas of competence listed,[23] (namely, (1) asylum policy, (2) rules governing the crossing by persons of the external borders of the Community and the exercise of controls thereon, and, above all, (3) immigration policy and policy regarding nationals of third countries in relation to (a) conditions of entry and movement on the territory of Member States, (b) conditions of residence, including family reunion and access to employment, and (c) combatting unauthorized immigration, residence, and work by nationals of third countries), the measure which, on a temporary basis, had a savage impact was the introduction, in isolation, of Article 100c (now repealed) into the wording of the EC Treaty.

In fact, the specific inclusion within the umbrella of Community competence of one of the aspects of point (2) relating to the conditions applicable to the crossing of borders, namely the issue of a *single visa*—that being the only matter on which there was agreement between the Member States and the Community—increased the degree of fragmentation, introducing new powers and procedures[24] which led, in turn, to an increase in the level of diversity, this time inside the Union. Thus, Article 100c, which was intended to function as a transitional provision affording a guaranteed means of access to the Community structure, via two 'linking' provisions which are interesting from a technical standpoint but too weak and too aleatory (Article 37 (*ex* Article K.9) of the Treaty on European Union and Article 100c(6) (now repealed) of the EC Treaty), for the other issues on the agenda concerning the Union's policy on aliens, has not helped to clarify the most contingent aspects of the field which it covers; its effects are centred on the efforts made to achieve its own success, and its implementation has remained precarious and open to dispute, as will be seen from the analysis appearing below.

Article 6(2) (*ex* Article F(2)) of the Treaty on European Union, which expressly imposes on the Union the obligation to respect fundamental rights, as guaranteed by the ECHR and as they result from the constitutional traditions common to the Member States, 'as general principles of Community law', is binding on all the institutions of the Union in the exercise of their respective powers. Having said that, there remains the familiar problem of the limited jurisdiction of the Court of Justice, which (in accordance with the provisions of Article 46 (*ex* Article L) of the Treaty on European Union) does not have powers of judicial review with regard to matters falling within the third pillar (save in respect of the Community conventions referred to in Article 31 (*ex* Article K.3)(2)(c)). We therefore find ourselves in an area in which, despite the fact that Article K.2 of the Maastricht Treaty (not reproduced in the Amsterdam Treaty) contained an express legal provision relating to the ECHR,[25] application of the provision in question is not formally subject to autonomous judicial review by the Union. This gives rise to further fragmentation, but it should none the less be borne in mind that, as regards the reservation of powers in matters relating to guaranteed freedom of movement for persons (Article 3(c) and the second paragraph of Article

---

[23] Paras. 1, 2, and 3(a) to (c) of Art. 29 (*ex* Art. K.1) TEU (1992).   [24] See note 14 above.

[25] 'The *matters referred to* in Article [29 (*ex* Article] K.1 shall be dealt with in compliance with the [European Convention on Human Rights] and the Convention relating to the Status of Refugees . . . and having regard to the protection afforded by Member States to persons persecuted on political grounds.'

14 (*ex* Article 7a) of the EC Treaty) and the policy on visas (Article 100c(1) to (7)), the Court of Justice fully retains its jurisdiction to review the application of fundamental rights as 'general principles of Community law'.

These inconsistencies, arising from an irrational fragmentation of the 'matters' concerned, may even occur within the framework of one and the same topic, as a result of the second constraint (specifically conferred powers) and of the 'pillar' structure discussed above. To take a classic example: in the case of the imposition of a visa requirement for nationals of third countries, competence clearly vests in the Community as regards the drawing up of the list of the third countries to which the common visa requirement is to apply, but it will be noted that such competence does not extend to cover transit visas in Community airports. Let us consider certain instances of this.

As regards the first of those issues, the Court of Justice has already confirmed, in its judgment in *Parliament* v. *Council*,[26] that it has jurisdiction to exercise its powers of review in so far as concerns the implementation of Article 100c of the EC Treaty. In bringing the proceedings in that case, the European Parliament contested its partial exclusion from participation in the procedure leading to the adoption of Council Regulation 2317/95 determining the third countries whose nationals must be in possession of a visa within the meaning of Article 100c(1) of the EC Treaty; the regulation was annulled by the Court. The second issue was the subject of a negative approach on the part of Advocate General Fennelly in his Opinion of 5 February 1998 in *Commission* v. *Council*,[27] in which the Commission, with the support of the European Parliament, sought annulment of a Joint Action adopted on the basis of Article 31 (*ex* Article K.3) of the Treaty on European Union, the Council being supported by France, the United Kingdom, and Denmark.[28]

In the latter case, the Commission, arguing on the basis of the approach adopted in its proposal for a regulation on the drawing up of a list of countries whose nationals require an entry visa (subsequently adopted as Regulation 2317/95), advanced a familiar argument, namely that Article 100c must be interpreted in the light of the concept on which it is based, namely the free movement of persons within the internal market. In the context of its proposal leading to the adoption of Regulation 2317/95, the Commission had made its position very clear, namely that Article 100c, which 'is clearly situated' in the chapter of the Treaty dealing with the internal market, was in line with the objectives pursued by Article 14 (*ex* Article 7a) of the EC Treaty, and that it was necessary to draw all the appropriate inferences from this.[29]

---

[26] Case C–392/95, *Parliament* v. *Council* (*Visa Directive*) [1997] ECR I–3213.

[27] Case C–170/96, *Commission* v. *Council* [1998] ECR I–2763.

[28] Opinion delivered on 5 Feb. 1998 in Case C–170/96, *Commission* v. *Council* [1998] ECR I–2763, at 2765.

[29] Thus, attention is drawn to Art. 100c(1), which requires unanimity, and, since 1 Jan. 1996, Art. 100c(3), which requires a qualified majority vote for the drawing up of the list of countries whose nationals must be in possession of a uniform visa (Reg. 2317/95 was adopted on 25 Sept. 1995, before the end of the period during which unanimity was required, and was the subject of the action brought by the European Parliament against the Council in Case C–392/95, *Parliament* v. *Council* (*Visa Directive*) [1997] ECR I–3213). The reg. laying down a uniform format for visas had its own legal basis, Art. 100c(3), and was adopted by a qualified majority. On the limitations on the Commission's powers in relation to initiatives by the Member States, see Art. 100c(4): 'the Commission shall examine . . .'. See the Communication from the Commission to the European Parliament and the Council on the possible application of Art. 37 (*ex* Art. K.9) TEU, COM(95)566 final.

How, then, was the term 'airport transit visa' to be defined? Did it fall within the scope of Article 100c, as the Commission and the Parliament claimed? Article 1 of the Joint Action of the Council which was contested in those proceedings defined the visa in question as authorizing 'transit through the international areas of the airports of Member States'. The Council and the Member States intervening in its support argued that, on a proper construction of the legislation, such a visa does not contemplate the crossing of the external borders of the Community or freedom of movement within the territory of the Member State concerned. The question arising, therefore, was whether it was possible for a person holding a transit visa to be transferred from one airport to another within the same Member State. That question was deliberately excluded from the scope of Regulation 2317/95 by its Article 5, thus suggesting that it should be answered in the negative. If, however, transit between two airports within the same Member State does not involve the crossing of external borders, that gives rise to a third regime, since it necessarily follows in such circumstances that nationals of third countries transferring between airports within the same Member State are not covered by either Regulation 2317/95 (relating to a uniform visa requirement) or the Joint Action (relating to transit visas). The Advocate General, in recapitulating several of the inconsistencies identified, seems to have been forced to acknowledge the possibility of such a situation and to consider that freedom of movement is not a relevant issue in this instance:

> While the traveller transferring between airports in a single Member State might well be present on the territory for a longer period than one who remains in the international zone of one airport, he still does not enjoy the benefits of the free movement of persons within the internal market, or even within the host Member State. Even if it were to be shown that the [airport transit visa] covered this category of air traveller, this would not suffice to bring the [airport transit visa] within the scope of Article 100c.[30]

The inconsistencies created by the internal factors mentioned above are necessarily supplemented by the diversity arising from the special regimes existing under the various Community agreements with the third countries of which the aliens concerned are nationals.[31] Applying the usual system of classification, it is necessary to distinguish between (a) co-operation agreements, (b) the Lomé regime, and (c) association agreements.

(a) The *co-operation agreements* operate, primarily, to the benefit of nationals of the Maghreb countries: Morocco, Algeria, and Tunisia. From the late 1970s onwards, the Community concluded a number of agreements the effect of which was to consolidate the situation regarding migration from northern Africa to Europe. The agreements in question are worded in very

---

[30] Para. 43 of the Opinion of Fennelly AG in Case C–170/96, *Commission* v. *Council* [1998] ECR I–2763, at 2780.

[31] See, in particular, the co-operation agreements with the Maghreb countries, most of which date from 1978: the 1978 Co-operation Agreement with Algeria, the 1978 Co-operation Agreement with Morocco and the 1988 Co-operation Agreement with Tunisia. See [1978] OJ L295/1. See also: M. Baldwin-Edwards, *The Politics of Immigration in Western Europe* (1994), 322 ff; M. Baldwin-Edwards, 'The Emerging European Immigration Regime: Some Reflections on Implications for Southern Europe' (1997) 35 *JCMS* 501–3; J. Handoll, *Free Movement of Persons in the EU* (1995) chap. 10, 313–43.

general terms; they seek to contribute to the economic and social development of the third countries concerned and to strengthen relations between those countries and the Community.[32] They also contain, however, provisions prohibiting discrimination as regards working conditions or remuneration, which are applicable by extension to other family members in the field of social security. The Court of Justice has based its decisions (particularly in *Kziber*[33] and *Yousfi*[34]) on a clear line of case law recognizing the repercussions for individuals of Article 41 of the Agreement with Morocco, inasmuch as that Article 'lays down in clear, precise and unconditional terms a prohibition of discrimination'.[35]

(b) Under the special regime provided for in the Lomé Convention, a substantial number of non-Community nationals who have legally entered the Community from former colonies and who are economically active there are entitled to rely on the principle of non-discrimination laid down in Article 5 and Annex VI to the Fourth Lomé Convention, particularly as regards the right to work and eligibility for social security, housing, education, health protection and social services.[36]

(c) In the context of the *association agreements*, and having regard to the current situation concerning immigration from third countries whose nationals are already present in considerable numbers within the Community, it is primarily Turkey and the countries of central and eastern Europe which are affected.

The agreement concluded with Turkey in 1963 has already produced a significant body of case law, attesting to the achievement of a certain amount of progress and, at the same time, the imposition of a number of restrictive qualifications.[37] That agreement has been the subject of various decisions of the Council of Association, almost all of them concerning Turkish workers resident in Germany. As long ago as 1987, when delivering its judgment in *Demirel*, the Court declared that the provisions of association agreements 'form an integral part of the Community legal system'.[38] In paragraph 21 of its 1994 judgment in *Eroglu*, the Court held that a young Turkish national seeking to join his father, who was legally working and residing in Germany, had the right to work and was entitled to renewal of his permit allowing him to reside in the Community; it stated that persons seeking employment must, as workers, be entitled to a residence permit in the Member State concerned, 'not only in order to accept offers actually made there, but also to look for employment

---

[32] Judgment of 31 Jan. 1991 in Case C–18/90, *Onem* v. *Kziber* [1991] ECR I–199; judgment of 20 Apr. 1994 in Case C–58/93, *Yousfi* v. *Belgium* [1994] ECR I–1353. For an analysis of the previous situation concerning the Maghreb countries, see A. Nadifi, 'Le statut juridique des travailleurs maghrebins résidant dans la CEE' [1983] *RMC* 289 ff.

[33] Case C–18/90, *Onem* v. *Kziber* [1991] ECR I–199.

[34] Case C–58/93, *Yousfi* v. *Belgium* [1994] ECR I–1353.

[35] Baldwin-Edwards, note 31 above, at 503.

[36] Handoll, note 31 above, at 340–5.

[37] See the 1963 Association Agreement and the Additional Protocol thereto of 1970, with regard to which the most important decisions have been Decs. 2/76 and 1/80 of the Council of Association.

[38] Judgment of 30 Sept. 1987 in Case 12/86, *Demirel* v. *Stadt Schwäbisch Gmünd* [1987] ECR 3719.

there'.[39] Unfortunately, in the case of *Bozkurt*, that case law was shown to be highly debatable and, in any event, inadequate.[40]

It should be borne in mind, moreover, that the *European* association agreements concluded with central and eastern European countries provide for a transitional period of ten years as regards access for workers originating from countries which are due in the future to accede to the Community; they facilitate both the establishment of self-employed workers and the establishment of, and competitive provision of services by, their undertakings by means of a workforce which is well trained but significantly less well paid than the Community workforce.[41]

One of the major issues concerning nationals of third countries is that of family reunification; this in fact constitutes their main access route to the territory of the Community. What is the legal regime governing that general means of access? In order to answer that question, it is necessary, first of all, to draw a basic distinction between the two groups of persons concerned. One of those groups is highly disparate, whilst the other is broadly homogeneous. The issue as regards the first group concerns family reunification for workers from third countries; in the case of the second, it is the reunification of family members who are not Community nationals with Community nationals exercising their right to freedom of movement. With regard to the first group, the applicable law (in the absence of any agreement with the Community or, alternatively, where no bilateral agreement is in force) is the national legislation of each of the Member States concerned, laying down the criteria for family reunification which need to be fulfilled in order to confer a right of residence.[42] In the case of the second group, the conditions are much more specific: the right of residence was extended to cover members of the families of Community nationals moving within the Community who are not themselves Community nationals as long ago as 15 October 1968, upon the adoption of Regulation 1612/68 of the Council (Article 10) and of Council Directive 68/360/EEC (Article 3). The principal right deriving from that legislation guarantees freedom of movement for workers who are Community nationals, irrespective of the nationality of their spouses. In addition, the right of residence for family members covers spouses of Community nationals moving within the Community who are not themselves Community nationals; in such cases, the legislation extends, from a formal standpoint, beyond the existing distinction between workers and non-workers.[43] The remaining lacuna relates, therefore, to spouses and relatives of Community nationals who continue to reside in their country of origin or who resettle there after spending time outside the Community; those persons fall within the first of the groups referred to above.

[39] Judgment of 5 Oct. 1994 in Case C–355/93, *Eroglu* v. *Land Baden-Württemberg* [1994] ECR I–5113.

[40] Judgment of 6 June 1995 in Case C–434/93, *Bozkurt* [1995] ECR I–1475.

[41] Baldwin-Edwards, note 31 above, at 501; see also the detailed analysis of those agreements in Handoll, note 31 above, at 327–8.

[42] L. Idot, 'Le regroupement familial dans l'Union européenne', in *Revue 'Europe'*, No. 6, at 5; A.M. Lopez Bellosta, 'El reagrupimiento familiar en la Union Europea' [1996] *Mémoire de Troisième Cycle*.

[43] Arts. 2 and 3 of the 1990 dirs. concerning persons not engaged in any occupational activity, note 19 above. See also the commentary on that point by Vila Costa in *Anuario CIDOB* 1996 (1997), 168. The measures concerned must be adopted within a mandatory time-limit, which does not apply in the case of the matters covered by Art. 63(3)(a) and (b) and (4) of the EC Treaty as amended by the Treaty of Amsterdam.

Does the wording of the Treaty of Amsterdam justify any real hopes that the regime governing legal aliens may be reconstituted under the umbrella of Community law?[44] It must be said that the surgical operation involved in separating the 'issues' of asylum, immigration, and the other policies concerning the free movement of persons, which are covered by the wording of Title IV of the EC Treaty (with a view to the creation of an area of freedom, security, and justice), from the other issues combined within Article 29 (*ex* Article K.1), as agreed at Maastricht (in particular, the fight against drug addiction, the fight against international fraud and the promotion of police co-operation, arranged in accordance with the powers of the ministers within the Council), cannot but inspire a positive reaction,[45] whilst at the same time confirming—albeit only partially—the importance of leaving a door open within the Treaty by means of Article 100c, relating to visas. However, the new Articles 61 to 63 of the EC Treaty also suffer from the same defect, in that they are 'dismembered' and split up pursuant to criteria which have been established not *ratione materiae* but *ratione auctoritatis*, in accordance with the Council's powers.

Thus, the new Article 61, laying down the measures to be adopted by the Council within a maximum period of five years,[46] draws a new structural distinction between (a) measures aimed at ensuring the free movement of persons in accordance with Article 14, which is to form its legal basis (formerly Article 8a of the EEC Treaty/Article 7a of the EC Treaty), (b) directly related flanking measures with respect to external border controls, asylum and immigration (dealt with in Article 62), and (c) other measures in those fields which do not relate to controls (which may also be adopted in the fields of asylum, immigration and the protection of the rights of nationals of third countries), dealt with in Article 63.

It will be seen from a closer examination of the provisions of Article 63 that paragraphs (3)(a) and (b) and (4) of that Article concern the adoption of measures on immigration policy and the rights of nationals of third countries who are legally resident in the Community. Save for the measures relating to illegal immigration and illegal residence, which must be adopted within the five-year period, those measures are not subject to that time-limit. What are those measures which are henceforth to fall within the scope of Community competence but in relation to which the Member States are to retain their powers to introduce compatible national provisions? The areas concerned relate to (a) conditions of entry and residence, and procedures for the issue by Member States of long-term visas and residence permits, including those for the purpose of family reunion; (b) illegal immigration and illegal residence; and (c), under Article 63(4), measures defining the rights and conditions under which nationals of third countries who are legally resident in a Member State may reside in other Member States.

[44] See, as regards the initial reactions to the text presented by the Irish Presidency in Dec. 1996 and the first document produced by the Dutch Presidency, Vila Costa, note 43 above, at 168.

[45] *Ibid.*, inasmuch as this will bring about a change which will help to 'unblock' the 'tranquil areas' of the third pillar.

[46] That time-limit is both binding (providing, as it does, for a fixed period of 5 years) and not immediate (inasmuch as its binding nature relates to the procedure by which the measures are to be taken, not the results which they are to achieve).

Despite the advantages afforded by this partial transposition of the various elements of the regime applicable to aliens in the European Union, the fragmentation brought about by this 'possible' re-working of the Treaty leads to two results:

- it gives rise to a 'structural' separation of the provisions concerning the free movement of persons from those relating to the system governing the status of the non-Community nationals concerned;
- all the indications are that, in consequence of the concentration on rules relating to the carrying out of controls, the measures adopted will primarily be aimed at achieving the objectives of establishing external border controls and ensuring the absence of controls at internal borders as a result of the absorption of the Schengen *acquis* into the Community sphere, as provided for by the new Treaty.

C. A Solely 'Political' Will to Tackle Matters which are of an Excessively Structural Nature

For the purposes of this analysis of what may be termed the 'inconsistency factors', and following on from the foregoing review of the technical/normative aspects, it is now appropriate to turn our attention to the ways in which the institutions have in the past manifested their will to tackle this subject, and to take stock of the different approaches revealed by the steps which have been taken. It should be stated at the outset that the greatest consistency is to be found, logically enough, in certain initiatives launched at various times by the Commission and, above all, by the European Parliament. The Council, on the other hand, swayed by the representations made by the governments of the Member States of which it is comprised, and by their eagerness to retain total control over their respective employment markets, affords a prime example of the inconsistency, imbued on occasion with feelings of guilt, which is under consideration here. Be that as it may, the political price paid, in historical terms, by the Commission with a view to the introduction, step by step, of piecemeal Community powers has been too high, and has had grave consequences.

The Commission's initiatives date, in fact, from the period when the problems of immigration began to affect certain highly sensitive labour markets; the situation was aggravated by factors connected with the third countries concerned (Mediterranean countries which had not yet joined the Community; former colonies, etc.) which necessarily contributed to the structural consequences arising from the impact, in the middle of an energy crisis, of the first enlargement of the Community. In the context of the implementation of its social action plan, the Commission submitted to the Council, as early as 1975 and 1976, two proposals for directives. The 1975 proposal for a directive on the education of children of migrant workers[47] encompassed the children of non-Community migrant workers; that aspect of it was rejected by the Council upon the adoption of the Directive in 1977, but a declaration

---

[47] The proposal for a dir. was published in [1975] OJ C213/2; the Parliament's resolution concerning that proposal, setting out the wording proposed by the Commission and the amendment requested by the Parliament, was published in [1975] OJ C280/48. For the dir. in the form in which it was finally adopted, see [1977] OJ L199/32.

was nevertheless annexed to the minutes, stating that the Council was manifesting the Member States' desire for an extension of those measures to cover that group of persons. A second proposal for a directive, submitted in 1976,[48] concerned the harmonization of laws in the Member States to combat illegal immigration and illegal employment in the Community; this was rejected by the Council.

In 1983 the European Parliament adopted a resolution concerning migrant workers, which sought to apply a codified, long-term approach to issues concerning their status, and which called for the existing problems to be resolved by (a) the elimination of discrimination between national workers and migrant workers in the fields of employment, remuneration, and vocational training; (b) the adoption of the Directive on illegal immigration; (c) the adoption by the Community and the Member States of the Council of Europe Convention on the Legal Status of Migrant Workers; and (d) the setting up of a proper body of Community rules governing that group of persons.[49]

In the context of the implementation of its 1984 social action plan, and on the highly precarious legal bases afforded by the Treaty provisions on social policy, in particular Articles 117 and 118 of the EC Treaty, the Commission adopted an extremely pragmatic, policy-oriented, and 'possibilist' approach in its 1985 'Guidelines',[50] in which it asserted that the Community should have simple competence with regard to consultation, experimentation, and information concerning the policies implemented by the Member States with regard to nationals of third countries and immigration from outside the Community. This prompted very strong criticism from the European Parliament in its 1985 resolution on those Guidelines,[51] in which it advocated a more codified and more radical approach. Lastly, the Commission's 'migration policy' decision[52] led to the conferring of binding powers in the field of the communication of information, consultation, and the procedures to be followed by the Member States with regard to migration policy; although that decision was analogous in its form to a set of guidelines, it imposed on the Member States various obligations as to the result to be achieved. It was contested before the Court of Justice by a number of Member States (France, Germany, the United Kingdom, the Netherlands, and Denmark) and partially annulled by the Court on the ground that

[48] [1976] OJ C277/2.
[49] Amongst the institutions, it is, in fact, the European Parliament which, since the early 1980s, has always adopted a broad, consistent position as regards the legal approach to be followed with a view to establishing the status of non-Community aliens. See the Dury/Maij-Weggen Report, together with the Resolution of 13 Mar. 1996 embodying (i) Parliament's opinion on the convening of the Intergovernmental Conference, and (ii) an evaluation of the work of the Reflection Group and a definition of the political priorities of the European Parliament with a view to the Intergovernmental Conference: Doc A4–0068/96, at 6–23.
[50] COM(85)48 final; see, in particular, Part V, paras. 44, 27.
[51] Text of the draft Council resolution, with the European Parliament's amendments, published in [1985] OJ C141/75.
[52] COM(85)310 final; see Commission Dec. 85/381/EEC [1985] OJ L217/25, in particular Arts. 1, 2, and 3. That decision proposed the adoption of preventive measures, involving the giving of advance notice of draft legislation and draft agreements, with a view to the establishment of a mandatory system of consultation between the Community and the Member States in matters concerning migration policies.

the legal basis afforded by Article 118 of the Treaty did not operate to confer on the Community sufficiently binding powers.[53]

From a strictly theoretical standpoint, the implementation of a real 'internal market', operating *inter alia* as an area offering freedom of movement for persons, should have facilitated Community action in all matters, including the migration of non-Community nationals, arising within that area; however, the 'intergovernmentalist' approach adopted and applied at the Intergovernmental Conference was bound to affect the outcome.

In fact, the White Paper on the Internal Market[54] provided for the co-ordination of national rules on residence, entry, and employment of nationals of third countries, together with the abolition of controls at the internal borders between the Member States, the establishment of a Community policy on visas, and the fixing of common rules concerning extradition. However, the adoption of the Single European Act, in particular the insertion by it of Article 18 (*ex* Article 8a) into the EEC Treaty and the definition of the internal market, was accompanied by a *general* declaration by the Conference stating that 'nothing in these provisions shall affect the right of Member States to take such measures as they consider necessary for the purpose of controlling immigration from third countries'[55] and by a *political* declaration by the governments of the Member States stating: '[i]n order to promote the free movement of persons, the Member States shall cooperate, without prejudice to the powers of the Community, in particular as regards the entry, movement and residence of nationals of third countries'. The Commission's broad approach to the very concept of the free movement of persons was counterbalanced by the Council's narrow approach, geared to controlling immigration from outside the Community; this resulted in the pursuit of the 'possibilist' line taken by the 1985 Guidelines.

It should nevertheless be noted that, in certain respects, the initial reactions of the European Councils of Hanover and Rhodes should not be read in a negative light. The Hanover European Council called for the submission by the Commission of a report on the social integration of migrants legally resident in the Community, whilst the Rhodes European Council drew attention in its Declaration to the need:

> to achieve . . . promotion of human rights and fundamental freedoms, free circulation of people and ideas and the establishment of more open societies; promotion of human and cultural exchanges between East and West.[56]

However, the Madrid European Council, held in June 1989, approved the so-called 'Palma document' prepared by the Co-ordinators' Group, defining, first and foremost, the five essential preconditions for the free movement of persons, namely: (1) the establishment of controls at external frontiers; (2) the common policy on visas; (3) the right to freedom of movement without the need to possess a visa; (4) the

---

[53] Judgment of 9 July 1987 in Joined Cases 281, 283–285 and 287, *Germany, France, Netherlands, Denmark and United Kingdom* v. *Commission* [1987] ECR 3203.

[54] COM(85)310 final.

[55] General Declaration on Arts. 13–19 of the SEA, published by the Office for Official Publications of the European Communities in *European Union: Selected Instruments taken from the Treaties* (1995), i, bk 1, 770.

[56] Political Declaration by the Governments of the Member States on the free movement of persons, *ibid.*, at 777; Conclusions of the Rhodes European Council, *Bull. EC* 12–1988, pt. 1.1.10.

abolition of controls at internal borders; and (5) determination of the Member State responsible for examining asylum applications which are submitted with a view to being able to exercise that right.[57] From the standpoint of the effectiveness of the action to be taken in the medium term and long term, that establishment of priorities was somewhat naïve, and it heralded subsequent developments of a negative nature which were destined to prevent the achievement of any tangible progress in the construction of a real regime governing the status of non-Community nationals.

At the request of the Hanover European Council, the Commission subsequently reverted to a codified approach in its 1989 'Report on the social integration of migrant workers' from third countries, based on a distinction applied to those possessing the legal and permanent status of persons resident in a Member State. That approach was adopted and developed in the 1990 Experts' Report on immigration policy and the social integration of migrant workers; and it was shared by the Community Charter of the Fundamental Social Rights of Workers, approved by the Strasbourg Council on 9 December 1989, at which the Member States recognized their obligation to guarantee to migrant workers and their families living and working conditions comparable with those enjoyed by national workers.[58]

The European Parliament decided to maintain a maximalist and unambiguous position; that approach was shared by the Economic and Social Committee, which, in its two opinions delivered in 1991, emphasized the need to establish a proper status for migrant workers and a migration policy.[59] Similarly, it was not until 1991 that the Commission took any significant steps in pursuance of a credible commitment to achieve progress in that direction, in the form of its communication of 23 October 1991, the objective of which was threefold: (1) the incorporation of migration, as a constituent element, into the external policy of the Communities; (2) control of the flow of migration; and (3) promotion of the integration of legally resident migrants within the Community.[60] 1991 marked, moreover, the commencement of a work programme instigated by the Report of the *Ad Hoc* Working Party on Immigration, which had been set up by the Luxembourg Council; that programme, relating to immigration policy, was subsequently submitted to the Maastricht European Council. It proposed greater harmonization of a number of principles in that field (harmonization of policy on the admission of persons for the purposes of employment, action with regard to aliens who, having already entered the Community, are resident there, and the creation of a category of 'persons permanently resident' in a Member State), and advocated the strengthening of the action to be taken in accordance with the extent to which a common institutional structure might henceforth exist within

[57] Conclusions of the Madrid European Council, *Bull. EC* 6–1989, pt. 1.1.7.

[58] Report on the social integration of migrant workers from third countries: SEC(89)924 final; experts' report on immigration policy and the social integration of migrant workers: SEC(90)1813; Community Charter of the Fundamental Social Rights of Workers, adopted in the form of a declaration by the Heads of State or Government at Strasbourg on 8 Dec. 1989; conclusions of the Strasbourg European Council published in *Bull. EC* 12–1989, pt. 1.1.9 (see, in particular, its para. 4).

[59] CES(91)560, CES(91)1122, and CES(91)1394.

[60] SEC(91)1855 final. Since 1990, the Commission has advocated the adoption of a more ambitious and consistent position: it maintains that the fundamental objective must be equality of treatment for legally resident aliens, as is clearly stated in its communications of 1991 and 1994.

the Union—even if that structure were divided up between the first and third pillars.[61]

In fact, following the entry into force of the Maastricht Treaty, the Commission affirmed its approach in its communication on immigration and asylum policies of 23 February 1994,[62] in which, in line with the objectives set out in its earlier communication of 1991, it structured the aims of Community action in terms of three familiar elements, namely: (1) action on the causes of migration; (2) control of migration flows; and (3) the integration of legal immigrants, to be achieved by promoting their successful integration into their host societies, by creating information and dialogue structures, and by combating racism and xenophobia.

The approaches adopted by the other Community institutions with regard to migration, taken as a whole, ultimately had a significant effect from a strictly political standpoint, prompting the Council to adopt five resolutions[63]—that is to say, instruments not possessing binding force—concerning the Community action planned for the period from 1993 to 1996. The resolutions in question are 'reconstruction' resolutions on family reunification (1993), on admission for the purposes of employment, admission of self-employed persons, and admission for study purposes (20 June 1994), and on the status of third-country nationals residing on a long-term basis in the territory of the Member States (1996).

It seems, therefore, that we may now be witnessing, to a certain extent, a transformation of the political will of the Member States of the Union into positive action on the terms advocated by the other institutions, and that the establishment of a distinct, properly codified status for the persons concerned may become legally possible in the near future.

However, the following question still remains to be answered: is it possible—as appears to be the political wish of all the institutions—for action to be taken on the basis of the 'reconstruction' of a coherent status for non-Community nationals in the light of the strategies hitherto pursued, namely:

- the inconsistency between the political approach of the Council (which has been broadly liberal, especially since 1991) and the *legal* approach which it has adopted (evidencing a marked concern to safeguard the national powers of the Member States in that sphere, if necessary by means of proceedings before the Court of Justice);
- increasing recourse to the only possible means of achieving the desired end, despite its ambiguous form and precarious solidity, that is to say, the inclusion within the areas of Community competence of the 'tranquil areas' comprised in the third pillar, in particular certain aspects of immigration policy;
- whilst, at the same time, the Community/Union remains, particularly in the aftermath of the Palma document and the good intentions expressed therein, a hostage to a problematic concentration on a particular issue, namely the bipartite distinction between external and internal frontiers and the division

---

[61] Report of the Immigration Ministers meeting within the Maastricht European Council on immigration and asylum policy, SN 2556/91 WGI 809, Brussels (31 May 1991).

[62] COM(94)23 final.   [63] Resolutions published in [1996] OJ C274 andC80.

of powers for the purposes of the exercise of controls by the Community and by the Member States, that being an issue which ought, from a naïve perspective, to have defined the remaining matters concerned?

III. DIAGNOSIS AND REMEDIES

A. Diagnosis of the Results: A Plurality of Confused Legal Solutions and an Asymmetrical and Purblind Policy

The existence, still disputed, of limited Community competence in the spheres of immigration policy and the status of non-Community nationals, combined with excessively fragmented techniques (too many specific 'issues' to be dealt with), constitute structural limitations, with the result that the Community is faced with real legal vacuums which cannot be filled without a transfer of sovereignty. In consequence of the division of powers and the 'possibilist' practices adopted by the institutions, we now have a diversity of authorities empowered to intervene; this in turn gives rise, internally, to a plurality of legal bases for action by the Union, inspired by a political will which is full of good intentions but which is wholly lacking in the practical effectiveness which would be afforded by a binding legal framework.

The picture is a disappointing one; it is appropriate, therefore, to undertake a brief review of the work accomplished since the first initiatives were launched, with a view to establishing the extent to which the methods used have met with success. It must be acknowledged that, outside the ambit of Community affairs *stricto sensu*, (1) the success of the Schengen Agreements[64] constitutes the most noteworthy achievement to date in the field of the free movement of persons. France, Germany, and the Benelux countries, which signed the original Agreement in 1985, were subsequently joined by Italy (1990), Spain, and Portugal (1991), Greece (1992), and Austria (1995), with the Scandinavian countries acting as observers; the Agreements (together with the 1990 Implementation Convention) entered into force in March 1995, the last countries to apply them being Italy and Greece (1997). The 1985 Agreement was inspired by the economic principles of the free movement of goods, services, and persons within the EC; its scope—following the establishment of the internal market resulting from the revision of the Single European Act—covers an entire range of procedures concerning checks at borders on Community nationals, nationals of third countries, and persons seeking asylum. As regards matters of immigration policy, however, the Agreements cover *inter alia* the following matters:

- common rules concerning checks at external borders;
- conditions concerning the crossing of internal borders and the policy on visas;
- the imposition of penalties on airlines which accept passengers who are not in possession of the requisite documents;

[64] See note 22 above.

- criteria concerning the determination of countries competent to examine asylum applications;
- exchanges of information regarding applicants for asylum.

Within the sphere of special areas of competence, mention should also be made of the Dublin Convention of 15 June 1990[65] determining the State responsible for examining applications for asylum lodged in one of the Member States of the European Communities. The Dublin Convention is the result of negotiations conducted within the *Ad Hoc* Working Party on Immigration; its objective is to guarantee the rights of persons seeking asylum in a Member State (in particular, by ensuring legal certainty). In pursuing that objective, it is clearly aimed at helping to reduce illegal immigration. Its guiding principle is the determination of the State possessing competence to examine an asylum application, that is to say, the State responsible for handling the matter. The Convention provides, lastly, that the State in which that responsibility rests is to be either (a) the State having the closest connection with the person seeking asylum, (b) the State through entry into which that person gains access to the territory of the Community, (c) the State which has issued him with an entry visa, or (d) the State with which the person seeking asylum shows that he has family connections.

Let us now consider the steps taken within the Community itself, taking as our starting-point the reforms introduced by the Maastricht Treaty on European Union, with its new legal bases:

- first, Article 14 (*ex* Article 7a) of the EC Treaty (formerly Article 8a of the EEC Treaty), aimed at the progressive establishment of an internal market for, *inter alia*, persons; Article 100c (now repealed) is not applicable for the purposes of achieving its objectives;
- next, Article 100c, laying down a visa requirement for nationals of third countries, a list of which is to be drawn up; this Article follows on from Articles 95 (*ex* Article 100a) and 100b (now repealed) concerning the internal market, and has always been interpreted by the Commission as an essential element of the very concept of the internal market;
- finally, and in particular, Article 31 (*ex* Article K.3) of the Treaty on European Union, which forms part of the third pillar and is contained in Title VI; that Article provides a basis for the adoption of joint positions and, more especially, the adoption of joint action and the drawing up of conventions.

What results have been achieved by the introduction of the above measures?

(a) On 10 December 1993 the Commission submitted a proposal for a regulation based on Article 100c; this was adopted on 25 September 1995 as Regulation 2317/95,[66] determining the third countries whose nationals must be in possession of visas when crossing the external borders of the Member States. Airport transit visas are excluded from its scope. That regulation formed the subject-matter of an action for annulment brought before the Court of Justice by the European Parliament and was annulled by the judgment of 10 June 1997.[67]

---

[65] Text published in *Bull. EC* 6–1990, pt. 2.2.2.
[66] See note 14 above.   [67] See above, Case C–392/95, *Parliament* v. *Council* [1997] ECR I–3213.

However, the specific issue of airport transit visas formed the subject-matter of an initiative launched in February 1995 by the French presidency of the Council, which led to the adoption—thus, without the participation of the Commission—of the Council's Joint Action of 4 March 1996, annulment of which was sought by the Commission in the proceedings before the Court of Justice.[68] The applicant institution pleaded that airport transit visas fell within the scope of Article 100c, and consequently claimed that the matter was amenable to the jurisdiction of the Court. However, the Court accepted the detailed reasoning contained in the Opinion delivered by Advocate General Fennelly, and held that the action was inadmissible.

A fortiori, the Commission was keen to see the adoption of Regulation 1683/95 of 29 May 1995 laying down a uniform format for visas, the legal basis of which was Article 100c(3) of the EC Treaty.[69]

(b) The Commission has presented two proposals for Council acts concerning the adoption of conventions, based on Article 31(2)(c) (*ex* Article K.3)(2)(c) of the Treaty. The first, dated 10 December 1993, relates to the crossing of the external frontiers of the Member States; this has not yet been adopted, and there is little chance of its adoption in the immediate future. The second, dated 30 July 1997,[70] concerns the rules for the admission of third-country nationals to the Member States; it is relatively broad in scope (covering both admission and residence), and is inspired by criteria which are clearly intended to promote the integration in Member States of groups of persons defined as 'legal residents' and 'long-term residents'.

(c) In addition, five joint actions have been adopted (pursuant to Article 31(2)(b) (*ex* Article K.3)(2)(b) of the Treaty on European Union) in relation to immigration within the framework of the third pillar:[71]

- a decision (adopted in 1994) on joint action concerning travel facilities for school pupils from third countries resident in a Member State;
- the decision referred to above (adopted in 1996) concerning airport transit visas for third-country nationals, which establishes a list of ten countries whose nationals must possess such visas for transit through the international areas of the airports of Member States, but which does not require them to possess a visa authorizing them to cross external borders;
- a decision (adopted in 1996) concerning burden-sharing with regard to displaced persons;
- a joint action (adopted in 1996, published in 1997) concerning a uniform format for residence permits for long-term residents;
- a joint action (adopted in 1997) on measures to combat trafficking in human beings and sexual exploitation of children.

---

[68] Case C–170/96, *Commission* v. *Council* [1998] ECR I–2763.   [69] See note 14 above.
[70] Communications from the Commission to the Council and the European Parliament concerning (a) a proposal for a decision based on Art. 31 (*ex* Art. K.3) of the TEU establishing the Convention on the crossing of the external frontiers of the Member States: COM(93)684 final; and (b) a proposal for a Council Act establishing the Convention on rules for the admission of third-country nationals to the Member States: COM(97)387 final.
[71] For a brief commentary on the contents of each proposal, see Baldwin-Edwards, note 31 above, at 503.

The question needing to be answered is as follows: has the common 'umbrella' under which the Union has accommodated, in three pillars, the diversified structure of the specific initiatives previously dealt with at an external or intergovernmental level, produced the results which were expected? In the author's view, the results which it has produced are exactly as feared. That answer has already been given not only by the Commission but also by the European Parliament and by the Intergovernmental Conference. For the purposes of attempting to change the situation, it is appropriate at this juncture to note three significant elements:

(1) a twofold obstacle, involving:

- the structural weaknesses inherent in the Treaty on European Union. The lack of progress in the implementation of the instruments available under Title VI is in fact due to those weaknesses rather than to any real lack of political will on the part of the Member States. Since decisions can be adopted only unanimously, the use of 'soft law' instruments and of resolutions has proved to be the only possible means of intervention in that sphere;
- the frustration of any hope of seeing the free movement of persons, including third-country nationals, established in consequence of the introduction of a real internal market. Article 100c of the EC Treaty has merely created one more legal frontier within the first and third pillars, by permitting the institution of proceedings before the Court of Justice to contest matters arising in certain very marginal areas, and without producing any result which really consolidates and codifies the status of third-country nationals.

(2) The obstacle created by a model dictated by political priorities (establishment of external frontiers) which were thought to constitute structural preconditions for an area within which persons could enjoy freedom of movement but which have conditioned and governed the development of other possible legal instruments. Those priorities are the result of decisions taken on various different legal bases; they characterize a confused and asymmetrical policy which takes pride only in its (disputed) power to exercise controls and to grant, on a unilateral basis, residence and work permits to aliens within the Community.

(3) The obstacle created by a model involving the application to persons of fragmented legal constructions which validly guarantee the free movement of goods and services in objective terms but which cannot easily be transposed as a method of ensuring a real and effective set of rights within a common area.

B. Possible Remedies?

It must be possible to remedy the situation. In September 1996 the Secretariat of the Council indicated that the demarcation line between the first and third pillars posed great problems for third-country nationals already legally residing in the Community.[72] The views expressed by the institutions in the course of the work carried out by the Intergovernmental Conference had a decisive effect: the Commission, the Parliament, the Court of Justice, and most of the Member States stated at the time that they were in favour of bringing certain areas—the 'tranquil areas' comprised in the third pillar, in particular asylum and immigration matters—within the sphere of Community competence. In addition, the approach adopted in the most recent proposal, dated 30 July 1997, for a Council Act[73] establishing the Convention on rules for the admission of third-country nationals to the Member States (presented pursuant to Article 31 (*ex* Article K.3) of the Treaty on European Union), which creates the status of 'legal resident' and 'long-term resident', appears in certain respects to constitute an extremely useful measure.

1. A Change of Method, Accompanied by Maximum Use of the Devices Currently Available, both Internally and under Existing Conventions   The substantive remedy involves a change of method. As we have seen, it is not possible, simply by bringing the matter within the sphere of Community competence, to resolve a problem, namely that of unsatisfactory situations, which is only too familiar, both within and on the fringes of Community law.

Consequently, it is necessary to determine the most appropriate method to be adopted in the legal treatment of the regime needing to be established with regard to non-Community nationals. In the circumstances, the following proposals are based on a line of reasoning which is aimed, in differing degrees, at the achievement of what is possible, whilst at the same time establishing certain 'layers' of modifications to be made the present system. Those proposals are as follows.

(1) First, as regards measures *de lege ferenda*, one would wish to see, in any future reform of the Treaty, an extension of Community citizenship to cover aliens who have been legally resident within the territory of the Community (even where they have resided in more than one Member State) for a sufficient length of time (say, seven to ten years). As matters currently stand, however, it is hard to envisage such a step being taken, particularly when one considers, in the light of the preparatory work leading to the conclusion of the Maastricht Treaty, the 'forceps delivery' which attended the birth of that idea in relation to Community nationals and the limited scope (notwithstanding the broad interpretations applied by the Court of Justice, for example in *Martinez Sala*[74]) of the specific areas in which the concept of citizenship of the Union plays an effective role. Ultimately, even though the concept of citizenship of the Union as it currently stands does not yet lend itself to the elimination of situations of the type which are referred to herein as 'unsatisfactory' or 'hamstrung', it offers, in this author's view, the advantage of indicating the method by which the rights of persons within the Union can be defined, inasmuch as it has the potential to compel the adoption of a parallel approach to the 'status of aliens' in the Union in terms going beyond the free movement of persons.

(2) Similarly, and on a parallel basis, the second proposal recommends that the benefits of freedom of movement enshrined in the former Articles 3(c) and 7a (now

---

[72] *Agence Europe*, 15 Sept. 1996.   [73] COM(97)387 final.
[74] Case C–85/96 [1998] ECR I–2691.

Article 14) of the EC Treaty and guaranteed by Articles 39, 43, and 49 (*ex* Articles
48, 52, and 59) in relation to the free movement of persons (employed and self-
employed workers) and services should be extended in any event to cover legally resident non-Community nationals once they are admitted into a Member State. Such
non-Community nationals should be able to enjoy those benefits in equal measure,
constituting as they do an indispensable, essential element of the reality of the internal market. As we know, however, the extension of those benefits is subject to certain
inherent limitations, and it cannot solve all the problems caused by the inconsistencies in the system unless it is accompanied by a real, effective legal regime applying in
parallel both to the citizens of the Member States and of the Union and to third-
country nationals (who do not currently enjoy such protection, either under the laws
of their country of residence or under Community law).

What are those limitations? The concept of a market has had the beneficial effect
of engendering a certain sense of reality: the reality of an 'area without frontiers', in
which freedom of movement is guaranteed by a total prohibition of all unjustified
obstacles and restrictions as well as all forms of discriminatory treatment. However,
the notion of discrimination, especially in relation to persons, has proved difficult to
apply in practice and has shown itself, above all, to be insufficiently broad in scope.
In particular, the concept of a market has proved incapable of providing any answers with regard to the following two types of situation: those involving human
rights, regardless of any question of cross-border movement; and those involving the
integration of certain distinguishing characteristics (relating to gender, race, physical handicaps, etc.; the list can be extended to include the status of a 'non-national'
of a Member State) within a competitive market scenario.

(3) The third proposal, likewise a parallel one, involves the adoption of a package
of measures in the form of secondary legislation, accompanied by immediate
ratification of the 1990 Council of Europe Convention on the Legal Status of Migrant Workers, the provisions of which must be applied in any event.[75]

As regards secondary legislation, the question which initially arises is a twofold
one: in order to bring about the creation of a coherent code of rights for aliens residing in the Community, is it necessary to bring the entire field of immigration policy
en bloc within the sphere of Community competence? And is it possible to arrive at a
coherent solution to the problem by bringing within the sphere of Community competence new areas deriving from the third pillar (in particular, those covered by Article 63(3)(a) (*ex* Article 73k) and (b) of the new Treaty, governing conditions of entry
and residence, procedures for the issue of long-term visas and residence permits, including those for the purpose of family reunion, and measures to combat illegal immigration and illegal residence) in respect of which the Member States remain
competent to adopt compatible national rules?

The author of this chapter is convinced that the question which really needs to be
asked is the second one, and that the answer to that question must be in the affirmative. However, careful reflection is needed: first, three 'tranquil areas' have already

---

[75] In particular, Chap. III of the Convention (Arts. 8–29), which lays down in their entirety the rights
of migrant workers from the standpoint of the principles of equal treatment and non-discrimination; see,
in particular, Art. 12 concerning family reunification.

been transferred, namely those concerning asylum, immigration policy (expressly covered by Article 63 (*ex* Article 73k)(3)(a) and (b)), and visa policy. Their incorporation within the Community sphere is immediate, even though it is not subject to the five-year implementation requirement. Secondly, the establishment of even a minimal code covering the status of citizenship of the Union, and the gradual implementation of such a code, will require an officially recognized terminology defining in express terms the rights attaching to such citizenship.

That solution draws its inspiration from certain statements made by the Reflection Group, within which certain States expressed their desire to see the Union adopt rules applying a common status to all legal residents. At the Intergovernmental Conference, Belgium and Italy, supported by the Commission, the Court of Justice, and, above all, the European Parliament, also evinced their desire to see the creation of a 'specific status' for legal residents and for the abolition of the preferential treatment accorded to such residents under the Community rules; they were opposed by the United Kingdom. The Immigrants' Forum[76] had fought resolutely for an effective right to family reunification, including the right to seek employment and occupational training in other Member States, on the ground that aliens resident in the Community play an economic role of major importance and that they should, 'in all fairness', be able to enjoy certain rights once they are established in the Community.

This author therefore shares the view expressed by the European Parliament in its 1996 resolution on the Maij-Weggen Report,[77] that aliens residing in the European Union should have guarantees regarding respect for human rights, equality of treatment and non-discrimination with regard to social, economic and cultural rights, and even, possibly, the right to obtain dual nationality, the right to vote and the right to stand as candidates in local elections, once they have been legally resident for five years. Moreover, such integrated treatment will avoid the difficult negotiations involved in the conclusion by the Community of bilateral agreements. Once the *acquis statutaire* is defined, the only matters still needing to be settled will be the system of access or, as the case may be, the fixing of new quotas (to be determined by the Member States of access or, subsidiarily, by the Community); flexibility will be required in resolving those matters, involving as they do policies affecting employment markets which are still too disparate. This will guarantee cohesiveness, first, between internal, intra-Community action and extra-Community action and, secondly, within the Community sphere, between secondary legislation and external agreements.

Thus, the ideal legal instrument for the proposed enactment of such secondary legislation would be a directive, that being the instrument which is most in keeping with the concept of subsidiarity and best able to provide the necessary degree of sensitivity in its treatment of the sectors concerned. However, the legal instrument in question would have to be of a twofold nature, separating into two distinct parts the

---

[76] *Ad Hoc* Working Party on Immigration: Report from the ministers responsible for immigration to the EC meeting in Maastricht on Immigration and Asylum Policy (SN4038/91), WGI–930; Report of the Reflection Group of 5 Dec. 1995, setting out the position of two groups of States on that point, in the 'Report of the Reflection Group on the convening of the Intergovernmental Conference to consider amendments to the Treaties', published in (1996) 32 RTDE 144–85. See also, as regards the position taken by the Immigrants' Forum, *Agence Europe*, 31 Jan. and 31 May 1995.

[77] See the resolution referred to in note 49 above, at 10–11.

two essential elements contained in the current proposal, presented on 30 July 1997 (pursuant to Article 31 (*ex* Article K.3) of the Treaty on European Union), for a Council Act on rules for the admission of third-country nationals, cited in the text following note 67 above.

This would involve, therefore, *two* directives:

(a) an initial directive concerning the introduction of co-ordinated rules for admission in the strict sense of the term, together with minimum standards for the grant of residence permits and work permits, these being matters which affect domestic labour markets to a highly sensitive degree in national terms. Such a directive could impose rigorous criteria requiring the different facts of each matter to be taken into consideration (e.g. the degree of actual integration of the person concerned and of his family, previous periods of long-term residence, etc.), with a view to limiting the discretionary powers of each national administration as regards the grant and renewal of permits and the justification of expulsion measures (the mere fact of a possible 'effect on the national employment market' being insufficient to justify the refusal of a permit in cases in which it is clear that the person concerned or his family are socially integrated to a very considerable degree);

(b) a second directive concerning the actual status of non-Community nationals: this would consolidate the rights accorded to aliens legally resident in the EC on the basis of their legal residence, extending those rights for the purposes of family reunification and laying down the conditions governing such reunification (see Articles 25 to 31 of the Commission proposal of 30 July 1997). It would also provide for the creation and express extension of certain economic and social rights enjoyed by Community nationals to cover long-term residents who have been legally resident for longer than the five-year minimum period (thus differing from Article 32 of the Commission proposal, which lays down, as a condition of inclusion within that category, the double requirement of residence on a regular basis for at least five years *and* of possession of an authorization permitting residence for a period of at least ten years from first admission).

In considering the technical aspects of the instruments of secondary legislation concerned, it would be necessary to circumvent the problems posed by certain legislative methods which have proved expedient in other areas relating to the internal market but which cannot, on account of their inevitably sensitive nature and the fact that they concern all the Member States, easily be transposed into areas involving 'human rights'. One would naturally wish to see the establishment of preventive control mechanisms governing all draft legislation to be adopted by the Member States, along the lines of those provided for by acts such as Directive 83/189.[78] It is in fact

---

[78] Council Dir. 83/189/EEC (28 Mar. 1983) laying down a procedure for the provision of information in the field of technical standards and regulations ([1983] OJ L109/8); this is known as the 'dir. for the prevention of technical obstacles' and has proved highly successful. It has twice been amended in order to extend its scope.

apparent from an examination of Commission Decision 85/381[79] that that decision sought to implement a system which was adequate to guarantee the desired result; according to the Court of Justice, the Commission, in enacting it, exceeded its powers under the former Article 118 (now Article 137) of the Treaty. Even though the situation now is not the same as it was in 1985, the absence of a timetable for the implementation of the new Article 63(3)(a) and (b) of the amended EC Treaty clearly indicates the problems involved in the immediate introduction of such a mechanism, provision for which will have to be deferred to the medium term.

2. Case Law which is Accessible and Integrationalist, Yet Limited in Scope It is to be hoped that, over the next few years, the Court of Justice and the Court of First Instance will be moved to ensure the greatest possible degree of accessibility and integrationalism in the development of their case law concerning the free movement of persons and citizenship of the Union,[80] and also in their interpretation of the co-operation agreements and association agreements with the various countries from which migrants originate (as the Court of Justice has already done with regard, in particular, to the agreements with Morocco and Turkey), and that they will continue to attempt to apply a codified approach to the rights and freedoms concerned.

However, one should not lose sight of the fact that, under the provisions of the Treaty of Amsterdam, the Court will henceforth be subject to severe constraints on its jurisdiction in the field of the free movement of persons, governed by the new Title IV of the EC Treaty. Apart from the provisions of the second paragraph of the new Article 9 of the Treaty on European Union (formerly Article H), Article 68, which follows on, in particular, from Articles 61 to 63, with which this chapter is concerned, stipulates that references for a preliminary ruling in matters governed by Title IV (i.e. those transferred from the third pillar) may be made only within certain limits: (a) jurisdiction to make such references (concerning questions of validity or interpretation) is restricted, as a measure of 'last resort', to the higher courts; (b) the Commission or a Member State may make a reference concerning a question of interpretation, but in such cases the ruling given by the Court of Justice shall not apply to decisions of national courts which have become *res judicata*; and (c) in any event, the Court of Justice shall not have jurisdiction to rule on any measure or decision relating to the maintenance of law and order or the safeguarding of national security (Article 62(1)).

In such cases, the spontaneity characteristic of references for a preliminary ruling will be absent from the questions referred to the Community judicature. It is necessary, moreover, to take into consideration the extremely strict approach sometimes adopted by the higher courts of the Member States, with the general exception of the

[79] Note 52 above. This formed the subject-matter of an action brought before the ECJ by various Member States, in which judgment was given on 9 July 1987.

[80] The matters under consideration here concern only the legislative measures to be adopted and their interpretation and review by the Court of Justice. It is also necessary to give consideration to an entire package of accompanying institutional measures, primarily designed to permit exchanges of information and the identification in advance of restrictions on the rights of aliens, and to ensure the effectiveness of the measures taken, in accordance with the principles of transparency and of sound administration. Those institutional measures should ideally include provision for the highly important role to be played by the European Ombudsman, supported wherever possible by his opposite numbers at national or even regional level, which would admirably serve to achieve the desired results.

constitutional courts or their equivalents, in areas concerning administrative matters and the employment of migrant workers who are not Community nationals, in
the absence of a codified status for aliens, several examples of which are given
above.[81]

That approach frequently results, in turn, from limitations restricting the jurisdiction of higher courts to questions of law and to a review of the application of the law
by the lower courts within the framework of the various types of legal proceedings
provided for by national law; the exercise of such jurisdiction very often involves a
complete disregard of the 'factual circumstances' of the case under consideration.

When all is said and done, the foregoing elements herald a future which is certain
to be plagued by difficulties. The Court of Justice will have to overcome those
difficulties if it wishes—otherwise than in applications brought by the Commission
(it is doubtful whether any Member State would have an interest in bringing before
the Court any case concerning possible limitations on the rights of individuals in that
field)—to make its mark on the development of the new Title IV of the EC Treaty following the amendments made by the Treaty of Amsterdam, and particularly on the
implementation of Community measures concerning the status of aliens, once these
have been enacted in the form of secondary legislation.

[81] See the introduction to this chap. and notes 8, 9, and 11.

D

Social Rights: European Union Perspectives

13

Striking the Elusive Balance Between Economic Freedom and Social Rights in the EU

MIGUEL POIARES MADURO

It has been repeatedly stated that European integration has promoted economic freedom while leaving social rights and policies in a secondary position. The impact of Community law on social rights has been as a function of economic integration, promoting economic freedom and deregulation, while challenging national social rights. This process has not been compensated by the development of European social rights. It has even been argued that the programme of European market integration is also a programme in favour of economic freedom and competition. In this light, the Treaty of Rome is conceived as an economic neo-liberal constitution whose aim is to protect market freedom from public power and whose underpinning legitimacy lies in voluntary market transactions and enhanced economic efficiency. On the other hand, European integration has also been conceived as a safeguard of the welfare state. In the latter perspective, the European Union is the new forum in which social rights, no longer viable at national level due to economic competition among States, are re-introduced. Moreover, European integration gives a stronger voice to the European States in shaping the rules of global economic competition and protecting the 'essentials' of the welfare state.

This chapter approaches these two constitutional perspectives of the European Union from both descriptive and normative perspectives, while reviewing the balance between economic freedom and social rights. In doing this, I will also attempt to highlight new forms of conceiving the relationship between economic freedom and social rights. The focus will be on the constitutional balance between economic freedom and social rights, and not on the treatment and status accorded to specific economic freedoms or social rights. This will allow me to take into consideration a very broad conception of social rights, including provisions that, arguably, do not have the status of fundamental rights in national constitutions. It will also allow me to work with three dimensions of social rights: first, as constitutional interpretative authority; secondly, as rights of participation and representation; thirdly, as social allocations.

The first section will review the concept of the European Economic Constitution arising from the case law of the European Court of Justice and the challenges it poses

to social rights. This will be related to the promotion of economic freedom through
market integration. In the second section, the focus will be on the issues regarding
the position of social rights in the 'European Constitution' by looking at the two
forms of fundamental rights discourse developed by the Court: on the one hand, the
judicial development of a EU fundamental rights catalogue based on international
law sources and the 'constitutional traditions common to Member States' to which
the Court refers;[1] on the other hand, the construction of the free movement and
other market integration provisions of the Treaty of Rome as fundamental rights.[2]
The third section of the chapter is of more general scope and ambition: it analyses the
relationship between the normative ideals of social rights and the process of European market integration in the context of the global process of economic competition among States. This will be done while addressing some of the key normative
questions faced by European economic integration, such as the choice or balance
between negative and positive integration, the 'regulation' of competition among
States, and the role of efficiency and redistribution goals in the European Union.

I. FROM MARKET INTEGRATION TO MARKET FREEDOM?

The core of the European Economic Constitution lies in market integration. It was
under the legitimacy granted by market integration and through the rules provided
in the Treaties for its achievement that the Court has developed the notion of a
European Constitution. I have explained elsewhere how this process took place,
highlighting the relationship between the process of constitutionalization[3] of the
Treaties and the rules of market integration (notably, free movement and competition rules).[4] Though the Treaty of Rome also contains social provisions (for example, Articles 117 to 119, now Articles 136–141), the core of market integration is the
free movement provisions promoting market access to the different national markets. However, the borderline between securing access to the market for further market integration and securing access to the market to enhance economic freedom is
thin and often non-existent. When reviewing national measures with an effect on

---

[1] See, e.g., Case 4/73, *Nold KG* v. *Commission* [1974] ECR 491 and Case 44/79, *Hauer* v. *Land Rhein-land-Pfalz* [1979] ECR 3727.

[2] See, e.g., Case C–55/94, *Gebhard* v. *Consiglio dell'Ordine degli Avvocati e Procuratori di Milano* [1995] ECR I–4165, at 37.

[3] The history and character of such process of constitutionalization of the Treaties are, by now, well known: the Court of Justice conceived Community law as an autonomous legal system, founded on the rule of law and based on principles such as supremacy, direct effect, fundamental rights, and the separa-tion of powers. In the words of J.H.H. Weiler, '[t]he Constitutional thesis claims that in critical aspects the Community has evolved and behaves as if its founding instrument were not a Treaty governed by inter-national law but, to use the language of the European Court of Justice, a constitutional charter governed by a form of constitutional law': 'The Reformation of Constitutionalism' (1997) 35 *J. Common Mkt. Stud.* 96. See also K. Lenaerts, 'Constitutionalism and the Many Faces of Federalism' (1990) 28 *AJCL* 205; E. Stein, 'Lawyers, Judges and the Making of a Transnational Constitution' (1981) 75 *AJIL* 1; J.H.H. Weiler, 'The Transformation of Europe' (1990–1) 100 *Yale LJ* 2403.

[4] See M. Poiares Maduro, *We the Court: The European Court of Justice and the European Economic Constitution* (1998).

free movement the Court of Justice is deciding both on the acceptable degree of restriction on trade and the level of market regulation.

The case law of the European Court of Justice on the market integration rules of
the EC Treaty (mainly free movement and competition rules) has, at times, appeared
to subscribe a neo-liberal, *'laissez-faire'*, conception of the European Economic
Constitution and promoted deregulatory consequences at national level with negative effects on social rights. Such deregulatory consequences *at the national level* are
not, however, a product of a neo-liberal vision of the economic constitution by the
Court but the functional result of the need to promote integration (requiring negative integration in the form of judicial review of divergent state regulations restricting
trade). Moreover, the Court has limited the effects of negative integration on national regulation whenever national regulations corresponded to a European majoritarian policy.[5] If a certain social regulation is shared by a majority of Member
States it has normally been upheld by the Court even if restricting trade. Thus, from
a European perspective, deregulation has been limited, and it will be more appropriate to talk of a judicial harmonization of national legislation. Nevertheless, the impact on national social rights exists, even if it is the combined result of the promotion
of market integration, through an expanded application of the free movement rules,
with a majoritarian review of national legislation. More protective national social
regulations which were not shared by a 'European majority' were normally considered incompatible with Community law and the objective of market integration. It
has been social protective regulation (corresponding to social rights) that has been
under attack as raising restrictions to trade while the promotion of common social
rights has not been used to the same extent in furthering trade under equal conditions of competition.

The fundamental rights character granted to the free movement provisions and
the widening of its scope of action in order to extend European supervision over national regulation and support the constitutionalization of Community law has led to
a spill-over of market integration rules into virtually all areas of national law. As a
consequence, many national social rights and policies have been challenged under
the free movement provisions. The balance between economic freedom and social
rights in the European Economic Constitution has largely been defined by the balance between market integration and national social rights.

The Court has long applied the free movement of goods (and, to a less extent, the
freedom to provide services) to national rules the effect of which on trade is not a
consequence of discrimination against imports, but simply a side-effect of the restriction imposed even on domestic trade as a consequence of market regulation.
This extension of the scope of the free movement of goods and services has raised
challenges to almost any regulation of the market and limited the social and economic policies of Member States. Several non-discriminatory national regulations
protecting or promoting social rights have been challenged as giving rise to restrictions on the free movement of goods or the freedom to provide services. That has

---

[5] I have coined the approach of the European Court of Justice in this area of the law as 'majoritarian
activism': *ibid.*, at 61–78.

been the case with legislation regarding working hours,[6] the organization of work, and the monopoly of workers' associations,[7] public systems of labour procurement services[8] or prices regulations,[9] all of which can be said to be related to social rights. In general, the application of some of the free movement rules has been seen as promoting deregulation and preventing Member States from pursuing national social policies, even without intents of protectionism.

At the same time, the Court has always denied that social arguments of an economic nature can be used to justify national regulations capable of restricting free movement. In particular, although the States can still justify some of those policies on the basis of social goals related to efficiency, redistribution became more difficult to pursue through regulation, since economic arguments cannot be used in the context of market integration rules. This approach has its basis on the Treaty rules, which allow only limited exceptions to the free movement provisions and do not authorize the use of economic arguments to justify national regulations in breach of those rules (such economic arguments are feared immediately to open the door to protectionism). However, that could be related to an understanding of the free movement provisions prohibiting only national measures which discriminate against foreign products and nationals. Since the Court of Justice broadened the scope of the free movement rules (notably, in a first stage, the free movement of goods) to include non-discriminatory national regulations with an impact on trade, it has itself extended the list of public goals that can justify a restriction on trade.[10] It can be argued that such an extension should include the protection of interests associated with social rights. In fact, this protection does not require express Treaty or legislative recognition, and should be conceived as part of the respect that the European Union legal order owes to fundamental rights (including fundamental social rights).

The Court has referred to the free movement provisions as 'fundamental freedoms',[11] granting them a status similar to that of fundamental rights in national constitutions. This conception of the free movement provisions as fundamental rights has played a key role both as an instrument of market integration (in co-operation with individual litigants and national courts) and, at the same time, as a form of legitimation of Community law and market integration. Community law was presented as a new source of individual rights and the integration process associated with a rights discourse supported by the participation of individuals and national courts. However, the character of such fundamental freedoms has long remained

---

[6] See the Sunday Trading cases, notably Case 145/88, *Torfaen Borough Council* v. *B&Q plc (Sunday Trading)* [1989] ECR 3851.

[7] Case C–179/90, *Merci Convenzionali Porto di Genova SpA* v. *Siderurgica Gabrielli SpA* [1991] ECR I–5889.

[8] Case C–41/90, *Höfner and Elser* v. *Macrotron GmbH* [1991] ECR I–197 and Case C–134/95, *USSL* v. *INAIL* [1997] ECR I–195.

[9] See, e.g., Case 65/75, *Tasca* [1976] ECR 291; Joined Cases 88–90/75, *Sadam* [1976] ECR 323; Case 13/77, *GB-INNO-BM* v. *ATAB* [1977] ECR 2115; and Case 82/77, *Openbaar Ministerie* v. *Van Tiggele* [1978] ECR 25.

[10] At least with regard to national regs. equally applicable to national and foreign goods: see Case 120/78, *Rewe-Zentral AG* v. *Bundesmonopolverwaltung für Branntwein (Cassis de Dijon)* [1979] ECR 649.

[11] See, e.g., Case C–55/94, *Gebhard* [1995] ECR I–4165, at para. 34.

grey. For some, they are an expression of the more general principle of non-discrimination: free movement of goods, services, and persons will be secured by protecting the different national companies, workers, and goods from being discriminated against by any Member State. Others have proposed a more far-reaching understanding of the fundamental rights character of the common market freedoms, arguing that they should be conceived as fundamental economic freedoms limiting public power and safeguarding competition in the free market. Underlying the latter interpretation is a neo-liberal conception of the European Economic Constitution whose legitimacy is derived from the individual rights granted against public power.[12]

The broad scope given by the European Court of Justice to the free movement of goods could suggest that the latter interpretation dominates the European Economic Constitution favouring economic freedom against social rights. The Court of Justice has, until the recent *Keck and Mithouard* decision,[13] adopted an interpretation of the rule of the free movement of goods that subjected almost any national regulation to a test of proportionality similar to a cost/benefit analysis.[14] Any rule with an impact on trade (even a non-discriminatory impact) was considered a measure having an equivalent effect to a quantitative restriction on imports (Article 28, *ex* Article 30 of the EC Treaty) and would only be upheld if necessary and proportional to one of the public goals set out in Article 30 (*ex* Article 36) or recognized by the Court in its *Cassis de Dijon* decision.[15] This brought virtually any public regulation of the market under close scrutiny and promoted deregulation of the market *at the national level*. That can be seen as a negative impact of European economic integration on social rights resulting from the spill-over of market integration rules into national economic and social regulations. Free movement provisions were granted fundamental rights status and used to promote access to the national markets, which sometimes became confused with a general right of access to the market. The expansion of market integration rules impacted on other areas of the law relating to social concerns and not trade protectionism. This process of spill-over raises conflicts between the values of market integration and/or free markets and the values embodied in social rights and policies. As stated by Davies, for example, a question then arises on how the Court 'has balanced the competing policies behind the free movement provisions of the Treaty, on the one hand, and the national labour law provisions on the other'.[16]

This 'negative' impact on social rights has been limited by the approach followed by the Court in the review of national regulations. The fact that national regulations

---

[12] See E.J. Mestmäcker, 'On the Legitimacy of European Law' (1994) 58 *RabelsZ* 615, and E.-U. Petersmann, 'Proposals for a New Constitution of the European Union: Building-Blocks for a Constitutional Theory and Constitutional Law of the EU' (1995) 32 *CML Rev.* 1123.

[13] Joined Cases C–267 and C–268/91, *Keck and Mithouard* [1993] ECR I–6097.

[14] See Poiares Maduro, note 4 above, at 61–8.

[15] Case 120/78, *Rewe-Zentral AG* v. *Bundes-Monopolverwaltung für Branntwein* (*Cassis de Dijon*) [1979] ECR 649. This extension of the list of public interest objectives that may justify *prima facie* invalid national measures under Community law is not exclusive of the free movement of goods and has also been established with regard to the free movement of persons or the principle of non-discrimination (Art. 12, *ex* Art. 6 of the EC Treaty).

[16] P. Davies, 'Market Integration and Social Policy in the Court of Justice' (1995) 24 *ILJ* 51.

were caught under the broad scope of Article 28 (*ex* Article 30), for example, did not establish an automatic violation of the free movement of goods. It would all depend on the test of necessity and proportionality applied by the Court in the review of those national rules. As mentioned above, such test has not been guided by concern about the limits to public intervention in the market but by an assessment of those rules in view of the majoritarian policy followed in the different EU Member States. The Court would normally strike down or uphold a national regulation depending on the regulatory policy followed in that regard in the majority of the Member States.[17] In fact, there have not been many circumstances in which the Court has struck down what could be foreseen as a fundamental social right (in particular, if one takes the majority in the European polity as the yardstick of such fundamental social rights). The extent to which economic freedom has been promoted at the cost of social rights depends, in this respect, on whether a national or European perspective is taken. The Court has imposed limits on State regulation, not public regulation. Deregulation has occurred only if one takes as the relevant level of analysis the national state and not the European Union. The Court has not promoted negative integration at the lowest common denominator but it has equally not accepted the highest levels of social regulatory protection if not shared by a European majority.

This reading of the Court's case law on the Economic Constitution is equally supported by its decisions on the review of Community legislation with regard to economic fundamental rights derived from the constitutional rules and practices common to the Member States or international sources such as the European Convention on Human Rights (ECHR).[18] The Court has recognized as fundamental rights protected in the Community legal order the right to property, the freedom to pursue a trade or business, and the freedom of economic activity,[19] but it has also been quite careful in applying these rights in the context of the review of Community legislation. It has never, to my knowledge, struck down Council legislation for violation of such economic rights and freedoms.[20] In other words, the Court has been quite generous towards the general interests pursued by the Community which restrict economic freedom. Moreover, it considers that such economic freedoms 'are not absolute but must be viewed in relation to their social function'.[21]

As a preliminary conclusion, one can state that the 'negative' impact of the European Economic Constitution on social rights has been limited and a function of mar-

[17] See Poiares Maduro, note 4 above, at 72–8.

[18] For a deeper analysis of the case law of the Court in the area of fundamental rights see the contribution of Bruno de Witte to this vol.

[19] See, for some recent examples of the Court of Justice and the Court of First Instance, Case C–44/94, *The Queen* v. *Minister of Agriculture, Fisheries and Food, ex parte National Federation of Fishermen's Organizations* [1995] ECR I–3115; Case C–280/93, *Germany* v. *Council* [1994] ECR I–4973; Case T–521/93, *Atlanta AG and others* v. *European Commission* [1996] ECR II–2109; Cases C–248/95 and C–249/95, *SAM Schiffahrt und Stapf* v. *Bundesrepublik Deutschland* [1997] ECR I–1167.

[20] In the same sense, see the contribution of Bruno de Witte to this vol. See note 24 below for a recent and rare case of Council legislation partially struck down as violating the fundamental right to non-discrimination.

[21] Case C–44/94, *The Queen* v. *Minister of Agriculture, Fisheries and Food, ex parte National Federation of Fishermen's Organizations and Others* [1995] ECR I–3115, at para. 28. This reference to the limits imposed on these economic rights by the general interest or the social function of the protected rights and activities is present from the outset in the *Nold* and *Hauer* decisions: see Case 4/73, *Nold* [1974] ECR 491, at para. 14; Case 44/79, *Hauer* [1979] ECR 3727. See also the other cases referred to above.

ket integration and judicial harmonization of national social and regulatory policies, not the result of a neo-liberal conception of the European Economic Constitution by the Court of Justice. The European majoritarian perspective followed by the Court means that the deregulatory effects have occurred only at the national level. If one takes the European majority polity as the yardstick by which to judge the impact of free movement rules on regulation, then there has been hardly any deregulation as a consequence of the application of free movement provisions. However, the fact remains that the broad scope granted to some free movement rules has allowed a growing litigation challenging national regulations protecting social rights. The free movement of goods and the freedom to provide services have been used by national litigants to favour economic freedom and change social policies at the national level. Moreover, the fact that the European Constitution is mainly a result of the judicial development of the Treaty rules supported by litigation means that the European Constitution will be a result of representation and participation in such a judicial process.

II. SOCIAL RIGHTS IN THE COMMON MARKET

Market integration has also promoted the development of European social rights. However, the functional use of market integration rules to further social rights has been more limited than in the case of economic freedom. At the same time, the development of social rights appears to be prisoner of the values of market integration and not a consequence of a political conception of the social and economic protection deserved by any European citizen.

The most representative example of a social right enshrined in the Treaty is Article 141 (*ex* Article 119 of the EC Treaty) that establishes 'the principle that men and women should receive equal pay for equal work'. The Court has interpreted this rule very broadly and has, in effect and in conjunction with Community secondary legislation, transformed it into a general principle of equality of treatment for men and women with regard to work.[22] The Court has picked up a norm the social content of which was, in its original construction, instrumental to the aim of protecting equal conditions of competition, and raised it to the status of a true fundamental social right. This social right also benefits from a unique status in the context of fundamental rights protection in the European Union, since it applies horizontally (i.e. among private parties) and to purely national situations.[23]

A more general principle of non-discrimination derived from the constitutional traditions common to the Member States is part of the EU legal order.[24] Such a

---

[22] In some cases going even further than this. See the contribution of Catherine Barnard to this vol.

[23] With the exception of the free movement provisions mentioned above, fundamental rights in the EU legal order only apply, in principle, to the review of Community legislation. There are, however, substantial and very important cases in which they, in fact, may apply to national legislation (see the contribution of Bruno de Witte).

[24] For a recent and rare example of Council legislation partially struck down as violating such a principle of non-discrimination see Cases C–364/95 and C–365/95, *Firma T. Port GmbH* v. *Hauptzollamt Hamburg Jonas*, [1998] ECR I–1023.

principle, however, does not apply in the case of purely internal situations of the Member States in conformity with the status of fundamental rights protection in the EU legal order. European fundamental rights are not incorporated into national legal orders and apply only to the review of Community acts and legislation (with some important exceptions).[25] The recent Treaty of Amsterdam has inserted in the EC Treaty a general principle prohibiting discrimination on the basis of sex, race, ethnic origin, religion, beliefs, disabilities, age, or sexual orientation.[26] But such principle does not appear to have direct effect and is more an empowering clause for future EU action in this area.

Non-discrimination has been, in any case, a driving force behind some of the most important developments on the protection of social rights in the European Union. The prohibition of discrimination on the basis of nationality (Article 12, *ex* Article 6 of the EC Treaty) has been used by the Court to extend the protection conferred by social rights in a given Member State to nationals of any Member State in that State.[27] Also in this case, market integration, through the free movement of workers, has been functional to the development of an important body of decisions extending social rights granted in one Member State to any worker in that State who is a national of another Member State. The Court has required the abolition of discrimination based on nationality among workers in one Member State with regard to many issues apart from those mentioned in Article 39 (*ex* Article 48): 'employment, remuneration, and other conditions of work and employment'. The Court included in the prohibition of discrimination related to the free movement of workers such things as a right to education or vocational training, or rights not to be discriminated against with regard to social security protection or family rights. This has been facilitated by the direct effect granted to the principle of non-discrimination on the basis of nationality established in Article 12 (*ex* Article 6 of the EC Treaty). Such principle is only effective within the scope of application of the Treaty but, once a certain social right can be conceived as instrumental to the protection of the free movement of workers, such right must be applied in a non-discriminatory manner, even though it may not directly concern 'employment, remuneration and other conditions of employment'. Once someone comes within the scope of Community law by virtue of the free movement of workers, the protection which is granted to him or her against non-discrimination is broader than would result simply from Article 39 (*ex* Article 48).

This process culminated in the recent *Martinez Sala* decision where the Court appears to confer almost absolute protection against discrimination by a Member State to a national of another Member State lawfully resident in that State. So long as that is the case, a national of any Member State in another Member State is

---

[25] See note 23 above.

[26] Art. 6A (now Art. 13) of the Treaty of Amsterdam, which is not yet in force.

[27] In the words of Carlos Ball: '[t]he Court of Justice has interpreted Community Law provisions that provide individuals with justiciable economic rights in a way that prohibits Member States from treating their own citizens better than the citizens from other Member States working within their borders. This has contributed significantly to the formation of a European social citizenship': 'The Making of a Transnational Capitalist Society: The Court of Justice, Social Policy, and Individual Rights Under the European Community's Legal Order' (1996) 37 *Harv. Int'l LJ* 314.

granted the same social rights and protection accorded by that State to its own nationals. The Court stated:

> Article 8(2) of the Treaty attaches to the status of citizen of the Union rights and duties laid down by the Treaty, including the right, laid down in Article 6 of the Treaty, not to suffer discrimination on grounds of nationality within the scope of application *ratione materiae* of the Treaty.
>
> It follows that a citizen of the European Union . . . lawfully resident in the territory of the host Member State, can rely on Article 6 of the Treaty in all situations which fall within the scope *ratione materiae* of Community law, including the situation where that Member State delays or refuses to grant to that claimant a benefit that is provided to all persons lawfully resident in the territory of that State on the ground that the claimant is not in possession of a document which nationals of that same State are not required to have and the issue of which may be delayed or refused by the authorities of that State.
>
> Since the unequal treatment in question thus comes within the scope of application of the Treaty, it cannot be considered to be justified: it is discrimination directly based on the appellant's nationality and, in any event, nothing to justify such unequal treatment has been put before the Court.[28]

The limit posed by the condition that the 'unequal treatment in question comes within the scope of application of the Treaty'[29] is much less significant than one could initially think, as the case in question confirms. In fact, it is difficult to conceive of any area which is still *ratione materiae* outside the scope of Community law,[30] much less when any unequal treatment among nationals of different Member States in a Member State can be said to restrict the free movement of persons. In this area, the scope of application *ratione materiae* of Community law will basically depend on its scope of application *ratione personae*. In other words, it will depend on the extent to which all European citizens are given a general right of free movement. If they are granted such general right, the logical consequence will be that they should not be discriminated against independently of the State in which they choose to live.

The limits imposed on the free movement of persons have however, been one of the main reasons for the secondary position of social rights with regard to economic freedom in the context of market integration. The Court has long interpreted the rules regarding the free movement of persons more strictly than those on the free movement of goods and (to a lesser extent) the freedom to provide services. As we have seen, in the field of the free movement of goods (and, to a more limited extent, services), the Court has for long considered as restrictions to trade national regulations that do not discriminate against imports, but may, nevertheless, affect trade by affecting market access in general. In this way, many national regulations limiting economic freedom (including regulations protecting social rights) have been challenged under Community rules since the limits to economic freedom are also conceived as limits to free trade and market access. The same broad scope has not been

---

[28] Case C–85/96, *Martínez Sala* v. *Freistaat Bayern*, judgment of 12 May 1998, at paras. 62–64.

[29] The Court establishes two conditions: that the facts of the case must fall within the scope *ratione materiae* and *ratione personae* of the Treaty. The latter is linked to the interpretation to be given by the Court to the general right of free movement of persons established in Art. 8A (now Art. 17) which the Court considered unnecessary to do in this case.

[30] It is not necessary for specific Community rules to address an issue for it to come within its scope of application. Otherwise, the Court would not need independently to apply Art. 6 (now Art. 12).

given to the free movement of workers, which could be used to challenge national regulations restricting certain social rights. In fact, in the same way that it is possible to argue that regulation of the market creates barriers to trade, it would be possible to argue that workers will need a minimal degree of protection effectively to exercise free movement. For example, it could be argued that a prohibition, in a Member State, on striking or becoming a Union member could deter workers from other Member States where those rights existed from moving to that Member State.[31] It may seem an argument quite distant from the original wording and intent of the Treaty rules on the free movement of workers, but it is in no way different from the arguments in favour of deregulation which have been accepted in the context of the free movement of goods.[32]

The broader scope granted to free movement of goods in comparison to the free movement of workers has favoured economic freedom litigation against social rights litigation. However, the recent case law of the Court signals a shift in the judicial activism of the Court which favours a limitation of the scope of the application of the free movement of goods and a broader application of the free movement of persons. The limits set in *Keck* to challenges, under Article 28 (*ex* Article 30), to national rules the effect of which is to limit the commercial freedom of traders[33] will reduce the impact of the free movement of goods on national legislation protecting social rights.

Instead, a broader use of the free movement of workers may now be available to promote social rights in the European common market. The recent *Bosman* decision is a good example, supporting a right to work and the freedom of workers to choose their work and employment.[34] This decision prohibited rules that, albeit not discriminating against workers of other Member States, reduced their free movement by imposing limits on their freedom to leave their employer and to choose between different employment contracts. The consequence of the recent expansion of the free movement of persons provisions beyond the simple prohibition of discrimination on

[31] Note that the two examples of social rights given do not require any type of legislative action (as normally happens with social rights of a programmatic character) and could be established simply by judicial recognition.

[32] It is sufficient to think of the arguments, regarding Art. 28 (*ex* Art. 30), used to challenge national regulations which prohibited shops from opening on Sundays, prevented certain marketing and advertising methods, or imposed the use of recyclable bottles.

[33] Joined Cases C–267 and C–268/91, *Keck and Mithouard* [1993] ECR I–6097. In this decision, the Court restricted the scope of application of Art. 30 (now Art. 28) with regard to national measures regulating 'selling arrangements' which do not discriminate against imports (no longer considered as capable of restricting trade in the context of the free movement of goods). The traditional interpretation of Art. 30 (now Art. 28) is, however, maintained with regard to national measures on product characteristics. On *Keck* see: S. Weatherhill, 'After *Keck*: Some Thoughts on How to Clarify the Clarification' (1996) 33 *CML Rev.* 885; L. Gormley, 'Two Years After Keck' (1996) 19 *Fordham Int'l. LJ*; J. Mattera, 'De l'arrêt "Dassonville" a l'arrêt Keck: l'obscure clarté d'une jurisprudence riche en principes novateurs et en contradictions' [1994] *RMUE* 117; D. Chalmers, 'Repackaging the Internal Market—The Ramifications of the *Keck* Judgement' (1994) 19 *EL Rev.* 385; M. Lopez Escudero, 'La jurisprudencia Keck y Mithouard: Una Revision del Concepto de Medida de Efecto Equivalente' [1994] *Revista de Instituciones Europeas* 379; N. Bernard, 'Discrimination and Free Movement in EC Law' (1996) 45 *ICLQ* 82; J. Higgins, 'The Free Movement of Goods Since Keck' (1997) 6 *IJEL*; and M. Poiares Maduro, 'Keck: The End? The Beginning of the End? Or Just the End of the Beginning?' (1994) 1 *IJEL* 30.

[34] Case C–415/93, *Union Royale Belge des Sociétés de Football Association ASBL* v. *Jean-Marc Bosman* [1995] ECR I–4921.

the basis of nationality may be the recognition of a set of European social rights required for effective protection of the free movement of persons.[35] Developments in this sense will depend much on the sophistication and capacity of social actors to raise litigation combining Community law arguments with fundamental social rights.[36]

The litigation that has helped to 'mould' the European Constitution has been based on market integration rules (notably free movement of goods) and dominated by some actors (notably companies that often appear as repeated litigants). Due to the character of those rules and to the information and organization costs involved in participating in the Community judicial process, it has been mainly companies which have started the discovery process of Community law and the European Constitution. The European Constitution (and its approach to fundamental rights) is a product of judicial construction fuelled by litigation arising from certain actors and free movement provisions. In particular, the 'preference' given to the free movement of goods has favoured litigation pushing for economic freedom. This pattern is reinforced by the character of the litigants who make use of Community rules. In the same way that formal constitutions are a product of representation and participation in the political process, the European Constitution is, to a large extent, a product of representation and participation in the judicial process.

The current shift in the Court's case law which restricts the scope of application of the free movement of goods and favours an extended application of the free movement of persons (including the free movement of workers) may help to redefine the actors and the interests promoted by litigation related to market integration. This may have important consequences on the balance between economic freedom and social rights in the European Economic Constitution.[37] It will be important for social rights to be inserted into the discourse of market integration and the European Economic Constitution. An important step will be the inclusion of social rights in the jurisprudential catalogue of social rights developed by the Court to be applied to Community legislation and, in some cases, national legislation (notably, whenever a national rule restricts one of the free movement rules).[38]

There is a hard core of social rights which have tentatively been developed by the Court in different circumstances and under different doctrines. We have already highlighted the development of the right not to be discriminated against, equality between men and women, free movement of persons (with some limits to be clarified[39]), the right to work, and the right freely to choose a job and employment. Other rights (such as those regarding worker participation) have been affirmed by the Court, but

---

[35] See section III A below.

[36] That has not been the case hitherto. In this sense, see E. Szyszczak, 'Future Directions in European Union Social Policy Law' (1995) 24 *ILJ* 31.

[37] However, it must be stressed that the shift towards a more restrictive interpretation of Art. 28 (*ex* Art. 30) (prohibiting mainly discriminatory restrictions on trade) will not prevent the use of the free movement of goods and services provisions to challenge national social rights. As mentioned by Davies (note 16 above, at 51), 'it is possible to construct arguments whereby protective social rules in a Member State are said to be directly or, more likely, indirectly discriminatory against imports' (and, it must be remembered, in some cases it will continue to be possible to challenge national rules restricting economic freedom and market access even where such rules do not discriminate against imports).

[38] See the contribution of Bruno de Witte to this vol. for a thorough explanation of the cases in which EU fundamental rights are applied by the Court of Justice to the review of national legislation.

[39] See section III A below.

following Community legislation[40] and without the recognition of a constitutional and fundamental rights status. The European courts have also referred to general sources of social rights protection, such as the European and Community Social Charters.[41] Such references have, however, been limited, and rarely has the Court of Justice affirmed, as general principles of Community law, some fundamental social rights, contrary to what has happened with regard to the rights to property and economic activity which have frequently been applied in the review of Community acts and legislation.[42] On the other hand, the Court of First Instance, in the *Comité Central d'Entreprise de la Société Générale des Grands Source* v. *Commission* decision,[43] was unclear about the status as fundamental rights of the rights of workers to the preservation of their jobs and the right of their representatives to be consulted and informed. The Court restrictively interpreted the rights of workers to be heard and informed by the Commission in the context of a decision declaring a concentration compatible with the common market and did not deal with the argument, advanced by the employees' representative organizations, that some fundamental social rights of the Community legal order were at stake (the rights of workers to the preservation of their jobs and the right of their representatives to be consulted and informed).

It is this uncertainty regarding the status and catalogue of fundamental social rights in the EU legal order that has led to calls for the introduction of a list of fundamental social rights in the Treaties.[44] This is reflected in the proposals of the *Comité de Sages* responsible for the report on a Europe of Civic and Social Rights prepared for the IGC leading to the Amsterdam Treaty. The Committee argued that it was necessary to provide the Court with a stronger legal basis in the Treaties empowering it to review Community legislation (and national legislation within the scope of Community law)[45] under the criteria of fundamental social rights. To this end, the Committee used a classical distinction in the realm of fundamental social rights between rights immediately effective and judicially enforceable and rights of a programmatic character expressing goals which are to be attained on a gradual basis.[46] The Committee proposed that both types of rights should be recognized and listed in the Treaties, but, at the first stage, only the first were to be given judicial protection. This first type of rights would constitute a hard core of social rights and were understood by the Committee as being shared by all Member States. They included:

---

[40] This is better developed and explained in the contribution of Silvana Sciarra to this vol.

[41] See, e.g., Case C–246/96, *Magorrian and Cunningham* v. *Eastern Health and Social Services Board and Department of Health and Social Services* [1997] ECR I–7153; Case C–191/94, *AGF Belgium* v. *European Economic Committee* [1996] ECR I–1859; Case T–135/96, *UEAPME* v. *Council*, judgment of 17 June 1998. See also Szyszczak, note 36 above, at 31 and the references therein.

[42] Carlos Ball notes 'the relative ineffectiveness of the social policy provisions found in the Treaty and in other sources of primary Community law': note 27 above, at 316.

[43] Case T–96/92, [1995] ECR II–1727.

[44] See B. Hepple, 'Social Values and European Law' (1995) 48 *Current Legal Problems* 39; R. Blanpain, B. Hepple, and S. Sciarra, *Fundamental Social Rights: Proposals for the European Union* (1996). See also the Molitor Group Report, section on labour law, proposal 1, *Agence Europe/Documents* No. 1947 (4 Aug. 1993).

[45] Thus, the degree of incorporation of EU fundamental rights into national legal orders would not be changed.

[46] European Commission, *For a Europe of Civic and Social Rights—Report of the Comité des Sages* (1996), 17–18. There is an old constitutional debate on the judicial protection of programmatic social rights. The Committee preferred not to raise that discussion at this stage in the European Union.

equality under the law; prohibition of any form of discrimination; equality between men and women; free movement within the Union; freedom to choose a profession and an educational system within the Union; freedom of association and the right to defend one's rights; and the rights to collective action and collective bargaining.[47] The Treaty of Amsterdam, however, has not included such list of rights. The steps taken were smaller than the Committee proposed. The Social Chapter was inserted into the Treaties and Article 136 (*ex* Article 117) in the title on social policy now includes a reference to 'fundamental social rights such as those set out in the European Social Charter signed at Turin on 18 October 1961 and in the 1989 Community Charter of the Fundamental Social Rights of Workers'. Contrary to the Committee's proposals no catalogue of fundamental social rights was inserted, neither were such rights given the same status as other fundamental rights whose respect by the Union is imposed immediately in Article 6 (*ex* Article F of the TEU). Moreover, the reference in Article 117 appears to share the programmatic character normally attributed to this norm.

Article 117 is, perhaps, the Treaty provision that most embodies and promotes social values. Even before the Amsterdam Treaty it stated: 'Member-States agree upon the need to promote improved working conditions and an improved standard of living for workers, so as to make possible their harmonization while the improvement is being maintained'. The Court of Justice has considered that such a provision 'is essentially in the nature of a programme'.[48] The Court has, in consequence, denied the application of such rule to the review of national regulation that would, arguably, reduce the level of social protection.[49] However, the Court has also stated:

> The fact that the objectives of social policy laid down in Article 117 are in the nature of a programme does not mean that they are deprived of any legal effect. They constitute an important aid, in particular for the interpretation of other provisions of the Treaty and of secondary legislation in the social field. The attainment of those objectives must nevertheless be the result of a social policy which must be defined by the competent authorities.[50]

This careful application of the social objectives enshrined in Article 117 coincides with the approach normally followed by national constitutional courts in the application of social rights of programmatic nature. Yet it is important that the fundamental social rights to which Article 117 now refers will not all be considered as dependent upon policy or legislative implementation. The right to collective bargaining, the freedom of association, the right to collective action, and the other rights of the first type mentioned in the report of the *Comité des Sages* are either expressly protected by other Treaty provisions or should be considered as part of the 'constitutional traditions common to the Member States'. Though certainty and coherence could have been gained by the introduction of a catalogue of fundamental rights into the Treaties the difficulty of reaching an agreement on a specific catalogue

---

[47] The second type of rights included the right to education, the right to work, the right to social security, etc.

[48] See Case 149/77, *Defrenne* v. *Sabena* [1978] ECR 1365; Case 170/84, *Bilka-Kaufhaus* v. *Weber von Hartz* [1986] ECR 1607; Case 126/86, *Gimenez Zaera* v. *INSS* [1986] ECR 2261, at para. 13.

[49] See *Gimenez Zaera* v, *INSS*, ibid.   [50] *Ibid.*, at para. 14.

has always prevented that from happening. This should not exclude from the concept of fundamental rights which has been developed by the Court a hard core of fundamental social rights which are either part of the common constitutional traditions of the Member States and/or referred to in other EU or international sources.[51]

Developments in the area of fundamental social rights protection will continue to be, to a large extent, dependent upon the judicial 'construction' of the European Economic Constitution. There are two main steps to be taken in this area: first, to free the fundamental rights discourse from the exclusive logic of market integration; secondly, to alter the patterns of litigation which have moulded the European Economic Constitution.

Social rights in the common market have been developed as a function of market integration, not as an element of European citizenship. This is visible in the conception of one of the most important social rights granted by European integration: the free movement of persons. Although the Court has extended the protection granted by Community law to students or job-seekers, there has been no general right of free movement of persons granted with direct effect.[52] The free movement of persons has been developed as a function of economic efficiency: the intent is an optimal allocation of labour under the mechanisms generated by market integration. There is no free movement of persons conceived as a right to choose between different models of life and regulatory regimes (including social protection). The potential that European integration has to grant to individuals a choice between different polities with different choices regarding efficiency, redistribution, and social protection has not yet been promoted in the European Union. Persons can move only as market agents: workers, self-employed persons, and companies. Everson has coined the form of citizenship arising from these rights as 'market citizenship'.[53] And, even in this capacity, there are many restrictions remaining as a result of the conditions upon which its practical implementation depends. In the main, contrary to the other areas of market integration, Community legislation regarding the free movement of persons and (in some cases) the rights of workers is still subject to the requirement of unanimous decision-making.[54]

Community legislation in the area of the free movement of persons should be enhanced by being subject to the same decision-making process that applies in the

[51] Such as the Community Charter of Fundamental Social Rights of Workers. See, for a recent international example, including some of the rights which it has been argued constitute fundamental social rights: the ILO Declaration on Fundamental Principles and Rights at Work, approved at the 86th Session, Geneva, June 1998. Available at http://www.ilo.org/public/english/10ilc/ilc86/com-dxt.htm.

[52] Much will depend on the reading to be made of Art. 8a (now Art. 18) introduced by the Maastricht Treaty that establishes that 'every citizen of the Union shall have the right to move and reside freely within the territory of Member States, subject to the limitations and conditions laid down in this Treaty and by the measures adopted to give it effect'. Of importance will also be the new title on free movement of persons, asylum, and immigration introduced by the Amsterdam Treaty.

[53] M. Everson, 'The Legacy of Market Citizen', in J. Shaw and G. More (eds.) *New Legal Dynamics of the European Union* (1995), 73.

[54] See Arts. 100A(2), 118, and 118A (the latter provisions will change after the entry into force of the Amsterdam Treaty, when they will become Arts. 95(2), 137, and 138 but several areas regarding labour and social law will continue to be subject to unanimity). The Court has interpreted the legal bases on social rights in a manner which favoured Community legislation under majority decision-making, therefore enhancing social rights legislation. See Case C–84/94, *United Kingdom* v. *Council* [1996] ECR I–5755. For a deeper analysis of European social policy see the contribution of Silvana Sciarra to this vol.

other areas of the creation of an internal market (majority decision-making). This would require a Treaty revision unlikely in the near future. In the meanwhile, the Court should continue the recent extension of the scope of the rules on the free movement of persons. The shift in activism in the Court's case law from the area of the free movement of goods to the area of the free movement of persons is perfectly logical if one has regard to the available alternatives to judicial intervention in those areas of market integration. Market integration in the area of the free movement of goods can, since the Single Act, be promoted through Community harmonizing legislation (which is subject to majority decision-making). The same does not happen in the area of the free movement of persons (still subject to the requirement of unanimity) which demands greater intervention by the Court to promote market integration in this area.

The Court of Justice should also focus its attention on the concept of European citizenship in developing fundamental rights. It should start by clarifying the status of the general right of free movement of persons introduced by the Maastricht Treaty.[55] In the *Martínez Sala* decision the Court did not consider it necessary to clarify the status of Article 8(1) (now Article 18(1)) and its direct effect (which was argued by the Commission).[56] For reasons which I will give more fully below, I am in favour of direct effect being granted to such provisions. Moreover, it would be particularly important for the rights arising from European citizenship to be interpreted as fundamental rights, restrictions on which should be interpreted in a limited and exceptional manner.

The process of economic constitutional litigation has remained prisoner to the constitutional limits of the Treaty and the formal and functional interpretation of market integration rules. The gap between negative and positive integration has generated spill-over effects favouring economic freedom against social rights at the national level. The recent developments in the case law of the European Court of Justice may help to balance economic litigation arising from market integration and its impact on the European Economic Constitution. They must be supported by a fundamental rights discourse which is no longer functionally attached to market integration. At the same time, the relationship between the fundamental rights arising from free movement rules and the classical economical and social fundamental rights has to be clarified. Moreover, the European Court of Justice must take into consideration broader social and economic values in the application of those rules. On the one hand, it must assume that conflicts will inevitably arise between the broad scope granted to the free movement rules and the economic and social values embodied in national regulations that, albeit not discriminating against foreign nationals or products, have an effect on free trade. In the same manner in which national rules restricting free movement should conform with fundamental rights, so too should the application of the free movement rules be made in light of fundamental rights, including validating otherwise invalid restrictions to trade.[57] On the other

---

[55] Art. 8a (now Art. 18).

[56] Case C–85/96, *Martínez Sala* v. *Freistaat Bayern*, judgment of 12 May 1998, at paras. 58–59.

[57] In this regard, it may be appropriate to accept that economic integration must still allow some sort of discrimination in favour of weaker social and economic groups. States' discrimination in favour of

hand, the Court should elevate the assessment of the reasonableness of public intervention in the market from market integration rules to the realm of classical social
and economic fundamental rights. In this respect, the time may be right for the Court
to develop a more sophisticated approach to the review of Community legislation
under economic and social fundamental rights. The growing importance of majoritarian decision-making in the EU legislative process may require a higher degree of
activism with regard to Community legislation.

Much of what has been argued for also depends on a clarification of the goals to
be pursued by European integration, in particular the balance between efficiency
and distributive justice. Equally or even more important are the choices and discourses between the different national and EU institutions entrusted with the pursuit of such goals. Accepting that the European Constitution and its fundamental
rights policy will continue to be, to a large extent, the result of a discursive process
between different EU and national actors, it is important to stress the need to discuss
such values and institutions and to reshape the European constitutional discourse so
as to broaden its basis of participation and representation and break the legal self-
referential character that has prevented the introduction of political debate in order
to safeguard the process of legal integration.

III. THE EUROPEAN SOCIAL DEFICIT?—MARKET
INTEGRATION, EFFICIENCY, AND DISTRIBUTIVE JUSTICE

The social rights deficit *vis-à-vis* economic freedom in European integration is more
a story of what has not been than what has been. As a result either of legal constraints
or the constraints of economic competition, European economic integration (in parallel with global economic integration) has generated pressures towards deregulation and challenged social standards and welfare. This has not been (at least totally)
compensated for by social policies arising at the level of the European Union. It is
easier to promote integration by reducing state legislation interfering with economic
activities (negative integration) than by creating common standards and regulatory
frameworks for economic agents (positive integration). The latter requires an agreement on social policies and rights normally expressed in the form of legislation, and
difficult to achieve in the EU context of different national interests and ideological
standpoints. The problems and successes in developing a European social policy are
dealt with in another paper.[58] Here, I will be concerned with the balance between
economic freedom and social rights that arises from the balance between negative in-

---

these groups is the consequence of a higher degree of solidarity that still supports national political communities. However, the expansion of the logic of market integration to all economic and social regulations
has hindered such forms of solidarity, since national exceptions on social-economic grounds are usually
seen as unacceptable forms of protectionism. The introduction of social rights into the EU legal discourse
requires the authorization of such types of discrimination. The safeguarding of some social rights is dependent on permission to discriminate in favour of a certain group of nationals. Social rights should be
the measurement and criteria of validity of this sort of discrimination.

[58] See the contribution of Silvana Sciarra to this vol.

tegration and positive integration and the institutional choices behind such mechanisms of decision-making.

Promotion of economic integration through free trade is understood to increase efficiency and wealth maximization. However, many fear that such gains may occur at the cost of weaker social groups or are not fairly distributed between all members of society. Underlying this discussion is the old conflict between efficiency and distributive justice or, in other words, between promoting competitiveness and wealth maximization and securing a certain degree of social protection to all members of the community. Among those who defend the welfare state, European integration is seen in different perspectives. For some, the European Union and its common market are just one more (albeit considerable) step in a current trend that tends to favour global economic competition and efficiency against the solidarity and distributive justice expressed in social rights and policies. For others, the European Union is an attempt to answer to those current global market competition trends by creating a new forum in which protective social rights and policies can be agreed and enforced. There are also those who highlight the freedom and efficiency gains of economic integration and see in the limits that such process imposes on public powers one of its greatest advantages. In this light, the political programme of European integration is the promotion of efficiency and the allocation of resources through free market transactions. The market will be the most efficient and, in many cases, the more just allocator of resources.

The balance between economic freedom and social rights in the European Union will be a consequence both of the model and ideal of European integration adopted and, in general, our preferences with regard to efficiency and distributive justice. There are two basic dilemmas that intersect in this issue: the first concerns the choice between wealth maximization and distributive justice; the second concerns whether we favour a model of economic integration or a model of political integration for Europe.

The impact of Community law on national social rights, through negative market integration, has generally been seen as 'negative' by social lawyers because it restricted the capacity of States to enact social provisions. Community law has been understood as favouring economic freedom against social rights. However, the opposite has normally occurred when Community law is addressed by social lawyers from the perspective of positive market integration in the form of social legislation enacted at the EU level. This is so, even though the competence of the EU on social issues has generally been limited and moved slowly. Community law has been seen, in particular among labour lawyers, as a source of the defence and promotion of social policies against predominant deregulatory ideologies at the national level. The ideology of deregulation is not uniform among the Member States and labour lawyers hope to mobilize the more 'social' States to push, at the European level, for social rights and policies that they are not able to establish at the national level. At the same time, the arguments in favour of deregulation often stress the need to be competitive in the European market, which requires States with more protective social rights to reduce their degree of protection. Thus, labour lawyers try to reinstate the primacy of social rights over the market through common regulations at the European level.

There are two strategies of European economic integration which lead to different conceptions of the balance between economic freedom and social rights: negative integration and positive integration. They reflect the broader debate between global economic competition and the protection of the welfare state: the viewpoint of negative integration stresses the function of European market integration in promoting efficiency through economic competition between the States; the viewpoint of positive integration stresses the value of European integration as a defence against such deregulated global economic competition and establishes a common level playing field and a hard core of social rights. Things are made even more complex in the European Union context by the introduction of the debate between economic integration and political integration. For those who argue in favour of a model of European integration restricted to economic integration, the goal is to maximize wealth (efficiency) through free trade and market integration. Social rights may be required, but only as a form of securing a level playing field and fair competition. For those who argue in favour of a model of political integration, wealth maximization has to be complemented by some criterion of solidarity and distributive justice in the new political community. Social rights will be a requirement independent of fair competition and arising from membership of that political community.

It is common to associate efficiency with resource allocation by the market and distributive justice with the establishment of social rights by the political process. However, that is not always the case, as a deeper analysis of those institutions would show.[59] In effect, market decisions may only represent the interests of some of those affected by them and that fact may produce inefficient decisions (since not all costs and benefits are taken into account). The problem that economists characterize as externality can also be conceived of as a problem of lack of representation of some of the affected interests in the decision-making institution (the market). Social rights can be forms of introducing that representation and enhancing efficiency.

The transfer of decision-making from the market to the political process can be advocated in two situations: either because there are market imperfections (such as those relating to externalities, transaction costs, or information costs); or because it is believed that distributive justice requires the replacement of the market efficient allocation of resources for a more just and equitable distribution of resources made by the political process, which takes into account interests which are not directly affected by the market transaction (the typical example would be redistribution through taxation). However, decision-making in the political process is also, to a large extent, a result of representation and participation in that process and is also subject to institutional malfunctions. In some cases, for example, the political process may be captured by interest groups, and what is presented as the protection of a social right aiming at a fair distribution of resources may be no more than the reinforcement of the interests of a few, with high costs both in terms of efficiency and distributive justice.

The balance between social rights and economic freedom in the European Union requires an analysis of the institutions of the market (responsible for negative inte-

---

[59] See Poiares Maduro, note 4 above, at 103–49. See also N. Komesar, *Imperfect Alternatives—Choosing Institutions in Law, Economics and Public Policy* (1994).

gration) and the EU political process (responsible for positive integration). It also requires a debate about the goals of European integration, notably the balance between efficiency and distributive justice. This cannot be undertaken within the limits of this chapter, but some suggestions will be advanced regarding the role and future of fundamental social rights in the European Union, taking into account goals of efficiency and distributive justice.

A. Social Rights and an Efficient Common Market

Market integration generates competition between the national economic and legal systems subject to the goal of efficiency. Even if normatively it is not imposed on States in order to lower their social standards, economic competition opens the national legal systems to competition and efficiency criteria, *de facto* subjecting normative ideals to economic reasoning. This also explains why economic freedom is enhanced without necessarily requiring the incorporation of economic fundamental freedoms into national legal systems.

The consequences of this process are deregulation at the national level and a reduction in political control over the economic sphere. The argument in favour of a European social policy attempts to reintroduce such political control over the economic sphere at the European Union level. The European Union would become the relevant level for the establishment and protection of social rights. Economic competition in the European Union should occur within a legal framework that includes a set of social rights. Those arguing against the development of a European social policy and European social rights prefer to subject those policies and rights to market competition itself. There is nothing new about this. When the EC Treaty was drafted there were two divergent opinions on whether the prior harmonization of social policy was necessary. One side (coinciding with French interests, France having the most protective social legislation), argued in favour of European legislative harmonization of social policies. The other side (namely Germany) opposed such harmonization, preferring to 'rely on normal competitive forces to achieve it in the long run'.[60] Article 141 (*ex* Article 119), requiring equal pay for men and women, is a result of the compromise reached in the Treaty.

In reality, both systems of managing economic and regulatory competition in integrated markets (negative and positive integration) generate harmonization of social rights and policies. The difference lies in the institutional framework through which such harmonization arises and its impact on the final outcome of harmonization. As stated by Trubek:

> Once economic interdependence reaches a certain point, and borders no longer serve as major barriers to economic movement, there is a pressure towards uniformity in economic policies. These pressures may come about to ensure fair competition and the smooth functioning of economic enterprises that span national borders ('level playing field'), or they may be the result of 'regulatory competition' among sovereignties in a unified space.[61]

---

[60] E. Haas, *The Uniting of Europe* (1968), 516.
[61] D. Trubek, *Social Justice 'After' Globalization—The Case of Social Europe*, typescript (Nov. 1996), 5.

The question we face in the context of the European Union is when or with regard to which issues we should accept competition between the different States with regard to social rights and policies or when we should establish common rights and policies to which such competition should conform.

Negative integration generates competition between States, but at the same time allows States to maintain their own policies (at least formally). On the contrary, common social rights are dependent on normative statements which need to be incorporated into the national legal systems affecting what are now considered purely internal situations. Thus, they require an extension of the reach of EU law in national legal orders, a process of complex legitimacy and effectiveness. For some, to impose common social standards will reduce the gains of efficiency arising from competition betweem States and will deprive the different States (and their citizens) from autonomy in deciding their preferred social model. For others, competition among States will lead to harmonization at the lowest common social denominator resulting in a 'race to the bottom'.

Those who focus on the European Union as an area of free trade and a common market envisage the Union as an instrument of efficiency and wealth maximization. The goal is to increase societal net gain through market integration without concerns about how such wealth is distributed within the Union. Many believe that the best way of achieving market integration and maximizing wealth is through the mutual recognition of national rules and the almost absolute free movement of goods, services, and factors of production. This will generate a process of regulatory competition subject to market choice. Companies and persons will move to where the regulatory environment is more favourable to their objectives (less regulation, lower taxes, more jobs, better social protection, etc.). Consumers could choose goods and services conforming to different national regulations and, in this way, those regulations will also be competing in the market. There are different economic analyses praising or criticizing such strategy of market integration and regulatory competition. Some stress the efficiency gains, others the risks of a 'race to the bottom'. This discussion will not be reviewed in depth here. Instead, I would like to call attention to some of the assumptions underlying this model and the role to be played by social rights in that context. Assuming we want to maximize wealth and efficiency, what is the role of social rights in a system in which the allocation of resources is left to the market?

There is much that is captivating in the notion of competition among States, but such a model subjects the different States' balances between social values and economic freedoms to market choice. This raises a key question: if we have social regulation and social rights which are normatively imposed on the market it is precisely because we do not trust the market. Why, then, should we submit that regulation to a decision of the market? Why should those that regulate the market trust in the market to judge that regulation? The answer is that the market which judges regulations is not the same as the regulated market. The market to which we are referring in this case is a political and economic market participation in which must be granted to all those affected by the regulation/deregulation choice (including labour, the unemployed; companies etc.). A market operating at its best will be a market in which decisions are the result of voluntary transactions in which all those affected participate, and in which all costs and benefits and alternative transactions are taken into account. Such a market would be an ideal decision-maker from the point of view of resource allocation efficiency. This is not incompatible with social rights and social justice. An ideal decision in terms of resource allocation efficiency must, for example, take into account the labour costs of the relocation of a company production site or the costs involved in the insecurity of more flexible labour legislation. Moreover, resource allocation efficiency will tend to favour social justice: this is so because, contrary to what is sometimes assumed, the measurement of efficiency does not value in the same manner the wealth of high-income and low-income people. The criteria depend on how much each person will value the protection of a certain interest or the use of a certain resource. If we were to have only one Euro available it would be more efficient to allocate it to a low-income person than to a high-income person (that latter values a Euro less than the former). What make people suspicious about resource allocation efficiency are two things: first, it is normally used to legitimize a decision that increases efficiency, although there could be alternatives that would promote a higher degree of efficiency; secondly, resource allocation efficiency is normally implemented through a narrow conception of the market conceived as the economic voluntary transactions market. In this market, people express their preferences by how much they are able to pay and, in consequence, this market tends to favour those with a higher income. However, in the conception of the market which supports competition among States generated by negative integration there are other forms of participation in the market beyond voluntary market transactions. The market responsible for choices in a competitive model is much more than the sum of voluntary market transactions. It also involves such things as 'voting with the feet', political votes, lobbying, or strikes.

Much of the economic jargon used in this area is about democratic questions and requires social rights. One may speak in this regard of the options of voice and exit,[62] and adjust these concepts to the different forms of expression people may have, either within the jurisdiction to which they are subject or by actually leaving that jurisdiction in favour of another jurisdiction. *Voice* refers to situations in which choices are made or stances taken which express a preference for a certain regulation but do not involve leaving the jurisdiction (this includes voting and lobbying, market transactions within that jurisdiction, but also, for example, worker participation and strikes). *Exit* refers to situations in which preferences for a certain regulation over another are expressed by moving to a different jurisdiction (and thus the relocation of factors of production but also consumers, taxpayers, and unemployed people).

---

[62] These concepts have been crafted by A. Hirschman in his well-known book, *Exit, Voice and Loyalty—Responses to Decline in Firms, Organizations and States* (1970). For two different examples of the use of these concepts see T.R. Dye, *American Federalism*, No. 102, at 17 and Weiler, 'The Transformation of Europe', note 3 above, at 2411. My use of these concepts, however, does not fully coincide with that of these authors or with the original definition given by Hirschman. In particular, I include all market transactions within a jurisdiction (e.g. both buying a product or stopping buying it) in the domain of voice.

When the efficiency of the market is assessed under the present constitutional analysis in order to choose the 'best' regulation, the possibilities of *exit* and *voice* in the market and in the political process should be taken into account for all the different interests affected by the regulation. In this respect, the system requires a set of social rights that can be said to guarantee participation and representation in market decisions and, by internalizing costs which tend to be ignored in those decisions, increase efficiency. Those social rights are related to forms of voice and exit in the market.

One of the first requirements of an effective system of regulatory competition among States is that of mobility. This is required not only for companies, capital, or workers but also for all those who are affected by the regulations and wish to express their preferences by choosing a certain jurisdiction in which to live. In the European Union, free movement of persons has been limited to workers or self-employed persons, and, even within these categories, it has been subject to many limits arising from national legislation. The greater development of the free movement rules relating to goods, services, companies, and capital means that those associated with the promotion of such rules are much more effective in expressing their preference or opposition to a certain social regulation. Workers, self-employed, and unemployed persons have few opportunities to choose between different jurisdictions with different social regulations. Thus, the results of competition between social regulations will tend to reflect the higher participation (through voice and exit) of companies and capital. An efficient and democratic process of competition between national regulations requires that free movement of persons be fully implemented and given equal status to that of the other free movement rules.

There are or may be other problems of representation in the market. Even among those that are able to move, not all have the same capacity for mobility: capital, for example, normally has much more mobility than labour. The same can be said of *voice*, where not all have the same opportunities: unemployed people have much less voice than unionized labour or organized capital, for example. Social rights will have an important role to play in this regard. Social rights of participation and collective action should constitute common ground on which the competitive process may take place. This system further requires forms of participation within some of these collective actors' decision-making. Thus, company decisions on where to move should allow for some sort of participation by the workers affected by that decision.

Free movement of persons and rights of participation and representation such as the freedom of association, the right to collective bargaining, and the right to collective action should be considered as instrumental to a fully functioning integrated market which can increase efficiency and wealth maximization. The argument in favour of these fundamental social rights arises not from the need for a level playing field but from the need of the competition system itself to achieve the goal of efficiency. At the same time, such rights will enhance the concept of European citizenship by providing new forms of participation and representation in a European forum of decision-making which is normally ignored in the debates regarding the democratic deficit: the European common market.

B. Social Rights and Redistribution

Another question remains: should the European Union protect only that limited set of social rights? Perhaps better, should European integration only be about wealth maximization, while distributive justice should and could be left to the States? Or does the European market needs to be complemented by some degree of distributive justice? Market integration increases efficiency and wealth, but it also diminishes the instruments for distribution of such wealth at national level. As we have seen, market integration has challenged the regulatory powers of the States, which are in many cases aimed at protecting or promoting social rights such as the rights to education, health, and social protection, fair working conditions, minimum income, and, in a broader sense, other 'social' rights, such as consumer and environmental protection. Many of these rights are recognized in the Treaties as goals of the European Union.[63] However, their status as fundamental rights and their interpretation varies among Member States. Maybe that explains their limited use as an interpretative authority in the European Court of Justice's application of market integration rules to the review of national legislation. This has meant that the internal logic of market integration has prevailed, even where conflicts with social rights arose. Yet it could be argued that States should be left sufficient policy autonomy to ensure 'the continuation of welfare states traditions, albeit under new economic constraints'.[64] It always becomes a question of where we draw the line. We want to ensure market integration and the efficiency gains it brings, but we also want to protect the States' autonomy to maintain their welfare states. Wherever we do come to draw the line, it appears that our conception of fundamental social rights must change and can no longer be opposed to economic freedom. We have come to distrust the law and realize the end of its normative empire. But we are yet to find the right balance between wealth maximization and distributive justice. Moreover, in the European Union, we are also yet to find the right balance between economic integration (promoting wealth maximization) and political integration (promoting an European entitlement to distributive justice).

The assumption of economic integration was increased growth without interference in the distribution function. But a viable and sustainable integration is only workable if economic growth is fairly distributed. Moreover, as was stressed earlier, economic integration has also challenged redistribution policies at the national level, since these policies can be argued either to restrict trade or to reduce the competitive ability of the national economies. Two further proposals are, in consequence, advanced: first, as mentioned in the first part of this report, fundamental social rights should be used as criteria for accepting national measures which restrict trade on social and economic grounds; secondly, a concept of distributive justice, including a redistribution policy, should be developed at the European Union level to compensate for the restrictions imposed on the redistribution function at national level and to legitimize the economic integration process with its gains in wealth and efficiency. The

---

[63] See, e.g., Arts. 2, 3, 117, and 118 of the EC Treaty, which are now Arts. 2, 3, 136, and 137.
[64] S. Silvana, *How Global is Labour Law? The Perspective of Social Rights in the European Union*, EUI Working Papers, Law No. 96/6, at 32.

The process of expanding social rights is an endless one. As such, it attracts the attention of all political actors and provokes the activism of institutions. It also represents for the writer the best historical link with the Universal Declaration of Human Rights,[1] which is at the origin of this collective effort to suggest a critical analysis and to advance new proposals, taking it as a source of inspiration for its 'universal' and 'positive' affirmation of rights addressed to all men, rather than to citizens of a country or of a region. The language adopted for universal human rights usefully applies to social rights: 'freedoms' rest on the assumption that States will abstain from intervening; 'powers' require active state policies for their enforcement.[2]

This chapter will concentrate on social rights and social policies resting within the domain of employment contracts: both the increasing activity of EC legislature and the attention paid to it by national labour law systems have opened up a wide research field. Active employment measures, as well as measures to fight unemployment, must be included in this wide angle of legal analysis. This will bring new evidence to the philosophical distinction between 'freedoms' and 'powers' and will transfer the practical consequences of this to the process of expansion and enrichment of a supranational legal order.

A. The Treaty of Paris and the Treaty of Rome: Two Early Visions of Social Rights

Looking back at the early days of the European Coal and Steel Community (ECSC) we find a valuable confirmation of the theory according to which European integration was oriented towards functional objectives, reflecting specific national interests rather than well-identified common interests. Furthering a broader political plan and achieving a more consistent interdependence of the economic systems appeared a very improbable objective because of the dominating strength of national interests. Specific peculiarities were nonetheless visible within the European Community; nothing but a 'false analogy' could be made when comparing the EC with other international organizations active at the same time, since none of them raised the problem of limiting national sovereignty while achieving co-operation.[3]

This is a crucial point in the understanding of social policies developments and must be read in conjunction with the introduction into the Treaty of Rome of unanimity as the golden rule in decision making within the European Council. If we go back to the Coal and Steel Community, we find an interesting key for the interpretation of early social measures, which can also be used in framing later developments in the field. As part of the aids addressed by the Community to the two industrial sectors in question, social measures were subordinate to the fact that major economic

---

[1] Adopted and proclaimed by GA Res. 217 A (III) (1948). In United Nations, *A Compilation of International Instruments* (1994), i, Part 1, 1.

[2] N. Bobbio, 'Presente e avvenire dei diritti dell'uomo' [1990] *L'età dei diritti* 17, and especially 41. Mengoni argues that social rights are an expansion of the principle of equality and are linked to emerging needs of the civil society, whereas fundamental freedoms are historically intended to protect the individual against political power. Unlike the latter, social rights do not bring about direct enforceability as individual subjective rights, but objectively bind the legislature: L. Mengoni, 'I diritti sociali']1998] *Argomenti di diritto del lavoro* 1.

[3] A.S. Milward, 'L'Europa in formazione', in M. Aymard, P. Bairoch, W. Barberis, and C. Ginzburg, *Storia d'Europa* (1993), 196.

choices had to be favoured within some nation States, in order to enhance the competitiveness of the newly born common market, by favouring free trade of coal and steel.

Restructuring or closure of activities brought with it unemployment benefits for coal miners, training for steel-workers made redundant, financial aid to move to other jobs, and similar measures which showed the purely instrumental nature of social protection. The main guarantee for workers had to do with the availability of resources allowing them to change occupation;[4] this was a quite extraordinary measure, when we think that at the time at which it was conceived, the prevailing pattern was that of permanent and never changing employment. Since the High Authority had no power to intervene in social policies, it was remarkable that it achieved all this through co-operation between nation States. What was favoured, in the absence of normative powers, was the gathering of information on national labour law systems which resulted in very interesting early attempts to build up a common legal culture, through comparative analysis.[5]

It can be maintained that a negative—albeit very pragmatic—rationale inspired social measures at that time, since social aids were considered to be a mere repercussion of broad industrial policies, lacking in continuity and in autonomy, linked as they were to decisions of a political and economic nature, taken at the national level. This explanation can also be read in the light of contemporary events and measured against the aforementioned inability of States to surrender sovereignty in favour of common social goals.

This is still a reality within the European Union, particularly, as we shall see later, when measures on employment are at stake.

In the Treaty of Rome, the debate on European social rights was influenced by the weakness and narrowness of the legal basis and by the strict connection established with mechanisms of market regulation, in order to avoid distortion in competition. These two points made the development of social policies largely dependent on competition rules; principles of fairness and efficiency within the market included only a limited number of social rules and made them functional to goals which would, otherwise, be considered outside the scope of national labour law systems.

The Spaak Report (1956)[6] is an illuminating document in this respect, inasmuch as it shows the theoretical inspiration which then led the founding fathers to draw a map of social rights within the borderlines of economic efficiency. The Report thought that a 'gradual coalescence' of social policies would become one of the elements of a well-functioning common market. The precondition was that harmonization could be furthered only where specific distortions of competition were visible. As a result of this the French government could ensure that labour law rules to be inserted into the Treaty would be measured against its own internal system, particularly with regard to parity of wages and social costs. It all resulted in the

---

[4] G. and A. Lyon-Caen, *Droit social international et Européen* (1993), 160.

[5] S. Sciarra, 'European Social Policy and Labour Law: Challenges and Perspectives' (1995) 4 *AEL* 312.

[6] Spaak Report: *Comité Intergouvernemental créé par la conférence de Messine, Rapport des Chefs de Délégations aux Ministères des Affaires Etrangères de 21 avril 1956*. The Committee, comprising the heads of delegations, was established at the Messina conference in June 1955 under the chairmanship of M. Paul Henri Spaak, then Belgian foreign minister

compromise of Article 136 (*ex* Article 117), characterized by its two sides, the first one being more prescriptive, the second more predictive.[7]

This analysis, albeit from the very specific and perhaps limited perspective of social rights, confirms the overall interpretation, highlighted above, which sees the creation of a common market as the outcome of strong national economic interests, particularly French ones. First with the ECSC, then with the EEC, national post-war reconstruction had to proceed and be favoured, without obstacles in its way.[8] It is not surprising that relevant Articles of the Rome Treaty would be inspired by this philosophy and produce a mechanism whereby assimilation of national legal systems should be the last resort and the Commission should only be given the power either to grant subsidies to correct distortions or to promote collaboration among Member States in the social field, as stated in Article 137 (*ex* Article 118).

Even Articles 141 and 143 (*ex* Articles 119 and 120)—the former then become a cornerstone for equality legislation—were inspired by French legislation and forced into the Treaty by the representatives of the French government. Both aimed at establishing equal rules governing contracts of employment, which would ensure the cohesion of the market.[9]

An important provision in the Treaty—regarded as the most significant achievement in the field[10]—was Article 51 (now Article 42), establishing the right of employees to social security measures, while moving freely within the common market. Both as the origin of very relevant legislation and as a fundamental principle established in order to counterbalance the risks inherent in labour mobility, this measure opens up a wide and complex scenario, the implications of which are still at the heart of institutional reforms both at a national and supranational level.

A strict unanimity rule had to govern the whole field, at least until the reforms brought about by the Single European Act in 1986. Before the timid derogation from such a principle, expressed in Article 138 (*ex* Article 118a) (introduced by the SEA), Article 100 (now Article 94) was the only legal basis for the approximation of social legislation. Unanimity was required for the directives on collective dismissals and transfers of undertakings adopted during the 1970s. No doubt this legislation must be included in the list of important achievements of the Commission in the framework of its social action programme. The attention shown towards important employees' rights had nevertheless to be ascertained against the background of economic instability and industrial restructuring; distortions in competition, even at that later stage of economic integration, had to be avoided, the result being that social rights were once again made adaptable to the prevailing interests of companies, put under pressure by new market demands.

The marginal position of social rights within the Treaties of Paris and Rome can fruitfully be compared with other international sources. A line is drawn between economic, social, and cultural rights on the one hand, and civil and political rights on

---

[7] O. Kahn-Freund, 'Labour Law and Social Security', in E. Stein and T.L. Nicholson (eds.), *American Enterprise in the European Common Market. A Legal Profile* (1960), i, 300.

[8] Milward, note 3 above, at 191–2.

[9] C. Barnard, 'The Economic Objectives of Article 119', in T.K. Hervey and D. O'Keefe (eds.), *Sex Equality Law in the European Union* (1996), 32.

[10] Kahn-Freund, note 7 above, at 320–1.

the other, in the United Nations human rights covenants of 1966.[11] Although a lot has been said on the generation gap dividing the former rights from the latter, pointing out that values inspiring all human rights are by definition 'variable' and open to absorb changes due to cultural and social factors,[12] it still remains true that the evolution of social rights continues to be much slower and highly controversial, even in advanced legal systems.

Various historical reasons are behind this assertion, some of which may prove central to the argument which is developed in this chapter, namely the importance of balancing national traditions against the supranational construction of social rights and of keeping this exercise in law-making within a multi-level framework of competencies and compatibility. It will be maintained throughout this chapter that when it comes to social rights, the process of European integration must not be such as to preclude national initiatives and obscure national traditions. In order to move in this direction, a digression will be necessary towards other international sources, different from Community sources and yet relevant for the understanding of current trends in the field.

Rather than attempting to offer a complete overview of relevant sources and of their enforcement, a few cases will be selected. This will be done in relation to one European country in particular, as far as ILO sources are concerned. The United Kingdom has in fact acquired a unique position in comparison to other countries of the Community, because of the drastic changes in labour legislation brought about by the Conservative administration from 1979 onwards.

Testing the new labour law regime against ILO standards proved to be a very important exercise, both for the quantity and the quality of condemnations undergone by the UK. The implications for European social rights are indirect and yet very relevant, as will be shown in the next section.

B. Renewed Centrality of ILO Standards—The Case of the United Kingdom

In the history of European social policies, the obstinate opposition shown by both the Thatcher and Major administrations to approving legislation in the social field leaves a very clear legacy. On the one hand the limits inherent in unanimity voting and the difficulties of operating on the narrow and contested terrain of Article 118a (now Article 138) became progressively more evident. This led to the Maastricht compromise which, by way of derogation from Article 148(2) (now Article 205) of the Treaty, excluded the United Kingdom from the scope of the agreement on social policies.

---

[11] See the International Covenants on Economic, Social and Cultural Rights and on Civil and Political Rights, adopted by GA Res. 2200 A (XXI) (1966): *International Instruments*, note 1 above, at 8 and 20; and A. Eide, 'Economic, Social and Cultural Rights as Human Rights', in A. Eide, C. Krause, and A. Rosas (eds.), *Economic, Social and Cultural Rights* (1995), 21. From this distinction, unlike the overall approach followed in the Universal Declaration of Human Rights, assumptions then followed that civil and political rights were to be considered 'absolute' and 'immediate', whereas social, economic, and cultural rights were 'programmatic' (Eide, at 22). Similar terms are adopted when describing the latter category of rights in Community sources. See below.

[12] Bobbio, note 2 above.

On a different—and yet connected—side of labour law policies, the UK showed its reluctance to ratify new ILO Conventions (only one of the twenty-five Conventions adopted between 1979 and 1996 was ratified) and its readiness to denounce previous Conventions.[13] While vetoing the approval of Community law, the UK wanted to prove the impenetrability of the system by international labour standards and, at the same time, wanted to show its ability to legislate against the mainstream of fundamental principles shared by the majority of countries within the Community.

Two conventions in particular were in the middle of the hurricane affecting the UK: conventions No. 87 (1948) and No. 98 (1949), dealing respectively with Freedom of Association and Protection of the Right to Organise and Right to Organise and Collective Bargaining.[14] Leading cases started in the public sector and had to do with the Government's attempt to exclude some categories of public servants from the scope of Convention No. 87.[15] They were intertwined with cases on the limitation of the right to strike,[16] with the result that the whole conservative legislation in collective labour law was put under regular scrutiny and led to a series of condemnations.

Later, the 1993 Trade Union Reform and Employment Rights Act, and particularly the narrow interpretation of this Act offered by the House of Lords,[17] kept all ILO bodies busy preserving freedom of association from the invasion of limiting employers' practices. It was held that Article 13 of the Act would 'discourage' collective bargaining if it were to be interpreted as allowing the payment of incentives for employees moving from collective agreed terms and conditions of employment to individual contracts. Annual condemnation by the ILO of the UK government became an exhausting ritual, in which the ILO showed its commitment and proved to have had a long-term perspective, waiting for substantial innovations to take place, once a change of government occurred.

In the early cases, the Committee on Freedom of Association and the Committee of Independent Experts were both called upon and made to play, each within its own competence, a very interesting institutional game, forcing the British government to amend legislation when in breach of ILO Conventions.[18] In the later cases too the

---

[13] B. Hepple, 'New Approaches to International Labour Regulation' (1996) 26 *ILJ* 356.

[14] In ILO, *International Labour Conventions and Recommendations* (1996), i, 435 and 524.

[15] The *Government Communications Headquarters (GCHQ)*, Case No. 1261, 234th Report of the Freedom of Association Committee, ILO, 87, on which see particularly Lord Wedderburn, *The Worker and the Law* (1986), 276. This case did not reach the Strasbourg Court due to the Commission on Human Rights' decision that the restrictions in question were justified under Art. 11(2), ECHR; on the consequences of this leading case and the still ongoing debate, see S. Mills, 'The International Labour Organisation, the United Kingdom and Freedom of Association: An Annual Cycle of Condemnation' (1997) 2 *EHRLR* 43. See also *Report of the Committee of Experts on the Application of Conventions and Recommendations* (1995) and (1996); and the *Schoolteachers' Pay and Working Conditions Case*, Case No. 1391, 256th Report of the Freedom of Association Committee, ILO, 39–89. As for GCHQ, the initiative was taken by the government in the summer of 1997 to restore the right to belong to a trade union, although with some restrictions. See briefly on this, Hepple, note 13 above, at 365.

[16] All analysed by B. Creighton, 'The ILO and Protection of Freedom of Association in the United Kingdom', in K. Ewing, C. Gearty, and B. Hepple (eds.), *Human Rights and Labour Law* (1994), 10.

[17] *Associated Newspapers Ltd* v. *Wilson* and *Associated British Ports* v. *Palmer* [1995] 2 AC 454, discussed in Mills, note 13 above, at 39.

[18] Creighton, note 16 above, at 11.

ILO was able to substantiate its position with wide and well argued criticism of the legislation in its entirety. As a consequence of this long and controversial confrontation, a critical ground has been prepared for the new Labour government; on its side, it would be hard to show scepticism and disregard towards international labour standards and to leave things as they are. There will be a need to go through previous legislation and revise it, while keeping very close scrutiny on new legislation to be adopted in the field. Furthermore, ratifying ILO conventions will appear as an opportunity to gain consensus in the international community.

The widespread and convincing opposition expressed in scholarly work to the lowering of ILO standards[19] was also accompanied by a militant view on the part of the unions. Such discovery of a new centrality for the ILO and for its labour standards has run parallel with a more balanced and inspired position of British academia towards the EC. The contribution of British scholars, particularly labour lawyers, in building up a critical—and yet constructive—evaluation of Community social policies was remarkable. An analogy can be drawn to a similarly active role of practising lawyers, interest groups, and specialized agencies in taking cases to the ECJ through preliminary ruling procedures.

Both examples show the misgivings of the British legal system about accepting structural changes in labour law and the wish to keep some of its characteristics intact, by referring to international and Community sources.

This was a test of some importance for the ILO, especially at a time when its political role appeared weaker, in the light of the new political order following the collapse of Eastern States, and because of the reduced weight of employees' representatives within it.[20] In a sense, the role played by the ILO with respect to British legislation went against both these elements and indicated that, despite its feeble capacity for imposing sanctions, an international organization can maximize its supervisory machinery and use its power to expose national governments to moral condemnation[21] and help them towards the implementation of international standards.

However, despite the peculiarities inherent in a tripartite organization like the ILO, in which standards are constantly revised and the voice of non-governmental organizations is regularly heard, the notion of 'best practice', as the final outcome of political options made in enforcing labour standards, might need to be revised.[22] This policy suggestion is also related to the ever stronger position of new organizations such as the WTO. The inclusion of labour standards within the regulation of

---

[19] K. Ewing, *Britain and the ILO* (1994); K.W. Wedderburn, 'Labour Standards, Global Markets and Labour Laws in Europe', in W. Sengenberger and D. Campbell, *International Labour Standards and Economic Interdependence* (1994), 245.

[20] A. Nussberger, 'Summary of Discussions: Is the International Labour Organization in a State of Transition?', in B. Maydell and A. Nussberger (eds.), *Social Protection by Way of International Law: Appraisal, Defecits and Further Development* (1996), 213–15.

[21] G. Gaja, 'Organizzazione internazionale del lavoro' (1981); XXXI *Enc. Dir.* 336; H. Bartolomei de la Cruz, 'Standard Setting Activities in the Field of Social and Labour Law: International Labour Law: Renewal or Decline?', in Maydell and Nussberger, note 20 above, at 46.

[22] L. Swepston, 'Supervision of ILO Standards' (1997) 13 *Int. Jour. of Comp. Lab Law and Ind. Rel.* 344.

free trade, despite the proclaimed commitment to the observance of ILO standards, may introduce dangerous limitations into the latter.[23]

Regional legal systems—like the Community system—need to be carefully evaluated, whilst also questioning the efficiency of international enforcement mechanisms. Homogeneity of technical standards can best be achieved at regional level, while maintaining a common core of fundamental principles. To take one example currently in the public eye, flexibility within the labour market must be measured against binding minimum rules rather than being left to national legislatures with wide options.

This exercise becomes even more crucial for the cultural identity of a regional legal system if we look at the very general and often vague indications addressed to governments by institutions such as the World Bank.[24] This is why the political and legal confrontation between the ILO and the UK becomes an exemplary case. It supports one of the main arguments in this chapter, namely the need to strengthen fundamental social rights—and in particular the right to organize—at Community level and to adopt specific monitoring mechanisms aiming at the convergence of international labour standards.

C. Article 11 of the ECHR: Shall We Listen to the Strasbourg Court?

In referring to the relevant sources of the Council of Europe, there is a tendency to confirm a separation of territories, historically significant, as well as politically remarkable: on one side the prevailingly individualistic approach of the 1950 European Convention on Human Rights, on the other the opening up of some collective rights in the 1961 European Social Charter.

Particularly if we take Article 11 of the ECHR, the most relevant within the general framework of this chapter, we are bound to see the close correlation with the provisions of the ESC and the way these two sources are made to function separately and yet in such a way that they can supplement each other.[25] The 'flavour of liberal principle combined with uncertainty of meaning',[26] which can be also tasted in reading Article 11, makes the Charter an essential supplement to the ECHR. First defined as a big footnote to the Convention,[27] the Charter has been constantly improving its moral and legal standing and acquiring a position of its own among international sources.

Dynamism in this development is confirmed first by the 1988 Additional Protocol, which had the merit of expanding the competence of the Charter to information and consultation rights, the most contemporary expression of the right to organize col-

[23] See, e.g., the Singapore Ministerial Declaration of 13 Dec. 1996. WT/MIN(96)DEC.
[24] The World Bank, *World Development Report 1995: Workers in an Integrating World* (1995); World Bank, *The State in a Changing World* (1997). A classification of labour standards is offered by K.E. Maskus, 'Should Core Labour Standards be Imposed through International Trade Policy?' [1997] *The World Bank Development Research Group* 8.
[25] D. Harris, *The European Social Charter* (1984); D. Gomein, D. Harris, and L. Zwaak, *Law and Practice of the European Convention on Human Rights and the European Social Charter* (1996).
[26] K.W. Wedderburn, 'Freedom of Association or Right to Organise? The Common Law and International Sources', in Lord Wedderburn, *Employment Rights in Britain and Europe* (1991), 140.
[27] O. Kahn-Freund, 'The European Social Charter', in F.G. Jacobs (ed.), *European Law and the Individual* (1976) 182.

lectively.[28] A protocol amending the Charter followed in 1991, bearing important consequences for a more effective functioning of the Committee of Ministers and for the sanctions to be applied in cases of non-compliance.

Finally, we should mention the innovations brought about by the 1995 Protocol on collective complaints, empowering NGOs, international and national organisations of workers, and employers to bring complaints directly. This 'model' can be particularly useful in the discussion following the incorporation of the Maastricht Social Agreement into the Amsterdam Treaty. If we take the words of Article 1 of the 1995 Protocol, we can see an analogy with the status of the European social partners, namely that of 'international organisations of employers and trade unions'. As much as the definitions coincide, the European organizations are given important tasks within the overall architecture of the Treaty without any power to complain. Indeed, the ECJ's competence to review collective agreements was debatable under the Maastricht Treaty[29] and still remains so, under the new provisions, in the absence of any explicit mention to this effect.

In May 1996 a new version of the ESC was adopted, which should be running in parallel with the previous one. New rights have been added at the end, in order to leave untouched the structure of the text and the division in parts I and II. Some of the new provisions are inspired by other international sources.[30]

The Council of Europe Parliamentary Assembly has expressed a strong commitment towards speeding up the process of ratification and introducing a distinct European Court of social rights to guarantee observance of obligations under the Charter.[31]

These recent developments should be kept in mind by observers of and commentators on Community law developments; in particular, after the reference to the ESC introduced in the Amsterdam Treaty, an approach oriented towards future changes should be adopted. While indirectly absorbing these new values into the ECJ's frame of reference, account should be taken of a process which will bring about innovation,[32] although the process of ratification of the new Charter may prove very slow and possibly disappointing. In particular, the new procedure for collective complaints should be looked at very closely, in view of the increasingly active role played by employers and labour organizations in the social policy field.

The paradox of the European debate, as we shall see later, is that two core social rights explicitly ousted from the Community competence—namely the right to organize and the right to strike—are those better enshrined in the Council of Europe

---

[28] Embarrassment at the non-ratification of the Protocol by the UK is reported by V. Shrubsall, 'The Additional Protocol to the European Social Charter—Employment Rights' (1989) 18 *ILJ* 39.

[29] S. Sciarra, 'Collective Agreements in the Hierarchy of European Community Sources', in P. Davies, A. Lyon-Caen, S. Sciarra, and S. Simitis, *European Community Labour Law Principles and Perspectives: Liber Amicorum Lord Wedderburn* (1996), 193.

[30] Some examples of convergence can be quoted. Protection of employees in the event of the employer's insolvency draws inspiration from ILO Convention No. 173, in ILO, *International Labour Conventions and Recommendations 1977–1995* (1996), 374. The right to be informed on conditions of work partially recalls EC Dir. 91/533 [1991] OJ L288/32.

[31] Council of Europe Parliamentary Assembly, *Future of the European Social Charter*, Doc. 7980 (1998).

[32] D. Harris, 'The European Social Charter and Social Rights in the European Union', in L. Betten and D. MacDevitt (eds.), *The Protection of Fundamental Social Rights in the European Union* (1996), 110.

sources. It is the interpretation of these rights which has given rise to interesting case law of the Strasbourg Court, in convergence with the activity of the Committee of Independent Experts.

We shall emphasize only a few aspects of this case law, in order to demonstrate to what standards in concrete terms the European Court of Justice would have to refer, should it want—or need—to take into account social rights kept outside the scope of European law.

Article 11 of the ECHR includes the rights to 'form and join trade unions' within the more general right to 'freedom of peaceful assembly and to freedom of association with others'. The most interesting outcome of the case law, for the limited purpose of this chapter, has to do with the negative freedom of association and with the possible expansion of the right to form a union in the direction of neighbouring rights, such as the right to bargain and the right to strike. Both developments, relevant in themselves, are marginal in the European debate and must be contextualized in the most current developments.

It is historically interesting to look at the impact of the *Young, James, and Webster* decision[33] on British academia and on British trade unions.[34] The strenuous defence of the closed-shop system, alien to the majority of continental systems, was so effective as to convince even the most determined critics and to prove that pluralism was a genuine and solid part of European traditions, in which it was possible to combine different forms of protection of the individual in exercising his/her right to join or not to join a union.

The Conservative administrations, from 1979 onwards, in some way pulled the plant out by its roots, progressively reducing the role and the function of the closed shop. The value of the negative freedom, even in the light of such legislative changes, remains incommensurable and needs to be kept alive within the Community, with particular emphasis on the constitutional traditions of Member States, which are also the result of deeply rooted practices in national labour movements.

If we look at the 1993 case of *Sibson*[35] (again a British case), we discover that it is not a violation of Article 11 to dismiss a vehicle driver from his union for dishonesty and to threaten him with strike action if he continued to work at the same depot, having joined another union. The employer requested the applicant either to rejoin the union or work in a different depot; both options were refused and dismissal followed, which gave rise to the claim. The European Court, declaring that there was no violation of Article 11, made a significant reference to *Young*, a case which dealt with the very substance of the freedom of association interfering with the freedom guaranteed by Article 11, thus implying that Sibson did not, and that it would be risky to expand the interpretation of the negative freedom.

Another series of cases touch upon breaches of Article 11 for lack of consultation with the unions. In *National Union of Belgian Police*[36] the claim was that the Belgian

[33] *Young, James and Webster* v. *United Kingdom* (1982) 4 EHRR 38.
[34] F. von Prondzynski, 'Freedom of Association and the Closed Shop: The European Perspective' (1982) 41 *Columbia LJ* 256 and 259; Wedderburn, note 26 above, at 144.
[35] *Sibson* v. *United Kingdom* (1995) 17 EHRR 193.
[36] *National Union of Belgian Police* v. *Belgium*, 1 EHRR 578 (1975).

government had refused to classify the union in question as representative, and had not consulted with it on some questions related to the contract of employment. The Court held that the union's freedom to present claims for lack of consultation was a sufficient sign of its presence and of its right to be heard. The same conclusion was reached in *Swedish Engine Drivers' Union*,[37] where the alleged violation of Article 11 was the refusal of the negotiating body to conclude agreements with the applicant. The Court indicated that the union, once excluded from the bargaining table, could engage in other activities and demonstrate that it was otherwise fulfilling an active role towards its members.

What emerges from this case law is how the Court succeeds in releasing the pressure to expand the scope of Article 11. The Court adopts a very narrow definition of freedom of association, proposing an individualistic rather than collective interpretation[38] which could have the effect of lowering the potential of the freedom itself. Article 11 is not seen as a supportive or auxiliary measure for trade unions, but rather as a source of individual guarantees. Intervention by the States is indispensable for the effectiveness of this right, which would otherwise remain an empty principle.

If we move on to cases dealing indirectly with the right to strike, we have a clear picture of the Court's self-restraint while engaging in interpretation which would overly broaden the horizon of Article 11. In *Gustafsson*,[39] the applicant, not bound by any collective agreement and having refused to sign one regarding a labour market insurance scheme, was hit by a boycott declared by the unions and by sympathy industrial action. The Court held—by twelve votes to seven—that Article 11 had not been violated for the lack of state protection against strikes, which, according to the applicant, would have limited his freedom of association.[40] The result of this case is that a refusal to enter negotiations and collective bargaining is implicitly admitted; quite a dangerous counter-effect to the justified self-restraint on the part of the State in not entering the delicate field of industrial relations.

In *Schmidt and Dahlström*[41] the crucial point was whether members of a union could be denied certain benefits, because of a strike in which they had not taken part. The Court had to confirm, as in previous cases, that the right to strike is only one of the many expressions of the freedom of association, having to choose whether to give flesh to a right which is not part of the ECHR, or whether to adopt a more moderate view which reduces the meaning of the expression 'for the protection of his interests', referred to in Article 11. The Court chose a minimalist interpretation.

Limited protection only is provided and the freedom of association is somehow unnaturally separated from its broader context. The Court was not prepared 'to read into the Convention a code of industrial relations law',[42] nor to invade the territory of the ESC.

[37] *Swedish Engine Drivers' Union* v. *Sweden*, 1 EHRR 617 (1976).
[38] This critique addressed to the Court and Commission is presented in D.J. Harris, C. Warbrick, and M. O'Boyle, *Law of the European Convention on Human Rights* (1995), 432.
[39] *Gustafsson* v. *Sweden* (1996) 22 EHRR 409.
[40] Critical remarks on the applicability of Art. 11 in T. Novitz, 'Negative Freedom of Association' (1996) 26 *ILJ* 86.
[41] *Schmidt and Dahlström* v. *Sweden*, 1 EHRR 632 (1976).
[42] J.G. Merrills, *The Development of International Law by the European Court of Human Rights* (1993), 142.

A tentative conclusion, following this brief account of the case law on Article 11, indicates that the lack of a fundamental social right in Community sources is not to-tally compensated for by reference to the ECIIR. The circulation of international labour standards also serves the purpose of showing that solutions internal to specific legal systems must be tailored, whenever they reflect specific traditions and practices.

On the road to Luxembourg new landscapes need to be discovered.

II. GLOBALIZATION VERSUS EUROPEANIZATION OF SOCIAL RIGHTS

A dilemma is at the centre of what has been described as the third period of post-modern legal pluralism.[43] Whereas in the first period it is relatively easy to distin-guish between legal orders, in the second it becomes more difficult to draw a line between state and non-state social regulation through law. In the third period, the state becomes a 'contested terrain': many external constraints are imposed on it by trans-national practices, while there is a need to expand and reproduce its own role. Globalization brings about a contrast between the local and the trans-national which may threaten the solidity of fundamental rights, as if a change in legal tradi-tion was an inevitable price to pay for the opening up of wider and more competitive markets.

The argument to be developed in this regard, when looking at Europe as 'the local' within 'the global', is that there is a specificity of European legal culture to be main-tained despite the impelling power of the external markets.[44] This specificity emerges in an even clearer perspective when dealing with social rights. The main reasons for this can be tentatively suggested.

(a) Social rights are 'embedded' in local traditions and reflect—possibly more than economic and political rights—the history of deeply rooted associations and interest-groups. The attempt is being made to co-ordinate more closely national organizations within European associations; significant in this regard is the reform of the statute of European Trade Union Confederation (ETUC), which aims at bal-ancing the power of national membership in order to specify the mandate of the supranational confederation. In spite of all this, and notwithstanding the active role of all interest organizations in proposing reforms and in achieving a well-informed presence in the institutional debate, there is no new supranational culture and noth-ing which yet resembles a European labour movement. The weight of national tra-ditions, very heavy for employers' organizations too, makes the search for a common core of interests to be defended a very challenging one.

---

[43] B. de Sousa Santos, 'State, Law and Community in the World System: An Introduction' (1992) 1 *SLS* 132.
[44] S. Sciarra, 'How Global is Labour Law?', in T. Wilthagen (ed.), *Advancing Theory in Labour Law and Industrial Relations in a Global Context* (1998), 99.

(b) The institutional role of the social partners, traditionally very strong in most European countries, is acquiring its own standing at a Community level. This quasi-public function of management and labour, when it comes to being interlocutors of the European institutions, has gained ground over the years, and it now results in a coherent attitude towards social policies, as well as towards macro-economic policies.

This latter attitude has been particularly visible since the Maastricht Treaty and the enforcement of Article 99 (*ex* Article 103), on economic policies and criteria for their convergence[45] and could, by analogy, have important consequences for the implementation of employment policies under the Amsterdam Treaty. The consultation of the social partners was started, beyond the requirement of the law but within a political climate, fostered at Community level, which also reflects national practices, accurately described as 'technical' concertation.[46]

The 1998 Employment Guidelines,[47] anticipating the implementation of the new provisions of the Treaty, openly indicate that social partners at all levels have an important contribution to make, the outcome of which will be assessed every six months—as was the case under the previous procedures for macro-economic policies. They are also urged 'to conclude as soon as possible agreements' at various levels, with a view to increasing all means indicated by the Council for 'employability', flexibility, improving work organization and the like.

(c) Rather than emphasizing an a-critical dependence of the social partners on macro-economics, in view of the achievement of monetary union, attention should be paid to the co-ordination established between national economic policies and supranational targets, through the active role of unions and employers' associations. The extraordinary opportunity offered to the social partners in the years to come is for them to be actors rather than spectators in the launching of the single currency, while monitoring very closely the first stage of implementation of the new Community measures on employment. The historical divide between monetary and social policies, whereby the latter would be graded on a lower scale and be rarely mentioned on the political agenda, still exists and has been criticized while looking at recent developments in Community law.[48] After the introduction of the single

---

[45] Sciarra, note 29 above, at 208. A recent resolution of the European Council of 13 Dec. 1997 ([1998] OJ C35/01) on economic policy co-ordination in stage 3 of EMU and on Treaty Arts. 109 and 109b (now Arts. 111 and 113) indicates that despite the likelihood of closer convergence of cyclical developments, as a consequence of EMU, wage determination should remain a national responsibility and yet be subject to Community surveillance should it influence monetary conditions. This is a meaningful indication of the implications that will be brought about by the single currency and by the new centralized powers of the Central European Bank. With regard to social partners and national collective bargaining the implications might be quite relevant, both in setting homogeneous wage standards in homogeneous sectors of the economy and in keeping inflation under control, in close co-ordination with the guidance which will no longer come from a national central bank.

[46] C. Crouch, 'The Unloved but Inevitable Return of Social Corporatism', in P. Kettunen and J. Valanta (eds.), *Hallinto ja Kansanvalta: Festskrift för Voitto Helander* (1997).

[47] COM(97)676 final. See also COM(98)316 final, at 2, for examples of countries which have adopted the method of consultation with social partners.

[48] A. Calon, L. Frey, A. Lindley, A. Lyon-Caen, A. Markmann, H. Perez Diaz, and S. Simitis, *The Social Aspects of Economic and Monetary Union*, Report prepared for DG V of the EC (1992).

currency, this divide deserves new attention and requires further action on the part of the social partners.[49]

(d) This analysis should be kept very central when writing an agenda of social rights for the new millennium. The argument developed in this chapter is that Europe is slowly and yet unceasingly searching for its own political and cultural identity; this implies the reconsideration of fundamental rights, as for the entitlement, function, and legal enforcement of the rights themselves. The specificity of social rights, within the broader definition of fundamental human rights, requires at times the adoption of different legal parameters and of a different legal language.[50]

If we take the points made in (b) and (c), we are made to face a practical reality, well beyond the black letter of the law. Spaces are opened up for actors—the social partners—which are not mentioned as among Community institutions. They interact with national governments as much as they do with the Commission, the Council, the Parliament, and possibly with the ECJ. Procedures are informal, and yet their transparency and proper functioning become a crucial element within the complex decision-making machinery which then leads to opting for one particular solution or for maintaining the *status quo*. It can be argued that procedures leading to the creation or consolidation of political consensus are a modern—and still mysterious— side of supranational collective labour law.

Because of the mysteries hidden behind this new practice of concertation and sometimes because of the limited impact the social partners may have on very relevant issues, it must be maintained that procedures can only function at their best when they rest on the solid ground of positive norms. Some of them constitute a precondition for the proper functioning of the procedures themselves,[51] others are to be viewed as a point of arrival. Social rights create the natural habitat in which procedures may flourish and be effective; on the other hand, ways of implementing social rights may at times be the content of procedures, thus representing the final result all actors should be jointly aiming at. We can project this last point into the new title on employment in the Amsterdam Treaty, and see whether it will generate similar procedures to those set in motion by economic and monetary policies.

(e) If we accept that consensus-building mechanisms and procedures to establish co-operation with the social partners are so very central for the furthering of politi-

---

[49] T. Padoa Schioppa, *The Genesis of EMU: A Retrospective View*, Jean Monnet Chair Papers 40, Robert Schuman Centre (1996). The argument in this paper is that the 'inconsistent quartet'—as the author describes the combination of fixed exchange rates, free trade, complete capital mobility, and national independence in monetary policies—is what the launching of EMU should consider, transforming inconsistency into the reconciliation of the four elements of the quartet. The argument to be added is whether in such reconciliation a fifth player should be included, making the quintet play the music of employment policies as well. This should be the implied indication when talking of co-ordination between the two relevant titles of the Amsterdam Treaty.

[50] It also forces labour lawyers fully to understand and adopt the distinction suggested in the so-called 'Limburg Principles', a guide for the interpretation of economic and social rights, as stated in the United Nations Covenant on Economic, Social, and Cultural Rights, as far as state obligations are concerned. Obligations of result imply an immediate justiciability, whereas obligations of conduct allow this to happen over time. See Eide, note 11 above, at 39. Interesting implications may be envisaged for the new title on employment in the Amsterdam Treaty.

[51] See below, Recommendation No. 3 arguing in favour of the introduction of the right to organize as a fundamental right in the EU.

cal and economic objectives within the Union, we should then look at other and inter-dependent sides of the same machine.

This procedural apparatus inevitably ties the social partners to the institutions; it almost confuses different actors' languages into a common expression of political intentions. In order to reconcile this quasi-institutional role of the social partners with well established legal traditions in Member States, it must be argued that rights exercised collectively and often built on a constitutional basis at a national level should not be infringed nor diminished. Although national collective bargaining machinery was asked to function in compliance with the Maastricht convergence criteria, adopting wage moderation as a leading criterion and helping to combat inflation, macro-economic policies should not invade the social partners' autonomous sphere of action, or impose on them pre-manufactured solutions.

At this point, it may be interesting to quote a complaint brought by the Federation of Public Services of the General Union of Workers (FSP–UGT) and the State Federation of Teachers (FETE–UGT) against the government of Spain for non-compliance with ILO conventions, in deciding unilaterally not to increase the salaries of public employees for 1997. The Committee on Freedom of Association, while analysing the case, mentions that the decision was taken 'to protect the predominant general interests which require moderation of the public deficit' and that the respect of the economic convergence criteria imposes a 'sacrifice painful but necessary'. The Committee's recommendation indicates to the Spanish government to return to the practice of 'mutual respect' in collective bargaining, stating, however, that no infringement of ILO Conventions had occurred.[52]

(f) One last example can be given from this non-exhaustive list, which should serve to identify some significant 'local' traditions and to strengthen the argument that the Europeanization of social rights is an open process, reactive towards globalization and 'emancipatory' in its own peculiar way.[53]

The debate on market efficiency, on the one hand, and the consolidation of workers' rights, on the other, have relit the flame of workers' participation at company level. Hidden in the dossier on the European Company Statute, this issue was at the centre of a long and passionate confrontation among Member States during the 1970s and onwards. The way the debate has been recently re-opened in the Davignon Report[54] shows that there may be an original way to introduce a social right, while furthering market integration and offering companies the opportunity to acquire a European statute.

Whereas information and consultation rights have already been absorbed into Community legal practice, through the Directive on the European Works Councils (the EWC Directive),[55] participation, even in the mild and flexible proposal put forward in the Davignon Report, still finds strong opponents in its way. The importance of this controversial innovation may be better understood if framed within the

[52] Case No. 1919, 308th Report of the Committee on Freedom of Association, ILO (1997).
[53] B. de Sousa Santos, 'Toward a Multicultural Conception of Human Rights' (1997) 24 *Sociologia del diritto*.
[54] Following the appointment by the Commission of a *Comité des sages* and the publication of the final report of the group of experts, *European Systems of Worker Involvement* (May 1997).
[55] Council Dir. 94/45/EC, [1994] OJ L254/64.

consensus-building scheme previously described. Participation could serve the purpose of establishing good practices of industrial relations at company level, while being part of a wider machinery of bargaining and concertation. The danger, never fully admitted by the proponents of these new rights, is that the way in which they will be exercised at Community level may tend to diminish the role of trade unions. The EWC Directive leaves the option open whether workers' representatives should be elected or appointed, and even attracts some criticism whether the exercise of information rights may, in the long run, pre-empt collective bargaining.[56]

Dilemmas faced by the advocates of new European social rights must also take into account the fear that some solid pillar in national towers of rights may be seriously shaken and even collapse. This is where legal theory can again help us to find the right way. It has been argued that progressive forces which resort to human rights reconstitute 'the language of emancipation' at a time when tensions occur between the State and civil society, as well as between nation States and wider legal orders, be they regional or global systems.[57] The aim should be to adopt the emancipatory potential of human rights theories, apply it to social rights as part of this larger family of rights, and prove that wherever one sees cultural fragmentation there must be attempts to reconstruct social relations around strong legal identities.

In the multicultural scenario of the European Union the Europeanization of social rights may create the basis for new emancipatory politics of rights: emancipation from the external impositions of the global market, emancipation from an approach to market-building which, as history proves, has often been the reflection of national interests, rather than the fulfilment of a common goal.

The European Union and the future stages of its integration constitute a peculiar and original response to globalization; the more we look at this process with the eyes of local legal traditions, the more we are likely to adopt emancipatory policies, for the very reason that they are closer to the needs of people and respectful of their cultures. The agenda of European human rights is now filled with new intentions and with universal aspirations; this allows us to turn to a more technical analysis of expected reforms and of changes occurring in the Amsterdam Treaty.

III. THE IGC AND THE TREATY OF AMSTERDAM

The debate preceding the IGC was fairly rich in relation to social rights and engaged both academic circles and European institutions. Some of the most relevant proposals will be presented in this section, the main purpose being to highlight points of convergence and to indicate further work that needs to be done. Despite the marginal impact of such proposals, some changes are visible in the overall philosophy inspiring the Amsterdam Treaty. If this perception of moderate—and yet progres-

---

[56] K.W. Wedderburn, 'Consultation and Collective Bargaining in Europe: Success or Ideology' (1997) 26 *ILJ* 1–2 and 6.
[57] De Sousa Santos, note 53 above, at 27–8.

sive—change is correct, some conclusions can be drawn for the future of social rights and some further projects can be pursued for the years to come.

In a pamphlet written by four academics and signed by a number of professors and experts in labour and social law from various countries of the European Union[58] a few suggestions were presented to the IGC. The main idea put forward in this proposal is that reformers of the Treaty could not ignore the revision of Article 117 (now Article 136) of the EC Treaty, whose inspiration and purpose appeared more and more to contrast with the evolution of social policies. Harmonization as a magical outcome of market integration could be envisaged in the early days of the Communities when, as previously indicated (section I.A, above), functional objectives were leading the most powerful nation States; that approach was the engine of a social policy which proved ancillary to market needs and never acquired a strong identity of its own.

It was emphasized that, because of the constraints caused by market building, the programmatic function of Article 117 proved of limited strength in favouring legislation,[59] despite the attempts made by the ECJ in leading cases. No mention of social policy was made in the activities of the Community (Article 3 EC), nor, later on in the Maastricht Treaty, among the objectives of the Union (Article B (now Article 2)). It is of some significance, therefore, that the suggestion was made to start the whole reform process by revising Article 117.

According to the authors of the proposal, ten fundamental rights should have been written into it. Some of them may appear provocative in their adopted wording and perhaps inconceivable even in a highly developed supranational legal system, whereby nation States would still be defending their sovereignty in adopting legislation (the right to work, the right to life-long education, the right to equitable remuneration); others may be seen as a completion and enlargement of existing provisions (the right to equality of opportunity and equality of treatment, without distinction of any kind, the right to health and safety in the working environment); yet others may be projected in the future, such as the right to protection for children, young persons, women who have recently given birth, and the elderly, the right to personal privacy.

The incipit of the suggested new Article 117, in particular, may attract criticism from the most disenchanted commentators, for its romantic reminiscence of the 1944 Philadelphia Declaration, which became part of the ILO Constitution. 'Labour is not a commodity', as has recently been proved in well-documented and enlightening scholarly work,[60] is much more than a principle or an aim set out in an international source. It has been powerful enough to inspire other sources and to favour the inclusion in them of the right to fair remuneration for workers, 'such as

---

[58] R. Blanpain, B. Hepple, S. Sciarra, and M. Weiss, *Fundamental Social Rights: Proposals for the European Union* (1996).

[59] S. Simitis and A. Lyon-Caen, 'Community Labour Law: A Critical Introduction to its History', in Davies, Lyon-Caen, Sciarra, and Simitis, note 29 above, at 4. References to relevant ECJ cases can be found in Poiares' contribution to this vol.

[60] P. O'Higgins, ' "Labour is not a Commodity"—An Irish Contribution to International Labour Law' (1997) 26 *ILJ* 225–34.

will give them and their families a decent standard of living', as in Article 4 of the 1961 European Social Charter, echoed later by the Community Charter.

The words 'rights' and 'principles' are used interchangeably in this document; the same semantic device is adopted in a later report, which will be examined shortly. Both documents, albeit with different forms of expression, draw a distinction between fundamental rights and other objectives of social policies or 'instrumental' rights, thus distinguishing between different levels and different stages of implementation.[61] This aspect of the overall proposal is a very delicate one[62] and could lead to the maintenance of the *status quo*, if no precise division of responsibilities was set between the States and the Community .

It is also indicated that the 1961 Social Charter of the Council of Europe is referred to in Article F(2) (now Article 6) TEU, together with the 1989 Community Charter of Fundamental Social Rights for Workers, following the already existing reference to the 1950 ECHR. As for expanding the competence of the Court of Justice, amending Article 46 (*ex* Article L) of the TEU, the proposal is intentionally weak. The proponents' self-restraint runs parallel to the consideration that the heat of very delicate institutional mechanisms could only be felt by political reformers, who could properly balance the expansion of judicial powers in this as well as in other fields of law.

The suggested new version of Article 136 (*ex* Article 117) is drawn upon common constitutional traditions of the Member States and existing international labour standards. This safety-net, built on the convergence of existing sources, is wider than Community law and is meant to be the reference point for the ECJ, whose responsibility will also be to indicate which fundamental rights are capable of having direct effect. In order to prove the dynamic nature of the same rights, a new method of implementation is envisaged in assigning to a committee of experts the power regularly to review the compliance of national laws with the obligations arising from Article 117.

Finally, while suggesting the incorporation of the Maastricht Social Agreement into the Treaty, the authors did not go into the details of how the Treaty should be consolidated, since the purpose of this concise publication was to air the problems and to promote discussion. They did, however, indicate the cumbersome presence of Article 2(6) (excluding Community competence for the right of association, the right to strike and lock out, pay) in the Social Agreement, and the need to abrogate this provision, while writing fundamental social rights in the Treaty.

In the second Social Action Programme, adopted in April 1995, the Commission decided to set up a *Comité des Sages*, with the particular aim of looking at the future of the Community Charter of Fundamental Social Rights of Workers, in the light of impending reforms of the Treaties. The *Comité*, chaired by Maria de Lourdes Pintasilgo and composed of leading figures from different countries, decided to extend the scope of its remit and to open up to the consideration of broader social-policy issues. The result was a very articulated and intense report,[63] which took into account

---

[61] This point is stressed in particular by M. Weiss, *Fundamental Social Rights for the European Union* (1996), at 14–15.

[62] As correctly pointed out by B. de Witte, 'Protection of Fundamental Social Rights in the European Union: The Choice of the Appropriate Legal Instrument', in Betten and MacDevitt, note 32 above, at 71.

[63] Comité des Sages, *For a Europe of Civic and Social Rights*, European Commission, Directorate General for Employment, Industrial Relations, and Social Affairs (1996). While this paper was still at the

a large range of topics and even indicated different stages for the implementation of social rights.

A point of similarity with the pamphlet examined before can once again be underlined, inasmuch as both documents are aware of the fact that for some social rights there is an urgent need to become visible in the treaties, whereas for others active intervention by individual Member States is necessary. Institutional reforms, such as those required to amend the treaties (expand qualified majority voting, insert a new chapter on employment, ban discrimination based on all grounds, and so on), should not be kept separate from other legislative reforms, which involve costs in order to provide benefits and services (training and education, health care, work and fair conditions of work and pay, minimum income, and pensions). The latter are, however, different kinds of reforms, based on the assumption of fundamental rights and dependent on them, but projected in the sphere of national legislative initiatives. A list of eight rights is indicated which should have 'full and immediate effect': together with equality of treatment, equality between men and women, ban on discrimination, freedom of movement, and the right to choose one's occupation, some collective rights—so described in the most common labour law terminology—make an appearance, namely the right to organize and the right to collective bargaining and action. The 'objectives', different from rights in terms of enforceability, are described as long-term projects which should be deferred to the second stage, like the definition of minimum standards and contents.[64]

The point of contact, in terms of feasibility of both plans, albeit in different stages, lies in the urgency and coherence of political choices which need to be made both at a supranational and at a national level. One of the original points of the report is the suggestion that, after the first stage, culminating in the work of the IGC preceding the Amsterdam summit, such choices should be the result of a widespread consultation across Europe, favouring the identification and the rise of new social rights from the bottom of civil society to the top of the institutions. This is an insightful suggestion, which may be linked to the idea that there should be regular opportunities to review European sources, making the IGC a safe point of arrival for an open process, during which other mechanisms for adjusting and improving the Treaty could be envisaged.[65]

While emphasizing the need to open up a broad and enriching process of amplification for social rights, the *sages* are aware of the judicial implications, in terms of the existing legal basis, with regard to the ECJ's competence. The report suggests, on the one hand, expanding the scope of Article 6 (*ex* Article F), including references to the Community Charter of Fundamental Social Rights of Workers and to other international agreements signed by the Member States; and on the other hand to free Article 6 (*ex* Article F) from the restrictions of Article 46 (*ex* Article L) which explicitly indicates the areas on which ECJ's competence is to be exercised and which does not include Article F.

proof stage the new expert group, chaired by S. Simitis, and entrusted by the Commission to follow up the debate started by the Pintasilgo Committee, published its Report: 'Affirming fundamental rights in the European Union—time to act', European Commission Unit V/D.2, Feb. 1999.

[64] Following the 'Limburg Principles', note 50 above, the 'objectives' indicated by the *sages* should form the content of an obligation of conduct on the part of the States.

[65] J.H.H. Weiler, 'Editorial: Amsterdam, Amsterdam' (1997) 3 *ELJ* 310.

Through these proposals, the report puts forward a very lively vision of social Europe, not only based on new rights and principles to be enforced, but also supported by real people, whose voices should be heard and taken into account. There are signs of innovation in this report which go beyond the rituals of exercising political pressure on law-makers. Since some of the proposals have now become part of Community law, there is a hope that a red thread has been thrown and will continue to be followed in pursuing social goals.

As well as the two proposals examined so far, a third one must be mentioned,[66] which occupies 'a particular place in this discussion', in between academics and institutions.[67] The manifesto, written by academics under the auspices of the European Trade Union Institute, expresses both the authors' concern for the separation of social from economic integration and their commitment to bringing about new approaches. Rather than engaging in detailed technical suggestions addressed to the IGC, they chose to offer a careful explanation of the changes that have occurred to work in the whole of Europe. The result is a collection of essays, attractive for a militant and well-documented style and for melding together different national and professional experiences.

The manifesto is built around the idea of incorporating the 1989 Social Charter into the Treaty, despite the fact that it originated as a contested political declaration—not signed by the UK—and was afterwards successfully referred to as a programme for social policies, rather than as a declaration of fundamental rights. The authors argue that the nature of social and economic rights has changed during the 1970s and 1980s in revised constitutions of the Member States, becoming essentially programmatic. In the light of this assumption, a series of alternatives is presented, as to whether the Charter should be 'Commission-oriented' or 'European Court' oriented, finishing with the indication that in both cases it would have to be deeply transformed in order to be addressed to 'non-standard' workers, not included within its present scope.[68]

Particularly in view of these changes, the technicalities of the incorporation remain unclear; the real aim of the authors is to prove the Charter's lasting validity as far as the fundamental principles enshrined within it are concerned. Even less clear—and perhaps slightly contradictory[69]—is the combination of this strategy with the incorporation of the Maastricht Social Agreement; the latter, it is said, should work as an implementation mechanism, whereas the programmatic fundamental rights would be provided for in the Charter.

One other publication must be mentioned, in connection with that specifically addressed to the IGC. In a book reporting the proceedings of a colloquium held in Amsterdam, several points of view are taken into account and an attempt is made to summarize the debate, while formulating a proposal, which does not come from all the authors in the book, but from the first of the two editors only.[70] According to Betten there should be a Bill of Rights in the TEU, enforceable throughout the

---

[66] B. Bercusson, S. Deakin, P. Koistinen, Y. Kravaritou, U. Muckenberger, A. Supiot, and B. Veneziani, *A Manifesto for Social Europe* (1996).

[67] This is the comment by A. Lo Faro, 'The Social Manifesto: Demystifying the Spectre Haunting Europe' (1997) 3 *ELJ* 300.

[68] Bercusson *et al.*, note 66 above, at 149–51.   [69] As implied by Lo Faro, note 67 above, at 303.

[70] Betten and MacDevitt, note 32 above.

Union by way of amendment to Article 46 (*ex* Article L); the 1961 European Social Charter should be mentioned in Article 6 (*ex* Article F). As one can see, even though the proposals came from different circles and groups of experts, not working together at the same time, a few points of convergence were the result of this intense and diversified research.

Some of the issues discussed so far were echoed during the IGC and even amplified, leading to reforms of the Treaty, which will certainly bring about further changes and will long be debated.

A reflection group chaired by Carlos Westendorp, at the time Spanish State Secretary for European Affairs, presented a report[71] at the Madrid Summit, in December 1995; the group was highly representative of national governments and European institutions and proved to be an open forum for discussion.[72] In this document the idea was put forward of rewriting Article 103 of the Maastricht Treaty and including employment among the objectives of the Union, as one of the economic choices to be shared by Member States.

The Swedish representative's proposal was more precise, suggesting that a new title on employment should be inserted into the Treaty and that social partners should be involved in its implementation, both at a Community and at a decentralised level. The Finnish position was even more straightforward, and indicated that the Union should have the obligation horizontally to examine employment policies and enact a European strategy, including in the Treaty specific provisions on monitoring the existing situation.[73]

At the European Council held in Turin in March 1996 the French '*Memorandum pour un Modèle Social Européen*'[74] was put forward and specified even more strongly the need to make employment the main priority for the European Union and use it as a 'criterion' of all European initiatives.

Furthermore, it is reported that the *Renault-Vilvoorde* case[75] had a tremendous political impact on the discussion and facilitated decision-making so that in the last two weeks the Growth and Stability Pact was completed by the employment side. A determined opposition was maintained to formally linking the new employment chapter with EMU;[76] this serious limitation to the reform of the Treaty must be taken as a starting point for current policies and for future revisions.

[71] General Secretariat of the Council of the European Union, *1996 Intergovernmental Conference: Reflection Group Report and Other References for Documentary Purposes* (1995).

[72] M. Petite, 'Le traité d'Amsterdam: ambition et réalisme' (1997) 3 *RMUE* 19–20, and 23.

[73] The Swedish position was expressed in a note of July 1995 on the fundamental interests of Sweden with a view to the 1996 Intergovernmental Conference, expressed in a Cabinet Office note. See also the report of the Finnish Government, 27 Feb. 1996 on Finland's objectives for the IGC. The overall role played by Nordic countries in the IGC seems to have led to a very positive contribution, coming from States with a longstanding tradition of efficient welfare states. The British position is taken into account by C. Barnard in 'The United Kingdom, the "Social Chapter" and the Amsterdam Treaty' (1997) 26 *ILJ* 275.

[74] See also the Commission's position on this matter in its opinion 'Reinforcing Political Union and Preparing for Enlargement', COM(96)90 final; and the European Parliament in its Resolution A4–0068/96 of 13 Mar. 1996 [1996] OJ C96/77.

[75] Whereby rights to information were infringed by the management of the Belgian company, and massive 'lay-offs' were announced: see M.-A. Moreau, 'A propos de "l'affaire Renault" ', (1997) 5 *Droit Social* 493–509.

[76] Observatoire social européen, *Analytical Review of the Treaty of Amsterdam*, Working Paper (Sept. 1997).

A. Innovations in the Treaty of Amsterdam

It is reasonable to believe that the widespread circulation of ideas, like that summarized above, had an impact on the IGC; this more policy-oriented discussion had indeed been preceded by solid academic research in all Member States, mainly oriented to prove the need for substantial changes in the Treaty and the limits suffered by social policies because of the still over-dominant unanimity principle.[77]

It is with this open-minded approach that we shall look at the main innovations in the Amsterdam Treaty; criticism of it for what has not yet been achieved must be placed within an ongoing discussion, which sees academic research oriented towards an expansion of social rights.

(a) The Treaty establishing the European Community and the Treaty on European Union have been consolidated and Articles have been renumbered (references will be made to this version).[78]

(b) Article 6 TEU (*ex* Article F) refers to the ECHR only. The choice made at Amsterdam confirms the previous position of the Community and of the Union with respect to the Convention: the Union is not subject to it, unlike all the Member States, but the Court of Justice has the power to review respect for fundamental rights by the Community institutions. The ECJ's judgment,[79] dealing with the accession by the Community to the ECHR, had a freezing effect on a long-lasting debate. The acknowledgement, on the part of the Court, of the 'constitutional significance' that the Community's entry into a distinct international system would have had, was not taken by the IGC as an invitation to amend the Treaty; the result is that, in the words of the judgment, the Community has no competence to accede to the ECHR.

This implies that some questions are left open. Would it still be desirable to establish better links between the Luxembourg and the Strasbourg Courts? Should the ECJ take into account the ECHR's principles in a dynamic perspective and consider the case law of the Court in Strasbourg as equally relevant? Would this be the only way to verify that the principles of the ECHR are truly incorporated into domestic legal systems? What should it do in cases of non-incorporation of the ECHR by Member States?[80]

[77] References cannot be exhaustive: W. Däubler (ed.), *Market and Social Justice in the EC—the Other Side of the Internal Market* (1991); K.W. Wedderburn, 'European Community Law and Workers Rights after 1992: Fact or Fake?', in Lord Wedderburn, *Labour Law and Freedom: Further Essays in Labour Law* (1995); A. Lyon-Caen and S. Simitis, 'l'Europe sociale à la recherche de ses références' (1993) 4 *RMUE* 109–22; M. Rodriguez-Piñero and E. Casas, 'In support of a European Social Constitution', in Davies *et al.*, note 29 above; Weiss, note 59 above; and A. Ojeda Aviles, *La calidad social europea desde la perspectiva de los derechos fundamentales* (1998).

[78] Research had been carried on in this direction, in order to enhance the readability of European primary law and the transparency of the Community legal system . See 'A Unified and Simplified Model of the European Communities Treaties and the Treaty on European Union in Just One Treaty' 1996, a report prepared under the auspices of the Robert Schuman Centre at the EUI and submitted to the European Parliament in Sept. 1996.

[79] *Opinion 2/94* [1996] ECR I–1759.

[80] For the Irish abortion case and for a thorough analysis of the open questions see G. De Búrca, 'Fundamental Human Rights and the Reach of EC Law' (1993) 13 *OJLS* 283–319. For the British debate on incorporation see T. Bingham, 'The European Convention on Human Rights: Time to Incorporate' (1993) 109 *LQR* 390–400. In general see B. Dickson, *Human Rights and the European Convention: The Effect of the Convention on the United Kingdom and Ireland* (1997).

(c) Following a suggestion of the Reflection Group, in view of the accession of new States with weaker democratic traditions (see the amendment to Article O (now Article 49), setting the conditions for applicant countries), Article 7 imposes penalties on Member States failing to respect fundamental rights. These measures, to be considered exceptional, even though the possibility of expelling a Member State is not envisaged, are—not surprisingly—kept within the competence of the Council.[81] It could be argued that a similar measure should be applied for the violation of the social rights enshrined in the Treaty, as well as of those protected by the ECHR and by the constitutional traditions of Member States.[82] It seems unlikely that the Council will interpret this norm extensively; therefore the issue should be raised in relation to the new agenda and to the new sanctions to be considered for the protection of social rights.

(d) Article 46 (*ex* Article L) in its new letter (d) includes Article 6.2 among the new areas of law within the competence of the Court. This amendment is little more than an optical illusion, if we consider that the respect for fundamental rights 'as general principles of Community law' will not much change the current situation. The Court now has such rights within the written sources to which it can refer; as general principles they can only inspire the Court's decisions, not bind it to precise enforcement mechanisms. This does not lead to an incorporation of the 'rights', but to a stronger relevance of the 'principles', albeit with two limits: the Court can only review the acts of the institutions and must remain within the bounds of its jurisdiction.

The voice of the *sages* has been—at least partially—listened to on this matter, although other Articles of the Treaty, which now introduce the reference to the 1961 ESC, will not be susceptible to judicial review. The indirect relevance of external international sources puts the Court in the position to choose how and when to take them into consideration, incorporating the principles in its judgments, without being bound by the source itself. This point will be considered again in the recommendations[83] as one of the most controversial items to be inserted into a new agenda for social rights.

(e) Article 13 (*ex* Article J.3) TEC introduces a new non-discrimination clause. It includes a very broad ban on discrimination based on the grounds of sex, racial or ethnic origin, religion or belief, disability, age, and sexual orientation. It does not have direct effect; furthermore secondary legislation based on it still requires unanimity. This choice reflects the ambiguities of the IGC as far as freeing new areas of social rights from the 'unanimity trap' is concerned.[84] In view of further steps to be taken, it is now the responsibility of the Member States to put flesh and bones on this innovative measure. Another weakness of this norm has to do with the merely consultative role of the Parliament, sought by national delegations for fear of being caught in co-decision mechanisms.[85]

(f) As expected after the change of government in the UK, the Maastricht Social Agreement has been incorporated into the Treaty, in Title XI, which also includes

---

[81] Petite, note 72 above, at 25–6.   [82] See below, Recommendation No. 1.   [83] *Ibid.*
[84] F. Scharpf, 'The Joint-Decision Trap: Lessons from German Federalism and European Integration' (1988) 66 *Public Administration* 239–78.
[85] Petite, note 72 above, at 26.

Articles on social policy. Some of these have been deleted, either because they are superfluous (as in the case of Article 118a on health and safety) or because they are replaced by a corresponding Article (Article 138, which also includes the former Article 118b on the so-called social dialogue). This new order in the relevant sources should also favour a more dynamic approach as regards the choice of the legal basis, although unanimity is still required for key subjects, such as legislation in the case of termination of an employment contract, representation, and collective defence of workers, including co-determination.[86]

Social exclusion makes its appearance among the subjects to be decided with a qualified majority, albeit not in the original wording, which included the elderly and the handicapped. This is a field of remarkable potential for development in social policies, considered very urgent, and to which a special heading of the financial perspective is addressed.

(g) Some incoherence can still be revealed: the last paragraph of Article 136 (*ex* Article 117) still mentions the harmonization of social systems as an outcome of the functioning of the common market; the first paragraph of the same Article proclaims that harmonization and improvement must be maintained while pursuing the objectives of promoting employment, living and working conditions, whereas Article 137(2) (*ex* Article 118) still mentions minimum requirements for gradual implementation. The impression is that two souls are kept alive inside one body; this can be intriguing at times, although it should not be too difficult to offer a systematic interpretation of the whole new Title.

Article 136 recalls the 1961 Social Charter and the 1989 Community Charter (see (b) above). This is an innovation of symbolic value which cannot be under-evaluated. It must be noted, however, that in the attempt to re-establish an equilibrium between all Council of Europe sources the choice of the *sedes materiae* seems to prove that even symbols are made to have a different impact: whereas the ECHR is mentioned in Title I on Common Provisions, the Social Charter is placed in the niche of social provisions. Furthermore, the exclusion of Community competence on the right of association, the right to strike and pay, confirmed in Article 137(6), is in sharp contrast to some of the fundamental social rights proclaimed by the Social Charter.[87] Again, we have to rely on the indirect relevance of international sources, which, particularly in the case of the right to organize and the right to strike, must be read in conjunction with the constitutional traditions of the Member States, which, even if not mentioned in the opening of Title XI, are always on the horizon of the ECJ.

(h) The new Title VIII on employment follows the Title on economic and monetary policy and introduces new procedures according to which Member States and

---

[86] A proposal to make qualified majority voting the rule when deciding on all Union policies was presented to the IGC by the Commission. On the contrary, the UK maintained strong opposition to the expansion throughout the IGC. See respectively Commission Opinion, note 72 above, and Foreign and Commonwealth Office, *A Partnership of Nations: The British Approach to the European Union Intergovernmental Conference 1996*. See also the Labour Party's *Business Manifesto* (1997) expressing unwillingness to change unanimity voting on key matters such as social security and co-determination.

[87] Similarly B. Ryan, 'Pay, Trade Union Rights and European Community Law' [1997] *Int. Jour. of Comp. Lab. Law and Ind. Rel.* 305.

the Community 'shall work' together for the co-ordination of new strategies, within the general objectives set in Article 2. A 'high level of employment' is now one of the objectives of the Union. Relevant in itself and also in view of future involvement of the social partners, as happened for economic and monetary policies (see above, Section II (b) and (c)), this Title is already being implemented, before the ratification of the Treaty. A special Employment Committee, with advisory status, has been created (Article130 (*ex* Article 109s)) to promote co-ordination between Member States and is indeed already operating, ideally in strict co-operation with the Economic Policy Committee. This is only an informal thread, which should bind together two key bodies, potentially very important in view of achieving formal co-ordination in the two policy fields. The Committee should also monitor employment initiatives in Member States, while consulting with the social partners. We are clearly facing a situation in which multi-level policy-making is conceived by a variety of institutional and quasi-institutional actors. This open-ended procedure, under which it is difficult to conceive of a 'right to work' in traditional terms, does not specify sanctions against Member States, or specific enforcement mechanisms for individual rights.

Activism on the part of the Commission is expressed through soft-law measures which have preceded the employment chapter[88] and which are now part of its implementation.[89]

IV. CONCLUSION: FURTHER PROPOSALS TO EXPAND SOCIAL RIGHTS IN THE HUMAN RIGHTS AGENDA FOR THE YEAR 2000

In the course of this chapter an empirical debate has been confronted with a more theoretical approach. The latter can be summarized as follows.

(1) The strategy of incorporating broad international legal principles into the European legal order is still a current one, as it results from some of the innovations in the Amsterdam Treaty. Especially when related to social rights, this strategy brings about the idea of adaptation of international sources to distinctly European legal traditions.[90] It also proves that Member States belonging to a wider international legal order have potential advantages in having recourse to sources other than Community sources. From Strasbourg to Luxembourg, passing through Geneva, the road is paved with good intentions, but travelling across these places may still not be an easy task for the individual citizen, whose rights are infringed or threatened.

---

[88] COM(95)273 final.   [89] COM(97)676 final.

[90] It would suffice to quote Art. 23 of the Universal Declaration (right to work, to free choice of employment, to just and favourable conditions of work, and to protection against unemployment, right to equal pay for equal work, right to just and favourable remuneration) in order to have a sufficiently broad basis of rights from which the European legislature should draw inspiration. The concept of adaptation of international sources is used in this chap. as equivalent to that of convergence: both concepts imply that initiatives should not be taken at the European level without consideration of the implications of wider international sources.

(2) The 'emancipatory' function of human rights, as opposed to their mere dependency on market mechanisms, helps legal scholarship to rediscover the centrality of social rights and to look ahead for new measures to strengthen their enforcement. In particular, the European Union represents a test of how to create internal coherence among principles and objectives, thus offering an answer to the dispersion of legal values and the weakening of rights within the global legal order.

Emancipatory theories should modify the definition of rights at the place of work, as well as the expansion of minimum standards world-wide.

In interpreting Community sources and in tracing new policies, the challenge is to reconcile the old and the new. Community sources are included in the wider circle of international sources and form a smaller circle, delimited by its own circumference.[91] In the process of European integration the adoption of new social rights is very slow and may not coincide with the emergence of new rights which expand the circumference of the wider circle.

It can be argued that an emancipatory theory of social rights in the European Union rests on all the rights referred to in the Treaty and on those indirectly included in it through the free and discretionary interpretation of the Court of Justice. The fact that the latter must also take into account the 'constitutional traditions common to the Member States' as a further and necessary criterion in its decisions forces the 'emancipatory' theory to go a step further and to insist on the peculiarities of the European debate. The most suitable suggestion for the years to come is that the concentric circles be kept as they are, the smaller included in the wider one and yet autonomous with regard to the implementation of social rights and for reviewing acts of the Community in breach of international standards. The area common to the two circles could become an even more homogeneous ground for the ECJ, if other reviewing mechanisms were introduced into the scene. These new bodies should have the function of filling in the ground with converging and coherent standards, through interpreting all relevant legal sources and closely following their implementation in Member States.

Out of the metaphor of the circles, we can obtain indications that we should strengthen those sources within the smaller circle, by way of inserting into the Treaty some fundamental social rights and by ensuring appropriate means of enforcement, especially through new monitoring mechanisms.

The remarkably rich and varied range of proposals circulated before the IGC and the innovations in the Amsterdam Treaty continues to leave several questions unanswered. Only a few points will be selected as urgent items to be inserted into the agenda for the year 2000, in the understanding that institutional reforms have wider priorities than those indicated in this chapter.

---

[91] The metaphor of concentric circles has been used by Lenaerts and re-interpreted here. See K. Lenaerts, 'Fundamental Rights to be Included in a Community Catalogue' (1991) 16 *EL Rev.* 367.

V. RECOMMENDATIONS

1. In the Amsterdam Treaty references are made to the ECHR and the ESC. This indirect inclusion of international sources in the Treaty—which could also be described as a tendency to convergence—leaves untouched the competence of the Strasbourg Court on the ECHR and the monitoring of the ESC by the Committee of Independent Experts, while expanding the standards to which the ECJ may refer. There is no indication in the Treaty that the concrete implementation of human rights should inspire the ECJ, still less bind it. The ECJ's judgment on accession by the Community to the ECHR reflects a careful internal balance between institutional powers and frees the ECJ from obedience to the rulings of institutions external to it.

Furthermore, the limited consideration shown by the IGC for amending Article L (now Article 46) TEU, with regard to the expansion of the ECJ's competence, is a strong political indication, inspired perhaps by realism. It is also in accord with the choice of the EU not to accede to the ECHR. The fear has prevailed that two legal orders governing fundamental rights, running parallel for quite some time, could suddenly collide and clash.

Rather than insisting on the politically impractical solution aimed at expanding the ECJ's competence, efforts should be concentrated on the creation of new bodies, similar to the European Social Charter's Committee of Independent Experts.[92] It has been emphasized correctly that when referring to a source external to the EU, its entire range should be retained, particularly with regard to its concrete translation into the living law of the States bound by it.[93] The suggestion is not to duplicate procedures, but to make them converge towards institutional co-operation. In concrete terms, the new body should have both monitoring powers and powers to refer to the Commission when infringements of social rights are discovered. It should be built into the Community legal order and include representatives from other international organizations, such as the Council of Europe and the ILO, thus enhancing convergence of international standards.

If an analogy with Article 7 (*ex* Article 4) of the Amsterdam Treaty were to be drawn, one could envisage that this monitoring mechanism might also bring, in exceptional cases, to the indication of sanctions to be applied to Member States failure to respect fundamental social rights.

2. References in the Amsterdam Treaty to the 1989 Social Charter cannot be compared to those made to Council of Europe sources. Notwithstanding the symbolic value attached to this innovation, we should not confuse the legal nature of these different sources. The Community Charter remains a programmatic and political document which has given flesh and bones to Community social policies; it will need to be revised also in the light of the achievements made so far in adopting legislation in various fields and in view of new emerging needs, especially related to active

---

[92] See the proposal by Blanplain *et al.*, note 58 above, and the further indications of the report by the *sages*, note 63 above.
[93] Harris, note 32 above.

employment policies. A careful reading of the Charter confirms the validity of the two levels of analysis previously suggested in the search for new and more efficient means of implementation of social rights. What the *sages* describe as different stages in what should be a new and beneficial reform of the Treaty are indeed different levels of legal analysis, and they force us to reconsider the distribution of powers among the Union and the Member States.

The Protocol on the application of the principle of subsidiarity and proportionality, annexed to the Amsterdam Treaty, should be interpreted in innovative terms when it comes to considering social rights. Article 5 indicates that Community action is justified when the objectives in question cannot be sufficiently achieved by Member States' action. This difficult balancing exercise is facilitated by some guidelines, which would need to be read in the light of a broad programme of action, a new social rights agenda for the Commission, with the indication of political priorities.

In particular, following Article 5 of the Protocol, in order to justify Community action, the transnational relevance of the issue should be recalled, as well as the possible conflict with the requirements of the Treaty, due to lack of Community action, such as to correct distortion in competition or to strengthen economic and social cohesion.

Employment is again the area to investigate for an innovative definition of the borderline between the powers of the Community and those of the Member States, in the light of Article 5 of the EC Treaty (*ex* Article 3b EC), which must be viewed as the most solid constitutional ground for subsidiarity. In this field a regime of shared competences, such as that which is taking shape in this early stage of enforcement of the new Title VIII, opens up space for yet another form of co-ordination of policies. It should be maintained, though, that an incumbent and unavoidable priority must be given to Community action, and such a power must be accompanied by precise monitoring mechanisms on national employment plans.

3. The peculiar nature of certain social rights (collective rights, procedural rights), confirms that the mere abstention of the nation States—or of the EC as such—could not suffice to guarantee its true enforceability. The right to organize and, more recently, the right to information and consultation are examples of individual rights to be exercised collectively, which, because of this peculiarity, can be enforced only through legislation at the national level. Emancipation consists in providing deep Community roots for social rights and, at the same time, assigning competencies to national and supranational legislatures.

It must be pointed out that what for some commentators appears to be the most daring reform of the Treaty and for others the most unnecessary, namely the insertion of the right to organize into the EU fundamental social rights, is indeed the most urgent and important one.

Two reasons support this recommendation:

- this right would acquire a new function in an evolving supranational legal order, in which private associations are asked to participate and be active and to fulfil quasi-institutional roles;

- this fundamental right, as suggested earlier,[94] does not receive sufficient support from the mere convergence of other international sources. Its specificity within the European legal debate can certainly be drawn from constitutional traditions in the Member States, but an even more specific function is emerging at Community level, where the right to organize appears as a precondition for exercising other collective rights (the right to bargain, the right to be informed and consulted) which at the moment lack full institutional legitimization. In again adopting the distinction between freedoms and powers, suggested earlier,[95] the fundamental right to organize would fall into the second category and require specific supportive legislation at Community level.

A renewed and stronger legitimacy of supranational associations, whose representativity should be ascertained following the criteria established in soft law, would also entitle them to new rights, such as introducing collective complaints when social rights are infringed by Member States, as well as when insufficient action is taken to permit the correct exercise of the rights themselves. It would be advisable for such complaints to be filed with the Commission, whose monitoring exercise on the state of enforcement of social rights should become even more critical and timely.

The Council of Europe Social Charter will undergo changes in the years to come, to which attention should be paid. In particular, the new procedure on collective complaints could prove a useful analogy and an occasion for bringing closer international standards and making them converge towards more cohesive measures of human rights protection.

[94] See the criticism of Art. 11 ECHR, which emerges from the case law of the Strasbourg Court. See Part I, Sect. C, above.

[95] See Sect. I, above, and Bobbio, note 2 above.

E

Additional Challenges for the Future

15

Human Rights and European Identity: The Debate about European Citizenship

ULF BERNITZ AND HEDVIG LOKRANTZ BERNITZ

I. INTRODUCTION AND PRESENTATION OF THE PROBLEMS

Citizenship in the traditional, national sense is a relationship of complete membership to a State, to which certain rights and duties have been attached. However, the nature and content of these civil rights have never been clear and have varied across time and place. For instance, expulsion and deprivation of citizenship are practices which have frequently been used. Rights vary among different legal systems. However, certain central civil rights connected to citizenship are found in most countries, such as specific political rights and the right to free movement.

Citizenship of the Union was introduced into the EU in the Treaty on European Union which was signed in Maastricht in 1992 and is principally regulated in Articles 17–22 (*ex* Article 8–8e) EC.[1] It appears to be a new type of citizenship, a *sui generis* creation. The Citizens of the Union are the nationals of the Member States, but they have rights only in the Member States and in the EC. Citizenship of the Union is apparently intended to provide an important step in the process of creating an ever closer union among the peoples of Europe. It constitutes a part of the endeavour to create a 'People's Europe'. The purpose is to bring the EU closer to the citizens in the Member States and to give the EU a new political and social dimension.[2] Moreover, it aims at giving the individual increased protection and strengthening individual rights both in the Community and in the Member States. However, the relationship between the protection of human rights within the EU context and the

---

[1] For some of the early and thoughtful analyses, see J. d'Oliveira, 'European Citizenship: Its Meaning, Its Potential', in R. Dehousse (ed.), *Europe After Maastricht: An Ever Closer Union?* (1994); C. Closa, 'The Concept of Citizenship in the Treaty on European Union' (1992) 29 *CML Rev.* 1137; E. Marias (ed.), *European Citizenship* (1994); S. O'Leary, *The Evolving Concept of Community Citizenship* (1996); D. O'Keeffe, 'Union Citizenship', in D. O'Keeffe and P. Twomey (eds.), *Legal Issues of the Maastricht Treaty* (1994).

[2] For a small selection of the broader political and philosophical explorations of European citizenship, see J. Habermas, 'Citizenship and National Identity: Some Reflections on the Future of Europe' [1992] *Praxis International* 1, and 'The European Nation State, Its Achievements and Its Limitations. On the Past and Future of Sovereignty and Citizenship' (1996) 9 *Ratio Juris* 125; J. Shaw, 'Citizenship of the Union: Towards Post-National Membership' (1995) 6 *AEL* 237; Y. Soysal, *Limits of Citizenship, Migrants and Postnational Membership in Europe* (1994); J.H.H. Weiler 'Does Europe Need a Constitution? Reflections on Demos, Telos, and the German Maastricht Decision' (1995) 1 *ELJ* 219.

newly constitutionalized status of EU citizenship remains unclear and problematic.[3] This chapter does not seek to explore that relationship in detail, but focuses primarily on one particular aspect of Union citizenship which raises human rights concerns: the dependence of EU citizenship upon possession of the nationality of a Member State and the consequent discrimination against third-country nationals.

The EU has no competence to decide who is a citizen of the Union. According to the main provision in Article 17 (*ex* Article 8) EC, every person holding the nationality of a Member State is also a citizen of the Union.

Citizenship of the Union to a large extent calls into question the issue of the sovereignty of the Member States. Indeed confrontations between the interests of the Member States and the EU are unavoidable. The conflicts are caused primarily by the differences of the laws on citizenship of the Member States, and it is against this background that the citizenship of the Union must be analysed and identified.

It is possible that the term 'European citizenship' can be used as a collective term to describe the laws on citizenship of the Member States. However, such a term has no clear content in itself. Citizenship in national terms varies considerably amongst the EC countries, above all concerning acquisition of citizenship and the legal consequences. In certain Member States it is quite easy to become a citizen; in others it is harder. Many individuals are affected by the obvious inequities and differences which arise due to the splintered laws on citizenship.

Consequently, no uniform rules on citizenship exist in the EU countries, nor do common rules on how a citizen of the Union may obtain citizenship of a Member State other than his country of origin. Differences between the laws on citizenship in the various Member States are reflected directly in the citizenship of the Union.

Thus, some of the problems concerning citizenship of the Union are connected to national citizenship in the EU countries and the great differences which exist between the national concepts on citizenship. Differences between the concepts of citizenship in the EU, which have arisen due to various political and legal traditions, can clearly be distinguished. For instance, in the Nordic countries, citizenship is founded on the principle of *jus sanguinis* (based on descent from a national). It is however relatively easy for an immigrant to acquire citizenship. The German concept of citizenship is also founded on a rather remote principle of *jus sanguinis*, but in contrast to the Nordic countries, it is much harder for immigrants to acquire German citizenship. German citizenship is founded on ethnical considerations and the 'people' is a concept which in history has been of a considerable importance for the law on citizenship.[4] Ethnical solidarity was of great significance during the unification of Germany in 1990, when all the citizens of the GDR were included in the Community without any changes to the Rome Treaty or formal decisions by the EC. According to a German declaration certain persons who have no personal or territorial connection with Germany are German citizens from the point of view of Community law.

[3] See S. O'Leary, 'The Relationship between Community Citizenship and the Protection of Fundamental Rights in Community Law' (1995) 32 *CML Rev.* 519; and also A. Rosas, 'Electoral Rights and the European Union: A Broader Human Rights Perspective' in N. Neuwahl and A. Rosas (eds.), *The European Union and Human Rights* (1995), 165.

[4] See D. Cesarani and M. Fulbrook, *Citizenship, Nationality and Migration in Europe* (1996).

British citizenship constitutes a mixture of *jus soli*, according to which place of birth is conclusive, and *jus sanguinis*. However any concept of citizenship and nationality stands out as quite vague. For example, different levels of citizenship apply to British subjects outside Great Britain. According to the British Nationality Act 1983, only British Citizens, certain British subjects without citizenship but with right to residence in Great Britain and who are exempted from immigration controls, and citizens of the British Dependent Territories with a connection to Gibraltar are British citizens in relation to Community law. Those with another type of citizenship are regarded as citizens of third countries and therefore cannot, for example, enjoy the Community right to reside in another EU country. In Italy, the principle of *jus sanguinis* is applicable. The principle of *jus soli* is used in exceptional cases where the child's parents are either unknown or stateless. Children born in Greece, who are without a foreign citizenship or of unknown nationality, also become Greek citizens. Accordingly, the principle of *jus soli* is used to fill in the gaps of the principle of *jus sanguinis*.

Moreover, laws on citizenship may differ, for example, as regards the issue of whether the child shall have the mother's or the father's citizenship, the approach to dual nationality, time limits, requirements of a special relationship to the Member State. Consequently, great differences exist between the laws on citizenship in the Member States.

For the individual, *citizenship of the Union* implies that he benefits, above all, from a number of specific rights. Nevertheless these rights are not at all as extensive as those conferred on him in his Member State under the legislation in force. These rights are of a different nature from national civil rights, in that they have been granted on a supranational level and confer on the individual rights beyond those rights he has in his own country. According to Articles 18–21 (*ex* Articles 8a–8d), the citizens of the Union shall have the right to move and to reside freely within the territory of the Member States, the right to vote and to stand as a candidate at municipal elections and in elections to the European Parliament, the right to diplomatic and consular protection in third countries, the right to petition the European Parliament, and the right to apply to the European Ombudsman. The most important rights are the rights to move and reside freely within the territory of the Member States. The right to petition the European Parliament and the right to apply to the European Ombudsman are even conferred on citizens from third countries who reside in the Union.[5] Of course, individuals within the EU—including in some cases non-EC nationals—enjoy many other rights which have been created over the years by Community law and practice, and which could be seen collectively as constituting a form of practical citizenship, albeit that they are not formally categorized as such under the Treaty.[6]

One of the main weaknesses of the citizenship of the Union is its lack of independence. This lack of independence is due to the fact that citizenship of the Union is

---

[5] The various rights need to be presented and discussed in more detail. Presentations can be found in a number of works. In particular, O'Leary, note 1 above, should be mentioned.

[6] See e.g. J. Shaw, 'The Interpretation of European Union Citizenship' (1998) 61 *MLR* 293; and more generally A. Wiener, *Citizenship Practice: Building Institutions of a Non-State* (1997).

totally founded on the splintered national concepts of nationality. The possibility of becoming a citizen of the Union varies according to where in the Union that person lives. A means of overcoming these differences, and thereby strengthening citizenship of the Union, would be to *harmonize the laws on citizenship* in the Member States. This is a very important and decisive question; however, in the present situation, harmonization seems to be a very remote possibility. Historical and ideological differences attached to notions of state sovereignty stand in the way. Thus, Professor Bruno Nascimbene writes that, despite common traditions and institutions and despite the independence of the systems, harmonization would, at present, be politically impossible.[7] However, partial harmonization has been achieved through the new European Convention on Nationality of 6 November 1997.

Nevertheless it appears less appropriate to establish the rights of the individual in the Union on the splintered national concepts of citizenship. Instead, as many writers have already suggested, an attempt to find another concept based specifically on Community law should be made, upon which EC law can be founded. It seems most appropriate to build the rights of the individual on the right of abode in the Union, conditional on either residence *tout court* or residence over a certain period of time. In order to be in a position to grant rights to the inhabitants of the Union on an objective and fair basis, it would be important to release citizenship of the Union from national rules on citizenship. This would correspond well with the EU rules on non-discrimination and moreover strengthen the rights of nationals from third countries in the Community.[8]

With regard to nationals from third countries who are resident in the Union, it is above all free movement and the right of residence which are of interest and which must be discussed. Such persons currently have the right to travel within the EU countries. However it is a vaguely developed right. Nevertheless, there has been a tendency to develop free movement for non-Community nationals.[9] The European Court of Justice has to a rather large extent granted rights to citizens from third countries. Certain groups have already been accorded rights within the Union. For instance, in principle, citizens from EEA countries enjoy the same right to free movement as citizens of the Union. In light of this, it cannot be justified that the great majority of nationals from third countries who live lawfully in a Member State are denied the right of residence in another Member State. In dealing with such issues the Community and the Union must respect human rights and other conventions to which the Member States are signatories. Of course, it is also a prerequisite that free movement is fully implemented for citizens of the Union, before nationals from third countries are taken into hand. Many of the issues which concern free movement are solved within the frame of the Schengen Agreement, according to which EU citizens, nationals of the Schengen countries, as well as non-Community nationals may move

---

[7] See B. Nascimbene, *Nationality Laws in the European Union* (1996), 11.

[8] On the specific issue of the human rights of third country nationals within the Community, see J. Weiler, 'Thou Shalt not Oppress a Stranger: On the Judicial Protection of the Human Rights of Non-Community Nationals—A Critique' (1992) 2 *EJIL* 65.

[9] See e.g. S. Peers, 'Towards Equality: Actual and Potential Rights of Third Country Nationals in the European Union' (1996) 33 *CML Rev.* 7; and M. Cremona, 'Citizens of Third Countries: Movement and the Employment of Migrant Workers Within the European Union' (1995) 2 *LIEI* 87.

freely within the Schengen area. Time limits are however imposed on this right for nationals from third countries. Nationals from third countries have the right to move freely for up to three months during a period of six months or, if a visa is required, as long as the visa is valid. Also, it should be observed that the United Kingdom and Ireland will stay outside the Schengen area.

The main issues concerning a reinforcement of the individual's rights in the Union and of citizenship of the Union appear to be the following:

- What is the object of citizenship of the Union and what aims are to be achieved?
- What is the relationship between human rights and EU citizenship? Are human rights a component part of EU citizenship, or does EU citizenship, conversely, represent only a cluster of the human rights which are protected in the European context?
- Is it justifiable that the present system is maintained where only nationals of the Member States are citizens of the Union?
- Should the EU accept the current strict differences between citizens of the Union and nationals from third countries, above all as regards the right to move to, live, work and pursue an economic activity freely in other EU Member States?
- Would it be possible to give nationals from third countries Community rights similar to the rights of the citizens of the Union?
- Should the EU develop a citizenship concept of its own or something similar which is legally independent from the legislation of the Member States on citizenship?

II. CITIZENSHIP

Citizenship is principally determined by the national rules of each State, but also by rules of international law and by rules on the protection of human rights and fundamental freedoms. It is very difficult to give a universal definition of the meaning of citizenship for the individual. It is above all decisive whether the citizen's country is a democracy and based on western principles, or is under a more totalitarian rule. *Civil rights and duties* should be regarded as exclusively associated with citizenship. The new European Convention on Nationality of 6 November 1997 (not yet in force) lays down in Article 4 that everyone has the right to a nationality. The UN's Universal Declaration of Human Rights[10] also provides that everyone has the right to a nationality. This right is, however, not addressed in the European Convention for the Protection of Human Rights and Fundamental Freedoms of 4 November 1950.

According to international law every country has the right to decide who shall be regarded as holding nationality of that State. In the 1930 Hague Convention

[10] Adopted and proclaimed by GA Res. 217 A (III) (1948). In United Nations, *A Compilation of International Instruments* (1994), i, Part I, 1.

Concerning Certain Questions Relating to the Conflict of Nationality, it is clear from Article 1 that 'it is for each State to determine under its own law who are its nationals'.[11] Nationality should be observed by other States on condition that it complies with international conventions, international customary law, and the principles of law generally recognized with regard to nationality. The Convention has been ratified by only twenty States, and within the EU only by Belgium, the Netherlands, the United Kingdom, and Sweden. However the Convention is considered as binding through custom. According to the International Court of Justice, a so-called 'genuine link' between the individual and the country of which he is a national is required in order for his nationality to have effect in international law.[12]

The Convention on Nationality of the Council of Europe lays down in Article 3 that every State decides 'under its own law who are its nationals'. This shall be accepted by other States 'in so far as it is consistent with applicable international conventions, customary international law and the principles of law generally recognised with regard to nationality'. The State cannot impose citizenship on foreigners against their wishes.

The rights and duties of citizens may vary considerably from one country to another. For the individual, citizenship is ultimately a question of being able to enter and reside freely in his country (*jus domicilii*). There are a number of other rights, however the principle of *jus domicilii* must always be regarded as fundamental. It is true that this right can be undermined, for example, if expulsion is allowed; however the core of citizenship is always the right to residence in that country. The State is considered to have a duty under international law to grant its citizens the right to reside in its territory. This right is usually described as the citizen's freedom of movement.

Freedom of movement consists of three elements: the right to enter, the right to stay, and the right to leave the territory. That the freedom of movement, in particular the right to stay in that country, is a central civil and even human right, has long been taken as granted. Historical documents from different periods confirm this point of view, even though exceptions have been extensive. The possibility of expulsion can be said to run contrary to the right to enter, and the right to leave one's own country has not always been recognized. Even the freedom of movement within the country can be limited, for example on grounds of defence policy. The freedom of movement can be seen as a uniform concept whereby all parts, the right to enter, the right to reside, and the right to leave, must be real rights in order for the freedom of movement to become a reality for the individual. It also indirectly protects the individual's possibility of exercising other rights i.e. freedom of speech, freedom of demonstration, etc.

In several international conventions freedom of movement has been adopted as a human right, in particular the UN's Universal Declaration on Human Rights, the European Convention for the Protection of Human Rights and Fundamental Freedoms of the Council of Europe, and the International Convention on Civil and Political Rights.[13]

---

[11] Adopted 12 Apr. 1930, 179 LNTS 89.
[12] *Liechtenstein* v. *Guatemala* (Nottebohm) (6 Apr. 1955) [1955] ICJ Reports 3.
[13] Adopted by GA Res. 2200 A (XXI) (1966). In *International Instruments*, note 10 above, at 20.

Article 13 of the UN's Declaration on Human Rights provides for the freedom of movement. The right for a national to enter his country is expressed in the second paragraph as the right for everyone to return to his country. Therefore such a right is reserved to nationals of a country. Similar wording is also found in the International Covenant on Civil and Political Rights. Article 12(2) prescribes that no one shall be arbitrarily deprived of the right to enter his own country. However, this provision gives the individual State extensive possibilities of deciding who shall have the right to enter the country, as long as this does not take place on arbitrary grounds.

Moreover, the European Convention lays down the national's right to enter his country. According to Article 3(2) of the Fourth Protocol, no-one shall be deprived of the right to enter the territory of the State of which he is a national. Since the word 'arbitrary' is not used, the provision has a more absolute content than the corresponding Article in the International Covenant on Civil and Political Rights. According to Article 3 of the Fourth Protocol the national is also guaranteed protection against expulsion. However, the Convention does not address the possibility of depriving individuals of their nationality.

Consequently, it can be said that the right to enter a State is generally dependent on citizenship. According to international agreements, every State has the duty to allow its own nationals to enter that country. It is clear that the EU countries must respect this. The European Court of Justice pronounced that 'it is a principle of international law, which the EEC Treaty cannot be assumed to disregard in the relations between Member States, that a State is precluded from refusing its own nationals the right of entry or residence'.[14] However, the State has no duty to grant non-nationals leave to enter the territory. Every country has sovereignty to decide whether a person who is not a national shall be granted leave to enter. Accordingly, the right to enter or reside in a foreign country is not an internationally recognized human right. Therefore, it is possible to treat nationals of a State and foreigners differently in this respect. From this perspective, the free movement of the citizens of the Union appears to be an exception to what usually applies to relations between States.

The right of abode in the State of which one is a national is generally recognized in the majority of countries and is an obvious condition for many other rights. It is a human right to be able to move freely in the country of abode. According to Article 13(1) of the UN's Declaration, everyone is entitled to this right, i.e. both nationals and non-nationals. According to Article 12 of the International Covenant on Civil and Political Rights and Article 2(1) of the Fourth Protocol to the European Convention, this right is granted only to those who are *lawfully* on the territory of the State, i.e. nationals and foreigners with permission. Under Article 2(3), restrictions are permitted only to the extent that they are in accordance with law and are necessary in a democratic society in the interests of national security, public order, the protection of health etc. In practice, this provision can give rise to quite extensive restrictions. The ability of foreigners to make use of the right of liberty of movement is dependant on the State's rules on entry.

---

[14] Case C–41/74, *Van Duyn* v. *Home Office* [1974] ECR 1337.

According to the European Convention on Nationality of the Council of Europe, Member States shall ensure that under national law rules exist on naturalization of persons who lawfully reside on their territory. Countries shall also facilitate acquisition of nationality, for example, for spouses and persons born in the country as well as for persons who lawfully abide there. Therefore, in certain circumstances it can be said to be a right to become a citizen in a country. However, there is no right to become a citizen of the Union. Only he who is a citizen of a Member State can be a citizen of the Union. As already described, it is not possible for an individual to become a citizen of the Union if he is not a national of one of the Member States.

The national concept of citizenship is thus a concept which differs greatly from the concept of citizenship of the Union. The national concept of citizenship is a status relationship between the individual and his State to which certain rights and duties have been attached. It is founded on a 'genuine link' between the individual and his country. In the new European Convention on Nationality of the Council of Europe it is stated that by the reference to nationality in the Convention it is meant 'the legal bond between a person and a state and does not indicate the person's ethnic origin'. On the other hand, citizenship of the Union stands out above all as a bundle of rights. The legal bond between the individual and the Union is much more tenuous than that which exists between the citizen and the State. It can therefore be called into question whether citizenship of the Union can be called a citizenship in the sense which has been outlined above. The person's rights under Community law are not, as they are in a State, attached to a firm status relationship between the individual and the Union. A citizenship of the Union founded on a status relationship between the individual and the Union does not, at present, seem very realistic.[15]

III. CITIZENSHIP OF THE UNION

As already mentioned, citizenship of the Union is a quite new phenomenon. It was introduced into the EC Treaty through the Treaty on European Union, which entered into force in 1993. Article 2 (*ex* Article B) of the Treaty on European Union lays down that the Union shall set itself the objective to strengthen the protection of the rights and interests of the nationals of its Member States through the introduction of a citizenship of the Union.

Citizenship of the Union has *two principal objectives*. On the one hand, it is intended to protect the individual and strengthen his rights. On the other hand, it aims at giving the Union a more state-like appearance, by allowing, for instance, citizens of the Union to participate in the political life of the Union, independently of where within the Union they live.

---

[15] The question whether the rights attached to the European citizenship have direct effect is not yet clear. It has been argued that, e.g., Art. 17 (*ex* Art. 8a) has direct effect (see D. Martin, *La libre circulation des personnes dans l'Union européenne* (1995), 123). See, however, the recent ruling by the ECJ on Art. 17 of the Treaty in Case C–85/96, *Martínez Sala* v. *Freistaat Bayern*, [1998] ECR I–269.

Thus, citizenship of the Union is intended to create a new relationship between the individual and the Union. The Commission wrote in a Report on Citizenship of the Union that 'the Treaty has created a direct *political* link between the citizens of the Member States and the European Union such as never existed with the Community, with the aim of fostering a sense of identity with the Union'.[16] Citizenship of the Union further aims at making the Union more public. The Commission has also pronounced that citizenship of the Union is part of the endeavour to strengthen the *Community's democratic legitimacy*, and consequently it constitutes a part of the development towards a more democratic EU. According to the European Court of Justice, Article 17 (*ex* Article 8) of the EC Treaty is not intended to extend the scope of Community law so as to include even internal, national situations which have no link to Community law: Therefore, Community law must first be activated.[17] For instance, for the rules on free movement to apply, a person must have migrated between two Member States.

Under the principal rule, every person who holds the nationality of a Member State is also a citizen of the Union. The insistence, in Article 17 (*ex* Article 8) of the EC Treaty, on citizenship in the Union makes it impossible for persons who lawfully live in a Member State but who are nationals of a third country to become citizens of the Union. The expression in itself, citizenship of the Union, suggests that the Union should have a certain ability to define who is a citizen of the Union, in conformity with how other concepts of Community law have been defined. However, this seems not to be the case. No competence has been transferred to the EC in this domain. The Member States seem to have considered that this would influence legislation on citizenship in the various countries to too great an extent. Thus, a fundamental principle within the EU is that every Member State defines which persons are citizens in the State.

This principle has been stressed by the Member States in the Declaration on Nationality of a Member State (annexed to the Treaty on European Union). According to this declaration 'wherever in the Treaty establishing the European Community reference is made to nationals of the Member States, the question whether an individual possesses the nationality of a Member State shall be solely settled by reference to the national law of the Member State concerned'. This was also laid down by the European Court of Justice in the *Micheletti* case.[18]

Mr Micheletti, who was a citizen of both Argentina and Italy, was refused leave to establish himself in Spain as he had lived in Argentina and therefore, according to Spanish law, was to be regarded as an Argentine citizen.

Since only an individual who is a national of a Member State can be a citizen of the Union, only the Member States decide unilaterally who is a citizen of the Union. Citizenship of the Union cannot be lost unless nationality of a EU country is lost at the same time. Citizenship of the Union does not replace national citizenship, but is

[16] COM(93)702 final. See also the Commission's 1997 report, COM(97)230 final.
[17] Cases 35–36/82, *Morson and Jhanjan* v. *Netherlands* [1982] ECR 3723, and see specifically on Art. 17 (*ex* Art. 8a), Case C–299/95, *Kremzow* v. *Austria* [1997] ECR I–2629; Cases C–64/96 and 65/96, *Land Nordrhein-Westfalen* v. *Uecker* and *Jacquet* v. *Land Nordrhein-Westfalen* [1997] ECR I–3171.
[18] Case C–369/90, *Micheletti* v. *Delegacion del gobierno en Cantabria* [1992] ECR I–4239.

conferred on the individual in addition to his national citizenship. A person is both a citizen of his own country and a citizen of the Union. How a person acquires his citizenship is irrelevant as regards the exercise of the rights in the EC Treaty. Moreover, it is of no significance when the person acquired citizenship.

The significance of the Court's judgment in *Micheletti* is that the Community and every Member State must accept that a person is a national of another Member State. The nationality of the individual cannot be called into question, nor can unilateral conditions be laid down in order for him to exercise his rights under Community law. This principle, the principle of *mutual recognition*, cannot be implemented on a national level, but only on a Community level. It has even been argued that the Member States have renounced the right, recognized under international law, to insist upon a 'genuine link' between the individual and the State in which he is a national.[19] Therefore, citizenship of the Union is entirely dependent on national law, which is its great weakness. However, it can be argued that there is in reality a mutual dependence. Certain writers have expressed the opinion that the right of Member States to decide on matters of citizenship is strongly affected when the Community adopts measures within its own competence.[20] The European Parliament has maintained that citizenship of the Union should be defined as an autonomous concept.[21]

For fear of encroachment of national sovereignty and identity, the Danish voted against the proposal on the introduction of the European Union in the 1992 Referendum. In the Edinburgh Agreement, a further clarification of citizenship of the Union was given, in order to convince the Danish to vote for the adoption of the Union in the following referendum. Denmark even had a unilateral protocol annexed to the Edinburgh Agreement, making it clear that citizenship of the Union is of a wholly different character from Danish nationality. Furthermore, it is clear that there is no obligation on Denmark to create a citizenship of the Union which is in line with nationality in a Nation State or that citizenship of the Union gives a right to Danish nationality or to rights, duties, privileges, or advantages resulting from Danish rules.

The Amsterdam Treaty, in an amendment to Article 17 (*ex* Article 8), reflects this conservatism and provides that citizenship of the Union shall complement and not replace national citizenship.[22]

Citizenship of the Union lacks several of the features characteristic of citizenship, including a specific, fundamental legal relationship between the individual and the Union. Citizenship of the Union stands out as an indirect status relationship, where the direct relationship lies on the one hand between the Member State and the Union, and on the other hand between the Member State and the individual. However, the term 'citizenship of the Union' seems to be aimed principally at the partic-

---

[19] R. Kovan and D. Simon, 'La citoyenneté européenne' (1993) *CDE* No. 3–4, 291.

[20] See, e.g. S. O'Leary, 'Nationality Law and Community Citizenship: A Tale of Two Uneasy Bedfellows' (1992) 12 *YEL* 353.

[21] *Report of the Committee on Institutional Affairs on Union Citizenship*. Doc. A3–0300/91.

[22] For a critical analysis of the EC citizenship provisions in the context of the IGC debate preceding the Amsterdam Treaty, see J. Weiler, 'Citizenship and Human Rights', in J. Winter *et al.* (eds.), *Reforming the Treaty on European Union: The Legal Debate* (1996).

ular rights to which the people of the different Member States are entitled, and not this indirect legal relationship. It seems very likely that Union citizenship could be regarded as a generic term for these rights. Citizenship of the Union is probably most accurately viewed as a distinctive type of citizenship, where the relationship between the Union and the citizens is not decisive, but where certain general rights, granted to several different ethnic groups, are the most characteristic feature. It is questionable, indeed, whether it should be called 'citizenship' at all. In order to be able to go further and fulfil more efficiently the objectives of Union citizenship of creating a relationship between the individual and the Union as well as strengthening the EU's democratic legitimacy, changes should be made.

Instead of nationality, the introduction of *permanent longer abode in the Union*, possibly conditional on permanent residence or residence over a certain period of time, as a starting point for building the individual's rights in the Community, would have several advantages. Naturally, the biggest advantage is that its scope could be defined by Community law. It would be more appropriate to base EC law on a concept defined by EC law than on the splintered national concepts of citizenship. It would lead to a clearer and more uniform application of the law and better correspond to the basic structure of Community law. It cannot be justified that a national from a third country, merely because he cannot become a national of the Member State in which he resides under the national rules, should be excluded from the application of Community rights. The concept based on abode is also well suited from the point of view of non-discrimination. Using a concept based on abode as a means of selection does not deprive the Member States of the right to decide who should be nationals in the individual Member States. The concept would only decide who shall have Community rights and would not affect the national standpoints on legislation on citizenship. The concept of citizenship of the Union could remain in use as a term, in as far as citizenship of the Union does not seem to amount to a real 'citizenship', as traditionally understood.

Another of the possible objectives of Union citizenship, that of giving the Union a more state-like dimension, is compatible with using a concept based on abode. Using a concept based on abode may in fact reinforce this objective, since a specific Community concept is created by which the Community can define who shall be entitled to rights in the Union independently from the Member States. The fact that, according to international law, a person cannot be given the status of a citizen against his will does not appear to be problematic, in that Union citizenship does not seem to amount to a citizenship of the same type as nationality of a State.

IV. THE RIGHTS OF THE CITIZENS OF THE UNION

Citizenship of the Union consists of two principal parts: on the one hand a part more concerned with public law, and on the other hand an economic part. Union citizenship itself is found in the part on public law, i.e. the relationship between the individual and the Union, as well as the question of who is a citizen of the Union. The majority of the rights of the citizens of the Union belong to this part. The economic part relates primarily to the citizen's right to move and reside freely in the Member States.

Citizenship of the Union has led to a reinforcement of the rights of the individual in the Community. As noted above, however, the relationship of these rights to the fundamental human rights which are part of the general principles of Community law remains unclear. The citizens of the Union have obtained rights both in relation to the Community and in relation to the Member States. Articles 18–21 (*ex* Articles 8a–d) of the EC Treaty regulate the rights, and since they are found in the EC Treaty they fall within the jurisdiction of the European Court of Justice.

Citizens of the Union have obtained certain *political rights* as a result of the Treaty on European Union: the rights to vote both at municipal elections and in elections to the European Parliament (Article 19, *ex* Article 8b).[23] These rights affect only a small proportion of the citizens of the Union, namely those who reside in a Member State of which they are not nationals. The right to vote amounts to a new right in Community law, and it is the first time that a direct political link has been created between the individual and the EC. It is a question of democracy on two levels: partly on the local level and partly in the European Parliament. The right to vote signifies a new feature in many Member States, whereas in other Member States this right already existed. The right to participate in municipal elections is above all of significance for the integration of citizens of the Union into the country in which they reside. However, citizens of the Union have no right under Community law to participate in national parliamentary elections.[24] Even the right to vote in elections for the European Parliament is important for the integration of the individual into the society, but is perhaps of greater importance in respect of the individual's own feeling of solidarity with the Union.

To extend the citizens of the Union's rights to vote in local elections and in elections to the European Parliament to apply even to those who abide in the Union without being a national of one of the Member States appears, for some Member States, to be a difficult step to take.[25] However, from point of view of non-discrimination it would be an important step forward. Nationals from third countries should be entitled to the right to participate in the political life of the country in which they live, a right granted to nationals of other EU Member States, on the same grounds and to the same extent. It would be desirable to fulfil the purpose of the rule, namely to give residents the right to participate in the political life which affects them to the greatest extent, in respect of nationals from third countries living permanently in a EU country. In Sweden, all foreigners, in addition to nationals from EU States and other Nordic countries, are granted the right to vote at municipal elections, as long as they have been registered in Sweden for three successive years before the day of election.

---

[23] See H. Lardy, 'The Political Rights of Union Citizenship' (1996) 2 *EPL* 611.
[24] See Rosas on the question whether this could be challenged for compatibility with international human rights law, note 3 above, at 165.
[25] R. Hansen, *Citizenship, Immigration and Nationality Law in the European Union: A European Citizenship or a Europe of Citizens?* (1998).

Furthermore, the citizens of the Union have the right to protection by the diplomatic or consular authorities of other Member States in third countries where their own country is not represented (Article 20, *ex* Article 8c). This departs from what usually applies in the relationship between Member States, whereby only the State in which a person is a national can give him diplomatic protection. The protection is provided for on an intergovernmental level and therefore is not granted by the Community. The right to diplomatic protection is a completely new right in Community law and, on the surface, appears to infringe the international law rule of a 'genuine link'. However, as the EU builds on the idea of a Union and on the principle of free movement, it is perhaps not so strange that this rule is not applied.

The right to petition the European Parliament and the right to apply to the Ombudsman (Article 21, *ex* Article 8d) constitute an important democratic contribution to the EU. The rights focus on the Community as such, and protect the rights of the individual citizen of the Union, giving him a stake in the activities of the Community. These rights are held not only by the citizens of the Union, but also by nationals from third countries who live in a Member State. The right to petition the European Parliament has long existed, whereas the right to apply to the Ombudsman was introduced in the Maastricht Treaty. It should also be noted, in this respect, that a concept based on abode without time limits has already been implemented, whereby all those who reside in the Union have the right to petition the European Parliament or apply to the Ombudsman. Thus rights in favour of all of the Union's inhabitants already exist. The same principle could well be used as regards other rights.

The rights, which previously already existed in the EC Treaty, have been completely changed through the implementation of Articles 18–21 (*ex* Articles 8a–d), as they have been 'constitutionalized' in the EC Treaty and moreover have been enlarged in order to include more people. The main focus amongst the rights of the citizens of the Union lies above all on free movement, the right to residence as well as the right to vote. The right to move and reside freely, the right to vote at municipal elections and in elections to the European Parliament and the right to diplomatic and consular protection must all be implemented by the Member States. However, two rights, namely the right to petition the European Parliament, and the right to apply to the Ombudsman, focus directly on the Community. They concern the relationship between the individual and the Community. The individual can address a petition to the European Parliament on matters which come within the field of activity of the Community. He can also lodge complaints with the Ombudsman concerning instances of maladministration in the activities of the Community institutions or bodies. When these rights are exercised, a direct legal relationship arises between the individual and the Community. The indirect legal relationship, which citizenship of the Union provides for, can therefore give rise to direct legal relationships between the individual and the EC. Nevertheless, this is only possible in the limited domain in which the Community has jurisdiction. A principle of non-discrimination applies to the right to vote and to diplomatic and consular protection. Free movement is also built on non-discrimination.

The European Court of Human Rights in Strasbourg has dealt with the question whether the EU Member States infringe the principle of non-discrimination in the

European Convention, when they treat citizens of the Union and other foreigners differently.[26] The Court held that 'as for the preferential treatment given to nationals of the other Member States of the Communities, there is objective and reasonable justification for it as Belgium belongs, together with those states, to a special legal order'. However, Evans considers that it is unclear whether citizenship of the Union always manifests this objective justification which is required.[27]

The most important rights for the individual are the right to move and to reside freely within the territory of the Member States (Article 18, *ex* Article 8a). Both these rights existed to a large extent before the entry into force of the Treaty on European Union. For those persons who pursue an economic activity, these rights are expressly addressed in Articles 39, 43, and 49 (*ex* Articles 48, 52, and 59) of the EC Treaty. Corresponding rights have gradually been developed for those individuals who do not fall within the scope of these Articles in the case law of the European Court of Justice[28] and in secondary legislation.[29] The most obvious difference, in comparison with the situation before the Treaty of European Union, is that all citizens of the Union are now granted the right to move and reside freely directly under the EC Treaty. Limitations or conditions to free movement are possible in as far as they are laid down in the EC Treaty (for example, on grounds of public policy, public security, or public health) and by measures adopted to give effect to the Treaty, which may in fact confine those rights to the existing 'economically active' or 'financially self-sufficient' categories covered by the EC Treaty and by secondary legislation.[30]

The EC Treaty only confers free movement on nationals of the Member States. According to Community law, nationals from third countries resident in the Union have no general right to free movement or residence. However, through association agreements and secondary legislation, certain nationals from third countries and family members of citizens of the Union have obtained free movement in the Union.[31] As a result of the Schengen Agreement, movement has increased as all inner borders between the Schengen Member States have been abolished, and all those who find themselves within the common outer border have the right to move freely. The Schengen Agreement is discussed at D in the next section.

V. FREE MOVEMENT AND THE RIGHT TO RESIDENCE OF NATIONALS FROM THIRD COUNTRIES

As a result of association agreements between the EC and third countries, certain categories of foreigners have the right to enter and reside in the Member States. Even

---

[26] *Moustaquim* v. *Belgium* ECHR (1991) Series A, No. 19, 20.

[27] A. Evans, 'Nationality Law and European Integration' (1991) 16 *EL Rev.* 214.

[28] See e.g. Cases 286/82 and 26/83, *Graziana Luisi and Giuseppe Carbone* v. *Ministero del Tesoro* [1984] ECR 377 and Case 186/87, *Ian William Cowan* v. *Trésor Public* [1989] ECR 195.

[29] E.g. Council Dirs. 90/364 [1990] OJ L180/26, 90/365 [1990] OJ L180/28, and 93/96/EEC [1993] OJ L317/59.

[30] Again, however, see the potential for a broader scope for Art. 17 (*ex* Art. 8a) introduced by the ECJ's ruling in *Martínez Sala*, note 15 above.

[31] See Cremona and Peers, note 9 above.

migrant families of citizens of the Union are regarded as an exception. Therefore, these specific categories of people can be regarded as a privileged group of non-Community nationals, a category in between citizens of the Union, who have at their disposal all Community rights, and third country nationals whose rights are principally based on national law in the Member States. Consequently, a distinction should be made between two categories of non-Community nationals: those who have and those who do not have rights in the Community.

A. Family Members

According to secondary legislation, family members, irrespective of their nationality, have the right to accompany and to install themselves with the citizen of the Union who is working in another Member State.[32] This right applies to spouses, relatives in the ascending or descending line of the migrant or his spouse (according to Directive 93/96 only spouses and children). The right does not, however, apply to co-habitants.[33]

Therefore, nationals from third countries have the right to migrate together with migrating citizens of the Union. Their rights are wholly dependent on the citizens of the Union and thereby cannot exist independently.[34] The Commission has nevertheless stated such a dependence is unsatisfactory and that a foreign spouse should be entitled to an independent right of residence after a certain period of time in the country.[35] An overhaul of the rules can therefore be expected. However, exceptions already exist. Thus, the spouse of a worker has the right to retain his right of residence in the event of the workers' death.[36]

B. Association Agreements

Under Article 310 (*ex* Article 238), the Community has the ability to conclude agreements establishing association with outside States and international organizations. The Community has concluded several such agreements concerning free movement. Certain agreements entitle non-Community nationals the right to move and reside freely. Others contain principally rules on non-discrimination.

The most developed association agreement is the EEA Agreement. It was concluded by the EFTA States (except Switzerland) and the EC and entered into force on 1 January 1994. Sweden, Finland, and Austria have now become EC States (since 1995) and not EFTA States, and a new EFTA State, Liechtenstein, has been established. At present, three EFTA States belong to the EEA: Norway, Iceland, and Liechtenstein. According to its preamble, the EEA Agreement aims at establishing a dynamic and homogenous European economic co-operation.[37] The EEA

[32] Council Reg. 1612/68 [1968] OJ L257/2, Council Dir. 73/148/EEC [1973] OJ L172/14), Council Dirs. 90/364 and 90/365, note 29 above, and Council Dir. 93/96, note 29 above.

[33] Case C–59/85, *Reed* [1986] ECR 1283.

[34] J. Wouters, 'European Citizenship and the Case-Law of the Court of Justice of the European Communities on the Free Movement of Persons', in E.A. Marias, *European Citizenship* (1994), 29.

[35] COM(94)23 final.

[36] J. d'Oliveira, 'Union Citizenship: Pie in the Sky?', in A. Rosas and E. Antola (eds.), *A Citizen's Europe* (1995).

[37] See M. Cremona, 'The "Dynamic and Homogenous" EEA: Byzantine Structures and Variable Geometry' (1994) 19 *EL Rev.* 508.

Agreement implies that the four freedoms, i.e. free movement of goods, workers, services, and capital, shall apply on the same conditions in the EEA as in the EC. The Articles of the EEA Agreement resemble to a large extent the Articles of the EC Treaty, both materially and linguistically. According to Article 6 of the EEA Agreement, measures which correspond with rules in Community law shall be interpreted in accordance with judgments of the European Court of Justice, passed prior to the signature of the EEA Agreement. Under Article 4 of the EEA Agreement, all discrimination on grounds of nationality is forbidden.

The EC has also concluded association agreements with other countries. These are however not as far-reaching as the EEA Agreement. For example the EC has concluded an agreement with Turkey on gradually developing free movement for workers.[38] The co-operation is inspired by Articles 39, 40, and 41 (*ex* Articles 48, 49, and 50) of the EC Treaty. Even obstacles to free establishment and the free provision of services shall successively be abolished.[39] A principle of non-discrimination, applying to conditions of work and remuneration, can be found in a protocol from 1970. The European Court of Justice has decided a number of cases concerning the agreement with Turkey. The Court has laid down that it has jurisdiction to interpret the provisions in the agreement which affect free movement of workers.[40] It has further stated that certain clear and unambiguous rules, which maintain the rights of Turkish workers, have direct effect.[41] The Turks' right to take up employment in a Member State implies that they also have a right of residence in that country.[42] The European Court of Justice has further placed on a par the ability of the Member States to limit the Turks' rights on grounds of public order, public security, and public health in accordance with Article 39(3) (*ex* Article 48(3)) of the EC Treaty.[43] In this respect, a Turkish worker who lawfully resides in a Member State shall be treated in the same way as a citizen of the Union. Further, although the measures have neither the same origin nor the same purpose, the ECJ has ruled that the interpretation of measures adopted under the Turkey–EC Association agreement should be informed by the principles in Articles 39–41 (*ex* Articles 48–50) of the EC Treaty.[44]

It can also be mentioned briefly that special arrangements apply to many former colonies and territories dependent on EU countries (OCT, Overseas Countries and Territories) in the EU, based on the principle of non-discrimination (Article 299(3), *ex* Article 227(3) of the EC Treaty). These are overseas countries and territories with special relations with Belgium, Denmark, France, Italy, the Netherlands, and the United Kingdom. For these countries and territories special arrangements for asso-

---

[38] Agreement establishing an Association between the EEC and Turkey, *Bull. EC* 8–1963, [1964] OJ 217/3685.

[39] *Ibid.*, Arts. 12, 13, and 14.

[40] Case C–12/86, *Demirel* v. *Stadt Schwäbisch Gmünd* [1987] ECR 3719.

[41] Case C–192/89, *Sevince* v. *Staatssecretaris van Justitie* [1990] ECR I–3461.

[42] Case C–237/91, *Kus* v. *Landeschauptstadt Wiesbaden* [1992] ECR I–6781. See also, more recently, Case C–171/95, *Recep Tetik* v. *Land Berlin* [1997] ECR I–329.

[43] Martin, note 15 above.

[44] See *Tetik*, note 42 above, and see S. O'Leary, 'Employment and Residence for Turkish Workers and their Families: Analogies with the Case-Law of the Court of Justice on Article 48 EC', in C. Gulmon (ed.), *Scritti in Onore di Giuseppe Federico Mancini* (1998), ii.

ciation apply. Freedom of movement between the EU and OCT shall be governed by agreements to be concluded subsequently with the unanimous approval of the Member States. In some cases, persons from OCT countries are also nationals in a Member State. However, it should be mentioned that these persons do not automatically have the right to free movement, as is conferred on citizens of the Union.[45]

C. Free Movement and the Right to Residence in the Union for Other Nationals from Third Countries

As shown above, there are nevertheless quite a few nationals from third countries who have certain rights in the Community. For those nationals from third countries who do not have rights in the Community, according to the rules on workers's families or according to association agreements, the right of residence is governed by the Member States, principally by national legislation in each country. It is true that the EC's jurisdiction concerning policies on refugees, immigration, and foreigners has been enlarged. However, the EC has no competence to govern freedom of movement in a general manner, for either those nationals from third countries who legally reside in a Member State or those who want to enter a Member State in the Union.[46] Immigration policies as such are considered as lying within the jurisdiction of the individual Member States.[47] Member States have been very reluctant to give up their right to self-determination in this domain. Nevertheless, Member States must co-operate with each other and with the EC, in order to co-ordinate their policies. However, harmonization of the Member States' legislation on nationals from third countries has in principle not yet happened. As a result of the Amsterdam Treaty, questions on asylum and immigration have come within the scope of the first pillar of the Union. Consequently, questions on asylum will be covered to a large extent by EC law. The Member States have already, within the framework of the third pillar, prepared agreements, corresponding partly to those adopted in the Amsterdam Treaty. The Dublin Convention determines which State is liable for the examination of an application for asylum made in a Member State.

The ability of the millions of refugees, foreign workers, and other nationals from third countries who live in the EU to reside and work in another Member State is governed by the national law of the Member States. Nevertheless, these persons shall, like all other persons, be entitled to protection of their human rights and fundamental freedoms. Both the EU and the Member States have undertaken to abide by these. On the other hand, substantial parts of the freedom of movement, and above all the right to enter a country, are limited, applying only to nationals of a State. The State has no duty to grant non-nationals leave to enter the territory of that State.

Consequently, many persons from third countries cannot invoke Community law in order to invoke the right to freedom of movement in a Member State. In the

---

[45] Evans, note 27 above, at 191.

[46] Refugees (defined in accordance with the 1951 Convention Relating to the Status of Refugees) are nevertheless given a special position in the EU. Those refugees who live in a Member State shall be treated favourably if they wish to seek employment in another Member State. However, no special rules exist: [1985] OJ C210/2.

[47] D. O'Keeffe, 'The Emergence of a European Immigration Policy' (1995) 20 *EL Rev.* 20.

majority of cases, a national from a third country cannot invoke the rules for protection of human rights in order to obtain the right to enter a Member State. Their rights are determined by national legislation. According to the rules for the protection of human rights, including the European Convention, persons lawfully within the territory of a State have the right to liberty of movement and freedom to choose their residence.

D. Schengen Agreement

Articles 3(c) and 14 (*ex* Articles 3(c) and 7(a)) of the EC Treaty lay down that all obstacles to the free movement of persons shall be abolished, aiming ultimately at the creation of an area without border controls and complete free movement for persons. This shall apply to all, both citizens of the Union and nationals from third countries, who have crossed the Member States' common outer border. Such a genuine freedom of movement is conditional on the abolition of requirements of nationality, which presently exist in the EC Treaty, for example in Article 17 (*ex* Article 8).

In order to accomplish complete free movement without internal borders and in order to avoid the negative consequences of an increasing number of asylum seekers, the Member States started co-operating on an inter-governmental level by means of the Schengen Agreement.[48] Only the United Kingdom and Ireland remain presently outside the scope of the co-operation under the Schengen Agreement. The Agreement entered into force on 26 March 1995. By virtue of a special agreement Norway and Iceland will be associated to the Schengen Agreement. As a result of a protocol linked to the Amsterdam Treaty, the Schengen Agreement shall be annexed to the Treaty on European Union and the EC Treaty. It is consequently incorporated into the EU and co-operation henceforth will take place within the framework of the EC. Thus, Community law applies to questions on asylum, immigration, and border control.

The principal objective of the Schengen Agreement is the abolition of border controls for persons crossing borders and the introduction of replacement measures. Even transport and the circulation of goods are treated. Both nationals of the Schengen States and the remaining EU countries as well as nationals from third countries, when within the territory of the Schengen States, have the right to move freely in the whole Schengen area. Nationals from third countries have the right to move freely for up to three months during a period of six months, or if a visa is required, as long as the visa is valid.

However, it should be observed that the Schengen Agreement does not address the ability of nationals of the Schengen States or of other States to reside or work in another Schengen State. EC law, the EEA Agreement, and national rules apply.

The Schengen countries maintain a common outer border with third countries. Entry into the Schengen countries may only take place at specific border controls, at which a control of persons shall be carried out. The control is concerned with

---

[48] See Protocol on Schengen attached to the EC and EU Treaties; and generally S. Peers, 'Human Rights and the Third Pillar', in this vol.

whether a person fulfils the requirements for entry, i.e. that the person carries acceptable travel documents, and where appropriate, a visa, and that he has adequate resources. Less desirable persons shall be entered into a black list. A national from a third country shall have the right to travel through the country if he has a residence permit or a visa issued for an other Schengen country. On entry into the Schengen Area, citizens of the Union shall be controlled less strictly than nationals from third countries.

The Schengen Agreement facilitates free movement for citizens of the Union who are tourists, travelling on business, or for any other similar short stay. It also facilitates free movement for persons from third countries, as visas apply to the whole Schengen area. A person who is required to have a visa can with one visa move freely in the whole area. A list exists of all countries whose nationals must have a visa. Currently, the list includes approximately 130 States. The Schengen countries shall strive at harmonizing their visa policies. As a counterpart to free movement, there is co-operation on legal and police matters.

E. Conclusion

The civil right to freedom of movement is reserved to the nationals of a country. Under the European Convention of Human Rights, no one shall be deprived of the right to enter the territory of which he is a national. By virtue of Community law, the freedom of movement and the right to residence have been introduced on a supranational level for all nationals of the Member States. As a result of association agreements, these rights have been further extended to include nationals of yet more countries. It is unjustifiable that certain nationals from third countries have the right to enter and reside in the Union according to Community law, whereas others already resident in a Member State are excluded from the scope of such rights. The Schengen Agreement, the objective of which is to confer on all persons who have crossed the common outer border the right to move freely, shows the clear intention to extend the right to free movement. Conditions as to nationality should therefore no longer be required.

VI. CONCLUSION

The fundamental differences between the EU Member States in respect of citizenship entail great tensions and legal problems within EC law, directly affecting many millions of people. Citizenship of the Union, which is an additional supranational citizenship conferred on all nationals of the EU Member States, is built on the splintered national concepts of citizenship. The main problem with Union citizenship is that it is a dependent concept, which is built on a completely different legal relationship, namely the national concept of citizenship. Neither the Union nor the Community has competence in the domain of nationality, and consequently no right to influence which persons are nationals of a Member State and thereby citizens of the

Union. Whilst the Union defines those categories of persons who are granted rights under Community law (for example workers), the Member States themselves decide who these persons are. In Europe, there are many millions of immigrants who are not nationals of the country in which they live. It is above all in relation to these persons, who actually constitute a substantial proportion of the population in the country in which they live, that Union citizenship appears to be most unreasonable and unjust.

Harmonizing measures, either through Community instructions or through an agreement between the Member States, in respect of the Member States' law on citizenship have not been taken and appear remote, despite mutual dependence and certain common traditions and institutions. Neither has Community law influenced national legislation on citizenship in any Member State to any considerable extent. In the long term harmonization of legislation on nationality would perhaps be desirable. However, the possibility of this is in all likelihood to a large extent limited, in as far as the notion of national sovereignty is so tied to the concept of citizenship. Consequently, Professor Bruno Nascimbe writes that, despite common traditions and institutions and despite the independence of the systems, harmonization would be difficult to achieve.[49] International conventions, and especially the 1930 Convention Concerning Certain Questions Relating to the Conflict of Nationality Laws, show the great difficulties which obstruct co-operation in this domain. This is clear in light of the quite vague wording and the small number of signatory States. The Convention has been ratified by only twenty States in the world, and within the EU only by Belgium, the Netherlands, the United Kingdom, and Sweden. However, a new Council of Europe Convention (European Convention on Nationality) has recently been agreed upon.

Citizenship of the Union came into existence as a result of the Maastricht Treaty and has a clear ideological background. Nevertheless, it appears that on the EU level that which was hoped for with the concept has not been achieved. It does not have the strength which was intended, and stands out as a weak and rather empty concept. Union citizenship, as it is today, does not take sufficiently into consideration the dissimilar formulation of the contents of the national laws on citizenship. As long as the national concept of citizenship serves as a basis for European co-operation in respect of people and their rights, the disparate rules on the acquisition of nationality mean that it is considerably easier to obtain the status and the advantages of European citizenship in certain EU countries than in others. However, there appears to be no reason why those rights which are presently conferred on citizens of the Union must be based on nationality, particularly in consideration of the fact that far-reaching rights have already been granted in the Union to nationals from third countries. The Union should therefore not accept that the Member States unilaterally have competence in deciding who shall be covered by the rights under Community law. Those rights which are granted to citizens of the Union cannot be put on a par with civil rights. They have been conferred on a different level and for a different purpose. In principle, Community rights can be granted to everyone, depending on which criterion

---

[49] See Nascimbene, note 7 above, at 11.

of selection is chosen. Free movement in Community law resembles to a certain extent the civil right of freedom of movement under Member State law. The Union should endeavour to grant this right to all residents.

On the present level of legal development, citizenship of the Union merely appears to be a generic term for certain specific rights. Seen from a global point of view, the insistence on nationality for many rights is increasingly being relaxed and, for example, free movement and the right to vote at municipal elections are being conferred, to a much greater extent, on all those who fulfil certain specified criteria such as a certain period of residence in a country. The rights are no longer exclusively reserved for nationals. Within the scope of Community law, the rights of the individual should, in accordance with this, be severed from national concepts of citizenship, so that free movement, the free work market, and other rights shall apply in favour of all those who lawfully reside in the Union. Important progress in this direction has already been made, for example nationals of EEA countries and family members of Union citizens enjoy free movement. Taking the step of allowing all those who are legally resident in the Union to enjoy the same rights does not appear too great. European citizenship does not distinguish sufficiently between nationals of the Member States and nationals from third countries for a distinction to be justifiably maintained. Neither does it appear reasonable that second and third generation immigrants into a Member State shall not have the right of residence in another EU country, due to the country's national laws on citizenship.

By virtue of the Schengen Agreement, free movement has further been extended. *All* who have crossed the common outer border have the right to travel freely, as long as they are not found on the common black list. However, Community law and national legislation apply with respect to the ability to reside and work in another Member State.

Within Community law, a tendency can be discerned for the solutions sought to use criteria other than nationality. Citizenship is a national concept and it can be discussed whether it is appropriate to create a supranational concept of citizenship. According to traditional international law, a state possesses three elements: a territory, a population, and a government. It is not always totally clear what constitutes a population. It either consists solely of the population of the State or of all those who live on the State's territory. It is not possible to give a clear answer to what constitutes a population when it is a question of a state in which more than one national group live. The creation of a supranational citizenship consisting of a number of state populations and other groups, which are not brought together on ethnical, religious, political, historical, sociological, or linguistic grounds, can therefore be doubted. This calls into question whether nationality is a suitable selection criterion of those groups of people for the benefit of which the rules on free movement, the free labour market, and other Community rights shall apply.

Citizenship is consequently a doubtful concept in the context of the EU, the application of which is in all likelihood not appropriate. As it is hardly going to be possible within a reasonable time to harmonize the widely differing laws on nationality in the Member States, the Union should have another starting point for distinguishing which persons are to benefit from Community law. An appropriate selection criterion appears to be to abode in the Union, possibly conditional on permanent residence or residence for a certain number of years.

The greater the development the Union makes in the integration process, the less significance would be attached to the concepts of nationality, in the context of the EU. Instead it should be possible that legal abode is the link between the individual in the Member State and the Union. Professor Bruno Nascimbene writes that nationality will gradually lose its significance in favour of the concept of abode, which will become 'the most appropriate standard to establish the link or tie between an individual and a civil or social community'.[50] The concept of abode appears to be a more objective basis for selection than the subjective national concepts of citizenship and corresponds with the EU's principle of equal treatment. This would be of greatest importance for nationals from third countries, residing legally in a Member State. They do belong to the population of the country, and from a perspective of democracy and non-discrimination it appears obvious that all inhabitants of the Member States should be allowed to participate in the cultural, political, and economic life of the Union. Equal treatment for inhabitants, irrespective of nationality, should be a target for the Union. It also creates a more direct relationship between the Union and its inhabitants. Therefore, against the background of what the EU wants to achieve in relation to the free work market and free movement for persons, abode in the Union should be the decisive factor, rather than nationality, in respect of Community rights.

Another considerable advantage of using a concept defined by EC law is that it would be possible to have a tradition of concepts common to the EU. This involves the creation of a specific concept based on Community law, and built on uniform and objective grounds for selection. Such a criterion of selection can be used without difficult attempts at harmonization of the Member States' legislation and is in line with the Member States' strong desire to define nationality themselves.

A common concept of abode could also be used for other areas within Community law. Free movement in Article 39 (*ex* Article 48) is currently based on nationality of the EU countries, but allowing for the right of nationals from EEA countries and family members of citizens of the Union to move freely within the Union. As a consequence the insistence on nationality is being increasingly relaxed. In this respect, legal abode could also be applicable. Foreigners today, other than those mentioned above, have no right to reside or look for employment in another Member State. This is also true under the Schengen Agreement. However, according to the Schengen Agreement, they are given a right to travel for a limited period. The Schengen Agreement applies above all to short stays, such as those of tourists or business travellers. The right to live and work is not touched upon. The Schengen co-operation illustrates that Member States are prepared, to a certain extent, to permit non-Community nationals right of free movement.

The same applies to the right of establishment, which according to Article 43 (*ex* Article 52) includes the right to take up and pursue activities as self-employed persons as well as the right to set up and manage undertakings within the Community.

---

[50] See Nascimbene, note 7 above, at 10.

The Article, which prohibits discrimination on grounds of nationality restricting the right of establishment, applies expressly only to nationals of a Member State. Whereas a national from a third country can establish himself in, for instance, Sweden according to national law without any requirement of nationality, it is impossible for him to establish himself within the Union under EU law. The suitability of this insistence on nationality can be to a large extent called into question. Instead a concept of abode based on Community law would be an appropriate way of deciding those persons to whom EC law applies.

The same applies to social policy. For instance, whereas the social policy of, for example, Sweden is in substance not dependent on nationality, the EU's social policy is mainly tied to nationality. Here, it can equally be called into question whether nationality is an appropriate concept to use in order to decide which persons shall come within the scope of EC law. Instead, the criterion of abode could be used.

The conclusion is that legal abode in the Union, possibly conditional on permanent residence or residence over a certain period of time, is a more appropriate criterion than nationality in respect of free movement and other Community rights. It enables the development of a tradition of concepts common to EC law and corresponds more with the EC's principle of non-discrimination. Abode is a more objective concept than the subjective notion of nationality. Using the concept of abode also appears appropriate with regards to the various conventions on human rights. The EU has undertaken to abide by the European Convention for the Protection of Human Rights, and therefore has a duty towards those persons on the territories of the Member States to ensure that the rules are respected in the context of the EU.

Union citizenship already provides for rights in favour of non-Community nationals. The right to petition the European Parliament and the right to apply to the Ombudsman apply to everyone who is resident in an EU country. This should be built on further so that all other rights apply in favour of all inhabitants. There is no doubt that citizenship of the Union as it is today must be overhauled and redefined.

16

The Future of Environmental Rights in the European Union

PAVLOS Z. ELEFTHERIADIS*

I. INTRODUCTION

The question of protection from environmental damage is not new. Roman law had rules protecting third parties from activities that could have such effects. But this old question has taken on a new significance in the last fifty or sixty years due to changes brought about by new technology and its massive use. These new problems cannot be fully covered by the traditional means of private law, e.g. property and tort law. It is very hard, for example, to establish private law remedies in the case of commonly held resources, like air or water, or to identify causal links betweeen victims and perpetrators, or even identify current victims at all (as opposed to those in future generations). As a result, we now require better focused tools of public environmental regulation, something that is reflected in the rapid expansion of environmental law over the past few decades.

The idea of human rights to the environment is relatively novel and raises many interesting theoretical and doctrinal questions. They have to do both with the very idea of a 'right to the environment' and the general place of human rights in the international legal order and the European Union. Given the absence of 'a right to the environment' in existing catalogues of human rights in international instruments, the first and obvious question is what such a right could possibly be. Can we formulate such a right with enough precision to make it practically relevant? Or should we say instead that there is only a cluster of other rights that jointly compose a set of human rights related to the protection of the environment? This is a difficult theoretical question that requires some discussion of issues of political and legal theory.

A second set of questions is about existing law. Does the international law of human rights recognize a right or a cluster of rights to the environment? And is a 'right to the environment' a right of the first, second, or third 'generation' of rights? Is it perhaps possible to interpret already existing civil, political, social, and economic rights in the light of new environmental concerns?

* Many thanks to Malgosia Fitzmaurice, Joanne Scott, and Stephanos Stavros for very helpful suggestions and discussion. I have benefited greatly from comments I received at the Brussels conference from Dan Bodansky, Joxe Ramon Bengoetxea, Claire Kilpatrick, Martti Koskenniemi, Gerard Quinn, Patrick Twomey, and Bruno de Witte.

A third, more specific, question is focused on the position of the European Union with regard to human rights. Assuming that the international law of human rights does recognize something along the lines of a right or a set of rights to the environment, what could its effect be in European Union law? Are human rights to the environment part of Community law and, if so, how do they operate? By what methods can such a right or set of rights best be protected in the Community legal order? Should it be mainly addressed at the State or the Community level? Should it be raised against private parties?

It is necessary for us to address these questions directly. Policy proposals and a new agenda will necessarily depend on one's perspective on such preliminary assumptions. The main task of this chapter is, therefore, to construct a basic framework of law and theory, within which it will be possible to outline a policy of environmental human rights in the EU. We shall construct this framework by addressing the three general questions raised above. First, could there be a legal right to the environment? Secondly, is such a right recognized by international law? And, thirdly, what could its effect be in the European Union, taking into consideration the current state of Community law? Only at the end of this excursion into law and theory will we be able to develop and defend a policy agenda on environmental human rights in the European Union.

II. SHOULD THERE BE A 'HUMAN RIGHT TO ENVIRONMENTAL PROTECTION'?

Can we consistently speak of a 'human right to the environment'? Traditionally, fundamental or human rights have been associated with constitutional law. They have been bundles of claims, liberties, powers, or immunities against the State.[1] For example, the right to free speech that every American has by virtue of the First Amendment of the US Constitution is a combination of liberties to speak freely and immunities against possible restrictions by Congress. These public law rights should be distinguished from private law rights, that are raised against private parties and do not carry an immunity against legislative interference. Hence, rights arising from contract and tort are addressed against any private actor equally, but may be amended as a result of legislative action. These private law rights are not necessarily fundamental, in the sense that constitutions (or international law) do not require that they are afforded unconditional protection by courts (domestic or international) or other implementing agencies.

The idea of fundamental constitutional rights goes hand in hand with judicial review of legislative action, an idea pioneered by the *Federalist Papers*[2] and Chief Justice Marshall in *Marbury* v. *Madison*.[3] Behind this institutional arrangement lies

---

[1] I am using the analysis of rights proposed by W. Hohfeld, *Fundamental Legal Conceptions as Applied in Judicial Reasoning* (ed. by W.W. Cook, 1923).

[2] J. Madison, A. Hamilton, and J. Jay, *The Federalist Papers* (ed. by I. Kramnick, 1987). See also N. Bobbio, *The Age of Rights* (trans. by A. Cameron, 1996).

[3] *Marbury* v. *Madison*, 5 US (1 Cranch) 137, 2 LEd. 60 (1803).

the assumption that some values are so important to everyone (all citizens or all human beings, depending on one's domestic or international point of view) that they should never be violated by state power—even if the current political leaders wished to violate them. This position also grounds the fact that, as a feature of many international human rights treaties since 1945, international adjudication may prevail over state sovereignty.[4]

Can the state-based, traditional model of fundamental rights leave room for a right to environmental protection? Can we, in other words, conceive of an area of action that could similarly be out of reach for governments in the interest of environmental policy? The problem here is that environmentally harmful activities are more often than not activities of industries in the private sector (although it is different in the few remaining state-run economies, like China, Cuba, or North Korea, and was different in the former Soviet bloc). Hence, the question of environmental protection appears to be mainly a private law issue. Yet, in the light of the mounting evidence for the ability of contemporary technology to have extraordinary and unpredictable effects on the natural world and the difficulty of establishing a causal link between polluters and victims, we could conceive of a fundamental duty of governments to put some system of administrative regulation in place that would protect citizens and future generations from particularly serious harm. This would require at least a system of standard-setting or prohibitions, the granting or withholding of licences for environmentally problematic activities and the adequate supervision of compliance. We could, therefore, construct a duty of governments not to remain inactive in the face of grave environmental threats posed by modern industry and engineering projects. Moreover, once a system of regulation was in place, its overall administration and direction should then fall under the ambit of fundamental public law rights, such as that of fair and equal treatment, as well as all kinds of conditions of fair administrative procedure. Hence, a fundamental right to environmental protection could be a right against governments and other state agencies, which would bear some corresponding duty effectively to regulate the economic exploitation of natural resources.

This approach is reflected in some of the existing proposals for a 'human right to the environment'. For example, the UN conference on the Human Environment in Stockholm in 1972 adopted the Stockholm Declaration on the Human Environment, the first principle of which stipulates that there is a general duty, presumably binding primarily on governments, to protect the environment:

> Principle 1. Man has the fundamental right to freedom, equality and adequate conditions of life, in an environment of a quality that permits a life of dignity and well-being, and bears a solemn responsibility to protect and improve the environment for present and future generations.[5]

---

[4] The philosophical justifications behind the elevation of a small number of moral values such as autonomy and dignity to a level that governments cannot reach vary with one's choice of political morality. But this difficulty in justification does not pose a serious threat to human rights law. It must be sufficient to say that fundamental human rights are selected in domestic or international fora on the basis of a shared view of what is morally fundamental. What kinds of disagreement on justification may lie behind this outward agreement on results may be an interesting topic in its own right but need not be dealt with here.

[5] *Declaration of the UN Conference on the Human Environment*, A/CONF/48/14/Rev. 1 (1972), reprinted in P.W. Birnie and A.E. Boyle, *Basic Documents on International Law and The Environment* (1995), 4.

The World Commission on Environment and Development (WCED), which was set up by the UN in 1983 as an independent Working Group, concluded in 1987 that there is a fundamental human right to environmental protection, which was spelt out as follows:

> Article 1. All human beings have the fundamental right to an environment adequate for their health and well-being.[6]

More recently, the Ksentini Report on behalf of the Sub-Commission on Prevention of Discrimination and Protection of Minorities included in a 1994 'Draft Principles on Human Rights and the Environment' the following provisions:

> 1. Human rights, an ecologically sound environment, sustainable development and peace are interdependent and indivisible.
> 2. All persons have the right to a secure, healthy and ecologically sound environment. This right and other human rights, including civil, cultural, economic, political and social rights, are universal, interdependent and indivisible.[7]

The problem with these simple constructions of an environmental human right (and a corresponding obligation for administrative action) is that, except in the most obvious cases of inaction and harm, it would be very difficult to ascertain what constituted a violation. There are at least two kinds of problems here. First, the definition of an 'adequate' state of the environment. What level of environmental degradation is required to constitute a violation?[8] And, secondly, even if we solved the first riddle, what level of inertia or incompetence or what kind of poor judgement on the part of the regulatory authorities would constitute a violation of the right (and not just a difference of opinion about priorities)? These problems of environmental standards and agency make one pessimistic about the determinacy and effectiveness of a direct 'right to environmental protection'. If such a right were to come about, it would lead to serious institutional problems regarding the formation of economic and environmental policy, because it would be very difficult to show that identifying violations of the right by courts was anything more than policy-making by other means. The main question is therefore one of legitimacy: who is to make sensitive decisions about the use of natural resources in modern democracies, the elected leaders of a national economic policy or the unelected domestic or international judges and other officials? The ambiguity of a proposed 'right to environment' makes it very easy for the latter to substitute their own judgement on environmental policy for that of more obviously legitimate policy-makers and very difficult for them to show that this was not in fact the case. The issue of striking a balance between environmental preservation and economic development is difficult

---

[6] World Commission on Environment and Development, *Our Common Future (The Brundtland Report)* (1987), 308, cited in I. Koppen and K-H. Ladeur, 'Environmental Rights', in A. Cassese, A. Clapham, and J. Weiler (eds.), *Human Rights and the European Community: The Substantive Law* (1991), 30.

[7] *Human Rights and the Environment. Final Report of the Special Rapporteur*, E/CN.4/Sub.2/1994/9 (1994), 74, cited in A.E. Boyle, 'The Role of International Human Rights Law in the Protection of the Environment', in A. Boyle and M. Anderson (eds.), *Human Rights Approaches to Environmental Protection* (1996), 43–69, at 66.

[8] For some of these problems see G. Winter, 'Standard-Setting in Environmental Law', in G. Winter (ed.), *European Environmental Law: A Comparative Perspective* (1996), 109–28.

and contested. How much should this question be removed from the political agenda, and taken to ostensibly non-political, legal processes?

That a general 'human right to environmental protection' leads to such institutional anomalies and tensions is also the position taken by Professor Alan Boyle in the most recent extensive discussion of the matter from the point of view of international law.[9] For Boyle, a right to a decent, healthy, or viable environment poses problems of uncertainty and redundancy. The problem of uncertainty consists of the 'definitional problems' that 'are inherent in any attempt to postulate environmental rights in qualitative terms', so that what 'constitutes a satisfactory, decent, viable, or healthy environment is bound to suffer from uncertainty and ambiguity'.[10] The problem of 'redundancy' amounts to the fact that a new right to the environment 'would add little to what already exists in international environmental law',[11] especially in terms of recent multilateral treaties and the work of international organizations. Existing law imposes duties on States without emphasizing a corresponding 'human right' on the part of all citizens.[12] For Boyle:

> given the now extensive scope of international environmental law and policy, and their intrusion into all aspects of environmental protection, including the reserved domain of domestic sovereignty, what is left for a substantive human right to a decent environment to do that has not already been done? It is scarcely necessary to labour the point that international law already offers rules, principles and criteria for ensuring environmental quality. It is far from certain whether much would be added by reformulating these rules in explicit human rights terms, or that nothing would be lost in the attempt to do so on an anthropocentric basis.[13]

Our brief account of the possibility of a 'right to environment' and the arguments offered by Boyle in particular lead us to end this discussion in a rather negative way. Environmental concerns cannot be served very well by the construction of a simple and general human right to environmental protection against the State.

There is a new avenue open to us, however, still within the law of human rights. This is the incorporation of environmental concerns into existing human rights, such as the rights to life, property, and privacy. Instead of talking of a single and new right to the environment we may speak of human rights, meaning existing civil, political, and economic rights, regarding the environment. We will explore this possibility in the next section, as we survey existing institutions of international law.

---

[9] Boyle, note 7 above. A different view is put forward by Dinah Shelton, who writes that 'although human rights and environmental protection represent separate social values, the overlapping relationship between them can be resolved in a manner which will further both sets of objectives'. Moreover '[a] clear and narrowly defined international human right to a safe and healthy environment, currently emerging in international law, can contribute to this goal': D. Shelton, 'Human Rights, Environmental Rights, and the Right to Environment' (1991) 28 *Stanford Journal of International Law* 106.

[10] Boyle, note 7 above, at 50. [11] *Ibid.*, at 53. [12] *Ibid.*, at 53–7.

[13] *Ibid.*, at 56.

III. HUMAN RIGHTS TO THE ENVIRONMENT:
INTERNATIONAL PROTECTION

Although there have been efforts to introduce a direct right to environmental protection into the international law of human rights, such efforts have been unsuccessful.[14] Neither the Universal Declaration of Human Rights (UDHR), nor the European Convention of Human Rights (ECHR), nor the International Covenant of Civil and Political Rights (ICCPR) has any reference to a human right to environmental protection. We find references to the environment only in the International Covenant on Economic, Social and Cultural Rights (ICESCR) of 16 December 1966, in Article 12:

1. The States Parties to the present Covenant recognize the right of everyone to the enjoyment of the highest attainable standard of physical and mental health.
2. The Steps to be taken by the States Parties to the present Covenant to achieve the full realization of this right shall include those necessary for:
a) The provision for the reduction of the still-birth rate of infant mortality and for the health development for the child;
b) The improvement of all aspects of environmental and industrial hygiene;
c) The prevention, treatment and control of epidemic, endemic, occupational and other diseases;
d) The creation of conditions which would assure to all medical service and medical attention in the event of sickness.[15]

However, due to the well-known problems of implementation of the Covenant and the ambiguity regarding its justiciability,[16] this provision has not done much to establish an international human right to environmental protection. Moreover, the wording of this Article puts clear emphasis on human health and hygiene, so that it does not really address the full range of environmental concerns, i.e. the problem of future generations, the possibility of as yet unknown effects on biodiversity, etc.

Nevertheless, environmental concerns have found their way into the interpretation and protection of existing human rights. At the level of civil and political rights, the right to private life and the right to property have been found to have at least some effects on environmental protection. The ECHR, for example, provides in Article 8 that 'everyone has the right to respect for his private and family life, his home and his correspondence'. Before 1994 the European Court of Human Rights occasionally entertained the thought that environmental damage could possibly constitute a breach of Article 8, although the threshold was so high that no actual breach

[14] See generally D. McGoldrick, 'Sustainable Development and Human Rights: An Integrated Conception' (1996) 45 *International and Comparative Law Quarterly* 796; M. Anderson, 'Human Rights Approaches to Environmental Protection: An Overview', in Boyle and Anderson, note 7 above; K. Tomaševski, 'Environmental Rights', in A. Eide, C. Krause, and A. Rosas (eds.), *Economic, Social and Cultural Rights: A Textbook* (1995), 257; and Shelton, note 9 above.

[15] International Covenant on Economic, Social, and Cultural Rights, adopted by GA Res. 2200 A (XXI) (1966). In United Nations, *A Compilation of International Instruments* (1994), i, Part 1, 8.

[16] See e.g., M. Scheinin, 'Economic and Social Rights as Legal Rights', in Eide, Krause and Rosas, note 14 above, at 41; P. Alston, 'Making Economic and Social Rights Count: A Strategy for the Future' (1997) 68 *Political Quarterly* 188, and 'Economic and Social Rights', in L. Henkin and J.L. Hargrove (eds.), *Human Rights: An Agenda for the Next Century* (1994), 137.

was found.[17] But in the landmark case of *Lopez-Ostra* v. *Spain* in 1994,[18] the Court declared that the Spanish government had violated the right when it failed to prevent environmental damage caused by a waste-treatment plant built near the applicant's home. The crucial issue was that, even though the plant was privately owned, it started operating without a licence and the government failed to implement its own regulations and procedures. A close link between the plant and the local authority could also be established because the local authority had allowed the plant to be built on its land and the State had subsidized its construction. The Court awarded Mrs Lopez-Ostra damages for the harm suffered in the period in which the plant operated before it was eventually scaled down.

The Court's decision distinguished the issue of private life from that of health and opened Article 8 to a broad construction, sensitive to environmental harm:

> 51. Naturally, severe environmental pollution may affect individuals' well-being and prevent them from enjoying their homes in such a way as to affect their private and family life adversely, without, however, seriously endangering their health.[19]

As a result of the national authorities' failure to take 'the measures necessary for protecting the applicant's right to respect for her home and for her private and family life under Article 8'[20] the Court concluded that:

> despite the margin of appreciation left to the respondent State, the Court considers that the State did not succeed in striking a fair balance between the interest of the town's economic well-being—that of having a waste-treatment plant—and the applicant's effective enjoyment of her right to respect for her home and her private and family life.
>
> There has accordingly been a violation of Article 8.[21]

It is clear that the Court considers that Article 8 creates a positive duty of regulation and protection on the part of the State, so that state tolerance of environmentally noxious activities may constitute a breach. The traditional civil right to private and family life is not, therefore, restricted to a negative claim that the State not interfere, but also leads to positive claims.[22]

This position has been strengthened in the recent decision of the Court in *Guerra* v. *Italy*, which was decided in February 1998.[23] This case was about the toxic emissions of a chemical factory in the Italian town of Manfredonia. The Court held that:

> although the object of Article 8 is essentially that of protecting the individual against arbitrary interference by the public authorities, it does not merely compel the State to abstain from such interference: in addition to this primarily negative undertaking, there may be positive obligations inherent in effective respect for private or family life.[24]

---

[17] See e.g., R. Churchill, 'Environmental Rights in Existing Human Rights Treaties', in Boyle and Anderson, note 7 above, at 92–3.

[18] *Lopez-Ostra* v. *Spain,* ECHR (1995), Series A, No. 303–C; (1995) 20 EHRR 277–300. See McGoldrick, note 14 above, at 816–18.

[19] *Lopez-Ostra* v. *Spain*, note 18 above, at 293.   [20] *Ibid.*, at 296.   [21] *Ibid.*, at 297.

[22] See also the Commission's view on the relevance of environmental considerations, *a propos* the French nuclear testing in the Pacific. See *Tauira* v. *France*, App. No. 28204/95 (1995) 83 D&R 112. The application was unsuccessful, however, because it was not shown that the applicants were in fact victims of any harm.

[23] *Guerra and Others* v. *Italy* (116/1996/735/932), 19 Feb. 1998, not yet reported.

[24] *Ibid.*, at para. 58.

The Court added that 'severe environmental pollution may affect individuals' well-being and prevent them from enjoying their homes in such a way as to affect their private and family life adversely'. Considering the State's failure to provide essential information that would have enabled the residents of Manfredonia to assess the risks they and their families might run in the event of an accident if they continued to live near the factory, the Court found that the State 'did not fulfil its obligation to secure the applicants' right to respect for their private and family life, in breach of Article 8 of the Convention'.[25] It must be therefore clear that on the basis of *Lopez Ostra* v. *Spain* and *Guerra* v. *Italy*, we can safely conclude that Article 8 provides a solid basis for claiming adequate environmental protection.

A similar possibility arises with regard to the right to private property, which is protected by Article 1 of Protocol 1 to the European Convention: '[e]very natural or legal person is entitled to the peaceful enjoyment of his possessions'. Although we do not have a case stating the principle as clearly as *Lopez-Ostra*, the Commission of Human Rights has found that if pollution and other environmental degradation resulted in a substantial fall in the value of the property which was not subsequently compensated for, there would be a breach. In *S* v. *France* the Commission stated that although Article 1 of the First Protocol does not 'guarantee the right to enjoy possessions in a pleasant environment', high levels of noise would affect the value of the property and therefore could amount to an unlawful interference with possession.[26]

A further possibility is the use of rights to political participation to allow individuals and groups—including NGOs—to press environmental interests through the political process.[27] This is a different avenue from that pursued above, because it seeks to further environmental concerns politically, not through judicial decisions. It uses judicial means, i.e. the right to political participation, only to gain access to the decision-making process. Relevant political rights in this respect are a right to information, to political participation, and to a fair judicial resolution of disputes. The United Nations World Charter for Nature, for example, provides that '[a]ll persons, in accordance with their national legislation, shall have the opportunity to participate, individually or with others, in the formulation of decisions of direct concern to their environment, and shall have access to means of redress within their environment has suffered damage or degradation'.[28] The Rio Declaration on Environment and Development, adopted on 14 June 1992 at Rio de Janeiro, includes principle 10, which states that '[e]nvironmental issues are best handled with the participation of all concerned citizens, at the relevant level', and not only that 'each individual shall have appropriate access to information concerning the environment that is held by public authorities . . . and the opportunity to participate in decision-making

---

[25] *Guerra and Others* v. *Italy* (116/1996/735/932), 19 Feb. 1998, at para. 60. The applicants were awarded compensation for 'non-pecuniary damage'.

[26] *S* v. *France*, App. No. 13728/88 (1990) 65 D&R 250, 261. See Churchill, note 17 above, at 95 and R. Desgagné, 'Integrating Environmental Values into the European Convention on Human Rights' (1995) 89 *AJIL* 277–80. However, in this case the threshold was too high for the kind of nuisance involved and, unlike *Lopez Ostra*, the application failed.

[27] See generally H. Steiner, 'Political Participation as a Human Right' (1988) 1 *Harvard Human Rights Yearbook* 77; and T. Franck, 'The Emerging Right to Democratic Governance', (1992) 86 *AJIL* 46, and 'Democracy as a Human Right', in Henkin and Hargrove, note 16 above, at 73.

[28] 'World Charter for Nature', UN GA Res. 37/7 (1982), in Birnie and Boyle, note 5 above, at 20.

processes' but also that '[e]ffective access to judicial and administrative proceedings, including redress and remedy, shall by provided'.[29]

The requirement for participation in decisions relating to the environment can be seen as just a specific application of a broader principle of political participation enshrined in the international law of human rights. The ICCPR[30] requires in Article 25 that every citizen shall have the right 'to take part in conduct of public affairs, directly or through chosen representatives', to 'vote and to be elected at genuine periodic elections' and to 'have access, on general terms of equality, to public service in his country'. The First Protocol to the ECHR provides in Article 3 that the Parties 'undertake to hold free elections at reasonable intervals by secret ballot, under conditions which will ensure the free expression of the opinion of the people in the choice of the legislature'. Under Article 10 of the Convention one may be able to ground a right to receive information, when the information is especially important for the person or group of persons seeking it.[31] Finally, the right to a 'fair and public hearing' under Article 6(1) should guarantee a right to access to a court, if all else fails.

In this brief survey I have looked only at the expansion of the right to private life, the right to property, and the rights to political participation into areas that affect environmental protection. Concluding his far wider study of the integration of environmental concerns in the European Convention, Richard Desgagné has stated that 'protection of the environment has been recognised as an important public interest and it appears, in this sense, to be a value protected by the Convention'.[32] However, Desgagné adds a note of caution, observing that the individualist nature of the human rights machinery is not always an adequate means for the protection of the environment. Problems of causation, sufficient levels of harm at the individual case, and the inability to represent future generations make the human rights avenue a limited one:

> Human rights litigation under the Convention presents limited opportunities to foster the protection of the environment in general. Environmental protection has an important public facet that cannot be translated into an individual perspective and involves social choices that cannot be dealt with piecemeal. A system of protection of human rights, given its individualist bias, is not the best forum to further objectives that go beyond individual interests.[33]

---

[29] The Rio Declaration on Environment and Development, A/CONF.151/5/Rev.1 (1992), reprinted in (1992) 31 ILM 874.

[30] International Covenant on Civil and Political Rights, adopted by GA Res. 2200 A (XXI) (1966). In *International Instruments*, note 15 above, at 20.

[31] *X* v. *Federal Republic of Germany*, App. No. 8383/78 (1980) 17 D&R 227, 228–9. However, no such general right exists. See Desgagné, note 26 above, at 288 and F.G. Jacobs and R.C.A. White, *The European Convention on Human Rights* (1996), 223. In *Guerra* v. *Italy* the Court held that the freedom to receive information as a corollary of the freedom of the press, is clearly distinguishable from the case of environmental information. Accordingly, the freedom to receive information 'cannot be construed as imposing on a State, in circumstances such as those of the present case [concerning failure to inform of major accident hazards of certain industrial activities], positive obligations to collect and disseminate information of its own motion': *Guerra* v. *Italy*, note 23 above, at para. 53. The Court did not find a violation of Art. 10.

[32] Desgagné, note 26 above, at 293.
[33] *Ibid.*, at 294 (footnote omitted).

IV. THE PRESENT STATE OF EU LAW

In the last two sections I argued, first, that a 'right to the environment' cannot be determinate enough to be of practical use for human rights purposes and that, secondly, it seems more promising to incorporate environmental considerations into the scope of protection of existing human rights, such as the rights to private life, property, and political participation. Even then, however, the scope of human rights fell far short of the kinds of requirements needed for an effective environmental policy. Rights, therefore, could not possibly exhaust the field of environmental law. In this section I shall look at the general issue of the position of human rights in the EU legal order and will comment on the relation of such human rights with the existing framework for environmental policy in the EU.

Even though the European Court of Justice considers the Treaties of the European Communities as the 'Constitution' of Europe,[34] these treaties do not contain a catalogue of fundamental rights and freedoms that we find (meaningfully or not) in most national constitutions of the post-war era. Initially, the Court of Justice interpreted this in a straightforward way as an invitation to apply Community law without subjecting it to a human rights review.[35] After the strong reaction to this view by national courts, however, the Court changed its position, and it now considers that 'fundamental rights form an integral part of the general principles of [Community] law'.[36] Faced with the problem that such rights do not appear anywhere in the Community's legal materials, the Court has declared that it 'is bound to draw inspiration from constitutional traditions common to the Member States' and that 'international treaties for the protection of human rights on which the Member States have collaborated or of which they are signatories, can supply guidelines which should be followed within the framework of Community law'.[37]

But this 'common tradition' does not amount to an extension of Community competences to a general human rights review of Member States' actions. It has been a constant, and in my view correct, position of the Court of Justice that human rights issues arise for the Community only within its existing area of competence. Hence, the Court cannot pass judgment on the compliance of national measures that lie outside the scope of EC law.[38] In the *ERT* case, though, the Court went further than this

---

[34] *Opinion 1/91 On the Draft Agreement on an European Economic Area* [1991] ECR I–6079 [1992] 1 CMLR 245 and Case 294/83 *Parti Ecologiste 'Les Verts'* v. *European Parliament* [1986] ECR 1339. On the doctrine of the 'European Constitution' see F. Mancini, 'The Making of a Constitution for Europe' (1989) 26 *CML Rev.* 595; E. Stein, 'Lawyers, Judges and the Making of a Transnational Constitution' (1981) 75 *AJIL* 1; K. Lenaerts, 'Constitutionalism and the Many Faces of Federalism' (1990) 38 *American Journal of Comparative Law* 205–63; and J.H.H. Weiler, 'The Transformation of Europe' (1991) 100 *Yale Law Journal* 2403. My own views on this development appear in P. Eleftheriadis, 'Aspects of European Constitutionalism' (1996) 21 *European Law Review* 32, and 'Begging the Constitutional Question' (1998) 36 *Journal of Common Market Studies* 255.

[35] Cf. Case 1/58, *Stork* v. *High Authority* [1959] ECR 17 and Case 40/64, *Sgarlata and Others* v. *Commission* [1965] ECR 215. See P. Craig and G. De Burca, *EC Law: Texts, Cases and Materials* (2nd edn., 1998), 296.

[36] Case 4/73, *Nold KG* v. *Commission* [1974] ECR 491, at 507.   [37] *Ibid.*

[38] See A. Clapham, *Human Rights and the European Community: A Critical Overview* (1991) 29–51 and J.H.H. Weiler, 'Methods of Protection of Fundamental Human Rights in the European Community: Towards a Second and Third Generation of Protection', in A. Cassese, A. Clapham, and J. Weiler (eds.), *Human Rights and the European Community: Methods of Protection* (1991), 555, at 595–617.

and affirmed that it will also review the compatibility with 'general principles of law and in particular . . . fundamental rights' of derogations to the freedom to provide services.[39] Hence, not just the implementation of Community law, but also legitimate derogations therefrom, are subject to a human rights review.[40]

Because of the structure of the European Union, human rights can play a role only in the areas of competence of the EU. Since the Single European Act the EU has had wide competences in the area.[41] After the Maastricht amendments one of the tasks of the Community under Article 2 of the EC Treaty is to 'promote throughout the Community . . . sustainable and non-inflationary growth respecting the environment'. Specific competences include the following objectives, enshrined in Article 174 (*ex* Article 130r):

> 1. Community policy on the environment shall contribute to pursuit of the following objectives:
>   —preserving, protecting and improving the quality of the environment;
>   —protecting human health;
>   —prudent and rational utilisation of resources;
>   —promoting measures at international level to deal with regional or world-wide environmental problems.

Article 174(2) (*ex* Article 130r(2)) adds that:

> 2. Community policy on the environment shall aim at a high level of protection taking into account the diversity of situations in the various regions of the Community. It shall be based on the precautionary principle and on the principles that preventive action should be taken, that environmental damage should as a priority be rectified at source and that the polluter should pay. Environmental protection requirements must be integrated into the definition and implementation of other Community policies.

The decision-making procedure for such measures is outlined in Article 175(1) (*ex* Article 130s(1)), which provides mainly for the co-operation procedure outlined in Article 252 (*ex* Article 189c).[42]

Community environmental policy seeks to attain a high standard of environmental protection, but also takes into consideration the aim of creating an integrated common market. There is a tension between these objectives, especially when Member States seek to take stricter environmental measures than those endorsed at Community level.[43] Trying to strike a balance between the two, the *acquis communautaire* now includes a complex body of law concerning water pollution, air pollution,

---

[39] Case 260/89, *ERT* v. *Dimotiki Etairia Pliroforisis and Sotirios Kouvelas* [1991] ECR I–2925, at 2964.

[40] A very lively debate has taken place on whether the protection of human rights by the Court of Justice is adequate or systematic enough. I consider this discussion vital for adequate preparation for a policy for the new millennium and I will return to it in the last section of this chap. See mainly J. Coppell and A. O'Neill, 'The European Court of Justice: Taking Rights Seriously?' (1992) 29 *CMLRev* 669–92; G. de Burca, 'Fundamental Human Rights and the Reach of EC Law' (1993) 13 *Oxford Journal of Legal Studies* 283; and J.H.H. Weiler and N. Lockhart, 'Taking Rights Seriously: The European Court and the Fundamental Rights Jurisprudence' (1995) 32 *CML Rev.* 51–94 (part I) and 579–627 (part II).

[41] See e.g., J. Scott, *EC Environmental Law* (1998), 3–23; L. Krämer, *E.C. Treaty and Environmental Law* (1995), 41; A. Kiss and D. Shelton, *Manual of European Environmental Law* (1993), 18; J. H. Jans, *European Environmental Law* (1995), 1–35.

[42] See Krämer, note 41 above, at 71; Jans, note 41 above, at 35–44 and J.H. Jans, 'The Competences for EC Environmental Law' in Winter, note 8 above, at 317.

[43] For an overview see Jans, note 41 above, at 197.

dangerous substances, toxic waste, nuclear safety, and nature conservation. Besides these sectoral measures there are also environmental provisions that apply across sectors, such as the Environmental Impact Assessment Directive,[44] the Directive on the freedom of access to information on the environment,[45] the Regulation on a Community eco-label[46] scheme, and the Eco-Audit Regulation.[47]

What is the relevance of these arrangements for the protection of a set of human rights to environmental protection? It is clear that, according to the case law of the Court of Justice, the environment is an area where a human rights review of state action, either as implementation or as derogation, can be practised by the Court. Hence we can expect litigation from the point of view of human rights in the course of the implementation of the Community's environmental policy. Thus far, however, there has not been much in the way of a human rights case law of the Court in the area of the environment. A recent study of environmental rights in the Union has observed that, despite the existing secondary legislation, there is not much scope for 'substantive rights to the environment under EC law' nor is this absence 'mitigated by truly effective participatory rights'.[48]

The Amsterdam Treaty of 1997 has not brought many changes in this field. The new Treaty has introduced a number of important changes to the environmental aspect of the Union Treaties but, despite specific proposals from the Commission and some Member States, it does not introduce a fundamental right to environmental protection. It changes only some of the institutional objectives and procedures.[49]

The Treaty introduces 'sustainable development' as a specific objective of both at the level of the Union and the Community. Article 2 (*ex* Article B) of the TEU will read:

> The Union shall set itself the following objectives: . . .
> —to promote economic and social progress and to achieve balanced and sustainable development. . .

Similarly, the new Article 2 of the TEC, will state that the Community shall promote 'balanced and sustainable development of economic activities' and 'a high level of protection and improvement of the quality of the environment'. The inclusion of a 'high level of protection' appears also in the new Article 95 (*ex* Article 100A), where it now forms one of the aims of all the Community institutions, Commission, Parliament, and Council, in the process of completing the internal market. Both the maintenance and the introduction of stricter national measures will be allowed according to the new conditions outlined in Article 95.

An important addition is the principle of integration of environmental protection into all sectoral policies. A new Article 3D of the TEC will read:

---

[44] Council Dir. 85/337/EEC [1985] OJ L175/40.

[45] Council Dir. 90/313/EEC [1990] OJ L158/56. On other information requirements see Jans, note 41 above, at 288.

[46] Council Reg. 880/92 [1992] OJ L99/1.   [47] Council Reg. 1836/93 [1993] OJ L168/1.

[48] S. Douglas-Scott, 'Environmental Rights in the European Union—Participatory Democracy or Democratic Deficit?', in Boyle and Anderson, note 7 above, at 128.

[49] For an excellent overview of the changes introduced by the Treaty of Amsterdam in the area of the environment see G. Van Calster and K. Deketelaere, 'Amsterdam, the Intergovernmental Conference and Greening the EU Treaty' (1998) 7 *European Environmental Law Review* 12–25.

Environmental protection requirements must be integrated into the definition and implementation of Community policies and activities referred to in Article 3, in particular with a view to promoting sustainable development.

The Treaty also introduces a change in the process of decision-making, according to which the procedure followed will be that of Article 251 (*ex* Article 189b), the new simplified co-decision procedure:

The Council, acting in accordance with the procedure referred to in Article 189b and after consulting the Economic and Social Committee and the Committee of the Regions, shall decide what action is to be taken by the Community in order to achieve the objectives referred to in Article 130r.

All in all, the new Treaty will change some aspects of European environmental law, will strengthen the environmental aspects of Community policy, and will simplify and clarify some procedures, but it is not likely to affect the protection of environmental human rights in the European Union.

V. A HUMAN RIGHTS POLICY: THREE VIEWS

When we try to think of a policy for human rights in general we are immediately confronted with the problem that there are many different approaches and preferences, not always consistent with one another. This variety arises because there are in fact great disagreements about rights and their mode of protection. Any policy proposal in the area of human rights has to face this diversity directly, because any proposal will itself depend on a set of assumptions about the content and purpose of human rights. Different strategies will, therefore, flow from different views regarding the content and purpose of human rights. These disagreements are particularly relevant in the case of rights to the environment, which are not an established part of the catalogue of human rights but rights of a new generation, requiring in the main positive state action. Here I shall take up this challenge directly and briefly outline three rival views on human rights that I think summarize well the available options for a human rights policy.

The first conception of human rights is an 'aggregative' view. According to this position, human rights are part of a policy for maximizing human welfare and serving important human interests. In other words, the general point of protecting human rights is part of the process of progressive and constant improvement of the conditions of life. Hence, a human rights policy ought to aim to 'maximize' in a straightforward aggregative sense the satisfaction of these important interests. This flexible position on rights is very popular among human rights activists. Among theorists it is taken mainly by indirect consequentialists in the tradition of John Stuart Mill and is also reflected in the view of the 'interest theory' of rights.[50]

---

[50] See J.S. Mill, 'Utilitarianism', in J. S. Mill and J. Bentham, *Utilitarianism and Other Essays* (ed. by Alan Ryan, 1987), 272. On the 'interest' theory of rights see J. Waldron, 'Introduction', in J. Waldron (ed.), *Theories of Rights* (1984), 9; J. Raz, *The Morality of Freedom* (1986), 165; N. MacCormick, 'Rights in Legislation', in P.M.S. Hacker and J. Raz (eds.), *Law, Morality and Society* (1977), 189; and

The second conception is a 'pluralist' view, according to which there is nothing to be maximized in the protection of human rights. Human rights seek to secure a minimum standard for the protection of a limited number of important values or interests. This view is pluralist in two senses. First, because it recognizes that there are plural rights that make sometimes conflicting claims. The conflict of rights makes it necessary carefully to balance one against others—for example, property against free speech, as in the case of picketing. Secondly, this view is pluralist because it recognizes also the co-existence of plural values and choices outside human rights such as democracy and self-government, and is therefore careful to restrict the scope of human rights to only one small range of important issues. What lies outside that scope should belong to the political process of government, which is better suited to resolving them. This view is reflected in the views of liberal theorists such as Ronald Dworkin, Jeremy Waldron, and Norberto Bobbio.[51]

The third conception is an 'exclusionary' view. It shares with the pluralist view the emphasis on minimum standards, but parts with it on the extent to which state action ought to be involved in the process. The exclusionary view introduces a vital distinction between negative and positive action. Whereas the pluralists would recognize that the idea of human rights is flexible enough to accommodate concerns that require positive governmental action, the exclusionary view would deny that. Human rights for this view are negative rights operating mainly as judicially imposed side-constraints on the State's action. This is the view of human rights taken, for example, by Maurice Cranston in his well-known *What Are Human Rights?* and by American constitutional theorists such as Richard Epstein and philosophers like Robert Nozick.[52]

It must be obvious that these rival views of human rights will end up proposing three different strategies for a human rights policy. The aggregative view will seek to promote human welfare through rights as much as it can. It will therefore always propose the expansion of rights into ever wider areas and will constantly work on the dynamic reworking of older ideas in the light of new circumstances of social life. The second view will maintain a narrower focus on adequate protection of minimum standards in as many cases as possible, but will not necessarily propose any ambitious expansion. The exclusionary view, similarly, will focus on minimum standards, but its focus will be even narrower. It will seek to ensure that the government does not transgress its permitted area of action.

These three views are not always presented coherently and systematically as theories of human rights. More often they form the implicit assumptions on which an interpretation of existing law or a policy proposal will be based. They are foundations,

---

L. W. Sumner, *The Moral Foundation of Rights* (1987), 45–53. The origins of this debate are in Jhering's attack on Savigny's 'will theory'. See e.g. R. von Jhering, *Geist des Römischen Rechts auf den verschiedenen Stufen seiner Entwicklung* (4th edn. 1888), iv, 327–50.

[51] See e.g., R. Dworkin, *Taking Rights Seriously* (1978), and *A Matter of Principle* (1986); J. Waldron, *Liberal Rights: Collected Papers 1981–1991* (1993), and 'A Rights-Based Critique of Constitutional Rights' (1993) 13 *Oxford Journal of Legal Studies* 18 and Bobbio, note 2 above.

[52] M. Cranston, *What Are Human Rights?* (1973); R. Nozick, *Anarchy, State, and Utopia* (1974); R. Epstein, *Takings: Private Property and the Power of Eminent Domain* (1985), and 'Two Conceptions of Civil Rights', in E.F. Paul, F.D. Miller Jr., and J. Paul (eds.), *Reassessing Civil Rights* (1991), 38.

rather than end-results, of arguments. But because they lead to different interpretations and policy proposals, they ought to be distinguished as different approaches to human rights law. Hence, in the next section we will survey some possible policy proposals for environmental human rights in the EU, bringing out into the open the link between particular proposals and the underlying, aggregative, pluralist, or exclusionary approaches to rights. I shall make it clear that my own preference is for a pluralist approach, and in the course of the argument I shall outline a pluralist position for environmental human rights in the EU.

VI. HUMAN RIGHTS TO THE ENVIRONMENT IN THE EU

How could the protection of human rights to the environment in the EU be improved? Obviously one should aim at reducing the number of violations or reducing their seriousness. In the late 1990s the situation is far better than it was a decade ago. Partly as a result of sustained pressure from environmental organizations and groups, governments and public opinion at large are now far more conscious of environmental risks than they were a few years ago. Nevertheless, the imperative for economic exploitation of natural resources cannot go away, and it will continue to pose serious environmental threats. Considering that private law measures, e.g. actions in tort or property law, are very rarely sufficient to prevent environmental damage, the key problem will remain the adequacy of national measures in the face of strong pressure from polluting industries and businesses.

A policy for human rights to the environment in the EU may take three forms. First, it may suggest constitutional changes, i.e. reform of the treaties in order to include a new set of fundamental principles or competences for the Union. Secondly, it may propose secondary legislation that may operate well under the current state of the Treaties. And, thirdly, there may be a plan of action under the existing primary and secondary law, by way, for example, of giving real effect to existing measures. The resourceful and imaginative use of already available legal means by organizations, activists, and ordinary citizens may prove far more effective in the way of protecting human rights to the environment than any new declarations from the top.

A. Constitutional Changes

Taking into account the changes brought about by the Amsterdam Treaty, there is little one would wish to add to the description of Community competences in the way of a comprehensive coverage of environmental protection and sustainable development. The most important question in this respect concerns a 'right to the environment' in a new Bill of Rights for the EU. The question whether such a right ought to be recognized depends first of all on one's general view on the desirability of a Bill of Rights for the EU.

Now, if the Treaties are going to be a real Constitution for Europe, they ought to have real constitutional provisions. In the present state of Community law, even though the European Court of Justice calls the Treaties a 'European Constitution', they do not look remotely like a constitution at all. They do not constitute a polity outlining fundamental institutions, powers, etc., but build on the existing institutions and constitutions of Member States. If this arrangement has served us well so far, there may be no need to change it. However, anyone who wishes to see a true federal European State should press for a European Constitution and therefore a new Bill of Rights. I shall not pass judgement on this issue here, since I am myself ambivalent about the need for a European Constitution. I will only suggest that all the values that European integration wishes to promote, such as peace and prosperity in Europe, a pan-European area of civil and political rights without discrimination, and a truly liberal and multi-cultural political community could be achieved without the erection of a European super-State.[53] Or, to put it even more cautiously, it has yet not been shown by anyone that a new 'European Constitution' is a necessary condition for the success of these objectives.

If a new Bill of Rights is proposed, should a right to the environment be part of it? In fact, the Commissioner for the Environment, Ritt Bjerregard, had proposed that 'the right to a clean and healthy environment' be included in the Treaty on the European Union as 'a fundamental citizen's right'.[54] This proposal was not endorsed, however, at the inter-governmental conference of 1996–7. But should the right be endorsed in a Community Bill of Rights of a future inter-governmental conference?

Here the choice between aggregative, pluralist, and exclusionary views is relevant. For the first position, the answer should be yes. For the other two, it must be no. For the aggregative view, nothing is to be lost by a 'dynamic' expansion of rights. If the objective is to maximize the protection of rights (and therefore maximize the protection of the interests that these rights serve) then nothing is lost by the new addition. A new avenue of legal argument will only help in the direction of expanding as far as possible the scope of the beneficial work of rights.

The exclusionary view will take the opposite view. Any expansion of 'positive' rights will damage the integrity of a human rights system and should be avoided. But this view is uninteresting because it is far too restrictive. It has not been a popular view in Europe and I shall not discuss it further.[55] For the pluralist view, however, which takes a narrower view of rights than the aggregative, but a wider view than the exclusionary, two problems may arise from such an expansion. First, the expansion of one range of rights may damage the protection of other rights. Secondly, the expansion to new areas of human rights may damage values other than individual rights and especially the institutional balance between courts and political bodies.[56] More judicial powers for scrutiny of environmental policies may upset the institutional equilibrium between legal constraints and democratically accountable

---

[53] See Garton Ash, 'Europe's Endangered Liberal Order' (1998) 77 *Foreign Affairs* 51–61.

[54] See Van Calster and Deketelaere, note 49 above, at 25.

[55] An avalanche of arguments have attacked the libertarian political theory that such a view draws on. See e.g., J. Paul (ed.), *Reading Nozick: Essays on Anarchy, State, and Utopia* (1981); J. Wolff, *Robert Nozick: Property, Justice and the Minimal State* (1991); and G. A. Cohen, *History, Labour and Freedom* (1988).

[56] For an argument along those lines see J. Waldron, 'Liberal Rights: Two Sides of the Coin' in Waldron, *Liberal Rights*, note 51 above, at 26.

processes. Here, Boyle's points are decisive.[57] This problem will necessarily arise if Boyle is right in pointing out the open-endedness and ambiguity to the notion of a 'right to the environment'. Hence, the pluralist view will be drawn to the position that environmental concerns are best protected as aspects of existing civil, political, and economic human rights, and not as a separate category altogether.

This was also the conclusion endorsed by Koppen and Ladeur in their 1991 contribution to the project on 'The Human Rights Challenge':

> A constitutionalization of environmental protection can take the form of a subjective individual right . . . or an objective Community goal. The disadvantage of the first option is its limited justiciability: the content of an individual right to environmental protection is hard to define in legal terms and does not fit within an existing structure of theoretically delimited legal concepts. This is true on the national level, but above all on the supranational level.[58]

B. Changes of Secondary Legislation

Should there be new secondary legislation to make rights to the environment more effective? Again, the disagreements between the aggregative and the pluralist views are significant. The first will outline a programme of appropriate legislation, reaching the outer limits of what is realistically possible in the present political climate. The pluralists will be more cautious.

Proponents of the aggregative approach would take this view because they probably considered the right to environmental protection along the lines of other rights to 'positive' state action, such as those we find in the catalogue of social, economic, and cultural rights. According to the principle of 'progressive realization' of these rights, one expects governments to undertake, as a matter of a human rights obligation, a programme of activities realizing the social, economic, and cultural rights outlined in the respective documents.[59] The focus here is on the 'needs' of the people involved and the end-result we seek to achieve in terms of the essential interests of those involved. Hence, any 'additional' protection of the environment by means of secondary legislation would contribute to a 'human rights policy'.

Here a pluralist view will invite us to be careful not to confuse human rights with policy in general. We are running the risk of forgetting the special and uncompromising nature of human rights standards. What matters from this point of view is the minimum standards that can or ought to be protected judicially.[60] Hence, there is a need to define carefully those areas that matter most from the point of view of human rights, and those that are open to the discretion of decision-makers. Note that the disagreement here is not between proponents of a 'first' as opposed to a 'second'

---

[57] See Boyle, note 7 above.   [58] Koppen and Ladeur, note 6 above, at 42.

[59] D. Trubek, 'Economic, Social and Cultural Rights in the Third World: Human Rights Law and Human Needs Programs', in T. Meron (ed.), *Human Rights in International Law: Legal and Policy Issues* (1984), 205, at 217. See also J. Häusermann, 'The Realisation and Implementation of Economic, Social and Cultural Rights', in R. Beddard and D. Hill, *Economic, Social and Cultural Rights: Progress and Achievement* (1991), 47.

[60] Such a view is taken, e.g., by Philip Alston, who proposes that more work is needed in order to establish 'benchmarks'—even on a voluntary basis by States—by which we could assess whether States are respecting economic and social rights or not: Alston, 'Making Economic and Social Rights Count', note 16 above, at 191.

generation of rights, nor of 'negative' and 'positive' obligations. The issue is clearly about positive obligations to provide environmental protection, and the disagreement is about an 'aggregative' or a non-aggregative view of the role of human rights. The general point was well made by Joseph Weiler when he pointed out that identifying 'low' and 'high' levels of protection—as if these things could be measured quantitatively—is false:

> However, this contradistinction of 'high' and 'low' standards is in my view erroneous. Almost invariably human rights issues posit a conflict between communal . . . and individual interest which must be balanced. Sometimes, the balancing is between conflicting individual interests . . . A so-called 'low' level of individual protection might signify a considered value choice *at the constitutional level* between collectivity and individuality with a corresponding stake in such a balance and an explicit or implicit rejection of the *values* underlying a different choice.[61]

Hence, from a pluralist point of view, a view that recognizes the value of self-government and autonomy, it is appropriate that environmental policy and the required 'balancing' of different values is in the hands of political institutions that are open to public scrutiny. Secondary legislation must balance the requirements of environmental protection on the one hand and economic development on the other. These choices are best made by political processes and not by courts. A human rights policy should rather be concerned with the kinds of violations that, because of their seriousness, lie beyond the 'margin of appreciation' and should therefore be outside the reach of governments.

From this perspective one would expect that secondary legislation should enhance procedures that would safeguard the continued respect of environmental rights. From this point of view one would expect a more developed system of representation in environmental decisions, through an improved flow of information and more active participation. It is important in this respect that the Amsterdam Treaty will introduce a new Article 255 (*ex* Article 191A) into the TEC, concerning a more transparent decision-making procedure for the Community as a whole:

> 1. Any citizen of the Union, and any natural or legal person residing or having its registered office in a Member State, shall have a right of access to European Parliament, Council and Commission documents, subject to the principles and the conditions to be defined in accordance with paragraphs 2 and 3.
> 2. General principles and limits on grounds of public or private interest governing this right of access to documents shall be determined by the Council, acting in accordance with the procedure referred to in Article 189b within two years of the entry into force of the Treaty of Amsterdam.
> 3. Each institution referred to above shall elaborate in its own Rules of Procedure specific provisions regarding access to its documents.

It is very important that the new provisions open up the decision-making process to outsiders and make it more transparent than it is today.

---

[61] Weiler, note 38 above, at 588.

C. Possibilities for Resourceful Litigation

There is a general problem with the existing case law of the Court of Justice. It was noted by Andrew Clapham in the following words:

It has to be admitted that although the Court has increasingly referred to the Convention, the European Social Charter, international treaties, and constitutional principles and traditions, the rights contained therein have hardly been developed by the Court, and they have rarely been relied on to give real concrete protection to an individual.[62]

Weiler has also noted the unease with the approach taken by the Court so far:

If there is distrust it is not distrust of a Court overreaching itself in protecting the individual, but of a Court not reaching far enough.[63]

A major debate took place over this issue, *a propos* a provocative study by Jason Coppel and Aidan O'Neill, who argued that the Court 'subordinates human rights to the end of closer economic integration in the Community' by treating 'human rights, and in particular their place in any normative hierarchy, in a confused and ambiguous way'.[64]

The only effective answer to such a criticism would be the gradual construction of a substantive human rights doctrine by the Court of Justice. In the area of the environment one hopes that examples such as the case of *Lopez Ostra* will inspire the Court into endorsing the existence of claimable positive obligations on the part of States and the Community. The rights to private life and to property are clear candidates for such development. Also, rights to information and participation should be vigorously defended. One hopes that cases with this content will arise in national courts and find their way into the Court of Justice through preliminary references. It is the responsibility of environmental activists to pursue these avenues systematically and with some imagination and resourcefulness.

A second major doctrinal issue with reference to environmental protection is that of the effect on third parties. Should the Court of Justice decide that it is a principle of EC law that human rights immediately cover private parties? Andrew Clapham has defended such a view in a number of writings.[65] He has said, for example, that in his view the Court should take a 'victim oriented approach to the question of rights'.[66]

Again, this can best be seen as a disagreement between an aggregative and a pluralist position. One could understand Clapham's thesis better if one took an aggregative view of rights that linked rights with persons' welfare or needs. It would be enough, for such a view, that a person had suffered some loss to trigger human rights concerns. By contrast for a pluralist position the question of agency, who did what

---

[62] Clapham, note 38 above, at 50.   [63] Weiler, note 38 above, at 570–1.

[64] Coppel and O'Neill, note 40 above. See also de Burca, note 40 above; and Weiler and Lockhart, note 40 above. Coppel and O'Neill made a good case for the weak commitment of the ECJ to human rights, but spoiled their argument with an irritating insistence that there is clearly such a thing as a 'fundamental right to life for the unborn'. Their certainty obscures the fact that this is clearly a very contested issue, both in moral philosophy and in constitutional law.

[65] See Clapham, note 38 above, and also *Human Rights in the Private Sphere* (1993) and 'The Privatisation of Human Rights' (1995) 1 *European Human Rights Law Review* 20–32.

[66] Clapham, note 38 above, at 103.

to whom, would be paramount. This is well illustrated by the fact that when people suffer a loss of their bodily integrity or liberty, this is not always a violation of their fundamental rights. A man in prison properly and fairly convicted for a crime is un-free, but his fundamental right to liberty is not thereby violated. Similarly, a poor man living in appalling squalor may be below the standard of 'adequate living conditions', but his social and economic rights need not thereby be violated, since he may either be on religious vows of self-sacrifice or just very lazy.

For this reason, pluralists would not begin from the 'victim's' perspective but would probably like to know who is acting. This is important in order to maintain the distinction between a public sphere, where more constraints and more powers apply, and a private sphere, where the main consideration is liberty. This means that duties of the public sphere should not burden private agents, whereas liberties of the private sphere should not benefit public bodies. Political morality is a special case of morals precisely because the exercise of political power is a unique phenomenon. We would lose our perspective on these issues—and weaken the principle of liberty—if we conflated public power with private actions and imposed as a matter of general policy stringent requirements of public responsibility on all private actors.

For the view supported here, the existence of fundamental constitutional rights means just that an area of action is taken away from the discretion of governments for the benefit of individuals or groups. Hence, governments cannot, for example, torture or arbitrarily imprison and kill their political opponents, nor can they restrict the free circulation of political ideas, however much this would promote their state 'interests'. This also means that, strictly speaking, if a terrorist group of deranged political radicals started torturing and imprisoning their own political 'opponents', this would not by itself constitute a violation of the victims' constitutional rights.[67] It would be a violation of other rights arising in private and criminal law. In fact, what is going on here, however despicable, has little to do with human rights, strictly speaking, since these enter the picture only when we are discussing the activity of state agents. The relevant law in cases of private actors is ordinary criminal or tort law, which should be sufficient and effective.

The question of agency is therefore paramount in any discussion of fundamental rights, and the issue of the bearer of the corresponding duties is crucial. The end-result of a private action may of course be a tragedy. Yet the violation of fundamental rights should not be confused with tragedies. Wrongs that private parties do may be as awful as those of government agents, but this is not sufficient to show that they constitute the same wrong. There are different reasons for condemning private and public violence.[68] To say this is not to say that private is in any way preferable or less blameworthy. It is only to say that there are different ways of assessing public and private actions. It must, therefore, be wrong to believe that human rights can have a monopoly over our legal, political, and moral thinking.

---

[67] Unless the government tolerates this activity by inactive or incompetent policing. It must be an element of the protection of fundamental human rights that there be an effective criminal justice system. A systematic policy of allowing crime to go unpunished would clearly be a violation of the autonomy and dignity of the actual and potential victims.

[68] In fact, public violence is often valuable, as in the case of law enforcement. It is very rarely the case that private violence is valuable (only in cases of self-defence and, perhaps, in sports).

VII. CONCLUSIONS

We have therefore outlined the following framework for environmental human rights in the EU. First, there is no compelling reason for introducing a new human right to environmental protection. Secondly, existing civil, political, and social rights may incorporate environmental concerns into their range of application. Recent case law of the European Court and Commission of Human Rights confirms this. Thirdly, the wide competences of the EU and the existing secondary legislation in this area, in conjunction with the existing provisions of international instruments regarding the rights to private life, to property, and political participation would allow for a substantive elaboration of fundamental principles of human rights regarding environmental protection by the Court of Justice. This has not yet happened, but could happen if sufficiently innovative and resourceful litigation was started within the Member States and was forwarded via preliminary references to Luxembourg. This is a responsibility of environmental activists as well as the Court for the years to come.

Finally, in this, as in other areas of law and morals, any policy proposals must not pursue an objective single-mindedly but must provide for a balance between a number of different priorities. In this case effectiveness of environmental protection must be balanced against economic growth and the right to self-government, i.e. the right of States and communities to do things their own way and draw the line where they see fit. It must be a mistake to believe that these conflicts can be reduced to a maximization of some elusive human 'welfare' or the satisfaction of human 'need'. The pluralism of values makes it necessary for us to seek the right balance between conflicting but equally pressing objectives.

F

Human Rights in External Relations

17

Holding Multinational Corporations Accountable for Human Rights Abuses: A Challenge for the EC

MENNO T. KAMMINGA*

If the [multinational enterprise] poses a threat to human freedom it is because of its peculiar effectiveness. Its capacity to pursue a centralized and coordinated strategy removes decision-making power far from the people affected by it.

D.F. Vagts, 'The Multinational Enterprise: A New Challenge for Transnational Law' (1970) 83 *Harv. L Rev.* 791.

I. INTRODUCTION

That the world's largest multinational corporations[1] (MNCs) are more powerful and influential than many States has been a cliché since the 1960s. However, it remains a point worth stressing because, if anything, the trend has intensified in recent years. By consistently privatizing and deregulating their own economies and by liberalizing international trade and capital movements States have substantially reduced their own influence on the daily lives of their citizens.[2] The decline of the nation State has been accompanied by the rise to power of the entities that have been able to take particular advantage of these developments: MNCs. These international actors increasingly escape control by States because they are able freely to move capital and investments to wherever conditions are most favourable. As a result, they are more and more becoming truly stateless, without loyalty to any

---

* I am grateful for the valuable research assistance provided by Serge Bronkhorst.

[1] The simplest definition of a multinational corporation is 'an enterprise which owns or controls production or service facilities outside the country in which it is based'. There is no generally accepted label for such an entity. The UN Economic and Social Council has for murky reasons embraced the term 'transnational corporation'. See P. Muchlinski, *Multinational Enterprises and the Law* (1995), 13. The OECD and the ILO on the other hand, continue to employ the term 'multinational' enterprise. The legal literature is divided between these two terms. This chap. sticks to the term 'multinational' because 'transnational' conjures up outdated images of the New International Economic Order and related ideological battles.

[2] The analysis contained in this para. is based on V.A. Schmidt, 'The New World Order, Incorporated: The Rise of Business and the Decline of the Nation-State' (1995) 124 *Daedalus* 75–106.

particular State. The international institutions through which these liberalization strategies have been pursued, such as the IMF, WTO, EC, and NAFTA, have generally neglected to give attention to the social effects of their measures. There has been no concerted effort to supplement the international supervisory system that has been directed at States, such as the international machinery for the protection of human rights, by a similar system focused on MNCs.

As a matter of fact, MNCs do not necessarily have a negative impact on human rights. In many cases foreign direct investment by MNCs has a positive effect on respect for social and economic rights in the host State, through the creation of jobs and by generally raising the standards of living. One statistical study also found a positive association between foreign direct investment and respect for civil and political rights.[3] However, the study does not demonstrate that respect for civil and political rights actually improves as a result of foreign direct investment. It merely shows that MNCs generally prefer to invest in States that respect civil and political rights. This seems self-evident, not only because such States provide a more stable investment climate but also because investment in such countries is less likely to result in negative publicity for the corporation.

The abuses can be divided into two broad categories: those committed in collusion with the home State and those committed in collusion with the host State. The former category now seems to belong to a bygone era. It includes the assistance by United Fruit in the coup against the government of Guatemala in 1954, the involvement of ITT in the overthrow of the government of Salvador Allende in Chile in 1973 and the role of Elf Aquitaine in the overthrow of the government of Congo-Brazzaville in 1997. These abuses, as well as lesser forms of interference into the internal affairs of the host State, are of course part of a long-standing tradition going back to the British and Dutch East India Companies.

These days, an MNC is much more likely to collude with the host State than with the home State. This is because host States now tend to take a very different attitude to MNCs. They are competing for their favours and they are actually begging them to come and invest in their territories. This phenomenon can be observed, for example, at the annual World Economic Forum in Davos where presidents and prime ministers come to pay their respects to the captains of industry and to explain the attractions of their investment climate. As a result of this new economic climate, the prohibition of interference in internal affairs that was propagated as an antidote against MNCs in the 1960s and 1970s has been turned round from a weapon of the critics into a weapon of the MNCs. The critics of Shell in Nigeria, for example, did not want the company to leave the country. They wanted it to stay and use its influence to protect the Ogoni people against the Nigerian government. Shell's response was that unfortunately it was unable to do so because that would amount to interference in Nigeria's internal affairs.[4] Cases such as this are currently the typical ones for which adequate accountability mechanisms need to be devised.

---

[3] W.H. Meyer, 'Human Rights and MNCs: Theory Versus Quantitative Analysis' (1996) 18 *HRQ* 368–97.

[4] S. Skogly, 'Complexities in Human Rights Protection: Actors and Rights Involved in the Ogoni Conflict in Nigeria' (1997) 15 *NQHR* 52.

Most likely to collude in repression with the host State are MNCs which engage in the extraction of raw materials.[5] This is because of the mutual dependence of the MNC and the host State in this branch of industry. Unlike other industries, MNCs engaged in the extraction of raw materials usually have a limited choice of location. In order to obtain the necessary concessions they require a close relationship with the host State, whether it has a repressive regime or not. As a result, an MNC involved in the extraction of raw materials and the host State often find themselves in the same boat together.

When a weak host State and a strong MNC share the same interests, for example the protection of the company's production facilities against perceived outside threats, there may be a strong temptation to have the MNC finance, and thereby closely control, the maintenance of law and order by the security forces around the production facilities. When such privatization or semi-privatization of state functions occurs, the obvious question that arises is whether an MNC that has taken over such functions should not be held accountable according to the same international human rights standards as the State from which it has acquired them.

A couple of examples from different parts of the world may illustrate this privatization process. In Nigeria, a massacre of some eighty people occurred at Umuechem in November 1990 after Shell had called in the Mobile Police Force, a paramilitary force, to protect its installations and personnel. Shell has also purchased handguns for the Nigerian police.[6] In Colombia, British Petroleum admitted in September 1996 that it had been paying the Colombian army to protect its installations in spite of the fact that the Colombian army has a notoriously had human rights record. BP has also been accused of providing lethal training to the Colombian police through the services of a private British security firm.[7] In India, the Dabhol Power Company (a joint venture between three US-based MNCs: Enron, General Electric, and Bechtel) has been paying the state police in order to provide police protection against demonstrators. The police officers in question have routinely used excessive force against the local villagers when they were peacefully protesting against the establishment of the power plant in their community.[8]

The problem is not that all MNCs consistently engage in serious human rights abuses. The problem is that almost three decades after Professor Vagts made his point quoted at the beginning of this chapter, MNCs still largely escape international legal scrutiny.[9] The temptation to boost profits by conspiring in human rights abuses with the host State may therefore prove irresistible. An MNC typically consists of a parent enterprise and a number of foreign affiliates. Because prescriptive jurisdiction is primarily exercised on the basis of territoriality it follows that an

[5] See D.L. Spar, 'Multinationals and Human Rights: A Case of Strange Bedfellows' (1998) 8 *Human Rights Interest Group Newsletter* No. 1, 13–16.

[6] Amnesty International, *Nigeria: Time to End Contempt for Human Rights*, Amnesty International Index: AFR 44/14/96 (Nov. 1996), 25.

[7] Amnesty International, *Colombia: British Petroleum Risks Fuelling Human Rights Crisis through Military Training*, Amnesty International Index: AMR 23/44/97 (June 1997).

[8] Amnesty International, *India: The 'Enron Project' in Maharashtra: Protests Suppressed in the Name of Development*, Amnesty International Index: ASA 20/31/97 (July 1997).

[9] O. Schachter, 'The Decline of the Nation-State and its Implications for International Law' (1997) 36 *Colum. J Trans. L* 8–12.

MNC is not governed by a single legal system. The parent company is subject to the laws of the home State while its foreign affiliates are subject to the laws of the various host States. It is still not widely accepted that, unlike an individual, an MNC has any obligations under international law. According to traditional legal doctrine, an MNC that is employing forced labour in connivance with the host State can therefore legitimately maintain that it is acting in full conformity with the law by complying with the laws of the host State. Under traditional international law, such a situation may amount to a breach of international law by the host State but not by the corporation.

The purpose of this chapter is to suggest ways in which the European Community could help to improve international accountability for human rights abuses by MNCs. The chapter starts with an analysis of the current accountability of MNCs under public international law. It then considers the same question from the perspective of European Community law. In principle, legal control over the conduct of MNCs may be exercised in three distinct ways: indirectly, by holding the home State or the host State responsible, and directly, by holding the MNC itself responsible. Naturally, a combination of these three avenues is also possible. The advantages and disadvantages of these three approaches will be assessed below.

II. MULTINATIONAL CORPORATIONS IN INTERNATIONAL LAW

Traditional international law does not have much to say about MNCs. If it has shown any interest at all, it has been more concerned with protecting the rights of corporations than with enforcing their duties. Since corporations were not recognized as having independent international legal personality discussions have focused on the question of which State may exercise diplomatic protection on behalf of a corporation. Accordingly, in the *Barcelona Traction* case the International Court of Justice pointed out that under traditional international law diplomatic protection of a corporate entity may be exercised by the home State, i.e. by the State in which it is incorporated and in which it has its registered office. However, the Court also recognized that no absolute test of the 'genuine connection' required between the corporation and the home State had found general acceptance.[10] The matter has not subsequently been authoritatively clarified by the Court or otherwise, so that it remains unclear precisely in what circumstances a home State may exercise diplomatic protection on behalf of a foreign affiliate of a parent company incorporated under its laws. In practice, this unclarity has not caused many problems, however, because, as will be shown below, MNCs have increasingly been able to act independently *vis-à-vis* their host States. They require less and less protection from their home States.

---

[10] *Case Concerning the Barcelona Traction Light and Power Company, Limited (Second Phase) (Belgium v. Spain)* [1970] ICJ Reports para. 70.

A. Rights of Multinational Corporations

The tendency of traditional international law to emphasize the rights of MNCs rather than their obligations reached a high point in the negotiations on the Multilateral Agreement on Investment (MAI) conducted in the context of the OECD.[11] The MAI is intended as an international bill of rights for investors. It seeks to guarantee them a 'level playing field' in host countries by embodying the principle of national treatment and most favoured nation treatment.[12] The underlying purpose of the MAI, therefore, is to offer legally binding guarantees to international investors, not to seek to ensure good corporate behaviour. Typically, among the few provisions on which no agreement could be reached are those which would make a perfunctory reference to international labour standards and environmental protection.

The MAI provisions are intended to become the key global standards applicable to MNCs. Although negotiated within the OECD, the MAI would be open for accession by non-OECD members. In the scramble to attract investors it is expected that pressure to accede to the MAI will be considerable. Argentina, Brazil, Chile, Hong Kong, and the Slovak Republic have already joined the negotiations as observers. While the MAI would not prevent host States from imposing human rights obligations on MNCs as long as this was done in a non-discriminatory manner, it would facilitate transfer of assets to other States if an MNC would consider these obligations as too onerous. The MAI has therefore been strongly criticized not only by environmental and human rights groups but also, for example, by the European Parliament.[13] Partly as a result of these criticisms, negotiations on the MAI reached deadlock in October 1998. It is, however, to be expected that the original underlying ideas of the MAI will survive and be incorporated in some future international instrument either in the context of the OECD or in the context of the WTO.

A crucial feature of the MAI is that it envisages the establishment of an international tribunal at which investors could sue States parties over alleged breaches of its provisions. The decisions of this tribunal would be binding. The MAI thereby builds on earlier dispute settlement procedures on the international plane between investors and States, such as the International Centre for the Settlement of Investment Disputes (ICSID) set up under the auspices of the World Bank.[14] One of the differences with the MAI, however, is that under the MAI only the investor would be able to sue the host State and not the other way around. Apart from the ICSID, companies are already able to sue States at several other specialized international judicial

---

[11] The latest negotiating text of the Multilateral Agreement on Investment may be found on the website of the OECD: www.oecd.org.

[12] See generally W.H. Witherell, 'The OECD Multilateral Agreement on Investment' (1995) 4 *Transnational Corporations* 1–14.

[13] *Agence Europe*, 11 Mar. 1998.

[14] Convention on the Settlement of Investment Disputes Between States and Nationals of Other States, 18 Mar. 1965, reprinted in (1965) 4 ILM 532.

bodies, including the Law of the Sea Tribunal,[15] the Iran–United States Claims Tribunal,[16] and the United Nations Claims Commission.[17]

If enforceability of claims on the international plane is taken as the decisive criterion for having international legal personality, the entry into force of the MAI would imply an important shift in favour of MNCs at the expense of the private individual. Unlike the investor investing in a State party to the MAI, the individual who claims that his rights have been infringed under a human rights treaty may only directly petition an international tribunal for a binding ruling in the regional context of the European Convention on Human Rights (since the entry into force of Protocol 11). If his complaint is against a State that is not a party to the European Convention on Human Rights this option is simply not available.

The MAI is therefore another nail in the coffin of the argument made by some authors that MNCs should not be regarded as addressees of international human rights obligations because this would risk granting them international legal personality.[18] Leaving aside the question whether this has ever been a valid proposition, it clearly no longer is because MNCs now have extensive rights under international law, and they are able to enforce these rights before international tribunals. A more realistic attitude to the status of MNCs under international law has been taken by authors such as Wolfgang Friedmann. He argued already in 1964 that private corporations should be regarded as 'participants' in the evolution of international law.[19] This approach has also been taken by Rosalyn Higgins.[20] Clearly, the time for strategies which try to cope with MNCs by simply ignoring them is now over.

B. Indirect Accountability of Multinational Corporations

International law can regulate MNCs by employing two distinct methods: indirect regulation by holding States responsible for the conduct of MNCs and direct regulation by addressing MNCs as such.[21] The traditional approach to controlling the conduct of MNCs is by way of the State. Conduct of private actors such as corporations which are not acting on behalf of the State is not attributable to the State.[22] However, there are two distinct ways in which a State may nevertheless be responsible.

[15] Set up under Annex VI of the UN Convention on the Law of the Sea, 10 Dec. 1982, reprinted in (1982) 21 ILM 1261.

[16] Set up under the Declaration of the Government of the Democratic and Popular Republic of Algeria Concerning the Settlement of Claims by the Government of the United States of America and the Government of the Islamic Republic of Iran, 19 Jan. 1981, reprinted in (1981) 20 ILM 230.

[17] Set up under SC Res. 692 (1991).

[18] See e.g. A. Cassese, *International Law in a Divided World* (1986), 103. See also F. Rigaux, 'Transnational Corporations', in M. Bedjaoui (ed.), *International Law: Achievements and Prospects* (1991), 129.

[19] W. Friedmann, *The Changing Structure of International Law* (1964), 230–1. For an argument that MNCs should be allowed to participate more actively in the drafting of international codes of conduct governing their behaviour, see J. Charney, 'Transnational Corporations and Developing Public International Law' (1983) 32 *Duke LJ* 748–88.

[20] R. Higgins, *Problems and Process: International Law and How We Use It* (1994), 50.

[21] For a useful discussion of the distinction, see D.T. Hamilton, 'Regulation of Corporations under International Environmental Law' [1989] *Proceedings of the Annual Conference of the Canadian Council on International Law* 72–92.

[22] Art. 11 of the draft arts. on state responsibility, *Report of the International Law Commission on its 48th Session*, UN Doc. A/51/10 (1998), at chap. III, reprinted in (1998) 37 ILM 440.

First, a State may be responsible under international law if it fails to exercise the required degree of due diligence with regard to the conduct of an MNC. The recently concluded OECD Convention on Combating Bribery, for example, obliges States parties to exercise jurisdiction in respect of the offence of bribery when committed abroad by companies possessing their nationality.[23] Another example may be found in Article 139(1) of the UN Convention on the Law of the Sea. According to this provision, States parties must ensure that enterprises which possess their nationality or are effectively controlled by them or their nationals act in conformity with the Convention. This language is interesting because it does not limit the responsibility of the home State to its territory or to companies which have its nationality. It imposes responsibility on the State for conduct of a foreign affiliate of a parent company incorporated in its territory if the parent exercises effective control over the affiliate. The question of the liability of parent companies for conduct of their affiliates will be further discussed in the text to note 43 below.

Secondly, if a corporation is exercising elements of governmental authority, either as a result of formal delegation by the authorities or *de facto*, the conduct of such a corporation may be attributable to the State.[24] In other words, if a State privatizes state functions which are subject to international human rights obligations by delegating them to a private corporation, the State in question remains responsible for the discharge of these obligations.[25] Accordingly, in *Costello-Roberts* v. *United Kingdom* the European Court of Human Rights observed that a State 'could not absolve itself of responsibility by delegating its obligations to private bodies or individuals'.[26] Privatization of state functions may occur in a formal manner, for example when police powers are delegated to a private railway company. This is the example given by the International Law Commission in its draft articles on state responsibility.[27] A contemporary example is the delegation of the operation of prison facilities to private industries. In the United States, 5 per cent of prison capacity is currently run by private companies. The largest of these companies, Corrections Corporation of America, is an MNC which also operates prison facilities in the United Kingdom and Australia.[28] The exercise of governmental functions may also occur without formal delegation, for example if an MNC maintains law and order in an area in which governmental authority has collapsed due to an armed conflict.

A corporation to which a state function has been delegated or which is exercising such a function *de facto* may also itself be responsible under international law for the manner in which it exercises this task. In domestic law this a familiar concept. Both in the United States and in India, for example, private parties that conduct themselves in a manner which resembles a State or pursuant to state authorization are

---

[23] Arts. 2 and 4 of the Convention on Combating Bribery of Foreign Public Officials in International Business Transactions, 17 Dec. 1997. Entered into force on 15 Feb. 1999. Text available on the website of the OECD: www.oecd.org.

[24] Arts. 7 and 8, draft-arts. on state responsibility, note 22 above.

[25] See A. Clapham, 'The Privatization of Human Rights' (1995) 1 *EHRLR* 20–1.

[26] *Costello-Roberts* v. *United Kingdom*, ECHR (1993), Series A, Vol. 247–C, para. 27.

[27] See, 2 *Yearbook of the International Law Commission*, Part One (1974), 277–82.

[28] See the website of Corrections Corporation of America at: www.correctionscorp.com.

subject to the same constitutional standards as public officials.[29] The obligations of MNCs under international law will be discussed in the next section.

C. Direct Accountability of Multinational Corporations

International law rarely addresses specific obligations directly to corporations. It is, however, quite capable of doing so. Article 137(1) and (3) of the UN Convention on the Law of the Sea, for example, provides that no juridical person may exercise sovereign rights over parts of the Area or its resources. This obligation obviously encompasses MNCs.

During the 1970s and 1980s several attempts were made to adopt international codes of conduct which directly address obligations to MNCs. The 1976 OECD Declaration on International Investment and Multinational Enterprises contains provisions on non-interference in the internal affairs of the host State, disclosure of information, competition, financing, taxation, employment and industrial relations, and science and technology.[30] A section on environmental protection was added in 1991.[31] The 1977 ILO Declaration of Principles Concerning Multinational Enterprises and Social Policy is more interesting from a human rights point of view.[32] It contains more detailed provisions on equality of opportunity and treatment, security of employment, wages, benefits and conditions of work, safety and health, freedom of association, and the right to organize and collective bargaining. A third instrument, the draft UN Code of Conduct on Transnational Corporations was never adopted due to ideological differences in the context of the New International Economic Order.[33] In any case, whatever the merits of the standards contained in these codes of conduct, the fact remains that they are not in themselves legally binding.

When an MNC exercises governmental authority it makes sense to hold it accountable by the same human rights obligations as a State. Such obligations would include not merely negative obligations but also positive ones. This line of argument finds some support in existing international legal instruments. The Universal Declaration of Human Rights, for example, provides in one of its preambular paragraphs that 'every organ of society' shall strive by teaching and education to promote respect for its provisions.[34]

On the other hand, if an MNC conducts itself in a manner which would amount to a crime under international law if committed by an individual, it would seem logical

[29] R. Kapur, 'From Human Tragedy to Human Right: The Accountability of Multinational Corporations for Human Rights Violations' (1990) 10 *Boston College Third World Law Journal* 24–32.

[30] OECD Declaration on International Investment and Multinational Enterprises, 21 June 1976, reprinted in (1976) 15 ILM 967. On its implementation, see S.C. Van Eyk, *The OECD Declaration and Decisions on Multinational Enterprises* (1995).

[31] See the OECD publication *The OECD Guidelines for Multinational Enterprises* (1994), 66–7.

[32] ILO Tripartite Declaration of Principles Concerning Multinational Enterprises and Social Policy, 16 Nov. 1977, reprinted in (1978) 17 ILM 422.

[33] For the latest text see UN Doc. E/1990/94. For an analysis of the difficulties encountered in the negotiations, see S. Dell, 'The United Nations Code of Conduct on Transnational Corporations', in J. Kaufmann (ed.), *Effective Negotiation* (1989), 53–74.

[34] Universal Declaration of Human Rights, adopted by GA Res. 217 A (III) (1948). In United Nations, *A Compilation of International Instruments* (1994), i, Part 1, 1.

to hold that MNC accountable by the same standards as an individual. There would appear to be no reason of principle why a corporation could not be criminally liable under international law. In the war crimes trials held after the Second World War, executives of certain German industries, rather than those industries themselves, were convicted of war crimes. For example, in the *Zyklon B* case, the owner of the firm which supplied the gas that was used for the extermination of the inmates of concentration camps, rather than the firm in question, was convicted of war crimes.[35] The International Criminal Tribunals for the Former Yugoslavia and Rwanda are not specifically competent to try corporations. However, there appears to be increasing support for the notion that corporations may be criminally liable under international law.[36] The draft Statute of the International Criminal Court, as submitted to the Rome Conference which adopted the final text of the Statute, would have provided the Court with jurisdiction to try not merely natural persons but also legal persons, which obviously includes corporations.[37] However, the Conference decided not to retain this option.

International criminalization of corporate conduct may be based on the criminal liability of corporations under municipal law, which is by now a well-established concept in most countries. Although corporations tend to be convicted of economic crimes, they may in fact be liable for any crime, including manslaughter.[38] The concept of corporate crime is especially prevalent in the United States, but Europe is not lagging far behind. Within the Council of Europe, the Committee of Ministers in 1988 recommended that member States should provide for the criminal liability of enterprises.[39] Within the European Community, preliminary efforts to harmonize national legislation in this field are currently under way.[40]

D. Case Law on Direct Accountability of Multinational Corporations

In the United States, some interesting cases are currently pending before US federal courts which attempt to hold MNCs accountable for violations of international human rights law committed abroad. If these courts were to accept that MNCs may indeed be sued for violations of international human rights law this would obviously constitute an important precedent that could have a considerable preventive effect. Jurisdiction in these cases is based on the Alien Tort Claims Act (ATCA) which provides: '[t]he district courts shall have original jurisdiction of any civil action by an alien for a tort only, committed in violation of the law of nations or a treaty of the United States'.

The most advanced of these lawsuits, *Doe* v. *Unocal*, is a class action by a group of Burmese citizens against the Californian energy corporation, Unocal. The citizens

[35] *In re Tesch and Others (Zyklon B Case)*, Hamburg, British Military Court, 8 Mar. 1946 (1946) 13 Annual Digest and Reports of Public International Law Cases 250.

[36] See T. Meron, 'Is International Law Moving Towards Criminalization?' (1998) 9 *EJIL* 19–20.

[37] Art. 23(5) of the draft Statute of the International Criminal Court, A/CONF.183/2/Add.1 (1998).

[38] G. Harding, 'Criminal Liability of Corporations—United Kingdom', in H. de Doelder and K. Tiedemann (eds.), *Criminal Liability of Corporations* (1996), 375; E.M. Wise, 'Criminal Liability of Corporations—USA', in *ibid.*, at 384.

[39] Recommendation (88) 18 (20 Oct. 1988).

[40] K. Tiedemann, 'La responsabilité pénale dans l'entreprise. Vers un espace judiciaire unifié? Rapport introductif' [1997] *Revue de science criminelle et de droit pénal comparé* 269.

allege that the Burmese government conspired with Unocal when subjecting them to forced labour and ill-treatment during the construction of a natural gas pipeline through their tribal lands. So far, the federal district court in Los Angeles has accepted that the ATCA provides it with the necessary jurisdiction to hear the claim.[41] In assuming jurisdiction, the Court apparently did not regard it as a problem that the claim for damages was directed against a corporate defendant rather than a private individual. In *Wiwa* v. *Royal Dutch Petroleum Company*, a case currently pending before a federal district court in New York, family members of former Ogoni leader Ken Saro-Wiwa are suing Royal Dutch Shell for damages because of the company's alleged co-responsibility for his hanging by the Nigerian authorities. The claim was later amended to include a woman who was shot by Nigerian troops called in by Shell when she was demonstrating against the construction of a pipeline by the company. At the time of writing, the Court has not yet finally decided whether it has jurisdiction over the claim.[42]

No similar cases against MNCs appear to have been brought so far in Member States of the European Community, perhaps because no equivalent of the ATCA is available in Europe.

The cases brought in the United States also raise the question whether a parent company may be liable for unlawful acts committed by its foreign affiliates. According to the traditional answer to this question, given in the United States and in most other countries, a parent company cannot be liable for the conduct of other members of a corporate group. This is because they constitute separate legal entities with limited liability.[43] However, in exceptional circumstances it is permitted to 'pierce the corporate veil' between the parent and the other components of a corporate group. Courts may be persuaded to do this on the basis of factual links of ownership or control by the parent over the foreign unit. In the *Amoco Cadiz* case, for example, the US District Court concluded that not only the subsidiaries directly involved in the accident but also their parent company, Standard Oil Co., were liable for the damage caused by the grounding of their tanker off the coast of Normandy. This was because of the close control exercised by Standard over its subsidiaries:

> 43. As an integrated multinational corporation which is engaged through a system of subsidiaries in the exploration, production, refining, transportation and sale of petroleum products throughout the world, Standard is responsible for the tortious acts of its wholly owned subsidiaries and instrumentalities AIOC and Transport.
>
> 44. Standard exercised such control over its subsidiaries AIOC and Transport, that those entities would be considered to be mere instrumentalities of Standard. Furthermore, Standard itself was initially involved in and controlled the design, operation and management of *Amoco Cadiz* and treated the vessel as if it were its own.[44]

The disadvantage of this traditional approach to the liability of corporate groups is its unpredictability. Liability of the parent depends on *ad hoc* decisions taken by

---

[41] *Doe* v. *Unocal*, 963 F.Supp. 880. US Dis. Ct., CD, Cal., 25 Mar. 1997. Summarized in (1998) 92 *AJIL* 309 with a note by W.J. Aceves.

[42] *Wiwa* v. *Royal Dutch Petroleum Company*, 96 Civ. 8389 (SDNY). See J. Green and P. Hoffman, 'Litigation Update', *ACLU International Civil Liberties Report* (May 1998), 51.

[43] J. Engrácia Antunes, *Liability of Corporate Groups* (1994), 475–6.

[44] *Amoco Cadiz*, US Dis. Ct., ND Ill. (ED), 18 Apr. 1984 [1984] 2 Lloyd's Rep. 338.

the courts. There are no straightforward criteria for allocating liability. This is why the European Commission has proposed a harmonization of legislation in the European Community based on a different approach. Under this 'enterprise' approach a parent company would be liable for the conduct of its subsidiaries on the grounds of the corporate control exercised by the former. This proposal (the so-called draft ninth directive) will be discussed in the text to note 64 below.

III. MULTINATIONAL CORPORATIONS IN EUROPEAN COMMUNITY LAW

Like MNCs in other parts of the world, MNCs based in the European Community have taken advantage of the new opportunities offered to international business. The outflow of foreign direct investment from the European Community has increased steeply from 106,372 million dollars in 1991 to 160,372 million dollars in 1996. The comparable figure for the United States in 1996 was only half of that, at 84,902 million dollars.[45] Of the world's twenty largest MNCs in terms of foreign assets, eight are based in the European Community, including No. 1: Royal Dutch Shell (United Kingdom/Netherlands). The others are No. 6: Volkswagen (Germany), No. 9: Bayer (Germany), No. 14: Elf Aquitaine (France), No. 16: Daimler-Benz (Germany), No. 17: Unilever (United Kingdom/Netherlands), No. 18: Philips (Netherlands), and No. 20: Fiat (Italy).[46]

Abuses by MNCs have long been on the agenda of the European Community. As early as 1973 the European Commission submitted a communication to the Council of Ministers entitled 'Multinational Undertakings and the Community' in which it proposed that a suitable legal framework should be created to guard against harmful effects of (multinational) undertakings.[47] At around the same time, however, under the influence of the economic crisis of the 1970s, the Community's attitude towards its MNCs became more protectionist.[48] It became primarily concerned with how it could best support its MNCs, for example with regard to foreign direct investment. No doubt, the corporate sector's own lobbying played an important role in this regard.[49] The Community's supportive approach is also the attitude which is predominantly reflected in the literature. Thus, an article on the 'problems of multinational enterprises' is more likely to be a sympathetic account of the difficulties encountered by MNCs than a critical account of the problems caused by them.[50]

---

[45] *World Investment Report 1997*, 308.   [46] *Ibid.*, at 29.

[47] 'Multinational Undertakings and the Community' (8 Nov. 1973), reprinted in J. Robinson, *Multinationals and Political Control* (1983), 231.

[48] G. Junne, 'Multinational Enterprises as Actors', in W. Carlsnaess and S. Smith (eds.), *European Foreign Policy: The EC and Changing Perspectives in Europe* (1994), 94.

[49] See A.H. McLaughlin, G. Jordan, and W.A. Maloney, 'Corporate Lobbying in the European Community' (1993) 31 *J Common Mkt. Stud.* 191–212.

[50] See T. Brewer and S. Young, 'European Union Policies and the Problems of Multinational Enterprises' (1995) 29 *Journal of World Trade* 33–52.

A. EC Action Against Apartheid in South Africa

The first, and so far only, attempt at a more critical EC policy towards MNCs was the adoption in September 1977 of a Code of Conduct for Community Companies with Subsidiaries, Branches, or Representation in South Africa. The text was drafted 'with almost indecent haste' at a time when the Community was under great pressure to step up its pressure on South Africa's apartheid regime.[51] It closely resembled a similar British Code of Practice, and called on companies investing in South Africa to treat their employees equally and to support trade unions for black South Africans. The Code did not contain any legal obligations. It merely requested companies doing business in South Africa to report annually on progress achieved in applying the Code and to submit a copy to their national governments. On the basis of the information received, a composite report was then published by the EC Presidency. Nevertheless, until 1984 it was in effect the Community's only foreign policy instrument *vis-à-vis* South Africa.[52] A new, slightly strengthened Code was adopted on 19 November 1985.[53] The Code was finally abolished in 1993 after firm election dates had been established in South Africa.[54]

Although it cannot be ruled out that the Code of Conduct may have had some positive impact on human rights in South Africa, it can hardly be considered a great success.[55] Most problematic was the system for monitoring the implementation of the Code. In effect, no EC body supervised the implementation of the Code. Since the Code was created as an instrument of European Political Co-operation the European Commission had no role to play. Because no common reporting format was agreed, the information supplied differed so considerably that comparisons were in effect impossible. Moreover, in view of the voluntary character of the Code, companies could not be forced too supply information. This compares poorly with the more elaborate forms of supervision created to monitor the implementation of the OECD Declaration on International Investment and Multinational Enterprises[56] and the ILO Declaration of Principles Concerning Multinational Enterprises and Social Policy.[57] The supervision of the implementation of these two instruments also leaves much to be desired. But although they are also non-binding, at least they provide for a standardized reporting format and a systematic periodic review by a competent body.

The Community's response to human rights abuses committed by its MNCs in South Africa also compares poorly to that of the other major home State of MNCs, the United States. The 1986 Anti-Apartheid Act required any US national that employed twenty-five or more persons in South Africa to respect a Code with respect to the employment of those persons.[58] This Code was based on the so-called Sullivan

---

[51] S.J. Nuttall, *European Political Co-operation* (1992), 135.

[52] M. Holland, *European Union Common Foreign Policy: From EPC to CFSP Joint Action and South Africa* (1995), 36.

[53] Code of Conduct for European Community Companies with Subsidiaries, Branches or Representation in South Africa, 19 Nov. 1985, reprinted in (1985) 24 ILM 1477.

[54] M. Holland, *The European Community and South Africa: European Political Co-operation Under Strain* (1988), 50.

[55] *Ibid.*, at 75.   [56] Note 30 above.   [57] Note 32 above.

[58] Comprehensive Anti-Apartheid Act of 1986, reprinted in (1987) 26 ILM 79.

Principles.[59] Unlike its EC counterpart, the American Act provided for systematic supervision and stiff penalties against violators.

B. Direct Accountability of Multinational Corporations

The impotent nature of the European Community's response to human rights abuses by MNCs is all the more disappointing because under EC law corporations are subject to direct regulation. Under Articles 81 and 82 (*ex* Articles 85 and 86) of the Treaty undertakings are prohibited from engaging in activities which prevent, restrict, or distort competition within the common market and from exploiting in an improper manner a dominant position within the common market. The European Commission has far-reaching powers to enforce these provisions *vis-à-vis* undertakings, including the authority to conduct house searches and to impose heavy fines. At the same time, undertakings are entitled to challenge decisions addressed to them before the European Court of Justice. In principle, the Community is therefore much better equipped to regulate the conduct of MNCs than other international organizations.

However, the Commission has shown little inclination to regulate or monitor the external conduct of MNCs based in the Community, in spite of pressure exerted in this direction by European Parliament. No follow-up has been given, for example, to a resolution adopted by the European Parliament after the Bhopal disaster, which requested the Commission to ensure that foreign subsidiaries of European MNCs would apply the same safety standards as in the European Community.[60] On 14 January 1999 the European Parliament decided to go a step beyond merely recommending that action ought to be taken by the Commission and the Council. Apart from recommending the establishment of a European Monitoring Platform by the Council, it decided to set up its own monitoring mechanism which would investigate alleged abuses by MNCs based in the European Community. The resolution envisages that public hearings would be held in which representatives of MNCs would be confronted with evidence of abuses committed by their companies.

It is true that at first sight Articles 81 and 82 (*ex* Articles 85 and 86) do not offer the necessary legal basis for regulating the external conduct of Community-based MNCs. After all, the scope of these provisions is restricted *ratione materiae* to the antitrust field and *ratione loci* to the common market area. But similar legal difficulties have never prevented the Commission from proposing legislative action in fields in which it was keen to act. In fact, the Commission appears to have made no creative attempts to get round these limitations by seeking to base proposals on Article 308 (*ex* Article 235) or by proposing an extension of its powers under the EC Treaty.

To some extent, the United States has a better record than the European Community in regulating the external conduct of its MNCs. One reason for this may be that the United States has traditionally been more inclined than the European Community to exercise prescriptive extra-territorial jurisdiction. An interesting example

---

[59] L. Sullivan, *Principles for US Corporations Operating in South Africa* (fourth amplification), 8 Nov. 1984, reprinted in (1985) 24 ILM 1496. See Sullivan, 'Agents for Change: The Mobilization of Multinational Companies in South Africa' (1983) 15 *Law & Policy in International Business* 427–44.

[60] European Parliament Resolution on the poison gas disaster in India, 13 Dec. 1984 [1985] OJ C12/84.

of the exercise of such jurisdiction with regard to companies is the 1977 Foreign Corrupt Practices Act which prohibits US corporations from making corrupt payments
to foreign government officials.[61] The competitive disadvantage thereby created for
US companies began to be eliminated only twenty years later with the adoption in
1997 by the OECD of the Anti-Bribery Convention.[62] With regard to the conduct of
US companies abroad, however, any tendency to exercise extra-territorial jurisdiction has, as in Europe, been much greater in areas in which the material interests of
the United States are at stake, such as antitrust law, than in areas in which such
material interests are lacking, such as the protection of human rights or the environment.[63]

It is also true that the possibilities for regulating the conduct abroad of subsidiaries of Community-based MNCs are complicated by the fact that attempts to
harmonize the law of corporate groups in the European Community have so far
been unsuccessful. The draft ninth directive on corporate groups submitted by the
Commission to the Council in 1985 would have strengthened the liability of a parent
company for wrongful acts committed by its subsidiaries.[64] Under Article 9 of the
draft, a parent company involved in the management of a subsidiary would have
been liable for any wrongful act resulting from such interference, thus weakening the
principle of limited liability of a parent company.[65] Although the proposal was
based on long standing German legislation, it caused such an outcry among MNCs
and among certain Member States that the Commission was forced to withdraw its
proposal.[66] This was after an earlier attempt by the Commission to introduce an optional system for 'European companies', under which the parent company would
have been liable for the debts and liabilities of dependent group members, had also
been defeated.[67]

However, this setback has not prevented the Court and the Commission from developing their own doctrine on corporate group liability when dealing with non-EC
parent companies suspected of anti-competitive conduct within the common market
area. According to this doctrine, the so-called enterprise approach, the mere existence of a subsidiary relationship is sufficient to establish jurisdiction over the parent

[61] Muchlinski, note 1 above, at 127.
[62] Convention on Combating Bribery of Foreign Public Officials in International Business Transactions, note 23 above.
[63] M. Gibney and R.D. Emerick, 'The Extraterritorial Application of United States Law and the Protection of Human Rights: Holding Multinational Corporations to Domestic and International Standards' (1996) 10 *Temple International and Comparative Law Journal* 140–1.
[64] The complete text of this draft proposal appears to have been published only unofficially and in German: 'Vorschlag für eine neunte Richtlinie auf der Grundlage von Artikel 54 Absatz 3 Buchstabe g) des
EWG-Vertrages über die Verbindungen zwischen Unternehmen insbesondere über Konzerne' (1985) 3
Zeitschrift für Unternehmens- und Gesellschaftsrecht 446. See K. Böhlhoff and J. Budde, 'Company
Groups—the EEC Proposal for a Ninth Directive in the Light of the Legal Situation in the Federal Republic of Germany' (1986) 6 *Journal of Comparative Business and Capital Market Law* 163–97.
[65] K. Hofstetter, 'Parent Responsibility for Subsidiary Corporations: Evaluating European Trends'
(1990) 39 *ICLQ* 588–9.
[66] D. van den Bulcke, 'Multinational Companies and the European Community', in B. Nelson *et al.*
(eds.), *The European Community in the 1990s* (1992), 111.
[67] Art. 239(1) of the amended draft proposal for a Council regulation on the Statute for European
companies, *Bull. EC Suppl.* 4/75.

company.[68] It would appear that in the absence of political will on the part of the Member States to accept harmonization of this area of the law, parent companies of MNCs based in the EC could be held responsible for human rights abuses by their foreign affiliates abroad on the basis of this judicial doctrine.

C. Indirect Accountability of Multinational Corporations

Apart from the possibility of regulating the behaviour of MNCs directly, EC law also offers opportunities to regulate the behaviour of MNCs indirectly, through their home and host States. Although Articles 81 and 82 (*ex* Articles 85 and 86) are primarily addressed to undertakings, for example, the European Court of Justice has determined that these provisions also create obligations for Member States. The Court has observed that Member States may not adopt or maintain in force any measure which could deprive these provisions of their effectiveness.[69]

More generally, the Court has recently indicated that Member States may violate EC law not only by their actions but also by failing to adopt adequate measures against unlawful conduct by non-state actors on their territories. In the *Spanish Strawberries* case (*Commission* v. *France*) the Court ruled that France had failed to fulfil its obligations under the EC Treaty to take all necessary measures to prevent French farmers from obstructing the free movement of Spanish strawberries.[70] Rather than basing itself on the public international law requirement of 'due diligence', the Court relied on Article 5 (now Article 10) of the EC Treaty (duty of faithful implementation of obligations).[71] The case demonstrates that when non-state actors commit abuses under EC law these can either be blamed on them directly or the territorial State can be blamed for failure to take remedial action. The Commission could conceivably have brought its action under Article 85 EEC (now Article 81) against the groupings of French farmers which organized the blockade, but it chose instead to hold the host state accountable under Article 30 EEC (now Article 28).

It is clear, however, that as a general rule it is more effective to hold MNCs accountable directly, without having to pass through their home or host states.

IV. CONCLUDING OBSERVATIONS AND RECOMMENDATIONS

There are three principal ways in which MNCs may be held accountable for human rights abuses.

[68] Muchlinski, note 1 above, at 137–8. See also P.J. Kuyper, 'European Community Law and Extraterritoriality: Some Trends and New Developments' (1984) 33 *ICLQ* 1016–17.

[69] Case 311/85, *Vereniging van Vlaamse Reisbureaus* v. *Sociale Dienst van de Plaatselijke en Gewestelijke Overheidsdiensten* [1987] ECR 3801. As a matter of fact, this ruling does not solve the problem of the limited material and territorial scope of Arts. 81 and 82 (*ex* 85 and 86) when trying to bring human rights abuses by EC based MNCs under the ægis of EC law.

[70] Case C–265/95, *Spanish Strawberries*, European Court of Justice, judgment of 9 Dec. 1997.

[71] In this sense also the conclusions of Lenz AG [1997] *EuGRZ* 391–2.

The traditional way is through the host State. This mechanism should be retained and strengthened. It offers no effective remedy, however, when, as is often the case, abuses are committed in complicity with the host State. In such circumstances the European Community should help to improve accountability of MNCs by providing financial and technical assistance to domestic watchdog groups that are able to investigate and expose such abuses. This approach should fit well within the European Commission's existing programme of assistance for human rights and democracy-building activities.

The second mechanism, holding MNCs accountable through their home States, should not be ruled out entirely. However, this approach is politically unattractive because it exposes home States to the legitimate criticism of jurisdictional imperialism. From the point of EC law, it also poses some serious difficulties because of the lack of a clear legal basis in the EC Treaty and because of enforcement problems. The European Monitoring Platform proposed in the 1999 European Parliament Resolution therefore offers an attractive, softer option.

The third and preferred way of confronting human rights abuses by MNCs is to subject companies to direct international obligations and international supervision on a worldwide basis. In view of the increasing strength of MNCs and the concomitant risk of abuses, it no longer makes sense that international law addresses obligations to respect human dignity to States and to individuals but not to corporations. At the domestic level, this anomaly has been corrected in most States by acknowledging that companies may be criminally liable and subject to constitutional standards. It is now time to take this step also at the international level.

The anomaly may be corrected either through the back door or through the front door. The back door approach would involve leaving it to municipal courts, for the time being this would mean US courts, to decide whether MNCs are subject to international human rights obligations. The front door option would be specifically to codify the human rights duties of MNCs in an international instrument. Such new provisions are needed because the scope of existing OECD and ILO codes of conduct for MNCs is too limited and because these codes put too much emphasis on the negative obligation of non-interference at the expense of the positive duties of MNCs. Such new texts would also offer much-needed clarity and a level playing field to the MNCs themselves.

At the same time, the uncontrolled mushrooming of voluntary codes of conduct— whether drawn up by MNCs themselves or otherwise—should be resisted because of their window-dressing tendency. Too often it is assumed that improvements will occur simply because another code of conduct has been proclaimed with some fanfare. What are needed instead are binding international standards accompanied by strong enforcement machinery.

A splendid opportunity to work towards this objective was presented by the draft Multilateral Agreement on Investment. Partly as a result of persistent criticisms made by environmental and labour groups progress on this instrument has been halted. The necessary time for reflection has thereby been created to consider the introduction of new provisions that would clearly state that corporations are subject to the same international human rights obligations as States and individuals (this is obviously on the assumption that negotiations on the MAI will continue one way or the other). It would mean that, like States, corporations could be held accountable for international crimes and, like individuals, they could be held accountable for crimes under international law. The MAI should also clearly provide that, like States, corporations have positive obligations to protect and promote human rights. Such provisions should be accompanied by an appropriate review machinery, including a reporting procedure for corporations and a mechanism for individual complaints.

The European Community is well suited to taking such an initiative to change the current one-sided nature of the MAI since it has played a leading role in the negotiations so far. The introduction of human rights provisions into the MAI would be roughly comparable to the human rights clauses the Community has been introducing into trade and co-operation agreements with third States in recent years. It would have the advantage of enabling the Community to take legislative action against corporate human rights abuses without having to face the political and legal difficulties inherent in home State regulation mentioned above. It would also help to meet some of the objections raised against the MAI by the European Parliament.

No attempt should be made to resuscitate the draft UN Code of Conduct on Transnational Corporations, because this would only help to revive the old North–South animosities. At the United Nations, work on human rights abuses by MNCs could instead be located at the Sub-Commission on Prevention of Discrimination and Protection of Minorities. The Sub-Commission in 1998 decided to form a sessional working group on transnational corporations.[72] This working group should provide a useful focal point for further analysis and discussion within the United Nations.

In sum, there are three concrete policy initiatives the European Community could now take to help to redress the imbalances caused by the sharply increased potency of MNCs on the world scene. First, it should provide financial and technical assistance to watchdog and consumer groups in host countries that attempt to investigate and redress abuses by MNCs. Secondly, it should insist that strong human rights obligations accompanied by a strong enforcement machinery be introduced into the MAI. Thirdly, it should set up the European Monitoring Platform recommended by the European Parliament.

The good news is that it may be easier to combat human rights abuses by MNCs than those committed by States. States often appear to think they can afford simply to ignore criticisms of their human rights record. In contrast, MNCs are unlikely to find they can get away with serious abuses for very long simply because they are more dependent on market forces. When offered a choice, most consumers, shareholders, and employees prefer not to be associated with companies which have an unsavoury reputation. Of these three categories of stakeholders, the impact of employees may be the most underestimated. The strongest incentive for an MNC to stop committing abuses may be provided by its need to continue to attract the brightest young graduates. Many of these young persons are unlikely to join an MNC which is known to be oblivious to basic standards of human decency.

---

[72] Sub-Comm'n Res. 1998/8.

18

Human Rights Considerations in the Development Co-operation Activities of the EC

BRUNO SIMMA, JO BEATRIX ASCHENBRENNER, AND CONSTANZE SCHULTE

INTRODUCTION

The Community launched its development policy in 1958, but, until the Maastricht Treaty, there was no explicit legal basis for conducting such a policy. Despite the delay in expressly authorizing development co-operation, the Community and its Member States together provide more than half of all development assistance given in the world today.[1] The Community has a widespread system of co-operation agreements with countries all over the world, and grants preferential trade relations and other forms of autonomous assistance to developing countries.[2] Because the Community deals with many developing countries, with a broad range of needs, no single strategy can be applied to all of them. Strategies differ based on the needs of the developing country receiving the aid. These needs range from open access to the markets of the Community to technical and financial assistance, and even to substantial food aid.[3] This chapter discusses the Community development policy of granting such assistance to developing States with the aim of promoting human rights and democracy. The provision of open markets through preferential trade relations and other aspects of contractual (economic, commercial) co-operation are dealt with elsewhere.[4] The present chapter deals exclusively with positive initiatives to link development co-operation to progress in the area of human rights. The activities of the European Investment Bank, the European Bank for Reconstruction and Development, and other international financial institutions would require a more extensive survey, therefore we limit ourselves to mentioning their considerable

---

[1] European Commission, Directorate-General for Development, *Understanding European Community Aid* (1997), 1.

[2] Economic co-operation is to create and reinforce a network of business and other economic links between the EU and its partners and to create an environment more favorable to investment and development.

[3] A. Hecker in C.O. Lenz (ed.), *EG-Vertrag* (1994). See Art. 130u(1).

[4] See the contribution of Rosas and Brandtner to this vol.

impact on development co-operation without going into the details of their work.[5] It is important to mention that the European Investment Bank manages Community loans, which primarily come from its own resources. The share of loans, however, is only 9.1 per cent in total EC aid.[6]

I. DEVELOPMENT CO-OPERATION AND POSITIVE WAYS OF PROMOTING HUMAN RIGHTS

The Community's development co-operation, in 1998, is global in reach, having shifted from a policy that paid scant attention to the observance of human rights in third countries to one that emphasizes human rights, democracy, and good govern-ance as core elements of development co-operation.

A. The Community's Development Co-operation

In contrast to Community policy in 1958, when preferential treatment and develop-ment assistance were restricted to associated countries,[7] the successive Lomé Con-ventions (Nos. I–IV) increased the number of recipient countries from the original eighteen of the Yaoundé Convention to seventy-one developing countries, including countries without ties to the Community as former colonies.[8] The EC and the Mediterranean countries launched co-ordinated co-operation in 1972 and amended the bilateral agreements (Mediterranean protocols, also called Maghreb and Mashraq agreements) already concluded in order to integrate these countries into the Community's system of preferential treatment. In 1976 the Community started its ALA Programme of financial and technical co-operation with Asian and Latin American countries. Thus, Community assistance spanned the globe by the early 1980s.

The countries of Central and Eastern Europe (CEEs), the New Independent States (NIS), and Mongolia do not fall within the category of 'developing countries',

---

[5] For a deeper analysis of related problems for the inclusion of human rights in the overall policies and the respective mandates of various international financial institutions, see I.F. Shihata, *The European Bank for Reconstruction and Development: A Comparative Analysis of its Constituent Agreement* (1990) and *The World Bank in a Changing World* (1995), Vol. II; S. Weber, 'Origins of the European Bank for Re-construction and Development' (1994) 48 *International Organization* 1–38; EBRD Memorandum, *Pro-cedures to Implement the Political Aspects of the Mandate of the European Bank for Reconstruction and Development* (28 May 1991); N.H. Moller, 'The World Bank: Human Rights, Democracy and Govern-ance' (1997) 15 *NQHR* 21–45; N.D. Bradlow, 'The World Bank, The IMF and Human Rights' (1996) 6 *Transnat'l L. & Contemp. Probs* 47.

[6] European Commission, note above, at 17.

[7] The so-called overseas countries and territories of the EEC Members. The Treaty provided special rules for dealing with these countries in Art. 131 EC. These agreements were later superseded by the Con-vention of Association with the Associated African States and Madagascar (Yaoundé Convention), signed on 20 July 1963, which adapted relations to the decolonization process, but still addressed only former colonies.

[8] This approach started in 1971 with the introduction of the GSP addressing a large group of develop-ing countries as beneficiaries. See K. Arts, 'Implementing the Right to Development?', in B.-A. An-dreassen and T. Swinehart, *Human Rights in Developing Countries Yearbook 1991* (1992), 41; GSP Regs. 3281/94 [1994] OJ L348/1 and 1256/96 [1996] OJ L160/1.

but the Community regards them as 'countries whose economies are in transition'.[9]
Thus, assistance to these countries, covered by the so-called Phare (CEEs) and Tacis
(NIS and Mongolia) assistance programmes of the Community, started in the late
1980s, only partially resembles what the term 'development' co-operation usually
means. The specific human rights-related initiatives promoted by these assistance
programmes will nevertheless be discussed to produce a more complete picture of
Community engagement in this field (see section III).

The overwhelmingly greater part of Community assistance, no less than 84 per
cent, goes to developing countries and therefore qualifies as Official Development
Assistance (ODA). The Community grants the remaining 16 per cent to economies
in transition, for example the CEEs and NIS, and labels it Official Assistance
(OA).[10] In regional terms, almost half of all Community assistance goes to the ACP
countries; the CEEs and NIS are the second largest recipients, receiving more than
twice the ALA's share,[11] and three times more than the Mediterranean countries.[12]
It will be crucial to observe how the progressive integration of the CEEs into the
European Union and the increasing use of conditionality in the field of human rights
and democratization influences the amount of assistance given to developing countries.

The instruments of Community assistance can be classified as follows:

- Programme aid (Stabex, Sysmin, Support for Structural Adjustment),
- Food aid (ECHO for emergency food aid),
- Humanitarian assistance (ECHO),
- Assistance to NGOs,
- Project aid (Natural Resources Productive Sectors, other Productive Sectors,
  Economic Infrastructure and Services, Social Infrastructure and Services,
  Governance and Civil Society, Multi-sector/Crosscutting),
- Unallocable.[13]

The Community usually defines positive measures to promote human rights and
democracy in third States as project aid, under the title 'governance and civil society'
or 'social infrastructure projects in education and training'. Less often the Community classifies these measures as 'assistance to NGOs' (see section IV D, 'decentralized
co-operation'). Positive measures of Community assistance include the promotion
of civil society as such, of human rights, support for electoral processes, and the rule
of law, as well as the independence of the media. The Community channels this assistance to the third States through relevant programmes in the form of financial and
technical grants. This type of operation, the focal point of this chapter, accounts for
only 2 per cent of total assistance given by the Community.[14]

---

[9] I. Macleod, I.D. Henry, and S. Hyett, *The External Relations of the European Communities* (1996),
348; K.J. Ners, 'Western Assistance to Post-Communist Countries in Central and Eastern Europe', in
J. Randel and T. German (eds.), *The Reality of Aid* (1997), 197.
[10] European Commission, note 1 above, at 3. Figures up to 1995.
[11] P. Burnell, *Foreign Aid in a Changing World* (1997), 161. Figures for 1996.
[12] European Commission, note 1 above, at 3. Figures up to 1995.
[13] *Ibid.*, at 28.   [14] *Ibid.*, at 43.

B. The Original Emphasis of Development Co-operation Activities

In the development policy of the early days, the Community failed to take into account the potential political dimension of development,[15] the possibility of influencing the political system of the recipient country. The role of human rights in development policy concerned only humanitarian relief (the basic needs approach).[16] Inclusion of democratic principles, as respected and understood by the Western World, and the promotion of human rights through development policies were not foreseen.[17] The international community believed that increases in economic wealth and industrialization, brought about by development assistance in the form of single (*ad hoc*) projects, would be sufficient to stimulate growth even among the poorest sectors of society. However, after several years of implementation of this policy, the situation of the poor was not improving.[18]

In response, aid donors moved their focus from project to programme aid in the early 1970s and started to concentrate on sectors of state infrastructure.[19] The commodity crisis influenced development policy within the Community considerably, turning its focus to the acquisition of rare resources.[20] Generally, development policy in the 1970s continued to underestimate the relevance of sustainable development and failed to promote self-sufficiency. The developing countries found themselves in an 'economic mess'[21] caused by, *inter alia*, exploding debts and a balance of payments deficit.

Accordingly, in the 1980s, the prevailing concerns of aid donors were crisis management and eco-political reform in recipient countries (leading to first generation conditionality[22]). Macro-economic structural adjustment programmes,[23] which centre around currency, trade liberalization, and stable public finances, were considered by many donors to be a panacea;[24] disagreements among the Member States

---

[15] Burnell talks about the 'modern politics of aid', note 11 above, at 187.

[16] S.A. Cunliffe, 'Economic Aid as an Instrument for the Promotion of International Human Rights', in D. M. Hill (ed.), *Human Rights and Foreign Policy* (1989), 117.

[17] This can also be explained by a reluctance to criticize newly independent states: W. Hammel, 'Entwicklungszusammenarbeit ist politischer geworden' (1997) 38 *E.+Z* 12.

[18] O. Stokke, 'Foreign Aid: What now?', in O. Stokke (ed.), *Foreign Aid Toward the Year 2000* (1996), 71.

[19] E.g., health, education, drinking water, and rural development. Stokke, note 18 above, at 93.

[20] Still an important issue in, e.g., the relations between the EU and Algeria. See 'Amnesty Asks EU to pressure Algeria on Human Rights', *Reuter EC Report*, 19 Nov. 1996. The dependency on Algeria for natural gas is insufficient reason not to pressure her on human rights issues.

[21] Stokke, note 18 above, at 94.

[22] It was generated by the Bretton Woods system and meant that the donor's intervention extended to the economic sphere of the recipient countries and assistance was made increasingly conditional on sound economic management.

[23] Due to the considerably negative effects of these programmes on society in the recipient countries, the SAPs were later refined and more emphasis was put on social and ecological requirements in the given state. Issues at stake were, for example, the liberalization of the market, which gave control to property owners instead of the people so far engaged in production. Secondly, environmentally sustainable production methods were neglected in response to the pressure to use natural resources. Thirdly, labour standards went down in certain industries because of increased competition. Fourthly, unemployment was fostered by driving small entrepreneurs from the market. Fifthly, costs of social services often increased due to privatization. See M. van Reisen, 'The EU and Africa', in Randel and German, note 9 above, at 181.

[24] For the role of SAPs in civil service reform, see J. Corkery and A. Land, *Civil Service Reform in the Context of Structural Adjustment: A Triangular Relationship*, ECDPM Policy Management Brief No. 7 (Sept. 1997).

were responsible for the Community's delay in introducing such programmes.[25] Despite the social drawbacks of structural adjustment, this macro-economic approach is now an essential element of a comprehensive development policy, because it lays the groundwork for sustainable economic development. However, hunger- and food-related catastrophes in the 1980s again directed the Community's attention towards humanitarian relief and food aid (basic needs), [26] even while the abovementioned economic concerns developed.

Thus, in the first thirty years of its existence, Community assistance changed its strategy from project to programme aid, relying on technical and financial co-operation alongside trade co-operation. However, the policy excluded forms of political co-operation concerning, *inter alia*, human rights and democracy. The next part of our chapter will investigate the process of discovery within the Community of the relationship between (economic) development and human rights issues.

C. The Change in Community Policy: Development Related to Democracy and Human Rights

In the early phase of Community development policy, the initiatives to include human rights considerations in general development policy in the 1970s were conducted *ad hoc* in most instances. These *ad hoc* initiatives had minimal impact on developing countries because they could neither respond effectively to violations nor significantly promote respect for human rights.[27] In other words, the Community took almost twenty years to begin to make serious efforts to include human rights considerations in its general development policy.[28] A Commission memorandum to the Council and the Parliament on human rights, democracy, and development co-operation policy, dated March 1991, paved the way in this direction, followed by a June 1991 European Council resolution which emphasized its dedication to the relationship between human rights and development.[29] The foregoing advances culminated in the Council resolution of 28 November 1991,[30] which officially included issues of human rights and democracy, and their observance in the recipient country, as essential elements in the overall development policy-making process, relying primarily on positive measures. The previous stage, in which human rights' observance

[25] Van Reisen, note 23 above, at 180. It was only in 1988 that the Community adopted a resolution on SAPs in which it finally addressed the social consequences of these programmes. Lomé IV then introduced an additional fund for structural adjustment. Finally, in its 1995 Resolution, the Council asked the Commission to implement the Lomé Convention with greater care regarding the negative social aspects of structural adjustment. Before, the Community had provided financial support through import support, i.e. STABEX and SYSMIN, and Balance of Payment Support (Lomé III Convention).

[26] Arts, note 8 above, at 42; *Bull. EC* 9–1981, points 1.2.1–1.2.8. Attention was directed towards simple food supply, food security, as well as agricultural and rural development.

[27] D. J. Marantis, 'Human Rights, Democracy and Development: The European Community Model' (1994) 7 *Harv. HRJ* 7; Arts (note 8 above, at 50) deals with the early stages of Community development action in favour of human rights, e.g. the case of Uganda in 1977. Moreover, human rights were already mentioned in Lomé III, but these references were still not part of an overall policy and appeared only in the Preamble and in Art. 4.

[28] Arts, note 8 above, at 49.

[29] European Council Resolution, June 1991, *Bull. EC* 6–1991, Annex V, *Declaration on Human Rights*, at 17–18: '[a]ll lasting development should be centered on man as the bearer of human rights'.

[30] Resolution of the Council and of the Member States meeting in the Council on Human Rights, Democracy, and Development of 28 Nov. 1991, *Bull. EC* 11–1991, at 122.

in third countries had played only a minor role in the process of formulation of development policy, gave way to a new era in which considerations of human rights and democracy have in fact become a central element.

Thus, the explicit inclusion of human rights as an aim of development policy was the first important change in Community policy. Previously, the human rights debate in development policy focused on the economic and social needs of the population and the improvement of its economic status as such, as in the basic needs approach discussed above.[31] Lomé Convention IV of 1989 recognized the importance of human rights for development, as reflected in the Preamble, Article 5, and several other Articles. These Articles deal mainly with economic and social rights,[32] probably because the drafters perceived these rights as more closely related to 'economic development'. In contrast, the 28 November Council Resolution explicitly puts equal emphasis on economic, social, and cultural rights and civil and political rights.[33]

The Resolution elevates democracy to a prominent place in development policy, in that the minimum requirement for democracy requires the observance of certain civil and political rights, which fall under the broader category of human rights.[34] Throughout the world, lessons taken from previous failures of development action have shown that growth does not come about by economic assistance alone, but is also closely linked to the organizational structure of society. In the overall context, the international community was discovering that there can be no development without a certain degree of democracy, no democracy without respect for human rights, and, finally, no democracy without development.[35] In short, it is now the accepted view that these concepts are interrelated and interdependent and constitute equal pillars of development co-operation (see also section IV A).

The Community attaches equal importance to the promotion of the rule of law in the recipient country, based on the realization that the rule of law is also closely related to development. The rule of law principle is not new, but played a role in development policy early on, albeit a limited one.[36]

The Maastricht Treaty affirms the Community's course taken regarding development policy, consolidation of democracy, the rule of law and respect for human rights and fundamental freedoms (inclusion of Article 177(2) (*ex* Article 130u(2)) in the EC Treaty). What is interesting, however, is that the notion of human rights, although a firm component of development policy, rarely appears in express terms.

---

[31] Supplying the people with humanitarian aid and guaranteeing the most basic economic and social rights first.

[32] Marantis, note 27 above, at 9. E.g. environmental protection (Title I), rural promotion (Art. 49), cultural development (Arts. 139–140), education and training (Art. 151), the advancement of women (Art. 153), and improved access to health care (Art. 154).

[33] Resolution of the Council, Nov. 1991, note 30 above. It remains to be seen whether the Community translates this focus into practice. See also sect. IV, and European Council resolution, June 1991, note 29 above, at para. 8.

[34] D. David, 'Dossier Human Rights, Democracy and Development', *The Courier* No. 128 (1991), 49; and the Resolution of the Council, Nov. 1991, note 30 above, in which the Council stressed its 'attachment to the principles of representative democracy'.

[35] For the relationship between human rights and economic development see, O. Schachter, *International Law in Theory and Practice* (1991), 348.

[36] Arts, note 8 above, at 52.

Rather, Commission documents[37] couch human rights in terms such as promoting and strengthening the rule of law, promoting a pluralist civil society, and providing initiatives for target groups. In the several technical and financial co-operation programmes, human rights activities are not listed as such;[38] the heading which comes closest is 'democracy and civil society'. Further, human rights and democracy are in practice often reduced to the latter, even if rhetoric pays equal attention to both.[39] Altogether, the Community refers to human rights as part of a 'larger set of requirements';[40] it builds human rights into a triptych consisting of human rights, democracy, and the rule of law, and seems to regard the term of 'good governance' as the primary, all-embracing principle.[41]

The notion of 'good governance' as used in development policy can be traced back to the 1989 World Bank Report,[42] which drew attention to this concept when the World Bank realized that sustainable development had not been achieved by countries receiving aid.[43] Seen in broad terms, a distinction can be made between the economic and political dimensions of governance: the former concerns prices, fiscal and exchange-rate policies, protectionism, subsidies, market liberalization, and the role of the State as an economic agent, while the latter includes the political system, the structure of government, general constitutional provisions, the nature of the electoral system, and the relations between State and civil society.[44] It is mainly the political aspect of good governance that pertains directly to promotion of democracy and support for human rights.[45]

[37] Implementation Report, SEC(92)1915 final; COM(95)191 final; and COM(96)672 final.

[38] See, e.g., COM(98)40 final for ALA; European Commission, *Tacis Interim Evaluation. Synthesis Report* (July 1997), and *The Phare Programme. An Interim Evaluation* (June 1997).

[39] K. Tomasevski, *Development Aid and Human Rights Revisited* (1993), 13.

[40] Resolution of the Council, Nov. 1991, note 30 above.

[41] According to K. Arts, 'European Community Development Cooperation, Human Rights, Democracy and Good Governance: At Odds or at Ease with Each Other?', in K. Ginther *et al.* (eds.), *Sustainable Development and Good Governance* (1995), 264. The Community's position is 'unnecessarily unclear and sometimes even confusing'.

[42] Stokke, note 18 above, at 80; Corkery and Land, note 24 above, at 4; World Bank, *Sub-Sahara Africa—From Crisis to Sustainable Growth* (1989): governance is the 'manner in which power is exercised in the management of a country's economic and social resources for development'.

[43] Stokke, note 18 above, at 81. The lack of good governance was taken to explain the failure of SAPs and economic policy reforms. In the subsequent discussion within the World Bank, 5 criteria of good governance, namely accountability, transparency, predictability, openness, and the rule of law, were elaborated. See Hammel, note 17 above, at 13. These terms are all related to representatives of the public sector: World Bank, *Governance and Development* (1992). The World Bank report was restricted to the economic side of good governance as this falls within its limited mandate. Stokke, at 81, notes 76 and 77; and Shihata, *The World Bank in a Changing World*, note 5 above, at chap. 19.

[44] F.J. van Hoek, 'Some Thoughts on Governance and Democratization', *The Courier* No. 128 (1991), 82.

[45] The Community's understanding of good governance is expressed in the Council's Resolution of November 1991 by stating that 'equitable development can only effectively and sustainably be achieved if a number of general principles of government are adhered to: sensible economic and social policies, democratic decision-making, adequate governmental transparency and financial accountability, creation of a market-friendly environment for development, measures to combat corruption, as well as respect for the rule of law, human rights and freedom of expression': Resolution of the Council, Nov. 1991, note 30 above.

D. The New Emphasis on Positive Measures

1. The November 1991 Resolution   In the 1990s, human rights, democracy, good governance, and the 'incentive'-based approach were officially included in the Community's development policy. The Lomé IV Convention of 1989 had already stipulated a positive approach to human rights when dealing with ACP countries (Article 5). On the other hand, the Commission's March 1991 memorandum[46] still followed traditional policy by emphasizing sanctions as a means of responding to human rights violations and disrespect for democratic principles.[47] The June 1991 European Council Resolution[48] evidenced a change in the Community's attitude. This change was further elaborated in the 28 November 1991 Resolution,[49] which clearly emphasizes positive measures in general development policy towards all recipient States. According to this Resolution 'the Community and its Member States will give high priority to a positive approach that stimulates respect for human rights and encourages democracy'.[50] Nevertheless, negative measures are still considered appropriate responses in the 'event of grave and persistent human rights violations or serious interruptions of the democratic process'.[51] Hence, along with the emphasis on positive measures, the so-called second-generation conditionality in aid was brought to the forefront of Community policy.

The Community can implement the positive approach on which the present chapter concentrates through active support for useful initiatives and through an open and constructive dialogue.[52] The emphasis of the positive approach is on creating an environment conducive to respect for human rights, supported by increased assistance to countries respecting these values.[53]

2. Why Positive Measures Instead of Sanctions?   Economic sanctions (which determined human rights policy in the early days of development co-operation[54]) have been the subject of many comprehensive studies,[55] most of which have been critical of the success of such sanctions.[56] Positive measures, on the other hand, display important advantages. The following paragraphs will discuss the main points of the argument, highlighting the advantages of positive measures without giving an exhaustive overview.

---

[46] *Bull. EC* 3–1991, point 1.3.41.
[47] Tomasevski, note 39 above, at 72. According to Marantis, donors have traditionally favoured punitive strategies to promote the links of human rights and development: Marantis, note 27 above, at 12.
[48] Resolution of the Council, June 1991, note 29 above—'actively promote human rights'.
[49] Resolution of the Council, Nov. 1991, note 30 above.   [50] *Ibid.*   [51] *Ibid.*
[52] COM(94)42 final; SEC(92)1915 final; COM(95)191 final; and COM(96)672 final.
[53] Resolution of the Council, Nov. 1991, note 30 above.   [54] Arts, note 8 above, at 50.
[55] See K. Tomasevski, *Between Sanctions and Elections* (1997); Kausikaan, 'Asia's Different Standard' (1993) 24 *Foreign Policy* 24; J. Nelson, *Encouraging Democracy: What Role for Conditioned Aid* (1992), 47–53. On trade and economic sanctions see Alston, 'International Trade as an Instrument of Positive Human Rights Policy' (1982) 4 *HRQ* 155, note 61; D. Baldwin, *Economic Statecraft* (1985); G. Hufbauer, J. Schott, and K. Elliot, *Economic Sanctions Reconsidered* (1985); D. Leyton-Brown (ed.), *The Utility of International Economic Sanctions* (1987); S. Hoffmann, *The Ethics and Politics of Humanitarian Intervention* (1996).
[56] Alston, note 55 above, at 155; G.A. Lopez and D. Cortright, 'Economic Sanctions in Contemporary Global Relations', in G.A. Lopez and D. Cortright (eds.), *Economic Sanctions: Panacea or Peacebuilding in a Post-Cold War World?* (1995), 6, and other contributions to that book.

Whereas negative measures are generally considered to be promising due to their capacity to exert pressure on governments and to express clear limits for state behaviour in the international context, it is exactly this component of negative measures which also leads to their first drawback: their infringement on state sovereignty. States, especially the newly independent states of the 1960s, were extremely reluctant to accept outside interference in their internal affairs because domestic policy was considered out of reach of other States.[57] Therefore, strong interference by one State in issues the target State considers part of its domestic policy could likely lead to a breakdown of communication between the States. Undeniably, such infringements of sovereignty (ranging from appeals to observe human rights to the cessation of aid and trade) are usually considered permissible in international human rights literature, nevertheless, the danger of deteriorating relations with the target State remains an obstacle to sanctions.[58] Positive measures, on the other hand, generally do not infringe upon the sovereignty of the State concerned, since they constitute measures of support and are increasingly based on consensus and co-operation through policy-dialogue.[59] This is not always the case, as exceptions can be found in which outside support of an anti-regime NGO, whose aim is to enhance the democratization of the country, can strongly infringe upon the sovereignty of the recipient country. The recent Mexican elections present just such an example. There the EU wanted to support a specific NGO before the elections, but was prevented from doing so by resistance of the Mexican government which felt the Community was infringing upon its sovereignty.[60] Algeria also rejected assistance from the EU. In January of 1998, when the EU *troika* visited Algeria, the Algerian authorities not only rejected the offer of inquiry into human rights by a special envoy of the United Nations, but also the proposition of humanitarian aid,[61] and any form of political dialogue regarding ongoing human rights violations.[62]

Another disadvantage of negative measures is that they do not address the actual causes of human rights violations, but only scratch the surface of much deeper issues.[63] Moreover, the victims of such measures are the members of the population of the State concerned, not its political leaders.[64] Accordingly, sanctions often mobilize the affected population to unite with the oppressive regime against the State

[57] Marantis, note 27 above, at 2–5.

[58] See e.g. the reluctance in this respect by the Chinese and the Indonesian governments. P. van Dijk, 'A Common Standard of Achievement: About Universal Validity and Uniform Interpretation of International Human Rights Norms' (1995) 13 *NQHR* 105.

[59] The flexible mechanism for identifying areas for funding and priorities for implementation.

[60] Interview with an EU official of DG I B; 'EU Cancels Funding for Human Rights Body's Election Observation', *BBC Summary of World Broadcasts*, 4 Apr. 1997. Mexico also opposed the inclusion of the human rights clause in a trade and co-operation agreement, but the EU insisted on the linkage and Mexico finally relented: Human Rights Watch, *Human Rights Watch World Report 1998: Events of 1997* (1998), p. xxv.

[61] A fact that was strongly regretted by European diplomats: 'EU Envoy Says Authorities Rejected Offer of Inquiry into Human Rights', *BBC Summary of World Broadcasts*, 23 Jan. 1998.

[62] J. van der Klaauw, 'Human Rights News: European Union' (1998) 16 *NQHR* 91.

[63] Alston, note 55 above, at 155.

[64] Marantis, note 27 above, at note 58. Surprisingly, sanctions are sometimes deemed 'effective' without regard to the consequences they have on the population.

imposing sanctions, contrary to the aim of negative measures.[65] However, the Community continues humanitarian assistance during the suspension of aid to counter the effect of sanctions on the poorest members of the population.[66] In comparison to negative measures, positive initiatives centred on humanitarian concerns are not targeted at governments, but are determined by the needs of the people.[67] This focus on the individual underlies the belief that change must come from within, not imposed from outside solely through coercive measures.[68]

Furthermore, negative measures, as applied by Western donors, usually promote the enforcement of civil and political rights only.[69] Sanctions such as withdrawal of aid or the termination of preferential trade arrangements have an undesirable effect on social and economic rights because a government's respect for these rights will not improve without outside assistance. Therefore, when the Community applies negative measures, they are unable to meet the objective of promoting both sets of rights equally, given the declared interdependence of these rights.[70] In theory, positive measures are meant to foster a broader range of rights as reflected in the guidelines of the November 28 Resolution which call for observation of economic and social and civil and political rights equally.[71] This chapter will show that Community programmes, in practice, still closely connect social and economic rights to the basic needs approach, especially in the lesser developed countries, and consequently these rights still lack equal standing with civil and political rights in Community programmes.

Another important factor in a critical assessment of negative measures is their close relationship to foreign policy considerations, which encourages more arbitrary action towards countries which range low on the 'foreign policy scale'. Since self-interest determines a state's external relations, a decision to apply economic sanctions can be a sign of low interest in the target country.[72] Positive measures remain more distinct from foreign policy considerations, enabling the donor governments to act more rationally and less arbitrarily. It is also easier to find common ground of action for a positive measure than for a negative one. In the case of Nigeria, France granted visas to several members of the Nigerian government despite the imposed EU sanctions, and thus contradicted a negative measure established by the Community.[73]

---

[65] J. Galtung, 'On the Effects of International Economic Sanctions: With Examples from the Case of Rhodesia' (1967) 19 *World Politics* 378–416. Galtung was the first to talk about the 'rally around the flag effect'.

[66] Resolution of the Council, Nov. 1991, note 30 above.

[67] Marantis, note 27 above, at 14.   [68] Alston, note 55 above, at 169.

[69] Marantis, note 27 above, at 14; Alston, note 55 above, at 155.

[70] *Vienna Declaration and Programme of Action*, A/CONF.157/23 (1993), para. 5.

[71] 'Development cooperation is based on the central place of the individual and has, therefore, in essence to be designed with a view to promoting—in parallel with economic and social rights—civil and political liberties by means of representative democratic rule that is based on respect for human rights': Resolution of the Council, Nov. 1991, note 30 above; Marantis, note 27 above, at 14.

[72] Alston questions this assumption, note 55 above, at 169.

[73] Human Rights Watch, note 60 above, at p. xxv. Human Rights Watch/Africa calls for control of the respect of visa restrictions: *Permanent Transition: Current Violations of Human Rights in Nigeria* (A803) (1996), 6, and *Transition or Travesty? Nigeria's Endless Process of Return to Civilian Rule* (A906) (1997), 6.

However, positive measures can have dangerous consequences if the donor fails to consider foreign policy interests. For example, in the case of Ethiopia, the Community allocated aid to the country between 1991 and 1994 at a time when it was devastated by civil war, led by a repressive regime and isolated by much of the rest of the donor community. The ongoing financial support for the regime might have enhanced its participation in the civil war.[74] The 'philosophy' of the positive approach was also maintained in Algeria when the European Community decided to continue to support the Algerian authorities in their fight against terrorism, despite ongoing violence and killings within the country, by pushing the early conclusion of a partnership agreement (but including a human rights clause).[75] In Albania, the EC uncritically supported the oppressive regime of Sali Berisha with $560 million from 1990, and thus the European Community indirectly fuelled the violent political upheaval there in 1997.[76] The EC granted preferential trade status as well as a new aid package to the Federal Republic of Yugoslavia in the spring of 1997 without regard to the human rights violations that were still going on there at that time. Human Rights Watch claimed that leverage, which could have been used to ensure compliance with the Dayton Agreement, was lost because of the European Community's actions.[77]

Finally, sanctions will have their intended effect only if the target government is willing to and capable of responding to pressure. Sanctions will have little effect on strong, undemocratic regimes and no effect on countries that do not have suitable institutions which can react to a situation and improve it.[78] In sum, although negative measures may help in very specific situations, sanctions are usually a sign of previous failure of aid to promote human rights and democratic institutions.[79] The promotion of human rights in a positive 'system' of measures adopts a preventive approach, addressing the roots of the problem instead of waiting for undesired results and then trying to 'repair' them.[80]

A very interesting example of combining a nominally negative instrument with a positive policy has been the case of Belarus. Using a human rights clause in the Tacis Regulation as its basis, the Commission has proposed to the Council the establishment of a Civil Society Development Programme for Belarus.[81] The Commission suggested this after the Council had signalled that, despite the *de facto* suspension of all Tacis assistance in response to the constitutional crisis in 1996, there was room for additional programmes.[82] At the time of writing, the status of the Civil Society

---

[74] Simon Maxwell, *Does European Aid Work? An Ethiopian Case Study* (1996) 13; IDS, Institute of Development Research, *An Evaluation of Development Cooperation between the European Union and Ethiopia, 1976–1994, Main Report* (June 1996), para. 279.

[75] Van der Klaauw, note 62 above, at 91. [76] Human Rights Watch, note 60 above, at p. xxv.

[77] Human Rights Watch/Helsinki, *Yugoslavia (Serbia and Montenegro). Discouraging Democracy: Elections and Human Rights in Serbia* (D911) (1997), 3.

[78] Marantis, note 27 above, at 13.

[79] Tomasevski, note 55 above, at 9. Tomasveski also questions, at 12, why a country that fulfills all the conditions linked to assistance should need assistance.

[80] Minister Spranger, 'Entwicklungspolitik im Zeichen der Zeitenwende', *Frankfurter Allgemeine Zeitung*, 19 Apr. 1997, at 5.

[81] COM(97)441 final, as amended by COM(97)602 final. See also the recommendations by Human Rights Watch/Helsinki, *Republic of Belarus: Crushing Civil Society* (D908) (1997).

[82] Council Conclusions of 24 Feb. 1997; Council Declaration of 29 Apr. 1997, *Bull. EU* 4–1997, point 1.4.6; and Council Conclusions of 15 Sept. 1997, all cited in COM(97)602 final.

Development Programme is still under negotiation with the Belarussian authorities.[83] This case is an example of the positive approach of the Community, which is generally reflected in the 'positive' interpretation of the human rights clauses by the Commission based on the wording of 'appropriate measures'.

3. Positive Measures Embraced by the New Approach   The aim of positive initiatives is to provide assistance to countries in need by building up society and establishing conditions for democracy, sustainable development, and human rights. In short, the goal is to develop an environment conducive to these elements and to assist governments and local organizations in their own efforts to obtain these goals. The Council listed examples of positive measures in its November 28 Resolution:

- support for countries which are attempting to institute democracy and improve their human rights performance;
- the holding of elections, the setting-up of new democratic institutions, and the strengthening of the rule of law;
- the strengthening of the judiciary, the administration of justice, crime prevention, and the treatment of offenders;
- promoting the role of NGOs and other institutions which are necessary for a pluralist society;
- the adoption of a decentralized approach to co-operation;
- ensuring equal opportunities for all.[84]

The November 28 Council Resolution's impact on Community policy has been twofold: first, the Community no longer views development in the recipient countries as independent from accountable government, democracy, and the observance of human rights; secondly, an integrated approach has been defined, including both negative and positive measures.[85]

In 1992, two major documents, the Commission Communication, 'Development co-operation policy in the run-up to the year 2000', and the Declaration of the Council and of the representatives of Governments of Member States meeting in the Council on aspects of development co-operation policy in the run-up to 2000 provided both guidelines for future action until 2000 and a résumé of three decades of Community policy.[86] These documents affirm that Community policy cannot replace national action, for example, good domestic policies or commercial trade outlets; rather the Community should use its development policy as a mechanism to foster economic and political reforms (including human rights and democracy) and sustainable development in the recipient country. The Council of Development Ministers has suggested broadening the scope of development policy by including such issues as freedom of the press, protection of minorities, and return of political exiles.[87]

---

[83] Interview with an EU official working on the case.
[84] Resolution of the Council, Nov. 1991, note 30 above.   [85] Marantis, note 27 above, at 2.
[86] SEC(92)915 final; Declaration of the Council and the Member States adopted in Brussels on 18 Nov. 1992, *Bull. EC* 11–1992, at 93. Reprinted in *The Courier* No. 137 (Jan.–Feb. 1993), 8–10.
[87] Declaration of the Council, note 86 above. See also Declaration of the Council in preparation for Vienna, *Bull. EC* 5–1993, at point 1.3.41.

II. LEGAL BASIS AND ADMINISTRATIVE FRAMEWORK OF DEVELOPMENT CO-OPERATION

A. *The General Competence of the European Community with regard to Development Co-operation*

The competence of the European Community to participate in development co-operation derives from several provisions of the Treaty establishing the European Community. Until the conclusion of the Treaty on European Union, no provisions existed specifically dealing with development policy. Nevertheless, Community competence was already established in this field, and was derived mainly from Articles 32 (*ex* Article 38) (common agricultural policy), 131 (*ex* Article 110) (common commercial policy), 182 (*ex* Article 131) (association of overseas countries and territories), and 310 (*ex* Article 238) (association agreements) respectively.

The Treaty on European Union introduced a title on development co-operation into the EC Treaty (Title XVII, Article 177 (*ex* Article 130u)). For the first time, common objectives of development policy were set out in express terms (Article 130u(1) and (2)):

- the sustainable economic and social development of the developing countries, and more particularly the most disadvantaged among them;
- the smooth and gradual integration of the developing countries into the world economy;
- the campaign against poverty in the developing countries (Article 130u (1));
- development and consolidation of democracy and the rule of law, respect for human rights and fundamental freedoms (Article 130u (2))[88].

Article 130u(1) EC clearly states that measures of the Community and those taken by Member States are to be complementary. Thus, Member States still furnish the lion's share of total assistance individually[89].

Article 180 (*ex* Article 130x) obliges Member States to co-ordinate their development efforts. This includes the framework of international organizations and conferences. Article 181 (*ex* Article 130y) states that the Community and the Member States have to co-operate with international organizations and third States within their respective spheres of competence.

The aim of Article 178 (*ex* Article 130v) is to achieve a coherent policy within the Community: the Community must take the above-mentioned objectives into account

[88] The legal service of the Council is of the opinion that Art. 130u(2) is merely an ancillary provision and that therefore no measures in the framework of development policy could be adopted on the basis of Art. 130w which only promote the objectives of Art. 130u(2) and do not fall under Art. 130u(1). It bases this interpretation on the ECJ's judgment in Case C–168/94, *Portugal* v. *Council* [1996] ECR I–6207. It may however be questioned if this is a correct interpretation of Art. 130u. The wording does not necessarily imply a subsidiary character of Art. 130u(2). The unsatisfactory results of traditional development policy have led to the new emphasis in EC development policy, acknowledging that structures securing human rights, the rule of law, and democracy are necessary to achieve sustainable development. Thus, measures to secure these aims *are* development policy and should not merely be regarded as ones which might merely accompany development policy. For further discussion, see the contribution of Weiler to this volume.

[89] European Commission, note 1 above, at 1.

in all policies which are likely to affect developing countries. We will take a closer look at these provisions in section V of the present chapter.

Article 179 (*ex* Article 130w) enables the Council of Ministers to adopt measures necessary to promote the objectives of development policies. The Development Council, i.e. the assembly of the Member States' Ministers for Development Co-operation, makes decisions regarding assistance policies by a qualified majority. The adoption of measures takes place under Article 251 EC, the joint legislative procedure with the European Parliament.[90] The European Parliament also has the power to influence development policy through its budgetary powers.

As for the special regime under the Lomé Convention, it remains untouched by Articles 177–179(3) (*ex* Articles 130u–130w(3)) EC.[91]

B. The Legal Basis of Concrete Programmes

The Community takes concrete action based on relevant EC legislation,[92] association agreements, and their financial protocols. Several programmes lack an express legal basis other than inclusion in the Community budget.[93] Alternatively, the Community can base its programmes on Articles 6 and 11(2) (*ex* Articles F.2 and J.1(2)) TEU in connection with Article 177(2) (*ex* Article 130u(2)) EC, the European Council declarations on human rights of 28 and 29 June 1991 and the Council resolution of 28 November 1991 on human rights and democracy in developing countries. These instruments include support for democratization processes and for organizations promoting human rights in particular fields.[94]

Thus far, the Community has determined its approach to human rights in terms of geography. Obviously, this does not facilitate the task of ensuring coherence. For these reasons, and in order to arrive at a global appreciation of human rights, the Commission has proposed a specific Council regulation on human rights.[95] The intent of this regulation is to provide the legal basis for all financial measures with regard to human rights and democracy that could represent a step towards more coherence. It will denominate the objectives and general principles of action for the

[90] Prior to the Treaty of Amsterdam, the procedure of co-operation was applicable: see *ex* Art. 130w. The rest of Title XVII remains unchanged.

[91] Relations with Eastern Europe and the NIS are not covered by this title either, since they are not part of 'development co-operation' in the strict sense. See above, sect. I.

[92] To name some of the most important regulations: ALA Council Reg. 443/92 [1992] OJ L52/1; Phare Council Reg. 3906/89 [1989] OJ L375/11, as last amended by Council Reg. 753/96 [1996] OJ L103/5; Tacis Council Reg. 2053/93 [1993] OJ L187/1; Council Reg. 1279/96 [1996] OJ L165/1; MEDA Council Reg. 1488/96 [1996] OJ L189/1. All these regulations have been based on Art. 235 EC.

[93] This does not pose a problem given that budgetization is sufficient to provide a legal basis even for agreements on financial help. Cf. C. Vedder, 'Commentary on Article 238', in E. Grabitz and M. Hilf, *Kommentar zur Europäischen Union* (1997), note 17a; ECJ, *Opinion 1/78, International Agreement on Natural Rubber* [1979] ECR 2871–918. In most cases, Art. 130w would provide a proper legal basis anyway.

[94] Budget Items B7–7020: support for promoting human rights and democracy in the developing countries with the exception of Latin America and the Mediterranean countries; B7–7030: democratization process in Latin America; B7–7050: programme for democracy in Mediterranean countries; B7–7040: support for organizations pursuing humanitarian aims and defence of human rights; B7–7070: for rehabilitation centres for torture victims and for organizations offering concrete help to victims of human rights abuses, all under Chap. B7–7 of the budget ('European initiative for democracy and the protection of human rights').

[95] COM(97)0357 final, SYN(97)0191.

promotion of human rights and democratic principles and will establish a unified procedure. An advisory committee, composed of representatives of the Member States and chaired by the representative of the Commission, is to assist the Commission. The Commission will submit annual reports. The proposal indicates Article 179 (*ex* Article 130w) as its legal basis. In light of the deliberations in the Council relating to the EC's external competence in this area, it seems possible that the draft regulation will be split up into two regulations, the first one applicable to developing countries (and based on Article 179 (*ex* Article 130w) EC), and the second one applicable to all other countries (based on Article 308 (*ex* Article 235) EC).[96] The Legal Service of the Council holds that the current proposal would not possess a proper legal basis. In its opinion, some of the measures contained therein could be included in a regulation based on Article 179 (*ex* Article 130w), others in existing acts such as Phare, Tacis, etc., and those remaining could only be adopted pursuant to Article 13 (*ex* Article J.3) TEU without recourse to Article 308 (*ex* Article 235) EC. This seems to be an unnecessarily restrictive interpretation of the European Court of Justice's Advisory Opinion 2/94.[97] Opinion 2/94 does not deny the existence of an EC human rights competence in external relations, but pronounces on the limits of that competence. These limits consist in acts bringing about fundamental changes to the institutional balance.[98] It is nowadays difficult to sustain the view that human rights do not represent an objective of the EC.[99] Given these facts, the Community should be deemed competent to adopt the proposal under Article 308 (*ex* Article 235) EC, and it should do that so as not to miss the opportunity towards more coherence. Even if the Community divided the proposal into two regulations, it would represent a decisive step in the right direction.

C. Procedure

The Council of Ministers (more precisely, the Development Council) makes decisions of EC development policy on the basis of Commission proposals. Those relating to the Lomé Convention are subject to special procedures: in most areas, the Community and the ACP countries share decision-making at the level of the Council of Ministers, the Committee of Ambassadors, and the Joint Assembly (Article 338 of Lomé IV).

The European Commission (with the participation of the management committees under ALA, Mead, Phare, and Tacis and the EDF committee under Lomé) manages the distribution of EC assistance, and the European Investment Bank manages its own resources. Within the Commission, four departments handle development co-operation[100]:

- DG VIII (Development)—ACP States;

---

[96] B. Brandtner and A. Rosas, 'Human Rights and the External Relations of the European Community: An Analysis of Doctrine and Practice' (1998) 9 *EJIL* 468, 489.

[97] *Opinion 2/94, Accession to the European Convention on Human Rights* [1996] ECR I–1.

[98] See the contribution of Weiler and Fries to this vol.

[99] Rosas and Brandtner, note 96 above, at 5.

[100] European Commission, note 1 above, at 18.

- DG I A (External Relations)—Central and Eastern Europe, former Soviet Union, Mongolia, Turkey, and other European countries outside the Union;
- DG I B (External Relations)—Mediterranean, Middle East, Latin America, most Asian developing countries;
- DG I (External Relations)—China, Korea, Taiwan.[101]

A separate Directorate General (the European Community Humanitarian Office) deals with humanitarian assistance, a complex area on which this chapter will not elaborate.

The regular Community Budget and the European Investment Bank provide the necessary financial means for development co-operation. Within the framework of Lomé, the European Investment Bank and the European Development Fund provide the financing (Article 220 of Lomé IV). Currently, the eighth European Development Fund covers the second phase of Lomé IV. It has been set up by an internal agreement concluded between the Community Member States on 20 December 1995 regarding financing and administration of community assistance, and is thus financed by the contributions of the individual States.

Because of the intergovernmental structure of spending under the Lomé Treaty, the European Parliament does not have the competence to exert control over the EDF, unlike in all other cases of assistance, where it has to approve the budget.

As far as allocation of funds from Community budget line B7–70 is concerned, the Standing Inter-departmental Human Rights Co-ordination Group has a decisive role in setting up general guidelines. The group is run by DG I A and is composed of representatives from a variety of departments: Secretariat-General, Forward Studies Unit, Legal Service, DGs I, I A, I B, II, V, VIII, X, XI, XII, XIII, XV, XIX, XXII, XXIV, XXIII, and ECHO.[102]

III. THE COMMUNITY'S REGIONAL PROGRAMMES TO PROMOTE HUMAN RIGHTS, DEMOCRACY, AND GOOD GOVERNANCE

A. ACP States

One of the priorities of the European Community's development policy has always been co-operation with ACP States. The Lomé Conventions represent a unique form of such co-operation, linking the Community and its Member States with seventy-one countries from Sub-Saharan Africa, the Caribbean, and the Pacific.[103]

---

[101] From the programmes mentioned above, DG I A manages Budget Items B7–7040, B7–7070, Phare, and Tacis; DG I B B7–7030, B7–7050, MEDA, and ALA; DG VIII B7–7020 and the Lomé Convention.

[102] European Parliament, *Report on setting up a single coordinating structure within the European Commission responsible for human rights and democratization (Lenz Report)*, A4–393/97, at 14.

[103] European Commission, note 1 above, at 9. South Africa joined the ACP States in Apr. 1997, but benefits from only some parts of the convention: *ibid.*, at 8.

The unique character of this framework of co-operation stems from three main characteristics. The first important element is the contractual relationship between the parties, in which rights and obligations exist for both sides. The principle of partnership is another important theme, stressing the equality and sovereignty of the partners, and encouraging dialogue between them. The third contributing factor is the inclusion of a combination of trade and aid provisions in a single agreement, creating a variety of possibilities.[104] Other contributors to the present volume are discussing trade issues,[105] therefore, we will limit the present analysis to the aid component of the Convention, i.e. financial and technical co-operation.

The various conventions have set different priorities: whereas Lomé I and II focused on industrial development and Lomé III on self-reliant development promoting self-sufficiency and food security, Lomé IV emphasizes human rights (Article 5), the status of women (Article 4), protection of the environment (Articles 6 and 14), decentralized co-operation (Articles 20–22), diversification of ACP economies (Article 18), and the promotion of the private sector.[106] The mid-term review of Lomé IV included human rights, democratic principles, and the rule of law as essential elements of the Convention and established a link between good governance and effective development (Article 5).[107] In practice, under EDF VII and VIII, the latter issues have not yet achieved priority status.[108]

The European Development Fund, established by financial protocols to the respective Convention, provides most of the funding for development co-operation with the ACP states.[109]

The large majority of development grants under the Lomé Conventions has been distributed as programmable aid,[110] defined as non-repayable grants which finance traditional development programmes on the basis of national or regional programmes. Although the largest share of aid is still programmable aid, the emphasis is gradually shifting to non-programmable aid, which is granted conditionally on a case-by-case basis. The benefit of non-programmable aid is that it elevates the importance of political dialogue between the EC and the ACP States. The procedure used by the Community to distribute aid to ACP States is as follows: first, the Community allocates a certain amount of its funds to each ACP State. The Community and the individual States then form agreements setting up a National Indicative Programme (NIP). This NIP agreement defines priority development objectives, principal sectors, potential projects, and programmes, etc. Finally, once all the terms have been agreed upon, the Community makes the finances available. The negotiation of the NIPs takes place entirely on the inter-governmental level. Civil society

---

[104] *Ibid.*, at 51. [105] Cf. Brandtner and Rosas, n. 96 above.

[106] European Commission, note 1 above, at 52.

[107] On the possibility of imposing sanctions in case of a violation of an essential element (Art. 366a(2)) see the contribution of Riedel and Will to this vol.

[108] ADE final report, *Evaluation of EU Aid to ACP Countries managed by the Commission, Phase I* (July 1997), 13–19.

[109] Humanitarian aid and aid for refugees are financed by resources from the EC budget as well as by Lomé funds (Arts. 254 and 255 of Lomé IV). Food aid and assistance to NGOs are not delivered by the EDF but by the EC budget. See European Commission, note 1 above, at 58. Furthermore, there exist several budget lines relating to specific purposes which are applicable also to ACP States.

[110] C. Piening, *Global Europe: The European Union in World Affairs* (1997), 185.

representatives are not substantially involved in this process. As a consequence, negotiators often fail to create an agreement reflecting accurately the entire spectrum of local needs.[111] Comprehensive country strategies are required. Since decentralization enhances knowledge and efficiency and might also enhance compatibility between NIPs and other Community instruments, it should be a priority in future negotiations. For example, the lack of an integrated aid strategy in the EC development programme in Ethiopia has been regarded as a serious shortcoming.[112]

However, progress is being made towards more efficiency. Lomé IV (revised) has introduced phased disbursal of funds to encourage their more efficient use. Until the mid-term review of Lomé IV, once funds were released, the respective country's subsequent performance in development and governance was, in principle, irrelevant to the availability of the grants, unless the Community completely suspended funding due to human rights violations. Phased disbursal under the current convention is divided into two parts. The first 70 per cent is made available upon conclusion of the NIP. The Community only releases the remaining 30 per cent after a positive evaluation of the implementation of the NIP has been made within 3 years (Article 282(3) and (4) of Lomé IV (revised)). If the receiving State has not properly implemented the NIP, the Community may spend the remaining 30 per cent for other development purposes (Article 282(5)). Article 284(3) requires the parties to submit annual reports on the progress of the NIP's implementation.

The dialogue leading to the adoption of a NIP has become an important mechanism for protecting human rights within the context of such agreements. Of course, the negotiating government plays the paramount role in all efforts to improve the human rights situation of its country. By discussion of development priorities and methods within the Community, human rights can become an integral part of the State's development programme, rather than being imposed on States by the donor.[113] Articles 4 and 5 now allow for the inclusion of human rights considerations within the framework of this dialogue, although the Community must attempt to realize the full potential of this approach.

The concept of decentralized co-operation, which can contribute effectively to the promotion of human rights, the rule of law, and good governance and has been formally included in Lomé IV, will be explained in section IV.

In view of the expiry of Lomé IV in the year 2000, the Community is currently discussing the future of the European–ACP relationship. On 27 October 1997, in a communication to the Council and the European Parliament, the Commission issued guidelines for the negotiation of new co-operation agreements with the African, Caribbean, and Pacific Countries.[114] These guidelines reflect the public debate which followed the release of the Green Paper on relations between the European Union and the ACP Countries on the eve of the twenty-first century.[115] Obviously, this demonstrates the Community's willingness to maintain a special relationship with the ACP States. The Community recognizes the benefits of its

---

[111] A. Cox, J. Healy, and A. Koning, *How European Aid Works: A Comparison of Management Systems and Effectiveness* (1997), 133.

[112] IDS, note 74 above, at 87.

[113] Marantis, note 27 above, at 22.   [114] COM(97)537 final.   [115] COM(96)570 final.

association (partnership, contractuality, predictability, security),[116] but also realizes that changes are called for.[117]

The Commission has emphasized the need for a new political dialogue, particularly taking into account human rights, democracy, the rule of law, and good governance.[118] Furthermore, the Commission proposes including good governance as an essential element in future agreements,[119] and suggests local capacity-building as a guiding principle of practical co-operation arrangements. Areas mentioned which should be given priority in such agreements are, among others, democratic reforms, the consolidation of the rule of law, good governance, the strengthening of civil society, and the creation of networks.[120] The Commission is also concerned with the promotion of gender equality.[121]

According to the Commission, programming is the best instrument available for policy dialogue and should therefore have a central role in all ACP States. Within the States, programming should be co-ordinated among donors and involve all non-governmental players as well.[122] Instead of automatic allocation, the Commission has proposed a system of rolling programming with annual reviews, in accordance with the position that the criterion of need must be complemented by the criterion of merit.[123]

The 1997 communication does not discuss the question of budgeting. In the Green Paper, the Commission reiterated its demand for incorporation of the European Development Fund into the Community budget.[124] From the point of view of coherence as well as democracy (the European Parliament controls the budget), such an inclusion should be welcomed. Whether enough political will can be created to abolish the inter-governmental structure of Lomé spending is doubtful.

B. The Mediterranean

The Community usually divides the Mediterranean region into two main geographical areas: the Northern Mediterranean countries (Malta, Cyprus, and Turkey) and the Eastern and Southern Mediterranean countries (Morocco, Algeria, Tunisia,[125] Egypt, Jordan, Syria, Lebanon,[126] and Israel). Iran, Iraq, Yemen, and the other countries of the Middle East, and the Palestinian Administrative Areas are dealt with separately.

The Barcelona Declaration, adopted by the European Council in 1995, for the first time introduced a political dimension to Community–Mediterranean relations. The Declaration formulated a 'Political and Security Partnership' and a 'Social, Cultural and Human Affairs Partnership' under the previously established Euro–Mediterranean Partnership.[127] The aim of these partnerships is to establish a

---

[116] *Ibid.*, at 7.   [117] *Ibid.*, at 29.   [118] *Ibid.*, at 12.   [119] *Ibid.*, at 13.
[120] *Ibid.*, at 19.   [121] *Ibid.*, at 20.   [122] *Ibid.*, at 27.   [123] *Ibid.*, at 28.
[124] *Ibid.*, at p. xv.   [125] Also known as Maghreb countries.
[126] Also known as Mashraq countries.

[127] It brings together the European Union, its 15 Member States and the 12 Mediterranean partners (Morocco, Algeria, Tunisia, Egypt, Jordan, Lebanon, Syria, Israel, Cyprus, Malta, Turkey, and the Occupied Territories) and complements the bilateral agreements with a region-wide strategy: European Commission, note 1 above, at 78. The third element is focused on economic and social partnership, and therefore of limited relevance to the present survey.

permanent forum for political dialogue between the parties.[128] This region-wide approach,[129] authorized until 2000, also includes a considerable increase in funds, raising the budget to 4.7 billion ECU.[130] Despite the inclusion of this new political orientation, the Euro–Mediterranean relationship continues to emphasize trade relations (under the third objective of the Barcelona Declaration on 'economic and financial partnership').

The partnership is given legal effect through bilateral Association Agreements.[131] Its financial and technical co-operation provisions are implemented through the Community's assistance programme for the Mediterranean countries. Article 2 of this new 'MEDA' Regulation, 1488/96,[132] includes respect for human rights and democracy within its main objectives. Thus, technical and financial measures can be used to promote human rights and democracy. The new MEDA Democracy Programme,[133] created in 1996 by an initiative of the European Parliament, finances specific human rights-related activities. In 1996, sixty-two human rights-related projects were financed with 9 million ECU, and 8 million ECU were allocated to fund such activities in 1997. Subsidies are granted to non-profit organizations, universities, and public bodies. Beneficiary states are all partners which adopted the Barcelona Declaration,[134] although 69 per cent of subsidies in 1996[135] were absorbed by support for the peace process in the Middle East.[136] The aim of MEDA

[128] This was new, as before there was 'no overall political framework for dialogue comparable to the CSCE': E. Mortimer, 'Europe and the Mediterranean: The Security Dimension', in P. Ludlow (ed.), *Europe and the Mediterranean* (1994), 118.

[129] The 'New Mediterranean Policy' in 1991 was the first attempt to apply a region-wide strategy in the Mediterranean. Before, the Community had to rely exclusively on bilateral agreements, as the differences between the given countries were too great and political tensions too prevalent: F. Nuscheler and O. Schmuck, *Die Süd-Politik der EG* (1992), 178; Special Association Agreements: Turkey 1963, Malta 1971, Cyprus 1973; Co-operation Agreements: Israel 1975, Algeria, Morocco, Tunisia, Egypt, Lebanon, Jordan, and Syria 1978; Yugoslavia 1980, accompanied by financial protocols to be renewed every 5 years.

[130] European Commission, note 1 above, at 10. 'The funds disbursed through the MEDA-regulation are wholly insufficient. They represent only a drop in the ocean. 4.685 billion ECU to spread between 12 countries is not enough. Portugal alone has received 3 billion dollars a year to promote economic and social integration', say Moroccan Employers: *Agence Europe*, No. 2176 (Nov. 1996) 8.

[131] Agreements were signed with Tunisia (17 July 1995), Israel (20 Nov. 1995), and Morocco (26 Feb. 1996). Negotiations have begun with Egypt, Jordan, Lebanon, Algeria, and an interim agreement has been signed with the PLO (24 Feb. 1997), Human Rights Watch/Middle East, *Lebanon. Restrictions on Broadcasting: In Whose Interest?* (E901) (1997), 5. HRW calls on the EU to use the conclusion of the Association Agreement to exert pressure on Lebanon to comply with its obligations deriving from Art. 19 of the International Covenant on Civil and Political Rights (adopted by GA Res. 2200 A (XXI) (1966). In United Nations, *A Compilation of International Instruments* (1994), i, Part 1, 20.

[132] [1996] OJ L189/1.

[133] Budget heading B7–705. The chap. B7–7 extends beyond the scope of technical and financial assistance in a narrow sense.

[134] See note 127 above.

[135] European Commission, *Information Note No. 2, Euro-Mediterranean Partnership, 'MEDA Democracy'*, Unit 1 B/A/1, Jan. 1997.

[136] The Community has a considerable self-interest in the whole region as far as stability and immigration are concerned. The Mediterranean region, besides its geographical and economic similarities, has always been characterized by a considerable difference in political systems (parliamentary democracies, military dictatorships, quasi-feudal monarchies). Moreover, the existence of a relevant number of minorities in some of the Mediterranean States, such as Egypt, Cyprus, Israel, and the different cultures and religions living together in a relatively close area (including Islamic states in the Middle East) pose particular challenges to a region-wide Community policy: A. Tovias, 'The Mediterranean Economy', in Ludlow, note 128 above, at 4. See also COM(97)715 final.

democracy in the future is to achieve a certain regional balance regarding the transfer of resources.[137]

C. Asia and Latin America

European Community assistance to the Asian and Latin American developing countries[138] was initiated relatively late in comparison to that to the ACP countries. The Treaty of Rome did not provide for any assistance to these countries. Despite this, mutual relationships have evolved quickly, and, in the 1990s, co-operation agreements with the Latin America countries have entered the 'third-generation'.[139] These 'third-generation' agreements include a clause designed to safeguard democratic principles and human rights. Concrete financial and technical co-operation assistance is provided under Council Regulation 443/92[140]. Article 1 of this Regulation states that the 'Community shall attach the utmost importance to the promotion of human rights, support for the process of democratization [and] of good governance'.[141]

Another source of financial assistance for the promotion of democracy and human rights activities in Latin America is provided under the budget line B7–7030, 'Democratization process in Latin America'. Like the other budget lines of Chapter B7–7, it is not confined to purely technical (and financial) assistance initiatives, but can be wider in scope.[142] The Commission has issued new guidelines for the relationship of the EC to the Latin American countries in the years 1996–2000.[143] It explicitly mentions the consolidation of the rule of law in the democratic process as essential for making the democratic process irreversible at the institutional level, forming one of the three priorities in the Community's strategy towards Latin America.

As for Asia, very few co-operation agreements between the Community and countries from this region include a reference to human rights.[144] The Community's

[137] European Commission, note 135 above.

[138] Regional groups: Andean Pact (Peru, Colombia, Equador, Venezuela, and Bolivia), Central America, MERCOSUR (Argentina, Paraguay, Uruguay, and Brazil, Chile since 1997); and the Association of South East Asian Nations, ASEAN.

[139] The so-called first and second generation agreements established technical and financial assistance but excluded any considerations of democracy, human rights, and good governance.

[140] See note 92 above.

[141] The envisaged technical and financial assistance to the ALA countries can even be increased when progress has been made (Art. 2(2)).

[142] The budget line was already set up in 1990 (then B7–5078) to support the democratization process in Central America and Chile but was extended soon afterwards to all Latin American countries: COM(95)191 final. Moreover, a working party on human rights in Latin America was set up and a multi-annual programme for promoting the observance of human rights in Central America was launched.

[143] COM(95)495 final.

[144] See the contribution of Riedel and Will to this vol. Problems with the inclusion of the clause are also reflected in the recent case between the Community and Australia. The latter has opposed the inclusion of the standard human rights clause in a new co-operation framework agreement with the Community and argued that this clause could not be mixed with a trade agreement. Pursuant to a Council Decision of May 1995 (*Bull. EC* 5–1992, at 82), such a clause is to be included in any new co-operation agreement. The parties finally only agreed on a political declaration instead of a binding agreement. Joint Declaration on EU–Australia relations (26 June 1997): *Bull. EU* 6–1997. See also *Agence Europe* No. 6903, 30 Jan. 1997, at 8; and No. 6905, 1 Feb. 1997, at 8; and 'EU Drops Human Rights Clause in Australia Accord', *Agence France Presse*, 6 May 1997.

ability to make Council Regulation 443/92 assistance conditional and to promote human rights thereby constitutes major progress. Relations with Asia are still strongly influenced by economic considerations. The Commission's Asia Strategy of July 1994 affirms the primary intention of the Community to raise its profile in Asia while establishing close economic links.[145] This bias is also strongly visible in EU relations with China[146] and in the EU's performance at the UN Commission on Human Rights in Geneva. However, in 1998 a new budget line for Asian countries is being created in order to support the process of democratization and respect for human rights there as well.[147]

D. Countries whose 'Economies are in Transition'

1. Central and Eastern European Countries   In 1989, the community established Phare[148] (Poland and Hungary Assistance for the Restructuring of the Economy) to support the reforms in Poland and Hungary, but extended its mandate soon after.[149] Phare began in 1989–90 providing emergency assistance (food aid, humanitarian aid, and priority import programmes) but it quickly grew to include assistance for economic and social restructuring (which continues for some countries), and now provides specific pre-accession assistance.[150] It is this focus of the assistance which explains the difference in the economic status of CEE countries compared to the developing countries discussed above. In June 1993, the European Council, meeting in Copenhagen, affirmed that in general the CEEs were eligible for accession,[151] but then defined the criteria they must meet in order actually to join. The December 1994 Essen summit confirmed the Copenhagen 'Pre-Accession Strategy' and determined that Phare should function as the main financial instrument to support the pre-accession strategies.[152] A country is eligible for assistance under this programme only if, in line with the Europe Agreements,[153] it meets the basic requirements of

---

[145]   COM(94)314. See also COM(98)40 final, at 17; and COM(98)181 final.

[146]   See COM(95)279 final; and COM(98)181 final.

[147]   Interview with an EC official of DG I B.   [148]   Phare Reg., note 92 above.

[149]   Macleod *et al.*, note 9 above, at 349. In Sept. 1990 Phare's mandate was extended to include Bulgaria, the former Czechoslovakia, the former GDR (until Dec. 1991), Romania, and the former Yugoslavia. In 1991 it was extended to include Albania, Estonia, Latvia, and Lithuania. In 1992 Slovenia was brought in, as was Croatia in June 1995, though the latter was again excluded soon after. The inclusion of Macedonia was opposed by Greece: European Commission, note 1 above, at 11.

[150]   C.R.N. Matthews, 'Phare-Tacis: EU cooperation with its Eastern Neighbours', *The Courier* No. 145 (1994), 68. Phare moved from a demand-driven to an accession-driven programme: European Commission, *Phare*, note 38 above, at 17. See also Ners, note 9 above, at 199.

[151]   Poland, Hungary, Bulgaria, the Czech Republic, Slovakia, Romania, Estonia, Latvia, Lithuania, and Slovenia. With all of them, Europe Agreements have either been concluded or are pending ratification. Albania does not pursue membership, but was nevertheless included in the Phare programme. European Commission, DG I A, *Relations of the EU with the Countries of Central Europe*, can be found at: http://europa.eu.int:80/comm/dg1a/cec/cec.htm. See also COM(98)53 final.

[152]   European Commission, DG I A, *The European Union's Pre-Accession Strategy for the Associated Countries of Central Europe* (1996), Doc. P/EN/02.96/01/04/32/B, at 5.

[153]   Except for the first agreements with Czechoslovakia, Hungary and Poland, in 1991, they now all include an explicit reference to regard for democratic principles and human rights, which are an essential element of the association. On 11 May 1992, the same day on which it authorized the Commission to open negotiations to conclude agreements with Romania and Bulgaria, the Council adopted a statement on the inclusion of these provisions in association agreements as being the rule from then on: *Bull. EC* 5–1992, at 82.

consolidation of democracy and human rights, and progress towards a market economy.[154] For the period 1995–9 the Cannes European Council allocated 6.7 billion ECU for the Phare Programme.[155] Through the recently approved 'Accession Partnerships' in Council Regulation No.622/98,[156] it was decided to pool all assistance to a country within one programme, and it now depends on consultation with the applicant State.

Since Phare is first and foremost a technical assistance programme, it focuses on institution-building and institutional reform.[157] As already touched upon in section I, successful economic changes are related to the establishment of democratic structures, and vice versa. Furthermore, an active citizenry is a basic prerequisite of a lasting democracy. To achieve this, the Phare Programme has developed two additional programmes: the civil society development programme (within mainstream Phare) and the Phare Democracy Programme[158] with an annual budget of 10 million ECU. Under the Phare Democracy Programme, the EC gives grants directly[159] to NGOs and similar organizations (macro and micro projects, complemented by *ad hoc* projects). It is also part of the European initiative for democracy and the protection of human rights (Budget Chapter B7–7)[160] and focuses on developing civil and political rights in the CEE countries.[161]

2. New Independent States and Mongolia   The unilateral assistance measures of the Community towards the New Independent States and Mongolia in the framework of the Tacis Programme (technical assistance to the Commonwealth of Independent States (and Mongolia)[162]) deal with a situation different from that facing the Phare Programme. The recipient countries are not foreseen for membership, nor for association, but merely for closer co-operation with the European Union (Partnership and Co-operation Agreements (PCA) providing for trade and economic co-operation).[163] The Tacis Programme was set up in 1993,[164] but had a predecessor in

[154] On the latter, see the White Paper, *Preparation of the Associated Countries of Central and Eastern Europe for Integration into the Internal Market of the Union*. On the former see statement of Commissioner Hans van den Broek at the Noordwijk Conference on the Rule of Law on 23 June 1997: if any of the conditions relating to democracy, respect for the rule of law, and human rights are not met, 'accession cannot be envisaged and negotiations for accession should not even be commenced': *European Report*, No. 2236 (June 1997), at 3.

[155] European Commission, note 1 above, at 12.   [156] [1998] OJ L85/1.

[157] European Commission, *Phare*, note 38 above, at 15. Typical outputs are trained staff, advisory documents, legal drafts, and organizational proposals.

[158] The Phare Democracy Programme is a complementary programme which was launched according to a European Parliament resolution in 1992. Set up as a pilot project, it includes 52 projects in 11 countries. They are: 10 in the field of parliamentary practice, 11 on promoting and monitoring human rights, 5 on independent media, 10 on development of NGOs and representative structures, 8 on local democracy and participation, and 8 on education and analysis: *ibid.*, at 54.

[159] European Commission, *Final Report. Draft. Evaluation of the Phare and Tacis Democracy Programme. 1992–1997*, Sept. 1997, at 3.

[160] A comprehensive evaluation of the Phare and Tacis Democracy Programmes can be found in the evaluation report: *ibid.*

[161] Matthews, note 150 above, at 69.

[162] The beneficiary states are Armenia, Azerbaijan, Belarus, Georgia, Kazakhstan, Kyrgyzstan, Moldova, Russian Federation, Tajikistan, Turkmenistan, Ukraine, Uzbekistan, and Mongolia.

[163] Since the mid-1990s concluded with Russia, Ukraine, Moldova, Kyrgyzstan, Belarus, Kazakhstan, Georgia, Armenia, Uzbekistan, and Azerbaijan. See COM(97)400 final, at 5; and European Commission, note 1 above, at 11 and 96.

[164] Tacis Reg., note 92 above.

Regulation 2157/91[165] which covered assistance for the then still existing Soviet Union. Tacis, like Phare, is a technical assistance programme, the aim of which is to support reform in the New Independent States by promoting their efforts to move from centrally planned economies to market economies, thereby encouraging democratic principles.[166] The first reference to democracy was included in the 1993 regulation and has been reinforced through the wording of the 1996 regulation which equally stresses 'transition to a market economy *and* reinforcing democracy' (emphasis added).[167] Some of the main priorities for funding are the reform of public administration, restructuring of the private sector and state enterprises, developing social services, and education. During the first six years (1991–6) of its existence, Tacis provided 2.807 million ECU for an increasing number of projects.[168] Over one-third of all assistance went to the Russian Federation alone; another third was regional, and nearly 10 per cent went to the Ukraine. In other words, the other NISs received less than 3 per cent.[169] At the time of writing, a successor regulation to replace the current Tacis programme, which expires at the end of 1999, is under negotiation. Key issues will be (1) the future relations between the Community and the Tacis countries in view of the Agenda 2000 package approved for the CEE countries; and (2) the proposal to link Tacis assistance to Partnership and Co-operation Agreements, as in the Phare Programme.[170]

As part of the European Initiative for Democracy and the Protection of Human Rights, the Tacis Democracy Programme has been operating since 1993 (in the beginning as a pilot project). Its aim is to strengthen pluralist democracy and the rule of law and to assist in the development of civil society in NIS countries.[171] With an annual budget amounting to 10 million ECU, it, like its Phare counterpart, is only a small part of the mainstream Tacis programme.

E. The Different Priorities of Financial and Technical Assistance in the Regions

The programmes described above all set different priorities regarding human rights activities and initiatives to support the process of democratization. Lomé states that 'support shall be provided . . . to achieve comprehensive self-reliant and self-sustained development . . . in order to promote the ACP States' social, cultural and economic progress'.[172] All human rights are to be fostered based on the realization that co-operation 'shall be directed towards development centred on man'.[173] The assistance to ALA countries stresses the important role of positive initiatives regarding human rights and democracy as preconditions for real and lasting economic

---

[165] [1991] OJ L201/2.
[166] Art. 4(I), Tacis Reg., note 92 above. Know-how is given through a wide range of public and private organizations in the form of policy advice, consultation teams, studies, and training and by developing and reforming legal and regulatory frameworks: European Commission, *Tacis Interim Evaluation*, note 38 above, at 15.
[167] Democratic principles and human rights even appeared as a conditional statement in Art. 3(11).
[168] European Commission, *Tacis Interim Evaluation*, note 38 above, at 16.
[169] European Commission, note 1 above, at 96.
[170] *European Report*, No. 2292 (18 Feb. 1998), at V–2.
[171] COM(95)191 final, at 5. See also European Commission, note 159 above.
[172] Art. 4 of the Lomé IV Convention.   [173] Art. 5 of the Lomé IV Convention.

and social development centred on human development,[174] as in ACP countries. The new Mediterranean Partnership focuses more on political stability in the region. Article 2 of the MEDA Regulation reflects this position by mentioning political stability as one of its main objectives. The Barcelona Declaration also reflects this focus in the establishment of a Political and Security Partnership which includes a Euro–Mediterranean zone of peace and stability meant to respect issues of human rights, democracy, good governance, and security (see the text to note 127 above).

Phare provides specific pre-accession assistance in accordance with the Copenhagen criteria. The criteria which a candidate country must have achieved are as follows: (1) stability of institutions guaranteeing democracy, the rule of law, human rights, and respect for the protection of minorities; (2) a functioning market economy, as well as the capacity to cope with competitive pressure and market forces within the Union; (3) the ability to take on the obligations of membership, including adherence to the aims of political, economic, and monetary union.[175] The focal point of the Tacis programme should be examined in the context of the break-up of the Soviet Union and the expressed will to continue support for the New Independent States.[176] The Tacis programme elected technical assistance as one of the first tools to support the economic transition and reform process because *financial* assistance and/or direct investments in infrastructure would be futile.[177] Support for the efforts to move from centrally-planned to market economies is seen as a reinforcing factor for democracy.[178]

In sum, all programmes have recognized the importance of human rights for development and established links to region-specific priorities. It is the practical component of implementation, however, which determines the seriousness of the promised commitments.

IV. POSITIVE INITIATIVES IN DEVELOPMENT CO-OPERATION: A THEMATIC PERSPECTIVE

As described above, the human rights objective of the Community, namely to promote human rights, democracy, and the rule of law in the world in a positive way, is being pursued through a wide variety of programmes. The following section will deal with the themes, or subject matters, of Community action (as opposed to the regional approach followed in section III) and focus on the following areas: support for democratic transition processes, rule of law, ensuring equal opportunities for all, measures aimed at the promotion of economic and social rights, decentralized co-operation[179], and the human rights dialogue between the partners of development

---

[174] Art. 2 of the ALA Reg., note 92 above.   [175] European Commission, note 152 above, at 5.
[176] A. Strub, 'Überlegungen anläßlich der neuen Tacis-Verordnung' (1997) 4 *Europäische Zeitschrift für Wirtschaftsrecht*, 105.
[177] European Commission, DG I A, *Tacis Programme: An Interim Evaluation* (May 1997), at 17.
[178] See Art. 4(I), Tacis Reg., note 92 above.
[179] The meaning of decentralized co-operation, which aims at the mobilization of all non-central actors, is explained in sect. IV d below. According to Heinz *et al.*, a strong 'concentration of projects in

co-operation. Finally, some concluding remarks on the efficiency of positive measures in general will be made.

A. Support for Democratic Transition Processes

1. General Aspects   'Development co-operation is based on the central place of the individual and has, therefore, in essence to be designed with a view to promoting—in parallel with economic and social rights—civil and political liberties by means of representative democratic rule that is based on respect for human rights.'[180] Two conclusions can be drawn from this statement: First, democracy in all its forms has become an essential focus of development co-operation, and, secondly, human rights are seen as a prerequisite and a part of democracy, as well as a concept of their own.

The human rights and democracy performance of a recipient country has become the focus of donors' and the Community's assistance in the 1990s, as has been described above.[181] This can be explained, on the one hand, with the end of the Cold War that, with its fundamental political changes, created a demand for democracy and human rights which came from within the developing countries,[182] and thus facilitated the process of launching the new policy of linking human rights to development co-operation. On the other hand, as already mentioned, sustainable development had not been reached in the target countries. Social structures, especially democratic ones, were from then on seen as crucial for economic development, and productivity was regarded as being dependent on the individual's possibility to control and to guide his work.[183] Human rights violations, large standing armies, and civil wars were deemed to be impediments to progress.[184]

Without going into the details of the different concepts, principles, and definitions of democracy,[185] which would be beyond the scope of the present chapter, some remarks about the understanding of it will be made. The proposed definition consists of two elements: a procedural and a substantive one. The first element deals with procedures and institutions of democracy (especially multi-party elections). The second concerns the degree of participation of the people in political life, the actual sharing of power among different groups in society, the possibilities for exerting con-

---

support of NGOs and elections' can be found: see W. Heinz, H. Lingnau, and P. Waller, *Evaluierung von Positivmaßnahmen der Europäischen Kommission zur Förderung von Menschenrechten und Demokratie (1991–1993)* (1995), at p. iii.

[180]   Resolution of the Council, Nov. 1991, note 30 above.

[181]   The basic hypothesis of Olsen is that 'when the Cold War ended, policy towards developing countries became increasingly—although far from exclusively—subject to moral and normative attitudes': G.R. Olsen, 'Public Opinion, International Civil Society and North-South Policy since the Cold War', in Stokke, note 18 above, at 334.

[182]   M. Marin, 'Democracy Cannot be Imposed from the Outside', *The Courier* No. 128 (1991), 50.

[183]   David, note 34 above, at 50. The Commission states that the Nov. Resolution stresses respect for human rights, democratic and pluralistic structures, and good governance to be the prerequisites for equitable and sustainable development: SEC(92)1915 final, at 2. See R. Barsh, 'Democratization and Development' (1992) 14 *HRQ* 124.

[184]   Interview with Dr. Erskine Simmonds in 'Dossier: Human Rights, Democracy and Development', *The Courier* No. 128 (1991), 53.

[185]   Barsh, note 183 above, at 120–34; W. Heinz, *Positive Maßnahmen zur Förderung von Demokratie und Menschenrechten als Aufgabe der Entwicklungszusammenarbeit* (1994), 2.

trol over the government, and in general influence on the situation in which citizens live (room for civil society programmes).[186]

2. Elections—A 'New Theme' in Development Co-operation According to an implementation report of budget chapter B7–7 of the Commission, support for transition to democracy, including the holding of free and regular elections, was one 'key element of external co-operation policy in favour of human rights and democratic principles' in 1995.[187] Operations which the Community/European Union supported between 1990 and 1995 concerned forty-four countries being given mainly technical assistance through specialized bodies in the pre- and post-election[188] phase. Rarely did the Community/EU participate in election observation missions by sending its own observers.[189] Election-related operations mainly concern the ACP and the Central and South American countries,[190] whereas in the CEEs, the NIS, and the MED co-operation partner countries 'democratic assistance', in the form of promotion of a pluralist civil society, has gained increased importance in the transition process. Additionally, the Community is increasingly involved in projects to strengthen the role of the media especially with a view to ensuring their independence and the quality of election coverage.[191]

The Community's/European Union's growing role in electoral assistance activities[192] provides another field where co-ordination between first and second pillar is needed, since the political dimension of the respective initiatives has given rise to action under the Common Foreign and Security Policy.[193]

---

[186] Barsh, note 183 above, at 121; European Commission, note 159 above, at 13; N. Thede, *The Democratic Development Exercise: Terms of Reference and Analytical Framework. A Discussion Paper* (June 1996), 3, which can be found at: http://www.ichrdd.ca/PublicationsE/ddfwkeng.html; Heinz, Lingnau and Waller, note 179 above, at 75.

[187] COM(96)672 final, at 7. The focus on democracy is more recent than that on human rights: Stokke, note 18 above, at 79.

[188] Pre- and post-election activities: specific support for the independence of the judiciary, the emergence of a civil society, the participation of women in political processes, civic education, and the formation of parliamentary structures, training of electoral bodies, assistance for modernizing the political parties, measures to encourage the exercise of political rights, funding to draft electoral laws.

[189] This was the case in the 1995 Palestinian elections. At a meeting organized by the ECDPM, the EU distinguished 4 types of international election-observation activities: (a) joint action under the CFSP (South Africa, Palestine); (b) provision of facilitation activities (Russia); (c) participation in observation missions co-ordinated by OSCE or UN; and (d) so-called European Political Co-operation actions: S. Mair, *Election Observation*, ECDPM Working Paper, No. 22 (June 1997), 6, which can be found at http://www.oneworld.org/ecdpm/pubs/wp22_gb.htm.

[190] E.g. organization of local, parliamentary (June 1995) and presidential elections (Dec. 1995) in Haiti; and activities in Kenya, Benin, Uganda, and Sierra Leone: COM(96)672 final, at 7; and support for the electoral tribunal in Panama in 1997: interview with an EC official from DG 1 B.

[191] COM(96)672 final, at 7; M. Braithwaite, E. Eberhardt, and T. Johnson, *The European Union's Phare and Tacis Democracy Programme: Compendium of Ad-hoc Projects 1993–1997* (1998), at 14, for further projects in Election Media Monitoring.

[192] See emphasis in COM(95)567 final, at 20. In 1997 a budget heading for electoral assistance/observers was created but has not been backed up with financial support: interview with an EC official at DG I A. The necessary means have therefore to be taken from other budget lines.

[193] Mair, note 189 above, at 6. Some of the first joint actions concerned electoral assistance to Russia in Dec. 1993, South Africa in May 1994, and support for the Middle East peace process in Apr. 1994. In 1996 the EU participated in the co-ordination and monitoring of the 1996 Palestinian elections: COM(96)672 final, at 7.

(a) Reasons for Election-monitoring Initiatives

Why have election-monitoring activities grown so much in the last seven years of development co-operation? One reason is that the wave of democratic change has heavily influenced these moves and directed international attention towards the issue of election monitoring.[194] The dispatch of observers and the disposal of technical assistance are no longer seen as an interference in internal affairs and breach of sovereignty.[195] As regards donors' budgets, elections are a relatively inexpensive technical tool and offer an easy option for developing a political surrounding conducive to the respect for human rights.[196] The number of countries that have become 'democracies' and the measurable success of this type of operation seem to present another incentive for electoral assistance.[197] It is far more difficult to assess the impact of long-term human rights activities, and to predict their possible outcome, let alone the immense costs related to them, than the result of elections, it is often argued. Finally, the assumption that democracies do not wage war against each other provides another argument for increased democracy activities, including election observation.[198]

(b) Objectives of Election Monitoring

Election-observation activities pursue five main objectives: legitimization of the electoral process; assistance in the creation of democratic institutions; enhancement of respect for basic political, civil, and other human rights; improvement of the prospects for the long-term building of democracy; and provision of a specific form of conflict resolution.[199]

Assistance in creating sustainable results of an election is especially important for countries in transition from one-party to multi-party systems where the newly elected government often does not have the necessary experience to rule the country effectively and might encounter problems in ensuring the progress and success of elections.[200] Moreover, post-election monitoring is essential to control the commitment of the newly elected government to improve the outstanding human rights issues as promised.[201] As for voters, they often need confidence-building in order to be able to make use of their rights, which they might not even know before.[202] Exercising the right to vote is also an endorsement of peace, hence the stabilizing function of an election should not be underestimated. Last but not least, election observation

---

[194] Mair, note 189 above, at 1. First post-communist elections were 1989 Poland, 1991 and 1992 Albania, 1990 Lithuania, Estonia, former East Germany, Hungary, Latvia, Slovenia, Croatia, Romania, Bulgaria, Czechoslovakia, Bosnia and Herzegovina, Macedonia, Serbia, and Montenegro. This wave of elections contributed to the popular view of elections according to which they constitute a means to disempower one-party States. See Tomasevski, note 55 above, at 164.
[195] A. Tostensen, D. Faber, and K. Jong, *Towards an Integrated Approach to Election Observation?*, ECDPM Policy Management Report, No. 7 (Sept. 1997), 3, which can be found at: http://www.oneworld.org/ecdpm/pubs/pmr7_gb.htm.
[196] Burnell, note 11 above, at 235.   [197] Tomasevski, note 55 above, at 157.
[198] *Ibid.*, at 158.   [199] Mair, note 189 above, at 4.
[200] Tomasevski, note 55 above, at 164.
[201] Human Rights Watch/Middle East, *Algeria* (E904) (1997). According to HRW, at 6, the EU should address the case of disappearances practised by Algerian authorities after the elections and in the framework of the new Association Agreement.
[202] Mair, note 189 above, at 5.

provides a highly recognized sign of legitimacy and enables the new government, on the one hand, to assert its position on the international scene, and, on the other hand, to affirm its legitimacy on the domestic level.[203]

3. Democratic Assistance   'Free elections and multi-party systems', Amnesty International states, 'cannot guarantee human rights on their own'.[204] Moreover, they are only a first step in the transition process to democracy.[205] It is therefore essential that assistance in this field also focuses on the substantial understanding of democracy. This form of operation enhances democratic values as such in the recipient countries and is based on the assumption that lasting development and democracy can only come about with the participation of an active and informed citizenry, and therefore focuses on the strengthening of civil society.[206] Initiatives include the promotion of the independence of the media, support for the freedom of expression and of the press, human rights education and public awareness-raising, promotion of equal opportunities for all members of society, and funding of NGOs (see also below on decentralized co-operation).[207] In this respect, special account should be taken of the Phare, Tacis, and MEDA Democracy Programmes.[208] But also under the mainstream technical co-operation programmes, civil society and governance as well as the social infrastructure have been promoted.[209] The mainstream Phare civil society programme, for example, includes support for political parties and training for accounting associations and so forth.[210]

4. The Impact of External Assistance on the Promotion of Democracy   As has been shown, the Community is providing considerable positive support to the transition to democracy (either electoral assistance or broader activities).[211] The questions then are which role can be foreseen for external assistance in promoting democracy and what is the interrelation between elections, the promotion of democracy, and human rights?

Surely, one important point is to provide people with the means of existence before they can think of democracy: that is, to fulfil basic needs first.[212] But, as

[203] *Ibid.*

[204] Amnesty International, 'The International Conscience for 30 years', *The Courier* No. 128 (July–Aug. 1991), 63.

[205] Tostensen, Faber, and Jong, note 195 above, at 3; Marantis, note 27 above, at notes 71 and 73.

[206] Thede, note 186 above, at 4.   [207] COM(96)672 final, at 34.

[208] European Commission, note 159 above, at 4. According to the Commission, at 3, the Phare and Tacis democracy programmes (PTDP) cover 8 areas of activity of which 5 can be directly related to democratic assistance: development of NGOs and representative structures; independent, pluralistic, and responsible media; awareness-building and civic education; promoting and monitoring human rights; equal opportunities and non-discrimination. The PTDP are based on active participation of NGOs and the important difference from other programmes of technical co-operation is that they can operate without the assent of the government. Links are directly established with NGOs.

[209] For the share of these activities compared to the total assistance spent in ALA countries, see COM(98)40 final, at 37: For Asia, 11 million ECU out of the total of 2,504 million ECU in 1991–5; for the Latin American countries, 70 million ECU out of 1,900 million ECU (commitments). The disbursements were even lower. For Phare, see COM(96)360 final, at 40. Civil society and democratization figured at around 10 million ECU per year between 1990–5; Tacis provided 443.84 million ECU in 1990–5 for public administration reform, social services, and education: COM(97)400 final, at 55.

[210] European Commission, *Phare*, note 38 above, at 53.

[211] Marantis, note 27 above, at 16. Democratic assistance began to flourish in the 1980s with the Latin American and African countries' transition to democracy: European Commission, note 159 above, at 28.

[212] S.M. Lipset, *Political Man: The Social Bases of Politics* (1960), 31–58. International IDEA, Stockholm, *Democracy in Burkina Faso*, issued by the Directorate General for Committees and Delegations of the European Parliament, Fdr 339466, PE 225–007, at 7.

discussed, the enjoyment of basic economic and social needs and the transfer of technology and financial means alone are not sufficient and do not lead to sustainable development. Development cannot be decoupled from observance of (all) human rights, and democracy and development are closely interrelated.[213] Hence, what is needed is a civil society that can respond to the exigencies of democracy and actively participate in political life. In this context, democracy forms an important condition of the lasting realization of economic and social rights,[214] but is certainly not the panacea. Moreover, the argument for fulfilling basic needs first represents an easy justification for totalitarian regimes to neglect civil and political rights before the enjoyment of economic and social rights has been accomplished. In line with the Concluding Document of the Vienna Conference on Human Rights, developing countries do not have an excuse for denying their people their human rights by saying that they want to guarantee basic needs first.[215] However, to impose western democratic models from the outside without respecting the country's background is no solution.[216] The promotion of democracy has to be effected on a case-by-case basis,[217] taking account of its stabilizing function in reaching equitable and sustainable development. Civic education and confidence building have to remain an essential part of democratic activities to ensure the active participation of the people.

There is a danger in donors' initiatives in that they seem inclined to equate democracy with multi-party elections for the abovementioned reasons. The risk of this equation is that countries are judged democratic as soon as they have conducted multi-party elections.[218] The change from a dictatorship to a democracy does not happen overnight, however, and has to be accompanied by pre- and post-election measures to prevent manipulation.[219] The sustainability of elections can only be guaranteed if substantive democracy remains the focus of donor activity,[220] and if elections are seen only as a first step. The Community appears to make a considerable effort not only to promote free and fair elections, but also to promote civil society. However, it is not enough only to accompany elections with democratic assistance to guarantee the success of election monitoring. If the Community/EU wants further to broaden its initiatives in the field of election observation as such, the following points are to be respected:

First, the time for election observation has to be right. It is only useful when the population does not favour the legitimacy of the existing regime. Secondly, observer

---

[213] Barsh, note 183 above, at 124. The crucial question is the direction of the arrow of causation.

[214] D. Beetham, 'What Future for Economic and Social Rights?', in D. Beetham (ed.), *Politics and Human Rights* (1995), 49.

[215] *Vienna Declaration and Programme of Action*, note 70 above, at para. 5. No set has priority: Beetham, note 214 above, at 49.

[216] Marin, note 182 above, at 50.

[217] Barsh, note 183 above, at 123; Heinz, Lingnau, and Waller, note 179 above, at 77. They refer to the 'central weaknesses' which have to be defined in each target country.

[218] Tomasevski, note 55 above, at 157. According to HRW, the international community often 'showed itself to be excessively preoccupied with elections as a surrogate for respect for human rights': HRW, note 60 above, at p. xxxiii.

[219] Heinz, Lingnau, and Waller, note 179 above, at 36: 'simply sending observation missions is far too fashionable at present'.

[220] *Ibid.* According to these authors, at 35, 'electoral support should be given as long as the full set of democratic institutions is in place'. Only then, is it time for other positive measures.

missions should apply identical criteria for when an election is fair and free.[221] Unfortunately, the assessments of different observers vary greatly.[222] Thirdly, election observation missions should not neglect the human rights dimension of their task,[223] even if human rights activities as such are de-emphasized and democracy occupies a far bigger place in assistance budgets.[224] Sometimes, the notion of human rights seems to have disappeared within the 'larger set of requirements' stated by the 28 November Resolution, or to form a part of good governance instead of being a concept in its own right.[225] This tendency neglects the fact that human rights are needed as a corrective to democracy, because newly elected governments do not necessarily respect these rights.[226] Human rights are necessary to ensure the electoral rights of the citizens (procedural norms regulating the exercise of political rights as a small part of human rights) and as a means to protect minorities disempowered in the political process.[227] In short, human rights and democracy are to be seen as mutually reinforcing, and neither of them should be given priority.

Finally, if these suggestions are respected, two problems remain: one is that democracy, despite its successes, has its own considerable weaknesses. The Council of Europe has acknowledged that 'democracies consolidated by decades of existence are suffering from the growing indifference of citizens to political life and the decline in the rate of citizens' participation in elections'.[228] Whoever seeks to export such a system has to be aware of the unforeseeable consequences this model can have in an unknown environment.[229] The other problem concerns the outcome of elections. The results of majority votes and the leaders elected do not always reflect the donors' views of a 'good government'.[230]

In conclusion, the recognition of the need for post-election projects, institution-building, and an active citizenry reflects the Community's understanding of democracy as being substantial—multi-party elections being only a first step. To enhance its effectiveness in electoral assistance, the Community should finally allocate means to the specific budget line created for such activities instead of continuing to take the resources from other budget lines.

B. Measures Aimed at Strengthening the Rule of Law

As the European Community has recognized, the implementation and strengthening of democratic and human rights norms and institutions require a concomitant

[221] Mair, note 189 above, at 1. Mair, at 18, also gives some criteria for free and fair elections: A free election is one in which basic human rights and constitutional freedoms are respected, a fair election involves the protection provided by consitutional, electoral and other legislative/ regulatory measures.

[222] Tomasevski, note 55 above, at 158.   [223] Tostensen, Faber, and Jong, note 195 above, at 7.

[224] Tomasevski, note 55 above, at 158. This author also submits that NGOs instead of governments are the main recipients of human rights assistance.

[225] Arts, note 41 above, at 259–73.

[226] T. Farer, 'Elections, Democracy, and Human Rights: Toward Union' (1989) 11 *HRQ* 508; Heinz, Lingnau, and Waller, note 179 above, at 80. Emerging democracies also need democratic assistance.

[227] Tomasevski, note 55 above, at 229.

[228] Council of Europe, Parliamentary Assembly Resolution 980 (1992) on citizens' participation in politics, at para. 3.

[229] Tomasevski, note 55 above, at 236.

[230] Tomasevski, note 39 above, at 15. Tomasevski cites the example of Algeria in 1991 where the Islamic Salvation Front had won the elections, but the process was interrupted by internal forces. The international community did not hinder this interruption.

strengthening of the rule of law.[231] The effective rule of law depends on the assurance of the supremacy of law, the independence of the judiciary, and the transparency of decision-making processes; it must also guarantee respect for citizens' rights.[232] In this regard, mechanisms for ensuring the reliable and impartial administration of justice are indispensable to the effective enforcement of human rights. Thus, the legal order must guarantee access to courts, must expunge arbitrariness and corruption, and must ensure that proceedings take place within a reasonable time.

Possibilities for effecting change through positive measures exist at a number of levels:[233] encouraging necessary legal reforms of the judiciary, securing that actual practice corresponds to respective legislation, etc. Practical measures include training of legal personnel (primarily judges, prosecutors, and lawyers) with an emphasis on national and international human rights standards; implementation of measures to strengthen judicial authority; facilitation of access to justice for the poor; assistance with legal reforms;[234] provision of administrative equipment; and the establishment of national human rights commissions and ombudsmen. In this regard, the European Community has financed several regional projects conducted by NGOs (particularly by the International Commission of Jurists, and also by the Inter-American Institute on Human Rights (IIDH) in Latin America) as well as national projects.[235] Although the Community's projects have focused on organizations, mobilization of the concerned government's political will to reform is a natural prerequisite to effective implementation, particularly as regards the independence of the judiciary.[236] But, given that the European Commission does not itself possess sufficient capacities for wholesale efforts to promote the rule of law, it should continue to rely on and maintain its existing co-operation with professional organizations in this field, namely the International Commission of Jurists.[237]

Efforts to reform the rule of law must focus on the executive as well as the judiciary. Positive measures taken by the Community can contribute to greater sensitivity towards human rights on the part of civil servants, in particular the police and military, thereby resulting in general behaviour that is more in accordance with the rule of law. The ultimate objectives of such measures are transparency, elimination of corruption, decentralization, democratic control of government, and observance of human rights.[238]

Thus, the European Community supports a number of projects on both the regional and national levels[239]—mainly provision of information and courses that educate civil servants about human rights. Programmes at the local level have been particularly important, and the Community has given priority to measures which enhance the synergy between civil society and the public sector.[240] Other Community projects provide assistance for reforms of public administration in general.[241]

---

[231] See sect. I D 3. See also *Vienna Declaration and Programme of Action*, note 70 above, at para. 8.
[232] COM(96)672 final, at 8.   [233] COM(96)672 final, at 9.
[234] E.g. under the Phare democracy programme, reform of the criminal code and criminal procedure in Ukraine has been supported. In Eritrea, assistance in the drafting of a constitution has been provided: see COM(96)672 final, at 12.
[235] Heinz, Lingnau, and Waller, note 179 above, at 42.
[236] *Ibid.*, at 46.   [237] *Ibid.*, at 49.   [238] *Ibid.*, at 37.   [239] *Ibid.*
[240] COM(96)672 final, at 12.   [241] *Ibid.*

The European Community has increased its financial commitment to activities aimed at strengthening the rule of law, which in 1995 reached 20 per cent of all initiatives under the budget heading B7–7. In the Latin American countries, it amounted to 36 per cent of the total budget from 1990–6.[242] Of course, the effects of these measures are difficult to assess and will depend on different factors. It is clear, however, that these programmes have often provided the only human rights education ever received by many of the affected civil servants.[243] Hence, such measures can have a fundamental, positive impact if the State itself is willing to and capable of executing reforms.[244]

C. Promoting Equal Opportunities for All and Support for Vulnerable Groups

Initiatives under this heading include not only those focused specifically on vulnerable groups in society, but also all means of fostering equal rights and equal dignity generally. Legal assistance and prevention through education and long-term measures are important tools for the implementation of both kinds of operations.[245] Target groups include women, younger generations, certain social groups, refugees, victims of torture, and prisoners.[246] The Phare and Tacis democracy programmes have placed growing emphasis on increasing the involvement of national minorities and women in civil, social, and political life. For example, the Community has created special programmes to promote women's rights and representation under an *ad hoc* Phare facility. The two existing projects involve the training of women as decision-makers and the combating of traffic in women brought about by the opening up of the CEEs.[247] Although this is certainly a laudable start, it remains deplorable that no comparable projects exist regarding Russia, where the widespread problem of violence against women has been largely ignored both internally and internationally.[248] 15 per cent of the MEDA democracy programme projects relates to women's issues, and another 15 per cent to children and youths.[249] Article 5 of the ALA regulation specifically recognizes the particularly vulnerable position of women and focuses development strategies on improving their active participation in the 'productive process and its results, and in social activities and decision making.' In Chile and Argentina, the Community has provided victims of torture with concrete medical and psychological care in specialized centres.[250]

Minority rights have thus far not been among the main priorities of EC engagement in human rights – a fact that might accrue from Western States' preferences for designating minority issues to the domestic domain.[251] As stated earlier, the

---

[242] European Commission, DG I B, *Construire une Culture de Justice et de Paix* (1995).

[243] Heinz, Lingnau, and Waller, note 179 above, at 40. [244] *Ibid.*, at 41.

[245] The overall aim should be to empower these groups and give them the ability to claim their rights: *ibid.*, at 69.

[246] COM(96)672 final, at 17 and 24.

[247] Braithwaite, Eberhardt, and Johnson, note 191 above, at 26.

[248] Human Rights Watch, *Russia. Too Little, Too Late: State Responses to Violence Against Women* (D913) (1997). HRW also proposes to raise the issue as a condition of the EU–Russia Partnership and Co-operation Agreement.

[249] European Commission, note 135 above. [250] *Ibid.*, at 33.

[251] Martín Estébanez, 'The Protection of National or Ethnic Religious and Linguistic Minorities', in N. Neuwahl and A. Rosas (eds.), *The European Union and Human Rights* (1995), 133.

Council in its 1992 Declaration expressed the desire to include minority issues in development policies *vis-à-vis* human rights concerns.[252] Recently, the Commission has stressed their relevance in regard to the candidate countries of the CEE, particularly Estonia and Latvia.[253] The new pre-accession strategy regulation affirms minority rights as part of the enlargement process by referring to the Copenhagen criteria.[254] The Treaty of Amsterdam does not include minority rights in its scope, but the new Article 13 (*ex* Article 6a) refers to discrimination based on racial or ethnic origin. Moreover, the new version of Article 151(4) (*ex* Article 128(4)) requires that signatories respect cultural difference and diversity.

According to Human Rights Watch, neither the EC nor the international community has dealt satisfactorily with the problem of Rwandan refugees.[255] In this context, the EC should provide all of its aid, including electoral assistance, on condition of a better human rights performance by the countries of the region.[256] Closer co-operation between the EC and the relevant organizations (the UN High Commissioner for Refugees, the Geneva Human Rights Centre, the OSCE's High Commissioner for National Minorities, and the Council of Europe) is likely to improve the overall cohesion and impact of development policies in this case as well as in general.[257]

Finally, the EC has not sufficiently addressed the problem of disappearances, which does not itself constitute a priority in budget chapter B7–7.

D. Measures Aimed Especially at the Promotion of Economic and Social Rights

According to the November Resolution, the Community must promote civil and political liberties by means of representative democratic rule 'in parallel with economic and social rights'. Whereas the new focus of the framework of development co-operation activities in 1991 concentrated specifically on civil and political rights and the concept of democracy as essential for sustainable development, economic and social assistance has itself been only an 'incomplete' aim of development co-operation. Because human rights theory presupposes a conception of human needs and human development,[258] the distinction between human needs and economic and social rights has become blurred in international politics. The internal discussion on the status and role of economic and social rights[259] raises the question whether Community development co-operation policy pays due respect to the indivisibility of human rights—i.e. whether it acknowledges the 'rights' component of social and economic rights (entitlements approach) rather than the 'basic needs approach' (charitable approach).

---

[252] See note 86 above.

[253] COM(97)2000 final, vols. i and ii; and COM(97)2001–2010 final, regarding individual candidate countries.

[254] See Council Reg. 622/98, [1998] OJ L85/1. See also Rosas and Brandtner, note 96 above, at 22.

[255] Human Rights Watch/Africa, *Zaïre: Attacked by All Sides* (A901) (1997), 2.

[256] Human Rights Watch/Africa, *Zaïre: Transition, War and Human Rights* (A902) (1997), 10.

[257] COM(96)672 final, at 40.

[258] J. Galtung, *Human Rights in Another Key* (1994), chap. 3; F. Stewart, 'Basic Needs Strategies, Human Rights and the Right to Development' (1989) 11 *NQHR* 347.

[259] See European Parliament, *Report on Human Rights within the Union*, discussed by J. van der Klaauw, 'European Union' (1997) 19 *NQHR* 204.

Financial and technical assistance aimed at reducing poverty, raising the standard of living, improving literacy rates, and providing primary health care and nutrition serves to support the promotion of economic and social rights as outlined in the International Covenant on Economic, Social, and Cultural Rights.[260] Article 11 of the Covenant, for example, recognizes 'the right of everyone to an adequate standard of living for himself and his family, including adequate food, clothing and housing, and to the continuous improvement of living conditions'. The rights proclaimed in the Covenant, which was ratified by 137 countries worldwide[261] including all Member States of the European Union, form a reference point for the Community.[262] Current sectoral spending on social development reflects the recognition that aid can most effectively eliminate poverty if it is targeted at basic health and education services, as well as clean water.[263] The Community contributes to the reduction of poverty through its main assistance programmes; however, it must realize that an effective policy for promoting economic and social rights requires more than merely the supplying of food, poverty alleviation, or the 'traditional analysis of the factual situation of nutrition, literacy or health care'.[264]

In the following, we examine the regional programmes of the Community and their attempts to conduct specific human rights projects related to the economic and social aims of development.

It is noteworthy in this context that budget chapter B7–7 is devoted only to the promotion of civil and political rights, whereas money for projects in the field of economic and social rights must be taken from other budget allocations[265]—a fact that is not particularly favourable to the indivisibility of both sets of rights.

In 1994, the Development Council issued a Resolution on support to Education and Training in Developing Countries,[266] emphasizing education as a fundamental right and stressing the need for enhanced education and training initiatives. Thus established, these principles apply to all Community assistance aimed at education and training.

Despite the recognized importance of social development, recent synthesis evaluations and reports by the European Court of Auditors suggest that the European Development Fund, with regard to the Lomé countries, has thus far failed to give high priority to investment in social development.[267] Despite encouraging statistics, the overall commitments in the social sector are still far below the 20 per cent level

---

[260] International Covenant on Economic, Social, and Cultural Rights, adopted by GA Res. 2200 A (XXI) (1966). In *International Instruments*, note 131 above, at 8.

[261] *Human Rights, International Instruments, Chart of Ratifications as at 31 December 1997*, ST/HR/4/Rev.16 (1998).

[262] See COM(95)567 final, at 9 and 10.

[263] For a more detailed discussion of the importance of social investment, see Eurostep, *Partnership 2000: Eurostep's Proposals on Social Developments* (1997).

[264] *Annual Report of the Committee on Economic, Social and Cultural Rights on its Tenth and Eleventh Sessions, 2–20 May 1994, 21 November–9 December 1994*, E/1995/22 (1995), para. 414. UNDP distinguishes the material dimensions of human development from human rights which it interprets exclusively as civil and political rights: see UNDP, *Human Development Report 1992* (1992), at 9.

[265] COM(95)191 final, at 3.

[266] It can be found at http://europa.eu.int:80/en/comm/dg08/recueil/en/en09/en092.htm; P. Bennel and D. Furlong, *Has Jomtien Made Any Difference? Trends in Donor Funding for Education and Basic Education since the late 1980s*', IDS, Working Paper No. 51 (Mar. 1997).

[267] ADE Report, note 108 above, at 11.

agreed at in Copenhagen,[268] and social sector allocations accounted for only 10.5 per cent of spending in project aid between 1990–5.[269]

For example, projects in the social sector in Ethiopia accounted for only 3 per cent of total commitments. Investments included some small-scale training activities, construction of a hospital in Mizan-Teferi, and other, smaller health projects. Despite the relevance of the particular projects, they were far from meeting Ethiopian needs.[270] Nevertheless, Lomé III marks an improvement over Lomé I and II in the integration of sectoral policies with regard to education and health.[271]

The European Special Programme on South Africa aimed at balancing the unequal distribution of education under apartheid. To this end, 41 per cent of the funds were committed to education.[272] In addition, the programme placed emphasis on the importance of furthering trade union rights in the implementation of the project.[273] Nevertheless, there was no overall objective for the health sector, and the programme never supported health projects on a large scale.[274]

Although the focus of financial and technical assistance to the ALA countries remains on food security, it now also integrates the role of women and the fight against drugs. A special budget line for population policies and programmes in developing countries (B7–631) is used to support innovative projects that are complementary to the larger programmes of support in the health sector. In July 1997, the Council approved a new Regulation (No. 1484/97)[275] which seeks to further the right of parents to choose how many children they wish to have and to help develop or reform health systems by improving the accessibility and quality of reproductive health care. Between 1990 and 1995 commitments for 'social infrastructure and services' projects in Asia reached 344 million ECU, compared to 386 million ECU in food aid, and 422 million ECU in humanitarian aid; in Latin America 223 million ECU, compared to 261 million ECU in food, and 188 million ECU in humanitarian aid.[276] Despite the considerable success of establishing democracy in Latin America, the protection of economic and social rights remains strongly underdeveloped, and the Community should increase efforts in this regard.[277]

In the Mediterranean countries, the Euro–Mediterranean Partnership has introduced an element of 'Social, Cultural and Human Affairs' co-operation as the 'third priority' for a work programme between the partners.[278] Resultant assistance allocations have been diverse, including contributions in areas of culture, religion,

---

[268] The assessment of the Court of Auditors on the use of EC funds [1996] OJ C340/311 ss. was still highly critical of the EC spending in basic education despite a major priority shift with EDF 8; the DAC has drawn up impact indicators for funding in the field of social development: DAC, *Shaping the 21st century: The Contribution of Development Cooperation* (1996), 2. A report to the EP Development Committee even suggests that a minimum of 50% of the funds should be spent in the social sector: G. Kinnock, *Opinion on the Discharge of the 1995 Financial Year concerning Title 7 of the General Budget of the European Communities and the EDF. Report to the EP Development Committee* (Feb. 1997), 4.

[269] ADE Report, note 108 above, at 20.

[270] IDS, Institute of Development Research, note 74 above, at p. xii and 47.   [271] *Ibid.*, at 49.

[272] SPM Consultants, *Evaluation of the European Special Programme on South Africa. Main Report* (Oct. 1996), 9.

[273] *Ibid.*, at 10. Financial assistance helped to ensure the survival of trade unions in South Africa: *ibid.*, at 72.

[274] *Ibid.*, at 56.   [275] [1997] OJ L202/1.   [276] COM(98)40 final, at 36–7.

[277] European Commission, note 242 above.   [278] See sect. III.

education, the media, and trade unions.[279] Some parts of the third 'work priority' are already achieved through the Community's decentralized co-operation programmes; other parts are entirely new. Assistance has thus far emphasized cultural heritage, drugs and organized crime, a conference on youth work, and initiatives within the dialogue between cultures and religions.[280] The gradual implementation of all three chapters of the Barcelona Declaration and programme of action is an important step in further stabilizing social and economic development in the region.[281] Thus, a priority of MEDA financial and technical assistance is the strengthening of the socio-economic balance, which is to be achieved by alleviating the short-term costs of economic transition with appropriate measures in the field of social policy.[282] Finally, the MEDA Democracy Programme also intends to apply the principles enshrined in the Barcelona Declaration and the new partnership, and will therefore focus on support for trade unions and training.[283] In Egypt, the Community is the largest contributor to the 'Social Development Fund', which was established in 1993 to smooth the transition from a state-run to a private economy by helping to balance the resultant social implications. It will contribute 155 million ECU for the 1997–2000 period.[284]

In the context of enlargement, the Commission has integrated economic and social rights in its assessment of whether the criteria for accession are fulfilled in each candidate country.[285] In its country-specific opinions, it examines adherence to the European Social Charter and the UN Covenant on Economic and Social Rights.[286] Although the Commission has mentioned specific social and economic rights in its opinions (e.g. trade union rights), such acknowledgement has been rather sparse in comparison to the discussions on civil and political rights.[287] The Phare assistance programme takes account of the considerable changes in the working environment resulting from the move from a planned to a competitive market economy, and gives support in areas such as education, training, and research (TEMPUS), social development and employment, and public health. This assistance comes from within mainstream Phare under the special category of 'civil society development programmes', which includes support for entrepreneur associations and trade unions. In Poland, Phare regional development programmes also assisted NGOs working in the social welfare field through technical support and training.[288] Education and training accounted for 13.2 per cent of Phare sectoral allocation funds between 1994

---

[279] European Commission, note 1 above, at 79.   [280] COM(97)68 final, at 11.

[281] Second Euro–Mediterranean Ministerial Conference, 15–16 Apr. 1997, Conclusions, Euro–Med 5/97 DG E II.

[282] European Commission, *Information Note No. 5, Euro-Mediterranean Partnership: 'The MEDA Programme'*; European Commission, DG I B, *Euro-Mediterranean Partnership* (Mar. 1997). Areas include basic education, health care, job creation, enhancement of public services, reducing gaps between urban and rural populations, and improving water supply.

[283] European Commission, note 135 above. In comparison, projects on trade unions acquired 8% of the budget in 1996, whereas support for civic rights amounted to 32%.

[284] European Commission, DG I B, note 282 above, at 17.

[285] European Commission, note 253 above.

[286] Rosas and Brandtner, note 96 above, at 20.   [287] *Ibid.*

[288] European Commission, *Phare*, note 38 above, at 53 and 58. See also Matthews, note 150 above, at 69.

and 1996, and social development, employment, and health accounted for only 3.2 per cent—compared to 36.1 per cent for infrastructure projects.[289]

Lastly, the Tacis assistance programme to the NIS countries and Mongolia contains a human resources and social development component. The interim evaluation report[290] identified training activities as the most important and most appreciated form of social infrastructure assistance. As for welfare issues, Tacis has contributed to easing the social consequences of sector and enterprise restructuring, and was one of the first donors to deal with the provision of services through NGOs. Between 1991 and 1996, initiatives in the field of human resources accounted for 12 per cent of Tacis sectoral allocation funds.[291]

On the whole, the Community has started to support economic and social rights by moving beyond the mere fulfilment of basic needs, and is now focusing on health and education. However, these projects still receive only a small portion of the overall budget, and they neglect the 'rights' component which entails an entitlement to demand the satisfaction of these rights.

E. Decentralized Co-operation

1. Concept and Background   Decentralized co-operation is more than a financial tool in the framework of development policy; the term also denotes a new developmental concept that envisages promoting democracy, the participation of civil society, and the rule of law, by shifting the focus of assistance to participative development.[292] The idea itself is of relatively recent origin and is becoming more widespread in the EU, on both the Member State and Community levels.[293]

Generally speaking, decentralized co-operation seeks to develop relations at the local and regional level and to draw together all components of civil society, thereby involving the particular population as much as possible.[294] Unlike traditional development co-operation, which mainly consisted of co-operation at the highest level, decentralized co-operation operates on the micro-level. This approach is closely connected to the new attitude in development policy that regards the human being as the central point of development,[295] and which realizes that top-down development requires complementary bottom-up development as well.[296] Central development has turned out to be rather illusory, and the role of the central State is now regarded more critically.[297] Moreover, development initiatives that offer external solutions

---

[289]   European Commission, *Phare*, note 38 above, at 64.

[290]   European Commission, note 177 above, at 52.

[291]   *Ibid.*, at 22. Matthews, note 150 above, at 70.

[292]   COM(96)70 final, at 1. Ryelandt (head of the decentralized co-operation unit, European Commission, DG VIII), 'Pourquoi la Communauté européenne travaille avec les ONG', *The Courier* No. 152 (July–Aug. 1995), 64.

[293]   COM(96)70 final, at 2.

[294]   European Parliament, *Report on the proposal for a Council regulation on decentralized cooperation*, COM(95)0290—C4–0327/95—95/0159 (SYN), at 10.

[295]   See Principle 1, *Rio Declaration on Environment and Development*, A/CONF.151/5/Rev.1 (1992); Art. 5 of Lomé IV.

[296]   J. Rhi-Sausi, 'El papel de las administraciones descentralizadas en la cooperación al desarrollo de la Unión Europea', *Revista Española de Desarrollo y Cooperación* (Spring 1997), 1, which can be found at: http://www.ucm.es/info/IUDC/rhi.htm.

[297]   European Parliament, note 294 above, at 10.

without accounting for specific local circumstances cannot succeed.[298] Sustainable development will be achieved only with sufficient support from the local population. Decentralized co-operation mobilizes additional capacities for development, tries to improve efficiency, and makes use of the specific know-how of respective local groups.[299] Decentralization trends, economic liberalization, the increasing number of NGOs in the south, and growing enthusiasm for democracy and civil society all contribute to this process.[300]

In sum, the objectives of decentralized co-operation are the implementation of a more participatory development process that satisfies the needs and initiatives of populations in developing countries, the diversification and reinforcement of civil society and the democratic underpinnings in these countries, and the mobilization of non-central actors in the developing countries and the EU.

2. Practice

(a) Tools

A clear-cut concept of decentralized co-operation does not yet exist. Because the idea is in the process of evolution, it is still rather broad.[301] The term 'decentralized co-operation' has been used to refer to three different phenomena.[302]

First, decentralized co-operation means horizontal co-operation. This entails the creation of co-operation and solidarity networks between entities operating below the central level (components of civil society), for example, local communities, universities, etc. These networks include North–South and South–South partnerships.

Secondly, decentralized co-operation comprises a policy that aims to incorporate the participation of citizens and their representatives in the process of development. It envisages civil society as an actor, rather than a mere profiteer, in development policy.

Thirdly, decentralized co-operation consists also in the granting of support to NGOs for carrying out official development projects that have been interrupted or cancelled for political reasons. This kind grounds itself in traditional development policy and focuses on provision of basic humanitarian needs rather than directly on the creation of structures to enhance human rights and a strong civil society. For this reason, and because it does not comport with the definition of decentralized co-operation outlined above, we will not further elaborate it here.

(b) Concrete Action

(i) Official Financial and Technical Co-operation Programmes

Most of the decentralized co-operation of the European Community falls within the official financial and technical co-operation programmes. Projects generally take one of three forms: programmes specifically intended to support grassroots initiatives, traditional programmes involving local groups, and horizontal instruments to promote the creation of networks.[303]

The Lomé IV Convention formally included decentralized co-operation for the first time (Articles 20–22), and almost all the national programmes refer to it.

---

[298] *Ibid.*, at 12.
[299] Rhi-Sausi, note 296 above, at 1.
[300] COM(96)70 final, at 1 and 3.
[301] Rhi-Sausi, note 296 above, at 6.
[302] COM(96)70 final, at 5 and 6. European Parliament, note 294 above, at 12–13.
[303] COM(96)70 final, at 8.

However, because the Lomé framework focuses on States, it raises difficulties regarding the translation of decentralized co-operation into practice. Nevertheless, Lomé IV put an end to the monopoly of central national units. The mid-term revision of Lomé introduced changes with a view to promoting co-operation between national authorizing officers and local partners, including making funds more accessible in the NIPs and attaching more importance to decentralized co-operation in traditional programmes. Even so, decentralized co-operation plays only a subordinate role within the rather traditional framework of the Lomé system; support for some micro-projects is based on decisions by the national authorizing officer and the delegations, whereas other programmes aimed at local development give more responsibility to local partners. Hence, a critical issue in the preparation of Lomé V will be the future role of decentralized co-operation.

The record of decentralized co-operation in other regions is different. The new Mediterranean policy primarily focuses on networks of North–South and South–South partnerships, through such programmes as Medurbs, Medcampus, Avicenne, and Medmedia.

The ALA Regulation, with its more flexible instruments (as compared to Lomé), permits making a greater number of decentralized actors eligible as partners for co-operation and recipients of assistance. Asia and Latin America both have a high degree of organization of civil society with a large variety of NGOs. These groups are in many cases involved as partners in implementation. Moreover, development strategy in the ALA countries incorporates network programmes, such as the Alfa programme directed at universities and other programmes similar to the Medurbs programme for the Mediterranean directed at city networks (Asiaurbs). Of course, we are still in the initial stages in this field, but the Community should certainly develop it further.

Phare and Tacis both attach central importance to decentralization. In particular, they contain programmes to build EU–East networks and to support NGOs in the recipient States.

(ii) Instruments Outside the Official Programmes
The Community Budget can also support a large variety of actions by decentralized actors outside the framework of the official programmes mentioned above.[304] These include development of North–South partnerships, reinforcement of non-governmental actors in the South, and initiatives by local groups or NGOs in the North or South.

3. Problems and Steps to be Taken   A fundamental problem of decentralized co-operation is that its success depends on the respective State's willingness to co-operate. Successful measures can only be implemented in countries with given decentralization tendencies and a readiness on the part of the government to introduce democratic reforms. Democratization is favourable to decentralized co-

---

[304] A compilation of the current Community resources in this field has been produced by the Commission: DG VIII, *Digest of community resources available for financing the activities of NGOs and other governmental and/or decentralized bodies representing civil society in the fields of development cooperation and humanitarian aid*, DG VIII/207/97 EN.

operation, and vice versa.[305] The degree of organization of civil society also plays an important role.

Horizontal co-operation with Eastern Europe has produced very positive results. The record is less favourable in other instances, however, especially in the framework of the Lomé Convention. Lomé emphasizes the role of the State, has an intergovernmental character, and does not provide adequate operative instruments. The secrecy surrounding EC programming directly conflicts with the objectives of decentralized co-operation. The inclusion of decentralized co-operation programmes in the NIPs depends on the national governments, and those programmes must be consistent with the respective NIPs' priorities. In practice, initiatives have met with resistance from governments. From the perspective of decentralized co-operation, there is an urgent need for more openness and participation in the process of adoption of NIPs.

Furthermore, civil society is generally not well developed in those regions. The Commission should place particular emphasis on developing an infrastructure of NGOs and civil society where it does not already exist.

The role to be played by the concerned State is a particularly difficult issue.[306] In most cases, support for NGOs is only possible if the government gives at least tacit consent. The inherent danger of supporting NGOs which are in reality not much more than government agencies is also an important concern. Community programmes should always attempt to achieve an effective balance between projects aimed at the private and at the public sector.

Lack of knowledge and capacities are also obstacles to effective implementation of decentralized co-operation.[307]

The diversity of instruments referred to as decentralized co-operation and the different interpretations of the concept have created confusion and uncertainty.[308] Hence, the Community should develop a firm conceptual basis.[309] A code of practice for decentralized co-operation should establish clear criteria for access to Community resources. It should include criteria for determining which NGOs from the ever-increasing NGO community should receive Community support; pseudo-NGOs, which are disguised government agencies or which pursue only commercial objectives, must be excluded.[310] Co-financing could serve as an instrument against abuse. Conversely, too rigid criteria might overburden NGOs with administrative tasks, thereby stripping them of much of their autonomy and independence. The Community should also take care that certain NGOs do not establish themselves at the expense of other local organizations.[311] Of course, the Community and NGOs must retain sufficient flexibility to deal adequately with all aspects of different local situations.[312]

Co-ordination and consistency are indispensable for efficient action. In 1995, the Commission issued a proposal for a Council regulation on decentralized

---

[305] European Parliament, note 294 above, at 11.

[306] European Parliament, *Report on the report from the Commission on the implementation of measures intended to promote observance of human rights and democratic principles (for 1995) (Imbeni Report)*, A4–381/97, at 13.

[307] Rhi-Sausi, note 296 above, at 3.

[308] COM(96)70 final, at 5.

[309] Rhi-Sausi, note 296, at 6.

[310] COM(96)70 final, at 5.

[311] Marantis, note 27 above, at 21.

[312] COM(96)70 final, at 6.

co-operation.[313] It sought to increase transparency and consistency by laying down the administrative modalities and defining priorities for decentralized co-operation. The Council has not yet adopted the proposal.[314] In any case, more research and evaluation is needed.

The Community should undertake a more intensive dialogue with the European decentralized actors. The Liaison Committee has already led a fruitful dialogue between the Commission and NGOs. A similar forum should be established for European local entities as well.[315] In this context, the Committee of Regions could also be included.

Because decentralized co-operation is an important factor in achieving sustainable development, as well as reinforcing of democracy and the rule of law, the Community should not limit it to certain financial instruments. Instead, the Community should adopt the necessary measures to make it a key element in all aspects of development co-operation.

F. Political Dialogue as a Positive Means of Promoting Human Rights

The Community's positive approach in development policy towards the respect of (all!) human rights and encouragement of democracy includes an 'open and constructive dialogue' between the Community, its Member States, and the governments of developing countries as one of the means for achieving comprehensive development.[316] The success of decentralized co-operation depends on the readiness and willingness of the concerned government to supply the necessary framework of action for NGOs and grassroots groups.[317] Political dialogue aims at easing oppressive, anti-NGO counter-reactions by governments that feel insulted by the donor community's support of anti-government or democratic NGOs. Development policy must, therefore, also focus on this type of action.

Political dialogue has been a part of all regional programmes since the 1980s.[318] Nevertheless, the Community has not used it extensively to raise issues of human rights or democratic principles.[319] In the case of the CEEs, however, common inter-

---

[313] COM(95)290 final.

[314] The European Parliament proposed some slight changes and adopted a 'legislative resolution embodying the Parliament's opinion on the proposal for a Council Regulation on decentralized cooperation' after the first reading in Dec. 1995, note 294 above.

[315] *Ibid.*, at 20.

[316] Resolution of the Council, Nov. 1991, note 30 above, at 122.

[317] Marantis, note 27 above, at 21.

[318] E.g. the Joint Assembly and Council of Ministers, Arts. 29–32 Lomé Convention, San José Dialogue with Central American countries, and structured dialogue with the CEEs politically to implement the Accession strategy. The dialogue was already included in the first Europe Agreements: *Bull.EC* 12–1991, point 1.3.2.

[319] In the case of Latin American countries, the only reference to human rights and democracy was made in 1992 in condemning the *coup d'état* in Peru: interview with an EU official of DG I B. Similarly, as regards the new Mediterranean Partnership, it has provided nothing more than a framework and affirmed the 'good intentions' of the partners to improve human rights and democratic issues. Neither of the two issues has been raised so far: COM(97)69 final, at 7. Nevertheless, in this Communication the Commission states the importance attached to the respect for human rights and fundamental freedoms and aims at encouraging the Mediterranean countries to sign the relevant international agreements (at 8). The action plan, set up to increase the efficiency of political dialogue, could be a first step in the right direction: European Commission, *Information Note No. 1, Euro–Mediterranean Partnership: 'Towards an area of peace and stability'*. The Community conducts a regional dialogue with ASEAN comprising

ests drive an exchange of views, which allow the CEEs to familiarize themselves with Community institutions and decision-making processes. It is this degree of co-operation that really distinguishes the Community/EU from all other international organizations.[320] Dialogue thus serves to prepare countries for membership, reflects common objectives, and accordingly extends to all areas of proposed accession (one condition for membership being the stability of institutions guaranteeing democracy, the rule of law, human rights, and respect for the protection of minorities[321]). Furthermore, unlike programmes targeting other developing countries, the Lomé Convention has presented a forum for discussing human rights violations and finding common solutions. The common institutions provide the necessary framework, and they have even attempted to define common criteria regarding how to respond to violations.[322]

Political dialogue is necessary to encourage mutual trust and to create a suitable environment in which topics of common interest can be addressed. An important condition for the success of such dialogue is that it be initiated as soon as possible without waiting until human rights violations have occurred.[323] Efficient follow-up is also necessary; often donor countries pay little attention to the dialogue once it has shown positive results.[324] Moreover, dialogue must be used in a sensitive way. Partners should refrain from blocking decisions by refusing to compromise and insisting on irreconcilable views. Unfortunately, the decisions of the Joint Assembly as regards the Lomé countries are neither binding nor always backed up by experienced and independent persons.[325]

Although it is not the only means of assuring respect for human rights and democratic principles, political dialogue does provide a necessary forum for discussing crucial points and exchanging views. Nevertheless, it serves only to complement other positive and negative measures in the field of human rights and democratic principles. It would be impossible to promote human rights and democratic values or provide effective responses to systematic human rights violations or interruptions of the democratic process through political dialogue alone.

G. Efficiency of Positive Measures in General

Recent evaluation studies on EC positive measures in favour of human rights and democracy arrived at positive assessments of such measures in the countries under

---

(rhetorical) discussions on human rights and democratic principles: see COM(98)40 final, at 17. The political human rights dialogue with China has entered a new phase with the recent statement of the EU Foreign Ministers to refrain from tabling a resolution at the UN Commission on Human Rights in Geneva, because relevant success is alleged to have been achieved in political dialogue: 'China Welcomes Decision on Human Rights', *Agence France Presse*, 24 Feb. 1998. The Tacis countries are only at a first stage concerning the establishment of a structured dialogue because the first Partnership and Co-operation Agreements have only recently been concluded, and many are pending ratification: COM(97)400 final, at 5.

[320] European Commission, DG I A, note 152 above, at 3.

[321] Since 1993, the Europe Agreements have all included a human rights clause, thus extending dialogue to these subject areas: *Bull. EC* 5–1992, at 82. According to COM(96)360 final, the dialogue covers all issues from cultural co-operation to foreign policy matters.

[322] Marantis, note 27 above, at 27.

[323] Interview with Dr Erskine Simmonds, note 184 above, at 53.   [324] *Ibid.*, at 53.

[325] Marantis, note 27 above, at 28.

review.[326] However, the Community has not yet carried out a truly comprehensive evaluation, and it is difficult to predict long-term effects in view of the relatively short history of these measures. The Commission must take account of numerous factors, in addition to those described above, in order to enhance the efficiency of positive measures.

Obviously, the overall political context is critically important to the possibilities and limits of positive measures aimed at promoting the rule of law, democracy, and human rights. It determines both the fields of action and the measures that can successfully be taken.

Hence, positive measures are most likely to succeed in countries where the government is committed to improving human rights and democracy. This is generally the case in countries in transition to democracy. In such cases, measures should be directed at the legislative system (electoral support), the executive branch, and the judiciary. In other cases, i.e. where such political will is lacking, the Commission should carefully examine the usefulness of positive measures. This situation arises in countries where the government (and parts of the population) rejects notions of human rights and democracy as Western interference and where authoritarian systems exist that are opposed to any process of opening or democratization. Positive measures face similar problems in countries with strong societal conflicts and a lack of common values. The situation becomes even more hopeless in countries that have lost their effective government and are disrupted by civil wars. In most of these cases, positive measures, if at all possible, should be limited to supporting NGOs and independent journalism and protecting vulnerable groups.[327]

It follows that the Community must carefully observe the situation in each country in order to create an appropriate strategy consisting of a variety of projects and taking into account the specific circumstances (country strategy papers). The question of the efficiency of positive measures cannot be answered *in abstracto*.

Also important is sustainability. The Community cannot effectively promote human rights if its projects are not designed for a longer period of time. On the other hand, there are dangers inherent in long-term financial support: the respective organizations might become too dependent on donors or lose contact with the individuals who are the intended beneficiaries.[328] Furthermore, monitoring is necessary to adapt Community engagement to changing circumstances. Effective evaluation of projects, however, encounters a number of difficulties stemming from the political character of positive measures. Any evaluation criteria must bear in mind the variety of factors that might be relevant to human rights situations; searching for a single cause would be misguided. Because no one project alone can have substantial influence on a given human rights situation, the Community must adopt a comprehensive strategy for the promotion of human rights that outlines objectives, time limits, and indicators for successful implementation. These indicators must also be evaluated before, during, and after the project. Evaluation techniques concerning positive measures are still evolving and need more research.[329] The Community should encourage comprehensive studies on their impact.

---

[326] Heinz, Lingnau, and Waller, note 179 above; ADE final report, note 108 above, at Annex 20.
[327] Cf. Heinz, note 185 above, at 40.   [328] *Ibid.*, at 44.   [329] *Ibid.*, at 45.

V. DEFICIENCIES IN PRACTICAL IMPLEMENTATION AND POSSIBLE IMPROVEMENTS

Unlike the preceding conceptual analysis of EC positive measures, this chapter will examine deficiencies relating to the practical modalities of EC development policy implementation in an effort to identify possible ways of improving the current state of affairs.

Despite its obvious successes, EC human rights and development policy suffers from a number of deficiencies. Critics have attacked EC decisions in this field for their lack of transparency. Some argue that the decision-making process is too time-consuming, collaboration within the EC administration and with Member States does not always function optimally, staff levels are not sufficient, and operations are not always conducted in a professional enough manner. Furthermore, a comprehensive global concept of development policy is still lacking, as is sufficient information, evaluation, and impact assessment.[330] Redress mechanisms also remain underdeveloped.

A. Visibility of EC Engagement, Dissemination of Information, and Openness Towards External Knowledge

To a certain extent, the EC suffers because its real role in development projects is not always visible enough.[331] One contributing factor is the Commission's general reluctance to make the entire process of aid management transparent through a dissemination of information.[332] As in other policy areas, the European taxpayer has a right to know how financial resources have been allocated. Moreover, when the Commission provides aid in secret, it forecloses on potentially valuable external incentives and expertise. We hardly need mention the irony of a donor that itself places so much importance on democracy and accountability disregarding its own obligations to ensure transparency concerning its own activities and spending. The Code of Conduct on Public Access to Council and Commission Documents, which aimed at providing the public with easy access to the widest possible extent, still keeps the system quite closed.[333]

DG VIII evaluation reports, as well as reports on aid expenditure, are already available,[334] but these reports focus far more on finances than on qualitative analysis. Access to country strategy papers and National Indicative Programmes is highly restricted in spite of their important function and the potential usefulness of discussing them with all the operators concerned.[335]

[330] Cf. the Scientific Council of the German Ministry of Economic Co-operation and Development, *Europäisierung der Entwicklungszusammenarbeit, Stellungnahme des wissenschaftlichen Beirats beim BMZ* (1993), 19.

[331] Imbeni report, note 306 above, at 11.

[332] The lack of readiness on the part of the Commission to make the entire process of aid management transparent must be highly criticized: see P. Feeney, *Accountable Aid: Local Participation in Development* (1998); and Imbeni report, note 306 above, at 9.

[333] Feeney, note 332 above.

[334] For further information see European Commission, DG VIII/A/6, Evaluation Unit G 12 6/05, *Evaluation Inventory*, 6th version (Dec. 1997).

[335] European Parliament, Martens Report, *Draft report to the European Parliament on the future of Lomé*, at 23.

In comparison, the World Bank pursues a far more progressive policy. In 1993 it adopted an Information Disclosure Policy, which became operative in 1994. It thereby introduced a network of public information centres that deliver a wide range of documents to the interested public.[336]

The Commission could hardly have a more legitimate reason for secrecy than the World Bank, especially given that the Community is not merely an international organization but a comprehensive legal community aimed at ever closer integration. Therefore, the Commission should provide information and receive external feedback to the largest extent possible. In particular, it should make use of the new information technologies that permeate existing borders, and thus publish a large variety of information on human rights on the Internet.[337] It should also strive for real co-operation with civil society and dialogue with all concerned actors (not only those in Brussels). It should open the lines of communication both by responding to requests for information and by remaining open to the expertise of NGOs.

The Commission should make use of advisory capacities. Many Member States have national advisory boards composed of independent experts. The Community should support the creation of a similar advisory unit at the European level and the building of communication networks between the present organizations.[338]

B. Evaluation

Although there is unanimity regarding the importance of evaluation for the improvement of development policy, satisfying strategies and methodology are still lacking. This is due in part to the extreme difficulty of assessing the impact of development measures from a broader perspective. It may be relatively easy to measure the success of a single project in economic terms, but the questions that we are eager to answer, i.e. how far EC development co-operation contributes to the creation of democratic and human rights-friendly structures, inevitably leave room for many doubts and much ambiguity. The large variety of relevant factors makes analysis difficult, and often statements on the ultimate success of executed measures can only be made years after implementation of a policy.

1. Scope Three types of evaluations must be distinguished: previous (pre-project phase), intermediate (implementation), and final evaluation (post-project phase). All three are equally important.

Pre-appraisal is often carried out rather superficially, and when deficiencies are identified during execution, the procedures are too inflexible to permit fast adaptation. Thus, the pre-project phase should not be disregarded.[339] Intermediate evaluation identifies changes to improve performance. Final evaluation can provide guidance for future policies and is often carried out several years after a project.

---

[336] World Bank, *The World Bank Policy on Disclosure of Information* (1994).

[337] Imbeni report, note 306 above, at 12; Lenz report, note 102 above, at 18.

[338] Netherlands Advisory Council for Development Cooperation, NAR secretariat, *Recommendation on Development Cooperation after the Treaty of Maastricht* (1993), 10, which can be found at: http://www.oneworld.org/euforic/nar/maas_gb.htm.

[339] P. Hoebink, *The Comparative Effectiveness and the Evaluation Efforts of EU Donors* (1995), 3, which can be found atat: http://www.oneworld.org/euforic/nar/hoeb95.htm.

As for human rights, the Commission must not limit evaluations only to specific human rights measures; rather, it should examine every measure of development policy in light of the objectives mentioned in Article 177(2) (*ex* Article 130u(2)) EC.[340] It should also undertake a general human rights impact assessment. However, the Commission must assure that decision-making takes place within a reasonable time.

2. Objectivity, Impartiality, and Transparency   If an evaluation is to be worthwhile, it should employ an objective, impartial, and open process. In order to increase objectivity and impartiality, the Commission should complement its own evaluation efforts with evaluations by independent experts. Such redundancy will guard against the danger that concerned officials might be too closely involved to give a critical view about deficiencies on the donor side.

These external evaluations should not be used, however, to shift evaluation responsibility away from the Commission itself.[341] This is especially true regarding assessment before and during projects, because it is the Commission that must act; the staff in the relevant DGs that deal with the relevant decisions are supposed to have the requisite expertise in the field of development co-operation. If they do not possess the special qualifications necessary to conduct regular evaluations, additional training should be provided; if the human resources are not sufficient or if there is a need of more specialized personnel, additional staff should be hired.

In any case, the process of evaluation must be made visible and transparent.

A central evaluation unit should concentrate on the following tasks:[342]

- co-ordination of the different studies;
- conclusion of subcontracts with selected experts, creation of independent expert panels composed according to the respective topic on an interdisciplinary basis, including participants of different backgrounds (i.e. universities, civil society, and perhaps even management consultancies if they can reasonably deal with the subject-matter—although this might be doubtful in the case of human rights impact assessments). The central evaluation unit should guarantee the independence and objectivity of the selected persons as much as possible;
- formulation of guidelines on the methodology to be used by these expert groups;[343]
- provision of information on the evaluations to interested persons;
- proposals for translating evaluation results into practice.

To avoid donor-centeredness, evaluations must include the recipient side. Greater participation of the recipients in all phases, including investment in institutional development and planning capacities within those countries, is indispensable because

---

[340] Imbeni report, note 306 above, at 6.   [341] *Ibid.*, at 10.

[342] F.M. Gudiño, *La evaluación de la cooperación al desarrollo en España: Un análisis de metodologías y organización institucional*, Universidad Complutense de Madrid, UCD Avances de Investigación (Oct. 1996), at 8, which can be found at: http://www.ucm.es/OTROS/IUDC/avances1.htm. The author mentions preconditions for successful evaluation in general.

[343] It must be secured that evaluation is not mere project-review without a clear methodology: Hoebink, note 339 above, at 7.

a lack of ownership is an impediment to successful project performance.[344] Of course, recipient evaluation should not be left solely with the government concerned. Rather, the Commission should make use of local evaluation capacities which partly already exist and partly need to be built.

Moreover, the Commission should utilize the expertise of civil society, for example by asking particularly interested NGOs to comment on the evaluation questions and results. Here again, transparency and publication facilitate constructive co-operation by third parties and could lead to a fruitful public discussion on objectives and methods. Thus far, evaluation of EC activities, be it pre-, post-, or mid-project, has hardly been a participatory process. NIPs Country Strategy Papers, mid-term reviews, annual reports from EC delegations, etc., are not readily available.

3. Subject Matter   In general, evaluation concentrates too closely on single projects while neglecting overall programme assessments, partly because the latter are much more difficult to appraise, and clear answers to the question 'does aid work?' can never be attained.[345] From the human rights perspective, however, it is essential that evaluations bear the overall context in mind. They should take thematic approaches to single questions concerning human rights, the rule of law, and good governance. The Commission has already introduced some cross-sectoral studies and should take further steps in that direction.

Additionally, the Commission should publish annual reports on the implementation of positive human rights measures that assess their over-all efficiency and clearly define the relevant criteria.[346]

C. Remedies Against Human Rights Violations by EC Development Policy

EC development projects may themselves result in infringements of human rights, democracy, and the rule of law. In Uganda, for example, massive human rights violations occurred during forcible evictions from the Kibale Forest and Game Corridor conducted under an EC-funded project. Although the Commission denies responsibility for these events, critics have identified the project itself with a policy of evictions and blamed EC staff for encouraging and planning them.[347]

Human rights impact assessments, the necessity of which has already been mentioned, are one possible method to identify and avoid problematic situations.

Another is to provide redress mechanisms that are open to the individuals concerned. One means is the implementation of judicial proceedings, which entail binding judgments and possibly compensation for the victims. In this setting, rules of procedure and rules on the burden of proof would need to be strictly observed, and the process leaves little space for flexibility. Hence, although an essential element for ensuring the protection of rights, judicial proceedings are not the best mechanism in all circumstances.

[344] Hoebink, note 339 above, at 4.   [345] *Ibid.*, at 9. See also Maxwell, note 74 above, at 3.
[346] Imbeni report, note 306 above, at 10.
[347] For a detailed discussion, see P. Feeney, *A Profile of European Aid: Natural Forest Management and Conservation Project, Uganda* (1996); LTS International Limited, *Evaluation of the EDF-Funded Natural Forest Management and Conservation Project. A Component of the World Bank Forestry Rehabilitation Project, Uganda (1988–1995)* (July 1996), i, at 70 and Annex 12.

One should not underestimate the potential of more flexible procedures that do not necessarily lead to binding decisions, but rather serve to draw the Commission's attention to the repercussions of its actions and introduce a fruitful discussion. However, without an institutional framework, there is a great risk that requests would get no attention at all. The Commission should, therefore, institute a procedure, albeit a more flexible one, which ensures that concerned individuals have a real forum for their complaints and that valid objections have a good chance of being translated into practice.

So far, though, redress mechanisms for human rights violations in the framework of development policy hardly exist on the EC level.

1. An Inspection Panel In order to provide remedies and identify potential conflicts, the Commission should establish an independent body through which affected individuals can request the EC to act in accordance with human rights standards in the framework of its development policy. This panel could handle tasks of inquiry and recommendation, and thereby assist the Commission. Again, the World Bank has set the example by establishing an inspection panel in 1993 through which people can request the Bank to act in accordance with its own policies and procedures.[348] This panel, which consists of three persons, conducts preliminary reviews of requests and carries out independent assessments and, if approved by the Bank Board, further investigations. It then sends its findings to the Bank Board and the Management; the latter then submits recommendations. After that, the Board makes the final decision on what should be done.[349]

Of course, such a panel does not wield the same power as a judicial body and cannot adopt binding decisions, but its potential influence is still great. The relevant officials cannot simply ignore the panel's findings, at least not in their deliberations. Such a body could be established without treaty amendment as a subsidiary organ of the Commission.

2. The European Ombudsman Another possibility for enabling affected individuals in beneficiary countries to raise objections would be to widen the competence of the European Ombudsman (Article 195 (*ex* Article 138e) EC), which at the moment only examines complaints by EU citizens or residents.

3. Recourse to the European Court of Justice Article 177 (*ex* Article 130u) EC *et seq.*, including the provision on human rights in Article130u(2), are generally subject to the jurisdiction of the European Court of Justice.

Individuals may bring non-contractual liability claims before the Court under Articles 275 and 288(2) (*ex* Articles 178 and 215(2)) EC—the competent body being the Court of First Instance. Such action is not restricted to EU nationals.[350] However, the conditions for success are rather strict.[351]

---

[348] IBRD Resolution No. 93–10 and the identical IDA Resolution No. 93–6, both of 22 Sept. 1993.

[349] World Bank, The Inspection Panel for the World Bank, *Overview September 1997*, which can be found at: http://www.worldbank.org/html/ins-panel/overview.html. For further information see I.F. Shihata, *The World Bank Inspection Panel* (1994).

[350] Case 145/83, *Adams* v. *Commission* [1985] ECR 3539; Case T–185/94, *Geotronics SA* v. *Commission* [1995] ECR II–2795.

[351] P. Feeney and T. Kenny, *EC Aid in Uganda and Kenya*, Oxfam Policy Department Briefing Papers (1996), 10.

First, the standard of proof is often very high. The relevant standard depends on whether a measure of a legislative nature or an administrative one is concerned. In the first case, the applicant has to demonstrate a sufficiently flagrant violation of a superior legal rule for the protection of the individual. In the second case, simple fault would be sufficient. If the Commission has already given a reason for a human rights violation in its initial decision relating to a project, the Court might well classify the decision as being of a 'legislative nature', thus implying that the high threshold would have to be passed, unlike in cases of maladministration and misconduct by Commission officials, where the requirement for liability would be simple fault.

The second concern is the influence of the recipient countries' liability on the liability of the EC. The fact that the Commission merely finances, whereas recipients implement, projects could lead to primary responsibility for the latter. The Court has not accepted this argument as a general bar to admissibility of a claim under Articles 275 and 288(2) (*ex* Articles 178 and 215(2)) EC.[352] However, the existence of fault on the part of the Commission is a crucial point. The relevant question is whether the Commission (and not exclusively another party) has failed to fulfil its responsibilities; the fault must relate to its competencies. Hence, if the Commission merely finances a project, the applicant would have to establish fault in the act of disbursing funds. Moreover, the Court seems to have adopted a very restrictive approach towards causation and has dismissed claims on the merits because of the primary responsibility of other parties.[353]

Thirdly, only physical injuries and clearly established economic loss are recoverable under Articles 275 and 288(2) (*ex* Articles 178 and 215(2)) EC. Therefore available compensation does not cover the entire range of possible human rights violations.

Finally, a valid claim can only be made by the individuals who suffered injury themselves. Representation, by interested NGOs for example, is not possible. This renders procedures in effect illusory because the victims of human rights violations in developing countries rarely have the means of instigating proceedings before the European Court of Justice on their own.

In view of all these considerations, recourse to the Court of Justice is adequate only in some exceptional cases.

Beyond the context of Articles 275 and 288(2) (*ex* Articles 178 and 215(2)) EC, the political will is not likely to exist to establish a general right of action in the field of maladministration with an extension of legal standing to, for example, interested NGOs. It is also questionable whether such a move would be ultimately desirable. Too broad an extension of legal standing might hamper an effective administration of justice, and the more flexible, non-judicial mechanisms outlined above might be more effective in many cases.

---

[352] Case 118/82, *CMC cooperativa muratori e cementisti and others* v. *Commission* [1985] ECR 2325; Case 33/82, *Murri Frères* v. *Commission* [1985] ECR 2759; Case 267/82, *Développement SA et Clemessy* v. *Commission* [1986] ECR 1907; and *Geotronics*, note 350 above.

[353] *Murri*, note 352 above, and Case T–175/94, *International Procurement Services* [1996] ECR II–729, at paras. 55–7.

D. On the Way to Consistency: Coherence, Co-ordination, and Complementarity

Inconsistency between the Community and the Member States' policies is an obstacle to greater efficiency.[354] Article 177 (*ex* Article 130u) EC *et seq.* lay down a threefold approach for achieving greater consistency based on the '3 Cs' (coherence, co-ordination, and complementarity), which are regarded as key elements of a successful development policy by the Community, over and above the provisions on co-operation contained in the Lomé framework.[355]

1. Coherence Coherence aims at consistency between development policy, other Community policies, and various instruments of development co-operation.[356] Article 178 (*ex* Article 130v) EC and Article C TEU establish a legal obligation to ensure overall coherence, but they do so without laying down mechanisms and procedures for implementation and without providing clear guidance on resolution of potential conflicts.[357]

(a) Problematic Areas

Areas most likely to conflict with development policy include the common commercial policy, the common agricultural policy, environmental policy, and common financial and monetary policy.[358] Conflicts might arise in connection with measures immediately directed at developing States, as well as with those which, despite their internal character, exert influence on the interests of developing States.[359]

A well-known and striking example of incoherence between development and agricultural policy was the dumping of EC beef in West Africa, which gave rise to a debate on coherence in 1993. The EC subsidized the export of beef surpluses to West Africa, creating unfair competition with local farmers, while at the same time maintaining development programmes for the livestock and meat processing industries in the region. Although attempts to reduce the inconsistency were made after it was identified, similar inconsistencies surfaced a few years later in the South African region.[360]

Coherence is also required between and within different development policies.[361] Many observers regard as inconsistent the preferential treatment given certain

[354] Cf. European Commission, note 86 above.

[355] Cf., e.g., the statement of Commissioner Pinheiro at the signing ceremony for revised Lomé IV in Mauritius, *The Courier* No. 155 (Jan.–Feb. 1996), 20–1.

[356] As regards the relationship of development policy and the foreign and security policy, Art. 3 (*ex* Art. C) TEU states: '[t]he Union shall in particular ensure the consistency of its external activities as a whole in the context of its external relations, security, economic and development policies.' The issue of the overall consistency of EU external actions, however, cannot be elaborated further in the given context.

[357] Cf. L. Box and A. Koulaimah-Gabriel, *Towards Coherence? Development Cooperation and the Development of Policy Cooperation* (1997), 2, at: http://www.oneworld.org/ecdpm/pubs/wp21_gb.htm.

[358] For further reading, see Y. Jadot and J.-P. Rolland, *Contradictions in European Policy Towards Developing Countries: Evidence from the Farm Sector and Proposals for Improving the Effectiveness of International Development Cooperation* (1996).

[359] An example of the latter category is the Chocolate Dir.: see A. Koulaimah-Gabriel and A. Oomen, *Improving Coherence: Challenges for European Development Cooperation* (1997), 5, which can be found at: http://www.oneworld.org/ecdpm/pmb/b9f_gb.htm.

[360] *Ibid.*, at 2.

[361] The planned reg. on human rights would be helpful in order to achieve more coherence. See above, sect. II.

developing States, most strikingly the privileges accorded to ACP countries, and many argue in favour of abolishing this discrimination and adopting a comprehensive horizontal approach instead.[362]

Of course, the issue of coherence is not limited to Community policy. Incoherence exists to a greater or lesser extent in each EU State. It is a general problem that is, to a certain degree, unavoidable in democratic societies. Therefore, the task cannot be to avoid conflicts of interests completely, but to manage them.[363] This requires, in addition to knowledge about the impacts of measures and potential conflicts, the commitment of the actors involved,[364] i.e. the willingness of Member States and the Community organs to implement coherent policies. The Community bureaucracy cannot ensure coherence on its own. Co-operation by the Member States and an open and constructive dialogue with the developing countries and the representatives of civil society will contribute to achieving greater horizontal consistency.

(b) Reasons for Incoherence

In many cases, incoherence results simply from a lack of information and co-ordination. Thus, measures are adopted without accounting for their potential impact on other policy areas. That is, evaluation does not play a sufficient role. Moreover, a lack of conceptualization inevitably leads to inconsistency.[365]

Conflicts of interest also contribute to incoherence— various competing interests have to be reconciled. To start with, 'the' interests of 'the' developing countries are impossible to define.[366] These countries do not represent a homogenous group and, even within a single State, opinions vary on which measures should be adopted to promote human rights and sustainable development. In many cases, the recipient State will bear responsibility for inefficiencies as well.[367]

The European Union faces a number of different interests and pressure groups. Lobbying by economic pressure groups will often be more successful than by those promoting development interests, thereby resulting in decisions that are more favourable to the Community's economic interests.

Incoherence is also a consequence of the decision-making system of the EC;[368] in the various sectors, the EC organs possess differing competencies and, therefore, different degrees of influence. Thus, development and human rights considerations will likely play a decisive role when the Parliament is involved; otherwise, economic interests will prevail.

In this framework, the problem of inconsistency of Member States' policies becomes relevant as well.[369] For instance, the Council of Ministers will adopt different positions when composed of the Ministers for Development rather than the Ministers for Agriculture or Economy. In this context, the success of development policy depends on the respective domestic minister's capacity to exert influence over the other policies. Cross-sectoral Council meetings would be helpful as well.

---

[362] Cf. Scientific Council, note 330 above, at 12; and Koulaimah-Gabriel and Oomen, note 359 above, at 6.

[363] Cf. the OECD Public Management Service Occasional Paper, *Building Policy Coherence* (1996), 1, which can be found at: http://www.oecd.org/puma/gvernance/strat/cohernc.htm.

[364] *Ibid.*, at 3.   [365] *Ibid.*   [366] NAR Secretariat, note 338 above, at 2.

[367] Koulaimah-Gabriel and Oomen, note 359 above, at 6.   [368] *Ibid.*, at 3.

[369] Scientific Council, note 362 above, at 7 and 13.

Difficulties of internal co-ordination within the Commission also create problems. Some have argued that collaboration between Brussels and the field does not always work optimally. A consequent horizontal approach is very difficult because of the various Directorates General which are involved in development policy and in the promotion of human rights in general. The tendency of geographic distribution within the Commission is reinforced by the fragmentation of the EC funds for human rights within the budget. The same kind of activity can be financed by different budget lines, which leads to confusion and a lack of transparency.

Although the concentration in one chapter of certain budget lines for the promotion of human rights represents progress, difficulties remain.[370]

Moreover, a change within the Commission structure would be welcomed, i.e. a single Directorate General for Human Rights or one department responsible for *all* aspects of co-operation policy. At the very least, the role of the inter-directorate group should be strengthened.

2. Co-ordination Co-ordination is obviously an important means for increasing assistance efficiency by avoiding overlaps and interference, sharing information about experiences, and reinforcing the effects of the Communities' and Member States' efforts.[371] The Commission distinguishes three levels of co-ordination, i.e. at the policy level, at the operational level, and within international fora.[372]

The Council has already approved several priority areas for policy co-ordination.[373] As regards operational co-ordination, the Council has proposed various methods, but has not provided for evaluation and monitoring.[374] The Council concluded that co-ordination within international fora has generally worked successfully,[375] though it may not in every case, as the Commission observed.[376] Because this question is closely tied to the common foreign and security policy dealt with in Professor Clapham's contribution, we will not elaborate on it further here.

The precondition for successful co-ordination is, first of all, prior agreement on the objectives of development policy.[377] The task of formulating these objectives must be performed at the Community level through a continuous process.[378] Since the entry into force of the Treaty on European Union, the Community possesses the competence to set standards binding on Member States in this regard, which should include rules for the evaluation of projects. Furthermore, the Community should establish a regular exchange of information and dialogue.

Important determinants of successful co-ordination include political will, the existence of national interests, the personal commitment of the individuals involved in

---

[370] Imbeni report, note 306 above, at 9.

[371] E.g., as regards Tacis subsidies to the Ukraine, lack of co-ordination between the actors involved has been deplored as being the worst obstacle to efficient action: European Parliament, *Report on the Court of Auditors Special Report No. 6/97 concerning TACIS subsidies allocated to the Ukraine. Rapporteur: M. Hoff*, A4–0063/98.

[372] COM(93)195 final.

[373] Namely, health, food security, education, and training: conclusion of the Council on Priority Areas for Co-ordination (25 May 1993), following the Communication from the Commission of 24 Mar. 1993, COM(93)123 final.

[374] Council Protocol 10802/93.

[375] Council document on co-ordination in international fora of May 94; Protocol 6449/94.

[376] COM(93)195 final.   [377] Cf. NAR Secretariat, note 338 above, at 4.

[378] Scientific Council, note 362 above, at 3.

co-ordination, and the existence of other frameworks for co-ordination.[379] Resolution of internal incoherence within Member States which hampers co-ordination is also critical.

Furthermore, administrative capacities can serve as limiting factors. At times when fewer personnel are employed by the Member States' assistance administrations, the Community must ensure the staff's ability to deal with the additional tasks connected with co-ordination and offer personal incentives in this field.[380] Co-ordination has so far been limited to the Community and Member States. It may be worth considering how the recipients could contribute to this process.[381]

It might be desirable to begin co-ordination of concrete action at ground level, i.e. to concentrate on related activities in the most concrete areas possible. As regards the promotion of human rights, the Council has stated that effective policy co-ordination already exists and that efforts should now primarily concentrate on implementation.[382] Nevertheless, the existence of a real consensus on particular issues of human rights policy is questionable. It might, therefore, be more efficient to focus policy co-ordination efforts on even more specific, well-defined areas. In this respect, the community delegations *sur place* play an important role.[383]

3. Complementarity   Though complementarity has frequently been emphasized as an important means of improving efficiency, the exact meaning of complementarity is still controversial, and the concept is difficult to make operational.[384] Complementarity is intrinsically connected with coherence and co-ordination, and depends on their effective implementation. It also seems clear that complementarity is not intended to replace subsidiarity.[385] Measures in the framework of development policy must be taken at the most appropriate level, which is not necessarily the Community level. The concept implies that competencies are to be used in a manner consistent with each other,[386] and that the division of tasks should be reasonable.

Implementation of the principle can take place on three different levels: Community, Member States, and international organizations.[387] For each type of measure, the Commission must consider which level provides the largest comparative advantage. The important role played by the Community level in co-ordination has already been discussed above.

As regards the operational field, the Commission's capacities are already inadequate to handle its current responsibilities. Hence the Commission should not be overburdened with new tasks. Rather, its role should be restricted to a mainly co-ordinating and conceptualizing function.

---

[379] C. Loquai, *The Europeanisation of Development Cooperation: Coordination, Complementarity, Coherence* (1996), 14, which can be found at: http://www.oneworld.org/ecdpm/pubs/wp13_gb.htm.

[380] *Ibid.*, at 14.   [381] *Ibid.*, at 15.   [382] Council conclusion of 25 May 1993, note 373 above.

[383] NAR Secretariat, note 338 above, at 5.   [384] Loquai, note 379 above, at 15.

[385] SEC(92)915 final, at chap. V, 1.

[386] M. Jorna, 'Complementarity Between EU and Member State Development Policies: Empty Rhetoric or Substantive New Approach?', *The Courier* No. 154 (Nov.–Dec. 1995), 78.

[387] It has been argued, e.g., that stabilization of export earnings can be dealt with more efficiently by the IMF and that the EC should thus refrain from acting in this field. See Scientific Council, note 330 above, at 11.

The full 'communitization' of development policy no longer seems to be an issue, not even for the Community organs.[388] Following Maastricht, a preference for bilateral assistance has been visible. The fact that treaty provisions for development co-operation have barely changed illustrates the Member States' reluctance to further 'Europeanize' development policy. Instead, the trend is to co-ordinate, divide the tasks reasonably, and continue to focus on bilateral measures as the primary means of development co-operation.

Of course, divergent national policies and administrative structures constitute obstacles to more integration; however, additional reasons for the Member States' reluctance exist as well. States are now regarding more critically the alleged advantage of communitization of development policy, i.e. its being less exposed to trade and foreign policy considerations. Doubts about the effectiveness of EC development co-operation have reinforced the desire to maintain national control. Bilateral instruments have various advantages, namely a stronger embodiment in society, greater flexibility, transparency, and broader acceptance in developing countries.[389] On the other hand, the large variety of actors inevitably creates problems. The broader scope for more effective policy dialogue and the economies of scale are advantages of EC action, as well as the clearer lines of political accountability and the avoidance of duplication of tasks.[390]

In any case, an improvement in EC aid quality could justify a call for greater financial engagement of and more competencies for the Community.

E. Bureaucratic Barriers

Several complaints have attacked the bureaucratic procedure within the Commission. First, the lack of transparency is a critical problem. The decision-making process takes far too long,[391] and the Commission provides no information in the interim.[392] This situation is unacceptable, especially since circumstances may change during the long period. One year after the submission of a project proposal, it may only be reasonable in a modified form, but modifications require further proceedings. Such a long delay creates many problems. Consideration of reform of the administrative process is, therefore, indispensable.

The Commission should, at the least, estimate upon receipt of an application how much time is required for processing, and determine if there exists a particular urgency. The Commission should also inform the applicant of the date on which a decision is to be expected. Intermediate replies should inform the applicant about the current state of affairs. This would contribute to both transparency and calculability.

One of the main reasons for delay is over-centralization. Field delegations, which are quite large compared to other donors, possess too few competencies in

---

[388] Loquai, note 379 above, at 11.
[389] Minister Spranger, 'Bilaterale Organisationen und Projekte sind stärker in der Gesellschaft verankert', *Der Überblick*, Feb. 1997.
[390] Maxwell, note 74 above, at 3.   [391] IDS, note 74 above, at 99.
[392] Imbeni report, note 306 above, at 11.

decision-making.[393] Project approval lies almost exclusively in Brussels; food aid and NGO decisions are all made there. Brussels must approve modifications as well.[394] It is recommended that the Commission follow the example of other organizations (World Bank, USAID, UNDP, etc.) and devolve more responsibilities to the delegates.[395] The present centralized structure both retards timely disbursal of funds and risks not paying enough attention to the respective local situation.

Field delegations, so far, are overburdened with administrative tasks and do not have enough time for policy analysis; they are understaffed, and too few local professionals are involved at the policy-making level.[396] For example, in Addis Ababa, the EC did not employ any local professional staff, whereas USAID employed twenty-five locals.[397] In view of the workload, the urgent need to be as well acquainted as possible with local needs, and the much lower costs of local professionals relative to expatriates, it is highly recommended that the Commission at least enlarge the local staff. Other critics have also questioned the lack of social development expertise and the fact that the EC, unlike other agencies, does not have a single line manager with overall responsibility for each project.[398]

Furthermore, the fragmentation within the budget may present an obstacle to flexible and reasonable aid management.[399] If financial means from one budget line exceed requirements or remain unspent, the budget should allow transfer into a budget line that pursues similar options instead of leaving the respective funds unused.

VI. CONCLUSION

Human rights, the rule of law, and democracy have become integral parts of EU development policy. However, the Community should take further steps to make them key elements of a consistent and efficient EU development policy. Of course, positive measures alone can neither ensure respect for human rights nor respond sufficiently to current patterns of gross and systematic human rights violations, but they can fundamentally contribute to building human rights-friendly structures.

[393] ADE report, note 108 above, at 53.
[394] IDS, note 74 above, at 99.
[395] *Ibid.*
[396] *Ibid.*, at 100.
[397] *Ibid.*
[398] *Ibid.*
[399] Imbeni report, note 306 above, at 12.

19

Where is the EU's Human Rights Common Foreign Policy, and How is it Manifested in Multilateral Fora?

ANDREW CLAPHAM

I. THE EUROPEAN UNION'S FOREIGN POLICY

A. Policy? What Policy?

In preparing this chapter I mentioned to a number of acquaintances that I was writing on the 'European Union's Foreign Policy'. The responses were invariably ironic: 'that'll be a short paper', 'is there one?', 'so it's a forward-looking paper?', and so on. As I cast my net more widely I realized that governments, commentators, and non-governmental organizations delight in pointing out the absence of a European Union foreign policy.[1] This caused me to ask some fundamental questions: why is the current EU foreign policy so invisible—or even risible? Why does the European Union need a common foreign policy at all? What are the interests that the Union needs to protect? Why is unity prized over diversity? Is the imperative of speaking with one voice hampering effectiveness in international organizations? Where has the European Union's common foreign policy enhanced the protection of human rights? And how can we strengthen these areas? These are some of the questions I hope to have tackled by the end of this chapter. But before embarking on this journey we need to explain some of the terms that we will be using.

The term 'European Union Foreign Policy' covers a whole gamut of activity in the public mind. Everything from the commitment by the Fifteen Heads of State and Government (the European Council) to 'keep up its efforts, within the framework of critical dialogue, to obtain a satisfactory solution in respect of the British writer

---

[1] Consider this passage from a recent introductory book on the European Union: '[o]f all the subjects covered in the Treaty on European Union foreign and security policy demonstrates the greatest divergence between rhetoric and reality. Art. J made the grandiloquent statement that "a common foreign and security policy is hereby established". However, neither within nor outside the Union is there any conception of what that means or what the policy contains other than a series of vague platitudes': S. Henig, *The Uniting of Europe: From Discord to Concord* (1997), 98. In a front page art. about the lessons to be drawn from the 'non-war' in the Gulf over the access of UN weapons inspectors Ignacio Ramonet concludes: '*[t]roisième leçon enfin: l'Europe n'existe pas. Sa politique extérieure et de sécurité commune est un fantôme*'. '*Leçons d'une non-guerre*', *Le Monde Diplomatique*, Mar. 1998, at 1.

Salman Rushdie',[2] through visits by Members of the European Parliament to Algeria, to decisions by the European Commission to suspend co-operation with Rwanda in the wake of the Kibeho massacre.[3] But EU foreign policy also includes action taken within the actual framework of the treaty-based 'Common Foreign and Security Policy' (also known as CFSP, or PESC in French, or GASP in German). This could be anything from the highly publicized conclusion by the EU Council in March 1998, that neither the Presidency nor Member States should co-sponsor a draft Resolution on China at the 54th UN Commission on Human Rights; through calls for clemency over prison sentences for individual young prisoners in Belarus;[4] to the little-noticed Declarations by the Presidency on behalf of the European Union welcoming the abolition of the death penalty in Azerbaijan,[5] and the Declaration on the release of prisoners in Cuba.[6] One should also mention the hundred or so confidential *démarches* undertaken by the Council each year.[7] But one should also go beyond the formal adoption of texts and include actions which are the practical follow-up to the conclusions and declarations adopted by the EU Council—even if these are not usually analysed as EU action. The EU Common Foreign and Security Policy was clearly being implemented when the EU Presidency insisted on visiting the disputed Jewish settlement in Jerusalem, Jabal Abu Ghneim/Har Homa, and meeting there with the Palestinian legislator, Mr Ta'amari. However headlines talked of '[a] British-Israeli spat'[8] even if it was clear to many that this was Europe speaking with one voice.[9]

---

[2] Madrid European Council conclusions, Dec. 1995: *Bull. EU* 12–1995, at 9. See also Florence European Council conclusions, June 1996: *Bull. EU* 6–1996, at 9.

[3] For details of how the EU Council (Development Ministers) and the Commission did not always see the priorities in the same way in Rwanda at this time see J. van der Klaauw, 'European Union' (1995) 13 *NQHR* 280.

[4] Statement by the Presidency on behalf of EU, 2 Mar. 1998.

[5] Declaration by the Presidency on Behalf of the European Union, 19 Feb. 1998.

[6] CFSP: Cuba/Release of Prisoners, 24 Feb. 1998.

[7] The nature and rationale of these *démarches* mean that their exact content may have to remain confidential. It is therefore difficult to assess their effectiveness. However, greater attention could be given to following up these *démarches* and evaluating their effectiveness. The frustration of the Parliament is evident from its *Report on the Role of the Union in the World: Implementation of the Common Foreign and Security Policy for 1997*, which ends with some comments on the document presented by the Council to Parliament on the '[m]ain aspects and basic choices of CFSP'. The Parliamentary report states: 'when we read (on page 14) that *A joint démarche EU/US was carried out on 29 July in Ankara, at the level of heads of Missions, concerning access by NGOs to North Iraq*, there seems to be no reason why we are not informed of its outcome. Démarches may be part of CFSP, but only successful démarches are part of a successful CFSP': Doc. A4–0169/98 (30 Apr. 1998), at 20.

[8] 'Visit to Project Sparks A British-Israeli Spat.': *International Herald Tribune*, 18 Mar. 1998, at 1. The art. quotes Robin Cook: 'I explained the role that the European Union can play in the peace process, the very substantial contribution that we can make to funding the peace process', and later mentions that he was '[s]hielded from driving rain by an umbrella bearing Britain's logo for its EU presidency'. But the thrust of the reporting concentrates on whether there was a dispute between the '*two countries*'.

[9] In contrast to the *International Herald Tribune*, some European newspapers presented the trip more as an affirmation of the EU's opposition to the settlements, and its seems clear that the fact that the Fifteen had agreed as the Union that the trip should go ahead actually reinforced the message. The AFP/AP report in the *Tribune de Genève* entitled '*[l]e Secrétaire au Foreign Office provoque la colère de Benjamin Netanyahou*' reported '*[l]e secrétaire au Foreign Office, dont le pays assure la présidence de l'Union européenne, a indiqué que sa visite visait à exprimer l'opposition des Quinze à l'expansion de la colonisation israélienne dans les territoires palestiniens occupés*': *Tribune de Genève*, 18 Mar. 1998, at 9. *Libération* quoted a spokesperson for the French Ministry of Foreign Affairs as saying that the meeting '*traduit la position de l'Union européenne, qui n'a jamais reconnu l'annexion de Jérusalem-Est en 1967—et l'occupation des*

With all these options available it seems odd that there is so little appreciation for the EU's foreign policy. Part of the answer lies in the fact that the EU is not a State but rather a collection of States with different interests and foreign policy organs. Foreign policy remains a carefully guarded instrument for use by sovereign governments. When the governments of Britain, France, Italy, and Germany explain their variegated foreign policy with regard to the issue of possible military action against Iraq, that is portrayed as confusion at the heart of EU foreign policy.[10] Confusion is compounded by the fact that, in a case such as this, the same person will have to represent national policy and the foreign policy of the European Union.[11] This lack of unity was seen by the newspaper *The European* to compromise the European project:

> Amid the rising diplomatic clamour which has been the inevitable prelude to the bombing of Iraq, one voice has remained silent: the European Union, quick to endorse the ideal of speaking with one voice, has been mute. Worse, its member states have adopted unco-ordinated, contradictory positions. Yet again, Euro-rhetoric, faced with real events, has proved empty. Following the inadequate European response to the 1990–91 Gulf War, the Bosnian fiasco and the latest useless handwringing over Algeria, it is depressingly predictable that Europe has nothing useful to say about the crisis in the Gulf.[12]

Even when the European Union acts together with a semblance of a human rights foreign policy the *démarches* have been greeted with derision in the same newspaper:

> There is a sense of *déjà vu* about the European Union's intervention in Algeria. The diplomatic mission which the EU is finally dispatching this week to investigate the massacres shows ominous signs of adding to the sorry string of failures that has marked the EU's common foreign and security policy (CFSP) since it came into existence with the signing of the Maastricht Treaty in 1991. The pattern is familiar. First the EU announces that a 'troika' of foreign ministers will travel to the country that is the object of concern. The government of that country initially demurs, before agreeing to receive the EU mission on terms designed to massage its own *amour propre*. The mission then flies in, holds talks, extracts promises that things will improve and departs. Nothing changes. In the seven-year history of the CFSP not a single success story has been chalked up by the EU.

territoires palestiniens'; similarly the secretary-general of the Israeli government was quoted as saying that the visit demonstrated that '*l'Europe a une politique trop favorable aux Palestiniens*': 18 Mar. 1998, at 12. *The Guardian* reports 'an extraordinary snub to Britain and the European Union' as well as reporting that the 'Foreign Secretary, representing the European Union, sheltered from the turbulent mix of elements and passions under a blue and white EU umbrella': 18 Mar. 1998, at 3 and 5.

10 Ramonet, note 1 above.
11 At the time of the Feb. 1998 Iraq crisis the British Foreign Secretary, Robin Cook, was of course also the personification of the foreign policy of the EU in his role as President of the Council of the EU.
12 'Growing up the hard way': *The European* editorial, 16–22 Feb. 1998, at 5. For a more 'realistic' appreciation of the potential of CFSP see C. Hill 'The CFSP and the National Foreign Policies of the Member States', *Quaderni Forum* (1996): '[n]o single actor, perhaps even no process of mediation, can "solve" savage and complex disputes like those in Yugoslavia, Northern Ireland, and Cyprus. Sometimes there are no "solutions", and even the passage of time only attenuates a conflict, without resolving it. The weight of a power like the United States, or a putative United States of Europe, might bring about some movement in a log-jam such as the Arab Israel dispute, but this is not at all the same as ending it. It therefore only muddies the waters of choice over the CFSP to claim that bigger must mean more effective. Effectiveness is relative to goals and to the opposition, which may be proportionate to the size of the actor taking the initiative': at 18. But we should not let these 'hard cases' lead us to the conclusion that CFSP could make no difference in the world of human rights. In fact there are plenty of reasons to believe that persistent intervention on human rights issues by the Union has considerable impact on governments around the world.

All attempts have failed because individual members of the EU cannot commit themselves to common decisive action.[13]

The European Parliament has also assessed the Common Foreign and Security Policy (CFSP) in particularly negative language. It began its critical analysis of the CFSP for 1996 in the following way:

> There is still a perception and feeling among the public at large in the Union that no progress has been made in developing a genuine CFSP. More than three years after its inception, this common policy ought still to be written in inverted commas in order to prevent its high-falutin name from giving rise to misunderstandings and unwarranted illusions.[14]

These harsh evaluations reveal the failure of the Union to demonstrate that the common policies which it does have can in fact bring concrete improvements. The truth is that hundreds of cables are sent between European missions around the world through a special EU cable network (COREU), and that the EU Council and individual ambassadors regularly intervene on human rights cases on the basis of Common Foreign Policy adopted in the form of confidential *démarches*. Furthermore, the CFSP has been heavily influential in ensuring EU support for the organization and monitoring of elections and human rights, and for developing policy in the context of international conferences.[15] We will deal with some of these issues in more detail below. For present purposes we need to understand the credibility crisis surrounding the CFSP in the field of human rights. Even those who closely follow these initiatives have difficulty in praising, or positively evaluating, the effectiveness of this foreign policy and its implementation. The sober assessment by Amnesty International seems remarkably unenthusiastic:

> Although formally CFSP is required to respect human rights and promote their protection by virtue of Article J.1 TEU, the implementation of this objective raises questions. The first question relates to transparency. CFSP is subject only to weak accountability by the European Parliament and is not effectively monitored by national Parliaments. There is insufficient information available publicly to make a full assessment of the application of human rights principles in this pillar. From the information which is available a picture of inconsistency and incoherence emerges. The whole sphere of Union external policy is riddled with competing competences, on the one hand among the Member States and the Union and on the other among the pillars of the Union. In such circumstances it is not surprising that the objective of human rights protection is not being fully served.[16]

[13] I. Mather and R. Fox, 'Adrift in a Vale of Tears', *The European*, 19–25 Jan. 1998, at 14.
[14] See para. 1. of part II.2 of the EP, *Report on Progress in Implementing the Common Foreign and Security Policy* for 1996, Doc A4–0193/97 (28 May 1997).
[15] The different types of future work likely to be carried out in CFSP can be gleaned from articles in the CFSP budget. The Interinstitutional Agreement on the financing of the CFSP, signed on 16 July 1997 by the Parliament, Council, and Commission, states in para. G. '[w]ithin the CFSP budget chapter, the articles into which the CFSP actions are to be entered, could read along the following lines: observation and organization of elections/participation in democratic transition processes; EU envoys; prevention of conflicts/peace and security processes; contributions to international conferences; urgent actions'. The institutions agreed 'that the amount for action entered under [urgent actions] cannot exceed 20% of the global amount of the CFSP budget chapter': *Bull. EU* 7/8–1997.
[16] Amnesty International's Memorandum: proposal for a strengthened protection of human rights by the European Union in the context of the Intergovernmental Conference 1996, RAC No. 04/96, I.1.c. The

This widely shared perception of inconsistency is compounded by the fact that Common Foreign and Security Policy is presented by a rotating Presidency. According to the article in *The European* (quoted above) : '[w]hen they do act, the six month rotation of the Union presidency makes it almost impossible to follow a consistent line because each country has its own priorities'.[17] We might add that not only does the rotating Presidency arrangement lead to inconsistencies but it also hinders any sort of meaningful follow-up to the initiatives and *démarches* undertaken by the Presidency in the name of the EU.

Before examining suggestions at reforming the CFSP in order to meet some of these criticisms, it is worth considering why unity is seen to be so important. Different governments have different policies which result from different national interests. We need to consider why nation States have foreign policy before we can understand why this policy is not easily harmonized. A number of reasons can be given why Member States have foreign policy: first, to protect that nation's foreign trading interests; secondly, to protect certain historical links which can arouse strong national sentiments; thirdly, to protect territorial sovereignty and the interests of nationals and national investment abroad; fourthly, to pursue international agreements to facilitate international co-operation; last (and probably least), we can add a commitment to development and the protection of human rights.

Most of the time there will be no spontaneous convergence of fifteen national interests around the EU Presidency. In fact a quick perusal of the decisions taken by the EU Council in the context of CFSP reveals that, where there is agreement, it is in fact around this last function of foreign policy: the protection of human rights and the promotion of development. Rather than belabouring the failure of the fifteen Member States to agree on the hard issues, we should try to reinforce what can be done in the area of human rights. But we need to think what are the special comparative advantages for the Union in this field. Although the European Union does not possess all the levers available to national governments, the Union does have some leverage which is special to the Union.

First, respect for human rights is now a condition for joining the Union. The 1993 Copenhagen European Council set out various human rights conditions which have to be fulfilled before joining the Union.[18] *Agenda 2000 for a Stronger and Wider Union*, prepared by the Commission, gives some indication of how the criteria can be met by prospective applicants and explicitly says that one State, Slovakia, did not satisfy these political conditions. This means that in dealing with prospective members, the Council, acting in the context of CFSP, can remind States that respect for human rights is not only an international obligation—but a *sine qua non* for different types of association and eventual membership.[19] Secondly, the options of certain

European Parliament has repeatedly complained about the failure to consult Parliament before common positions and joint actions are adopted (see below), and that the Council makes no response to the recommendations addressed to it by Parliament.

[17] Note 13 above.

[18] 'Membership requires that the candidate country: has achieved stability of institutions guaranteeing democracy, the rule of law, human rights, and respect for the protection of minorities.'

[19] See e.g. the Declaration by the Presidency on the situation in Slovakia, 10 Mar. 1998. 'The decision by Prime Minister Meciar to exercise the presidential powers to grant amnesties in these cases brings into

sanctions or the suspension of aid remain far more meaningful than individual measures, when taken following a binding decision of the Council. Not only will all
fifteen States be bound by the measures, but sanctions may in some cases be more
likely, as States which stand to lose may be more convinced of their effectiveness.
Thirdly, and in a similar vein, rules governing the arms trade are clearly central to
any human rights foreign policy. The European Union has the legal and political
framework to design binding regulations to ensure that action by one group of States
within the Union is not undermined by arms trading through other States. Fourthly,
retaliatory steps are harder to take against the whole Union than against one or two
European States that stick their necks out to criticize certain governments. This
means that States that might be unwilling to promote an antagonistic foreign policy
can shelter under the EU 'umbrella'.

The present report focuses on the Common Foreign and Security Policy (CFSP)
of the European Union as regulated by the relevant treaties. Issues such as the development and technical assistance policies of the European Commission, the insertion of human rights clauses into co-operation agreements with non-EU States,[20]
scrutiny of minimum labour standards abroad with regard to the Generalized System of Preferences (GSP), and the general role of the European Parliament will be
touched on only to the extent that they are relevant for our discussion of EU Common Foreign and Security Policy. They are all components of the EU's human rights
foreign policy, but they are dealt with in detail elsewhere in this project. In the second part of this chapter we will examine how the European Union's foreign policy is
manifested in multilateral fora.

B. The Formation of EU Foreign Policy on Human Rights under the Treaties

What then is the legal framework for the execution of a common human rights
foreign policy? And who are the players that contribute to its formulation and implementation?

Member States co-operated on issues of foreign policy outside any particular legal
framework until the 1970 report adopted by Foreign Ministers, whereby they undertook regularly to consult, harmonize views, and, where possible, undertake joint action. Increased consultations meant that during the Helsinki Conference on Security
and Co-operation in Europe (CSCE) from 1973–4 the Member States were, according

---

question his commitment to commonly accepted principles of good governance and the rule of law. These
actions do not make a positive contribution to Slovakia's efforts to prepare for EU membership'. In response to the failure of President Tudjmann to meet the Troïka in Zagreb the EU Presidency stated to the
press: '[i]f Croatia wishes to proceed with closer ties to the European Union, it itself must accept the dialogue that the European Union wishes to have with it and listen to the concerns [regarding President
Tudjmann's speech appealing to ethnic confrontation] that we wish to express': Press conference, 13 Mar.
1998, Edinburgh.

[20] The EU Commission has elaborated new clauses for insertion in co-operation agreements with third
countries which refer to human rights as an 'essential element' of co-operation: COM(95)216 final. For
the significance of the 'essential element' nomenclature, see the contribution of Riedel to this vol. and note
Art. 60(1) and (3)(b) of the Vienna Convention on the Law of Treaties (1969) which state that the violation of a provision essential to the accomplishment of the object and purpose of a treaty shall be a ground
for terminating or suspending the operation of a treaty in whole or in part. Therefore, violations of
human rights will theoretically trigger a legal entitlement for the Commission to suspend or terminate co-
operation agreements as they see fit.

to one commentator, '[r]esolved to assert their common identity in a context where deliberations concerned the future of the continent, the Community countries took no initiative in Helsinki without first discussing it together'.[21] One of the first hints of a collective foreign policy in the specific area of human rights came in 1978 at the Copenhagen European Council meeting. The Nine Heads of State or Government solemnly declared 'that respect for the maintenance of representative democracy and human rights in each Member State are essential elements of membership of the European Communities'. Greece was admitted in 1981 and Spain and Portugal in 1986. The process of inter-governmental foreign policy-making was formalized in the Single European Act (1986) which also gave a further push to the role of human rights in foreign policy by including two preambular paragraphs.[22] The Single European Act included a Title on 'European Cooperation in the sphere of foreign policy' and stated that '[t]he High Contracting Parties, being members of the European Communities, shall endeavour jointly to formulate and implement a European foreign policy'. This relatively weak legal commitment to co-operation was followed up in the same year by an important statement on human rights by the Foreign Ministers meeting in the framework of political co-operation and as the Council. A key paragraph reveals the extent of the Member States' public commitment to a human rights foreign policy:

> The Twelve seek universal observance of human rights. The protection of human rights is the legitimate and continuous duty of the world community and of nations individually. Expressions of concern at violations of such rights cannot be considered interference in the domestic affairs of a State. The major United Nations instruments in the field of human rights should be universally ratified as soon as possible. States should cooperate with intergovernmental organizations which monitor implementation of human rights and of which they are a member. Respect for human rights is an important element in relations between third countries and the Europe of the Twelve.[23]

One can parse four guiding principles from this one paragraph. There is an obligation on States to work for the protection of human rights worldwide. Voicing concern about human rights violations in other countries is a legitimate exercise of state sovereignty and does not violate the non-intervention principle of international law. Universal ratification of UN human rights treaties is a pressing goal, and not just a long term option. The Twelve expect all States to co-operate when their own intergovernmental organizations are engaged in monitoring human rights.

[21] C. Duparc, *The European Community and Human Rights* (1993), 20.

[22] The third preambular para. includes the following passage: '[d]etermined to work together to promote democracy on the basis of the fundamental rights recognized' and the fifth preambular para. reads in part: '[a]ware of the responsibility incumbent upon Europe to aim at speaking ever increasingly with one voice and to act with consistency and solidarity in order more effectively to protect its common interests and independence, in particular to display the principles of democracy and compliance with the rule of law and with human rights to which they are attached'.

[23] 21 July 1986, *Bull. EC* 7/8–1986, and reproduced in full in A. Clapham, *European Union: The Human Rights Challenge* (1991), i, Annex II at 164. See also the Declaration on Human Rights adopted at the European Council, 28–9 June 1991: '[t]he Community and its Member States undertake to pursue their policy of promoting and safeguarding human rights and fundamental freedoms throughout the world. This is the legitimate and permanent duty of the world community and of all the States acting individually or collectively. They recall that the different ways of expressing concern about violations of rights, as well as requests designed to secure those rights, cannot be considered as interference in the internal affairs of a State, and constitute an important and legitimate part of their dialogue with third countries. For their part, the Community and its Member States will continue to take up violations wherever they occur.'

Some of these principles later found their way into the 1990 CSCE Moscow document, and the 1993 Vienna Declaration and Programme of Action,[24] but they are important for present purposes because they clearly bind the Member States of the European Union to a set of principles which demand an active, rather than reactive, approach. Furthermore, the advocacy of a human rights policy became de-linked from 'the responsibility incumbent on Europe to aim at speaking with one voice . . . in order more effectively to protect its common interests'.[25] The protection of human rights had by 1986 become an end in itself, rather than simply a tool for the protection of European interests.

Six years later the Treaty on European Union (1992)[26] boldly stated in Article J.1: '[a] common foreign and security policy is hereby established'. The Treaty makes quite clear that the obligation is no longer one of endeavour and co-operation, but that the 'Union and its Member States shall define and implement' this common policy. The Treaty on European Union also stated that one of the objectives of the newly coined common foreign and security policy shall be 'to develop and consolidate democracy and the rule of law, and respect for human rights and fundamental freedoms'. This Common Foreign and Security Policy represents a stronger commitment to ensure that the Member States' 'combined influence is exerted as effectively as possible by means of concerted and convergent action' (Article 12, *ex* Article J.2) The Article explains that the Council may 'define a common position' and that Member States shall ensure that their national policies conform to these common positions. In addition Member States are to co-ordinate their action in international organizations and uphold common positions in these fora.

In addition to creating this legal obligation with regard to national policy, the Treaty outlined a framework for agreeing to 'joint action'. It is the EU Council of Ministers which is to decide that a matter should be the subject of joint action on the basis of general guidelines from the European Council (the Heads of State and Government).[27] Under this procedure some qualified majority voting may be foreseen for certain follow-up decisions and the Member States are committed not only to the joint action in their activity, but also to provide information to the Council on any national action which may be planned in this context. Although the Common Foreign and Security Policy cannot be reviewed in the European Court of Justice,[28] obligations undertaken by governments in this context are actually binding interna-

---

[24] *Vienna Declaration and Programme of Action*, A/CONF.157/23 (1993).

[25] See the fifth preambular para. of the Single European Act (1996) reproduced above, note 22.

[26] The stronger commitments in the Union Treaty can be found in Art. 11 (*ex* Art. J.1(2)) and Art. 177 (*ex* Art. 130u) of the EC Treaty. For a general evaluation of some of the changes brought about by the Union Treaty in the context of CFSP see R. Morgan, 'How Common Will Foreign and Security Policies Be?', in R. Dehousse (ed.), *Europe After Maastricht: An Ever Closer Union* (1994), 189–99.

[27] In this chap. the term 'Council' will always refer to the Council of Ministers of the European Union. Other Councils such as the European Council, the Security Council, and the Council of Europe will always be referred to by their full title.

[28] Although arguably any impingement in the context of the CFSP on the Community pillar could trigger a case which might have to consider the actual CFSP decision or action in question, as Art. 47 (*ex* Art. M) which safeguards the Community treaties is justiciable under Art. 46 (*ex* Art. L). See M. Eaton, 'Common Foreign and Security Policy' in D. O'Keeffe and P.M. Twomey (eds.), *Legal Issues of the Maastricht Treaty* (1996), 221.

tional legal obligations and theoretically 'justiciable' before the International Court of Justice.[29]

But we should not judge the relevance of this treaty framework by its potential to generate international litigation. As Dehousse and Weiler pointed out when European foreign policy was first codified in treaty form: 'international commitments are frequently deprived of enforcement measures other than reciprocity and counter-measures. The interesting thing is precisely that in spite of this weakness, most states generally observe their international legal obligations.'[30] In fact one can go further and admit that it is not really the status of the legal obligation in public international law that is important, but rather the process of continually bringing together the Member States to thrash out a common position. Dehousse and Weiler take a sociological approach to the question of the legal effects of the foreign policy-making process and conclude:

> It is widely acknowledged that since 1970, European Political Cooperation has gained credibility owing essentially to its efficiency as a socialization process. Member States have got used to consulting each other on major international issues, to profiting from each other's advice and paying attention to each other's concerns. Such a collegial spirit would not have been possible had they not had reasonable hopes to see their partners follow the mutually agreed code of conduct.[31]

Most importantly for present purposes, Article J.1 also defined the institutional arrangements for consultation, consideration, definition, representation, implementation, association, contribution, and assistance in this context. The European Parliament is to be consulted on 'main aspects and basic choices', and the Presidency is to ensure that Parliament's views are taken into consideration. The European Council is to define the principles and general guidelines for the policy, but it is the Council that will take the decisions for the defining and implementation of the policy. The Presidency is to represent the Union in this context and express the position of the Union in international organizations and conferences. The Commission is to be fully associated with the work. The Political Committee (the Political Directors from the Member States' Ministries of Foreign Affairs) (COMPOL) is to monitor the international situation and contribute to the definition of policies. The Presidency is assisted by the previous and next Presidencies in its representational tasks.[32] This tryptich, together with the associated Commission, is commonly known as the Troïka.

Having clarified a little the legal framework and the institutional arrangements for the moulding of this common policy we can start to consider how to ensure these are

[29] *Ibid.*, at 222.

[30] R. Dehousse and J.H.H. Weiler, *EPC and the Single Act: From Soft Law to Hard Law?*, EUI Working Paper EPU No. 90/1 (1990), 17. See also E.-U. Petersmann, 'How to Reform the UN System? Constitutionalism, International Law, and International Organizations' (1997) 10 *LJIL* 421–74 who sees constitutional/Community type approaches, rather than 'power-orientated' foreign policies, as the way to achieve CFSP (at 460).

[31] *Ibid.*

[32] This arrangement is to change under the Amsterdam Treaty. The Presidency is to be assisted by the Secretary-General of the Council (who will exercise the function of High Representative of CFSP). The Commission remains associated with the representation and implementation of CFSP by the Presidency, and, if need be, the Presidency is to be assisted in these tasks by the next Presidency. New Art. 18(3) and (4) TEU (*ex* Art. J.8).

best used in the context of the protection of human rights.[33] We will then offer some recommendations for reform in the context of the changes foreseen by the Amsterdam Treaty.[34]

In any discussion of effectiveness we have to look at what effect we are trying to produce. The Treaty of the European Union itself sets out a number goals in this regard. The Treaty states that one of the objectives of the Common Foreign and Security Policy shall be 'to develop and consolidate democracy and the rule of law, and respect for human rights and fundamental freedoms'.[35] In this context the Treaty also states that: '[t]he Council shall ensure the unity, consistency and effectiveness of action by the Union'.[36] The requirement of consistency at the time was seen to demand not only consistency of action taken by various bodies within the Union, but also that the Union and the different Member States act in a consistent way.[37]

C. Quest for Consistency

In the run-up to the 1996 Inter-Governmental Conference in Amsterdam there was considerable concern over the disarray and perception of failure which seemed to surround the Common Foreign and Security Policy. If one reads some of the documents prepared at this time one can encapsulate the discontent around three conceptual concerns: the concern for credibility, the concern for coherence, and the concern for consistency. These concerns may seem self-evident, but closer inspection reveals layers of complexity.

If one dissects the Reflection Group's final report before the Inter-Governmental Conference, one finds that the word 'consistency' appears thirty-one times,[38] and is used in almost a dozen different ways. Despite the stress on coherence it is the concept of consistency which seems to have caught the imagination of the Reflection Group. It is not obvious why consistency should be seen as such an overriding goal of foreign policy. If one were to present a national Minister for Foreign Affairs with such a lodestar, the response might be: 'but I want a foreign policy based on flexibility, activity and efficacity—the world is changing we need to be reactive and even proactive. Calling for consistency is just another way of doing nothing new'. It is here that we again find differences between the dynamics of European foreign policy

---

[33] The annual reports by the European Parliament on 'progress in implementing the CFSP' provide an overview of the common positions and joint actions taken and assess the progress towards greater visibility and identity for the EU on the international scene. The report for 1996 contains an annex with all common positions and joint actions since the establishment of the CFSP. See Doc A4–0193/97. With regard to human rights these reports tend to focus on the general issue (lack of unity over China at the UN Commission, or lack of action from the Council over Algeria) rather than addressing detailed human rights recommendations to the Council for their inclusion in future CFSP. Ways of including greater attention to the human rights perspective might be considered by the Parliament.

[34] Signed 2 Oct. 1997, in force 1 May 1999.

[35] See Art. 11(1) indent 5 (*ex* Art. J.1) of the newly consolidated TEU incorporating the changes made by the Amsterdam Treaty. Unless otherwise indicated all references are to this new version of the TEU.

[36] Art. J.8(3) of the old TEU now Art. 13(3) in the new TEU as renumbered by the Amsterdam Treaty.

[37] See N. Neuwahl, 'Foreign and Security Policy and the Implementation of the Requirement of "Consistency" under the Treaty on European Union', in O'Keefe and Twomey, note 28 above, at 235.

[38] Reflection Group Report (RGR), Brussels (5 Dec. 1995). This count includes instances where the Group was concerned to combat 'inconsistency'.

and what characterizes national foreign policies. It is suggested that at the level of the European Union we can discern *eight different concerns for consistency*.

1. Concern for Consistency between the Union's Economic Influence and its Foreign Policy The Reflection Group has lamented the fact that there is no consistency between the fact that '[a]lthough an economic power today, the Union continues to be weak in political terms, its role accordingly often confined to financing decisions taken by others'.[39] Its report included the suggestion that there be a High Representative for the Common Foreign and Security Policy (now commonly known as Monsieur or Madame PESC after the acronym for CFSP in French). There was a perceived need to bring the different elements of the external dimension of the Union closer together so that they function as a 'coherent whole'. 'This greater political role for the Union in the world should be consistent with its external influence as the premier trading partner and premier humanitarian aid donor.'

With regard to the setting up of a proposed analysis unit, again the Group immediately highlighted the need to 'avoid an inconsistency between the political dimension and the external economic dimension of the Union'. A large majority therefore suggested that this unit should include Commission staff as well as staff from national foreign ministries. This intermingling of *fonctionnaires* would be aimed at marrying the external economic power of the Union to the forces that determine the Union's political foreign policy.

We will return to these proposals in Part III, which contains our recommendations. For the moment we are simply highlighting the preoccupations which led to their formulation.

2. Concern for Consistency between Pillars This is similar to the concern addressed above but relates more to how those on the inside of the EU bureaucracy feel frustrated by the isolated preparation and the lack of co-ordination surrounding CFSP discussion. The Reflection Group was concerned about inconsistency between the pillars and saw the existing problems as a question of co-ordination between the Community (first pillar) and the CFSP framework (second pillar).[40] For those attempting to devise human rights policies the pillars do indeed get in the way. Despite the imagery of a Union constructed on three pillars, institutional actors still find it hard to move from pillar to pillar. Human rights as a specific field of activity are not yet considered either as part of the solid foundations of the Union or as a pediment firmly fixed over the three pillars. Discussion of issues arising in all three pillars is hampered not only by the impossibility of easily moving from pillar to pillar, it is debilitated by the failure to create any kind of forum to tackle policies to ensure

[39] RGR, 'Common Foreign Policy' and III, 'Giving the Union greater capacity for external action'. See also para. 149.

[40] See RGR, note 38 above, at paras. 150 and 151. Some members of the Reflection Group were more worried to reinforce the structural separation of the pillars to emphasize the different types of decision-making rather than harmonizing procedures to emphasize that decisions under all pillars are taken within a single institutional framework. See para. 148: '[a]ccording to some, recent practice shows that the current functioning of the "pillars" does not make for increased consistency between actions undertaken under them but that, on the contrary, there is a risk of spillover from the second "pillar" to the first, which reduces the efficiency of the Union and which could weaken the "acquis". Some are equally concerned by the opposite effect.'

coherence throughout the European Union's activities. One example may help to illustrate the point. In the run-up to the Beijing World Conference on Women, there was no opportunity to develop a policy which was discussed in the context of the Commission's development activities (first pillar), the Common Foreign and Security Policy and positions taken at the United Nations (second pillar), and issues as they related to refugees, asylum-seekers, and third-country nationals (third pillar—as it then was).

3. Concern for Consistency between the Different EU Bodies   Again this may seem like a similar point, but the diagnosis and cure are of a different order. Even if the pillar structure remains, there is seen to be room for greater 'structural coordination between the Presidency and Commission'.[41] These are issues that can be addressed through simple bureaucratic formulae rather than demanding demolition of the pillar structure. Similarly the need for consistency was invoked as part of a concern that there was confusion about the relationship between the Committee of Permanent Representatives (Coreper) and the Political Committee (the fifteen Directors of Political Affairs from the Fifteen Foreign Ministries) (COMPOL).[42] Of course there are reasons, beyond simple bureaucratic competition, why these different bodies remain in a state of tension and mutual distrust. The Member States are not yet ready to cede the initiative to the Union as the issues are of considerable national sensitivity.

4. Concern for Consistency with Regard to Different Non-Member States   Here the issue is how to ensure that the same standards and actions are used against different non-Member States. The Reflection Group pointed to the importance of defining the difference between common positions and joint actions so as to strengthen the consistency of the Union's external action. In the European Parliament Mrs Lenz and Mr Rocard have been even more explicit about the need to place decision-making in a 'clear framework to ensure that human rights policy is consistently formulated and the human rights instruments are consistently applied'.[43]

---

[41] RGR, note 38 above, at para. 150.

[42] 'The need for greater consistency should also inform preparations for Council proceedings, clarifying the relationship between Coreper and the Political Committee. In that sense some members consider that Coreper's coordinating and central role as the preparatory committee for the whole of the areas within the Council's competence should be reinforced in the Treaty': RGR, note 38 above, at para. 151. This reinforcement did not find a place in the Treaty of Amsterdam.

[43] *Report on setting up a single co-ordinating structure within the European Commission responsible for human rights and democratization (Lenz Report)*, A4–393/97. Rocard addresses the related point concerning the importance of similar consistency of approach between different non-Member States in the area of the Community's human rights work in the context of development: 'consistency in the implementation of this policy must be the Community's first priority: with a solid political commitment and a range of instruments and substantial resources at its disposal, the Community must focus its efforts on shaping and implementing a strategy capable of ensuring that its activities are coherent, effective and efficient and guaranteeing transparency and nondiscrimination in the use of the instruments available. Such consistency should enable the Union's activities to be effective in the medium and long term and enable the Union to provide a suitably effective response to emergency situations. It rules out the adoption of different approaches depending on the relative economic or political importance of the countries concerned, and requires that the principles laid down in the area of democracy, human rights and development be applied to all spheres of Community foreign policy, including commercial relations': 'Letter from the committee chairman to Mr Soulier, chairman of the Subcommittee on Human Rights', included in the Lenz report.

In addition to suggesting a high-level personality to redress the inconsistency between the external economic and political roles, the Group makes further suggestions for recalibration within the institutional balance of the Union. It successfully argued that the Commission, as well as the Council, should be responsible for ensuring consistency of external action decided in both the Community and CFSP frameworks.

5. Concern for Consistency over Time This point follows from the previous one but is not identical to it. Some measure of predictability is important for other States to be able to know how the European Union is going to act and what sort of follow-up to expect with regard to the implementation of CFSP decisions. The time dimension highlights the revolving nature of the Presidency and the tendency for policy to change depending on the interests and competence of the Presidency. Reorganizing the rotation so that it lasts for, say, eighteen months has been proposed as an option, but the Amsterdam Treaty has tackled the issue by strengthening the role of the Council secretariat and the Commission in the Troïka rather than changing the rules concerning the duration of the rotating Presidency.

6. Concern for Consistency between Dealing with Human Rights at Home and Abroad This is clearly the key factor for ensuring credibility.[44] We have already alluded to the legal difficulties involved with admitting that the Community has general competence with respect to human rights issues within the Union. In Part II below we will explore this issue in more detail, looking in particular at the inconsistency, inherent in the CFSP, whereby the Union decries violations of human rights abroad yet has no voice with regard to human rights problems at home. We will suggest in Part III that, following Amsterdam, there are new reasons to admit that the Commission has to have competence in this area and that the Union can easily ensure that it uses its voice to address human rights violations committed within the Union. This inconsistency is probably the most troubling—yet probably the easiest to remedy.

7. Concern for Consistency between the Existing International Monitoring of Member States and the Absence of International Accountability for EU Institutions This point is different from the previous one as here we are not talking about violations committed by EU Member States but rather by the Council, Commission, or Parliament. We might also add the European Court of Justice, as an institution, could act in violation of international human rights.[45] This is not the place to rehearse the complex doctrine on the legal avenues for holding the institutions accountable in Community or international law. Some of the issues will be discussed in more detail in Part III below. Suffice it to state here that, with the advent of international treaties that include human rights clauses, which allow for suspension of agreements

---

[44] For a recent articulation of this concern see the Rocard letter (note 43 above): '[t]he need for the Union to be both consistent and credible in the eyes of its interlocutors also means that the Union must adopt a consistent approach to the internal and external dimension of human rights'.

[45] See the RGR, note 39 above, at para 34: '[a]s for the possibility of complaints by individual natural persons concerning human rights, the great majority of members of the Group makes the point that there is at present an inconsistency in the fact that, while the Member States are subject to the monitoring mechanisms of the European Convention on Human Rights, the Institutions of the Union and Community law remain exempt from such control. The protection of individual human rights has hitherto been ensured solely by the Court of Justice in Luxembourg.'

between the European Community and non-Member States, the question arises how to judge violations of human rights by the Community and its Member States. The Amsterdam Treaty means that the EU institutions can in the future be held accountable for violations of human rights before the European Court of Justice. But the bigger issue is to ensure that the Community can be held internationally accountable in the same way that the EU demands that non-Member States submit to international procedures and reporting. This is dealt with in Part III below in the section on accession to human rights treaties by the Community.

8. Concern for Consistency between Ambitions and Available Funds   This is the perennial concern for anyone looking at the decision-making processes in the Union. There are multiple inconsistencies relating to the Union's ambitions and the limited funds available from Member States, as well as the inconsistency between Parliament's budget powers and its limited role with regard to revenue. For present purposes it is enough to note that the Union has often taken decisions in the context of its common foreign policy on human rights with no corresponding available funds to make the decision meaningful. For example support for UN resolutions recommending human rights monitors in Burundi and Sudan meant very little in the absence of significant available funding. In the end the Commission stepped in for the Burundi office and provided some funds, but the delays and uncertainly undermined what could have been an important contribution to the protection of human rights in Burundi. The problems associated with the Commission's support of UN human rights field operations will be dealt with in more detail below.

These eight concerns for consistency are a good introduction to the current inadequacies of the EU's human rights foreign policy. They also provide a useful gauge of whether our recommendations are likely to resolve some of the fundamental schisms at the heart of the EU's policy. The recommendations in the final part of this report are aimed at ameliorating some of the effects of these inconsistencies. It would be impossible to resolve all of them through institutional reform. Some of the inconsistencies simply reflect the current stage of European integration. As suggested above, consistency can never be the ultimate goal. An effective foreign policy will need room to be reflexive and flexible. This analysis of the consistency imperative is interesting, as it helps us to understand perceptions of the Union's foreign policy problems. We are not suggesting that consistency be the overriding aim of EU human rights foreign policy. On the other hand, we could say that coherence and credibility are 'essential elements' for the effectiveness of the EU's human rights foreign policy.

Summarizing our conclusions so far with regard to the EU's foreign policy, we can say that: first, there is some cynicism regarding the failure of the EU to solve the big crises in the former Yugoslavia, Algeria, the Great Lakes region in Africa, Iraq, and the Middle East. However, failure in such areas should not mask the potential for success in other contexts. Secondly, the fact that different Member States have different national interests, that cannot be simply combined to create 'common foreign policy', should not deter us from concentrating on areas where EU policy can do things that multiple national policies can not. Thirdly, those who have made suggestions with regard to improving the EU's foreign policy have emphasized multiple inconsistencies as the cause of the policy's weakness. These inconsistencies can be resolved through institutional reform. They do not really relate to differences in national policies.

The second part of this chapter will examine EU foreign policy through its manifestation in multilateral fora. Today, the EU's visible human rights foreign policy *tout court* (rather than human rights as part of trade, aid, or development policy) is usually executed by the EU at the UN or with regard to developments in other fora.[46] The EU's commitment to the UN and multilateral co-operation demands that it attempt to work with its partners through these fora.

II. THE MANIFESTATION OF EU FOREIGN POLICY IN MULTILATERAL FORA

A. The Importance of Coherence and Credibility

If one considers for a moment the issue of human rights violations occurring within the territory of the EU one is reminded that the history of European integration is a history of economic integration. Hitherto, the European Community's actual competence over civil and political rights issues within the Union has been rather limited. The Member States have not empowered the Commission of the European Community to act and speak out on human rights violations within the Union (where they do not fall within the scope of fundamental Community rights found in the Treaty of Rome).[47] This has in turn meant that, despite the legal obligations to pursue development and foreign policy in accordance with human rights objectives, the Union's arrangements for discussing or protesting human rights issues within the territory of the Union are only now being developed in the aftermath of the Amsterdam provisions for suspension and expulsion of a Member State for persistent human rights violations. But in less dramatic circumstances it is difficult to see how the Member States' 'common foreign policy' can critically address violations by an actual Member State of the Union. Any such criticism could hardly be a 'common policy' of the Fifteen! The result is human rights policy which is skewed, and which, to most observers, seems solely focused on the behaviour of non-European States.

[46] As already pointed out, the CFSP human rights work also includes action taken through direct diplomatic contacts between foreign ministries and third countries. This invisible work is almost impossible to evaluate, analyse and improve due to the failure of the Council to report in any detail on this work. However it does seem that better follow-up and evaluation by the Council itself is called for. The solution may be in demanding that the secretariat of the Council that is privy to this sort of information be empowered to remind the Council, and the other institutions, of their successes, failures, and ongoing work. This task might arguably be entrusted to the new secretariat in the Policy Planning and Early Warning Unit or to the staff who will be working most closely with the new High Representative for the CFSP (Mr or Mme PESC). One could describe the EU's human rights CFSP as resembling an iceberg. The invisible part being the collection of *démarches* that are never publicly discussed—the visible part being the public disagreements and common positions taken in multilateral fora.

[47] On the distinction between universal human rights and fundamental Community rights see A. Clapham, 'A Human Rights Policy for the European Community' (1991) 10 *YEL* 320.

The human rights policy of the EU as expounded at the UN therefore lacks coherence in the eyes of the rest of the world—as EU policy fails to consider human rights issues within. Human rights violations are committed outside by 'non EU people' or '*extracomunitari*' or 'others'.

This part of the report considers how the EU foreign policy on human rights is implemented through its participation in multilateral fora and in the fieldwork of those organizations. The success of any EU initiative aimed at strengthening the human rights role of the United Nations will depend on how the EU and its Member States are seen by the rest of the UN membership. Unity and consistency will not be enough in this context. Only when the EU's human rights policy is coherent and credible will the EU have a chance successfully to enhance the role of the UN and pursue its human rights policy in that forum.

We have to point out that the same schism that was referred to above, whereby external policy is divorced from internal policy and different considerations apply inside and outside the European Union, currently contributes to the credibility deficit in the context of UN human rights debates. Although one does not expect virulent self-criticism from governments during the UN human rights debates, at the UN General Assembly and Commission on Human Rights, it can hardly be acceptable that the longest, and arguably most important, survey of the situation of human rights in the world never really touches on the actual human rights violations occurring in any of the fifteen countries that comprise the European Union (a Union with more than 363 million inhabitants). This is particularly striking at a time when the rest of the world is waiting to see how the European Union will explain its treatment of non-EU nationals and asylum-seekers. It is disconcerting for the rest of the world to have to absorb harsh human rights criticism when it knows that its nationals, and European Union citizens, are enduring a series of human rights violations in the workplace, at the police station, and at the borders of the European Union. To respond that the institutional arrangements of the Union generally preclude such self-criticism and accountability, due to the fact that these issues are divided amongst the three pillars, is unsatisfactory.[48] There are precedents for European States taking a self-critical look at their own records in the context of the human rights debate at the United Nations. Before joining the Union Austria was prepared to dedicate a whole intervention at the United Nations General Assembly to details of criticism levelled at its own human rights record. There are signs of change, for example at the 1998 Commission on Human Rights, the EU joint statement referred to action planned by the EU to promote the right to work and efforts to tackle racism. This is an important step, but the EU could go further. To downplay human rights problems in Europe is to reinforce the notion that human rights issues arise in far away places and that human rights law has little to say about the future arrangements in Europe.

In some ways this preference for 'extrospection' over introspection is not so different from the situation in other polities. Departments of Foreign Affairs only

---

[48] The three pillars are: first: European Community 'area without internal frontiers' economic and monetary union, economic and social cohesion, citizenship of the Union, aspects of visa policy, development co-operation; second: CFSP, third: Justice and Home Affairs (immigration, control of external borders, police, judicial and customs co-operation).

rarely enter into self-critical international discussions of human rights abuses occurring within their own jurisdiction. But it is suggested that the success of any EU human rights foreign policy will be partly dependent on the ability of the Union to discuss and remain accountable for its own record. Only this sort of self-critical coherent approach can build the sort of credibility needed to ensure that the Union's position in multilateral fora is taken seriously and has some impact. For any human rights foreign policy to be truly effective, the way in which the policy is executed will have to be not only consistent, but coherent and credible as well. These are all important qualities for any human rights foreign policy. Consistency can help to inject a measure of predictability into the action of the European Union, and thus can serve to prevent human rights violations as governments become aware of the scope and meaning of the European Union's commitment to human rights. Paying attention to coherence and credibility can help to ensure that the European Union can protect itself from accusations of selectivity, arbitrariness, and double standards.

It is worth briefly referring to the role that the United States has played in the field of human rights foreign policy, and the problems which that State has had with regards to enforcing a credible policy. Since the 1970s the USA has been hampered in its human rights foreign policy due to a credibility deficit as a result of its failure to ratify any of the human rights treaties. Only in 1992 did the United States join the other States parties to the International Covenant on Civil and Political Rights (ICCPR),[49] and then albeit with an implied admission that it was done to bolster its foreign policy, rather than enhance human rights protection at home. (The United States entered reservations, declarations and understandings in order to preclude the Covenant taking effect in national law[50]). The fact that some aspects of the reservations are contrary to the object and purpose of the Covenant has also detracted from any authority that ratification might have brought, and has currently diminished the ability of the United States to speak with moral authority in the human rights arena.[51] These issues go beyond the technical examination of treaty obligations by expert bodies. Countries which are singled out for criticism of their human rights record are nowadays less likely to appeal to the blanket defence that the reporting is 'an interference in internal affairs'. Victim States rather point to the dubious records of the accusers and the selectivity involved in choosing to highlight the

[49] International Covenant on Civil and Political Rights, adopted by GA Res. 2200 A (XXI) (1966). In United Nations, *A Compilation of International Instruments* (1994), i, Part 1, 20.
[50] For the Human Rights Committee's reaction to the US first report and the attendant reservations, declarations, and understandings see Docs. CCPR/C/SR.1401–02 and SR.1405–06. The Committee's concluding comments includes the following para.: '[t]he Committee regrets the extent of the State party's reservations, declarations and understandings to the Covenant. It believes that, taken together, they intended to ensure that the United States has accepted only what is already the law of the United States. The Committee is also particularly concerned at the reservations to Art. 6, paragraph 5, and Art. 7 of the Covenant, which it believes to be incompatible with the object and purpose of the Covenant.' See *Annual Report of the Human Rights Committee to the General Assembly*, A/50/40 (1995), at para. 279.
[51] In particular the United States have reserved the right to execute juvenile offenders in violation of Art. 6(5) of the Covenant which expressly prohibits this. On the effects of this incompatibility see W. Schabas, 'Invalid Reservations to the International Covenant on Civil and Political Rights: Is the United States Still a Party? (1995) 22 *BJIL* 277–325. The UN Human Rights Committee stated: that it was 'particularly concerned at reservations to Art. 6, paragraph 5, and Art. 7 of the Covenant, which it believes to be incompatible with the object and purposes of the Covenant': CCPR/C/79/Add. 50 (1995), at para. 14.

issue in question.[52] If the European Union is to have a credible foreign policy in the field of human rights it has to be able to show that the Union is taking steps to promote and protect all human rights within the Union.

During the Cold War the risk of such a credibility deficit was less pronounced as the human rights discourse was often part of a rhetorical flourish, brandished as part of the politics of alignment and the pressure on developing countries to become a superpower client or strategic partner. In the 1990s the West will need to present its human rights policies with conviction and credibility if they are going to have any effect. Nothing undermines a human rights foreign policy more that the tendency to tell others abroad how to behave while refusing to subject one's own human rights record to international scrutiny. In contrast to the United States, all fifteen Members States of the European Union have undertaken legal obligations which subject them to an international jurisdiction with binding results. All members of the European Union are subject to the jurisdiction of the European Court of Human Rights concerning human rights complaints brought against them under the European Convention on Human Rights (ECHR). Such a submission to international scrutiny is important, but does not go far enough. In order for the European Union to hold third States to account for breaches of standards such as those found in the International Covenant on Civil and Political Rights, the Member States need to demonstrate greater commitment to the legal standards found in that treaty. All fifteen Member States of the European Union are parties to the ICCPR,[53] but only fourteen have allowed for individual communications to the Human Rights Committee under the First Optional Protocol.[54] With regard to economic, social, and cultural rights we should note that all fifteen are parties to the International Covenant on Economic, Social, and Cultural Rights (ICESCR).[55]

It is suggested that the success of any human rights foreign policy developed by the EU at the United Nations will be partly dependent on the ability of the Union to discuss and remain accountable for its own record. This is not just a question of avoiding charges of hypocrisy and double standards. The rise of racism, police brutality, the restrictions on asylum-seekers, and the treatment of immigrants are all of intense interest to non-EU countries. Nowhere is the lack of self-criticism more marked than in the joint EU statements made on the human rights situation in the world at the UN. It is to this topic that we now turn.

B. Statements by the EU Presidency and Commission during Human Rights Debates at the United Nations

The European Union statements on human rights in the world, made in fora such as the UN Commission on Human Rights or the General Assembly, represent an overview of the 'countries of concern' to all fifteen Member States.[56] A joint state-

---

[52] 'In Riposte, China Cites "Plight of U.S. Children" ', *International Herald Tribune*, 23 Feb. 1996, at 4.

[53] Greece became the last EU Member State to become a Party in 1997.

[54] The United Kingdom is the only Member EU State not to have ratified this Protocol.

[55] International Covenant on Economic, Social and Cultural Rights, adopted by GA Res. 2200 A (XXI) (1966). In *International Instruments*, note 49 above, at 8.

[56] We are dealing here with the joint statements by the Fifteen and not any statements made by the Commission (such as the one made in Mar. 1996 at the UN Human Rights Commission). It is the

ment like this has disadvantages and advantages. On the one hand, this statement is more diluted in its criticism than if the individual Member States were each making their own foreign policy statements. Certain Member States may have political ties with the State being criticized and will seek to water down the joint statement. On the other hand, the combined weight of the statement lends it greater force and, in some instances, the concerns of one State will be endorsed by the other fourteen, thus highlighting a human rights issue that might otherwise have been dismissed as of limited interest. Overall we can say that the power of these statements lies in their use as instruments for leverage. Considerable lobbying takes place in order to ensure inclusion or exclusion of country references in the EU statement. Criticism by the EU, in a public multilateral forum, still counts for something. This is the forum where co-operation with the UN or with humanitarian organizations will be scrutinized. Non-co-operation can result in an EU rebuke and inclusion of the country in a statement primarily aimed at States with a record of on-going serious human rights violations.

At the 1996 UN Human Rights Commission, the EU Commission itself made an intervention explaining how it spent its 1995 human rights budget. It is to be hoped that the Commission will develop its own participation at United Nations meetings and continue to explain some of the details of its human rights projects. The Commission had over $100 million at its disposal in 1998 and its projects can make a considerable impact. These projects are basically aimed at developing countries as well as programmes such as TACIS and PHARE for the former Soviet Union and Eastern and Central Europe. However a greater profile for the EU Commission at UN human rights meetings would balance the image currently projected by the European Union as a hectoring, lecturing actor at the UN human rights debate. The statement made by Mme Emma Bonino, the Member of the EU Commission responsible for humanitarian affairs and the EU humanitarian agency ECHO, at the 1998 UN Commission on Human Rights, demonstrated how the EU Commission can have a constructive role in this context. Not only did she highlight the key issues facing the UN, including the need for greater political support from the Member States on issues such as the International Criminal Court, the protection role of UNHCR, the need for funds for the human rights programme, and the threat to women's rights in Kabul under the Taliban, she also highlighted to the UN Commission the possibility, enshrined in the Amsterdam Treaty, for the Council of the EU to sanction a Member State of the EU for a serious and persistent breach of human rights.[57]

C. *The Issue of Resolutions on Country Situations and the Role of the EU*

The Unionization of the Member States' human rights foreign policy has arguably watered down the commitment of some of the more radical Member States. Consider the case of action to secure a resolution at the UN Human Rights Commission on the human rights situation in China. In 1996 the EU Member States did not make a co-ordinated effort to lobby other States to ensure a successful resolution, and failed to

Member States of the Union and the Council's secretariat that have to formulate this policy. At the present stage of integration the Commission has less of a role here.

[57] Statement to the UN Commission on Human Rights, 17 Mar. 1998.

secure the votes for a resolution. The economics of the European Community are never very far from the surface as the foreign policy on human rights is executed. But the EU rarely admits that trade concerns affect human rights foreign policy with a State such as China. Rather, the policy is presented as a tactical choice. In a revealing passage, Sir Leon Brittan, Vice-President of the EU Commission, stated in 1995:

> A commitment to human rights and fundamental freedoms is at the heart of EU policy worldwide. Violations are not only a cause for concern in their own right, but because the EU believes that espousal of international standards of human rights and acceptance of political liberalization is vital for long-term social and political stability. The key criterion for pursuing human rights initiatives must be effectiveness, the impact that an initiative would have on the ground. For this reason, there is a danger that relying solely on frequent and strident declarations will dilute the message or lead to knee-jerk reactions from the Chinese government. To make progress, all the EU institutions should pursue human rights issues through a combination of carefully timed statements, formal private discussions and practical cooperation.[58]

Effectiveness is important, but human rights policy cannot be primarily determined by the reaction of the impugned State. The capacity of China to react is given as a justification for muting criticism. The credibility of the European Union's policy will be further damaged if it drops objective statements, and *démarches* based on the human rights situation, and tailors its action to selective action based on the perceived sensitivities of States. Moreover there are continuing tensions over the commitment to human rights and the perceived conflict with the commercial interests of the Member States. Where this combines with the fear of giving offence (which we highlighted in the case of China above) human rights concerns seem to diminish to vanishing point. Muting human rights concern when delicate commercial or other advantages are at stake has been defended as 'constructive engagement' and the basis of a more effective strategy. The obvious recent examples where this approach is being followed is with respect to China, Algeria, and Turkey. The risk in such situations is that this common commitment to this sort of engagement weakens the base of those States prepared to take a tough confrontational approach.[59]

---

[58] Communication of the Commission, 'A Long-term Policy for China-Europe Relations': COM(95)279 final. Sir Leon Brittan is responsible for external relations with China, as well as the common commercial policy, and relations with OECD and WTO. Cited with approval by Roberto Toscano, 'EU-China Relations and Human Rights', paper presented to a workshop on Europe and China: The Implications of Growing Economic Interdependence and the Evolving Political/Security Dialogue, Exploring the Link Between Interdependence and Security' 6 June 1996, Centro Studi di Politica Internazionale. Toscano goes on, at 6: '[i]n a way, this spells out what should be a EU human rights policy *vis-à-vis* any country and any issue: a combination of pressure (involving a denunciation of the most blatant cases of human rights violations) dialogue and technical assistance to help countries address problems affecting human rights. Until now, with China, the first aspect has been predominant (and, one may add, ineffective). It seems that now the path of dialogue (to be sure, not a new one) will be tried with more time, intensity, and political commitment. Certainly, about dialogue one may say what can be said about public, condemnatory declaration: it is not an end in itself; on the contrary, it has to be judged on the basis of results. But for that both sides to a dialogue have to show their good will.'

[59] *The Economist* has suggested that the Chinese government is using this governmental enthusiasm for exports to China as a way to 'divide one western ally from another' and that the price for such negotiated exports is not worth paying 'whether in economic or diplomatic terms'. See 'Don't be Salesmen', 1 Feb. 1997, at 17–18. Little attention is being paid to the importance of ensuring an independent judiciary and the rule of law, even as an instrument to ensure that foreign investors build confidence in the Chinese business environment.

Of course commercial considerations do not always mitigate against taking a human rights stance. With regard to Cuba the European Union has been prepared to speak out as the Union and include a desire to see respect for human rights in Cuba in its 14 December 1996 Dublin European Council Conclusions. This has been seen in some quarters as a position engineered to appease the United States at a time when a trade war was looming over European opposition to US domestic legislation designed to isolate Cuba.[60]

The logic for standing together to negotiate and adopt resolutions seems unassailable.[61] But one problem is that the framework for adopting Common Foreign and Security Policy can also be used for preventing States from taking initiatives at the UN. It is disturbing that the first time the Council formalized its position with regard to an impending country resolution at the UN, it was to announce that the Union would not be acting, and nor would its Member States. At the General Affairs meeting of the Council on 23 February 1998 the Council concluded, '[i]n view of the first encouraging results of the EU–China human rights dialogue, the Council agreed that neither the Presidency nor Member States should table or co-sponsor a draft Resolution at the next UN Commission on Human Rights'.

This formal 'levelling down' of the EU foreign policy on human rights at the UN seems at first glance to represent a drastic self-imposed reduction of sovereignty for those States that might choose to table or co-sponsor a resolution. In any event it certainly weakens the position of those seeking to pressure the Chinese government in the run-up to the UN Commission session. The official position of the EU is that trade had nothing to do with the decision, which was taken with respect to an assessment of the improvements in China's human rights policy. However, this has not satisfied human rights advocates, who see European interest in the Chinese markets and little concrete improvement on the ground in China.[62]

In fact, individual States could have introduced a resolution should they have wanted to do so. The injunction states that Member States 'should' not introduce a resolution or co-sponsor a text. The door is left open for eventual action. This may seem like a rather strained interpretation of the paragraph, but apparently one government insisted on revising the draft from 'would not' to 'should not' in order to leave itself the option of action later on. This episode, according to the European Parliament's report on the role of the Union in the world, has highlighted the 'absence of any common policy on human rights in China'.[63]

---

[60] See 'European Union Pushes for Democracy in Cuba', *New York Times*, 15 Dec. 1996, at A17, 'the Union's response is partly a response to the United States' Helms Burton law, which seeks to isolate Cuba'.

[61] For a detailed analysis of the EU practice in the UN Commission on Human Rights and the General Assembly with regard to human rights resolutions see M. Fouwels, 'The European Union's Common Foreign and Security Policy and Human Rights' (1997) 15 *NQHR* 291–324.

[62] See 'Outcome of Wei Jingsheng's visit to Brussels 12–17 March 1998: Agreement on seriousness of human rights situation and the need for a public approach—disagreement on change in EU Policy': Amnesty International European Union Association, 18 Mar. 1998. Wei Jingsheng saw the decision of the EU in the following way: '[t]he EU has made concrete concessions to China by letting China off the hook in Geneva, while in return China has only expressed intentions without clear prospects for improvements of the ground.' Amnesty International's assessment of the EU policy is harsh: '[t]his decision by the EU seems to have more to do with policy splits in the EU and chasing lucrative markets than with changes on the ground in China. The EU is putting markets before morality.'

[63] EP Doc. A4–0169/98 at 18.

However we might draw some rays of hope from the fact that at least one State is prepared to leave its options open. First, Member States do indeed take their responsibilities seriously under the human rights CFSP and consider even 'conclusions' to have some legal effect in international law.[64] Secondly, States are not always looking for an excuse to hide behind the EU 'shield'; human rights policy at the national level will continue to drive the foreign policy of some governments, even if they end up having to break ranks with the rest of the EU. Thirdly, by publicly stating that they are prepared to stand together on the question of a country resolution, States subject to possible scrutiny at the UN Human Rights Commission are under notice that the unity of the EU cannot easily be undermined. Should the EU use this procedure actually to put states on notice that they *will* be presenting a resolution, we may have taken a step forward in the creation of an effective CFSP human rights policy. States under notice will see that it is better therefore to try to accommodate the EU demands than to play one State off against another in a competitive marketplace. The fact is that the drive towards a common policy can take us down two different roads. The EU can choose to be more or less active on human rights. In some contexts acting together will mean a less activist approach. But this is not inevitable.

Some of those concerned with the EU decision to give notice that Member States should ease off the pressure on China feel vindicated due to the subsequent announcement that China will sign the ICCPR. They feel that not having a resolution allowed the Chinese government to make improvements without seeming to be buckling under Western pressure. The strong statement from the Council regarding CFSP, according to this line of thinking, allowed the Chinese to see that dialogue on human rights and *rapprochement* with regard to the international legal regime will be respected. The ultimate test for this new type of human rights foreign policy decision will be whether the situation in China will actually improve and whether the commitment to the Civil and Political Rights Covenant will result in signature, ratification, and implementation. We might also look forward to the EU Council taking similar decisions where it announces, in advance of UN meetings, that the Presidency will be introducing a resolution and that all Member States will be co-sponsoring the resolution. At this point 'speaking with one voice' could mean a definite 'leveling up' of human rights foreign policy.

D. Negotiating International Texts Together in International Fora

Another issue should be addressed in the context of international negotiation of texts. The recent round of world conferences and global summits has reinforced the profile of the EU as a key Western negotiator. Negotiations in Vienna, Copenhagen, and Beijing depended on the EU Presidency being recognized as the voice of the Fifteen (and in many cases representing the position of associated States from Eastern and Central Europe as well). This has considerable advantages as, contrary to popular perceptions, these negotiations can move very fast indeed. The leverage at-

---

[64] See Dehousse and Weiler, note 30 above, and note the point made earlier that the ECJ has no jurisdiction in this field, so it is the international legal order which is exercising some sort of pull in this sphere rather than fear of sanctions in European law under the treaties.

tached to the European vision has been considerably increased due to the coherence of the negotiating positions. The only other blocs currently capable of demonstrating such cohesion are the 'G 77' developing countries in the economic context, and the Non-Aligned Movement (NAM) in the political context. On the one hand, EU cohesion has meant that EU policy has become apparent and important in a context such as the elaboration of the right to development or the integration of human rights throughout the UN system. On the other hand it can be argued that it is precisely because the EU has achieved some conceptual coherence on such issues that the debate has become polarized: because the EU represents an ideological and powerful bloc, other blocs may have to redefine their identity and ideology in counter-position to the EU. There is division in the debate, not despite EU consistency, but *because of* EU coherence. For example the drafting of a single resolution by the Working Group of the Third Committee of the UN General Assembly has dragged on for nearly five years. The dynamic is that suggestions made by the EU are almost automatically opposed by the NAM and vice versa. This is the sort of discussion where EU unity may have to be forsaken for a less threatening constellation. Proposals could then perhaps be judged on their merit, rather than part of a points-scoring exercise. There are plenty of examples of drafting exercises where no attempt at consistent EU unity has been made.[65] The flexibility and constructive atmosphere which resulted are instructive.

E. European Union Commission Assistance to the UN's Human Rights Field Operations

The European Community Monitoring Mission (ECMM) in the former Yugoslavia states that one of its 'main tasks' is to 'monitor and report on the humanitarian and Human Rights situation'.[66] With over fifty personnel in the field, this monitoring represents an important contribution to the protection of human rights,[67] and clearly can be considered part of the human rights foreign policy of the EU. The ECMM is fully integrated into the complex international organigramme in the former Yugoslavia and it has a liaison officer in the Human Rights Co-ordination Centre organized by the Office of the High Representative. This sort of 'stand alone' mission organized by the European Community has however become the exception to the rule.

[65] E.g. there is no consistent EU co-ordination or unity in the discussions on the drafting of the statute of the International Criminal Court which started in the General Assembly in 1995. Exceptionally in 1998 the UK Presidency communicated to the Preparatory Committee the view of the EU on the procedure for adoption of the Rules of Procedure for the proposed Court. This sort of flexibility, whereby there are Member State positions and EU positions within the same drafting exercise, seems helpful.

[66] European Community Monitoring Mission: 'Status Report' in *International Round Table on Human Rights in Bosnia and Herzegovina* (Austrian Federal Ministry for Foreign Affairs) (1996), 45.

[67] The Amnesty International report on the international community's operation in Bosnia and Herzegovina praises the fact that the 'ECMM Humanitarian Bi-Weekly Reports' are widely distributed and suggests that: '[a]lthough these regional reports rarely contain any in-depth analysis or reports of investigations of reported human rights violations, they sometimes contain remarkably frank assessments of the situations in their areas of responsibility': *Bosnia-Herzegovina: The International Community's Responsibility to Ensure Human Rights* (AI Index: EUR 63/14/96) (June 1996), 59.

In 1995 and 1996 the EC Commission became more and more involved in the UN's human rights field operations. Sending human rights field officers to countries is a relatively new type of activity for the United Nations, and in the context of countries like Rwanda and Burundi it poses special challenges due to the scale of the killing which engulfed those countries, and because of the ever-present threat of further violence. The UN High Commissioner for Human Rights' operations in Rwanda and Burundi failed to attract the initial necessary finance and logistical support to make them work. In response to the High Commissioner's appeals for voluntary funding the EU Commission promised financing for both operations, and, in the context of the Rwanda operation, became involved in the recruitment of 'EU Contributed Observers' and the co-ordination of certain policy questions.

In a 'mixed operation', such as the UN's Human Rights Field Operation in Rwanda (HRFOR), the fact of having some field officers paid for by the European Commission in Brussels, with a separate administrative structure, led to considerable tension and unnecessary bad feeling within the mission. A number of studies have looked at the new problems surrounding human rights monitoring operations in the field. Most conclude that with proper selection, training, management, and political support, such operations can make a useful contribution. However, whether or not there is scope for a separate European Union profile within United Nations operations remains problematic, and it is hoped that lessons will be learned from the Rwanda experience. This following passage from a report commissioned for the Human Rights and Justice Division of the Canadian Department of Foreign Affairs reflects some of the worst aspects of the European Union/United Nations dynamic in the Rwanda UN human rights field operation:

> The EU team retained separate insignia [their vehicles carried both UN and EU logos], separate radio frequencies, and there were computer compatibility problems with the rest of HRFOR. In principle the EU observers were to be paid at UN rates, but they ended up being paid more than the UN monitors and this also caused some friction. In addition it sounds as if some of the EU contingent had felt superior to the UN team proper, and did not hide it very well. Also at times it appeared that the EU was retaining a degree of distance from the rest of HRFOR partly for European media profile. Positive publicity about EU efforts *per se* were perceived to be more likely if the EU component was distinct and almost separate.[68]

It is in some ways understandable that officials are interested in increasing the image of the European Union's efforts and that they demand visibility as well as a certain amount of accountability from the UN for how EU money is spent.[69] But the conclusion of the most recent evaluation by Ingrid Kircher and Paul LaRose-

[68] Paul LaRose-Edwards, *UN Human Rights Operations: Principles and Practice in United Nations Field Operations* (1996), available from the Human Rights and Justice Division of the Canadian Department of Foreign Affairs.

[69] The EC Commission assigned R. Von Meijenfeld to produce an evaluation of the EU participation in the UN human rights field operation in Rwanda. The report, *At the Frontline for Human Rights*, of Oct. 1995 is positive and concluded that '[t]he presence of the contingent of HRFOs provided excellent visibility for the European Union' (recommendation 12) but complains that the EU contribution should be 'more prominently acknowledged'. Based on questionnaires filled out by the EU field officers the evaluation also concludes that 'there exists confusion and differences in interpretation of whether or not the assignments of EU HRFOs differ from those of the UN HRFOs'. Executive summary, at 25.

Edwards was that, while the input of the European Commission was absolutely essential for the creation of the initial operation, the EU contingent should be eliminated as a separate group and be integrated into the UN structure. There should then be guaranteed EC funding to the UN High Commissioner for Human Rights for their salaries for at least six months.[70]

Turning from the role of the EU Commission to the role of the Member States of the European Union in the wake of the Rwanda genocide, we have to conclude that their performance was extremely disappointing. The Member States of the European Union failed from the start to give the UN's human rights operation in Rwanda the sort of political and financial support which was needed to make it work. The comparison with the United States' support for a similar operation in Haiti is instructive. Despite the fact that the Haiti operation was a combined operation between the UN and the Organization of American States, diplomatic activity by the USA at the UN in New York led to a proper assessment of the challenges, a proper budget, and the kind of political support which at times meant that human rights were taken seriously in discussions of the future of Haiti. By contrast, at the start of the crisis there seemed to be little attempt by EU Member States to engage in efforts at the UN to support the UN Human Rights Field Operation in Rwanda. There was neither political support nor a concerted effort to ensure a regular funding base from the UN budget. It was almost as if the European Commission's early activity had absolved the Member States from their responsibilities.[71]

The most recent initiative by the EU Commission has been its support for the establishment of the Permanent Office of the UN High Commissioner for Human Rights in Colombia. The Commission is paying the salaries of five observers, and their role is currently restricted to providing the finance as the recruitment and

[70] 'Evaluation of the European Union Contingent to the UN Human Rights Field Operation in Rwanda—Commissioned by the European Commission' (1997) (unpublished), recommendation 32. The evaluation also recommends that the European Commission's Kigali Office should provide a small and flexible 'funding window' for the UN's HRFOR 'micro projects', and points out that actors such as UNDP and donors such as the European Commission are likely to remain long after the withdrawal of HRFOR and that some of the human rights and justice programmes already 'dwarf HRFOR's efforts'. An examination of the complementary role of technical assistance by the EU when the UN has a technical assistance programme on the ground is outside the scope of the current chap. but see the contribution of Bruno Simma to the present vol. for more details of the Commission's work in this area. Suffice it to say that the Commission's work in this context is extremely important for the promotion and protection of human rights around the world. The leverage which the Commission exerts through funding NGOs is different from the sorts of controls the UN has over its own technical co-operation projects. Some of the advantages for NGOs are discussed in D. Marantis, 'Human Rights, Democracy, and Development: the European Community Model' (1994) 7 *Harv. HRJ* 1.

[71] The UK and the Netherlands later made large *donations* to ensure the success of the operation. However, the problem of speedy response to UN appeals for the funding of human rights operations remains. In Burundi the EU Commission promised to pay for a team of 35 human rights monitors. Nearly a year later in Mar. 1996 the agreement had only just been signed and by June 1996 there was still little evidence of any concrete action on the ground. Again European promises generated false hopes and prevented alternative plans developing. Although this was a generous offer and not tied to an EU 'profile' the result has been disappointing. It is to be hoped that the new arrangements for a budget within the Council of the EU for CFSP will allow for rapid disbursement of funds in the event of an appeal from the UN High Commissioner for Human Rights for a human rights field operation. CFSP budget has sometimes been charged to the European Community budget in the past. In theory this can give the European Parliament a greater role. See D. McGoldrick, *International Relations Law of the European Union* (1997), 157–8 and 172–3.

administration of the salaries has been sub-contracted to an international non-governmental organization, the International Commission of Jurists. This Permanent Office is to provide technical assistance as well as to report on the human rights situation to the UN Commission on Human Rights through the UN High Commissioner for Human Rights. The recent activity of the Office and the 1998 report to the UN Commission on Human Rights have been generally seen by Colombian human rights organizations, and by European Union Member States, to be an important contribution to the fight against human rights violations in Colombia.[72] The support of the European Commission for the Office has turned an idea into a reality at a time when there would be little chance of securing funding through the regular United Nations budget. The support of the Commission of the European Union for this project is important and should be welcomed. However, concerns about selectivity remain. We have to admit that unpopular issues for the European Union may not attract funding from the Commission, and then there will be little chance of a United Nations field presence for those countries. So far projects for UN human rights field offices for Liberia, Angola, Sierra Leone, Sudan, and Somalia have attracted little attention from the Commission of the European Union (or from the Member States of the EU).

F. The European Union and the Issue of Core Labour Standards at the World Trade Organization and International Labour Organization

The European Union has asserted its commitment to human rights and the rule of law. The regulation of world trade and the establishment of the World Trade Organization have ignited a series of divisions in the international community over the question of inserting a 'social clause' into international trade agreements.[73] The discussion relating to this topic turns on two sets of suspicions. Developing countries suspect that the European Union position of insisting on respect for basic workers' rights could be disguised protectionism designed to restrict imports and protect European farmers, industries, and commerce. Some members of the European Union are apparently worried about suspicions from the general public that unregulated free trade will not only perpetuate violations of workers' rights in the developing world, but also threaten European jobs due to the competitive advantage of abusing workers' rights. This last sentiment emerges from the position of one European Union Member State presented to the Singapore Ministerial Conference in June 1996:

> It is essential to ensure widespread public support for the multilateral trade system. To achieve this the WTO must be seen by the general public to be concerned about problems of paramount importance. The same idea has been put brilliantly by Vice President of the Commission, Sir Leon Brittan: 'If free traders are not seen to tackle concerns that the man in the street regards as legitimate, we shall lay ourselves open to protectionist

---

[72] *Report by the UN High Commissioner for Human Rights*, E/CN.4/1998/16 (1998).
[73] See V. Leary 'Workers' Rights and International Trade: The Social Clause (GATT, ILO, NAFTA, US Laws)' in J. Bhagwati and R. Hudec (eds.), *Fair Trade and Harmonization: Prerequisites for Free Trade?* (1995), 177–230.

demagogy, for example to the effect that other countries deliberately exploit child labour in order to increase European unemployment'.

In addition to the competing suspicions there are a number of misunderstandings and exaggerations. The European Union has ruled out imposing higher wage levels or demanding European working conditions in the developing world as conditions for trade. The human rights which are considered relevant in this context are: the prohibition of slavery and forced labour, freedom of association and the right to collective bargaining, elimination of discrimination in employment, and the suppression of the exploitation of child labour. But the reaction to this position is that these human rights are vague and easily manipulated for political and selective reasons.

Work has started on defining the exact scope of these human rights in order that they may be reaffirmed as legally binding obligations and monitored at the international level. The European Commission has set out the internationally recognized labour standards which are to form the framework for its policy in the context of international trade. They are conveniently listed in the Commission's communication of July 1996.[74] The Communication goes on to outline action taken by the European Union in this context and some of the future schemes which will enter into force in the coming years:

> Given the principles underlying the European Union's own policy, what action can it take in this matter? We need to act on a broad canvas, because different social problems will require a different unit of EU policy instruments. For example, in the field of child exploitation, we must bear in mind that, while a small minority of children are exploited in export-driven industries, many more are being found in subsistence farming or local construction projects.
>
> The issue of human rights and, more specifically, labour standards is already a feature of the new GSP [Generalized System of Preferences] arrangements, which provide for two types of measures. The first concerns the possibility of withdrawing some or all preferences granted to countries which countenance slavery or forced labour. The possibility of withdrawing GSP benefits as a punitive measure is in itself not new. It is inherent in the unilateral character of the GSP and has been used in the past to sanction discriminatory commercial practices or fraud. In such cases, specific reference is made to forced labour in all its forms, as defined in the Geneva Conventions of 25 September 1926 and 7 September 1956 and in ILO Conventions 29 and 105. The withdrawal of benefits is decided by the Council on a proposal from the Commission following an enquiry into the

[74] 'Freedom of association and the right to form and to join trade unions are recognized in the Universal Declaration of Human Rights and the ILO Constitution. Two ILO Conventions in particular, Nos. 87 and 98, as well as the International Covenants of 1966, provide more detailed rules on the subject, including the right to collective bargaining. At least the general principles expressed in these instruments are part of the general principles of international law. The elimination of discrimination is generally recognized in virtually all international human rights instruments . . . It is beyond doubt that, for instance, the formal exclusion of segments of the population from the labour market on the basis of race or sex would be a violation of general international law. As to the question of the exploitation of child labour, Art. 10(3) of the International Covenant on Economic, Social and Cultural Rights and Art. 32 of the 1989 Convention on the Rights of the Child provide that children must be protected from economic exploitation and from performing work of a hazardous or harmful nature. States are asked to provide for a minimum age for admission to employment. ILO Convention No 138 contains more specific rules in this respect': Commission Communication to the Council, 'The Trading System and Internationally Recognized Labour Standards': COM(96)402 final.

matter. This procedure gives each party concerned the opportunity to state his case after evidence has been taken by the management committee.

The second type of measure consists of 'special incentive schemes' the main aim of which is to help beneficiary countries improve the quality of their development by adopting more advanced social and environmental policies. Thus, in the area of labour standards, additional preferences may be granted from 1 January 1998 to countries which so request and which comply with ILO Conventions 87 and 98 on freedom of association and the right to collective bargaining and with Convention 138 on child labour. The implementation procedures and the degree of preferences granted (supplementary margin) will be defined on the basis of a Commission report which will take into account the results of studies carried out by other international bodies such as the ILO, WTO and OECD.

At bilateral level the cooperation agreements concluded between the EU and third countries cover economic and social cooperation. Thus, in collaboration with other international bodies (World Bank, ILO), the Union is organizing and financing financial and technical assistance programmes to promote education and jobs for women. These programmes include: a) the building of schools; b) vocational training; c) training for secondary school teachers (where positive discrimination in favour of women is common); d) 'informal' education (targeting children who left school at a very early age, adults, people in rural areas, etc.). This assistance may be granted either to governments or to non-governmental organizations. In the light of the international commitments entered into at the World Summit in Copenhagen and following the example of the recent agreements concluded with, for instance, Pakistan and Bangladesh, the Union intends to incorporate social development objectives into its cooperation agreements with third countries, making specific reference to the need to safeguard workers' basic rights as laid down in the relevant ILO instruments, including those banning forced labour and child labour and upholding the right to association and collective bargaining and the principle of non-discrimination.[75]

These passages are cited at length to highlight the importance and complexity of the issue of the EU's human rights foreign policy in the area of trade and the core labour standards. Not only will action in this area have serious effects in economic terms, but decisions will affect the quality of life and right to work for a large number of children, family members, and other workers around the world. For present purposes the point we need to consider is the plethora of multilateral fora to which the communication refers: UN, WTO, ILO, OECD, World Bank.[76] Suffice it to say that the EU has no 'consistent' form of representation in these bodies. The Commission, which is in the driving seat for this field of human rights foreign policy, plays a key role at the WTO, and will be fully aware of developments there; but the Commission is often irrelevant in the other fora. Even if there is some participation there seems to be no coherence within the Commission on an issue such as child labour.

The Commission's human rights unit might be involved in approving grants for education programmes, but would be entirely absent from discussions surrounding

[75] 'The Trading System and Internationally Recognized Labour Standards': COM(96)402 final.
[76] We might also add some of the international organizations and other fora which are not mentioned: the European Bank for Reconstruction and Development (BERD) (of which the European Community is actually a member), the UN Conference on Trade and Development (UNCTAD), the UN Children's Fund (UNICEF), the International Monetary Fund and many others. The issue of better co-ordination for the integration of human rights into the EU's work with these and other organizations is dealt with below and in the conclusions and recommendations.

the monitoring of the core labour standards at the International Labour Organization (ILO).[77] It seems likely that the debate concerning workers' rights and international trade will continue to rage in the ILO and around the edges of the World Trade Organization (WTO). Until the issue is regulated in either or both fora, the European Union and individual Member States will continue to find regional or bilateral solutions to the quandary of how to encourage human rights in the context of trade without using these solutions as illegal instruments of protectionism. It is suggested here that a successful strategy must do two things. First, the rights that are at the centre of the policy have to be clearly defined by reference to the existing international standards. Secondly, the international treaty bodies which currently monitor and interpret these standards need to be drawn into the process and strengthened, so that the applicable international norms are accessible and clear, and States and employers will know exactly what behaviour constitutes a violation of the international norm—and hence could be subject to complaints or even jeopardize a trade agreement. The Treaty on European Union contains the injunction that Member States shall co-ordinate their action in international organizations, yet there seems to be little EU co-ordination on this issue, at least as it was dealt with before the Governing Board of the ILO.[78] This in fact is not unusual when the action at an international organization involves what can really be described as international law-making. There is no attempt to co-ordinate positions over the drafting at the UN of the statute for a permanent international criminal court. Commentators often cite the fact that on 90 per cent of UN General Assembly Resolutions the EU Member States vote the same way. But in fact when it comes to important legally binding texts, national interests are considered too important to be surrendered to a co-operative position for the purposes of negotiation.

We should not be too surprised by this, and in fact it is probably healthier that each State retains a degree of control over this sort of law-making. National interests will vary, and a State that becomes isolated in the negotiation can always decline to ratify any eventual treaty. As long as it is the Member States that are the international actors who are going to ratify and implement treaties, the tug of co-operation will remain relatively weak. Nevertheless, the area of core labour standards is likely to develop within a treaty framework, and is probably an area which demands a clearly articulated EU position. It would certainly strengthen consistency, coherence, and credibility if States were aware that the standards and approach used for

[77] See the 'Draft of a Possible Declaration of Principles Concerning Fundamental Rights and its Appropriate Follow-up for Consideration at the 86th Session (1998) of the International Labour Conference': ILO Doc. GB.271/3/1, discussed at the Governing Body, 271st Session, Mar. 1998. The issue of the division of competence between the Community and the Member States over the negotiation and implementation of conventions drawn up at the ILO was brought by the Commission to the ECJ in *Opinion 2/92 (Re ILO Convention 170)* [1993] ECR I–1061. Member States and the Commission are in this field under a duty to co-operate. However, our concern is for consistency between the agreed positions adopted in this forum and the human rights policy developed elsewhere.

[78] However governments were prepared to co-ordinate around an IMEC position (industrialized market economy countries). In other agencies positions are taken in accordance with the agreements reached within the 'Geneva group'. This is a group of major contributors to the UN budget who meet to formulate their position on budgetary issues within the UN agencies and organizations. Inevitably these positions will have implications for the substantive shape of the UN work in the various fields. Again there is no visible EU policy making.

granting trade privileges under the Community's GSP were the same as those invoked by the Union in the context of the ILO, or even the WTO.

G. Policy with Regard to International Financial Institutions and the European Community's own Development Assistance Projects

Space does not permit a detailed discussion of the effects on the enjoyment of human rights of the policies of the various international financial institutions. As is well known the World Bank considers itself prevented by its Articles from 'political interference', and there is resistance to allowing a dominant political ideology to determine the Bank's policies. Nevertheless there is a general acceptance that where human rights considerations affect the efficiency of the Bank's policies then they should be taken into account.[79] Another chink in the Bank's armour has appeared, through the admission that 'an extensive violation of individual political rights which takes pervasive proportions could impose itself as an issue in the Bank's decisions. This would be the case if the violation had significant direct economic effects or if it led to the breach of international obligations relevant to the Bank, such as those created by the UN Security Council.'[80] It seems that the barriers which have prevented discussion of human rights issues in the context of the World Bank are gradually crumbling. It is probably only a question of time before interest from the human rights movement will finally introduce greater accountability for the effect on human rights of the Bank's activity. Indeed, in recent years new procedures to determine environmental damage and impact have been developed to make the Bank more accountable.[81]

We might briefly also mention that, with regard to issues of human rights and international financial institutions, the United States has concrete legislation which calls on the government to 'advance the cause of human rights' in 'connection with its voice and vote' in the international financial institutions. This includes 'seeking to channel assistance toward countries other than those whose governments engage in ... a pattern of gross violations of internationally recognized human rights'.[82] In the

[79] I.F.I. Shihata, 'Human Rights Development, and International Financial Institutions' (1992) 8 *Am. U J Int'l L & Pol'y* 32–3.

[80] I.F.I. Shihata, 'The World Bank and Human Rights' in *Österreichische außenpolitische Dokumentation,* Special Issue 'The Universal Protection of Human Rights: Translating International Commitments into National Action', 40th International Seminar for Diplomats, Helbrunn Castle, Salzburg, Austria, 28 July–1 Aug. 1997, 197. Shihata discusses whether States should consider amending the Articles of the Bank to give the Bank a clear political mandate 'as in the case of the BERD' and points out in his conclusion at 198 that 'if the political situation in a country is so repugnant to internationally acceptable behaviour or if the violation of political rights in such country is so pervasive, there will inevitably be *economic* repercussions to these political events which the Bank may have no choice but to take into account as relevant economic considerations.'

[81] See I.F.I. Shihata, *The World Bank Inspection Panel* (1994). In conclusion at 124 Shihata states the purpose of the new panel as 'protecting the rights and interests of those parties which may be unintentionally undermined by bank actions or omissions, and improving the very process of development'. The panel already has before it a case concerning Nepal. Greater accountability in this area should lead to a certain sensitivity to avoiding Bank actions that 'undermine' the economic and social rights of individuals in countries receiving loans or assistance from the Bank. One might also hope that those policies that 'unintentionally' discriminated against women by favouring so-called 'productive sectors' will be reviewed and adjusted before they are implemented.

[82] 22 USC § 262d (1994). 'The United States Government, in connection with its voice and vote in the International Bank for Reconstruction and Development, the International Development Association,

determination of such violations the government is to give consideration to how the country under consideration is co-operating with human rights investigations, including by the International Committee of the Red Cross, Amnesty International, and the International Commission of Jurists. The US Executive Directors are authorized and instructed to oppose 'any loan, any extension of financial assistance, or any technical assistance', to any country committing such violations unless 'such assistance is directed specifically to programs which serve the basic human needs of the people of such country'. In the European context not only might Parliament consider similar scrutiny over World Bank Executive Directors voting on behalf of EU countries,[83] but the policy of the European Bank for Reconstruction and Development might be examined more closely, and the references in its statute to human rights, democracy, and pluralism[84] more fully developed, so that clear policies are adopted, and prospective clients are aware of which human rights considerations will be pertinent in this context. According to an 'indicative list' developed by the European Bank the rights which it considers relevant are 'those which, in accordance with international standards, are essential elements of multiparty democracy, pluralism and market economies'.[85]

H. Discussion of the Community's Own Human Rights Record in Multilateral Fora

It is in the field of development loans and assistance that the Community has some of the biggest impact yet the lowest degree of accountability for the impact of its policies in terms of their effect on human rights in developing countries. So far we have discussed how different forms of participation in multilateral bodies can reinforce the foreign policy of the Union. This section considers how to ensure international accountability, not only for non-member States and the Fifteen, but also for the acts of the legal entity which is the European Community.

the International Finance Corporation, the Inter-American Development Bank, the African Development Fund, the Asian Development Bank, and the African Development Bank, the European Bank for Reconstruction and Development, and the International Monetary Fund, shall advance the cause of human rights, including by seeking to channel assistance toward countries other than those whose governments engage in (1) a pattern of gross violations of internationally recognized human rights, such as torture or cruel, inhumane, or degrading treatment or punishment, prolonged detention without charges, or other flagrant denial to life, liberty, and the security of the person.'

[83] The voting power of the EU as percentages is as follows: Austria 0.74%, Belgium 1.92%, Denmark 0.69%, Finland 0.55%, France 4.58%, Germany 4.78%, Greece 0.08%, Ireland 0.36%, Italy 2.97%, Luxembourg 0.13%, Netherlands, 2.35%, Portugal 0.38%, Spain 1.58%, Sweden 1%, United Kingdom, 4.58%.

[84] For a discussion of the relevance of these references see J.V. Louis, 'La Banque européenne pour la reconstruction et développement: aspects juridiques' (1992) 2 *AEL* 251–302.

[85] Quoted by Katarina Tomaševki in *Development Aid and Human Rights Revisited* (1993), at 9. She also lists some of the rights developed by the Bank in a May 1991 memorandum: free elections; representative and accountable government; rule of law; separation between the State and political parties; independence of the judiciary; equal protection under the law, including for minorities; fair criminal procedure; freedom of speech, association and assembly; freedom of conscience and religion; freedom of movement; the right to private property; the right to form trade unions and to strike. 'Procedures to implement the political aspects of the mandate of the European Bank for Reconstruction and Development', memorandum BDS91–16, 28 May 1992, at 4. Tomaševski points out that the list pays little attention to economic, social, and cultural rights. One might ask if this policy fits with the Union's stated commitment to the promotion and protection of all human rights and its assertion about the interdependence of democracy and development.

Let us look at a concrete example of alleged violations of economic, social, and cultural rights by the policies and projects of the European Commission. The following details are taken from a submission to the UN Economic, Social, and Cultural Rights Committee.[86] In January 1988 the EC agreed to finance a Natural Forest Management and Conservation Project as part of a forestry rehabilitation project devised by the World Bank:

> The principal objectives were the demarcation of forest boundaries, replanning, and the establishment of management plans, increasing the conservation area to 50% of the total of 1,400,000 hectares of natural forest. These measures not only failed to contribute to the effective progressive implementation of the Covenant but also contributed to the violation of certain rights enshrined within the Covenant.
>
> On 31 March/1 April 1992 around 35,000 people were evicted from the Kibale Game Corridor and the Kibale Game Reserve. The latter was an area covered by the EC funded Project. There were reports of serious human rights violations during the evictions to include rape, beatings, looting, and the destruction of belongings and crops. A number of people died as a direct result of the manner in which the evictions were carried out. The Ugandan Government later launched a Cabinet enquiry into the evictions.[87]

In devising a human rights policy for the European Union it is important to find a legal framework to guide the work of the Commission as it devises and executes development projects around the world. The European Community is not a party to the International Covenant on Economic, Social, and Cultural Rights. However in addition to the commitment in Article 6(2) (*ex* Article F(2)) TEU, it is suggested that the Community is bound by the norms contained in the Covenant. All the Member States of the European Union are parties to the ICESCR. Because competence for development projects, such as the one referred to above, comes under the Commission there is room for the argument that international obligations regarding economic, social, and cultural rights attach to the Commission when it executes development projects.[88] The Chairman of the Committee has asked both organizations to account for the effects of their joint project in order to prepare the annual report to the UN Economic and Social Council.[89] It is hoped that this process will lead

---

[86] 'The advisability of international measures adopted by the European Commission and the World Bank which facilitated evictions from the Kibale Forest and Game Corridor in Uganda in March/April 1992', submitted by Ugandan Rural Development and Training Programme (URDT), Bugangaizi Resettlers Association (BRA) and Oxfam (UK/Ireland), 12 Apr. 1996 (on file with the author).

[87] *Ibid.*, at I of the summary.

[88] Cf. P. Pescatore, 'La Communauté est liée par la Convention en vertu de la doctrine de succession d'Etat' in F. Matscher and H. Petzold (eds.) *Protecting Human Rights: The European Dimension* (1988), 450–5. Pescatore argues that the doctrine of succession found in international law and applied in the context of GATT to the Community can be applied to the Community even though the succession is neither territorial nor general, but rather functional and limited. He argues that the organs of the European Convention could take decisions which recognize that the Community is bound by the substantive provisions of the Convention. By analogy we could say that the UN Committee on Economic, Social, and Cultural Rights could decide to ask for reports from the EC Commission with regard to their promotion of rights and their efforts to ensure that their development projects enhance the rights in the Convention.

[89] See also Art. 22 of the International Covenant on Economic, Social and Cultural Rights which states that the Economic and Social Council (ECOSOC) may bring to the attention of other organs of the United Nations, their subsidiary organs, and specialized agencies concerned with furnishing technical assistance any matters arising out of the reports referred to it in order to assist those bodies in deciding on the advisability of international measures likely to contribute to the effective progressive implementation of the economic, social and cultural rights in the Covenant. The annual report of the Committee to

to new procedures within the European Commission so that projects are constantly evaluated for their compatibility and conformity with human rights guarantees. One way to ensure that this evaluation is consistently undertaken, and properly applied in conformity with the evolving interpretation of international human rights law, would be for the Commission of the Community to volunteer reports to the United Nations treaty bodies and to the relevant treaty monitoring mechanisms of the Council of Europe.[90]

Apart from ensuring greater accountability at the international level it is suggested that the Community needs to address the effects of its aid and development through careful impact assessment studies. Only if the Community is prepared to look at its own human rights record can it retain the necessary credibility to enforce the promise that human rights are essential elements in co-operation or trade agreements with third countries.[91] This issue goes beyond the seemingly technical question of accountability for Commission action before UN bodies. It goes to the heart of the image of the EU Human Rights Foreign Policy. As one delegate from a developing country involved in the negotiation of such an agreement put it to me: '[w]e are all in favour of cooperating to promote human rights. We are all in favour of human rights. But we can't stand the EU taking the moral high ground and thrusting it down our throats.'[92]

ECOSOC can make recommendations of a general nature. See provisional rules of procedure rules 57 and 64 (E/1989/22) and Arts. 19 and 23 of the Covenant.

[90] In addition to the International Covenant on Economic, Social, and Cultural Rights mentioned above, all the EU Member States are parties to two other UN human rights treaties: the Convention on the Elimination of All Forms of Discrimination Against Women (adopted by GA Res. 34/180 (1979), in *International Instruments*, note 49 above, at 150) and the Convention on the Rights of the Child (adopted by GA Res. 44/25 (1989), *ibid.*, at 174). In the context of the Council of Europe's treaty monitoring system all Member States are parties to the European Convention on Human Rights (1950) and the European Social Charter (1961). Although not all Member States are bound by all the provisions of these Council of Europe treaties the EC Commission could provide reports on the rights which bind the Fifteen (and therefore arguably the Commission in certain sectors). The European Convention is usually seen as a complaints mechanism rather than a monitoring mechanism. However under Art. 57 ECHR the Secretary-General of the Council of Europe may request a High Contracting Party to furnish an explanation of any of the provisions of this Convention. Although the Community has not acceded to this Convention and the Social Charter, the Commission could submit reports on its activities and efforts to ensure conformity with the provisions of the treaties. It would be interesting to submit such reports to scrutiny by the Parliamentary Assembly of the Council of Europe. This would be a way to make the Commission accountable to the people of Europe (as represented by the parliamentarians from the different European Member States).

[91] Although the insertion of the 'essential element' clause has been widely accepted by the third countries in the adoption of their co-operation agreements this situation is starting to change as agreements are being drawn up with countries that resent the implication that they may violate human rights in a systematic way and that human rights are more than aspirations in the trade context. See 'Canberra Resists Rights Clause', *Guardian*, 14 Sept. 1996, at 5.

[92] Compare the attitude of Ghebray Berhane, Secretary-General of the African Caribbean and Pacific (ACP) countries, during the negotiation of the review of the Fourth Lomé Convention, when the European Commission proposed a clause providing for partial or total suspension in case of serious violation of human rights: 'we certainly don't want EC officials judging us': quoted by Tomaševski in *Between Sanctions and Elections: Aid Donors and their Human Rights Performance* (1997), 43, citing J. Samboma, 'ACP Countries Cry "Foul" ', *New African*, Dec. 1993, at 26. The issue could be seen to be not so much the issue of accountability for human rights, but who is doing the judging. 'EC officials' seem to lack the legitimacy or accountability. Furthermore human rights issues are still seen as a stick with which to beat countries rather than as a legitimate topic for dialogue. A theme of the present chap. is that only when the EU/EC can show that it is prepared to discuss issues of human rights within the Union, as well as those outside it, that attitudes towards the human rights dialogue will change.

I. Asylum and Refugee Policy and the Relationship with UNHCR

Asylum policy has remained a closely guarded privilege for Member States of the Union. This is an area which, until the Treaty of Amsterdam came into force, remained outside Community law and was left to inter-governmental decision-making under the old Treaty on European Union's Article K. But the move towards the internal market and the reduction in border controls within the Community have obviously forced the need to co-ordinate a more harmonized asylum policy for Member States. Furthermore, the fall of the Berlin Wall and the disintegration of the Soviet Union and the former Yugoslavia led to increased pressure at the borders of the European Union. In the 1970s there were about 30,000 asylum-seekers a year in Europe, this rose to about 160,000 by 1987, peaked at 670,000 in 1992, and was down to about 300,000 by 1994.

As some States started to introduce new forms of control and accelerated procedures for dealing with the influx of asylum-seekers at the beginning of the 1990s this resulted in other EU States feeling forced to adopt similarly stringent measures. Some EU States, which had remained more generous in their acceptance policies, found themselves fielding an increasing number of applications, as asylum-seekers gravitated to the point of least resistance. Despite the fact that most asylum policy is not covered by Community law, Resolutions, Joint Positions, and Conclusions of the European Union's Council of Ministers have started to take on considerable importance. Some States concretized their policies at the European level, and other States adapted their legislation to ensure greater harmony with the European resolutions and the policies of their European neighbours. In effect this has resulted in a certain amount of 'levelling down' of protection.

Although this area has not been strictly governed by European Community law but rather by governments working at the inter-governmental level to achieve consensus, the impression is rather different. The world perceives the shifting policy on asylum as evidence of a move towards 'fortress Europe', with Euro-decisions being taken behind closed doors. In an article entitled 'EU slams the door on fleeing victims' Leonard Doyle presented the process as follows:

> The EU's draconian new approach was hatched in secret by a group of officials from home affairs and interior ministries who meet under the auspices of the K4 Committee. Responsible for running inter-governmental co-operation for justice and home affairs, the K4 committee has the luxury of never having to face parliamentary scrutiny, whether at national or European level.[93]

He describes the plight of those being deported from European Union countries and asserts that 'in the rush to deport the economic migrants many genuine refugees are being pushed out as well without even getting a hearing'.

We encounter here the same problems of divergence between the Union's position with regard to its own refugee policy and what is expected from other governments. This inconsistency has made the United Nations High Commissioner for Refugees (UNHCR) uncomfortable. In the words of its representative to the European Union:

---

[93] *Guardian Weekly*, 31 Mar. 1996, at 7.

On the one hand [European governments are] asking UNHCR to give assistance and protection to victims of conflict, with the complete political support of European funding countries. But on the other hand, when these same victims of conflict attain the territory of the countries of the European Union, the response is completely different: the people under UNHCR protection are all of a sudden no longer recognized as refugees.[94]

Perhaps the European governments' attitude can be understood as exceptional in the face of the Yugoslav tragedy—where UNHCR has been asked to shoulder the burden of assisting refugees before they leave the territory of the Former Yugoslavia. But the issues run much deeper. And the changing attitude of European countries risks threatening the foundations of the legal regime for refugees.

Today, Europe is at a crossroads. If it was in Europe that asylum was born, it is also in Europe that the principle is now most menaced. Will the warning be heard? If not, the consequences will be felt not just in the region but worldwide. How can poor countries be convinced to accept refugees if the richest nations close their doors to the few still knocking? One thing is certain: If Europe sets the example, the rest of the world will follow.[95]

Let us turn to some of the decisions taken at the European level and their relevance for the human rights of those outside the Union. A series of resolutions adopted at the end of 1992 aimed at the harmonization of issues such as 'manifestly unfounded applications for asylum', 'minimum guarantees for asylum procedures', and a 'harmonized approach to questions concerning host third countries'.[96] European Union Immigration Ministers also adopted their 'Conclusions on Countries in which there is generally no serious risk of persecution'. The effect has been to reduce the scope of the right to a hearing, so that in some cases this right is almost eliminated. UNHCR has analysed the effects of these changes as the resolutions get converted into national legislation. And UNHCR has protested that notions such as 'safe country of origin' are contrary to the 'necessary individual determination of refugee status'.[97]

But UNHCR looks to the EU Commission and the Members of the European Union as important contributors to its budget.[98] UNHCR is torn between responding to the humanitarian demands made on it in crisis situations and forcing donor governments to look for lasting solutions. With a total of $11.6 billion spent on processing and reception of asylum-seekers by Western European governments in 1993, one can see why European governments are seeking ways to save money in this

---

[94] Cécil Kpenou, quoted in Berthiaume, 'Asylum under Threat', *Refugees*, No. 101 (1995), 9.

[95] *Ibid.*, at 10. Other regions currently have more generous regimes for admission of refugees, e.g. the OAU Convention Governing the Specific Aspects of Refugee Problems in Africa, in force since 1974, and the OAS Cartagena Declaration of 1985 both recognize flight from serious disturbances of public order. Reprinted in J.P. Colombey (ed.), *Collection of International Instruments and Other Legal Texts Concerning Refugees and Displaced Persons* (UNHCR, 1995).

[96] See 'Resolution on Manifestly Unfounded Applications for Asylum' and 'Resolution on a Harmonized Approach to Questions Concerning Host Third Countries', both adopted in London, 30 Nov. and 1 Dec. 1992.

[97] *An Overview of Protection Issues in Western Europe: Legislative Trends and Positions Taken by UNHCR*, Vol. 1, No. 3 (Sept. 1995).

[98] In 1995 the European Commission contributed $208,302,155 to the UNHCR total budget of $979,650,176. In addition the 15 Member States of the EU contributed $302,073,706 (all figures reflect the situation at 24 July 1996). The combined contributions therefore make up more than half the contributions to UNHCR during 1995.

sphere. However, in the rush to streamline applications, and increase intergovernmental co-operation over protection in transit States and 'safe countries', the
fundamental principle of protection from persecution is being threatened. At a time
when individuals around the world face horrific violence and persecution the European Union ought to be reinforcing the protection principle, rather than undermining it. One example should suffice to illustrate the point.

> In January 1993, a 29-year-old Liberian named Thomas arrived in Germany with his
> wife. Back home, his father had been killed by one of the largest of the armed factions
> which have been tearing Liberia apart since the government collapsed in 1990. Shortly
> afterwards, Thomas was forcibly recruited by the same faction. Subsequently, suspected
> of spying for a rival group, he was made to watch as his wife was raped. As another test
> of his loyalty, he was forced to kill a number of children who had also been accused of
> spying. Fearing that their days were numbered, Thomas and his wife managed to stow
> away on a cargo ship which took them to Italy. They then traveled by car to Germany,
> where they applied for asylum. Their experience would appear to qualify them as
> refugees. Or so one might think, given the very reasonable fears they expressed for their
> personal safety and the fact that, by 1993, the system of 'national protection'—a func-
> tioning police force and judicial system—was extinct in Liberia . . . [I]n September 1993
> the German Federal Office for the Recognition of Foreign Refugees rejected Thomas'
> and his wife's asylum claims as 'manifestly unfounded'.[99]

They were victims of a 'European interpretation' of the concept of 'refugee' under
the 1951 Geneva Convention.[100] Under this interpretation: where the threat comes
from 'non-state agents', which are outside the control of governments, then the victims are not eligible for refugee status and risk being sent back to imminent danger.
In 1995, in the context of harmonizing asylum policy, the Members States of the European Union adopted a joint position on the 'definition of the term "refugee"'.
This document includes a paragraph on 'persecution by third parties' which effectively limits the scope of the term refugee.[101] Its effect is that people fleeing persecution in countries where the State has collapsed, or people fleeing factions that have
no state-like qualities, will be excluded from refugee status. UNHCR has expressed
its concern that the new position of the definition of the term 'refugee' adopted by the
European Union on 23 November 1995 will 'allow states to avoid recognizing as
refugees people persecuted by "non-state agents"—such as rebel groups or extremist organizations.'[102] At a time when flight is increasingly generated by civil war, and,

[99] M. Colville, 'Persecution Complex', *Refugees*, No. 101 (1995), 16–21.

[100] Convention relating to the Status of Refugees, adopted on 28 July 1951 by the UN Conference of
Plenipotentiaries on the Status of Refugees and Stateless Persons convened under GA Res. 429 (V)
(1950). In United Nations, *A Compilation of International Instruments* (1994), i, Part 2, 638.

[101] The whole para. reads: '[p]ersecution by third parties will be considered to fall within the scope of
the Geneva Convention where it is based on one of the grounds in Art. 1A, is individual in nature and is
encouraged or permitted by the authorities. Where the official authorities fail to act, such persecution
should give rise to individual examination of each application for refugee status, in accordance with national judicial practice, in the light in particular of whether or not the failure to act was deliberate. The persons concerned may be eligible in any event for appropriate forms of protection under national law.' The
Danish and Swedish delegations appended the opinion that 'persecution by third parties falls within the
scope of the 1951 Convention where it is encouraged or permitted by the authorities. It may also fall
within the scope of the Convention in other cases, when the authorities prove unable to offer protection.'

[102] 'UNHCR Expresses Reservations over EU Asylum Policy', *Update on Europe*, 24 Nov. 1995; see
also European Council on Refugees and Exiles, 'ECRE Condemns Agreement by European Ministers'

in some cases, the complete collapse of the State, those in danger are going to find it hard always to point to a state actor as persecutor. Furthermore, the use of rape as a weapon against women and the recognition of other forms of 'gender based persecution',[103] which result from women transgressing social mores, mean that a narrow reading of the definition of refugee is not only endangering the lives of those at risk, but is discriminatory as well.

European human rights law prohibits the extradition or expulsion of anyone where there are substantial grounds for believing that the person faces a real risk of being subjected to torture, or to inhuman or degrading treatment, in the receiving country. The European Commission on Human Rights has suggested that this principle applies where the individual faces threats from non-state actors.[104] While there is no judicial review by the European Court of Human Rights of asylum policy decisions taken by the Council of the EU, we risk the development of a policy which is at variance with European human rights law as developed under the organs of the European Convention on Human Rights.

Following the entry into force of the Amsterdam Treaty, one might have expected the communitarization of asylum policy (so that it is dealt with under the first pillar) to have resulted in greater international judicial scrutiny in this area.[105] However, the new Article 68(2) (originally numbered Article 73p(2)) of the new EC Treaty means that governments and the EU could escape scrutiny in difficult cases under the familiar excuse that these could be issues of 'internal security'.[106] Article 68(2) reads: '[i]n any event, the Court of Justice shall not have jurisdiction to rule on any measures or decision taken pursuant to Article 62(1) relating to the maintenance of law and order and the safeguarding of internal security'.[107] Excluding judicial

23 Nov. 1995, press release. See also the UNHCR *Handbook on Procedures and Criteria for Determining Refugee Status*, at para. 65, which includes non-governmental persecution as part of the definition of persecution *inter alia* where the authorities prove unable to offer effective protection.

[103] See the conclusions of the UNHCR seminar, 23 Feb. 1995, Reuters, 25 Feb. 1995. Note the resolution of the European Parliament of 13 Apr. 1984 suggesting gender discrimination be included among the grounds for granting refugee status: *Bull. EC* 4–1984, at pt. 2.4.11.

[104] See A. Clapham, *Human Rights in the Private Sphere* (1993), 193–6. See also 'The Potential of the European Convention on Human Rights in Securing International Protection to Forcibly Displaced Persons', unpublished Colloquy paper by Sara Egelund (UNHCR) Oct. 1995.

[105] Art. 68 of the new EC Treaty allows for interpretation by the ECJ of the Title covering asylum, as well as for references to the ECJ where there is a question before certain national courts of the validity or interpretation of acts of the institutions of the Community based on Title IV. The actual conditions are complex and need not be discussed here. Suffice it to say that Art. 63 mentions that measures on asylum are to be adopted by the Council 'in accordance with the Geneva Convention of 28 July 1951 and the Protocol of 31 January 1967 relating to the status of refugees and other relevant treaties'. An interpretation by the ECJ of the compatibility of a measure with the Geneva Convention or a human rights treaty therefore seems hypothetically possible. This is a double edged sword as the process of ensuring compatibility could result in a 'European' ruling on the scope of the Geneva Convention. An overly restrictive ruling could result in further friction with UNHCR.

[106] Another way to fill the democratic deficit in this context would be to grant greater roles for the Commission and European Parliament in the sphere of EU agreements on refugee and asylum issues. See S. O'Leary, *European Union Citizenship: Options for Reform* (1996), p. viii. Five years after the entry into force of the Amsterdam Treaty the Commission will have the sole right of initiative over asylum issues. At this time the Council will decide whether the European Parliament will be granted the right to amend or veto Community legislation in this field. See Arts. 67 (*ex* Art. 73o) and 251 (*ex* Art. 189b) of the new TEC.

[107] The European Council on Refugees and Exiles (ECRE), a non-governmental organization, has pointed out that this exclusion seems to fly in the face of the jurisprudence of the European Court of Human Rights which adheres to the notion of an absolute right not to be subjected to torture 'even where

review in this way does not represent a good precedent for the protection of human rights worldwide. More dramatically we could say that if this sort of measure is copied outside Europe it is hard to see how the Union can, with any credibility, protest similar disregard for the rule of law. It is a shame, to put it mildly, that the EU's human rights foreign policy will eventually be weakened by this sort of internal compromise.

If there is cause for disquiet over this evasion of judicial scrutiny, there is cause for real alarm over the 'Protocol on Asylum for Nationals of Member States of the European Union'. This Protocol was adopted under pressure from the Spanish government following a 'dispute with the Belgian authorities, who in the recent past, had admitted in the Belgian asylum procedure Spanish citizens suspected of having been associated with terrorist acts perpetrated by the ETA'.[108] The 'sole article' starts: '[g]iven the level of protection of fundamental rights and freedoms by the Member States of the European Union, Member States shall be regarded as constituting safe countries of origin in respect of each other for all legal and practical purposes in relation to asylum matters'. The Article then goes on to outline a number of exceptional cases where the application for asylum made by a national of a Member State may be considered by another Member State.[109] This Protocol, even though not fully endorsed by all fifteen Member States, has been met with protests from UNHCR. It creates a precedent that is obviously extremely dangerous. It suggests that other regions might one day decide that their adherence to human rights treaties similarly allowed them to suspend existing international law on asylum. It is easy to see how the EU could have difficulty pronouncing a human rights foreign policy that demanded open borders for asylum-seekers, in accordance with the Geneva Convention, when the EU itself has suspended the application of that same Convention for its own nationals moving across international borders in the EU. In order to dispel the impression that the EU is undermining the application of the Geneva Convention the preamble states: 'WHEREAS this protocol respects the finality and the objectives of the Geneva Convention of 28 July 1951 relating to the status of refugees'. However the Protocol has been roundly criticized in the following terms by UNHCR:

> We are very concerned at the EU decision. If the EU applies limitations to the Convention, others can follow and could weaken the universality of the instrument for the international protection of refugees. We do not, therefore, share the position taken in the preamble stating that the protocol respects the Convention.[110]

internal security issues are at stake. So a different standard of judicial control is being applied to Community law than that which is binding upon the member States as parties to the ECHR; notwithstanding the Treaty's own references to the ECHR': 'Analysis of the Treaty of Amsterdam in so far as it relates to asylum policy' 10 Nov. 1997, at 5.

[108] J. van der Klaauw, 'European Union' (1997) 15 *NQHR* 87.

[109] Where the State of which the applicant is a national has declared a state of emergency in accordance with Art. 15 of ECHR; where the Council is considering whether there exists a serious and persistent breach of human rights by the member state of which the asylum seeker is a national under the procedure in the new Art. 7 (*ex* Art. F.1) of TEU; and where a Member State has decided unilaterally in which case the application is to be dealt with on the basis of the presumption that it is manifestly unfounded. The actual implementation of these exceptions is not of real importance here the issue is the message which the general geographical exclusion sends.

[110] 'UNHCR Concerned about Restricted Access to Asylum in Europe', *Update on Europe*, 20 June 1997.

Considering that the EU Commission will eventually have the sole right of initiative over asylum matters, and that the EU and UNHCR may be on a real collision course, it would seem appropriate to consider the formal role of the Community on the Executive Committee of UNHCR. Until there is greater synergy between the Community and UNHCR there is a risk that EU human rights foreign policy will become something which fails to protect the legal entitlements of refugees in Europe, and eventually undermines the protection of refugees in the rest of the world. Ironically this is perhaps an area where the EU's economic power is consistent with its effect on human rights protection: it is because UNHCR is so dependent on the Commission and the fifteen Member States that it finds it hard aggressively and effectively to confront the EU. It is a shame that the EU is not using its economic privilege to strengthen rather than undermine the regime for refugee protection established by the 1951 Geneva Convention

III. RECOMMENDATIONS FOR ENSURING CONSISTENCY, COHERENCE, AND CREDIBILITY

A. Special Commissioner for Human Rights as Vice-President of the EU Commission

We have already seen that several Commissioners have to deal with human rights issues. It falls under four different Commissioners with different regional responsibilities. So East and Central Europe fall under one Commissioner; developing countries (ACP) under another; Latin America, the Middle East and part of Asia under a third; and China the USA and a number of developed countries under a fourth Commissioner. In addition, human rights issues cut across thematic portfolios such as development, social issues, humanitarian affairs, migration, foreign policy, commercial policy, and even tourism. Of course the importance of integrating human rights into everyone's activities, and mainstreaming human rights work to prevent it being sidelined, is well understood, but there needs to be direction and responsibility for ensuring this happens. It is suggested that the current arrangements are inadequate, as no one Commissioner is clearly associated with human rights. And no one is visible as the face of human rights within the Commission and outside. Secondly, the secretariat is similarly dispersed in its attempts to develop human rights policy and implement this policy through European Union activities. It is suggested that one Commissioner be given the human rights portfolio and be designated the Commissioner for Human Rights. This Commissioner would not be responsible for any other thematic or country issues, but would have authority to ensure that human rights were truly mainstreamed into the activity of the other Commissioners. It is worth opening a parenthesis to remark that human rights only started to become properly mainstreamed into the different sectors of United Nations activity once a UN High Commissioner for Human Rights was created at the level of Under-Secretary-General and empowered by the Secretary-General to ensure that the agencies, funds, programmes, and departments were actually incorporating attention to respect for human rights into their work, and taking this obligation seriously. The European Commissioner for Human Rights should be a Vice-President of the Commission, and should have a secretariat which would be clearly authorized to ensure that work carried out in the various directorates not only conformed to the Commission's policy on human rights, but was also informed by the appropriate expert opinion and experience in the relevant domain.

The idea of having human rights activity focused on one single Commissioner is not new. The European Parliament has formally proposed this on various occasions. In 1996, Commissioner Van den Broek announced, in response to the Lalumière report, presented in the European Parliament, that he had been given responsibility for the horizontal and thematic issues relating to human rights, while the President of the Commission, Mr Santer, had personally taken on the delicate issue of human rights.[111] The issue came around again in December 1997. Sir Leon Brittan re-stated the 1996 position to the European Parliament. Human rights remain an integral part of the work of several directorates general (DGs) in the context of their work in the different geographical regions. We should mention in this context the 'Declaration on the Organization and Functioning of the Commission' adopted by the Member States at the Amsterdam Conference. The last sentence of the Declaration 'notes in particular the desirability of bringing external relations under the responsibility of a Vice-President'.

Our position is that human rights and external relations should come under the authority of such a Vice-President. Of course the dangers of isolating human rights should be borne in mind. No one wishes to see human rights issues languish in obscurity, isolated from the real work of the Commission. But to have a consistent, coherent, and credible human rights policy, the work needs to be driven by one Commissioner, and one department, so that a viable and authoritative policy can develop across departments, across directorates, across Commissioners, across pillars.

Of course the reorganization of any bureaucracy gives rise to suspicion and resentment. The quandary for any reformer was artfully explained by Machiavelli in *The Prince*, published in 1537:

> It must be considered that there is nothing more difficult to carry out, nor more doubtful of success, nor more dangerous to handle, than to initiate a new order of things. For the reformer has enemies in all those who profit by the old order, and only lukewarm defenders in all those who would profit by the new order, this lukewarmness arising partly from fear of their adversaries, who would have the laws in their favour; and partly from

---

[111] Response to Mme Lalumière, *rapporteur* of the Annual Report of the European Parliament on human rights in the world in 1995–6 and on EU policy in the area of human rights, 11 Dec. 1996, plenary session at 80: '*U weet dat voorzitter Santer persoonlijk de verantwoordelijkheid voor het gevoelige terrein van de mensenrechten op zich heeft genomen. En mij werd onder zijn autoriteit de verantwoordelijkheid toevertrouwd voor de thematische en horizontale aspecten hiervan.*' The Lalumière report A4–0400/96 included a motion for a resolution which included a para. whereby the Parliament reaffirmed 'its belief that the Commission should appoint from among its members a Commissioner responsible for human rights, in order to guarantee consistency between the Commission's various areas of action which have a bearing on human rights and that this Commissioner, working in close contact with the President of the Commission, should be able to take initiatives in the field of human rights in the same way as the UN High Commissioner for Human Rights'.

the incredulity of mankind, who do not truly believe in anything new until they have had actual experience of it.[112]

B. A New Human Rights Department in the Administrative Structure of the Commission

Funding from the European Community budget for human rights rose from 59.1 million ECU in 1994 to 64 million ECU in 1995,[113] and 97.4 million ECU ($107 million) for 1998.[114] This money is spent by the European Commission in the form of grants. Suffice it to say that this is a large amount of money compared to the resources available to other international organizations. The UN Centre for Human Rights has an annual budget of around $22 million, which is largely allocated to paying the salaries for the staff.[115] In contrast the European Commission's staff are not paid out of the $107 million which is spent on projects and assistance. The details of how this budget is spent in any one year can be found in the Commission's 'Report on the implementation of measures intended to promote observance of human rights and democratic principles',[116] and is tabulated on a monthly basis in the *EU Bulletin*.

The European Parliament has recently called attention to fact that there are a 'bewilderingly large number of departments' taking part in the Standing Inter-Departmental Human Rights Co-ordination Group.[117] No fewer than nineteen different parts of the Commission are represented. The quest for consistency and transparency has led to an unmanageably complicated co-ordination structure which is still failing to satisfy Parliament's request for accessible information on the results of projects and how Community policy on human rights and democracy is being implemented.[118] Part of the complaint is the absence of any institutional arrangement for co-ordination with the Parliament on the Commission's initiatives.[119] We might add

[112] N. Machiavelli, *The Prince* (trans. L. Ricci, revd. by E.R.P. Vincent, 1935).

[113] 'Commission refines its Human Rights Strategy', IP/95/1265, 22 Nov. 1995.

[114] *Bull. EU* 12–1997 at 134. This is the total for the budget line B7–7.

[115] In addition there are voluntary funds which can attract considerable sums, in 1998 there was more than $30m available for different projects concerning technical co-operation with States.

[116] COM (95)191 final (for 1994).

[117] Established under Note 114903 of 24 Sept. 1994 from Mr Williamson, the Group's role is to '[i]mprove internal coordination to ensure consistency in Community policies, including the use of budget resources'. See COM(96)672 final, Report from the Commission on the implementation of measures intended to promote observance of human rights and democratic principles (for 1995). The Group met seven times in 1995.

[118] The 1997 Lenz Report, note 43 above, on setting up a single co-ordinating structure within the European Commission responsible for human rights and democratization contains the following complaints: '[t]he allocation of funds from B7-70 is based on general guidelines which have been laid down since 1991 in the interest of consistency by the Standing Inter-Departmental Human Rights Coordination Group, run by DG IA; a bewilderingly large number of departments take part in the Group's meetings: the Secretariat-General, the Forward Studies Unit, the Legal Service, DGs I, IA, 1B, II, V, VIII, X, XI, XII, XIII, XV, XIX, XXII, XXIV, XXIII, and ECHO . . . The Commission itself comments on the difficulty of procedures for selecting projects and allocating support. The ensuing delays in funding are frequently counterproductive, in terms not only of their intentions but also of the important role the EU plays as a source of funding. Technical and financial management within the Commission absolutely must be improved.'

[119] See the Lenz Report, note 43 above: '[t]he cause of interinstitutional coordination between the Commission and Parliament would be served by ensuring that Parliament was represented on the Inter-Departmental Human Rights Group. As for coordination between the Council and Commission, it should be said that there is at present no interinstitutional coordination between the Commission

that with the prospect of a more consolidated common foreign and security policy following the entry into force of the Amsterdam Treaty, with the advent of common strategies and a reinvigorated Council secretariat in the field of foreign policy, a strong case can be made for this new Commission department to be more closely integrated and involved with the work of the Council. In the end it is the committee work of bodies such as COHOM (Committee on Human Rights) or the working groups such as COASIA or COAFRI which will be most closely associated with the political possibilities available to the EU and its Member States with regard to third countries.

The new human rights department will have to deal not only with human rights affairs as they affect the rest of the world, but also with the human rights dimension of the European Union's own legislation and administrative action. The need to consolidate the existing expertise in this area has been dramatically increased by the new possibilities for judicial review created by the Amsterdam Treaty. Following the entry into force of the Amsterdam Treaty the acts of the Council, Commission, and Parliament will be reviewable for violations of human rights.[120] Working with the Commission's legal service the Department would have to take on the role of protector of human rights within the Community legal order. In the same way that national officials currently scrutinize national legislation to ensure that it does not violate constitutional guarantees of fundamental freedoms and international obligations on human rights, so too the new human rights department will have a role in raising human rights issues as they relate to Community action in order to prevent an eventual ruling by the European Court of Justice that institutions of the Commission have violated human rights as defined in Article 6(2) of the newly-numbered EC Treaty.[121]

A further role for the new department is suggested by the Amsterdam Treaty. The Treaty creates a new procedure for suspension of voting and other rights of Member States in the event of a determination that there has been a 'serious and persistent breach' of the 'principles of liberty, democracy, respect for human rights and fundamental freedoms, and the rule of law'. The procedure specifically allows for the Commission to propose that the Council meet to make such a determination. Clearly for the Commission to make such a procedure it must have some administrative unit empowered to consider information on persistent violations of human rights, and to develop guidelines so that its actions in this sphere are at least consistent over time, and with regard to different Member States. Unless there is some established methodology, the Commission's entire human rights programme could become seen as partisan and selective. At this point it would seem to be no answer to

and Council in the Community context, whereas there is a Human Rights/CFSP Working Party. The establishment of a working party comprising Commission and Council representatives, on which ideally Parliament was also represented, is recommended.'

[120] This is the effect of Art. 6(2) and Art. 46 of the new TEU (or Arts. F(2) and L as amended by the Amsterdam Treaty).

[121] Art. 6(2) reads: '[t]he Union shall respect fundamental rights, as guaranteed by the European Convention for the Protection of Human Rights and Fundamental Freedoms signed in Rome on 4 November 1950 and as they result from the constitutional traditions common to the Member States, as general principles of Community law.'

respond that the Commission has no mandate to consider human rights issues as they arise in the Member States. By explicitly granting, in the Amsterdam Treaty, the Commission the right to bring a Member State before the Council for persistent human rights violations, the Member States have obviously admitted that the Commission will have a role in monitoring serious human rights violations in the Member States of the European Union.

C. Annual EU Report on the State of Human Rights in the World

Since the mid-1970s when the US Congress enacted a series of provisions which outlined procedures and policy, with regard to US foreign policy and human rights, the Secretary of State has been responsible for the preparation of an annual report on human rights in other UN Member States.[122] The origins of this report lie in the need for the Congress to be informed of the human rights situation in countries receiving development assistance. Congress needs to ensure compliance with the legislation which demands that no assistance be provided to a government which 'engages in a consistent pattern of gross violations of internationally recognized human rights . . . unless such assistance will directly benefit the needy people in such country'.[123] Although there is no identical procedure in European Union law, we have seen that the EU is moving towards the inclusion of human rights violations as a factor which could lead to the rupture of legally binding agreements, as well as a host of other measures. It is suggested that in order to take a fair, transparent, and informed decision on the suspension or termination of such agreements, the Union should start to prepare human rights reports in a similar way to the manner in which the US State Department reports are compiled.

Although the Department of State reports were initially criticized for their bias and poor methodology, they are generally recognized to have vastly improved. Critiques of these reports have been offered over the years, and one group in particular, the Lawyers' Committee for Human Rights, has worked to highlight the strengths and weakness of these reports. By 1989 Human Rights Watch and the Lawyers' Committee were prepared to hold up the Department of State's reports on Chile, South Africa, Sudan, and Czechoslovakia as models because they:

—include detailed accounts of specific cases;
—cite information and statistics from a variety of sources, especially from non-governmental groups and court records, where applicable;
—describe comprehensively the context surrounding an event or issue;
—distinguish between rights and freedoms theoretically guaranteed by law and the actual observance of such rights and freedoms.[124]

Such reports are drawn up by the diplomats and others working for the Department of State working in Washington and in the different embassies around the world.

---

[122] S. 116 of the Foreign Assistance Act of 1961, as amended 22 USCA §2151n, sub-para. (d).

[123] *Ibid.*, sub-para (a): '[v]iolations barring assistance; assistance for needy people'.

[124] Human Rights Watch & Lawyers Committee for Human Rights, *Critique: Review of the Department of State's Country Reports on Human Rights Practices for 1988* (1989), reproduced in part in F. Newman and D. Weissbrodt, *International Human Rights* (1990), 523–6.

For the European Union a comparable process would have to be executed by diplomats from the fifteen Member States and the officials of the Commission, with a secretariat 'harmonizing' and taking overall responsibility for the final compilation. Although this sounds like a nightmare as the fifteen Foreign Affairs departments of the Member States do not operate with the same coherence as the US State Department, the exercise should be considered. The co-ordination could be carried out either by the new merged Political Co-operation Secretariat and General Secretariat of the Council or perhaps by the new Department within the Commission.

The task is probably less awesome than imagined as the Fifteen and the Commission do actually already compile human rights situation reports which circulate internally. An interesting precedent has now been set. In May 1998 the Council decided to publish a summary of its report on the Israeli Occupied Territories. This two-page summary included the conclusion that there had been 'no substantial improvement in Israel's human rights record' in the period from November 1997 to 20 March 1998. It referred to the facts that '[u]nder Israeli law, the Israeli security services are allowed to use "moderate physical pressure" on detainees to obtain information in so called ticking bomb cases', and that Israeli methods of interrogation have been considered to constitute torture by the UN Committee Against Torture. The second half of the summary deals with the Palestinian Authority and states that '[m]istreatment of detainees remains routine and torture continues to occur' and notes some improvements in prison conditions and the record of the civil police.[125] If this exercise can be accomplished for such sensitive areas as the human rights situations in Israel and Palestine, then it could surely be executed for other countries. Furthermore, consistency would seem to demand a potentially more universal approach to such human rights situation reports.

One could legitimately ask what such an exercise would add to the current report produced by the Department of State. A number of advantages of a European report present themselves. First, in the event of a decision to suspend co-operation this should be done on the basis of a *European* investigation and description of the human rights violations. Secondly, in the event of a common asylum policy, and in order to make better assessments of claims for refugee status, there should be a clear statement of the European evaluation of the human rights situation in the countries in question.[126] Thirdly, communication between the Fifteen on human rights matters remains more problematic than one might expect, and such an exercise could only reinforce channels of communication even if heated disagreements were to surface. Fourthly, the US report suffers from the fundamental flaw that it contains no entry on the human rights situation in the United States. Although internal and external competencies are strictly defined within the European Union's legal and po-

---

[125] *Middle East EU Human Rights Watch Report Occupied Territories*, Brussels, 15 May 1998, 8680/98 (presse 155). The fact that the EU has chosen to call their reports 'Human Rights Watch' may lead to some unfortunate confusion in the future as these reports are nothing to do with the reports of the human rights organization Human Rights Watch based in New York.

[126] Arguably, such an annual report could prejudice the chances of individual asylum-seekers, or might even be disapproved by governments which would not wish to find themselves stopped from arguing later that there was no danger. Because asylum applications have to be considered on their individual merits, it is suggested that the advantages of such an annual report outweigh the disadvantages.

litical order, there is no overriding reason why the diplomats of the Fifteen should not compile reports on each other within the context of such an annual report. The Dutch Embassy in Paris would contribute, as would the Irish Embassy in London. Of course this is a radical and ambitious proposal, but it would demonstrate a certain courage and consistency in the field of human rights foreign policy. It would also ensure that diplomats gained some sort of training in the standards that Europe finds acceptable within its borders before Europe starts to apply international standards to others. Fifthly, the rights which the US State Department examines in its report represent a number of core civil and political rights[127] but skew the appreciation of the human rights picture at a time when the international community is committed to the promotion of all human rights, including economic, social, and cultural rights as well as the right to development. In 1991 the Community and its Member States recognized the importance of a consistent approach towards human rights, democracy, and development, and stated in a resolution that '[d]evelopment cooperation is based on the central place of the individual and has, therefore, in essence to be designed with a view to promoting—in parallel with economic and social rights—civil and political liberties by means of representative democratic rule that is based on respect for human rights'.[128] Sixthly, the fact that the report was being compiled would give the Union and its individual representatives around the world greater leverage. Not only would structures, practices, and laws inimical to human rights be clearly identified, but some individual cases would arguably be resolved in favour of the individual before the need arose to highlight them in an annual report.

D. The European Parliament's Report on Human Rights in the World

Again the EU's internal institutional arrangements create a schism between the examination of human rights within and outside the EU. The EP Committee on Civil Liberties and Internal Affairs considers with some delay an 'Annual report on respect for human rights in the European Union'.[129] The adoption of this report has been delayed in the past due to what the Christian Democrat group consider its overemphasis on social rights and issues relating to immigration and asylum.[130] There is seemingly little institutional or other connection with the 'Report on human rights in the world 1993–1994 and the Union's human rights policy' adopted by the EP Committee on Foreign Relations and Security. It is quite clear that a coherent policy on asylum and immigration would ensure that issues of human rights abroad and the right to seek asylum in Europe are dealt with at the same time, by some of the same people. Moreover, when Parliamentarians meet their opposite numbers in the developing world, the request has come from 'the South' for joint discussions on racism in Europe.

---

[127] The legislation specifically refers to 'torture or cruel, inhuman, or degrading treatment or punishment, prolonged detention without charges, causing the disappearance of persons by the abduction and clandestine detention of those persons, or other flagrant denial of the right to life, liberty and the security of the person.'

[128] Resolution on Human Rights, Democracy and Development by the Council and Member States, meeting within the Council, 28 Nov. 1991, para. 3: *Bull. EC* 11–1991.

[129] The most recent report, for 1996 is contained in Doc A4–0034/98 (28 Jan. 1998).

[130] See J. van der Klaauw, 'European Union' (1994) 12 *NQHR* 178.

Continually dividing external from internal competencies may seem to make sense for those steeped in the history of European integration, but inevitably smacks of hypocrisy when discovered by outsiders.[131] It is suggested that the European Parliament consider finding a way to produce an annual report on human rights in the world which combines the internal and external dimensions of the issue.

It is further suggested that a way be found for Parliament to co-operate with the preparation of the EU annual report on human rights proposed in the previous section. This could be in the form of furnishing information and debating the results. These Parliamentary voices can clearly represent the views of the people of Europe and drive the EU's human rights foreign policy. It is to be expected that the Parliament's view on human rights in the Union will remain more critical than that drawn up by foreign office diplomats as part of the proposed EU annual human rights report. Nevertheless it is suggested that such a confrontation could set up a healthy dialectic and eventually lead to human rights improvements, both within the EU and abroad, as the actors involved gain greater credibility and experience.

E. Parliamentary Scrutiny of Arms Exports

In 1991 and 1992 the European Council agreed on a set of eight common criteria for arms exports. These conditions are non-binding and are supposed to guide decisions by Member States of the Union on whether to issue licences for the export of arms and ammunition. One condition is the 'respect for human rights in the country of final destination'. So far the institutions of the European Union have not been involved in the vetting and issue of export licences, or in the impositions of fines and penalties. Amnesty International has suggested that the joint action procedure be used to draw up lists of proscribed arms and police security forces which should not be provided with certain goods and services.[132] The fact is that small arms and equipment are often excluded from international arms control agreements, and that this means that Member States often grant export licences without regard to the Member States' obligations towards the protection of human rights around the world. The most common categories of such equipment are: machine guns and submachine guns, sniper and automatic rifles, hand grenades, landmines, automatic handguns, electronic weapons, unusual or exploding ammunition, mortars, bazookas, shoulder-fired/hand held rockets and missiles, 'machine guns, and riot control equipment.'[133] The European Parliament has already called for the deletion

---

[131] See generally A. Clapham, *Human Rights and the European Community: A Critical Overview* (1991), 71–89, especially notes 236 and 237.

[132] 'EU Member States should use the Joint Action procedures to draw up common lists of (i) proscribed military, security and police equipment and technology, the sole or primary use of which is to contribute to human rights violations; (ii) sensitive types of military, security and police equipment and technology which has been shown in practice to be used for human rights violations; and (iii) military, security and police units and forces which have been significantly responsible for human rights violations and to whom sensitive goods and services should not be provided': Amnesty International's Memorandum, *Proposals for a Strengthened Protection of Human Rights by the European Union in the Context of the Intergovernmental Conference 1996*, RAC no. 04/96.

[133] *Ibid.*, at 26.

of Article 296 (*ex* Article 223) EC in order to bring the arms industry under EU law and policy.[134]

On 25 May 1998 the Council adopted a Code of Conduct for Arms Export. The Code states that '[e]ach EU member State will assess export licence applications for military equipment made to it on a case-by-case basis against the provisions of the Code of Conduct'. The Code includes eight criteria. One of these relates to respect for human rights in the country of final destination. Member States will not issue export licences 'if there is a clear risk that the proposed export might be used for internal repression'. The Code of Conduct contains operative provisions which outline procedures for information sharing and consultation between Member States where one Member State has refused a licence for the export of certain arms.

The adoption of the Code has been seen as a 'welcome first step' by NGOs working in this sector, but its actual mechanisms have been criticized for failing to include full multilateral notification and consultation procedures, and for introducing the ambiguous concept of 'internal repression'.[135] More generally the Code is criticized for the failure to meet the stated objective of transparency, by failing to include any procedure for Parliamentary scrutiny. Although the Code is intended to operate through consensus by the Fifteen, rather than as some sort of binding procedure, it seems worth thinking about a future role for the European Parliament.[136]

The European Parliament would be in a very good position both to gather information on how arms are being used, and also to debate the political support for arms being used. A co-decisional procedure might therefore be imagined whereby a majority vote in the Parliament would trigger a decision to legislate to suspend arms, or security assistance, to countries where that was shown to be contributing to human rights violations. In addition to the European Parliamentarians, it is quite clear that the diplomats of the Member States and the Commission posted abroad usually have a very good idea of the use that materials are being put to in various countries. Some of these observations could be built into the suggested annual reports on human rights in the world. The adoption of the Code of Conduct therefore represents

[134] See *Report on Disarmament, Arms Export Controls, and Non-proliferation of Weapons of Mass Destruction*, Committee on Foreign Affairs and Security, PE 206.753, and the comments of Van der Klaauw, note 130 above, 207. Art. 223(1)(a) and (b) of the EC Treaty (now Art. 296) read: '[t]he provisions of this Treaty shall not preclude the application of the following rules: (a) no Member States shall be obliged to supply information the disclosure of which it considers contrary to the essential interests of its security; (b) Any Member State may take such measures as it considers necessary for the protection of the essential interests of its security which are connected with the production of or trade in arms, munitions and war material; such measures shall not adversely affect the conditions of competition in the common market regarding products which are not intended for specifically military purposes.'

[135] Briefing by ISIS Europe, 26 May 1998. See also the Analysis by Amnesty International, Basic, Oxfam, and Saferworld of 12 Feb. 1998 with regard to the draft Code circulating at that time.

[136] There is instructive experience in the legislation covering security assistance enacted in the United States whereby information is presented to Congress. See Sect. 502B as amended, 22 USC § 2304 (1994) (reprinted in F. Newman and D. Weissbrodt (eds.), *International Human Rights: Law, Policy, and Process—Selected International Human Rights Instruments and Bibliography for Research on International Human Rights Law* (2nd edn., 1996), 193–6. Note para. (a)(2) reads in part '[e]xcept under circumstances specified in this section, no security assistance may be provided to any country the government of which engages in a consistent pattern of internationally recognized human rights'. The sect. defines security assistance and internationally recognized human rights as well as reporting obligations and a role for Congress. For a review of the US practice in this field see the annual report of Amnesty International USA, *Human Rights and US Security Assistance*.

an important element in the eventual implementation of a coherent EU foreign policy on human rights.[137]

Even if concrete legal embargoes were impossible to implement at the European level a more open discussion, over which arms were being used where, would assist in the process of obtaining better information on emerging human rights crises. It would also mean that those States which operated with less accountability with regard to their arms exports would eventually lose some of their competitive advantage within the European Union. Furthermore multinational enterprises are exploiting the variations in national laws to export through associated companies situated in Member States with weaker export controls. If Europe is serious about the prevention of human rights violations abroad, then proper scrutiny of its weapons exports must be a crucial step.

F. Formalizing Diplomatic Arrangements for the Protection of EU Nationals Abroad

Article 17 (*ex* Article 8) TEC boldly states: '[c]itizenship of the European Union is hereby established. Every person holding the nationality of a Member State shall be a citizen of the Union.' However, it is unlikely that this has altered the international law which protects access by Consular officials to nationals in detention abroad. Article 20 (*ex* Article 8c) grants European citizens, who are in the territory of a third country in which the Member State of which they are nationals is not represented, protection by the diplomatic or consular authorities of any Member State on the same conditions as the nationals of that State. However, it is not clear that a third State would feel obliged under existing international law to allow this access.[138] Consideration could be given to ensuring that this new form of protection is recognized as part of a third country's legal obligations. Of course one solution would be to create EU nationality. But this is a radical step, and gives rise to myriad legal implications. Because dual or multiple nationality is increasingly accepted, it would seem possible to reinforce the concept of EU citizenship so that it worked as a form of second nationality, at least in the context of the protection of nationals abroad. We might at this point open a parenthesis and mention the recent case of Mr Breard, a Paraguayan national who was being detained and charged with murder in the United States. The US authorities failed to inform Mr Breard of his right to consular assistance. The Paraguayan government eventually claimed before the International Court of Justice that '[h]ad a Paraguayan consular official been permitted to assist Mr. Breard, the officer would have provided Mr. Breard with information that would have enabled him to make more informed decisions in the conduct of his defence'.[139] In short it was

---

[137] See the editorial of *The Independent*, 'Arms and the Rhetoric of Ethics' 26 May 1998, at 20 which cautions against exaggerating the ethical advances but rather suggests that a realist would say '[f]ine, it [the Code] does imply there will be some consistent, albeit minimal, application of human rights doctrine to non-EU countries and in turn that might lead to the growth of common positions in EU foreign policy.'

[138] See McGoldrick, note 71 above, at 180, who mentions Council Decision 95/553/EC [1995] OJ L314/73, *Bull.EU* 11–1995, pt. I.I.I, but adds that: '[a]s of July 1996, no agreements had been reached with third states on diplomatic and consular protection'.

[139] *Case concerning the Application of the Vienna Convention on Consular Relations (Paraguay v. United States of America), Request for the Indication of Provisional Measures,* verbatim record, 7 Apr. 1998.

suggested that such decisions would have enabled Mr Breard to avoid the death penalty. Despite the International Court of Justice's indication of provisional measures to be taken by the United States so that Mr Breard not be executed pending the final decision of the Court, the execution went ahead five days later on 14 April 1998.

This dramatic killing has reminded us that access to consular officials could be a life-and-death issue. The likely rationalization of European Union representation abroad could leave EU citizens without proper diplomatic and consular protection if the third countries remained unaware of the intention to provide EU protection to EU citizens. It is suggested that preventive steps are taken to ensure that all third countries realize and accept that they have legal obligations to the EU Member States represented in that country. A strict reading of the nationality condition could work to deprive EU citizens of protection by EU embassies and consulates. The EU Council should consider what initiatives need to be taken in this field to ensure that the EC Treaty's provisions for diplomatic protection actually work in practice, and that no EU citizen is left at the mercy of a legal loophole.

G. *Accession by the European Community to Human Rights Treaties and the Council of Europe*

Accession by the European Community to human rights treaties is not a panacea for greater protection of human rights inside or outside the Union. Nevertheless there are a number of points worth making in this context.

First, accession, if accompanied by steps to allow individual complaints, would benefit those people who are able to obtain satisfaction through these new procedures for a violation of their rights resulting from Community action. The present study concentrates on the external dimension of EU policy, and it may seem fanciful to imagine accession to a treaty such as the European Convention on Human Rights giving rise to new rights of complaint arising out of action undertaken in countries outside the EU. But as the EU moves into new spheres, such as deploying personnel abroad into the middle of human rights crises and conflict zones (such as the former Yugoslavia), the concept of an EU employee violating the rights of an individual or group is no longer an abstract problem. Human rights treaties such as the European Convention on Human Rights have been interpreted to give rise to jurisdiction even when the action relates to events outside the territorial jurisdiction of the Contracting Party, and the violation in this context could be a violation of the positive obligation to protect rights such as the right to life.[140] Secondly, by becoming a party to a treaty which demanded reporting obligations, the Union, or at least the Community, would have to report on steps it had taken in various fields related to human rights. This would aid transparency and could even inspire a certain amount of human rights education. Thirdly, accession could theoretically give rise to the possibility of the European Union (or whichever legal entity were to accede) bringing

---

[140] See Clapham, note 104 above, at 203, but see the limitations on the duty of diplomatic agents to protect people abroad in D.J. Harris, M. O'Boyle, and C. Warbrick, *Law of the European Convention on Human Rights* (1995), 642–4. For a judgment of the European Court of Human Rights which deals with the actions of state agents acting outside the territorial jurisdiction see *McCann and Others* v. *United Kingdom*, ECHR (1985), Series A, No. 325, and *Loizidou* v. *Turkey*, ECHR (1995), Series A, No. 310, 27.

'inter-state' cases against other Contracting Parties: an ambitious but not impossible option. Such a possibility, of course, represents a leap forward in developing the range of options available to the Union/Community in terms of its human rights foreign policy.

Accession is usually discussed purely in the context of the European Convention on Human Rights. However Community accession to the European Social Charter has been recommended in the past, and such action would again demonstrate the seriousness of the Union's commitment to social and economic rights. Unfortunately, during the recent drafting of the revised Social Charter, efforts to include a clause which would allow for Community accession were stymied—suggesting that there is little political support for this at the moment. However, when considering the question of accession, the option of acceding to the Social Charter ought to be borne in mind, especially now that complaints mechanisms are being added.[141]

A blow to moves for proponents of accession to the European Convention on Human Rights has come in the form of an opinion from the European Court of Justice in Luxembourg. The Council of the European Union had requested under Article 228(6) (now Article 300(6)) of the EC Treaty[142] an opinion in response to the question 'would the accession of the European Community to the Convention be compatible with the Treaty establishing the European Union?'. The Court ruled that it was not in a position to give its opinion on 'compatibility', as it did not have enough information on how exactly the Community would become a party to the Convention system, and what its relationship would be with the European Court of Human Rights; however, it went on to give an opinion on whether the Community was 'competent' to accede to the European Convention. The Court started by referring to Article 3b (now Article 5) of the EC Treaty, which states in part that '[t]he Community shall act within the limits of the powers conferred upon it by this Treaty and the objectives assigned to it therein'. The Court stated that the principle of 'conferred powers' must be respected in both the internal and international action of the Community. However, the Court recalled its own case law, which admits that where Community law had created Community powers to obtain a specific Community objective, then the Community was empowered to enter into international commitments necessary to attain that objective—even in the absence of an express provision to that effect.[143] As there was no general power to enact rules on human rights or conclude treaties in that field, and the Court determined there were no implied powers in this field, the Court moved on to examine Article 235 (now Article 308) of the

---

[141] For details on how the complaints mechanism will work see R. Brillat, 'The European Social Charter: A New Protocol' (1996) 1 *EHRLR* 53–62. Accession to this Charter or other Social and Economic Rights treaties could be accomplished through a protocol to those treaties. For a discussion of the advantages and disadvantages of accession to the European Social Charter see B. Hepple, *Memorandum presented to the House of Lords Select Committee on the European Communities*, Session 1992–3, 3rd Report 'Human Rights Re-Examined', at 41–6.

[142] Art. 228(6). The Council, the Commission, or a Member State may obtain the opinion of the ECJ on whether an agreement envisaged is compatible with the provisions of this Treaty. Where the opinion of the Court of Justice is adverse, the agreement may enter into force only in accordance with Art. 48 (*ex* Art. N) TEU. Art. 48 outlines the procedure for amending the Treaties on which the Union is founded. Article N stated that in 1996 there is to be an inter-governmental conference (IGC) to revise provisions of the Maastricht Treaty on European Union.

[143] *Opinion No 2/91* [1993] ECR 1–1061, at para. 7.

EC Treaty.[144] The Court felt that accession to the human rights treaty would, in effect, amend the EC Treaty without following the correct procedure. It reasoned that joining the European Convention system would have two significant effects. First, it would mean that the Community itself would become part of an institutional system (the European Commission and Court of the Council of Europe). Secondly, the provisions of the Convention would become part of the Community legal order. The constitutional significance of these fundamental changes meant that the Court felt that accession could only be brought about by way of Treaty amendment. The Court therefore concluded that the present state of Community law meant that 'the Community had no competence to accede to the Convention for the Protection of Human Rights and Fundamental Freedoms'.

Therefore if the EU Member States want the Community to accede to the Convention they have to follow the procedure for Treaty amendment. The interesting point which emerges from the Court's opinion is that accession would apparently alter the legal status of the Convention in the Community legal order. On the one hand, the Court reiterates its established case law by stating that 'it is well settled that fundamental rights form an integral part of the general principles of law whose observance the Court ensures . . . Respect for human rights is therefore a condition of the lawfulness of Community acts.' But, on the other hand, the Court, having repeated its well-known explanation of how it discerns these 'fundamental rights',[145] goes on to state that accession would involve a 'substantial change', because it would entail 'integration of all the provisions of the Convention into the Community legal order'. It is worth pausing to study what exactly this change of status would imply.

Under Community law, individuals may be able to use provisions of international treaties binding on the Community to challenge the validity of Community measures in the national courts.[146] But the provision of the treaty (in our case the European Convention on Human Rights) must be 'capable of conferring rights on

---

[144] Art. 235 (now Art. 308): '[i]f action by the Community should prove necessary to attain, in the course of operation of the common market, one of the objectives of the Community and this Treaty has not provided the necessary powers, the Council shall, acting unanimously on a proposal from the Commission and after consulting the European Parliament, take the appropriate measures.'

[145] At considerations 33 and 34 of *Opinion 2/94* of 28 Mar. 1996: 'the Court draws inspiration from the constitutional traditions common to the Member States and from the guidelines supplied by international traditions common to the Member States and from the guidelines supplied by international treaties for the protection of human rights on which the Member States have collaborated or of which they are signatories. In that regard the Court has stated that the Convention (ECHR) has special significance'.

[146] *International Fruit Company NV et al.* v. *Productschap voor Groenten en Fruit* [1972] ECR 1219 and see P.J.G. Kapteyn and P. VerLoren van Themaat, and L.W. Gormley (ed.), *Introduction to the Law of the European Communities* (2nd edn., 1990), 345–6 who also suggest that according to Case 65/777, *Razanatsimba* [1977] ECR 2229 individuals can challenge national measures incompatible with such national agreements. With regard to the European Convention it already forms part of European Community law and national courts are obliged to have regard to it in the sphere of Community law as a result of the ECJ's jurisprudence. Several commentators have stressed that accession would not therefore change the status of the Convention at the national level: see P. Allott, *Memorandum to the House of Lords Select Committee on the European Communities*, Session 1992–3, 3rd Report, 'Human Rights Re-examined', at 41; in fact this was also the conclusion of the Select Committee at para. 94. See also J.P. Jacqué, 'The Convention and the European Communities', in R.St.J. Macdonald, F. Matscher, and H. Petzold (eds.), *The European System for the Protection of Human Rights* (1993), 903–4. The Commission communication and annexes assert that the provisions of the Convention already 'rank as Community law in the law of the Member States in the areas in which Community law is applicable. Community accession to the Convention would not change this situation in any way': Communication 10555/90, annex II, para. 4.

citizens of the Community which they can invoke before the courts'.[147] This sounds circular but means that the provision has to be considered 'self-executing' by the national courts.[148] The European Court of Justice seems to have seen this as a major change for the status of the Convention in the realm of Community law. Secondly, accession would reinforce the legal argument that the Convention could be used as part of Community law to challenge national legislation at the national level. Although, strictly speaking, such challenges would have to be confined to national legislation implementing community obligations, or measures taken in the sphere of Community law, this kind of creeping Europeanized judicial control over national legislation would be likely to set alarm bells ringing in some quarters. Thirdly, accession would seem to imply greater standing to challenge Community acts before the European Court of Justice for conformity with the Convention (and any protocols that the Community acceded to). These legal developments could be important for the following reason. It may be that, by becoming a party to the Convention, the Community would take on extra substantive obligations other than those it has assumed through Article 6 (*ex* Article F) of the TEU. This is because the Convention demands that parties 'secure', rather than merely 'respect', the rights and freedoms contained in the Convention. The obligation to 'secure' implies positive obligations, and the failure to undertake these would conceivably be justiciable before the European Court of Justice in Luxembourg.

Whether or not accession would make such a big change to the status of the Convention in the Community legal order remains a complex question. But this issue obscures the more important advantages of accession. The fact that accession would entitle individuals and groups to challenge Community acts (or national acts in pursuance of community obligations) before the European Court of Human Rights is obviously important as the Community sphere of influence touches more and more spheres. But the debate is confusing, as accession would affect only the accountability of the European Community (first pillar), not the European Union as such, and therefore there would be no change as regards legal control over the European Union's foreign policy (second pillar), nor would the current proposals for accession affect the accountability of the European Union for its activities in the field of police and judicial co-operation in criminal matters.

As the Union looks eastwards towards the rest of Europe, it is increasingly couching its dialogue in the language of human rights and fundamental freedoms, and urging reform along these lines. As we have seen, as long ago as 1978, the European Council 'solemnly declare[d] that respect for and maintenance of representative democracy and human rights in each Member State are essential elements of membership of the European Communities'.[149] Nowadays there are innumerable projects aimed at adjusting national laws in Eastern and Central European countries so that they conform with the standards contained in the European Convention on

---

[147] Communication 10555/90, annex II, para. 4 at 1226.

[148] Whether or not a provision of the Convention is considered self-executing is complex and varies from State to State: see A.Z. Drzemczewski, *European Human Rights Convention in Domestic Law: A Comparative Study* (1983).

[149] Declaration on democracy, Copenhagen European Council, 8 Apr. 1978: *Bull. EC* 3–1978, at 5.

Human Rights and its case-law.[150] As long as the Community remains outside the European Convention system, its efforts at reform for countries 'in transition' will be less convincing. Even with regard to States that are not potential Member States of the Union, the Community maintains a dialogue in its co-operation, development, and humanitarian assistance work which places considerable emphasis on human rights. As is well known, many agreements with third countries now contain clauses which make respect for human rights an 'essential element' of the agreement. As long as the Community (as the Community) remains unbound in law by human rights treaties, such clauses will retain an aura of lopsidedness. The Community demands respect for human rights, yet remains immune from legal challenges to its own human rights record. Moreover should human rights issues become included in the form of a 'social clause' in international trade agreements, then the Community (at times the designated legal actor in the field) ought to be obliged to reflect and report on those human rights norms which are binding in the Community context. Accession to human rights treaties, including the European Social Charter, would help not only to deepen the understanding of social and economic rights in the Community context, but it would also diminish the force of the attack which paints Community concern for social rights abroad as mere protectionism.

Finally, one must mention some hidden effects of accession. Accession would highlight the importance of a text, such as the European Convention on Human Rights, as a living text. Officials from the European Union would become aware of the human rights norms and principles. Not only would this give them a better insight into useful measures that could be taken at the national level, but they ought to be able better to evaluate the possible harmful effects of their own projects. This sort of closer co-operation could arguably also be achieved by bringing the Community closer to the Council of Europe in other ways. One idea which seems worth resuscitating is that the Community should become a member of the Council of Europe. First, this would give it a formal status in many of the Council's activities and should result in a better working relationship, as well as a more efficient division of labour. Secondly, this could provide an important injection of resources and political *appui* into the Council of Europe system. Thirdly, the law-making process could be considerably simplified as EU officials could contribute to the European norms elaborated in the Council of Europe so that they are then more suitable for adoption as Community law.

As we have seen, the European Community already has a parallel role alongside the Member States in the UN Commission on Human Rights, and in fact the Community has membership along with EU Member States in organizations such as the

---

[150] The International Commission of Jurists has made the point that '[b]y acceding to the ECHR, the Communities would recognize the importance of this document as the basic European "code of conduct" in the field of civil and political rights': *The Accession of the European Communities to the European Convention on Human Rights*, Position Paper (1993), at 11. The EC Commission made the point in the following way: '[a]t a time when public opinion is becoming increasingly aware of the human rights issue, as can clearly be seen at the level of the CSCE, it is hard to imagine the Community sitting on the sidelines, particularly as the Community will be taking an active part in the development of the CSCE, which must include the development of pluralist democracy, the rule of law, human rights, better protection of minorities, and human contacts': Communication 10555/90, at para. 3.

European Bank for Reconstruction and Development, the Food and Agriculture Organization, and the World Trade Organization. In these contexts one is often dealing with matters falling within the exclusive competence of the European Community, and the Community will wield the fifteen votes of the Member States. With regard to the Council of Europe, there might be issues which fall under the exclusive competence of the Community, but in the sorts of foreign policy issues which call for a vote in that forum it is more likely that the Community would have no formal vote.

It seems incongruous that the area where the Community and Commission have the weakest formal links is in the Council of Europe, a European Inter-Governmental Organization with a substantial human rights programme and various legal regimes concerned with human rights. The Council of Europe is mentioned in the Treaty of the European Community which states in Article 303 (*ex* Article 230) that '[t]he Community shall establish all appropriate forms of co-operation with the Council of Europe'. It is suggested that the appropriate form of co-operation for the year 2000 is membership. As a prelude to membership, steps should be taken to ensure observer status for the Community in the Council of Europe.

H. A Review of Membership for the EU and EC of Various International Bodies

As we have seen, EU membership, representation, and participation in international bodies is complex but important. To explain the position in detail would require a whole book. Suffice it to state here that our recommendation is that there be established a working group to re-examine all the different models of representation and co-operation. This working group should examine how the different arrangements are facilitating or hindering the elaboration of a coherent and effective human rights foreign policy. It is not really enough continually to emphasize mainstreaming human rights throughout the UN system if the EU Member States are not prepared to mainstream human rights within their own representation within the UN system. This is an area where concerted effort by the EU Member States could bring large rewards in terms of the orientation of the different parts of the UN system. We are not suggesting that all representation be harmonized or brought under a Community umbrella. In fact, there may be situations where it makes more sense to draw up guidelines which allow for more freedom of action by individual Member States. We are only suggesting that a thorough look at EU representation within the UN system, with a view to reinforcing the representation of EU human rights foreign policy, would reap considerable rewards in terms of mainstreaming attention to human rights within the system. The issue is complicated due to the mixed competence, which invariably exists in UN fora, and the way in which Member States still jealously guard their competence over foreign affairs and policy-making in international organizations. Consequently, the *ad hoc* arrangements for co-ordination between Member States or between Member States and the Community can be criticized for their lack of transparency and for the turf battles that inevitably waste everyone's time. In fact one detailed analysis of the different arrangements introduces the applicable rules in the following way: '[t]he precise terms of such coordination vary from forum to forum, and owe as much to habit and history as to law or logic'.[151]

It is suggested that the review could potentially cover representation in all international bodies but should at least cover the following key bodies: the Council of Europe, the Organization of Security and Co-operation in Europe, the European Bank for Reconstruction and Development, the International Monetary Fund, the World Bank, the World Health Organization, the International Labour Organization, the World Trade Organization, the UN Economic and Social Council and its subsidiary bodies, the UN General Assembly, and, most pertinently, the UN Security Council. The Security Council is so special in the context of any human rights policy that we will discuss this issue in more detail in a separate last recommendation.

I. The Work of the UN Security Council and the New EU Policy Planning and Early Warning Unit

As is well known, neither the EU nor the European Community is a member of the Security Council. Two Member States, France and the United Kingdom, have permanent seats on the Council, and other Member States can be elected during the annual elections. Special provisions of the Treaty of European Union attempt to deal with ensuring that the Common Foreign and Security Policy is applied in the context of the Security Council. Article 19(2) TEU states the position:

> Member States which are also members of the Security Council will concert and keep the other Member States fully informed. Member States which are permanent members of the Security Council will, in the execution of their functions, ensure the defence of the positions and the interests of the Union, without prejudice to their responsibilities under the provisions of the United Nations Charter.

We have already seen instances where there is no common position or interest of the Union (for example, over the mobilization of force against Iraq in 1998). It would be futile to rail against inconsistency in this context. Different Member States sometimes have different national policies. This was evident with regard to EU foreign policy expressed at the UN towards China and Algeria. It may sometimes be better to allow these differences to emerge and express themselves than to demand a consistently harmonized approach (which, for example in the case of action on Algeria, has resulted in harmonized inaction).

In fact, most of the time the CFSP is closely linked to the policy of the Security Council, and is often used to implement Security Council mandatory sanctions.[152] This is not the place to discuss the options for reform of the Security Council and the prospects of 'Unionizing' the EU membership of this organ. What is important in the present context is the fact that human rights are now regularly part of the

---

[151] I. Macleod, I.D. Hendry, and S. Hyett, *The External Relations of the European Communities* (1996), 172. See also J. Sack, 'The European Community's Membership of International Organizations' (1995) *CML Rev.* 1227–56.

[152] The European Parliament pointed out in 1997 that '[a]ll the CPs [common positions adopted by the Council as part of CFSP] intended to restrict trade and financial dealings with various parts of former Yugoslavia or Haiti have been adopted in implementation of United Nations Security Council resolutions, a fertile source of "inspiration" for CPs during [1996]': Doc A4–0193/97, note 14 above, at 14.

Security Council's work, and that reforms within the EU with regard to foreign policy need to take this into account. This is really only a question of ensuring that EU human rights policy is incorporated into EU security policy. But this is not as obvious as it sounds. The diplomats dealing with security issues are unlikely to be conversant with the EU's human rights foreign policy. Co-ordination and co-operation within delegations completely break down in this area. As the Presidency and the Commission have only a minimal role here, we should consider a different approach. It is suggested that the 'Policy Planning and Early Warning Unit' agreed to at the Amsterdam Conference should have a specific orientation towards the Security Council. Before detailing how this might work we may consider the current situation in a bit more detail.

The European Union does in fact address the Security Council during meetings. For example the Dutch Presidency of the Union delivered a 'statement on behalf of the European Union' at the Security Council meeting on the situation in Liberia on 27 March 1997. The statement explains the Union's plans for EU electoral observers as well as appealing for respect for human rights. What is really needed in this context is for the EU Council's working group on human rights (COHOM) to become more involved in presenting warnings and proposals for post-conflict peace-building to the Security Council. So far the EU's human rights foreign policy is focused around the UN Commission on Human Rights and the General Assembly. To return to the Liberia example: despite the fact that the Security Council had requested human rights reports from its peace-keeping operation UNOMIL, and despite the fact that there were concrete proposals for a post-electoral human rights operation, no EU human rights foreign policy was ever attempted for these issues. EU human rights policy is currently almost entirely sealed off from discussion of human rights in the UN Security Council.

The Declaration on the Establishment of a Policy Planning and Early Warning Unit adopted by the Member States at the Amsterdam Conference outlines a number of functions for the unit. These include: monitoring, analysis, suggesting future areas for CFSP focus, and 'providing timely assessments and early warning of events or situations which may have significant repercussions for the Union's foreign and security policy, including potential political crises'. The Unit is to be established in the Council of the EU under the responsibility of the new 'High Representative for the CFSP'. It is suggested that there be a specific focus on the role of the Security Council, and that this new unit should be closely associated with those responsible for the EU's human rights foreign policy. The drive to mainstream human rights as part of the follow-up to the Vienna World Conference has had significant effects. But the burden of mainstreaming human rights in the field of peace and security will fall on the Member States. Building this sort of organic link between EU human rights foreign policy and the work of the Security Council would be an important step towards creating a truly effective Common Foreign and Security Policy. It is not just that the foreign policy and the security policy need to be consistent. What is really essential is that discussions in the Security Council are actually informed by human rights reports, and that solutions are devised that respect human rights and ensure better protection for human rights. It is in this forum that the greatest possib-

ilities for protecting human rights are being squandered. It is in this forum that the
EU has little or no human rights policy.

IV. CONCLUSION

The theme of this report has been a recurring appeal for the European Union to take
steps to achieve greater coherence and credibility in its human rights policy. This appeal does not stem from an abstract attachment to consistency, coherence, and credibility. These are obviously desirable qualities for any policy. The importance of
evaluating EU human rights foreign policy for its coherence and credibility is
grounded in a search to create a more *effective* human rights protection. We have
seen that the Union's policy lacks coherence in a number of spheres: it criticizes the
human rights records of States outside the Union, without acknowledging the
human rights violations which take place within the Union; it treads softly with some
countries where their capacity to react is greater than others; and it seems to have no
benchmarks for comparing different countries' human rights records.

An effective human rights policy will flow from European recognition of Europe's
diversity and the need to respect difference and human dignity within the Union. The
re-emergence of identity politics, and new emphases on the ties that bind, can over-
emphasize the identification of 'the other' as a force to battle with and an opposition
to rally against.[153] Identities do not have to be forged in opposition to others—but it
is a lot easier. A deep and resonant human rights foreign policy will not be tempted
to follow the easy route; it will eschew the symbolism of Europe (flags, uniforms, and
anthems) and celebrate what links Europe to the rest of the world. It will explore
with others the fundamental values that human rights law seeks to protect. Common
concerns about racism and asylum need to be explored in a common normative
framework. If the rest of the world feels that Europe is prepared to take its human
rights discourse seriously at home—then we may have the beginnings of a credible
human rights foreign policy.

> We have made little progress if the *Us* becomes European (instead of German, French or
> British) and the *Them* becomes those outside the Community.'[154]

[153] Consider the following passage from Kwame Anthony Appiah: '[t]o accept that Africa can be in
these ways a usable identity is not to forget that all of us belong to multifarious communities with their
local customs; it is not to dream of a single African state and to forget the complexly different trajectories
of the continent's so many languages and cultures. "African solidarity" can surely be a vital and enabling
rallying cry; but in this world of genders, ethnicities, and classes, of families, religions, and nations, it is as
well to remember that there are times when Africa is not the banner we need': 'African Identities' in L.
Nicholson and S. Seidman (eds.) *Social Postmodernism: Beyond Identity Politics* (1995), 113.

[154] J.H.H. Weiler, 'Thou Shalt Not Oppress a Stranger: On the Judicial Protection of the Human
Rights of Non-EC Nationals—A Critique' (1992) 3 *EJIL* 65–91.

G

Human Rights 'Conditionality', Both Internal and External

20

Human Rights 'Conditionality' in Relation to Entry to, and Full Participation in, the EU

MANFRED NOWAK

I. THE EUROPEAN UNION AND HUMAN RIGHTS

The promotion and protection of human rights does not figure among the objectives of the European Union (EU) as listed in Article 2 of the Treaty on European Union (TEU).[1] Nevertheless, the European Court of Justice (ECJ) during the last thirty years developed jurisprudence which established that measures adopted by the institutions of the three European Communities, as well as measures adopted by Member States either to implement Community measures or which, in one way or another, fall within the scope of Community law, must be in accordance with minimum human rights standards.[2] Although the EU neither adopted its own Bill of Human Rights nor acceded to the European Convention on Human Rights (ECHR), the ECJ developed its human rights jurisprudence on the understanding that *basic human rights*, as guaranteed by the ECHR and as they result from the constitutional traditions common to the Member States, *are general principles of Community law*. This understanding was affirmed by the Member States and laid down explicitly in Article F(2) of the 1992 Maastricht Treaty on the European Union (now Article 6(2) TEU). Once the ECJ in March 1996 expressed its opinion that 'as Community law now stands, the Community has no competence to accede' to the ECHR,[3] optimists expected the Intergovernmental Conference of 1996–7 either to adopt an EU Bill of Rights or to amend the TEU in order to authorize the EU to

---

[1] The Amsterdam Treaty (ToA) of 2 Oct. 1997 entered into force on 1 May 1999. This chap. will use the revised and consolidated version of the TEU.

[2] Cf, in particular, Case 29/69, *Stauder* v. *Ulm* [1969] ECR 419; Case 4/73, *Nold* v. *Commission* [1974] ECR 491; Case C–5/88, *Wachauf* v. *Federal Republic of Germany* [1989] ECR 2609; Case C–260/89, *ERT* v. *DEP* [1991] ECR I–2925. With respect to literature cf, e.g., A. Cassese, A. Clapham, and J. Weiler (eds.), *European Union: The Human Rights Challenge*(1991), i–iii; C.O. Lenz, 'Der europäische Grundrechtsstandard in der Rechtsprechung des Europäischen Gerichtshofes' [1993] *EuGRZ* 585; H.W. Rengeling, *Grundrechtsschutz in der Europäischen Gemeinschaft* (1993); J. Iliopoulos-Strangas (ed.), *Grundrechtsschutz im Europäischen Raum* (1993); N.A. Neuwahl and A. Rosas (eds.), *The European Union and Human Rights* (1995); L. Woods, 'The European Union and Human Rights', in R. Hanski and M. Suksi (eds.), *An Introduction to the International Protection of Human Rights: A Textbook* (1997), 283.

[3] *Opinion 2/94* [1996] ECR I–1759, at para. 36.

accede to the ECHR. Both initiatives failed. Only by virtue of Article 46(d) was the jurisdiction of the ECJ extended to cover the observance of human rights as laid down in Article 6(2) TEU 'with regard to action of the institutions, insofar as the Court has jurisdiction under the Treaties establishing the European Communities and under this Treaty'. It has rightly been pointed out that this amendment of Amsterdam was not a revolutionary one, as it merely 'put into law what has happened *de facto* for some 30 years'.[4] Since the case law of the ECJ in connection with the 'first pillar'[5] has already been extended to national implementation of Community law, one might even argue that Article 46(d) TEU is a step backwards, as it only applies to 'action of the institutions'.[6] We will come back to this question later.

In addition to its obligation to respect human rights in internal matters, the EU, by virtue of Article 6(2), is bound to respect *human rights in external relations*.[7] In fact, for many years, human rights have played an important role in EC and EU external policies. Without any explicit legal basis, the EC organs have since the early 1970s applied human rights in the framework of the European Political Co-operation (EPC) in their relations to third States.[8] In Article J.1(2) of the 1992 Maastricht Treaty (now Article 11(1) TEU) the development of respect for human rights and fundamental freedoms was explicitly laid down as one of five objectives of the Common Foreign and Security Policy (CFSP), the so-called 'second pillar' of the EU. By means of autonomous foreign policy instruments (declarations, *démarches*, common positions, and joint actions) and in the framework of international organizations, above all the UN and the OSCE, the EU attempted to develop a distinctive and consistent human rights image. In view of the disastrous human rights policy of the EU *vis-à-vis* the former Yugoslavia[9] and the dispute between its Member States over the EU resolution on human rights abuses in China during the 1997 session of the UN Commission on Human Rights, the Union has been criticized for being 'torn between its moral ambitions and its economic interests', and the CFSP as

---

[4] European Policy Centre, *Making Sense of the Amsterdam Treaty* (1997), 90, at para. 15; cf also A. Duff (ed.), *The Treaty of Amsterdam: Text and Commentary* (1997), 162; C. Thun-Hohenstein, *Der Vertrag von Amsterdam, Die neue Verfassung der EU* (1997), 22; F. Sudre, 'La Communauté Européenne et les Droits Fondamentaux après le Traité d'Amsterdam' [1998] *La Semaine Juridique* 11; Manin, 'The Treaty of Amsterdam' (1998) 4 *Columb. JEL* 22.

[5] The ECJ still has no jurisdiction in relation to the 'second pillar', i.e. the Common Foreign and Security Policy, and only limited jurisdiction in relation to the 'third pillar', i.e. Police and Judicial Co-operation in Criminal Matters. Cf. Arts. 35 and 46(b) TEU as well as the new Title IV on the free movement of persons, visa, asylum, and immigration in the EC Treaty (Arts. 61 to 69) which has been transferred from the third to the first pillar.

[6] M. Bulterman, 'The Chapter on Fundamental Rights and Non-Discrimination of the Draft Treaty of Amsterdam' (1997) 17 *NQHR* 399.

[7] Even if the ECJ has no jurisdiction to review EU measures adopted in the context of the 'second pillar', there can be no doubt that the common provision of Art. 6 TEU binds the Union in all actions, including external relations. Cf, e.g. N.A. Neuwahl, 'The Treaty on European Union: A Step Forward in the Protection of Human Rights?', in Neuwahl and Rosas, note 2 above, at 13ff; Thun-Hohenstein, note 4 above, at 22; M. Fouwels, 'The European Union's Foreign and Security Policy and Human Rights' (1997) 17 *NQHR* 294.

[8] Cf, e.g., M. Zwamborn, 'Human Rights Promotion and Protection through the External Relations of the European Community and the Twelve (1989) 7 *NQHR* 11; E. Boumans and M. Norbarts, 'The European Parliament and Human Rights' (1989) 7 *NQHR* 37.

[9] Cf, e.g., M. Nowak, 'Lessons for the International Human Rights Regime from the Yugoslav Experience', in *AEL* (forthcoming).

'an insufficiently adequate framework for the promotion and protection of human rights'.[10]

The relevance of human rights for the external policies of the EU, however, extends far beyond the CFSP. In addition to Article 130u of the EC Treaty (now Article 177 TEC) which provides that Community policy in the area of development co-operation shall contribute to the general objective of respecting human rights and fundamental freedoms, the EC in the framework of the 'first pillar' developed an external human rights policy by, *inter alia*, insisting on the insertion of specific human rights clauses in all agreements concluded with third countries, imposing economic sanctions, linking human rights to unilateral trade preferences, and carrying out comprehensive programmes on technical (financial) assistance for democracy—and human rights—building activities.[11]

II. HUMAN RIGHTS AS A PRECONDITION FOR EU MEMBERSHIP

It has been argued that 'the biggest innovation of the Treaty of Amsterdam was to substantiate the competences of the European Union in the field of civil liberties'.[12] Indeed, the progressive development of the EU into an 'area of freedom, security and justice' has now been recognized as one of the five objectives of the Union enlisted in Article 2 TEU. In the Common Provisions of the TEU (Title I), the central provision on human rights, Article 6 (former Article F), has been substantially revised. Instead of the first paragraph referring to the national identities of the Member States (which is now found in paragraph 3) Article 6(1) TEU reads as follows:

> The Union is founded on the principles of liberty, democracy, respect for human rights and fundamental freedoms, and the rule of law, principles which are common to Member States.

The second paragraph, which obliges the Union to respect fundamental rights, remained unchanged, but the EU institutions' compliance with it was explicitly subjected to the jurisdiction of the ECJ by virtue of Article 46(d) TEU. In view of these changes it has been suggested that 'it seems more and more difficult to argue that human rights are not an objective of the EC'.[13]

Whether or not human rights are regarded as an objective, or only as one of the basic principles of the EU, they had gradually achieved such importance in the Union's internal and external policies that they were proclaimed in the Amsterdam

---

[10] Fouwels, note 7 above, at 324.

[11] Cf, e.g., D. Napoli, 'The European Union's Foreign Policy and Human Rights', in Neuwahl and Rosas, note 2 above, at 297; E. Decaux, 'La PESC et la diplomatie des droits de l'homme', in A. Fenet and A. Sinclair-Cytermann (eds.), *Union européenne: intégration et coopération* (1995) 232; B. Brandtner and A. Rosas, 'Human Rights and the External Relations of the European Community: An Analysis of Doctrine and Practice' (1998) 9 *EJIL* 468; E. Riedel, 'Human Rights Clauses in External Agreements of the European Communities', in this vol.

[12] Duff, note 4 above, at 8. See also J. Wachsmann, 'Les droits de l'homme' [1997] *RTDE* 175.

[13] Rosas and Brandtner, note 11 above, at 472.

Treaty as explicit preconditions for EU membership. According to a newly inserted passage into Article 49 TEU (former Article O) only a European State 'which respects the principles set out in Article 6 (1) may apply to become a member of the Union'.

III. SUSPENSION OF MEMBERSHIP RIGHTS AS A RESULT OF SERIOUS AND PERSISTENT HUMAN RIGHTS VIOLATIONS

The new Article 7 (*ex* Article F.1) TEU (as well as Article 309 (*ex* Article 236) of the TEC) for the first time establishes a procedure for the suspension of rights of Member States (including voting rights) in the case of a 'serious and persistent breach by a Member State of principles mentioned in Article 6(1)'. The procedure consists of two steps. First, the Council, meeting in the composition of the Heads of State or Government and acting unanimously (without participation of the Member State concerned) on a proposal by one third of the Member States or by the Commission, after obtaining the assent of the European Parliament (by a two thirds majority of the votes cast), may determine the existence of a serious and persistent breach. In a second step, the Council, acting by a qualified majority as laid down in Article 205(2) (*ex* Article 148) TEC,[14] may decide to suspend certain of the rights deriving from the application of the TEU to the State in question, including the voting rights in the Council. According to the new Article 309 (*ex* Article 236) TEC and corresponding amendments to the treaties on the ECSC (Article 96) and Eurotom (Article 204), voting rights shall automatically also be suspended with regard to these treaties, too.

In contrast to Article 8 of the Statute of the Council of Europe, Article 7 (*ex* Article F.1) TEU stops short of excluding a Member State,[15] but it authorizes the Council to apply appropriate and potentially far-reaching sanctions, as, for example, the withdrawal of structural funds and other financial support, the suspension of a Member State's participation in scientific or educational programmes,[16] or the suspension of the government's voting rights in the Council. In doing so, the Council shall, however, take into account the possible consequences of such suspension on the rights and obligations of natural and legal persons, which leaves open a possible legal challenge by individuals, non-governmental organizations, or companies which are affected by the imposition of any such sanction.[17] The obligations of the Member State concerned under the TEU and the other Treaties of the EC shall, however, continue to be binding on that State.[18]

---

[14] The qualified majority is defined as the same proportion of the weighted votes of the Member States as in other areas where qualified majority voting is authorized, i.e. 62 out of 87 weighted votes.

[15] Cf Duff, note 4 above, at 10; Sudre, note 4 above, at 16.

[16] Cf European Policy Centre, note 4 above, at 90, para. 17.

[17] *Ibid.*, at para. 18. For the possibility of judicial review see Part VII below.

[18] Arts. 7(2) TEU, 309(2) TEC, 96(2) ECSC, and 204(2) Euratom.

IV. THE COPENHAGEN POLITICAL CRITERIA FOR ACCESSION TO THE EU

By virtue of Article 49 (*ex* Article O) TEU accession of new members to the EU needs the unanimous approval of the Council and an absolute majority of the European Parliament. In assessing whether a candidate country meets the requirements for membership, the Opinion of the Commission plays an important role. Until the Amsterdam Treaty entered into force, Article O TEU did not contain any formal requirements, apart from to be a European State. In addition to the relevant economic and legal criteria (above all, the acceptance of the *acquis communautaire*), the European Council decided in June 1993 in Copenhagen on a number of 'political criteria' for accession to be met by candidate countries in Central and Eastern Europe. These countries must have achieved 'stability of institutions guaranteeing democracy, the rule of law, human rights and respect for and protection of minorities'.[19] The Council asked the Commission to give its opinion on all ten candidate countries in Central and Eastern Europe. In carrying out the required assessment, the Commission, in its Opinions published in July 1997, has drawn on a number of sources of information: answers given by the respective authorities to questionnaires sent to them in April 1996, bilateral follow-up meetings, reports from Member States' embassies and the Commission's delegations, assessments by international organizations (including the Council of Europe and the OSCE), NGO reports etc.[20] The assessment of the political criteria was divided into three parts: 'Democracy and the Rule of Law', 'Human Rights and the Protection of Minorities', and 'General Evaluation'. The chapters on human rights contain brief overviews of the situation of civil and political, as well as economic, social, and cultural rights. The analysis seems, however, rather superficial and relates more to the *de jure* than the *de facto* situation. Only the chapters on the protection of minorities contain a more comprehensive and critical assessment.

On the basis of this evaluation, the Commission expressed its opinion that only five Central and Eastern European countries (the Czech Republic, Estonia, Hungary, Poland, and Slovenia) already fulfilled the requirements, and that accession negotiations could therefore begin with these five alone. Four countries (Bulgaria, Latvia, Lithuania, and Romania) did not qualify for negotiations on economic grounds, and Slovakia was considered not yet to fulfil the democratic and human rights standards required by the Copenhagen criteria. Similarly, Turkey is generally also considered not to fulfil the political criteria of Copenhagen, and there might, of course, be problems with respect to Cyprus. Despite differences of opinion between the Commission and some Member States the European Council decided on 12 and

---

[19] *Bull. EC* 6–1993, pt. I.13. Cf, e.g., M. Bulterman, 'European Union Membership and Political Conditionality', in M. Bulterman, A. Hendriks, and J. Smith (eds.), *To Baehr in Our Minds*, SIM Special No. 21 (1998), 129.

[20] COM(97)2000 final, i and ii ('Agenda 2000'); COM(97)2001–2010 final (Commission Opinions on the individual candidate countries). Cf. also Brandtner and Rosas, note 11 above, at 16ff; Dutch Advisory Council on International Affairs (AIV), *An Inclusive Europe—Advisory Report on the Enlargement of the European Union* (1997), 10ff; M. Berger, 'Ein Europa der Freiheit, der Sicherheit und des Rechts', *Europa Perspektiven* (1/98), 5.

13 December 1997 in Luxembourg that negotiations should start on 11 March 1998 in principal with all ten Central and East European States and Cyprus, but the speed of negotiation procedures will certainly vary among those candidate countries.

V. THE AMSTERDAM HUMAN RIGHTS CRITERIA FOR ACCESSION TO THE EU

The principles enumerated in Article 6(1) (*ex* Article F(1)) of the Amsterdam Treaty are widely regarded as confirmation of the Copenhagen political criteria within the text of the TEU.[21] They are, however, not identical. While in Copenhagen special emphasis was laid on the protection of minorities, this criterion was not explicitly included in Article 6(1), which applies to all Member States, i.e. even to those which do not recognize minorities, such as France.[22] On the other hand, the Amsterdam Treaty includes the principle of liberty. In general, the Union principles resemble those laid down in Article 3 of the Statute of the Council of Europe. The admission practice and monitoring procedure of the Parliamentary Assembly and the Committee of Ministers, as well as the compatibility review of domestic law with the European Convention on Human Rights carried out by the Directorate of Human Rights of the Council of Europe should, therefore, be taken into account by the organs of the European Union when assessing the situation in countries applying for membership.[23] On the other hand, the recent admission practice of the Council of Europe in respect of countries such as Albania, Croatia, the Russian Federation, or the Ukraine, raises doubts about the seriousness of the Council of Europe in applying its own membership criteria.[24] Membership of the Council of Europe, therefore, no longer necessarily means that the political admission criteria in Article 6(1) TEU are met.

What does the term 'human rights and fundamental freedoms' in Article 6 (1) mean? A systematic interpretation of Article 6 as a whole indicates that, as a mini-

---

[21] As early as 8 Apr. 1978, the European Council solemnly declared in Copenhagen that 'respect for and maintenance of representative democracy and human rights in each Member State are essential elements of membership of the European Communities'. See 'Declaration on Democracy', *Bull. EC* 3–1978, at 5ff. Cf. Bulterman, note 6 above, at 398.

[22] Cf, e.g., the reservation of France to Art. 27 of the International Covenant on Civil and Political Rights. For the text and interpretation of this reservation see M. Nowak, *CCPR Commentary* (1993), 485ff and 755.

[23] Cf. the Declaration of the Committee of Ministers of 10 Nov. 1994 on Compliance with Commitments Accepted by Member States of the Council of Europe as well as Council of Europe Documents, H(96)12 (23 May 1996) and Monitor/Inf(97)2 rev. (26 June 1997). Cf. also A. Drzemczewski, 'Ensuring Compatibility of Domestic Law with the European Convention on Human Rights Prior to Ratification: The Hungarian Model' (1995) 17 *HRLJ* 241.

[24] Cf, e.g., M. Nowak, 'Entwicklung der Menschenrechte seit der Wiener Weltkonferenz', in H. Alefsen *et al.* (eds.), Menschenrechte im Umbruch: 50 Jahre Allpemeine Erktarung der Menschenrechte, Neuwied 1998, 87, at 88. One of the most outspoken critics of this admission practice is the former deputy Secretary General of the Council of Europe, Peter Leuprecht, who resigned in 1997 because he did not wish to continue to serve an organization that had become 'feeble and flabby' in its role as the standard-bearer of democracy, rule of law, and human rights in Europe: see, e.g., *Daily Telegraph*, 28 June 1997, at 13; and *Frankfurter Rundschau*, 3 July 1997.

mum, the term includes all rights and freedoms guaranteed by the European Convention on Human Rights, which is explicitly referred to in Article 6(2), to which all Member States of the Union are parties, and the ratification of which is today a precondition to membership of the Council of Europe. But what about the Additional Protocols to the Convention in the light of the fact that neither Greece, Spain, nor the United Kingdom is a party to the Fourth Additional Protocol, and that the United Kingdom is not a party to the Sixth Additional Protocol? On the other hand, in Amsterdam a Declaration to the Final Act on the abolition of the death penalty has been adopted, which notes with reference to Article 6(2) TEU that the death penalty has not been applied in any Member State of the Union since the signature of the Sixth Additional Protocol in 1983. It has, therefore, been suggested that an application for EU membership by a State where the death penalty is still used could be refused, and an existing Member State which returned to the use of the death penalty might be subject to sanctions in accordance with Article 7.[25]

Furthermore, are economic, social and cultural rights included in the term 'human rights and fundamental freedoms'? All Union Member States are parties to the European Social Charter (ESC) of 1961, and in the new fourth preambular paragraph to the TEU the attachment to fundamental social rights, as defined in the ESC and in the 1989 Community Charter of the Fundamental Social Rights of Workers, was confirmed. Since most Member States have, however, not yet inserted this 'second generation of human rights' as fundamental rights into their constitutions, it would be difficult to assert that the respect for these rights 'result[s] from the constitutional traditions common to the Member States', as stated in Article 6(2) TEU. In addition, the Austro-Italian proposal of October 1996, which contained the original draft for Articles 6 and 7 TEU and which explicitly provided that the Union should respect the political, economic, social, and other fundamental rights, as guaranteed by the European Convention and other international treaties to which the Member States are parties, was not accepted in Amsterdam.[26] On the other hand, the Commission had already assessed economic, social, and cultural rights when applying the Copenhagen political criteria to candidate countries from Central and Eastern Europe. It has, therefore, rightly been suggested that 'the *acquis* may well include other human rights conventions [than the ECHR], including those dealing with economic and social rights'.[27]

Even more difficult to answer is the question whether *collective rights* of the so-called 'third generation of human rights' fall within the definition of Article 6(1). Under the Copenhagen criteria, the protection of minorities was at least explicitly referred to, but this was deleted from the text of Article 6(1). The European Charter for Regional or Minority Languages of 1992 has been ratified only by Finland, Germany, and the Netherlands, and the European Framework Convention for the Protection of National Minorities of 1995 hitherto only by Austria, Denmark, Finland, Germany, Italy, Spain, and the United Kingdom. On the other hand, the most

[25] European Policy Centre, note 4 above, at 90, para. 14; cf. also Duff, note 4 above, at 10 who considers this Declaration as 'one of several insurances against reversion by a yet-to-enter state to barbarism'.

[26] Information provided to the author by a member of the Austrian delegation.

[27] Brandtner and Rosas, note 11, at 17; cf. also E. Szyszczak, 'Social Rights as General Principles of Community Law', in Neuwahl and Rosas, note 2 above, at 207; L. Betten and D. MacDevitt (eds.), *The Protection of Fundamental Social Rights in the European Union* (1996).

comprehensive statement on the protection of minorities, which is contained in the Copenhagen Document of the CSCE Human Dimension Conference of June 1990, was adopted unanimously by all CSCE participating States.

The interpretation of the term 'human rights and fundamental freedoms' in Article 6(1) TEU is, therefore, not an easy task. In view of the fact that the *indivisibility and interdependence of all human rights* have repeatedly been confirmed by EU Member States, most importantly in the Vienna Declaration and Programme of Action of 1993,[28] we would nevertheless conclude that the term 'human rights and fundamental freedoms' in Article 6(1) goes beyond the narrower term, 'fundamental rights', in Article 6(2) and, in principle, includes all human rights presently recognized by EU Member States in the context of the United Nations, the OSCE, and the Council of Europe.[29] 'Respect' for these rights means that they shall be recognized in the legal (not necessarily the constitutonal) systems of the respective countries and that they shall by and large be observed in practice. But in the assessment of the human rights situation, certain priority needs to be accorded to compliance with the ECHR. Individual cases of violations, as established, for example, in the case law of the European Commission and Court of Human Rights or of the UN Human Rights Committee, however, do not mean that the State in question is violating the general principle as laid down in Article 6(1) in conjunction with Article 49 (*ex* Article O) TEU.

VI. SERIOUS AND PERSISTENT BREACH OF HUMAN RIGHTS AND FUNDAMENTAL FREEDOMS

As was pointed out in the preceding chapter, the assessment of 'respect for human rights and fundamental freedoms' as an admissibility criterion transcends individual cases and must address the overall legal and factual situation in candidate countries. The requirements for the suspension of membership rights are, of course, even more stringent and depend on the determination of 'the existence of a serious and persistent breach' of human rights and fundamental freedoms. This term resembles to some extent the expressions of 'grave breaches of the Geneva Conventions of 1949' as found, for example, in Article 2 of the Statute of the International Criminal Tribunal for the former Yugoslavia, and of 'consistent pattern of gross and reliably attested violations of human rights' in ECOSOC Resolution 1503 (XLVIII) of 1970 (and similar expressions in ECOSOC Resolution 1235 (XLII) of 1967, Article 3(2) of

---

[28] Cf. M. Nowak (ed.), *World Conference on Human Rights* (1994), 168ff.

[29] This broader understanding of human rights, which goes beyond the classical concept of civil and political rights, is also confirmed by the practice of the EU in securing human rights in the economic and social field (e.g. equality between men and women with regard to labour market opportunities and treatment at work, social security, and social protection of workers as laid down in Arts. 136–145 TEC) and in adopting human rights clauses in bilateral trade and co-operation agreements. Cf. Brandtner and Rosas, note 11 above; see also W. Obwexer, 'Status quo des Grundrechtsschutzes in der Europäischen Union', in W. Hummer and M. Schweitzer (eds.), *Österreich und das Recht der Europäischen Union* (1996), 53.

the UN Convention against Torture[30] of 1984, or Article 58(1) of the African Charter on Human and Peoples Rights[31] of 1981). While the term 'grave breaches' refers to individual criminal responsibility for serious violations of international humanitarian law, the concept of 'gross and systematic violations of human rights', as applied by the UN Commission on Human Rights and its Sub-Commission under the confidential and public procedures provided for in the two above-mentioned ECOSOC Resolutions, extends to state responsibility for violations of international human rights law. As in the procedure envisaged by Article 7 (*ex* Article F.1) of the TEU, the UN Commission on Human Rights first has to determine whether there exists in a specific country a situation of gross and systematic human rights violations, and only on the basis of such determination can it take action, such as to pass a country-specific resolution, to initiate a thorough study of the situation, or to appoint a Special Rapporteur or Working Group.[32]

It is, therefore, suggested that the practice of the UN Commission and its Sub-Commission, as well as that of the UN Committee against Torture,[33] shall be taken into account when developing criteria for the application of Article 7 TEU. Although the expression 'gross and systematic violations' has never been legally defined, the voluminous practice of the United Nations since the early 1970s clearly sheds light on it. The term 'gross violations' can be equated with 'serious breach' in Article 7(1) TEU and usually refers to the severity and intensity of a particular human rights violation.[34] Although the indivisibility and interdependence of all human rights exclude a hierarchical order of more or less 'important' human rights, it cannot be denied that certain human rights violations are more serious than others. For example, the arbitrary execution, enforced disappearance, or torture of a human being or the phenomena of slavery, apartheid, and absolute poverty constitute more severe or intense human rights violations than the delay of court proceedings in civil matters. One indicator for this type of particularly important human rights, which should however not be over-estimated, is the list of non-derogable rights, as enumerated, for example, in Article 15(2) of the European Convention on Human Rights and Article 4(2) of the International Covenant on Civil and Political Rights.[35] Another indicator is the list of thematic mechanisms established by the UN Commission on Human Rights under the '1235-procedure' since 1980 and which

[30] Convention Against Torture and Other Cruel, Inhuman or Degrading Treatment or Punishment, adopted by GA Res. 39/46 (1984). In United Nations, *A Compilation of International Instruments* (1994), i, Part 2, 293.
[31] African Charter on Human and Peoples Rights, adopted on 27 June 1981. OAU Doc. CAB/LEG/67/3 Rev. 5.
[32] On these procedures see, e.g., H. Steiner and P. Alston, *International Human Rights in Context* (1996), 374ff; P. Alston, 'Appraising The United Nations Human Rights Regime' in P. Alston (ed.), *The United Nations and Human Rights* (1992), 1; D. Weissbrodt and F. Newman, *International Human Rights* (1996), 173ff; M. Nowak, 'Country-Oriented Human Rights Protection by the UN Commission on Human Rights and its Sub-Commission' (1991) 22 *NYIL* 39.
[33] Cf. W. Suntinger, 'The Principle of Non-Refoulement: Looking Rather to Geneva than to Strasbourg?' [1995] *ÖZÖRV* 203; M. Nowak, 'Committee against Torture and Prohibition of Refoulement' (1996) 14 *NQHR* 435.
[34] Cf, e.g., C. Medina Quiroga, *The Battle of Human Rights: Gross, Systematic Violations and the Inter-American System* (1988); H. Hey, *Gross Human Rights Violations: A Search for Causes* (1995).
[35] International Covenant on Civil and Political Rights, adopted by GA Res. 2200 A (XXI) (1966). In *International Instruments*, note 30 above, at 20.

refers to gross violations, such as: enforced disappearances, arbitrary executions, torture, racism and xenophobia, religious intolerance, sale of children, arbitrary detention, freedom of opinion and expression, the independence of the judiciary, and violence against women. Only recently, thematic mechanisms were also established in the field of economic, social and cultural rights, such as violations of the right to education and extreme poverty.

The term 'systematic violations' or 'consistent pattern' can be equated with 'persistent breach' in Article 7(1) TEU and limits the scope of this procedure to widespread and/or systematic violations, thereby excluding specific individual cases. One indicator of the practice of the United Nations in this regard is the 'black list' of countries which have been addressed in country-specific resolutions under both the 1235 and 1503 procedures. For the application of the procedure under Article 7 TEU the relevant practice of the OSCE and the Council of Europe seems to be even more relevant. The respective procedures in both organizations for suspending membership rights have, however, almost never been applied. Only in the Greek case of the late 1960s was the Committee of Ministers of the Council of Europe close to expelling Greece as a sanction for particularly serious and systematic human rights violations under the then military regime;[36] and the CSCE in July 1992 suspended the Federal Republic of Yugoslavia from participation for similar reasons.[37] More important for assessing whether a serious and persistent breach of human rights and fundamental freedoms exists in a present or future Member State of the EU are, therefore, relevant decisions and recommendations of independent expert monitoring bodies, such as the European Commission and Court of Human Rights (since 1 November 1998 the Single European Court of Human Rights), the European Committee for the Prevention of Torture, the Committee of Independent Experts monitoring compliance with the ESC, the OSCE High Commissioner on National Minorities, and the respective expert bodies of the United Nations, above all the Human Rights Committee, the Committee against Torture, and the various Working Groups and Special Rapporteurs of the UN Commission on Human Rights. In addition, the organs of the EU should also establish one or more independent expert bodies in order to guarantee an objective, impartial, and non-selective procedure for the application of the sanctions envisaged in Article 7 TEU as well as for other procedures, above all in the Union's foreign relations, which assess the legal and factual situation of human rights in Member and non-member States. Such an independent EU human rights expert body might eventually be affiliated to the newly established Observatory on Racism in Vienna.

---

[36] In fact, under the imminent threat of expulsion, the Greek military government decided to leave the Council of Europe.

[37] Decision of the CSCE Committee of Senior Officials of 7 July 1992. Cf. A. Bloed, *The Conference on Security and Co-operation in Europe* (1993), 115 and 951.

VII. JUDICIAL REVIEW OF THE ACCESSION AND SANCTIONS PROCEDURES

According to Article 46 TEU the powers of the ECJ under the EC Treaties shall apply only to selected provisions of the TEU, including Articles 6(2) and 46 to 53 (*ex* Articles F(2) and L to S). These provisions cover the accession procedure in Article 49 (*ex* Article O). While the principles enumerated in Article 6(1) as such seem to fall outside the jurisdiction of the ECJ, that Court may nevertheless review decisions of the Council, the Commission, and the European Parliament determining in accordance with Article 49 whether a candidate State respects these principles or not. Since non-member States have no *locus standi* in Article 230 (*ex* Article 173) TEC, the probability that infringement proceedings will be initiated in relation to accession procedures seems, however, rather limited.[38]

The sanctions procedures in Article 7 TEU are not covered by Article 46 TEU and, therefore, do not fall within the jurisdiction of the ECJ. If the Council determines the existence of a serious and persistent breach of human rights and fundamental freedoms pursuant to Article 7(1) TEU, it may also apply sanctions on the basis of Article 309 TEC, Article 96 ECSC, and Article 204 Euratom. These decisions may lead to infringement proceedings under Article 230 TEC on the initiative of the Member State concerned. It seems, however, that only the decision of the Council to suspend certain membership rights might be subject to review and not the decision determining whether a Member State committed a serious and persistent breach of human rights.[39] It is in our opinion regrettable that such important decisions are not subject to judicial control.[40]

VIII. CONCLUSIONS AND RECOMMENDATIONS

With the European Union gradually developing from an economic into a political organization, human rights are becoming more and more important, both in the internal and external relations of the Union. Amsterdam was a significant step in this direction. Although the promotion and protection of human rights do not yet figure among the main objectives of the Union, the TEU for the first time provides that the Union is founded on the principles of liberty, democracy, human rights, and the rule of law, i.e. on principles which are closely interlinked, and which all find their legal expression in current European and international human rights law. Secondly, the obligation of the Union to respect fundamental rights, which was for the first time officially recognized 1992 in Maastricht, was explicitly made subject to judicial

[38] Cf., however, Bulterman, note 19 above, at 131ff, with reference to Case 93/78, *Mattheus* v. *Doego Fruchtimport und Tiefkühlkost EG* [1978] ECR 2203.

[39] Cf. Manin, note 4 above, at 23, notes 95 and 96; see, however, European Policy Centre, note 4 above, at 90, para. 17: '[w]hile it is clear that the requirements of "serious" and "persistent" breach are cumulative, and therefore that a one-off breach (no matter how serious) would not suffice, the precise ambit of these criteria is not defined and could lead to considerable argument and challenge before the Court of Justice by the member state in question'.

[40] See also Bulterman, note 19 above, at 137.

review by the ECJ. Thirdly and most importantly, respect for human rights is now an essential precondition for accession to the Union, and in the event of serious and persistent human rights violations by a Member State, sanctions can be applied against that State. At the same time, the European Union is still suffering from a number of shortcomings in the field of human rights. First, its constitution lacks a written Bill of Rights. Secondly, the Union did not accede to the European Convention on Human Rights, the European Social Charter, the UN Human Rights Covenants, or any other human rights treaty, and its constitution, according to the jurisprudence of the ECJ, at present does not even permit accession to such treaties. Thirdly, the competence of the ECJ to review the human rights 'conditionality' in the accession and sanctions procedures is currently very limited and unclear. Finally, the actual practice of the Union in applying a policy of human rights 'conditionality' towards third countries seems to be somewhat selective and is often based on economic and political, rather than on purely legal, grounds.

If the Union wishes to prove that its policies are really founded on the principle of human rights (Article 6(1) TEU) it is not enough for its organs by and large to respect the rights guaranteed by the European Convention on Human Rights. The Union has to make sure that all human rights are effectively protected by its Member States, by candidate countries with which accession negotiations are under way, and by third countries with which the Union maintains close economic and political relations. In order to achieve such a moral position as a key actor within the international community, the following criteria need to be fulfilled:

- The Union and its Member States need to take the *indivisibility and interdependence of all human rights* seriously, i.e. accord economic, social, cultural, and other rights equal status to civil and political rights, both in internal and external policies;
- The implementation of the policy of *human rights 'conditionality'* at all levels, i.e. *vis-à-vis* Member States in the sanctions procedure under Article 7 TEU, *vis-à-vis* candidate countries in the accession procedure under Article 49 TEU, and *vis-à-vis* third countries in the context of all three 'pillars', *needs to be based on legal and judicial rather than on economic and political criteria*;
- To this end the relevant organs of the Union, i.e. the Council, the Commission, and the European Parliament, should establish one or more *independent and impartial fact-finding bodies* in order to monitor the human rights situation in all countries concerned and make their respective decisions in the field of human rights 'conditionality' subject to *judicial review by the ECJ*;
- The Union should define the concept of human rights in Article 6(1) TEU by either adopting a comprehensive *EU Bill of Rights* which, as the legal basis for the 'EU Human Rights Agenda for the Year 2000', should reflect all fundamental human rights presently codified in European and international human rights law; or by acceding *to all major European and international human rights treaties* and, thereby, making the measures taken by its organs subject to review by the competent European and international human rights monitoring bodies.

21

Trade Preferences and Human Rights

BARBARA BRANDTNER AND ALLAN ROSAS

I. INTRODUCTION

While linking trade and human rights easily provokes controversy, it seems impossible to keep the two completely separate. This is because the 'right to pursue a trade'
has some human rights connotations, as can be seen in the case law of the European
Court of Justice (ECJ).[1] Private traders see sanctions and embargoes as threats to
their property and their acquired rights to continue 'business as usual'.[2] In addition,
there is the question of the implications of sanctions for the economic and social
rights of the population of the targeted State.[3]

However, trade and human rights have also become linked in a way which suggests *conditionality* of trade preferences and other trade measures on respect for
human rights and fundamental freedoms in general, including rights and principles
which transcend property rights, such as the principle of democracy and political
rights and freedoms.

At the world level, and in the context of the World Trade Organization (WTO) in
particular, the issue of conditionality is controversial. Existing WTO law, notably
Article XX of the General Agreement on Tariffs and Trade (GATT), seems to
permit trade restrictions prompted by human rights concerns only to a very limited

---

[1] This right was recognized by the ECJ as forming part of the general principles of Community law as
early as in Case 44/79, *Hauer* v. *Land Rheinland Pfalz* [1979] ECR 3727 (together with the right to prop-
erty); more recent case law includes Case 265/87, *Schräder* v. *Hauptzollamt Gronau* [1989] ECR 2237, Case
C–84/95, *Bosphorus Hava* v. *Minister of Transport* [1996] ECR I–3953, Case T–390/94, *Schröder et al.* v.
Commission [1997] ECR II–501, and Case T–113/96, *Dubois* v. *Council and Commission* [1998] ECR
II–125.

[2] In Case T–184/95, *Dorsch Consult*, judgment of 28 Apr. 1998, a private company, having done business with Iraq and allegedly been affected by the sanctions, invoked, *inter alia*, property rights to support
its compensation claim against the Community under the principle of non-contractual liability as recognized in Art. 288 (*ex* Art. 215) of the EC Treaty. The claim was not successful in the CFI, however. See
also Case C–162/96, *Racke* v. *Hauptzollamt Mainz*, judgment of 16 June 1996, where a trader relied on
trade concessions stemming from the 1983 Co-operation Agreement with Yugoslavia (cf below, text to
notes 14–17). It seems that, hitherto, no claim relating to the freedom to pursue a trade or profession or to
the right to property has ever been successful in the Community courts. See, more generally, F. Campbell-
White, 'Property Rights: A Forgotten Issue under the Union', in N.A. Neuwahl and A. Rosas (eds.), *The
European Union and Human Rights* (1995), 249–63.

[3] See e.g., Committee on Economic, Social and Cultural Rights, General Comment No. 8, *The Relationship Between Economic Sanctions and Respect for Economic, Social and Cultural Rights*,
E/C.12/1997/8 (1997).

extent, if at all.[4] The question of a 'social clause' or 'core labour standards' has been discussed in the WTO context, but the Singapore Ministerial Conference of 9–13 December 1996 could agree only on a general statement noting that the International Labour Organization (ILO) is 'the competent body to set and deal with these standards' and affirming its support for the ILO's work in promoting them.[5] In a recent Declaration on Fundamental Principles and Rights at Work, the International Labour Conference advanced the normative foundation of core labour standards but avoided establishing any conditionality between respect for them and trade rules.[6]

This has not prevented the major traders, notably the European Community (EC) and the United States (USA), from introducing links between trade preferences and human rights in their bilateral and unilateral trade policy instruments adopted outside the WTO framework. From an EC perspective at least, it appears too late to ask whether such a link can be made. The former insistence on a complete separation of trade and human rights has been overtaken by events. With the developments of the 1990s, it is more pertinent to consider how the link between trade and human rights has been established in legal and practical terms, what the implications of recent practice are, and what main tendencies and prospects for the future may be extrapolated therefrom.

The following dimensions can be observed in this context:

1. *Legal instrument*: unilateral ('autonomous') trade measures *v.* bilateral (or multilateral) agreements;
2. *Trade measure*: incentives ('positive' measures or the 'carrot') *v.* sanctions ('negative' measures or the 'stick');
3. *Human rights standard*: fundamental *v.* less fundamental human rights and serious *v.* less serious human rights violations;
4. *Decision-making*: flexible *v.* cumbersome procedures;
5. *International legal context*: the WTO dimension.

[4] Art. XX allows, under certain strict conditions, derogations from the other provisions of the Agreement (such as Most Favoured Nation (MFN) and national treatment, or the prohibition of quantitative restrictions); see below, part II.

[5] WTO Ministerial Conference, Singapore, 9–13 Dec. 1996, Singapore Ministerial Declaration, adopted on 13 Dec. 1996, WT/MIN(96)/DEC of 18 Dec. 1996, at para. 4. This para. reads as follows: '4. We renew our commitment to the observance of internationally recognized core labour standards. The *[ILO] is the competent body* to set and deal with these standards, and we affirm our support for its work in promoting them. We believe that economic growth and development fostered by increased trade and further trade liberalization contribute to the promotion of these standards. *We reject the use of labour standards for protectionist purposes*, and agree that the *comparative advantage* of countries, particularly low-wage developing countries, *must in no way be put into question*. In this regard, we note that the WTO and ILO Secretariats will continue their existing collaboration' (emphasis added).

[6] See the 'Declaration on Fundamental Principles and Rights at Work' adopted by the International Labour Conference on 18 June 1998, and in particular its para. 5. Also note the close similarity between this Declaration and the Singapore Ministerial Declaration (note 5 above). In fact, the adoption of this para. proved most controversial during the negotiations and led to the Declaration finally being adopted by a *vote* (273 in favour, 0 against, 43 abstentions), contrary to the generally stated objective of having the Declaration adopted by consensus. Para. 5 reads as follows: '5. [the International Labour Conference] stresses that labour standards should not be used *for protectionist trade purposes*, and that nothing in this Declaration and its follow-up shall be invoked or otherwise used for such purposes; in addition, *the comparative advantage* of any country *should in no way be called into question* by this Declaration and its follow-up' (emphasis added).

This chapter will focus on trade preferences provided in both *unilateral* Community instruments and *bilateral agreements*, especially the 'human rights clause' included in such agreements (point 1). A basic theme running through the chapter is an analysis of whether, and to what extent, the development of the Community's recent practice corresponds to a development from a 'stick' towards a 'carrot' approach, as exemplified by the concept of 'conditionality' (notably with respect to the countries of former Yugoslavia) and the 'special incentive arrangements' introduced through amendments to the EC Generalized System of Preferences (GSP) of May 1998 (point 2).

This will be linked to the human rights standards involved, and the question will be asked whether the 'stick' approach has been limited to what is sometimes called the 'first generation' of human rights, that is, mainly civil and political rights, and in this context whether it is conceived as applying to 'serious' human rights violations only, while the 'carrot' might be considered more appropriate for 'second generation' human rights, notably economic and social rights[7] (point 3). Some consideration will also be given to the relevant decision-making procedures, such as the right of initiative of the European Commission, unanimity versus qualified majority in Council, and the role of the European Parliament (point 4). Finally, the section on bilateral agreements in particular will pay some attention to the WTO context and the limits it contains on the right to take trade measures in response to human rights violations (point 5).

The discussion, which will draw upon these five dimensions, will be structured in the following way: first an account will be given of the relevance of the human rights clause included since the early 1990s in bilateral agreements on trade and co-operation. The main part of the discussion will then be devoted to the question of conditionality in the context of unilateral trade preferences granted to individual countries (notably those of ex-Yugoslavia), and to an analysis of the evolution of the GSP regime. A final section will endeavour to combine the different elements and draw the necessary conclusions.

II. THE HUMAN RIGHTS CLAUSE

The 'human rights clause' that the EC has been including in its bilateral trade and co-operation agreements since the early 1990s will be more extensively discussed in other contributions to this volume.[8] Here, the clause will be seen in the specific context of trade preferences, by paying attention to the five dimensions outlined above

---

[7] As will be explained below, the distinction between these two 'generations' is not free of problems and the EC human rights approach seems to stress the indivisibility of human rights. See also B. Brandtner and A. Rosas, 'Human Rights in the External Policy of the European Community: An Analysis of Doctrine and Practice' (1998) 9 *EJIL* (forthcoming).

[8] See, in particular, the contribution of E. Riedel. See also P. J. Kuijper, 'Trade Sanctions, Security and Human Rights and Commercial Policy' in M. Maresceau (ed.), *The European Community's Commercial Policy after 1992: The Legal Dimension* (1993), 420–36; D. Napoli, 'The European Union's Foreign Policy and Human Rights', in Neuwahl and Rosas, note 2 above, at 306–8; Brandtner and Rosas, note 7 above.

(legal instrument, trade measure, human rights standard, decision-making, WTO context) and taking account of recent Community practice.

More than fifty Community agreements[9] negotiated during the 1990s have a clause stipulating that respect for democratic principles and fundamental human rights (often by reference to the Universal Declaration of Human Rights[10] of 1948 and, in a European context, the Helsinki Final Act[11] of 1975 and the Charter of Paris for a New Europe[12] of 1990) inspires the internal and external policies of the Parties and constitutes an 'essential element' of the agreement. In more recent agreements, a final clause (non-execution clause) spells out the ability to take 'appropriate measures' (including suspension of the agreement) if a Party considers that the other Party has not fulfilled its obligations under the agreement.[13]

Hitherto, the human rights clause has never been used as a ground for suspending or otherwise not executing trade preferences granted by a Community agreement.[14] Does this mean that the human rights clause is simply window-dressing? We believe such a conclusion would be premature, and this for several reasons.

First, the human rights clause is a child of the 1990s, and many of the agreements providing for such a clause have not even entered into force. Secondly, recent Community practice seems to suggest that the EC is not ruling out taking measures when human rights are violated. While this has mainly occurred with respect to *unilateral* trade preferences (see parts III and IV below) or financial or development *assistance*,[15] one cannot rule out that this practice might also be extended to the formal suspension of bilateral trade arrangements.

[9] The term 'Community agreement' here also includes the so-called mixed agreements, that is, agreements with both the EC and its Member States as Contracting Parties (on the problem of mixture; see e.g., A. Rosas, 'Mixed Union—Mixed Agreements', in M. Koskenniemi (ed.), *International Law Aspects of the European Union* (1998), 125–48). For instance, all the Europe Agreements concluded with Central and Eastern European countries and the Partnership and Co-operation Agreements concluded with the countries of the former USSR are mixed.

[10] Universal Declaration of Human Rights, adopted by GA Res. 217 A (III) (1948). In United Nations, *A Compilation of International Instruments* (1994), i, Part 1, 1.

[11] Helsinki Final Act, adopted at Conference on Security and Co-operation in Europe, 1 Aug. 1975, reprinted in 14 ILM 1292.

[12] Charter of Paris for a New Europe, adopted by Heads of State or Government of the participating States of the Conference on Security and Co-operation in Europe, Paris, 21 Nov. 990, reprinted in 30 ILM 190.

[13] There is a Council decision of May 1995, which spells out the basic modalities of this clause in order to ensure consistency in EC treaty practice. This decision was accompanied by a Communication from the Commission on the inclusion of respect for democratic principles and human rights in agreements concluded between the Community and third countries, COM(95)216 final. Art. 5 of the Lomé Convention, as revised by an Agreement signed in Mauritius on 4 Nov. 1995 ([1998] OJ L156/1), is somewhat more elaborate than the standard clause used in bilateral treaties (see also Art. 366a on non-execution and below, text to notes 16, 42, and 52).

[14] On 2 Dec. 1991, the Council decided that a trade embargo should be imposed on Haiti. This decision was never followed up by any formal suspension of the Lomé Convention: Kuijper, note 8 above, at 433–5. An Agreement with Yugoslavia was suspended in 1991, but that agreement contained no human rights clause (notes 18–19 below). While development co-operation with some African countries has from time to time been *de facto* suspended or restricted (partly because of civil war situations), that part of the Lomé Convention has not so far been formally suspended either (see notes 16, 42, and 52 below). See also the contribution of Riedel to this vol.

[15] On 18 Dec. 1997 ([1998] OJ L1/6), the Council resorted to the human rights clause of the TACIS Regulation (No. 1279/96 of 25 June 1996 concerning the provision of assistance to economic reform and recovery in the New Independent States and Mongolia [1996] OJ L165/1) in order to enact a special Tacis Civil Society Development Programme for Belarus; see Brandtner and Rosas, note 7 above. On the *de*

In fact, in July 1998, the Council, at the initiative of the Commission, decided to request consultations with Togo on the basis of the human rights clause of the Lomé Convention (invoking irregularities in the presidential elections of 21 June).[16] At the time of writing, these consultations have not yet been held. It is therefore too early to say what specific measures, if any, the EC will take. However, at least in principle, they may well cover the trade part of the Lomé Convention.

Nevertheless, there are reasons why the non-execution of bilateral trade arrangements seems less likely to occur than the suspension of unilateral trade preferences or the suspension of development assistance. These reasons can be related to the five dimensions of legal instrument, trade measure, human rights standard, decision-making, and WTO context outlined above.

As regards the legal instrument involved, it should be recalled that the non-execution of an agreement (treaty) always poses a problem of international law, notably the fundamental principle of *pacta sunt servanda*.[17] This question was raised in the case of *Racke* between a private company and a national customs authority, which became the subject of a preliminary ruling by the European Court of Justice.[18]

The company argued that a Council regulation (Regulation 3300/91 of 11 November 1991), which suspended the trade concessions granted to the Socialist Federal Republic of Yugoslavia (SFRY) by a Co-operation Agreement of 1983, was invalid,[19] since there was no justification in general international law for proceeding with the suspension in the manner in which this had been done by the Community. In fact, the 1983 Agreement contained no human rights clause, and thus no non-execution clause. Therefore, the main legal question concerned the relevance of general (customary) international law, in particular the clause *rebus sic stantibus* (fundamental change of circumstances) which had been invoked by the Community, for the validity of Community legal acts aiming at the suspension of contractual relations with third countries.

The Court held, on the one hand, that an individual relying on rights which he derived directly from an agreement[20] could not be denied the chance of challenging the

facto suspension of development co-operation with countries party to the Lomé Convention, see note 14 above.

[16] Communication from the Commission to the Council on the opening of consultations with Togo pursuant to Art. 366a of the Lomé Convention, SEC(1998)1189 final. The General Affairs Council accepted this initiative by a decision of 13 July; on the same day, letters signed on behalf of the Council and the Commission were sent to Togo and to the President of the ACP Council of Ministers.

[17] See Art. 26 of the Vienna Conventions on the Law of Treaties (the 'Vienna Conventions'), according to which 'every treaty is binding upon the parties to it and must be performed by them in good faith'. In its judgment of 16 June 1998 in Case C–162/96, *Racke* v. *Hauptzollamt Mainz*, 16 June 1998, not yet reported, the ECJ characterized the *pacta sunt servanda* principle as 'a fundamental principle of any legal order and, in particular, the international legal order' (para. 49). See also Case 104/81, *Hauptzollamt Mainz* v. *Kupferberg* [1982] ECR 3641, at para. 18, and the judgment of the International Court of Justice of 25 Sept. 1997 in the *Case concerning the Gabcikovo-Nagymaros Project*, reprinted in 37 ILM 162, notably paras. 104, 114, and 142–3.　　　　[18] Judgment of 16 June 1998 in Case C–162/96, *Racke*.

[19] Co-operation Agreement between the EEC and the SFRY, signed 2 Apr. 1980; concluded by Council Reg. 314/83 of 24 Jan. 1983 [1983] OJ L41/1. The Agreement was suspended 'with immediate effect' by Council Decision 91/586/ECSC/EEC of 11 Nov. 1991 [1991] OJ L315/47. On the same day, the Agreement's trade concessions were suspended by Council Reg. 3300/91 (*ibid.*, 1). Both suspensions thus became effective on the day of their publication, i.e. on 15 Nov. 191.

[20] In fact, the Court found that the relevant provision of the 1983 Agreement had direct effect, i.e. was 'capable of conferring rights upon which individuals may rely before national courts' (para. 34).

validity of an EC act suspending those rights by invoking customary international law. On the other hand, only 'manifest errors of assessment' concerning the conditions for applying the rules of customary international law should be subject to judicial review. The Court therefore concluded that, in view of the change of circumstances in the former Yugoslavia which took place during 1991, no factor had been disclosed of such a kind as to affect the validity of the suspending regulation.

While this case concerns the application of general international law as a ground for suspending an agreement, it serves to illustrate the general problems which may arise from the non-execution of agreements in force. Even if the human rights and non-execution clauses make it legally easier to take measures of non-execution,[21] and even if the clause *rebus sic stantibus* is not the only ground that general international law offers for non-execution of treaty obligations,[22] the fact that the act to be suspended is a treaty involving mutual rights and obligations between two subjects of international law may set a serious legal and political barrier against taking such measures.

A further barrier may follow from the more specific trade implications of the arrangements concerned. In fact, trade and co-operation agreements can be concluded either with WTO Members or with non-members, and they may contain unilateral or reciprocal trade concessions. However, the ability to grant specific trade preferences which would go beyond the WTO schedules is limited by the Most-Favoured-Nation clause (MFN), one of the cornerstones of the WTO, which implies that even preferences granted to WTO non-members should normally be extended to all WTO Members.[23]

While there are a number of exceptions to the MFN principle,[24] including the ability to obtain waivers[25] and to conclude, among a group of countries, a customs

[21] See also Case C–268/94, *Portugal* v. *Council* [1996] ECR I–6177, where the Court held (para. 27) that an important function of the human rights clause may be to secure the right to suspend or terminate an agreement if the third State has not respected human rights.

[22] For instance, suspension of treaties can take place on the basis of the principles enshrined in Art. 60 of the Vienna Conventions. The law of countermeasures (reprisals) may offer an additional ground: see Arts. 30 and 47–50 of the Draft Arts. on State Responsibility drawn up by the International Law Commission (ILC) (*Report of the ILC on the Work of its Forty-eighth Session 6 May–26 July 1996*, A/51/10 (1996), at 125 and L. Boisson de Chazournes, *Les contre-mesures dans les relations internationales économiques* (1992). In his Opinion in *Racke* (note 17 above), Jacobs AG, while noting that it was not necessary to consider the invocation by the Commission of such additional grounds as impossibility of performance and the 'right of retorsion' (since *rebus six stantibus* provided a sufficient ground for suspending the agreement), nevertheless observed that 'those arguments, too, have some force' (para. 99). Meanwhile, following a common position (CFSP) adopted on 29 June 1998 on the basis of Art. J.2 (now Art. 12) of the TEU ([1998] OJ L190/3), the Council adopted Reg. 1901/98 of 7 Sept. 1998 concerning a ban on flights by Yugoslav carriers between the Federal Republic of Yugoslavia and the European Community ([1998] OJ L248/1). This measure, which is based on Art. 301 (*ex* 228A) of the EC Treaty, has been conceived as a reprisal; in fact, a preambular para. recalls the FRY's 'use of indiscriminate violence and brutal repression against its own citizens, which constitutes serious violations of human rights and international humanitarian law'.

[23] See Art. I(1) GATT, which provides that with respect to a number of trade measures, including customs duties and other charges, 'any advantage, favour, privilege or immunity granted by any Contracting Party to any product originating in or destined for any other country shall be accorded immediately and unconditionally to the like product originating in or destined for the territories of all other Contracting Parties'.

[24] See e.g. M. Trebilcock and R. Howse, *The Regulation of International Trade* (1995), 76–7; and J. Jackson, *The World Trading System* (2nd edn., 1997), 163–5.

[25] In 'exceptional circumstances', the Ministerial Conference may grant a waiver (derogation) from a WTO obligation: see Art. IX(3) of the Marrakesh Agreement Establishing the World Trade Organization (1994) and Art. XXV GATT.

union or a free-trade area aiming at liberalizing 'substantially all trade' between its constituent countries,[26] the WTO system limits the right of its members, including the EC, to grant trade preferences beyond the WTO schedules. In any case, both WTO and—to the extent that they would pose a MFN problem—extra-WTO preferences are subject to challenge in the WTO dispute settlement system, which since 1995 has been a compulsory system comprising trade panels, an Appellate Body, and a Dispute Settlement Body with authority to take legally binding decisions.[27] This system is based on the principle that WTO obligations can be suspended only upon authorization of the Dispute Settlement Body, following a determination, by a panel or Appellate Body report adopted by it, that there has been a violation of obligations stemming from the WTO.[28]

Moreover, the WTO system is based on the principle that members can derogate from their obligations only by recourse to one of the exceptions allowed in the GATT or other agreements covered.[29] While the 1948 draft Havana Charter of the abortive International Trade Organization (ITO) contained a clause on fair labour standards,[30] there is nothing comparable in the GATT/WTO. Under normal circumstances, only Article XX GATT (or its counterpart, Article XIV GATS) seems to offer some chance of restricting GATT obligations for reasons somewhat related to human rights. The exceptions that could be cited in this context are measures 'necessary to protect public morals' (Article XX(a) GATT),[31] 'necessary to protect human, animal or plant life or health' (Article XX(b) GATT), or 'relating to the products of prison labour' (Article XX(e) GATT). However, as can be seen, none of these provisions addresses human rights *per se*. It is thus not very probable that the WTO dispute settlement bodies, which have stressed the need to interpret these exceptions narrowly,[32] and have placed the burden of proof on the party invoking them,[33] would, save perhaps in exceptional circumstances, accept human rights considerations as a ground for trade restrictions.

This said, one cannot totally rule out the possibility, for instance, of interpreting the reference to prison labour to include slavery and forced labour.[34] There is no

[26] Art. XXIV GATT. See also Art. V of the General Agreement on Trade in Services (GATS), which contains comparable rules.

[27] See the Understanding on Rules and Procedures Governing the Settlement of Disputes (Dispute Settlement Understanding—DSU).

[28] See, in particular, Arts. 22(2) and 23 of the DSU, and Jackson, note 24 above, at 24, who notes that no dispute involving the GATT has ever been taken to the International Court of Justice and concludes that 'it can be argued that the parties have agreed in the WTO treaty that the WTO dispute-settlement procedure is the exclusive recourse for disputes concerning any of the WTO texts'.

[29] See e.g., Boisson de Chazournes, note 22 above, at 148–9 and 184.

[30] V. Leary, ' "Workers" Rights and International Trade: The Social Clause (GATT, ILO, NAFTA, U.S. Laws)', in J. Bhagwati and R. Hudec (eds.), *Fair Trade and Harmonization: Prerequisites for Free Trade?*, Vol. 2: *Legal Analysis* (1996), 197–8.

[31] Art. XIV GATS provides for an exception for measures necessary not only to protect public morals but also to 'maintain public order'. A footnote explains that the public order exception may be invoked 'only where a genuine and sufficiently serious threat is posed to one of the fundamental interests of society'.

[32] See e.g. *United States—Restrictions on Imports of Tuna*, panel report circulated on 16 June 1994, not adopted, DS29/R, at paras. 5.26 and 5.38.

[33] See e.g. *United States—Standards for Reformulated and Conventional Gasoline*, Appellate Body report of 29 Apr. 1996 (AB–1996–1), adopted on 20 May 1996, WT/DS2/9, 22–3.

[34] The GATT, *Analytical Index: Guide to GATT Law and Practice* (6th edn., 1994) does not even contain an entry concerning Art. XX(e), which probably means that this exception has not so far been

GATT or WTO case law on such issues.[35] Nor is there any express case law on the interpretation of Article XXI GATT, which allows a member to take 'any action which it considers necessary for the protection of its essential security interests' if taken, *inter alia*, 'in time of war or other emergency in international relations'.[36] As this clause seems to leave the members a wide margin of discretion,[37] one cannot rule out the possibility of interpreting the references to 'essential security interests' and 'emergency in international relations' to include serious human rights violations, such as genocide, given the broader concept of security that has become fashionable during the 1990s.[38]

Subject to these exceptions, suspension or other non-applicability of treaty-based trade preferences should normally happen only with respect to agreements concluded with States which are not members of the WTO or preferences that go beyond the WTO obligations. In the latter case, the WTO rules may still limit the right to suspend preferences.[39] And even when suspension can take place without being called into question by the WTO rules, suspension of *mutual* preferences will often not be considered feasible, as they will equally affect the Community's market access to the country concerned.

To be sure, one could envisage suspension, not of the agreement itself (as a treaty-law measure),[40] but of the preferences granted to the third state as a unilateral countermeasure.[41] One might recall in this context that the standard human rights clause

invoked by any WTO member. However, in the light of the general requirement of Art. XX (*chapeau*) that 'such measures are not applied in a manner which would constitute an arbitrary or unjustifiable discrimination . . ., or a disguised restriction on international trade', a more 'economically oriented' interpretation of this exception would seem difficult to reconcile with this Art.'s general requirement. Of course, Art. XX(e) also states that measures may relate only to the '*products*' of prison labour, but to qualify prison labour, forced labour, or slavery as a 'production method' would seem difficult anyway.

[35] The situation is different with respect to environmental considerations (Art. XX(g) GATT). See, e.g., the *Tuna II* and *Gasoline* cases referred to in notes 32 and 33 above, and *United States—Import Prohibition of Certain Shrimp and Shrimp Products*, Panel report circulated on 15 May 1998, WT/DS58/R (at the time of writing subject to appeal). It is significant that in all these cases the measures taken by the defendant have been held incompatible with the GATT.

[36] See also Art. XIV bis GATS and 73 TRIPS.

[37] Jackson, note 24 above, at 229–32. See also text to note 61 below.

[38] See also Cases C–70/94, *Werner* v. *Germany* [1995] ECR I–3189 and C–83/94, *Criminal Proceedings against Leifer* [1995] ECR I–3231, where the Court (paras. 26 and 27 in *Werner*, paras.27 and 28 in *Leifer*), citing its AG (Jacobs), noted that 'it is becoming increasingly less possible to look at the security of a State in isolation, since it is closely linked to the security of the international community at large, and of its various components. So, the risk of a serious disturbance to foreign relations or to peaceful coexistence of nations may affect the security of a Member State'.

[39] For instance, it can be asked whether a member can suspend preferences which, in the context of a free trade area or customs union to which it belongs, are part of the 'substantially all trade' requirement of Art. XXIV GATT, and still be recognized as such, and thus exempt from the MFN obligation as regards the remaining benefits granted under the free trade area or customs union.

[40] Art. 60 of the Vienna Convention, which regulates the conditions for suspension, is probably reflective of customary international law; see e.g. the *Gabcikovo-Nagymaros case* referred to in note 17 above, at para. 46. According to Art. 72(1)(a) of the Vienna Convention, the suspension of the operation of a treaty 'releases the parties between which the operation of the treaty is suspended from the obligations to perform the treaty in their mutual relations during the period of suspension'. Formal suspension thus implies that the treaty is not applied between *either* party.

[41] Art. 60 of the Vienna Conventions does not seem to rule out the taking, under certain conditions, of countermeasures (reprisals) under the general international law on state responsibility. See e.g. L.A. Sicilianos, 'The Relationships Between Reprisals and Denunciation or Suspension of a Treaty' (1993) 4 *EJIL* 341–59; A. Rosas, 'Reactions in the Event of Breach' in D. Bardonnet (ed.), *The Convention on the*

refers to 'appropriate measures'. It is thus not limited to the formal suspension of a treaty, as envisaged by the Vienna Conventions. However, were the Community to derogate unilaterally from its obligations stemming from an agreement, the other party might retaliate. Even if this were illegal retaliation, it could diminish or even extinguish the dissuasive effect of the original (unilateral) measure. Suspension of trade preferences is thus more likely to cover preferences enjoyed exclusively by the Community's trading partner.

A further requirement for taking 'punitive' trade measures relates to the nature of the human rights violations committed by the other side. The standard human rights clause refers to 'democratic principles' and 'fundamental human rights', and uses the Universal Declaration of Human Rights as a frame of reference. This suggests that suspension is envisaged to take place only in cases of serious human rights violations. In a Joint Declaration on Article 366a (the suspension clause) of the Lomé Convention, the Contracting Parties declare that they will not have recourse to the provision of 'special urgency' in Article 366a, other than in 'exceptional cases of particularly serious and flagrant violations that, because of the response time required, render any prior consultation impossible'.[42] While this Declaration is limited to the Lomé context, and, even within this context, to cases of special urgency, it is submitted that its wording is indicative of a more general tendency to focus the possibility of suspension on serious violations.

Further guidance is provided by a theoretical consideration which seems to underlie the human rights clause. As we have argued elsewhere,[43] the reference to the Universal Declaration (a formally non-binding instrument), combined with the legal uncertainties surrounding the Community's competence to enact new rules in the field of human rights, arguably implies that the standard envisaged in the human rights clause is the general international law standard, be this articulated as customary law or as general principles of law recognized by civilized nations.[44] The Community's human rights policy thus seems to be based on the assumption that the Universal Declaration, at least at the level of its general principles, has become reflective of general international law in the field of human rights. Now, by necessity, such general principles are fundamental in nature. They thus seem not to cover details concerning, say, the functioning of the judicial system or the protection of family life, which would be regulated in particular by human rights conventions or stem from individual case law.

The only initiative for the formal suspension of a Community agreement based on the human rights clause which has existed to date, the request for consultations with Togo of July 1998, concerns alleged irregularities in general elections, that is political rights and 'internal self-determination' as a 'right to democracy'.[45] The 1991

Prohibition and Elimination of Chemical Weapons: A Breakthrough in Multilateral Disarmament, Hague Academy Workshop 1994 (1995), 577–91; M.M. Gomaa, *Suspension or Termination of Treaties on Grounds of Breach* (1996), 69. See also the discussion by the International Court of Justice in the *Gabcikovo-Nagymaros* case referred to above, note 17, at para. 196.

[42] *The Courrier*, No. 155 (1996), 195.   [43] Brandtner and Rosas, note 7 above.

[44] See Art. 38 of the Statute of the International Court of Justice.

[45] Cf. note 16 above. On 'internal' self-determination, see the articles by A. Rosas, 'Internal Self-determination' and J. Salmon, 'Internal Aspects of the Right to Self-determination: Towards a Democratic Legitimacy Principle?' in C. Tomuschat (ed.), *Modern Law of Self-Determination* (1993), 225 and 253.

suspension of the Co-operation Agreement with Yugoslavia (which did not contain an express human rights clause) was based on a fundamental change of circumstances, including 'war' (or at least, serious internal armed conflict) and the dissolution of the former SFRY. Finally, the 'conditionality' applied in the context of unilateral trade preferences seems mainly to focus on basic civil and political rights (see below, section III).

While it can thus be surmised that the suspension of trade preferences based on the human rights clause would be likely to concern violations of the 'right to democracy' and basic civil and political rights (military groups, genocide, crimes against humanity, etc.), it should be underlined that the human rights clause is not, in principle, limited to civil and political rights. The Universal Declaration, as well as the Community's human rights policy, is based on the principle of indivisibility of human rights.[46] In many cases, it is difficult to draw the line between civil rights on the one hand and economic and social rights on the other. This is illustrated, for example, by the overlap between the right to life (as a civil right) and the right to basic subsistence and security (as an economic and social right), or by the dual nature of workers' and trade union rights.[47]

Whether, and to what extent, the human rights clause will be used to suspend trade preferences or other parts of Community agreements also depends on the pertinent decision-making procedures. While the procedure for resorting to 'embargoes' has been a controversial one,[48] things have been clarified by the Maastricht and Amsterdam Treaties. Article 301 (*ex* Article 228a) of the EC Treaty, which was introduced by the Maastricht Treaty, provides for a general possibility to 'interrupt or reduce, in part of completely, economic relations with one of more third countries' (and Article 60 (*ex* Article 73g) spells out that this may include the movement of capital and payments). However, the new version of Article 300(2) (*ex* Article 228(2)) as amended by the Treaty of Amsterdam clarifies that suspension of a Community agreement does not have to follow the procedures of Article 301 (*ex* Article 228a) which presuppose a common position or joint action adopted according to the provisions of Title V of the Maastricht Treaty), but can be taken by the Council, on a proposal from the Commission, on the basis of Article 300 (*ex* Article 228).

If total suspension of an agreement is envisaged, the legal basis for such measure should be the legal basis used when concluding the agreement. If only partial suspension is envisaged, the legal basis depends on the subject matter. If, for instance, trade in goods is suspended, or measures to restrict the trade preferences of the other party taken, the legal basis would be Article 133 (*ex* Article 113) of the EC Treaty (common commercial policy).[49] That would entail qualified majority voting in

[46] Brandtner and Rosas, note 7 above, notably sect. 3.2. The Universal Declaration also covers some economic, social, and cultural rights, in particular the right to social security (Art. 22), the right to work (Art. 23), the right to rest and leisure (Art. 24), the right to an adequate standard of living (Art. 25), the right to education (Art. 26), and the right to participate in cultural life (Art. 27).
[47] These and other examples are discussed in A. Eide, C. Krause, and A. Rosas (eds.), *Economic, Social and Cultural Rights: A Textbook* (1995).
[48] See e.g. Kuijper, note 8 above; M. Kaniel, *The Exclusive Treaty-Making Power of the European Community up to the Period of the Single European Act* (1996), 76–8.
[49] If services or trade-related intellectual property rights are envisaged as well, that is, matters regulated in the GATS and TRIPS agreements of the WTO family, this could, in light of *Opinion 1/94* of the

Council and no formal consultation of the European Parliament, in other words, a relatively flexible procedure.[50]

To suspend other parts of an agreement could lead to difficult questions concerning the necessary legal base, including the role of the European Parliament. The new Article 300 (*ex* Article 228) of the EC Treaty clarifies that the Parliament need only be informed, not formally consulted. Even with this provision, however, there will remain the problem of how to involve the Member States if suspension concerns a mixed agreement.[51] If trade in goods is suspended in the context of a mixed agreement, this can arguably be done by a Council Decision alone, based on Article 133 (since the Community's trade competences are exclusive). Therefore, the Commission's proposal to provide procedures for suspending the Lomé Convention (a mixed agreement) would, if adopted, provide much needed clarification, especially as regards the non trade-related parts of this Convention.[52]

III. THE COMMUNITY'S AUTONOMOUS TRADE MEASURES IN FORMER YUGOSLAVIA

One of the most striking examples of the Community's 'stick and carrot' approach as regards trade concessions and respect for fundamental human rights probably lies in the Community's policy towards certain countries of south-east Europe (most of which have emerged from the former Yugoslavia). The matter is best known under the heading of 'conditionality'.[53]

As will be recalled, relations between the Community (and its Member States) and the SFRY had since 1983 been governed by a Co-operation Agreement (EC) and an

ECJ (*Opinion 1/94* of 15 Nov. 1994 [1994] ECR I–5267), be done on the basis of Art. 113 (now Art. 133 EC) only to a limited extent.

[50] This procedure could arguably have been followed when the trade preferences of the 1983 Agreement with Yugoslavia were suspended in 1991. However, the peculiarity of this Agreement was that its act of conclusion did not formally mention a legal base, even though the Community's intention (as evidenced by the act of conclusion of the Additional Protocol of 1987 [1987] OJ L389/72) had apparently been to conclude an association agreement (Art. 310 of the EC Treaty (*ex* Art. 238)). It therefore seems probable that both the act of suspension of the Agreement, and Reg. 3300/91 suspending the trade preferences (note 19 above) were adopted by consensus. In Case C–124/95, *Centro-Com* [1997] ECR I–81, the ECJ reaffirmed that political motives behind a trade embargo are not a sufficient reason to remove them from the ambit of Art. 133. See also Cases C–70/94 *Werner* and C–83/94 *Leifer*, note 38 above.

[51] See Rosas, note 9 above, at 135–6.

[52] Proposal for a Council Decision on a framework procedure for implementing Art. 366a of the Fourth Lomé Convention, COM(96)58 final, submitted by the Commission on 26 Feb. 1996 [1996] OJ C119/7. This proposal is based on Art. 310 (*ex* Art. 238) of the EC Treaty, the same legal base as that retained for the Lomé Convention itself (association agreement). It thus requires the European Parliament's assent before being adopted by unanimity in Council.

[53] See also Brandtner and Rosas, note 7 above, at section 2.3. Particularly in the light of the new provisions introduced by the Treaty of Amsterdam, the concept of 'conditionality' may now also be said to cover matters relating to entry to, and full participation in, the EU; for this aspect of the question, see the contribution to this vol. by M. Nowak.

Agreement on coal and steel matters (ECSC).[54] In November 1991, because of the continuation of hostilities between the SFRY's various ethnic communities, these Agreements were first suspended,[55] then denounced.[56] Even though the legal motivation for these acts consisted of a fundamental change of circumstances,[57] their political motivation probably lay in the fact that the Community had been diplomatically very active in the months preceding the suspension, trying to bring the parties to the conflict together in a 'peace conference' and mediating various cease-fire agreements. None of these was respected. The Community thus decided to use the 'stick' it had, and unilaterally suspended the two Agreements' trade preferences.

However, within weeks, the EC preferences were reintroduced with respect to those republics which then actively contributed to the peace process.[58] Soon after, these 'positive selective measures' were even extended to cover the 'Yugoslav Republic of Montenegro', in line with a Declaration accepted by the Community and its Member States in the context of European Political Co-operation (the precursor of today's CFSP).[59] The measures had to be partially revoked, however, following the promulgation, on 27 April 1992, of the creation of the 'Federal Republic of Yugoslavia' (FRY) between Serbia and Montenegro, and UN Security Council Resolution 757 (1992) of 30 May 1992 imposing an economic embargo on the FRY under Title VII of the UN Charter.[60]

Both the suspension/denunciation of the Agreements and their trade preferences and the selective reintroduction of these preferences in favour of certain parties to the conflict were notified to the GATT Contracting Parties in November/December 1991, recourse being had to Article XXI GATT and the Community's essential security interests.[61] In fact, the Community had not been the only party to withdraw trade preferences after the outbreak of the Yugoslav crisis: among others, the United States, Canada, Australia, New Zealand, and Japan had done so too.

[54] Co-operation Agreement between the EEC and the SFRY (note 19 above); Agreement between the Member States of the ECSC and the ECSC, on the one hand, and the SFRY, on the other hand [1983] OJ L41/113.

[55] As regards the suspension of the 1983 Co-operation Agreement and its trade preferences, cf. note 19 above. The ECSC Agreement, for its part, was denounced, and its trade concessions suspended, by Decisions 91/587/ECSC and 91/588/ECSC of the Representatives of the Member States meeting within the Council [1991] OJ L315/48–9). All these measures thus became effective on the same day (the date of their publication), 15 Nov. 1991.

[56] Council Decision 91/602/EEC of 25 Nov. 1991 denouncing the Co-operation Agreement between the EEC and the SFRY [1991] OJ L325/23. As regards the denunciation of the ECSC Agreement, cf. note 55 above.

[57] This motivation was validated by the ECJ in Case C–162/96 *Racke*, note 17 above.

[58] The first such Reg. was Council Reg. 3567/91 of 2 Dec. 1991 concerning the arrangements applicable to imports of products originating in the Republics of Bosnia-Herzegovina, Croatia, Macedonia and Slovenia [1991] OJ L342/1.

[59] See Council Reg. 545/92 of 3 Feb. 1992 concerning the arrangements applicable to imports into the Community of products originating in the Republics of Croatia and Slovenia and the Yugoslav Republics of Bosnia-Herzegovina, Macedonia and Montenegro [1992] OJ L63/1, and in particular its second and last preambular paras.

[60] Council Reg. 1433/92 of 1 June 1992 amending, *inter alia*, Reg. 545/92, with respect to the Republics of Bosnia-Herzegovina and Montenegro [1992] OJ L151/7; Council Reg. 1432/92 of 1 June 1992 prohibiting trade between the EEC and the Republics of Serbia and Montenegro, *ibid.*, 4. As regards SC Res. 757 (1992), see 'Documents regarding the conflict in Yugoslavia' and the Introductory Note by Paul C. Szasz, in 31 ILM 1421, 1427.

[61] See the GATT, *Analytical Index*, note 34 above, re. Art. XXI, 558–62. On Art. XXI, cf text to notes 36–8 above.

In February 1992, the SFRY requested the establishment of a panel under Article XXIII(2) GATT (nullification or impairment) against the Community, stating in particular that 'the positive compensatory measures applied by the EC to certain parts of Yugoslavia [were] contrary to the MFN treatment of products originating in or destined for the territories—taken as a whole—of all contracting parties'.[62] A month later, a panel was indeed established. However, by April 1992, the 'transformation' of the SFRY into the FRY had also been notified, which reoriented the debate on the question of the FRY's succession to the former SFRY's GATT rights. In May 1992, the GATT Council finally decided that the representative of the FRY should refrain from participating in its work, as long as no decision had been taken on the succession issue. To the authors' knowledge, the dispute has not been resumed (nor settled) since. The question of an eventual succession to the rights of the former SFRY thus remains to be solved in the WTO.

The autonomous trade measures introduced in 1991 were thereafter annually renewed without major changes until, at the end of 1996, the Council adopted Regulation 70/97.[63] Its application was again limited to one year (until 31 December 1997), but the reason for this now was that the benefits contained in it would be 'renewed on the basis of *conditions established by the Council* in relation to the development of relations' between the Community and each of the countries concerned, which should 'permit a regular review of compliance, without prejudice to the possibility of modifying the geographical coverage of this Regulation'.[64] From simply adapting its trade regime to the political developments of the day, the Community had moved to defining its own coherent strategy, in a 'carrot and stick' approach, to future relations with the countries concerned.

The Council Conclusions of 29 April 1997 on 'conditionality', which embody the new strategy with respect to those countries of south-east Europe with which association agreements have not yet been concluded (Bosnia-Herzegovina, Croatia, FRY, FYROM, and Albania), introduce a clear link between these countries' performance as regards, *inter alia*, democracy, the rule of law, and higher standards of human and minority rights (in line with some of these countries' commitments under the Dayton Peace Agreements) and the Community's willingness not only to grant autonomous trade measures, but also economic and financial co-operation, and even to enter into new contractual relations.[65]

---

[62] DS 27/2, dated 10 Feb. 1992, cited in GATT, *Analytical Index*, note 34 above, at 558.

[63] Council Reg. 70/97 of 20 Dec. 1996 concerning the arrangements applicable to imports into the Community of products originating in the Republics of Bosnia-Herzegovina, Croatia, and the former Yugoslav Republic of Macedonia and to imports of wine originating in the Republic of Slovenia [1997] OJ L16/1. The main modifications introduced by its predecessors were the progressive recognition of the 'former Yugoslav Republic of Macedonia' (FYROM) and the progressive elimination of Slovenia from the autonomous trade regime after a co-operation agreement was signed with Slovenia on 5 Apr. 1993 [1993] OJ L189/1.

[64] See the last preambular para. of Reg. 70/97, note 63 above (emphasis added); Council Reg. 825/97 of 29 Apr. 1997 [1997] OJ L119/4, which extended the benefits of Reg. 70/97 to the FRY for part of 1997, constitutes the first example of an interim modification of the Reg.'s geographical coverage.

[65] Council Conclusions on the principle of Conditionality governing the development of the EU's relations with certain countries of south-east Europe, adopted on 29 Apr. 1997, *Bull. EU* 4–1997, points 1.4.67 (commentary) and 2.2.1 (full text).

The underlying human rights standard, which is contained in an Annex to the Council Conclusions, may be qualified as 'hybrid'. For example, the concept of 'human rights [and] rule of law' (which would generally be considered as belonging to 'civil and political rights') encompasses matters such as the 'right of assembly and demonstration', the 'right of association', the 'right to privacy', and even the 'right to property' (some of which have elements of 'economic, social, and cultural rights'). In the same vein, the concept of 'minority rights' not only comprises the cultural rights of minorities (the 'right to establish and maintain their own educational, cultural and religious institutions, organizations, or associations'), but also the protection of refugees and displaced persons. In the authors' view, this corresponds not only to a certain amount of pragmatism on the Community's part (retaining those rights most endangered on the ground rather than drawing dogmatic distinctions), but also serves as an example to the interrelatedness and indivisibility of the Community's human rights approach.[66]

Compliance is supervised by the Commission by means of bi-annual 'conditionality reports' (and legislative proposals based on these reports), while the Council remains in charge of drawing the political conclusions and possibly adopting the legislative proposals stemming therefrom. As regards the renewal (or withdrawal) of trade preferences, the legal base is Article 133 (*ex* Article 113) of the EC Treaty (in line with the legal base retained for Regulation 70/97 and its predecessors since Regulation 1433/92),[67] which means qualified majority in Council and no formal consultation of the European Parliament. Extension (or withdrawal) of economic and technical/financial co-operation is subject to the voting requirements governing the pertinent technical assistance regulations.[68] Finally, the legal basis to be retained for the conclusion of a Community agreement obviously depends on the subjects covered therein. The voting requirements will thus vary, in line with the extent of co-operation envisaged.[69]

The practical application of conditionality can best be evidenced by the Community's recent practice. When, in December 1997, the Council decided to extend the application of the trade preferences of Regulation 70/97 for 1998,[70] this extension was

[66] Cf. part II above, text to notes 46–7. See also Brandtner and Rosas, note 7 above, at section 3.2.

[67] Cf. notes 60 and 63 above.

[68] See in particular, Council Reg. 3906/89 of 18 Dec. 1989 concerning economic assistance to the Republic of Hungary and the Republic of Poland (PHARE) [1989] OJ L375/11, as last amended by Reg. 753/96 of 22 Apr. 1996 [1996] OJ L103/5, and Council Reg. 1628/96 of 25 July 1996 relating to aid for Bosnia and Herzegovina, Croatia, the Federal Republic of Yugoslavia, and the former Yugoslav Republic of Macedonia (OBNOVA) [1996] OJ L204/1, as last amended by Reg. 851/98 of 20 Apr. 1998 [1998] OJ L122/1. Both PHARE and OBNOVA are based on Art. 308 (*ex* Art. 235) of the EC Treaty, which means unanimity in Council and (simple) consultation of the Parliament. For an analysis of the PHARE Reg. from a human rights perspective, see Brandtner and Rosas, note 7 above, at section 2.4. OBNOVA, for its part, contains a 'human rights clause' in Art. 2, which even explicitly refers to the Council's conditionality criteria.

[69] e.g. the recent co-operation agreement with FYROM (note 72 below) has been concluded on the basis of Arts. 113 (now Art. 133) and 308 (*ex* Art. 235) of the EC Treaty. However, due to its financial implications and since it creates joint institutions, the conclusion of this Agreement has required the Parliament's assent (Art. 300(3), second subpara. (*ex* Art, 228) of the EC Treaty). By contrast, the slightly older Trade and Economic Co-operation Agreement between the EC and Albania [1992] OJ L343/1), while also based on Arts. 133 and 308, only required the Parliament's consultation.

[70] Council Reg. 2536/97 of 29 Dec. 1997 [1997] OJ L356/16.

based on the Commission's first report on compliance with the conditionality criteria, in which the Commission noted a general lack of improvement in the FRY's
human rights performance, in particular as regards 'a credible commitment to
democratic reform' and 'compliance with *generally recognized standards of human
and minority rights*'.[71] Regulation 2636/97 thus applies to imports from Bosnia-
Herzegovina and Croatia and to imports of wine from FYROM[72] and Slovenia. The
FRY has been excluded from the preferential regime because of a significant lack of
performance as regards conditionality.[73] This seems to correspond to the EC's overall tendency to limit recourse to the 'stick' to *serious* human rights violations.[74]

The Commission's (second) conditionality report of 15 April 1998 which highlighted severe deficiencies in Croatia's performance as regards 'the *fundamental principles of human and minority rights*' and 'democratic procedures',[75] was followed by
a rather harsh assessment of this country's deteriorating human rights performance
by the General Affairs Council (GAC) of 27 April 1998. The matter almost 'exploded' once since then, Croatia having failed to produce a long-awaited reconstruction programme concerning in particular refugee return. In its Conclusions of
25 May 1998, the GAC therefore recalled its Conclusions of 27 April and even invited the Commission to submit a proposal, possibly aiming at Croatia's withdrawal
from the autonomous trade measures, for the 29 June GAC.[76] Croatia produced the
programme at the very last minute. The GAC of 29 June 1998 therefore reversed its
approach and indicated that the Community would even be disposed to participate
in a Croatian Reconstruction Conference, should the implementation of the global
refugee programme meet its expectations.[77] The 'stick' (or, at least, the threat of the
'stick') having apparently worked, the Council could thus resume offering 'carrots'.
This was confirmed in October 1998 when the Council decided, on the basis of the
(third) conditionality report,[78] not to withdraw the Community's autonomous trade
preference from Croatia.

IV. THE GSP SYSTEM

The third example to be analysed in the context of this chapter concerns the Community's unilateral scheme of generalized tariff preferences (the 'GSP'), as currently
laid down in Regulations 3281/94 and 1256/96 in respect of certain industrial and

---

[71] This report was transmitted to the General Affairs Council of 6 Oct. 1997 as a Commission Services
Paper (emphasis added).
[72] FYROM's remaining products are covered by a new co-operation agreement which entered into
force on 1 Jan. 1998 [1997] OJ L348/1.
[73] This motivation was spelled out in the penultimate preambular para. of the Commission's proposal,
cf COM(97)637 final. It has however not been included in the Reg.'s final version.
[74] Cf. part II above, text to notes 42–4.   [75] COM(98)237 final, at 3.
[76] *Agence Europe*, 27 May 1998, at 4.
[77] *Agence Europe*, 1 July 1998, at 4. By 29 June, the Commission's proposal was in fact ready, and it
would have been formally presented to the Council during this very session of the GAC. Croatia was apparently fully aware thereof: the 'good news' of the Croatian Parliament's approval of the refugee programme thus literally 'hit' the Commission a (working) day before the GAC.
[78] COM(98)618 final of 28 Oct. 1998.

agricultural products originating in developing countries.[79] This concerns human rights—and more precisely, fundamental workers' rights—'conditionality' provided in *unilateral* (autonomous) Community instruments. In this realm, the Community has recently moved from a 'carrot and stick' to a 'more carrots' approach.

As regards the GSP's WTO dimension, any such scheme necessarily conflicts with the MFN requirement laid down in Article I of GATT, since it grants *unilateral* trade preferences to a certain number of countries qualified as 'developing countries', without extending the same benefits to all other WTO Members.[80] This is also the reason why, inspired by work done in the context of the first (1964) United Nations Conference on Trade and Development (UNCTAD I), the GATT Contracting Parties decided in 1971 to grant a 'waiver' to all 'industrialized' countries, enabling them to establish their own GSP system, as long as this benefited all 'developing countries'.[81] However, this original waiver was restricted to a ten-year period. In 1979, during the Tokyo Round negotiations, the Parties therefore adopted a new Decision, the so-called 'enabling clause', basically aimed at prolonging the effects of the 1971 waiver.[82]

These Decisions have been carried over into the WTO as part of the GATT 1994.[83] They are therefore still applicable today, even though the Uruguay Round negotiations have resulted in the introduction of numerous specific 'developing country' preferences in the WTO's various instruments. Whether these Decisions, and in particular the 'enabling clause', could cover so-called 'graduation' mechanisms remains debatable. However, the Community is certainly not the only entity practising 'graduation' in the sense in which this will now be described. The USA may well have 'pioneered' this particular course of action.[84] In any event, to the authors' knowledge, no challenge of (any form of) 'graduation' has ever been brought before the GATT or WTO.

---

[79] Council Reg. 3281/94 of 19 Dec. 1994 applying a four-year scheme of generalized tariff preferences (1995 to 1998) in respect of certain industrial products originating in developing countries [1994] OJ L348/1, as last amended by Council Reg. 2623/97 of 19 Dec. 1997 [1997] OJ L354/9; Council Reg. 1256/96 of 20 June 1996 applying multiannual schemes of generalized tariff preferences from 1 July 1996 to 30 June 1999 in respect of certain agricultural products originating in developing countries [1997] OJ L160/1, as last amended by Council Reg. 2623/97 of 19 Dec. 1997 [1997] OJ L354/9.

[80] Cf. part II, text to notes 23–6 and 29–33. See also Jackson, note 24 above, at 322–4.

[81] *Generalized System of Preferences*, Decision of 25 June 1971 L/3545 of 28 June 1971; GATT, BISD 18 Supp. 24 (1972).

[82] *Differential and More Favourable Treatment, Reciprocity and Fuller Participation of Developing Countries*, Decision of 28 Nov. 1979, L/4903 of 3 Dec. 1979; GATT, BISD 26 Supp. 203 (1980); as regards the classification of this 'Decision' as a 'Declaration' and a more differentiated analysis than is possible in the context of the present chap., see Jackson, note 24 above, at 323–4; see also J. Jackson, W. Davey, and A. Sykes, *Legal Problems of International Economic Relations* (3rd edn., 1995), chap. 24.

[83] See the General Agreement on Tariffs and Trade 1994 (GATT), included in Annex I.A of the Marrakesh Agreement establishing the WTO (1994).

[84] By 'graduation', one commonly understands measures aimed at differentiating between developing countries according to their respective levels of development, with the aim of progressively eliminating those countries which have reached a certain (objectively quantifiable) level, to the benefit of 'less developed countries'. The last amendment to the Community's GSP (note 79 above), which withdrew Hong Kong, Singapore, and South Korea from the Community scheme, is a pertinent example of this 'classical' form of graduation. This is also the reason it is uncertain whether the temporary withdrawal of GSP preferences or the 'special incentive arrangements' belong to 'graduation'. However, see Jackson, note 24 above, at 324–5, in particular as regards the US' GSP system.

A. Temporary Withdrawal of Trade Preferences—the 'Carrot and the Stick'

By virtue of Article 9 of the GSP Regulations, benefits granted to a particular country may be temporarily withdrawn, in whole or in part, if the country is found to export any goods made by prison labour or to practise any form of forced labour, as this term is defined in the Geneva Conventions on slavery of 1926 and 1956[85] and ILO Conventions 29 and 105 relating to forced labour.[86] While the reference to 'goods made by prison labour' is inspired by Article XX(e) GATT,[87] the reference to forced labour (and slavery) as a ground for suspension is more of a human rights clause *per se*. The prohibitions of slavery and forced labour are in fact examples of fundamental human rights (perhaps of *ius cogens* character),[88] which transcend the distinction between civil and political and economic, social, and cultural rights.

Temporary withdrawal of tariff preferences is not automatic, however. In fact, before withdrawing any part of the GSP, the Community must follow a detailed (and according to some, quite cumbersome) procedure.

According to Article 10 of the Regulations, complaints concerning the circumstances referred to in Article 9 may originate not only from Member States, but also from 'any natural or legal persons, or associations not endowed with legal personality' if they can show an interest in the withdrawal. If the Commission finds, following consultations in the GSP Committee, that there is sufficient evidence to initiate an investigation, this fact is announced in the Official Journal of the European Communities and a period set during which interested parties may communicate their views in writing, and ask to be heard if they are likely to be affected by the proceedings' outcome (Article 11).

While private actors thus have a right of initiative as regards investigations under the GSP, and while they may submit written evidence and 'plead their case' in an oral hearing, the Commission has a margin of appreciation as regards the 'interest' of the actors concerned. It also decides whether or not to initiate an investigation, whether to terminate the investigation, or to propose the temporary withdrawal of tariff concessions. Nevertheless, the final responsibility for any withdrawal lies with the Council, acting by qualified majority (Article 12(3) of the GSP Regulations).

The first (and thus far, only) successful application of this procedure happened during the course of 1996, when, on 16 January, the Commission initiated an investigation against the *Union of Myanmar (Burma)* for alleged use of forced labour.[89] This was based on a joint complaint by two Trades Union Confederations (made in June 1995), which originally concerned only the industrial GSP.

---

[85] Slavery Convention, signed at Geneva on 25 Sept. 1926, and Supplementary Convention on the Abolition of Slavery, the Slave Trade, and Institutions and Practices Similar to Slavery, adopted on 7 Sept. 1956, reprinted in *International Instruments*, note 10 above, at 201 and 209.

[86] Forced Labour Convention No. 29 and Abolition of Forced Labour Convention No. 105 of 1957, in ILO, *International Labour Conventions and Recommendations 1919–1991* (1992), ii, 115 and 618.

[87] See part II above, text to note 34.

[88] See generally L. Hannikainen, *Peremptory Norms (Jus Cogens) in International Law: Historical Development, Criteria, Present Status* (1988), 425–520.

[89] Notice of initiation of an investigation of forced labour practices being carried out in Myanmar in view of a temporary withdrawal of benefits under the GSP, Notice No 96/C15/03 [1996] OJ C15/3.

During the investigation, the Commission collected written and oral statements, in consultation with the GSP Committee, and even attempted to conduct an 'on-site inspection', which was however refused by Burma. Having thus found, on the basis of the facts available,[90] that the condemned practices were 'routine and widespread', the Commission on 19 December 1996 proposed the temporary withdrawal of all industrial tariff concessions.[91] This finding was apparently based on the understanding that preferences can be suspended under the GSP if the country concerned is found to practise forced labour, regardless of whether or not the products exported have been produced by such labour.

On 2 January 1997, the Trades Union Confederations notified the Commission that they were extending the scope of their complaint to the agricultural GSP. The Commission considered that the evidence gathered under the initial investigation and the resulting conclusions were 'broad enough in scope to provide a valid basis for examining the extended complaint', thus 'rendering a specific investigation of the agricultural sector unnecessary'. On 17 February 1997, the Commission therefore also proposed the temporary withdrawal of Myanmar from the agricultural GSP.[92]

All concessions were finally suspended on 24 March 1997 *uno actu* by means of a Council Regulation.[93] Even though the Regulation's legal base is Article 12.3 of the GSP Regulations, both the European Parliament and the Economic and Social Committee were consulted before its adoption, in line with the Commission's proposals, although this is not foreseen in Article 12.3. Apart from conforming to the procedure originally retained for adopting the GSP Regulations, this may well reflect the strong interest expressed by the Parliament in the opening and conduct of the investigation.[94]

The Parliament's Resolutions and debates on Myanmar reveal another interesting feature. Around the same time, the same Trades Union Confederations had launched a complaint against *Pakistan* for the use of forced child labour.[95] Appar-

[90] A possibility expressly foreseen in Art. 11(5) of the GSP Regulations if 'information requested by the Commission is not provided within a reasonable period or the investigation is significantly impeded'.

[91] COM(96)0711 final [1997] OJ C35/14.

[92] See COM(97)0058 final [1997] OJ C80/18, and in particular its 2nd and 3rd preambular paras.

[93] Council Reg. 552/97 of 24 Mar. 1997 temporarily withdrawing access to generalized tariff preferences from the Union of Myanmar [1997] OJ L85/8.

[94] See the Parliament's Resolution on the application of social clauses within the framework of the multiannual programme for generalized tariff preferences *inter alia* with respect to Pakistan and Myanmar (Burma), adopted on 14 Dec. 1995 [1996] OJ C17/201 (in which it asked the Commission to clarify the procedures applying to such complaints and to be notified of any action taken during the various stages of the procedure, and even requested the Commission to proceed immediately to the 'second stage', the investigation proper); see also the Resolution on human rights violations in Burma (Myanmar), adopted on 23 May 1996 [1998] OJ C166/201 (where the Parliament welcomed the opening of the Commission's investigation, 'with a view to possible suspension of GSP privileges').

[95] This is apparent from the Parliament's Resolution of 14 Dec. 1995, note 94 above, in particular from preambular paras. B and C and point 4 of the Resolution (where the Parliament asked for the immediate opening of an investigation against Pakistan). However, a number of written questions put to the Commission by MEPs in late 1996 and early 1997 suggest that this request may not have been uncontroversial; see in particular Written Question 1728/96 by Ms. Larive MEP (European Liberal Democrat and Reform Party (ELDR)) of 3 July 1996 on 'child labour' and the Commission's answer of 22 July 1996]1996] OJ C305/122, where the MEP asks whether a 'simple ban on this practice 'the use of child labour in Pakistan's football industry] would have a disastrous effect on the children concerned'; see also Written Questions 2468/96 of 23 Sept. 1996 by Ms. Maij-Weggen MEP (European People's Party (PPE)) on 'support for the ILO's IPEC' and the Commission's answer of 21 Nov. 1996 [1997] OJ C91/6; and 3404/96 of 5 Dec. 1996

ently, this complaint never proceeded beyond its 'first stage' (the Commission's assessment, following consultations inside the GSP committee, whether there is sufficient evidence to justify the initiation of an investigation), probably because the Commission reached the conclusion that a ban on imports was not the best way of addressing the problem. At the request of the government of Pakistan, and in collaboration with the ILO and UNICEF, the Commission therefore decided actively to support projects in Pakistan under the ILO's international programme for the eradication of child labour (IPEC).[96]

The 'first stage' of the Pakistan proceedings continued well into 1997. This may have enabled the Commission to elaborate a new approach to the question. In fact, the Commission preferred 'a policy of encouraging compliance with social standards through *incentives* rather than coercive measures'.[97] In addition, Pakistan had introduced legislation to outlaw child labour, and it kept the Commission regularly informed of its authorities' efforts to implement this legislation. For the Commission, it was therefore enough 'to follow developments closely, without moving on to the second stage of the procedure'.[98] The following Commission statement may sum up its thinking on the matter:

> The overriding objective of the procedure, during which contacts are established with the authorities of the countries concerned, is *to bring about progress on the ground* by encouraging the countries concerned to pursue a qualitative social development, a process the Community backs up with complementary schemes. Preferences are *withdrawn as a last resort*, if the first two stages have come to nothing.[99]

From a human rights perspective, the distinction drawn by the Community in its treatment of Myanmar and Pakistan may well be questioned. After all, is 'forced (adult) labour' more serious than 'forced child labour'? Probably, the answer to this question lies in the merits of each particular case. According to the results of the Commission's investigation, there was 'forced labour' in Myanmar, and its use was 'routine and widespread'. The Community may thus have reacted to what it considered as a *serious* human rights violation.[100]

As regards Pakistan, however, and while the use of child labour may always be considered as 'serious', the case was not so unequivocal. Child labour as such is not mentioned in Article 9 of the GSP Regulations and the international rules on the subject are less than clear.[101] Finally, the Commission soon realized that the only

---

by Mr. Fernàndez-Albor MEP (PPE) on the 'ILO programme to combat child labour in Latin America' and the Commission's answer of 21 Jan. 1997 [1997] OJ C105/71.

[96] See the Commission's answers to Written Questions 1728/96, 2468/96 and 3404/96, note 95 above.

[97] Commission's answer of 6 June 1997 to Written Question 1491/97 of 30 Apr. 1997 by Mr. Robles-Piquer MEP (PPE) on 'alleged crimes of a multinational' [1998] OJ C45/41.

[98] Commission's answer of 20 June 1997 to Written Question 1590/97 of 6 May 1997 by Mr. Kaklamanis MEP (Union for Europe (UPE)) on 'violation of human dignity by Pakistan' [1998] OJ C45/56; Commission's answer of 18 July 1997 to Written Question 2368/97 of 1 July 1997 by Mr. Holm MEP (Green Group (V)) on the 'generalized system of preferences'; [1998] OJ C21/148.

[99] Answer to Written Question 2368/97, note 98 above (emphasis added).

[100] Cf. part II above, text to notes 42–4.

[101] See e.g. the Commission's Communication to the Council on Trade and Internationally Recognized Labour Standards, COM(96)402 final, at 13. This is also the reason the ILO has started work on a new convention, which would clarify what exactly constitutes illegal exploitation of child labour.

immediate consequence of an eventual withdrawal of tariff preferences would be the children's lay-off. From a development perspective, this was not, and could not be, in the Community's interest. The Community's 'differential' treatment of Pakistan seems therefore justifiable both from a development and from a human rights perspective. The factual situation was not clear-cut enough to warrant the use of the 'stick', at least not at this stage.

B. 'More Carrots'—the Special Incentive Arrangements

The development of the Commission's thinking, as evidenced in the case of Pakistan, did not come totally unexpectedly. In fact, as early as 1994, at the time of presenting its orientations for the future 'decennial'[102] GSP, the Commission advocated the introduction of certain social and environmental incentives—in a *'sustainable development'* perspective.[103] As a result, Article 7 of the GSP Regulations (as originally adopted) already provided for the establishment, by January 1998, of a system of additional preferences, the so-called 'special incentive arrangements', to be granted to countries honouring the standards laid down in ILO Conventions 87 and 98 concerning freedom of association and protection of the right to organize and to bargain collectively and Convention 138 concerning the minimum age for admission to employment.[104]

The standards retained concern workers' and trades union rights, which again transcend the dichotomy between civil and political rights on the one hand and economic and social rights on the other. The core ILO Conventions referred to in the GSP's 'special incentive arrangements' contain elements of both civil rights and freedoms (such as the freedom of association) and economic and social rights (such as the right to bargain collectively).

At the Community level, the GSP is the first instrument to contain a social incentive clause with concrete potential benefits. However, its implementation proved slightly more complex (and lengthy) than expected. The procedure's first step was completed on schedule, the Commission having sent, on 2 June 1997, a report to the Council on the results of studies carried out in international fora such as the ILO, the WTO, and the OECD on the relationship between trade and labour rights.[105] On 30 October 1997, the Commission tabled its proposal for a Council Regulation implementing Articles 7 and 8 of the two Regulations,[106] but it took the Council until the

---

[102] The Community's GSP is strategically conceived in 'decades'. Its implementation is reduced, however, in line with the Community's (quadrennial) budget perspectives.

[103] Cf. the Commission's Communication to the Council and the European Parliament, Integration of Developing Countries in the International Trading System—Role of the GSP 1995–2004 COM(94)212 final, at 10ff. Conscious of the strictures imposed by the WTO 'waiver' and 'enabling clause' (part IV above, text to notes 80–4), the Commission considered that the future incentive arrangements had to be voluntary and additional to the preferences 'normally' granted. These arrangements were thus clearly intended as an instrument of development co-operation. Social progress and environmental protection were considered as 'components' of sustainable development, and not as its 'precondition'.

[104] Similar 'special incentive arrangements' were also foreseen, and have meanwhile been implemented, with respect to countries ready to honour 'the substance of the standards laid down by the ITTO (International Tropical Timber Organization) relating to the sustainable management of forests' (cf. Art. 8 of the GSP Regs.). This aspect is not further elaborated upon in the context of this chap.

[105] COM(97)260 final.   [106] COM(97)534 final [1997] OJ C360/9.

end of May 1998 finally to approve this Regulation.[107] Among others, its adoption had been overshadowed by a serious controversy over general management short-comings in preferential tariff regimes.[108]

The additional preferences, which were introduced by the Incentives Regulation, are quite impressive in size.[109] Moreover, they may be granted to certain sectors, and not only to entire countries, which may increase their practicability.[110] However, because of the very cumbersome procedures that were laid down for their granting and monitoring, it seems improbable that the 'special incentive arrangements' will become popular in the near future.

According to Article 3 of the Incentives Regulation,[111] special incentive arrangements may only be granted upon written request by the authorities of a beneficiary country, which must contain, in particular: (a) their domestic legislation *already incorporating* the substance of the abovementioned ILO Conventions, including its full text (and authentic translation into a Community language); (b) details of measures *already taken* to implement and monitor the application of this legislation, including sectoral limits, breaches observed, and a breakdown of such breaches by production sector; and (c) a commitment to take *full responsibility* for monitoring the application of this regime, including all administrative procedures.

Upon receipt of such a request, the Commission must publish a notice in the Official Journal, inviting the interested parties (natural or legal persons) to provide any useful information and setting a period during which they may submit observations (Article 3(2)). The Commission has in principle one year within which to complete the investigation (by putting further questions to the country concerned, seeking additional information from the interested persons, and conducting on-the-spot

[107] Council Reg. 1154/98 of 25 May 1998 applying the special incentive arrangements concerning labour rights and environmental protection provided for in Arts. 7 and 8 of Regs. 3281/94 and 1256/96 applying multiannual schemes of generalized tariff preferences in respect of certain industrial and agricultural products originating in developing countries, [1998] OJ L160/1 (hereinafter referred to as 'the Incentives Reg.').

[108] Before proposing the Incentives Reg., the Commission had transmitted to the Council a Communication on the Management of Preferential Tariff Arrangements COM(97)402 final, in which it analysed the difficulties of the Community's numerous preferential regimes (high diversity, lack of transparency, serious risk of customs fraud, in particular as regards origin certificates) and laid the responsibility for this state of affairs, among others, on those Community importers benefiting from fraudulent use of these regimes and on national customs authorities overwhelmed by their number and complexity. This provoked a strong reaction from Member States, since some of them believed that 'simplification' would lie in exonerating Community importers from their responsibilities. (Importers are free to choose preferential import regimes; therefore, they are also fully responsible for the accuracy, veracity, and authenticity of the documentation presented to national customs, in particular as regards origin certificates). This debate is reflected, *inter alia*, in recital 10 and Art. 7 of the Incentives Reg. However, an in-depth analysis of this problem would exceed the scope of this chap.

[109] Cf. Art. 2 of the Incentives Reg. As indicated in recital 11 to this Reg., the various percentages amount to doubling the preferential margin for industrial products, increasing the preferential margin for agricultural products by two thirds, and granting specific preferential margins to industrial and agricultural sectors subject to 'graduation'. However, countries excluded from the GSP because of their advanced level of development (cf. Art. 6 of the GSP Regs.) and countries/sectors whose exports to the Community exceed 25% of all GSP-exports in the same sector (cf. Art. 5(1) of the GSP Regs.) are not entitled to the special incentive arrangements. On 'graduation', cf. note 84 above.

[110] Cf. Art. 5(2) of the Incentives Reg. This point seems very important from a development perspective. In fact, if preferences could only be granted once a given country fulfilled all criteria, no developing country would ever become eligible, or at least, become eligible before being 'too developed' for the GSP.

[111] Which, in this context, expands upon the general rules already foreseen in Art. 7 of the GSP Regs.

checks) and submit its findings to the GSP Committee (Article 4). Once the Committee has voted by qualified majority, the Commission may decide to grant the special incentive arrangements either to the entire country, or to certain sectors, or not to grant them at all.[112] The requesting country must be notified of this decision. Where the request is rejected in whole or in part, the decision must also be reasoned. The ensuing 'dialogue' with the requesting country is to be carried out 'in close co-ordination' with the GSP Committee (Article 5(3) and (4)).

From the date of entry into force of a positive decision, products originating in the country (or sector) concerned will be eligible for the additional tariff reductions. However, this is subject to production of a statement, made by the authorities 'duly identified during the examination of the request' and certifying that the products concerned '*and their components* manufactured in that country or in a country entitled to regional cumulation' have been manufactured in compliance with the domestic legislation incorporating the relevant social standards.[113]

Moreover, the Commission must establish a non-exhaustive list of criteria specifying cases of 'reasonable doubt', to be published in the Official Journal, as well as notices containing details of the 'products, producers, and exporters' concerned or cases whose lack of qualification as 'a particular product from particular producers and exporters' has already been established. Community importers do not incur customs debt until after the notice is published and unless the debt concerns a 'product, producer and exporter specifically mentioned therein'.[114]

The special incentive arrangements may also be temporarily withdrawn, in whole or in part, if there is 'sufficient evidence' that the country concerned has not fulfilled its obligations (legislation, implementation, and administrative co-operation). This is without prejudice to a possible application of Article 9 of the GSP Regulations (see above, section IV, A). However, in contrast to the latter, the temporary withdrawal of special incentive arrangements seems not to be subject to any specific procedure.[115]

Where does this leave the 'special incentive arrangements'? It is certainly too early to pass judgement on the Incentives Regulation. What may safely be said, however,

[112] Cf. Arts. 5(1) and (2) and 16 of the Incentives Reg. Should the Committee reject the Commission's proposal, this is then submitted to the Council, which has a further three months in which to adopt or reject the Commission's proposal. If the Council fails to act within this period, the measure is approved by the Commission (a normal 'comitology', type 3A, procedure; the question whether to replace this with the even more cumbersome, type 3B, procedure, also proved very controversial).

[113] Cf. Art. 6 of the Incentives Reg. The cited passages, which were introduced by the Council in the Commission's original proposal, reflect the 'customs controversy' referred to in note 108 above. They will certainly not ease the arrangements' application, since they demote certification from the 'product' level to the level of 'components', and from (normal) origin certification to the verification of 'regional cumulation'.

[114] Here again, cf. note 108 above. In this context, 'reasonable doubt' principally means doubts concerning the authenticity, veracity, and accuracy of the origin—and 'incentives'—certification. What this boils down to is a clear shift in the burden of proof from the Community importers to the national customs authorities and the Commission, with the effect that a Community importer cannot be held liable for customs fraud (apparently even if fully aware of it) unless and until the competent authorities have completed their investigation.

[115] Cf. Art. 15 of the Incentives Reg. In fact, the only procedure referred to in this context is the normal 'comitology' procedure (note 112 above). However, in the absence of a complaints (and investigation) procedure, it is difficult to imagine how the necessary evidence could be obtained.

is that its procedural subtleties risk making it a very cumbersome tool for the purposes of fostering compliance with fundamental social standards (or, even, for a gradual improvement of the beneficiary countries' social rights performance). It is difficult to avoid the conclusion that a country advanced enough to understand all the rules will probably no longer benefit (nor, indeed, need to benefit) from the 'special incentive arrangements', and possibly not even from the GSP. Nevertheless, and even though this is not mentioned in the Incentives Regulation, its shortcomings may in time be overcome through intelligent use of the good old tools of 'classical' development co-operation.[116]

V. CONCLUSION

The link between trade preferences and human rights is here to stay. This does not mean that this link will be free from difficulty. Limiting trade may have unfavourable implications for the interests of traders (who may also be stakeholders in a human rights discourse) or for the situation of the affected population (and its economic and social rights).

As the above discussion has shown, trade benefits are more likely to be suspended by the Community (the 'stick') if they have been granted unilaterally, if they are based on unilateral rather than bilateral instruments, and if they go beyond obligations stemming from the WTO. Suspending bilateral agreements may pose a number of problems, including the possible reaction (retaliation) of the other party and the procedural difficulties of suspending mixed agreements. However, limiting suspension to trade in goods may enable the Community to proceed on the basis of Article 133 of the EC Treaty (exclusive Community competence), and thus trigger qualified majority voting in Council.

The above discussion also shows that the 'stick', whether used in the context of bilateral agreements (ex-Yugoslavia in 1991) or in the context of unilateral acts (Myanmar in 1996), is more likely to be resorted to if fundamental rights and values are at stake—and if there has been a *serious* human rights violation. However, the combination of 'sticks and carrots' (*'conditionality'* in ex-Yugoslavia) and emphasis on 'more carrots' (the *'special incentive arrangements'* in the context of the GSP) make it easier to bring in a wider range of human rights. While it is sometimes taken for granted that the sole focus is on civil and political rights, a closer analysis reveals that any dichotomy between 'categories of human rights' should be avoided, an observation which is particularly pertinent with respect to labour and trade union rights.

While Article 133 of the EC Treaty offers a fairly flexible procedural framework for Community action in this area, additional procedural hurdles have been set up,

---

[116] Note that this seems to leave the Community with exactly the same tools as already used in the case of Pakistan (cf. part IV, A, above). This being said, however, should the IPEC programme be successful, Pakistan (or at least, some sectors of its economy) might one day qualify for special incentive arrangements.

especially in the GSP context. The WTO dimension provides further restraints, particularly between WTO members and as regards trade concessions covered by the WTO. Nevertheless, it is the authors' impression that the substantive and procedural limitations inherent in its 'sticks' will not prevent the Community from using trade *sanctions for human rights goals*. The 'stick' will certainly not be in daily use, however. While trade sanctions may sometimes fulfil an important symbolic function and may be reasonably effective (as the prospect of economic loss does have a dissuasive effect), they should not be resorted to lightly. Resorting to 'carrots' may well prove to be a more attractive way of 'forcing people to be free'.[117]

[117] J.J. Rousseau, *The Social Contract* (1762), bk. 1, chap. 7.

22

Human Rights Clauses in External Agreements of the EC

EIBE RIEDEL AND MARTIN WILL

I. SUSPENSION AND TERMINATION OF TREATIES UNDER GENERAL INTERNATIONAL LAW

The unsatisfactory situation with regard to suspending or terminating agreements between the European Communities (EC) and third States or groups of third States in the event of grave human rights breaches was one of the main reasons human rights clauses became incorporated in such agreements from Lomé IV (1989) onwards. Massive human rights violations in States like Uganda or Equatorial Guinea immediately after Lomé I had come into force on 1 April 1976 had underlined the moral and legal dilemma of the EC: They had increasingly found themselves facing payment obligations arising from treaties *vis-à-vis* regimes perpetrating human rights violations.[1] The fact that payments, such as the payment of seven million ECU to the Idi Amin regime out of STABEX funds were not halted altogether, despite such violations, had its root-cause not least in the limited possibilities for reaction which general international law offered.[2]

A. Termination and Suspension of Treaties under the Vienna Convention on the Law of Treaties (VCLT) of 1969

The VCLT of 23 May 1969[3], Articles 54 ff, contains detailed rules for the termination and suspension of treaties. Technically, the EC are signatories neither to the VCLT (open for ratification only by States according to Article 83 in conjunction with Article 81 VCLT) nor to the Vienna Convention on the Law of Treaties between States and International Organizations or between International Organizations. That means that these treaties are not directly binding for the EC under Article 300(7) (*ex*

---

[1] Cf. G. Oestreich, *Menschenrechte als Elemente der dritten AKP-EWG-Konvention von Lomé* (1990), 45ff.; K. Arts, 'European Community Development Cooperation, Human Rights, Democracy and Good Governance: at Odds or at Ease with Each Other?', in, K. Ginther, E. Denters, and P. de Waart (eds.), *Sustainable Development and Good Governance* (1995), 267ff.

[2] Cf. the Commission's statement answering Written Question 943/77 from a MEP in [1978] OJ C74/17ff.

[3] 1155 UNTS 331.

Article 288(7)) of the EC Treaty (EC)[4]. However, as subjects of international law the EC are bound by the provisions of the VCLT and the second treaty just mentioned, in that the provisions of those conventions, except for some rare points, have by now become part of general customary international law, and as such are binding on States and international organizations, even without specific treaty ratification.[5]

1. Termination and Suspension Resulting from a Breach of an Essential Treaty Provision   Articles 54(a) and 57(a) VCLT start by stating the obvious, namely that termination and suspension of a treaty are possible following the relevant treaty provisions. In addition, suspension or termination is possible under Article 60(1) and (2) VCLT in cases of material breaches of a treaty. Such material breaches may consist, for example, in the violation of a provision essential to the accomplishment of the object or purpose of the treaty (Article 60(3)(b) VCLT). This means that treaty suspension or termination on account of human rights violations is justified only if such possibilities arise either under specific treaty provisions, or if respect for human rights may be regarded as an essential element of the object and purpose of the treaty as such.[6]

Even though the external treaties of the EC until Lomé IV (1989) increasingly contained passages about the importance of human rights in the preambular phrases or in general clauses, respect for human rights nevertheless did not form part of the operative components of those treaties regarded as fundamental and essential for the achievement of the object and purpose of the treaty in question. Thus, suspension or termination of treaty obligations on account of human rights violations was effectively excluded.[7]

2. Termination on Account of Subsequent Impossibility of Performance or Fundamental Change of Circumstances   In many cases where the EC considered suspending treaty obligations, the party concerned found itself in a state of turmoil, emergency, or even civil war or secession. In such situations it was—depending on the specific circumstances of the individual conflict—possible to consider termination or suspension of the relevant treaties on grounds of subsequent impossibility of treaty fulfilment or on the grounds of a fundamental change of circumstances (*clausula rebus sic stantibus*).

There is plenty of factual evidence for the EC to have suspended treaty obligations *vis-à-vis* third States due to the impossibility of treaty performance. It is obvious that in times of civil war or other major crises projects geared to improve infrastructure cannot be continued. Nor can co-operation be maintained if the government in question no longer exercises effective control. Article 61(1) VCLT clearly elaborates

---

[4]   La Pergola AG fails to notice this in Case C–268/94, *Portugal* v. *Council* [1996] ECR I–6177, at 6191; the Court more carefully speaks in the same case not of Art. 60 VCLT, but more generally of a suspension or termination under international law.

[5]   Concerning the binding force of customary international law for the Community cf. e.g. Case C–286/90, *Anklagemyndigheden* v. *Poulsen und Diva Navigation Corp.* [1992] ECR I–6019, at 6053; K. Lenaerts and E. de Smijter, 'The European Community's Treaty-Making Competence' (1996) 16 *YEL* 46.

[6]   Cf. the final pleadings of La Pergola AG in Case C–268/94, *Portuguese Republic* [1996] ECR I–6177, at 6191; Lenaerts and De Smijter, note 5 above, at 46.

[7]   Oestreich, note 1 above, at 465ff.

the general principle of 'impossibility of performance' in such a way that a temporary impossibility of treaty performance allows for the suspension of treaty obligations, while treaty termination is only permissible if the impossibility follows from the permanent disappearance or destruction of an object indispensable to the execution of the treaty.

Likewise, a fundamental change of circumstances under Article 62(1) VCLT may only be invoked as a reason for suspension or termination of a treaty if such circumstances constituted an essential basis for the consent of both parties in the first place and, furthermore, if such changed circumstances would radically transform the extent of obligations still to be performed under the treaty. The International Court of Justice (ICJ) has emphasized this by stating that Article 62 in many ways could be regarded as codifying existing customary international law.[8] Even though Article 62(1) VCLT thus has to be interpreted narrowly, it has been relied upon by the EC Council and Commission in a case under Article 177 (now 234) EC still pending, regarding the suspension of the co-operation treaty with the Socialist Federalist Republic of Yugoslavia of 1991.[9] Both EC organs argued that suspending the treaty implementation by way of decisions of the Council and of the 'Representatives of the Governments of the Member States meeting within the Council' of 11 November 1991 rested on the *clausula rebus sic stantibus* exception.[10] Advocate-General Jacobs more or less accepted this line of argument in his final opinion of 4 December 1997;[11] at the time of treaty suspension there was a clear case of *clausula rebus sic stantibus* affecting the basis of co-operation between the Community and Yugoslavia. The Community organs, in his opinion, were also entitled to assume that this change of circumstances had reached a point where it fundamentally affected the remaining treaty obligations.

While the *clausula rebus sic stantibus* thus seems to be applicable in a number of situations, a word of warning seems, however, warranted: a final decision by the European Court of Justice (ECJ) is still outstanding and the Advocate-General merely examined an evident violation of rules of customary international law. An automatic extensive application of the principle to all kinds of grave human rights violations does, therefore, not appear to be possible.[12]

B. Suspension and Termination as Reprisals

Suspension and termination of treaties based on human rights violations may also be invoked for reasons of reprisal,[13] where an illegal act is met by an illegal answer that is justified as an exception. In the Yugoslavian case referred to above the

---

[8] *Fisheries Jurisdiction Case (United Kingdom v. Iceland)*, Jurisdiction of the Court, Judgment [1973] ICJ Rep. 3, at para. 36 and *Fisheries Jurisdiction Case (Federal Republic of Germany v. Iceland)*, Jurisdiction of the Court, Judgment [1973] ICJ Rep. 49, at para. 36.

[9] [1991] OJ L315/1, 47, 49.

[10] Opinion of Jacobs AG, 4 Dec. 1997 Case C–162/96, para. 51ff, 60ff.

[11] *Ibid.*, at para. 92ff.

[12] Cf. Oestreich, note 1 above, at 409 and the Commission's answer of 18 July 1978 to question 115/78 [1978] OJ C199/27.

[13] Generally on the right of the Community to take reprisals cf. C. Tomuschat, 'Völkerrechtliche Grundlagen der Drittlandsbeziehungen der EG', in M. Hilf and C. Tomuschat, *EG und Drittstaatenbeziehungen nach 1992* (1991), 153.

Commission by way of auxiliary argument characterized the suspension of treaty obligations, in response to the prior illegal acts committed by Yugoslavia, as a measure of retorsion. While in theory it may be doubted whether the acts in question really were measures of retorsion or rather of reprisal, the more interesting question seems to be whether reprisals are a legitimate answer to human rights violations. Since the EC is not a party to the relevant human rights treaties, only violations of the minimum standards of human rights protection recognized in customary international law as valid *erga omnes* would provide a possible justification for retorsion or reprisals by the EC.[14] There is much controversy about all the other modalities of reprisals,[15] and in particular about the necessity of meeting the requirements of the proportionality principle regarding the violation of international law and the reprisal taken.[16] However, generally this will justify the partial or complete suspension rather than the termination of the treaty.

II. DEVELOPMENT AND TYPOLOGY OF HUMAN RIGHTS CLAUSES

A. Article 5 Lomé IV (1989)

Despite massive human rights violations by member States of Lomé I in the 1970s (for example, by Uganda) it took until 1989[17] before Article 5 of Lomé IV could spell out a first human rights clause.[18] However, closer scrutiny of Article 5 reveals that the strong emphasis which is placed on human rights merely takes the form of programmatic principles, not one of concrete human rights guarantees capable of being employed as conditions for the fulfilment of the Treaty. The closest approximation to a specific conditionality clause can be found in Article 5(2)(2) stating: '[e]very individual shall have the right, in his own country or in a host country, to respect for his dignity and protection by the law'. It seems problematic that Lomé IV does not

---

[14] *Case Concerning the Barcelona Traction, Light and Power Company, Ltd.*, Judgment, [1970] ICJ Rep. 3, at paras. 33–4; for a more detailed discussion cf. Oestreich, note 1 above, at 411ff; I.E. Hörndler, *Menschenrechte und Entwicklungshilfe—Eine Koppelung der Vergabe von Entwicklungshilfe an die Beachtung der Menschenrechte* (1996), 217ff; J. Frowein, 'Die Verpflichtungen erga omnes im Völkerrecht und ihre Durchsetzung', in R. Bernhardt *et al.*, *Festschrift für Hermann Mosler* (1983), 241–62.

[15] Cf. M. Akehurst, 'Reprisals by Third States' (1970) 46 *BYIL* 1–18; Y. Dinstein, 'The Erga Omnes Applicability of Human Rights' (1992) 30 *ArchVR* 16–21; Oellers-Frahm, 'Comment: The Erga Omnes Applicability of Human Rights' (1992) 30 *ArchVR* 32ff; B. Bryde, 'Verpflichtungen Erga Omnes aus Menschenrechten', in Berichte der Deutschen Gesellschaft für Völkerrecht 33, *Aktuelle Probleme des Menschenrechtsschutzes*, 177ff.

[16] Cf. J. Delbrück, 'Proportionality' (1997) III *EPIL* 1141ff.

[17] Cf. concerning the importance of human rights in Lomé III, particularly in its preamble, Art. 4, and the joint declaration on Art. 4 in Annex No. I: N. White, 'Structural Adjustment with a Human Face and Human Rights in Development: New Approaches in the Fourth Lomé Convention', in R.S. Pathak and R.P. Dhokalia (eds.), *International Law in Transition—Essays in Memory of Judge Nagendra Singh* (1992), 52ff; Arts, note 1 above, at 269.

[18] D. Marantis, 'Human Rights, Democracy, and Development: The European Community Model' (1994) 7 *Harv. HRJ* 7ff; Lenaerts and De Smijter, note 5 above, at 45.

contain an explicit suspension clause for cases of violation,[19] nor does it clarify whether any such violation amounts to an essential breach of a treaty obligation under Article 60(3)(b) VCLT. Even if one were to assume that this was the case, bearing in mind Article 5(1)(1) of Lomé IV (1989), whereby 'co-operation shall be directed towards development centered on man, the main protagonist and beneficiary of development, which thus entails respect for and promotion of all human rights',[20] legal doctrinal advantages in respect of termination or suspension gained by the formulation of Article 5 would be slender, compared with the position under general international law.[21] The minimum standards of human rights protection would not be enhanced significantly by mere reference to human dignity, and would not add substantially to the *erga omnes* rights and guarantees prevailing under existing customary international law, whereby suspension or termination of a treaty can be effected as a measure of reprisal. Article 5 of Lomé IV (1989) thus did not constitute an adequate basis for treaty suspension in cases of serious human rights violations.[22]

B. The 'Basis Clause'

Repeated attempts by the European Parliament (EP) to achieve the insertion of a human rights clause in treaties with non-ACP (African, Caribbean, and Pacific) States remained unsuccessful until 1990.[23] When consensus about such a clause eventually was reached in the Council and in the Commission, a simple extension of Article 5 of Lomé IV (1989) to treaties with non-ACP States was ruled out.[24] Article 5 was seen as the outcome of a singular and protracted negotiation process with the ACP States, not capable of generalization. The particular emphasis on economic and social rights in sub-paragraphs (2) and (3) and references to the *apartheid* regime found in subparagraph (2), sub-subparagraph (4) made that position quite clear.[25]

[19] A. Clapham, 'A Human Rights Policy for the European Community' (1990) 10 *YEL* 349 refers to the general possibility of termination in relation to an ACP State in Art. 367 of Lomé IV (1989), which, however, requires six months' notice.

[20] This seems possible in relation to the respect for human rights in a very general sense. Cf. White, note 17 above, at 49: '[f]or the first time in a Lomé Convention the parties have agreed to declare their commitment to respect for and promotion of all human rights as an essential element in the objectives and principles of ACP-EC co-operation'.

[21] F. Hoffmeister, *Menschenrechts—und Demokratieklauseln in den vertraglichen Außenbeziehungen der Europäischen Gemeinschaft* (1998), chaps. 6, I.2.

[22] Lenaerts and De Smijter, note 5 above, at 45ff, note 284; European Parliament, Committee on Development and Co-operation, 'Interim Report on the Proposal for a Council Decision on a Framework Procedure for Implementing Article 366a of the Fourth Lomé Convention (COM(96)0069)', PE 222.307/fin, at 8; European Parliament, 'Report on the Communication from the Commission on the Inclusion of Respect for Democratic Principles and Human Rights in Agreements between the Community and Third Countries' (COM(95)216), Opinion of the Committee on External Economic Relations', PE 216.714/fin., at 24; cf. Arts, note 1 above, at 259 and K. Tomasevski, *Between Sanctions and Elections—Aid Donors and their Human Rights Performance* (1997), 42ff.

[23] Cf. concerning the general trend towards human rights conditionality in international relations, O. Stokke, 'Aid and Political Conditionality: Core Issues and State of the Art', in O. Stokke (ed.), *Aid and Political Conditionality* (1995), 28ff.

[24] In its resolution on human rights, democracy, and development of 22 Nov. 1991 [1991] OJ C326/259, the Parliament called on the Council and the Commission to ensure that due account is taken of the letter and/or spirit, as appropriate, of Art. 5 of Lomé IV (1989) in future agreements with third States.

[25] For the specific human rights content of Art. 5 of Lomé IV (1989) cf. White, note 17 above, at 56ff.

Instead, in the framework treaty with Argentina, signed on 2 April 1990,[26] a clause entitled 'democratic basis for co-operation', was introduced in Article 1(1) stipulating:

> Cooperation ties between the Community and Argentina and this Agreement in its entirety are based on respect for the democratic principles and human rights, which inspire the domestic and external policies of the Community and Argentina.

Although this so-called *basis clause,* which was later also used in agreements with Chile, Uruguay, and Paraguay, may be regarded as an important stepping stone for the introduction of human rights clauses into all external agreements of the Community, the basis clause on its own, not unlike Article 5 of Lomé IV (1989), does not represent an unambiguous foundation for the termination or suspension of a treaty on the grounds of human rights violations or infringements of democratic processes, even if some commentators see this differently.[27] Again, there is no express suspension clause, and the formulation of the clause, as requested by Argentina, remains vague. The imprecise formulation, '*based* on respect for the democratic principles and human rights, which *inspire* the domestic and external policies of the Community and Argentina' leaves much room for interpretation. This makes it easy to assert that 'respect' for human rights and for democratic principles cannot be regarded as a provision essential for the fulfilment of the object or purpose of the treaty under Article 60(3)(b) VCLT. The basis clause may therefore be regarded as an improvement on the clause in Article 5 of Lomé IV (1989);[28] however, it did not entirely remove all doubts about its effect on suspension and termination of treaties in the event of human rights violations.

C. The 'Essential Element Clause'

The disputed suspension of the co-operation agreement with Yugoslavia in 1991 convinced the Council of the need for agreements concluded by the Communities with third States to contain an express human rights conditionality clause. As a first step towards this it emphasized in its declaration of 11 May 1992 concerning relations of the EC with Conference on Security and Co-operation in Europe (CSCE) States[29] that the respect for democratic principles, as set out in the Helsinki Final Act[30] 1975 and in the Charter of Paris for a New Europe[31] 1990, forms an essential and integral part of agreements between the Communities and their CSCE partners. From May 1992 (new agreements with the Baltic States[32] and with Albania[33]) onwards, further agreements with other Organization for Security and Co-operation in Europe (OSCE) States and with other third States such as Brazil included a clause specifically stressing that respect for democracy and for human rights henceforth

---

[26] [1990] OJ L295/67.   [27] Cf. Arts, note 1 above, at 259, 266.
[28] For a detailed analysis of the scope of protection of the different types of human rights clauses cf Hoffmeister, note 21 above, at chap. 7.
[29] *Bull. EC* 5–1992, pt. 1.2.13.
[30] Helsinki Final Act, adopted at the Conference on Security and Cooperation in Europe, Helsinki, 1 Aug. 1975, reprinted in 14 ILM 1292.
[31] Charter of Paris for a New Europe, adopted on 21 Nov. 1990, reprinted in 30 ILM 190.
[32] [1992] OJ L403/2 (Estonia), 11 (Latvia), 20 (Lithuania).   [33] [1992] OJ L343/2.

constituted an essential element of the respective agreements in the sense used in Article 60(3)(b) VCLT.[34] In OSCE treaties additional reference was made to the Helsinki Final Act and to the Charter of Paris for a New Europe, and sometimes also to the principles of market economy:

> Respect for the democratic principles and human rights established by [the Helsinki Final Act and the Charter of Paris for a New Europe] [as well as the principles of market economy] [as defined at the Bonn CSCE conference] inspire the domestic and external policies of the Community and of [third countries] and constitute an essential element of this agreement.

This *essential element clause* unequivocally spells out the conditions as provided by Article 60(3)(b) VCLT[35] and subsequently can be used as a proper justification for suspension or termination of such treaties in cases of grave human rights violations,[36] as well as serious breaches of democratic processes. In such cases Article 60(1) in conjunction with Article 60(3)(b) VCLT can justify a total or partial suspension or termination of the treaty, provided that the procedural steps to be followed under Article 65 VCLT are respected.[37]

The effect of the essential element clause was further enhanced by so-called specific *non-compliance clauses*, enabling recourse to specified modes of reaction in the event of non-compliance by the treaty partner, without reference to Article 60 VCLT,[38] the application of which might otherwise remain in doubt.

A first type of non-compliance clause, the so-called *Baltic clause*, emerged in the treaties with the Baltic States[39] and Albania:[40]

> The parties reserve the right to suspend this Agreement in whole or in part with immediate effect if a serious breach of its essential provisions occurs.

This Baltic clause may well be characterized as a sharp sword with a limited range. On the one hand, suspension with immediate effect offers pertinent options for reaction that might even bypass the procedures prescribed by Article 65 VCLT. On the other, its application is limited to *serious* violations of essential provisions, even if these undoubtedly include respect for human rights as the unambiguous formulation of the essential element clause makes clear. As from 1993 the Baltic clause was increasingly replaced by the so-called *Bulgarian clause*. The Bulgarian clause was first used in agreements with Romania[41] and Bulgaria[42] in February and March 1993, and opened up both, a broader scope of implementation as well as more flexible possibilities for response:

---

[34] Gilsdorf, 'Die Außenkompetenzen der EG im Wandel—Eine kritische Auseinandersetzung mit Praxis und Rechtsprechung' (1996) 31 *Europarecht* 164.

[35] Cf. e.g. the arguments brought forward by the Council and the parties intervening on its behalf in Case C–268/94, *Portuguese Republic* [1996] ECR I–6177, at 6216, and the final pleadings by La Pergola AG in the same case, at 6191.

[36] Communication from the Commission on the inclusion of respect for democratic principles and human rights in agreements between the Community and third countries, COM(95)216 final, at 7–8.

[37] Final conclusions by La Pergola AG in Case C–268/94, *Portuguese Republic* [1996] ECR I–6177, at 6191, para. 28.

[38] Lenaerts and De Smijter, note 5 above, at 46.   [39] Art. 21(3).   [40] Art. 21(4).

[41] [1994] OJ L357/2, Art. 119(2).   [42] [1994] OJ L358/3, Art. 118(2).

> If either party considers that the other Party has failed to fulfil an obligation under this agreement, it may take appropriate measures. Before so doing, except in cases of special urgency, it shall supply the Association Council with all relevant information required for a thorough examination of the situation with a view to seeking a solution acceptable to the Parties.
>
> In the selection of measures, priority must be given to those which least disturb the functioning of this Agreement. These measures shall be notified immediately to the Association Council and shall be the subject of consultations within the Association Council if the other Party so requests.

It is noteworthy that the second paragraph expressly picks up the proportionality principle as a precondition for the operation of the clause. The danger soon became apparent that the requirement for such a thorough situational analysis by the Association Council to proceed to unilateral action by either party might easily render the *non-compliance clause* ineffective or even inoperative. Thus, when concluding the Partnership Treaty with the Russian Federation on 24 June 1994, 'cases of special urgency' entitling suspension of the treaty were consequently expressly defined by way of a joint interpretative declaration, which was later copied for other treaties with members of the CIS.[43] According to that joint interpretative declaration both parties are agreed that cases of special urgency are made up of grave breaches of the treaty by either party. For cases of special urgency to be assumed, it suffices that violations of the essential elements of the treaty as laid down in Article 1 are in question. Thus, any infringement of democratic principles or of the human rights therein enshrined constitutes a case of 'special urgency' entitling the other party to take any suitable counter-measures without the need of prior examination by the Association Council.

D. Article 5 of Lomé IV (1995)

A combination of the essential element clause as outlined, and a non-compliance clause of the Bulgarian type was later utilized in treaties with other world regions, such as those with Vietnam and South Korea, and the Association Agreements with Tunisia and Morocco in 1995. Naturally, all OSCE references were dropped in these clauses. Instead, at least in some agreements, the Universal Declaration on Human Rights[44] (UDHR) of 1948 took their place. The negotiations about the revision of the Lomé Treaty starting in May 1994 showed broad consensus on both, the acceptance of an essential element clause with extended scope of protection and the addition of a non-compliance clause (Article 366a). While also copying parts of Article 5 Lomé IV (1989) Article 5(1) Lomé IV (1995) in its new sub-subparagraph 3 stipulates:

> Respect for human rights, democratic principles and the rule of law, which underpins relations between the ACP States and the Community and all provisions of the Conven-

---

[43] Kazakhstan [1994] OJ C319/6; Ukraine, COM(94)226; Kyrgyzstan, COM(94)412; Moldavia, COM(94)477; Belarus, COM(95)44.

[44] Universal Declaration of Human Rights, adopted by GA Res. 217 A (III) (1948). In United Nations, *A Compilation of International Instruments* (1994), i, Part 2, 1.

tion, and governs the domestic and international policies of the Contracting Parties, shall constitute an essential element of the Convention.

While on the one hand the EC managed to insert a reference to the rule of law into the clause, the ACP States, on the other, succeeded in eliciting from the Community a formulation of the non-compliance clause (Article 366a of Lomé IV (1995)) which puts much stronger emphasis on consultation mechanisms than even the Bulgarian clause:

> 2. If one Party considers that another Party has failed to fulfil an obligation in respect of one of the essential elements referred to in Article 5, it shall invite the Party concerned, unless there is special urgency, to hold consultations with a view to assessing the situation in detail and, if necessary, remedying it.
> For the purposes of such consultations, and with a view to finding a solution:
>
> —the community side shall be represented by its Presidency, assisted by the previous and next Member States to hold the Presidency, together with the Commission;
> —the ACP side shall be represented by the ACP State holding the Co-Presidency, assisted by the previous and next ACP States to hold the Co-Presidency. Two additional members of the ACP Council of Ministers chosen by the Party concerned shall also take part in the consultations.
>
> The consultations shall begin no later than 15 days after the invitation and as a rule last no longer than 30 days.
> 3. At the end of the period referred to in the third subparagraph of paragraph 2 if in spite of all efforts no solution has been found, or immediately in the case of urgency or refusal of consultation, the Party which invoked the failure to fulfil an obligation may take appropriate steps, including, where necessary, the partial or full suspension of application of this Convention to the Party concerned. It is understood that suspension would be a measure of last resort.
> The Party concerned shall receive prior notification of any such measure which shall be revoked as soon as the reasons for taking it have disappeared.

In contrast to the joint declaration of interpretation with the CIS States, Lomé IV (1995) included a joint declaration of interpretation of Article 366a, contained in annex LXXXIII, which is much more restrictive *vis-à-vis* unilateral measures, stating in no uncertain terms:

> 1. In the practical application of this Convention, the Contracting Parties will not have recourse to the provision of 'special urgency' in Article 366a, other than in exceptional cases of particularly serious and flagrant violations that, because of the response time required, render any prior consultation impossible.
> 2. In the event that either Contracting Party has resort to this measure, the relevant Party undertakes to make arrangements to consult with the other expeditiously with a view to assessing the situation in detail and, if necessary, remedying it.

E. The 'Standard Clause'

The human rights clause in external agreements of the Communities now also included in Lomé IV (1995) has since served as a model for future treaties of the Communities as proposed by the Commission[45] and adopted by the Council[46] in its

---

[45] COM(95)216 final.   [46] *Bull. EU* 5–1995, pt. 1.2.3.

universal systematic guidelines of 29 May 1995. Accordingly, human rights are referred to in the preamble as well as in the operative provisions, which in turn contain a combination of the essential element clause — referring to OSCE documents where applicable—and a non-compliance clause. The latter is to be seen in conjunction with an interpretative declaration of the CIS type where called for. By the end of 1995 in addition to the seventy ACP States twenty OSCE States, fifteen Latin-American States, two Mediterranean States, six Asiatic States, as well as South Africa, had contractually agreed to such a human rights clause.[47] In this way a *standard clause* has evolved which has been utilized in all subsequent framework treaties of the Community with third States, thus constituting the '*acquis communautaire*' in this area.

III. THE LEGAL BASES IN THE EC TREATY

The question now arises where the legal foundations for the application of the *standard clause*, in combination with the Bulgarian *non-compliance* clause and an interpretative declaration of the CIS-type, can be found. Such legal justification is essential, bearing in mind the paramount principle of limited attribution, as laid down in Article 3b (now Article 5) EC, which also applies to the external relations treaty-making power of the Community.[48]

A. Possible Legal Bases

1. Article 181 (ex Article 130y) in Conjunction with Article 177 (ex Article 130u) EC—Development Co-operation   The Treaty of Maastricht introduced a new title XX (*ex* title XVII) on development co-operation into the EC Treaty including Articles 181 (*ex* Article 130y) and 177 (*ex* Article 130u). The latter two Articles might be regarded as the first ones to lay clear foundations for human rights clauses in external agreements of the Community. Article 181(2) EC contains an express competency of the Community to conclude agreements with third States relating to development co-operation and Article 177(2) EC provides:

> Community policy in this area shall contribute to the general objective of developing and consolidating democracy and the rule of law, and to that of respecting human rights and fundamental freedoms.

The question immediately arises whether the Community can find an implied competence to introduce human rights clauses into agreements with third States, forming part of development co-operation measures following Article 181 EC. This issue constituted the basis of a dispute between Portugal and the Council, and was decided by the ECJ on 3 December 1996.[49] In an attempt to create a precedent for a

---

[47] Hoffmeister, note 21 above, at chap. 4, V.
[48] *Opinion 2/94* [1996] ECR I–1759, at 1787; Lenaerts and De Smijter, note 5 above, at 5.
[49] Case C–268/94, *Portuguese Republic* [1996] ECR I–6177; cf J. van der Klaauw, 'Human Rights News—European Union' (1997) 15 *NQHR* 206ff.

pending agreement with Indonesia, Portugal *inter alia* argued that the co-operation agreement between the EC and India should have been based on Article 308 (*ex* Article 235) EC. They insisted on the applicability of Article 308 EC because, unlike Article 181 in conjunction with Article 300(2) (*ex* Article 228(2)) EC it presupposes unanimity in the Council. Portugal claimed that Article 181 EC might merely be used for agreements containing fairly general human rights references only, since Article 177(2) (Article *ex* 130u(2)) itself referred to respect for human rights simply as a general objective of Community policy.[50] A co-operation agreement in which respect for human rights constituted an essential element of the agreement, such as the one with India, should always be based on Article 308 EC.

The Court, however, found that the essential element clause was fully covered by Article 177(2) EC. The ECJ elaborated its decision by saying that the wording of Article 177(2) EC clearly revealed the importance of respect for human rights and democratic principles. Adjusting co-operation policies to the respect for human rights presupposes the creation of a relationship of subordination.[51] Consequently, a provision which declares respect for human rights and democratic principles as essential elements of the Treaty does not exceed the aim laid down in Article 177(2) EC.[52] The Court did not go as far as Advocate-General La Pergola, who in his final conclusions even argued that the renunciation of such a clause would, on the contrary, eliminate the legal basis of Community action, as a guarantee for the observance of the clear provision contained in Article 177 EC would then be lacking.[53] The Court did, however, clarify in its decision that Article 177(2) EC justifies the inclusion of a human rights clause of the essential element type in a treaty following Article 181 EC, even if such a clause entitles the Community to suspend or terminate the Treaty.

While the Court's dictum thus clearly endorsed the inclusion of an essential element clause in a treaty based on Article 181 EC as being fully covered by Article 177 EC, the question remains which states may be regarded as legitimate parties under Article 181 EC. Title XX (*ex* XVII) of the EC Treaty does not provide explicit and unambiguous criteria to answer the question which countries qualify as developing countries in order to become partners in such development co-operation. At most, one could, by means of inverted inference, bring into play the conditions development co-operation is meant to bring about, as have been set out in Article 177(1) EC. The absence of such conditions in a specific country might then indicate the status of a 'developing country' in the sense of title XX. However, criteria such as poverty or a lack of integration into the world economy remain general to the point of rendering a clear-cut decision impossible. Moreover, there is a general lack of definition of what constitutes a developing country. Development indicators like those produced by the World Bank, by UNCTAD, OECD, or by other institutions (usually based on the gross national product per citizen, the literacy rate, etc.[54]) could be used, yet they,

---

[50] Case C–268/94, *Portuguese Republic* [1996] ECR I–6177, at 6215, para. 15ff.

[51] *Ibid.*, at 6217, para. 26.   [52] *Ibid.*, at 6217, para. 24.

[53] *Ibid.*, at 6192, para. 29. More cautiously, Lenaerts and De Smijter, note 5 above, state at 14: '[i]t [Art. 177 EC] moreover requires the Community to condition its co-operation policy on the respect for human rights and democratic principles'.

[54] Cf. J. Hecker, in C.O. Lenz (ed.), *Kommentar zu dem Vertrag zur Gründung der Europäischen Gemeinschaften* (1994), Art. 130u, No. 1ff.

too, are seen controversially and do not provide clear answers in respect of all States. South Africa, for example, represents a borderline case in this regard. The Community concluded a co-operation treaty with that State in 1994, based on Article 181 EC. On the other hand, the Community did not infer provisions on development co-operation with regard to agreements with Central and Eastern European States, even where they clearly showed the criteria characteristic for developing states, rather seeing them as 'States in transition'.[55] By not utilizing title XX for these States, the Community evidently wishes to stress *ratione personae* that title XX is reserved for classical development functions.

*2. Article 133 (*ex *Article 113) EC*   Apart from Article 181 (*ex* Article 130y) in connection with Article 177 (*ex* Article 130u) there is no other legal basis for the conclusion of external agreements which contain express human rights references in the EC Treaty. The question therefore arises whether such inclusion may be implied. Article 133 EC, empowering the Community to conclude treaties within the common commercial policy is a case in point. A number of treaties, such as the free trade agreements with the Baltic States of 1995[56] and the interim agreements with CIS States, have been based entirely on Article 133 EC.[57] One might argue that the competence to include human rights clauses in such agreements might be deduced from an overall assessment of the *acquis communautaire* of the Community pervading the whole treaty and thus also Article 133 EC. This may, for one, be justified considering the various occasions on which human rights are mentioned in the preamble to the Single European Act (SEA), the preamble to the EU Treaty, as well as in Articles 6(2) (*ex* Article F(2)), 11(1) (*ex* Article J.1(2)), fifth indent, and K.2(1) of the EU Treaty, and, of course, Article 177 EC. More importantly, however, the jurisprudence of the ECJ according to which human rights form part of the general principles of law, the respect for which has to be safeguarded by the Court, might be added in support of this implied powers argument.

Tempting as such a line of argument may be, it must, however, not be overlooked that the cases decided by the ECJ in its expanded human rights jurisprudence primarily concern the protection of individual rights of market citizens. Also to deduce from this jurisprudence an external competence of the Community could easily undercut the Court's jurisprudence as regards the emergence of unwritten external competences first established by its *AETR* decision[58] and later fine-tuned in decisions such as *Kramer*,[59] *Opinion 2/91*,[60] and *Opinion 1/94*.[61] Another reason why it would seem problematic to rely on provisions of the EU Treaty to establish an external competence of the Community lies in the fact that the latter represents only one pillar of the Union. This argument applies in particular to Articles such as Articles K.2(1) and 11(1) (*ex* Article J.1(2)) fifth indent, which concern the other two pillars of the Union. It has therefore to be concluded that such a wide and unwritten

---

[55] I. MacLeod, I.D. Hendry, and S. Hyett, *The External Relations of the European Communities* (1996), 341.

[56] [1994] OJ L373/1; L374/1; L375/1.

[57] e.g. the interim agreement with the Russian Federation [1995] OJ L247/1.

[58] Case 22/70 [1971] ECR 263.   [59] Joined Cases 3, 4, and 6/76 [1976] ECR 1279.

[60] *Opinion 2/91* [1993] ECR I–1076ff, at para. 7ff.   [61] *Opinion 1/94* [1994] ECR I–5267.

human rights treaty-making power, concerning both the internal and external area, would exceed the bounds set by the limited attribution principle of Article 5 (*ex* Article 3b) EC.

Another justification for the insertion of human rights clauses, applying principles of general international law, seems more promising. Suspension of a treaty or of some of its provisions is the reverse of the treaty conclusion. Thus, to the extent that the Community is entitled to conclude a treaty based on Article 133 (*ex* Article 113) EC, it must also be empowered to suspend it. General international law permitting the suspension of a treaty as a measure of reprisal in certain cases of breach of human rights naturally also applies to the EC. Seen as mere tools for suspension human rights clauses might thus be covered implicitly by the material provisions of the respective treaty.[62] Doubts remain, though, that human rights clauses unduly expand the scope of *erga omnes* norms, recognized as part of customary international law, thereby enlarging the generally accepted minimum standards of human rights protection, since they cannot be limited to a purely negative function. However, the specific reference to the Universal Declaration of Human Rights (UDHR) or OSCE documents in many agreements can be used to counter these arguments. Admittedly with a few exceptions, the provisions of the UDHR as part of the Universal Bill of Rights in the last fifty years have gradually hardened into binding customary international law.[63] The 1966 Covenants[64] have since been ratified by more than two thirds of all States, and many of the provisions of the UDHR have been incorporated into national constitutional documents, particularly during the decolonization process. Regional human rights have elaborated its guarantees, and the UN Charter legitimizes a view whereby respect of human rights, as established in the UDHR, spells out membership duties of States. Moreover, numerous references in national and international courts have bolstered its legal significance. While the UDHR, even in 1976 when the two Human Rights Covenants came into force, could merely be regarded as a legally non-binding declaration of great political and moral impact, this has certainly changed since, owing to the practice of States and the nearly universal acceptance of its binding nature. The UDHR now marks a 'common standard of achievement', as Inis Claude aptly put it, but one that has crossed the lines from non-binding to binding rules of international law.

Thus, it is submitted, that the inclusion of human rights clauses in agreements which are based on Article 133 (*ex* Article 113) EC is justified.

However, Commission officials point out that the real significance of human rights clauses lies not so much in their negative function as in the positive conditional effects they produce by binding treaty partners indirectly. The fact that so far there

---

[62] Hoffmeister, note 21 above, at chap. 9, V.1.a.

[63] B. Simma and P. Alston, 'The Sources of Human Rights Law: Custom, Use Cogens, and General Principles' (1992) 12 *AYBIL* 102ff, argue that the UDHR reflects binding general principles of law. For some provisions of the UDHR as *ius cogens* norms cf. L. Hannikainen, 'Peremptory Norms (Ius Cogens)' [1988] *International Law* 425ff; O. Schachter, 'International Human Rights' (1982) V *RdC* 334ff, regards some but not all UDHR norms as binding in customary international law. It is submitted that this reflects the pre-1980 period and has since been superseded by more recent developments of customary law.

[64] International Covenant on Economic, Social, and Cultural Rights, and the International Covenant on Civil and Political Rights, proclaimed by GA Res. 2200 A (XXI) (1966), in *International Instruments*, note 44 above, at 8 and 20.

have been no real suspension cases based exclusively on the application of a human rights clause, even though in many instances there would have been ample reasons to do so, supports this point of view. Given that human rights clauses in practice reveal their beneficial effect mainly in the realms of diplomacy, that is to say prior to a decision on the suspension of an agreement, it seems doubtful whether the effect of human rights clauses can really be reduced to mere means of suspension and termination of treaties. Critics might thus still question whether the inclusion of human rights clauses in external agreements can indeed be based on provisions such as Article 133 EC. To remove all doubt it would therefore be desirable to insert a provision into the EC Treaty explicitly stating that all Community policy in its external relations shall contribute to the general objective of respect for human rights and fundamental freedoms.

3. Article 308 (ex Article 235) EC   A reserve competence for stipulating human rights clauses in external agreements may be deduced from Article 308 EC, provided the insertion proves necessary to attain, in the course of the operation of the common market, one of the objectives of the Community. In *Opinion 2/94*, concerning the competence of the Community to accede to the European Convention on Human Rights (ECHR), it was argued that the protection of human rights despite the lack of clear references in the EC Treaty forms part of the general objectives of the Community.[65] The protection of human rights was seen to be a general principal, applying horizontally to all Community activities. In favour of these arguments the Articles and preambular provisions cited above were raised as well as the Court's own developing human rights jurisprudence. As is well known, the ECJ for different reasons rejected accession to the ECHR system, mainly because it felt that accession would constitute an essential change in the present Community system of human rights protection and thus cause fundamental institutional implications for the Community as well as for the Member States.[66] Such a step was seen to imply a constitutional law dimension exceeding the scope of Article 308 EC and, therefore, to necessitate an amendment of the EC Treaty. Protection of human rights as a Community goal was thus not the issue. On the contrary, the Court specifically pointed out that fundamental rights belong to the general principles of law which the Court must protect, and that human rights represent crucial preconditions for the legality of Community actions.[67]

The result of this is that the protection of human rights has indeed become an unwritten general objective of the Community. Since they represent an essential means towards the attainment of respect for human rights in the external relations of the Community, human rights clauses are covered by Article 308 EC. Article 308 EC was therefore a sufficient basis for Community action with regard to developing countries before title XX (*ex* title XVII) on development co-operation came into force on 1 November 1993, and it is still a reserve basis for the insertion of human rights clauses in external agreements of the Community with countries other than the developing countries.

---

[65] *Opinion 2/94* [1996] ECR I–1773ff, para. 28.   [66] *Ibid.*, at 1789, para. 34ff.
[67] *Ibid.*, at 1789, paras. 33–34.

4. Article 310 (ex Article 238) EC Association agreements with third States or international organizations, such as the Lomé treaties, Europe Agreements, and the new agreements with some Mediterranean States containing human rights clauses, could be concluded on the basis of Article 310 EC. Article 310 EC aims to associate the Community with partner States by spelling out reciprocal rights and obligations, joint actions, and particular procedures geared towards harmonization and progressively bringing the partner State's legal and economic system in line with the Community legal order. Such association treaties may encompass all Community law areas,[68] and also the *acquis communautaire*, including the jurisprudence of the ECJ.[69] Human rights clauses may therefore be made a condition precedent for the conclusion of association treaties based on Article 310 EC.

B. Application of Human Rights Clauses in Mixed Agreements

In mixed agreements concluded by the Community and one or more Member States, as was the case with the Lomé Treaty, the question invariably arises who is entitled to suspend or terminate such an agreement for human rights reasons. In the absence of a specific provision to the contrary under public international law any of the treaty parties may rely on the human rights clause[70] in order to suspend or terminate treaty relations. Yet this is clearly not a question of international law treaty competence, but exclusively a problem of European law, as the Community may act only in accordance with the principle of limited attribution (Article 5 (*ex* Article 3b) EC). If a provision of a mixed treaty is to be suspended, the Community may act only to the extent that the Community competence for establishing the provision in question exists. The Member States which are parties to a mixed treaty may suspend those provisions falling in their sphere of competence. Theoretically, termination and complete suspension of a mixed agreement must be effected jointly by the Community and the Member States.[71] However, if only individual treaty provisions are affected, then either the Community or individual Member States may act on their own, provided the provision falls within their respective sphere of competence. Straightforward as this rule may appear, in practice it turns out to be difficult. In mixed treaties clear attribution of competence to the Community or to Member States is usually missing, if not impossible. This spells out the danger that different opinions may be reached regarding the question of competence.[72]

---

[68] Case 12/86, *Demirel* v. *Stadt Schwäbisch Gmünd* [1987] ECR 3719, at 3751, para. 9.

[69] Lenaerts and De Smijter, note 5 above, at 17.

[70] Cf. e.g. Art. 32 of the Interregional Framework Co-operation Agreement of 15 Dec. 1995 between the EC and its Member States, on the one part, and the Mercado Común del Sur and its member countries, on the other part, '[f]or the purposes of this Agreement, the term "the Parties" shall mean, on the one hand, the Community or its Member States or the Community and its Member States, in accordance with their respective spheres of competence, as deriving from the Treaty establishing the EC and, on the other hand, Mercosur or its party States, in accordance with the Treaty establishing the Southern Common Market'.

[71] A. Rosas, 'Mixed Union—Mixed Agreements', in M. Koskenniemi (ed.), *International Law Aspects of the European Union* (1998), 135.

[72] J. Sack, 'The European Community's Membership of International Organizations' (1995) 32 *CML Rev.* 1256.

The ECJ in its *Opinions 2/91*[73] and *1/94*[74] has held that the necessity for unity in the international representation of the Community in cases where competence falls in part on the Community and in part on Member States requires close co-operation between Member States and the Community organs, in negotiating, concluding, and executing mixed agreements.[75] Such joint action of the Community organs and of Member States was also emphasized in the Court's dictum in *Opinion 1/94*, where it was held that such duty of co-operation applies to agreements such as the GATS and TRIPS appended to the WTO Treaty, because in this sphere the possibility of reciprocal measures of retorsion provides a compelling reason for joint actions, since otherwise the Community or a Member State might not be able to make use of an effective retaliatory measure. This means that co-operation between the Community organs and the Member States involved is a prerequisite to every suspension case. Unilateral action thus is excluded *a limine*. The story is different if Member States have already either generally or for particular types of cases delegated the decision-making power to the Community. It is also possible that in cases of insoluble dispute between the Member States and the Community organs the power unilaterally to suspend a mixed treaty reverts back to the Community on account of its Union competence. This also follows from the general principle that Member States have a duty to act faithfully in the Community interest.

IV. COMPETENCY OF COMMUNITY ORGANS FOR THE APPLICATION OF THE CLAUSE

The European Parliament (EP), the Council, and the Commission are each empowered to make statements concerning the human rights situation in countries with which the Community maintains treaty relations, and each of them is *a priori* entitled to object to the conclusion of a treaty with a third State on the grounds of human rights violations, and to prevent it. The question whether this also applies to the suspension or termination of treaties is problematical. While hitherto no specific provisions existed, the Treaty of Amsterdam now expressly provides such a possibility in Article 300(2) (*ex* Article 228) EC. Suspensions of treaties or of some of their provisions clearly transcends mere administrative execution of treaties and therefore cannot be left to the Commission alone. Instead, following the *actus contrarius* idea, the organ that is entitled to conclude the treaty in the first place should be empowered also to effect the suspension. This seems convincing when one bears in mind that treaty suspensions have an international law dimension, and, if unjustified, entitle affected States to measures of reprisal or retorsion. As with the former Article 228(2) EC (now Article 300) suspension thus has to be determined by the Council on a prior proposal of the Commission. The question of the necessary Council majorities will

---

[73] *Opinion 2/91* [1993] ECR I–1061, at 1083, para. 36.
[74] *Opinion 1/94* [1994] ECR I–5267, at 5420, para. 108.
[75] Cf. also M. Hilf, 'EG-Außenkompetenzen in Grenzen—Das Gutachten des EuGH zur Welthandelsorganisation' [1995] *EuZW* 8.

then depend on the legal bases for the treaty provisions to be suspended. Treaty provisions based, for example, on Article 181 (*ex* Article 130y) EC will require only a qualified majority, while those based on Article 308 (*ex* Article 235) EC or on Article 310 (*ex* Article 238) EC require unanimity.

One complication arises, however, with the new Article 300(2) (*ex* Article 228) of the Treaty: that Treaty merely requires that the European Parliament (EP) is informed about the suspension decision (Article 300(2)(3) EC). It is doubtful whether the rights of the EP in relation to treaty suspension were confined to mere subsequent information prior to the Amsterdam Treaty coming into force. This inter-temporal problem will not be pursued here, as the participation rights and consent requirements of the EP in cases of complete treaty suspension will become obsolete when the Amsterdam Treaty comes into force.

In cases of termination of a treaty the *actus contrarius* idea may be resorted to again. Thus by analogy with Article 300 (*ex* Article 228(2) EC, termination is decided by the Council on a prior proposal from the Commission. Such a decision must be taken unanimously, if based on Article 308 (*ex* Article 235) EC or if it applies to an Association Treaty under Article 310 (*ex* Article 238). One might argue that, with the exception of treaties based on Article 133(3) (*ex* Article 113) EC, by analogy with Article 300(3) EC the EP is to be heard prior to a Council decision, and that in cases of termination of association treaties the prior consent of the EP is required. However, the better point of view seems to be that no renewed participation of the EP is required, as this reflects the treaty termination practice in most constitutional law settings of Member States.[76] The parliamentary act of consenting to a particular treaty implicitly includes the possibility of future termination or renunciation.

V. HUMAN RIGHTS CLAUSES IN EC PRACTICE

EC practice concerning the application of human rights clauses will necessarily be limited since such clauses have evolved only slowly, and have culminated only very recently in the standard clause outlined above. As far as can be ascertained not a single suspension case exists today which was decided entirely and solely on the basis of a human rights clause. However, this does not mean that human rights clauses were completely without effect. On the one hand, the insistence on including a human rights clause in all external framework treaties of the Community has effectively prevented the conclusion of various agreements. Examples of this are the follow-up agreement with China the conclusion of which was postponed indefinitely, or the negotiations with Australia where the conclusion of an agreement foundered on Australia's refusal to accept a human rights clause. On the other hand, human rights clauses also have anticipatory effect. Between signature and ratification of a treaty containing a human rights clause the party to the treaty is often confronted with this anticipatory effect obliging it to show respect for human rights. However,

[76] H. Von der Groeben *et al.*, *Kommentar zum EWG-Vertrag* (1991), iv, Art. 228, No. 44.

ratification of the treaty is not always made dependent on respect for human rights.[77]

In respect of relationships with States that have acccepted a human rights clause, there is a rich practice of referring to obligations arising from it. The EP has passed numerous resolutions denouncing violations of human rights and demanding or threatening the imposition of sanctions. In addition, confidential *démarches* are frequently employed before the Community raises public criticism of the human rights situation in a particular State.[78] In particular, in relation to ACP States there are numerous instances where fulfilment of obligations under the Lomé Treaty were, in effect, discontinued,[79] even if not purely and solely on account of human rights violations. This was rather done for a mixture of unspecified reasons, usually related to the impossibility or uselessness of treaty performance in combination with violations of human rights and democratic processes. The emergence of a coherent Community policy towards human rights violations is made more difficult because of the mixture of measures adopted by the Community on the one hand and measures adopted within the Common Foreign and Security Policy (CFSP)[80] in the framework of the European Union on the other.

A. ACP States

In relation to ACP States there have been some examples where treaty obligations of the Community under the Lomé IV Treaty have been discontinued due to serious human rights violations.[81] However, the path chosen was not a formal suspension on the basis of Article 5 of Lomé IV (1989), in any event being inadequate for that purpose, but rather an informal suspension of the performance of treaty obligations. Cases like Rwanda, Somalia, Liberia, and Sudan, where undoubtedly civil wars ruled, demonstrate quite clearly that the borderline between suspension due to human rights violations and non-performance of treaty obligations due to actual impossibility or pointlessness is quite fluid. It is hard to identify a rational pattern of behaviour of the EC concerning human rights violations by a party to the Lomé Treaty. An analysis of relevant cases reveals rather a frequently incoherent mixture of Community statements regarding the decision on treaty suspension, as well as of Member States in the context of the CFSP.[82]

In the case of Rwanda[83] the Commission, reacting to the genocide committed between April and June 1994, informally suspended Lomé payments. In July 1994

---

[77] Cf. the example of Russia below, and European Parliament, 'Bericht über die Menschenrechte in der Welt im Zeitraum 1995/96 und über die Menschenrechtspolitik der Europäischen Union, Ausschuß für auswärtige Angelegenheiten, Sicherheit und Verteidigungspolitik', PE 218.638/end, 9, at para. 10.

[78] D. Vignes, 'Communautés Européennes et Pays en Voie de Développement' (1988) III *RdC* 320ff.

[79] Cf. the answer by Mr Pinheiro on behalf of the Commission in relation to question E–0670/96 [1996] OJ C280/60; Hoffmeister, note 21 above, at chap. 11; Tomasevski, note 22 above, at 43; PE 216.714/fin., note 22 above, at 10.

[80] Cf. M. Fouwels, 'The European Union's Common Foreign and Security Policy and Human Rights' (1997) 15 *NQHR* 291–324.

[81] PE 222.307/fin., note 22 above, at 8; *ibid.*, Opinion of the Committee on External Economic Relations, at 21ff.

[82] Cf. the examples given by Rosas, note 71 above, at 136, note 52.

[83] Cf. Hoffmeister, note 21 above, at chap. 11, I.4.

reconstruction aid amounting to 22 million ECU was earmarked, stemming from Lomé assignments. In October 1994, the EC countries made payments of aid subject to respect for human rights and to progress in the national reconciliation process. In November of that year, the Council, which had thus far been blocked by France, decided to take up aid payments for Rwanda again, by setting aside 7 million ECU for the execution of an action programme. When the Rwandan army forcibly evacuated a refugee camp, causing several thousands Hutu to die, the EC ministers requested the Rwandan government to investigate the facts immediately and to impose sanctions, as a precondition for the payment of reconstruction aid. The aid for reconstruction programme was subsequently suspended for a while; humanitarian aid, however, was continued, furthering human rights protection and similar measures. When the Rwandan government agreed to prosecute members of the army responsible for the massacres, aid for Rwanda was finally fully reinstated following a decision by the Commission taken in July 1995.

B. OSCE States: The Russian Example

For treaties with OSCE States, as outlined above, the Baltic clause is sometimes, and the Bulgarian non-compliance clause often, chosen, supplemented in the case of CIS States by the CIS interpretive declaration.[84] Thus in theory suitable instruments exist to facilitate an adequate reaction of the Community to human rights violations or infringements of democratic principles. However, although in a number of cases such human right clauses might well have been applicable, there has not been a single formal suspension of a treaty as a result of them. The treaty relationship may be characterized as one of soft political co-ordination rather than one of strict conditionality. One of the main reasons for this undoubtedly is that most States concerned are potential candidates for full membership of the Community. Therefore many critical remarks by Community organs emphasize the standards to be fulfilled for achievement of EC membership rather than focus on the violations of a particular human rights clause.

The main usefulness of the human rights clause may thus be seen in its anticipatory effects. The Community may decline to conclude a treaty on the basis of a lack of respect for human rights and democratic principles. Between signing and ratifying the treaty in question the Community can thus count on foresight. It is much easier to use the pending ratification of a treaty as a means of persuasion than to rely on the human rights clause after ratification, when the legal bases have to be named quite clearly. A good case in point for anticipatory effect (albeit for political reasons inconsequentially applied) is the time before the partnership agreement with the Russian Federation actually came into force.[85]

After President Yeltsin had signed the partnership agreement in June 1994, and subsequently, in December 1994, initialled an interim agreement about the trade policies to be applied, relations between the EC and Russia deteriorated by reason of the Chechenian crisis. In January 1995, the EP passed a resolution pointing to the

---

[84] See above, Part II, section E.
[85] Cf. Hoffmeister, note 21 above, at chap. 13, III.3; Tomasevski, note 22 above, at 52ff.

human rights clause and endorsing the Commission's decision to suspend ratification of the interim agreement. The Council and Commission were requested to halt ratification until military attacks and massive human rights violations against the Chechenian people had ceased. The EU Troika in early March 1995 made ratification of the interim agreement dependent upon the permanent presence of the OSCE in Chechenia, on allowing humanitarian aid to enter the country, on a cease-fire, and on a serious search for political solutions to the conflict. However, although the OSCE mission stated at the end of March 1995 that serious violations of human-itarian law continued, the EU indicated at the beginning of April that it would be satisfied with Russia undertaking to honour its obligations soon. In mid-July 1995, the EP found that Common Article 3 of the Geneva Conventions, as well as several OSCE principles and principles of the partnership agreement, were still being vio-lated, effectively making the signature to the interim agreement as well as the ratification of the partnership agreement inconceivable. In spite of this, the Euro-pean Council formally decided at the end of June to sign the interim agreement, ar-guing that progress had been made in Chechenia. The interim agreement was eventually signed in mid-July 1995, and came into force on 1 February 1996. The co-operation treaty came into force on 31 December 1997 after the EP had consented to it in November 1995 because of the continuing cease-fire.

VI. ASSESSMENT AND FUTURE PERSPECTIVES

A. Status Quo*: Adequate Clause, Inadequate Application?*

The human rights clause in the form of the standard clause established by the uni-versal systematic guidelines of the Council in 1995, which has since been inserted in all framework treaties of the EC, in principle offers an adequate tool for sanctioning persistent, serious breaches of human rights by treaty parties.[86] Yet its theoretical potential is in conspicuous contrast to its utilization in practice. So far, not a single formal suspension of a treaty or of some treaty provisions has been based solely on human rights violations, even though there was ample occasion for it. However, this does not result from the formulation of the human rights clause itself. It offers, on the one hand, sufficient scope for protection by referring to human rights generally, to the UDHR, or to OSCE documents, and an essential element clause in combina-tion with a non-compliance clause and the CIS interpretative declaration of ade-quate mechanisms for suspension, on the other. If at all, the problem therefore lies in the application of the clause in practice.

In this context, it must be remembered that the essential element clause has only very recently been adopted as a standard clause for all treaty relations. Whether and how such clauses will operate in practice will depend on future developments. It is of the utmost importance that the significance of the human rights clause in practice

---

[86] Fouwels, note 80 above, at 309.

should not be reduced to a mere potential of treaty suspension.[87] One of the main functions of the human rights clause will be to raise respect or attention to violations of human rights from the domestic to the international level, and to make them a legitimate subject of reciprocal relations. Respect for human rights by the parties to the treaty can be made an issue within the confines of the treaty relationship, and conditionality may well be utilized to put pressure on the treaty partner or as a means of persuasion, without amounting to an inadmissible intervention in the domestic affairs of the States concerned. This is exactly how Community policy is shaped. Usually the Commission will first seek confidential dialogue, reverting to an open dialogue with States violating clause protected human rights only in a second stage. Suspension of treaty obligations thus represents only a means of last resort, marking the ultimate failure of such dialogue. One could even argue that the human rights clause has missed its point, if it actually has to be applied by way of treaty suspension.

B. Flexibility of the Human Rights Clause

The standard clause could be seen as a satisfactory solution and it could be assumed that its defects lie not so much in its normative scope, but rather in the way it is being applied in practice.[88] But the standard clause is not likely to mark the end of any definitional development. Even today small variations in its formulation can be detected, usually due to imprecision of translation. In the agreements with Georgia, Azerbaijan, and Armenia of April 1996[89] the respect for the principles of international law was added:

> Respect of democracy, principles of international law and human rights as defined in particular in the United Nations Charter, the Helsinki Final Act and the Charter for a New Europe . . . underpin the internal and external policies of the Parties and constitute an essential element of partnership and of this Agreement.

This addition to the clause may have been caused by the Nagorny–Karabach conflict. It allows such events to become matters of concern for the Community in its relations with these States, but the follow-up question is whether the clause should, in fact, always be attuned to specific situations of particular States.

The idea of non-discriminatory treatment for all treaty parties opposes this. If the Community insists on including the standard clause in all its framework treaties with other States, then this strengthens its negotiation position considerably. The States concerned cannot feel discriminated against, as the clause is in fact operative *vis-à-vis* all States. Moreover, the choice is between acceptance of the clause or non-conclusion of the treaty. Applied sensibly, the clause offers no incentive to try to change the wording of the clause.

---

[87] Conditionality by human rights clauses on the one hand and diplomacy with the aim of promoting human rights on the other are often effectively treated as a pair of opposites. Cf. e.g. Fouwels, note 80 above, at 309.

[88] In the light of the anticipated revision of Art. 5 of Lomé IV (1989), Arts, note 1 above, at 273, argued that—instead of revision—one should first of all and for a longer period concentrate on the application of the clause including suitable mechanisms.

[89] [1997] OJ L129/3 (interim agreement Armenia); L129/23 (interim agreement Georgia).

On the other hand, it may be argued that failure of the entire treaty is disproportionate, if—as happened in the case of Mexico—reference to the UDHR is declined
for constitutional reasons, while reference to the UN Covenants remains possible. A
more flexible application of the clause might have led to the conclusion of treaties
with Australia or even with China. Thus it may very well be that in the longer run a
more flexible attitude towards the formulation of the clause will prevail. Close attention will, however, have to be paid to the maintenance of the spirit of the clause
which a reference to the UN Covenants would undoubtedly achieve. To fall back on
the status of the standard clause would thwart the human rights policies of the Community in its external relations and would eliminate the advantages to be gained by
the standard clause in relation to non-discrimination and enforceability. It may well
be argued that a more flexible utilization of the standard clause might at the same
time cause the genie to escape the bottle, which should be avoided at all costs.

C. The Social Clause

Among the possibilities currently being discussed for developing the human rights
clause the introduction of a social clause attracts most attention. The hope is to create conditionality as regards certain social rights and standards.[90] Quite a variety of
possibilities are being discussed, ranging from assuring certain fundamental rights
like the prohibition of child labour or forced labour all the way to a reference to particular International Labour Organization (ILO) conventions, the effectiveness of
which might thereby be enhanced considerably.[91] While the EP[92] as a motor for in-
tensifying the Community human rights policies has, on a number of occasions, declared itself in favour of a social clause,[93] the Commission gave up its right to initiate
the development of such a social clause for external agreements.

Various reasons are advanced for rejecting social clauses.[94] It is argued that not
only Article 5 of Lomé IV, but also the standard clause with its reference to human
rights or to the UDHR or to documents of the OSCE, already embraces social
human rights. A specific mention of social human rights would run counter to the
idea of the indivisibility of rights. There could also be an implicit threat to the general concept of social human rights, as one could gain the impression that the Community was of the opinion that social human rights do not belong to the canon of
universally recognized human rights.

Another fear is that social clauses might carry the danger of protectionism in the
guise of human rights formulations, i.e. demanding application for standards which

[90] Cf. for the corresponding discussion within the WTO, where in the final Ministerial Declaration of
the Ministerial Conference in Singapore in Dec. 1996 the link between labour standards and trade was referred to for the first time in an official WTO document: V. Leary, 'The WTO and the Social Clause: Post-
Singapore' (1997) 8 *EJIL* 118–22.

[91] Cf. E.H. Riedel, *Theorie der Menschenrechtsstandards* (1986), 165ff, 291ff.

[92] Cf. e.g. European Parliament Resolution on Human Rights in the European Union's Foreign Policy [1994] OJ C128/370; Resolution on the Introduction of a Social Clause in the Unilateral and Multilateral Trading System [1994] OJ C61/89; PE 216.714/fin., note 22 above, at 24ff.

[93] Cf. Tomasevski, note 22 above, at 44ff; Fouwels, note 80 above, at 312ff; PE 218.638/end., note 77
above, 16ff, at para. 67.

[94] Cf. N. Malanowski and C. Scherrer, *International Trade Agreements and Social Standards—The
North American Experience* (1996), 37ff; Hoffmeister, note 21 above, at chap. 15, II.

could negate the comparative advantages of the developing countries.[95] This fear was clearly highlighted by the World Trade Organization's Singapore Ministerial Declaration:[96]

> We reject the use of labour standards for protectionist purposes and agree that the comparative advantage of countries, particularly low-wage developing countries, must in no way be put into question . . .

Another problematic issue lies in the fact that in relation to social standards states cannot be treated alike. An individualized social clause could again provoke allegations of inequality of treatment, and might thereby, as a side-effect, eliminate the uniform standard clause. Mere reference to ILO conventions or the elaboration of detailed social standards might be problematical too. After all, state practice in relation to ratification of ILO conventions and the state of development of social standards and social rights amongst Member States varies a great deal.[97] For all these reasons, the introduction of a social clause seems very unlikely at the moment.[98]

It may well be asked whether a general broadening of the human rights clause is indeed advisable, considering that no adequate application practice has yet been developed. In a medium-term perspective there appears to be no need for an explicit social clause, as most social rights can be subsumed under the essential element clause and, what is more, the advantages of introducing a social clause could even be outweighed by its disadvantages. Instead, the Commission should follow a *bottom-up approach* and emphasize the idea that any human rights clause embraces social rights. It could do so by actively applying the existing clause to social rights situations in treaty States, where such rights and standards are systematically and seriously violated. A bottom-up approach would mean that the general clause should first be applied to flagrant breaches of the most important and undisputed social rights. Once this practice is established, application could be widened to an increasing number of social rights and standards. Following a bottom-up approach of this kind would promise the development of a satisfactory scope of protection for social rights and standards under the roof of the general human rights clause.

However, if the Commission in the medium term fails to translate the social rights potential of the human rights clause into reality the very idea of the indivisibility of human rights might require the introduction of an explicit social clause. In that case, much will depend, on the one hand, on whether the Council will be able to reach consensus about the respect for certain social rights and standards, and, on the other, that these may gain a level of importance warranting a general approval of conditionalities for trade relations. If such a social impetus were to develop, arguments to the contrary might well evaporate or be regarded as purely academic. A specific

---

[95] P. Alston, 'Linking Trade and Human Rights' (1980) 23 *GYIL* 148ff.

[96] World Trade Organization, Singapore Ministerial Declaration, para. 4. WT/MIN(96)/DEC/W (13 Dec. 1996).

[97] The opposition of the UK—together with developing countries—to the linking of trade and labour standards within the WTO at the Ministerial Conference of the WTO in Dec. 1996 is characteristic in this context, cf. Leary, note 90 above, at 119ff.

[98] In a short-term perspective the idea of a code of conduct for European companies abroad is interesting in this context. Cf. PE 216.714/fin., note 22 above, at 24ff, and PE 218.638/end., note 77 above, 10, at para. 19.

social clause, spelling out in detail what would otherwise have to be deduced from a more generally phrased human rights clause, might have a signal effect, marking the determination of the Community to take social rights seriously and to implement them effectively. Fears that such an explicit social clause might create the impression that the human rights clause on its own did not cover social rights could be dispelled by a clarifying formulation in the clause.

To start with, only few non-controversial fundamental rights should be spelled out (like the prohibition of forced or child labour[99]) which Member States of the EC consider essential to safeguard their universal respect even by sanctions, should the need arise. Reference to a small group of indispensable social rights and standards might muster more consent and could pave the way for the formulation of a universally applicable, general social clause, thus obviating non-uniform application in state practice.[100] Ultimately, it would be up to the political decisions by Member States or by the Council members whether full implementation of certain social rights and standards should be insisted upon, and thus deserve express formulation of a social clause.

D. Procedural Rules for Suspension

One reason for the lack of implementation of human rights clauses so far might be that no unambiguous rules relating to suspension procedures have existed.[101] Clearly such procedures and the necessary majorities can be deduced from the EC Treaty. However, different opinions can be voiced with regard to necessary majorities in the Council and the extent of the participation rights of the EP. Moreover, if one makes the suspension of parts of a treaty subject to the legal basis of the provision to be suspended, then there will be cases where even this basis is in dispute. Establishing uniform rules about procedures and *quorum* questions could thus contribute to replacing the present practice of reacting to serious human rights violations by treaty partners with *de facto* non-application of treaty provisions by the Commission or measures taken in the framework of the CFSP, by a practice which more closely mirrors the spirit of human rights clauses as well as the Community organ balance.

The new Article 300(2)(2) (*ex* Article 228(2)) EC now contains express clauses about procedures and Council *quora*. But here, too, the relevant legal bases determine those questions, as was pointed out above. Thus, in practice, unanimity in the Council will be the rule, apart from very obvious cases. The veto right following from this position might turn out to be a major stumbling block for developing a rational, uniform, and thus non-discriminatory application practice for human rights clauses. In the past numerous cases demonstrated how special interests of individual Member States could undermine the emergence of a consistent and rational human rights policy of the Community.[102] It would, therefore, be highly desirable if the

---

[99] Cf. PE 216.714/fin., note 22 above, at 24.   [100] Alston, note 95 above, at 145.
[101] Lenaerts and De Smijter, note 5 above, at 47; Rosas, note 71 above, at 136.
[102] Fouwels, note 80 above, at 309; Tomasevski, note 22 above, at 48ff; PE 222.307/fin., note 22 above, at 10.

Council by way of decision renounced the unanimity rule in treaty suspension matters and opted for a qualified majority.[103]

It is doubtful whether hesitant or opposing States would often have to face being overruled. The practice of qualified-majority voting in the Council in general has shown that the danger of being overruled creates pressure to consent, frequently leading to unanimous decisions, where in theory qualified majorities would suffice.

Renunciation of the unanimity rule thus has two clear advantages. On the one hand, eliminating the veto possibilities would pave the way for the effective and consistent implementation of human rights clauses. At the same time, the influence of hesitant or opposing States would be forced back into the time prior to taking the suspension decision, where weighing the pros and cons of the suspension issue might more easily lead to a modification or mitigation of the suspension decision. This way a compromise agreed by all could evolve.

One attempt to introduce a qualified majority for the suspension of a treaty can be found in the Commission proposal for a Council decision of 1996 on the procedure to be adopted for implementing Article 366a of Lomé IV (1995).[104] The proposal has so far been blocked by the United Kingdom, but since the change of government in 1997, there has been a real likelihood that the Council will decide positively before long. Article 2 of that Commission proposal stipulates that suitable measures to be taken on the legal basis of Article 366a in conjunction with Article 5 of Lomé IV may be decided upon by a qualified Council majority. The EP, in its turn, is only to be informed *ex post* about the decision taken. It may well be argued that the EP should be accorded broader participation rights,[105] or at least be consulted. However, the establishment of a qualified Council majority affecting suspension decisions under the Lomé Convention would clearly be a most rational step which should be extended at a later stage to other categories of Community treaties.[106]

In cases of mixed treaties, the prerogative powers of Member States relating to the suspension of particular treaty provisions might counteract the increase in procedural effectiveness aimed for by the establishment of qualified-majority voting in the Council, simply on account of the amount of time the co-ordination of the positions of the Member States would require.[107] A solution could be that the 'representatives of the Governments of the Member States meeting within the Council' took a decision in parallel to the decision by the Council on the introduction of qualified-majority voting, entitling the Community to act in accordance with the adopted procedure on behalf of the Member States as well. Only in this way could an effective procedure be created, facilitating consistent implementation of human rights clauses

---

[103] Cf. the Opinion of the Economic and Social Committee on 'The European Union and the External Dimension of Human Rights Policy' [1977] OJ C206/117, at para. 3.2.2; PE 216.714/fin., note 22 above, at 13; PE 222.307/fin., note 22 above, Opinion of the Committee on External Economic Relations, at 21ff.

[104] COM(96)69.

[105] PE 216.714/fin., note 22 above, at 13, suggests that the Parliament be consulted; PE 222.307/fin., note 22 above, at 5, claims that the assent of the Parliament ought to be necessary in implementing Art. 366a of Lomé IV (1995).

[106] PE 222.307/fin., note 22 above, at 17ff, notes that this is necessary simply to counteract the impression that ACP States were put at a disadvantage.

[107] Fouwels, note 80 above, at 312.

in practice. However, whether all Member States are willing to empower the Community likewise remains to be seen.

E. Rationality and Transparency in Implementing Human Rights Clauses: The Role of Objective Criteria and Country Reports

1. Criteria for the Implementation of Human Rights Clauses   Apart from the lack of unambiguous procedural rules concerning the interaction of Community institutions in implementing human rights clauses, another major cause of the discrepancy between the adequate legal potential of the standard clause and the inadequacy of its implementation might be the lack of objective criteria for applying the clause.[108] If the Community seeks to implement a consistent human rights policy in its external relations, objective criteria for applying the human rights clause would have to be established.[109] Although such objective criteria have frequently been called for,[110] no unequivocal statements to this effect have so far been issued.[111] Marantis in this respect resorted to deducing three more or less general principles from a publication by the Commission:[112]

- measures taken must be guided by objective and equitable criteria;
- measures must be tailored to the circumstances and graduated according to the gravity of each case;
- negative measures should avoid penalizing the population of the country in question and particularly its poorest sections.

But obviously these criteria are not sufficiently specific. And as the first principle amply shows, the claim for objective criteria has to this day not been fulfilled. In order to meet this challenge the criteria would have to be formulated in such a way that a balance can be struck between objectivity and consistency of implementation of the human rights clauses, on the one hand, and the potential for flexibility and discretion in Commission practice, on the other. If one is of the opinion that human rights clauses reveal their beneficial effect mainly prior to a possible decision on suspension, then the Commission needs adequate scope for action in order to persuade EC treaty partners by means of political dialogue that human rights positions must be respected. Naturally, every case will be unique, and so the individual, unique situation each treaty party is facing will have to be borne in mind. The response to grave breaches of certain human rights must not automatically and invariably entail measures such as suspension of specific treaty obligations.

The elaboration of objective procedures would be an important step towards a rational and transparent implementation of human rights clauses. The Commission will have to be quite clear about how it is to apply human rights clauses, from the recognition of a rights violation to actually applying a counter-measure.[113]

[108] PE 222.307/fin., note 22 above, at 8.
[109] Arts, note 1 above, at 266; PE 222.307/fin., note 22 above, at 9, 10.
[110] Cf. e.g., European Parliament, Resolution on Human Rights, Democracy, and Development of 22 Nov. 1991 [1991] OJ C326/259, at 260, para. 5; Clapham, note 19 above, at 365; PE 216.714/fin, note 22 above, at 19; Fouwels, note 80 above, at 311ff; PE 222.307/fin., note 22 above, at 10.
[111] Lenaerts and De Smijter, note 5 above, at 46ff.
[112] Marantis, note 18 above, at 23ff.   [113] PE 222.307/fin., note 22 above, at 21ff.

This will for one require drafting a catalogue of the very human rights covered by the clause. Although, as was shown above, EC human rights clauses have so far found at least three different shapes by referring either generally to human rights or to the UDHR or the OSCE documents, an intersecting core area can be determined. The synthesis struck is more or less covered by the Universal Bill of Rights containing the UDHR in combination with the 1966 Covenants. In addition, the various modes of reaction to grave breaches of human rights should be listed and a graded hierarchy of such measures established. In this respect, one might refer to the communication issued by the Commission '[o]n the inclusion of respect for democratic principles and human rights in agreements between the Community and third countries',[114] which forms the basis of the universal systematic guidelines of the Council adopted in May 1995. Annex 2 to the communication lists nine modalities that might be applied in cases of grave human rights violations:

(1) alteration of the contents of co-operation programmes or the channels used;
(2) reduction of cultural, scientific, and technical co-operation programmes;
(3) postponement of a Joint Committee meeting;
(4) suspension of high-level bilateral contacts;
(5) postponement of new projects;
(6) refusal to follow up partners' initiatives;
(7) trade embargoes;
(8) suspension of arms sales, suspension of military co-operation;
(9) suspension of co-operation.

The number of such reaction modalities might easily be increased and their implications detailed more precisely. In the case of the Lomé Convention, one might well outline which aspects could be envisaged for partial suspension: National Indicative Programme, Regional Indicative Programme, STABEX, Sysmin and Market access provisions, tendering, cumulation of rules of origin, and trade protocols.[115] Also, a loose hierarchy might be established between measures, always bearing in mind that such a hierarchical list merely represents a yardstick.

2. Country Reports as Catalysts   Apart from these modes of action with regard to human rights violations by treaty partners regular country reports about the human rights situation in all States with which the EC has concluded agreements containing a human rights clause could be drafted.[116] Such reports might be structured along the lines of the US State Department's annual report to the Senate, systematically surveying the human rights situation in all partner States and highlighting developments since the previous report. This should be followed by an outline of modes of reaction that the Community has chosen, and to what extent such measures were

---

[114] COM(95)216 final.   [115] PE 222. 307/fin., note 22 above, at 21ff.
[116] Cf. the Opinion of the Economic and Social Committee, note 103 above, at para. 3.2.4; European Parliament, 'Report on the Report from the Commission on the Implementation of Measures Intended to Promote Observance of Human Rights and Democratic Principles (for 1995) (COM(96)0672–C4–0095/97), Opinion of the Committee on Development and Co-operation, PE 223.610/fin., at 16.

successful. Such an approach might also provide the foundation of a comprehensive evaluation system for the implementation of human rights clauses.[117]

(1) Such a system of regular country reports might produce a more coherent and more transparent human rights policy of the Community in its external relations, and could thereby render it more effective. First, the country reports would force the Community to draw up a catalogue of rights to which the reports are to refer. Furthermore, the Community would find itself under pressure to optimize its fact-finding procedures. To obtain the relevant data, the Community could draw on information received from EU diplomatic missions and Member State missions in the countries concerned, as well as make use of information provided by UN institutions and NGOs.[118]

(2) It would be desirable to have one institutional focus for the fostering of human rights within the structure of the EC. Given the increasing importance of human rights in the internal and external dimension of the EC one could imagine one of the Commissioners being made responsible exclusively for human rights affairs.

(3) Publishing the database on the human rights situation in a specific country causing certain Community actions would allow NGOs to point out possible discrepancies in their own assessment of facts and thus make an input into the viewpoint held by the EC.[119]

(4) The existence of country reports might further contribute to lowering the threshold for taking sanctions in specific cases. As practice has shown, the Community and Member States tend to be reluctant to envisage sanctions where this would mean stigmatizing a powerful State as a human rights violator. The existence of objectively formulated country reports on all treaty partners does not in itself stipulate any sanctions, but can induce comments by NGOs. It might thus further suggest moving from mere pillorying to finding the most suitable sanction. At any rate, it would fulfil a publicity function before any concrete sanctions are envisaged, and might thus in itself lead to changes in conduct by States concerned. That this lesser form of reproof can work in practice was demonstrated when the UN Human Rights Commission declined to make a resolution condemning China's human rights practices in exchange for that country ratifying one of the 1966 Covenants and promising to sign the other one soon afterwards.

(5) Publishing country reports might also compel the Community as well as the Member States to adopt more consistent non-discriminatory implementation of the human rights clause. The general public would not understand

---

[117] Cf. the Opinion of the Economic and Social Committee, note 103 above, at para. 3.2.2.

[118] *Ibid.*, at para. 3.2.4; PE 216.714/fin., note 22 above, at 13.

[119] For the function of NGOs within the human rights policy of the Community cf. COM(96)672 final, Report from the Commission on the Implementation of Measures Intended to Promote Observance of Human Rights and Democratic Principles (for 1995), at 19ff. For the possible function of NGOs in the application of human rights clauses cf. P. Robinson, 'Political Conditionality: Strategic Implications for NGOs', in Stokke, note 23 above, at 373ff.

an unequal application of sanctions treating weaker States and more influential States differently.

(6) The credibility of Community action in the field of human rights protection might thus be enhanced through published country reports revealing uniform practice, based on objective and adequate criteria.

(7) The Community could be empowered to draw up reports on all countries with which it has concluded treaties containing a human rights clause, although the EC still lacks overall competence on human rights in all external relations, as shown above. Wherever it is entitled to draw up human rights clauses and implement them, it is also entitled to draw up country reports. They represent an important element of fact-finding in a preliminary phase of action, and are therefore to be considered as covered by the relevant competence of the Community.

However, the Community currently does not possess a general association power to draw up country reports on all States, particularly not on those with which no treaties or only treaties not containing a human rights clause exist. Legally, the compilation of reports on these States could be justified on the basis of the Common Foreign and Security Policy of the European Union under title V of the EU Treaty. At present, one could thus envisage an annual Community country report covering all States with which the Community has concluded treaties containing human rights clauses, supplemented by a European Union country report founded on the CFSP of title V of the EU Treaty for all other States. However, splitting the reports could be criticized as being artificial or reducing the authority of either report. Therefore, it would seem more advisable to draw up one general human rights report on all countries within the framework of the CFSP of the EU, which could then cover measures taken by the EC as well as such within the CFSP.

Regular country reports could thus properly underpin the human rights clauses in the external agreements of the European Community, and lead to a more rational, consistent, and uniform application by the Community.

VII. SUMMARY OF RECOMMENDATIONS

(1) The theoretical potential of the standard clause seems to be in conspicuous contrast to its utilization in practice. Yet it should be appreciated that the standard clause was introduced only a short time ago. Also, the significance of the human rights clause in practice should not be reduced to a mere potential of treaty suspension. The human rights clause reveals its beneficial effect mainly in the diplomatic phase prior to its application as a means of suspension of an agreement. One might therefore even argue that the human rights clause has missed its point, if it actually has to be applied by way of treaty suspension.

(2) Variations in the formulation of human rights clauses could undermine the advantages of a standardized clause and should therefore be avoided. However, if a variation should prove necessary, for example, in order to safeguard the conclusion of a certain agreement, close attention will have to be paid to the maintenance of the spirit of the clause.

(3) No explicit social clause should be established in external agreements of the Community. Instead, the Commission should translate the social rights potential of the existing human rights clauses into reality. Following a bottom-up approach the Commission should increasingly apply the general clauses to situations where social rights and standards are systematically and seriously violated by treaty partner States. Should the Commission, however, fail to put the social potential of the clauses into action, in a medium-term perspective, the very idea of indivisibility of human rights, which is often put forward as an argument against a specific reference to social rights, might in itself necessitate the introduction of a social clause.

(4) Unambiguous procedural rules to be followed for the suspension and termination of external agreements of the Community should be established. Qualified-majority voting in the Council could pave the way for the coherent and consistent application of human rights clauses and should consequently replace the requirement of unanimity. In cases of mixed agreements, the 'representatives of the Governments of the Member States meeting within the Council' should entitle the Community to act in accordance with the adopted procedure on behalf of the Member States as well.

(5) Objective criteria for applying the human rights clauses should be established. They should be formulated in such a way that a balance can be struck between objectivity and consistency of implementation of the human rights clauses, on the one hand, and the potential for flexibility and discretion of Commission practice, on the other. No automatisms must be introduced. Both a list of protected human rights and one of potential reaction modalities should be worked out.

(6) Annual country reports about the human rights situation in States with which the EC has concluded agreements containing a human rights clause should be published. These reports could, right by right, survey the human rights situation in the partner States and outline the modes of reaction the Community has chosen. A system of regular country reports might contribute considerably to a more consistent, coherent, and transparent human rights policy of the Community in its external relations by, *inter alia*, forcing the Community to draw up a catalogue of rights to which the reports refer, to optimize its fact-finding procedures, and to apply the clause equally to all partner States.

(7) It would be desirable to have one institutional focus for the fostering of human rights within the structure of the EC. Given the increasing importance of human rights in the internal and external dimension of the EC one could imagine one of the Commissioners being made responsible exclusively for human rights affairs.

ANNEX

I. Formulations of Human Rights Clauses

A. The 'Basis Clause' Co-operation ties between the Community and (Argentina) and this Agreement in its entirety are based on respect for the democratic principles and human rights, which inspire the domestic and external policies of the Community and (Argentina).

B. The 'Essential Element Clause' Respect for the democratic principles and human rights established by (the Helsinki Final Act and the Charter of Paris for a New Europe) (as well as the principles of market economy) (as defined at the Bonn CSCE conference) inspire the domestic and external policies of the Community and of (third countries) and constitute an essential element of this agreement.

C. Non-Compliance Clauses

1. The *'Baltic Clause'*
The parties reserve the right to suspend this Agreement in whole or in part with immediate effect if a serious breach of its essential provisions occurs.

2. The *'Bulgarian Clause'*
If either party considers that the other Party has failed to fulfil an obligation under this agreement, it may take appropriate measures. Before so doing, except in cases of special urgency, it shall supply the Association Council with all relevant information required for a thorough examination of the situation with a view to seeking a solution acceptable to the Parties.

In the selection of measures, priority must be given to those which least disturb the functioning of this Agreement. These measures shall be notified immediately to the Association Council and shall be the subject of consultations within the Association Council if the other Party so requests.

D. Lomé IV (1995)

1. Article 5(1)(3) of Lomé IV (1995)
Respect for human rights, democratic principles and the rule of law, which underpins relations between the ACP States and the Community and all provisions of the Convention, and governs the domestic and international policies of the Contracting Parties, shall constitute an essential element of the Convention.

2. Article 366a(2) of Lomé IV (1995) (Non-compliance Clause)
2. If one Party considers that another Party has failed to fulfil an obligation in respect of one of the essential elements referred to in Article 5, it shall invite the Party concerned, unless there is special urgency, to hold consultations with a view to assessing the situation in detail and, if necessary, remedying it.

For the purposes of such consultations, and with a view to finding a solution:

—the Community side shall be represented by its Presidency, assisted by the previous and next Member States to hold the Presidency, together with the Commission;

—the ACP side shall be represented by the ACP State holding the Co-Presidency, assisted by the previous and next ACP States to hold the Co-Presidency. Two additional members of the ACP Council of Ministers chosen by the Party concerned shall also take part in the consultations.

The consultations shall begin no later than 15 days after the invitation and as a rule last no longer than 30 days.

3. At the end of the period referred to in the third subparagraph of paragraph 2 if in spite of all efforts no solution has been found, or immediately in the case of urgency or refusal of consultation, the Party which invoked the failure to fulfil an obligation may take appropriate steps, including, where necessary, the partial or full suspension of application of this Convention to the Party concerned. It is understood that suspension would be a measure of last resort.

The Party concerned shall receive prior notification of any such measure which shall be revoked as soon as the reasons for taking it have disappeared.

H

The Role of Key Institutions and Actors

23

Human Rights Case Law in the Strasbourg and Luxembourg Courts: Conflicts, Inconsistencies, and Complementarities

DEAN SPIELMANN*

I. INTRODUCTION: HUMAN RIGHTS IN THE EUROPEAN AND INTERNATIONAL CONTEXTS

The European Convention for the Protection of Human Rights and Fundamental Freedoms (the ECHR) was signed in Rome on 4 November 1950. It entered into force on 9 September 1953. Originally signed by twelve States the Convention has now been ratified by most European States, and pursuant to recent changes in Eastern Europe, its territorial scope has been extended considerably. Thus, at the present moment, all forty one member States of the Council of Europe have ratified the Convention.[1]

It covers with its various Protocols mainly civil and political rights.[2] The Convention has proved to be a very successful treaty, a 'constitutional instrument of European public order in the field of human rights'.[3] The Convention provides for the right to life (Article 2); prohibition of torture (Article 3); prohibition of slavery and forced labour (Article 4); right to liberty and security (Article 5); right to a fair trial (Article 6); no punishment without law (Article 7); right to respect for private and family life (Article 8); freedom of thought, conscience and religion (Article 9); freedom of expression (Article 10); freedom of assembly and association (Article

---

* The author is deeply indebted to Georges Friden, M.Phil. (Cantab.), Legal Secretary at the ECJ for valuable comments on an earlier draft of this chap.

[1] The member States having signed/acceded to and ratified the Convention are: Albania, Andorra, Austria, Belgium, Bulgaria, Croatia, Cyprus, Czech Republic, Denmark, Estonia, Finland, France, Georgia, Germany, Greece, Hungary, Iceland, Ireland, Italy, Latvia, Liechtenstein, Lithuania, Luxembourg, Malta, Moldova, Netherlands, Norway, Poland, Portugal, Romania, Russia, San Marino, Slovakia, Slovenia, Spain, Sweden, Switzerland, the Former Yugoslav Republic of Macedonia, Turkey, Ukraine, and the UK.

[2] Economic and social rights are covered in the European Social Charter (1961). M. N. Shaw, International Law (1997) 257.

[3] J. Polakiewicz and V. Jacob-Foltzer, 'The European Human Rights Convention in Domestic Law: The Impact of Strasbourg Case-Law in States where Direct Effect is given to the Convention' (1991) 12 *HRLJ* 65. See also, most notably, C. Gearty, 'The European Court of Human Rights and the Protection of Civil Liberties: An Overview' (1993) 52 *Cambridge LJ* 89–127.

11); the right to marry (Article 12); the right to an effective remedy (Article 13) and the prohibition of discrimination (Article 14). Protocol I provides for the protection of property (Article 1); the right to education (Article 2) and the right to free elections (Article 3). Protocol IV provides for prohibition of imprisonment for debt (Article 1); freedom of movement (Article 2); prohibition of expulsion of nationals (Article 3) and prohibition of collective expulsion of aliens (Article 4). Protocol VI provides for the abolition of the death penalty and Protocol VII provides for procedural safeguards relating to expulsion of aliens (Article 1); the right of appeal in criminal matters (Article 2); compensation for wrongful conviction (Article 3); the right not to be tried or punished twice (Article 4) and equality between spouses (Article 5).[4]

Those are very briefly the main rights guaranteed by the Convention and its protocols.[5]

The European Court of Human Rights has emphasized that:

unlike international treaties of the classic kind, the Convention comprises more than mere reciprocal engagements between contracting states. It creates, over and above a network of mutual and bilateral undertakings, objective obligations, which in the words of the preamble, benefit from a 'collective enforcement'.[6]

This clear statement by the European Court echoes the famous *obiter dictum* of the International Court of Justice distinguishing:

between the obligations of a State towards the international community as a whole, and those arising *vis-à-vis* another State in the field of diplomatic protection. By their very nature the former are the concern of all States. In view of the importance of the rights involved, all States can be held to have a legal interest in their protection; they are obligations *erga omnes*.

Such obligations derive, for example, in contemporary international law, from the outlawing of acts of aggression, and of genocide, as also from the principles and rules concerning the basic rights of the human person, including protection from slavery and racial discrimination.[7]

More recently, the European Court of Human Rights, in a landmark judgment of 23 March 1995 referred to the Convention as 'a constitutional instrument of European public order (*ordre public*)'.[8]

---

[4] Shaw, note 2 above at 257–8. For more detail see among many monographs, D.J. Harris, M. O'Boyle, and C. Warbrick, *Law of the European Convention on Human Rights* (1995); D. Gomien, D. Harris, and L. Zwaak, *Law and Practice of the European Convention on Human Rights and the European Social Charter* (1996). See also the various contributions in R.St.J. Macdonald, F. Matscher, and H. Petzold (eds.), *The European System for the Protection of Human Rights* (1993).

[5] Besides the Convention, the two UN Covenants are often relied on before national courts, especially in systems where international treaties are directly applicable: International Covenants on Economic, Social and Cultural Rights and on Civil and Political Rights, adopted by GA Res. 2200 A (XXI), in United Nations, *A Compilation of International Instruments* (1994), i, Part 1, 8 and 20.

[6] *Ireland* v. *United Kingdom*, ECHR (1978), Series A, No. 25, 90–1, cited in Shaw, note 2 above, at 258.

[7] *Barcelona Traction, Light and Power Company, Limited* [1970] ICJ Rep. 3, at 32. See S. Schwebel, 'Human Rights in the World Court' (1991) 24 *Vand.J.Trans.L.* 965.

[8] *Loizidou* v. *Turkey (Preliminary Objections)*, ECHR (1995), Series A, Vol. 310, 27, at para. 75. See further J. Cohen-Jonathan, 'L'affaire Loizidou devant la Cour européenne des droits de l'homme. Quelques observations' [1998] *RGDIP* 123. See also, F. Sudre, 'Existe-t-il un ordre public européen?', in P. Tavernier (ed.), *Quelle Europe pour les droits de l'homme* (1996), 39. It is worth recalling that in this case

Although the Convention does not define how the States parties are to implement internally the relevant obligations, a majority of the High Contracting Parties have incorporated the Convention, giving it direct effect and allowing domestic courts to interpret it under the supervision of the Strasbourg institutions.[9]

At present, the European Community is not party to ECHR.[10] It is not bound by it and *Opinion 2/94* of 28 March 1996 of the European Court of Justice (ECJ)[11] makes it unlikely that an accession will be foreseeable in the near future. However, Article 6(2) (*ex* Article F) of the TEU, as amended by the Amsterdam Treaty of 1 October 1997 clearly concretizes the obligation to ensure respect for fundamental rights. The Maastricht Treaty in Article F(2) already provided that:

> The Union shall respect fundamental rights, as guaranteed by the European Convention for the Protection of Human Rights and Fundamental Freedoms signed in Rome on 4 November 1950 and as they result from the constitutional traditions common to the Member States, as general principles of Community Law.[12]

The Amsterdam Treaty,[13] however, added an important first paragraph promulgating general principles underlying the Union:

the European Court of Human Rights held that the Turkish restriction (Turkey accepting the jurisdiction of the Court only subject to a restriction concerning happenings in the Turkish-controlled part of Cyprus) was not permissible under the law of the Convention, and that the World Court precedents (concerning the so-called 'optional clause' under Art. 36 of the Statute of the ICJ which served as a model for Art. 46 of the Convention) were inapposite to the wholly different Strasbourg Court, which had different purposes and functions. See R. Jennings, 'The Judiciary, International and National, and the Development of International Law' (1996) 45 *ICLQ* 5. In the context of the present contribution, it is interesting to note that the European Court of Human Rights deliberately takes a different approach from that of the Permanent Court of International Justice and the International Court of Justice. See also H. Thirlway's intervention, 'The Proliferation of International Judicial Organs and the Formation of International Law', at the conference on *The Hague, Legal Capital of the World*, organized by the TMC Asser Instituut on 2–4 July 1998 in The Hague, Netherlands. See also J. Cohen-Jonathan, 'Les réserves dans les traités institutionels relatifs aux droits de l'homme. Nouveaux aspects européens et internationaux' [1996] *RGDIP* 915; J. Andriantsimbazovina, ' "Chronique Droits de l'homme": L'élaboration progressive d'un ordre public européen des droits de l'homme. Réflexions à propos de la jurisprudence de la Cour européenne des droits de l'homme de 1988 à 1995' (1997) 33 *CDE* 670.

 [9] Concerning the future incorporation of the Convention into English law, see, amongst many comments, B. Emmerson, 'This Year's Model—The Options for Incorporation' (1997) 2 *EHRLR* 313.

 [10] There have, however, been various attempts to formalize accession of the EC to the Convention. See e.g. the Joint Declaration of 5 Apr. 1977, [1977] OJ C103/1; the Memorandum of the Commission of 1979, *Bull. EC Suppl.* 2/79; the Communication of the Commission of 10 Nov. 1990, SEC(90)2078 final; and the Resolutions of the European Parliament of 17 Dec. 1993, [1994] OJ C20/546 and 18 Jan. 1994, [1994] OJ C44/32. The first explicit reference to the Convention was made in the Preamble to the Single European Act (1986) [1987] OJ L169/1.

 [11] *Opinion 2/94* [1996] ECR I–1759. On this opinion, see amongst many articles the case-note by C. Adams and P. Sands (1997) 46 *ICLQ* 220 and O. de Schutter and Y. Lejeune, 'L'adhésion de la Communauté à la Convention européene des droits de l'homme. A propos de l'avis 2/94 de la Cour de Justice des Communautés' (1996) 32 *CDE* 555. See also the conclusion to this chap.

 [12] It is submitted that the reference to the Convention also includes the various additional prots. Indeed, if Art. 6 (*ex* Art. F) is a *coup de chapeau* to the pioneering action of the ECJ, as Bruno de Witte rightly puts it in his contribution to this vol., it should be emphasized that the jurisprudence of the Luxembourg Court includes references to the additional protocols of the Convention. See e.g. the judgment in Case 44/79, *Hauer* v. *Land Rheinland-Pfalz* [1979] ECR 3727, referring to the right of property as laid down by Art. 1 of Prot. I to the Convention.

 [13] Concerning human rights in the context of the Amsterdam Treaty, see J. Wachsmann, 'Les droits de l'homme' (1997) 33 *RTDE* 884; F. Sudre, 'La Communauté européenne et les droits fondamentaux après le traité d'Amsterdam: Vers un nouveau système européen de protection des droits de l'homme' [1998] *La*

The Union is founded on the principles of liberty, democracy, respect for human rights and fundamental freedoms, and the rule of law, principles which are common to the Member States.

More fundamentally, under the modification of Article L,[14] the European Court of Justice will have jurisdiction to supervise acts of the European institutions concerning co-operation in the fields of justice and home affairs as to their consistency with international human rights norms. Moreover, fundamental rights as defined by the Convention will be monitored by the European Union and sanctions will be imposed on Member States which systematically violate these rights.

It is also obvious that the European Union enters into competition with the Council of Europe in so far as fundamental rights referring to a political model, 'the democratic society' are concerned. As Frédéric Sudre rightly puts it:

> the triptych, human rights–democracy–rule of law is erected by Article 6 para. 1 as a founding socle of the European Union and thus of the three pillars composing it, i.e. the Communities, cooperation in the fields of justice and home affairs, common foreign and security policy.[15]

The European Court of Justice[16] has protected fundamental rights within the Community sphere as being part of the unwritten general principles of Community law.[17] Indeed, many cases decided by it concern fundamental rights, in particular

Semaine Juridique I–100. See also K. Lenaerts and E. de Smijter, 'Le traité d'Amsterdam' (1998) 46 *Journal des Tribunaux Droit Européen* 33; R. Dehousse, 'Le traité d'Amsterdam, reflet de la nouvelle Europe' (1997) 33 *CDE* 265; C.-D. Ehlermann, 'Différenciation, flexibilité, coopération renforcée: les nouvelles dispositions du Traité d'Amsterdam' [1997] *RMUE* 53; J.V. Louis, 'Le Traité d'Amsterdam, une occasion perdue?' [1997] *RMUE* 17.

[14] Art. 46 of the Amsterdam Treaty (*ex* Art. 38).

[15] Sudre, note 13 above.

[16] The generic term 'ECJ' includes in this chap. the ECJ properly speaking and the CFI.

[17] However in its early days, the ECJ refused to take into account fundamental rights. See J.-P. Jacqué, 'Cours général de droit communautaire' (1990) 1–I *AEL* 279. Early restrictive case law includes Case 1/58, *Stork* v. *High Authority* [1958–9] ECR 41 and Joined Cases 16, 17, & 18/59, *Ruhr* v. *High Authority* [1960] ECR 47. An important step was taken by the ECJ in Case 29/69, *Stauder* v. *City of Ulm* [1969] ECR 419. Since then the ECJ has developed a considerable body of case law referring to fundamental rights: Case 11/70, *Internationale Handelsgesellschaft mbH* v. *Einfuhr- und Vorratsstelle für Getreide und Futtermittel* [1970] ECR 1125; and the Convention: Case 4/73, *Nold KG* v. *Commission* [1974] ECR 491; Case 36/75, *Rutili* v. *Minister for the Interior* [1975] ECR 1219; Case 44/79, *Hauer* v. *Land Rheinland-Pfalz* [1979] ECR 3727. Cf. Joined Cases 60 & 61/84, *Cinéthèque SA et al.* v. *Fédération nationale des cinémas français* [1985] ECR 2605; Case 12/86, *Demirel* v. *Stadt Schwäbisch Gmünd* [1987] ECR 3719. Among countless comments on the subject, see, *inter alia*, T. Hartley, *The Foundations of European Community Law* (1998) and J. Verhoeven, *Droit de la Communauté européenne* (1996). See also, amongst numerous articles on the subject, P. Pescatore, 'The Context and Significance of Fundamental Rights in the Law of the European Communities' (1981) 2 *HRLJ* 295 and 'La Cour de justice des Communautés européennes et la Convention européenne des Droits de l'homme', in F. Matscher and H. Petzold (eds.), *Protecting Human Rights: The European Dimension: Studies in honour of Gérard J. Wiarda* (1988), 441; M. Mendelson, 'The European Court of Justice and Human Rights' (1981) 1 *YEL* 125 and 152; M. Dauses, 'La protection des droits fondamentaux dans l'ordre juridique communautaire' (1984) 20 *RTDE* 401; J.H.H. Weiler, 'The European Court at Crossroads: Community Human Rights and Member State Action', in F. Capotorti *et al.* (eds.), *Du droit international au droit de l'intégration* (1987), 821; N. Foster, 'The European Court of Justice and the European Convention for the Protection of Human Rights' (1987) 8 *HRLJ* 245; R. Lecourt, 'Cour européenne des Droits de l'Homme et Cour de justice des Communautés européennes', in F. Matscher and H. Petzold, above, at 441; H. Schermers, 'The European Communities Bound by Fundamental Human Rights' (1990) 27 *CML Rev.* 249; F. Mancini and V. di Bucci, 'Le développement des droits fondamentaux en tant que partie du droit communautaire' (1990) 1–I *AEL* 27; J.-P. Jacqué, 'Communauté européenne et Convention européenne des droits de l'homme', in J. Boulouis (ed.), *L'Europe et*

those guaranteed by the Convention, and fundamental rights are frequently referred to as a guideline[18] denoting a special category of general principles of Community law.[19] It is thus inevitable that divergent or inconsistent interpretations between the two European Courts is possible,[20] especially as the Luxembourg Court is

le droit: Mélanges en Hommage à Jean Boulouis (1991), 325; J.H.H. Weiler, A. Cassese, and A. Clapham (eds.), *Human Rights and the European Community: Methods of Protection* (1991) and *Human Rights and the European Community: The Substantive Law* (1991); A. Clapham, *Human Rights and the European Community: A Critical Overview* (1991), 51; J. Coppel and A. O'Neill, 'The European Court of Justice: Taking Rights Seriously?' (1992) 29 *CML Rev.* 669 and the response by J.H.H. Weiler and N. Lockhart, "Taking Rights Seriously" Seriously: The European Court and its Fundamental Rights Jurisprudence' (1995) 32 *CML Rev.* 51 and 579; F. Jacobs, 'The Protection of Human Rights in the Member States of the European Community: The Impact of the Case-law of the Court of Justice', in J. O'Reilly (ed.), *Human Rights and Constitutional Law: Essays in Honour of Brian Walsh* (1992), 243; J. Pipkorn, 'La Communauté européenne et la Convention européenne des droits de l'homme' (1993) 4 *RTDH* 221 and (1994) 4 *Actualités du droit* 464; Jacqué. 'The Convention and the European Communities' in R. St J. Macdonald, F. Matscher and H. Petzold (eds.), note 4 above, 889–907; the various remarks and interventions at a panel chaired by Schermers on 'Human Rights Protection in Europe: The Court of Justice of the European Communities and the European Court of Human Rights', in *Contemporary International Law Issues: Opportunities at a Time of Momentous Change* (Proceedings of the Second Joint Conference of the ASIL & NVIR held in The Hague, The Netherlands, 22–24 July 1993) (1994), 22; J. Kokott, 'Menschenrechtsschutz im Rahmen der Rechtsordnung der Europäischen Gemeinschaften', in A.A. Cançado Trindade (ed.), *The Modern World of Human Rights: Essays in Honour of Thomas Buergenthal* (1996), 135; Andriantsimbazovina, 'La Convention européenne des droits de l'homme et la Cour de Justice des Communautés européennes après le traité d'Amsterdam: de l'emprunt à l'appropriation?', *Europe* (Oct. 1998), 3. For a detailed survey and analysis, see Bruno de Witte's contribution to this vol.

[18] Notable cases include Case 36/75, *Rutili* [1975] ECR 1219; Joined Cases 46/87 and 227/88, *Hoechst AG* v. *EC Commission* [1989] ECR 2859, and, more recently, Case C–84/95, *Bosphorus Hava Yollari Turizm ve Ticaret AS* v. *Minister for Transport, Energy and Communications e.a.* [1996] ECR I–3953, Opinion of Jacobs AG, as well as the Aids test case concerning the right to keeps a person's state of health secret and Art. 8 of the European Convention on Human Rights, Case C–404/92, *X* v. *EC Commission* [1994] ECR I–4737, (1995) 16 HRLJ 54, Opinion of Van Gerven AG. Cf. Case C–62/90, *EC Commission* v. *Federal Republic of Germany*, [1992] ECR I–2575. In more recent cases, the ECJ has taken into account the case law of the European Court of Human Rights. See Case C–13/94, *P* v. *S & Cornwall County Council* [1996] ECR I–2143; Case C–129/95, *Criminal Proceedings* v. *X* [1996] ECR I–6609, and Case C–368/95, *Vereinigte Familiapress Zeitungsverlags und -vertriebs GmbH* v. *Heinrich Bauer Verlag* [1997] ECR I–3689. For a complete overview, see Sudre (ed.), 'Droit communautaire des droits fondamentaux. Chronique de la jurisprudence de la Cour de Justice des Communautés européennes' (1998) 9 *RTDE* 675. See below for comments.

[19] See, *inter alia*, the judgment in Case 4/73, *Nold* [1974] ECR 491; and the judgment in Case 136/79, *National Panasonic (UK) Limited* v. *EC Commission* [1980] ECR 2033.

[20] In some cases, the problems arising under the Convention have been left undecided. See e.g. Case 136/79, *National Panasonic* [1980] ECR 2033. See comments on this case by J. Cohen-Jonathan, 'Respect for Private and Family Life', in R. St. J. Macdonald, F. Matscher, and H. Petzold, note 4 above, at 428. See also the judgment of the Court in Joined Cases 46/87 and 227/88, *Hoechst* [1989] ECR 2924. See also the famous *Spanish Fishermen* Cases, Joined Cases 50–58/82, *Administrateur des affaires maritimes à Bayonne & Procureur de la République* v. *José Dorca Marina et al.* [1982] ECR 3949 and comments by R. Churchill and N. Foster, 'Double Standards in Human Rights? The Treatment of Spanish Fishermen by the European Community' (1987) 12 *EL Rev.* 430. Other cases include Case C–168/91, *Christos Konstantinidis* v. *City of Altensteig, Standesamt, & Landratsamt Calw, Ordnungsamt* [1993] ECR I–1191 and the Opinion of Van Gerven AG on Art. 10 of the Convention in Case C–159/90, *The Society for the Protection of Unborn Children Ireland Ltd* v. *Stephen Grogan and others* [1991] ECR I–4685. See also Joined Cases 100–103/80, *SA Musique Diffusion française et al.* v. *EC Commission* [1983] ECR 1825 and comments by D. Spielmann, 'Deux conséquences du caractère pénal des amendes prononcées par la Commission des Communautés européennes dans le domaine du droit de la concurrence', in F. Tulkens and H-D. Bosly (eds.), *La Justice pénale et l'Europe. Travaux des XVe journées d'études juridiques Jean Dabin* (1996), 509, as well as the judgment in Case 374/87, *Orkem* v. *EC Commission* [1989] ECR 3283.

not legally obliged to follow the interpretation of the European Court of Human Rights.[21]

II. THE POTENTIAL SITUATIONS WITHIN THE COMMUNITY SPHERE

It is traditionally admitted that the protection of human rights by the ECJ can only arise within the scope of EC law. Where the field within which such rights are claimed falls outside the Community's competence, Community law has no relevance.[22] The European Court of Justice has taken a broad view of when it may legitimately respond to claims based on the protection of fundamental rights, but has been careful to require that the applicability of EC law to the facts must be established before the issue of human rights is examined.[23]

Community acts and national measures under review by the ECJ may be inconsistent with the Convention. National measures within the Community sphere and/or implementing European Community acts, including judgments of the ECJ and the Court of First Instance (CFI) may also be contrary to the Convention. Let us briefly consider both situations and case law dealing with the problems.

A. *Community Acts under Review by the European Court of Justice*

Community acts are frequently challenged before the CFI and the ECJ. It is also frequent that the Convention is invoked in order to have such acts annulled.

Historically, in developing its fundamental rights jurisprudence, the ECJ limited itself to reviewing the validity of Community acts, referring to fundamental rights as general principles of Community law derived from the human rights commitments of the Member States.[24] This clear commitment of the ECJ can be observed in a consistent body of case law and has contributed to a positive development of the interpretation of certain human rights provisions. For example, in a landmark judgment of 5 October 1994,[25] the ECJ overruled a judgement of the CFI of 18 September 1992[26] concerning an individual's refusal to undergo an Aids test for pre-

---

[21] See Opinion of Darmon AG in Case 374/87, *Orkem* [1989] ECR 3351. For comments, see the major contribution of R. Lawson, 'Confusion and Conflict? Diverging Interpretations of the European Convention on Human Rights in Strasbourg and Luxembourg', in R. Lawson and M. de Bloijs (eds.), *The Dynamics of the Protection of Human Rights in Europe: Essays in Honour of Henry G. Schermers* (1994), iii, 219 at 228, a contribution that has been of considerable help for the preparation of this chap. See also Andriantsimbazovina, note 8 above, at 670.

[22] Case 12/86, *Demirel* [1987] ECR 3719.

[23] Case C–168/91, *Christos* [1993] ECR I–1191. However, in Case C–13/94, *P* v. *S and Cornwall County Council* [1996] ECR I–2143, the ECJ seems to take a far more liberal approach, reversing the standard test declaring that fundamental human rights include the principle of equality, and that this non-discrimination principle extends to transsexuals. On this evolution see the case-note by L. Flynn (1997) 34 *CML Rev.* 384.

[24] Lawson, note 21 above, at 224.

[25] Case C–404/92, *X* v. *EC Commission* [1994] ECR I–4737, (1995) 16 HRLJ 54.

[26] Joined Cases T–121/89 and T–13/90, *X* v. *Commission* [1992] ECR II–2195.

recruitment purposes and the right to keep one's state of health secret pursuant to Article 8 of the ECHR.[27]

Article 46 (*ex* Article L) of the Amsterdam Treaty defines the scope of the jurisdiction of the ECJ and refers expressly to Article 6(2) of the Amsterdam Treaty (*ex* Article F of the Maastricht Treaty) concerning acts by the institutions in so far as the Court is competent by virtue of the treaties.[28] The respect for fundamental rights by the institutions is thus enshrined,[29] and their implementation through the ECJ is guaranteed.[30]

B. *National Measures under Review by the European Court of Justice*

Going beyond the mere respect for fundamental rights by the institutions, the ECJ has insisted that *national measures within the Community sphere, scope, field, or area*[31] must comply with fundamental rights[32] and that the Convention can be used as a yardstick for review.[33]

This may occur when a State is acting for and/or on behalf of the Community and implementing a Community policy and when the State relies on a derogation from fundamental market freedoms. In the *ERT* judgment of 18 June 1991,[34] the ECJ insisted that:

> where (national) rules do fall within the scope of Community law, and reference is made to the Court for a preliminary ruling, it must provide all the criteria of interpretation needed by the national court to determine whether those rules are compatible with the fundamental rights the observance of which the Court ensures and which derive in particular from the European Convention on Human Rights.[35]

Such rules may be subject to scrutiny by the ECJ.

The same applies as indicated above to *national measures implementing Community acts*, as indeed it should be, given the lack of strong parliamentary procedures during enactment of EC legislation.[36] Robust judicial review as advocated by

---

[27] See also text to note 124 below.   [28] Wachsmann, note 13 above, at 888.

[29] In its *Opinion 2/94*, the ECJ had already made it crystal clear that respect for human rights is a condition of the legality of Community acts.

[30] A parallel non-judicial remedy is offered through Art. 190(e) (*ex* Art. 138(e)) EC: the ombudsman. See de Witte's contribution to this vol. and his suggestion for reform allowing the ombudsman to bring a complaint about a breach of fundamental rights, after having tried to reach a solution using existing mechanisms, before the CFI (or directly before the ECJ). See also J. Söderman, 'Rapport général on Citizenship of the Union', XVIII FIDE Congress Stockholm (June 1998), forthcoming.

[31] Different formulae are used. See Weiler and Lockhart, note 17 above, at 62.

[32] See above. On this, see most notably, *ibid.* On the recent evolution see also Flynn, note 23 above, at 384.

[33] Weiler and Lockhart, note 17 above, at 62, note 26.

[34] Case C–260/89, *Elliniki Radiophonia Tiléorassi AE & Panellinia Omospondia Syllogon Prossopikou* v. *Dimotiki Etairia Pliroforissis & Sotirios Kouvelas & Nicolaos Avdellas et al.* [1991] ECR I–2925. Cf. Case C–159/90, *Grogan* [1991] ECR I–4685; and Case C–168/91, *Christos* [1993] ECR I–1191, in which the ECJ ignored the ECHR. See also Case 12/86, *Wachauf* [1989] ECR 2609. Cf. i.e. where national measures were not taken in pursuance of powers granted under Community law, Case 12/86, *Demirel* [1987] ECR 3719; Joined Cases 60 and 61/84, *Cinéthèque SA et al.* v. *Fédération nationale des cinémas français* [1985] ECR 2627. See also Case C–326/88, *Anklagemyndigheden* v. *Hansen & Soen I/S* [1990] ECR I–2911 and comments by J. Cohen-Jonathan, 'L'adhésion de la Communauté européenne à la Convention européenne des droits de l'homme' (1995) 3 *Journal des Tribunaux Droit Européen* 49.

[35] Case C–260/89, *ERT* [1991] ECR I–2925, at 2964, cited in Lawson, note 21 above, at 233.

[36] Weiler and Lockhart, note 17 above, at 62.

leading authorities[37] inevitably creates the risk of potential conflicts between both European Courts.[38] In *Wachauf*, the Court explicitly held that 'the requirements of the protection of fundamental rights in the Community legal order' are 'also binding on the Member States when they implement Community rules'.[39]

Recent developments concerning the implementation of Community decisions, including judgments of the European Court of Justice, show that international obligations might collide and impose a considerable dilemma on Member States.[40] A warning shot has now been fired by the Strasbourg Court in the *Cantoni* judgment of 15 November 1996.[41] The Strasbourg Court held in this case that the principle of legality implies that an offence must be clearly defined in the law, and that the fact that a domestic provision is based almost word for word on a Community Directive does not remove it from the ambit of Article 7 of the Convention.[42]

Moreover, it seems that the European Commission on Human Rights has agreed to reconsider the position it initially took in the *Melchers* case,[43] declaring admissible by its decision of 24 February 1997 an application concerning refusal of access to court with regard to an action against the European Space Agency.[44]

III. CONFLICTS AND INCONSISTENCIES

A. Leaving Fundamental Rights Questions Undecided

In some cases, the ECJ decided on the issue whilst leaving the Convention dimension aside. The *National Panasonic* case, leading to a judgment of 26 June 1980,[45] is particularly interesting in this respect. The case concerned a search that was carried out under the competition rules of the EC Treaty and Regulation 17. The EC Commission inspected the premises of the undertaking without a search warrant and in the absence of the company's lawyer. Moreover, no advance notice had been given. If it is understandable that no notice be given in investigatory proceedings, most Member States provide, however, for the intervention of a judicial authority delivering a search/seizure warrant. *National Panasonic* relied on Article 8 of the Convention which reads as follows:

[37] Weiler and Lockhart, note 17 above, at 62

[38] See, e.g., the situation involving an EC dir. and subsequent Member State action in *Cantoni* v. *France*, ECHR Reports, 1997–V, 1614 (1997) 8 *RTDH* 685, note by Spielmann. On this case, see below.

[39] Case 5/88, *Wachauf* [1989] ECR 2609 at 2639, cited in Lawson, note 21 above, at 224.

[40] *M and Co.* v. *Germany* (1990) 64 D&R 138, (1991) 2 *RTDH* 395, note by F. Rigaux. See also *Procola* v. *Luxembourg*, Decision of 1 July 1993 (1993) 1 *Bulletin des droits de l'homme* 3.

[41] *Cantoni*, ECHR Reports, 1997–V, 1614; Spielmann, note 38 above.

[42] *Ibid.*, at paras. 29–30. Cf. the ECJ's judgment in Case 64/83, *Regina* v. *Kent Kirk* [1984] ECR 2689; Joined Cases C–206/88 and 207/88, *Criminal Proceedings* v. *G. Vessoso & G. Zanetti* [1990] ECR I–1474. See D. Spielmann, 'Principe de légalité et mise en œuvre communautaire' (1997) 8 *RTDH* 694 and 710. On the principle of legality see also H. Sevenster, 'Criminal Law and EEC Law' (1992) 29 *CML Rev.* 32.

[43] *M. and Co.* v. *Germany* (1990), 64 D&R 138; Rigaux, note 40 above.

[44] Appl. No. 26083/94, *R. Whaite et al.* v. *Germany*, cited by G. Ress, 'Menschenrechte, europäisches Gemeinschaftsrecht und nationales Verfassungsrecht', in H. Haller *et al.* (eds.), *Staat und Recht, Festschrift für Günther Winkler* (1997), 921.

[45] Case 136/79, *National Panasonic* [1980] ECR 2057; Lawson, note 21 above, at 237.

1. Everyone has the right to respect for his private and family life, his home and his correspondence.

2. There shall be no interference by a public authority with the exercise of this right except such as is in accordance with the law and is necessary in a democratic society in the interests of national security, public safety or the economic well-being of the country, for the prevention of disorder or crime, for the protection of health or morals, or for the protection of the rights and freedoms of others.

The European Court left most problems undecided by holding that while Article 8(2), 'in so far as it applies to public persons', provides that public authorities should not interfere with the exercise of the rights referred to in Article 8(1), it also acknowledges that such interference is permissible to the extent to which it is 'in accordance with the law and is necessary in a democratic society for the economic well-being of the country'. The Court held that the powers given to the Commission by Article 14 of Regulation 17 are to enable the Commission to carry out its duty under the EEC Treaty of ensuring that the rules on competition are applied in the common market—rules which aim to prevent competition from being distorted to the detriment of the public interest, individual undertakings, and consumers. As such, the Commission's exercise of those powers:

> contributes to the maintenance of the system of competition intended by the Treaty which undertakings are absolutely bound to comply with. In these circumstances, it does *therefore* not appear that Regulation No. 17, by giving the Commission the powers to carry out investigations without previous notification, infringes the right invoked by the applicant.[46]

As Rick Lawson in his major contribution to the subject[47] points out, the ECJ left open whether a legal person could rely on the right to privacy and more importantly applied a very general and abstract test to determine if the Commission had respected this right, arguing merely that the interference with the assumed private life of Panasonic had a 'legitimate aim' as required by the Convention.[48]

The author continues that:

> Whether the investigation had actually 'been necessary in a democratic society' was left unanswered. As a separate issue, the ECJ did entertain the complaint that the investigation had been disproportionate, but dismissed it on essentially the same ground as the complaint under Article 8 ECHR:
>
> > Considering that the contested decision *aimed* solely at enabling the Commission to collect the necessary information to appraise whether there was any infringement of the Treaty, it does *therefore* appear that the Commission's action in this instance was disproportionate to the objective pursued and therefore violated the principle of proportionality.[49]

Again, the Court applied a very general and abstract test. Apparently, the way in which the search was actually executed was not a relevant factor in its assessment.[50]

---

[46] *Ibid.*, at 2957. Emphasis added. Cited by Lawson, note 21 above, at 238.
[47] Lawson, note 21 above.   [48] *Ibid.*
[49] Case 136/79, *National Panasonic* [1980] ECR 2033 at 2060. Emphasis added.
[50] Lawson, note 21 above, at 238, quoting the judgment of the ECJ at 2060. Cf. the *Funke*, *Crémieux* and *Miaille* cases concerning French customs law: ECHR (1993), Series A, Vols. 256–A, 256–B, and

The ECJ did not take into account human rights issues in various other cases. For example, in the so-called *Spanish Fishermen Cases*[51] involving alleged retrospective law, the Court did not meet the argument based on Article 7 of the Convention[52] and in *Dorca Marina*[53] misinterpreted Article 14 of the Convention.[54] Similarly, in *Konstantinidis*,[55] concerning the right to a name, the ECJ left the human rights dimension undecided.[56] The same occurred in *Grogan*[57] concerning medical termination of pregnancy and prohibition on distribution of information about clinics in other EEC States, where the Court left the question open concerning freedom to receive and impart information as protected by Article 10 of the Convention.[58]

This careful approach of the ECJ, of avoiding the human rights dimension, can thus be observed in cases where no Strasbourg case law exists and where the Strasbourg Court is about to decide a rather controversial issue.[59] This reluctant approach should be distinguished from situations where the ECJ for policy reasons in competition cases declined to decide the fundamental rights issue, as in *National Panasonic*, or even embarked on an open conflict line as may be observed in subsequent cases.

B. Open Conflict

Flagrant conflict as to the case law of the two European Courts can be ascertained in the context of major cases concerning Articles 8 and 6 of the Convention where the Luxembourg Court took a restrictive view.[60]

256–C respectively. In those cases no warrants had been issued. The European Court of Human Rights found a breach of Art. 8 of the Convention. For comments see, *inter alia*, Cohen-Jonathan, note 20 above, at 428.

[51] Joined Cases 50–58/82, *Administrateur des affaires maritimes à Bayonne & Procureur de la République* v. *José Dorca Marina et al.* [1982] ECR 3949. See on this Lawson, note 21 above, at 234.

[52] Art. 7 of the Convention reads:

'1. No one shall be held guilty of any criminal offence on account of any act or omission which did not constitute a criminal offence under national or international law at the time when it was committed. Nor shall a heavier penalty be imposed than the one that was applicable at the time the criminal offence was committed.

2. This Article shall not prejudice the trial and punishment of any person for any act or omission which, at the time when it was committed, was criminal according to the general principles of law recognised by civilised nations.'

Cf. Case 63/83, *Regina* v. *Kent Kirk* [1984] ECR 2689.

[53] Joined Cases 50–58/82, *Administrateur des affaires maritimes à Bayonne & Procureur de la République* v. *José Dorca Marina et al.* [1982] ECR 3494.

[54] The ECJ discussed the merits of Art. 14 after having regarded all the other human rights arguments advanced as irrelevant. See comments by Churchill and Foster, note 20 above.

[55] Case C–168/91, *Christos* [1993] ECR I–1191; Lawson, note 21 above, at 247.

[56] Cf. Strasbourg case law: *Cossey* v. *United Kingdom*, ECHR (1990), Series A, Vol. 184; *B* v. *France*, ECHR (1992), Series A, Vol. 232; *Burghartz* v. *Switzerland*, ECHR (1994), Series A, Vol. 280–A; and *Stjerna* v. *Finland*, ECHR (1994), Series A, Vol. 299–B.

[57] Case C–159/90, *Grogan* [1991] ECR I–4685. Van Gerven AG however, construed the case as a conflict between two fundamental human rights, i.e. the right to life and that to freedom of expression, concluding that individual States must be allowed a fairly considerable margin of discretion in defining public policy and morality.

[58] See also Van Gerven AG's opinion on Art. 10 which proved to be inconsistent with the Strasbourg Court's judgment of 29 Oct. 1992, *Open Door and Dublin Well Woman* v. *Ireland*, ECHR (1992), Series A, Vol. 246–A. See also Lawson, note 21 above, at 234–5.

[59] Joined Cases 50–58/82, *Administrateur des affaires maritimes à Bayonne & Procureur de la République* v. *José Dorca Marina et al.* [1982] ECR 3494, might be an exception in this respect.

[60] In some cases, the ECJ took a more liberal view than its Strasbourg counterpart. See e.g. the

Firstly in *Hoechst*,[61] where a Commission investigation into several undertakings and their refusal to co-operate were at stake, the ECJ held that Article 8 of the Convention *does not* apply to companies. Hoechst had relied on the inviolability of the home, arguing that for the search to be lawful, it was necessary for the Commission to have a court order, issued by the ECJ and specifying the limits of the search in detail.[62]

The ECJ, in its judgment of 21 September 1989 and without taking account of the *Chappell* judgment of the European Court of Human Rights of 30 March 1989,[63] held that although the existence of a fundamental right to the inviolability of the home must be recognized in the Community legal order as a principle common to the laws of the Member States in regard to private dwellings of natural persons:

> the same is not true in regard to undertakings, because there are not inconsiderable divergencies between the legal systems of the Member States in regard to the nature and degree of protection afforded to business premises against intervention by the public authorities.[64]

For the Court, the protective scope of Article 8(1), according to which 'everyone has the right to respect for his private and family life, his home and his correspondence':

> is concerned with the development of man's personal freedom and may not therefore be extended to business premises. Furthermore, it should be noted that there is no case-law of the European Court of Human Rights on that subject.[65]

The Court continued, however, that in all the legal systems of the Member States, any intervention by the public authorities in the sphere of private activities of any person, whether natural or legal:

> must have a legal basis and be justified on the grounds laid down by law, and, consequently, those systems provide, albeit it in different forms, protection against arbitrary or disproportionate intervention. The need for such protection must be recognized as a general principle of Community law.[66]

applicability of the fair trial principles as laid down in Art. 6 in relation to staff cases. See Case 257/85, *Dufay* v. *European Parliament* [1987] ECR 1561 and Case 22/84, *Marguerite Johnston* v. *Chief Constable of the Royal Ulster Constabulary* [1986] ECR 1651, and compare with Strasbourg case law, in particular with *Neigel* v. *France*, ECHR Reports, 1997–II, 399; *Lombardo* v. *Italy*, ECHR (1992), Series A, Vol. 249–B; and *Massa* v. *Italy* ECHR (1993), Series A, Vol. 265–B.

  [61] Joined Cases 46/87 and 227/88, *Hoechst* [1989] ECR 2859.
  [62] See, Lawson, note 21 above, at 239. This is also the view of Mischo AG in his opinion in the *Hoechst* case, *ibid.*, at 2900, referring to the report of 15 May 1984 of the Select Committee on the European Communities of the House of Lords (*Commission's Powers of Investigation and Inspection*, House of Lords, Session 1983–4, 18th Report). On the Commission's investigatory powers, see G. Friden, 'Les garanties procédurales en droit communautaire de la concurrence', in Tulkens and Bosly, note 20 above, at 473.
  [63] *Chappell*, ECHR (1989), Series A, Vol. 152. It should however be stressed that in *Chappell* the applicants' business premises and private home were in the same building. The Strasbourg Court found no violation of Art. 8 of the Convention. See also Lawson, note 21 above, 241.
  [64] Joined Cases 46/87 and 227/88, *Hoechst* [1989] ECR 2859 at 2924. Cited by Lawson, note 21 above, 240.
  [65] *Ibid.*
  [66] Joined Cases 46/87 and 227/88, *Hoechst* [1989] ECR 2859 at 2924. Cf. also Case 85/87, *Dow Benelux NV* v. *EC Commission* [1989] ECR 3137 and Joined Cases 97–99/87, *Dow Chemical Ibérica SA et al.* v. *EC Commission* [1989] ECR 3165. Cited by Lawson, note 21 above, 240. On the principle of proportionality see, R-E. Papadopoulou, *Principes généraux du droit et droit communautaire* (1996).

The European Court of Human Rights did not share this view in *Niemietz*,[67] a case concerning the search of a lawyer's office pursuant to a warrant drawn in very broad terms in the absence of an independent observer and impinging on professional secrecy. According to the Court, on the basis that respect for private life must also comprise to a certain degree the right to establish and develop relationships with other human beings, there appeared to be no reason of principle why this understanding of the notion of 'private life' should be taken to exclude activities of a professional or business nature 'since it is, after all, in the course of their working lives that the majority of people have a significant, if not the greatest, opportunity of developing relationships with the outside world'[68]—a view supported by the fact that 'it is not always possible to distinguish clearly which of an individual's activities form part of his professional or business life and which do not'.[69]

Furthermore, the Court held that to deny the protection of Article 8 on the ground that the measure complained of related only to professional activities—as suggested by the complainant government—could 'lead to an inequality of treatment, in that such protection would remain unavailable to a person whose professional and non-professional activities were so intermingled that there was no means of distinguishing between them'.[70]

The Court also discussed the meaning of the word 'home' as it appears in the English text of Article 8, observing that in certain Contracting States, notably Germany, the word has been accepted as extending to business premises. The Court went on to observe that such an interpretation is, moreover, fully consonant with the French text, since the word '*domicile*' has a broader connotation than the word 'home' and may extend, for example, to a professional person's office. In this context the Court also noted how it may not always be possible to draw precise distinctions, since activities which are related to a profession or business may well be conducted from a person's private residence and activities which are not so related may well be carried on in an office or commercial premises. 'A narrow interpretation of the words "home" and "*domicile*" could therefore give rise to the same risk of inequality of treatment as a narrow interpretation of the notion of "private life" '.[71]

More generally, the Court ruled that to interpret the words 'private life' and 'home' as including certain professional or business activities or premises 'would be consonant with the essential object and purpose of Article 8, namely to protect the individual against arbitrary interference by the public authorities',[72] noting that such an interpretation:

---

[67] *Niemietz*, ECHR (1992), Series A, Vol. 251–B. See comments by P. Lambert (1993) 4 *RTDH* 470 and F. Rigaux (1993) 4 *RTDH* 480.

[68] *Ibid.*, at para. 29.   [69] *Ibid.*

[70] 'In fact, the Court had not heretofore drawn such distinctions; it concluded that there had been an interference with private life even where telephone tapping covered both business and private calls (see the *Huvig* v. *France* judgment of 24 Apr. 1990, Series A, No. 176–B, 41, para. 8, and 52, para. 25); and, where a search was directed solely against business activities, it did not rely on that fact as a ground for excluding the applicability of Art. 8 under the heading of "private life" (see the *Chappell* v. *United Kingdom* judgment of 30 Mar. 1989, Series A, No. 152–A, 12–13, para. 26, and 21–22, para. 51)'; *ibid.*

[71] *Ibid.*, at para. 30.

[72] See e.g. *Marckx* v. *Belgium*, ECHR (1979), Series A, No. 31, 15, para. 31.

would not unduly hamper the Contracting States, for they would retain their entitlement to 'interfere' to the extent permitted by paragraph 2 of Article 8; that entitlement might well be more far-reaching where professional or business activities or premises were involved than would otherwise be the case.[73]

The Court found that the search was disproportionate in this particular case and insisted on the fact that the warrant was drawn in broad terms and the search carried out with no independent observer in the office of a lawyer bound to professional secrecy emphasizing his important role in the context of Article 6, guaranteeing the right to a fair trial.

Although the ECJ was prepared in *Hoechst* to afford protection from arbitrary or disproportionate intervention as a general principle of Community law,[74] Rick Lawson submits rightly that the 'level of protection offered under Community law as interpreted by the ECJ in *Hoechst* is in danger of falling below the requirements of Article 8 ECHR'.[75]

In *Orkem*,[76] concerning the right not to give evidence against oneself, the ECJ ruled in the context of a European competition investigation that:

> As far as Article 6 of the European Convention is concerned, although it may be relied upon by an undertaking subject to an investigation relating to competition law, it must be observed that neither the wording of that Article nor the decisions of the European Court of Human Rights indicate that it upholds the right not to give evidence against oneself,[77]

whereas the European Court of Human Rights in *Funke*[78] found a breach of Article 6(1) of the Convention[79] ruling that:

> The special features of customs law . . . cannot justify . . . an infringement of the right of anyone 'charged with a criminal offence', within the autonomous meaning of this expression in Article 6, to remain silent and not to contribute to incriminating himself.[80]

---

[73] *Niemietz*, ECHR (1992), Series A, Vol. 251–B, para. 31. This case law has been confirmed in the *Funke, Crémieux* and *Miaille* cases concerning French customs law. ECHR (1993), Series A, Vols. 256–A, 256–B, and 256–C.

[74] Joined Cases 46/87 and 227/88, *Hoechst* [1989] ECR 2924.

[75] Lawson, note 21 above, at 245.

[76] Case 374/87, *Orkem* [1989] ECR 3283; Lawson, note 21 above, at 234.

[77] *Ibid.*, at para. 30. However, the ECJ recognized the right not to supply information capable of being used in order to establish, against the person supplying it, the existence of an infringement of the competition rules as being part of the rights of the defence. See also Case 27/88, *Solvay & Cie* v. *EC Commission* [1989] ECR 3355.

[78] *Funke*, ECHR (1993), Series A, Vol. 256–A. See also the report of the European Commission of Human Rights in *K* v. *Austria* (Appl. No. 16002/90) and comments by P. Kinsch, 'Le droit de ne pas contribuer à sa propre incrimination' (1993) 1 *Bulletin des droits de l'homme* 47.

[79] Art. 6(1) of the Convention reads as follows:
'In the determination of his civil rights and obligations or of any criminal charge against him, everyone is entitled to a fair and public hearing within a reasonable time by an independent and impartial tribunal established by law. Judgment shall be pronounced publicly but the press and public may be excluded from all or part of the trial in the interest of morals, public order or national security in a democratic society, where the interests of juveniles or the protection of the private life of the parties so require, or to the extend strictly necessary in the opinion of the court in special circumstances where publicity would prejudice the interests of justice'.

[80] Para. 44.

Leaving aside the difficult and highly controversial question of the applicability of Article 6 of the Convention to European competition investigations,[81] the decision of the ECJ is now inconsistent with the Strasbourg case law in so far as the applicability of Article 6 of the Convention is concerned, even though the ECJ concluded that the impugned right is part of the rights of the defence.

On the other hand, the principle decided in *Walt Wilhelm*[82] involved the cumulative effect of domestic and European Community competition penalties. The ECJ took a restrictive approach, accepting to a certain extent such a cumulative effect, subject now to reconsideration in the light of the *Gradinger* judgment of the European Court of Human Rights.[83] This case concerned criminal and administrative criminal proceedings for causing death by negligence and driving under the influence of alcohol. The Strasbourg Court found a violation of Article 4 of Protocol VII to the Convention guaranteeing the *non bis in idem* principle,[84] as the impugned decisions had been based on the same conduct.

It seems that the ECJ would be prepared to take into account relevant case law from the European Court of Human Rights.[85] After all, in *Hoechst*, it took for granted 'that there is no case-law of the European Court of Human Rights on the subject'[86] and in *Orkem* it reached a similar conclusion.[87]

Not taking into account Strasbourg case law because there was none, or because the ECJ inadvertently believed that there was none, should thus not lead to an overestimation of inconsistency, and there is good reason to believe that the Luxembourg Court would not adopt conflicting solutions to the problems at stake if there were relevant case law from Strasbourg. Moreover, it is submitted that in very specific areas such as competition law, the protective standard might vary in the light of policy considerations specific to the European Community legal order. Future case law will show us if the ECJ continues to adopt an *in dubio pro integrationem* approach.

---

[81] In Joined Cases 100–103/80, *SA Musique Diffusion française et al.* v. *EC Commission* [1983] ECR 1825, the ECJ held that Art. 6 does not apply to competition cases as the Commission is not to be considered to be a tribunal within the meaning of this provision. This seems to be inconsistent with Strasbourg case law. On this problem, see Spielmann, note 20 above, at 509.

[82] Case 14/68, *Walt Wilhelm* [1969] ECR 1. For comments see N. Colette-Basecqz, ' Une conséquence de la nature pénale de la sanction communautaire au niveau des garanties procédurales: L'application du principe *non bis in idem*', in Tulkens and Bosly, note 20 above, at 463. Cf., however, with Joined Cases 18 and 35/65, *Max Gutmann* v. *Commission of the EAEC* [1967] ECR 61, cited in Weiler and Lockhart, note 17 above, at 92. In this judgment, the ECJ annulled a Commission decision in a staff case as violating the *non bis in idem* principle.

[83] *Gradinger*, ECHR (1995), Series A, Vol. 328–C.

[84] Art. 4(1) of Prot. VII reads:
'No one shall be liable to be tried or punished again in criminal proceedings under the jurisdiction of the same State for an offence for which he has already been finally acquitted or convicted in accordance with the law and penal procedure of that State'.

[85] To believe a statement made by Mr Moitinho de Almeida, judge of the ECJ, on the occasion of the official visit paid by a delegation of the ECJ to the European Court of Human Rights on 14 Mar. 1997. See (1997) 7 *Bulletin des droits de l'homme* 280.

[86] Joined Cases 46/87 and 227/88, *Hoechst* [1989] ECR 2859 at 2924, para. 18.

[87] Case 374/87, *Orkem* [1989] ECR 3283 at 3350, para. 30.

C. The Procedure Before the European Court of Justice

In a series of landmark decisions the European Court of Human Rights insisted on the principle of equality. In *Lobo Machado*,[88] it ruled that Article 6 of the Convention, guaranteeing the right to adversarial proceedings, had been violated in a case concerning the impossibility for the plaintiff in proceedings relating to social rights to obtain a copy of the written opinion of a representative of the Attorney-General's department at the Supreme Court or to reply to it, and the presence of that representative at the court's private sitting. The Court of Human Rights took a similar view in the *Vermeulen* case delivered the same day[89] and concerning a plaintiff in civil proceedings in the Belgian *Cour de cassation* who was unable to reply to submissions made at the hearing by a member of the *Procureur Général's* department who participated in the Court's deliberation.[90]

The right to adversarial proceedings has been restated in *Nideröst-Huber*[91] concerning a cantonal court's observations not communicated to either of the parties in dispute, and in *Van Orshoven*[92] concerning the impossibility for a plaintiff in disciplinary proceedings in the *Cour de cassation* to reply to submissions made at the hearing of the *Procureur Général's* department at the *Cour de cassation*.

As the parties to the proceedings do not have the opportunity to comment on the conclusions of the Advocate General, it has been submitted that the procedural rules governing the intervention of the Advocate General at the ECJ,[93] might be inconsistent with the Strasbourg principles.[94] It has also been rightly submitted that this procedural problem could eventually lead to considerable difficulty if a national authority refused to give effect to a judgment of the ECJ notwithstanding Article 256 (*ex* Article 192) of the EC Treaty, especially as for most of the Member States Article 307 (*ex* Article 234) of the Treaty imposes primacy of the European Convention.[95]

Other potential problems include the length of procedure concerning preliminary references pursuant to Article 234 (*ex* Article 177) of the EC Treaty and the lack of *locus standi* of the individual concerning human rights questions within the Community sphere.[96]

---

[88] *Lobo Machado*, ECHR Reports, 1996–I, 195.

[89] *Vermeulen*, ECHR Reports, 1996–I, 224.

[90] See also *Borgers*, ECHR (1991), Series A, No. 214–B.

[91] *Nideröst-Huber*, ECHR Reports, 1997–I, 101.

[92] *Van Orshoven*, ECHR Reports, 1997–III, 1039. See also the Court's judgment in *Reinhardt and Slimome-Kaïd*, ECHR Reports, 1998.

[93] Pursuant to Art. 59 of the rules of procedure. See e.g. the judgment of the ECJ in Case 206/81, *José Alvarez* v. *European Parliament* [1982] ECR 3369.

[94] See G. Ress, note 44 above, at 922, note 118; L. Weitzel, 'A propos des arrêts *Vermeulen* et *Lobo Machado*' (1996) 6 *Bulletin des droits de l'homme* 140 and (1997) 7 *Bulletin des droits de l'homme* 282; J. Cohen-Jonathan, 'Conclusions générales', in *Les nouveaux développements du procès équitable au sens de la Convention européenne des droits de l'homme* (1996), 190.

[95] Weitzel, note 94 above, at 142.

[96] See Ress, note 44 above, at 922, note 118.

IV. COMPLEMENTARITIES AND CONSIDERATION
OF STRASBOURG PRECEDENT

A. Taking Strasbourg Case Law into Account

In four cases, the ECJ expressly took into account the case law of the Strasbourg Court. In *P* v. *S and Cornwall County Council*,[97] concerning dismissal of a transsexual for a reason arising from the gender reassignment of the person concerned, the ECJ expressly referred for the first time to the case law of the European Court of Human Rights. It relied on the *Rees* judgment of 17 October 1986[98] to consider that:

> The European Court of Human Rights has held that the term 'transsexual' is usually applied to those who, whilst belonging physically to one sex, feel convinced that they belong to the other; they often seek to achieve a more integrated, unambiguous identity by undergoing medical treatment and surgical operations to adapt their physical characteristics to their psychological nature. Transsexuals who have been operated upon thus form a fairly well-defined and identifiable group (judgment of 17 October 1986, in *Rees* v. *United Kingdom* . . .).[99]

The ECJ therefore ruled that Directive 76/207/EEC, being the expression in the relevant field of the principle of equality, which is one of the fundamental principles of Community law,[100] also applies to discrimination arising from the gender reassignment of the person concerned. The Court decided that such discrimination is based, essentially if not exclusively, on the sex of the person concerned, and where a person is dismissed on the ground that he or she intends to undergo, or has undergone, gender reassignment, he or she is treated unfavourably by comparison with persons of the sex to which he or she was deemed to belong before undergoing gender reassignment.[101] The fact of tolerating dismissal of a person because he or she is a transsexual or because he or she has undergone a gender reassignment operation would be tantamount, as regards such a person, to a failure to respect the dignity and freedom to which he or she is entitled, and which the Court has a duty to safeguard.[102] It came to the conclusion that dismissal of such a person must be regarded as contrary to Article 5(1) of the Directive.[103]

This judgment is interesting as the ECJ takes a liberal approach, reversing the standard test to discover if a human rights matter falls within its jurisdiction, by starting with the declaration that fundamental human rights include the principle of equality and that this non-discrimination principle extends to transsexuals, and con-

---

[97] Case C–13/94, *P* v. *S and Cornwall County Council* [1996] ECR I–2143. See also the case-note by Flynn, note 23 above, and C. Barnard, 'The Principle of Equality in the Community Context: *P, Grant, Kalanke* and *Marshall:* Four Uneasy Bedfellows?' (1998) 57 *Cambridge LJ* 352.

[98] *Rees* case, ECHR (1986), Series A, No 106.   [99] *Ibid.*, at para. 16.

[100] Case C–13/94, *P* v. *S and Cornwall County Council* [1996] ECR I–2143, at para. 18. The Court ruled in para. 19 that the right not to be discriminated against on grounds of sex is one of fundamental human rights whose observance the Court has a duty to ensure. It relied on earlier case law, i.e. Case 149/77, *Defrenne* [1978] ECR 1365 and Joined Cases 75/82 and 117/82, *C. Razzouk and A. Beydoun* v. *EC Commission* [1984] ECR 1509.

[101] Case C–13/94, *P* v. *S and Cornwall County Council* [1996] ECR I–2143, at para. 21.

[102] *Ibid.*, at para. 22.   [103] *Ibid.*, at para. 23.

cluding that the scope of the Directive must be read in the light of this principle.[104] It is also of the greatest interest in that the Court takes into account the expertise of the European Court of Human Rights referring to the description of 'transsexual'.

Concerning the principle of legality in the context of implementing EC law by national legislation, the Luxembourg Court, in *Criminal Proceedings* v. *X*[105] discussed the Strasbourg case law and ruled that in the present case which concerned the extent of liability in criminal law arising under legislation adopted for the specific purpose of implementing a directive:

> the principle that a provision of the criminal law may not be applied extensively to the detriment of the defendant which is the corollary of the principle of legality in relation to crime and punishment and more generally of the principle of legal certainty, precludes bringing criminal proceedings in respect of conduct not clearly defined as culpable by law. That principle, which is one of the general legal principles underlying the constitutional traditions common to the Member States, has also been enshrined in various international treaties, in particular in Article 7 of the [Convention] (see, *inter alia*, the judgments of the European Court of Human Rights in *Kokkinakis* v. *Greece* . . . and in *SW* v. *United Kingdom* and *CR* v. *United Kingdom* . . .).
>
> The national court must therefore ensure that that principle is observed when interpreting, in the light of the wording and the purpose of the Directive, the national legislation adopted in order to implement it.[106]

This ruling echoes the *Cantoni* judgment of the European Court of Human Rights.[107] As indicated above, firing a warning shot to Luxembourg nearly a month before, the Court in Strasbourg ruled that the fact that a national provision was based almost word for word on a Community directive did not remove it from the ambit of Article 7 of the Convention.[108]

In the *Familiapress* judgment of 26 June 1997,[109] the Luxembourg Court relied on the *Lentia* judgment, delivered in Strasbourg on 24 November 1993.[110] The Court ruled, concerning the right to freedom of expression as enshrined in Article 10 of the Convention, that:

> A prohibition on selling publications which offer the chance to take part in prize games competitions may detract from freedom of expression. Article 10 of the [Convention] does, however, permit derogations from that freedom for the purposes of maintaining press diversity, in so far as they are prescribed by law and are necessary in a democratic society (see the judgment of the Court in *Informationsverein Lentia and Others* v. *Austria* . . .).[111]

[104] See Flynn, note 23 above, at 384 who claims that the traditional approach would have been to have looked first to the scope of the dir. and then to find that the principle of equality applied within its scope and that the reasoning of the Court quite literally overturns its earlier perspective on this point.

[105] Case C–129/95, *Criminal Proceedings* v. *X* [1996] ECR I–6609.   [106] *Ibid.*, at paras. 25–6.

[107] *Cantoni*, ECHR Reports, 1996–V, 1614, (1997) 8 *RTDH* 685. See comments by Spielmann, note 42 above.

[108] *Cantoni, ibid.*, at para. 30.

[109] Case C–368/95, *Familiapress* [1997] ECR I–3689. Compare with Case C–260/89, *ERT* [1991] ECR I–2925 and Case C–353/89, *EC Commission* [1991] ECR I–4069, as well as Case C–148/91, *Vereiniging Veronica Omroep Organisatie* v. *Commissariaat voor de Media* [1993] ECR I–487. For a commentary on the *Familiapress* judgment, see J. Kühling, 'Grundrechtskontrolle durch den EuGH: Kommunikationsfreiheit unde Pluralismussicherung im Gemeinschaftsrecht' [1997] *EuGRZ* 296.

[110] *Lentia*, ECHR (1993), Series A, No. 276.

[111] Case C–368/95, *Familiapress* [1997] ECR I–3689, at 3717, para. 26.

The Luxembourg Court also referred to the proportionality test in order to appraise whether the national prohibition, i.e. the prohibition under domestic competition law on publishers of periodicals inviting consumers to take part in draws, was proportionate to the aim of maintaining press diversity, and whether that objective might not be attained by measures less restrictive of both intra-Community trade and freedom of expression.[112]

Finally, in the recent *Grant* case[113] concerning the question of equal treatment of men and women and the refusal of travel concessions to cohabitees of the same sex, the ECJ rather surprisingly cited various decisions of the European Commission on Human Rights and judgments of the European Court of Human Rights but took a very restrictive view with regard to the latter, analysing only the *Rees*[114] and *Cossey*[115] judgments in the context of Article 12 of the Convention guaranteeing the right to marry.

As far as the European Commission on Human Rights is concerned, the Court observed that despite the modern evolution of attitudes towards homosexuality, the Commission considers that 'stable homosexual relationships do not fall within the scope of the rights to respect for family life under Article 8 of the Convention',[116] and that national provisions, which, for the purpose of protecting the family, accord more favourable treatment to married persons and persons of the opposite sex living together as man and wife than to persons of the same sex in a stable relationship, 'are not contrary to Article 14 of the Convention, which prohibits, *inter alia*, discrimination on the ground of sex'.[117]

Regarding the European Court of Human Rights, the ECJ held that the former has interpreted Article 12 of the Convention as applying only to the traditional marriage between two persons of opposite biological sex.[118]

According to the ECJ therefore:

> It follows that, in the present state of the law within the Community, stable relationships between two persons of the same sex are not regarded as equivalent to marriage or stable relationships outside marriage between persons of opposite sex. Consequently, an employer is not required by Community law to treat the situation of a person who has a stable relationship with a partner of the same sex as equivalent to that of a person who is married to or has a stable relationship outside marriage with a partner of the opposite sex.[119]

The ECJ omitted to have a close look at the Strasbourg Court's case law on Article 8.[120] It is certainly true that a situation similar to that in *Grant* has not yet been

[112] Case C–368/95, *Familiapress* [1997] ECR I–3689, at 3717, para. 27.
[113] Case C–249/96, *Lisa Jacqueline Grant* v. *South-West Trains Ltd* [1998] ECR I–621.
[114] *Rees*, ECHR (1986), Series A, No. 106.   [115] *Cossey*, ECHR (1990), Series A, No. 184.
[116] Case C–249/96, *Grant* [1998] ECR I–621, at 647, para. 33. The Court cited the decisions in, in particular, *X and Y* v. *United Kingdom* (1983) 32 D&R 220; *S* v. *United Kingdom* (1986) 47 D&R 274, at para. 2; and *Kerkhoven and Hinke* v. *The Netherlands* (1991), not yet reported, at para. 1.
[117] *Ibid.*, at para. 33. Citing the Commission's decision in *S* v. *United Kingdom*, at para. 7; *C and LM* v. *United Kingdom* (1989), not yet reported, at para. 2; and *B* v. *United Kingdom* (1990) 64 D&R 278, at para. 2.
[118] *Ibid.*, at para. 34, and citing the *Rees* judgment (1986), Series A, No. 106, 19, at para. 49, and the *Cossey* judgment (1990), Series A, No. 184, 9, 17, at para. 43.
[119] *Ibid.*, at para. 35.
[120] See e.g. *Dudgeon* v. *United Kingdom*, ECHR (1981), Series A, Vol. 45; *Norris* v. *Ireland*, Series A, Vol. 142; and *Modinos* v. *Cyprus*, ECHR (1993), Series A, Vol. 259, cited in Barnard, note 97 above, at 357–8.

adjudicated by the European Court of Human Rights. But it is equally true that the so-called 'positive obligations' theory imposing concrete action on public authorities might have been of valuable assistance in this respect.[121] The reason the ECJ took a restrictive approach is difficult to appraise. Perhaps, as Catherine Barnard puts it, 'extending the word "sex" to include sexual orientation was a bridge too far in terms of literal interpretation'.[122]

B. Contribution of the European Court of Justice to the Development of Human Rights Protection

The ECJ has in recent cases had the opportunity to make a significant contribution to the development of human rights protection within the Community legal order.[123] In the aforementioned landmark judgment of 5 October 1994,[124] the ECJ overruled a judgment of the CFI of 18 September 1992[125] concerning an individual's refusal to undergo an Aids test for pre-recruitment purposes and the right to keep one's state of health secret. This judgment is a major contribution to the jurisprudence on Article 8 of the Convention.

With regard to Article 8, the Court observed that the right to respect for private life, as embodied in Article 8 and as derived from the common constitutional traditions of the Member States, is one of the fundamental rights protected by the Community legal order,[126] and includes, in particular, 'an individual's right to keep his state of health secret'.[127] That said, the Court further observed that restrictions may be imposed on fundamental rights provided that they 'correspond to objectives of general public interest and do not constitute, with regard to the objectives pursued, a disproportionate and intolerable interference', infringing upon the very substance of the protected right.[128]

The Court then dealt with the relevant provisions of the conditions of employment, observing that Article 13 thereof provides that, before being engaged, a member of the temporary staff must undergo a medical examination in order that the institution may be satisfied that he fulfills the requirements of Article 12(2)(d) concerning physical fitness. According to the latter provision, no one may be engaged as a member of the temporary staff unless he satisfies the conditions of physical fitness laid down for the performance of his duties.[129]

---

[121] See D. Spielmann, 'Obligations positives et effet horizontal des dispositions de la Convention' , in F. Sudre (ed.), *L'interprétation de la Convention européenne des droits de l'homme, Actes du colloque de Montpellier des 13 et 14 mars 1998* (1998) 133–74.

[122] Barnard, note 97 above, at 357. The author continues: 'or perhaps the Court was concerned about the potential number of people affected by the judgement and the cost of extending equality to homosexuals in terms of pensions and health insurance. Nevertheless, the Court ducked the challenge presented by *Grant* and put the matter into the hands of the legislature. The new Article 6a introduced by the Amsterdam Treaty now provides a legal basis for Community action to combat discrimination based, *inter alia*, on sexual orientation. This was expressly noted by the Court': *ibid.*, at 357 (footnotes omitted).

[123] For a complete overview, see the case law review by L. Weitzel published on a regular basis in the *Bulletin des droits de l'homme*.

[124] Case C–404/92, *X* v. *EC Commission* [1994] ECR I–4737, (1995) 16 HRLJ 54.

[125] Joined Cases T–121/89 and T–13/90 [1992] ECR II–2195.

[126] See Case C–62/90, *Commission* v. *Germany* [1992] ECR I–2575, at 2609, para. 23.

[127] Case C–404/92, *X* v. *EC Commission* [1994] ECR I–4737, at 4789, para. 17.

[128] *Ibid.*, at para. 18. See Case C–62/90, *Commission* v. *Germany* [1992] ECR I–2575, at 2609, para. 23.

[129] *Ibid.*, at para. 19.

Although the pre-recruitment examination serves a legitimate interest of the Community institutions, i.e. to be able to fulfill their tasks, the Court also observed that that interest does not justify the carrying out of a test against the will of the person concerned.[130] However, if the person concerned withholds his consent to a test which the medical officer considers necessary in order to evaluate his suitability for the post for which he has applied, 'the institutions cannot be obliged to take the risk of recruiting him'.[131]

The Court then dealt with the CFI's interpretation of these provisions, observing that the latter had interpreted them as imposing an obligation to respect a refusal by the person concerned only in relation to the specific test for Aids but as allowing any other tests to be carried out which might merely point to the possible presence of the Aids virus.[132] To the contrary however, the ECJ held that:

> the right to respect for private life requires that a person's refusal be respected in its entirety. Since the appellant expressly refused to undergo an Aids screening test, that right precluded the administration from carrying out any test liable to point to, or establish, the existence of that illness, in respect of which he had refused disclosure.[133]

However, additional tests had been carried out which provided the medical officer with sufficient information to conclude that the candidate might be carrying the Aids virus, and which had formed the basis for the Commission's decision that the appellant did not satisfy the conditions of physical fitness required for recruitment.[134] Consequently, the ECJ annulled both the judgment of the CFI to the extent to which it held that, in view of the abnormalities found in the medical examination, the medical officer was entitled to request additional tests, and therefore dismissed the applicant's claim that the Commission's decision be annulled, without it being necessary to consider the other pleas in law advanced by the applicant, as well as the Commission's decision itself.[135]

V. CONCLUSION: AN APPRAISAL

A behaviouristic explanation for why the Luxembourg Court left human rights questions undecided, faced open conflict, or adopted a constructive approach is very difficult to provide.[136] The history of the human rights jurisprudence of the ECJ shows that a progressively more courageous approach took precedence over a restrictive view avoiding far-reaching decisions. Conflicts and inconsistencies should indeed be distinguished from cases where the ECJ left human rights questions undecided. This happened in some cases, and it might be considered astonishing that the Luxembourg Court took such a reluctant approach, avoiding facing the problem,

---

[130] Case C–62/90, *Commission* v. *Germany* [1992] ECR I–2575, at 2608, para. 20
[131] *Ibid.*, at para. 21.   [132] *Ibid.*, at para. 22.   [133] *Ibid.*, at para. 23.
[134] *Ibid.*   [135] *Ibid.*, at paras. 24–5.
[136] Coppel and O'Neill, note 17 above, claim that the ECJ refused to take the discourse of fundamental rights seriously. This conclusion is, however, strongly criticized by Weiler and Lockhart, note 17 above.

whereas in other later cases it took a very strong view, rejecting the fundamental rights argument in favour of an efficient implementation of Community (especially competition) law.

A survey of the case law leads to the conclusion that divergent interpretation is possible in certain areas such as European competition law[137], although the ECJ, in recent cases, seems to have taken a similar line to the European Court of Human Rights, referring not only to the Convention as the minimum standard, but taking into account the Strasbourg jurisprudence.

The best way to avoid inconsistent case law would of course be for the Community to accede formally to the Convention. On 28 March 1996, the ECJ gave its *Opinion 2/94* that as Community law now stood the Community had no competence to accede to the Convention.[138] It is unlikely that in the near future the question will again be put on the political agenda. Moreover, formal accession presupposes the submission by the Community to present and future judicial control machinery under the Convention,[139] and thus, at least indirectly, submission by the Luxembourg Court to the Strasbourg Court. Future changes in this direction would of course be in the

---

[137] To avoid interference and inconsistent approach, it has been suggested on various occasions to create a net of bridges between the specialized courts in Europe. As Professor Schermers puts it in the context of the future role of the International Court of Justice: 'the most effective bridge developed so far is that of the so-called "preliminary ruling" of Article 177 of the EC Treaty. This provision permits national courts to obtain authentic interpretations from the regional court on the rules of regional law, which they can subsequently apply in their national court decision. Even though the regional court cannot overrule the domestic court, its ruling obtains force of law in the national legal system through the co-operation of the national court which makes it part of its own decision. This system has worked well and could be expanded to the relationship between other legal systems. Apart, perhaps, of problems of workload and efficiency, there is no fundamental objection against preliminary rulings between all different systems. . . . *When faced with questions of human rights any court could ask a preliminary ruling of the European Court of Human Rights on the interpretation of such a right.* Thus, a network of relationships between courts could be established': see Schermers, 'The International Court of Justice in Relation to Other Courts', in A.S. Muller *et al.* (eds.), *The International Court of Justice. Its Future Role after Fifty Years* (1997), 261, at 265 (emphasis added). See also by the same author, 'Prejudiciele Vragen Voor het Europese Hof Voor de Rechten van de Mens', in *Rechter en Mensenrechtenbeleid* (1985), 47–58; M. Janis, 'Fashioning a Mechanism for Judicial Cooperation on European Human Rights Law among Europe's Regional Courts', in Lawson and de Bloijs, note 21 above, 211 at 217; Ress, note 44 above, at 924. See also J. Cohen-Jonathan, 'La problématique de l'adhésion des Communautés européennes à la Convention européenne des droits de l'homme', in *Mélanges Pierre Henri Teitgen* (1984), 95. For earlier views, see K. Vasak, *La Convention européenne des droits de l'homme* (1964), 248. See also, D. Spielmann, 'Quelques réflexions au sujet d'un recours préjudiciel éventuel devant la Cour européenne des droits de l'homme' (1987) 31–32 *DDC* 531. Leaving aside the difficult question of uniformity in the Convention context, avoiding inconsistent case law through the creation of a preliminary reference network would however presuppose that the Luxembourg Court is a domestic court. Support for this view of the hierarchy is already given by the European Commission of Human Rights in relation to the exhaustion of local remedies principle. See the decision of 19 Jan. 1989 in the *Dufay* case (Appl. No. 13539/88, not yet reported). This is also the view expressed by Mr Weitzel, Member of the European Commission of Human Rights, in an intervention made on the occasion of the official visit paid by a delegation of the ECJ to the European Court of Human Rights on 14 Mar. 1997. See (1997) 7 *Bulletin des droits de l'homme* 280. See also M. Mendelson, *L'incidence du droit communautaire sur la mise en œuvre de la Convention européenne des droits de l'homme* (1984). See also, most recently, R. St. J. Macdonald, 'The Luxembourg preliminary ruling procedure and its possible application in Strasbourg' in *Mélanges en hommage à Louis Edmond Pettiti* (1998) 593 and by the same author, 'Supervision of the execution of the Judgments of the European Court of Hhuman Rights', in *Mélanges en l'honneur de Nicolas Valticos* (1999) 417 at 435–7.

[138] *Opinion 2/94* [1996] ECR I–1759. On this opinion, see Adams and Sands, and de Schutter and Lejeune, note 11 above.

[139] *Ibid.*, at para. 21.

interest of the most efficient protection of the individual's rights as a citizen of the European Union.[140]

It should be emphasized that human rights questions do arise with increasing frequency within the European Community context and that the individual asks generally for broader access to the ECJ. In May 1995 the ECJ published its initial contribution to the debate surrounding the intergovernmental conference (IGC)[141] and opposed any immediate reform. However, the Court expressed concern about whether the restrictive *locus standi* rules under Article 230 (*ex* Article 173) for natural and legal persons are sufficient to protect their fundamental human rights. Any change of the *locus standi* provision granting direct action and broader access to the Court[142] would of course increase the risk of divergent interpretation concerning the Convention. Indeed the opening of the floodgates would lead to more clashes, especially in the (at this moment unlikely) event of an extension of European Community competence to co-operation in the fields of justice and home affairs, the so-called 'third pillar'.[143] Although Community action might be challenged indirectly under the reference procedure pursuant to Article 234 (*ex* Article 177) of the EC Treaty, there is strong theoretical evidence that a direct action is always preferable. Indeed, an Article 234 reference implies long delays and a certain lack of predictability, as it is always subject to the domestic judge's discretion. Of course, the number of cases concerning individuals might grow as litigants try all avenues to succeed and rely inevitably on human rights arguments and the huge body of Strasbourg case law, which turns out to be of great help in formulating the arguments. If the ECJ wants to play a greater role itself in the protection of fundamental rights, the *in dubio pro integrationem* approach adopted in competition cases[144] might be qualified in the potential (now so-called) 'third-pillar' cases, taking into account the valuable body of Strasbourg precedent characterized by a strong civil liberties approach. Express reference to Strasbourg jurisprudence in recent cases denotes that the Luxembourg Court is willing to embark upon this route.

However, divergent interpretation should not necessarily be ruled out.[145] A dis-

---

[140] Efficient protection also includes *provisional* protection. Under the Convention's control machinery, it has been decided that provisional measures are not binding. See *Cruz Varas* v. *Sweden*, ECHR (1991), Series A, Vol. 201. On this case, see R. Macdonald, 'Interim Measures in International Law, with Special Reference to the European System for the Protection of Human Rights' (1992) 52 *ZaöRV* 703; D. Spielmann, 'Les mesures provisioires et les organes de protection prévus par la Convention européenne des droits de l'homme', in *Présence du droit public et des droits de l'homme. Mélanges offerts à Jacques Velu* (1992), 1293. See also D. Spielmann and D. Spielmann, 'La Cour unique et permanente et les mesures provisoires. (La nécessité d'une réforme)', in *Mélanges Rolv Ryssdal* (forthcoming, 1999). For comments on provisional measures in the European Community context, where such measures are binding, see de Schutter and Lejeune, note 11 above, at 603.

[141] *Proceedings of the Court of Justice*, No 15/95. See the comment by Beaumont in [1997] 46 *ICLQ* 205.

[142] Concerning this issue, see most notably J. Nihoul, 'La recevabilité des recours en annulation introduits par un particulier à l'encontre d'un acte communautaire de portée générale' (1994) 30 *RTDE* 71. See also H. Rasmussen, 'Why is Article 173 Interpreted Against Private Plaintiffs?' (1980) 5 *EL Rev.* 112; and P. Greaves, '*Locus Standi* under Article 173 EEC When Seeking Annulment of a Regulation' (1986) 11 *EL Rev.* 119.

[143] For a proposal in this sense see J.H.H. Weiler, 'Les droits des citoyens européens' [1996] *RMC* 51.

[144] e.g. Joined Cases 46/87 and 227/88, *Hoechst* [1989] ECR 2859.

[145] A different approach by different international courts concerning similar problems is indeed possible. Compare the case law of the World Court with the approach taken by the European Court of Human Rights in *Loizidou* v. *Turkey (Preliminary Objections)*, ECHR (1995), Series A, Vol. 310. See note 8 above.

senting or merely separate voice from Luxembourg could indeed be a valuable input, especially as the Strasbourg Court is accustomed to separate opinions coming from its own members.[146] Moreover, in systems where the Convention is self-executing, divergent interpretation of domestic courts is possible and even frequent,[147] and sometimes local courts go even far beyond the minimum standards set by the European Court of Human Rights. The rich national jurisprudence, especially of constitutional courts, has proved to be of greatest value to the European Court of Human Rights and the ECJ.[148] The *Solange* saga, for instance, has turned out to be an impetus for the Luxembourg Court, acknowledged eventually by the German Constitutional Court in its decision of 22 October 1986,[149] stating that the protection of fundamental rights on the Community level had reached a degree essentially comparable to the standard set by the *Grundgesetz*.[150]

The Luxembourg Court and the Strasbourg Court are courts of equal dignity, important institutions responsible for judicial functions in two international legal systems.[151] The Luxembourg Court now has the opportunity to make major contributions to the efficient protection of human rights and the Strasbourg Court, in exercising its control function over national measures, has the power to contribute to the efficient implementation of EC law[152] in a continuous stream of authoritative decisions.

European judges, adopting a comparative attitude should favour a mutual sensibility bearing in mind the particular contexts involved[153] and the fact that human rights questions might be formulated in different terms in Luxembourg, albeit that

---

[146] On separate opinions at the European Court of Human Rights, see M.-A. Eissen, 'Discipline de vote à la Cour européenne des droits de l'homme?', in O'Reilly, note 17 above, at 71. See also, de Bloijs, 'The Fundamental Freedom of the European Court of Human Rights' in Lawson and de Bloijs, note 21 above, at 35; L. Wildhaber, 'Opinions dissidentes et concordantes des juges individuels à la Cour européenne des droits de l'homme', in *Mélanges en l'honneur de Nicolas Valticos* (1999) 529. It is thus of paramount importance that an appropriate geographic balance should be upheld in each chamber of the future Strasbourg Court. See generally on this issue and the Court's practice since 1995, N. Valticos, 'Quels juges pour la prochaine Cour européenne des droits de l'homme', in *Liber amicorum Marc-André Eissen* (1995), 427.

[147] See Lawson, note 21 above, at 230. See also A. Drzemczewski, *The European Human Rights Convention in Domestic Law. A Comparative Study* (1983); Polakiewicz and Jacob-Foltzer, note 3 above.

[148] See M.-A. Eissen, 'Les juridictions constitutionnelles nationales dans la jurisprudence et la pratique de la Cour européenne des droits de l'homme' (1987) 25–26 *DDC* 385, and 'L'interaction des jurisprudences constitutionnelles nationales et la jurisprudence de la Cour européenne des droits de l'homme', in D. Rousseau and F. Sudre (eds.), *Conseil constitutionnel et Cour européenne des droits de l'homme* (1990) 138; 'Cours constitutionnelles nationales et Cour européenne des droits de l'homme' (1991) 2 *RTDH* 167.

[149] BVerfG, 22 Oct. 1986 [1987] 3 CMLR 259–63.

[150] See W.-H. Roth, 'The Application of Community Law in West Germany: 1980–1990' (1991) 28 *CML Rev.* 143.

[151] Janis, note 137 above, at 213. See also Andriantsimbazovina, note 17 above, at 7.

[152] e.g. in *Hornsby* v. *Greece*, ECHR Reports, 1997–II, 495, the European Court of Human Rights held that Art. 6 of the Convention had been infringed, for delay by the administrative authorities in taking the necessary measures to comply with two judgments of the Supreme Administrative Court implementing a judgment of the ECJ. Similarly, the refusal by a judge to make a preliminary reference to Luxembourg could be in breach of Art. 6 of the Convention subject to Strasbourg control. See e.g. Sudre, note 13 above. See also Andriantsimbazovina, note 8 above, at 732.

[153] Regular mutual visits of both Courts prove to be very beneficial in this respect. For a recent example see the official visit paid by a delegation of the ECJ to the European Court of Human Rights on 14 Mar. 1997. See (1997) 7 *Bulletin des droits de l'homme* 274.

they might be better decided in Strasbourg. A possible circulation of judges between Luxembourg and Strasbourg and *vice versa* could be of the utmost benefit in the event that national governments are willing to propose as candidates personalities with considerable judicial expertise gained as members of one of the two European Courts.[154]

The question of who is invested with the final word on a particular issue will then soon become obsolete.

---

[154] Concerning the background of the judges composing the future 'single' Court, see J.-F. Flauss, 'Radioscopie de l'élection de la nouvelle Cour européenne des droits de l'homme' (1998) 9 *RTDH* 435.

24

New Instruments and Institutions for Enhancing the Protection of Human Rights in Europe?

GIORGIO GAJA

I. THE NEED FOR A REASSESSMENT OF EXISTING INSTRUMENTS

There is a great variety of systems applying in Europe for the protection of human rights, operating at the universal, regional, and national levels. This variety largely reflects historical developments for reasons that at least in part no longer hold good. For instance, the Council of Europe was established as an organization comprising only States of (politically) Western Europe, while its membership—currently forty-one States—now approaches that of the Organization for Security and Co-operation in Europe (OSCE), the main distinction being the presence of the United States and Canada in the latter organization. Moreover, there is nowadays a much greater political homogeneity throughout Europe. The prospective enlargements of the European Union will gradually bring the composition of the Union into line with that of the Council of Europe. This may take some time and never become a complete process; for instance, Russia's accession to the European Union seems at the moment a very remote possibility. However, one could say that all the major European organizations will substantially encompass the same members. The extant differences in membership would anyway hardly justify the existence of different European levels of protection of human rights.

The Council of Europe, the European Union, and the OSCE are all concerned with ensuring that human rights are protected. With regard to the same organization, certain types of rights are covered by different instruments, each with its respective treaty body supervising compliance with the relevant obligations. This is due in part to historical reasons. All these instruments add to those that have been established at a universal level for the same rights. The ensuing result gives a fairly complex picture.

Many instruments overlap at least in part. To take just one example, the right to information is covered by Article 19 of the Universal Declaration of Human

Rights,[1] Article 10 of the European Convention of Human Rights (ECHR), Article 19 of the UN Covenant on Civil and Political Rights (ICCPR),[2] Article 15 of the UN Covenant on Economic, Social and Cultural Rights (ICESCR),[3] Article 5 of the Convention on the Elimination of All Forms of Racial Discrimination,[4] Article 17 of the Convention on the Rights of the Child,[5] the Final Act of the Helsinki Conference,[6] etc. Each of these texts has some distinctive elements. Very often, when a new text is adopted, the rewording of a rule concerning a given right finds its origin in the drafters' perception of the importance of some aspects that may have previously been less evident. Thus one could say that the number and variety of provisions concerning the same rights are also a product of historical developments.

Once an instrument is adopted and a machinery for monitoring its implementation is put into action, there is an understandable reluctance on the part of those more directly concerned with its functioning—whether it is States, institutions, or officials—to resist any change that one may wish to introduce. This occurs irrespective of the fact that certain features of the system may be due to a specific reason that no longer holds good.

Since any suggestion of changes—even for the sole purpose of streamlining the existing systems for the protection of human rights—is likely to run into political difficulties, one could find some justification in limiting oneself to a description of what has been achieved so far. However, the interest in discussing the existing systems for the protection of human rights is not simply theoretical. In view of enhancing that protection and making a better use of resources, a reassessment appears of some use even if only a few minor changes to the present systems will be regarded as politically expedient. Moreover, the production of texts for the protection of human rights is far from being concluded. An evaluation of the existing systems appears to be essential before any new initiative is taken in order to establish yet another instrument. A further text should be adopted only if it serves an appreciable purpose that prevails over the disadvantages that would be caused by making the systems for protecting human rights even more complicated.

---

[1] Universal Declaration of Human Rights, adopted by GA Res. 217 A (III) (1948). In United Nations, *A Compilation of International Instruments* (1994), Vol. I, Part 1.

[2] International Covenant on Civil and Political Rights (ICCPR), adopted by GA Res. 2200 A (XXI) (1966), in *International Instruments*, note 1 above, at 20.

[3] International Covenant on Economic, Social, and Cultural Rights (ICESCR), adopted by GA Res. 2200 A (XXI) (1966), in *International Instruments*, note 1 above, at 8.

[4] International Convention on the Elimination of All Forms of Racial Discrimination, adopted by GA Res. 2106 A (XX) (1965), in *International Instruments*, note 1 above, at 66.

[5] Convention on the Rights of the Child, adopted by GA Res. 44/25 (1989), in *International Instruments*, note 1 above, at 174.

[6] Helsinki Final Act, adopted at the Conference on Security and Co-operation in Europe, Helsinki, 1 Aug. 1975, reprinted in (1975) 14 ILM 1292.

II. POSSIBLE CONFLICTS BETWEEN HUMAN RIGHTS TREATIES

One current justification of the large number of existing instruments for the protection of human rights is that they are all intended to increase protection and are therefore compatible with one another, and also with national legislation having a similar purpose. Generally, this feature is expressly stated in human rights treaties. For instance, Article 60 (as from 1 November 1998, Article 53) of the ECHR says that '[n]othing in this Convention shall be construed as limiting or derogating from any of the human rights and fundamental freedoms which may be ensured under the laws of any High Contracting Party or under any other agreement to which it is a Party'. Similarly, Article 5(2) of the ICCPR provides that '[t]here shall be no restriction upon or derogation from any of the fundamental human rights recognized or existing in any State party to the present Covenant pursuant to law, conventions, regulations or custom on the pretext that the present Covenant does not recognize such rights or that it recognizes them to a lesser extent'.

While one may assume that in principle the various systems that protect human rights are therefore consistent with each other, this is not always true. Some provisions of human rights treaties do not set only minimum standards: for instance, under Article 20(1) of the ICCPR '[a]ny propaganda for war shall be prohibited by law'; this conflicts with treaties or national rules providing for freedom of expression without making an exception for war propaganda.

A second type of conflict stems from the fact that a few treaty provisions give rights to different individuals in relation to a given issue. These rights may be conflicting in a given situation. Thus, under Article 2 of the First Protocol to the ECHR, '[i]n the exercise of any functions which it assumes in relation to education and to teaching, the State shall respect the right of parents to ensure such education and teaching in conformity with their own religious and philosophical convictions'. Article 18(4) of the ICCPR similarly protects the parents' right 'to ensure the religious and moral education of their children in conformity with their own convictions'. Again, according to Article 13(3) of the ICESCR, States parties 'undertake to have respect for the liberty of parents and, when applicable, legal guardians to choose for their children schools, other than those established by the public authorities, which conform to such minimum educational standards as may be laid down or approved by the State and to ensure the religious and moral education of their children in conformity with their own convictions'. It is clear that all these provisions tend to ensure respect for the parents' or legal guardians' convictions, irrespective of the child's own convictions. This appears to reflect the conception of the parental role that prevailed when the above-quoted texts were adopted. The more recent Convention on the Rights of the Child takes a different approach. As its Article 3 says, 'the best interests of the child shall be a primary consideration'; under Article 14(1) and (2), 'States Parties shall respect the right of the child to freedom of thought, conscience and religion', and 'the rights and duties of the parents and, when applicable, legal guardians, to provide direction to the child in the exercise of his or her right in a manner consistent with the evolving capacities of the child'. Thus, under the Convention on the Rights of the Child, should a teenager have religious or philosophical convictions that conflict with his or her parents', a State party would be required to take conduct which is inconsistent with what the previously mentioned treaties provide. A State party to all these treaties would have to take the child's convictions as paramount under the Convention on the Rights of the Child, while it would be under an obligation to give decisive weight to the parents' convictions according to the earlier treaties.

A third, and more frequent, type of conflict may derive from the fact that under a human rights treaty, especially one of those concerning social and economic rights, a right—for instance, the right to strike under Article 8(1)(e) of the ICESCR—may be granted to a person in a way that negatively affects the position of another person. This person may enjoy for his or her position a right under the same or another human rights treaty. The balance between the relevant rights may be differently placed in the various treaties. Therefore by giving maximum protection to one person's economic or social rights, an infringement of another person's rights may well occur.

The various types of conflict which have been illustrated may not have had a great impact so far. However, there seems to be little justification for ever imposing obligations that require conflicting conduct in a given situation on States parties to human rights treaties.

In order to prevent conflicts when establishing a new instrument, it cannot be assumed that by inserting in the text a general clause providing for consistency with other treaties one would always prevent the new instrument from causing conflicts. A careful assessment of the risk of conflicts should be made. The multiplication of instruments no doubt increases that risk.

Some existing conflicts may be resolved through contextual interpretation. However, if the import of treaty provisions cannot be corrected through evolutive interpretation, some revision of the existing texts could usefully be undertaken, especially in order to make the older treaties conform to the tendencies that are reflected in the more recent instruments. This should not create too many political difficulties when the conflicting treaties are situated at the same level—whether universal or regional—and, therefore, one can assume that values incorporated in recent treaties are generally shared by parties to the older ones. Thus, in the example given above concerning the education of minors, the UN Covenants could be revised in order to make them tally with the highly successful Convention on the Rights of the Child.

III. UPDATING HUMAN RIGHTS TREATIES

The need for a revision of existing human rights treaties does not appear only in connection with the conflicts that may arise among them. With regard to most treaties there is a marked discrepancy between the way in which the texts were written and the meaning that has come to be attributed to them, mainly through the work of bodies entrusted with supervising their implementation. While none of the human rights treaties has endowed any of these bodies with the power to interpret the treaty in a binding way, these bodies' case law exerts an undeniable influence on the interpretation of the respective treaties. States that are parties to a treaty tend to acquiesce to the interpretation given by the treaty body. Anyway, all serious discussion of the meaning of the various texts has to consider what those bodies say, at least as a starting-point. Influence of judgments of the European Court of Human Rights with regard to the interpretation of the ECHR is especially high, although Article 53 of the Convention (Article 46 (1) as from 1 November 1998) states only that '[t]he High Contracting Parties undertake to abide by the decision of the Court in any case to which they are parties'. General comments by the Human Rights Committee concerning the ICCPR are also widely regarded as authoritative. An exception has to be made when those comments are challenged by some States parties to the Covenant, as was General Comment No. 24 on reservations.[7]

One of the results of this abundant case law is that the wording of the various instruments conveys only to a limited extent the meaning that the texts have acquired. It would for instance be difficult to infer from reading Article 11 of the ECHR, which establishes the workers' 'right to form and join trade unions for the protection' of their interests, that their union is thereby granted the right to be consulted over collective disputes, as the European Court held in the *National Union of Belgian Police* case[8] and in the *Swedish Engine Drivers' Union* case.[9] Similarly, it would be hard to derive from the text of Article 6(1) of the same Convention that determination of 'civil rights and obligations or of any criminal charge' may also cover disciplinary actions.[10]

States that are parties to the European Convention are no doubt aware of the Court's judgments, and therefore may feel that they have to comply with obligations under the Convention as defined by the Court. However, the formal inclusion in an amending protocol of some of the specifications and additions resulting from the Court's judgments would contribute to the effective protection of the relevant rights. Moreover, potentially interested persons would be better informed of the precise scope of their rights under the Convention.

What has been said here about the ECHR applies to other treaties, whenever the interpretation given by the respective bodies diverges from the wording of the relevant text and can be taken as sufficiently significant to affect the meaning of the treaty provision.

The older human rights treaties may need revising also for a different reason. Parts of their text reflect outdated conceptions and may not appear capable of lending themselves to an interpretation that would satisfy contemporary exigencies. Thus, the European Court of Human Rights and other bodies may feel that they

---

[7] The critical comments that were made by the Governments of the USA and the UK are reproduced in (1995) 16 *HRLJ* 422 and 424. For the text of General Comment No. 24 see (1994) 15 *HRLJ* 464.

[8] *National Union of Belgian Police*, ECHR (1975), Series A, No. 19, 18. The Court then said that 'the members of the trade union have a right, in order to protect their interests, that the trade union should be heard'.

[9] *Swedish Engine Drivers' Union*, ECHR (1976), Series A, No. 20, 15.

[10] See in particular the *Engel* case, ECHR (1977), Series A, No. 22, 34 5.

cannot provide all the necessary updating and that a formal amendment to the treaty is therefore required.

Supplementary protocols have sometimes been used to add new rights to those guaranteed under a treaty. They could be used more extensively also for incorporating some elements of the case law and therefore ensuring a greater transparency in the meaning that the various provisions have acquired. New dimensions to the protection of rights already guaranteed could also be added in order to take into account some important developments that have taken place at the national level in respect of the same rights.

The adoption of amending protocols may, however, involve the risk that governments take the opportunity of concluding a protocol for settling questions of interpretation in a way that does not conform to the solution which has been adopted by the treaty body. This may likely be in the direction of giving more limited protection to human rights. Thus, while the adoption of a new instrument may appear to be useful for enhancing the protection of human rights, this move could be counterbalanced by the current political attitude towards those rights.

The adoption of an amending protocol or an additional treaty covering the same rights that are already protected in a treaty may sometimes involve a further risk. The adoption of the protocol or the treaty giving a wider protection of a right could be understood as implying that a corresponding protection was not given under the original treaty. Should this attitude prevail, the adoption of a new protocol or treaty could have a negative effect on the interpretation of the original treaty in cases when the amending protocol or the additional treaty is not yet in force or is not applicable for some other reason.

A similarly negative conclusion could be reached when the new protocol or treaty does not grant a certain right to the same extent that is arguably ensured by an earlier treaty. For instance, in the *National Union of Belgian Police*[11] and *Swedish Engine Drivers' Union*[12] cases, mentioned above, the European Court of Human Rights found that Article 11 of the ECHR could not be interpreted as having granted some rights that had not been recognized by the later European Social Charter, which was also concluded within the framework of the Council of Europe.[13] While the risk of a negative effect of the new instrument being established has to be highlighted, it should be said that, as a general approach, the European Court's argument does not seem convincing. Even if adopted by the same group of States, a new instrument does not necessarily intend to provide a standard that is equal to, or higher than, the standards that have already been accepted. A new protocol or treaty may have as its purpose that of enriching the protection of some human rights only under certain circumstances.

Anyway, the entry into force of a new instrument does not necessarily imply that the previously accepted rules have been replaced in their entirety, when these are not formally repealed. Provisions that are generally included in human rights treaties —

---

[11] Note 8 above, at 18.   [12] Note 9 above, at 15.
[13] With regard to relations between the ECHR and one of its additional Prots., a similar argument was developed by the European Commission of Human Rights in its decision on the admissibility of App. No. 21072/92, *Gestra*, 80 D&R 89 (1994).

like Article 60 (now Article 53) of the ECHR and Article 5(2) of the ICCPR (both quoted in the previous paragraph)—seem to reinforce this conclusion.

IV. ENSURING THAT HUMAN RIGHTS ARE EFFECTIVELY PROTECTED

A. Examining Petitions or Communications from Victims of Violations

No doubt protection of human rights as required by treaties is primarily ensured through national laws and institutions. State authorities are generally bound by treaties either directly or through implementing legislation. Moreover, in many cases compliance with obligations under human rights treaties is effected through the application of national rules which have been enacted independently from the treaty.

Judicial and administrative remedies generally existing under national laws extensively provide means for making the protection of human rights effective. This does not imply that adequate remedies are available for all human rights, as remedies tend to be limited for some rights, especially most economic and social rights. Moreover, for several victims of violations, remedies may be open only nominally because their cost is prohibitive.

National systems tend to rely on the use of remedies by affected physical or legal persons and do not generally provide effective machinery for monitoring compliance with existing legislation. Moreover, at the national level, institutions for promoting the protection of human rights either do not exist or operate selectively for some rights only.

At the international level, treaty bodies provide supplementary protection. This supplementary character is clearly evident with regard to remedies: when national remedies are available, and may be considered adequate, they have to be exhausted before remedies at the international level may be used. This is expressly provided, for instance, by Article 26 (as from 1 November 1998, Article 35(1)) of the ECHR, Article 2 of the Optional Protocol to the ICCPR, Article 22(5)(b) of the Convention against Torture and other Cruel, Inhuman or Degrading Treatment or Punishment,[14] and Article 14(7)(a) of the Convention on the Elimination of All Forms of Racial Discrimination. The last provision makes an exception where 'the application of the remedies is unreasonably prolonged', but this appears to be implied by the local remedies rule in international law.[15] The same may be said of the above-mentioned provision of the Convention against Torture, which excepts the case where 'the application of the remedies is unreasonably prolonged or is unlikely to bring effective relief to the person who is the victim of the violation of the Convention'.

While remedies for the protection of human rights at the international level are no doubt very significant within the system of the ECHR, and probably has been

[14] Convention against Torture and Other Cruel, Inhuman or Degrading Treatment or Punishment, in *International Instruments*, note 1 above, at 293.

[15] See C.F. Amerasinghe, *Local Remedies in International Law* (1990), 203–6.

enhanced since direct access to the European Court has become available to victims of violations as a consequence of the entry into force of the Eleventh Protocol, the other systems for the protection of human rights that give some means of recourse to physical or legal persons do not lead to binding decisions, and also appear in practice to be considerably less effective. One reason for this is that the resources of personnel and time of treaty bodies like the Human Rights Committee are inadequate, even if the total number of communications from victims is still limited. Given this situation, it is of little importance that some systems, especially the one provided by the Optional Protocol to the ICCPR, appear to be more tilted in the victims' favour than the system of the ECHR—especially with regard to the way in which conditions of admissibility are assessed and rules of evidence applied.[16]

To ensure a better protection of human rights, the efficacy of most systems providing for petitions or communications on the part of victims of violations clearly needs to be enhanced. This would essentially require that treaty bodies be given more resources and that their decisions acquire a binding character.

The opportunity for victims of violations to put their grievances to treaty bodies needs to be considerably widened, especially with regard to economic, social, and cultural rights.[17] A timid step in this direction was made by the 1995 Additional Protocol to the European Social Charter, which entered into force on 1 July 1998; however, under this instrument remedies do not lead to a binding decision and are open only to international workers' and employers' organizations and to other NGOs.

Providing remedies for economic, social, and cultural rights at the international level does not necessarily presuppose that the same rights may be invoked before national courts or administrative authorities. When rights are not so invocable, there would be no local remedies to exhaust. Anyway, as the Committee for Economic, Social, and Cultural Rights noted in its General Comment No. 3, a number of provisions in the Covenant 'would seem to be capable of immediate application by judicial and other organs in many national legal systems'.[18]

Remedies at the international level may sometimes be used cumulatively. Thus, while under Article 27(1)(b) (Article 35(2)(b) as from 1 November 1998) of the ECHR a petition is inadmissible if it 'has already been submitted to another procedure for international investigation or settlement and if it contains no relevant new information'—and this includes the fact that a communication has been made under the Optional Protocol to the Covenant—Article 5(2)(a) of the Optional Protocol only prevents the admissibility of a communication when '[t]he same matter is . . . examined under another procedure of international investigation or settlement'. Thus, a communication would become admissible when a parallel petition is no longer being examined under the system of the ECHR. While some States that are parties

---

[16] See, however, for a list of advantages—other than procedural ones—that may be attributed to the Optional Protocol system, M. Nowak, 'The Inter-relationship Between the Covenant on Civil and Political Rights and the European Convention on Human Rights', in S. Vassilouni (ed.), *Aspects of the Protection of Individual and Social Rights* (1995), 131.

[17] This statement is only affected in part by the fact that, as the European Court said in the *Airey* case, '[w]hilst the Convention sets forth what are essentially civil and political rights, many of them have implications of a social or economic nature': *Airey*, ECHR (1980), Series A, No. 32, 15.

[18] The text of this comment is also reproduced in M. Craven, *The International Covenant on Economic, Social and Cultural Rights* (1995), 373.

both to the ECHR and the Optional Protocol have sought to avoid having to defend themselves first against a petition and then against a communication and made a reservation to the Optional Protocol to this effect, other States have not done so. This may lead to opposite results in individual cases. For instance, in the *Coeriel and Aurik* case,[19] two years after the European Commission of Human Rights had found that the claimants' petition was manifestly ill-founded and therefore inadmissible, the Human Rights Committee expressed its view that the Netherlands had committed an infringement of the claimants' rights in denying them the right to change their surnames for religious reasons.

While Article 22(5)(a) of the Convention against Torture considers that a communication is admissible only if '[t]he same matter has not been, and is not being, examined under another procedure of international investigation or settlement', other treaties, such as the Convention on the Elimination of All Forms of Racial Discrimination, do not require that a communication has not previously been made to another body. This could lead to a petition being successively addressed to three or more treaty bodies. With regard to the UNESCO human rights procedure, it has even been held that 'UNESCO was not legally bound to suspend the examination of a communication in accordance with 104 EX/Decision 3.3 on the grounds that it was already being examined by the Human Rights Committee'.[20] Thus, even simultaneous proceedings are possible.

From the point of view of the victim, the possibility of addressing first a petition under the system of the ECHR and later a communication under the Optional Protocol may appear to be a welcome result. There is no contradiction between the findings of treaty bodies when they reach opposite conclusions on the basis of the different way in which the governing treaties protect the relevant right. In other cases of opposite conclusions there may be a contradiction, but this is not necessarily an evil. On the other hand, when both proceedings concern the alleged infringement of the same right because of the same facts, it does not seem reasonable that a State should be required to defend itself in different venues, also in view of the fact that both systems, and particularly that of the Optional Protocol, are overburdened. Giving the victim the choice between the two sets of proceedings then seems an adequate solution. This would imply an amendment to the Optional Protocol so as to bar the possibility of addressing a communication when the alleged infringement of the same right has already been examined by the European Court. It is true that victims do not generally possess the necessary knowledge for making an appropriate choice, and that they are free to address a communication or petition without a lawyer's assistance. However, in most cases victims should be encouraged to seek a lawyer's specialized knowledge as it considerably enhances the prospects of an outcome that is in the petitioner's favour.

A similar solution could be advocated for the other treaties that allow petitions to be successively addressed to various treaty bodies. However, a different solution would seem more appropriate whenever an examination by a specialized treaty body

---

[19] The Commission's decision on App. No. 18050/91 and the Committee's views on Communication 453/1991, both concerning this case, are reproduced in (1994) 15 *HRLJ* 448 and 422.
[20] UNESCO Doc. 107/EX/34, para. 45.

ensures better protection of the relevant right. In that case it might be preferable to envisage this treaty body's competence as prior or exclusive. However, it would be too complicated to adopt the necessary amendments to the other treaties providing for a system of petitions or communications. Identifying one particular venue as the most adequate would no doubt give rise to many objections.

B. Monitoring States' Compliance

While States should not be required to defend themselves over the same facts and rights before different treaty bodies, there seems to be little inconvenience in the overlapping of monitoring activities by treaty bodies. This type of supervision currently takes a large amount of time and attention of treaty bodies on the basis of provisions such as Article 40 of the ICCPR, Articles 17 to 21 of the ICESCR, Articles 19 and 20 of the Convention against Torture, Article 9 of the Convention on the Elimination of All Forms of Racial Discrimination, or Articles 21 to 29 of the European Social Charter. All these procedures require States to submit periodic reports, that are subsequently examined by the relevant body. Generally there is an oral discussion of the report with the participation of one or more representatives of the State; the treaty body is empowered only to make recommendations. The contribution that these procedures make to the effective protection of human rights should not be over-emphasized also in view of the fact that many States do not comply with their obligations to submit reports. Moreover, treaty bodies are greatly encumbered by reports, so that, by considering their work, one may reach the paradoxical conclusion that timely examination of reports is only possible because many States fail to submit them, and therefore those States' conduct cannot be properly monitored. However, the procedure serves some useful purpose, so much so that it would be an important addition in those systems for the protection of human rights that do not provide for periodic monitoring of compliance.

One vital purpose of the procedure under discussion is that it places an obligation on States that are parties to a treaty periodically to submit to the scrutiny of the treaty body their compliance with all their treaty obligations. The ECHR, which does not provide for a general monitoring system, only gives the Committee of Ministers the task of supervising the execution of the Court's judgments (Article 54; Article 46(2) as from 1 November 1998). This has been understood in practice as covering State conduct similar to that revealed in the case which is the object of the judgment, so that in several instances States have been prompted to modify their legislation in order to bring it into line with the ECHR. However, no initiative is taken with regard to States for which a similar need appears to exist; parallel action towards these States presupposes that petitions are taken against them and that the Court delivers judgments which contain findings of non-compliance.

It is clear that giving an institution the task of monitoring the way in which the obligations under the ECHR are complied with would greatly contribute to the effective protection of the corresponding rights. As it would be impractical to give this type of role to the European Court of Human Rights, monitoring could be entrusted to a new body that would work either independently or under the authority of the Committee of Ministers. The main requirement would be that monitoring activities are consonant with the Court's case law. The proposed new body should be bound to take the Court's judgments as the basis for solving problems of interpretation.

A second function of a monitoring system is to complement petitions and applications when these cannot be made because access to remedies under the human rights treaties is in practice not open to some persons who are victims of infringements.

Moreover, treaties on human rights do not provide for remedies that natural or legal persons may use against other natural or legal persons, infringing their rights in the case that those rights have a horizontal effect (*Drittwirkung*). At the international level creating remedies in this case would raise obvious problems of due process. With regard to rights having this type of effect, national remedies can be supplemented only by methods other than remedies—in the first place by monitoring activities.

In playing their monitoring role, treaty bodies serve another vital purpose. The examination of State reports provides treaty bodies with an opportunity of expressing their opinion on the meaning of treaty obligations. This is better done when issues are considered in depth, after an extensive examination of State practice, as in most general comments of the Human Rights Committee or of the Committee on Economic, Social, and Cultural Rights.

While the function of interpreting the ECHR is currently fulfilled by the European Court when giving judgments, the possibility of addressing issues out of the context of individual cases would provide the Court with the opportunity of considering those issues in a wider context, after an extensive analysis of practice concerning all the States parties. This may be achieved by giving the European Court the power to deliver opinions on the import of all rights and obligations under the Convention, going beyond the limited scope of the advisory jurisdiction under Protocol No. 2 (as from 1 November 1998, Article 47 of the Convention). Article 64 of the American Convention on Human Rights[21] could serve as a model for introducing a provision granting States parties, and possibly some organs of the Council of Europe, the power to request advisory opinions from the Court. Should a new monitoring institution be established within the ECHR system, as was suggested above, this body could also be entrusted with the task of requesting the Court's opinion.

C. Examining Inter-State Claims

In order to protect human rights under treaties, one State may submit claims that another State has not complied with its treaty obligations. Few treaties on human rights provide for effective machinery for settling inter-State disputes. Article IX of the Genocide Convention, which was recently invoked by Bosnia against the Federal Republic of Yugoslavia,[22] gives the International Court of Justice competence

---

[21] American Convention on Human Rights, adopted at San José, Costa Rica, on 22 Nov. 1969, reprinted in United Nations, *A Compilation of International Instruments*, Volume 2, *Regional Instruments* (1997), 14.

[22] *Case concerning application of the Convention on the Prevention and Punishment of the Crime of Genocide (Bosnia-Herzegovina* v. *Yugoslavia) (1996)*, [1996] ICJ Rep. 595. In Dec. 1997 an order by the Court declared that a counterclaim by Yugoslavia was admissible: [1997] ICJ Rep. 243.

over 'the interpretation, application or fulfilment' of the Convention. Some treaties give a role to treaty bodies with regard to 'any alleged breach of the Convention' by another State, as set out in Article 24 (as from 1 November 1998, Article 33) of the ECHR. Article 41(1) of the ICCPR makes the Human Rights Committee's competence—with regard to one State's communication 'to the effect that another State Party is not fulfilling its obligations under the present Covenant'—conditional on declarations accepting the Committee's competence on the part of both States; moreover, even a State communication according to this procedure cannot lead to a binding decision. Many human rights treaties do not say anything about State complaints; on the other hand, the Concluding Document of the Vienna Meeting of the CSCE (now OSCE) Conference,[23] which is not a treaty, provides that a participating State may follow a procedure which could lead to the submission of information, 'including information concerning situations and specific cases, at the meetings of the Conference of the Human Dimension as well as the main CSCE Follow-up Meetings'.

The various procedures for settling inter-State claims that are provided in human rights treaties are not exclusive of other procedures that may have been agreed upon by the claimant State and the State that is alleged to have committed an infringement. It would be difficult to maintain that human rights treaties intend to establish self-contained regimes.[24] However, States are not likely to use procedures that are not provided in the relevant treaty for ensuring the protection of human rights on the part of other States. Even the use of procedures open to States under the human rights treaties is relatively rare, and mainly concerns cases in which the claimant State has a special interest due to the victim's nationality or ethnic origin.

In order to increase the contribution that inter-State claims may make to the protection of human rights, it would first of all be necessary to provide some more effective procedures for the compulsory settlement of disputes over alleged infringements of human rights. Should the States that are parties to the dispute fail to agree on its solution, a binding decision at the end of the procedure would no doubt enhance the protection of human rights. Involving treaty bodies in the procedure would have the advantage of ensuring that any decision is coherent with the treaty body's case law. Thus, the existing procedure for State claims under the ECHR system would require no modification.

Even if the competence of treaty bodies with regard to State claims were substantially increased, this would be of little avail if States did not overcome their traditional reluctance in raising claims against other States over infringements of obligations under human rights treaties. This is likely to be a slow development and will always be less important for the overall compliance with treaty obligations than the use of remedies on the part of victims and the treaty bodies' monitoring activities.

---

[23] Concluding Document of the Vienna Meeting 1986 of representatives of the participating States of the Conference on Security and Co-operation in Europe, reprinted in I. Brownlie (ed.), *Basic Documents on Human Rights* (1992), 450.
[24] See B. Simma, 'Self-Contained Regimes' (1985) 16 *NYIL* 111.

D. Actively Promoting Respect for Human Rights

The protection of human rights often requires the assumption by treaty bodies of a role of promotion that goes well beyond the instruments considered hitherto. This may involve a constant dialogue with a variety of State authorities, sometimes in view of conciliation—to be reached through confidential methods—with natural or legal persons that invoke certain rights. A human rights High Commissioner has recently been cast in this role at the United Nations level; a proposal to introduce a similar figure within the Council of Europe was made by the Government of Finland and has been adopted in May 1999.[25] A rather successful experience has been provided so far by the OSCE High Commissioner on National Minorities, especially with regard to the rights of minorities in Slovakia and in the Baltic States.[26] The OSCE High Commissioner's role was recently described as ' first, to try to contain and de-escalate tensions involving national minority issues, and, second, to act as a "tripwire" '.[27]

Inevitably, the chances of success depend on political elements that may exist only in certain sets of circumstances. However, the much more general use of a High Commissioner and his or her methods may well yield significant results. Alongside the OSCE High Commissioner on National Minorities, one or two more High Commissioners could operate in Europe, under the auspices of either OSCE or the Council of Europe. Overlapping of activities would not be desirable, since it would be likely to undermine the High Commissioner's role.

V. PRESENT SCOPE OF PROTECTION OF HUMAN RIGHTS UNDER COMMUNITY LAW

The survey made here has considered existing treaties for the protection of human rights in relation to States. While some aspects of possible developments have already been discussed, more comprehensive proposals concerning enhanced protection in Europe require a specific analysis from the European Union's perspective.

As is well known, the European Community is not party to any of the human rights treaties. According to *Opinion 2/94* of the European Court of Justice, accession to the ECHR 'could be brought about only by way of Treaty amendment' because of its 'constitutional significance'.[28] A similar conclusion may well have to be reached with regard to accession to most other human rights treaties, although the Court of Justice (ECJ) may have been particularly concerned with the way in which its own role would have been affected by that played by the European Court of Human Rights within the Convention system.[29] The ECJ also mentioned the

---

[25] A similar proposal has been made by Judge Pettiti in his intervention in A. Cassese, A. Clapham, and J. Weiler (eds.), *Human Rights and the European Community: Methods of Protection* (1991), 179.

[26] See The Foundation on Inter-Ethnic Relations, *The Role of the High Commissioner on National Minorities in OSCE Conflict Prevention* (1997), 52.

[27] *Ibid.*, at 19.   [28] *Opinion 2/94* [1996] ECR I–1759, at para. 35.

[29] See my annotation to *Opinion 2/94* in (1996) 33 *CML Rev.* 988–9.

'integration of all the provisions of the Convention into the Community legal order',[30] but this could hardly mean that by acceding to the Convention the Community would exert powers outside its competence. For instance, a human right concerning criminal proceedings would generally have little to do with conduct regulated by Community law; should the Community bind itself to recognize that right, it would do so only in so far as the same right became relevant with regard to Community acts or to State acts that are governed by Community law. Therefore, the fact that one or the other human right is granted under a treaty would not seem in principle to affect the issue of whether the Community is entitled to accede to the treaty without an amendment to the EC Treaty.

The ECHR has acquired special significance among human rights treaties in the case law of the ECJ and even more so in Article 6(2) (*ex* Article F(2)) of the Treaty on European Union (TEU), which does not refer to any treaty other than the ECHR. Under this provision the 'Union shall respect fundamental rights, as guaranteed by the European Convention for the Protection of Human Rights and Fundamental Freedoms signed in Rome on 4 November 1950'. The third preambular paragraph of the Single European Act also referred to 'the fundamental rights recognized in . . . the European Social Charter'. The Single European Act applies to Community law and to co-operation in the field of foreign policy, while Article 6(2) concerns all three pillars.

As the second and third pillars mainly concern intergovernmental action, and Member States' action is of course subject to human rights treaties that the various States have ratified, the main question concerns the relevance for the first pillar of human rights treaties other than the ECHR.[31] The ECJ has often referred in more general terms to 'international treaties concerning the protection of human rights on which the Member States have collaborated or to which they have acceded'.[32] This wider reference to treaties has not become obsolete once Article 6(2) of the TEU has singled out the ECHR.[33] Since Article 6(1), as amended by the Treaty of Amsterdam, refers more generally to 'respect for human rights and fundamental freedoms', it would seem reasonable in future to amend Article 6(2) to include a reference to human rights treaties other than the ECHR, and thus give also to those treaties a higher status within EC law.

Both the case law of the ECJ and Article 6(2) TEU draw part of the standards for the protection of human rights also from 'the constitutional traditions common to the Member States'.[34] No conflict between human rights as they are protected under the treaties and those which result from constitutional traditions has as yet appeared; besides, 'constitutional traditions' is a sufficiently vague concept to allow the

---

[30] Note 28 above, at para. 34.

[31] This question also relates to the Prots. to the ECHR as they are not mentioned in Art. 6(2) TEU. For a discussion of this point see G. Gaja, 'The Protection of Human Rights under the Maastricht Treaty', in D. Curtin and T. Heukels (eds.), *Institutional Dynamics of European Integration. Essays in Honour of Henry G. Schermers* (1994), 556–7.

[32] The quotation is taken from Case 5/88, *Wachauf* v. *Germany* [1989] ECR 2609, at para. 17.

[33] Case C–249/96, *Grant* v. *South-West Trains* [1998] ECR I–621, at para. 44.

[34] The first reference to those 'traditions' appeared in Case 11/70, *Internationale Handelsgesellschaft mbH* v. *Einfuhr- und Vorratsstelle für Getreide und Futtermittel* [1970] ECR 1125, at para. 4.

ECJ to even out potential conflicts. The scope of application of Community law standards concerning the protection of human rights has been defined rather narrowly by the ECJ. As was said in *SPUC* v. *Grogan*, the Court:

> when requested to give a preliminary ruling, must provide the national court with all the elements of interpretation which are necessary in order to enable it to assess the compatibility of the legislation with the fundamental rights—as laid down in particular in the European Convention on Human Rights—the observance of which the Court ensures. However, the Court has no such jurisdiction with regard to national legislation lying outside the scope of Community law.[35]

Thus, the standards for the protection of human rights that are provided by Community law apply only to Community legislation and to national measures that either implement Community legislation or are otherwise situated within the framework of Community law.[36] While it may be argued that the Community law standards extend to the whole area of the Community's exclusive competence, they do not apply to matters within the Community's concurrent competence until this has been exercised. These same standards both affect the validity of Community acts and integrate existing rules, some of which—especially in the field of social rights—can be regarded as directly providing the protection of specific rights.

This approach tends to assimilate the protection of human rights under Community law to that which is granted under national laws. The Community law standards basically apply to Community acts; they do not affect all national measures, but concern only a certain number of them: those that come within the scope of Community law. This may explain why conflicts of Community and national standards for the protection of human rights have not so far appeared with regard to national measures.

The German and Italian Constitutional Courts have dealt with a different type of conflict—that between a rule of Community law requiring certain behaviour from physical or legal persons, on the one hand, and the national standards for the protection of human rights on the other. In this set of cases,[37] the rule of Community law may have not been contravening any Community law standard protecting human rights, but generally cannot be regarded as implementing one of those standards.

While some parts of the Community law standards for the protection of human rights may be considered as not being totally adequate, the remedy sought for this by

---

[35] Case C–159/90, *SPUC* v. *Grogan* [1991] ECR I–4685, at para. 31. A similar assertion was made more recently in Case C–299/95, *Kremzow* v. *Austria* [1997] ECR I–2629, at para. 15. The scope of the protection of fundamental rights under Community law will arguably not be affected by the amendment made by the Treaty of Amsterdam to Art. L (now Art. 46) TEU, to the effect that the ECJ's exercise of its powers will be extended to 'Article 6 (2) with regard to actions of the institutions, insofar as the Court has jurisdiction under the treaties establishing the European Communities and under this Treaty'. Although this text refers only to 'actions of the institutions', it does not necessarily imply that State conduct within the scope of Community law will no longer come under the Court's review: see G. Rodríguez Iglesias, 'La protección de los derechos fundamentales en la Unión europea', *Scritti in onore di Giuseppe Federico Mancini* (1998), Vol. II, 845.

[36] This criterion may be difficult to apply when it is not clear how far Community law reaches. For instance, in *Bickel and Franz*, the Court held that Art. 6 EC also gives protection in criminal proceedings against discrimination based on nationality: Case C–274/96, *Bickel and Franz*, [1998] ECR I–7637.

[37] These may be exemplified by Cases 4/73, *Nold KG* v. *Commission* [1974] ECR 491 and 44/79, *Hauer* v. *Land Rheinland-Pfalz* [1979] ECR 3727.

a few national courts, namely to resort to national law standards, is clearly unsatisfactory. It impinges on the uniform application of Community law and implies an infringement by the relevant Member State of its obligations under Community law. The proper remedy to the perceived inadequacy of the Community law standards lies elsewhere, beyond the powers of national courts. It clearly consists in correcting and completing the Community law standards. However, while these could be improved, they will not be able to include all national standards. The idea of maximizing protection of human rights by this technique is not viable: even if all the national standards were considered to be acceptable at the Community level, the differences and even conflicts between them would prevent their global inclusion in the Community law standards. Thus, some discrepancies and even conflicts between national and Community standards for the protection of human rights would remain possible. The practical importance of these potential conflicts would depend on the way the Community law standards are developed, and especially on their scope of application: should they be applied in the future to a much larger number of national measures, conflicts would become more frequent. In order not to jeopardize the uniform application of Community law, national law standards should anyway not prevail, whether the conflicting Community rule implements standards for the protection of human rights or not.

VI. ENHANCING PROTECTION OF HUMAN RIGHTS UNDER COMMUNITY LAW

Within their scope of application, the Community law standards concerning the protection of human rights seem comprehensive. The reference to treaties and to common constitutional traditions potentially encompasses all the civil, political, economic, social, and cultural rights. Given the matters governed by Community law, one would expect in the ECJ's judgments a wealth of references to economic and social rights. This is not so. Only very rarely is a treaty other than the ECHR mentioned in the Court's judgments.[38] References to constitutional principles are rare, especially with regard to economic and social rights.[39] This phenomenon may be partly explained by the fact that economic and social rights are often protected only under fairly general provisions.

The absence of an adequate set of rules to which the ECJ can refer may be remedied by enriching the ECHR and the European Social Charter with regard to economic and social rights or by concluding a separate treaty under the auspices of the Council of Europe. Another way would be to adopt binding rules—or at least rules to which the ECJ would have to refer—within the European Union. As was noted

---

[38] e.g. in *Defrenne III*, the Court mentioned both the European Social Charter and ILO Convention No. 111: Case 149/77, *Defrenne III* [1978] ECR 1365 at para. 28: In *Orkem* the Court referred to Art. 14(3)(g) of the ICCPR: Case 374/87, *Orkem* [1989] ECR 3283 at para. 31. The European Social Charter was also referred to in Case 24/86, *Blaizot* [1988] ECR 379 at para. 20.

[39] One instance of a relatively thorough reference to these principles is given by the *Hauer* case, note 37 above.

above, to adopt parallel treaties concerning the same rights within the Council of Europe and the European Union would create some difficulties, because even identical texts would no doubt acquire different meanings in their respective contexts, if only through the respective roles of the European Court of Human Rights and the ECJ.

Recent developments in Europe appear to add some elements in favour of choosing the Council of Europe as a framework for enhancing the protection of human rights. As noted above, a clear trend exists towards progressively enlarging the European Community so as to encompass nearly all the European States, while there will be an increasing political homogeneity between some of the States which will become Community members and the majority of European non-member States. Thus, a significant difference in the level of protection of human rights would not be justified.

Should the choice be made in favour of building on the ECHR and the European Social Charter, it would be reasonable for the ECJ to interpret the new treaty according to the meaning that the relevant treaty body would give to its provisions, especially if that body was empowered to give binding decisions, albeit with regard to specific cases. This is what the ECJ already tends to do—although not always accurately—when it refers to judgments of the European Court of Human Rights when considering provisions of the ECHR concerning civil rights.[40]

One practical advantage of the suggested approach is that the interpretation of provisions granting human rights would be entrusted to a specialized body, which may acquire much wider experience and will be more sensitive to the need for the protection of human rights; there would be only one standard, at the European level, with regard to each right, so that it would be easier for State authorities to apply it, while moreover the risk of conflicts between rights would diminish.

The suggested solution does not necessarily imply the adoption of a system of preliminary references from the ECJ to the treaty body so that new questions of interpretation of the human rights standards could be examined by the relevant treaty body as they arise in judicial proceedings. The ECJ could continue to decide on the significance of the human rights standards in individual cases. What is important is that the ECJ should progressively adjust its case law to the interpretation given by the treaty body.

It is useful at this point to consider in greater detail the alternative solution of enacting binding rules for the protection of economic and social rights, and possibly other rights as well, within the European Union. As was noted above, this solution may well imply a higher standard of protection, but not a significantly higher one. The idea that the Union should adopt a catalogue of fundamental rights has drawn considerable support; for instance, the Pintasilgo Committee suggested that the

---

[40] e.g. references to the judgments of the European Court of Human Rights may be found in Joined Cases 209–215 and 218/78, *Van Landewyck* v. *Commission* [1980] ECR 3125 at paras. 79–80 (albeit in the summary of the parties' arguments), in Joined Cases 46/87 and 227/88, *Hoechst AG* v. *Commission* [1989] ECR 2859 at para. 18, and in *Orkem*, note 38 above, at para. 30. For some critical comments on the way in which the ECJ interpreted the ECHR see J.P. Jacqué, 'Communauté européenne et Convention européenne des droits de l'homme', in *L' Europe et le Droit. Mélanges en hommage à Jean Boulouis* (1991), 330–1, and G. Gaja, 'Aspetti problematici della tutela dei diritti fondamentali nell'ordinamento comunitario' (1998) 71 *RDI* 585.

Intergovernmental Conference did this through amendments to the EC Treaty. A catalogue included in the TEU or in the EC Treaty would probably be intended to apply to all Community and national measures, and thus be juxtaposed to national rules on the protection of human rights. The system for the protection of human rights existing within the Council of Europe, or even its further development, would apparently not be affected by a European Union catalogue, but—apart from the risk of conflicts—the effectiveness of the Council of Europe system would most likely be undermined, to the detriment of the protection of the same rights in the States that are not members of the European Union.[41] Another disadvantage would be the fact of giving the decisive role in the interpretation of the catalogue to a non-specialized court, that would moreover become overburdened, unless one accepted the idea of creating a new human rights court within the European Union—a solution that would be politically difficult and would complicate the position of national courts when confronted with an issue of the validity of Community acts.

Short of creating a court for the protection of human rights within the European Union, there is the need to provide an adequate remedy to physical or legal persons when one of their human rights is infringed by European Union institutions—particularly when redress cannot be obtained from the ECJ. If one adopts the first alternative, and therefore one builds on the ECHR and on the European Social Charter, it would seem logical to provide for remedies before the European Court of Human Rights or to any other body to be established within the Council of Europe. In the well-known *Melchers* case the European Commission of Human Rights ruled out the admissibility of a petition concerning a State act implementing a decision given by a Community institution in view of the equivalence of protection that supposedly was granted within the Community system.[42] The Commission's view was widely criticized;[43] it may well be that the principle stated in *Melchers* will be reversed by the European Court of Human Rights. Should this occur, the compatibility of a Community act with the ECHR could be assessed, albeit indirectly, when a petition concerns a State measure implementing the Community act.

For envisaging a direct remedy against a Community act at an international level, accession by the Community to the ECHR would be required—an event that seems unlikely after the ECJ's *Opinion 2/94*.[44] Apart from the addition of a remedy that would be especially valuable when there is no parallel remedy under the EC Treaty, the main interest in ensuring an external review of Community acts, according to a standard incorporating a revised ECHR which would already be applicable under

[41] This consequence would be even more serious should the EU Member States withdraw from the ECHR, as was suggested by G. Toth, 'The European Union and Human Rights: The Way Forward', (1997) 34 *CML Rev.* 491.

[42] App. No. 13258/87, (1990) 64 D&R 138. See also App. No. 21090/92, (1994) 76–B D&R and (1994) 77 *RDI* 810, with a comment by Vitucci, *ibid.*, at 737. The latter decision concerned the European Patent Office.

[43] See, among the critical comments, J. Rigaux, 'L'article 192 du Traité CEE devant la Commission européenne des droits de l'homme' [1991] *RTDH* 399; J. Cohen-Jonathan and J.P. Jacqué, 'Activités de la Commission européenne des droits de l'homme' (1989) 35 *AFDI* 512; G. Gaja, 'Gli atti comunitari dinanzi alla Commissione europea dei diritti dell'uomo: di nuovo Solange?' (1990) 73 *RDI* 388. A similar view was expressed by D. Curtin, 'EU Police Cooperation and Human Rights Protection: Building the Trellis and Training the Vine', in *Scritti in onore di Guiseppe Federico Mancini*, note 35 above, at 250.

[44] Note 28 above.

Community law, lies in making the same standard more effective in its internal dimension. In particular, the ECJ would no doubt strive, more than it has done so far, to interpret the ECHR consistently with the European Court of Human Right's case law.

Some of the difficulties that concern accession to the ECHR would no doubt also exist if a monitoring system along the lines suggested above were adopted within the Council of Europe through a treaty and the Community wished to accede to it. As is implied in *Opinion 2/94* of the ECJ, an amendment to the EC Treaty would be required in order to do this .[45]

However, an effective monitoring system could also be established without a treaty. There would then be no obligation under international law for the Community periodically to submit reports; however, if the Member States and the political institutions of the European Union were willing to accept supervision, such a system could be established on a voluntary basis and there would arguably be no need to amend the EC Treaty.

The same applies if the High Commissioner to be established within the Council of Europe is given a role also with regard to the European Community. As is well known, the OSCE system does not rest on treaties and, in principle, the OSCE High Commissioner on National Minorities is already entitled to act in relation to the European Community.

All these steps concerning the external supervision of Community acts would add to the credibility of the European Union when it insists that non-member States accept the inclusion of obligations concerning the protection of human rights in their association or trade agreements with the European Community.

Should an external control of the type suggested here be politically unacceptable, a supervisory system and a High Commissioner could be established within the European Union.[46] A Treaty amendment would be required in order to provide a more generally available remedy before the ECJ for the protection of human rights. Even if this were limited to Community acts and to the Member States' conduct within the scope of Community law, a considerable strain would then be imposed on the Community's judicial system. On the other hand, *Opinion 2/94*[47] does not appear to imply that the Treaty be amended in order to establish within the European Community a monitoring system concerning the respect of human rights by Community institutions and by Member States within the scope of Community law. However, if such a system is created it will be necessary to see that the monitoring body does not impinge on the ombudsman's role. Establishing a monitoring system within the European Community may not provide a solution as effective as creating a similar system within the Council of Europe; however, it would represent progress for the protection

---

[45] Accepting an external monitoring system by treaty could be understood as implying, in the language of *Opinion 2/94*, 'a substantial change in the present Community system for the protection of human rights in that it would entail the entry of the Community into a distinct international institutional system': *ibid.*, at para. 34.

[46] A first initiative in this line is Council Reg. No. 1035/97 establishing a European Monitoring Centre on Racism and Xenophobia [1997] OJ L151/1. Monitoring under this instrument concerns the Member States.

[47] Note 28 above.

of human rights within the European Community. If limited as suggested above, it would not necessarily prevent a parallel initiative by the Council of Europe covering the behaviour of States that are members of the latter organization, including Member States of the European Community. In this case, in order to avoid the overlapping of the monitoring systems, it would be preferable for the Council of Europe's system to leave out Member States' conduct within the scope of Community law.

VII. CONCLUSIONS

It may be useful at this stage to summarize the main reflections and proposals that have been made. In order to enhance the protection of human rights in Europe the main option appears to be whether to reinforce the Council of Europe system or adopt a solution within the European Union. Pursuing both courses at the same time would create the risk of conflicts between human rights that are protected by different instruments; it would also be likely to weaken the Council of Europe system.[48] The preferable way would appear to be to build on the expertise that the Council of Europe has already acquired, in order both to extend the protection of human rights and to establish effective supervision.

The protection under the ECHR, the European Social Charter, or a parallel treaty should be extended in order more comprehensively to cover economic, social, and cultural rights. The protection of civil and political rights should also be increased. Furthermore, a monitoring system and an institution entrusted with actively promoting the respect of human rights should be established within the Council of Europe.

Any progress towards these goals, will mainly depend on the political initiative of the European Union and its Member States. Accession by the European Community to the ECHR and the additional treaties to be adopted within the Council of Europe would be preferable, but not essential. What is required is that the pivotal role of the European Court of Human Rights and of additional treaty bodies, were they established for certain types of rights, should be recognized both within the Council of Europe system and within the European Community.

---

[48] As H. Schermers recently put it, '[f]or Europe as a whole . . . there would also be a considerable loss. Europe would be split with regard to human rights, most certainly to the detriment of non-members of the Union. The system of the Council of Europe would suffer enormously if the Members of the European Union were to go their own way in protecting human rights': see 'The New European Court of Human Rights' (1998) 35 *CML Rev.* 5.

25

The Role of the European Parliament: Past and Future

REINHARD RACK AND STEFAN LAUSEGGER

I. THE ACTIVITIES OF THE EUROPEAN PARLIAMENT

A. *Introduction*

This chapter reviews the work of the European Parliament in the field of human rights both within and outside the European Union and provides some proposals for improvements.[1] Parliament, as the only democratically elected Community institution, has long deemed itself to have a particular vocation for the promotion of human rights—even prior to the first direct elections in 1979—and, over the years, it has developed its own policy approach in this field. As human rights were not of primary concern in the early stages of the European Communities, this provided an opportunity for Parliament to bring human rights within its own sphere of influence, as it regarded human rights protection as an essential part of the activities of the European Union. There was a special reason for Parliament's activities in this field: by making human rights a sphere of activity, and by linking them to other policies, the European Parliament could expand its powers and responsibilities to topics which did not actually fall within its normal remit. A good example of this is the role played by Parliament in the introduction of the policy of conditionality, on which it has exerted a major influence.

Human rights have increasingly gained in importance during recent decades. After World War II, various countries acted together in order to adopt texts based on the basic values of international society. The texts drawn up shortly after the end of the war therefore set out rights which had been under threat during the Nazi era in Germany. By underpinning these civil and political rights with a clear legal basis, Europe has created a very sophisticated system of human rights protection, based upon the establishment of the Council of Europe and the adoption and subsequent ratification of the European Convention on Human Rights (ECHR) in 1950.

But the conventional civil and political rights enshrined in the ECHR are not the only rights. As a result of growing prosperity following the years of rebuilding in

---

[1] This report does not necessarily reflect the opinion of the European Parliament. Nonetheless, it is based on the records and documentation of the Parliament itself rather than on analyses and evaluations made by external commentators.

Europe, lists of economic and social rights were established (such as the 1966 International Covenants on Economic, Social, and Cultural Rights (ICESCR),[2] and Civil and Political Rights (ICCPR),[3] the 1961 European Social Charter (ESC), and the 1989 Community Charter of the Fundamental Social Rights of Workers). This has added a second category to the discussion on human rights. However, the fact remains that while the rights guaranteed by the ECHR may be the subject of direct complaints even from individuals, this is not possible in the case of infringements of the second category of human rights. This also clearly shows that we are a long way off reaching a consensus on these rights.

The above texts all refer to individual rights. In recent years, however, group rights have constituted a subject for wider discussion. This category of rights may also include human rights that must be dealt with in the context of the European Union and its enlargement and the cultural rights of minorities. They must not be taken for granted, although they have been recognized by the United Nations, OSCE, and the Council of Europe, and they are not being incorporated into legally binding texts, as are, for example, the rights covered by the provisions of the ECHR. Nonetheless, in accordance with the Copenhagen criteria, countries applying for accession to the EU are being asked to guarantee a high level of protection in the field of minority rights.[4] Respect for these rights is a very important part of the democratic principle: neglecting them very often results in ethnic conflicts. As tensions between ethnic groups are a problem in many of the countries of Central and Eastern Europe, they represent a risk for the security of Europe in general, as we may currently see once again in the former Yugoslavia, where the most fundamental rights are being denied to the ethnic Albanian 'minority'.

It has been one of the outstanding achievements of the European Parliament that human rights are nowadays taken into account in many different spheres of activity of the European Union. From the outset, the absence of a list of human rights at Community level has been a topic for constant discussion, one to which more and more attention has been paid as the EU has developed into something much more complex than a purely economic Community, and as it is now moving towards a new and innovative kind of a federal order of States. Over the years, the various reports and resolutions on this subject have exerted a major influence on this discussion, one which must not be underestimated. After Maastricht and Amsterdam, there is no doubt that the introduction of a list of human rights is becoming increasingly necessary, although the most appropriate way of doing so has still to be defined.

Although the Treaties of Rome made no specific reference to human rights (only the principles of equal pay for men and women—Article 141 (*ex* Article 119) of the EC Treaty—and of the prohibition of discrimination on grounds of nationality—Article 7—had been included), the subsequent treaty revisions began to pay more attention to human rights. As a first step, human rights were referred to in the Preamble to the Single European Act in 1986. Human rights standards achieved more

---

[2] International Covenant on Economic, Social and Cultural Rights, adopted by GA Res. 2200 A (XXI) (1966). In United Nations, *A Compilation of International Instruments* (1994), i, Part 1, 8.

[3] International Covenant on Civil and Political Rights, adopted by GA Res. 2200 A (XXI) (1966). In *ibid.*, at 20.

[4] *Bull. EC* 6–1993, at I.13.

commensurate status when the Treaty on European Union (TEU) entered into force. For the first time in the history of the European Union, human rights were incorporated in the body of the treaties, with Article 6(2) (*ex* Article F(2)) stating that: '[t]he Union shall respect fundamental rights, as guaranteed by the [ECHR] and as they result from the constitutional traditions common to the Member States, as general principles of Community law'.

On its entry into force, the Treaty of Amsterdam will constitute another step forward in the development of human rights, strengthening the commitment to human rights in Article 6 (*ex* Article F) TEU, defining them as a fundamental principle on which the European Union is based. Furthermore, it establishes a procedure whereby the existence of a serious and persistent breach by a Member State of those principles may be determined and a decision taken to suspend certain rights of the Member State in question, after the assent of the European Parliament has been obtained (Article 7 (*ex* Article F.1) TEU and Article 309 (*ex* Article 236) (TEC). These provisions certainly have to be interpreted in the light of the enlargement. However, human rights have not only become an important matter to be dealt with inside the Union, they are also referred to in the context of the Common Foreign and Security Policy (CFSP) (Article 11(2) (*ex* Article J.1(2)), fifth indent TEU) and of development co-operation policy (Article 177(2) (*ex* Article 130u(2)) TEC). In its external relations, the European Community has progressively developed a human rights policy, using Europe's economic power to foster the promotion of human rights throughout the world. Today, every agreement with a third country includes a human rights clause, defining respect for human rights and democracy as an essential part of the agreement. Unfortunately, the human rights aspect depends to a very great extent on the economic strength of the partners with which we are dealing. Accordingly, the notion of human rights in the context of the Union's relations with China[5] differs greatly from the human rights approach which has been selected in the case of the accession negotiations with the applicant countries of Central and Eastern Europe.[6] Parliament has often deplored these differing and, to some extent, discriminating human rights approaches.

Nonetheless, with a view to the negotiations with the applicant countries, Parliament has on several occasions pointed out the importance of high standards of human rights protection, especially in a European Union of twenty-one or more Member States. In the case of Slovakia, the lack of an adequate commitment to human rights and to the democratic principle is one of the main obstacles impeding its accession to the Union,[7] and has led the Commission to deliver a negative

---

[5] The European Parliament has on several occasions criticized the Union's policy towards China and has repeatedly called on the Council and the Commission to take human rights into account when dealing with China. Furthermore, it has urged China to pursue a more satisfactory policy in the field of human rights. See Resolution on the Communication from the Commission on a long-term policy for China–Europe Relations (COM(95)0279—C40288/95) [1997] OJ C200/158.

[6] See e.g. the Proposal for a Council Reg. on assistance to the applicant countries of Central and Eastern Europe in the framework of the pre-accession strategy, Art. 5. (COM(97)0634—C4–0010/98–97/0351(CNS)).

[7] See, e.g., the Resolution on the need to respect human and democratic rights in the Slovak Republic [1995] OJ C323/116, where the European Parliament calls upon the Slovak government to respect human rights.

opinion[8] on Slovakia's application. A similar statement may be made in the case of Turkey, where the human rights situation has given rise to a very large number of resolutions[9] and constitutes the most cogent argument for delaying negotiations.

During the negotiation process, the European Parliament will closely monitor the requirement that applicant countries must guarantee a satisfactory level of human rights protection.

It is obvious that the European Union guarantees a level of human rights protection that has not yet been attained by most of the rest of the world. Parliament has always promoted human rights, regarding them as one of the main objects of its activities and making use of a broad range of instruments. It made a major contribution to the human rights policy of the European Union by ensuring that the value of human rights and democracy was not being underestimated within the sphere of activities of the Communities. This commitment will become more, rather than less, significant in the future.

Parliament's approach to human rights is based on the following key principles:

- a broad concept of human rights;
- the indivisibility of human rights, prohibiting any distinction between civil and political rights on the one hand and economic, social, and cultural rights on the other;
- the universality of human rights, which implies that no provision of a national, cultural, or religious nature may override the principles enshrined in the Universal Declaration of Human Rights;[10]
- a close connection with development policy and democratic principles in general, bearing in mind the interdependence of these fields.

Furthermore, Parliament has always stressed that the principle of non-interference in the field of human rights is relative, since it does not regard them as a part of the internal affairs of a State. On the contrary, they constitute an important and legitimate part of the dialogue with third countries.[11] The general feeling nowadays is that not only does the right of intervention exist, there is an actual duty to intervene when human rights seem to be seriously threatened.[12] Needless to say, the implementation of this principle is largely contingent on political and—unfortunately—economic considerations.

The European Parliament considers human rights in a number of contexts, the most important of which are the following.

[8] COM(97)2004 final.

[9] See, *inter alia*, Resolution on the freedom of the media in Turkey [1997] OJ C167/156; Resolution on human rights and the situation in Turkey [1996] OJ C198/208; Resolution on the human rights situation in Turkey [1996] OJ C17/46.

[10] Universal Declaration of Human Rights, adopted by GA Res. 217 A (III) (1948). In *International Instruments*, note 2 above, at 1.

[11] See also the Declaration on Human Rights, Luxembourg European Council, June 1991: *Bull.EC* 6–1991, at Annex V, 17.

[12] That topic has already been the subject of a report by Parliament. See Report on the right of humanitarian intervention, Doc. A3–227/94.

B. Constitutional Affairs

In an extensive series of political papers, the European Parliament has tried to contribute to and influence the constitutional development of the Union. In this context, the issue of human rights has, of course, always played a major role.

1. Joint Declaration on Human Rights of the European Parliament, Council and Commission, 5 April 1977 As Parliament's powers and responsibilities increased during the 1970s, it began to show more concern for human rights issues. Its increasing concern resulted in this Declaration, with which the other main institutions soon associated themselves.[13] The reason for the Declaration also lay in the fact that, by 1977, all the Member States had ratified the ECHR (the final Member State to do so was France on 3 March 1974, which prompted the European Court of Justice (ECJ) to base its judgments in cases involving claims related to human rights issues partly on the ECHR). The Court of Justice had begun developing a body of case law relating to human rights in the late 1960s, basing its judgments on the common principles of the constitutional law of the Member States on the one hand and on international conventions for the protection of human rights on the other, using them as guidelines which should be followed within the framework of Community law. This Joint Declaration at least gave some sort of political support and democratic legitimacy to the Court's case law, as it represented the recognition of the basic rights which had been developed by the Court of Justice.[14] Although not legally binding, it constituted the first step towards giving human rights a Community dimension.

2. Parliament's Draft Treaty on European Union (Spinelli Report), 14 February 1984 As European integration progressed, the notion of a European constitution was introduced into the political and academic debate. Needless to say, the European Parliament had and still has an important role to play in these matters. The Spinelli Report was adopted as a draft Treaty establishing the European Union.[15] As respect for human rights and democracy was considered indispensable for the legitimacy of a European Union, Article 4 referred to human rights, the first of which was the dignity of every human being. According to this draft treaty, the EU would respect human rights both political and civil (ECHR) and economic, social, and cultural (ESC). The Spinelli Report also included a clause providing for possible accession to other international conventions concerning human rights.

3. Parliament's Declaration on a List of Fundamental Rights (De Gucht Report), 12 April 1989 The Single European Act had pointed out the importance of human rights in its Preamble. By adopting the resolution based on the De Gucht Report in 1989, Parliament again took a qualitative step towards the creation of a legally

---

[13] [1977] OJ C103/1.

[14] The main specific rights recognized so far by the Court are: human dignity (Case C–9/74, *Casagrande* v. *Landeshauptstadt München* [1963] ECR 773); equal treatment (Joined Cases C–17 & C–20/61, *Klöckner Werke AG and others* v. *High Authority* [1962] ECR 653); non-discrimination (Case C–43/75, *Defrenne* v. *Sabena* [1976] ECR 455); freedom of religion (Case C–130/75, *Prais* v. *Council* [1976] ECR 1589); property and freedom of profession (Case C–44/79, *Hauer* v. *Land Rheinland-Pfalz* [1979] ECR 3727); privacy (Case C–136/79, *National Panasonic* v. *Commission* [1980] ECR 2033, 2056 ff); respect for family life (Case C–249/86, *Commission* v. *Germany* [1989] ECR 1263).

[15] [1984] OJ C77/33.

binding, basic Community instrument guaranteeing fundamental rights.[16] Human rights standards attained a new dimension at the European level. Whereas the Spinelli Report dealt only with human rights in the context of a European constitution, for the first time a complete list of human rights was now being drawn up by a Community institution. Drawing on research which has been carried out by the European University Institute since its foundation in 1976 as part of its project on human rights, the resolution on the one hand set out the basic rights protected by the ECJ, and, on the other, introduced social rights as well as the rights deriving from citizenship of the Union and the principles of the rule of law. In short, the resolution covers every aspect of human rights as they derive from the common constitutional orders of the Member States.[17]

Given that the extent of the notion of human rights has been the subject of controversial debates, it is important to note that the final resolution reflects the scope of the notion of human rights on which it was possible to obtain a fairly broad consensus in Parliament. It is, therefore, regrettable that other European institutions did not follow Parliament's Declaration and did not associate themselves with it. Accordingly, the practical outcome in the following treaty revisions is less than overwhelming.

4. The Committee on Institutional Affairs' Draft Constitution (Herman Report), 10 February 1994   This report, which deals with a draft constitution of the European Union, also sets out in Title VII a list of human rights and—in addition—an enumeration of the fundamental freedoms of the Union's citizens.[18] With regard to social rights, it includes the right to work, and therefore covers a broader notion of human rights than the 1989 De Gucht Report. Subsequently, although the Draft Constitution was adopted by the Committee on Institutional Affairs, the House merely noted it. This once again reflected the course of the debate on the notion of human rights, a debate which has been going on for several years now and which is yet to be concluded.

5. Report on the Treaty of Amsterdam, 5 November 1997 (report by Mr Mendez de Vigo and Mr Tsatsos)[19]   In its resolutions on the Intergovernmental Conference, the European Parliament had continued to stress the need for a list of human rights to be drawn up at Community level and also called for accession to the ECHR. In its resolution of 18 January 1994,[20] the European Parliament stated that the Commission should be authorized by the Council to negotiate with the Council of Europe in

---

[16] [1989] OJ C120/51.

[17] The rights enumerated in this document are in Art. 1: Dignity; Art. 2: Right to life; Art. 3: Equality before the law; Art. 4: Freedom of thought; Art. 5: Freedom of opinion and information; Art. 6: Privacy; Art. 7: Protection of family; Art. 8: Freedom of movement; Art. 9: Right of ownership; Art. 10: Freedom of assembly; Art. 11: Freedom of association; Art. 12: Freedom to choose an occupation; Art. 13: Working conditions; Art. 14: Collective social rights; Art. 15: Social welfare; Art. 16: Right to education; Art. 17: Principle of democracy; Art. 18: Right to access to information; Art. 19: Access to the courts; Art. 20: *Non bis in idem*; Art. 21: Non-retroactivity; Art. 22: Death penalty; Art. 23: Right of petition; Art. 24: Environment and consumer protection; Art. 25: Field of application; Art. 26: Limits; Art. 27: Degree of protection; Art. 28: Abuse of rights;

[18] [1994] OJ C61/155.   [19] Doc. A4–0347/97.

[20] Resolution on Community accession to the European Convention on Human Rights, [1994] OJ C44/32.

respect of accession to the ECHR. The Treaty of Amsterdam, however, did not result in the corresponding improvements. Parliament's resolution[21] deplores this, because it would have been appropriate to create at least a legal basis for accession to the ECHR (the ECJ had rejected this possibility under the provisions of the treaties, finding that Article 235 (now Article 308) TEC was not the appropriate basis for such a step, since accession to the ECHR would change the institutional system of the Union and would therefore have effects of constitutional dimensions, not to mention the provisions of the Statute of the Council of Europe[22]).

Nevertheless, by amending Article L (now Article 46) TEU, the Treaty of Amsterdam confirms the body of case law concerning fundamental rights developed to date by the ECJ and confers upon it jurisdiction to review respect for fundamental rights by the institutions, a development which has been approved not only by the European Parliament but also by the Commission and the Court of Justice itself.

C. Reports Drawn up on Human Rights

1. Regular Annual Reports on Human Rights in the World and/or the Community

Regular reports have been drawn up on the human rights situation both in the world and in the European Union itself.

(a) Human Rights in the World

Reports on human rights in the world were first introduced in 1983, with a view to monitoring the human rights situation throughout the world and to providing the Parliament with a proper basis for establishing priorities in its activities. Those priorities are mainly expressed in resolutions but also result in specific measures which have a practical impact. The tabling of questions to the Council and/or Commission, for example, may and frequently does have a real impact on Union policies, as in the case of Burma (see the text to note 40 below).

The reports generally cover different subjects, depending on current events and the preferences of the *rapporteur*. However, topics recur in nearly all of them. Combating racism and the abolition of the death penalty are very often discussed. A call for a more coherent and co-ordinated human rights policy in external relations is made in each of the reports. This request is based upon the idea that human rights are closely linked to development and democracy and must therefore be secured through a more sophisticated foreign policy. On the other hand, the various *rapporteurs* have dealt with specific issues because of their topicality or for other reasons. In the annual report covering 1993–4 drawn up by Mr Imbeni,[23] special attention was paid to the rights of minorities, in the light of the cruelties perpetrated on the territory of the former Yugoslavia.

The subsequent report on 1995–6 by Mrs Lalumière[24] was geared to the Intergovernmental Conference (IGC) on the revision of the treaties and therefore dealt in

---

[21] Resolution on the Amsterdam Treaty, [1997] OJ C371/99.

[22] *Opinion 2/94* [1996] ECR I–1759.

[23] Annual Report on human rights throughout the world in 1993–4 and the Union's human rights policy (Doc. A4–0078/95) [1995] OJ C126/15.

[24] Annual Report on human rights throughout the world in 1995–6 and the Union's human rights policy (Doc. A4–0400/96) [1997] OJ C20/161.

particular with the improvement of the European Union's system for the protection of human rights. It included a number of suggestions concerning the CFSP (*inter alia*, the call for the inclusion of the democracy clause in all agreements which do not as yet contain such a clause and the creation of appropriate legal mechanisms in order to guarantee their effectiveness) and also dealt with improvements regarding the institutions which are responsible for human rights (for example, it referred to the introduction of qualified majority voting in the Council in respect of the suspension of agreements with third countries found guilty of human rights violations).

(b) Human Rights in the European Union

In 1993 Parliament introduced this second type of report, reflecting the opinion that human rights violations outside the Union may be criticized only if the human rights situation on the territory of the Member States is also monitored, thereby ensuring that there is no possibility of any tit-for-tat criticism of the human rights situation inside the Union.

Similarly, certain topics recur, combating racism and xenophobia being a case in point. Furthermore, a very important issue is the notion of equal rights and non-discrimination between men and women, which had figured in the primary legislation of the Community from the outset, and the right to freedom from bodily harm. Parliament has constantly and consistently condemned the use of violence against and torture of persons under arrest or being held in detention by security forces. Reports also concern specific topics. This may reflect the field of interests of the *rapporteur*, but in most cases it results from the large number of amendments tabled to the original report.

The report on 1993[25] was very controversial and therefore, as an exception to the rule, was rejected by Parliament, failing to secure the majority required for the adoption of a resolution. The subsequent report, which covered 1994 and was drawn up by Mrs De Esteban Martín,[26] dealt in particular with the fight against poverty and with economic, social and cultural rights on the basis of the indivisibility of human rights. It must be said that, in this instance, the resolution[27] was radically altered by the large number of amendments tabled to the draft report, although the draft report had closely followed the ECHR. The subsequent *rapporteur* was Mrs Roth. Her report laid special emphasis on the rights of the child and the rights of persons held in detention or appearing before a court.[28] It also dealt with the mechanisms for strengthening human rights, calling on the IGC to confer separate legal personality on the European Union in order to enable it to accede to the ECHR. Furthermore, a large section of the resolution[29] dealt with asylum and immigration policy. For example, it called on the Council and the Member States to grant asylum also to applicants claiming to be the victims of persecution by non-governmental actors in so far as their country could not provide the required protection. This may be taken as an

---

[25] Annual Report on respect for human rights in the European Union 1993 (Doc. A4–124/94) [1995] OJ C068/3.

[26] Annual Report on respect for human rights in the European Union 1994 (Doc. A4–0223/96).

[27] [1996] OJ C320/36.

[28] Annual Report on respect for human rights in the European Union 1995 (Doc. A4–0112/97).

[29] [1997] OJ C132/31.

example of Parliament's criticism of the Council's somewhat restrictive interpretation of the 1951 Convention relating to the Status of Refugees.[30]

Based on a very broad conception of human rights, the 1996 report by Mrs Pailler[31] paid special attention to human rights which are not incorporated in legally binding instruments. That was in sharp contrast to the rights enumerated in the ECHR and concentrated on economic, social, and cultural rights on the one hand and on the right to asylum on the other. The report reflected the innovative role of Parliament, being one step ahead of generally accepted and legally enforced rights. As a result, the debate at the Strasbourg part-session in February 1998 demonstrated the various positions on the notion of human rights, and the final vote was a very close-run thing.

2. Report on Setting up a Single Co-ordinating Structure within the European Commission Responsible for Human Rights and Democratization (Mrs Lenz) A very recent report, which does not actually belong to the reports drawn up every year on human rights in and outside the EU, is the report by Mrs Lenz on setting up a single co-ordinating structure within the European Commission responsible for human rights and democratization.[32] Bearing in mind the growing complexity of EU activities concerning human rights, be it at the internal institutional level or in the context of the large number of budget items involved, the report once again calls for improvements in the structure.

Under Article 3(2) (*ex* Article C(2)) TEU, the Union is required to ensure the consistency of its external relations. Nevertheless, given the large number of departments concerned with the policies on human rights and democratization, consistency and coherence are far from being achieved. In conclusion, the resolution[33] based on the report proposed the setting up of a 'European Agency for Human Rights and Democratization', under the responsibility of a Commissioner, which would administer programmes and co-ordinate the guarantees and sanctions policy. It is, therefore, clear that Parliament believes that there should be a common internal administrative structure. Nonetheless, the option also exists for the establishment of an external agency if the internal agency should fail to produce the desired results (not unnaturally, the opinions of Parliament and the Commission differ on this subject).

As regards the complexity of the budgetary issues, the report called for a concentration of funds under chapter B7–70 in order to highlight the thematic approach since, as things stand, various Directorates General have to deal with human rights issues within their geographical remit.

Another important point of the report is the introduction of a European network for human rights and democratization under the responsibility of the Commission.

---

[30] Convention relating to the Status of Refugees, adopted on 28 July 1951 by the UN Conference of Plenipotentiaries on the Status of Refugees and Stateless Persons convened under GA Res. 429 (V) (1950). In United Nations, *A Compilation of International Instruments* (1994), i, Part 2, 638.

[31] Annual Report on respect for human rights in the European Union 1996 (Doc. A4–0034/98) [1998] OJ C80/43.

[32] Doc. A4–0393/97.   [33] [1998] OJ C14/402.

3. Report on the European Commission's Report on the Implementation of Measures Intended to Promote Observance of Human Rights and Democratic Principles (for 1995) (Imbeni Report)   This report tackles the financial and institutional aspects of promoting human rights. Given the Union's substantial financial contributions to the implementation of democracy and human rights projects, the visibility of EU funding needs to be improved.[34] Parliament has often deplored the complexity and diversity of the budgetary proceedings and the decision-making process in the field of human rights projects. Therefore, as regards support for and monitoring of elections, a specific budget item should be created outside the CFSP (taking into account the rather scant powers of Parliament in the field of the third pillar), just to give one example.

Furthermore, an important point of the resolution[35] based on the report is the call for a better evaluation of the effectiveness of Community activities in the field of the promotion of human rights and democracy. The evaluation of the Union's activities in the field of human rights has always been a problem, it being difficult to establish comparable criteria.

D. Ad Hoc *Resolutions on Human Rights*

In 1973, the European Parliament adopted its first resolutions on human rights. During that first year, only five resolutions were forwarded to other EU institutions, but that number—which has never been exceeded before or since—rose in 1988 to 117 resolutions, of which 116 concerned human rights issues outside the Community.

Whenever human rights seem to be threatened, the European Parliament draws up *ad hoc* resolutions. The reactions of the countries criticized often demonstrate the fragility of their human rights situation. The topics of these *ad hoc* resolutions are many and varied. For example, between September 1997 and March 1998, Parliament adopted resolutions concerning the human rights situation in countries such as Mongolia, Afghanistan, Djibouti, and the Democratic Republic of Congo; executions in Abu Dhabi, the United States, and South Korea; free elections in Bahrain and Kenya; agricultural reform in the Philippines; and Nicaragua's foreign debt.

The impact and/or success of these *ad hoc* resolutions varies. Sometimes, they are of immediate help to the person concerned (for example, in the case of the release of prisoners), but this is not always the case.

E. *Questions Concerning Human Rights*

Individual Members of Parliament regularly express their concern about human rights, and the failure of third countries to respect human rights, in the questions they table to the Commission or the Council. These questions have proved to be very useful in securing information on Union policies. Various types of questions may be tabled pursuant to Parliament's Rules of Procedure.

---

[34] Doc. A4–0381/97.   [35] [1998] OJ C14/399.

1. Questions for Oral Answer, Rule 40   Under Rule 40, questions may be put to the Council or the Commission by a committee, a political group, or at least twenty-nine Members. Recently, questions have been put to the Commission concerning the human rights situation in Turkey,[36] Union policy on human rights and democracy as an aspect of Community development policy,[37] and Union policy on human rights in general.[38] Questions to the Council normally address the positions taken by the Union in its relations with third countries. In this regard, questions have been tabled on, for example, the EU's position at the 54th meeting of the UN Commission on Human Rights,[39] the human rights situation in Burma,[40] and human rights in Iran and the *fatwa* against Salman Rushdie.[41]

2. Questions for Answer at Question Time, Rule 41   According to Rule 41, every Member of the Parliament may table questions to either the Council or the Commission. As questions of this type are not dependent on the support of another twenty-eight Members, a political group, or a committee, they have frequently been used to have a subject related to human rights entered onto the agenda. The Commission has been asked for information about the establishment of an International Criminal Court and human rights,[42] the Commission's human rights commitment,[43] human rights in Colombia[44] and environmental protection and human rights in co-operation between Canada and the European Union under the Canada–EU action plan.[45] As concerns questions to the Council, the human rights situation in China[46] and Nigeria[47] has been raised, as has the violation of the basic rights of the population trapped in the occupied part of Cyprus.[48]

3. Written Questions, Rule 42   Under Rule 42, every Member of Parliament may put a question for written answer to the Commission or the Council. Such questions are forwarded to the institution concerned by the President of Parliament. The questions and the answers thereto are published in the Official Journal of the European Communities. Written questions to the Commission have concerned human rights in the European Union following the IGC,[49] the action of the Turkish authorities in blocking European Union funds intended for the Turkish Human Rights Association,[50] compliance with the ECHR,[51] and the human rights clause in treaties

---

[36] Oral Question with debate by Mrs Catherine Lalumière to the Commission, B4–1438/95.

[37] Oral Question with debate by Mr Saby on behalf of the Committee on Development and Co-operation, B3–1694/91.

[38] Oral Question on behalf of the Committee on Foreign Affairs, Security and Defence Policy to the Commission, B3–0017/94.

[39] Oral Question with debate by Mr José Barros Moura, B4–0140/98.

[40] Oral Question with debate by Leonie van Bladel, B4–0139/98.

[41] Oral Question with debate by Marlene Lenz, Arie Oostlander, and Ria Oomen-Ruijten, B4–0132/96.

[42] Question 41 (H–0739/96) by Gianfranco Dell'Alba.

[43] Question 65 (H–0131/97) by Otto von Habsburg.

[44] Question 62 (H–1004/97) by Richard Howitt.

[45] Question 78 (H–0171/97) by Wilfried Telkämper.

[46] Question 37 (H–0146/98) by Graham Watson.

[47] Question 21 (H–0041/98) by David Martin.

[48] Question 15 (H–0956/96) by Konstantinos Hatzidakis.

[49] Written Question No. 1095/97 by Jesús Cabezón Alonso [1997] OJ C373/65.

[50] Written Question No. 1724/97 by Alexandros Alavanos [1997] OJ C391/125.

[51] Written Question No. 283/97 by Riccardo Nenceni and Ernesto Caccavale [1997] OJ C186/255.

concluded with third countries.[52] Questions to the Council have addressed human rights violations in the United States (especially regarding the death penalty),[53] human rights in general,[54] human rights in Russia,[55] human rights violations in the United Kingdom—the case of Roisin McAliskey,[56] and EU action on China with regard to the UN Commission on Human Rights.[57]

The topics raised recently and the large number of questions dealing with human rights in many different contexts covering situations both inside and outside the Union demonstrate Parliament's concern with human rights. Furthermore, by making use of these various procedures, Parliament draws the attention of the other institutions of the Union to its determination to promote human rights. This is very important in the field of relations with third countries and accordingly, a large proportion of the questions put to the other institutions concern human rights in China or Turkey, where respect for human rights still needs to be improved. With regard to Turkey, a third country which has particularly close ties with the European Union because of the custom union, Parliament continues to call upon the Council and Commission to highlight human rights in the context of economic relations with Turkey. The situation of the Kurds in south-eastern Turkey constitutes an important aspect, which is also closely linked to the European asylum and immigration policy.[58]

In the case of China, the prevalence of economic interests over respect for human rights has, in recent years, been sharply criticized by Parliament. Unfortunately, Union policy towards China recently has not been very consistent, and it has proved impossible to establish a common position on human rights violations in that country which could be supported by all the Member States.

F. Other Activities

1. Committees of the European Parliament   The broad spectrum of Parliament's concern about human rights issues is also reflected by the fact that almost every standing committee deals with human rights in one way or another. The following committees are chiefly involved in human rights activities:

- Subcommittee on Human Rights;
- Committee on Civil Liberties and Internal Affairs;
- Committee on Development and Co-operation;
- Committee on Petitions;
- Committee on Foreign Affairs, Security, and Defence Policy;
- Committee on Legal Affairs and Citizens' Rights;

[52] Written Question No. 2990/96 by Inigo Méndez de Vigo [1997] OJ C96/120.
[53] Written Question No. 1150/97 by Lucio Manisco [1997] OJ C373/77.
[54] Written Question No. 765/96 by Nikitas Kaklamanis [1997] OJ C11/2.
[55] Written Question No. 681/97 by Gijs de Vries [1997] OJ C373/27.
[56] Written Question No. 1148/97 by Lucio Manisco [1997] OJ C319/96.
[57] Written Question No. 422/97 by Olivier Dupuis [1997] OJ C319/73.
[58] See in this context e.g. the Commission's Report on the developments in relations with Turkey since the entry into force of the customs union (COM(96)491), where the Commission states that, while the customs union functions in a satisfactory manner, much remains to be done in the field of human rights, the situation in the prisons, and the treatment of NGOs by the Turkish government.

- Committee on Women's Rights;
- Committee on External Economic Relations.

Of these, the most heavily involved in human rights issues are the Subcommittee on Human Rights and the Committee on Civil Liberties and Internal Affairs. While human rights issues outside the EU fall within the remit of the former, the latter deals with human rights inside the Community.

Since Parliament's powers have grown constantly over the years, as have its activities regarding human rights, the Committees deal with human rights in many contexts. A report on women in advertising[59] naturally has to deal with the human right to dignity. In the same way, a report drawn up on the impact of new technologies upon the press in Europe[60] has to do with the right of expression. The right to non-discrimination is reflected in a report on the Commission proposal for a Council directive concerning the framework agreement on part-time work concluded by UNICE, CEEP, and ETUC,[61] just as the report on the common position established by the Council with a view to the adoption of a European Parliament and Council directive to facilitate the practice of the profession of lawyer on a permanent basis in a Member State other than that in which the qualification was obtained[62] is strongly linked to the right to choose an occupation and the right of establishment.

2. Individual Support for Human Rights in the Context of Petitions—Committee on Petitions The right to petition Parliament constitutes a basic right of every European citizen and resident. Since the Committee on Petitions was established as a separate committee in 1987, it has received some 10,000 petitions which represent the views, opinions, and requests of more than ten million signatories. Parliament's Committee on Petitions naturally deals with breaches of individual human rights whenever not only EU citizens but also citizens of third countries ask for help. The examples range from a Belgian who argues that the Union should ban the smuggling of women from Eastern Europe into the Union for the purposes of prostitution, to Zaïreans calling for the recognition of all Zaïrean refugees as victims of the Mobutu dictatorship.

In addition to the type of petitions referred to above, which concern human rights only to a certain extent, petitions relating to human rights in the strict sense of the term have been received, concerning, for example, discrimination in the exercise of the right to freedom as enshrined in the ECHR;[63] the situation of threatened minorities in Romania;[64] social constitutional rights;[65] and the violation of human rights in the prison in which the petitioner is being detained.[66]

Many of the petitions forwarded to the Committee deal with discrimination on the grounds of nationality. If this proves to be the case, the Committee's interventions normally result in a satisfactory solution for the petitioner concerned.[67]

---

[59] Doc. A4–0258/97. [60] Doc. A4–0289/97.
[61] (COM(97)0392–C–40551/97), Doc. A4–0352/97. [62] Doc. A4–0337/97.
[63] No. 0122/88 by Mr Günther Meinzer.
[64] No. 0441/88 by the Siebenbürgische Weltorganisation, Sektion BR, Deutschland.
[65] No. 0697/93 by Mr Adalberto Paulo Linia. [66] No. 0870/94 by Mr Manuel Jesus Rodrigues.
[67] See, e.g., the Report on the deliberations of the Committee for Petitions for the parliamentary year 1996–7 (Doc. A4–0190/97) [1997] OJ C200/26.

3. Public Hearings   Pursuant to Rule 151(3) of the Rules of Procedure, a committee may organize public hearings in order to secure information about a certain topic. Securing information from independent experts, for example staff of non-governmental organizations (NGOs), has proved to be very important. Topics may be discussed from very different points of view. To date, a number of public hearings have taken place, providing Parliament with up-to-the minute information. Among many other public hearings related to human rights, the following rate a mention:

- Public hearing on the serious situation in Tibet in April 1990, where the Dalai Lama described the human rights situation in Tibet (Political Affairs Committee);
- Public hearing on human rights and foreign policy, on 2 and 3 June 1993 (Committee on Foreign Affairs, Subcommittee on Human Rights and Committee on Development and Co-operation);
- Public hearing on free speech/free media: Rights under threat?, on 25 April 1996 (Subcommittee on Human Rights);
- Public hearing on impunity: the need for an international response, on 30 and 31 October 1996 (Subcommittee on Human Rights);
- Public hearing on the use of European Union resources for the development and consolidation of democracy and the rule of law and respect for human rights, on 19 March 1998 (Committee on Foreign Affairs);

4. Sakharov Prize   Every year since 1988, following a resolution adopted on 13 December 1985,[68] the Sakharov Prize has been awarded to a person who has undertaken activities in one of the following fields:

- development of relations between East and West, taking into account the Helsinki Final Act;
- protection of the liberty of scientific research;
- defence of human rights and respect for international law;
- ensuring the compliance of governments with their own constitution.

Among others, the Prize has been awarded to Nelson Mandela (1988), Alexander Dubcek (1989), Las Madres de la Plaza de Mayo (1992), and Taslima Nasreen (1994). The defence of freedom of speech has been one of the main considerations for Parliament when selecting the Prize winner, since this is a basic human right and the first prerequisite of a pluralistic democracy. The award of this Prize gives Parliament the opportunity to draw the attention of a wider public to human rights issues outside the Community.

G. Specific Questions Concerning Human Rights in the Context of Asylum and Immigration

Because of the increase in the number of asylum seekers during the early 1990s, European countries have tightened up their asylum and immigration policies. Germany, the classic asylum country within the European Union, was the first Member

---

[68] [1985] OJ C352/304.

State to make access to its territory more difficult, because the right to asylum laid down in the Constitution, unique among the constitutions of European countries, had led to a mass influx. Other Member States had to follow in order to avoid any spill-over to their countries. The result may be classified both as an attempt to introduce measures which are designed to protect the very principle of asylum and as a downward spiral of restrictive measures which may be divided into two categories. On the one hand, measures have been introduced which are intended to reduce the number of applications which have to be considered. On the other hand, Member States have adopted very innovative procedures in order to reduce the time required for the consideration of such applications. An assessment of the situation depends on the ideological orientation of the person making that assessment.

Be that as it may, this development has often been criticized by all kinds of human rights activists, especially by NGOs. Parliament has also expressed its reservations in respect of the activities of the Member States on various occasions.[69] According to Parliament, changing asylum problems cannot be solved by making access to EU territory more difficult or by interpreting the 1951 Convention relating to the Status of Refugees in a restrictive manner. Better co-ordination is required between Member State policies, a point of view which is also shared by other institutions.[70]

While the intergovernmental procedures covering the third pillar have not proved to be very effective for various reasons, the Treaty of Amsterdam constitutes major progress towards a more consistent asylum policy at Community level, in that it provides the EU with a legal basis on which to bring within the Union's remit the main areas covered by the third pillar of the European Union. Parliament called for this both before as well as after the 1996 Intergovernmental Conference.[71]

Parliament's approach to asylum and immigration policy is defined by three considerations outlined in the Wiebenga Report: prevention, admission and integration:[72]

- Prevention: in accordance with its broad approach to immigration and asylum policy, the opinion adopted by the European Parliament also stresses the importance of the measures to be taken in the context of development co-operation and under the second pillar of the Union (CFSP), which includes the promotion of peace.
- Admission: in this context, it is important to stress Parliament's call for harmonization or alignment of Member State legislation. Furthermore, a system of burden-sharing should be devised, taking into account the different roles that Member States have played and are still playing as regards the number of asylum-seekers for whom they are responsible. A strong commitment to counter illegal immigration also forms part of this approach.

---

[69] See, e.g., the Resolution on the Council Resolution on minimum guarantees for asylum procedures [1996] OJ C362/270.

[70] See, e.g., the Report by the Commission for the Reflection Group, 19 May 1995.

[71] See, e.g., the Resolution on the functioning of the Treaty on European Union with a view to the IGC 1996 [1995] OJ C151/56.

[72] (COM(94)0023—C3–0107/94), Doc. A4–0169/95.

• Integration: Parliament has expressed its willingness to combat racism in the EU. Racism has recently become a serious problem in the Union once again. According to Parliament, the integration of immigrants and refugees cannot be achieved under these circumstances. Accordingly, the resolution[73] based on this report draws the attention of the other institutions of the Community and—under the principle of subsidiarity—of the Member States to their responsibilities in combating racism.

The report deals with the basic issues of immigration and asylum policy, since the Communication from the Commission reflects the major areas where action is required at Community level.

It is clear that asylum and immigration are areas that are closely linked with individual human rights issues. Furthermore, asylum and immigration constitute the interface between human rights inside and outside the EU. Indeed, Parliament emphasizes that the asylum and immigration policy and the CFSP are interdependent. The latter should be used as an instrument to promote human rights and democratization and, hence, to prevent immigration and new flows of refugees all over the world. It is, therefore, necessary to improve the procedures under the second pillar in order to make the CFSP more consistent and effective.

Another demand made by Parliament is for the full integration of immigrants who are legally resident in a Member State of the European Union, since that would enable them to enjoy the fundamental freedoms deriving from Union citizenship.[74] Parliament has been making these demands since the early 1990s when it began to address asylum and immigration issues. Two resolutions[75] have been tabled on each of these topics, based upon two major committee reports,[76] and they reflect the sharp distinction between them.

Sometimes, fundamental rights such as the right to life, to equality before the law, or to the protection of the family are involved. The European Parliament is fully aware of this and has, over the years, been dealing with this problem, in relation to issues concerning the treatment of citizens of Morocco when applying for visas or in the context of illegal immigration for example, and petitions.

According to the Parliament's opinion, the substance of the Council regulations in the field of asylum and immigration constitutes a topic where Parliament's opinion differs completely from those of the other institutions. They are almost without exception repressive, in that they provide principally for a reduction in the number of applications for asylum.[77] Furthermore, the legal instruments used are often ineffective since they are not legally binding, because of their questionable legal standing, and are not subject to the control of Parliament.[78]

---

[73] [1995] OJ C269/156.

[74] See in this context the recent Report on the Report of the High Level Panel on the free movement of persons chaired by Mrs Simone Veil—Committee on Civil Liberties and Internal Affairs, Doc. A4–108/98, drawn up by Mrs AnneMarie Schaffner.

[75] [1992] OJ C337/94 and 97.

[76] Report on the European Immigration Policy, Doc. A3–0280/92; Report on the harmonization within the European Communities of Asylum Law and Policies, Doc. A3–0337/92.

[77] See the Resolution on the Council Reg. on minimum guarantees for asylum procedures ([1996] OJ C362/270), which criticizes the existing exceptions to the minimum guarantees provided for in the Reg.

[78] See, e.g., the Resolution on the Schengen Agreement and political asylum [1995] OJ C109/169.

Another complaint which has been made but which has had little impact concerns the fact that, on occasions, the Council and the Commission have failed to consult Parliament in accordance with Article 34 (*ex* Article K.6) TEU. Given that the right of asylum must indubitably be considered as one of the Council's principal spheres of activity, Parliament must also be involved: such involvement is enshrined in the treaties. Nonetheless, it has to be said that, as regards the increased powers of the European Parliament under the provisions of the Treaty of Amsterdam, the Council is already anticipating their implementation and increasing the number of its consultations with Parliament.

The very recent Report on the proposal for a Joint Action based on Article 31(2)(b) (*ex* Article K.3(2)(b)) TEU concerning temporary protection of displaced persons[79] is of special interest because it represents the first consultation of the European Parliament as part of a joint action proposed by the Commission. This legal instrument is binding but, given the fact that ECJ has no powers in this field, its classification as fully-fledged legislation remains doubtful, to say the least. Despite this uncertainty, Parliament tabled various amendments in its resolution, thereby showing its determination to take part in the decision-making process in accordance with the provisions of the TEU.

Another recent report on a related topic is the Report on the draft Council Act drawing up the Convention concerning the establishment of Eurodac for the comparison of fingerprints of applicants for asylum on the basis of Article 31 TEU.[80] As Parliament has to be consulted on this topic, it has forwarded several amendments to the Council which have been included in the resolution. In the amendments, Parliament calls on the Commission to operate the system, which is designed to provide the requisite information about applicants for asylum in order to determine which Member State is responsible for the consideration of the application in accordance with the Dublin Convention.[81] This reflects Parliament's criticism of intergovernmental co-operation which has, in the past, resulted in Community activities being reduced to the lowest common denominator. Furthermore, data protection is to be given wider consideration.

It must not be forgotten that, as regards asylum and immigration, the European Parliament is divided along ideological lines, a division which is comparable to the one which has been shown in the context of the debates on the annual reports on human rights in the Union.

Given that most of the third-pillar issues will be incorporated into the Community framework within five years after the entry into force of the Treaty of Amsterdam, there is no doubt that the European Parliament will make use of its legislative powers in order to promote human rights in this field.

---

[79] Doc. A4–0284/97. One of the report's main criticisms concerned the woolly approach to the notion of burden-sharing in the context of displaced persons, a matter which proved to be one of the crucial points during the debate.

[80] Doc. A4–0402/97.

[81] Convention Determining the State Responsible for Examining Applications for Asylum Lodged in One of the Member States of the Community, Dublin, 15 June 1990, entered into force, 1 Sept. 1997 [1997] OJ C254/1.

H. The European Parliament and Human Rights in External Relations

The TEU states that one of the overriding principles of the CFSP is to develop and consolidate democracy and the rule of law, and respect for human rights and fundamental freedoms. The European Parliament has played a very important role in introducing the notion of conditionality into the field of agreements with third countries and development co-operation policy, with humanitarian aid being excluded from this requirement (see the text to note 88 below).

1. Humanitarian Aid   Based upon Article 179 (*ex* Article 130w) TEC, the Community's humanitarian aid policy is closely linked to the promotion of human rights. The European Community is the world's principal donor of humanitarian aid. The financial resources made available for humanitarian aid have greatly increased since 1990. One of the main reasons for the increase was the situation in the former Yugoslavia following the war, when immediate help was necessary.

In the context of a reform of the Community's humanitarian aid in the early 1990s, the European Parliament played a major role in introducing the idea of setting up a body within the Commission to co-ordinate humanitarian aid. This led to the creation of the European Community Humanitarian Office (ECHO) on 1 April 1992, which has helped to improve the co-ordination, effectiveness, and visibility of EU measures in the field of humanitarian aid. ECHO acts not only when there is a genuine crisis; it also intervenes in order to prevent any deterioration in the situation. It deals with humanitarian aid in general, as well as with emergency humanitarian aid, aid for refugees, and disaster prevention. In 1997, ECHO was endowed with a budget of 438 million ECU, which it allocated to aid programmes all over the world. The budget for 1998 has an endowment of more than 380 million ECUs in the relevant budget chapter (B7–21). According to the Court of Auditors' Special Report No. 2/97, some 45 per cent of the funds were channeled by way of NGOs, and some 30 per cent were distributed through the UN and its specialized agencies.

The European Parliament is extremely active in the field of humanitarian aid and in its capacity as one arm of the budgetary authority, Parliament has, every year, pushed through an increase in the funds earmarked for humanitarian aid and allocated them to specific regions or countries. Parliament has also drafted a large number of reports on this topic (for example, the Sauquillo Report on a Council regulation concerning humanitarian aid,[82] the Howitt Report on refugees,[83] the Baldi Report on rehabilitation,[84] the Fassa Report on the role of ECHO,[85] the Goerens Report on the effectiveness of aid,[86] and the Vallés Report on the Special Report of the Court of Auditors concerning humanitarian aid from the EU between 1992 and 1995[87]).

It should be noted that, according to the Parliament's opinion, conditionality must not be applied in the field of humanitarian aid, provided that there is no doubt about the effectiveness of Community action.[88] Another point which has been

---

[82] Doc. A4–0125/96.   [83] Doc. A4–0344/96.   [84] Doc. A4–0136/96.
[85] Doc. A4–0021/97.   [86] Doc. A4–0388/97.   [87] Doc. A4–0391/97.
[88] See, e.g., the Resolution on the Communication from the Commission on the inclusion of respect for democratic principles and human rights in agreements between the Community and third countries [1996] OJ C320/239.

stressed since 1993[89] is the need to co-ordinate Community policies with measures taken by the Member States in order to avoid any counterproductive effects.

2. Community Development Co-operation Policy   Before the Treaty on European Union came into force, there was no specific legal basis for development policy. Accordingly, Community activities in this field were based on other general provisions of Community law which actually had nothing to do with development co-operation policy, for example Article 133 (*ex* Article 113) (Generalized Scheme of Preferences (GSP) and Co-operation Agreements), Article 308 (*ex* Article 235) (Financial and Technical Assistance to Asian and Latin American Developing Countries), and Article 310 (*ex* Article 238) (Lomé). The post-Maastricht Treaty contains a special chapter which deals with development policy. Among the relevant articles (Articles 177–181 (*ex* Articles 130u–130y) EC), Article 177 recognizes respect for human rights as one of the general objectives of the Community's development co-operation policy on the grounds of the interdependence of development, democratization, and human rights.

As long ago as November 1991, a resolution of the European Parliament had already called for a connection to be made between the promotion of democracy and respect for human rights on the one hand and development policy on the other.[90] This interdependence has often been emphasized by Parliament. Accordingly, one good example of practical results of the efforts made by Parliament is the withdrawal of the GSP from Burma. After Parliament had tabled a large number of questions on the human rights situation in Myanmar (Burma) to both the Commission and the Council,[91] the latter withdrew GSP entitlement from that country because of its forced-labour practices. This is only one of many achievements of Parliament in the field of development policy and human rights.

According to Parliament, co-ordination between national and Community measures should be improved in order to achieve complementarity between them.[92] In addition, as consistency between co-operation policy and other Community measures and national policies has to be taken into account, the role of the external effects of policies must not be underestimated. During all these years, Parliament has repeatedly emphasized these facts.[93]

3. Agreements with Third Countries   Taking account of human rights in contractual relations with third countries has become an important instrument for the promotion of human rights throughout the world. While agreements with countries outside the EU were long considered inappropriate for the inclusion of human rights

---

[89] Resolution on increased co-ordination of development aid [1993] OJ C315/250.

[90] Resolution on human rights, democracy, and development [1991] OJ C326/259.

[91] See, e.g., Written Question No. 1879/96 by Glenys Kinnock to the Council on EU relations with Burma [1997] OJ C83/3, and Written Question No. 1770/97 by Iñigo Méndez de Vigo to the Commission on European investment in Burma [1997] OJ C391/129. Since 1996, there have been more than 30 questions on this topic.

[92] See the Resolution on the Communication from the Commission to the Council and the European Parliament on complementarity between the Community's development co-operation policy and the policies of the Member States (COM(95)0160—C4–0178/95) [1997] OJ C85/178.

[93] See, e.g., the Report on improving the effectiveness of Community aid drawn up by the Committee on Development and Co-operation (Doc. A4–0388/97) and the corresponding resolution of 16 Jan. 1998 [1998] OJ C34/192.

commitments, the commitment to human rights in external relations is today only comparable with the US 'Foreign Assistance Act 1996' which also provided for the possibility of economic relations with the third country being suspended in the event of permanent human rights violations.

The idea that international agreements have to be fulfilled in accordance with the principle of *pacta sunt servanda* previously precluded any possibility of suspending or even denouncing such a treaty on the grounds of an unsatisfactory human rights situation in the territory of one of the parties. Therefore human rights were referred to only in the preamble of such treaties (or not at all). This changed in 1989, when Article 5 of the Fourth Lomé Convention included the first reference to human rights within the body of a contractual document. Although Article 5 did not provide a clear legal basis for the suspension or denunciation of agreements in the event of serious human rights violations or interruptions of the democratic process, a clause defining democratic principles and human rights as an 'essential element' was introduced in 1992. This was followed by the 'Baltic clause' (an explicit suspension clause), and the 'Bulgarian clause' (a general non-execution clause, providing for a consultation procedure in the event of the parties not fulfilling their obligations).

The European Parliament has often exercised its powers regarding agreements with third countries. Between January 1992 and December 1993 it refused its assent to the third and fourth financial protocols of the Co-operation Agreement between the EU and Syria and did not give its assent until both Syria and the Commission had agreed to put human rights on the agenda of the Co-operation Council.[94] In 1995, Parliament delayed the conclusion of the treaty on a customs union between the EU and Turkey for several months because of the unsatisfactory human rights situation in Turkey.[95] As a result, the customs union with Turkey did not enter into force until 31 December 1995. In a resolution on the political situation in Turkey adopted in September 1996, Parliament urged the Commission to block all appropriations set aside under the MEDA Democracy Programme for projects in Turkey.[96] Nevertheless, the credibility and, hence, the effectiveness of such clauses depends to a great extent upon a non-discriminatory approach.[97]

By amending Article 300 (*ex* Article 228) EC, the Treaty of Amsterdam introduces a simplified procedure for Council decisions concerning the suspension of the application of an international treaty in the event of infringements and breaches of contract. It remains to be seen whether this procedural improvement will prevail over the political obstacles which, in the past, have made it difficult for the requisite measures to be taken rapidly.

---

[94] Resolution on the financial protocols with Syria, Morocco, Algeria, Egypt, Tunisia, Jordan, Lebanon, and Israel and these countries' respect for human rights and international agreements [1992] OJ C39/50.

[95] Resolution on the draft agreement on the conclusion of a customs union between the EU and Turkey [1995] OJ C56/99.

[96] Resolution on the political situation in Turkey [1996] OJ C320/187.

[97] See, e.g., the Resolution on the Communication from the Commission on the inclusion of respect for democratic principles and human rights in agreements between the Community and third countries [1996] OJ C320/261.

4. The Lomé Convention   The Convention is a very important instrument of co-operation policy which shows the interdependence of development, democratization, the rule of law, and human rights. As noted, Article 5 of the Convention emphasizes the importance of human rights. As a result of the mid-term review, Article 366a was introduced which provides for a suspension clause and a very sophisticated procedure to be followed in the search for a solution based on the principle of parity, a notion that has been one of the crucial commitments throughout the history of the Convention.

According to the provisions of the Single European Act, Parliament's assent was required for the conclusion of the Fourth Lomé Convention, and it was given on 16 May 1990.[98] In addition, Parliament had already influenced the Convention by setting out in its resolution of 20 May 1988,[99] the guidelines which were to be used in the Convention, based on the report on the Fourth ACP–EEC Convention and drawn up on behalf of the Committee on Development and Co-operation.[100]

Another way of influencing co-operation under the Lomé Convention is through the ACP–EU Joint Assembly, a consultative body set up within the institutional system of the Convention. The Assembly consists of seventy MEPs and seventy members from the ACP States (of whom currently about two-thirds are Members of Parliament). It may set up working parties on specific topics and may also put questions to the Council or the Commission. The Joint Assembly also deals explicitly with human rights. A resolution which is worth noting in this context was adopted at the Windhoek meeting in 1996.[101] Although there was no provision for a secret ballot in the Rules of Procedure, a secret ballot was requested after the Nigerian regime had intensively 'lobbied' the members of the Joint Assembly. The resolution condemning the Nigerian regime for serious human rights violations was adopted after both 'sides' of the Joint Assembly agreed on a motion for a resolution tabled by the Europeans.

Every year, a report on the outcome of the proceedings of the ACP–EU Joint Assembly is drawn up by the Committee on Development and Co-operation in order to provide Parliament with the latest information.[102] This gives Parliament the opportunity to take the latest developments into account when dealing with Lomé-related subjects.

Over the past few years, the European Parliament has continued to call for the integration of the European Development Fund into the development co-operation section of the general budget of the European Communities. Although the European Parliament has no budgetary or legislative powers to control this large amount of money, it is obliged to give an annual discharge in respect thereof, a situation which, on several occasions, has been deemed to be extremely unsatisfactory.[103]

---

[98] [1990] OJ C149/71.

[99] Resolution on the Fourth ACP–EEC Convention [1988] OJ C167/429.

[100] Doc. A2–0049/88.　　　　　　　　　　　　　　　　　　[101] Resolution of 20 Mar. 1996.

[102] See, e.g., the Report on the outcome of the proceedings of the ACP–EU Joint Assembly in 1997 by Mr Robles Piquer, Doc. A4–0080/98.

[103] See in this context the Resolution of 17 Apr. 1996 refusing discharge to the Commission in respect of the implementation of the European Development Fund for the 1994 financial year ([1996] OJ L148/56), in which Parliament once again criticizes the fact that the EDF is not managed in accordance with regular budgetary provisions.

Given that a human rights clause was introduced only in 1989, the opportunities to enforce the promotion of human rights in the ACP States were, until then, few and far between. Because of the importance of this subject, a special report thereon was drawn up by the Committee on Budgets[104] and a corresponding resolution adopted in July 1995.[105]

Parliament has also stated its opposition to any denationalization of development aid and to any further reductions being made in the funds earmarked for the developing countries so that more funds may be made available to the countries of Eastern Europe.[106]

5. Parliamentary Delegations   Parliamentary delegations, defined as interparliamentary delegations and Joint Parliamentary Committees, are important instruments for dialogue between the European Parliament and parliamentarians from third countries with which the European Union has treaty-based ties. Human rights have become a fixed item on the political agenda for joint meetings.

The Joint Parliamentary Committees, which were set up under the Europe Agreements with the associated States of Central and Eastern Europe, are now playing a leading part in the process of preparing the ground for enlargement. They enable Members of the European Parliament to discuss with their partners the principle of the rule of law and the Western European understanding of democracy. In addition, these parliamentary committees can make recommendations to the relevant Association Council; in accordance with the objective of meeting the political criteria laid down in Copenhagen, these may concern all matters relating to human rights, minority rights, democracy, and the rule of law. This joint commitment can and must be developed. It is precisely in the enlargement process that a consistent approach by MEPs will undoubtedly have an effect (it is worth recalling its determined stance with regard to Slovakia).

However, parliamentary delegations do not exist solely to bring third countries closer to our understanding of human rights. They are also an important forum for discussing concerted action that will serve to protect human rights. At the last meeting of the EP–US delegation, for instance, discussions took place with representatives of Congress concerning a joint strategy for future treaty rounds under the WTO, so that Europe and the US will not be played off against each other by third countries, and can co-operate in the benefit of their human rights promotion in this multilateral forum.

What are known as *ad hoc* delegations also play an important role where observation of the human rights situation in third countries is concerned. The most recent examples of this are the *ad hoc* delegations that the European Parliament sent to Algeria and Albania. More use should be made of these instruments and developed into genuine parliamentary diplomacy,[107] since this offers Parliament wide-ranging opportunities to discuss even the most sensitive issues with representatives of third countries.

---

[104] Report on the integration of the EDF in the budget of the Union, Doc. A4–0157/95.
[105] [1995] OJ C249/68.
[106] Resolution on the renewal of the European Development Fund [1995] OJ C129/53.
[107] *Ibid.*

I. Parliament's Budgetary Powers and the Promotion of Human Rights

Parliament adopts the Union budget each year, and the signature of the President of Parliament signals its entry into force. A distinction is made between compulsory and noncompulsory expenditure, on which Parliament and the Council have different views: it is the Council which decides on the former, while Parliament has the final say on the latter since 1 January 1975. Over the years, Parliament's 'power of the purse' has grown significantly.

The European Parliament has often made use of its right to amend the remarks entered against budget lines concerning human rights and democratization. An interesting example in this context is the history of chapter B7–70 in the 1998 budget. The preliminary draft budget drawn up by the Commission allocated an appropriation of 78,625,000 ECUs, but that figure was reduced by the Council to 70 million ECUs at first reading. After the first reading in Parliament, the amount was increased to 97,400,000 ECUs. Although the Council tried to reduce it again to 74 million ECUs at the second reading, Parliament finally adopted the budget chapter as proposed at first reading. This clearly shows that Parliament has promoted the human rights activities of the European Union more than the other institutions.[108]

Most of the human rights measures are financed from the endowment of chapter B7–70 ('European initiative for human rights and democratization'), which was created at the instigation of the European Parliament in 1994[109] (B7–52 in 1995, becoming B7–70 thereafter). This budgetary heading covers both geographical and thematic items.

Chapter B7–70 contains all the funds whose aim is, *expressis verbis*, the promotion of democratization and human rights. The European Parliament has, in the past, supported the provision of increased budgetary resources for the activities in question. Chapter B7–70 acts, furthermore, as a catalyst designed to promote innovative actions. These may be subsequently supported by other financial instruments, once they have proved successful. Similarly, the amount spent, for example, under the Phare and Tacis Democracy Programme represents just a small part of the whole Phare and Tacis budget (approximately 1 per cent), although it has increased constantly since the programme began in 1992 (5 million ECUs in 1992, 20 million ECUs in 1997). Nonetheless, these programmes (like the MEDA Democracy Programme) have a big political impact and show the Union's commitment to human rights and democracy. In this context, it should also be noted that, following the resolution adopted on 19 September 1996,[110] 53 million ECUs of the amount entered for financial co-operation with Turkey was put into the reserve and will be released only when the human rights situation in Turkey improves. Other resources are taken from financial and technical assistance and co-operation appropriations and are used to attain the same objectives.

---

[108] European Commission, *General Report on the Activities of the European Union 1997* (1998), 386.
[109] Resolution on a European Democracy Initiative [1992] OJ C150/281.
[110] [1996] OJ C320/187.

II. EVALUATION AND PROPOSALS FOR IMPROVEMENTS

To end, possible improvements in the protection of human rights by the European Union and European Parliament are set out below.

A. Internal Affairs

1. The Issue of Political Consensus on the Notion of Human Rights   A closer look at the many different positions adopted in Parliament reveals that there is no real common definition of human rights because of ideological and national preferences. The overview of the various and somewhat diverging positions expressed by Parliament in the field of human rights seems to show the absence of any political consensus on these matters. Indeed, the results of the votes on this topic appear to be quite different and are obviously dependent on what is required to secure a majority. The extent to which human rights are taken into account in resolutions adopted with a qualified majority (under the co-decision and assent procedures) differs greatly from the human rights element in subjects where the decision-making procedure requires a simple majority (in the case of consultations and own-initiative reports). In the first case, the need to secure a majority of the component Members of Parliament results in a major left-right coalition. In other cases, a simple majority may be and often is secured by a centre-left coalition. Accordingly, the European Parliament has at least two views on human rights: a centre-left (Socialist, Green, and Liberal Groups) simple majority in most areas and a major left–right qualified majority in matters under the co-decision procedure at second and third reading. In order to complete the information on the various majorities, it should be noted that, in economic affairs, Parliament acts with a simple centre-right majority. This results from the fact that, as a rule, the Liberal Group votes centre-right on economic matters, but in the field of human rights or civil liberties, it shares the centre-left point of view.

The fact that there is political controversy in Parliament on human rights issues should not, however, be misinterpreted or seen as a demonstration of the absence of political consensus. On the contrary, there is a very broad consensus on the basic notion of human rights derived from the conventional liberal view of human rights, to which certain additions have been made in order to cope with the challenges of modern society. Furthermore, the importance of Parliament's activities has always been emphasized by every single political group in the European Parliament.[111]

Nevertheless, the debate about the concept of human rights as such should move into the background. There are several opinions concerning the question of which concept of human rights Parliament should uphold. In the past, the ideological dif-

---

[111] As we have already seen, the scale of this understanding of human rights is reflected in the 1989 De Gucht Report and in the list of human rights set out in the corresponding resolution. Furthermore, there is certainly a broad consensus on the fact that the level of human rights protection should be no lower than that set out in that Declaration. In addition to the basic agreement on the subject, there are other opinions on the centre-left of Parliament which call for these rights to be supplemented by others, e.g. in the field of social protection or the environment. There is also some discussion of the question whether the fundamental rights guaranteed by the European Union should be enforceable only with regard to acts adopted under the law of the Union or whether it should be possible to challenge any act of an authority of a Member State on the grounds that it is in breach of a fundamental right of the European Union.

ferences about the question of the appropriate scope of that concept have led repeatedly to heated debates in plenary. These have harmed Parliament's reputation rather than benefiting human rights. It is much more important to grasp the fact that there is a broad consensus: a consensus, first, about the high priority that should be accorded to human rights in Parliament's day-to-day work, and, secondly, a consensus about the fact that traditional human rights are fully recognized by all political movements. These rights are clearly defined and described and are enshrined in law and protected, while for various reasons other rights do not enjoy such protection. This does not mean that human rights of the second and third generation should be left out of the debate. On the contrary: it was, in fact, one of the achievements of the Treaty of Amsterdam to incorporate into the Preamble the European Union's declaration of support for fundamental social rights as enshrined in the 1961 European Social Charter and the 1989 Community Charter of the Fundamental Social Rights of Workers. If we recall the Preamble to the 1986 Single European Act, we can be optimistic that fundamental social rights will follow the same course until, when the time comes, they achieve the same status as traditional human rights.

Developing the protection of such rights and establishing a system of legal protection for them has been a major concern for Parliament. This development will continue. In addition, environmental rights have become increasingly relevant to Parliament's work. If it is borne in mind that substantial areas of environmental legislation are subject to the co-decision procedure, Parliament has a great opportunity to protect European citizens' rights in this respect. This is unfortunately not the case where the European Union's employment policy is concerned, although the Treaty of Amsterdam basically marks a great step forward in this area, even though co-decision is envisaged only where incentive measures are concerned, while Parliament only has to be consulted on measures to co-ordinate the Member States' policies.

2. The Issue of Powers   While Parliament has been strongly committed to human rights and has often taken its declarations of belief in their protection more seriously than the other Community institutions, its powers in the Union's institutional framework with regard to both external relations and the fields of justice and home affairs (the so-called second and third pillars) are inadequate, making it more difficult for it to exercise influence in these policy areas. That said, Parliament's powers have grown steadily over the years, and the consultation, co-operation, co-decision, and assent procedures enable Parliament to have what in some cases is a decisive say in European 'laws'. As a result, human rights feature on a daily basis.

However, one important and, to some extent, disillusioning fact must be taken into account if we seek to evaluate the European Parliament's future role: Parliament has long since ceased to be little more than a consultative assembly. It now has a quite different, and stronger, position in the European Union's institutional framework and power structure. If we look at the development of the European Parliament's role, we can see that Parliament started out as a consultative assembly. Anything could be debated and resolutions were adopted without difficulty (even when they were on controversial topics), since there was no 'risk' of them having a genuine impact on the Community's policies. This situation made it easy for MEPs to agree on texts which were in stark contrast to the views of the other institutions.

Reinhard Rack and Stefan Lausegger

Parliament's role now is completely different. It has a very substantial say in legislation, and takes a line with a view to achieving a consensus with the other institutions. This does not mean that Parliament must be of the same opinion as the Council and the Commission (although that would certainly make the lives of those institutions easier). It means something quite different, namely co-operation in the legislative process, rather than visionary resolutions. It is simple to put forward a sweeping, generous approach to asylum policy, if it is a question of telling others how they should deal with a constantly expanding number of applicants for asylum. It nonetheless remains to be seen whether Parliament will maintain its criticism of the Council's and Commission's possibly negative approach to and narrow interpretation of asylum and immigration issues when the time comes to co-operate with those institutions. From our point of view it is more likely that the frequently criticized principle of agreement on the lowest common denominator will also be found to apply to Parliament.

This fact can also be explained when it is considered from another angle. Not only is Parliament now aware of its powers and responsibility; it also knows their source: they come from the Member States, which have given more and more powers to Parliament when the Treaties have been revised. The involvement in the Community's legislative process of representatives of the people has increased as the powers of the European Union and the European Community have been extended. Alongside this reason for Parliament's involvement there is a second factor which enables Parliament gradually to move towards the role that national parliaments play. In the past, Parliament has managed to co-operate with the other Community institutions to an increasing extent without hampering their joint work by striking visionary attitudes. It has obtained genuine decision-making powers only through this conformist—almost opportunistic—behaviour.

Parliament, as the body representing the citizens of the European Union, has always grasped the need to protect the rights of those whom it represents. It is therefore a pity that its role is still far from being comparable to that played by its national counterparts. Although European Parliament resolutions always generate a wide public response, they cannot make up for the absence of legislative powers.

The provisions of the Amsterdam Treaty will bring some improvements by extending the co-decision procedure to areas in which Parliament is currently involved in the decision-making process only through the co-operation procedure. In addition to other areas, which have only an indirect and limited bearing on the area of fundamental and human rights, the following provisions, in particular, are worth highlighting:

- Article 12 (*ex* Article 6) EC: rules to prohibit discrimination on grounds of nationality, where the co-operation procedure (Article 252 (*ex* Article 189c)) currently applies;
- Article 46(2) (*ex* Article 56(2)): co-ordination of provisions laid down by law, regulation, or administrative action for special treatment of foreign nationals (right of establishment);
- Article 141 (*ex* Article 119): equal opportunities and equal treatment;

• Article 153 (*ex* Article 129a): consumer protection;
• Article 286 (*ex* Article 213b): establishment of an independent advisory authority on data protection (right to privacy).

Furthermore, there are a number of new areas for consultation with Parliament, among them, for example, the new Article 13 (*ex* Article 6a) on discrimination on grounds other than nationality. These areas will generate new opportunities for Parliament with regard to the protection of fundamental rights. As Parliament is drawn more deeply into the legislative process its opportunities to exercise a positive influence over the promotion of fundamental and human rights will increase. If the European Union's activities are extended to embrace social and employment policy, cultural policy, and education and training matters, this development will also present a significant opportunity for Parliament, operating in the context of the provisions of the Treaties, to play its part fittingly as the representative assembly within a Union which is closer to its citizens.

One demand which was made, *inter alia*, in the run-up to the Intergovernmental Conference, was for the introduction of a right for Parliament to take legislative initiatives, so that it would no longer be dependent on action by the Commission, or on the latter's failure to act. This request has not been met in the new Treaty, not least because Parliament has the option anyway of using resolutions to prompt action by the Commission. Parliament has certainly made use of this instrument in the past. In this way, the Commission retains its role as the motive force behind Community legislation.

A greater failure, however, was the on-going one of not giving Parliament a general, active right to institute proceedings before the ECJ. If we want to do away with the inequalities between the European institutions, this will be an indispensable step.

Qualified progress has been made with regard to the budget. Parliament's influence has been strengthened, because operational expenditure under the third pillar has been incorporated into the Community budget and classified as non-compulsory expenditure. This will allow Parliament to use the allocation of resources and the annual discharge to have an indirect say in this intergovernmental policy area. All the same, this was only one step towards a more satisfactory budgetary procedure, since the distinction between compulsory and non-compulsory expenditure will be retained even after the Treaty of Amsterdam comes into force.

There is a close connection between this and the moves to bring major areas coming under the third pillar within the Community system. The transfer of these policy areas to the first pillar, and the consequences with regard to the procedures that must then be used, constitute an important stage in the development of the European Union. Criticism is nonetheless due: there will be a five-year transitional period, during which the principle of unanimity and the consultation procedure will be retained, before Article 251 (*ex* Article 189b) TEC is applied. Even then, the transfer will still be conditional on a unanimous vote in the Council (with the exception of two provisions concerning visas). In a nutshell, qualified majority voting and the use of the co-decision procedure have been put off for as long as possible. If we consider the uncertainty about the European Parliament's involvement in these policies, the extension of the powers of the ECJ brought about by the new Article 46 (*ex* Article L) is welcome (even if we consider the fact that national courts which constitute the final court of appeal unexpectedly have the right to decide whether a case must be brought before the ECJ for a preliminary ruling or not. In the interests of a uniform application of Community law national courts do not have this option under Article 234 (*ex* Article 177) EC. It therefore remains to be seen whether Community law enacted in this area will be applied uniformly in all fifteen (or more) Member States if the national courts are not obliged to seek clarification from the ECJ in cases of uncertainty).

3. The Issue of Fundamental Rights in the Union   As noted, on many occasions Parliament has called for the Community to accede to the ECHR, just as it has stressed the importance of the European Union having its own list of fundamental rights. It is vitally important that European citizens are clear about what their rights comprise. Given the lack of a list of fundamental rights, it is very difficult to predict judgments by the ECJ. The scope or precise nature of a protected right is not defined (this shortcoming must be taken into account when evaluating the extension, by Article 46 of the TEU, of the ECJ's jurisdiction to cover the actions of the institutions' bodies in terms of its compatibility with fundamental rights. The access to the ECJ that is thereby also provided under primary law will remain just a fine gesture (which will, moreover, make no change to the ECJ's long-standing practice) if the protected corpus of rights is not adequately defined). As part of the process of constructing a Union citizenship, which consists, after all, of individual citizens' duties and, of course, rights *vis-à-vis* the Union, drawing up a list of fundamental rights is an obvious step.

It is difficult to imagine how the Treaty of Amsterdam's new Article 7(1) (*ex* Article F.1(1))[112] might be applied. Its introduction is to be welcomed, however, as a declaration of the European Union's attachment to the protection of human rights in respect of itself, and not just where its external relations are concerned.

B. External Relations

1. The Institutional Framework   The protection of human rights is both an objective of development policy, which falls within the sphere of Community competence, and an objective of the CFSP, which lies outside Community competence. This has led the Council to propose a dual legal basis for measures to protect human rights, namely Article 179 (*ex* Article 130w) EC for Community measures in favour of developing countries (particularly the ACP States) and Article 308 (*ex* Article 235) EC for other countries. The Commission, on the other hand, in its initial draft Council Regulation,[113] advocated a single legal basis (under Article 179 EC), in order to

---

[112] Art. 7(1) states: '[t]he Council, meeting in the composition of the Heads of State or Government and acting by unanimity on a proposal by one third of the Member States or by the Commission *and after obtaining the assent of the European Parliament*, may determine the existence of a serious and persistent breach by a Member State of principles mentioned in Article F(1) [now Art. 6(1)], after inviting the government of the Member State in question to submit its observations' (emphasis added).

[113] Proposal for a Council Reg. (EC) on the development and consolidation of democracy and the rule of law and respect for human rights and fundamental freedoms (COM(97)357 final).

bring about a more consistent Community approach in the field of human rights policy. The Council's stance means that this plan is no longer certain and Parliament will have to reach agreement with the Council.

As Parliament has always pointed out the importance of consistency and equal treatment of third countries, from its point of view the creation of a single legal basis would be more appropriate (all the more so since, under Article 308 EC, Parliament has merely to be consulted!). Nonetheless, if legal problems should preclude this solution, consideration should be given to the drawing up of two regulations with identical wording but different legal bases. Either way an agreement is urgently needed, especially in view of the judgment of the ECJ of 12 May 1998 regarding the lack of a legal basis for the action programme to combat poverty. In the year of the fiftieth anniversary of the signing of the Universal Declaration of Human Rights that judgment resulted in the Commission, in its capacity as guardian of the Treaties, temporarily blocking the budget lines relating to the protection of human rights and the promotion of democracy (including the Phare and Tacis democratization programmes).

An institutional agreement reached on 17 July 1998 has managed to secure the financing of projects for 1998 until a legal basis is adopted. In any event, the adoption of a unified legal basis would place the Union's activities relating to measures to promote human rights on a substantially more coherent footing.

2. Parliament's Role in the Implementation of the CFSP In addition to its demand for the CFSP to be brought within the Community system, Parliament has called for all policies relating to external relations—the CFSP, trade, development, and co-operation—to be consolidated in a single chapter of the Treaty, in order to make Community action more consistent and coherent. This has not happened so that, post-Amsterdam, external relations continue to be determined by the EU's tripartite structure. The CFSP continues to be separate from external economic relations, which fall under the first pillar. This is all the more regrettable, in that trade policy and foreign policy will in future be increasingly intertwined (examples are the policies *vis-à-vis* China and Turkey), and ought to be an integral element of European preventive diplomacy, which includes the promotion of human rights as a priority.

The main reason for the failure to transfer the CFSP to the first pillar is to be found in the Member States' unchanging, traditional reluctance when it comes to giving up powers in this area, which for them is so important in national terms. They prefer to leave this policy as a matter for intergovernmental co-operation, thereby accepting both the disadvantages entailed, for instance, by the requirement of unanimity, and the democratic deficit constituted by the non-involvement of the European Parliament.

The most recent revision of the Treaties has left Parliament's role unchanged. A single improvement can be pointed to: operational expenditure under the CFSP, which continues to be classified as non-compulsory expenditure, will in future be charged to the Community budget, in the same way as the changes regarding operational costs coming under the third pillar (Justice and Home Affairs). Parliament's role in monitoring CFSP expenditure has been confirmed in an inter-institutional agreement, which also sets out more visibly the CFSP's spheres of action.

Amsterdam has thus demonstrated, once again, that the Member States are un-willing to involve Parliament in the conduct of the CFSP to a greater extent than at present. Its powers continue to be limited, essentially, to the right to be informed and consulted and the right to make recommendations to the Council. An inter-institutional agreement on a formal consultation procedure to ensure that Parliament's views are duly taken into account by the Council would be a major step forward. What will count in the future, too, is the way in which Parliament manages to use inter-institutional agreements to arrive at a parliamentary practice which makes up, as far as possible, for the limitations placed on its powers by the Treaties. Within the bounds of its possibilities, Parliament must continue its endeavours to in-crease its influence over the CFSP by means of the intelligent use and extension of ex-isting instruments and the development of new instruments and procedures with regard to parliamentary practice. In doing so, the protection of human rights as an integral part of the European Union's foreign policy will remain a key concern of Parliament.[114]

3. The Notion of Human Rights in External Relations   One of the most important demands in the field of human rights and third countries is for a coherent, consistent policy *vis-à-vis* the European Union's partners. The concept of human rights is based on the principle of universality, indivisibility, and interdependence. Any deviation from this concept harms the credibility and thus the effectiveness of the European Union's human rights policy.

While the Central and Eastern European countries which have applied for mem-bership must meet a high standard of human rights, based on the political criteria laid down by the Copenhagen European Council in 1993[115] (a standard which in some ways is higher than the level of protection provided in the current Member States[116]), the concept of human rights in relations with Asia, and China in particu-lar, is becoming increasingly fuzzy. Parliament has often criticized this development, since the European Union must be all the more serious and determined in seeking to protect human rights in respect of those countries in which human rights violations are the order of the day.

4. Assessment and Sanction Mechanisms   Now that the importance of human rights has been irrevocably enshrined in relations with third countries, by being included in all agreements with them, the time has at last come to work out transparent mechan-isms for evaluating human rights violations in third countries.[117] The transition to the 'Bulgarian' clause, moreover, has led to a situation which does not preclude dis-criminatory, unequal treatment of the European Union's partners. Consequently, in

---

[114] See the most recent Report on the role of the European Union in the world (Doc. A4–0169/98—the Spencer Report), in which the subject of human rights is considered as being of outstanding importance and open to the instruments of the second pillar.

[115] Art. 49 (*ex* Art. O) TEU, as amended by the Treaty of Amsterdam, now explicitly makes compli-ance with the principles of liberty, democracy, respect for human rights and fundamental freedoms, and the rule of law a condition of accession.

[116] We need only recall the difficulties encountered in the process of drafting European legislation on ethnic groups, or the precise definition of the concept of 'minority'.

[117] See the Resolution on human rights in the world in 1993 to 1994 and the Union's human rights pol-icy ([1995] OJ C126/15) which, with a view to the 1996 IGC, makes 10 proposals for the improvement of the promotion of human rights by the Union.

1995 the Commission agreed on formulations which are intended to 'improve the consistency, transparency and visibility of the Community approach and to make greater allowance for the sensitivity of third countries and the principle of non-discrimination'.[118]

A non-discriminatory approach must be found for dealing with human rights violations in third countries. The measures that the Community has hitherto taken in cases of human rights violations make it clear that the lack of an objective assessment system has led to the divergent treatment of third countries.[119]

The development of an objective scale of sanctions should be seen as being closely linked to this. It would make it possible to respond to human rights violations in a non-discriminatory manner, without any degree of arbitrariness. It would also mean that, from the outset, third countries would have to take clearly defined sanctions into account, a situation which would undoubtedly provide an incentive to respect human rights. It has thus become a necessity to establish a scale of sanctions, so that human rights clauses in international agreements can be implemented effectively. The scope of sanctions to be applied by the Community must be predictable.

5. Social Clauses   The time has now come, moreover, to include effective instruments for implementing social rights in our treaty relations with third countries.[120] As became clear in the case of Burma (suspension of the GSP), persistent failure to respect social rights can lead to sanctions on the Community's part. If we really want to be serious in promoting such rights they must, like traditional human rights, be included in international agreements. The objection that this would constitute hidden protectionism is a weak argument where the abolition of child labour is concerned. That objection is equally unconvincing in connection with rights relating to environmental protection, if pollution caused by industry is on such a scale as to endanger human life. In future, Parliament must place greater emphasis on achieving these objectives, too.

The Council Regulation of 25 May 1998,[121] which introduces a new social clause into the GSP, is an initial step in this direction. The Regulation is not based on the

[118] Communication from the Commission on the inclusion of respect for democratic principles and human rights in agreements between the Community and third countries (COM(95)0216—C4–0197/95).

[119] See, among other documents, the Resolution on the Communication from the Commission on the inclusion of respect for democratic principles and human rights in agreements between the Community and third countries (COM(95)0216—C4–0197/95) ([1996] OJ C320/261), in which Parliament calls on the Commission to 'draw up a report listing all countries to which sanctions have so far been applied by the Union and a further communication, to address, *inter alia*, criteria, procedures, forms of sanctions, and their method of application, in particular with regard to the implementation of the democracy and human rights clause included in agreements with third countries'.

[120] Parliament has adopted a specific Resolution on the introduction of a social clause in the unilateral and multilateral trading system ([1994] OJ C61/89), in which it 'considers it essential that a social clause designed to combat child and forced labour and to encourage trade union freedoms and the freedom to engage in collective bargaining on the basis of the ILO conventions mentioned above be introduced in the multilateral and unilateral framework (GSP) of international trade', 'considers that the introduction of a social clause in international trade must not become a means of increased protectionism directed against developing countries' and 'calls on the Commission to introduce a social incentive clause as a means of combating underdevelopment in the new ten-year arrangement for the Community's [GSP]'.

[121] Council Reg. (EC) 1154/98 applying the special incentive arrangements concerning labour rights and environmental protection provided for in Arts. 7 and 8 of Regs. (EC) 3281/94 and (EC) 1256/96 applying multi-annual schemes of generalized tariff preferences in respect of certain industrial and agricultural products originating in developing countries [1998] OJ L160/1.

concept of sanctions, but on the principle of incentives (which also appears appropriate in view of the sensitivity of the issue). This means that countries which are basically eligible for the benefits of the GSP will be granted additional trade advantages in their economic relations with the European Union if they can prove that they comply with the relevant social and environmental criteria (primarily ILO Conventions Nos. 87, 98 and 138,[122] and the criteria laid down by the International Convention on the Protection of Tropical Timber). This approach must be pursued further outside the GSP.

6. The Role of Parliament in External Economic Relations   Since the agreements with third countries are now the most important instrument in the promotion of human rights by the European Union, as a result of the systematic inclusion in them of human rights clauses, Parliament's lack of powers in the field of external economic policy is regarded as being particularly serious. However, the results of Amsterdam must generally be described as disillusioning. No consolidation of Articles 133, 300, and 310 (*ex* Article 113, 228 and 238) EC was achieved, and nor was an enhanced role for Parliament in the conclusion of agreements with third countries.[123]

Specifically, Parliament is demanding to be consulted formally on agreements coming under Article 133, to be informed systematically about all the stages concerning the preparation and adoption of guidelines for the negotiation of agreements and about the progress of negotiations, in the case of external agreements with a significant financial impact, and to have a general right of assent before international agreements are concluded. Only if its participation is enhanced in this way will Parliament be able to use its opportunities to promote human rights in third countries with the aid of the European Union's economic strength.

At present, agreements with third countries which are based on Article 133 EC (trade policy), unlike other international agreements, do not require either prior consultation (Article 300) or assent (Article 310). The result of this is that in areas in which the opportunities provided by the co-decision procedure are available to Parliament where internal policy is concerned, Parliament has absolutely no opportunity to have any say when they are the subject of external agreements.[124]

---

[122] Convention No. 87, Freedom of Association, Convention No. 98, Right to Organize and Collective Bargaining, and Convention No. 138, Minimum Age. In ILO, *International Labour Conventions and Recommendations 1919–1991* (1992), ii.

[123] In its Resolution on the functioning of the TEU with a view to the 1996 IGC—Implementation and development of the Union ([1995] OJ C151/56), Parliament proposed that 'the Articles of the Treaty dealing with international agreements should be consolidated, and the respective roles of the Commission and the Council should be clarified (notably as regards the arrangements for participation by the Union in international economic organizations), and the democratic role of the European Parliament before, during and after the negotiating process should be reinforced, with the assent of Parliament being required for all international agreements entered into by the Union (without prejudice to the powers of national parliaments)'.

[124] Report on improvements in the functioning of the institutions without modification of the Treaties—making EU policies more open and democratic, in which Parliament 'regrets that its role in the field of external economic policy has not been improved by the Amsterdam Treaty, notably the fact that the European Parliament is not even formally consulted on agreements based on Art. 133 (*ex* Art. 113), especially considering the role Parliament has as an arm of the budgetary authority': Doc. A4–0117/98.

Inter-institutional agreements should make good this lack of powers by the time of the next revision of the Treaties, which it is to be hoped will remove this democratic deficit.[125]

The mistrust of Parliament where external relations are concerned can likewise be discerned in the provisions of Article 300 of the Amsterdam Treaty. Parliament is only informed after the event of any decision concerning the provisional application or suspension of agreements on account of human rights violations, or failure to comply with democratic rules.

The prospects for Parliament are similarly discouraging with regard to the application of Article 366a of the Lomé Convention, where the Council does not want to give Parliament any powers in the decision-making process.[126] The Council Decision therefore makes no provision for the possibility of an initiative by Parliament in connection with the planned mechanism for consultation with the partner State in which a human rights violation has occurred. Similarly, there is no provision for Parliament to be consulted, as it has demanded, prior to suspension of the agreement. If it is recalled that the Lomé Convention is based on Article 310 EC and thus requires Parliament's assent, Parliament's exclusion from the application of Article 366a of the Lomé Convention is clearly a step in the wrong direction.

It is incomprehensible that Parliament, which has an important role to play in the ACP Assembly as the interlocutor for the representatives of the Lomé Convention's contracting States, should not be entitled to play any part in monitoring compliance with the human rights clause. This practical example, however, shows only the Council's general unwillingness to involve Parliament in matters with an external policy dimension to a greater extent than the minimum laid down in the Treaties.

However, the more Parliament is drawn into all areas of external economic policy, and the more it is thus able to colour the various policy areas with its human rights thinking, the greater the progress that will be made by the European Union in terms of consistent action.

7. Development Policy   The shortcomings regarding uniformity and consistency between the first and second pillars in connection with international relations also apply to development policy. On the one hand, there is non-exclusive Community competence in the field of development co-operation, but on the other, the restriction that this policy complements the policies of the Member States has been retained in the Treaty of Amsterdam. National policies therefore need to be co-ordinated in this area, too, if effective Community action is to be ensured. The Union's concept of the indivisibility of democracy, human rights, and development must find expression in a unified policy on the part of the Union and its Member States towards the developing countries. In this area, in which the promotion of human rights and democracy is playing an increasingly prominent role (see the Council's most recent Common Position on the new strategy regarding relations

---

[125] *Ibid.*
[126] See the Interim Report on the proposal for a Council Decision on a framework procedure for implementing Art. 366a of the Fourth Lomé Convention (COM(96)0069—C4–0045/97—96/0050(AVC)) and the Interim Report on the draft Council Decision on the procedure for implementing Art. 366a of the Fourth Lomé Convention (5644/98—C4–0156/98—96/0050(AVC)).

with Africa[127]), it is once again regrettable that no adequate steps were taken as part of the Amsterdam revision of the Treaties to harmonize the provisions of the CFSP with those concerning trade, development, and co-operation policy.

8. Increased Consistency and Visibility in Connection with Co-operation

(a) Interinstitutional Co-operation and the Role of Parliament

One weak point, which has been on the agenda for a long time, is indicated by the call for consistency in the European Union's activities with regard to measures under the first and second pillars concerning external relations. Parliament has been pointing out the negative effects of this for many years, and has repeatedly called for the situation to be remedied and improved. As a result of the Treaty of Amsterdam, the new version of Article 3 TEU now explicitly requires the Council and the Commission to co-operate on measures concerning external relations, security, economic and development policies; with regard to consistency, this is a very welcome provision, but what it will mean in practice will continue to depend on the will of the parties concerned. The inclusion in the new Troika of the Member of the Commission with responsibility for the CFSP also holds out the hope of improved co-ordination, consistency, and visibility.

. As regards the Commission, it has to be said that the continuing division on geographical lines, where human rights matters are concerned, makes it very difficult to pin down the body which is actually responsible within the Commission structure (at present at least five Commissioners, under the authority of the President of the Commission, deal with human rights issues). Parliament is therefore calling for a single Commissioner to be made responsible in future for policy concerning the promotion of human rights and democracy; this would raise the profile of the European Union's human rights policy and might also lead to improved co-operation with Parliament.[128] Parliament wishes to establish close working relations using the new instruments which have been introduced by the revision of the Treaties in connection with the CFSP. The new High Representative for the CFSP (a function exercised by the Secretary-General of the Council), who will contribute to the formulation, preparation, and implementation of policy decisions,[129] together with the special representative, now enshrined in the Treaty, who will if necessary have a mandate in relation to particular policy issues,[130] offer new opportunities for institutional co-operation.

Following the logic of analysis at European level, the mandate of the Council's Policy Planning and Early Warning Unit should explicitly include monitoring of

---

[127] Common Position of 25 May 1998 concerning human rights, democratic principles, the rule of law and good governance in Africa [1998] OJ L158/1.

[128] See, e.g., the Resolution on human rights throughout the world in 1995–6 ([1997] OJ C20/161), in which Parliament 'reaffirms its belief that a member of the Commission should be appointed to be responsible for human rights, in order to guarantee consistency between the Commission's various areas of action which have a bearing on human rights and that this Commissioner, working in close contact with the President of the Commission, should be able to take initiatives in the field of human rights in the same way as the UN High Commissioner for Human Rights'; see also the Resolution on setting up a single coordinating structure within the Commission responsible for human rights and democratization [1998] OJ C14/402.

[129] New Art. 18, which amends Art. 15 by inserting a new para. 3.

[130] Para. 5 of the new Art. 18.

human rights. In this connection the work of the Council's working party on human rights/CFSP should be mentioned. Commission representatives take part in it, but Parliament is excluded from participation. It would be desirable for Parliament representatives also to be able to take part in this body's deliberations, even if Article 3 (*ex* Article C) TEU, as amended by the Treaty of Amsterdam, obliges only the Council and the Commission to co-operate in the areas with a bearing on external relations.

A further major aspect of co-operation is the provision of regular, comprehensive information for Parliament. Although there has been some progress in recent years, the flow of information should be improved. The reports already submitted by the Commission should become more comprehensive and easier to compare. Forward projections of effectiveness and assessments of the effectiveness of completed projects are essential for the practical implementation of human rights policy. They are an important source of information for Parliament, not least with regard to the exercise of its powers of scrutiny.[131]

Parliament's demand to be informed about measures implemented by the Commission and the Council in response to its resolutions follows the same line of thinking. It is important for it to learn in what way parliamentary resolutions are actually acted upon by the other institutions, and what the results are in practice.

With regard to the Council, it must further be said that it appears to have other priorities than co-operation with Parliament. The Council's memorandum on the European Union's activities in the field of human rights in 1996 was forwarded to Parliament only at the beginning of 1998. It is rather unlikely that it has taken the Council a long time to draft this document and it by no means reflects the importance that now attaches to the promotion of human rights by the European Union. The transmission of this document is, however, a step in the right direction.

The conclusion of an inter-institutional agreement on improved information for Parliament would be conceivable.

(b) The European Union and its Member States

In the field of human rights policy, in particular, improved co-ordination between the Union and its Member States to ensure greater consistency and visibility has frequently been called for.[132] Co-ordination does not mean that the European Union and its Member States must do the same thing. It means that both sides must pursue the same objectives while taking on different individual tasks. The effectiveness of

---

[131] See, for instance, the Resolution on the Commission report on the implementation of measures intended to promote observance of human rights and democratic principles (for 1995) ([1998] OJ C 14/399), in which Parliament calls on the Commission to address the following issues in future reports: the effectiveness of operations undertaken by organizations specifically named in human rights budget lines; the ratio of administrative to operational expenditure in the grants given under chapter B7–70; the extent to which projects were co-funded through other sources, in order to allow closer scrutiny of the benefits and shortcomings of co-operation with other actors; the breakdown of funding between official or government activities, semi-state activities, and non-governmental initiatives, and to seek to achieve a proper balance between government-run and non-governmental projects; and the compilation of comparative figures on expenditure on democratization by EU Member States, other States such as the US, and other international organizations.

[132] Cf. for instance, the Resolution on human rights throughout the world in 1995–6 and the Union's human rights policy [1997] OJ C20/161.

the Union's policy undoubtedly depends on the extent to which its members are capable of presenting a united front to the outside world.

The instruments of common positions and joint actions, which were introduced by the Maastricht Treaty, have increasingly been used to heighten the external profile of the European Union. The new instruments introduced as a result of the Amsterdam revision of the Treaties provide the opportunity to make further progress towards a genuine common foreign policy.

For third countries it is important to have good relations with the European Union as a dependable entity, and not to be confronted with fifteen different views. This is particularly vital for healthy political dialogue, and hence, of course, for the effective promotion of human rights, when we are cultivating bilateral contacts with partners.

The option of constructive abstention provided for in the Treaty of Amsterdam could be a valuable instrument, in that the European Union will remain capable of acting externally, even if not all its Member States hold exactly the same view internally.

United action by the European Union is equally important where international organizations (the UN, the WTO, etc.) are concerned. Achieving such unity and exploiting the resulting opportunities to exercise influence present a difficult but promising challenge. The fact, for instance, that the European Union is represented on at least two seats on the UN Security Council (France and the United Kingdom are permanent members) gives it a not insignificant opportunity to influence the activities of that international organization. It would be a pity not to make use of the prospects that that opens up.

The fact that, even post-Amsterdam, the European Union has no legal personality will continue to diminish its international standing, its external unity, and its negotiating strength. However, the power of the Presidency to negotiate or conclude international agreements on behalf of the Union (Article 24 (*ex* Article J.14) of the TEU) does constitute a first step towards making co-operation with third countries easier.

(c) Co-operation with International Organizations

Further improvements must be made with regard to co-operation with international organizations. Significant synergies can be achieved through division of labour and the avoidance of duplication. The UN, the Organization for Security and Co-operation in Europe, and the Council of Europe have a long and impressive tradition with regard to the protection of human rights. Co-operation with these and other institutions has produced positive results in the past (for instance, the European Union's contribution to the establishment of an independent international criminal court, its commitment regarding the concept of the human dimension within the OSCE process or its co-operation with Council of Europe bodies in the work of establishing the rule of law and Western European standards of democracy in the countries of Central and Eastern Europe).

Consideration has to be given to ways of improving co-ordination and mutual support between European organizations (OSCE/Council of Europe/EU) and international organizations (EU/UN) in the field of human and civil rights policy. The question arises whether longer-term decisions on structural and co-operation issues should be sought which will safeguard the character of each organization, contribute to their mutual strengthening, and simultaneously prevent overlaps.

The electoral observation operations conducted jointly with the OSCE, the Council of Europe, or the UN are worth mentioning, in particular. On 29 June 1998 the Council adopted general guidelines and a code of conduct for electoral observation by the European Union. To cover international electoral observation operations, the code of conduct should be supplemented by an agreement with the organizations referred to above, with the aim of increasing the visibility of the role played by the European Union, and in particular by the European Parliament.

III. CONCLUSIONS

These are some—but far from all—of the areas in which there is a need for united action by the European Union and its institutions. The European Parliament has repeatedly brought up most of these points in its standing committees and in plenary. Unfortunately, for reasons which are well known Parliament can often only utter warnings, especially where the Common Foreign and Security Policy is concerned. In addition, it can only repeatedly call on the other institutions to involve it to a greater extent, in a legitimate fashion, in the activities of the European Union, and to that extent it is dependent on their political will.

The European Parliament's role in the interplay among the institutions is unfortunately a long way from reaching that of an elected representative assembly. Although Parliament's powers have been steadily extended, it still has a long way to go before a genuinely democratic Union which is close to its citizens becomes a reality.

The European Parliament is guided by the vision of a European institutional order based on democracy, liberty, and human rights, the rule of law, social justice, and solidarity. This vision shapes the political and institutional demands still being made by the European Parliament, post-Amsterdam.

The fiftieth anniversary of the signing of the Universal Declaration of Human Rights must be the occasion for us to renew our efforts to secure the widest possible implementation of that universal yardstick of human rights. Fifty years after the signing of the Universal Declaration a clear signal must be given to strengthen human rights as a factor in international politics.

26

Reflections on the Human Rights Role of the European Parliament

KIERAN ST C. BRADLEY

I. INTRODUCTION

The present chapter examines, for the most part, institutional aspects of the activity of the European Parliament in connection with human rights[1] protection, rather than attempting to evaluate its positions on substantive issues, or its overall contribution in this area. In some respects, adopting a highly critical approach to the Parliament's initiatives in favour of human rights might seem like taking a crowbar to a cloud. Though its activity, as demonstrated by Rack and Lausegger,[2] is both considerable as to its volume and extensive as to its subject matter, the impact of its positions is not always easy, or even possible, to evaluate;[3] while the evidence is necessarily anecdotal, a parliamentary resolution condemning violations of human rights in some far-flung corner of the globe, for example, may have effects which bear no discernable relation to the Union's general influence in that region, as if in application of chaos theory[4] to political behaviour.

Human rights may be universal and indivisible; the powers of the European Union,[5] and of the institutions charged with carrying out its tasks, are not.[6] This underlying consideration is of particular significance in examining the role of the European Parliament, whose influence on policy outcomes depends in any given case on a number of variables. Though its actions can take different forms, most of these fall into two main categories, to wit, *a priori* control over policy decisions, and

---

[1] The terminology 'human rights', as distinct from say, 'fundamental rights', which more clearly benefit legal persons, is borrowed from that of the EUI project; it also corresponds with that employed in Parliament's rules of procedure. The distinction is not in any case material to the present discussion.

[2] See their contribution to this vol.

[3] See also J. Touscoz, 'Actions de la Communauté européenne en faveur des droits de l'homme dans les pays tiers' in A. Cassese, A. Clapham, and J. Weiler (eds.), *Human Rights and the European Community: Methods of Protection* (1991), 507 at 530; the author describes the Parliament as exercising 'a sort of messianic mission' in relation to human rights in third countries (at 529).

[4] See J. Gleick, *Chaos: Making a New Science* (1988).

[5] While the distinction between 'European Union' and 'European Community' is legally significant, the former term will be used throughout to refer to both the Community and the non-Community activities of the Union, the latter being reserved specifically for the Community pillar.

[6] The revised numbering of the EC and European Treaties is used throughout, with the old numbering in brackets as appropriate.

positions[7] on alleged systemic or individual violations of human rights. As regards policy scrutiny, the Parliament is under a legal and political duty[8] to ensure, in so far as it is able, that the action of the Union authorities respect the human rights of those affected, regardless of the pillar under which the Union is acting, and of whether this action deploys its effects in the Member States or in third countries.

A distinction may be drawn between violations allegedly committed (by institutions, Member States, or third countries) within the field of application of Community law, and other violations, whether by Member States or third countries. The former are under the supervisory jurisdiction of the Community institutions, and the Treaties expressly allow for concrete sanctions to be adopted against the institutions,[9] the Member States,[10] and third States.[11] The Parliament has not drawn back from taking positions on human rights issues arising within the territory of the Union but outside its jurisdiction *ratione materiae*, sometimes to the considerable chagrin of the Member State concerned. [12] The fact that the Parliament's powers in relation to the Union's external relations, particularly under the common foreign and security policy, are rather limited does not prevent its taking a very active interest in alleged human rights violations in third countries, as if seeking to compensate through the quantity and scope of its activity for its lack of formal clout.

II. THE PECULIAR POSITION OF THE EUROPEAN PARLIAMENT

Any discussion of the role of the European Parliament in the protection of human rights should take account *in limine* of a number of institutional considerations which influence, and may even distort, the terms of such discussion. The student of, say, the protection of human rights and the US Congress would not usually feel obliged to explain the American constitutional context or the role of Congress within that context, or to justify congressional concern with the protection of such rights. The situation is quite other as regards the European Parliament. These considerations may be as much difficulties of discourse as substantive problems, but

---

[7] The term is deliberately open-ended, and may include, e.g., a finding that human rights have been breached, a condemnation of those responsible, and a call for action by the Community institutions and/or the authorities of the (Member) State concerned.

[8] See further sect. III. B.2. below; the scope of this duty does, of course, reflect the universality and indivisibility of human rights.

[9] Notably by an action in damages, of which the most dramatic illustration is probably that by the unfortunate whistleblower Stanley Adams against the Commission (Case 145/83 [1985] ECR 3539); one of Adams' legal representatives was an MEP, though acting in his private capacity. Parliament had examined the matter on a number of occasions (see S. Adams, *Roche versus Adams* (1984), especially chaps. 11 and 14).

[10] A 'sufficiently serious' breach by a Member State of a rule of Community law which confers rights on individuals, including in principle those which seek to protect human rights, may give rise to liability (Joined Cases C–46/93 and C–48/93, *Brasserie du Pêcheur SA* v. *Germany* [1996] ECR I–1029).

[11] See sect. III. B.2. below.

[12] See, e.g., its resolution of Feb. 1997 calling upon the Juppé government to withdraw the Debré bill then before the French parliament ([1997] OJ C85/150), and the immoderate response of certain members of the government ([1997] OJ C115/1).

should not be overlooked in any critical evaluation of the Parliament's role and capacities.

In the first place, the European Parliament operates in a system of government which is limited as to the scope of its powers, according to its founding instruments.[13] The powers of the Union to take action in relation to the protection and the promotion of fundamental rights were not clearly established until recently, and even now these powers are fragmentary and open to very divergent interpretations. As a result, the exercise by the Union of such powers would be vulnerable to legal and political challenge,[14] even by parties who in principle favour a seamless and effective protection of human rights.[15]

Secondly, the system suffers from a certain lack of 'social legitimacy' even within its own jurisdiction,[16] in the sense that the public is often reluctant to accept the right of the Union to legislate, particularly in as sensitive an area as human rights. The institutions are frequently accused of usurping the powers of the Member States which established the Union, without regard to the rights and interests of the citizens of which the Members States are still considered the ultimate defenders.[17] Furthermore, amongst the reasons the Union system suffers from a low social legitimacy rating[18] is its institutional system, which does not correspond to the image of parliamentary democracy which prevails in the Member States of the Union. Through membership of the Union, governmental and legislative powers are transferred out of the ambit of scrutiny of the national parliaments, but are not, or not always, within that of the European Parliament.

It is important in the present context not to lose sight of the historical dimension, and in particular the evolution over the last two decades[19] of the Parliament's position within this institutional system. For most of its existence, the Parliament has been able to play only a very modest role, with a right, considered practically unusable, to dismiss the Commission as the principal means of enforcing its institutional prerogatives, and no powers to control the principal legislator, the Council; though important, its powers in determining Community expenditure in the budget are

---

[13] It has been argued that the demarcation of competences between the Community and the Member States has not always been respected in practice. See J.H.H. Weiler, 'The Transformation of Europe', (1991) 100 *Yale LJ* 2403. This would exacerbate the problem of the legitimacy of the Union system of government adumbrated below.

[14] The 1979 proposal that the Communities accede to the European Convention on Human Rights (ECHR), revived in 1990, failed through a combination of these. See *Opinion 2/94* [1996] ECR I–1759; a positive opinion of the ECJ would not have guaranteed accession, owing to the strong opposition of a number of Member States.

[15] That a cause may be worthy does not protect it from such challenge: see Case C–106/96, *United Kingdom* v. *Commission* [1998] ECR I–2729, where the Court struck down certain Commission initiatives to combat social exclusion for lack of the requisite legislative authorization.

[16] Weiler, note 13 above, at 2469.

[17] To make matters worse, political parties or even governments have been known to play on this lack of public acceptance for their own domestic purposes, without in any way questioning the overall benefits to their Member State of membership of the Union.

[18] There are others, real and apparent, such as the lack of any political accountability of the Council (except, perhaps, where it co-decides with the Parliament), the lack of transparency of the decision-making process, and the alleged remoteness of the Union institutions.

[19] In 1978, the Parliament was still not directly elected, had just acquired significant budgetary powers, and only participated in the adoption of legislation through the delivery of a consultative opinion which was considered, at least in some Community circles, a non-essential formality.

closely circumscribed by Treaty rules and procedures. The contours of the institutional system, at least as regards the Parliament's role, have probably still not been determined definitively; the Member States have a tendency, when reforming the institutions, to stay close to existing political practice, rather than striving for an optimal solution which might be valid in the long term. Thus, even after Amsterdam, the Parliament's role in decision-making in the outer pillars is minimal, and even within the Community pillar, it will, for example, only be consulted on immigration matters (at least for the first five years) and will not even be consulted on the urgent imposition of economic sanctions against a third country.[20]

Parliament also suffers from something of an image problem in the Member States, especially compared to the other institutional actors of the Union (Council, Commission, national governments). None of these suffers from the same difficulty in providing a simple explanation to the public of its role, or in adopting and presenting a clear and, if need be, consistent position. Nor does the Parliament operate as a collegiate body, and its decisions are subject to majorities which may fluctuate from one vote to the next, for reasons which are not always clear to the outside world.[21] Responsibility within the Parliament for human rights matters is distributed amongst a bewildering variety of officers, committees, political authorities, and services; unlike most of the other institutional considerations mentioned above, the solution to this diffusion of internal responsibility is a matter for the Parliament itself.

III. WHY SHOULD THE EUROPEAN PARLIAMENT BE CONCERNED WITH HUMAN RIGHTS?

A number of reasons have been advanced to justify the Parliament's general interest in the protection of human rights. The fact that people ask it to play a role in this field and the existence of a consensus 'that the democratic institutions have a special duty to take care of fundamental rights' have been suggested as a sufficient explanation.[22] Its status as 'the world's only directly elected international parliament',[23] 'the only democratically elected Community institution',[24] 'a major symbol of democracy',[25] and 'a tribune for the defence and promotion of human rights [which encourages] Community policy makers to take these fundamental rights into account' has also been proposed.[26] Less rhetorically, and more realistically, it has been suggested that

[20] Arts. 67 and 301 EC, respectively.
[21] R. Rack and S. Lausegger explain some of the subtleties of Parliament's voting on human rights matters in their contribution to this vol., at sect. II. A. 1.
[22] E. Boumans and M. Norbart, 'The European Parliament and Human Rights' (1989) 7 *NQHR* 37.
[23] EP Human Rights Unit, 'The European Parliament, Human Rights and the EU's External Policy', information note, 20 Jan. 1998; see also G. de Vries ' Human Rights and the Foreign Policy of the European Union', unpublished paper presented to the Netherlands Institute of Human Rights (University of Utrecht), 24 Apr. 1998, at 10.
[24] See Rack and Lausegger, this vol., sect. II. A., Introduction.   [25] De Vries, note 23 above.
[26] D. Napoli, 'The European Union's Foreign Policy and Human Rights' in N. Neuwahl and A. Rosas (eds.), *The European Union and Human Rights* (1995), 302.

the Parliament has used the issue of human rights protection to 'expand its powers and responsibilities' beyond its 'normal remit', though the claim that it has 'obtained genuine decision-making powers' through 'striking visionary attitudes' in co-operating with the other Community institutions in this area remains to be verified.[27] Its attention to such matters has also been justified, at least in certain fields of Union activity, by the consideration that there is no other Community institution which is as involved in this topic as the Parliament.

Whatever degree of conviction these views may carry, they provide little guidance as to the proper role of the Parliament in this regard, and what, if any, limits it should set on its activities. There are a number of structural, formal, and political consider-ations which, in the author's view, are pertinent in this regard.

A. Structural

Governments abuse human rights. Acts which, if perpetrated by private citizens or groups, would constitute criminal offences or civil wrongs, acquire the status of vio-lations of human rights when carried out, often under cover of positive law, by gov-ernments. While it is true that the legislature and judiciary may be formally responsible within the State for such acts, they will normally only be adopting or ap-plying, respectively, laws which reflect the policy of the executive branch; moreover, it is the executive which represents the State under international law, and which is re-sponsible for ensuring that such acts are not carried out by private agencies. In a well-functioning democratic polity, opposition political parties, public opinion, and NGOs, and an independent judiciary applying constitutional restraints on the exer-cise of public power, should, in principle, be able to prevent or, in case of a violation, provide redress for, any such abuses. Within such a polity, these political forces can also seek to pressurize the government to sanction notorious breaches of human rights standards by foreign governmental actors.

The European Union does not conform to this constitutional model. While there exists an independent judiciary for the Community, its human rights jurisdiction is limited *ratione materiae* and, according to some, timidly or ineffectually exercised.[28] The existence of a 'European public opinion', as distinct from fifteen distinct na-tional public opinions, remains controversial. Perhaps most significantly of all, the only formal political opposition in the governing structures of the institutions is that exercised by the European Parliament. Even after three rounds of substantive Treaty amendment, the membership of the political institutions and ancillary organs of the Community, with the sole exception of the European Parliament, reflects the will of the national governments; only the Parliament, more or less of political necessity, contains representatives of opposition parties, and of minority groups whose human rights are most at risk from government policies.[29] It is true that the Parliament may

---

[27] See Rack and Lausegger, this vol., sect. II. A. 2.

[28] N. Foster, 'The European Court of Justice and the European Convention for the Protection of Human Rights' (1987) 8 *HRLJ* 245; J.H.H. Weiler and N. Lockhart, 'Taking Rights Seriously: The Eu-ropean Court and its Fundamental Rights Jurisprudence', (1995) 32 *CLMRev.* 51 and 579, provides an incisive critical analysis of the relevant case law.

[29] While opposition politicians may be appointed, e.g., to the Commission and to the Committee of the Regions, governments are under no obligation to ensure such representation.

now play a decisive role in determining the composition of the Commission and, as from May 1999, when it approved the nomination of Mr Prodi, the choice of its President; none the less, it is the national governments which select the candidate Commissioners, often from among their own ranks, and which appoint the Commission by common agreement at the end of the procedure.

The governments have not relinquished their iron grip on either the process of Treaty reform, subject to a possible repudiation of the entire text by a national parliament or judiciary, or the people in a referendum, or on the definition of foreign policy and co-operation on law and order. Thus, despite its partly supranational character and framework, decision-making remains to a large degree in the hands of governments, particularly in those areas of Union activity where the mechanisms for judicial review are weakest and where the threats to human rights could arguably be said to be most serious. It is therefore somewhat unrealistic to think that the Commission and the Council, other than in the most extreme circumstances, would seek to pass judgement on human rights violations occurring in the Member States. Moreover, in adopting positions in relation to violations alleged to have been committed in third countries, they may be more amenable to economic considerations than, say, a national parliament or the European Parliament.

The costly realization that 'States [meaning essentially governments] generally are not the best watchdogs of [the] implementation' of human rights law[30] is now widely accepted, as is the notion that '[e]xpression of concern at violations of such rights cannot be considered interference in the domestic affairs of a State'.[31] One of the major achievements of the European Convention was to remove ultimate supervision of respect for human rights in the High Contracting Parties to a supranational level, out of the hands of the individual national governments, and to vest it in independent judicial or quasi-judicial organs, or political review by majority vote. Given the partial exclusion of the jurisdiction of the Court of Justice in the outer pillars,[32] and the hands-off approach heretofore adopted by the organs of the European Convention,[33] the Parliament can plausibly claim, in the context of the European Union, to be the 'international institution which is able to distinguish between the individual interests of the States and the common interests of mankind'.[34]

It does not follow, of course, that the Commission and the Council are not sensitive to human rights concerns; on the contrary, they are both under certain obligations to respect such concerns as a matter of Community law. The Commission is politically responsible to the European Parliament, while individual members of the Council are theoretically under the tutelage of their respective national parlia-

---

[30] P. van Dijk, 'The Law of Human Rights in Europe—Instruments and Procedures for a Uniform Implementation' (1997) VI (2) *AEL* 22.

[31] Declaration of the Foreign Ministers of the European Community of 21 July 1986: *Bull. EC* 7/8–1986.

[32] Art. 35 TEU does, however, allow for an optional jurisdiction to provide preliminary rulings on certain matters (see [1999] OJ L 114/56) concerning co-operation in criminal matters.

[33] See, e.g., the decision of the European Commission of 3 May 1990 on App. No. 13258/87, *M* v. *Germany*; as this is a self-limiting ordinance, it could of course be abandoned if need be (see, further, K. Bradley, 'Fundamental Rights and the European Union: A Selective Overview' (1994) 21 *Polish Yearbook of International Law* 204–8 and *Matthews* v. *United Kingdom*, see note 103 below).

[34] Van Dijk, note 30 above.

ments.[35] It is nonetheless the case that, as the only non-governmental institution in the political structures of the Union, the Parliament provides the principal counter-balance to the collective will of the governments.

B. Formal Powers and Responsibilities

Like the other institutions, the Parliament is under a legal injunction to 'act within the limits of the powers conferred upon it' by Article 7 (*ex* Article 4) of the EC Treaties. No single Treaty provision grants the Parliament an overarching jurisdiction to investigate and adopt positions on human rights matters; nonetheless a number of provisions may be relied on to justify the exercise of such a power in different areas of Community and Union activity.

1. Treaty on European Union   Article 5 (*ex* Article E) of the TEU provides, *inter alia*, that the Parliament 'shall exercise [its] powers under the conditions and for the purposes provided for . . . by the other provisions of this Treaty', while Article 6 (*ex* Article F) both notes that '[t]he Union is founded on . . . respect for human rights and fundamental freedoms' and requires the Union to 'respect fundamental rights . . . as general principles of Community law'. It follows that, for the purposes of Article 6, Parliament is obliged, and not merely empowered, to take account of the necessity to respect human rights in the exercise of its advisory, supervisory, and budgetary powers under the Union and Community Treaties. This view is consistent with that implicitly adopted by the Court of Justice, for example, in *T-Port* v. *Bundesanstalt für Landwirtschaft und Ernährung*, where it held that '[t]he Community institutions are required to act in particular when [an existing Community rule] infringes certain traders' fundamental rights protected by Community law'.[36]

More specifically, the conferring on the Parliament of a power of veto over the accession of new States to the Union (Article 49 (*ex* Article O) TEU), and the finding that a Member State has been guilty of a 'serious and persistent breach' of the principles set out in Article 6(1) TEU, in each case implies that it is entitled to take an interest in the human rights situation in both categories of State. That the Parliament should take such matters into account in exercising its modest prerogatives in relation to the common foreign and security policy arises from the very wording of Article 11(1) (*ex* Article J.1(1)) TEU, fifth indent, though this element is most inherent in the area of police and judicial co-operation in criminal matters.

2. EC Treaty   Clearly, where a human rights violation occurs within the jurisdiction of the Union, whether in a Member State (acting within the scope of Community law as defined by the court's case law[37]) or where committed by a Community institution in a third State[38] or with effects in a third state, the act would,

---

[35]. Weiler opined in 1991 that '[d]irect democratic accountability . . . remains vested in national parliaments to whom the members of the Council are answerable': note 13 above, at 2430. There was, however, little evidence at the time that the national parliaments, with the possible exception of the Danish *Folketing*, were able or willing to exercise any meaningful control over the acts of their ministers in Brussels; see now P. Norton (ed.), *National Parliaments and the European Union* (1996).

[36] Case C–68/95, *T-Port* v. *Bundesanstalt für Landwirtschaft und Ernährung* [1996] ECR I–6065, 6100, at para. 40.

[37] See, e.g., Case C–260/89, *ERT* [1991] ECR I–2963.   [38] See further sect. III. D. below.

presumably, constitute a 'contravention of . . . Community law' which Parliament could investigate '[i]n the course of its duties' by setting up a temporary committee of inquiry.[39] In so far as it directly concerns[40] the complainant(s), such a violation could be examined as a petition or, where committed by a Community institution or body, by the Ombudsman who is appointed by, and reports to, Parliament.[41] Apart from these supervisory mechanisms of horizontal application, different provisions of the Treaty also require the institutions, including Parliament in its legislative role, to have special regard to the promotion of the respect for human rights generally, though only in relation to development co-operation,[42] or to particular aspects of human rights protection, such as the prohibition of discrimination.[43]

As regards human rights violations committed outside the Union's direct jurisdiction, the Court of Justice has recognized that Parliament enjoys an inherent right 'to discuss any question concerning the Communities, to adopt resolutions on such questions and to invite the Governments to act'.[44] In so far as the Communities have established, or may establish, trade relations with most third countries in the international community, the respect by third countries of human rights may be said to concern the Communities. Where the matter is not yet of concern to the Communities, the Parliament could, arguably, be entitled at the very least to make it so. On the same occasion, the Court noted that Article 142 (now Article 199) of the Treaty granted the Parliament 'the power to determine its own internal organization',[45] a provision which could serve to justify Rule 54 of the Parliament's rules of procedure, according to which '[d]uring the examination of a legislative proposal, Parliament shall pay particular attention to whether the proposal respects . . . the fundamental rights of citizens'.[46]

C. Political Considerations

The courts are often seen as the primary defenders of fundamental rights in a constitutional polity. This view is particularly prevalent in relation to the European Community, though obviously not as regards the European Union in its non-Community manifestations. Hence, with a few notable and mostly recent exceptions,[47] the literature on this subject is overwhelmingly devoted to analysing, and occasionally criticizing, the case law of the Court of Justice, with almost no attention being given to

[39] Art. 193 (*ex* Art. 138c) EC and Decision 95/167 [1995] OJ L113/1.

[40] The Parliament interprets this phrase as requiring that the object of the petition represent a real and effective concern of the petitioner, though not that he necessarily have an individual personal interest in the matter (see S. Baviera, 'Essai de division de compétences entre le médiateur et la commission des pétitions du Parlement européen', in M. Epaminondas (ed.), *The European Ombudsman* (1994), 115).

[41] Arts. 193–195 (*ex* Arts. 138c–138e) EC.

[42] Hence outside the territorial jurisdiction of the Community, Art. 177 (*ex* Art. 130u(2)) EC.

[43] Generally, Arts. 12 and 13, and more specifically, in relation to, e.g., agricultural production and migrant Community workers, Arts. 34(2) and 39(2) (*ex* Arts. 40 and 48(2), respectively).

[44] Case 230/81, *Luxembourg* v. *Parliament* [1983] ECR 255, 287, at para. 39.

[45] *Ibid.*, at para. 38.

[46] While it is difficult to discern how the Parliament applies this provision, which is rarely, if ever, mentioned in legislative resolutions, the restriction to fundamental rights of *citizens* appears rather anomalous.

[47] Of which the present project is one; see also the works cited at the beginning of part III, above, and Cassese, Clapham, and Weiler, note 3 above.

the activities of the Community's political institutions. It is surely the case, however, that the legislative and executive branches of government should be considered the primary defenders of human rights. The definition of the rights to be protected, and especially the balance to be struck between conflicting values in a given situation, and of the methods of protection, falls in the first place to the legislature, possibly in accordance with guidelines established by a written constitution, while their implementation on the ground, where the citizen is first in contact with the State, is the task of the administration.

In any case, recourse to the judiciary may not always provide a practical or efficient remedy. Beneficiaries may not be aware of their rights, the breach of a right may give rise to fragmented damage no individual has *locus standi* to challenge, or a right may be inherently inadequate or impossible to enforce.[48] Moreover, an international court may be somewhat reluctant to give priority to a human right which would directly contravene the provisions of the instrument upon which its jurisdiction is founded.[49] Judicial forms of protection should therefore be seen as a solution of second-last resort,[50] in cases of disputes concerning the existence or scope of a particular right or rights; in short, prevention is better than cure.

This analysis of the proper division of responsibilities amongst the branches of governments applies with particular force in the European Union, given the limited access of the citizen to direct judicial review of the acts of the Community institutions, and its exclusion as regards foreign policy decisions and co-operation on law and order matters. This responsibility, first affirmed in the Joint Declaration of 5 April 1977[51] and confirmed by Article 6 (*ex* Article F) TEU, is shared amongst the political institutions of the Union. Parliament is, however, particularly well placed, given its relative accessibility by the public and its variegated composition, to exercise a certain *a priori* control of legislative proposals for possible fundamental rights problems, and to respond to the concerns, for example, of NGOs and other interest groups. It may also be able to adopt the 'self-critical coherent approach' to the Union's human rights foreign policy which it has plausibly been suggested is necessary for the Union's credibility on the international stage.[52] Furthermore, in situations where the generally accepted standards of democratic process are not fully respected, there may be no effective judicial or other remedy for alleged breaches of human rights, and a parliamentary resolution may indeed be better than nothing.

A number of other functions have been attributed to parliaments in general, such as those of educating and informing the public,[53] and of setting the political agenda, where the European Parliament could usefully promote the protection of

[48] J.H.H. Weiler, 'Methods of Protection: Towards a Second and Third Generation of Protection', in Cassese *et al.*, note 3 above, at 561.

[49] Thus neither citizens nor associations have a remedy against breaches by the institutions of even directly applicable legislative provisions, where the contested decision is deemed only to affect their interests indirectly. See Case C–321/95, *Stichting Greenpeace Council (Greenpeace International)* v. *Commission* [1998] ECR I–1651.

[50] The preamble to the Universal Declaration describes 'rebellion against tyranny and oppression' as the last resort: Universal Declaration of Human Rights, adopted by GA Res. 217 A (III) (1948). In United Nations, *A Compilation of International Instruments* (1994), i, Part 1, 1.

[51] [1977] OJ C103/1.   [52] See the contribution of Andrew Clapham to this vol.

[53] W. Bagehot, *The English Constitution* (1867), cited in P. Norton (ed.), *Legislatures* (1990), 38.

fundamental rights. Indeed, its Declaration on Fundamental Rights and Freedoms of 12 April 1989 was motivated by both these concerns.[54] The importance of education 'directed . . . to the strengthening of respect for human rights and fundamental freedoms' is, moreover, expressly recognized in the Universal Declaration of Human Rights, the application of which is incumbent on 'every organ of society', and in the designation of 1995–2005 as the Decade for Human Rights Education, matters to which the Parliament should not be insensitive.[55]

One final matter in this regard is that scrutiny of human rights issues may be more palatable where undertaken by public representatives who are answerable to an electorate, rather than by 'unelected bureaucrats'.[56] This is as true of issues arising in the Member States, where MEPs are elected, as of those concerning third States, whose officials are reported to object to being judged by 'EC officials'.[57] The Parliament's interest in the Union's external human rights policy may be justified by the limited, or non-existent, supervisory role played by the national parliaments.[58] Generally speaking, the Parliament's intervention could serve to relativize the appreciations of the governments involved and to democratize the process of human rights protection in the Union.

D. A Case in Point: Sex, Lies, and Red Tape

The Community's concern with the respect for human rights within its own legal order, particularly respect by the institutions themselves, might at first blush appear to be something of a luxury, 'an indulgence of the affluent'.[59] The handling of the petition of Mrs H[60] is instructive in demonstrating how the system operated in one instance where the institution was the accused, not the accuser, and where no judicial intervention was in effect possible.

Mrs H, a British national, was employed in a Commission delegation to a third country on a contract of unlimited duration. In February 1983, her immediate superior, Ms J, proposed that, in view of her 'outstanding qualities', this 'highly qualified, extremely devoted secretary' be promoted. That summer, the petitioner claims to have been the victim of sexual harassment by Mr R, the head of delegation.[61] In October 1983, Ms J proposed that Mrs H's contract of employment be terminated. While the official responsible at the Commission's personnel department in Brussels expressed surprise at the sudden reversal in the appreciation of her work, an *ad hoc* committee was set up to investigate the complaints made against Mrs H; Ms J and Mr R both

---

[54] [1989] OJ C120/56; the Parliament's 1988 white paper on the subject was intended to be 'a valuable source of information for the people of Europe and the everyday exercise of their rights' (PE 115. 274/fin., at 3).

[55] Van Dijk, note 30 above, at 114.

[56] Editorial comment on P. Alston and J.H.H. Weiler, 'The European Union and Human Rights: Final Project Report on an Agenda for the Year 2000' (see Chap. 1 of this vol.), entitled 'Rights Wrongs', *Wall Street Journal*, 13 Oct. 1998.

[57] See Clapham's contribution to this vol. at note 92 and the text thereto.   [58] *Ibid.*

[59] The phrase is Weiler's; he goes on to show why this is not the case. See Weiler, note 48 above, at 555.

[60] Given the lapse of time and the nature of the allegations, the names of the parties concerned are withheld. 'Neither this incident nor that recounted in sect. IV.4 below reflects the very valuable work of Parliament's petitions committee in protecting human rights.'

[61] The graphic detail and language used to recount this incident prefigures that of the Starr report which so inspired the admiration of publisher Larry Flynt.

refused to give evidence. The committee concluded that the allegations of sexual harassment were not material to the complaints against Mrs H and were outside its remit, and, on two grounds,[62] the committee recommended that she be downgraded.[63]

Six weeks later, the Commission informed the petitioner that her contract was being terminated, because of a reduction in the number of local staff; she was offered a posting in London. This offer was withdrawn two days later, when it was learnt that she had contacted a staff representative in Brussels concerning the allegations of sexual harassment; Mrs H was ordered to stay away from the office. Her contract was terminated with effect from 31 December 1985.

In April 1986, Mrs H commenced proceedings against the Commission and Mr R in the local court on nine counts; her action was dismissed on all counts but one because of the defendant's diplomatic immunity, which the Commission declined to waive. The court found in favour of the Commission on the count concerning breach of contract, as the plaintiff had failed to provide any evidence to substantiate her claim. In answer to a parliamentary question some months later, the Commission declared that its 'attitude . . . in this lawsuit corresponds to the diplomatic practice of States and international organizations in similar circumstances' and that 'there is a forum available to the plaintiff (the Court of Justice) that is competent to hear the plaintiff's non-contractual claims'.

In submitting a petition to Parliament in June 1989, Mrs H complained that she had no other means of recourse for the solution of her dispute with the Commission concerning her wrongful dismissal and the sexual harassment to which she had allegedly been subjected. The Commission declared to the petitions committee that the competent local court had given 'full and final judgment' in its favour as regards the alleged breach of contract, and claimed that it was justified in dismissing the petitioner 'in view of the disruption caused to the functioning and management of the Delegation by [Mrs H's] case'. The committee was not satisfied with the Commission's responses, particularly as regards the justification proffered for relying on diplomatic immunity, and concluded that the complaint was justified; after more than two years of correspondence with the Commission, during which the Commission neither budged from its initial position on the substance nor provided any more complete explanation of its action in this matter, the committee closed its examination of the petition in February 1993 without any further action.

By relying on its diplomatic immunity, the Commission denied Mrs H the possibility of pursuing her claims, including those concerning wrongful dismissal and sexual harassment, in the local court. As a matter of Community law, the Commission's reliance on its diplomatic immunity, especially as regards Mr R, was, in the circumstances, somewhat doubtful.[64] It was also in apparent contradiction with Article 81 of the Staff Regulations, under which '[a]ny dispute between the institution and a member of the local staff shall be submitted to the competent court in accordance

---

[62] These related to the conduct of private business during working hours and unauthorized absences from the delegation.

[63] The petitioner claims to have only been given access to an incomplete version of the report.

[64] See Art. 23 of the Staff Regulations of the European Communities; Case 5/68, *Sayag* [1968] ECR 395, and Case C–2/88, *Imm Zwartveld and Others* [1990] ECR I–3365 and I–4405.

with the laws in force in the place where the servant performs his duties'. Perhaps not entirely by coincidence, shortly after the petitioner's legal action, the Commission proposed an amendment to the Staff Regulations denying local staff in third countries access to the courts.[65]

Most significantly in the present context, however, it is difficult to believe that the petitioner had been afforded a 'fair and public hearing within a reasonable time by an independent and impartial tribunal established by law', as required by Article 6 of the European Human Rights Convention (ECHR), in respect of eight of the claims made against the Commission and all of her claims against Mr R. In particular, as regards the allegations of sexual harassment, the Commission's noncontractual liability would only arise if the acts complained of were 'acts which, by their nature, represent a participation of [Mr R] in the performance of the tasks of the institution to which he belongs',[66] which the Commission expressly denied. It follows that the Court of Justice would not, as the President of the Commission had unblushingly informed Parliament in 1987, have been 'competent to hear the plaintiff's non-contractual claims'.[67]

A number of lessons may be drawn from this sorry saga. In the first place, the Commission failed to provide the petitioner with any internal avenue for the resolution of her complaint against Mr R, and this despite its self-proclaimed solicitude regarding victims of such behaviour. At the same time as it was stonewalling the petitions committee, the Commission issued a recommendation 'on the protection of the dignity of women and men at work'; the accompanying code of conduct urges employers, *inter alia*, to establish a complaints procedure, and to handle internal investigations with sensitivity.[68] The fact that the complaint, according to the Commission, was only raised in the course of disciplinary proceedings against the petitioner, seems an insufficient justification for denying her any effective judicial remedy, especially against the head of delegation; part of the petitioner's complaint was that her dismissal was intimately linked to the (alleged) incident of sexual harassment. Whatever the disadvantages of thrashing the matter out in open court (though this would have enabled Mr R to clear his name), these were surely outweighed by the lingering suspicion of a cover-up and a denial of a fundamental right.

Secondly, in its dealings with both the Parliament (in answer to the written question) and its petitions committee, the Commission's answers were so far short of the whole truth as to be capable of misleading. It is doubtful that the Commission could escape so lightly today, when the Parliament has a wider selection of supervisory mechanisms and, as illustrated by the BSE inquiry, is willing to use them imaginatively.[69] Thirdly, and rather exceptionally, in the absence of any other judicial or political solution, the

[65] COM(88)776 final; oblivious to the consequences, the Parliament approved the modification without demur ([1990] OJ C295/203).

[66] Case 5/68 [1968] ECR 395, 402.

[67] In any case, to claim that a court based several thousand kilometers away, and applying rules, principles, and procedures of Community law, was 'available' in any meaningful sense to a local employee recently dismissed from her employment and complaining of a violation of local laws against sexual harassment beggars belief.

[68] Recommendation 92/C 27/04 of 27 Nov. 1991 [1992] OJ C27/4.

[69] See K. Bradley, 'Legal Developments in the European Parliament' (1997) 17 *YEL* 395, 411–2 (1998), and of course, the events leading to the resignation of the Santer Commission in Mar. 1999.

Parliament was arguably the most, or even sole, appropriate body to investigate and, if need be, condemn the Commission's attitude in this affair. Instead, the Commission was able to act as policeman, jury, judge, and executioner in its own cause.

Two postscripts may be added, though no clear conclusion suggests itself. In February 1993, in the same month as the petitions committee closed its file on Mrs H, the Commission conducted an inquiry into allegations of sexual harassment against the head of delegation of, presumably, another of its delegations. Following disciplinary proceedings, the official was removed from his post on the ground of having committed 'very serious misconduct' which amounted to 'an offence under ordinary law, which cannot be excused by the applicant's state of health or by any other circumstance'; the Commission action was upheld by the Court of First Instance and, on appeal, by the Court of Justice.[70] More recently, however, the Commission has been accused of failing to take action in the face of sexual harassment allegedly committed by an official's hierarchical superior; the matter is now pending before the Court of First Instance.[71]

IV. WHY THE EUROPEAN PARLIAMENT SHOULD NOT CONCERN ITSELF WITH HUMAN RIGHTS

The same types of reason which serve to justify the Parliament's assuming responsibilities in the area of human rights protection may indicate the limits of its proper role.

A. Structural Considerations

The caricature of a parliament as 'a big meeting of more or less idle people' with unlimited time, vanity, (assumed) comprehension, and curiosity[72] is one which the European Parliament would do well not to dismiss out of hand. Not only does it shoulder vast amounts of legislative work, but the Parliament and its Members on their own initiative devote a great deal of time and energy to other topics which happen to interest them. In order to pursue an effective human rights policy, it seems logical that the Parliament would need the human and material resources, and decisional capacity, to match its appetite.

It is true that a large number of MEPs participate directly in the work of the various bodies within the Parliament which deal with human rights, either as their principal task (subcommittee on human rights, civil liberties committee) or incidentally. It is unlikely, given the other calls on MEPs' attention, that this work occupies a major place in the political activity of more than a handful of members. The same is almost certainly true of their personal and political group staffs, while the role of committee secretariats is primarily one of organization, rather than, for example, extensive research into and direct verification of, alleged or possible human rights

---

[70] Case T–549/93, *D* v. *Commission* [1995] ECR-SC I-A-13 and (in French) II–43; Case C–89/95 [1996] ECR I–53.

[71] Case T–136/98, *G* v. *Commission* [1998] OJ C327/33.

[72] W. Bagehot cited by M. Westlake, *A Modern Guide to the European Parliament* (1994), frontispiece.

violations. The Parliament's directorate general for committees does include a human rights unit, though at the last count this boasted just three A-grade staff, who can hardly be expected to exercise *a priori* control over all the stances the Parliament adopts on human rights matters. Unlike the governments which comprise the Council, the Parliament does not have a fully staffed foreign service with the necessary contacts to ascertain and analyse what is really happening in a given State, or a very extensive network of third country delegations, such as those of the Commission.[73]

This relative paucity of resources should not impinge seriously on the Parliament's capacity to evaluate the human rights dimension in legislative proposals, which may surface in the general political debate,[74] or in relation to alleged human rights violations in the Member States, where the MEPs live, work, and for the most part have available to them the resources of their political party and of the national administrations. Equally, where a parliamentary resolution is based on the work of a committee, such as the annual reports on human rights throughout the world, and on respect for human rights in the European Union,[75] the Parliament's position will have been the subject of detailed and careful scrutiny and considered judgement.[76] The same may not necessarily be so of resolutions following 'debates on topical and urgent subjects of major importance'; though restricted to five in number every session week,[77] they systematically include one or more resolutions on human rights violations. The underlying motions for resolutions are drafted, tabled, debated, and voted within a very short timescale, and necessarily run the twin dangers of factual error or platitudinous posing to a much greater extent than the general run of the Parliament's political initiatives. While factual error may be more of a potential than a real problem—most of the resolutions deal with notorious and well-documented breaches or potential breaches, while 'repeat resolutions' revisiting problem situations which have been the subject of previous resolutions are not uncommon—there is no fail-safe mechanism to stop the Parliament making hasty judgements on the basis of mistaken, or perhaps deliberately distorted, evidence. In accordance with a principle of 'institutional subsidiarity', the Parliament might be well advised to reconsider its rather liberal attitude to the adoption of 'urgent' human rights resolutions.[78]

B. Formal Constraints

The formal constraints on the Parliament's human rights activities are most explicit where its formal powers are strongest, to wit, in the area of the application of Community law. Outside the ambit of the application of the codecision and assent procedures, the Parliament is unable to enforce its views on whether an item of draft

[73] The delegations play a role, e.g., in the monitoring of the implementation of budget heading B7–7020, European initiative for democracy and the protection of human rights (written question E–1036/98, [1998] OJ C323/108).

[74] The opponents of the tobacco advertising ban, e.g., relied *inter alia* on its impact on the freedom of commercial speech (Dir. 98/43/EC, [1998] OJ L213/9; see also Case C–377/98, *Germany* v. *Parliament and Council*, pending).

[75] See respectively, [1999] OJ C98/270 (world 1997–8) and 279 (EU 1997).

[76] And, by all accounts, a good deal of lobbying by the governments concerned in many cases.

[77] The right to table such a motion is also limited to the political groups or 29 members (Rule 47).

[78] There are of course many cases where such urgency is well justified, e.g. where a notorious breach is on-going or likely to occur in the near future.

legislation respects human rights standards, and, unlike the other political institutions or the Member States, would in any case be unable to initiate legal proceedings to test the matter. Parliamentary initiatives in this area are subject to judicial review, at least where they are 'intended to produce legal effects *vis-à-vis* third parties'. While the Court has on occasion appeared to adopt a rather flexible interpretation of Article 7 (*ex* Article 4) EC,[79] the Parliament did have the dubious honour of being the first Community institution to see one of its acts, *in casu* a resolution of uncertain legal effect, struck down by the Court of Justice for lack of competence.[80] Similarly, the Parliament's supervisory mechanisms for promoting human rights protection within the Community are subject to specific limitations which are, in principle, amenable to judicial review: no inquiry committee may investigate matters which are *sub judice*, a petitioner may only complain of a 'matter which comes within the Community's fields of activity', the Ombudsman may only investigate maladministration by Community institutions or bodies.[81] The underlying principle was formulated by the Court of Justice as being that '[in] accordance with the balance of powers between the institutions provided for by the Treaties, the practice of [one institution] cannot deprive the other institutions of a prerogative granted to them by the Treaties themselves'.[82]

In matters outside the direct jurisdiction of the Community, the formal constraints are weaker; the lack of judicial control over the outer pillars, now mitigated by the optional system of preliminary rulings under Article 35 (*ex* Article K.7) TEU, is well-known. In this area, other forms of constraint may come into play: by analogy with the principle of the institutional balance so dear to the Parliament in its Community manifestation, it should take care to show due respect for the legal and political prerogatives of the governmental actors involved in a given human rights issue, whether those of the Community, the Member States, or third countries.

C. Political

The effectiveness of the Union's initiatives in favour of human rights protection is both a political and a moral imperative, and is rightly attracting increasing attention from the institutions, as witness the Commission's 1996 report on the implementation of measures intended to promote observance of human rights and democratic principles and the Parliament' s resolution thereon. [83] In this regard, the Parliament might well give some consideration to whether the pursuit of what appears to be an autonomous human rights policy, particularly in regard to third countries, necessarily contributes to the effectiveness of the efforts of the other institutions, and particularly the Council. While condemnatory resolutions may sound well in the media, and may well give some comfort to oppressed groups and individuals, it is difficult to deny that the most effective human rights protection is assured when the government of the country concerned is persuaded to co-operate.[84] Governments listen to

[79] See in particular its judgment in Case C–248/91, *Parliament* v. *Commission* [1993] ECR I–3685.
[80] Case 108/83, *Luxembourg* v. *Parliament* [1984] ECR 1945.
[81] Arts. 193, 194, and 195 (*ex* Arts. 138c, 138d, and 138e) EC, respectively.
[82] Case 149/85, *Wybot* v. *Faure* [1986] ECR 2391, 2409, at para. 23.
[83] COM(96)0672 (covering the year 1995) and [1998] OJ C14/399.
[84] N. Valticos, 'Droits fondamentaux de l'homme et compétence des Etats', in J. O'Reilly (ed.), *Human Rights and Constitutional Law* (1992), 50.

governments, and the Council is rather better placed than the Parliament to conduct 'strategies based on political decision-making, pressure and exposure' which are more likely to produce results.[85]

Internal considerations may also militate in favour of the Parliament channelling its efforts towards influencing, and co-operating with, the other institutions. Under the Community Treaties, in those areas where it does not enjoy co-decisional powers the Parliament can exert the most influence on decisional outcomes where it acts in concert with the Commission. It is true that the Union's foreign policy is conducted under different rules which reserve a much less important place for these institutions; however, if the Parliament wishes to see this policy (which includes a major human rights element) brought into the Community fold, it will almost certainly have to accept that the Council be empowered to act on behalf of the Union (perhaps with a concomitantly greater degree of parliamentary scrutiny), and thereafter respect that distribution of competences. In its resolution of 19 December 1997 on the implementation of human rights measures, the Parliament has already expressly recognized the necessity for 'the closest possible cooperation' between the three institutions 'if endeavours on behalf of human rights are to be successful'.[86] That said, if the Council wants the Parliament to show a greater degree of self-restraint in order not to encroach on its activities,[87] the Council should in turn show itself willing both to consult the Parliament and accord its views due weight.

One final consideration is that where it is clear that the Parliament will not, in fact, be able to make any contribution to preventing or remedying a breach, it should abstain from taking a position on the matter rather than nourishing expectations it cannot hope to fulfil.

D. 'Give a Dog a Bad Name'—A Cautionary Tale

It is the summer of 1989, on the eve of the third elections to the European Parliament. The Thatcher government has been in power for ten years and is deeply unpopular in certain quarters, including some outside the United Kingdom. On 20 June, the President of the European Parliament receives a letter from an MEP, who also happens to be a *député* at the *Assemblée nationale* and mayor of a small town near Paris, raising a surprising incident with overtones of racial discrimination. Some weeks before, a group of primary-school children, who had been issued a French collective passport, had received a letter refusing the issue of a visa for an intended educational visit to the United Kingdom; the refusal was based on the grounds that most of the children were of Maghreb origin, and that Her Majesty's government had decided, with effect from the end of April and for an indefinite period, to limit the entry of Maghreb nationals onto British territory. The letter is referred to the petitions committee; the Commission, asked to supply information, replies in September that the

[85] P. van Dijk, note 30 above, at 111, citing Van Boven. De Vries (note 23 above, at 12) notes that the Council has conducted an active policy of 'quiet diplomacy', by means of several dozen confidential démarches per year since 1981, and, more recently, has resorted to public declarations to express human rights concerns.

[86] [1998] OJ C14/399.

[87] A Council official, presumably speaking in his own name, made a remark to this effect at the Vienna conference launching the Agenda of the *Comité des Sages* on 9 Oct. 1998.

conditions of entry and the presence of third-country nationals on the territory of the Member States is a matter of national competence.

The committee is not satisfied; before taking the matter further, it invites the petitioner, now no longer an MEP, to provide a copy of the United Kingdom regulations. On 30 January 1990, the petitioner sends by fax a copy of the letter refusing the visa request; the item is included on the committee's agenda of the following day.

In preparation for the meeting, a parliamentary official rings the British Embassy in Paris for a copy of the offending regulations. The call elicits two interesting pieces of information. In the first place, the letter refusing the visa is wholly false, and neither emanated from the UK authorities nor represents its position. Secondly, and perhaps even more striking, the fact that the letter is false had been communicated to the school in the first week of June by the British Embassy (by telephone and by letter), and to the petitioner by the British Embassy (letter of 21 June), by the French Minister of Education, a certain Lionel Jospin (letter of 24 June), and by the French Ministry of Foreign Affairs (letter received at the petitioner's office on 6 July).[88]

High drama at the petitions committee that afternoon; members' indignation at the UK government's intolerance of innocent schoolchildren is now turned on the petitioner, who is invited to comment on the matter. With cheek enough for two faces, the petitioner replies in April 1990, that 'it now clearly appears that . . . the letter was false . . . the petition can no longer be considered well founded'. Consideration of the petition is closed, though it leads to a spat in plenary between two British members during the debate on the committee's annual report.[89]

The false letter incident is clearly untypical; it may nonetheless serve as a warning in a number of respects. Scathing condemnations of apparent breaches of human rights, whether within the Member States or in third States, may, in political and organizational terms, cost the Parliament little or nothing; there is a danger, if these are not firmly based on fact, that that is what they are worth. In the present case, the curiosity or scepticism of an official helping the committee, perhaps less consciously and certainly less heroically, than the Dutch boy who stuck his hand in the dyke, probably rescued the Parliament from adopting just such a condemnation. The Commission is under a moral duty at least[90] to assist the committee, though it does not consider itself bound, or did not in this case, to verify the facts on which a petition is based. Whether such a restricted approach would be justified in the normal case of a complaint submitted by a member of the public, it is certainly more understandable regarding one raised by a triple-mandate elected public representative. While the murky origins of the incident will probably never be clarified, it is difficult to find a charitable explanation of the petitioner's maintenance of the complaint after June 1989, or to see it as anything other than an attempt to score a political point at the expense of both the European Parliament and the UK government. The Parliament's blushes were spared largely because the matter was dealt with by a committee; had

---

[88] It also transpired that a collective passport may not be issued in France in respect of persons of other nationalities.

[89] Debates of the European Parliament, 14 June 1990, Annex to OJ No 3-391/311.

[90] Under the interinstitutional agreement on petitions of 12 Apr. 1989 [1989] OJ C120/43 and 90, the legal effects of which are unclear.

the matter arisen just a month or so earlier, the petitioner would have been able to propose that the matter be dealt with as a topic for urgent debate, with who knows what consequences.

V. WHEN SHOULD THE PARLIAMENT CONCERN ITSELF WITH HUMAN RIGHTS PROTECTION?

It may not be easy to synthesize the various arguments for and against the Parliament's taking an active interest in human rights protection, or to establish a generally applicable bright line test. The main thesis of the present chapter is however that the Parliament should, at least on a case-by-case basis, consider whether it can and should take a position on a human rights issue. As noted above, there are a number of circumstances in which it is under a legal and political duty to do so. This is particularly the case where human rights matters arise in the context of proposed Community legislation, such as the protection of the right to commercial speech, in regulating aspects of advertising,[91] or the right to bodily integrity in relation to the use of biotechnological techniques.[92] While, in most of these areas, Parliament disposes of sufficient internal mechanisms and formal powers to take and enforce a human rights position, it does not follow that this will take priority over other economic and political considerations. In any case, the Parliament should be particularly vigilant where a Community institution is alleged to be responsible for either an individual or a systemic violation of human rights.[93]

The fact that the Court of Justice will generally be able to exercise its powers of review in these areas does not deprive parliamentary scrutiny of its utility, for the reasons adumbrated above.[94] Furthermore, where the Court of Justice is seised of human rights questions of a general character, the Parliament should consider making greater use of its (limited) powers of intervention in legal proceedings.[95] Its well-argued intervention in the transparency decision case, for example, rescued the main issue from the unfortunate procedural context in which it had been placed by the application, and encouraged the Court to go some way towards recognizing the fundamental nature of the right of access to administrative documents.[96] It has been suggested by a judge of

[91] Apart from tobacco advertising mentioned above, the preamble to the 1989 Television Broadcasting Dir. notes that the right to provide television services is a specific manifestation of the freedom of expression enshrined in Art. 10 ECHR (Dir. 89/552/EEC [1989] OJ L298/23).

[92] Owing to a quirk in the institutional system for the adoption of implementing legislation, neither the Council nor the Parliament was able in 1997 to prevent the marketing of genetically modified foodstuffs (see K. Bradley, 'Alien Corn, or the Transgenic Procedural Maze', in M. van Schendelen (ed.), *EU Committees as Influential Policy-Makers* (1998).

[93] The H case outlined above is a probable example of the former; for an example of the latter see Case C–37/89, *Weiser* v. *Caisse nationale des Barreaux français* [1990] ECR I–2395.

[94] Sect. III. B. 3.

[95] The Parliament has no general right to intervene either in the preliminary ruling procedure, where the majority of such questions arise, or in the procedure for rulings on the compatibility with the Treaty of international agreements.

[96] Case C–58/94, *Netherlands* v. *Council* [1996] ECR I–2169; see K. Bradley 'La transparence de l'Union européenne: une évidence ou un tromp l'oeil?', *CDE*, forthcoming, sect. VI(b).

the English High Court that *amicus* and *Brandeis* briefs would be appreciated in the context of constitutional adjudication on human rights questions,[97] and it seems likely that the Court of Justice could also benefit from such submissions. Consideration could also be given of importing into the Community judicial system a mechanism equivalent to that in France, whereby a fixed number of members of the *Assemblée nationale* or the *Sénat* may refer to the *Conseil constitutionnel* the question of the constitutional validity of a law; even if restricted to human rights matters, this would enable the European Parliament to raise potential breaches before they occur, particularly in those areas where it does not enjoy co-decisional powers.[98]

Where a systemic breach of human rights arises from the provisions of the Treaty itself, or of other legal instruments of the Union having treaty status, the jurisdiction of both the Court of Justice and the European Court of Human Rights is, for different reasons, excluded in principle. While deprived of formal powers in relation to amending the Treaty, the Parliament may draw attention to such matters and press for their inclusion on the Union's agenda for reform. It has recently been suggested, for example, that the fact that the parties in cases before the Court of Justice are unable to respond to the opinion of the Advocate General may constitute a violation of Article 6 of the ECHR, as interpreted by the European Court of Human Rights in *Vermeulen* and its progeny.[99] In the exercise of its general supervisory functions, the Parliament could examine the problem and, should the view that there is a breach prevail,[100] propose a remedy. Closer to home, in October 1997 the European Commission examined a complaint, submitted by a British citizen resident in Gibraltar unable to vote in European Parliament elections,[101] alleging a breach of Article 3 of Protocol No. 1 to the European Convention which guarantees 'free elections . . . under conditions which will ensure the free expression of the opinion of the people in the choice of the legislature'.[102] The Commission decided, by eleven votes to six, that Article 3 does not apply to 'supranational bodies which exercise functions in a legislative process having direct impact within the State concerned'.[103] By virtue of the principle of *audi alteram partem*, it would seem only correct that the Community should be able to present its point of view on the question before a final decision is taken, though neither the Parliament nor the other institutions have so far shown any interest in the case.[104]

---

[97] S. Sedley, 'Human Rights: a Twenty-First Century Agenda' [1995] *PL* 398.

[98] As the question would, in principle, only arise where the Commission and the Council are of the view that there is no risk of a breach, one can assume that such a mechanism would be sparingly used.

[99] *Vermeulen*, judgment of 20 Mar. 1996, *Reinhardt and Slimane-Kaïd*, judgement of 31 Mar. 1998.

[100] In the author's personal opinion, this view is based on an unjustified identification of the role of the various national legal officials (who, despite their independence, derive their authority from the executive) considered by the Human Rights Court, with that of the AG at the ECJ (whose function is judicial and whose independence is structural).

[101] The exclusion of Gibraltese voters arises from Annex II to the 1976 Act on the direct elections to the European Parliament, which has effectively the same status as a Treaty provision.

[102] App. No. 24833/94, *Matthews* v. *United Kingdom*, decision of 29 Oct. 1997.

[103] The Commission thereby avoided the issue of which Community institution(s) should be considered its legislature. On 18 Feb. 1999, the Court of Human Rights by a large majority found the UK to be in breach of Art. 3 of Prot. No. 1.

[104] In principle the Commission should represent the Community for these purposes, though the question is of primary interest to the Parliament. The Community has no *locus standi* before the European

As the Union's institutional system is founded on the representation of interests, the Parliament should pay particular attention to possible or actual violations of the human rights of those categories of persons who enjoy no direct representation in this system, such as third-country citizens within the territory of the Member States and, depending on the circumstances, in third countries. While such parliamentary action would normally be concerned with systemic violations, there is no reason to exclude individual cases where action by the Parliament would have some chance of improving an existing or potential situation; in this regard, and in accordance with the spirit of the age, the Parliament may wish to consider doing less, but doing it better. Similarly, in its capacity as policy initiator, the Parliament should promote those categories of human rights which are inadequately catered for in the Treaties,[105] and itself draw up the outlines of an autonomous human rights policy[106] which the Commission could then propose formally.[107]

To end on a more philosophical note, it is clearly not sufficient, in the European Union or in any other polity, simply to establish human rights standards and ensure their respect by well-functioning legal and political mechanisms, if substantive equality before the law is not also guaranteed. It has been observed in this regard that:

> [t]he notion that the prime function of human rights and indeed of the rule of law is to protect the weak against the strong is not mere sentimentality. It is the child of an era of history in which equality of treatment and opportunity has become perceived . . . as an unqualified good, and of a significant recognition that you do not achieve equality by proclaiming it but only by levelling up from the inherited and systemic inequalities which make some social actors too weak to make use of their rights and others strong enough to stifle their aspirations.[108]

Along with the other institutions, the Parliament must base its action not only on fine principles and worthy objectives but the necessity to achieve concrete outcomes; not just the protection of rights, but the empowerment of individuals and groups. It is thus that the Parliament can best remain true to its vocation as 'the indispensable means of expression' of 'the democratic peoples of Europe'[109] and 'secure the universal and effective recognition and observance' of the rights deemed universal by the international community fifty years ago.

Court of Human Rights; under rule 36(2) of the Court's rules of procedure, however, the President may invite any interested person to present written observations or take part in the oral hearing in a case.

[105] At the Vienna Conference in Oct. 1998, Mrs Lalumière proposed that economic and social rights be treated equally with civil and political rights, and stressed the need to take account of the possible threat to human rights posed by scientific innovation.

[106] The Parliament's regular resolutions on human rights throughout the world refer in their title to 'the Union's human rights policy'; see also Weiler, note 48 above, at 629–42.

[107] Under the second para. of Art. 138b, the Parliament enjoys a half-baked 'right of initiative' which still requires a formal Commission proposal.

[108] Sedley, note 97 above, at 399.

[109] According to the preamble to the Single European Act.

The Past and Future Role of the European Court of Justice in the Protection of Human Rights

BRUNO DE WITTE

The question of the role of the European Court of Justice in protecting human rights within the Community legal order is an evergreen of EC legal studies. It is dealt with by all the textbooks on EC law and has also been analysed in a large number of special doctrinal studies. There is no need to repeat here what has so often been written before. In the light of the overall perspective of the present research project, the emphasis will rather be on a *critical evaluation* of the European Court's performance in this field so far (Part II), on an examination of the *new perspectives* opened up by the likely entry into force of the EC and EU Treaty revisions agreed in Amsterdam (Part III), and on a discussion of possible *proposals for change* so as to improve the protection of human rights in the European Union legal order (Part IV). Those Parts will be preceded by a recapitulation of the evolution so far (Part I); again, the intention of that first Part is not to march along well-trodden paths but to offer an *aide-mémoire* which may help the reader through the rest of this chapter.

I. THE PLACE OF HUMAN RIGHTS IN THE CASE LAW OF THE EUROPEAN COURT OF JUSTICE

A. Defining the Scope of this Chapter

In this first section, I shall set out to clarify the overall subject of this chapter, in its own terms and also with respect to other chapters in this book dealing with related topics, by considering in turn the terms 'European Court of Justice', 'case law', and 'human rights'.

Attention will be centred, throughout this chapter, on the role of one particular institution of the European Union, namely the 'European Court of Justice'. This generic term includes the ECJ properly speaking as well as the Court of First Instance. The latter is not a separate institution but rather a new judicial body which, in the words of Article 225 (*ex* Article 168a) of the EC Treaty, is 'attached' to the

Court of Justice.[1] In this chapter the term 'European Court of Justice' or simply 'Court of Justice' will be used with reference to both judicial bodies taken together, whereas the abbreviation 'ECJ' will be used to refer to the upper *échelon* specifically; the term 'Court of First Instance' and the abbreviation 'CFI' will both be used with specific reference to the lower of the two courts.

The analysis of the *case law* of the Court of Justice will not be limited to the actual cases involving the application of human rights, but also includes rulings of the Court which have had an indirect effect on the guarantee of human rights in the European Union, for instance by defining the duties of national courts in this field, or by defining the scope of the competence of the EU's political institutions in the field of human rights.

The most difficult preliminary definition is that of the term *human rights* itself. The term appears only rarely in the case law of the European Court. It is used when reference is made to international treaties for the protection of human rights, more particularly the European Convention on Human Rights.[2] It is also used with reference to the 'human rights clauses' which the European Community has inserted in agreements with third countries.[3] The European Union itself is bound, according to Article 6(2) (*ex* Article F(2)) of the EU Treaty, by *fundamental rights*: '[t]he Union shall respect fundamental rights, as guaranteed by the European Convention for the Protection of Human Rights and Fundamental Freedoms signed in Rome on 4 November 1950 and as they result from the constitutional traditions common to the Member States, as general principles of Community law'.

The wording of Article 6(2) makes it clear that 'fundamental rights' should not be seen as a narrower sub-category of human rights, but rather as a potentially broader notion. Beyond the rights recognized in international documents (at least, those included in the ECHR), it also embraces those recognized in the *constitutional law* of the Member States of the EU; in fact, the term 'fundamental rights' is more commonly used in constitutional law than the term 'human rights'. Things are complicated, however, by the final words of Article 6: 'as general principles of Community law'. This is, in part, a *coup de chapeau* to the pioneering action of the European Court of Justice. Many years before the Member States had resolved, in Maastricht, to insert an express reference to fundamental rights in the EU Treaty, the ECJ had decided that fundamental rights were part of the unwritten general principles of Community law which it enforces; and, even after the enactment of Article 6, it is still as general principles that fundamental rights are enforced by the ECJ today.[4]

The problem with this, for the present purpose of definition, is that the Court of Justice does not clearly distinguish between fundamental rights and *other general principles of Community law*. Indeed, it had recognized what could be called 'princi-

[1] L.N. Brown and T. Kennedy, *The Court of Justice of the European Communities* (1994), 81.

[2] The most obvious example is *Opinion 2/94 (Accession by the Community to the European Convention for the Protection of Human Rights and Fundamental Freedoms)* [1996] ECR I–1759.

[3] The human rights clause in one such agreement, the Co-operation Agreement with India, was considered by the ECJ in Case C–268/94, *Portugal* v. *Council* [1996] ECR I–6177.

[4] This does not only result from the wording of Art. 6 itself, but also from the fact that Art. 46 of the same Treaty of Maastricht did not extend the jurisdiction of the ECJ to Art. 6, so that the Court, even after Maastricht, could only continue to apply its doctrine of unwritten general principles.

ples of administrative law' already in the early days of the Community, in judgments about the Coal and Steel Community,[5] long before it decided to include fundamental rights in the general principles category. In order not to stray away from the overall subject of this book (which is human rights), I will not deal with the general principles of Community law as a general category, but only with those general principles that can be ranged within the sub-category of 'fundamental rights'.[6] Within the latter category, one should put first those principles for which the Court of Justice itself uses the language of 'rights' and 'freedoms', such as *freedom of expression*, the *right to privacy*, the *right to property*, the *freedom to pursue one's trade or business*. To those rights and freedoms one should certainly add the *principle of equality*; although it is not described as a 'right', it is a traditional, and indeed extremely important, part of international human rights documents and constitutional rights chapters.

In contrast, the *principle of proportionality* is more of a borderline case. Proportionality is used as a *criterion* for deciding whether an interference with fundamental rights is legitimate; to that extent, it must be considered here. But the ECJ also, and more often, applies proportionality as a *general principle in its own right*, quite apart from any other fundamental right that may be affected;[7] such broader use of proportionality is part of the administrative law systems of some European countries (foremost among them, Germany and France) but is not part of human rights treaties. I shall not deal directly with such 'autonomous' application of the proportionality principle in the case law of the ECJ and CFI.[8]

On the other hand, it should be emphasized that the analysis of the case law of the Court of Justice on the general principles of law, which is the primary focus of this chapter, does not exhaust the question of judicial protection of human rights in the EC legal order. Indeed, certain *specific human rights* are guaranteed by *written EC law*, namely by the text of the EC Treaty and by secondary acts of Community law.

The most obvious cases are three specific embodiments of the *principle of equality,* or *non-discrimination*, all of which have given rise to a large number of Court cases, which in turn have had a major impact on the evolution of EC law and have provided appreciable benefits to large categories of persons. Despite their importance, and despite the fact that the doctrinal approach of the ECJ to the interpretation of those specific equality principles resembles that which it uses with regard to the general

---

[5] Thus, the principle of proportionality was recognized by the ECJ in Case 8/55, *Fédéchar* v. *High Authority* [1954–56] ECR 245, at 299; and the principle of legal certainty in Cases 42 and 49/59, *SNUPAT* v. *High Authority* [1961] ECR 53, at 87.

[6] For a recent survey of the role of general principles of EC law as a *general category*, see J.A. Usher, *General Principles of EC Law* (1998).

[7] For an example in which the ECJ examines the alleged breach of the principle of proportionality as a separate ground, *in addition to* the grounds based on a violation of fundamental rights, such as non-discrimination, the right to property, and the freedom to pursue one's trade, see Case C–280/93, *Germany* v. *Council* [1994] ECR I–4973, at 5068.

[8] I refer, for a detailed analysis, to G. de Búrca, 'The Principle of Proportionality and its Application in EC Law' (1993) 13 *YEL* 105; N. Emiliou, *The Principle of Proportionality in European Law: A Comparative Study* (1996); and A. de Moor-van Vugt, *Maten en gewichten: het evenredigheidsbeginsel in Europees perspectief* (1995).

principle of equality,[9] I will leave aside two of those specific principles because they are sufficiently dealt with elsewhere in this volume:

(a) *Gender equality*, as guaranteed by Article 141 (*ex* Article 119) EC Treaty and by several EC Directives, is covered by Catherine Barnard's contribution to this volume.

(b) *Non-discrimination on the ground of nationality* is guaranteed, in general, by Article 12 (*ex* Article 6) EC and, more specifically, by provisions of the EC Treaty such as Article 39 (*ex* Article 48) and by acts of secondary EC law, such as Regulation 1612/68 on the rights of migrant workers and their families. This principle has gradually developed, not least due to the generous reading adopted by the ECJ, into an almost universal right to equal treatment for nationals of Member States residing in a Member State other than their own.[10] By its wording, Article 12 could also be read as prohibiting discrimination against *third-country nationals*. But the European Court of Justice has, so far, never challenged the interpretation adopted by the other EC institutions that Article 12 only applies to nationals of EU Member States.[11] On the other hand, the European Court of Justice gave due recognition to the limited forms of equal treatment for third-country nationals which it found in external agreements concluded between the EC and such third States as Turkey or the Maghreb countries.[12]

(c) The third written recognition of the non-discrimination principle is to be found in Article 34(3) (*ex* Article 40(3)), second sentence of the EC Treaty, which states that the common organization of the *agricultural markets* to be set up by the Community 'shall exclude any discrimination between producers or consumers within the Community'. The rich practice of the Court of Justice about this provision blends so smoothly with the application of the general principle of equality in other fields of EC activity that it can easily be included within the scope of this chapter.[13]

[9] For a cross-cutting analysis of the many forms of the equality principle in EC law, see K. Lenaerts, 'L'égalité de traitement en droit communautaire—Un principe unique aux apparences multiples' [1991] *CDE* 3; Usher, note 6 above, at chap. 2.

[10] The scope of the equal treatment rights thus guaranteed to EU nationals is described by S. O'Leary, *The Evolving Concept of Community Citizenship* (1996), chaps. 5 to 7. Although, technically, the equal treatment rights are not part of the Treaty chap. on Citizenship of the Union (Art. 17 EC), in substance, equality is, together, with the right of residence, the core element of Citizenship of the Union. See further discussion in other chaps. of this vol.

[11] One could also argue that unequal treatment of third-country nationals, while not contrary to Art. 12 EC, can be contrary, depending on the context, to the *general principle of equality*. This argument is developed, with specific reference to the exclusion of third-country nationals from the social security benefits granted in Reg. 1408/71, by H. Verschueren, 'EC Social Security Coordination Excluding Third Country Nationals: Still in Line with Fundamental Rights after the *Gaygusuz* Judgment?' (1997) 34 *CML Rev.* 991.

[12] See the survey by S. Peers, 'Towards Equality: Actual and Potential Rights of Third-Country Nationals in the European Union' (1996) 33 *CML Rev.* 7. The human rights of third country nationals are discussed in more detail elsewhere in this vol.

[13] For a *separate* discussion of the Court of Justice's case law on this written principle of non-discrimination, see R. Barents, *The Agricultural Law of the EC* (1994), chap. 17.

Finally, there are the common market freedoms (free movement of goods, persons, services, and capital), which have gradually been turned by the Court of Justice into *fundamental freedoms* which have, according to some authors, a quasi-human rights character.[14] Those fundamental freedoms, particularly the free movement of persons, have been important vehicles for the affirmation of individual rights but also appear, at times, to be a threat to national constitutional values and rights.[15]

Any conclusions reached here with regard to the 'general principles' case law should be counterbalanced by looking at the central role played by the Court of Justice in shaping the more specialized areas of human rights protection just mentioned. Indeed, it is largely due to the European Court of Justice that the full human rights potential of those provisions has been revealed.

B. The Nature of Human Rights as Court-based 'General Principles of Community Law'

Having defined the central subject of this chapter as being the role of the European Court of Justice in promoting human rights *as a general category*, I will start by briefly reconsidering the way in which those human rights were introduced by the Court into the EC legal order. The ECSC and EEC Treaties, as adopted in the 1950s, did not contain a chapter listing the fundamental rights which the Community institutions should respect. The silence of the Treaty may have been deliberate, indicating possibly the drafters' intention that the courts of each individual Member State should be 'the ultimate protection of that country's citizenry against an unlawful intrusion of the Community into the realm of its (national) protected rights'.[16] But, if that was the intention, it soon became incompatible with the principle of the supremacy of Community law, as it was formulated in the 1960s by the European Court of Justice; if Community acts were to prevail over national law, including national *constitutional* law, then judicial review of those Community acts could only be based on Community law itself. The Court of Justice therefore decided to fill a threatening gap in the legal protection of individuals by formulating its own doctrine of the protection of fundamental rights as an unwritten part of the *Community* legal order. This dialectic relationship between the question of the supremacy of EC law and that of the protection of fundamental rights is well expressed by two subsequent paragraphs of the *Internationale Handelsgesellschaft* judgment of 1970:

> [T]he validity of a Community measure or its effect within a Member State cannot be affected by allegations that it runs counter to either fundamental rights as formulated by the constitution of that State or the principles of a national constitutional structure.

[14] For a doctrinal exposition of the similarity between those fundamental freedoms and the 'traditional' fundamental rights, see A. Bleckmann, *Europarecht* (1997), 269–78 (building on a much earlier article by the same author: 'Die Freiheiten des Gemeinsamen Marktes als Grundrechte', in R. Bieber *et al.* (eds.), *Das Europa der Zweiten Generation; Gedächtnisschrift für Christoph Sasse* (1981), ii, 655). The Court of Justice itself has called the free movement of workers a 'fundamental right' (see, among other judgments, Case 222/86, *Unectef* v. *Georges Heylens* [1987] ECR 4097, at 4117).

[15] The role of those freedoms, and the tension between economic integration and social welfare, are analysed elsewhere in this vol.

[16] H. Rasmussen, *On Law and Policy in the European Court of Justice* (1986), 390. See also, on the reasons for the absence of a Declaration of Rights in the EC Treaties, J.H.H. Weiler, 'Methods of Protection: Towards a Second and Third Generation of Protection', in A. Cassese, A. Clapham, and J. Weiler (eds.), *Human Rights and the European Community: Methods of Protection* (1991) 571–5.

However, an examination should be made as to whether or not any analogous guarantee inherent in Community law has been disregarded. In fact, respect for fundamental rights forms an integral part of the general principles of Community law protected by the Court of Justice. The protection of such rights, whilst inspired by the constitutional traditions common to the Member States, must be ensured within the framework of the structure and objectives of the Community.[17]

In 'filling the gap', the ECJ made use of *general principles*, a source of law which both international and national courts have traditionally used to fill perceived lacunae in their legal system. Yet, whereas Article 38(I)(c) of the Statute of the International Court of Justice allows that Court, in general terms, to make use of 'general principles of law' in its judicial determinations, the EEC Treaty explicitly allowed the ECJ to apply 'general principles common to the laws of the Member States' only within the specific context of the non-contractual liability of the Community (Article 288(2) (*ex* Article 215(2)). Despite this, it could be argued that the signatories of the Treaty had accepted that Community law could include more than written rules alone. Article 230 (*ex* Article 173) of the Treaty refers, among the grounds for annulment of Community acts, to 'infringement of this treaty *or of any rule of law relating to its application*'. This formula, in addition to the fact that Article 220 (*ex* Article 164) describes the general function of the Court to be that of ensuring that 'in the interpretation and application of this Treaty *the law* is observed', may justify the European Court's early, and by now firmly established, doctrine that general principles of law form a source of Community law in their own right. Today, the express reference to general principles in Article 288 (*ex* Article 215) is seen as merely one application of a wider rule that the Community is bound by the general principles common to the laws of the Member States.

Those general principles of law have now become a very frequent ground for the review of the legality of Community acts by the Court of First Instance and the European Court of Justice, each within the limits of its powers. And fundamental rights are at the core of those general principles. They are a vivid testimony to the influence of national constitutional law on the development of the European Community legal order. In this respect, it has often been noted that the recognition, by the European Court of Justice, of the existence of an unwritten 'Community Bill of Rights' was, to a large extent, the result of a direct challenge by the German Constitutional Court (and, to a lesser extent, the Italian Constitutional Court) of the idea that Community law could prevail over national constitutions.[18] But it is less often appreciated how closely the doctrine of the general principles of Community law itself and its application to fundamental rights are closely modelled on, and possibly inspired by, developments in French constitutional law.

---

[17] Case 11/70, *Internationale Handelsgesellschaft mbH* v. *Einfuhr- und Vorratsstelle für Getreide und Futtermittel* [1970] ECR 1125, at paras. 3 and 4 of the judgment.
[18] The story of this conflict between courts has often been told. See G.F. Mancini, 'The Making of a Constitution for Europe' (1989) 26 *CML Rev.* 608 ff; Rasmussen, note 16 above, at 393ff; R.M. Dallen, 'An Overview of European Community Protection of Human Rights with some Special References to the UK' (1990) 27 *CML Rev.* 766–72; with special reference to the attitude of the Italian Constitutional Court, see M. Cartabia, *Principi inviolabili e integrazione europea* (1995), 95ff.

The French Constitution of 1958 resembled the EEC Treaty in being a 'Constitution without a Bill of Rights', which, even at the time of its adoption, formed an anomaly in the panorama of European constitutions. There are a few fundamental rights (such as the right to equal protection) in the text of the Constitution itself, and apart from that the Preamble refers to the rights to be found in the Declaration of Rights of 1789 and the Preamble to the previous French Constitution, that of 1946.[19] It is clear that, in the view of those who adopted the Constitution of the Fifth Republic, the Preamble 'was to be the expression of pious intentions, fine words, and possibly political obligations without any clear legal consequences';[20] the oblique references to fundamental rights which it contained were not meant to be binding on Parliament and enforceable by the *Conseil constitutionnel*. Yet, in its famous decision of 1971 on *Liberté d'association*, the *Conseil* held that it could review legislation (if only before its enactment) for breach of fundamental rights; in that landmark case, the right protected by the *Conseil* was freedom of association, which is not even mentioned in the 1789 Declaration of Rights, nor in the 1946 Preamble, but which the *Conseil* held to be one of the 'fundamental principles recognized by the laws of the Republic' to which the Preamble of the 1946 Constitution briefly refers. In one stroke, the *Conseil constitutionnel* created an extremely broad *bloc de constitutionnalité* incorporating a wide variety of sources of fundamental rights. The attitude of the *Conseil constitutionnel* (which may itself have been inspired in 1971 by the case law of the German Constitutional Court on the binding nature of the Preamble of the Constitution[21]) resembles the European Court's fundamental rights case law in two ways: first, by its creative *'manipulation' of the sources of law*, making fundamental rights part of the 'higher law' of the system, whereas that had not been intended by those who created the system (the drafters of the French Constitution and the Member States signing the Treaty of Rome); secondly, by the *importance assumed by general principles* which cannot be found with so many words in any specific Declaration of Rights but are derived by the Court itself from a variety of relevant sources. Particularly striking is the parallel between the *Conseil's* use of the 'fundamental principles recognized by the laws of the Republic' which allow it to delve freely in the vast mass of pre-1946 legislation and beyond, and the European Court's reference to the 'common constitutional traditions of the Member States', a large category which, again, leaves the final selection in the hands of the Court itself.

Clearly, by using unwritten principles instead of, or in addition to, rights expressly contained in the constitution, supreme courts enlarge their scope for creative lawmaking. One may note that even constitutional courts that, unlike the European and French courts, *did* have the benefit of an extensive catalogue of fundamental rights,

---

[19] Preamble to the 1958 Constitution, para. 1: '*Le peuple français proclame solennellement son attachement aux droits de l'homme et aux principes de la souveraineté nationale tels qu'ils sont définis par la Déclaration de 1789, confirmée et complétée par le Préambule de la Constitution de 1946.*'

[20] J. Bell, *French Constitutional Law* (1992), 66.

[21] P. Häberle, 'Theorieelemente eines allgemeinen juristischen Rezeptionsmodells', [1992] *Juristen Zeitung* 1037.

have nonetheless constitutionalized a number of rights that were not expressly laid down in the Constitution.[22]

Yet, a major difference between the European Court and the *Conseil constitutionnel* remains. Whereas the latter's fundamental rights *jurisprudence* effectively transformed its role in the French constitutional system, from the limited function of being a 'watchdog' protecting the executive against the parliament to that of a central institution of the French constitutional system,[23] the fundamental rights case law of the European Court of Justice caused a less profound transformation of its role. It was clear from the beginning that one of its main functions was to control the legitimacy of Community acts; the general principles of law were 'simply' added to the grounds of review provided by the text of the EEC Treaty.

Looking back at the development, it is undeniable that part of the ECJ's motivation for creating its Community doctrine of fundamental rights was to protect the supremacy of EC law from being rejected at the national level. The, at times, sceptical attitude of some national courts is a continuing spur for the Court of Justice to continue taking fundamental rights seriously. But the Court's activism must also be seen as a straightforward response to a problem that was revealed in the course of the 1960s, namely the Community's growing capacity to affect fundamental rights to an extent unforeseen at the time the European Communities were created.[24]

The bold move of the Court of Justice to read into the EC Treaty a 'Bill of Rights' which was not put there by the drafters of the Treaty was approved, afterwards, by the Member States, first in an informal way[25] and later formally through the adoption of Article 6 (*ex* Article F) of the EU Treaty. Although this Article F definitively sealed the legitimacy of the ECJ's doctrine, it also constituted an important setback. The new areas of co-operation organized by the EU Treaty outside the Community framework, namely Common Foreign and Security Policy and Justice and Home Affairs, were not made subject to the Court's jurisdiction (Article 46 (*ex* Article L) TEU), so that the Court was also precluded from extending its general principles doctrine to those new areas. The reluctance of the Member States to accept the discipline of judicial review in those sensitive areas has often been criticized. The Treaty of Amsterdam offers some improvement in this respect (see Part III below).

The Treaty of Maastricht (and the Treaty of Amsterdam) have left the European Union with an unwritten set of human rights, which is very unusual from a compar-

---

[22] In Germany, this occurs by means of the right to the 'free development of the personality' (Art. 2 of the *Grundgesetz*) which has become the receptacle for a number of unwritten individual rights; in Italy, the Constitutional Court has repeatedly held that the reference in Art. 2 of the Constitution to the 'inviolable rights of persons' means that there is an 'open list' of fundamental rights including, apart from the rights spelled out in the text of the Constitution, also a number of unwritten rights to be discovered by the Court on a case-by-case basis. An interesting comparative study of French and Italian case law in this matter is proposed by M.Cl. Ponthoreau, *La reconnaissance des droits non-écrits par les cours constitutionnelles italienne et française* (1994).

[23] Y. Mény, *Le système politique français* (1993), 150: '*organe marginal et technique, le Conseil Constitutionnel est devenu une pièce centrale du dispositif politique et constitutionnel*'. See also A. Stone, *The Birth of Judicial Politics in France: The Constitutional Council in Comparative Perspective* (1992), 230: '[t]he Council's current role and its terms of reference . . . have virtually no relation to the framers' intentions'.

[24] S. Weatherill, *Law and Integration in the European Union* (1995), 105–6.

[25] See the Joint Declaration by the European Parliament, the Council and the Commission on fundamental rights of 5 Apr. 1977, [1977] OJ C103/1.

ative perspective, and which makes the Court of Justice bear a particularly heavy task in developing those rights. It must be said, though, that the Court of Justice seems to relish this responsibility. In denying, in its famous *Opinion 2/94*,[26] that the European Community has the competence to accede to the European Convention on Human Rights, it has not facilitated the formal incorporation into EC law of that written and authoritative European Bill of Rights.

C. The Present State of the 'General Principles' Case Law

The detailed story of the development of the ECJ's case law on general principles of Community law and fundamental rights has been told many times, not least in the earlier European University Institute project on Human Rights in the European Union.[27] It may be recalled, in a nutshell, that the ECJ broke the 'silence of the Treaty' in the *Stauder* judgment of 1969 where it hinted at the fact that fundamental rights might be part of the general principles of Community law.[28] This was solemnly confirmed shortly afterwards in the *Internationale Handelsgesellschaft* judgment, where the ECJ added that it would draw inspiration from the common constitutional doctrines in shaping its general principles of Community law.[29] In 1974, the *Nold* case offered the occasion for the ECJ to add that also international human rights could provide inspiration,[30] and the Court considered the ECHR and national constitutional law in some detail in the *Hauer* judgment of 1979.[31] The next important moves took place around 1990, when the ECJ stated, in cases like *Wachauf*[32] and *Elliniki Radiophonia*[33] that its review powers also extended to *Member States'* acts, but only to the extent that those acts came within the sphere of Community law.

---

[26] *Opinion 2/94* [1996] ECR I–1759. The Opinion has been criticized by many commentators (and, in my view, rightly so) for its inadequate reasoning on the scope of Art. 308 (*ex* Art. 235) EC (see, among others: O. de Schutter and Y. Lejeune. 'L'adhésion de la Communauté à la Convention européenne des droits de l'homme—A propos de l'Avis 2/94 de la Cour de Justice des Communautés' [1996] *CDE* 567–78; G. Tiberi, 'La questione dell'adesione della Comunità alla convenzione europea dei diritti dell'uomo al vaglio della Corte di giustizia' [1997] *Rivista italiana di diritto pubblico comunitario* 450–8).

[27] *European Union—The Human Rights Challenge* (1991), 3 vols, more particularly: A. Clapham, *Human Rights and the European Community: A Critical Overview* (1991), i, 29–61, and Weiler, note 16 above, at 575–620. Other important surveys (each containing further bibliographical references) include: M. Hilf, 'The Protection of Fundamental Rights in the Community', in F. Jacobs (ed.), *European Law and the Individual* (1976), 145; M. Mendelson, 'The European Court of Justice and Human Rights' (1981) 1 *YEL* 125; I. Pernice, 'Gemeinschaftsverfassung und Grundrechtsschutz—Grundlagen, Bestand und Perspektiven' [1990] *NJW* 2409; H.-W. Rengeling, *Grundrechtsschutz in der Europäischen Gemeinschaft* (1993); N. Neuwahl, 'The Treaty on European Union: A Step Forward in the Protection of Human Rights?', in N.A. Neuwahl and A. Rosas, *The European Union and Human Rights* (1995), 1; R-E. Papadopoulou, *Principes généraux du droit et droit communautaire—Origines et concrétisation* (1996) 137–65; J. Kokott, 'Der Grundrechtsschutz im europäischen Gemeinschaftsrecht' [1996] *Archiv des öffentlichen Rechts* 599; B. Beutler, 'Artikel F—Der Grundrechtsschutz in der Union', in H. Groeben, J. Thiesing, and C.-D. Ehlermann (eds.), *Kommentar zum EU-/EG-Vertrag* (1997), i, 86–129; W. Hins and J.L. de Reede, 'Grondrechten, Europese integratie en nationale soevereiniteit', in L. Besselink, *Europese Unie en nationale soevereiniteit* (1997), 1; P. Craig and G. de Búrca, *EU Law—Text, Cases and Materials* (1998), 296–348.

[28] Case 29/69, *Stauder* v. *City of Ulm* [1969] ECR 419, at 425.

[29] Case 11/70, *Internationale Handelsgesellschaft* [1970] ECR 1125, at 1134.

[30] Case 4/73, *Nold* [1974] ECR 491, at 506.   [31] Case 44/79, *Hauer* [1979] ECR 3727, at 3744–7.

[32] Case 5/88, *Wachauf* [1989] ECR 2609, at 2639.

[33] Case 260/89, *Elliniki Radiophonia Tileorassi AE* v. *Dimotiki Etairia Pliroforissis and Sotirios Kouvelas* [1991] ECR I–2925, at 2964.

The present state of the general principles doctrine may best be summarized by quoting the account given recently by the ECJ itself, in a judgment of 29 May 1997:

> [A]s the Court has consistently held . . . fundamental rights form an integral part of the general principles of Community law whose observance the Court ensures. For that purpose, the Court draws inspiration from the constitutional traditions common to the Member States and from the guidelines supplied by international treaties for the protection of human rights on which the Member States have collaborated or of which they are signatories. The Convention [i.e. the ECHR] has special significance in that respect. As the Court has also held, it follows that measures are not acceptable in the Community which are incompatible with observance of the human rights thus recognized and guaranteed. . .

In the next paragraph of that same judgment, the Court specified the extent to which its doctrine extended to *Member State* measures as well:

> It is also apparent from the Court's case law . . . that, where national legislation falls within the scope of Community law, the Court, in a reference for a preliminary ruling, must give the national court all guidance as to interpretation necessary to enable it to assess the compatibility of that legislation with the fundamental rights—as laid down in particular in the Convention—whose observance the Court ensures. However, the Court has no such jurisdiction with regard to national legislation lying outside the scope of Community law.[34]

As for the *content* of fundamental rights protection, the following have been recognized by the Court of Justice to be part of the general principles of Community law: freedom of expression,[35] freedom of religion,[36] freedom of association,[37] the right to privacy, family life, and protection of the home,[38] the right to property,[39] the freedom to pursue one's trade or business,[40] the principle of non-retroactivity of penal measures,[41] the right to a judicial remedy for the protection of one's rights,[42] a group of connected rights known as the 'rights of defence',[43] and, of course, the principle of equality which has been applied in very many cases. But, given the nature of general principles, the list is not closed. One should certainly add all other rights that can be found in the ECHR as well as rights to be found in national constitutions. In

---

[34] Case C–299/95, *Friedrich Kremzow* v. *Austrian State* [1997] ECR I–2629, at 2645. The Court went on to hold that, in this particular case, the Member State measure was *not* within the scope of Community law. See discussion below, Part II, sect. A.

[35] The *Elliniki Radiophonia* judgment, cited at note 33 above.

[36] Case 130/75, *Vivien Prais* v. *Council* [1976] ECR 1589, at 1599 (a staff case).

[37] Case C–415/93, *Union Royale Belge des Sociétés de Football Association and Others* v. *Jean-Marc Bosman and Others* [1995] ECR I–4921, at 5065.

[38] Case 136/79, *National Panasonic* v. *Commission* [1980] ECR 2033, at 2056; Case 249/86, *Commission* v. *Germany* [1989] ECR 1263, at 1290; Case C–404/92P, *X* v. *Commission* [1994] ECR I–4737, at 4789.

[39] The *Nold* and *Hauer* judgments cited at notes 30 and 31 above.

[40] *Ibid.*

[41] Due to its inclusion in the European Convention of Human Rights, this 'principle' was declared to be a 'fundamental right' in Case 63/83, *Regina* v. *Kirk* [1984] ECR 2689, at 2718.

[42] Case 222/84, *Johnston* v. *Chief Constable of the Royal Ulster Constabulary* [1986] ECR 1651, at 1682.

[43] Case 374/87, *Orkem* v. *Commission* [1989] ECR 3283, at 3351. Rights of the defence are often invoked, and applied, in appeals against administrative decisions of the European Commission in fields like competition law, external trade, or state aid. For a comprehensive view, with references to the Court's case law, see K. Lenaerts and J. Vanhamme, 'Procedural Rights of Private Parties in the Community Administrative Process' (1997) 34 *CML Rev.* 531.

fact, the Court has seldom refused to include an alleged right into its capacious bag of general principles; but it has been more cautious in finding an actual violation of those rights.

II. EVALUATION OF THE ROLE OF THE COURT OF JUSTICE

The evaluation will be conducted, here, in terms of the contribution of the Court's doctrine and case law to the *protection of human rights*. Yet, one should not forget that the Court's case law in this field has other important functions than the protection of rights *per se*, such as the promotion of European integration and, more specifically, the safeguarding of the supremacy of EC law before domestic courts.

A starting point for the evaluation could be a crude quantitative observation: in terms of *numbers of cases* decided by the European Court of Justice (including the Court of First Instance), its role in the field of human rights protection is incomparably more limited than that of national constitutional courts in countries such as Germany, Italy, or Spain. Such a comparison with constitutional courts is not frivolous. The ECJ itself stated that its examination of 'whether fundamental rights and general principles of law have been observed by the institutions, and by the Member States when their actions fall within the scope of Community law' is part of 'its constitutional role'.[44] In view of the fact that the scope of activity of the EU institutions has been expanding continuously, it seems reasonable to consider the relation between these institutions and 'their' court in the same terms as the relation between national political institutions and their constitutional courts: in both cases, the protection of fundamental rights seems to be one of the primary objects of attention. And yet, compared to the thousands of cases of alleged fundamental rights violations dealt with every year by the constitutional courts of Germany, Italy, and Spain, there are only a handful before the ECJ and CFI every year,[45] and the cases in which an actual breach of fundamental rights is found are extremely rare indeed.

Part of the explanation is, no doubt, that the scope of the fundamental rights review by the Court of Justice is more limited. It covers actions of the EU institutions only within the framework of the *EC Treaty*, and not actions under the second and third pillars. But, above all, acts of the *Member States* are reviewed only to the extent that those acts fall 'within the scope of Community law'. It is as if the *Bundesverfassungsgericht* or the Spanish Constitutional Tribunal could scrutinize all central state acts and those acts of the regional and local authorities which those authorities perform as 'agents' of the central State, but not the autonomous acts performed by those authorities. The merits of this self-imposed limit to the role of the European Court of Justice will be evaluated first in section A below.

[44] *Report of the Court of Justice on Certain Aspects of the Application of the Treaty on European Union*, submitted to the European Council in preparation of the IGC (May 1995) at 4.
[45] The exact number depends on the definition of 'fundamental rights' (on which, see above Part I, sect. A) and on whether one chooses to include, in the comparison, cases brought by the employees of EU institutions (the 'staff cases'). The latter are dealt with by the CFI (and by the ECJ in appeal) whereas, at the national level, they tend to be dealt with by lower courts.

Yet, even when allowing for this structural difference with national constitutional courts and leaving aside review of Member State action, the effective role of the Court of Justice in protecting human rights appears still very limited. Possible explanations for the paucity of cases could be the following:

—There are fewer occasions for EU institutions than for national institutions to adopt acts raising concern for human rights; or, even if there are, the few 'leading cases' have had an irradiating effect on the activity of the European institutions so as to make them strongly aware of the human rights dimension, and thereby to obviate the need for judicial review;

—The judicial procedures do not allow for human rights to be raised in all cases where that would be appropriate, because standing to sue is too limited or because of insufficient control by the ECJ over the activity of national courts;

—Private parties (and national courts, in the case of the Article 234 (*ex* Article 177) procedure) fail to raise human rights issues, even where the existing procedures would allow to raise them, because of a lack of visibility of the Court's general principles case law;

—The European Court of Justice and Court of First Instance are too timid in enforcing human rights in the cases that reach Luxembourg, thereby discouraging future potential applicants.

The first and third of those explanations are almost impossible to test. Their plausibility may, however, be appraised better after a discussion of the second and fourth explanations, which will be considered in sections B and C, below.

A. The Scope of Protection: Sufficiently Extensive Review of National Measures?

The European Parliament does not hesitate to comment on the human rights performance of the Member States without bothering whether their actions are connected with their Community obligations or not.[46] Not so with the Court of Justice. Its general principles doctrine was designed to fill a gap in the legal protection of individuals *against the action of the Community institutions*, and not against the Member States. Yet, since the end of the 1980s, the European Court has started to add an 'offensive' dimension to its fundamental rights doctrine, by assuming the power to assess the compatibility of *certain national rules* (and not just Community rules) with the general principles of Community law. It exercises such judicial control when the national rules fall 'within the scope of Community law', that is, when the Member States implement Community rules (the *Wachauf* line[47]) and when they restrict the exercise of one of the common market freedoms (the *ERT* line[48]). In this way, 'a two-

---

[46] See, for instance, its recent Resolution on the Human Rights Situation in the European Union of 17 Feb. 1998, published in *Agence Europe—Documents*, No.2074/75 of 26 Feb. 1998. In fact, the Resolution focuses *more* on the action of the Member States than on the EU institutions.

[47] Case 5/88, *Wachauf* v. *Germany* [1989] ECR 2609, at 2639; Case C–2/92, *The Queen* v. *Ministry of Fisheries, Agriculture and Food, ex parte D.C. Bostock* [1994] ECR I–955, at 983; Case C–63/93, *Fintan Duff et al.* v. *Minister for Agriculture and Food, Ireland, and the Attorney General* [1996] ECR I–569, at 610.

[48] Case 260/89, *Elliniki Radiophonia Tileorassi* [1991] ECR I–2925, at 2964; Case C–159/90, *Society for the Protection of Unborn Children* v. *S. Grogan* [1991] ECR I–4685, at 4741; Case C–23/93, *TV 10 S.A.* v. *Commissariaat voor de Media* [1994] ECR I–4795, at 4833.

way traffic has been created; the Court looks at national constitutional laws to see if a given right should be regarded as protected by Community law, and if so all Member States are obliged to respect that right in the sphere of Community law'.[49]

The extent to which the sphere of protection of fundamental rights has thus been expanded by the European Court of Justice has been explained in some detail in the literature, particularly in a number of contributions by Joseph Weiler.[50] Three judgments of the ECJ in 1997 allow a reassessment of this matter. They show that the Court of Justice is, and remains, careful to check whether national measures allegedly breaching Community fundamental rights are indeed within the scope of EC law and, in checking this, the Court is exercising commendable self-restraint. In two of the cases, *Kremzow*[51] and *Annibaldi*,[52] it declined jurisdiction to review Member State measures in the light of Community fundamental rights, whereas in the third case (*Bauer Verlag*), it did exercise control over the respect of fundamental rights from the side of national authorities.

In *Kremzow*, the applicant had been convicted of murder in Austria, but the criminal proceedings had subsequently been held to be in breach of the European Convention on Human Rights. In an action for damages against the Austrian state, Kremzow argued that the national court was bound by the judgment of the European Court of Human Rights *because* of Austrian membership of the European Union. Kremzow also argued that the prison sentence prevented him from exercising his right of free movement under the EC Treaty. The ECJ refused to accept jurisdiction because the situation of Mr Kremzow was 'not connected in any way with any of the situations contemplated by the [EC] Treaty'.[53] The deprivation of liberty, although it actually prevented him from moving to other EU countries, was not sufficiently connected with free movement as to bring the case within the scope of EC law.[54]

In *Annibaldi*, the applicant alleged violation of his right of property by the refusal of local authorities to allow the planting of an orchard within the perimeter of a nature and archaeological park. Although the national measure relates to agricultural activity, the European Court held that it did not affect the common organization of

---

[49] J. Temple Lang, 'The Sphere in which Member States are Obliged to Comply with the General Principles of Law and Community Fundamental Rights Principles' (1991) 2 *LIEI* 34.

[50] J.H.H. Weiler, 'The European Court at a Crossroads: Community Human Rights and Member State Action', in F. Capotorti *et al.* (eds.), *Du droit international au droit de l'intégration. Liber Amicorum Pierre Pescatore* (1987), 821; J.H.H. Weiler and N. Lockhart, ' "Taking Rights Seriously" Seriously: The European Court and its Fundamental Rights Jurisprudence' (1995) 32 *CML Rev.* 59–82; J.H.H. Weiler, 'Fundamental Rights and Fundamental Boundaries: On Standards and Values in the Protection of Human Rights', in Neuwahl and Rosas, note 27 above, at 66–74. See, in addition, Clapham, note 27 above, at 33–55; Temple Lang, note 49 above; Craig and de Búrca, note 27 above, at 317–31; M. Ruffert, 'Die Mitgliedstaaten der Europäischen Gemeinschaft als Verpflichtete der Gemeinschaftsgrundrechte' [1995] *EuGRZ* 518; T. Jürgensen and I. Schlünder, 'EG-Grundrechtsschutz gegenüber Maßnahmen der Mitgliedstaaten' [1996] *Archiv des öffentlichen Rechts* 200; A. Duijkersloot, 'Nationale maatregelen, communautaire grondrechten en de vrij verkeersjurisprudentie' [1997] *SEW* 218.

[51] Case C–299/95, *Kremzow* [1997] ECR I–2629.

[52] Case C–309/96, *Daniele Annibaldi* v. *Sindaco del Comune di Guidonia and Presidente Regione Lazio* [1997] ECR I–7493.

[53] Case C–299/95, *Kremzow* [1997] ECR I–2629, at 2645.

[54] As La Pergola AG observed (at 2635), the criminal sanction was but the consequence of the application of a norm defining the crime of murder which itself has no connection with the free movement of persons.

the agricultural markets and therefore was not within the scope of Community law. In other words, the fact that the national measures deal with a policy area, such as agriculture, in which the European Community is actively involved is not sufficient to bring the measure within the scope of EC law for the purpose of fundamental rights review. What is needed is a narrower link between the national measure and a particular rule of Community law: the national measure must purport to implement a rule of Community law or else impinge on the effective application of that rule.

In *Bauer Verlag*,[55] the Commercial Court of Vienna had referred to the ECJ the question whether a provision of Austrian law prohibiting the sale of periodicals containing prize competitions was compatible with the free movement of goods as guaranteed by Article 28 (*ex* Article 30) EC. The effect of the measure was that foreign publications containing prize competitions (such as those of the defendant, Bauer Verlag, a German publishing house), while perfectly lawful under the laws of the country of origin, could be banned in Austria. The Court of Justice held that, in assessing whether this restriction of the movement of goods could be justified, one should examine whether Austria could invoke overriding requirements in the sense of the *Cassis de Dijon* case law, and added that 'where a Member State relies on overriding requirements to justify rules which are likely to obstruct the exercise of free movement of goods, such justification must also be interpreted in the light of the general principles of law and in particular of fundamental rights. . . . Those fundamental rights include freedom of expression, as enshrined in Article 10 of the European Convention' (paragraph 24 of the judgment).

The fundamental right of freedom of expression acts here as an additional hurdle for the Member State in trying to justify a measure which is, at the same time, a derogation from one of the common market freedoms. In fact, the test to be used by the national court is similar for both hurdles: is the national prohibition proportionate to the aim which it seeks to achieve and could that aim not be 'attained by measures less restrictive of both intra-Community trade and freedom of expression' (paragraph 27). Interestingly, the most convincing 'overriding requirement' that could justify the Austrian measure was the maintenance of press diversity, which is *also* a value protected by Article 10 ECHR. What the ECJ is doing here (and what it requires the national court to do) is the balancing of two sides of the same fundamental right of freedom of expression: the right of publishers to sell their products regardless of frontiers (combined with the right of readers to receive that information), as opposed to the value of protecting press diversity so as to allow for effective freedom of expression.[56] What appeared to be a banal trade restriction is thus transformed into a delicate balancing act of opposed aspects of an important fundamental right, to be performed by the national courts under the guidance of the European Court of Justice.[57]

---

[55] Case C–368/95, *Bauer Verlag* [1997] ECR I–3689.

[56] This aspect of the case is emphasized in the commentary by J. Kühling, 'Grundrechtskontrolle durch den EuGH: Kommunikationsfreiheit und Pluralismussicherung im Gemeinschaftsrecht' [1997] *EuGZ* 302.

[57] One may note that the referring Austrian court had not raised the fundamental rights issue, which was dealt with by the ECJ *of its own motion* (although formally, as part of its ruling on the correct interpretation of Art. 30 (*ex* Art. 28) EC).

The *Bauer Verlag* judgment is perfectly in line with the *ERT*-style review of Member State measures, but it also shows that this strand of the ECJ's fundamental rights doctrine may raise delicate questions in the relationship between the national and Community legal orders. It requires any national court to act as a 'constitutional court' ensuring respect by the national authorities of the fundamental rights of EC law, which may even require them to disregard national constitutional rights as they are normally understood.[58]

Although the 1997 judgments show some of the potential tensions which the Court's doctrine may cause, they are solidly argued and do not break any spectacular new ground. The prudent attitude of the Court of Justice is commendable. There is no justification for going beyond and undertaking the full-scale 'incorporation' of Community fundamental rights into the national legal orders, as happened in the United States.[59] Indeed, there is no glaring human rights deficit in the legal orders of the Member States, which the ECJ should set out to remedy. In some of them, such as Germany, Italy, and Spain, there are sophisticated systems for the judicial protection of constitutional rights; in others, such as France, Belgium, and the Netherlands, the European Convention on Human Rights is enforced by the courts as a quasi-constitution. Also, all Member States are (unlike the EU) subject to the supervision of the European Convention organs in Strasbourg.

Still, some of the implications of the existing case law remain to be spelled out. The question whether the *Wachauf* line (Member States are bound by Community fundamental rights when they implement EC law) also applies to the transposition and implementation of *directives* (as opposed to the mere execution of *regulations* as in *Wachauf* and *Bostock*) remains unclear. In several cases, the ECJ has held that the specific duties imposed by a directive on the Member States should be read *in the light of* the general principles of Community law,[60] but has never declared those general principles to be binding *as such* on the States when they are adopting measures for the transposition of a directive. Yet, one would think that the 'choice of form and methods' left to the States according to Article 249 (*ex* Article 189) EC does not include the choice whether or not to violate fundamental rights, and, vice versa, that respect for fundamental rights is an implicit part of the 'result to be achieved' under the directive. So, the extension of the *Wachauf* line to directives (and, indeed, to the application by Member States of external agreements concluded by the EC) would seem logical.

A complete evaluation of this strand of the ECJ's case law would require a careful analysis of *national court judgments* as well. In addition to the (relatively few) human

---

[58] The possibility that 'fundamental rights' review of Member State derogations could lead to open conflict with *national* constitutional values had been narrowly avoided by the ECJ in *Grogan*, the Irish abortion case (Case C–159/90 [1991] ECR I–4685). But that case had prompted speculation on the question of value conflicts in the legal literature. See, in particular, S. O'Leary, 'Aspects of the Relationship between Community Law and National Law', in Neuwahl and Rosas, note 27 above, at 23.

[59] The contrast with the US experience with incorporation of constitutional rights is described by K. Lenaerts, 'Fundamental Rights to be Included in a Community Catalogue', in (1991) 16 *EL Rev.* 368–72; and by Weiler, note 16 above, at 595–6.

[60] Case 36/75, *Rutili* [1975] ECR 1219; Case 222/84, *Johnston* [1986] ECR 1651; the same principle of interpretation applies, obviously, to regs.: Case 249/86, *Commission* v. *Germany* [1989] ECR 1263. See discussion of those cases in Craig and de Búrca, note 27 above, at 318–20.

rights cases that have reached the ECJ through the preliminary reference procedure, there may be other (more numerous) cases in which national courts simply apply the general principles of Community law to strike down national measures without making a preliminary reference first. A study of domestic court practice in this respect would be welcome.

One issue that has not emerged at all in the general principles case law so far is the extent to which violations of Community fundamental rights *by private individuals or firms* may also be sanctioned. After all, some of the most dangerous threats to human rights, today, originate from activities by private groups. The question of the 'horizontal' effect of Community law has been amply discussed in the context of the enforcement of directives; it has also arisen, in a more directly relevant way, in connection with the fundamental freedoms of the common market. In principle, those freedoms involve duties for the State authorities and should therefore not display horizontal direct effect, except in the case of collective regulation by private organizations such as a sports federation (as in the *Walrave* and *Bosman* cases). Normally, the Treaty rules on the free movement of goods, and on other freedoms, may not be relied upon against private parties.[61] The same must be true, *a fortiori*, of the general principles of Community law. In view of the fact that these principles are unwritten, and that the constitutional law of most Member States does not recognize the *direct* horizontal effect of constitutional rights, it must be assumed that Community fundamental rights do not directly bind private parties.[62]

If one accepts that, for the time being, private individuals and groups do not have a direct obligation to respect the general principles of Community law (including fundamental rights), that still leaves the question where to draw the line, in borderline cases, between 'State action' and 'private action'. That issue has, again, received most attention in the context of the direct effect of directives. The findings in that area could be transposed to the question of fundamental rights.[63]

Obviously, the lack of horizontal effect of the EC fundamental rights *per se* does not prevent the Community institutions from taking legislative action for combating private abridgements of those rights. To the extent that such action is adopted, the Court of Justice acquires its usual role of interpreting and, where possible, amplifying those rights through its case law.

---

[61] See, for general discussion of the Court's case law on the matter, which is not entirely consistent: W.H. Roth, 'Drittwirkung der Grundfreiheiten?', in O. Due, M. Lutter, and J. Schwarze (eds.), *Festschrift für Ulrich Everling* (1995), 1231. A strong criticism of the European Court's decision to give horizontal effect to Art. 48 (now Art. 39) EC in the *Bosman* case was made by W. Kluth, 'Die Bindung privater Wirtschaftsteilnehmer an die Grundfreiheiten des EG-Vertrages—Eine Analyse am Beispiel des Bosman-Urteils des EuGH' [1997] *Archiv des öffentlichen Rechts* 557.

[62] Yet, the ECJ took a different view about Art. 119 (now Art. 141) in its famous *Defrenne I* judgment (Case 43/75, *Defrenne* v. *Sabena* [1976] ECR 455, at para. 39). One might argue that the particular nature of the right at stake there (equal pay for equal work), which normally applies in *horizontal* relations, justifies its direct horizontal operation.

[63] See Craig and de Búrca, note 27 above, at 194–8; and V. Kvjatkovski, 'What is an "Emanation of the State"? An Educated Guess' (1997) 3 *EPL* 329.

B. *Access to the European Courts: Adequate Mechanisms for Litigating Human Rights Violations?*

Private litigants can challenge Community acts which, in their opinion, violate their fundamental rights, before the European Court of First Instance. According to Article 230 (*ex* Article 173), fourth paragraph, of the EC Treaty, such actions are admissible only if they are brought within two months after publication or notification of the act, and if the act was addressed to the applicant or is 'of direct and individual concern' to him. Much ink has flown about the way in which the Court of Justice and the Court of First Instance have interpreted the words 'direct and individual concern', but the main point is that, except in really exceptional circumstances, there is no right of action against breaches of fundamental rights committed through general normative acts of Community law.[64] To put it in simple (albeit slightly over-simplified) terms: the legality of EC regulations and directives cannot be challenged before the CFI by individual citizens and firms.

The Court of Justice has argued, though, that there is no real lacuna in judicial protection and that, in fact, the EC Treaty does create a complete system of remedies, because general normative acts can be contested by means of the preliminary rulings procedure of Article 234 (*ex* Article 177) EC. In the *Les Verts* judgment of 1986, the Court drew an overall picture of the available remedies in the following terms:

[T]he European Economic Community is a Community based on the rule of law, inasmuch as neither its Member States nor its institutions can avoid a review of the question whether the measures adopted by them are in conformity with the basic constitutional charter, the Treaty. In particular, in Articles 173 and 184, on the one hand, and in Article 177, on the other, the Treaty established a complete system of legal remedies and procedures designed to permit the Court of Justice to review the legality of measures adopted by the institutions. Natural and legal persons are thus protected against the application to them of general measures which they cannot contest directly before the Court by reason of the special conditions of admissibility laid down in the second paragraph of Article 173 of the Treaty. Where the Community institutions are responsible for the administrative implementation of such measures, natural or legal persons may bring a direct action before the Court against implementing measures which are addressed to them or which are of direct and individual concern to them and, in support of such an action, plead the illegality of the general measures on which they are based. Where implementation is a matter for the national authorities, such persons may plead the invalidity of general measures before the national courts and cause the latter to request the Court of Justice for a preliminary ruling.[65]

So far the ECJ, when adjusting this general statement to the particular case of human rights violations and to the European Community as it has developed since

---

[64] Among the many surveys of the case law on the admissibility of Art. 173 (now Art. 230) actions by individuals, see Craig and de Búrca, note 27 above, at 461–90; A. Arnull, 'Private Applicants and the Action for Annulment under Article 173 of the EC Treaty' (1995) 32 *CML Rev.* 7; C. Soulard, 'Cour de Justice—Recours en annulation—Conditions de recevabilité', *Juris-Classeur Europe*, Fasc. 330 (1995); A. Albors-Llorens, *Private Parties in European Community Law: Challenging Community Measures* (1996), chap. 4; N. Neuwahl, 'Article 173 Paragraph 4 EC: Past, Present and Possible Future' (1996) 21 *EL Rev.* 17.
[65] Case 294/83, *Parti écologiste 'Les Verts'* v. *European Parliament* [1986] ECR 1339.

1986,[66] the picture thus traced by the Court of Justice seems, indeed, to provide a coherent and formally complete system for the protection of human rights against Community acts. As implementation of normative EC acts is usually a matter left to the Member States, the last hypothesis mentioned in the *Les Verts* statement, the one involving national courts, is particularly important. An example may illustrate this. The Regulation on the common organization of the market in bananas[67] has been at the origin of the so-called 'banana saga',[68] which will be considered repeatedly in the following pages. German banana importers, who thought that their fundamental rights had been infringed by some provisions of the Regulation, first brought a direct action for its annulment, but this action was declared inadmissible by the ECJ, for lack of direct and individual concern.[69] Yet, those banana importers were able, subsequently, to challenge the implementing measures of the Regulation taken by German customs and administrative authorities before German administrative courts, who then referred questions to the ECJ about the validity of the Regulation, to be assessed in the light of the general principles of EC law.[70]

Legal protection through the intermediary of the national court system is, however, not always so straightforward. Take for instance Article 13 of the Television without Frontiers Directive, which prohibits all forms of television advertising for tobacco products.[71] The Directive could not be challenged directly by tobacco producers or advertisers for violation of freedom of expression or economic rights, due to the standing requirements of Article 173 (now Article 230). Moreover, this provision of the Directive was transposed into the relevant legislative regimes of the Member States, often without any additional specific measures of implementation. This raises a problem in terms of judicial review: in most countries, statutory provisions cannot be challenged directly by private persons, and individual measures, which could be challenged, have not been taken. It would seem that, in this hypothesis, access to a court would require, first, an infringement of the prohibition on advertising, and then the fundamental rights arguments could be used as a defence in ensuing proceedings. An additional difficulty is that such a 'test case' could only be brought by tobacco producers or advertisers with the active collaboration of some broadcasting station.

This example merely serves to show that, in terms of effective access to justice, the preliminary reference procedure may, in fact, not be a perfectly suited alternative for a (non-available) direct action under Article 230 (*ex* Article 173). There are other reasons why this is so.[72] To force individuals to make a détour along the Member

---

[66] The main change, since *Les Verts*, has been the creation of the CFI, which has taken over from the ECJ the task of dealing (in first instance) with actions for annulment brought by private parties. But the ECJ retains sole competence to give preliminary rulings on the validity of EC law.

[67] Council Reg. 404/93 [1993] OJ L47/1.

[68] See the intermediate survey of the various European and national court decisions by N. Reich, 'Judge-made "Europe à la carte": Some Remarks on Recent Conflicts between European and German Constitutional Law Provoked by the Banana Litigation' (1996) 7 *EJIL* 103.

[69] Case C–286/93, *Atlanta Fruchthandelsgesellschaft* v. *Council and Commission*, Order of 21 June 1994 (not published in ECR), available from the ECJ Information Service.

[70] Case C–466/93, *Atlanta Fruchthandelsgesellschaft and Others* v. *Bundesamt für Ernährung und Forstwirtschaft (No 2)* [1995] ECR I–3799.

[71] Dir. 89/552 [1989] OJ L298/23.

[72] See also, for elaboration of some of the following arguments: M. Waelbroeck and A.-M. Verheyden, 'Les conditions de recevabilité des recours en annulation des particuliers contre les actes normatifs

State courts when the real issue is not about the administrative measure which is being contested but about the underlying Community regulation or directive, is a waste of the time, energy, and money of litigants (and of the domestic courts involved in the proceedings);[73] would it not be much simpler to allow litigants to contest the Community measure directly before the Court which is, anyway, the sole competent authority to decide on the validity of the measure?[74] Another problem with the Article 234 (*ex* Article 177) route is that individual litigants cannot decide themselves that a preliminary reference about the validity of Community law should be made, but depend on the willingness of national courts to find that there is enough doubt about that validity to warrant a prolonged interruption of the proceedings during which the European Court of Justice prepares its preliminary ruling. There is no remedy against national court rulings which fail to raise issues of human rights violations by Community acts.

Given this state of affairs, some scepticism is permissible about whether the present system of remedies offers watertight protection to individuals suffering human rights violations by the Community. Some potential cases might never reach the European Court. The problem is compounded by the fact, which has often been emphasized by legal commentators[75] and even by some members of the Court themselves,[76] that the condition of 'direct and individual concern' is interpreted rather strictly by both the ECJ and the CFI, so that standing to sue under Article 230 is in fact considerably narrower than standing to sue in the Member States' systems of administrative justice[77] and narrower also than before the European Commission of Human Rights.[78] I will therefore assume that there may well be a lacuna in access to justice (although it is difficult to provide the 'negative proof' that cases would be brought to Luxembourg if it were not for the restrictions in the system of remedies) and will consider, in Part IV of this chapter, some possible remedies.

communautaires à la lumière du droit comparé et de la Convention des droits de l'homme' [1995] *CDE* 433–6; Albors-Llorens, note 64 above, at 188–95.

[73] The loss of time may be illustrated by the *Atlanta* cases mentioned above. The direct action by the German banana importers contesting the legality of the Banana Reg. was lodged with the Court of Justice and declared inadmissible on 21 June 1994. The preliminary reference about the validity of the same Reg. was made by the Administrative Court of Frankfurt on request of the same banana traders on 1 Dec. 1993, and was decided by the ECJ only on 9 Nov. 1995.

[74] The same is true for *interim protection* in urgent cases of fundamental rights violations. The CFI can order interim measures in the framework of an Art. 230 action (in accordance with the general power accorded by Art. 243 (*ex* Art. 186) EC); national courts can also order interim measures against the Community, but the conditions are defined more strictly and the European Court is, obviously, better situated to decide on this (on the criteria which national courts must follow in offering interim relief against Community measures, see Case C–465/93, *Atlanta Fruchthandelsgesellschaft and Others* v. *Bundesamt für Ernährung und Forstwirtschaft (No 1)* [1995] ECR I–3761, at 3790–5).

[75] See, among others: A. Barav, 'Direct and Individual Concern: An Almost Insurmountable Barrier to the Admissibility of Individual Appeal to the EEC Court' (1974) 11 *CML Rev.* 191; H. Rasmussen, 'Why is Article 173 Interpreted against Private Plaintiffs?' (1980) 5 *EL Rev.* 112; Craig and de Búrca, note 27 above, at 479–89.

[76] G.F. Mancini and D.T. Keeling, 'Democracy and the European Court of Justice' (1994) 57 *MLR* 188–9.

[77] For a comparative survey of a number of Member States' systems, accompanied by a critique of the European Court's narrowly drawn standing requirements, see Waelbroeck and Verheyden, note 72 above.

[78] De Schutter and Lejeune, note 26 above, at 582–3.

C. The Standard of Protection: Sufficient Recognition of Human Rights by the European Court?

Some authors have argued that the European Court of Justice is not really interested in offering effective protection for human rights, but uses its 'general principles' case law in an instrumental way, namely to affirm the authority of Community law (and its own authority) against the Member States.[79] More concretely, it has been argued that the reference made to the international human rights treaties and to the common constitutional principles of the Member States is rather ritual and does not denote a willingness of the Court of Justice to subject itself to the human rights standards developed elsewhere.

The text of the European Convention on Human Rights is cited very often by the ECJ as evidence for the existence of a fundamental right which is to be incorporated into the general principles of Community law. But the case law of the European Court or Commission of Human Rights, which is the flesh and blood of the Convention, was not cited or taken into account until recently.[80]

As for the *common constitutional principles*, Andrew Clapham suggested in 1991 that 'the Court's method so far has been to selectively distill common practices from *some* Member States . . . and even then these only offer "inspiration" or "guidelines" '.[81] This remains equally true today. One could even say that the Court of Justice is not genuinely interested in finding out whether there is a 'common tradition' among the Member States concerning the legal regime of a particular rule. References to specific national legal systems are perfunctory and haphazard.[82] A national constitutional court judgment has never been cited.

It is therefore abundantly clear that international human rights treaties and national constitutions (and their respective case law applications) do not bind the European Court of Justice. In the Court's own words, they merely provide 'inspiration' and 'guidelines'. This has prompted misgivings among commentators, who have argued that the standard of human rights protection used by the Court of Justice falls short of the level of protection mandated by the ECHR or the constitutions of the Member States. Among the cases most often cited as examples of the ECJ failing to reach the appropriate level are the *Hoechst* judgment[83] and the 'Bananas' cases

---

[79] The most elaborate critique of this sort was written by J. Coppel and A. O'Neill, 'The European Court of Justice: Taking Rights Seriously?' (1992) 29 *CML Rev.* 669; a lengthy rebuttal of their views was published by Weiler and Lockhart, note 50 above, at 51 and 579.

[80] Specific references to judgments of the European Court of Human Rights were made in four cases: in Case C–13/94, *P* v. *S and Cornwall County Council* [1996] ECR I–2143, at 2164; in Cases C–74/95 and 129/95, *Criminal Proceedings against X* [1996] ECR I–6609, at 6637; in Case C–368/95, *Bauer Verlag* [1997] ECR I–3689, at 3717; and in Case C–249/96, *Lisa Jacqueline Grant* v. *South-West Trains Ltd.* [1998] ECR I–621, at paras. 33 and 34. All four judgments were delivered after the Court's *Opinion 2/94* on accession to the ECHR, as if the Court wanted to console the many commentators that deplore its refusal to recognize an EC competence to accede to the ECHR.

[81] Clapham, note 27 above, at 50–1.

[82] The *Hauer* judgment (Case 44/79 [1979] ECR 3727) is often cited as an example of concrete examination of national constitutional law. In fact, the ECJ examined the constitutional protection of the right of property in only three of the (then) nine Member States and did not delve deeply into them (para. 20 of the judgment).

[83] Joined Cases 46/87 and 227/88, *Hoechst* v. *Commission* [1989] ECR 2859.

(foremost of which is the judgment in *Germany* v. *Council*).[84] Two elements are criticized about the *Hoechst* ruling: the fact that the European Court applied the ECHR without taking due account of the case law of the organs of the ECHR and the fact that it failed to give protection to an interest which, under German constitutional law, was considered as a fundamental right. The former issue, that of the consistency between the ECJ's use of the European Convention and the interpretation of that Convention by the Convention organs themselves, is considered in Dean Spielmann's contribution to this volume. The latter criticism, that the European Court of Justice failed to reach the standard of human rights protection reached at the national level, is also at the heart of the criticism of the Court's performance in the bananas cases, where German authors, mainly, have argued that the European Court was paying lip-service to fundamental rights and general principles, without giving them the same scrupulous attention as German courts are used to give.[85]

Let us consider for a moment what I will call the German problem (although similar issues may exist, potentially, with regard to other States). On a closer look, two aspects may be distinguished: the fact that the rights identified as being part of the unwritten European catalogue may not include all the rights protected at the national constitutional level; and the fact that the rights that *are* included among the general principles of Community law may be taken 'less seriously' by the European Court than they ought to be according to national constitutional traditions. The first argument may be illustrated by the *Hoechst* case; the second one by the *Bananas* case. In *Hoechst*, the Court of Justice found that, although in German law the right to the inviolability of the home was granted to 'legal' as well as to 'natural' persons, it could be invoked in Community law only in relation to private homes and not to business premises.[86] This was the clearest affirmation, so far, of the fact that the common constitutional standard does not comprise the rights protected in each country separately. But this occurs very rarely.

A more consistent divergence can be found in the *interpretation* of fundamental rights. In the main 'bananas' judgment, *Germany* v. *Council*, the applicant government argued that the Regulation was in breach (among other things) of the principle of non-discrimination, the right of property, and the freedom to pursue one's business or profession. The ECJ accepted that all those rights were, indeed, general principles of Community law, but denied that they had been violated. With regard to non-discrimination, it reiterated its traditional doctrine that differentiations could be made when there was an objective justification for them; as there was an objective difference between German banana importers and those from other countries prior to the Regulation (due to the free trade regime which Germany alone had under the

---

[84] Case C–280/93, *Germany* v. *Council* [1994] ECR I–4973.

[85] An authoritative criticism is that voiced by a former judge of the ECJ, U. Everling, 'Will Europe Slip on Bananas? The Bananas Judgement of the Court of Justice and National Courts' (1996) 33 *CML Rev.* 401.

[86] Criticism was expressed, among others, by G. Ress and J. Ukrow, 'Neue Aspekte des Grundrechtsschutzes in der Europäischen Gemeinschaft.Anmerkungen zum Hoechst-Urteil des EuGH' [1990] *EuZW* 499. As far as the criticism is based on a German constitutional perspective, it has recently acquired an ironic twist because of the reform of Art. 13 of the *Grundgesetz* adopted in 1998 by the German Parliament, which considerably reduces the right to the inviolability of the home for *all persons*, both 'natural' and 'legal'.

old rules), the difference in treatment between categories of economic operators appeared 'to be inherent in the objective of integrating previously compartmentalized
markets' (paragraph 74).

The claim of a breach of the right to property was summarily dismissed by the
Court with the argument that 'no economic operator can claim a right to property in
a market share which he held at a time before the establishment of a common organization of a market' (paragraph 79). However, the invocation of the freedom to pursue a trade or business was the occasion for a more searching analysis. The Court
readily admitted that it had been restricted by the Community legislator, but added
that there were valid justifications for this restriction. The regime of acceptable restrictions to fundamental rights was defined by the following formula:

> the exercise of the right to property and the freedom to pursue a trade or profession may
> be restricted, particularly in the context of a common organization of a market, provided
> that those restrictions in fact correspond to objectives of general interest pursued by the
> Community and do not constitute a disproportionate and intolerable interference, im-
> pairing the very substance of the rights guaranteed.[87]

This formula combines the criteria used by the European Court of Human Rights
(existence of a public interest and proportionality of the restriction with regard to
that public interest) with an additional criterion directly taken from German constitutional law where it is known as the *Wesensgehaltsgarantie*:[88] the 'very substance'
of a right may not be impaired. Despite this impressive doctrinal apparatus, the
Court was not particularly severe in its actual examination of the Banana Regulation, and accepted that all the restrictive features of the Regulation could appear to
the Community legislator to be necessary means for establishing the common market of bananas. The proportionality test, applied in conjunction with those rights,
was quite lenient.[89]

On all those points, the position of the ECJ fits very well with its earlier case law in
which it favoured a hands-off approach in matters of economic regulation.[90] Yet,
German authors have unfavourably compared the Court's ruling with the way German courts would deal with the same fundamental rights.[91] It may well be that the

---

[87] *Germany* v. *Council*, note 84 above, at 5065. The same, or a very similar, formula is used in many
other fundamental rights cases. See, for a recent example, Case C–200/96, *Metronome Musik* v. *Music
Point Hokamp*, judgment of 28 Apr. 1998 (not yet reported), at para. 21. Sometimes however, the Court
is, for reasons unknown, much more laconic and simply states that fundamental rights 'may be subject to
restrictions justified by objectives of general interest pursued by the Community', without further
qualifications (Case C–84/95, *Bosphorus Hava Yollari Turizm ve Ticaret AS* v. *Minister for Transport, Energy and Communications, Ireland, and the Attorney General* [1996] ECR I–3953, at 3985).

[88] Art. 19(2) of the German *Grundgesetz*. See P. Lerche, 'Grundrechtsschranken', in J. Isensee and
P. Kirchhof (eds.), *Handbuch des Staatsrechts* (1992), v, 791–5.

[89] See particularly para. 94 of the judgment: '[w]hile other means for achieving the desired result were
indeed conceivable, the Court cannot substitute its assessment for that of the Council as to the appropriateness or otherwise of the measures adopted by the Community legislature if those measures have not
been proved to be manifestly inappropriate for achieving the objective pursued'.

[90] The comparison with earlier cases is developed by M. Dony, 'L'affaire des bananes' [1995] *CDE* 461,
at 471–87. The hands-off approach with regard to claims based on a breach of the right of property is described, in general terms, by Usher, note 6 above, at chap. 6.

[91] In addition to the article by Everling, note 85 above, see also P. Huber, 'Das Kooperationsverhältnis zwischen BVerfG und EuGH in Grundrechtsfragen', (1997) *EuZW* 517; T. Stein, 'Bananen-Split?
Entzweien sich BVerfG und EuGH über den Bananenstreit?' [1998] *EuZW* 261. A more balanced view is
taken by M. Nettesheim, 'Grundrechtliche Prüfdichte durch den EuGH' [1995] *EuZW* 106.

Court of Justice, generally speaking, exercises much more restraint when examining the respect by the Community legislator for fundamental rights than the German Constitutional Court would do in relation to the German legislator. But this should not be a decisive consideration. It is not the proper role of the European Court of Justice to enforce the combined and consolidated constitutions of the Member States, but rather to observe a European standard of protection which is inspired by the common constitutional traditions of those Member States. In doing so, the European Court is showing an awareness of the limits of its institutional role and of the constitutional autonomy of the Member States. Indeed, the definition, in each country, of which rights shall be considered to be fundamental (and, hence, beyond the reach of the legislator) reflects the value preferences of the citizens of that country as well as their views on the appropriate division of roles between the legislator (or government) and the courts. The degree to which the national legal system is 'constitutionalized', that is, the degree to which legislative choices are scrutinized on their compatibility with fundamental rights, varies enormously between, say, Germany and Sweden.[92] By choosing a 'maximum standard' of protection, the Court of Justice would in fact be privileging the German over the Swedish approach, and there is no obvious reason why this should be so.[93]

Although it is argued here that the Court of Justice should not strive to enforce the combined constitutional rights of all Member States, this does not mean that its actual record in the scrutiny of Community measures is beyond reproach. Perhaps it should exercise a somewhat stricter review even in economic regulation disputes such as *Germany* v. *Council*. Indeed, in its latest 'banana' judgments of 10 March 1998, the Court does exercise a close scrutiny of a Council regulation which had amended the original Banana Regulation, and this time holds that certain of that Regulation's provisions are in breach of the general principle of non-discrimination.[94] Yet, these recent judgments do not necessarily announce a generally more active human rights scrutiny by the ECJ. They rather fit with earlier case law, in the sense that agricultural legislation has, so far, been the only area in which Community *legislative acts* (as opposed to an individual decision, in staff or competition cases) have been held invalid for breach of a fundamental right of Community law, namely the non-discrimination principle.[95]

---

[92] In Swedish law, there is judicial review of the constitutionality of legislation, but it is exercised with much caution by the courts who are traditionally deferential to parliament. See I. Cameron, 'Protection of Constitutional Rights in Sweden' [1997] *PL* 488.

[93] In a recent essay, Besselink developed an elaborate argument in favour of the contrary thesis, namely that the ECJ should adopt the *maximum standard* in the field of fundamental rights, because this would provide optimal protection for the rights themselves and, at the same time, avoid conflicts with the constitutional laws of the individual Member States: L. Besselink, 'Entrapped by the Maximum Standard: On Fundamental Rights, Pluralism and Subsidiarity in the European Union' (1998) 35 *CML Rev.* 629. Despite the logical strength of many of his arguments, I do not agree with the conclusion, for the reasons mentioned in the text; see also, for a considered rejection of the maximum standard solution, Weiler, note 50 above, at 56–66.

[94] Case C–122/95, *Germany* v. *Council* [1998] ECR I–973, paras. 54–72, and Joined Cases C–364/95 & C–365/95, *T. Port GmbH* v. *Hauptzollamt Hamburg-Jonas* [1998] ECR I–1023, paras. 74–89. The Court's ruling on the general principle of non-discrimination is identical in both judgments.

[95] Earlier such judgments included: Cases 117/76 & 16/77, *Ruckdeschel and Hansa-Lagerhaus Ströh* v. *Hauptzollamt Hamburg-St Annen* and *Diamalt* v. *Hauptzollamt Itzehoe* [1977] ECR 1753; Cases 124/76 & 20/77, *Moulins et Huileries de Pont à Mousson* v. *ONIC* and *Providence Agricole de la Champagne* v. *ONIC*

The ECJ's case law on human rights is, in fact, still developing. It has dealt only quite recently with another well-known issue of the fundamental rights doctrine of both national constitutional courts and the European Court of Human Rights, namely the question whether fundamental rights also impose *positive duties* on government (in our case, on the Community institutions as well as on the Member States acting within the scope of EC law).[96] In the *Port-I* judgment of 26 November 1996 (another of the 'banana' cases), the European Court of Justice held, in an obiter dictum, that the failure by the Community institutions to take action for preventing breaches of fundamental rights could be sanctioned by the Court.[97] This is a dimension of fundamental rights protection which the Court will probably be called to develop further in the years to come.

D. Conclusion

Let us now return to the question put at the beginning of this Part: what does it mean that so few cases involving possible breaches of fundamental rights reach the European Court: that there is no significant problem of human rights protection in the EC legal order, or that there is a vast mass of hidden human rights issues which the legal system fails to account for? The considerations above do not allow for a simple answer to this fear of the 'iceberg syndrome'. Still, two worries have emerged so far.

One worry is about the *standards of review* applied by the Court of Justice. It is true that many potential litigants may be discouraged by the lack of sympathy displayed by the Court towards arguments based on economic rights, such as the right of property or the right to pursue one's trade, and towards arguments of alleged discrimination directed against economic regulations adopted by the EC. But this, as I argued above, is not a bad thing in itself. It is wise for the Court not to adapt the 'maximum standard' of protection but to exercise some judicial restraint in applying fundamental rights. That being said, the ECJ and CFI could take extra care in developing more detailed and persuasive arguments about why they reject pleas of human rights breaches in a particular case. They could also more directly and unambiguously acknowledge the authority of the European Convention of Human Rights. They could, finally, be less vague about the 'common constitutional traditions' by venturing, when a case so warrants, into a genuine comparative evaluation of Member State constitutions; this would make a rejection of arguments taken from the law of

[1977] ECR 1795; Cases 103 & 145/77, *Royal Scholten Honig* v. *Intervention Board* [1978] ECR 2037; Case C–309/89, *Codorniu* v. *Council* [1994] ECR I–1853. Still, it should be emphasized that the cases in which the ECJ has found a violation of the principle of non-discrimination are only a very small proportion of the cases in which applicants argued that the EC's agricultural legislation was in breach of the principle, so that Barents is led to conclude that the non-discrimination principle, although it constitutes a fundamental right, has 'a rather limited significance for the protection of the operator vis-à-vis the Community legislature': Barents, note 13 above, at 352.

[96] For an analysis focusing on this 'lacuna' (from a comparative perspective) in the ECJ's fundamental rights jurisprudence, see G. Gersdorf, 'Funktionen der Gemeinschaftsgrundrechte im Lichte des Solange II-Beschlusses des Bundesverfassungsgerichts' [1994] *Archiv des öffentlichen Rechts* 400.

[97] Case C–68/95, *T. Port GmbH & Co. KG* v. *Bundesanstalt für Landwirtschaft und Ernährung* [1996] ECR I–6065, at 6100 (para. 40): '[t]he Community institutions are required to act in particular when the transition to the common organization of the market infringes certain traders' fundamental rights protected by Community law, such as the right to property and the right to pursue a professional or trade activity'.

just one State more compelling. Those are, in fact, more matters of style than of substance. But justice must also be seen to be done, particularly in the field of human rights.

The second, and major, worry is that a number of possible human rights violations may, in fact, never reach the European Court of Justice at all. This might be the result of the combination of the following factors: the lack of visibility of Community fundamental rights due to their unwritten state of general principles of law; the narrow standing rules for individual complaints under Article 230; the wide discretion left to the national courts as to whether they will raise issues of human rights breaches by Member State authorities; and finally, the classical access to justice problem that litigation is both costly and time-consuming, which means that fundamental rights issues tend to be raised, typically, by business firms with time in hand, rather than by the ordinary citizen. In the EC, more than in other legal contexts such as the ECHR or national constitutional litigation, one can say that 'those invoking the language of rights are often not the oppressed minorities or individuals as might be expected'.[98]

These are considerations relating to the need of ensuring *effective protection for human rights* in the Community legal order. But one should not forget that there are other dimensions to this problem than the plight of individual citizens and firms. The fundamental rights case law of the ECJ has played, and continues to play, a central role in the articulation between the EC and the national legal orders, and in the acceptance of the authority of the Court of Justice by the national (constitutional) courts. The affirmation of fundamental rights can be a means of bolstering the integration process by convincing citizens and national courts that cherished constitutional values are in safe hands with the Court of Justice. But the same case law may also be a divisive force, if it appears that the ECJ is not taking rights seriously enough or when the affirmation of Community fundamental rights upsets strongly held national policy preferences.

III. NEW PERSPECTIVES AFTER AMSTERDAM

Before examining possible reforms for the more or less distant future, I will examine the probable reforms of the immediate future, namely the changes which the Treaty of Amsterdam is making to the role of the European Court of Justice in the human rights field.

One might start the survey of the legal effects of the entry into force, probably some time in 1999, of the Treaty of Amsterdam by mentioning what the Treaty does *not* do in matters of human rights. It does not provide the EC or the EU with the power to accede to the European Convention on Human Rights which, due to the position adopted by the ECJ in *Opinion 2/94*, means that the EC will not be able to become a party to the Convention in the coming years. The Treaty does not, either,

---

[98] G. de Búrca, 'The Language of Rights and European Integration', in J. Shaw and G. More (eds.), *New Legal Dynamics of European Union* (1995), 51.

enact a Community catalogue of fundamental rights, it does not create special procedures for the judicial enforcement of existing fundamental rights and it does not
modify the existing standing requirements for individual applications to the European Court of First Instance, as they are formulated in Article 230 (*ex* Article 173)
EC.

Yet, the Treaty of Amsterdam contains other changes, some of which will have
important consequences for the role of the Court of Justice. A first change, which
looks spectacular but will not meaningfully affect the work of the ECJ, is the mechanism of *sanctions against Member States* that seriously and persistently breach fundamental rights, as established by Article F.1 of the EU Treaty (to be renumbered as
Article 7 TEU).[99] The Court of Justice does not play any role in either the assessment
of the serious and persistent breach or the imposition of the sanctions themselves; all
this is left in the hands of the Council. This seems to be a wise decision. The Court of
Justice, while well equipped to deal with ordinary breaches of fundamental rights in
the context of specific cases and controversies, should not be drawn into the highly
political and largely subjective exercise delineated by Article 7.

Another innovation in the Treaty of Amsterdam that draws the immediate attention, is the new Article 6a (renumbered as Article 13) of the EC Treaty which allows
the Council to 'take appropriate action to combat discrimination based on sex,
racial or ethnic origin, religion or belief, disability, age or sexual orientation'. The
Member States were careful to draft this *anti-discrimination provision* as a 'competence clause' and to avoid any implications that it could contain a directly effective
prohibition, to be used by the Court of Justice as a standard for reviewing either
Community or Member State actions.[100] This intention emerges from the, no doubt
deliberate, contrast with the older 'sister provision', Article 12 (*ex* Article 6), which
deals with non-discrimination on grounds of nationality (only), and which contains
both a directly effective prohibition *and* the conferment of a power for the Council to
adopt further measures designed to prohibit such discrimination. If and when the
Council will adopt 'appropriate measures' on the basis of Article 13 (which will not
be easy, due to the requirement of unanimity included in the Article), the European
Court of Justice will obviously have the power to interpret and enforce those measures. If the 1976 Directive on equal treatment of women and men is a precedent to go
by, then the Court of Justice may, indeed, considerably enhance the potential effect
of a Council measure designed to combat, say, racial and ethnic discrimination.[101]
Apart from that, the new Article 13 could also play an indirect role by affecting the
interpretation given by the Court to Justice to the *general principle of equality*.
Henceforth, differentiations (made by the EC institutions or Member States within
the scope of Community law) based on the grounds listed in Article 6a might be examined with greater suspicion than other differentiations.

A less apparent but more immediately important change is the fact that the application and interpretation of Article F(2) TEU (renumbered as Article 6(2)) is

---

[99] This new mechanism is analysed elsewhere in this vol.

[100] That this formulation aims at 'avoiding any direct effect' was expressly stated by the Dutch Presidency's 'Non-Paper' No. 6 ('Fundamental Rights and Non-Discrimination') of 26 Feb. 1997,
CONF/3827/97—not made public, but available at http://www.eel.nl/docs/nonpape6.htm.

[101] The 1976 Directive is examined by Catherine Barnard in her contribution to this vol.

brought within the jurisdiction of the Court of Justice thanks to an amendment of Article L. The new text of Article L (renumbered as Article 46), states that the provisions of the Treaties concerning the powers of the Court of Justice shall apply, among others, to 'Article F(2) with regard to action of the institutions, insofar as the court has jurisdiction under the Treaties establishing the European Communities and under this Treaty'.

The main function of this amendment of Article 46 is to correct the anomaly created by the Treaty of Maastricht which had proclaimed, in Article F (now Article 6), that the EU should respect fundamental rights as general principles of Community law, but had failed, in Article L, to allow the Court of Justice to use this new clause as a written basis for its fundamental rights case law. Through the correction made now, the Court of Justice will henceforth be able to refer to the text of the (EU) Treaty itself, rather than to unwritten general principles, when applying its fundamental rights doctrine. The irony, however, is that Article 6 states that fundamental rights are protected 'as general principles' so that, in fact, nothing much will change.

The new Article 46(d), contains two qualifying clauses which deserve closer attention. The words 'with regard to action of the institutions' are somewhat enigmatic. They might be read as an attempt to overrule the *Wachauf/ERT* case law of the ECJ that extended its supervision to the action of the *Member States* when acting within the scope of Community law,[102] but nothing in the *travaux préparatoires* of the Treaty, as far as they are available, indicates that this was the Member States' intention when inserting those words.[103] They probably serve only as an introduction to the other qualifying clause ('insofar as the Court has jurisdiction under the Treaties establishing the European Communities and under this Treaty'), which does have a precise meaning: it is intended to confirm that the Court will have to apply Article 6 in the framework of the existing procedures and that this Article does not, as such, allow the Court to review measures under the second and third pillars that fall generally outside the jurisdiction of the Court.

So far, the Court has been excluded from considering *any* second and third pillar measures, with the only exception of Conventions in the field of justice and home affairs which *can* provide for a competence of the Court (Article 31 (*ex* Article K.3) TEU, final sentence).[104] But the Treaty of Amsterdam changes this picture quite radically by providing that, in principle, the Court shall have jurisdiction to review and interpret third-pillar measures (Article K.7, renumbered as Article 35 TEU). The nature of that jurisdiction is rather different from, and globally more restricted, than that under the EC Treaty. Preliminary references will be possible if the individual Member States so allow, and individuals cannot bring direct actions to the CFI.[105] Still, the reform opens the opportunity to subject the future measures on police and judicial co-operation to judicial review based on Article 6(2) (*ex* Article F(2)). Equally, if not more, important is the fact that the entire part of Justice and Home

---

[102] See above, Part II, sect. A.

[103] The same view is taken by P. Wachsmann, 'Les droits de l'homme' [1997] *RTDE* 181.

[104] On the use made of this optional competence clause, see C. Groenendijk, 'The European Court of Justice and the Third Pillar', in H. Meijers (ed.), *Of Democracy, Migrants and Police in the European Union: The 1996 IGC and Beyond* (1997), 45.

[105] See H. Labayle, 'Un espace de liberté, de sécurité et de justice' [1997] *RTDE* 874–6.

Affairs dealing with immigration and movement of persons is going to be transferred to the EC Treaty, where it will form a Title of its own,[106] with its own characteristics, including special rules on the European Court's jurisdiction that are
somewhat different from the general rules of the EC Treaty. For present purposes,
the most important difference is that only national courts of final appeal will be able
(but not bound) to make preliminary references on the interpretation and validity of
this part of EC law. The intention was probably to avoid a flood of cases coming from
lower national courts about asylum issues.[107] Yet, although lower courts will not be
able to refer cases themselves, they will certainly be able to apply to those cases the
general principles of Community law as interpreted by the ECJ in previous rulings.

The role which the Court of Justice will play in the area now covered by the third
pillar will be of crucial importance. The credibility of the EU's external human rights
policy generally depends on how seriously human rights are taken as an internal EU
matter, and questions of immigration and asylum are particularly meaningful in the
eyes of third countries.

Apart from the consequences of the changes made to the text of the EC and EU
Treaties, the post-Amsterdam years may also bring new challenges of a more general
nature for the ECJ's fundamental rights case law. One could mention three of those:

(a) The protracted dispute with a number of German courts on the Community organization of the banana market, although only partially related to
fundamental rights, is certainly having a negative effect on the authority of
the ECJ's case law on fundamental rights. The Court will have to display
considerable caution and sensitivity in order to restore the situation and
avoid other judicial guerrillas from breaking out elsewhere in the Union.[108]

(b) Increasing reference is made, recently, to 'civil and political rights' a trend
which is naturally linked to the increased scope of the European Union's
activity, away from the core area of economic regulation. One could cite, as
an example, the multiplication of freedom of expression issues within the
EC legal order. Apart from the actual judgments of the Court dealing with
this freedom (*ERT, TV 10, Bauer Verlag*), free speech issues arise in
connection with the 'Television without Frontiers' Directive,[109] with the
Data Protection Directive of 1995,[110] and with the actions taken or envisaged by the European Union to combat racism and to regulate the use of
the Internet.

---

[106] Title IIIa of Part 3, Arts. 73i–73q (now Title IV, Arts. 61–69).

[107] Labayle, note 105 above, at 861.

[108] Awareness of this problem is shown in a recent article co-authored by the President of the Court of
Justice: G.C. Rodriguez Iglesias and A. Valle Galvez, 'El Derecho comunitario y las relaciones entre el
Tribunal de Justicia de las Comunidades Europeas, el Tribunal Europeo de Derechos Humanos y los Tri-
bunales Constitucionales nacionales' [1997] *Revista de Derecho Comunitario Europeo* 329.

[109] Namely, with regard to the restrictions of the freedom of broadcasting contained in the Dir., such
as the total ban on advertising for tobacco (on which, see above Part II, sect. B) and the 'European quota'
requirements (on which, see B. de Witte, 'The European Content Requirement in the EC Television Directive—Five Years After' [1995] *The Yearbook of Media and Entertainment Law* 116–17).

[110] See S. Rasaiah and D. Newell, 'Data Protection and Press Freedom', *The Yearbook of Media and
Entertainment Law* Vol. III (1997–8), 209.

(c) The Court of Justice will probably be called on to play a more important role with regard to the outside world. In 1996, it already decided a case of alleged fundamental rights violations caused by the EU sanctions against *ex*-Yugoslavia.[111] If the human rights clauses included in so many external agreements of the EC start being activated, legal disputes might arise before the ECJ there as well. And the announced accession of Central and Eastern Europe may require a strengthening of the judicial enforcement of human rights in the EU legal order beyond what the Treaty of Amsterdam has been able to achieve.

IV. AN AGENDA FOR THE FUTURE

In its recent Resolution on the Human Rights Situation in the European Union, the European Parliament approved no fewer than 140 recommendations and calls for action addressed to the Member States and to various EU institutions. Only one of them was also addressed to the European Court of Justice, and even that one was put in very generic language.[112] The least one can say after that is that the role of the ECJ in human rights affairs is not a prime object of public discussion. Does the absence of exhortations to the Court also mean that its present performance in the human rights sphere is perfect and that nothing needs to be changed? That would be going too far. There may be more pressing issues on the EU's human rights agenda, but the 'unspectacular' question of human rights protection by the ECJ and CFI requires some further thought too.

One general point should be taken into account, when considering the reforms relating to the role of the Court of Justice that are discussed in the following pages. Most, if not all of them, would increase the workload of the Court of First Instance and European Court of Justice. This, in itself, is no good reason for not undertaking reforms which would strengthen the rule of law in the EC legal order. But it means that any reforms should be accompanied by structural reforms of the European 'judicial architecture' and the present procedures. Indeed, increasing the possibility for some parties to have access to the European Courts would be of no avail if all parties had to wait even longer than today for a ruling from those Courts. Already during the preparation of the previous intergovernmental conference, Jacqué and Weiler had emphasized the serious consequences of the Court's backlog of cases, and made some imaginative proposals of reform.[113] Two IGCs have passed since, and nothing much has been accomplished, although the problem itself has not gone away. It

---

[111] Case C–84/95, *Bosphorus* [1996] ECR I–3953, at 3985–7.

[112] Resolution on the Human Rights Situation in the European Union of 17 Feb. 1998, published in *Agence Europe—Documents*, No. 2074/75 of 26 Feb. 1998, point 47: '[the EP] urges the Council, the Commission and the Court of Justice of the European Communities to devote special attention, in their own decisions, to the above mentioned Declaration of fundamental rights and freedoms adopted by the European Parliament on 12 April 1989 . . .'.

[113] J. Jacqué and J.H.H. Weiler, 'On the Road to European Union—A New Judicial Architecture: An Agenda for the Intergovernmental Conference' (1990) 27 *CML Rev.* 185.

would lead too far to examine here how such a structural reform of the European adjudication system should look. Others have made useful suggestions in this respect.[114] But it should be emphasized that most of the proposals discussed in the following pages would have to be accompanied by reforms of the present system of European adjudication.

When coming, now, to the 'agenda' for the role of the Court of Justice, an important formal distinction should be kept in mind, namely the procedure to be followed in order to bring about desirable changes:

—Major changes, such as accession of the European Community and/or the European Union to the European Convention on Human Rights or the adoption of a fundamental rights catalogue for the European Union, require an amendment of the EC or EU Treaty in accordance with Article 48 (*ex* Article N), that is to say, an intergovernmental conference crowned by the common accord of all fifteen Member States and followed by ratification by all of them according to their constitutional requirements. Now that the Treaty of Amsterdam has just been agreed, there is no immediate perspective for a new treaty revision. Changes requiring treaty amendment can therefore only be envisaged within the framework of the next 'regular' IGC which will take place in connection with the enlargement of the EU.[115]

—Other measures could be adopted in a simpler way. They could involve the adoption of an act of Community law (a regulation or a decision) by the institutions of the EU, or action taken by the European Court of Justice or the Court of First Instance itself. In this connection, it should be recalled that the ECJ is not the master of its own Rules of Procedure. Article 188 EC (renumbered as Article 245) provides: '[t]he Court of Justice shall adopt its rules of procedure. These shall require the unanimous approval of the Council.'

Against this background, I will now turn to the following suggestions for reform:

—a redefinition of the *formal sources* of human rights protection, by either the accession to the European Human Rights Convention or the adoption of additional (written) human rights;

---

[114] See, in addition to Jacqué and Weiler's article mentioned in the previous note, W. van Gerven, 'The Role and Structure of the European Judiciary Now and in the Future', in J. Winter, D. Curtin, A. Kellermann, and B. de Witte (eds.), *Reforming the Treaty on European Union—The Legal Debate* (1996), 221; D. Scorey, 'A New Model for the Communities' Judicial Architecture in the New Union' (1996) 21 *EL Rev.* 224; various contributions in Lord Slynn of Hadley (ed.), *The Role and Future of the European Court of Justice* (1996); A. Tizzano, 'Il ruolo della Corte di giustizia nella prospettiva dell'Unione europea' (1994) 73 *RDI* 922; J.L. da Cruz Vilaça, 'Le système juridictionnel communautaire', in A. Mattera (ed.), *La conférence intergouvernementale sur l'Union européenne: répondre aux défis du XXIe siècle* (1996), 219; U. Everling, 'Die Zukunft der europäische Gerichtsbarkeit in einer erweiterten Europäischen Union' [1997] *Europarecht* 398; F. Emmert, *Der Europäische Gerichtshof in Luxemburg als Garant der Rechtsgemeinschaft*, Ph.D thesis at the University of Maastricht, Apr. 1998, Part V.

[115] See Prot. (No. 7) to the Treaty of Amsterdam 'on the institutions with the prospect of enlargement of the European Union'. In that Prot., the States Parties agree (in Art. 2) that '[a]t least one year before the membership of the European Union exceeds twenty, a conference of representatives of the governments of the Member State shall be convened in order to carry out a comprehensive review of the provisions of the Treaties on the composition and functioning of the institutions'. Thus, the date for the next IGC is not indicated with precision, although it is not likely to be started before 2001 at the earliest. Although the protection of human rights is not expressly mentioned, nothing would prevent the Member States from dealing with that subject at that future IGC, if they choose to.

—a relaxation of the *standing requirements* for individuals before the European Court of Justice in cases of human rights violations;

—the creation of a *new course of action* before the European Court of Justice (including the CFI), namely a 'human rights complaint' or 'European *amparo*';

—provision for a right of action or intervention for *public interest organizations*, such as the European Ombudsman.

One could, of course, also consider changes in the human rights *doctrines and review standards* applied by the European Court of Justice. But this is a matter for the Court itself to decide, in a dialogue with the Member State courts and (perhaps) with the legal literature; also, the evaluation of the Court's present performance in this respect is rather controversial and does not allow for firm recommendations.[116]

Finally, it must be emphasized that the 'agenda' described in the following pages is limited to reforms which would directly affect the role of the European Court of Justice. They have to be seen within the context of the overall picture drawn by the chapters of this book dealing with the various EU institutions. For instance, if a stronger *preventive control* of the respect for human rights by EU institutions were set up, that would alleviate the review function of the Court of Justice.[117] If, to mention another example, a new section were added to the EC Treaty providing the Community with the competence to develop a *human rights policy*[118] (that is, a more general recognition of the power limited, in the new Article 13 EC, to certain forms of discrimination), this would allow progress in domains where the Court cannot act, such as improving non-judicial mechanisms of human rights advocacy, and laying down new human rights obligations, in certain well-defined areas, for the *Member States* and for *private actors*. Such a human rights competence would not immediately affect the Court of Justice, but *au fur et à mesure* that the institutions would develop such a human rights policy, the Court could usefully make its contribution in enforcing those new rules.

A. Accession to the ECHR and an EU Catalogue

These two 'spectacular' reforms have been on the agenda for many years now, to no avail so far. They seem like two Loch Ness monsters of EU human rights protection: attractive to some and repulsive to others but intriguing to all, and yet ever so elusive. They have also been likened to 'tired old horses which have over the years been

---

[116] But see my observations in the Conclusion to Part II, above.

[117] For instance, one could envisage the creation of the European equivalent of the French *Conseil d'Etat*, as was suggested by the *Conseil d'Etat* itself in its *Rapport Public 1992* (Etudes et Documents No. 44, at 31). The role of the *Conseil d'Etat* in preventing fundamental rights violations is emphasized by N. Questiaux, 'Administration and the Rule of Law: The Preventive Role of the French Conseil d'Etat' [1995] *PL* 249. For a sceptical view on whether this model would make sense in the European Union, see C. Timmermans, 'How Can One Improve the Quality of Community Legislation?' (1997) 34 *CML Rev.* 1247–8.

[118] See the proposal submitted, prior to the Treaty of Amsterdam, by J.H.H. Weiler, 'European Citizenship and Human Rights', in Winter *et al.*, note 114 above, at 81–6. From the legal point of view, it might be argued that a global human rights policy would *not necessarily* require Treaty amendment, but could also be based on Art. 308 EC. In my view, the ECJ's *Opinion 2/94* on accession to the ECHR does not rule this out.

flogged practically to death';[119] their advantages have repeatedly been described but the masters of the Treaty, the Member States acting together within an IGC, have never let themselves be convinced so far.

Accession of the European Community to the European Convention of Human Rights through the relatively informal route of a Community act based on Article 308 (*ex* Article 235) (followed, obviously, by the necessary modifications of the Convention itself) was sealed off by the European Court of Justice in its *Opinion 2/94*. There is no sign that the ECJ would reconsider its view in the future, nor is there any inclination among the EU institutions or the Member States to ask its opinion again. The ECJ hastened to add, in its *Opinion 2/94*, that accession to the ECHR could be made possible by way of an amendment of the EC Treaty. During the recent IGC, that option was duly considered, but there was no general consensus (nor even a majority) among the Member States in favour of inserting a provision into the Treaty which would allow accession. Therefore, until a new IGC for the revision of the Treaties is convened, the accession of either the EU or the EC[120] to the Convention is no longer under consideration. Is the idea definitively killed or will it be worth opening up the whole discussion once again on that future occasion? Several commentators, disappointed by the ECJ's *Opinion 2/94* and the lack of progress achieved in the Treaty of Amsterdam, have expressed the opinion that accession remains the best way to enhance the legal protection of fundamental rights in the EU legal order.[121]

Their main argument is one of congruence. All Member States of the EU are parties to the ECHR and subject to the jurisdiction of its organs. By transferring powers to the EC and the EU, at each Treaty revision again, they are in fact reducing the scope of their own actions that are subject to ECHR review; it would seem logical that the beneficiary of those transfers of powers, the EU, should be subject to the same human rights standards as they are. The problem is not so much that the standard of protection for Convention rights, offered by the Court of Justice, would be lower than that offered in Strasbourg; as I indicated before, there may not be a real problem there.[122] But the existence of a check by 'outsiders' on the human rights performance of the EU institutions would be a sign of self-confidence and a useful message to those third countries whose human rights performance is monitored by the EU. As for the limit to the ultimate authority of the ECJ which accession would

---

[119] Weiler, note 118 above, at 77.

[120] The question whether the EU or the EC would be the appropriate Contracting Party to the ECHR raises difficult issues in terms of the current understanding of EU law. Obviously, it would be of utmost importance that *all EU actions*, not just those of the EC pillar, should be subject to human rights review. In my view, the European Union should now be considered as the encompassing organization (of which the EC is a part) and will have, after the entry into force of the Treaty of Amsterdam, the capacity to conclude international agreements, so that accession of the European Union (without separate accession by the EC) would seem appropriate (for arguments supporting this view, see B. de Witte, 'The Pillar Structure and the Nature of the European Union: Greek Temple or French Gothic Cathedral', contribution to the proceedings of the 40th Anniversary Colloquium of the Europa Institute Leiden, Nov. 1997.

[121] Wachsmann, note 103 above, at 902; D. Curtin and Y. Klerk, 'De Europese Unie en het Europees Verdrag voor de Rechten van de Mens' [1997] *Nederlands Juristenblad* 202; R. Gosalbo Bono, 'Reflexiones en torno al futuro de la protección de los derechos humanos en el marco del derecho comunitario y del derecho de la Unión: insuficiencias y soluciones' [1997] *Revista de Derecho Comunitario Europeo* 56–8.

[122] See above, Part II, sect. C. But see also the contribution of Dean Spielmann to this vol.

entail, one can simply say that 'there is no loss of prestige for the ECJ to be in the same position as the highest courts in all Member States'.[123]

The adoption of a *catalogue of rights* (or 'Bill of Rights'), tailor-made for the European Union itself, remains a very divisive issue. Although the idea was considered during the recent IGC, it never came very far, as none of the Member State delegations even bothered to submit a draft catalogue of its making. The European Parliament, on its part, has adopted such a catalogue in its Declaration on Fundamental Rights of 1989,[124] and its institutional committee adopted a slightly different version as part of its Draft Constitution of the European Union of 1994.[125] Both texts are inspired by the ECJ's judgments and by its general attitude of drawing from national constitutions and the European Convention on Human Rights rather than trying to reinvent the wheel. Due to its moderate approach, the European Parliament's effort forms a useful starting-point for any future attempts to formulate a binding EU catalogue of rights. But, even if the Member States could find agreement on the text of a catalogue, the question remains whether such a new EU-centred Bill of Rights would serve any discernible purpose in view of the existing national, European and worldwide instruments. Is there not in Western Europe today a situation of rights saturation rather than rights deprivation?[126]

The main advantage of a written Bill of Rights would be to make the existing regime of protection of human rights in the EC legal order more *visible*. This symbolic move could strengthen the legitimacy of the European Union in the eyes of European citizens, which may precisely be the reason why the Member States have been reluctant to adopt such a catalogue. Beyond these political considerations, a written catalogue would also make the European citizens, and other aggrieved persons, somewhat more aware of their rights. At least, one would no longer have to suspect that the small number of fundamental rights cases reaching the CFI and ECJ is simply due to the esoteric nature of the 'general principles' doctrine. Also, written rights could better reverberate through the whole EC legal order and serve as a policy objective for the legislator and as an interpretive device for the Court of Justice. Those are reasons which could justify the adoption, on a future occasion of Treaty revision, of a Treaty Article or chapter enumerating the fundamental rights by which the EC and the EU are bound (as well as the Member States acting within the scope of EC

[123] Weiler, note 118 above, at 79. A rather different view was defended recently by A. Toth, 'The European Union and Human Rights: The Way Forward' (1997) 34 *CML Rev.* 491. He proposes the incorporation of all Convention rights into the EU Treaty, combined with the withdrawal of all EU States from the European Convention, so that the task of protecting human rights (including protection against the Member States) would be transferred from Strasbourg to Luxembourg. This would be a decisive step towards a federal European Union and, already for that reason, quite unacceptable for the Member States in their present mood. But, apart from that, the present situation in which responsibility for the protection of human rights is divided over the European Court of Human Rights, the ECJ, and national constitutional courts, each within the limits of their competence, seems preferable to me.

[124] [1989] OJ C120/51. A detailed commentary on the Declaration was published recently: R. Bieber, K. de Gucht, K. Lenaerts, and J. Weiler (eds.), *Au nom des peuples européens—In the name of the peoples of Europe* (1996).

[125] The Draft Constitution was not formally adopted by the plenary of the European Parliament but was published as an Annex to its Resolution on the Constitution of the European Union of 10 Feb. 1994, [1994] OJ C61/155.

[126] Those expressions are used by Weiler, note 118 above, at 79–81. Yet, this author goes on, in his article to support the adoption of a catalogue.

and EU law).[127] At the same time, it should be clear that such a step would have major institutional consequences, way beyond the human rights question itself. The adoption of a catalogue of fundamental rights would be seen by many, and correctly so, as a decisive step towards a federal Europe. A consensus on this matter seems therefore very remote, for reasons which are not directly related to the question of devising the optimal system of protection for human rights in Europe. It is important, therefore, to put on the 'agenda' some other reforms that would be (slightly) less controversial, while being as useful, if not more, for the effective protection of rights.

B. Relaxation of the Standing Requirements under Article 230(4) EC Treaty

One of the criticisms of the present case law of the ECJ and CFI is that those courts have taken an unnecessarily narrow view of the condition, imposed by Article 230(4) (*ex* Article 173(4)) EC, that individuals should be 'directly and individually concerned' by an act of Community law in order to have standing to sue the Community. The ECJ itself showed some uneasiness about this *locus standi* rule in its Report to the recent IGC, where it wrote:

> It may be asked . . . whether the right to bring an action for annulment under Article 173 [now Article 230] of the EC Treaty (and the corresponding provisions of the other Treaties), which individuals enjoy only in regard to acts of direct and individual concern to them, is sufficient to guarantee for them effective judicial protection against possible infringements of their fundamental rights arising from the legislative activity of the institutions.[128]

If this was an invitation to the Member States to modify paragraph 4 of Article 173, it went unheeded; the Treaty of Amsterdam has not dealt with this question.

Yet, perhaps the ECJ (and, under its ægis, the CFI) could remedy, to some extent, this deficit on its own initiative. When examining standing requirements in national law, it appears that similar expressions as those of 'directly and individually concerned' are often used in order to limit the possibilities of access to courts, but the interpretation given to those expressions is invariably more liberal.[129] So, the ECJ could overrule, or bend, its case law and allow, more liberally than before, private parties to challenge the legality of normative acts of EC law, while staying within the formal limits of Article 230 as it stands today.[130] Perhaps a method for reaching that

---

[127] For more elaborate pleadings in favour of a Community catalogue of rights, see, for instance, L. Diez-Picazo, 'Una constitución sin Declaración de Derechos? (Reflexiones constitucionales sobre los derechos fundamentales en la Comunidad Europea)' (1991) 32 *Revista Española de Derecho Constitucional* 135; M. Hilf, 'Ein Grundrechtskatalog für die europäische Gemeinschaft' [1991] *Europarecht* 19; P. Twomey, 'The European Union: Three Pillars without a Human Rights Foundation', in D. O'Keeffe and P. Twomey (eds.), *Legal Issues of the Maastricht Treaty* (1994), 128–31; U. Preuss, 'Grundrechte in der Europäischen Union' (1998) 31 *Kritische Justiz* 1.

[128] *Report of the Court of Justice on Certain Aspects of the Application of the Treaty on European Union*, note 44 above, at 11.

[129] Waelbroeck and Verheyden, note 72 above, at 399.

[130] The ECJ was formally invited to overrule its earlier case law and allow standing more widely in a 'test case' brought by Greenpeace: Case C–321/95P, *Stichting Greenpeace Council and Others* v. *Commission*, judgment of 2 Apr. 1998 (not yet reported). The Court, while extensively quoting from the arguments submitted by the applicants, decided to stick to its established case law but without offering extensive arguments for doing so (paras. 27–35), a fact which, perhaps, is due to disagreement among the judges on this question.

result could be to interpret Article 230, paragraph 4, in the light of Articles 6 and 13 of the European Convention on Human Rights which require that a judicial remedy should be available for the protection of 'civil rights' (Article 6) and for the 'rights granted by the Convention' (Article 13).[131]

There are limits to the possibility for the Court of Justice to stretch the terms 'direct and individual concern'. A clear-cut solution could be offered by a revision of Article 230, paragraph 4, which would make the basic test of standing whether the applicant has been *adversely affected* by the contested act,[132] a term which is inspired by the liberal standing rules in US and UK administrative law, and by the *intérêt à agir* criterion of French administrative law. It does not seem very practical to reserve such a broader right of access just to cases of fundamental rights violations; a general extension of the right of action under Article 230 would be preferable, although one could imagine that victims of fundamental rights violations would more easily be able to show that they were 'adversely affected' by a given measure.

One could go even one step further by recognizing the *locus standi* of associations and public interest groups.[133] In a number of countries in Europe, such forms of group litigation are facilitated through legislative reforms and court doctrine. The recognition of their standing rights is a traditional demand of the access to justice movement whose time may have come in the European Union, and particularly in the human rights field.[134]

C. Creation of an Individual Human Rights Complaint Procedure (the 'European Amparo')

In the first progress report on the Intergovernmental Conference, submitted by the Italian Presidency at the end of its term, in June 1996,[135] one of the options in the area of fundamental rights was described as follows: 'extending the scope for bringing actions before the Court of Justice by enabling individuals to bring actions directly before the Court of Justice for violation of a fundamental right'. The Italian government added cautiously that this option attracted little support, so far, among the Member State delegations. And, indeed, the subsequent draft submitted by the

---

[131] Waelbroeck and Verheyden (note 72 above) even argue that the present case law of the ECJ is actually in breach of those Arts. of the Convention. From the standpoint of the EC legal order, though, the ECHR (merely) provides guidelines for developing the general principles of Community law. Those general principles cannot prevail over the text of the EC Treaty itself, but nothing surely prevents the Court from *interpreting* that Treaty *in the light of* the general principles.

[132] This term was proposed by Arnull, note 64 above, at 49. A similar suggestion was made by G. Vandersanden, 'Pour un élargissement du droit des particuliers d'agir en annulation contre des actes autres que les décisions qui leur sont adressées' [1995] *CDE* 535, who proposed (at 551) the following text of a new para. in Art. 173: '*[t]oute personne physique ou morale peut former, dans les mêmes conditions, un recours contre les actes autres que ceux dont elle est destinataire, dans la mesure où elle est suffisamment affectée par de tels actes*'.

[133] For the distinction between associational and public interest standing, together with a description of the very liberal practice in the United Kingdom, see P. Cane, 'Standing up for the Public' [1995] *PL* 276. For a comprehensive panorama of the present state of the law, covering national and EC law, see H.-W. Micklitz and N. Reich (eds.), *Public Interest Litigation before European Courts* (1996).

[134] Elaborate arguments in favour of increased public interest representation before the ECJ can be found in C. Harlow, 'Towards a Theory of Access for the European Court of Justice' (1992) 12 *YEL* 213.

[135] Conference of the Representatives of the Governments of the Member States, Conf. 3860/1/96, 17 June 1996.

Irish Presidency (the so-called 'Dublin-II document') avoided any reference to this option, and it was no longer on the agenda during the final stages of the negotiations leading to the adoption of the Treaty of Amsterdam.

In reconsidering this option for the future, one should note its close relationship with the question addressed above, of the standing to sue under Article 230, paragraph 4, EC. Obviously, what was meant by the Italian suggestion is a *special* procedure for the judicial protection of *fundamental rights* which would go beyond what is offered by Article 230 for the protection of private interests *in general*.

The model for this suggestion is formed, undoubtedly, by the constitutional complaint procedure (*Verfassungsbeschwerde*) in German law and by the slightly different *recurso de amparo* procedure in Spanish law. Without going into a detailed comparison, those two procedures have a few important common features. First, they are *subsidiary* procedures. A direct complaint to the Constitutional Court is available only to the extent that the ordinary courts have failed to uphold the applicant's constitutional rights. And secondly, the applicant must show that he is directly and individually[136] concerned by the measure. A so-called *Popularklage* is not allowed, and complaints directed against *legislative acts*, although possible in German law, are only very rarely declared admissible. Normally, such acts will harm the applicant only through their application by the administrative authorities; the complaint can then be raised against this administrative act or, rather, against the court judgment which failed to provide a remedy against that administrative act. Despite those conditions of admissibility, there are thousands of *amparo* and *Verfassungsbeschwerde* complaints every year, and those found admissible do constitute the majority of cases dealt with by the constitutional courts of those two countries.[137]

In considering the value of incorporating the *Verfassungsbeschwerde* or *amparo* model into EU law,[138] one should distinguish between protection against European Union acts and protection against Member State acts.

As for protection against EU acts, an individual complaint procedure modelled on the *amparo* or the *Verfassungsbeschwerde* procedures would not serve, at first sight, any discernible purpose. In German as well as in Spanish law, the ordinary judicial remedies must have been exhausted and the applicant must show that he is directly concerned by the act which he is challenging. In practice, this means that the vast majority of *amparo* or *Verfassungsbeschwerde* complaints are directed against judicial decisions which, allegedly, failed to protect the applicant's constitutional rights. Under the existing system of judicial review of EC acts, the issue of their validity is not to be decided by the 'ordinary' courts first, but directly by the European Courts themselves, either the ECJ (when the validity of an EC act is questioned by a

---

[136] In one of its first judgments, the German Constitutional Court used the formula that the applicant must be affected personally, directly, and presently (*selbst, unmittelbar, und gegenwärtig*): 1 Entscheidungen des Bundesverfassungsgerichts 97. This formula has been used ever since.

[137] And even though only 2% of the *Verfassungsbeschwerden* are successful on the merits, according to the latest figures, that still amounts to some hundred cases a year (*Süddeutsche Zeitung*, 13 Dec. 1997).

[138] The most elaborate argument in favour of its introduction into EC law was made by H.-W. Rengeling, 'Brauchen wir die Verfassungsbeschwerde auf Gemeinschaftsebene?', in Due, Lutter and Schwarze, note 61 above, at 1187.

national court) or the CFI (when the legality of the act is challenged directly by an individual). Moreover, judgments of the Court of First Instance can be appealed to the European Court of Justice on points of law, which obviously include failure to give due recognition to fundamental rights. In other words: the result that the *recurso de amparo* and the *Verfassungsbeschwerde* seek to achieve, namely allowing individuals direct access to the constitutional court for deciding human rights issues, seems to be in place already in EC law. But that conclusion is not quite true, due to two characteristics of the EC system which have been mentioned before: the fact that the admissibility criterion of being 'directly and individually concerned', although formally similar, is given a much narrower reading by the European Courts than by the constitutional courts of Germany and Spain; and the fact that the individual, after having exhausted domestic remedies, cannot bring himself a complaint to the European Court of Justice, but depends on the willingness of the national court to refer a question of validity. If access to the CFI under Article 230 were made broader, in accordance with the proposal made above, then introducing a new 'constitutional complaint' procedure would not be useful. In the absence of such a broadening of standing under Article 230, it could be envisaged as a second-best solution.

Things are rather different with regard to the *judicial review of Member State acts* for violation of Community fundamental rights. Even within the present limits of the application of those fundamental rights ('within the scope of Community law'; see above Part II, Section A), a 'European *amparo*' would radically transform the existing judicial architecture as it would allow the European Courts to decide upon the compatibility of national measures with Community fundamental rights on the initiative of aggrieved individuals and not, as is the case today, through the intermediary of national courts formulating a preliminary reference. Today, where a national court, deciding a case at final appeal, fails to address an issue of violation of Community rights, or decides this issue in the wrong way, there is no further remedy for the individual invoking those rights. A European *amparo* procedure would allow such an individual to raise the issue directly in Luxembourg. This would alter the present 'sacrosanct' division of tasks, whereby individual challenges to Member State action are to be decided by the courts of that Member State.

In order to protect the Court from being overwhelmed, the conditions for the admissibility of the European *amparo* should be clearly circumscribed. Inspiration could be found in the conditions of admissibility of the similar actions in Germany and Spain:

(a) The case should involve the alleged violation of fundamental rights. This is a difficult point. Both in Spain and in Germany, the complaint procedure may be used for the protection of a closed number of expressly identified constitutional rights. In the European Union, as there is no pre-existing catalogue of fundamental rights which potential applicants may consult, there would be considerable uncertainty as to which breaches are cognizable by the Court of Justice, at least as long as the Court had not developed a full list through its case law. Here again, as is obvious, the adoption of a Treaty-based catalogue of fundamental rights would facilitate things considerably.

(b) The national measure which allegedly violates fundamental rights should fall within the scope of Community law. The creation of a new individual remedy would be an extra reason for the Court of Justice to be careful not to extend its review to national measures which are unconnected with EU law.

(c) The applicant should be 'directly' or at least 'sufficiently' affected by the measure.

(d) The national remedies should have been exhausted.

If one adds up all those conditions of admissibility, they are, in fact, very similar to the requirements for bringing an application to the European Commission of Human Rights (from November 1998 on: the European Court of Human Rights itself) in Strasbourg. In substance, the human rights standard to be applied by the CFI and ECJ would also be similar to that applied in Strasbourg. One might argue that it is not worth the trouble of creating an entirely new procedure, with the danger of increasing the workload of the Court of Justice and disturbing the delicate relationship between national and European courts, for the duplication of a procedure which is already provided by the European Convention.[139]

Our conclusion is that, despite its *prima facie* appeal, the creation of a European *amparo* is not to be recommended.

D. Access to Court for Public Interest Institutions?

The European Ombudsman deals with *maladministration* by the EC institutions. This term includes breaches of fundamental rights, or at least breaches through individual administrative acts. When a complaint is made, the Ombudsman must, first, try to find an amicable solution; if that is not possible, he can direct a draft recommendation to the EC institution involved and, in the absence of a satisfactory reaction by the latter, make a final recommendation to the European Parliament on the measures to be taken. The Ombudsman is not allowed to seise the European Court of Justice.

The action of the European Ombudsman seems to be taken seriously by the EU institutions. This may justify a reform moving one step further by allowing the Ombudsman to bring a complaint about a breach of fundamental rights, after having tried to solve it according to the existing mechanisms, before the CFI (or directly before the ECJ). This option could be an attractive 'lighter' alternative to the introduction of an individual constitutional complaint of the *amparo* type. The sieve mechanism, which an *amparo* procedure must expressly provide in order to prevent submersion of the Court, would be naturally provided here by the prior conciliation efforts of the Ombudsman and his discretionary evaluation whether the case is serious enough to put it before the Court of Justice.

The European Ombudsman is not competent to consider the activities of *national authorities* acting under Community law. The present Ombudsman expressed the

---

[139] Things would be slightly different if the ECJ were able to waive the condition of exhausting available national remedies if the case raises important questions of general interest. This exception to the exhaustion rule exists in the regime of the German *Verfassungsbeschwerde*.

view that, rather than extending the scope of his powers, one could rely on the emerging network of national ombudsmen who can, each for their own country and within the remit of their existing powers, check instances of national 'maladministration' in Community affairs.[140] Those national ombudsmen could also be given the right to bring to the CFI (or the ECJ) complaints about violations of Community fundamental rights by Member State authorities. Such a procedural innovation, although rather incisive, might seem less threatening to the Member States than the option, considered above, of allowing *individuals* to bring complaints against them directly before the European Court. The creation of a right of action for the European Ombudsman and for the various national ombudsmen would, in both cases, require a revision of the EC Treaty.[141]

Apart from the ombudsmen, one could encourage other bodies and institutions to play a role in facilitating access to justice for the vindication of human rights. For instance, it is worth meditating on the active role played by the British Equal Opportunities Commission (EOC) in furthering the elimination of gender discrimination.[142] The EOC brought a series of test cases as part of a litigation strategy, both by funding individual litigants and bringing cases in its own name before British courts; these actions before British courts, combined with the preliminary reference procedure of Article 234 (*ex* Article 177) EC, have allowed the ECJ to give many of its important rulings in this field which have brought concrete benefits to millions of women in Britain and, indirectly, elsewhere in Europe. This example could be a source of inspiration for improving access to justice in the field of fundamental rights generally. A European human rights agency could be set up, independently of the EU institutions, which could be given, alongside its other tasks, the right to fund selected human rights applications by individuals and to intervene in relevant cases before the Court of Justice, or even (the most far-reaching reform) to bring cases of alleged human rights violations itself.

[140] The European Ombudsman, *Annual Report 1996,* [1997] OJ C272/1, at 46.

[141] The powers of the European Ombudsman are described in relatively detailed terms by Art. 195 EC and do not include the right to start an action before the Court of Justice. Another problem with the reform advocated here is that one Member State, Italy, does not yet have a national Ombudsman.

[142] See C. Barnard, 'A European Litigation Strategy: The Case of the Equal Opportunities Commission', in Shaw and More, note 98 above, at 253.

28

Human Rights and Civil Society

EMMANUEL DECAUX

Human rights concern us all. The European Union is not just a framework of institutions or the area confining a fragmented European citizenship. It is strange how the very meaning of the word 'community' seems gradually to have become a platitude, although it was at the heart of the founding fathers' project. As the heading of one of the chapters of his political writings, Robert Schuman wrote: '[r]ather than a military alliance or an economic entity, Europe must be first and foremost a cultural community in the loftiest sense of the word'.[1] It is this cultural community that we must regain if the building of Europe is to achieve its full significance.

Today, however, the European Union tends to define itself more in relation to the static description of the various elements which constitute the State than in a relationship of discourse between individuals and the community. Even though the framework of the State is still the model of an organized 'political society', the part played by the individual in collective life is made far richer and more complex through the various forms of 'civil society'.

I. INTRODUCTION

1. Population and Space

Beyond the States, it is the idea of 'peoples' which has been put forward, going with the grain of the Treaty of Rome, now undoubtedly referring more to 'populations' in the macro-economic aggregate than to 'peoples' as agents of history. Thus, in the preamble to the Treaty on European Union the Member States refer in passing to 'the solidarity between their peoples', the strengthening of 'their economies', 'economic and social progress for their peoples', 'the safety and security of their peoples. . .'.

The Treaty contains numerous references to the basic elements of the classic State, territory, population, and government, as though the only reference model were still that of the State. Article 11 (*ex* Article J.1) of the Amsterdam Treaty amends the Maastricht Treaty by making the Union the sole mover of the common foreign and

---

[1] R. Schuman, *Pour l'Europe* (1963), 35.

security policy and no longer 'the Union and its Member States', which gives a different meaning to the objectives entrusted to it, in particular to safeguard the 'independence and integrity of the Union in conformity with the principles of the United Nations Charter', although this concerns attributes of sovereignty belonging to the States themselves and the Charter itself refers only to the States.[2] It has all come about as though, by some legal sleight of hand, the Union meant to steal into the cast-offs of the State, if not a super-State, but yet not to challenge the rights and duties of its Member States.

Odder still is the afterthought about the principles and undertakings of the Organization on Security and Co-operation in Europe ('OSCE'), since Article 11 (*ex* Article J.1) uses terms foreign to the highly coded vocabulary of the OSCE, speaking of 'objectives', but above all it refers to an unknown concept, that of 'external borders', whereas the principles of the OSCE, like those of the UN, recognize sovereign States alone.

Individuals themselves are taken into account in the preamble to the Treaty which seeks to 'establish a citizenship common to nationals of their countries', which applies only to nationals, reproducing on a different scale the state model, 'national treatment' being replaced by 'European treatment', at the risk of involving more discrimination against nationals of European non-member countries and still more against nationals of non-European countries who may have been living on that territory for a long time. Here I must stress how different is the approach of the Council of Europe in 1992 concerning the participation of foreigners in public life at local level.[3] Citizenship is perceived as one of the elements of European identity *vis-à-vis* the external world. At the same time, the new Article 2 (*ex* Article B) states that the Union is intended 'to strengthen the protection of rights and interests of the nationals of its States through the introduction of a citizenship of the Union'.

Only in the field of 'freedom of movement for persons' does the individual as such, almost abstract, nameless, and stateless like a Folon character lost in space,[4] finally make an appearance in the Treaty, rather than 'peoples' *en masse*. According to the new Article 2 (*ex* Article B), one aim is to 'maintain and develop the Union as an area of freedom, security and justice, in which the free movement of persons is assured in conjunction with appropriate measures with respect to external border controls, asylum, immigration and the prevention and combating of crime'. The unspoken logic underlying this list is to associate indiscriminately foreigners and emigrants, asylum-seekers and refugees, with criminals, as external threats without mentioning the fight against terrorism, treated more directly in Title VI of the Treaty of Amsterdam.

Confronted with this macro-political approach, emphasizing peoples and drawing a new boundary between within and without, 'them and us', it seems that there is

---

[2] Apart from Chap. VIII, which is not under consideration here.

[3] ETS No 144. The Convention entered into force on 1 May 1997, after 4 ratifications, those of Italy, the Netherlands, Norway, and Sweden. Only 3 other States are signatories: Cyprus, Denmark, and the United Kingdom.

[4] It is not by chance that it was the artist Folon who illustrated an edition of the Universal Declaration for its 40th anniversary in 1988 for *Libération (Folio)*.

very limited space for individual persons. People, who are the object of 'human rights', are only mentioned behind the ramparts of the law, in so far as the party States confirm 'their attachment to the principles of liberty, democracy and respect for human rights and fundamental freedoms and the rule of law'.

The last recital in the preamble attempts to perfect the ideal of the founding fathers, calling for 'an ever closer union among the peoples of Europe, in which decisions are taken as closely as possible to the citizen in accordance with the principle of subsidiarity'. Can another zone of democracy be discovered in between the union among peoples and the Europe of nation States?

2. *Individual and Community*

Does the principle of subsidiarity[5] apply only to the dialectical discourse between the Union and the Member States, or is it spilling out like a waterfall through ever more vital decentralization? Not just the geographic decentralization of a 'Europe of the regions', but decentralization at yet greater depth through a social and 'cultural' democracy which still remains to be invented, for the most part. The choice is not simply between the capital cities and Brussels, the European executive, or even Strasbourg, the seat of parliamentary 'legitimacy'. Like each of our democracies, Europe more and more needs stages, balances, and mediation, contact points, counterweights, and 'intermediate bodies', that is to say, it needs a genuine civil society, both global and diversified.

There is no question of denying or diluting Europe by favouring a 'centrifugal' Europe at the expense of a 'centripetal' Europe, or of splitting up Europe in full view of its rivals, by seeking a 'formless', as opposed to a 'uniform' Europe or by promoting a Europe of separate pieces, possessing neither political will nor federal dream, but, on the contrary, of wondering whether the European Union should not first be a 'community' with a destiny of becoming a 'powerful Europe' instead of being content with being a 'powerless Europe'? The 'message to Europeans' adopted by the Congress of the Hague in 1948 had already put forward that argument:

> Without a freely agreed union our present anarchy will expose us tomorrow to forcible unification, whether by the intervention of a foreign empire or usurpation by a political party within . . . Europe's mission is clear. It is to unite her peoples in accordance with their genius, which is diversity, and in the conditions of the twentieth century, which are those of the community, so as to open up the path which the world is seeking, the path of organised freedoms.[6]

By using the term 'community', the founding fathers of Europe were not simply looking for a convenient means of transcending the debate between federation and confederation; they were translating a profound philosophy in which the individual person is at the heart of the community.[7] 'The ever closer union among the peoples of Europe' means gradually moving beyond state monopolies in order to allow a real

---

[5] Cf. C. Millon-Delsol, *Le principe de subsidiarité*, Que sais-je? No 2793 (1993).

[6] The Hague Congress (1948), *Verbatim Report*, Closing Plenary Session, 38.

[7] The influence of Emmanuel Mounier's personalism is especially significant, as is the reference to the idea of community in the early works of Paul Reuter. It would be interesting to compare the concepts of 'commonwealth' and 'community' as bases of the social pact.

'European society', alive and rich in its diversity, to see the light of day. To this effect, rather than calling on the 'citizens of Europe' every five years through a political citizenship which remains largely symbolic, like the anthem and the flag, would it not be better to appeal to active citizens, amongst whom the individual is perceived in all his dimensions, no longer 'man in the abstract' confronting the State, but 'man centred' in society.

This multiple democracy is certainly to be found in economic democracy, that of workers and consumers, and social democracy, that of the world of associations. One misunderstanding to avoid is that of the guild mentality which tends to oppose any actual representation of social man confronted with the matchless 'citizenship' of political democracy, by reducing 'social democracy' to the protection of special interests.[8] Too often intermediary bodies represent new fiefdoms, overlapping bureaucracies, or interest groups, to the prejudice of that fundamental democracy whose exemplary beginnings Tocqueville had witnessed in the United States:

> Americans of all ages, all conditions, and all dispositions, constantly form associations . . . Wherever at the head of some new undertaking you see the government in France, or a man of rank in England, in the United States you will be sure to find an association . . . Unhappily, the same social condition that renders associations so necessary to democratic nations renders their formation more difficult among those nations than among all others. . . . A government can no more be competent to keep alive and to renew the circulation of opinions and feelings among a great people than to manage all the speculations of productive industry. . . . Among the laws that rule human societies there is one which seems to be more precise and clear than all others. If men are to remain civilized or to become so, the art of associating together must grow and improve in the same ratio in which the equality of conditions is increased.[9]

Since it is impossible to conjure up the 'United States of Europe' by *Diktat* from on high, have we attempted to create from the bottom up that associative life with its 'intellectual and moral associations' which, for Tocqueville, were not merely the safeguard of liberty in the face of a 'guardian power' determined to be ever more omnipresent but also the very condition for what he called 'civilization'? Beside the Europe of the regions or the Europe of the lobbies, it is time to make space for a Europe conceived of as a community of citizens, rich in ideas and initiatives, closely binding the 'good neighbourhood' ideal to the wider idea of 'community', civilization in daily life.

3. Political Society, Private Society, Civil Society

The importance of civil society as such has for long been obscured by high political stakes. The battle for democracy favoured the role of 'political society', whereas the primacy given to the economy has stressed the role of 'industrial society'. As Raymond Aron, highly representative of that brand of liberal sociology which is fascinated by Marxism, remarked in a study called 'Social Class, Political Class, Ruling Class', power is not only political:

---

[8] Historical examples may be found in abundance, from 'Latin' corporatist regimes to the tripartite composition of the Supreme Soviet in the Gorbachev era.

[9] *Democracy in America* (1840), ii, 106–10.

Today, equality before the law is hardly ever challenged in theory any more and the universality of political participation through the right to vote is no longer a cause of conflict. All members of the community are citizens. But citizens, at the level of what Hegel called 'civil society', at the level of economic activity, all have an occupation . . . East or West, those who hold the reins of state power are connected (it remains to be demonstrated exactly how) to the men of economic power and the men of intellectual or moral standing'.[10]

Raymond Aron goes beyond the purely economic vision of 'civil society' as opposed to political society, which has been traditional since Plato's *Republic*,[11] to describe four antitheses, successively contrasting 'temporal and spiritual power, civil and military power, political and administrative power, and political and economic power'.

But while Raymond Aron concentrated his study on 'élites', we can, I believe, broaden the scope of the question by noting that this differentiation is to be found throughout modern society wherever the State is no longer omnipresent or omnipotent. Thus he connects with Robert Dahl's arguments concerning 'polyarchy'.[12] Confronted with totalitarian societies, pluralism is still the best guarantee of freedom in a global society.

> No ruling class or élite rules in the polyarchic model or in the societies which come closest to it, such as the United States: there, on the contrary, leaders representing the interests of the various groups are seen to compete under the control of the people. The latter exercises its rights both through elections and by its compliance with the 'rules of the game' which the various ruling categories must also observe. It is this free competition between rival groups which, within the limits imposed by consensus, gives rise to spontaneous equilibrium which is the more stable as society itself becomes more diversified.[13]

Without wishing to prolong a theoretical debate concerning political sociology, we may at this juncture recall the existence of a civil society, separate from political society, but which can neither be reduced to the economic sphere alone nor confined to a mere self-sufficient 'private society' turned in on itself.[14] Admittedly, it frequently happens that, through the networks of influence, lobbies, or examples of professional interests, the different types are confused, but 'the intellectual and moral associations' spoken of by Tocqueville must be taken into full consideration.

There is no question of calling in aid some scholarly privilege or 'republic of wise men' which would run the risk of turning into a 'dictatorship of the intelligentsia'. Nor should it be confined to an expression of special interests and lobbies. Sociological analysis of 'interest groups'[15] clearly reveals all the ambivalence of pressure groups, and the profound differences between the American tradition, which perceives the public interest as resulting from private interests, and the European tradition, which allies the monopoly of representative democracy with distrust of all forms of protection of professional interests.

---

[10] R. Aron, 'Classe sociale, classe politique, classe dirigeante' in *Archives européennes de sociologie* (1960), 260–81, reprinted in P. Birnbaum and F. Chauzel, *Sociologie politique* (1971), i, 124 at 134.
[11] A. Bloom, *The Republic of Plato* (2nd edn., 1991), paras. 369–72.
[12] R. Dahl, *A Preface to Democratic Theory* (1956).   [13] Birnbaum, n. 10 above, 121.
[14] J. Rawls, *A Theory of Justice* (1971).
[15] Cf. in particular the works of Y. Mény, *Politique comparée* (1988), 121.

Development of civil society remains essential if the social fabric is to be strengthened, given that the State is increasingly distant, and the construction of Europe contributes to this effect by further distancing the governors from the governed. An embryonic civil European society must be given all the space it needs; it must be envisaged not just as a 'counterbalance', a sphere of autonomy, but above all as a field of participation. Naturally, the freedom which is expressed in autonomy is to be respected, through a wholly secular society, based in particular on the separation of the political arena from the spiritual or religious domain, or on the opposition between the public domain and the private sphere, even beyond 'public freedoms'. However, the freedom which comes through participation, by means of new forms of commitment, a 'social movement' impossible to reduce to the traditional forms of political or trade union involvement, has yet to be discovered.

The spontaneous growth of NGOs (voluntary or non-governmental organizations) in the world would seem to reflect this deep need for freely offered commitment, of collective contemplation, of a watchful sense of citizenship. Since 'civil society' in itself cannot be envisaged here, in its rather rigid totality or by means of somewhat simplified categories, it appears appropriate to take into consideration its most dynamic element through the NGOs. Even in processes centred on the European Union, we must not lose sight of the various dimensions of this question, with the major role played by NGOs in each of the Member States of the Union and having regard to the European Union as such, but also the potential role of NGOs in non-member countries, especially in the field of co-operation where the existence of a flourishing civil society is a sign of development, good governance, and democratic process.

The Declaration of the World Conference on Human Rights in Vienna in 1993 stressed this, emphasizing programmes concerning 'the establishment and strengthening of national legislation, national institutions and related infrastructures which uphold the rule of law and democracy, electoral assistance, human rights awareness through training, teaching and education, popular participation and civil society'.[16] Accordingly '[s]pecial emphasis should be given to measures to assist in the strengthening and building of institutions relating to human rights, strengthening of a pluralistic civil society and the protection of groups which have been rendered vulnerable . . . Equally important is the assistance to be given to the strengthening of the rule of law, the promotion of freedom of expression, and the administration of justice, and to the real and effective participation of the people in the decision-making process'.[17]

Far from being opposed, political democracy and civil society enrich and reinforce each another within a 'society governed by the rule of law'. Taking part in election is on a par with social commitment. By turning their backs on the danger of depoliticization and withdrawal in a 'private society' with no foundation other than selfish calculation, NGOs introduce a new area of good citizenship, participation, and solidarity.

---

[16] United Nations, Vienna Declaration and Programme of Action (1993), part I, para. 34.
[17] *Ibid.*, part II, para. 67.

The Commission itself has described NGOs as the kingpins of our democracy:

> There is no doubt that voluntary organizations and foundations make a profound and indispensable contribution to the democratic life of Europe. Indeed, the existence of a well-developed association and foundation sector is an indication that the democratic process has come of age . . . The contribution [of that sector] to the effectiveness with which representative democracy functions should not, however, be underestimated. Above all, they now play an essential part as intermediaries in the exchange of information and opinion between governments and citizens, providing citizens with the means with which they may critically examine government actions or proposals, and public authorities in their turn with expert advice, guidance on popular views, and essential feedback on the effects of their policies.

The Commission did, however, immediately issue a stern warning:

> That voluntary organizations and foundations are important to the democratic process does not mean that they could ever take on the role occupied by elected representatives. There are, indeed, some dangers in the sort of 'single issue' lobbying which some voluntary organizations tend to espouse. Their preoccupation with particular causes or with particular individuals or groups can make them unjustifiably impatient with the balance between competing interests which all democratically elected governments seek to achieve.[18]

Undoubtedly matters seem different with regard to NGOs active in the field of human rights, inasmuch as they do not plead one special interest against another, but refer to the legal values which are the very foundation of our societies and confer legitimacy on our democracies. That is to say that, however interesting the Commission study quoted above may be, it can only, by reason of its very generality, refer back to the classic debates already mentioned, without taking account of the special aspect of human rights. It is, however, precisely this dimension which I shall now attempt to highlight.

Democratic Europe is reflected in the vitality of its 'civil society', not just in the efficiency or even the transparency of the various centres of 'power', whether political, economic, or financial. Thus Europe, in its turn and in its own fashion, must find ways and means of developing its own 'European civil society' beyond the measurements and polls of a 'European public opinion' not easily to be discovered. Admittedly it cannot impose its agenda on its interlocutors, for that would be a contradiction in terms in creating dependence where the NGOs are fiercely defending their independence, but it can explain its intentions, put forward initiatives, or support acts of solidarity within the scope of Europe as well as at international level.

II. CONSOLIDATING THE STATUS OF NGOS

If social democracy is the responsibility of each of us, we cannot shrug it off with a liberal *'laissez passer, laissez faire'*, or be content simply to declare the neutrality of States or international organizations. At the meetings concerning the human

---

[18] *La promotion du rôle des associations et fondations en Europe*, Communication from the Commission, COM(97)241 final, paras. 9.1 to 9.3.

dimension of the Conference on Security and Co-operation in Europe ('CSCE'), the United States, loyal to that ideal, refused to define NGOs, taking the view that 'every individual is an NGO' in their eyes. That maximalism, which goes from all to nothing, does not take sufficient account of international life. If they are to win full acceptance as participants, NGOs must be defined in order to prevent 'bad money driving out good' in the shape of associations which have nothing in common with NGOs but the name.[19] Above all, however, an undifferentiating system would render multilateral diplomacy ineffective, sinking as it is already under the weight of the States.[20] It would appear essential to strengthen the legal status of NGOs, without challenging their independence.

1. The Legal Position of NGOs

The Member States possess widely diverse statutes for associations and foundations. In some cases, for example France, old law, such as the 1901 Act on freedom of association, has received constitutional blessing. We may, none the less, wonder whether those systems are always well adapted to the situation of our societies at the turn of the century. The question arises for humanitarian organizations, defined in France under the old terminology as *'associations d'assistance et de bienfaisance'* (welfare and charitable associations). *A fortiori*, the international dimension of NGOs ought to be taken into account.

Besides the standard theoretical definitions,[21] NGOs have been made the subject of special statutes by international organizations. It is, however, only the members of the Council of Europe which have tried to provide a common definition of a general system, through the 'European Convention on the recognition of the legal personality of international non-governmental organizations' adopted on 24 April 1986.[22] It must be acknowledged that this convention has not met with the success expected: it entered into force in 1991, but after three ratifications, it is binding on only seven of the forty members of the Council of Europe: Austria, Belgium, Greece, Portugal, Slovenia, Switzerland, and the United Kingdom. Admittedly, from a qualitative point of view, the participation of States which are host to the seats of many NGOs, starting with Belgium, Switzerland, and the United Kingdom, is significant. France itself signed the convention on 4 July 1996 and undertook to ratify it in December 1998.[23] The process should, however, be relaunched, particularly as Convention No 124 was designed to be a 'treaty susceptible of revision'.

[19] Only too often governmental NGOs (the celebrated GONGOs) or 'sects' take part in certain international meetings. The ultimate was surely the seminar on tolerance organized jointly by ODIHR of the OSCE and the Council of Europe in 1995.

[20] At the UN there is an obvious tactic which consists of silencing NGOs by dividing a frequently derisory amount of speaking time among a multitude of competing associations. The States and experts make short work of denouncing those who wear two hats, when one spokesman speaks several times for a series of NGOs, even if only for practical reasons.

[21] Cf. M. Bettati and P.-M. Dupuy, 'Les ONG et le droit international' (1986), 3.

[22] ETS, No 124.

[23] Although the draft Law was put before the National Assembly on 7 May 1997, it took 2½ years to accomplish a single reading in the two chambers. Authorization for ratification was given by Law No. 98–1166 of 18 Dec. 1998 and the Secretary of State for Health, Bernard Kouchner, indicated that ratification would be undertaken promptly: Journal Officiel de l'Assemblée Nationale, Débats, 17 Dec. 1998, 10–777.

Clearly the convention is of interest. In the preamble, the States declare that they desire 'to establish in their mutual relations rules laying down the conditions for recognition of the legal personality of these organizations in order to facilitate their activities at European level'. This pragmatic aim is underlined by the lack of any lyricism in the recital referring to the contribution of NGOs, since the States confine themselves to recognizing that international NGOs 'carry out work of value to the international community, particularly in the scientific, cultural, charitable, philanthropic, health and education fields and that they contribute to the achievement of the aims and principles of the United Nations Charter and the Statute of the Council of Europe'.

In accordance with the definition given in Article 1, the Convention applies to:

associations, foundations and other private institutions (hereinafter referred to as 'NGOs') which satisfy the following conditions:

   a. have a non-profit making aim of international utility;
   b. have been established by an instrument governed by the internal law of a Party;
   c. carry on their activities with effect in at least two States; and
   d. have their statutory office in the territory of a Party and the central management and control in the territory of that Party or of another Party.

Application of the Convention entails significant legal and financial consequences, which no doubt explains the reservations of technical departments, in particular the tax authorities, with respect to ratification which should, one might have thought, have been automatic. In fact the Convention provides that 'the legal personality and capacity, as acquired in the Party in which it has its statutory office, shall be recognized as of right' (Article 2). Safeguards are provided for, since the application of the Convention may be excluded if, 'by its object, its purpose or the activity which it actually exercises', an NGO:

   a. contravenes national security, public safety, or is detrimental to the prevention of disorder or crime, the protection of health or morals, or the protection of the rights and freedoms of others; or
   b. jeopardizes relations with another State or the maintenance of international peace and security [Article 4].

These protective restraints are not unnecessary when one considers the possibilities of 'delocalizing' and reconstituting 'dissolved factions', parties, or prohibited sects within a State. It is less easy to understand the NGOs specifically referred to in (b), for how is an NGO which seeks to protect a national minority or an oppressed people to be proscribed, if it is not a threat to public order in a 'democratic society', solely for the sake of good 'diplomatic relations' with a regime which, for its part, may well be highly undemocratic? If the aim is to prohibit subversive movements or disguised terrorist groups, those seem to be amply covered in (a). It would have been wiser to omit paragraph (b) so as to be able legitimately to tell a non-member country that free speech is an element of democracy, withdrawing in advance any justification for gagging public opinion.

At this juncture, Convention No 124 provides a system of mutual recognition which would make it easier for NGOs to become fully established within Europe. At the very least, it is to be hoped that the fifteen Member States of the Union and the associate States will ratify the convention without further delay. We might also ask whether it would be possible and appropriate for the European Union to adhere to that instrument as a body.

2. *The Tax Regime Applicable to NGOs*

Legal recognition should go hand-in-hand with a suitable tax regime favourable to the activity of NGOs financed by individual donations. Here, too, the position varies greatly from one Member State to another and is highly complex. Thus it is established that at 30,000 million francs, the amount of donations made to NGOs in the United Kingdom was three times greater than the amount of French donations, which came to 10,000 million francs. Gifts in the Netherlands also came to 10,000 million francs, that is to say, five times more per person than in France.[24] These striking discrepancies may no doubt be explained by sociological reasons having to do with the civic tradition and militant commitment to grand causes, with Amnesty International in the humanitarian domain or with Greenpeace in the environmental, but also, perhaps, by vagaries of taxation.

While the Sixth EEC Directive on VAT[25] sought harmonization of indirect taxation, and exonerated NGOs (Article 13), and while the same tendency towards relief from direct taxation may be observed (except for the tax on wealth in France), the most widely divergent situations are to be found under the rules governing gifts and legacies made by individuals. Apart from the isolated case of Finland, which provides no possibility of deducting gifts, we see two situations. In the majority of Member States, tax may be deducted in full: that is the case in Austria, Belgium, Denmark, Germany, Ireland, Italy, Luxembourg, the Netherlands, Sweden, and the United Kingdom. In two countries, gifts may be set against tax only in part: that is the case in France (50 per cent) and Spain (20 per cent). In most cases, very different ceilings are set on deductibility.

It is clear that public generosity could be directly encouraged if there were a general system exempting gifts made to NGOs by deducting the tax, subject to ceilings to be determined. Such harmonization might be provided for either at Community level, or by spontaneous alignment of the four or five States 'dragging astern' on the more favourable system already put in place by some ten other States.

One condition which would have to be settled beforehand is a sufficiently precise definition of the associations in question: benevolent and charitable associations, voluntary organizations with a humanitarian or philanthropic object, depending on the various terminologies, with the limit possibly set at ordinary public interest or non-profit making organizations whose object may be merely the protection of professional interests or one of mutual assistance. *A fortiori*, what must be prevented is any tendency among undertakings or individuals to use the cover of such an organization in order to avoid taxation under the ordinary law.

---

[24] See the annex on tax systems to the Communication from the Commission, note 17 above.
[25] Dir. 77/388/EEC [1977] OJ L145/1.

3. The Implications of Legal Personality

Redrawing the definition of an NGO would also make it possible to specify certain implications of legal personality. Those facts depend on the NGOs themselves. In many countries they have adopted guiding principles, charters, or guidelines to define their internal operations. Internal democracy goes hand in hand with civic responsibility, the managers' duty of 'accountability' towards the members of the association, without any interference by the State in the democratic life of the organization. Public or private audit systems can, however, be very useful in ensuring that a NGO is properly run and the funds collected properly managed.[26]

Too frequently the planning of NGOs remains the subject of separate groups, sometimes rivals or born of schisms, such as the '*collectif Agen*', the '*collectif Nord/Sud*' and the 'CLONG' in France. The partners in ECHO are grouped together in the collective VOICE, but the quest for a European dialogue should go beyond the sphere of local humanitarian NGOs to attain a genuine code of ethical rules for NGOs, widely accepted and disseminated among the public. It would be interesting to clarify in that manner the relations of NGOs with the public, as with the members, and above all with their staff.[27]

One important aspect of legal personality is the capacity to sue or be sued. In this area NGOs may have an essential part to play at national level. In France, associations may, within the confines of their special field, sue for civil injury (concurrently with a criminal action) instead of or alongside the victims. The State no longer possesses a monopoly on public action with regard to certain crimes or misdemeanours, in particular in the area of racial discrimination. It would be helpful to carry out a comparative study of the various NGOs' capacity to sue in order to recommend appropriate solutions for strengthening their role.

Similarly, NGOs should more often play a part in the sphere of international legal action, particularly before European courts: setting up a new European Court of Human Rights could create a new bridgehead in this domain, either by extending the concept of 'a legal interest in bringing proceedings', or by developing the use of the *amicus curiae*. Here there is a gap to be filled, having regard to the fact that there are no inter-State cases to be considered *ultima ratio* with respect to a State which has failed to fulfil its obligations, either because the States hesitate in the face of a step they perceive as an 'unfriendly act' or because the solidarity of circumstance unites the States, those 'cold monsters' only too aware of their own failings. Between non-existent inter-State legal action and risky individual actions, there is a loophole the NGOs could fill by helping 'class actions' or 'test cases', with a genuine 'judicial policy' targeting questions of principle likely to help develop human rights jurisprudence. They could also play a specific part in the new non-contentious methods of

---

[26] Thus, in France, large humanitarian organizations, such as Médecins sans Frontières, are audited by the Cour des Comptes.

[27] The law of 1901 makes no provision for the payment of a salary to the people responsible for running an association, whereas it is becoming a full-time occupation. The requirements of the voluntary sector and of professionalism should be studied in detail, especially as during periods of crisis public authorities tend to subcontract some of their responsibilities to voluntary organizations, so adding to the insecurity, and sometimes even the exploitation, of the voluntary sector.

settling disputes: the Ombudsman of the European Parliament, the future 'High Commissioner for Human Rights' at the Council of Europe.

III. ESTABLISHING A PARTNERSHIP WITH NGOS

In addition to those judicial or financial technical measures intended to make it easier for NGOs to operate, a really dynamic measure ought to be promoted. At European level, the legitimacy of NGOs has never been fully recognized. In this respect the attitudes adopted by European organizations remain very frosty, as we see in the Recommendation of the Committee of Ministers of the Council of Europe on national institutions in 1997 or even the recent document of principle of the ECRI called 'Declaration of policy and action concerning the relations of the ECRI with non-governmental organizations'.[28] It seems that the European Union itself also regards NGOs as merely 'auxiliary' from a certain paternalistic point of view, rather than as true partners with legitimacy in their own right.

It is paradoxical that the least 'homogeneous' international organizations, such as the UN or the OSCE, should be the most favourable to NGOs, whether in declarations of principle or in practice: NGOs have the right to speak within the Economic and Social Council of the United Nations and its subsidiary bodies, just as within the OSCE meetings on the human dimension in which they participate on an equal footing with the States and are largely responsible for any animation in the agenda. Where are human rights NGOs recognized as such in Brussels or Strasbourg, except in information meetings?

Admittedly, for the first time a short declaration annexed to the Maastricht Treaty stresses the importance of co-operation with 'charitable associations' by a reference to Article 117 on 'social policy'. The dialogue remains confined, however, to the classic forms of 'social democracy', as with the organization in March 1996 of the 'First European Forum on Social Policy' which refers to 'the building over time of a strong civil dialogue at European level to take its place alongside the policy dialogue with national authorities and the social dialogue with the social partners'. The main aims are 'to ensure that the views and grassroots experience of the voluntary sector can be systematically taken into account by policy-makers at European level' and, conversely, 'to disseminate information from European level down to the local level so that citizens are aware of developments, can feel part of the construction of Europe and can see the relevance of it to their own situation, thus increasing transparency and promoting citizenship'.[29] This dialogue is evidently self-interested, as is the dialogue with NGOs concerning co-operation, in which they are frequently perceived as intermediaries or even impermanent and cheaper subcontractors.

By contrast, after the endeavours of years, the declaration on 'defenders of human rights',[30] adopted by consensus by the General Assembly in December 1998 is par-

---

[28] CRI(98)32, of 6 Mar. 1998.   [29] Communication from the Commission, note 17 above, para. 9.7.

[30] Declaration on the Right and Responsibility of Individuals, Groups and Organs of Society to Promote and Protect Universally Recognized Human Rights and Fundamental Freedoms, GA Res. 53/144 (1998).

ticularly substantial. The European organizations have never adopted so ambitious a document. Optimists will be tempted to say that it is because the process of achieving the desired goal was in any event already under way, even though the number of repetitive or trite declarations has never dissuaded European decision-makers. Is it not rather the truth that the European States are the first to fear the vigilance of counter-powers perceived as 'irresponsible'?

The European institutions should officially recognize NGOs' political legitimacy by setting up a genuine action programme together. Several opportunities to collaborate might thus be explored while fully respecting the respective powers, objectives, and roles of each.

1. Consulting NGOs

A first, quite empirical stage, could be to organize formal consultation of the NGOs, whether through the troika or the Commission or the Parliament.

As regards the Parliament, such an opening-up would be very useful in taking account of the experience gained by NGOs in the field with their networks of activists and experience of investigation reports. Two instances will suffice to demonstrate that the quality and 'efficiency' of Parliamentary work could be greatly increased thereby. It cannot be said that the European Parliament's mission to Algeria took place in the best conditions possible: a mixed delegation, giving places to NGO representatives, would have allowed a better 'division of roles', whereas the Parliamentary mission appeared to be split, prone to one-upmanship and showing off, and above all willing to impugn the detailed work of the 'Western' NGOs challenged by the Algerian government. Furthermore, the only public conclusion of the Parliamentary mission was to announce the fact that an Algerian report would be examined by the Human Rights Committee, thus interfering with the monitoring work carried out by the independent experts of the United Nations under the Covenant.[31]

Internally, it would be in the interests of the European Parliament to take fuller account of the in-depth work done by the NGOs. The way in which the 'Annual Report on respect for human rights within the European Union (1996)' was prepared within the 'Public Freedoms and Internal Affairs Committee', and then adopted on 26 January 1998 by thirteen votes to twelve, may appear derisory in view of the stakes involved.[32] The vote by a Parliament, in itself highly divided, has only accentuated the politicization of a question which goes beyond partisan allegiances. The report, particularly prolix and confused, possessing neither legal coherence nor political structure, would appear to be a 'hold-all' in which special groups have endeavoured to insert their preoccupations without any overall vision. Is it not imperative to organize wide, prior consultation of NGOs, at European and at State level, to make this annual report a public 'barometer' and a navigational instrument fixing priorities and time-limits, instead of a belated, unreadable catalogue of pious wishes marred by faults in law.

---

[31] In this connection, the position taken by the UK presidency, on behalf of the EU, was much more consistent and, it is to be hoped, effective: see the speech made by Ambassador Audrey Glover, UN doc. E/CN.4/1998/SR.58, para. 15, 22 Apr. 1998.

[32] Report by A. Pailler, doc. A4/0034/98 of 28 Jan. 1998.

2. Co-operation Structures

Furthermore, it is important to develop institutional co-operation. That calls for a structured dialogue between European bodies and organs of civil society. Several instances of partnership have already been set up in sensitive areas, with committees composed of independent experts or qualified 'personalities'. This is the case in the field of bioethics, in which NGOs have always played a large part,[33] with the development of ethics committees. The 'Advisory Body on the Ethics of Biotechnology' was created in November 1991 on the initiative of the Commission, in response to a report seeking to encourage the conditions for competitiveness for industrial activity based on biotechnology in the Community. Its very title demonstrates that the approach adopted, as often happens with the European Union, was at the outset commercial, and so was the directive on the 'patentability' of the genome and the directive on protection of data privacy in the field of data processing. The creation of the Advisory Body has none the less enabled emphasis to be placed on the moral aspects of those scientific implications. Curiously, it is the Commission itself which nominates the nine 'wise men' *intuitu personae* and puts matters before them, even though the experts have an autonomous power in that regard.

Recently the Parliament called for the Advisory Body to be transformed into the 'Ethics Committee of the European Union', under the procedure provided for by Article 251 (*ex* Article 189b) of the EC Treaty, insisting that it should be 'constituted with full respect for transparency and democratic principles, and that all appropriate interested groups [should be] represented within it'.[34] Instead of appearing to be a mere vehicle for the exercise of powers, simply 'advisers to the prince', in a close alliance of knowledge and power, the members of the Committee would thus possess greater moral legitimacy and would produce greater effect on public opinion in elucidating the 'social issues' in the name of ethical principles.

A second structure was set up more recently, with the establishment of the European Monitoring Centre on Racism and Xenophobia by a Council Regulation of 2 June 1997, in response to the recommendations of the Consultative Committee charged with making recommendations on combating racism and xenophobia, itself set up at the European Council meeting in Corfu in June 1994. The regulation states that:

> [I]n order to carry out this task of collecting and analysing information on racism, xenophobia and anti-Semitism as well and as independently as possible and in order to maintain close links with the Council of Europe, it is necessary to establish an autonomous body, the European Monitoring Centre on Racism and Xenophobia, at Community level with its own legal personality.[35]

It notes in passing that 'in the Member States there are numerous outstanding organizations which study racism and xenophobia' and that 'the coordination of research and the creation of a network of organizations will enhance the usefulness and effectiveness of such work'.

---

[33] N. Lenoir, *Les normes internationales de la bioéthique*, Collection Que sais-je? No 3356 (1998).
[34] Resolution on cloning, 11 Mar. 1997 [1997] OJ C115/92.
[35] Council Reg. 1035/97 of 2 June 1997 [1997] OJ L151/1.

More specifically, Article 2 of the regulation names as principal sources of information, besides the States and international organizations, 'research centres' and 'non-governmental organizations' (Article 2). The Monitoring Centre is to set up and co-ordinate a European Racism and Xenophobia Network (RAXEN) to 'co-operate with national university research centres, non-governmental organizations and specialist centres set up by organizations in the Member States or international organizations . . .'. Finally, there is a reference to 'existing standing advisory bodies'.

The (Management Board of the) Monitoring Centre, established in Vienna in early 1998, is 'composed of one independent person appointed by each Member State, one independent person appointed by the European Parliament, one independent person appointed by the Council of Europe . . . and a representative of the Commission'. It is of course much too soon to take stock for the first time of such an institution at the crossroads of the European institutions and the 'active forces' of civil society.

Both those examples, however, demonstrate the need to go beyond a purely internal approach to great social issues, whether bioethics or racism, by having recourse to independent persons, known as 'wise men', but in particular by providing for a large measure of co-operation with NGOs and grassroots activists, scientists, or committed members of the associations.

3. For a European Human Rights Forum

Is it possible to go further, making a close connection between NGOs that goes beyond the standard forms of consultation and co-operation? Can original forms of joint decision-making be imagined? The idea is less 'revolutionary' than we might be tempted to believe, if we recall the old tripartite model with which the ILO succeeded representatives of unions and employers' groups alongside representatives of the States. At the beginning, UNESCO made room for intellectuals to be represented as such by the States, with great names sitting in the UNESCO Council, and then it replaced the writers and scientists with officials. Even within the United Nations, some of the Commission of Human Rights' proposed reforms draw their inspiration from those illustrious precursors.

Would it not be possible for European decision-makers to set an example and allow room for a new kind of tripartism? The most ambitious scheme would undoubtedly be to reform the Economic and Social Committee, which at present 'consist[s] of representatives of the various categories of economic and social activity, in particular, representatives of producers, farmers, carriers, workers, dealers, craftsmen, professional occupations and representatives of the general public' (Article 257 (*ex* Article 193)). Even while it may well be asked who is really able to represent the public interest in the face of this procession of special interests, the list is closer to the economic life of the nineteenth century than to the information society of the dawning twenty-first century. In point of fact, in its composition the Economic and Social Committee is a legacy of the Treaty of Rome, with the sector-based interests of the common market. In its 1996 Rules of Procedure, the 'Groups' reflect that unchanged stratification in a way that is almost a caricature: Group I 'employers', Group II 'workers', and the 'other categories of economic and social activity' in Group III 'other activities'. At the very least, it would be useful to set up in the Economic and Social Committee a new section with responsibility for matters of human rights, ethics, or the fight against racism. It is equally essential to widen the composition of the Committee so that these new responsibilities are not reduced to mere consumerism.

Even without challenging the present establishment, inspiration could be drawn from the experiences of 'national organizations for the promotion and protection of human rights' which have sprung into vigorous action in the world. Those organizations may be quite disparate, they may be consultative bodies, with internal and/or international powers, or Ombudsmen or similar institutions, or committees specializing in particular in the field of racial non-discrimination.[36] As a result of the first 'international meeting' organized in Paris in 1991 under the ægis of the United Nations, the network has been created on the basis of guiding principles (the Paris principles) given force by the General Assembly in Resolution 48/134 of 20 December 1993. These are the principles of independence and pluralism which enable national institutions to function as a meeting-point for the public authorities and the 'active forces' of civil society, such as churches, trade unions, or NGOs.

Oddly enough, the decision-makers in Brussels do not seem to understand the special nature of national organizations. Thus the proposal for a Council regulation 'laying down the detailed rules for the implementation of cooperation action' with non-member countries in the sphere of human rights referred in particular in Article 2(1)(d) to 'supporting local, national, regional or international institutions involved in the protection or defence of human rights, including support of Ombudsmen and defenders of human rights'. In a more recent version, Article 2(1)(e) mentions 'supporting local, national, regional or international institutions, including NGOs, involved in the protection or defence of human rights', while Article 2(2)(c) refers to 'promotion of pluralism both at political level and at the level of civil society by strengthening the institutions needed to maintain the pluralist nature of that society, including non-governmental organizations (NGOs) . . .'.[37]

In one sense, Ombudsmen constitute a model unto themselves, a secular form of that justice, appertaining to the royal prerogative, intended to right wrongs, rather than a social forum based on pluralism and the search for a consensus. This is not the place to assess the performance of the Union Ombudsman,[38] but clearly he cannot on his own fulfil the role of permanent dialogue between public authorities and the elements of civil society, any more than can the future 'High Commissioner for Human Rights' with which the Council of Europe intends to equip itself.[39] Mary Robinson, the United Nations High Commissioner for Human Rights, has frequently stressed the importance she attaches to such intermediaries, considering that

[36] See United Nations Human Rights Centre, series on vocational training No 4, *Institutions nationales pour les droits de l'homme* (1996).
[37] Doc. No 101/98 (DEVGEN), Apr. 1998.
[38] The Ombudsman, Jacob Söderman, received 298 complaints in 1995, 842 in 1996, and 1181 in 1997, i.e. an increase of 40%: *International Herald Tribune*, 22 Apr. 1998, 5.
[39] The second summit of the Council of Europe ratified a Finnish initiative to this effect, final declaration of 11 Oct. 1997, see http://www.coe.fr/summit/edeclaration.htm.

this is an issue for the future, especially before the Committee for co-ordination of national organizations which met in Geneva in April 1998.

Only a tripartite structure enables an institutional dialogue to be established. It might be helpful to consider the experience of the French national advisory committee.[40] In this committee meet the representatives of the various ministerial Departments in a purely advisory capacity, representatives of NGOs and humanitarian associations, and a series of 'qualified persons', judges, academics, United Nations experts, and also representatives of religions and intellectual trends. Consequently, the system may appear rather cumbersome, but it does take into account the need to ensure the most open exchange of information possible, while respecting everyone's own responsibilities, before reaching opinions, fully aware of the stakes involved, in both the national and international arenas.[41]

It is strange that the 'consultative function' and the role of continuous assessment to be found in various forms in many Commonwealth countries have been neglected within Europe. The adoption of reference texts within the Steering Committee on Human Rights of the Council of Europe has been much more difficult than at the UN. Furthermore, some of the major partners, in their distrust of NGOs, have attempted to challenge the principles established in the documents of the United Nations. Others, calling on 'balanced information', expressed concepts that were in circulation at the time of peaceful coexistence. More worrying, certainly, was the idea that specialist parliamentary committees would make it unnecessary to set up national organizations whereas, without challenging the democratic legitimacy of parliamentary representation at national and supranational level the object of national organizations is to make it possible to engage in a debate which transcends political differences.[42] It would be a step forward to encourage, within the Fifteen, the creation of national organizations, as recommended by the Human Rights Committee of the United Nations as long ago as 1946.[43] It would also be progress to try to establish, either independently or as an intermediate stage for the various national organizations, a European human rights forum with three classes of member: representatives of the European institutions, representatives of NGOs, and qualified persons.

If that body is not to be too awkward and formal, it is important that the NGOs should achieve a better structure or group themselves into grand 'international federations', as the FIDH, Amnesty International, Helsinki Watch, or the CIJ have already done, and avoid purely national representation, but yet not dismiss the 'little'

---

[40] The Committee, which was set up in 1948, is governed today by a decree of 30 Jan. 1984, amended several times, most recently on 11 Sept. 1996. For an assessment, see E. Decaux, '*Utile Cassandre . . . ou le rôle de la Commission nationale consultative des droits de l'homme*' in *Pouvoir et liberté: Etudes offerte à Jacques Mourgeon* (1998), 589.

[41] These opinions are made public as soon as they are adopted and are then published in the Committee's annual report. See *La Lutte contre le racisme et la xénophobie* (Combating racism and xenophobia): La Documentation française, 1998.

[42] The idea of setting up a 'national human rights commission', which was considered by a study group for the Labour party, seems to have been abandoned in favour of a mere parliamentary committee. See Institute for Public Policy Research, *Consultation Paper: A Human Rights Commission for the UK: The Options*, Dec. 1996.

[43] It would be interesting to go further into a comparison with national committees for UNESCO, which have gone in quite a different direction.

NGOs, which they managed to do so well in the anti-personnel mine campaign or the coalition for the international criminal court, thus showing the States that 'there is strength in unity'.[44]

This dedication of space to NGOs, in an open society in which States no longer hold a monopoly on information or negotiation, would be of great importance in bestowing full credibility on the European Union. The conduct of the Union *vis-à-vis* the external world too often appears unilateral and paternalistic, linked to economic considerations and fostering double standards. Recognition of the crucial role of NGOs nationally as in the field of international co-operation would give a signal that the Union is intent, first and foremost, on the internal promotion of human rights. Such an example would be one more argument to use against critics in certain third-world countries who tend to see NGOs that criticize them as 'western' organizations, or to attack national sections of international NGOs, as though they were remote-controlled by their country of origin.

Above all, greater collective involvement of NGOs in European life would have the merit of providing a more concrete and coherent approach to the issues. Too frequently the unthinking invocation of 'human rights' is not enough to disguise the lack of political visibility: the very fact that the Commissioner responsible for humanitarian matters is also responsible for consumers and fisheries clearly demonstrates that 'human rights' were initially perceived as the fifth wheel on the carriage. We might acknowledge that human rights cannot be separated from the other major areas, so much do they inform training and employment, foreign trade or European diplomacy, but it is hard to prove any actual connection. Now the Community approach seems to combine bureaucratic management of resources, which means NGOs alternate between penury and uncertainty,[45] with a form of amateurism when confronted with events, as we see only too often, regrettably, when crises have to be dealt with. Diplomatic bluff-calling and technocratic ponderousness consort oddly.

Apart from spontaneous action and indignation, what long-term activity is provided for nationally and internationally in the domain of human rights? What are the priorities, the material and human resources mobilized, the stages and time-limits in the time-table, the criteria and the methods of evaluating the results? Co-operation with the NGOs would certainly make it possible to supply a better definition of the objectives to be attained and jointly to try to find the best means of attaining them. The critical dialogue for drawing up a report on the present situation must begin without more ado within the European Union and lead to an annual report enabling progress to be measured.

---

[44] In the absence of a proper handbook of NGOs in the field of human rights, it is noteworthy that the EC Commission has published a directory of European Non-Profit Organizations in order to enable officials to consult more systematically and as widely as possible (Communication from the Commission, note 17 above, 13, note 5). On the other hand, the Development Centre of the OECD has disseminated a thematic directory among the public at large: *Directory of NGOs in OECD Countries: Human Rights, Refugees, Migrants and Development* (1993).

[45] The idea that Community aid should be used for 'projects' and not for operating budgets would require reassessment in the light of the importance of a permanent solid base from which to launch pinpoint operations with the necessary flexibility.

At that initial stage I have envisaged civil society participating by means of the major NGOs, but clearly a more targeted approach would be necessary too, having regard to specific needs and possibilities:

The media and the new information society. The creation in 1998 of an OSCE representative for the freedom of the media has already been imitated by the countries of the OAS at their recent summit meeting. The role of information about infringements of human rights and early warnings through the networks, and also the battle against delocalization of infringements such as public denial of the Holocaust or racial hatred on websites merit separate study;

The legal professions, access to the law for the most disadvantaged, the role of lawyers who in some countries have to devote part of their time to social or humanitarian activities *pro bono publico*;

A place for the young, both through training and information on human rights and in combating the social crisis with the development of the 'caring' and associated professions, apprenticeship in new forms of citizenship and civic activity faced with the rebellion or despair of too many young people.

But here again, it is the NGOs with their grassroots experience that are best placed to propose 'good practice' and inspire decentralized initiatives. The entire European Union would gain in credibility and effectiveness. The impossible human rights diplomacy run by States must give way to the mobilization of civil society. Recourse to NGOs or 'foundations' must not be merely a matter of sub-contracting, a mixture of illegitimate favours and preserves in order to escape administrative and budgetary constraints, but must become a political priority, an action model for a fully democratic modern society, a new 'social pact' at the base of a community of responsible citizens.

Europe must not become a fortress in its conception of citizenship based on exclusion, but must on the contrary be an open society, rich in its diversity while remaining true to itself, and one based on participation.

Annex

Leading by Example: A Human Rights Agenda For the European Union for the Year 2000

This Agenda was launched at a Conference held in Vienna on 9–10 October 1998 which was opened by the Austrian Vice-Chancellor and Minister for Foreign Affairs, Dr Wolfgang Schüssel.

The Agenda was adopted by a *Comité des Sages* consisting of:

- *Judge Antonio Cassese*, President from 1993 to 1997, and currently Presiding Judge of Trial Chamber II of the International Criminal Tribunal for the former Yugoslavia, and former President of the European Committee for the Prevention of Torture;
- *Mme Catherine Lalumière*, Member of the European Parliament (and President of its ARE Group), and former Secretary-General of the Council of Europe;
- *Professor Peter Leuprecht*, Professor and Dean of the Faculty of Law, McGill University, Montréal, and former Deputy Secretary-General and Director of Human Rights of the Council of Europe, and
- *Mrs. Mary Robinson*, United Nations High Commissioner for Human Rights, and former President of Ireland.

A. WHY THE EUROPEAN UNION NEEDS TO DEVELOP ITS HUMAN RIGHTS POLICY

1. The European Union is committed to human rights. Its achievements to date are considerable, both within the Union and outside. Nevertheless, much remains to be done and the time for action is now.

2. A European Union which fails to protect and promote human rights consistently and effectively will betray Europe's shared values and its long-standing commitment to them. However, the Union's existing policies in this area are no longer adequate. They were made by and for the Europe of yesterday; they are not sufficient for the Europe of tomorrow. The strong rhetoric of the Union is not matched by the reality. There is an urgent need for a human rights policy which is coherent, balanced, substantive and professional.

3. There are many reasons why the European Union cannot remain without a comprehensive and effective internal human rights policy. They include:

- the rapid movement towards an 'ever closer Union' and towards a comprehensive single market;

- the adoption of a single currency for close to 300 million people;
- the increasing incidence of racism, xenophobia and ethnic hatred within Europe;
- the tendency towards a 'fortress Europe' which is hostile to 'outsiders' and discourages refugees and asylum-seekers;
- the growing cooperation in policy and security matters, which is not matched by adequate human rights safeguards;
- the increasingly complex political and administrative system that governs the Union and is supported by a bureaucracy with extensive powers; and
- the aspiration to bring at least five and perhaps as many as thirteen countries within the Union's fold in the years ahead.

4. These developments call for a Union which must be adequately equipped to protect and promote the human rights of all its residents.

5. Similarly, human rights must be a key part of the EU's policies towards the rest of the world. An integrated policy is essential for a European Union that:

- recognizes that respect for human rights among its neighbours and partners has an enormous impact on its own security;
- has been taught by history that respect for human rights is the only enduring foundation for building peace and harmony;
- is forging a common foreign policy, within which human rights must be a core element;
- has cooperation and other agreements with a vast number of other countries;
- plays a key role in many international organizations concerned with human rights; and
- spends well over a billion euros every year on development assistance and humanitarian aid.

6. The EU must conduct an informed, consistent, credible and effective human rights policy. But it cannot do so in the absence of an authentic commitment, one underpinned by appropriate political, financial and administrative support. Instead, the Union's present approach to human rights tends to be splintered in many directions, lacks the necessary leadership and profile, and is marginalized in policy-making.

7. The EU has devoted a great deal of energy and resources to human rights, both in its internal and its external policies. Yet the fragmented and hesitant nature of many of its initiatives has left the Union with a vast number of individual policies and programmes but without a real human rights policy as such.

B. WHAT ARE OUR PRINCIPAL OBJECTIVES?

8. EU human rights policy should be guided by these objectives:

  a. *Recognition of legal obligations*. Even the most minute actions on behalf of the Union should be conducted with full respect for human rights. EU Member States should always comply with their international human rights obligations, deriving both from treaties and general norms, as well as the policy commitments they have undertaken in the Vienna Declaration and Programme of Action. They should explore the extent to which their cooperation within the EU context provides opportunities to honour those obligations, both within and outside the Union as well as at the national level.
  b. *Universality*. The EU should always uphold the principle that human rights are universal in nature and must be respected by all States and applied to all individuals.
  c. *Indivisibility*. Civil and political rights cannot be separated from economic, social and

cultural rights. All these rights are both a means of promoting the common good and ends in themselves.

d. *Consistency between internal and external policy.* These two dimensions of human rights must be seen as two sides of the same coin. A Union which is not prepared to embrace a strong human rights policy for itself is highly unlikely to develop a credible external policy, let alone to apply it with energy or consistency. As long as human rights within Europe are considered to be an area in which the Union has only a very limited role, their status in the Union's external policy will remain tenuous.

e. *A sound policy requires a strong information base.* Especially in this field, informed, consistent and transparent policy-making is impossible in the absence of accurate and up-to-date information. Yet the Union currently lacks any systematic approach to the collection of information on human rights, either within or outside Europe.

f. *Mainstreaming.* Human rights must not be put to one side as a separate or specialized concern. They should be an integral part of, and fully permeate, all the activities of the EU.

9. Leading by example must become the *leitmotif* of a new European Union human rights policy. If these objectives are respected, the EU will be well placed to provide such leadership.

C. WHAT ARE OUR MAIN CONCERNS?

10. There are many concerns which should be prominent on the European Union's human rights agenda. We call attention to some that seem especially pressing, but our list is not intended to be comprehensive.

11. Within the Union, large-scale discrimination persists in various forms. *Racism and xenophobia* are thriving. EU efforts to combat these phenomena should be broadened and reinforced. Important strides have been made in the quest for *gender equality*, but there is considerable scope for broader-based efforts to promote non-discrimination and equality in all of the relevant fields of Community law, including the internal market, the workplace, in access to education and training, in structural funds, and in public procurement. The promotion of gender equality and the fight against racism and discrimination should also be accorded a higher priority in the EU's development cooperation programmes.

12. EU policy towards *persons with disabilities* should reflect a human rights-based approach which aims to eliminate barriers to full participation and equal opportunities within society. Protection of the *rights of members of minority groups* should also become a more prominent focus of the Union's policies, both internally and externally. *Discrimination based on sexual orientation* continues to be widespread and should be more systematically addressed through a Commission action plan and the development of a draft directive on equal treatment.

13. The need to combat *inhumane conditions of detention* should be an important element in the context of development cooperation. Unfortunately, it is also a growing concern within the EU, where it increasingly has a discriminatory racial and ethnic dimension as well. While prison conditions are not matters of Community competence, there is scope for the Union to encourage its Members to address this issue more systematically.

14. The quality of justice within the EU is inevitably, and rightly, judged in part by our response to the plight of *refugees* fleeing persecution. Yet within Europe we see pressures to shape asylum policy to accommodate nationalism and to weaken accepted international protection standards in the name of greater 'efficiency' or the need to meet 'new' challenges. Both

the EU and the European Court of Justice must take seriously the explicit commitment in the Amsterdam Treaty to those standards.

15. There is much scope for improving the treatment of *third country nationals* within the EU. Consistent with appropriate measures to preserve law and order, xenophobia must not be permitted to curtail the enjoyment of the human rights of such individuals.

16. No human rights policy is complete in the absence of measures designed to ensure respect for basic *social rights*. Continuing large-scale unemployment, very high levels of youth unemployment, and growing poverty and social exclusion continue to blight the picture within the EU. The development and adaptation of the European social model, in response to new trends, must be based on respect for human rights in general, and social rights in particular. In external policy as well, there is a need for far greater attention to social rights than has been the case to date.

17. The revolution being wrought by the emergence of the 'Information Society' must be shaped and regulated in accordance with human rights and the values that inspire them. This will require efforts to enhance democracy through appropriate uses of information technology, using that technology to build a more inclusive society and economy, and using appropriate forms of regulation to prevent abuses of that technology while ensuring freedom of expression. The EU's external policies should also seek to ensure that these new technologies are used to enhance the capacity of human rights defenders in third countries. The Union also needs to devote increased attention to the threats posed to human rights by breakthroughs in bio-technology and related developments.

18. Very valuable human rights initiatives have been promoted within the EU's development cooperation programmes and we welcome the development of the European Master's Course in Human Rights undertaken by a consortium of universities led by the University of Padua. Nevertheless, these initiatives remain limited in scope and human rights has yet to be fully integrated into the development programme as a whole. International aid flows are diminishing rapidly precisely at a time of great instability and widespread suffering and when many of the gains achieved since the early 1990s are at risk in a backlash against policies that have failed to meet expectations. The EU must continue to develop a comprehensive aid policy in which the promotion of human rights is a central element.

D. WHAT INITIATIVES ARE REQUIRED TO ACHIEVE THESE OBJECTIVES?

19. Based on the many studies and analyses which have been prepared for our consideration in the context of this project, we have identified the following initiatives which we believe warrant urgent consideration. While many are institutional in nature, they are designed to provide the foundation stones upon which the human rights policies that we are calling for can be built and applied.

    a. The Commission should appoint a Commissioner for Human Rights; he or she should play a central coordinating role to ensure that all Commission activities are consistent with, and contribute as much as possible to the realization of, human rights. By the same token, this approach must coincide with, and not be at the expense of, a systematic effort to mainstream human rights within all the services of the Commission.

    b. The Council should establish a specialist Human Rights Office to inform the work of the new High Representative for the Common Foreign and Security Policy ('Monsieur PESC').

c. European Community law should be developed in such a way as to enable individuals and public interest groups alleging serious human rights violations to get more ready access to the European Court of Justice.

d. A European Union Human Rights Monitoring Agency, with a general information-gathering function in relation to all human rights in the field of application of Community Law, is essential. One option for this purpose would be to expand the existing European Monitoring Centre on Racism and Xenophobia in Vienna. Another is to establish a new and separate Agency.

e. Balanced and objective surveys of the human rights situation both within the EU and in the world at large are an indispensable basis for informed analysis and policy-making. The Commission, in consultation with the Council, should develop a global report for this purpose, while the new Monitoring Agency should develop such a report in relation to the EU and its Member States. Action would then be taken at whatever level is appropriate in light of the principle of subsidiarity.

f. The European Parliament should be seen as an important force for promoting respect for human rights by and within the Union. An effort should be made to reinforce the specialist human rights expertise available to the secretariat of the Parliament; better coordination should be sought between the Committee on Civil Liberties and Internal Affairs and the Sub-Committee on Human Rights of the Committee on Foreign Affairs, Security and Defence Policy; and there should be greater interaction with the human rights committees in national parliaments. Parliament should strive to achieve a more coherent and better focused approach to human rights, with improved cooperation on the part of the Commission and the Council. The two annual reports we propose would provide an ideal basis upon which to build that approach.

g. Despite continuing reluctance, the Community should accede to the European Convention on Human Rights, even if this requires a Treaty amendment, as well as to the European Social Charter.

h. In addition to the work of the Council's Committee on Human Rights (COHOM), there should be greater interaction within the EU among Government Ministers with major human rights responsibilities.

i. The human rights aspects of the Commission's development cooperation programmes should be expanded, the details of those programmes should be made more transparent, and more systematic evaluations should be undertaken. Measures should also be taken to ensure that the Union is obliged to investigate allegations that specific development cooperation projects have had a negative human rights impact.

j. In view of the rapidly growing impact of non-State actors on the enjoyment of human rights, the Commission should evaluate existing voluntary codes of conduct and prepare a study on the ways in which an official EU code of conduct for businesses could be formulated, promoted and monitored.

k. The human rights clauses that are now included in over 50 Community agreements should be a standard feature of all such agreements. However, more detailed criteria, designed to balance consistency and flexibility in the application of those clauses, are required. Clear procedures for the suspension and termination of external agreements are also needed and the powers of the Commission and the European Parliament in this respect should be clarified.

l. The Commission should undertake a study of the procedures to be applied in considering whether to suspend the rights of a Member State for a serious and persistent breach of human rights under the new provisions in the Amsterdam Treaty.

m. The various institutions of the Union should develop a more effective system of consultation with non-governmental organizations and should consider the possibility of establishing a permanent forum to facilitate more systematic and productive interaction with them.

n. Human Rights education should be given a high priority within the Union as a whole. Building a culture of mutual respect, understanding, and harmony represents a long-term challenge. Since it is a process that may take decades and even generations, the earlier it begins the better.

E. DO THE INITIATIVES REQUIRE CHANGES IN THE BASIC LEGAL FRAMEWORK?

20. This Agenda is based upon policies and institutions that are already in place. We do not call for the recognition of new rights and the increase in resources required is not great. Very few of the proposals imply a Treaty amendment and we do not seek to alter either the existing institutional balance within the Union or the constitutional balance between the Community and its Member States.

21. Since legal sophistry is too often used to circumvent the need for an EU human rights policy, this Agenda is based upon a thorough and cautious legal analysis of the existing competences of the Union in this field. We reject the view that is sometimes expressed that the Community has, or should have, full authority with respect to all human rights matters of any significance. This view is out of touch with the legal and constitutional realities of the Union. However, neither do we accept the more commonly held, contrary view that human rights should be matters solely for Member States. The Union is already legally obligated to 'respect fundamental rights', including those guaranteed by the European Convention on Human Rights. And there are already many areas of major and direct human rights relevance in which the competence of the Community is unquestionable. The cross-cutting nature of these issues also justifies a prudent use of the powers inherent in the Community under Art 308 (formerly Art 235) of the Treaty Establishing the European Community. Moreover, a Community human rights policy is not only consistent with the principle of subsidiarity, but is in some measure a necessity required by it.

22. Finally, there is absolutely no legal or constitutional barrier to the Union's common foreign and security policy taking full account of human rights. Indeed, the European Council has made precisely that commitment.

23. It is clear therefore that the existing legal competences of the Community and the Union are sufficient to support the proposals contained in this Agenda.

AN APPEAL TO THE EUROPEAN COUNCIL

As the century and the millennium draw to a close, we call upon the European Council to restore human rights to the central role they enjoyed at the dawn of the European construction: that of the cornerstone upon which the fabric of a united Europe must rest.

To renew this fundamental commitment, the European Union can no longer limit itself to grand philosophical statements. It must commit the political, legal, administrative and financial resources needed to fulfill this ideal. Otherwise, the European idea risks losing both its force and its main *raison d'être*.

We therefore call upon the European Council, meeting in Vienna exactly 50 years after the proclamation of the Universal Declaration of Human Rights, to:

1. Adopt a solemn statement confirming the Union's commitments to a human rights policy based on the principles and objectives outlined above.

2. Call for the appointment of a Human Rights Commissioner in the next Commission.
3. Request the Commission to prepare a detailed study, including budgetary implications, on the proposal to establish a fully-fledged European Union Human Rights Monitoring Agency. The study should be transmitted to the European Parliament by December 1999.
4. Call upon the Commission and the Council to study the Agenda of the *Comité des Sages* along with the Final Report of the Project and present their proposals in light of the recommendations made therein.

SELECT BIBLIOGRAPHY

BOOKS

ALBORS-LLORENS A., *Private Parties in European Community Law: Challenging Community Measures* (Oxford, Clarendon Press, 1996)

BALDWIN-EDWARDS M., and SCHAIN M. (eds.), *The Politics of Immigration in Western Europe* (Ilford, Frank Cass, 1994)

BARNARD C., *EC Employment Law* (Chichester, Wiley, 1995)

BERCUSSON B., DEAKIN S., KOISTINEN P., KRAVARITOU Y., MUCKENBERGER U., SUPIOT A., and VENEZIANI B., *A Manifesto for Social Europe* (Bruxelles, European Trade Union Institute of the ETUC, 1996)

BETTEN L. and MACDEVITT D. (eds.), *The Protection of Fundamental Social Rights in the European Union* (The Hague, Kluwer Law International, 1996)

BLANPAIN R., HEPPLE B., and SCIARRA S., *Fundamental Social Rights: Proposals for the European Union* (Leuven, Peeters, 1996)

BOYLE A. and ANDERSON M. (eds.), *Human Rights Approaches to Environmental Protection* (Oxford, Clarendon Press, 1996)

CANÇADO TRINDADE A. A. (ed.), *The Modern World of Human Rights: Essays in Honour of Thomas Buergenthal* (San Jose, Inter-American Institute of Human Rights, 1996)

CARTABIA M., *Principi inviolabili e integrazione europea* (Milan, Giuffrè, 1995)

CASSESE A., CLAPHAM A., and WEILER J.,(eds.), *European Union The Human Rights Challenge* (Baden-Baden, Nomos, 1991)

CESARANI D. and FULBROOK M., *Citizenship, Nationality and Migration in Europe* (London, Routledge, 1996)

CLAPHAM A., *Human Rights and the European Community: A Critical Overview* (Baden-Baden, Nomos, 1991)

—— *Human Rights in the Private Sphere* (Oxford, Clarendon Press, 1993)

COLLINSON S., *Migration, Visa and Asylum Policies in Europe* (London, H.M.S.O.,1995)

CRAIG P. and DE BÚRCA G., *EU Law—Text, Cases and Materials* (2nd edn., Oxford, Oxford University Press, 1998)

CRAWLEY H., *Women as Asylum Seekers: A Legal Handbook* (London, Immigration Law Practitioners' Association, 1997)

DASHWOOD A. and O'LEARY S. (eds.), *The Principle of Equal Treatment in EC Law* (London, Sweet & Maxwell, 1997)

DÄUBLER W. (ed.), *Market and Social Justice in the EC—the other Side of the Internal Market* (Guetersloh, Bertelsmann Foundation, 1991)

DAVIES P. and LYON-CAEN A., (eds.) *European Community Labour Law Principles and Perspectives, Liber Amicorum Lord Wedderburn of Charlton* (Oxford, Clarendon Press, 1996)

DE MOOR-VAN VUGT A., *Maten en gewichten: het evenredigheidsbeginsel in Europees perspectief* (Tilburg, Schoordijk Instituut, 1995)

DEHOUSSE R. (ed), *Europe After Maastricht: An Ever Closer Union?* (München, Beck, 1994)

DRZEMCZEWSKI A., *European Human Rights Convention in Domestic Law: A Comparative Study* (Oxford, Clarendon Press, 1983)

DRZEWICKI K., Krause C. and Rosas A. (eds.), *Social Rights as Human Rights: A European Challenge* (Turku/Åbo, Institute for Human Rights, 1994)

DUPARC C., *The European Community and Human Rights* (Luxembourg, Office for Official Publications of the EC, 1993)

ELLIS E., *European Community Sex Equality Law* (Oxford, Clarendon Press, 1991),

EUROPEAN DISABILITY FORUM, *Guide to the Amsterdam Treaty* (Brussels, 1998)

EUROPEAN HUMAN RIGHTS FOUNDATION, *The First Fifteen Years*, Report 1995 (Brussels, 1995)

FENET A. and SINCLAIR-CYTERMANN A. (eds.), *Union européenne: intégration et coopération* (Paris, Presses universitaires de france, 1995)

FINES F., *Etude de la responsabilité extracontractuelle de la Communauté economique européenne : De la reférence aux "principes généraux communs" à l'edification jurisprudentielle d'un système autonome* (Paris, Librairie Générale de Droit et de Jurisprudence, 1990)

GUILD E. and NIESSEN J., *The Developing Immigration and Asylum Policies of the European Union* (The Hague, Kluwer Law International, 1996)

HANSKI R. and SUKSI M. (eds.), *An Introduction to the International Protection of Human Rights: A Textbook* (Turku, Åbo Akademi University, 1997)

HARGREAVES A. and LEAMAN J. (eds.), *Racism, Ethnicity and Politics in Contemporary Europe* (Aldershot, Elgar, 1995)

HARLOW C. and RAWLINGS R., *Pressure Through Law* (London, Routledge, 1992)

HARRIS D. *et al., Law of the European Convention on Human Rights* (London, Butterworths, 1995)

HARTLEY T., *The Foundations of European Community Law*, (4th edn., Oxford, Oxford University Press, 1998)

HATHAWAY J. and DENT J., *Refugee Rights: Report on a Comparative Survey* (Toronto, York Lanes Press, 1995)

HENDRICKS A., *The Concepts of Non-Discrimination and Reasonable Accommodation, in European Day of the Disabled: Disabled Persons' Status in the European Treaties—in Invisible Citizens*, (Brussels, 1995)

HERVEY T. and O'KEEFFE D. (eds.), *Sex Equality Law in the European Union* (Chichester, Wiley, 1996)

HUGHES J. and LIEBAUT F. (eds.), *Detention of Asylum Seekers in Europe: Analysis and Perspectives* (The Hague, Nijhoff, 1998)

JACOBS F. (ed.), *European Law and the Individual* (Amsterdam, North-Holland, 1976)

JADOT Y. and ROLLAND J-P., *Contradictions in European Policy Towards Developing Countries: Evidence from the Farm Sector and Proposals for Improving the Effectiveness of International Development Cooperation* (Brussels,1996)

JONES P. and PULLEN J., *Inside We Are All Equal: A Social Policy Survey of Deaf People in the European Community* (Brussels,1989)

JOUBERT C. and BEVERS H., *Schengen Investigated: A Comparative Interpretation of the Schengen Provisions on International Police Cooperation in the Light of the European Convention on Human Rights* (Hague, Kluwer Law International, 1996)

KOULAIMAH-GABRIEL A. and OOMEN A., *Improving Coherence: Challenges for European Development Cooperation* (Brussels, 1997)

LASSEN N. and HUGHES J., *Safe Third Country Policies in European Countries* (Copenhagen, Danish Refugee Council, 1997)

LAWSON R. and DE BLOIJS M. (eds.), *The Dynamics of the Protection of Human Rights in Europe: Essays in Honour of Henry G. Schermers, Vol. III* (Dordrecht/London, Nijhoff, 1994)

LOQUAI C., *The Europeanisation of Development Cooperation: Coordination, Complementarity, Coherence* (London, Overseas Development Institute, 1996)

LUCCHINI A., *Cooperazione e diritto allo sviluppo nella politica esterna dell'unione europea* (Milan, Giuffrè, 1999)

LYON-CAEN G. and LYON-CAEN A., *Droit social international et Européen* (Paris, Dalloz, 1993)

MACDONALD R.ST.J., MATSCHER F. and PETZOLD H., (eds.), *The European System for the Protection of Human Rights* (Dordrecht, Nijhoff, 1993)

MACHADO S. and DE LORENZO R., *European Disability Law* (London, 1997)

MARIAS E. (ed.), *European Citizenship* (Maastricht, European Institute of Public Administration, 1994)

MATSCHER F. and PETZOLD H. (eds.), *Protecting Human Rights: The European Dimension: Studies in honour of Gérard J. Wiarda* (Köln, Heymanns, 1988)

McCRUDDEN C. (ed.), *Women, Employment and European Equality Law* (London, Eclipse, 1987)

McGOLDRICK D., *International Relations Law of the European Union* (London, Longman, 1997)

MEIJERS H. *et al.*, *Schengen: Internalisation of Central Chapters of the Law on Aliens, Refugees, Privacy, Security and Police* (Leiden, Stichting NJCM-Boekerij, 1992)

MEIJERS H. *et al.*, *Democracy, Migrants and Police in the European Union. The 1996 IGC and Beyond* (Utrecht, Forum, 1997)

MENDELSON M., *The impact of European Community law on the implementation of the European Convention on Human Rights* (Strasbourg, Council of Europe, 1984)

MICKLITZ H-W. and REICH N. (eds.), *Public Interest Litigation before European Courts* (Baden-Baden, Nomos, 1996)

MOSSE G., *Towards the Final Solution. A History of European Racism* (London, Dent, 1978)

NASCIMBENE B. (ed.), *Nationality Laws in the European Union* (Milan, Giuffrè, 1996)

NELSON B. *et al.* (eds.), *The European Community in the 1990s* (New York/Oxford, Berg, 1992)

NEUWAHL N. and ROSAS A. (eds.), *The European Union and Human Rights* (The Hague, Nijhoff, 1995)

O'KEEFFE D. and TWOMEY P., (eds.), *Legal Issues of the Maastricht Treaty* (London, Chancery Law Publishing, 1994)

O'LEARY S., *European Union Citizenship: Options for Reform* (London, Institute for Public Policy Research, 1996)

OESTREICH G., *Menschenrechte als Elemente der dritten AKP-EWG-Konvention von Lomé* (Berlin, Duncker & Humblot, 1990)

OJEDA AVILES A., *La calidad social europea desde la perspectiva de los derechos fundamentales* (Madrid, 1998)

PAPADOPOULOU R.-E., *Principes généraux du droit et droit communautaire—Origines et concrétisation* (Bruxelles, Bruylant, 1996)

PEERS S, *Mind the Gap! Ineffective Member State Implementation of European Union Asylum Measures*, (London, Immigration Law Practitioners' Association and the Refugee Council,1998).

PIENING C., *Global Europe: The European Union in World Affairs* (Boulder, Lynne Rienner, 1997)

PRECHAL S. and BURROWS N., *Gender Discrimination Law of the European Community* (Aldershot, Dartmouth, 1990)

RENGELING H., *Grundrechtsschutz in der Europäischen Gemeinschaft* (München, Beck, 1993)

RIEDEL E., *Theorie der Menschenrechtsstandards* (Berlin, Duncker & Humblot, 1986)

ROSAS A., and ANTOLA E. (eds.), *A Citizen's Europe* (London, Sage, 1995)

ROUSSEAU D. and SUDRE F. (eds.), *Conseil constitutionnel et Cour européenne des droits de l'homme* (Paris, Editions STH, 1990)

SAMOY E., *Sheltered Employment in the European Community* (Brussels, 1992)

Scritti in onore di Giuseppe Federico Mancini, Volume II (Milan, Giuffrè, 1998)

SENGENBERGER W. and CAMPBELL D. (eds.), *International Labour Standards and Economic Interdependence* (Geneva, International Institute for Labour Studies, 1994)

SHAW J. and MORE G. (eds.) *New Legal Dynamics of the European Union* (Oxford, Clarendon Press, 1995)

SLAUGHTER A.-M, STONE SWEET A. and WEILER J., *The European Courts and National Courts: Doctrine and Jurisprudence* (Oxford, Hart Publishing, 1998)

SOYSAL Y., *Limits of Citizenship, Migrants and Postnational Membership in Europe* (Chicago, Univ of Chicago Press, 1994)

STOKKE O. (ed.), *Aid and Political Conditionality* (London, Frank Cass, 1995)

SUDRE F., *Droit international et européen des droits de l'homme* (Paris, Presses universitaires de France, 1989)

TULKENS F. and BOSLY H.-D., (eds.), *La Justice pénale et l'Europe. Travaux des XVe journées d'études juridiques Jean Dabin* (Brussels, Bruylant, 1996)

WADDINGTON L., *Disability, Employment and the European Community* (Antwerpen, Maklu, 1995)

WEISS M., *Fundamental Social Rights for the European Union* (Amsterdam, Hugo Sinzheimer Institute, 1996)

WRENCH J., *European Compendium of Good Practice for the Prevention of Racism at the Workplace* (Dublin, European Foundation for the Improvement of Living and Working Conditions, 1997)

—— and SOLOMOS J. (eds.), *Racism and Migration in Western Europe* (Oxford/Providence, Berg, 1993)

ARTICLES AND CHAPTERS

ABRAHAM R., 'Les principes généraux de la protection juridictionnelle administrative en Europe: L'influence des jurisprudences européennes', 9 EPLR (1997) 577

ANDRIANTSIMBAZOVINA J., ' "Chronique Droits de l'homme": L'élaboration progressive d'un ordre public européen des droits de l'homme. Réflexions à propos de la jurisprudence de la Cour européene des droits de l'homme de 1988 à 1995', 33 CDE 670

ARNULL A., 'Private Applicants and the Action for Annulment under Article 173 of the EC Treaty', 32 *CMLRev.* (1995) 7

ARTS K., 'European Community Development Cooperation, Human Rights, Democracy and Good Governance: at Odds or at Ease with Each Other?', in K. Ginther, E. Denters and P. de Waart (eds.), *Sustainable Development and Good Governance* (Dordrecht /London, Nijhoff, 1995)

BALL C., 'The Making of a Transnational Capitalist Society: The Court of Justice, Social Policy, and Individual Rights Under the European Community's Legal Order', 37 *Harv. Int'l LJ* (1996) 314

BARAV A., 'Direct and Individual Concern: An Almost Insurmountable Barrier to the Admissibility of Individual Appeal to the EEC Court', 11 *CMLRev.* (1974) 191

BARNARD C., 'A European Litigation Strategy: the Case of the Equal Opportunities Commission', in J. Shaw and G. More (eds.) *New Legal Dynamics of the European Union* (Oxford, Clarendon Press, 1995)

—— 'The Principle of Equality in the Community Context: P, Grant, Kalanke and Marschall: Four Uneasy Bedfellows?', 57 *Cambridge LJ* (1998) 352

BERGER M., 'Ein Europa der Freiheit, der Sicherheit und des Rechts', 1/1998 Europa Perspektiven, 5

BERNARD N., 'Discrimination and Free Movement in EC Law', 45 *ICLQ* (1996) 82

BESSELINK L., 'Entrapped by the Maximum Standard: on Fundamental Rights, Pluralism and Subsidiarity in the European Union', 35 *CMLRev.* (1998) 629

BINDER D., 'The European Court of Justice and the Protection of Fundamental Rights in the European Community: New Developments and Future Possibilities in Expanding Fundamental Rights Review to Member State Action', 4/95 Harvard Jean Monnet Working Paper Series

BOUMANS E. and NORBARTS M., 'The European Parliament and Human Rights', 7 *NQHR* (1989) 37

BRADLEY K., 'Administrative Justice: A Developing Human Right?', 1 *EPL* (1995) 347

BRANDTNER B. and ROSAS A., 'Human Rights in the External Relations of the European Community: An Analysis of Doctrine and Practice', 9 *EJIL* (1998) 468

BREWER T. and YOUNG S., 'European Union Policies and the Problems of Multinational Enterprises', 29 Journal of World Trade (1995) 33

BULTERMAN M., 'The Chapter on Fundamental Rights and Non-Discrimination of the Draft Treaty of Amsterdam', 17 *NQHR* (1997) 399

—— 'European Union Membership and Political Conditionality', in M. Bulterman, A. Hendriks, and J. Smith (eds.), *To Baehr in Our Minds: Essays on Human Rights from the Heart of the Netherlands*, SIM Special No. 21 (SIM [Netherlands Institute of Human Rights], Utrecht, 1998) 129

BYRNE R. and SHACKNOVE A., 'The Safe Country Notion in European Asylum Law', 9 *Harv. HRJ* (1996) 185

CAMPBELL-WHITE F., 'Property Rights: A Forgotten Issue under the Union', in N. Neuwahl and A. Rosas (eds.), *The European Union and Human Rights* (The Hague, Nijhoff, 1995)

CHURCHILL R. and FOSTER N., 'Double Standards in Human Rights? The Treatment of Spanish Fishermen by the European Community', 12 *ELRev.* (1987) 430

CLAPHAM A., 'A Human Rights Policy for the European Community', 10 *YEL* (1990) 349

CLOSA C., 'The Concept of Citizenship in the Treaty on European Union', 29 *CMLRev.* (1992) 1137

COHEN-JONATHAN J., 'La problématique de l'adhésion des Communautés européennes à la Convention européenne des droits de l'homme', in *Mélanges Pierre Henri Teitgen* (Paris, Pédone, 1984)

—— 'L'adhésion de la Communauté européenne à la Convention européenne des droits de l'homme', 3 Journal Tribunaux Droit Européen (1995) 49

—— 'Les réserves dans les traités institutionels relatifs aux droits de l'homme. Nouveaux aspects européens et internationaux', Revue générale de droit international public (1996) 915

—— and JACQUÉ, J.-P. 'Activités de la Commission européenne des droits de l'homme', 35 *AFDI* (1989) 512

COPPEL J. and O'NEILL A., 'The European Court of Justice: Taking Rights Seriously?', 29 *CMLRev.* (1992) 669

CREMONA M., 'Citizens of Third Countries: Movement and the Employment of Migrant Workers Within the European Union', 2 *LIEI* (1995) 87

CROMACK V., 'The EC Pregnancy Directive: Principle or Pragmatism', 15 *JSWL* (1993) 261

CURTIN D., 'EU Police Cooperation and Human Rights Protection: Building the Trellis and Training the Vine', in *Scritti in onore di Giuseppe Federico Mancini, Volume II* (Milan, Giuffrè, 1998)

—— and GEURTS M, 'Race Discrimination and the European Union Anno 1996: From Rhetoric to Legal Remedy?', 14 *NQHR* (1996) 155

—— and KLERK Y., 'De Europese Unie en het Europees Verdrag voor de Rechten van de Mens', Nederlands Juristenblad (1997) 202

D'OLIVEIRA H., 'European Citizenship: its Meaning, its Potential', in R. Dehousse (ed.), *Europe After Maastricht: An Ever Closer Union?* (München, Beck, 1994)

——, 'Union Citizenship: Pie in the Sky?', in A. Rosas and E. Antola (eds.), *A Citizen's Europe* (London, Sage, 1995)

DALLEN R. M.,'An Overview of European Community Protection of Human Rights with some Special References to the UK', 27 *CMLRev.* (1990) 766

DAUSES M., 'La protection des droits fondamentaux dans l'ordre juridique communautaire', 20 *RTDE* (1984) 401

DE BÚRCA G., 'Fundamental Human Rights and the Reach of EC Law', 13 *OJLS* (1993) 283

DE SALVIA M., 'L'élaboration d'un "ius commune" des droits de l'homme et des libertés fondamentales dans la perspective de l'unité européenne: l'oeuvre accomplie par la Commission et la Cour européennes des droits de l'homme', in F. Matscher and H. Petzold (eds.), *Protecting Human Rights: The European Dimension: Studies in honour of Gérard J. Wiarda* (Köln, Heymanns, 1988)

DE SCHUTTER O. and LEJEUNE J., 'L'adhésion de la Communauté à la Convention européene des droits de l'homme. A propos de l'avis 2/94 de la Cour de Justice des Communautés', 32 CDE (1996) 555

DE SOUSA SANTOS B., 'Toward a Multicultural Conception of Human Rights', 18 Zeitschrift für Rechtssoziologie (1997) 2

DE WITTE B., 'Protection of Fundamental Social Rights in the European Union: The Choice of the Appropriate Legal Instrument', in L. Betten and D. MacDevitt (eds.), *The Protection of Fundamental Social Rights in the European Union* (The Hague, Kluwer Law International, 1996)

DECAUX E., 'La PESC et la diplomatie des droits de l'homme', in A. Fenet and A. Sinclair-Cytermann (eds.), *Union européenne: intégration et coopération* (Paris, Presses Universitaires de France, 1995)

DÍEZ-PICAZO L., 'Una constitución sin Declaración de Derechos? (Reflexiones constitucionales sobre los derechos fundamentales en la Comunidad Europea)', 32 Revista Española de Derecho Constitucional (1991), 135

DOCKSEY C., 'The European Community and the Promotion of Equality', in C. McCrudden (ed.), *Women Employment and European Equality Law* (London, Eclipse, 1987)

—— 'The Principle of Equality between Men and Women as a Fundamental Right Under Community Law', 20 *ILJ* (1991) 258

DUIJKERSLOOT A., 'Nationale maatregelen, communautaire grondrechten en de vrij verkeersjurisprudentie', Sociaal-economische wetgeving (1997) 218

EVANS A., 'Nationality Law and European Integration', 16 *ELRev.* (1991) 214

FENWICK H. and HERVEY T., 'Sex Equality in the Single Market: New Directions for the European Court of Justice', 32 *CMLRev.* (1995) 445

FITZPATRICK B., 'Towards Strategic Litigation? Innovations in Sex Equality Litigation Procedures in the Member States of the European Community', 8 *Int. J of Comp. Lab. L and Ind. Rel.* (1992) 8

FORDER C., 'Abortion: A Constitutional Problem in European Perspective', 1 *Maast. J. Eur & Comp. L.* (1994) 56

FOSTER N., 'The European Court of Justice and the European Convention for the Protection of Human Rights', 8 *HRLJ* (1987) 245

FOUWELS M., 'The European Union's Common Foreign and Security Policy and Human Rights', 15 *NQHR* (1997) 291

FREDMAN S., 'European Community Discrimination Law', 21 *ILJ* (1992) 121

GAJA G., 'Aspetti problematici della tutela dei diritti fondamentali nelltordinamento comunitario', 71 *RDI* (1988) 585

—— 'Gli atti comunitari dinanzi alla Commissione europea dei diritti dell'uomo: di nuovo Solange?', 73 *RDI* (1990) 388

—— 'The Protection of Human Rights under the Maastricht Treaty', in D. Curtin and T. Heukels (eds.), *Institutional Dynamics of European Integration. Essays in Honour of Henry G. Schermers* (Dordrecht, Nijhoff, 1994)

GEARTY C., 'The European Court of Human Rights and the Protection of Civil Liberties: An Overview', 52 *Cambridge LJ* (1993) 89

GOSALBO BONO R., 'Reflexiones en torno al futuro de la protección de los derechos humanos en el marco del derecho comunitario y del derecho de la Unión: insuficiencias y soluciones', [1997] Revista de Derecho Comunitario Europeo 56

GREAVES P., 'Locus Standi under Article 173 EEC When Seeking Annulment of a Regulation', 11 *ELRev.* (1986) 119

HÄBERLE P., 'Theorieelemente eines allgemeinen juristischen Rezeptions modells', Juristen Zeitung (1992) 1037

HABERMAS J, 'The European Nation State, its Achievements and its Limitations. On the Past and Future of Sovereignty and Citizenship', 9 Ratio Juris (1996) 125

—— 'Citizenship and National Identity: Some Reflections on the Future of Europe', Praxis International (1992) 1

HARDING C., 'Who Goes to Court in Europe? An Analysis of Litigation against the European Community', 17 *ELRev.* (1992) 105

HARLOW C., 'Towards a Theory of Access for the European Court of Justice', 12 *YEL* (1992) 213

HARRIS D., 'The European Social Charter and Social Rights in the European Union', in L. Betten and D. MacDevitt (eds.), *The Protection of Fundamental Social Rights in the European Union* (The Hague, Kluwer Law International, 1996)

HATHAWAY J., 'Harmonizing for Whom? The Devaluation of Refugee Protection in the Era of European Economic Integration', 26 Cornell International Law Journal (1993) 719

HEPPLE B., *Memorandum presented to the House of Lords Select Committee on the European Communities*, Session 1992–93, 3rd Report 'Human Rights Re-Examined'

—— 'Social Values and European Law', 48 Current Legal Problems (1995) 39

HERVEY T. and SHAW J., 'Women, Work and Care: Women's Dual Role and Double Burden in EC Sex Equality Law', 8 Journal of European Social Policy Law (1998) 43

HILF M., 'Ein Grundrechtskatalog für die europäische Gemeinschaft', Europarecht (1991) 19

HUBER P., 'Das Kooperationsverhältnis zwischen BVerfG und EuGH in Grundrechtsfragen', EuZW (1997) 517

JACOBS F., 'The Protection of Human Rights in the Member States of the European Community: The Impact of the Case-law of the Court of Justice', in J. O'Reilly (ed.), *Human Rights and Constitutional Law: Essays in Honour of Brian Walsh* (Dublin, Round Hall Press, 1992)

JACQUÉ J.-P., 'The Convention and the European Communities', in R.St.J. Macdonald, F. Matscher and H. Petzold (eds.), *The European System for the Protection of Human Rights* (Köln, Heymanns, 1988)

—— 'Communaute européenne et Convention européenne des droits de l'homme', in *L' Europe et le Droit. Melanges en hommage a Jean Boulouis* (Paris, Dalloz, 1991)

—— and WEILER J., 'On the Road to European Union— A New Judicial Architecture: An Agenda for the Intergovernmental Conference', 27 *CMLRev.* (1990) 185

JANIS M., 'Fashioning a Mechanism for Judicial Cooperation on European Human Rights Law among Europe's Regional Courts', in R. Lawson and M. de Bloijs (eds.), *The Dynamics of the Protection of Human Rights in Europe: Essays in Honour of Henry G. Schermers, Vol. III* (Dordrecht/London, Nijhoff, 1994)

JORNA M., 'Complementarity Between EU and Member State Development Policies: Empty Rhetoric or Substantive New Approach?', The Courier No. 154 (November-December 1995) 78

JÜRGENSEN T. and SCHLÜNDER I., 'EG-Grundrechtsschutz gegenüber Massnahmen der Mitgliedstaaten', Archiv des öffentlichen Rechts (1996) 200

KOKOTT J., 'Menschenrechtsschutz im Rahmen der Rechtsordnung der Europäischen Gemeinschaften', in A.A. Cançado Trindade (ed.), *The Modern World of Human Rights:*

Essays in Honour of Thomas Buergenthal (San José, Inter-American Institute of Human Rights, 1996)

KUIJPER B., 'Trade Sanctions, Security and Human Rights and Commercial Policy', in M. Marescu (ed.), *The European Community's Commercial Policy after 1992: The Legal Dimension* (Dordrecht, Martinus Nijhoff, 1993)

LABAYLE H., 'Un espace de liberté, de sécurité et de justice', *RTDE* (1997) 874

LARDY H., 'The Political Rights of Union Citizenship', 2 *EPL* (1996) 611

LAWSON R., 'Confusion and Conflict? Diverging Interpretations of the European Convention on Human Rights in Strasbourg and Luxembourg', in R. Lawson and M. de Bloijs (eds.), *The Dynamics of the Protection of Human Rights in Europe: Essays in Honour of Henry G. Schermers, Vol. III* (Dordrecht/London, Nijhoff, 1994)

LECOURT R., 'Cour européenne des Droits de l'Homme et Cour de justice des Communautés européennes', in F. Matscher and H. Petzold (eds.), *Protecting human rights: the European dimension—studies in honour of Gerard Jwiarda* (Köln, Heymanns, 1988)

LENAERTS K., 'Fundamental Rights to be Included in a Community Catalogue', in 16 *ELRev.* (1991) 368

—— 'L'égalité de traitement en droit communautaire—Un principe unique aux apparences multiples', CDE (1991) 3

—— and VANHAMME J., 'Procedural Rights of Private Parties in the Community Administrative Process', 34 *CMLRev.* (1997) 531

LENZ O., 'Der europäische Grundrechtsstandard in der Rechtsprechung des Europäischen Gerichtshofes', EuGRZ (1993) 585

LO FARO A., 'The Social Manifesto: Demystifying the Spectre Haunting Europe', 3 *ELJ* (1997) 300

LUNDBERG E., 'The Protection of Social Rights in the European Community: Recent Developments', in K. Drzewicki, C. Krause and A. Rosas (eds.), *Social Rights as Human Rights: A European Challenge* (Turku/Åbo, Institute for Human Rights, 1994)

MADIOT Y., 'Un statut européen de l'étranger dans la jurisprudence de la CEDH', Annales de la Fac. de Droit de Poitiers (1992)

MANCINI G., 'The Making of a Constitution for Europe', 26 *CMLRev.* (1989) 608

—— and DI BUCCI V., 'Le développement des droits fondamentaux en tant que partie du droit communautaire', Vol. I, 1 AEL (1990) 27

—— and KEELING D., 'Democracy and the European Court of Justice', 57 *MLR* (1994) 188

MARANTIS D., 'Human Rights, Democracy and Development: The European Community Model', 7 *Harv. HRJ* (1994) 7

McCRUDDEN C., 'The Effectiveness of European Equality Law: National Mechanisms for Enforcing Gender Equality Law in the light of European requirements', 13 *OJLS* (1993) 320.

MENDELSON M., 'The European Court of Justice and Human Rights', 1 *YEL* (1981) 125

MORE G., 'Equal Treatment of the Sexes in European Community Law: What does "Equal" Mean?', 1 Feminist Legal Studies (1993) 45

—— 'Reflections on Pregnancy Discrimination under European Community Law', 14 *JSWL* (1992) 48

MORGAN R., 'How Common Will Foreign and Security Policies Be?', in R. Dehousse (ed.), *Europe After Maastricht: An Ever Closer Union?* (München, Beck, 1994)

NAPOLI D., 'The European Union's Foreign Policy and Human Rights', in N. Neuwahl and A. Rosas (eds.), *The European Union and Human Rights* (The Hague, Martinus Nijhoff, 1995)

NEUWAHL N., 'Article 173 Paragraph 4 EC: Past, Present and Possible Future', 21 *ELRev.* (1996) 17.

—— 'The Treaty on European Union: A Step Forward in the Protection of Human Rights?', in N. Neuwahl and A. Rosas (eds.), *The European Union and Human Rights* (The Hague, Martinus Nijhoff, 1995)

NOLL G., 'Prisoners' Dilemma in Fortress Europe: On the Prospects for Equitable Burden Sharing in the European Union', 40 GYIL (1997) 405.

O'KEEFFE D., 'The Emergence of a European Immigration Policy', 20 *ELRev.* (1995) 20

O'LEARY S., 'Nationality Law and Community Citizenship: A Tale of Two Uneasy Bedfellows', 12 *YEL* (1992) 353

—— 'The Court of Justice as a Reluctant Constitutional Adjudicator: An Examination of the Abortion Information Case', 17 *ELRev.* (1992) 138

—— 'The Relationship between Community Citizenship and the Protection of Fundamental Rights in Community Law', 32 *CMLRev.* (1995) 519

PEEBLES G., 'A Very Eden of Innate Rights of Man? A Marxist Look at the European Union Treaties and Case Law', 22 Law & Soc. Inquiry (1997) 592.

PEERS S., 'Towards Equality: Actual and Potential Rights of Third Country Nationals in the European Union', 33 *CMLRev.* (1996) 7

PESCATORE P., 'La Communauté est liée par la Convention en vertu de la doctrine de succession d'Etat', in F. Matscher and H. Petzold (eds.), *Protecting Human Rights: The European Dimension: Studies in honour of Gérard J. Wiarda* (Köln, Heymanns, 1988)

—— 'La Cour de justice des Communautés européennes et la Convention européenne des Droits de l'homme', in F. Matscher and H. Petzold (eds.), *Protecting Human Rights: The European Dimension: Studies in honour of Gérard J. Wiarda* (Köln, Heymanns, 1988)

—— 'The Context and Significance of Fundamental Rights in the Law of the European Communities', 2 *HRLJ* (1981) 295

PETERSMANN E.-U., 'Proposals for a New Constitution of the European Union: Building-Blocks for a Constitutional Theory and Constitutional Law of the EU', 32 *CMLRev.* (1995) 1123

PHELAN D., 'Right to Life of the Unborn v. Promotion of Trade and Services: the European Court of Justice and the Normative Shaping of the European Union', 55 *MLR* (1992) 670

PIPKORN J., 'La Communauté européenne et la Convention européenne des droits de l'homme', 4 *RTDH* (1993) 221

PREUSS U., 'Grundrechte in der Europäischen Union', 31 Kritische Justiz (1998) 1

REICH N., 'Judge-made "Europe à la carte": Some Remarks on Recent Conflicts between European and German Constitutional Law Provoked by the Banana Litigation', 7 *EJIL* (1996) 103

RESS G., 'Menschenrechte, europäisches Gemeinschaftsrecht und nationales Verfassungsrecht', in H. Haller *et al.* (eds.), *Staat und Recht, Festschrift für Günther Winkler* (Vienna, 1997)

—— and UKROW J., 'Neue Aspekte des Grundrechtsschutzes in der Europäischen Gemeinschaft. Anmerkungen zum Hoechst-Urteil des EuGH', EuZW (1990) 499

RHI-SAUSI J., 'El papel de las administraciones descentralizadas en la cooperación al desarrollo de la Unión Europea', Revista Española de Desarrollo y Cooperación (Spring 1997) 1

RIEDEL E., 'Menschenrechte der dritten Dimension', EuGRZ (1989) 10

RIGAUX F., 'L'article 192 du Traite CEE devant la Commission européenne des droits de l' homme', *RTDH* (1991) 399

RODRIGUEZ IGLESIAS G., 'La proteccion de los derechos fondamentales en la Union europea', in *Scritti in onore di Giuseppe Federico Mancini, Volume II* (Milan, Giuffrè, 1998)

—— and VALLE GALVEZ A., 'El Derecho comunitario y las relaciones entre el Tribunal de Justicia de las Comunidades Europeas, el Tribunal Europeo de Derechos Humanos y los Tribunales Constitucionales nacionales', [1997] Revista de Derecho Comunitario Europeo 329

RODRIGUEZ-PIÑERO M. and CASAS M., 'In support of a European Social Constitution', in
P. Davies, and A. Lyon-Caen (eds.) *European Community Labour Law Principles and Perspectives, Liber Amicorum Lord Wedderburn of Charlton* (Oxford, Clarendon Press, 1996)

ROSAS A., 'Electoral Rights and the European Union: a Broader Human Rights Perspective'
in N. Neuwahl and A. Rosas (eds.), *The European Union and Human Rights* (The Hague,
Nijhoff, 1995)

RYAN B., 'Pay, Trade Union Rights and European Community Law', *Int. Jour. of Comp. Lab.
Law and Ind. Rel.* (1997) 305

SCHERMERS H., 'The European Communities Bound by Fundamental Human Rights', 27
CMLRev. (1990) 249

SCHWARZE J., 'Developing Principles of European Administrative Law', *PL* (1993) 229.

SCIARRA S., 'European Social Policy and Labour Law: Challenges and Perspectives', 4 AEL
(1995) 312

SPIELMANN D., 'Deux conséquences du caractère pénal des amendes prononcées par la Commission des Communautés européennes dans le domaine du droit de la concurrence', in F.
Tulkens and H-D. Bosly (eds.), *La Justice pénale et l'Europe. Travaux des XVe journées d'é-
tudes juridiques Jean Dabin* (Bruxelles, Bruylant, 1996)

STEVER, T. 'Protecting Human Rights in the European Union: an argument for treaty reform',
Vol 20 *Fordham Intl.* LJ 919

SUDRE F., 'La Communauté européenne et les droits fondamentaux après le traité d'Amsterdam: Vers un nouveau système européen de protection des droits de l'homme', La Semaine
Juridique (1998) I-100.

SZYSZCZAK E., 'L'Espace Sociale Européene, Reality, Dreams or Nightmare', 33 GYIL (1990)
298

—— 'Social Rights as General Principles of Community Law', in N. Neuwahl and A. Rosas
(eds), *The European Union and Human Rights* (1995)

TEMPLE LANG J., 'The Sphere in which Member States are Obliged to Comply with the General Principles of Law and Community Fundamental Rights Principles', 2 *LIEI* (1991) 34

TIBERI G., 'La questione dell'adesione della Comunità alla convenzione europea dei diritti
dell'uomo al vaglio della Corte di giustizia', Rivista italiana di diritto pubblico comunitario
(1997) 450

TOTH A., 'The European Union and Human Rights: The Way Forward', 34 *CMLRev.* (1997)
491

TWOMEY P., 'The European Union: Three Pillars without a Human Rights Foundation', in D.
O'Keeffe and P. Twomey (eds.), *Legal Issues of the Maastricht Treaty* (London, Chancery
Law Publishing, 1994)

VAN DEN BULCKE D., 'Multinational Companies and the European Community', in B. Nelson
et al. (eds.), *The European Community in the 1990s* (New York/Oxford, Berg, 1992)

VAN DER KLAAUW J., 'European Union' 13 *NQHR* (1995) 280

—— 'European Union', 16 *NQHR* (1998) 91

—— 'Refugee Protection in Western Europe: A UNHCR Perspective', in J.-Y. Carlier, and
D. Vanheule (eds.), *Europe and Refugees: A Challenge?* (The Hague, Kluwer Law International, 1997)

VERSCHUEREN H., 'EC Social Security Coordination Excluding Third Country Nationals: Still
in Line with Fundamental Rights after the Gaygusuz Judgment?', 34 *CMLRev.* (1997) 991

VON PRONDZYNSKI F., 'Freedom of Association and the Closed Shop: the European Perspective', 41 *Columbia LJ* (1982) 256

WEDDERBURN of CHARLTON K., 'Labour Standards, Global Markets and Labour Laws in Europe', in W. Sengenberger and D. Campbell (eds.), *International Labour Standards and Economic Interdependence* (Geneva, International Institute for Labour Studies, 1994)

—— 'Consultation and Collective Bargaining in Europe: Success or Ideology', 26 *ILJ* (1997)

WEILER J., 'The European Court at Crossroads: Community Human Rights and Member State Action' , in F. Capotorti *et al.* (eds.), *Du droit international au droit de l'integration : Liber amicorum Pierre Pescatore* (Baden-Baden, Nomos, 1987)

—— 'Thou Shalt Not Oppress a Stranger: On the Judicial Protection of the Human Rights of Non-EC Nationals—A Critique', 3 *EJIL* (1992) 65

—— 'Les droits des citoyens européens', RMC (1996) 51

—— and LOCKHART N, ' "Taking Rights Seriously" Seriously: The European Court and its Fundamental Rights Jurisprudence', 32 *CMLRev.* (1995)

WOODS L., 'The European Union and Human Rights', in R. Hanski and M. Suksi (eds.), *An Introduction to the International Protection of Human Rights: A Textbook* (Turku, Åbo Akademi University, 1997)

ZWAMBORN M., 'Human Rights Promotion and Protection through the External Relations of the European Community and the Twelve', 7 *NQHR* (1989) 11

REPORTS

Affirming Fundamental Rights in The European Union: Time to Act, Report of the Expert Group on Fundamental Rights (Brussels, European Commission, Employment, Industrial Relations and Social Affairs, Feb. 1999)

AMNESTY INTERNATIONAL, *Memorandum: Proposal for a strengthened protection of human rights by the European Union in the context of the Intergovernmental Conference* 1996. RAC No. 04/96, I.1.c.

ECONOMIC AND SOCIAL COMMITTEE, Opinion on 'The European Union and the external dimension of human rights policy', OJ 1997 C 206/117

EUROPEAN COMMISSION AGAINST RACISM AND INTOLERANCE, *Legal measures to combat racism and intolerance in the Member States of the Council of Europe: A Report prepared by the Swiss Institute of Comparative Law*, Lausanne (1996)

EUROPEAN COMMISSION, *Annual Report on Equal Opportunities for Men and Women in the EU* (1997)

EUROPEAN COMMISSION (DGV), *For a Europe of Civic and Social Rights, Report by the Comité des Sages chaired by Maria de Lourdes Pintasilgo*, (Luxembourg, Office for Official Publications of the EC, 1996)

EUROPEAN COMMISSION, (DGV), Working Paper, *Raising Employment Levels of People with Disabilities— The Common Challenge* (Luxembourg, Office for Official Publications of the EC, 1998)

EUROPEAN COMMISSION, *The European Institutions in the Fight against Racism: Selected Texts* (Luxembourg, Office for Official Publications of the EC, 1997)

European Declaration of Business Against Exclusion (Brussels, 1995)

EUROPEAN PARLIAMENT, Annual report on human rights throughout the world in 1993–1994 and the Union's human rights policy (Doc. A4–0078/95). OJ 1995 C 126/15

—— Annual report on human rights throughout the world in 1995–1996 and the Union's human rights policy (Doc. A4–0400/96). OJ 1997 C 20/161

—— Annual report on respect for human rights in the European Union 1993 (Doc. A4–124/94). OJ 1995 C 068/3

—— Annual Report on respect for human rights in the European Union 1994 (Doc. A4–0223/96 (1996))

—— Annual Report on respect for human rights in the European Union 1995 (Doc. A4–0112/97 (1997))

EUROPEAN PARLIAMENT, Annual Report on respect for human rights in the European Union 1996 (Doc. A4–0034/98). OJ 1998 C 80/43

——— *Committee of Inquiry into the Rise of Fascism and Racism in Europe. Report on the Findings of the Inquiry (The Evrigenis Report)* (1985)

——— *Committee of Inquiry on Racism and Xenophobia. Report on the Findings of the Inquiry (The Ford Report)* (1991)

——— Council of the European Union and European Commission *Joint Declaration on fundamental rights,* 5 April 1977, OJ 1977 C 103/1

——— *Report on the report from the Commission on the implementation of measures intended to promote observance of human rights and democratic principles (for 1995) (Imbeni Report),* A4–381/97/13 (1997)

——— Report of the High Level Panel on the free movement of persons chaired by Mrs Simone Veil—Committee on Civil Liberties and Internal Affairs, Doc. A4–108/98 (1998), drawn up by Mrs Anne-Marie Schaffner

——— Report on the communication from the Commission on racism, xenophobia and anti-semitism and on the proposal for a Council decision designating 1997 as European Year against Racism (*Rapporteur*: Mr Arie Oostlander), Doc. A4–135/96/37 (1996)

——— Report on the European Immigration Policy, Doc. A3–0280/92 (1992)

——— Report on the harmonization within the European Communities of Asylum Law and Policies, Doc. A3–0337/92 (1992)

——— Report on the proposal for a Council Regulation establishing a European Monitoring Centre for Racism and Xenophobia (*Rapporteur*: Mr Glyn Ford), Doc. A4–110/97/29 (1997)

——— Report on the resurgence of racism and xenophobia in Europe and the danger of right-wing extremist violence (*Rapporteur*: Mr Cesare De Piccoli), Doc. A3–0127/93 (1993)

——— Report on the situation of gypsies in the Community (*Rapporteur*: Mr Juan de Dios Ramirez Heredia), Doc. A3–124/94/11 (1994)

——— Report on the status of nationals of non-member countries in the European Union (*Rapporteur*: Mrs Djida Tazdait), Doc. A3–332/93/25 (1993)

HELIOS I (Second) Community Social Action Programme for Disabled People, OJ 1988 L 104/38.

HELIOS II (Third) Community Social Action Programme to Assist Disabled People, OJ 1993 L 56/30.

HUMAN RIGHTS WATCH/HELSINKI, '*Germany for Germans'. Xenophobia and Racist Violence in Germany* (1995)

HUMAN RIGHTS WATCH/HELSINKI, *Racist Violence in the United Kingdom* (1997)

STARTING LINE GROUP, The New Starting Line: Proposal to the European Parliament, Council and Commission, and to the member states of the European Community for a Draft Directive Concerning the Elimination of Racial and Religious Discrimination (Brussels, 1998)

UNITED NATIONS HIGH COMMISSIONER FOR REFUGEES, *Detention of Asylum Seekers in Europe* (1995)

INDEX

ACOSTE. LACROIX. LAGERFELD. LALIQUE. VAN LAMSWEERDE. LANCETTI. LANE. LANG.
ANVIN. LAPIDUS. LAROCHE. LAUDER. LAUREN. LÉGER. LEIBER. LELONG. LENOIR.
LEPAPE. LEONARD. LEROY. LESAGE. LESER. LESTER. LEVINE. LEY. LIBERMAN. LIBERTY.
LINDBERGH. LLOYD. LOEWE. LOUBOUTIN. LOUIS. LUTENS. MCCARDELL. MCCARTNEY.
MCDEAN. MACDONALD. MCFADDEN. MCGRATH. MACKIE. MCKNIGHT. MCLAREN.
MCLAUGHLIN-GILL. MCQUEEN. MADONNA. MAINBOCHER. MALTÉZOS. CARPENTIER.
MANDELLI. MAN RAY. MARAMOTTI. MARGIELA. MARTEANS. MATSUDA. MATSUSHIMA.
MAXWELL. MAZZII. MEISEL. MESEJEÁN. DE MEYER. L. MILLER. N. MILLER. MILNER.
MISSONI. MIYAKE. MIZRAHI. MODEL. MOLINARI. MOLYNEUX. MONTANA. MOON.
MOREHOUSE. MO. MORRIS. MORTON. MOSCHINO. MOSES. MOSS. MUGLER. MUIR.
MUNKACSI. NARS. NAST. NEWTON. NORELL. NUTTER. OLDFIELD. OLDHAM. ORRY-
KELLY. OUDEJANS. OZBEK. PAGE. PALEY. PALMERS & WOLFF. PAQUIN. PARKER.
PARKINSON. PATOU. PAULETTE. PAULIN. PEARL. PENN. PERETTI. PERINT PALMER.
PERTEGAZ. PERUC. PFISTER. PIGUET. PINET. PINGAT. PIPART. PITA. PLATT LYNES.
POIRET. POLLOCK. PORTER. POZO. PRADA. PRÉMONVILLE. PRESLEY. PRICE. PUCCI.
PULITZER. QUANT. RABANNE. RAYNE. REBOUX. REDFERN. DE LA RENTA. REVILLON
FRÈRES. REVSON. RHODES. DE RIBES. RICCI. RITTS. M. ROBERTS. T. ROBERTS. ROCHA.
ROCHAS. RODRIGUEZ. ROEHM. ROSIER. ROTTEN. ROUFF. ROVERSI. RUBINSTEIN.
RYKIEL. SAINT LAURENT. SANDER. SANT' ANGELO. SARNE. SASSOON. SCAASI. SCAVULLO.
SCHERRER. SCHIAPARELLI. SCHIFFER. SCHÖN. SCHUBERTH. SHRIMPTON. SIEFF.
SIMPSON. SIMS. SITBON. G. SMITH. P. SMITH. W. SMITH. SNOW. SNOWDON. SOULEIMAN.
SPROUSE. STEELE. STEICHEN. STEIGER. STEPHEN. STERN. STEWART. STIEBEL.
STOREY. STRAUSS. SUI. SUMURUN. SYBILLA. TALBOT. TAPPÉ. TARLAZZI. TATSUNO.
TELLER. TENNANT. TESTINO. THIMISTER. THOMASS. TIFFANY. TOLEDO. TOMMASO.
TOPOLINO. TORIMARU. TOSKAN. TRAN. TRAVILLA. TREACY. TREE. TRIGÈRE. TROUBLÉ.
TURBEVILLE. TURLINGTON. TWIGGY. TYLER. UEMURA. UNDERWOOD. UNGARO. VON
UNWERTH. VALENTINA. VALENTINO. VALLHONRAT. VAN BEIRENDONCK. VAN CLEEF &
ARPELS. VAN NOTEN. VANDERBILT. VENET. VENTURI. VERDURA. VERSACE. VERTÈS.
VERUSCHKA. VIONNET. VIRAMONTES. VIVIER. VREELAND. VUITTON. WAINWRIGHT.
WANG. WARHOL. WATA. WESTWOOD. WILDE. WILLIAMSON.
WINDSOR. WINSTON. WOLF. YAMAMOTO. YANTORNY. ZORAN.

THE FASHION BOOK

Phaidon Press Limited
Regent's Wharf
All Saints Street
London N1 9PA

First published 1998
©1998 Phaidon Press Limited

ISBN 0 7148 3808 X

A CIP catalogue record for this book
is available from the British Library.

Library of Congress Cataloging in
Publication Data available.

Printed in Singapore

Abbreviations

ALG = Algeria
ARG = Argentina
ASL = Australia
AUS = Austria
BEL = Belgium
BR = Brazil
CAN = Canada
CHN = China
CI = Canary Islands
CU = Cuba
CYP = Cyprus
CZ = Czechoslovakia
DOM = Dominican Republic
DK = Denmark
EG = Egypt
FR = France
GER = Germany
GR = Greece
HK = Hong Kong
HUN = Hungary
IRE = Ireland
IT = Italy

JAM = Jamaica
JAP = Japan
KEN = Kenya
KOR = Korea
LUX = Luxembourg
MAL = Malaysia
MEX = Mexico
MON = Monaco
MOR = Morocco
NL = Netherlands
PER = Peru
POL = Poland
PR = Puerto Rico
ROM = Romania
RUS = Russia
SA = South Africa
SING = Singapore
SP = Spain
SW = Switzerland
SWE = Sweden
SYR = Syria
TUN = Tunisia

TUR = Turkey
UK = United Kingdom
USA = United States of America
YUG = Yugoslavia

THE FASHION BOOK takes a fresh look at the fashion world and the people who created and inspired it. Spanning 150 years, the whole industry is represented; from pioneering designers including Coco Chanel and Issey Miyake to influential photographers such as Richard Avedon and Helmut Newton and the people they photographed. Easy to use and filled with inspirational images, it is an A-Z guide to 500 clothes and accessory designers, photographers, models and those iconic individuals who instigated or symbolize a whole fashion movement. It cuts through the usual classifications and creates juxtapositions that make fascinating and unlikely partnerships: René Lacoste sits opposite Christian Lacroix while Kate Moss rubs shoulders with Thierry Mugler. Each entry is illustrated with a photograph or drawing which shows a quintessential aspect of their work. An accompanying text describes where they fit into the fashion story and includes essential biographical information about the creator. In addition, THE FASHION BOOK uses a comprehensive cross-referencing system and glossary which explain the many collaborations and techniques used in fashion, that singular business which lives somewhere between art and commerce.

Φ

Abbe James

Photographer

James Abbe's choice of a simple, uncluttered backdrop and soft use of lighting accentuates the seductiveness of Gilda Gray, a dancer in *Ziegfeld Follies* and other Broadway revues. Like many fashion photographs of its time, it promotes a feeling that we are privy to something intimate – as if Gray has been captured unawares, dreamily caught up in her own thoughts with her eyes turned away from the lens. Taken in Paris in 1924, the photograph seizes the essence of mid-1920s eveningwear – a plumb line dress, possibly by Lanvin or Patou, in filmy, sensuous fabric trimmed with fringed tiers. In the early twentieth century, American photographer James Abbe favoured taking portraits of stage and screen actresses. His well-mannered work for American *Vogue* represented what Alexander Liberman called '...an underlying dream of a world where people act and behave in a civilized manner'.

☛ Lanvin, Liberman, Patou

James Abbe. **b** Alfred, ME (USA), 1883. **d** San Francisco, CA (USA), 1973. **Gilda Gray, Paris**. 1924.

Abboud Joseph

Designer

A Mao jacket cut from rough linen is worn over a hand-knitted waistcoat and collarless shirt. The buttons on each garment have a natural, artisanal quality which defies the urban slant used by most American designers. Of Lebanese descent, Joseph Abboud makes clothes for men and women which are an unusual combination of American sportswear and North African colours and textures. In the 1960s Abboud collected Turkish kilims and these have inspired his natural palette and the stylized symbols that recur in his work. He began his career as a buyer and in 1981 joined Ralph Lauren, later to become associate director of menswear design. He emerged four years later with a similar philosophy to Lauren: that clothing is as much about lifestyle as it is about design. In 1986 Abboud launched his own label and found a niche for his understated clothes with their rich colours and unusually crafted textures.

☛ Alfaro, Armani, Lauren, Ozbek

Joseph Abboud. b Boston, MA (USA), 1950. **Linen menswear. Spring/summer 1995.** Photograph by Randall Mesden.

Adolfo

Designer

This impromptu snap of society figures Mr and Mrs Wyatt Cooper is one of Adolfo's favourite pictures, and not just because both are wearing his refined clothes. He says, 'Getting dressed and going out is fun only because we don't do it often – it's good to feel glamorous once in a while.' But his glamour never strays into the realms of vulgarity. Adolfo worked first as a milliner, then trained at Chanel and Balenciaga, before setting up his New York salon. There, Adolfo provided his famous knitted suits, one of which is worn here by Gloria Cooper (aka Gloria Vanderbilt). Inspired by Coco Chanel's jersey sportswear and famous suits, they were bought by New York's old society. When his salon closed in 1993 his wealthy clientele were distraught, not least Nancy Reagan, the former First Lady, who had worn Adolfo's clothes for two decades. She, perhaps more than anyone, embodied his assertion that, 'An Adolfo lady should look simple, classic and comfortable.'

☛ Balenciaga, Chanel, Galanos, Vanderbilt

Adolfo (Adolfo Sardinia). b Havana (CU), 1933. **Mr and Mrs Wyatt Cooper**. Photograph by Bill Cunningham, American *Vogue*, 1972.

Adrian Gilbert

Designer

Joan Crawford wears Adrian's famed 'coat hanger look': a suit with padded shoulders and slim skirt which produces an 'inverted triangle' silhouette that has since intermittently returned to fashion – not least in the 1980s. Here, that shape is exaggerated further by triangular lapels which reach over the shoulders and taper, pointing at the waist. As Adrian told

Life magazine in 1947, 'American women's clothes should be streamlined in the daytime.' He is also known for long, elegantly draped dinner gowns, like those he designed for Joan Crawford in *Grand Hotel,* and for his silver satin bias-cut dresses for starlet Jean Harlow. As a costume designer at Metro-Goldwyn-Mayer in the 1930s and 1940s, Adrian found a vast audience for his work

and became an influential fashion designer. In 1942 he retired as a costume designer to open his own fashion house, continuing to create his trademark suits and gowns.

☞ Garbo, Irene, Orry–Kelly, Platt Lynes

Gilbert Adrian. b Naugatuck, CT (USA), 1903. **d** Los Angeles, CA (USA), 1959. **Joan Crawford.** c1940.

Agnès Madame   Milliner

During the 1930s, hats were literally the pinnacle of fashion, and a lady would no sooner go out without her hat than she would without her dress. In France millinery was an exclusively female occupation and Madame Agnès was the most popular milliner, famous for cutting her elegant brims while they were worn by her clients. Trained under Caroline Reboux, she established her own salon in 1917 on the rue du Faubourg Saint-Honoré in Paris among all the great couturiers. She worked in the same understated manner and combined this discrimination with an awareness of art and of the artistic trends of the 1930s, especially Surrealism. In particular, Madame Agnès brought a Surrealistic touch to that traditional millinery trim: the plumage of birds, as seen here. The feathery touch and lightness of flight which represent Madame Agnès's spirited interpretation of the movement is put into an eveningwear context with a spangled jacket by Maggy Rouff.

☞ Hoyningen-Huene, Reboux, Rouff, Talbot

Madame Agnès. **b** (FR), late 1800s. **d** (FR). (Active 1910s–1940s.) **Hat of blue paradise plumes.** Photograph by George Hoyningen-Huene, *Harper's Bazaar*, 1935.

Alaïa Azzedine   Designer

Amazonian models in skintight dresses and high-heeled shoes embody the slick sex appeal of the dress-to-kill 1980s. Each wears an outfit from Azzedine Alaïa's 1987 spring/summer collection. 'The base of all beauty is the body,' says Alaïa, who was inspired by Madeleine Vionnet. 'There is nothing more beautiful than a healthy body dressed in wonderful clothes.'

The 'King of Cling' is an expert manipulator of the female form, having studied sculpture when he was younger. He moved to Paris and worked briefly for Dior and Guy Laroche, and by the end of the 1960s had his own couture business on the Left Bank. Alaïa went on to produce the prototype for Yves Saint Laurent's famous Mondrian dress and worked for Thierry Mugler. In the

early 1980s, his own stretchy dresses and bodysuits, constructed from thick knitted panels, came to define the Lycra revolution.

☛ Audibet, Bettina, Coddington, Léger, M. Roberts, Vionnet

9

Azzedine Alaïa. b (TUN), c1940. **Paris presentation**. Photograph by Arthur Elgort, British *Vogue*, 1987.

Albini Walter   Designer

Striking disco poses, two women wear the Walter Albini hallmarks: fast, glamorous clothes which recall shapes from the 1930s. Albini started his luxury sportswear business in 1965 and became known for his fundamental allegiance to the early styles of Chanel and Patou, which were counterpointed by the global influences of the 1970s. Bold colours from Asian and African art, as well as bright tartans, were employed on the jackets, skirts and other basic silhouettes. As much as any 1970s designer, Albini energized anti-establishment hippie layering and ethnicity and mixed it with the sophistication of the urbane sportswear pedigree. Albini's motto was 'Enjoy today and leave unpleasant things for tomorrow'. Ironically, premature death obviated any tomorrows, but Albini's exuberant, aggressive and youthful sportswear was a significant contribution to the 1970s.

☛ Barnett, Bates, Chanel, Ozbek, Patou

Walter Albini. b Busto Arsizio (IT), 1941. d Milan (IT), 1983. **Black crepe outfits**. Photograph by Chris von Wangenheim, Italian *Vogue*, 1971.

Alexandre

Hairdresser

Alexandre de Paris, or 'Monsieur Alexandre', as he likes to be known, attends to Elizabeth Taylor's hair during the filming of *Cleopatra* in 1962. Many legends surround the hairdresser, whose clients included the Duchess of Windsor, Coco Chanel and Grace Kelly. His parents, it is said, had wanted him to study medicine, but after a fortune-teller predicted that 'the wife of a king will do everything for you', they relented and let him pursue his ambition to become a hairdresser. He was apprenticed to Antoine, the Parisian stylist who invented the urchin cut. Alexandre took on his mantle and became the hairdresser of the stylish European social set. His motif, a sphinx, was designed for him by Jean Cocteau in gratitude for the perm which rescued him from his despair that he no longer had 'the curly hair of a true poet'. In 1997, Jean Paul Gaultier persuaded Alexandre out of retirement to design the hair for his first couture show, as he had done for Coco Chanel, Pierre Balmain and Yves Saint Laurent.

☛ Antoine, Cocteau, Gaultier, Windsor, Winston

11

Alexandre (Louis Alexandre Raimon). b St Tropez (FR), 1922. **Alexandre de Paris with Elizabeth Taylor.** On the set of *Cleopatra.* Photograph by Eric Adjani, 1962.

Alfaro Victor　Designer

Victor Alfaro's first collection, launched in 1991, was dubbed by *Cosmopolitan* magazine 'a series of heat-seeking glamour missiles'. Reputedly the heir to Oscar de la Renta and Bill Blass, Alfaro has never sought to philosophize through his offerings; on the contrary, his mission is as simple as making the wearer look beautiful. This image shows a quintessential Alfaro creation in which vulgarity is proscribed, leaving room for bare simplicity skilfully counterbalanced by sexy, luxurious silk. The combination of a ball skirt and strapless top is typical of Alfaro's use of separates for cocktail- and eveningwear, acquired while working for American ready-to-wear designer Joseph Abboud. He uses slub silk as others use cotton, in keeping with the American sportswear tradition of evening clothes that quietly forgo decoration for practical statements, even on a ball gown.

☛ Abboud, Blass, de la Renta, Tyler

Victor Alfaro. b Chihuahua (MEX), 1965. **Satin bustier and evening skirt.** Spring/summer 1996. Photograph by Chris Moore.

Amies Sir Hardy   Designer

Her Majesty the Queen is photographed during the Silver Jubilee celebrations in 1977. She wears an eye-catching pink silk crepe dress, coat and stole by Sir Hardy Amies, dressmaker to Her Majesty since 1955 and the architect of her vivid, feminine and simple style. Sir Hardy, knighted in 1989, was designer and manager at Lachasse, a traditional British couture house, from 1934 to 1939. As well as being lieutenant-colonel in charge of special forces in Belgium, he designed clothes under the Utility rationing scheme. In 1946 he founded his own dressmaking business, designing for Princess Elizabeth and eventually holding the royal warrant. In 1950, Sir Hardy started ladies' ready-to-wear and in 1961 began working with menswear chain Hepworths. His remark, 'A man should look as if he bought his clothes with intelligence, put them on with care, then forgot all about them', defines the Englishman's approach to fashion.

☛ Clements & Ribeiro, Hartnell, Morton, Rayne, Stiebel, Tran

Sir Hardy Amies. b London (UK), 1909. **Her Majesty Queen Elizabeth II wears pink Royal Jubilee outfit**. 1977.

Antoine

Hairdresser

Josephine Baker was one of Antoine's many famous clients – she wore his wigs like skullcaps for her stage performances. Born in Russian Poland, Antoine moved to work in the Parisian salon of hairdresser Monsieur Decoux. He acquired a following and, cannily, Decoux took his star stylist to the fashionable seaside town of Deauville; there Antoine was introduced to the society he would coif for decades. On his return to Paris, Antoine set up his own salon, selling his own haircare and cosmetics range – the first to do so. Although he is famed for his 'Eton crop', he always maintained he could not claim it as his own. At the time he said he was simply carrying out the orders of a client who returned three times to have her short bobbed hair cut progressively shorter to suit the increasingly sporty lifestyle enjoyed by women of that era. The peak of Antoine's career was the coronation of George VI, when he supervised 400 coiffures in one night.

☛ Alexandre, G. Jones, Kenneth, de Meyer, Talbot

Antoine (Antak Cierplikowski). b Sieradz (POL), 1884. d (POL), 1977. **Josephine Baker.** Photograph by Baron de Meyer, c1925.

14

Antonio

Illustrator

Antonio's watercolour model embraces a deconstructed mannequin for Italian *Vogue* in 1981. This surreal element, a tradition created by Dalí, Cocteau and Bérard in the 1930s, was a theme used by Antonio throughout his career. Texan Jerry Hall was painted with Lone Star emblems and cacti growing from her stetson and Pat Cleveland was metamorphosed into a stiletto boot. Despite this visual play, Antonio worked from life, building sets as a photographer would. Antonio was inspired by the drawings of Boldini and Ingres, which becomes clear when looking at the fine finish on his pencil drawings. His work dominated fashion illustration for a decade, encouraging a discipline that had diminished throughout the 1950s. Antonio worked with a clique of international models and high-profile friends who converged on Paris in the 1970s. Tina Chow, Grace Jones and Paloma Picasso were regular sitters.

☞ Chow, G. Jones, Khanh, Versace

15

Antonio (Antonio Lopez). b (PR), 1943. d (PR), 1987. **Gianni Versace editorial**. Italian *Vogue*, 1981.

Arai Junichi

Textile designer

Junichi Arai has been described as the 'truly *enfant terrible* of Japanese textiles...a naughty boy playing with high-tech toys'. His favoured toys are the jacquard loom and digital computers. The fabric illustrated here is typical of his work, which commonly uses metallic fibres and turns them into exquisite works of art destined only to be admired. The son and nephew of weavers,

Arai was born in Kiryu, an historic centre for textiles. He initially worked with his father on kimono and obi cloths, which he developed, eventually acquiring three dozen patents for new fabrics. From 1970 Arai worked experimentally and began long-standing collaborations with Rei Kawakubo and Issey Miyake, who would suggest phrases such as 'like clouds', 'like stone' or

'driving rain' which Arai would magic into a representative fabric by using his idiosyncratic weaving techniques.

☞ **Hishinuma, Isogawa, Jinteok, Kawakubo, Lloyd, Miyake**

16

Junichi Arai. b Kiryu (JAP), 1932. **Crush-pleated fabric. Spring/summer 1990**. Photograph by Masanao Arai.

Arden Elizabeth   Cosmetics creator

In one of Baron de Meyer's famous advertisements for Elizabeth Arden, a model resembling a figure from a Modigliani painting wears the Arden face. The name behind one of the century's greatest cosmetic houses was inspired by Tennyson's poem *Enoch Arden* and a love of the name Elizabeth. Her real name was Florence Nightingale Graham and she worked as a beauty treatment girl for Eleanor Adair in New York where, in 1910, she opened her own salon on Fifth Avenue with her signature red door (it would later sell couture by Charles James). One of the first beauty gurus to encourage exercise, she opened a spa and health retreat in Maine in 1934, and was passionate about horses. Arden developed a range of make-up for Hollywood which wouldn't melt under the lights and was later used by women when they were out dancing. In 1935 she launched the legendary Eight Hour Cream, which remains to this day a cult beauty product for professional make-up artists and millions of women worldwide.

☛ C. James, de Meyer, Morris, de la Renta, Revson

17

Elizabeth Arden. b Woodbridge, ONT (CAN), 1878. **d** New York (USA), 1966. **Advertising campaign.** Photograph by Baron de Meyer, c1927.

Armani Giorgio
Designer

A man and woman wear the hallmarks of a great modernist: tailoring that trades stiff formality for assured relaxation. Giorgio Armani laid the groundwork for the easy, minimalist working uniform of emancipated 1980s women and blazed the trail for designers such as Calvin Klein, Donna Karan and Jil Sander. His menswear was equally mould-breaking: taking the stuffing and stiffness out of the suit, he made the laid-back style of southern Europe coveted around the world. Armani was assistant to Nino Cerruti before starting his own business in 1973. His name came to the fore in 1980 when he dressed Richard Gere for the film *American Gigolo*. Every scene was choreographed to work for Armani's clothes, prompting Gere to ask, 'Who's acting in this scene, me or the jacket?' A good question. Giorgio Armani's fashion shows never use famous models, the designer preferring that his clothes receive the audience's unclouded attention.

☛ Abboud, Cerruti, Dominguez, Etro

18

Giorgio Armani. b Piacenza (IT), 1934. **Unstructured tailoring. Spring/summer 1995.** Photograph by Peter Lindbergh.

Arnold Eve

Photographer

Eve Arnold's camera picks up the gold beaded skullcap, glossed lips and lacquered nails of a model backstage at a Lanvin show in 1977. Arnold rarely uses studios, relying instead on natural light and she is dependent on her hand-held Nikon. Her work is always respectful and sympathetic to its subject, background details are never an afterthought, and Arnold insists, 'You have to take advantage of the variables. It might be the smile, the gesture, the light. None of which you can predict'. She took pictures of black women modelling in Harlem fashion shows in 1948 and continued the project for two years, until *Picture Post* published her story. As a result, she was offered a job as the first female stringer for the Magnum photographers' agency. A long friendship with Marilyn Monroe produced some of her best-known images. But Arnold's work covers a broad spectrum – 'everything from serious disaster to Hollywood hoop-la'.

☛ Lanvin, Lapidus, L. Miller, Stern

Eve Arnold. b Philadelphia, PA (USA), 1913. **Lanvin model at Mappins, Paris**. French *Vogue*, 1977.

Ascher Zika

Textile designer

In the long tradition of artists turning fabric designers, such as Dufy and Cocteau, the unmistakable sketches of Henry Moore are applied to silk by Zika Ascher. This design, which combines screen printing with batik painting, was selected for use by Nina Ricci. When *Vogue* asked in 1962, 'Which comes first, the chicken or the egg? The fabric or the fashion?' it could have had Ascher in mind. His innovative approach to fabrics revolutionized fashion from the 1940s. He started his own production company and silk-screen print works in London in 1942. In 1948 he approached artists such as Moore and Henri Matisse to design prints. His own inventive approach to textiles acted as a catalyst for fashion designers of that time: in 1952 his highly original large-scale floral prints were used by Dior and Schiaparelli, and in 1957 his shaggy mohair inspired Castillo to create huge enveloping coats.

☞ Castillo, Etro, Pucci, Ricci, Schiaparelli

Zika Ascher. b Prague (CZ), 1910. **Fabric designed by Henry Moore, 1945 (detail).** Photograph by Daniel McGrath.

Ashley Laura · Designer

A Victorian-inspired, white cotton dress worn under a floral pinafore sums up the mood of romantic rural idyll which made Laura Ashley a household name. She once said that she designed for women who wanted to look 'sweet': 'I sensed that most people wanted to raise families, have gardens and live as nicely as they can.' She used puffed sleeves, sprig prints, pin-tucking, lace trims and high collars to make romantic references to a pastoral lifestyle which in reality was a hard one for most. In a way that only fashion can, the look reinvented history and enabled women to dress for a role. It precipitated a movement known as 'milkmaidism'. In 1953, Ashley and husband Bernard began silk-screen printing textiles by hand in a small workshop in Pimlico, making table mats and napkins. In 1968 they opened their first shop, selling the basic Laura Ashley dress for £5. By the 1970s, it had become a symbol of femininity.

☛ **Ettedgui, Fratini, Kenzo**

Laura Ashley. b Merthyr Tydfil (UK), 1926. **d** Coventry (UK), 1985. **Dress with pinafore.** c1970.

Audibet Marc Designer

This design is entirely about 'stretch'. There are no hooks, no eyes, no buttons and no zippers. It is a seamless, asymmetrical creation that clings to the body, following the lines of the model's figure. Audibet is both a fashion designer and an industrial designer, and is celebrated in the fashion world for his research into stretch fabrics. His expertise was acquired working as an assistant for Emanuel Ungaro and then as a designer for Pierre Balmain, Mme Grès and Nino Cerruti. An admirer of the work of Mme Vionnet and Claire McCardell, Audibet believes that fashion is a matter of anatomy and that innovation starts with fabrics. In 1987 he became textile adviser to the fabric and fibre company DuPont and together they created and launched single- and two-way stretch fabrics made from DuPont's 'Lycra' – the most important development in fashion in the 1980s.

☛ Alaïa, Bruce, Godley, Grès, Ungaro, Zoran

22

Marc Audibet. b Boulogne-sur-Seine (FR), 1958. **Stretch column**. Photograph by Tyen, American *Elle*, 1987.

Avedon Richard   Photographer

Penelope Tree is suspended in space, frozen in a joyful leap by Richard Avedon. It is an image that epitomizes the motion and emotion Avedon introduced into fashion photography, resisting the prevailing tradition of static poses. Instead he prefers the mood of street reality; a woman glimpsed on a busy sidewalk or the unexpectedness of the famous Dovima With Elephants.

Influenced by photographer Martin Munkacsi, who explored the principle of the fashion figure in motion, Avedon established his images of dancing and swinging frenzy which have retained their freshness to this day. Avedon joined *Harper's Bazaar* in 1945, moving to *Vogue* in 1965. He has never forsaken fashion but, through his keen convictions in politics and intense interests in subcultures, Avedon has become a photographer in service to a vision larger than fashion *per se*.

☛ Brodovitch, Dovima, Moss, Parker, Tree, Ungaro

Richard Avedon. b New York (USA), 1923. **Penelope Tree in Ungaro suit**. Paris studio, 15 January, 1968.

Bailey David   Photographer

Jean Shrimpton, the face of the early 1960s, shares a confidence with Cecil Beaton, photographer, illustrator, costume designer and writer whose influence on fashion spanned forty years. The photograph is by David Bailey. His shots of Jean Shrimpton, who he first met in 1960 and with whom he had a relationship for four years, let the world into an intimate relationship between photographer and model. Bailey, who was regarded as a bad boy, used few models and developed long working relationships with them. His reluctance to be categorized as a fashion photographer is justified by time: those fashion shots now stand as legendary portraits in themselves. As Marie Helvin, model and former wife, put it, '...the very essence of Bailey's style is his refusal to allow his models to be simply clothes hangers or his pictures moments of fashion. He photographs women wearing clothes.'

☞ Beaton, French, Horvat, Shrimpton, Twiggy

David Bailey. b London (UK), 1938. **Jean Shrimpton and Cecil Beaton**. British *Vogue*, 1965.

Bailly Christiane   Designer

Christiane Bailly was part of the *prêt-à-porter* revolution of the 1960s. Her radical methods included experimenting with synthetic fabrics such as silver plastic and 'cigarette paper'. She took the stiff interlinings out of jackets for a more supple silhouette, and cut close-fitting clothes from black ciré in 1962. Bailly began her career as a model for Balenciaga, Chanel and Dior in 1957. Her interest in fashion developed and she entered design, working on more approachable clothes than those she had been wearing at the grand couture houses. In 1961 she started designing for Chloé and, after two years, moved on to work with Michèle Rosier. In 1962 Bailly formed a company with Emmanuelle Khanh whom she had met at Balenciaga, and both were assisted by a young Paco Rabanne. Their label, Emma Christie, produced revolutionary designs to critical acclaim and poor commercial success, but their role in the birth of French *prêt* was an important one.

☛ Bousquet, Betsey Johnson, Khanh, Lenoir, Rabanne, Rosier

Christiane Bailly. b Lyons (FR), 1932. **Bouclé jacket and black wool skirt**. Photograph by Tim Jenkins, *Women's Wear Daily*, 1979.

Bakst Léon

Illustrator and designer

The overall effect of this costume is both classical and oriental. It reflects the current fashionable silhouette in its long, columnar shape. However, this severe line is softened by the lavish surface decoration, reminiscent of the East. Léon Bakst's contribution to the history of fashion came through the theatre. He collaborated with Sergei Diaghilev in the creation of the Ballets Russes which

came to Paris in 1909. As its artistic director, Bakst designed the vibrantly coloured and exotic costumes. It was his designs for *Schéhérazade* which caused a sensation when it was performed in Paris in 1910. Orientalism in haute couture had already been successfully promoted by Paul Poiret. It was given further impetus by Bakst's sensual costumes, which had an extraordinary

impact on Parisian fashion houses such as Worth and Paquin, who used his designs from 1912 to 1915. Bakst, like Erté, was a designer and an illustrator, and was acclaimed for the technical excellence of his draughtsmanship.

☛ Barbier, Brunelleschi, Dœuillet, Erté, Iribe, Poiret

26

Léon Bakst. b St Petersburg (RUS), 1866. d Paris (FR), 1924. **Design for Paquin**. Illustration, 1913.

Balenciaga Cristobal   Designer

Layered bells form the sleeves of this cape, worn over a matching dress. They exemplify the shapely simplicity that made Cristobal Balenciaga a great couturier. His genius lay in cut. The sack dress, the balloon dress, the kimono-sleeve coat and a collar cut to elongate the neck were a few of his fashion innovations, although his clothes also came with a disclaimer: 'No woman can make herself chic if she is not chic herself,' said Balenciaga. His Spanish severity, in the tradition of Velásquez and Goya, contrasted with the light femininity of French designers; his favourite fabric was silk gazar, diaphanous but stiff, which satisfied his instinct for the sculptural. As early as 1938, Balenciaga's modern vision was influential, explained by *Harper's Bazaar* thus, 'Balenciaga abides by the law that elimination is the secret of chic.' In 1968, after a battle against what he saw as the tide of vulgarity flowing through fashion, Balenciaga bowed out with the words, 'It's a dog's life.'

☛ Chow, Penn, Pertegaz, Rabanne, Snow, Thimister, Ungaro

Cristobal Balenciaga. **b** Guetaria (SP), 1895. **d** Valencia (SP), 1972. **Dress and cape. Autumn/winter 1964.** Photograph by Kublin.

Balla Giacomo   Designer

Although flat on the surface, this suit fuses movement, line and colour in a representation of the excitement of speed. Intrinsically forceful, the green jagged strokes on the jacket, like storm-strewn palm leaves, mark high velocity, converging in a vortex of patterns, which transmit energy. It gives us an image of an experimentalist at work. Balla, like fellow Futurists Severini and Boccioni, felt a positive need to extend his interests from the canvas to his environment, in this case exploring the subject of dress as a medium for expressing his Futurist ideas. Focusing more on male clothing, he stated the tenets of modernity in his 'Manifesto of Anti-Neutral Clothing', which aimed to bring disorder to the logic and communication of clothing. His ideas were based on asymmetry, clashing colours and juxtaposed forms that opposed the notion of tradition and convention. 'The past I so fiercely reject,' he said, embracing the industrial dynamics of modern art in his perception of fashion.

☛ Delaunay, Exter, Warhol

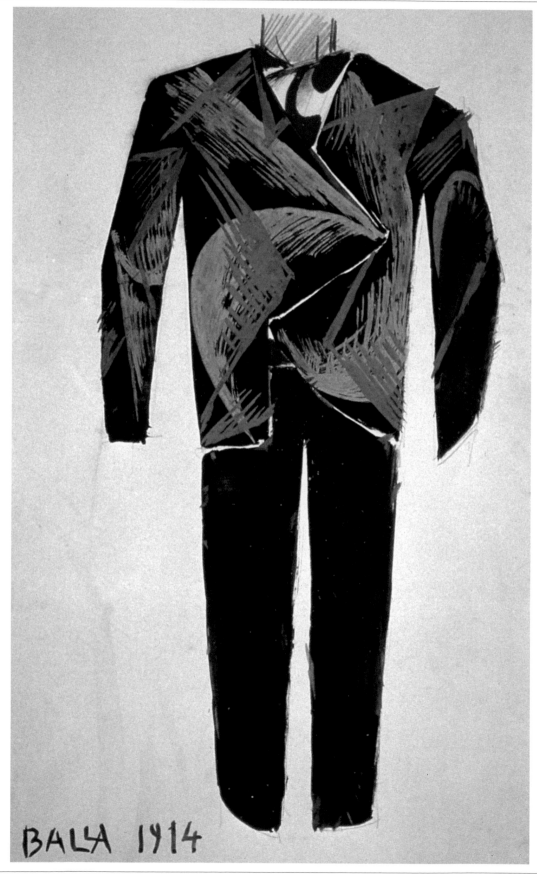

Giacomo Balla. **b** Turin (IT), 1871. **d** Rome (IT), 1958. **Sketch for men's suit, 1914.** Photograph by Giuseppe Schiavinotto, Rome.

28

Bally Carl Franz

Shoe designer

The continuity of fashion is illustrated by two examples of Bally's Mary Jane shoes, which are separated by fifty years. The delicacy of red suede, gold leather trim and diamond button was replaced by serviceable leather for the 1990s. Carl Franz Bally decided to mass-produce high-quality footwear after falling in love with a pair of shoes he found for his wife in Paris. The son of a silk ribbon weaver, Franz had taken over the family business, expanding the company to include an elastic tape that was used by shoemakers. While visiting one of his clients in Paris, he saw the inspirational shoes and bought the entire stock. 'Papa Bally' continued buying such shoes for his wife and later started to manufacture his own collections in his factory. The Bally style is a classic one and in the 1920s its Swiss quality made it an important player in the burgeoning ready-to-wear shoe market.

☞ Chéruit, Steiger, Vivier

Carl Franz Bally. b Schönenwerd (SW), 1821. **d** Schönenwerd (SW), 1898. **Scarlet evening shoe, 1930, and brown leather reinterpretation, 1998.**

Balmain Pierre Designer

Mlle Laure de Noailles wears her debutante gown, with foaming tulle skirt, by Pierre Balmain. *Vogue* declared that 'eventful skirts' were his speciality; they were often embellished with embroidered motifs such as leaves (ivy in this case), cherries or scrolls. Balmain, who trained as an architect, believed that both professions worked to beautify the world, declaring couture to be 'the architecture of movement'. In 1931 he was appointed junior designer at Molyneux. He sold sketches to Robert Piguet, then worked at Lucien Lelong where he was later joined by Christian Dior; they collaborated for four years. The pair nearly went into partnership together, but in 1945 Balmain left to establish his own house. Like Dior's New Look of 1947, Balmain's full-skirted silhouette was part of the new postwar luxury. His dresses were always carefully constructed. Signature details included drapery or a bow across the shoulders and fur hoods, muffs or trims.

☞ Cavanagh, Colonna, Dior, Lelong, Molyneux, Piguet, Pipart

Pierre Balmain. b St-Jean-de-Maurienne (FR), 1914. **d** Paris (FR), 1982. **Mlle Laure de Noailles.** Photograph by Cecil Beaton, American *Vogue*, 1945.

Bandy Way   Make-up artist

Model Gia wears the perfect work of Way Bandy. Her light, translucent make-up was delivered with very few products. Usually working with liquid cosmetics, Bandy would mix his colours at home and tie them up in two small Japanese baskets – accessories for his elegant, black working outfits. He was visionary in the formulations he used: his foundations were blended with eye drops that would tighten the pores, promoting the flawlessness he worked for. Blending was also very important to his work and Bandy named his dog Smudge after his refining technique. He was always perfectly made-up himself, turning up for fashion shoots wearing inconspicuous base and powder. For one night, however, Bandy demonstrated his skill with grander schemes by arriving at a Halloween party thrown by his friend Halston wearing the full, traditional kabuki face. As a friend remembered, 'He loved beauty and from those little bottles could come perfection in the form of lightness or the bizarre'.

☞ **Halston, Saint Laurent, Uemura**

Way Bandy. b Birmingham, AL (USA), c1941. **d** (USA), 1986. **Gia**. Photograph by Arthur Elgort, 1978.

31

Banton Travis   Designer

Travis Banton's costume for Marlene Dietrich is from the film *Shanghai Express* (1932). He disguised her as a black swan in a costume of feathers, veiled and hung with ropes of crystal beads. Her handbag and gloves were specially made for her by Hermès. Banton regularly visited Paris; on one occasion, he bought up an entire stock of bugle beads and fish-scale paillettes reserved for Schiaparelli. In reparation, he sent her enough trim to complete her line for the season. Banton worked in couture in New York; his break came when he designed the costumes for Paramount's *The Dressmaker from Paris* in 1925, after which he became Paramount's designer-in-chief. He designed for Dietrich, Mae West, Claudette Colbert and Carole Lombard. One of his signatures was dressing women in men's clothes. He continued to run his successful couture business alongside costume designing.

☞ **Carnegie, Hermès, Orry-Kelly, Schiaparelli, Trigère**

Travis Banton. **b** Waco, TX (USA), 1894. **d** Los Angeles, CA (USA), 1958. **Marlene Dietrich**. Still from *Shanghai Express*. 1932.

Barbier Georges   Illustrator

This fashion illustration shows two of Paul Poiret's models in a setting that represents one of his fashion houses. The evening coat on the right has a long train which falls from the shoulders and drops back at the sides like huge wings. It has an intricate design representing a stylized tree. A similar coat designed by Paul Poiret and called Battick was photographed by Edward Steichen and appeared in *Art et Décoration* in April 1911. The required headwear to be worn with the coat and equally exotic dress (with its high waistline reminiscent of the 'Directoire' line of late eighteenth-century France) was the turban, trimmed with pearls and surmounted by an aigrette. Barbier has united Poiret's simple classical line with the bold colours and design elements of his oriental style. Barbier was one of the great fashion artists, together with Paul Iribe and Georges Lepape, commissioned by Poiret to illustrate his fashions.

☞ Bakst, Drian, Iribe, Lepape, Poiret, Steichen

Georges Barbier. b Nantes (FR), 1882. d Nantes (FR), 1932. **Exotic coat and dress**. Cover of *Les Modes*. April 1912.

Barbieri Gian Paolo   Photographer

A woman in full, glamorous make-up wears the uniform of a meat market trader. It could be a reference to the model's work, but in a practical sense it is advertising a mesh vest which parodies the string version worn by working men. It is a typically dramatic example of Gian Paolo Barbieri's work. In 1997, he directed Vivienne Westwood's first-ever campaign which was based on the work of the sixteenth-century painter Holbein. For Barbieri this was more than fashion work. It was the creation of a filmic tableau which indulged all his passions: proportion, minute detail and a desire to seal the moment. In 1965 Barbieri photographed the first cover of Italian *Vogue*. His work for that magazine and others opened doors to advertising work for designers such as Valentino, Armani, Versace and Yves Saint Laurent. In 1978 the German magazine *Stern* named him as one of the fourteen most important image-makers of the time.

☛ Bourdin, Valentino, Westwood

Gian Paolo Barbieri. b Milan (IT), 1938. **Meat Market**. 1985.

Bardot Brigitte   Icon

Actress Brigitte Bardot sits under a tree, smoking moodily, her deshabille hair and *au naturel* appearance the epitome of amoral French sensuality. British *Vogue* called her 'the sensuous idol, a potent mixture of the sexy and the babyish, a seething milky bosom below a childish pout'. She was known simply as BB (the French pronounced it '*bébé*' – French for 'baby'), and the phrase 'sex kitten' was invented to describe her. Her narrow trousers and tight black sweater reflect the nonchalant beat style. She also popularized flat ballet pumps and set a trend for not wearing socks in her film *And...God Created Woman* (1956), for ruffles and ringlets, petticoats and prettiness in *Les Grandes Manoeuvres* (1955), and for Edwardian dress in *Viva Maria* (1965). Jeanne Moreau wrote that Bardot, 'was the real modern revolutionary character for women'.

☞ Bouquin, Esterel, Féraud, Frizon, Heim

Brigitte Bardot. b Paris (FR), 1934. **Brigitte Bardot**. Photograph shot during the filming of *La Vie Privée*. 1961.

Barnett Sheridan Designer

A cool bride is transported to the church on a Harley Davidson. Her wedding outfit is by Sheridan Barnett, who graced the 1970s with lean, uncontrived fashion. Her cream jacket and skirt are spare of any detail other than Perspex buttons to fasten her jacket and patch pockets to carry her handkerchief. Barnett was almost architectural in his approach to clothes, demanding function and purity of line at a time when all around him were making additions with embroidery, printing and appliqué fighting for space on dresses everywhere. Because function is more commonly found on menswear, Barnett often used it as a central theme. Although the bride's cloche hat is trimmed with net, a black pussy-cat bow is tied at her neck and her stockinged legs end in a pair of wedge sandals, that clean, masculine theme comes through in a jacket which is modelled on a classic, double-breasted blazer.

☛ Albini, Bates, Wainwright

Sheridan Barnett. b Bradford (UK), 1951. **Cream blazer and skirt**. Photograph by Peter Knapp, British *Vogue*, 1971.

36

Baron Fabien   Creative director

Fabien Baron's clean, clear layouts, allowing tangled graphics to float luxuriantly in vast areas of space, recall the power of Alexey Brodovitch's work and have set new standards in modern design. The son of a graphic designer, Baron started his career at *New York Woman* in 1982 and moved quickly to Italian *Vogue*. His first issue, September 1988, is now a collector's item. He worked for eighteen months at *Interview* before being appointed creative director at Brodovitch's old home, *Harper's Bazaar*, of which he said, 'this was the only magazine left to do'. His style has been widely influential and Baron acknowledges, 'the look doesn't belong to me any more'. He directed Madonna's *Erotica* video and designed her metal-covered book, *Sex*. The frosted vodka-bottle shape for Calvin Klein's unisex CK One perfume was also his creation. Klein says, 'We are on the same wavelength, except Fabien goes way beyond my capabilities of aestheticism'.

☞ Brodovitch, W. Klein, Madonna

Fabien Baron. b Antony (FR), 1959. **Collage of spreads**. From *Harper's Bazaar*, *Interview* and Italian *Vogue*. 1998.

Barrett Slim

Jewellery designer

In this swathe of chain links by Slim Barrett, jewellery becomes a garment with a piece which suggests both a draped necklace and a hood. Pierre Cardin and Paco Rabanne both used this theme by expanding dresses to become hybrids of fashion and jewellery, and here Barrett has done the same from his perspective as a jewellery designer. He returns intermittently to medieval themes – he helped Karl Lagerfeld by developing silver wire so fine that it could be knitted – and, in the 1990s, Barrett was responsible for the tiara's rise in popularity (particularly among brides). In his quest to extend the realm of costume jewellery, other catwalk collaborations (including those for Chanel, Versace, Montana and Ungaro), have resulted in the creation of plated body armour, waistcoats and skullcaps as vehicles for Barrett's work.

☞ Lagerfeld, Morris, Rabanne

Slim Barrett. b Galway (IRE), 1960. **Chain mail torso in sterling silver.** Photograph by Philip Newton, British *Elle*, 1990.

Barthet Jean

Milliner

In a café scene from 1955, two women wear feminized boaters by Jean Barthet. They are coquettish yet formal accessories for tailored suits worn with gloves and pearls; a very proper combination for the period. While he designs in the traditional manner of the great French hat makers such as Caroline Reboux, who place the emphasis on purity of line and structure, he also embellishes his creations with trimmings that reflect his own imagination, in this case restrained velvet ribbons and bows. Barthet showed his first collection in 1949 and rose to become the most successful milliner in Paris, dressing the heads of Sophia Loren and Catherine Deneuve. His success was underlined by his membership of the Chambre Syndicale de la Couture Parisienne. He has long collaborated with his colleagues, the fashion designers, including Claude Montana, Sonia Rykiel, Emmanuel Ungaro and Karl Lagerfeld.

☞ Deneuve, Hirata, Reboux

Jean Barthet. b The Pyrénées (FR), 1930. **'Café Hats'.** *La Donna*, 1955.

Bartlett John Designer

A shirt is laid open at the throat and left untucked in the style of the 1950s. John Bartlett's aesthetic is a relaxed one. He thinks about clothing pictorially and his fashion shows have profound themes and narratives, often becoming essays in style. Bartlett trained at Willi Smith, a label historically known for its democratic attitude towards fashion, and he has developed a natural feel for sportswear. He began his menswear collections in 1992, adding womenswear five years later when he told *People*, 'My mission is to make women look sexy', just as it is for men. He is said to be the American version of Thierry Mugler in sexy stories, but Bartlett adds something extra with his relish for the rhetoric of fashion, introducing his menswear collection for 1998 with the words, 'Imagine a world where *Forrest Gump* is directed by Otto Fassbinder...'

☞ Matsushima, Mugler, Presley, W. Smith

John Bartlett. b Cincinnati, OH (USA), 1963. **White open-neck shirt**. Photograph by Enrique Badulescu, *Arena*, 1997.

Bassman Lillian   Photographer

'I almost always focus on a long, elegant neck,' said Bassman of this photograph featured in *Harper's Bazaar*. Her shadowy, sensual pictures are known for their gentle intimacy: 'Women didn't have to seduce me the way they did male photographers. There was a kind of inner calm between the model and myself.' Her dream-like images were created by innovative printing techniques such as bleaching areas to give results that resembled charcoal drawings, recalling Bassman's early career as a fashion illustrator before being apprenticed to art director Alexey Brodovitch. Bassman's work is more evocative of moods than subjects and has not always been understood. Carmel Snow, editor of *Harper's Bazaar*, once berated Bassman for photographing a diaphanous Piguet gown to resemble butterfly wings, saying, 'You are not here to make art, you are here to photograph buttons and bows' – an early landmark in the debate about the purpose of fashion photography.

☛ Brodovitch, Parker, Piguet, Snow

Lillian Bassman. b New York (USA), 1917. **Barbara Mullen.** *Harper's Bazaar*, c1950.

Bates John Designer

John Bates is photographed with two dramatic outfits from a 1979 collection. They both use jersey cutaway to reveal the torso – a charismatic theme based on shapes from the 1930s and 1940s. The black dress uses a geometrically bared midriff in a modern take on Carmen Miranda's trademark – a feature Bates had used in 1965 with his 'bikini dress', the two halves of which were joined with transparent netting. These squared-off shoulders minimize the hips and spaghetti ties are used as suggestively available fastenings. Decorative cocktail hats finish both outfits and lend them the highly co-ordinated, polished look of the 1930s. In the 1960s, Bates created 'the smallest dress in the world' and the black leather wardrobe for *The Avengers* television series. His wide range of eveningwear, much of it ethnically inspired in the 1970s, was skilfully made and had a sophisticated youthfulness.

☛ Albini, Barnett, Burrows, N. Miller, Wainwright

John Bates. b Ponteland (UK), 1938. **John Bates with models. Spring/summer 1979**. Photograph by Chris Moore.

42

The Beatles

Icons

The Beatles are credited with marketing the 'youthquake' look around the world. In 1962, while touring Germany, Stuart Sutcliffe's photographer girlfriend Astrid Kirchherr gave the group a co-ordinated image: matching 'moptop' haircuts like her own beatnik-style gamine cut. The following year, the Beatles' manager Brian Epstein contacted Soho tailor Dougie Millings, who recalled, 'I'd been experimenting with round collars. I did a sketch of one, showed it to Brian, and that was that. I've never claimed to have entirely "invented" it, I just came up with the suggestion.' In fact, the neat, collarless, high-neck, grey jackets with black trim had been inspired by Pierre Cardin. They became a trademark for the Beatles, worn with whip ties and pointed chelsea boots. The Beatles hit the USA the following year and their girlfriends were credited with introducing America to the miniskirt.

☛ Cardin, Leonard, McCartney, Sassoon, Vivier

43

The Beatles. John Lennon. b Liverpool (UK), 1940. d New York (USA), 1980; Ringo Starr (Richard Starkey). b Liverpool (UK), 1940; Paul McCartney. b Liverpool (UK), 1942; George Harrison. b Liverpool (UK), 1943. The Beatles, 1963.

Beaton Sir Cecil Photographer

Eight models in a spectacular neoclassical interior are wearing ball gowns by Charles James in this 1948 American *Vogue* editorial by Cecil Beaton. Its dramatic mood of elegant grandeur captures the spirit of Dior's New Look, which revolutionized fashion with its feminine romanticism and state-of-the-art construction. Dior claimed James had inspired the New Look and

Beaton and James were lifelong friends. Beaton – photographer, illustrator, designer, writer, diarist and aesthete – captured the nuances of fashion and the fashionable from the 1920s until his death in 1980. In 1928 he began a long relationship with *Vogue*. Always in touch with the Zeitgeist, he developed accordingly, photographing the Rolling Stones, Penelope Tree and Twiggy in

the 1960s. He was as much a part of Swinging London as they were. 'Fashion was his cocaine. He could make it happen. He sought the eternal in fashion,' wrote a friend after his death.

☞ Campbell-Walters, Coward, Ferre, Garbo, C. James, Tree

Sir Cecil Beaton. b London (UK), 1904. d Broadchalke (UK), 1980. **Dresses by Charles James, 1948.**

Beene Geoffrey

Designer

Geoffrey Beene is pictured with an outfit from 1975. His ivory shirt with no closings lies flat against the throat. The pleated trousers are 'not too wide, not too narrow' and the perfect coat to throw over it is a 'trench coat in beige cotton'. With their soft wrapping and pared-down functionality, Beene's creations are the epitome of simple elegance. While his exquisitely made dresses are sometimes seen as the American version of couture, Beene is ultimately a designer with a sportswear sensibility. Comfort is paramount and has been since his label was launched in 1963. His first collections used an easy fit for clothes that were designed for active women. Combining the simplicity of Vionnet with whimsy, he often works with humble materials, including cotton piqué and sweatshirt fleece. Beene freely borrows from menswear – collections have included versatile vests and fanciful ties – whilst the pragmatic West meets the East in his use of quilting, obi belts and layering.

☛ Blass, Miyake, Mizrahi, Vionnet

Geoffrey Beene. b Haynesville, LA (USA), 1922. **Geoffrey Beene with model wearing stone mac and silk trousers**. Photograph by Deborah Turbeville, American *Vogue*, 1975.

Benetton Luciano, Giuliana, Gilberto and Carlo

Retailers

Unusually for fashion advertising, the clothes in this photograph can barely be seen and are not the central focus of the picture. Two people of different races are handcuffed together but it is not clear who is handcuffed to whom, and why. 'I am not asked by Benetton to sell clothes' claims the photographer and creative director Oliviero Toscani, 'The communication is a product in itself.' Such advertisements were an iconoclastic method of selling fashion, placing clothes in real contexts rather than overestimating their central importance. In the early 1980s Benetton's adverts had featured smiling young people of all nationalities, the 'United Colors of Benetton' catchline referring to both the cosmopolitan customers of their worldwide stores and the rainbow spectrum of knitwear and clothing. Luciano Benetton, the family-run company's founder, admits these 1990s images contrast with its design philosophy: 'It is true our clothes are not at all extreme or controversial'.

☞ **Fiorucci, Fischer, Strauss**

Benetton. Luciano. **b** Treviso (IT), 1935; **Giuliana. b** Treviso (IT), 1937; **Gilberto. b** Treviso (IT), 1941; **Carlo. b** Treviso (IT), 1943. **Handcuffed**. Photograph by Oliviero Toscani, 1985.

Benito

Illustrator

Benito, one of the masters of fashion illustration of the Art Deco period, captured through his simple, supple strokes the statuesque women in their extravagant gowns who epitomized the 1920s. His outstanding characteristic was the extreme elongation of the figure to emphasize the elegance of the silhouette. His style was reminiscent of sixteenth-century Mannerist painting and of the Cubist paintings of Picasso and the sculptures of Brancusi and Modigliani. Benito was also noted for his inventive vignettes. The close links between fashion and interior decoration are shown with perfect clarity and create an Art Deco harmony of design, colour and line. Born in Spain, Benito went to Paris at the age of nineteen, where he established himself as a fashion artist. Along with Lepape, his illustrations for *Vogue* reflected the *haut monde* of the Jazz Age.

☛ Bouché, Lepape, Patou, Poiret

Benito (Eduardo García Benito). b Valladolid (SP), 1892. **d** Paris (FR), 1953. **Afternoon dress by Paul Poiret**. Drawing from *La Gazette du Bon Ton*, 1922.

Bérard Christian   Illustrator

As his painted caption reports, Bérard's subject in this rich watercolour sketch wears the train of her ruby velvet gown draped over a medieval chain slung around her hips. Like his close friend, Cocteau, Bérard was a master of many artistic media. He designed the stage-sets and costumes for several of Cocteau's plays. During the 1930s he turned his artistry to designing fabrics and to fashion illustration, becoming associated with Schiaparelli and Surrealism in fashion. His drawings appeared in *Vogue* for the first time in 1935. They were so well received that he worked for *Vogue* until his death in 1949. Also like Cocteau, Bérard's draughtsmanship is immediately recognizable by its very stumpy, spidery line that is liberally imbued with vivid colours. It was this lush style, enhanced by his vision of fashion as a kind of theatre, that he brought to his graphic work for *Vogue*. It was defined as romantic expressionism.

☞ Bouché, Cocteau, Creed, Dalí, Rochas, Schiaparelli

At Patou's Opening
Velvet draped low on a chain

Christian Bérard. b Paris (FR), 1902. d Paris (FR), 1949. **Dress by Patou**. American *Vogue*, 1938.

Berardi Antonio   Designer

Karen Elson wears a pale blue, crepe dress smattered with astral embroidery. Its fluted, bias-cut skirt dips to the right to end in an asymmetric drape. Berardi's cutting techniques and decorative detailing have led him to be compared to John Galliano, with whom he trained for three years before finally being accepted as a student at Central Saint Martin's College of Art and Design in London (on his fourth attempt). Berardi's Italian roots manifest themselves in his love of traditionally crafted leather and hand-worked lace and macramé; one lace dress took a Sicilian village of lacemakers three weeks to make. Berardi's stunning leather pieces are decorated with embroidery and pierced with cutwork, specialist techniques that were reintroduced at a time when simplicity was being championed elsewhere. His light-as-air, lingerie-style pieces are intended to be flirtatious rather than vulgar. He describes his style as 'sensual, sexy and thought-provoking – and intrinsically feminine'.

☛ Chalayan, McDean, Pearl

49

Antonio Berardi. b Grantham (UK), 1968. **Karen Elson wears pale blue, crepe dress**. Photograph by Craig McDean, Italian *Vogue*, 1997.

Beretta Anne-Marie   Designer

In an abstract, graphic, red, white and black scheme, two leather coats are trimmed with Bs to signify the work of Anne-Marie Beretta. Her trademark is a play on proportions, from wide-collared coats to mid-calf-length trousers and asymmetrical lines, used here to break the conformity of these coats. The upper part of each letter is larger, throwing the emphasis onto the shoulders and thereby minimizing the widths of the models' hips. Beretta has used these techniques for many different collections, including ski-wear, but when she opened her own boutique in 1975 it was with business-like tailoring, similar in style to those collections she has since designed for the Italian label, MaxMara. Beretta wanted to pursue a career in fashion from an early age – by the time she was eighteen she was designing for Jacques Esterel and Antonio Castillo. In 1974 she established her own label.

☛ Castillo, Esterel, Maramotti

Anne-Marie Beretta. b Béziers (FR), 1937. **Leather 'B' coats.** *L'Officiel*, 1980.

Bergère Eric   Designer

These spare wrap dresses represent the self-assured work of Eric Bergère. Briefly apprenticed to Thierry Mugler, he arrived at Hermès aged just seventeen. It was Bergère who gave modernity to Hermès' luxury, using the then passé snaffle and H logo to add wit. In doing so, he famously created a camp, mink jogging suit. Bergère blends European humour and respect for tradition with the American sportswear sensibility. He has said, 'I like the work of Americans, like Anne Klein...very simple clothes, very elegant,' and he keeps detail to a minimum, using a thin tie belt or a tiny bow on a knitted camisole top. His first collection under the Bergère label was tightly edited: twelve pieces of knitwear in three colours and one jacket in three different lengths. 'I want the jackets to be like cardigans, I try to make everything lighter – the finishings, the linings, the foundations – but they must still have a definite shoulder.'

☛ Evangelista, von Furstenberg, Hermès, A. Klein, Mugler

Eric Bergère. b Troyes (FR), 1960. **Shalom Harlow and Linda Evangelista wear black dresses**. Photograph by Mario Testino, *Visionaire*, 1997.

51

Bernard Augusta (Augustabernard)   Designer

During the 1930s there was a revival of interest in classical art and an evening gown was especially suitable garment for re-creating the flowing movement of the draperies of Ancient Greek statues. It is this sculptural form and the long, floating line billowing out at the bottom of the evening dress that Man Ray captures and emphasizes in his photograph. Augusta Bernard

enjoyed a successful career during the first half of the 1930s. A neoclassical evening gown she designed in 1932 was chosen by *Vogue* as the most beautiful dress of that year. Augusta Bernard belonged to that eminent band of couturières between the two World Wars which included Chanel, Vionnet, Schiaparelli, Louiseboulanger and the Callot Sœurs. Like Vionnet, she was a

technician with a mastery of the bias cut. By cutting the fabric of the dress on the cross-grain, she achieved a fluidity which gave the evening gown great elasticity and a refined, draping quality.

☞ Boulanger, Callot, Chanel, Man Ray, Schiaparelli, Vionnet

52

Augusta Bernard. b Provence (FR). (Active 1930s.) **Bias-cut dress**. Photograph by Man Ray, *Harper's Bazaar*, 1934.

Berthoud François   Illustrator

François Berthoud's startling illustration presents a woman in a stovepipe hat, her demonic eyes watching from the shadows. Berthoud uses linocuts and woodcuts for his melodramatic work. They are brave and unusual methods for fashion illustration, which usually demands flowing lines. But these approaches suit the sharp contours of contemporary fashion, lending strength and drama to the simplest garment. Berthoud studied illustration in Lausanne and, after receiving his diploma in 1982, moved straight to Milan where he worked for Condé Nast. He later became heavily involved in the visual appearance of *Vanity* magazine, a publication that showcased illustration, designing many of their covers. In the 1990s Berthoud's enduring illustrations have appeared in the New York–based style quarterly *Visionaire*.

☛ Delhomme, Eric, S. Jones

François Berthoud. b Lausanne (SW), 1961. **Woman with hat**. Woodcut, *Mondi*, 1993.

Bettina

Model

Wearing a sharply constructed black dress by Christian Dior, the consummate French model gives a pose of polished *froideur*. Bettina's gamine beauty is unique in having inspired three designers over two generations. Born in Brittany, the daughter of a railway worker, Simone Bodin dreamed of becoming a fashion designer. She took her drawings to the couturier Jacques Costet, who took her on as his model and assistant. When the house closed, she moved to Lucien Lelong, employer of the young Christian Dior, who then invited her to join him in his own house. She refused, choosing to work for Jacques Fath instead. He renamed her Bettina and made her 'the face' of his scent Canasta, which was launched in 1950. Her fame took her to America where *Vogue* loved her 'Gigi' looks, and 20th Century Fox offered her a seven-year contract which she declined. In 1955 she left modelling, returning three decades later as muse (and best friend) of Azzedine Alaïa.

☞ **Alaïa, Dior, Fath, Lelong**

Bettina (Bettina Grazziani). b Laval (FR), 1925. Christian Dior cocktail dress. Autumn/winter 1952. Photograph by Frances McLaughlin-Gill.

54

Biagiotti Laura

Designer

The fluid spirit of Italy's 'Queen of Cashmere' is illustrated by René Gruau in 1976. His easy lines imitate the composed chic for which Laura Biagiotti is known: the sweater worn with lean tailoring and an open-necked shirt. Biagiotti read archaeology at university in Rome and worked in her mother's small clothing company after graduation. In 1965 she founded her company, with partner Gianni Cigna. It manufactured and exported clothing for the eminent Italian fashion designers Roberto Capucci and Emilio Schuberth. As the company grew, so did Biagiotti's aspiration to design herself. She presented a small but successful womenswear collection for the first time in 1972. Designing with comfort as a priority, Biagiotti became known for working with fabrics of exceptional quality, especially cashmere in the most subtle colours – a blueprint later used by Rebecca Moses.

☛ Capucci, Gruau, Moses, Schuberth, Tarlazzi

Laura Biagiotti. b Rome (IT), 1943. **Daywear.** Illustration by René Gruau, 1976.

Bikkembergs Dirk   Designer

'A classic suit which a businessman wears has nothing to do with fashion. For me, fashion should not be about business,' says Dirk Bikkembergs, whose own suits use unconventional cut and fastenings. This jacket has an asymmetric cut fastened with two distant buttons which suggests both militaristic and workwear themes. Having graduated with avant-garde contemporaries Ann

Demeulemeester and Martin Margiela, Bikkembergs started out as a shoe designer in 1985. He made his name with a sturdy boot which has no eyelets and whose laces are threaded through the sole, a play on closures that can still be seen today. The Bikkembergs aesthetic uses dark colours and heavy fabrics for his solid silhouettes, which lend them an urban appeal. He says, 'I

design strong clothes for strong individuals rather than wrapping up pretentious nerds in sophisticated cashmere,' and his visual references often include macho stereotypes, from motocross bikers to soldiers.

☞ Demeulemeester, Fonticoli, Margiela, Van Noten

56

Dirk Bikkembergs. b Bonn (GER), 1959. **Suit.** Photograph by Michel Comte, 1997.

Birtwell Celia   Textile designer

Actress Jane Asher sits amidst the jumble of accessories and kooky paraphernalia of a London boutique in 1966. She wears a printed paper minidress by Ossie Clark, another variation of which hangs on the wall behind her. The print is by Celia Birtwell, who decorated the fabric used by her husband Clark, and the 'paper' is a prototype of that used by Johnson & Johnson for J-cloths. Birtwell's stylized, sometimes psychedelic, florals with striped borders were also used for flowing fabrics resurrected from the 1930s, such as crepe and satin. Her lavish, two-dimensional style, which suited the fantastical and semi-historical fashion of the late 1960s and early 1970s, was part of a print explosion. Birtwell's bohemian mixture of Indian and traditional English themes was an expression of the wealthy, young Chelsea society around her, which was exploring the trail to Goa at the same time as inheriting the English countryside.

☛ **Clark, Gibb, Pollock**

57

Celia Birtwell. b Bury (UK), 1941. **Jane Asher wears screen-printed paper minidress.** Photograph by Brian Duffy, 1966.

Blahnik Manolo   Shoe designer

Rude and nude, but executed with as much refinement as a queen's coronation slipper, Manolo Blahnik's sexy sandal is made out of black leather. The transforming powers of Blahnik's shoes have become legendary. They are said to lengthen the leg from the hip all the way down to the toe cleavage. The secret lies in balance and taste; neither proportion nor degree of fashionability ever stray into vulgarity, thereby upsetting Blahnik's careful blend of beauty, style and function. He left the Canary Islands to study literature at the University of Geneva and art at the Ecole du Louvre in Paris. During a trip to New York in 1973, an appointment with famous American *Vogue* editor Diana Vreeland inspired him to settle in London and open his first shop. Blahnik's influential shoe designs are, for many fashion designers such as John Galliano, the sole choice for catwalk collections.

☛ Coddington, Galliano, Tran, Vreeland

Manolo Blahnik. b Santa Cruz (CI), 1942. **'Lara'. Autumn/winter collection 1997**. Illustration by Manolo Blahnik.

Blair Alistair

Designer

With deftness, Alistair Blair turns satin and velvet into a gracious evening outfit. The jacket rolls outward with the help of quilted facings and is cleverly cut to follow the waist inwards. Blair trained with Marc Bohan at Christian Dior, before moving on to assist Hubert de Givenchy and Karl Lagerfeld at Chloé. After six years in Paris, his ready-to-wear had taken on the quality and glamour of continental couture. Of his first own-label collection in March 1989, Blair said, 'The designing was absolutely the easiest part – it's what I enjoy'. He provided grown-up glamour during the eccentric streetwear boom of the 1980s. His use of luxurious fabrics such as cashmere, duchesse satin, grey flannel and kid leather brought a nostalgic quality to his carefully edited designs. Since 1995 he has designed for Louis Féraud, claiming, 'Today women want more than adoration from a designer – they want insight'.

☛ Bohan, Cox, Féraud, Tran

59

Alistair Blair. b Helensburgh (UK), 1956. **Quilted satin evening jacket**. Photograph by Ian Thomas, *Harpers & Queen*, 1987.

Blass Bill

Designer

Three distinctly American graces capture the essence of Blass's high-style sportswear. Urbane and Europe-aware, but definitely easy to wear and pared-down in ornament, Blass's separates for day and evening and his dresses for what used to be called the cocktail hour capture the American spirit in functional, elegant clothing. Blass perpetuates the traditions of Norman Norell and Hattie Carnegie in providing smart, simplified sophistication for American women. Sweater dressing, even for evening gowns, is a Blass signature; layering and the harmony of rich materials, from silk to cashmere, are favoured. Witty references to menswear or vernacular dress are also frequent in Blass. Often referred to as the 'dean of American designers', Blass is one of the last of the designers consistently delivering classic good taste, filtering fashion's fluctuations through a fine sieve.

☛ Alfaro, Beene, Roehm, Sieff, Underwood

Bill Blass. b Fort Wayne, IN (USA), 1922. **Heavy, white, silk crepe dresses with bugle beads. Spring/summer 1984.** Photograph by Gideon Lewin.

Blumenfeld Erwin   Photographer

Legs are wrapped in damp muslin; this is not a fashion image but a beauty one. This photograph by Erwin Blumenfeld is reminiscent of his first art success which was a suite of collages and altered images in the style of Berlin Dada. His late work in New York was equally cryptic and artistic, often obscuring the nude with smoke, mirrors and shadows and implying spiritual forms through reference to the body. In between, in a prodigious series of photographs in *Vogue* and *Harper's Bazaar* in the 1930s through to the 1960s, he addressed fashion, but often subjected icons of beauty to his own obscurities and emendations. He allowed body parts to stand for the whole (most famously in a cover image of lips and eye for *Vogue* in January 1950), rendering fashion misty and mystical. Blumenfeld came to fashion at the relatively advanced age of forty-one. He was an experimenter who reserved his admiration, and film, for the work of great designers such as Balenciaga and Charles James.

☛ **Dalí, Hoyningen-Huene**

61

Erwin Blumenfeld. b Berlin (GER), 1897. **d** Rome (IT), 1969. **Solarized Legs.** Paris, c1937.

Bohan Marc — Designer

In the preamble to Marc Bohan's show for Christian Dior, the designer and his model, wearing a slim cardigan jacket over a belted dress, pose for American *Vogue*. Bohan won plaudits for restoring haute couture to the tradition set by the grand couturiers, when he was appointed chief designer and artistic director of the house of Dior in succession to Yves Saint Laurent in 1960. He was of his time, however, and was able to communicate a youthful spirit His dramatic collection for winter 1966, influenced by the film *Doctor Zhivago*, was acclaimed and started the craze for fur-trimmed, belted tweed coats worn with long, black boots. Marc Bohan gained valuable practical experience in fashion from his mother, who was a milliner. Between 1945 and 1958 he worked for the fashion houses of Piguet, Molyneux and Patou. Having left Dior in 1989, he moved to London where he was enlisted in an attempt to revive the fortunes of the house of Norman Hartnell.

☛ Blair, Dior, Hartnell, Molyneux, Patou, Piguet

Marc Bohan. b Paris (FR), 1926. **Marc Bohan and model**. Photograph by Deborah Turbeville, American *Vogue*, 1975.

Bouché René

Illustrator

Working in pen and ink, Bouché was a master at blending fashion and society. Two attenuated figures are silhouetted against an empty background like a *tableau vivant*. They are linked by their large, fur muffs. With his vivacious and witty line, Bouché has revealed these fashionable women and their elegant clothes and has expressed their character, their manner and a sense of occasion. It is a throwaway style but the informal virtuosity of Bouché as a fashion illustrator was combined with a skilful training in painting, drawing and portraiture. Bouché illustrated the pages of *Vogue* during the 1940s, 1950s and early 1960s, and had a particular flair for communicating the relationship between clothes and wearers with accuracy and humour. The prestige of *Vogue* was due in large measure to the revival of fashion illustration by artists of the calibre of Benito, Eric, Christian Bérard, René Gruau and René Bouché.

☛ **Balmain, Benito, Bérard, Eric, Gruau**

René Bouché. b (FR), 1906. **d** 1963. **Two suits by Pierre Balmain**. Illustrated in American *Vogue*, 1945.

Boué Sylvie and Jeanne (Boué Sœurs) Designers

A delicate lace and embroidered lawn tea gown is caught up on the hips with a threaded silk sash. Roses decorate the shoulders and, as was customary, the hem dips either side to create the impression of swags. The Paris couture house of the Boué Sœurs flourished at the beginning of the twentieth century, together with those of Paul Poiret, the Callot Sœurs and Mme Paquin.

During the First World War the Boué Sœurs moved to New York, where John Redfern and Lucile had already opened branches of their businesses. The Boué Sœurs, who contributed much to the city's high fashion, were renowned for their romantic designs which often borrowed details from costume found in historical paintings. Their garments, sometimes reminiscent of underwear

as here, were made in luscious fabrics such as paper taffetas and silk organdies and were ornately decorated.

☞ Callot, Duff Gordon, de Meyer, Paquin, Redfern

Boué. Sylvie. b (FR), 1880; Jeanne. b (FR), 1881. (Active 1910s–1930s.) (Boué Sœurs.) Tea dress. c1920.

Boulanger Louise (Louiseboulanger) Designer

Lace and tulle is projected as the backdrop for a dress whose bodice is so fine that it appears almost gaseous. Louise Boulanger was very much influenced by the work of her contemporary, Madeleine Vionnet. She imitated with finesse Madame Vionnet's use of the bias, cutting diagonally across the grain of the fabric to achieve a seamless, flowing movement.

She was noted for launching graceful evening gowns that had skirts which were knee-length in front and reaching to the ankles at the back. Another of her trademarks was elegantly tailored suits worn with hats designed by Caroline Reboux. Louise Boulanger learned her craft as a thirteen-year-old apprentice with Madame Chéruit. In 1923 she opened her own

fashion house whose name was an amalgam of her first and last names. With her svelte figure, she was a couturière in the manner of Coco Chanel.

☞ Bernard, Chéruit, Reboux, Vionnet

Louise Boulanger. b Paris (FR), 1878. **d** c1950. (Louiseboulanger.) **Black tulle and corded silk dress.** Photograph by Cecil Beaton, British *Vogue*, 1935.

Bouquin Jean   Designer

'Hippie deluxe' is the phrase which will forever be linked with Jean Bouquin's clothes and lifestyle. Although he dabbled in fashion for just seven years, Bouquin captured the bohemian spirit of St Tropez's jet-set society at the end of the 1960s. This photograph from French *Vogue* epitomizes Bouquin's vision: a natural woman, draped with beads, who lives an ironically

privileged hippie life wearing a luxurious interpretation of the nonconformist's uniform, all sold in Bouquin's boutique. Her printed panne velvet minidress uses drawstrings, borrowed from Indian pyjamas, at the cuffs, and ends just shy of the bikini bottoms she might have worn underneath it. After his success in St Tropez, Bouquin opened a second shop in Paris called Mayfair,

which continued his theme of relaxed 'non-dressing'. He retired from the fashion business in 1971 to enjoy his social life.

☞ Bardot, Hendrix, Hulanicki, Porter, Veruschka

66

Jean Bouquin. b Paris (FR), 1936. **Panne velvet dress with beads.** Photograph by Henry Clarke, French *Vogue*, 1970.

Bourdin Guy   Photographer

An overt exercise of self-satisfaction, stimulated by the looks of John Travolta, mirrors the 1970s obsession with sex, individuality and status. The hard-edged glamour of sheer fabrics and flashing make-up serves as a canvas for Guy Bourdin's strangely cold yet unmistakably sexual vision. Daringly showing the symbiosis between savvy disco decadence and stardom as a stimulus to the senses, this image is finely in tune with the psyche of Bourdin's times. A Pop-Surrealist, he began to work for French *Vogue* in 1960, recommended by photographer Man Ray and couturier Jacques Fath. He concentrated on editorial work for this publication alongside advertising campaigns for Charles Jourdan shoes and Bloomingdales' lingerie range. An obsessive master colourist, Bourdin is said to have left actress Ursula Andress lying naked on a glass table for six hours while searching around Paris for the right shade of rose petals to match her skin.

☛ Barbieri, Fath, Jourdan, Man Ray

67

Guy Bourdin. b Paris (FR), 1928. d Paris (FR), 1991. **Advertising campaign for Charles Jourdan.** 1979.

Bourjois Alexandre Napoléon   Cosmetics creator

The fashionably blanched face of the 1920s is given colour by one of the first cosmetics companies, Bourjois, which was launched in Paris in 1863. Alexandre Napoléon Bourjois originally created his powders with the theatre in mind, and he sold them from a barrow. The dusty texture of his Rouge Fin de Théâtre was completely different to the greasepaint available at the time, and soon he was the official supplier to the Imperial theatres. Fashionable Parisiennes, taking their cue from actresses and courtesans, began to use his cosmetics. Bourjois repackaged his rice powder, Fard Pastels, in little card pots stamped with the legend 'Fabrique Spéciale pour la Beauté des Dames'. Bourjois set a precedent for printing phrases and quotes on the boxes and, famously, in 1947 it was 'Women will Vote'. One of the original colours, Cendre de Roses Brune, is still a bestseller, and the distinctive rose-water scent remains unchanged.

☞ Brown, Factor, Uemura

68

Alexandre Napoléon Bourjois. b Tours (FR), 1845. d Paris (FR), 1893. **Pastel face**. Illustration, 1927.

Bousquet Jean (Cacharel) Designer

In a bizarre scene created by photographer Sarah Moon, a plaid pinafore by Cacharel is worn by a doll-like figure who lies on a vast sewing machine. The designer of the pinafore was Jean Bousquet, who named his company Cacharel after a species of wild duck. The company's aim was to represent a wild, free image which rejected the formality of clothing favoured by older generations. As such, Bousquet was part of the new ready-to-wear scene in Paris along with Christiane Bailly and Michèle Rosier. Emmanuelle Khanh, who went on to succeed in her own right, styled for Cacharel. In 1961 the company produced a woman's blouse constructed without bust darts. The result was a best-selling fitted shirt. In 1965 Bousquet signed an agreement with Liberty to use its floral designs in his own contemporary colourways. Cacharel became known for semi-casual, matching separates which captured the Zeitgeist by bringing relaxed styles into broader use.

☞ Bailly, Khanh, Liberty, Moon, Rosier, Troublé

Jean Bousquet. b Nîmes (FR), 1932. (Cacharel.) **Plaid dress. Fashion show invitation, spring/summer 1982.** Photograph by Sarah Moon, 1982.

Bowery Leigh   Icon

Leigh Bowery approached dressing as a creative, artistic act, although whether his 'Redbeard with Aerosol Tops' from winter 1987 is 'art' or not is a matter of opinion. Part voodoo, part clown, Bowery's surreal and often disturbing costumes were always highly creative. 'I am in this odd area between fashion and art,' he said. He described his work as 'both serious and very funny'. Bowery arrived in London in 1980 during the New Romantic era. He dressed up for the first time at an Alternative Miss World contest, and was delighted to find himself the centre of attention. Later he hosted the gay nightclub Taboo, continually reinventing himself and always trying to 'improve' on his previous outfit. An expert tailor, Bowery collaborated with Rifat Ozbek, although posterity will remember him as a sitter for the painter Lucian Freud.

☛ N. Knight, Ozbek, Van Beirendonck

Leigh Bowery. b Melbourne (ASL), 1962. d London (UK), 1994. **Leigh Bowery**. Photograph by Nick Knight, *i-D* magazine, 1987.

Bowie David   Icon

Wearing a glittering knitted unitard, David Bowie plays Aladdin Zane. He used clothes as costumes for his stage personae, each one representing a phase and an album: from *Ziggy Stardust*'s tight metallic spacesuits and wild plastic quilted bodysuits by Kansai Yamamoto to a sleek suit and tie for his 'plastic soul' disco album, *Young Americans*. He said of his inventions, 'The important fact is that I don't have to drag up. I want to go on like this long after the fashion has finished...I've always worn my own style of clothes. I design them. I don't wear dresses all the time either. I change every day. I'm not outrageous. I'm David Bowie.' At times he was a sexually ambiguous figure, using make-up and hair dye to achieve these characters and in doing so inspiring the New Romantic movement. Bowie's interest in fashion continued in the 1990s with his slightly less theatrical outfits designed by Alexander McQueen and his marriage to model Iman.

☛ Boy George, Iman, McQueen, K. Yamamoto

David Bowie (David Jones). b London (UK), 1947. **David Bowie**. Photograph by Bill Orchard, 1973.

Boy George

Icon

Boy George holds a home-made George doll given to him by a Japanese fan. Like him, it wears a theatrical outfit from 1984. With his Hasidic Jew's hat, dreadlocks, face of a Geisha, loose-fitting Islamic-style shirt, checked trousers and hip hop shoes by Adidas, George represented an eclectic, home-styled approach invented in the squats and clubs around London. It was a fashion born of necessity. Students and the unemployed spent their days making ever-more exotic outfits to wear at night. The clubs, such as Taboo, had rigorous door policies – issuing humiliating rejections for those who had not made the effort – and they became a spawning ground for designers such as Body Map, John Galliano and John Flett. George, who was a central character, had been inspired by the androgynous costumes of David Bowie. He styled himself 'Boy George' to clear the confusion his dresses created amongst the wider public.

☞ Bowie, Dassler, Flett, Forbes, Stewart, Treacy

72

Boy George (George O'Dowd). b Bexleyheath (UK), 1961. **Boy George wears Dexter Wong**. Photograph by Brian Aris, 1984.

Brodovitch Alexey   Art director

Two demure cotton dresses are made exciting by placing them against a speeding foreground and background, like lambs playing amongst the rush-hour traffic. Alexey Brodovitch, the art director who commissioned and laid out these pictures, brought a new informality and spontaneity to magazine design. Based on European graphic modernism, his years as art director of *Harper's Bazaar* (from 1934 to 1958), brought movement and life to fashion photography. By creating complementary typographic images to put next to a picture, producing animated two-page spreads and using multiple images (a single woman photographed several times running across the page), Brodovitch invented the modern lexicon of art directors. His credo was 'Astonish me!' Richard Avedon, Hiro and Lillian Bassman were a few of his favoured photographers and his Design Laboratory in Philadelphia was a workshop 'for studying new materials, new ideas...in order to establish new devices for the future'.

☛ Avedon, Baron, Bassman, Hiro, Snow

Uncommon Cottons—Embroidered and Marbled

• It takes an uncommonly knowing eye, these days, to know what's cotton and what isn't. The coat on our Junior cover, for instance: cotton looking uncommonly like tweed. And here, cotton embroidered so thickly it stands by itself or, above, cotton piqué, waffled and printed in marbly whorls. There's more here than just new surfaces, too: these cottons are ready to start spring now, ride on through Indian summer.
• The overall dress, opposite, in coppery red, encrusted with embroidery. About $25. And the properly workmanlike striped shirt that goes with it, about $7. Both by Loomtogs; Wamsutta cotton. Altman; Harzfeld's; Joseph Magnin; Sakowitz. Hat by Madcaps; M M satchel. The traffic: new 1955 Dodges.
• Print in three dimensions, above, black and white waffle piqué bound off in cotton satin. By Lanz Originals; cotton piqué by Everfast. About $35. Bonwit Teller; L. S. Ayres; Sakowitz. Hat by Madcaps.

HARPER'S BAZAAR, MARCH 1955

Alexey Brodovitch. b (RUS), 1898. **d** Le Thor (FR), 1971. **Fashion spread**. Design for *Harper's Bazaar*, 1955.

Brooks Daniel, John, Elisha and Edward (Brooks Brothers)   Retailers

From Wall Street to Capitol Hill the oldest retail clothing company in America has been catering to the Establishment since 1818. Brooks Brothers pioneered men's ready-to-wear, with an emphasis on soft construction and ease. Its unmistakable air of traditionalism, so alluring to its predominantly Wasp clientele, has not prevented Brooks Brothers from introducing some of the principal innovations in American men's clothing. Bermuda-length shorts and the classic pink shirt first hit the American shores through their stores. Brooks also brought over the button-down shirt collars worn by polo players in England, instituted madras fabric for shirts (originally designed for British officers in India), and introduced the Brooks Shetland sweater and their trademark Polo coat in white, camel or grey with mother-of-pearl buttons and a full belt. Ralph Lauren's early work experience for Brooks Brothers was a crucial influence in shaping his own label's style.

☛ Burberry, Hilfiger, Lauren

Brooks. Daniel. b New York (USA), 1809. **d** (USA), 1884; **John. b** New York (USA), 1813. **d** (USA), 1899; **Elisha. b** New York (USA), 1815. **d** (USA), 1876; **Edward. b** New York (USA), 1821. **d** (USA), 1875. (Brooks Brothers.) **Button-down collars. Spring/summer 1998.**

Brown Bobbi

Cosmetics creator

In the early 1990s, Bobbi Brown provided an antidote to the exotic colours used throughout fashion. From beige to bitter chocolate, her earthy colours reflect natural beauty. They are achieved through a whole range of cosmetic products, without camouflaging ethnicity, age or skin tone. It is a method that looks to the skin for its lead: eye shadow that does exactly that and lipstick which accentuates rather than masks natural colour. Brown is simple, straightforward and basic. 'Make-up is not rocket science', she says, downplaying the hype of make-up as an art form. With her degree in theatrical make-up and extensive catwalk and editorial work, Brown started on a small scale with ten neutral-toned lipsticks. While the beauty colourscape has radically altered, Brown remains true to her plain-spoken philosophy.

☛ Bourjois, Lauder, Page

Bobbi Brown. b Chicago, IL (USA), 1957. **Bridget Hall**. Photograph by Walter Chin, 1995.

Bruce Liza   Designer

Lisa Lyon, bodybuilding champion of 1979 and inspiration for Liza Bruce, braces herself in a strongwoman pose. Stretched across her muscular body is 'Liza', a black Lycra bikini which uses futuristic, graphic shapes to section her body. From the outset, Bruce determined to make experimentation a central theme of her work and her career has been punctuated by innovations which have found their way onto the high street. Initially a swimwear designer, she made a thick lustre crepe, designed by textile specialist Rosemary Moore, her signature material. They later developed a 'crinkle' crepe fabric which was widely copied throughout the swimwear business. Bruce is also credited with introducing leggings in the 1980s. Sport has been an enduring theme for Bruce, with function conspicuously dominating the design of everything from cycling shorts in the 1980s to an evening dress in 1998.

☞ Audibet, Godley, di Sant' Angelo

Liza Bruce. b New York (USA), 1955. **Lisa Lyon wears 'Liza' bikini**. Photograph by Robert Mapplethorpe, 1984.

76

Brunelleschi Umberto   Illustrator

Around the time of this drawing, a Paris critic wrote of Brunelleschi, 'His art has nothing realistic about it. He would not know how to evoke modern life with its huge factories and streets full of people. But the world of fiction, which is so much more beautiful than the world of men, that he makes real.' Parisian by adoption, Brunelleschi worked as a costume and set designer in the theatre, where the effects of the innovations made by Bakst and Poiret were still very much alive. The hallmarks of a Brunelleschi theatrical costume drawing are clear, strong, calligraphic lines, derived from his sound training at the Accademia di Belle Arti in Florence, and brilliant, jewel-like colours that bring a fairy-tale world to life, the influence of Bakst and Poiret. Like Bakst and Erté, Brunelleschi was both a designer and illustrator, making him a leading figure in the history of twentieth-century fashion.

☛ Bakst, Erté, Poiret

Umberto Brunelleschi. b Montemerio (IT), 1879. **d** Paris (FR), 1949. **'Danseuse Orientale'.** c1920.

Bruyère Marie-Louise   Designer

The model wears a windbreaker coat from the Bruyère salon in the place Vendôme. It has a more feminine look than the simple, tailored styles seen in London in 1944. The shoulders have a softened, draped line, the waist is narrow, the sleeves are full, as is the hemline which has a swing to it. She is photographed outside the salon, opened in 1937 and decorated by Bruyère herself. The window has been strafed with bullets and temporarily mended with brown paper, a detail that places this photograph between fashion photography and wartime reportage. Lee Miller, the photographer and journalist, was one of the first people to arrive in Paris on the liberation of the city in August 1944. Recording her impressions in *Vogue*, she wrote that, 'The French concept of civilized life has been maintained.' Bruyère trained with the Callot Sœurs and worked as an apprentice with Jeanne Lanvin.

☞ Callot, Drecoll, French, Lanvin, L. Miller

Marie-Louise Bruyère. b (FR). (Active 1920s–1950s.) **Bruyère windbreaker coat**. Photograph by Lee Miller, 1944.

Bulgari Sotirio

Jewellery designer

A Bulgari collar and earrings modelled by Tatjana Patitz makes a statement worthy of a Medici, although the jewellery is a blend of traditional Italian forms and contemporary style. Andy Warhol once called the Bulgari store on Rome's via Condotti 'the best gallery of contemporary art'. Bulgari is regarded as a great house because of its modern approach. The company was founded in Rome by silversmith Sotirio Bulgari. His sons, Constantino and Giorgio, developed the jewel and precious stone side of the business in the first decades of the twentieth century. In the 1970s, Bulgari drew on their Art Deco themes, in particular the rectangle-cut baguette work, to develop modern, graphically spare jewellery that put diamonds in geometric settings. Precious jewellery was thus placed in the domain of young, fashionable society. In 1974, Sotirio's grandson, Gianni Bulgari, told W, 'The business will only survive if it shows tremendous creativity...if it presents itself as a form of art'.

☞ Cartier, Lalique, Warhol

Sotirio Bulgari. b (IT). (Active 1880s–1930s.) **Tatjana Patitz wears a diamond collar and earrings**. Photograph by Fabrizio Ferri, 1989.

Burberry Thomas

Designer

A geometric layout illustrates all the features that have made the Burberry check as British as the Liberty print or Scottish tartan. Thomas Burberry, a country draper, developed a water- and wind-proof fabric which he called gabardine; his first raincoat went on sale in the 1890s. Originally designed for field sports, the garment was used by officers in the trenches in the First World War and was dubbed the 'trench coat'. Many of the original features, from epaulettes and storm flaps to the metal D-rings, still appear on the coat today. The coat's shape slowly evolves to keep pace with broad fashion movements. Humphrey Bogart and other Hollywood stars later invested it with an aura of glamour. The distinctive beige and red check lining was first used in the 1920s. Given new life by the Japanese Burberry-fever of the 1980s, it has since been applied to everything from umbrellas to silk underwear.

☛ Brooks, Creed, Jaeger

Thomas Burberry. b Dorking (UK), 1835. d Hook (UK), 1926. **Classic trench coat**. 1995.

Burrows Stephen   Designer

A matte jersey dress by Stephen Burrows is decorated with his trademark 'lettuce' edging. Deliberately caused by closely spaced zig-zag stitching on raw seams, it is an example of how Burrows sparingly used machine techniques to decorate his fluid, sexy vision of modern femininity. The full cut of this dress will have produced a wake of rippling fabric, giving it sinuous movement.

Customers who visited his store-within-a-store, Stephen Burrows' World at Henri Bendel, in the 1970s, came for simple jersey and chiffon outfits which then defined New York style. In 1971, Halston told *Interview* magazine that Burrows was 'one of the unrecognized geniuses of the fashion world...Stephen gives the most original cut in America today. And the thing is really

the cut.' One of Burrows' favourite cuts is the asymmetric (where the hem is cut on the diagonal), about which he said, 'There's something nice about something wrong'.

☞ Bates, Halston, Munkacsi, Torimaru

81

Stephen Burrows. b Newark, NJ (USA), 1943. **Electric blue jersey wrap and matching pants**. Photograph by Oliviero Toscani, American *Vogue*, 1974.

Butler Nicky and Wilson Simon (Butler & Wilson)   Jewellery designers

A face is framed by glittering diamanté jewellery, one eye obscured by an amusing lizard. Recognizing the potential for antique costume jewellery in the late 1960s, antique dealers Nicky Butler and Simon Wilson started selling Art Deco and Art Nouveau treasures at London's most fashionable markets. By the time they opened their first shop in 1972, Butler and Wilson had started designing themselves. Their eponymous period-inspired and often witty creations raised the profile of costume jewellery. The change in conventional attitudes towards genuine takes, however, was never more conspicuous than in the opulently ornamental 1980s, when glamorous ambassadors of Butler & Wilson's style included Jerry Hall, Marie Helvin, Lauren Hutton and the Princess of Wales, who often wore their bejewelled designs for formal evening occasions.

☞ Diana, Hutton, Lane

Nicky Butler. b (UK), c1950; Simon Wilson. b Glasgow (UK), 1950. (Butler & Wilson.) Twenty-first birthday celebratory cover for Rough Diamonds: The Butler & Wilson Collection. Photograph by John Swanell, 1989.

82

Callot Marie, Marthe, Regina and Joséphine (Callot Sœurs) Designers

This panniered taffeta evening dress, supported by a hoop, represents the exotic work of the Callot Sœurs. Its sheer vest is wrapped over a taffeta bodice and caught into a rose on the hip. The petalled skirt, inspired by an eighteenth-century dress, is appliquéd with green billows reminiscent of designs painted by Erté. The sisters worked with exquisite and unusual materials, including antique lace, rubberized gabardine and Chinese silks, with *Orientalisme* a favourite theme. They are remembered for introducing the fashion for the gold and silver lamé evening dresses which were popular in the 1910s and 1920s. The Callots were influential into the 1920s when Mme Marie Callot Gerber, the eldest sister, was referred to as the backbone of the fashion world of Europe. Madeleine Vionnet said of her training at Callot Sœurs, 'Without the example of the Callot Sœurs, I would have continued to make Fords. It is because of them that I have been able to make Rolls-Royces.'

☛ **Bernard, Boué, Bruyère, Dinnigan, Duff Gordon, Erté, Vionnet**

Callot. Marie, Marthe, Regina, Joséphine. (Callot Sœurs.) (Active 1890s–1920s.) Ivory and chartreuse evening dress. 1920s.

Campbell Naomi   Model

Herb Ritts casts Naomi Campbell as Pan, representing eternal spring. Her athletic body is regarded as being as near perfect as it is possible for a body to be – even in the fashion industry, a demanding audience. Azzedine Alaïa realized her potential early and dressed Campbell in his clothes, which are as equally demanding of perfection. She sought stardom from an early age, attending stage school in London, and has rarely been out of the news since she was hailed as a supermodel. Known for her diva-like qualities, she has a demanding, star-like ability to dominate a picture or catwalk. She was dubbed 'the black Bardot' for her full lips and sexy demeanour, although she claims to have encountered racial prejudice, saying, 'This is a business about selling – and blonde, blue-eyed girls are what sells.' However, Naomi Campbell's success has coincided with, and contributed to, a broader conception of the feminine ideal.

☛ Clements & Ribeiro, Jacobs, Kamali, Keogh, Lindbergh, Peretti

Naomi Campbell. b London (UK), 1970. **Norma Kamali bikini bottoms**. Photograph by Herb Ritts, British *Vogue*, 1990.

Campbell-Walters Fiona   Model

Fiona Campbell-Walters wears the duchesse satin ball gown, stole and full-length gloves of an aristocrat, the society she represented in the 1950s. Born the daughter of an admiral in the Royal Navy, she was encouraged by her mother to become a model and was photographed by Henry Clarke while still a teenager. She attended modelling school and soon became a *Vogue* regular, chosen for her aristocratic looks. She was also Cecil Beaton's favourite. Always in the gossip columns, Campbell-Walters married Baron Hans Heinrich Thyssen, heir to Germany's biggest steel-manufacturing company, in 1956. Together they were prolific art collectors, living mainly in Sicily. They had two children but divorced in 1964. In January 1993 she married Archduke Karl de Habsbourg-Lorraine in Austria and she now devotes herself to animal welfare. The high point of her modelling career was featuring on the cover of *Life* magazine on 12 January 1953.

☛ Beaton, Clarke, McLaughlin-Gill

Fiona Campbell-Walters. b (UK), c1932. **Duchesse satin ball gown**. Salle des Glaces, Versailles. Photograph by Frances McLaughlin-Gill, 1952.

Capasa Ennio (Costume National)   Designer

Described as a 'mix of couture and the street', Ennio Capasa's dress uses cutaway armholes to reveal the shoulders and a simple tie at the neck. These are its only details. Its focus is the fabric: fine, shimmering Lurex which highlights the angles and curves of the body below it. Capasa's work is dictated by material. 'I always start designing a collection from the fabrics,' he says. 'I love the interplay between matt and shine. The fabrics are where you really experiment in fashion.' He trained with Yohji Yamamoto in Japan in the early 1980s, where the practice was to pare details away from a design and to take inspiration from traditional cutting techniques. On his return to Milan in 1987, Capasa started his own label, Costume National. It combines his perception of Japanese purism with a sexier, more close-fitting silhouette which is influenced by street fashion – a 1990s imperative epitomized by Helmut Lang and Ann Demeulemeester.

☛ Demeulemeester, Lang, Y. Yamamoto

Ennio Capasa. b Lecce (IT), 1960. (Costume National.) **Lurex dress. Spring/summer 1997**. Photograph by Nathaniel Goldberg.

Capucci Roberto   Designer

Two immense ball gowns are assembled from an acre of pleated rainbow taffeta. The backs are constructed in such a way that they appear to be shoulder-to-floor bows. They are an example of engineering from Roberto Capucci who, in 1957, was called the 'Givenchy of Rome' by fashion writer Alison Adburgham. She continued, 'He designs as though for an abstract woman, the woman we never meet.' Such is the extravagance of some experiments that the wearer becomes secondary to the gown. For ten years Capucci showed in Rome before decamping for six years to Paris in 1962, and showing alongside fashion's other architect, Cristobal Balenciaga, with whom he is often compared. The purity of Capucci's work extended to his selling technique. His fashion shows would be conducted in silence and he refused to replicate an outfit, so that any woman buying from him would have to do so from the show collection.

☛ Biagiotti, Exter, Givenchy, W. Klein

Roberto Capucci. b Rome (IT), 1929. **Pleated gowns. 1985.** Photograph by Fiorenzo Niccoli.

Cardin Pierre   Designer

In what could be a still from *Star Trek*, men, women and even a boy, strike exaggerated poses to accentuate their tomorrow's wardrobe. In the mid-1960s Pierre Cardin spun off into deep space with Courrèges and Paco Rabanne. He offered utopian clothes to a new generation. Graphic symbols were cut from his jersey tunics; men's jackets were given military epaulettes. The silver shine of asymmetric zips, steel belts and buckles brought couture into the space age. Cardin's training had been a traditional one – at the houses of Paquin, Schiaparelli and Dior – but his mind was on the future. In 1959 he was the first couturier to design ready-to-wear and was expelled from the Chambre Syndicale. Cardin became fashion's scientist, developing his own material, Cardine, a bonded fibre that would rigidly hold his geometric shapes, and experimenting with metals to produce dresses suspended from metal bodices. In later years, Cardin put his name to everything from pens to frying pans.

☛ Beatles, de Castelbajac, Courrèges, Rabanne, Schön, Ungaro

88

Pierre Cardin. b Sant'Andrea di Barbarana (IT), 1922. **'Space' collection. Autumn/winter 1967/8.** Photograph by Yoshi Takata.

Carnegie Hattie   Retailer

C.Z. Guest, an American social figure, wears a simple creamy silk gown by Hattie Carnegie. Although she has a reputation as a revered designer, Carnegie never actually made a dress. She was a retailer who delivered a current look, such as this strapless, wasp-waisted silhouette derived from Dior, a shape that formed the hourglass figure of the 1950s. Carnegie's reputation was legendary. She employed designers of the calibre of Norman Norell, Travis Banton, Jean Louis and Claire McCardell; the 'Carnegie look' was a reliably sophisticated simplification of European design that was favoured by American society and high-profile clients such as the Duchess of Windsor. In 1947, *Life* declared Carnegie (née Kanengeiser, but she took the name of the richest American of the time) to be the 'undisputed leader' of American fashion, with more than one hundred stores selling her product and her imprimatur the keenest sign of prestige in American clothing.

☛ **Banton, Daché, Louis, Norell, Trigère, Windsor**

Hattie Carnegie. b Vienna (AUS), 1889. **d** New York (USA), 1956. **C.Z. Guest**. Photograph by Cecil Beaton, 1952.

Cartier Louis François

Jewellery designer

This brooch, designed as a flamingo in characteristic pose, has plumage set with calibré-cut emeralds, rubies and sapphires. Cabochon citrine and sapphire are used for the beak, a sapphire for the eye, with the head, neck, body and legs pavé-set with brilliant-cut diamonds. It was created in 1940 by Jeanne Toussaint for the jewellery firm Cartier, founded in Paris in 1847 by Louis François Cartier. This jewel was designed for the Duchess of Windsor, who owned one of the finest jewellery collections of the 1940s. It was chosen for her by the Duke of Windsor, who spent a great deal of time choosing jewels to adorn her clothes, often designed as a setting for a particular gem. Pieces such as this one (resold in 1987 for $470,000) were still considered avant-garde many years after their design and were the precursors of a new vocabulary in *bijouterie* after the Second World War.

☛ **Bulgari, Tiffany, Windsor**

Louis François Cartier. **b** (FR), 1819. **d** Paris (FR), 1904. **Flamingo brooch created for the Duchess of Windsor, 1940**. Photograph by Louis Tirilly.

90

Cashin Bonnie   Designer

A capacious, grey cashmere poncho trimmed in leather typifies Bonnie Cashin's distinctive contribution to American sportswear. Attuned to dancers and their motion, the variable weather and outdoor life of California, and to Hollywood and the movies (she was a designer for 20th Century Fox in the 1940s), Cashin created ingenious sportswear. She often used global references but always remained faithful to the pragmatic and contemporary woman. Separates were versatile and luxurious; sizing was easy, given that most tops, dresses, skirts and trousers wrapped or tied, allowing for accommodation for many body types. Cashin used layering before it became an accepted and expected part of women's lives. Toggles and luggage hardware became practical fastenings for her bags, leather-trimmed wools and cocoon-like mohair covers. Cashin's reputation is such that she is regarded, along with Claire McCardell, as the mother of American sportswear.

☛ A. Klein, McCardell, Schön

Bonnie Cashin. b Oakland, CA (USA), 1915. **Cashmere shawl**. Photograph by Francesco Scavullo, 1966.

Cassini Oleg   Designer

In the 1960s, Cassini was the American designer most identified with Jacqueline Kennedy as First Lady, an evening dress for whom is illustrated here. Stung by criticism of her costly wardrobe (largely from Balenciaga and Givenchy), even before her husband was elected president, Mrs Kennedy chose to consider Cassini her official designer. Although her mother-in-law and aides secretly helped Mrs Kennedy to continue to acquire clothes by Grès, Chanel and Givenchy, Cassini's sleek minimalism supplemented that elite wardrobe and the American designer was publicly acclaimed. By the conspicuous association with Kennedy, Cassini became a powerful figure in 1960s style, offering youthful, smooth modernity; his A-line dresses and suits of a semi-fitted top over a slim skirt corresponded to contemporary Parisian designs. Cassini respected Mrs Kennedy's demureness, while letting each garment stand out in a manner appropriate for a First Lady.

☞ Givenchy, Grès, Kennedy

Oleg Cassini. b Paris (FR), 1913. **Evening dress for Jacqueline Kennedy.** 1961.

De Castelbajac Jean-Charles   Designer

The deadpan expression on the model's face contradicts Jean-Charles de Castelbajac's joke: a square-cut dress that imitates the front-opening of a huge pair of blue jeans. De Castelbajac uses a deceptively childlike sense of form in this way – bearing in mind Cervantes' phrase, 'Always hold the hand of the child you once were.' His simple, enveloping clothes remain true to the uncut cloth. Thick, felt-like fabrics have preoccupied him since he was at boarding-school when he cut his first garment out of a blanket. He was one of France's new age of ready-to-wear designers in the 1960s and has worked with Pop Art themes such as Warhol's Campbell's soup can, which he printed onto a cylindrical dress in 1984. Inspired by the work of Paco Rabanne and Pierre Cardin, which he said surpassed the work of artists working on the theme of futurism, he has been called 'the space-age Bonnie Cashin'.

☛ Cardin, Ettedgui, Farhi, Rabanne, Warhol

93

Jean-Charles de Castelbajac. b Casablanca (MOR), 1950. **'Jeans' dress**. Photograph by Denis Malerbi, 1984.

Castillo Antonio

Designer

The risqué potential of the black lace used in Castillo's A-line dress is at once removed by its stately aura. A black hat, moulded into the shape of a mantilla comb, lends grace, while the model maintains an imperial pose, turning her back to the camera as if to shake hands with foreign heads of state. Born of a noble Spanish family, regality and dignity surround every one of

Antonio Castillo's designs – his training was as accessory designer for Chanel and as designer at the distinguished fashion houses Piguet and Lanvin. Castillo left Spain for France in 1930 at the onset of the Spanish Civil War. He was no Courrèges, indulging in avant-garde couture for the younger generation of customers in the1960s; instead, he subtly instilled a sense of

innovation into mature, seemingly classic looks, which resulted in a quiet, exceedingly tidy style.

☛ Ascher, Beretta, Lanvin, Piguet, G. Smith

Antonio Castillo. **b** Madrid (SP), 1908. **d** c1984. **Lace Cage.** Photograph by Seeberger Brothers, 1965.

94

Cavanagh John   Designer

John Cavanagh is photographed in 1962 with a model wearing his full, yet immaculately tailored, wool coat. Its black cuffs, plain collar and geometric configuration of buttons are its only details beyond top-stitched, princess-line seams into which the pockets disappear. His was an international training, firstly with Molyneux on his return from Paris and then at Pierre Balmain. In 1952 Cavanagh opened his own couture house in London, making clothes which had that international appeal and understood the mores of British life. He noted, 'A couturier worth his name must design in the world-stream of design change, but direct it to the lives of his clients that make this business exist.' Cavanagh was at the centre of London's small made-to-measure society which continued to dress the English season, despite becoming engulfed by cheap imitations. In 1964 he said, 'Couture will and must continue. It is the lifeblood of the ready-to-wear.'

☞ Balmain, Molyneux, Morton

John Cavanagh. b (IRE), 1914. John Cavanagh and model wearing cream wool coat. Photograph by John French, 1962.

Cerruti Nino   Designer

Jack Nicholson wears loose pink and white linen separates by Cerruti in the film *The Witches of Eastwick*. 'Fashion, ultimately, is a way of describing the world we live in,' says Cerruti, a philosophy that applies itself not only to the world of fashion but also to film – Cerruti has designed costumes for over sixty movies. Cerruti initially studied philosophy and had wanted to become a writer, but in 1950 he took over the family textile business in northern Italy. His launch of a menswear range, Hitman, in 1957 was the start of the company's transformation into a luxury label. A women's ready-to-wear collection followed in 1977. Epitomizing the aspirational dressing of the 1980s, the Cerruti label was used in films such as *Wall Street* and *Baby Boom*. In the 1990s, Cerruti's womenswear enjoyed a period of success while it was designed by Narciso Rodriguez, a young designer who introduced contemporary themes such as transparent, embroidered fabrics worn with precise tailoring.

☛ Armani, von Etzdorf, Rodriguez

Nino Cerruti. b Biella (IT), 1930. **Jack Nicholson.** Still from *The Witches of Eastwick.* 1987.

Chalayan Hussein   Designer

Katerina Jebb, known for her photocopier art, depicts a dress trimmed with gold chains by Hussein Chalayan. He describes his innovative designs as 'an evolution of ideas'; his first collection was made from reinforced paper which he had buried with iron filings in his back garden to create a rusted effect. Chalayan is known for his intricate detail – be it delicate beading, glittery flight-pattern charts or flashing LED lights. Each of his collections is based around a narrative plot and customers are provided with booklets outlining the story. There is often a darkness to his themes: vampires, tombs and constriction have all featured in the past. Chalayan maintains that, 'Trends are boring and transient. I am interested in clothes, not fashion.'

With McQueen and Berardi in the 1990s, he pioneered the sharp, angular tailoring that became known as the 'London look'.

☛ Berardi, Clements & Ribeiro, Dell'Acqua, Isogawa, McQueen

97

Hussein Chalayan. b Nicosia (CYP), 1970. **'Lands Without'. Spring/summer 1997**. Photograph by Katerina Jebb.

Chanel Gabrielle   Designer

Coco Chanel is strolling in the Tuileries in Paris, a short distance from the rue Cambon where she lived and had her maison de couture, which she closed in 1939 and re-opened in 1954. She is wearing all the hallmarks of her signature style: suit, blouse, pearl jewellery, scarf, hat, gloves and handbag with gilt chains. She was a perfectionist, and the way she gestures to Alexander Liberman with her right arm manifests one of her fixations – a comfortable arm movement. She would rip off the sleeves of her suit time and again to get a perfect fit. The basic idea for her suits came from the concept of military uniforms. As the mistress of the Duke of Westminster, she had taken many trips on his yacht where the crew wore uniforms. The essence of her style was rooted in a masculine model of power, a direction that has dominated twentieth-century fashion.

☞ Cocteau, Dalí, Lagerfeld, Liberman, Parker, Perint Palmer, Verdura

98

Gabrielle (Coco) Chanel. b Saumur (FR), 1883. d Paris (FR), 1971. Coco Chanel wearing Chanel suit. Photograph by Alexander Liberman, 1951.

Charles Caroline

Designer

In an early design, Caroline Charles uses a chequerboard pattern jacket, worn with long socks. During the 1960s, Charles also worked as a broadcaster and journalist but she stayed with fashion. 'Does it fit? Is it useful? Does it create the feeling that someone wants to get close to you?' These are the practical questions which are considered for every piece of Caroline Charles clothing. Charles recalls wanting to be a dress designer from an early age. After graduating from Swindon Art School, she headed to London, which was in full 1960s swing. Following a spell at Mary Quant, she launched her own collection in 1963. Charles's occasion- and eveningwear were an instant hit with the entertainment trendsetters of the day, including Cilla Black and Barbra Streisand. However, it has been her knack of creating very British clothes – and, latterly, accessories and interiors – that has allowed her career to span three decades.

☞ Courrèges, Foale & Tuffin, Quant

99

Caroline Charles. b Cairo (EG), 1942. **Check weave wool jacket and black wool skirt.** *Tatler*, 1964.

Chéruit Madeleine   Designer

Monochromes forge a vintage ambience, illuminated by the flush of porcelain skin set against dazzling sequins crystallized under transparent organza. Marion Morehouse wears a deep V neckline, then considered risqué, that runs down to a beltless waist, indicating the move away from the curvaceous prewar silhouette to a more relaxed contour. Trained in the 1880s at the couture house Raudnitz, Chéruit was a Parisian designer who, like Lelong and Louiseboulanger, transformed high fashion into the reality of ready-to-wear. Based in place Vendôme, she refined the excessiveness of couture for her aristocratic Parisian clientele, who favoured her richly ornamented dresses. Fascinated by the effect of light on fabric, she worked with lustrous taffeta, glowing lamé and silvery gauze. With Chanel's move towards simple fashions in the 1920s, her opulent taste lost appeal. She retired in 1923, but her design house continued until 1935 when Schiaparelli famously took over her premises.

☛ Bally, Boulanger, Lelong, Morehouse

100

Madeleine Chéruit. b (FR). (Active 1900s–1930s.) Marion Morehouse. Photograph by Edward Steichen, 1927.

Choo Jimmy

Shoe designer

A powder-blue suede sandal is trimmed with feathers, an example of the dainty, seductive work of Jimmy Choo, who was born into a family of shoemakers and made his first pair aged eleven. All Choo shoes are handmade and his perfectionist craftsmanship is displayed in their simple details. They are never overtly fashionable, yet are equal in elegance to the designer clothes they are usually worn with. He attended London's Cordwainer's Technical College with a fresh generation of cobblers, including Patrick Cox and Emma Hope. Of his style, Choo says, 'There is an elegance, a femininity, maybe a sexiness.' It was one that came to be favoured by the Princess of Wales, who would buy one style in several colours for eveningwear and to co-ordinate with her day suits. Choo's Malaysian roots account for his signature palette: a range of crystalline colours which includes aqua blue, fuschia pink and bright orange.

☛ Cox, Diana, Hope

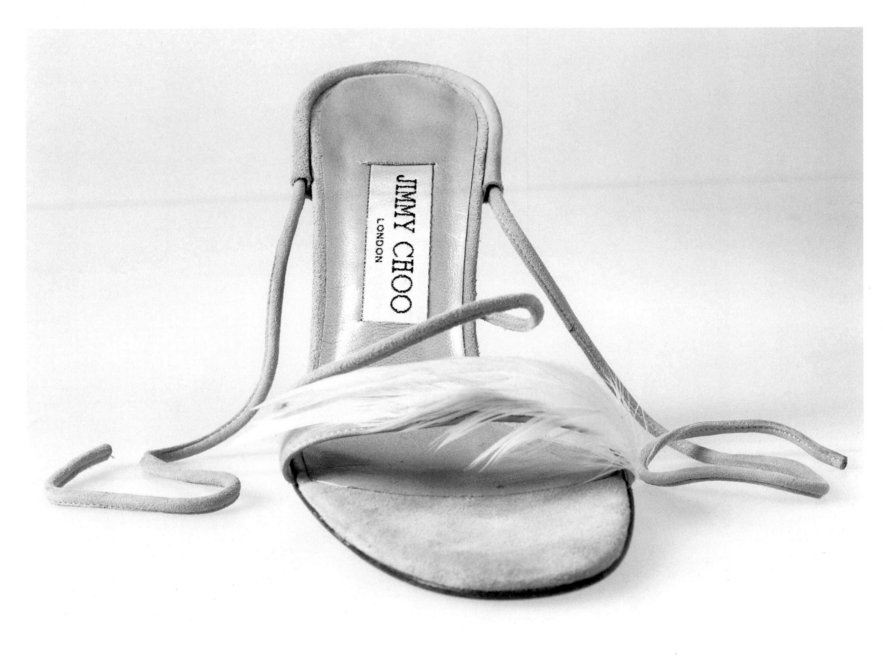

Jimmy Choo. b Penang (MAL), 1961. **Feathered sandal. Spring/summer 1997**. Photograph by Simon Archer, *E.S.* magazine, 1998.

Chow Tina   Icon

Tina Chow strikes an elegant, demure pose. A supreme model in the 1970s, she went on to become one of the great fashion connoisseur-collectors of the twentieth century. An Asian-American, Chow represented the new diversity and universalism of modern beauty, but her fashion intelligence was even greater than her beauty. One of the most important collectors of couture clothing, Chow's practised eye is still regarded as the paradigm of collecting and connoisseurship. Chow knew the great designers of her time, but demonstrated her interest in the past by choosing works by Madeleine Vionnet, Cristobal Balenciaga and Christian Dior for her astute collection. Her initial collecting interest was Mariano Fortuny, whose 'Delphos' dresses, capes and mantles were a syncretist interpretation of East and West.

☛ Antonio, Balenciaga, Fortuny, Vionnet

Tina Chow. b Cleveland, OH (USA), 1950. **d** New York (USA), 1992. **Tina Chow**. Photograph by Arthur Elgort, 1982.

Clark Ossie

Designer

In this wild scene photographed at London's Chelsea Town Hall in 1970, Ossie Clark shows his clothes under the name Quorum, a company set up by Alice Pollock. It was, said *Vogue*, 'more a spring dance than a show'. The spaced-out models wear Clark's chiffon dresses (each with a secret pocket into which a key and a £5 note would fit – his trademark), both printed by his wife, textile designer Celia Birtwell. The couple were immortalized in a portrait entitled *Mr and Mrs Clark and Percy* by their friend, painter David Hockney, who can be seen on the far right of this picture. 'I'm a master cutter. It's all in my brain and fingers,' Clark had said, and that talent became one of the most sought-after in the late 1960s and early 1970s. Singer Marianne Faithfull and Anita Pallenberg, then the girlfriend of the Rolling Stones guitarist Keith Richards, shared an 'Ossie' snakeskin suit, now one of the most precious reminders of the age.

☞ Birtwell, Fratini, Hulanicki, Pollock, Sarne

Ossie Clark. b Liverpool (UK), 1942. **d** London (UK), 1996. **Printed chiffon dresses.** Photograph by Annette Green, 1970.

Clarke Henry   Photographer

The citrus colours of summer are given a fresh, literal interpretation. Photographer Henry Clarke was first drawn to fashion photography by watching Cecil Beaton photograph Dorian Leigh. He created animated photographs, but Clarke was also naturally inclined to elegance, and his images of French fashion in the 1950s, in particular, exemplify the balance he sought between the formal, almost statuesque, dress of the epoch and the casual effect of snapshot instantaneity. Artful and artless at the same time, Clarke's photographs benefited from the licence given him by Diana Vreeland at *Vogue* and the exotic locations they used for photo shoots. Skilfully moving from 1950s high style to the dazzling colours and layering of the 1960s, he made the flamboyant and ethnographic clothes come alive in the context of Mayan archaeological sites and various settings in India, Sicily and around the world.

☞ Campbell-Walters, Goalen, Pertegaz, Vreeland

104

Henry Clarke. b Los Angeles, CA (USA), 1918. **d** Le Cannet (FR), 1996. **Fruit sweaters**. *French Vogue*, 1957.

Clements Suzanne and Ribeiro Inacio (Clements Ribeiro)

Clements Ribeiro's graphically patterned cashmere has become its trademark: from bold rainbow stripes to this striking Union Jack insignia, worn by Naomi Campbell, which symbolized the 1990s upswing in British fashion fortunes known as 'Cool Britannia'. Ribeiro has said, 'We do simple cuts with strong fabrics; we call it clumsy couture.' Bright, multicoloured prints define the themes of each collection; from traditional tartans and windowpane checks to bohemian paisleys and mottled florals. Luxurious materials are used for daywear – dusty-coloured suedes, cashmere, silk taffeta and sequins. Clements Ribeiro favour neat, almost prim, separates and simple styling. Their collections are inspired by an ever-changing female role model: punk, gypsy, suburban housewife or mermaid. Inacio Ribeiro and Suzanne Clements met at Central Saint Martin's College of Art and Design, married and moved to Brazil after graduating. They designed their first joint collection in London in 1993.

☞ **Amies, Campbell, Chalayan**

Suzanne Clements. b London (UK), 1969; **Inacio Ribeiro. b** São Paulo (BR), 1963. (Clements Ribeiro.) **Union Jack cashmere sweater. Autumn/winter 1997.** Photograph by Chris Moore.

Cobain Kurt

Icon

Cobain was to grunge what Johnny Rotten was to punk. His greasy, bleached hair, pale waify body and thrift-shop clothes created the image of a strung-out, moody adolescent. The garments of grunge bands such as Cobain's Nirvana, Pearl Jam and Alice in Chains were cheap and casual; washed-out jeans and rock T-shirts. It started as an anti-fashion formula that dressed a generation of disaffecteds known as Generation X, but, predictably, was 'cleaned up' to become a mainstream movement known as 'Heroin Chic': an affected representation of an addict's wardrobe, influenced by Cobain's. Rebelling against his upbringing among homophobic blue-collar lumberjacks in his home town, he would sometimes try harder by wearing his partner's flowery dress and painting his nails red. That partner, Courtney Love, came to personify a feminized version of the look which inspired Marc Jacobs to create his 'grunge' collection of 1993: a mishmash of florals, laddered knits and army boots.

☞ Dell'Acqua, Jacobs, Rotten

106

Kurt Cobain. b Hoquaim, WA (USA), 1967. **d** Seattle, WA (USA), 1994. **Kurt Cobain and daughter, Frances Bean.** Photograph by Stephen Sweet, 1994.

Cocteau Jean   Illustrator

The legend on this fashion drawing reads, 'Paris 1937. Schiaparelli made this tapering sheath dress for dining and dancing. Jean Cocteau drew it for the readers of *Harper's Bazaar*'. Cocteau was a writer, film-maker, painter, print-maker, stage-, fabric- and jewellery-designer and fashion illustrator. His entrée into the world of fashion came through the theatre.

Cocteau met Diaghilev when the Ballets Russes came to Paris in 1910 and he designed posters for him. Some of Cocteau's most important work for the theatre and fashion included his collaborations with Chanel. Between 1922 and 1937 she designed costumes for a whole cycle of his plays, including *Le Train Bleu* of 1924 which had an impact on sportswear. He

often sketched her and her fashions in his characteristic form of outline drawing with its sharp line and elegant simplicity. Cocteau was also closely associated with Surrealism and fashion. For Schiaparelli he designed fabrics, embroideries and jewellery.

☞ Bérard, Chanel, Dessès, Horst, Rochas, Schiaparelli, Viramontes

107

Jean Cocteau. b Paris (FR), 1889. **d** Paris (FR), 1963. **Schiaparelli dress**. Illustrated in *Harper's Bazaar*, 1937.

Coddington Grace | Editor

'Grace Coddington is the eye – the eye...I never saw a wrong dress she chose...Grace was without a doubt the fashion editor.' says Manolo Blahnik. Coddington has influenced fashion in many different ways, from modelling to styling and designing. In 1959 'The Cod', photographed here wearing all-over prints by Jacques Heim, was spotted by Norman Parkinson. She constantly reinvented her image by changing her distinctive red hair from a chunky Vidal Sassoon bob to a halo of frizzy curls – a formula that would later be used by Linda Evangelista. In 1968 she moved to British *Vogue*, taking Calvin Klein's modern aesthetic to a 1970s European audience. Her style inspired designers such as Kenzo and Pablo & Delia and she later championed the talents of Azzedine Alaïa and Zoran. Coddington moved to American *Vogue* in 1987. She said of her time there, 'You're either having dinner with 300 people or grovelling on the floor with pins in your mouth.'

☛ Alaïa, Blahnik, Heim, C. Klein, Mesejeán, Sassoon, Zoran

108

Grace Coddington. b Holyhead (UK), 1941. **Grace Coddington wears Jacques Heim.** Photograph by John French, 1965.

Coffin Clifford

Photographer

For the June 1949 issue of American *Vogue*, Clifford Coffin photographs four models wearing American swimsuits as polka-dots on a sand dune in a customarily strong composition. Coffin's main contribution to fashion photography in the 1950s was his use of ring-flash lighting – a circular bulb which wraps around the lens and casts a directional frontal light onto the model, thereby creating an indistinct shadow. A dramatic technique which 'blasts' light onto the subject, highlighting shiny fabric and make-up, it was widely used in tandem with a wind machine in the 1970s and again in the 1990s. Coffin was a fashion personality whose early ambition was to be a dancer. He was also an 'out' homosexual, who was close to society writer Truman Capote. His work for American, British and French *Vogues* secured his own position in that society and he was described as 'the first photographer to actually think fashion, sometimes more than fashion editors'.

☞ Gattinoni, Gernreich, Goalen

Clifford Coffin. b IL (USA), 1913. **d** Pasadena, CA (USA), 1972. **Swimsuits**. American *Vogue*, 1949.

Colonna Jean   Designer

Imagine the dark backstreets of Paris, a flashing neon sign and a hidden door opening to an underground world inhabited by women who sleep during the day and dress for the night in leopard prints, stretchy sheer lace, skimpy skirts and little else. This is the world of French designer Jean Colonna, whose fashion shows conjure up the world of the Pigalle district after dark. He came to prominence during the 'deconstruction' trend of the early 1990s, upsetting the establishment by creating clothes that people could actually afford. The manufacturing methods that allowed him to do this included overlocked hems and edges, doing away with the need for finishing. He also used unashamedly cheap fabrics such as PVC. Colonna trained in Paris and spent two years at Balmain, before launching his own label in 1985. Colonna's philosophy has always been that 'a piece of clothing must be simple – to make, to sell and to wear'.

☛ Balmain, Dolce & Gabbana, Topolino

Jean Colonna. b Oran (ALG), 1955. **Backstage. Spring/summer 1998**. Photograph by Thierry Ledé.

Connolly Sybil   Designer

Photographed in her Dublin home, Sybil Connolly wears a dress made from her famous pleated linen. The tailored shawl covers a simple bodice and typically understated skirt. The doyenne of Irish fashion in the 1950s, Connolly specialized in adapting traditional Irish fabrics for modern, easy dressing. Her forward-thinking designs transformed thick mohair, Donegal tweed and linen, which she hand-pleated for delicate blouses and dresses. Like her American contemporary, Claire McCardell, she was a pioneer in the creation of smart shapes that used informal fabrics and a relaxed attitude during the 1950s and 1960s. Connolly moved to London to learn dress design, but returned to Ireland upon the outbreak of the Second World War. At the age of twenty-two she became design director of the Irish fashion house Richard Alan, going on to launch her own couture label in 1957 at the age of thirty-six.

☞ Leser, McCardell, Maltézos

111

Sybil Connolly. b Swansea (UK), 1921. **d** Dublin (IRE), 1998. **Sybil Connolly at home, Merrion Square, Dublin**. Photograph by Perry Ogden, 1987.

Conran Jasper   Designer

In an exercise in contrast, a scarlet poppy hat, designed with Philip Treacy, explodes above an unadorned black dress designed for a touring production of *My Fair Lady*. Jasper Conran regarded Jean Muir as his mentor and his own work carries her hallmarks of modern sophistication. Lit from behind, his dark dress comes to life as a silhouette, a graphic sculpture beneath an organic one. Having studied at Parson's School of Design in New York, Conran set up his own label at the age of nineteen. He relies on a monochrome palette interspersed with stimulating bursts of striped fabric or salvos of colour: bold orange, cerise or cobalt blue. He likes his clothes to have 'speed and life... For me it's always about the cut and the shape.' Conran's work is also wearable. Some garments, such as a fitted leather jacket reminiscent of Marlon Brando's 'biker' jacket, have remained in his collection for ten years because of their flattering shapes.

☞ Muir, Treacy

112

Jasper Conran. b London (UK), 1959. **'Poppy'**. Hat designed with Philip Treacy worn with dress for *My Fair Lady* stage production. Photograph by Tessa Traeger, 1992.

Courrèges André   Designer

A former civil engineer, André Courrèges placed the meticulous cut of fashion he had practised in Balenciaga's atelier in the 1950s in the service of the 1960s idealism of youth and the future. Along with Pierre Cardin and Paco Rabanne, Courrèges led the cult of visionary fashion design in Paris. It was a movement that cut away superfluous material, banned decoration and established geometry and new materials for fashion in the mid-1960s. 'I think the women of the future, morphologically speaking, will have a young body,' said Courrèges at the time. His miniskirts were stiff and square and advocated a minimum of body coverage, enjoying those 'young' bodies that became visible in the 1960s. His most characteristic symbol, often covering his dresses and bare body parts, was the youthful daisy. Unisex was another Courrèges theme. He predicted that womenswear would become at least as practical as menswear.

☞ Cardin, Charles, Frizon, Quant, Rabanne, Schön, Ungaro

André Courrèges. b Pau (FR), 1923. **Space-age designs**. Photograph by William Klein, 1964.

Coward Noel   Icon

The playwright and entertainer Noel Coward strikes a classic pose in this photograph by Horst. A flawless Prince of Wales check, accessorized with polka-dot silk and woven checks, epitomizes his peerless sophistication. After his first theatrical success in 1924, Coward remarked, 'I was unwise enough to be photographed in bed wearing a Chinese dressing gown as an expression of enhanced degeneracy. I indulged in silk shirts, pyjamas and underclothes...coloured turtleneck jerseys...and started a fashion.' It was the look for the glamorous, brittle 1920s aesthete. For the first time since Oscar Wilde, a writer's appearance seemed as important as what he wrote. 'All sorts of men suddenly wanted to look like Coward – sleek and satiny, clipped and well groomed,' observed Cecil Beaton. Cary Grant was one of them, remarking that he based his own urbane style on, 'a combination of Jack Buchanan and Noel Coward'.

☞ Beaton, Horst, Wilde

114

Noel Coward. b London (UK), 1899. d Blue Harbour (JAM), 1973. **Noel Coward. Paris, 1934.** Photograph by Horst P. Horst.

Cox Patrick

Shoe designer

A model wears the python-skin Wannabe shoe that became an icon and raised the average male spend on footwear. In 1993 Patrick Cox realized that his collection needed a lightweight summer shoe. His answer was the Wannabe, a moccasin-constructed loafer. In 1995 his Chelsea shop was besieged by customers wanting a pair, some of whom attempted bribery. When he launched the range in 1993, Cox acknowledged his debt to the white loafers worn by the American comedian Pee Wee Herman. An indispensable accessory of the rave culture, the Wannabe is one half of Cox's shoe business – the other comprises a collection of styles that develops seasonally with fashion trends. Born in Canada, Patrick Cox moved to London in 1983 to study at Cordwainer's Technical College. His first success was a customized Dr Marten shoe (its toe stripped to reveal a steel toe cap), and he went on to work with a long list of designers, starting with Vivienne Westwood in 1984 and including John Flett, John Galliano, Richard James and Alistair Blair.

☞ Blair, Choo, Flett, Galliano, R. James, Marteans, Westwood

115

Patrick Cox. b Edmonton, AB (CAN), 1963. 'Python' Wannabe loafer. Autumn/winter 1995. Photograph by François Rotger.

Crahay Jules-François   Designer

Jules François Crahay poses with Jane Birkin who wears a matte jersey dress pulled into a lazy handkerchief knot at the shoulder. Crahay learned the techniques of dressmaking at his mother's shop in Liège and at the fashion house of Jane Régny in Paris. After these apprenticeships he became a designer at Nina Ricci in 1952, then at the house of Lanvin in 1963. While he was fêted for his refined eveningwear, Crahay was also one of the leading fashion designers to promote the peasant and gypsy styles which dominated fashion at the end of the 1960s. As early as 1959, his collections contained full, flounced skirts worn with low-cut, elasticated blouses and scarves worn around the head, neck and waist. All were made in vividly coloured, lightweight materials which produced the light, feminine style for which Crahay is remembered. He characterized his own work by saying that he wanted to have fun making his dresses.

☞ Lanvin, Pipart, Ricci

116

Crawford Cindy   Model

Cindy Crawford works on her multi-million-dollar body, the marketing of which is controlled by its owner, who says, 'I see myself as a president of a company that owns a product, Cindy Crawford, that everybody wants.' Her defined physique, honed in the fitness market, welded the connection between health and beauty for a generation of women. A shoot for *Playboy* was also part of the business strategy: 'I wanted to reach a different audience...let's face it, most college guys don't buy *Vogue*.' While conservative in the fashion sense (she has kept the same hairstyle for ten years), Crawford is the most commercial supermodel. Her popularity is attributable to her clean sex appeal and indefinable 'multicultural' appearance: olive skin, brown eyes and brown-to-blonde hair. It adds up to the perfect cover face: a beauty that alienates nobody. Crawford remains a pragmatist, an example of the new model breed that has learned to separate fact from fantasy.

☛ P. Knight, Lindbergh, Schiffer

117

Cindy Crawford. b De Kalb, IL (USA), 1966. **Cindy Crawford**. Still from *Shape your Body* workout video. Photograph by Tim Rooke, 1992.

Creed Charles

Designer

This outfit is typical of the 1930s. The suit has a boxy-style jacket with a broad shoulder line and wide lapels, while the skirt is straight and the hemline stays well below the knees. It foreshadows the masculine, military style of the Second World War, but details such as the buttons and the hat anchor the outfit firmly in the prewar era. Charles Creed belonged to an English family of tailors who were known for their understated tweeds, popular in nineteenth-century Paris. The family established a tailoring firm in London in 1710 and in Paris in 1850, launching womenswear in the early 1890s. During the Second World War, Creed designed women's suits and coats while on leave from the army and was also involved in the Utility scheme. He set up his own fashion house in London in 1946 and enjoyed success in America where his restrained English tailoring found a ready market.

☞ Bérard, Burberry, Jaeger, Morton

Charles Creed. b Paris (FR), 1906. d London (UK), 1966. **Travel coat**. Illustration by Christian Bérard, 1935.

Crolla Scott

Designer

Using rich colours, opulent brocade and blooming prints, Scott Crolla's early work was an historical fantasy. Crolla trained in art and sculpture, but grew bored of the discipline, moving to fashion because it is 'the honest side of the whole artistic discourse'. In 1981 he formed a partnership with fellow artist Georgina Godley. This tableau, styled by Amanda Harlech, who went on to work for John Galliano and Chanel, suggests the ecstasy of an eighteenth-century poet – a scene that epitomizes Crolla's fanciful work. Brocade trousers worn with silk stockings and tail coats dominated a time when fashion became costume and men rediscovered the vain pleasure of peacockery – a historical tendency that puts this outfit into context. Despite its fancy-dress connotations, Crolla's work was instrumental in encouraging men and women to wear ruffled shirts and brocade trousers.

☛ Godley, Hope, Wilde

Scott Crolla. b Edinburgh (UK), 1955. **Ruffled shirt**. Photograph by Andrew Macpherson, *The Face*, 1984.

119

Daché Lilly   Milliner

Lilly Daché decorates a half-hat with feathers, autumnal berries and dried flowers for this sitting for American *Vogue*. Towering turbans, draped toques and snoods, and knitted or openwork nets which enclosed the hair at the back of the head were other millinery confections characteristic of Daché. Trained at Caroline Reboux's atelier in Paris, she emigrated to the United States and in 1924 became, like Hattie Carnegie before her, an assistant in the millinery department at Macy's in New York. Two years later she set up her own establishment in New York and became one of the most eminent milliners in America, challenging Paris for the title of millinery capital. She adorned the heads of New York high society and of Hollywood stars such as Betty Grable and Marlene Dietrich – as well as creating Carmen Miranda's turbans. Her most outstanding discovery was Halston, who designed pillbox hats for Jacqueline Kennedy before moving into fashion.

☞ Carnegie, Halston, John-Frederics, Kennedy, Reboux, Sieff, Talbot

120

Lilly Daché. b Bégles (FR), 1907. **d** Louveciennes (FR), 1989. **'Autumnal Berry' hat**. Photograph by Edward Steichen, American *Vogue*, 1946.

Dahl-Wolfe Louise   Photographer

Beneath the Cairo sun, model Nathalie shades herself in a white cotton robe by Alix Grès. Louise Dahl-Wolfe, the photographer, often cast her images in bright sunlight. Beaches, deserts and sunny plains were her natural domain, first for compositions in black and white and later for some of the most sumptuous photographs ever taken of swimwear, playsuits and the exoticism of modern fashion. Her most frequent editor-stylist was Diana Vreeland. The unpretentious Dahl-Wolfe and the extravagant Vreeland were an odd couple in style, but together they became collaborator-adventurers in seeking out an ambient naturalism for the emerging modern woman. Vreeland's flamboyance and artifice were sweetly tempered by Dahl-Wolfe's interest in portraiture and in landscape. Even in the most glamorous image, Dahl-Wolfe displays her inquiring mind and analytical insight, giving photography not just models, but character and idiosyncrasy.

☛ Grès, Leser, McCardell, Maxwell, Revillon, Snow, Vreeland

Louise Dahl-Wolfe. b San Francisco, CA (USA), 1895. **d** New York (USA), 1989. **Grès coat, Egypt.** 1950.

Dalí Salvador   Illustrator

In this dream sequence by Salvador Dalí, the spectator's attention is fixed on the svelte figure wearing a bold red dress very fashionably cut on the bias, the fabric falling in smooth, vertical folds from the hips. Dalí described his pictures as 'hand-painted dream photographs' and his juxtaposition of the real and unreal presented fashion in a new imaginative way, bringing out its decoration, elegance and seduction. During the 1930s, with economic and political pressures mounting, fashion and fashion illustration took an escapist route, venturing into Surrealism, the dominant art movement of the decade. Cecil Beaton, Erwin Blumenfeld and George Hoyningen-Huene, house photographers at *Vogue*, captured Surrealism's bizarre elements in their work.

Vogue also commissioned artists such as Dalí, who collaborated with Schiaparelli in the design of fabrics and accessories, to make 'photo-paintings', presenting fashion's relationship with Surrealism.

☛ **Bérard, Blumenfeld, Cocteau, Man Ray, L. Miller, Schiaparelli**

122

Salvador Dalí. **b** Figueres (SP), 1904. **d** Figueres (SP), 1989. **I Dream About an Evening Dress**. Illustration for American *Vogue*, 1937.

Dassler Adi (Adidas)   Designer

Sport met fashion and music in 1986 when hip hop group Run DMC recorded its devotion to streetwear on the track 'My Adidas'. Sweatshirts, track pants and trainers were appropriated by a generation of men and women who threw away the laces and decorated themselves with heavyweight gold jewellery. In the 1970s, Adidas trainers had been an anti-establishment fashion statement worn with jeans, but in the defiant, label-aware 1980s branding took over and an unsuspecting sportswear company found itself at the heart of a fashion movement. In the 1936 Olympics, Jesse Owens, a black American runner, won four gold medals wearing a pair of trainers made by cobbler Adi Dassler and his brother, Rudolf. They had seen a gap in the market for high-performance athletic shoes in 1920 and they started to build what was to become a label as important to street fashion as it was to sport.

☛ Boy George, Hechter, Hilfiger, P. Knight, Lacoste

Adi (Adolf) Dassler. b Herzogenaurach (GER), 1900. **d** Herzogenaurach (GER), 1978. (Adidas.) **Run DMC in 'Superstar' shoes**. Photograph by Michael E. Heeg, 1986.

Day Corinne   Photographer

In this picture, from the series that introduced Kate Moss to the world, photographer Corinne Day aims to capture 'A teenage sexuality which I love. I want to make my images as documentary as possible, an image of life that is real'. Day's style rejects everything that fashion photography has traditionally stood for – glamour, sexiness, sophistication – by shooting skinny girls in cheap nylon knickers amidst squat-like squalor. Her anti-fashion attitude exemplifies the mood of the 1990s. Herself an ex-model, Day discovers her subjects in the street, preferring 'cocky English girls with a strong identity'. She launched the career of Kate Moss by photographing her aged fifteen for *The Face*, shown here. The best known of the 'grunge' photographers, Day is credited with starting the trend for pre-pubescent-looking waifs. *Vogue* editor Alexandra Shulman, however, defended her work as 'a celebration of vulnerability and joyousness'.

☛ **Moss, Page, Sims**

Corinne Day. b (UK). (Active 1980s–1990s.) **Kate Moss**. 1990.

Dean James   Icon

James Dean, the original teenage rebel, leans against a wall smoking. Dean was the role model for generations of disaffected youth who immediately related to his portrayal of lost adolescence and emulated his wardrobe because of it. Andy Warhol called him 'the damaged but beautiful soul of our time'. His status as a handsome movie star far outshone his acting

talents, and in his short-lived career he made only three films: *East of Eden* (1955), *Rebel Without a Cause* (1955) and *Giant* (1956). Dean said, 'Being a good actor isn't easy; being a man is even harder. I want to do both before I'm done'. But, tragically, he was killed at the age of twenty-four, crashing his Porsche Spyder on the way to a race meeting. He is now suspended

forever in adolescence. The basics that Dean wore are still popular today as the uniform of youth: Levi's jeans, white T-shirt and zip-up bomber jacket.

☞ Presley, Strauss, Warhol

James Dean. **b** Fairmount, IN (USA), 1931. **d** Route 466 CA (USA), 1955. **Bomber jacket and Levi's**. *Rebel Without a Cause* publicity shot. 1955.

Delaunay Sonia

Designer

Brilliantly coloured and sharply patterned geometric designs are lavishly displayed on this 'simultaneous' coat worn by Gloria Swanson. Sonia Delaunay, a leading Parisian artist of Orphism, a movement which developed out of Cubism and which made colour the primary means of artistic expression, has here merged art with fashion. In 1912 she began a series of non-figurative paintings called *Contrastes simultanés*, combining geometric forms with bright, prismatic hues. This work was based on the theory of the simultaneous contrast of colours of the nineteenth-century chemist Michel-Eugène Chevreul. Her simultaneous fashions had their origins in these paintings, since she moulded the fabric to the shape of the garment to ensure that the application of the colours remained intact. Her new concept of fabric pattern, whereby the cut and decoration of the garment were created at the same time, perfectly complemented the unstructured clothes of the 1920s.

☛ **Balla, P. Ellis, Exter, Heim**

126

Sonia Delaunay. **b** Odessa (RUS), 1884. **d** Paris (FR), 1979. **Embroidered 'simultaneous' coat created for Gloria Swanson.** 1923.

Delhomme Jean-Philippe   Illustrator

The supermodel, the hairstylist, the photographer and the assistant interact in a familiar scene from the fashion world. Such familiarity, however, becomes a novelty when painted in the form of a comic-style strip. An accessory to Jean-Philippe Delhomme's wit, fashions are blurred in favour of visually comforting satires of the affectations of those who lead their everyday lives in this industry. This bright, hand-painted gouache, which belongs to Delhomme's own one-page column published monthly in French *Glamour* since 1988, reveals a knowing artist. While drawing inspiration from his friends in the fashion trade, he claims to operate in, 'a *décalage*, a kind of jet lag, that appears between life written up in magazines and what's happening in the real world'. Delhomme's highly stylized and spontaneous caricatures recall the work of Marcel Vertès who, in the 1930s, fondly satirized the foibles of fashionable society.

☛ Berthoud, Vertès

Jean-Philippe Delhomme. b Nanterre (FR), 1959. **Modes de Vie.** Illustrated for *Glamour*, 1993.

Dell'Acqua Alessandro   Designer

How to make something delicate and romantic appear hard-edged and punky: this dilemma is at the centre of Alessandro Dell'Acqua's work. While his clothes have a softness and sensuality defined by materials such as chiffon, shown here on a T-shirt with fluted, bias-cut sleeves, his outfits are often styled with aggression. Long leather gloves and broad sweeps of violet eye shadow lend edge to what would otherwise be a dainty shirt. Dell'Acqua claims rock star Courtney Love, widow of Kurt Cobain, as his heroine and her own style reflects his blend of aggressive femininity. His mix-and-match, layered pieces are modern in their versatility and wearability. His signature palette is contrasting colours (nude and black being two of his favourites). Initially Dell'Acqua specialized in knitwear and he worked with a small group of artisans in Bologna. His collections carry reminders of this period through fragile knits of delicate, lacy mohair.

☞ Cobain, Chalayan, Sarne

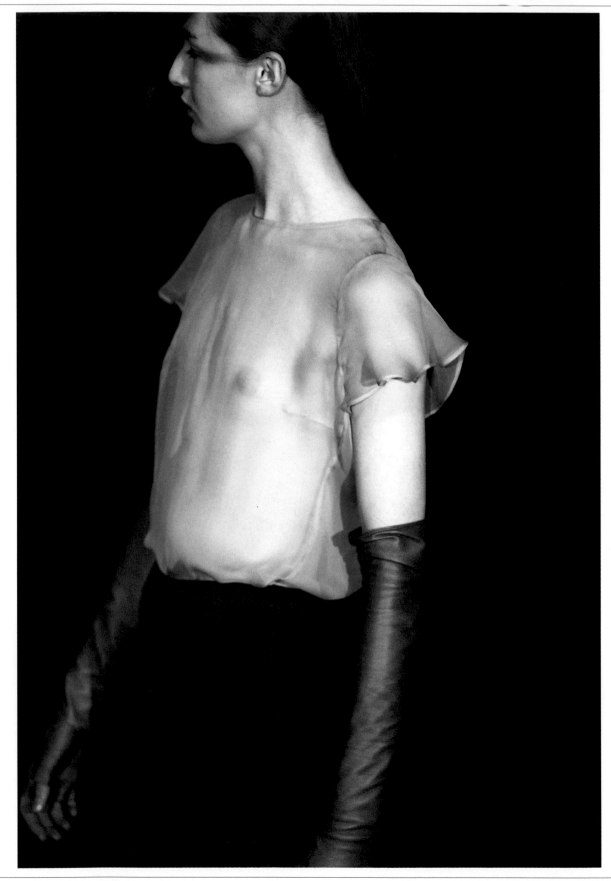

128

Alessandro Dell'Acqua. b Naples (IT), 1963. **Silk chiffon T-shirt. Autumn/winter 1997/8**. Photograph by Chris Moore.

Dell'Olio Louis

Designer

Dogtooth check and black leather is a blend of fashion and function, sass and shrewdness by Louis Dell'Olio, called 'the designer for everywoman'. The fitted, single-breasted jacket follows a body-conscious line without alienating his conservative clientele. This outfit was created under Anne Klein's label which he had taken over with Donna Karan, a friend from college, after Klein's death in 1974. Dell'Olio said of the experience, 'We didn't know enough to be terrified' but together they forged a style that suited the working women of America. In 1984 Karan left to set up her own label and Dell'Olio continued what they had started until Richard Tyler took over the company in 1993. One fan of Dell'Olio's work told *Vogue*, 'I don't want to be gussied up to the ears...the jackets hide a multitude of sins, the pants have a fabulous fit, the clothes are clean.'

☛ Karan, A. Klein, Tyler

129

Louis Dell'Olio. b New York (USA), 1948. **Dogtooth check and black leather for Anne Klein**. Photograph by Chris Moore, 1988.

Demarchelier Patrick   Photographer

Patrick Demarchelier catches Nadja Auermann mid-spin, her aigrette adding to an aura of costume history. Though relentlessly modern, Demarchelier's work also has a grand quality usually associated with the great couture photographers of the 1950s. He left Paris for New York in 1975 and started a long relationship with America's magazines, in particular the Condé Nast titles *Vogue*, *Glamour* and *Mademoiselle*. In 1992 he joined Hearst's *Harper's Bazaar*, recruited by Liz Tilberis, its new editor, for his clear, graphic photographs. It was the perfect material for the spreads designed by creative director Fabien Baron. Though dealing largely with the vicissitudes of fashion, Demarchelier's work has also explored other territories, especially portraiture. *Harper's Bazaar* said of his work, 'For people who want to look really beautiful, Demarchelier has become the photographer of choice, perhaps the most sought-after shooter of the 1990s'.

☛ Baron, Chanel, Lagerfeld, Wainwright

130

Patrick Demarchelier. b Le Havre (FR), 1943. **Nadja Auermann wears haute couture by Karl Lagerfeld for Chanel.** *Harper's Bazaar*, 1994.

Demeulemeester Ann   Designer

It could be a music video, or a science fiction film: the subject's hard-edged image, punk make-up and black leather dress alienate her from the natural environment she inhabits. Belgian designer Ann Demeulemeester's 1970s rock star-style tailoring and leatherwear draw inspiration from strong female icons of music, such as Patti Smith, Janis Joplin and Chrissie Hynde. 'The things that meant something to you when you were sixteen stay with you forever. They are your roots,' she says. From cobweb knitwear to oversized masculine 'slouch' suits, Demeulemeester designs clothes with attitude. Jackets are worn back to front or have just one sleeve; trousers are oversized, slung around the hips; knitwear is shrugged off the shoulder. In the same way that Helmut Lang has earned his copyists, Demeulemeester's ideas have been translated onto many other catwalks. Her work has that highly marketable quality: cool.

☛ Bikkembergs, Capasa, Kerrigan, Thimister, Van Noten

131

Ann Demeulemeester. b Courtrai (BEL), 1954. **Black leather draped tunic dress and jersey shirt.** Photograph by Philip-Lorca diCorcia, *Harper's Bazaar*, 1997.

Deneuve Catherine   Icon

Catherine Deneuve leaps for Francesco Scavullo's camera, a consummate model as well as an icon of French elegance, *froideur* and sensibility. Deneuve is also a long-term muse to Yves Saint Laurent, whom she met when he dressed her for *Belle de Jour*. Saint Laurent says of her, 'She is a woman who makes me dream... As a friend she is the most delightful, warmest, sweetest and most protective.' As French *Vogue*'s most featured cover face, Deneuve represents the legendary chic femininity of French womanhood and as such was also the face of Chanel No.5. Here, she wears a suit made of calfskin printed with cheetah spots and trimmed with mink, a powerful combination brought together by Arnold Scaasi. When she talks about the de-feminized roles played by actressses in modern films, Deneuve outlines her own style, 'Superficially, it may appear that the women now are stronger, but they are not stronger, only more masculine.'

☞ Barthet, Chanel, Saint Laurent, Scaasi, Scavullo

132

Catherine Deneuve. b Paris (FR), 1943. **Calfskin and mink cheetah print suit by Arnold Scaasi.** Photograph by Francesco Scavullo, 1970.

Dessès Jean   Designer

The roses at the hem of this chiffon dress were only usually exposed as the wearer walked. They are a charming addition to a classically inspired gown. The fashions of Dessès were inspired by his Greek heritage and Egyptian place of birth. He was a master of draped chiffon and muslin evening dresses that were derived from ancient robes. He was also noted for dresses made in the form of fitted jackets in plain colours with voluminous skirts in a contrasting patterned print. He established his own maison de couture in Paris in 1937. Dessès participated in the Théâtre de la Mode, the fashion doll exhibition organized by the Chambre Syndicale de la Couture Parisienne under its president, Lucien Lelong. Some forty couturiers designed haute couture in miniature for these little mannequins made of wire. They were placed in sets depicting scenes of Parisian life designed by artists involved in fashion, such as Cocteau and Bérard.

☛ Cocteau, Laroche, Lelong, McLaughlin-Gill, Valentino

133

Jean Dessès. b Alexandria (EG), 1904. **d** Athens (GR), 1970. **Black chiffon dress with pink silk roses on underskirt.** Photograph by Frances McLaughlin-Gill, American *Vogue*, 1952.

Diana Princess of Wales Icon

'Clothes are now not as essential to my work as they used to be,' Diana, Princess of Wales, told *Vogue* in 1997. It was a confident statement from a woman who had come to realize that a pair of jeans wouldn't compromise her effectiveness. And it showed. Towards the end of her life, Diana's wardrobe finally took a back seat to the person she was and the work she did; an utterly modern concept. Here she wears an artfully uncomplicated navy lace dress by Catherine Walker for a charity film premiere in 1997. From the day Lady Diana Spencer was first caught on film in the early 1980s wearing archetypal British upper-class clothing, the ensuing developments in her wardrobe and the colour of lipstick she chose were closely watched and widely copied. Particular attention was given to her hair, sleeked and simplified in the 1990s by Sam McKnight.

☛ Choo, Emanuel, Fratini, McKnight, Oldfield, G. Smith, Testino

134

Diana, Princess of Wales. b Sandringham (UK), 1961. **d** Paris (FR), 1997. **Catherine Walker dress**. Photograph by Kelvin Bruce, 1997.

Dinnigan Colette   Designer

Colette Dinnigan's dress has the charm of an antique gown, yet possesses a modern sensuality, suspended as it is from two fragile spaghetti straps. Its lace tiers and train belong to the romantic, early twentieth-century designers such as Paquin, Lucile and Dœuillet. As the latter had done before her, Dinnigan launched her career designing and selling delicate lace and chiffon lingerie. Her success allowed her to open a shop in 1992, and begin designing a ready-to-wear line. Her use of womanly fabrics and attention to the female form resulted in clinging slip dresses which gave sophistication to the trend for wearing underwear-as-outerwear. The preciousness of her designs is reminiscent of haute couture detailing and was a contrast to the prevailing use of undecorated fabrics cut into graphic forms. The simple shapes of underwear are wrought in lace and placed over contrasting satins to achieve the luminescence illustrated here.

☛ Dœuillet, Duff Gordon, Moon, Oudejans, Paquin

Colette Dinnigan. b Durban (SA), 1965. **Satin dress overlaid with lace**. Photograph by Gerald Jenkins, *Australian Style*, 1997.

Dior Christian   Designer

Reading the faces of this salon audience, it is possible to gauge the breadth of reaction which greeted Christian Dior's first collection, which was dubbed the 'New Look' after this show by Carmel Snow, editor of *Harper's Bazaar*. As they gaze at an hourglass jacket of cream tussore over a skirt constructed from a decadent yardage of black wool, the audience registers shock, disapproval and deep yearning. At a time of postwar austerity, the New Look tempted women back into the nostalgic femininity of corsets and, most controversially, flowing skirts that would use up to fifty yards of material. Dior, who had wanted to be an architect but turned to fashion, working for Piguet, Lelong and Balmain, said that it was one of the happiest moments of his life:

'I created flower women with gentle shoulders and generous bosoms, with tiny waists like stems and skirts belling out like petals.'

☞ Bohan, Ferre, Galliano, Gruau, Molyneux, Saint Laurent, Snow

136

Christian Dior. b Granville (FR), 1905. d Montecatini (IT), 1957. **New Look parade.** 1947. Photograph by Bellini.

Dœuillet Georges   Designer

The fashion plates of André Marty have a very evocative quality. Fastidiously stylish, Marty has created a pictorial witticism to depict the character of the dress. He has juxtaposed the delicacy and fragility of the *robe de lingerie* against the foreboding figure of Cupid and the dark, sinister landscape. It is an example of haute couture providing a stimulating atmosphere for the

rejuvenation of fashion illustration, a combination of luxurious design and texture with artistic excellence that captured the spirit of the times. The exquisitely intricate workmanship of this immaculate dress came from the Paris couture house of Dœuillet, which was founded in 1900. Noted for its use of magnificent fabrics, Dœuillet was a prestigious fashion house

that provided the *bon ton* with some of the most opulent clothes of the early years of the twentieth century. It merged with the salon of Jacques Doucet on his death in 1929.

☞ Bakst, Dinnigan, Doucet, Poiret

Georges Dœuillet. d (FR), 1929. (Active 1890s–1920s.) **Broderie anglaise boudoir dress.** Illustration by André Marty, *La Gazette du Bon Ton*, 1913.

Dolce Domenico and Gabbana Stefano (Dolce & Gabbana) Designers

This photograph of Italian actress/model Isabella Rossellini could almost be a still from one of her father, Roberto Rossellini's, black-and-white films of the 1940s. This cinematic sensuality is typical of Dolce & Gabbana's style. Their idealistic vision of Italy revolves around specific themes: 1940s screen sirens (leopard prints and corsetry *à la* Sophia Loren), Catholicism (Sunday best suits and rosary beads) and various Italian stereotypes, from Mafioso machismo (pinstripe suits and trilbys) to the simplicity of Sicilian widows (little black dresses, headscarves, fishing village baskets). But beneath this puritanical patriotism there are also hints of subversion: cross-dressing and suits cut with integral corsetry or lace panels are favourites. Although the religious imagery is strong, it is glamorized almost to the point of pastiche, from sequined icons to rosary beads worn as jewelled necklaces.

☞ Colonna, McGrath, Matsushima, Meisel, Nars

Domenico Dolce. b Palermo (IT), 1958; **Stefano Gabbana. b** Milan (IT), 1962. (Dolce & Gabbana.) **Isabella Rossellini wears leopard-print coat. Autumn/winter 1994.** Photograph by Michel Comte.

Dominguez Adolfo   Designer

A bodice is formed from a loosely wrapped swathe of iridescent fabric, the only decoration being the shine picked out by the light on its folds. As with the work of Mitsuhiro Matsuda, the material dictates the shape and creates an indistinct garment somewhere between shawl and jacket. Adolfo Dominguez is the Spanish answer to Giorgio Armani. In the 1980s he was famously called 'King of the Wrinklies' for his tailored but unpressed, crinkled suits for men. Like Armani, he is known for using fabrics that direct his work and lend themselves to a simpler, softer look. These visual preoccupations come from the fact that he is not a traditionally trained fashion designer. Dominguez studied cinematography and aesthetics in Paris, before returning to his father's drapery shop in Orense, northern Spain. He is also an author and film-maker. Dominguez launched his first men's ready-to-wear collection in Madrid in 1982, and followed it with womenswear in 1992.

☛ Armani, Matsuda, del Pozo

Adolfo Dominguez. b Orense (SP), 1950. **Metallic shawl jacket.** Photograph by Manuel Madarnas, 1988.

Doucet Jacques   Designer

Doucet's gown is beautifully illustrated by Magnin for *La Gazette du Bon Ton* in 1914. The illustration reflects not only the high-waisted style in vogue before the First World War but also the way Doucet worked with artists. Together with his contemporary Poiret, he helped revive the art of fashion illustration in France. He was also a patron of the fine arts and

in 1909 bought Picasso's avant-garde painting *Les Demoiselles d'Avignon*, installing it at the head of a crystal staircase in a specially built wing of his house. The grandson of a lace merchant, Doucet expanded the family business by opening a couture department in 1871. With his gowns of rare gros-point de Venise, bodices of paper-thin ivory chamois and opera capes

lined with swans' down or chinchilla, Doucet's style epitomized the opulent femininity of the *belle époque*.

☛ Dœuillet, Iribe, Poiret

Jacques Doucet. b Paris (FR), 1853. **d** Paris (FR), 1932. **Afternoon dress.** Illustrated by J. Magnin for *La Gazette du Bon Ton*, 1914.

Dovima

Model

Dovima, made-up with the painted kohl lids and expressive pencilled brows of the 1950s, strikes an artful pose from behind white tulle. She and Richard Avedon broke new ground in fashion photography. Modelling with elephants or in front of the Pyramids, they took fashion out of the whitewashed studio and into the 'real' world for the first time. Dovima was talent-spotted on the street outside the offices of *Vogue* in New York and was soon in front of Irving Penn's lens. She told him her name was Dovima (the first letters from her real names, Dorothy Virginia Margaret) because that was how she signed her paintings. Charging an hourly rate of $60, she became known as the dollar a minute girl. After twelve years at the top, she appeared alongside Audrey Hepburn in one of the most famous fashion films, *Funny Face*. Dovima's graceful, arch poses are now regarded as the *sine qua non* of haute couture presentation.

☛ Avedon, Lauder, Penn

141

Dovima (Dorothy Virginia Margaret Juba). b New York (USA), 1927. **d** Fort Lauderdale, FL (USA), 1990. **Dovima behind tulle.** Photograph by Cecil Beaton, 1950s.

Von Drecoll Baron Christoff   Designer

The house of Drecoll spanned the years from 1905 to 1929 and shows two distinct styles. In the *belle époque* period, Drecoll specialized in promenade gowns and evening dresses with boned bodices, tight waists and full skirts, which produced the S-shaped figure of the period. Photographs in *Les Modes* show that Drecoll ensembles were fussier and trimmed with more confection than comparable outfits from other couture houses. In the 1920s the house was known for chic, short, low-waisted gowns teamed with the cloche, a tight fitting hat shaped like a bell and pulled low over the forehead. These flapper outfits were illustrated in luxury fashion magazines such as *Art, Goût* and *Beauté*. The house of Drecoll was founded by Christoff von Drecoll in Vienna. It opened in Paris in 1905 under the ownership of M and Mme de Wagner, a Belgian couple, who also supported Marie-Louise Bruyère.

☛ **Bruyère, Gibson, Poiret, Redfern, Rouff**

142

Baron Christoff von Drecoll. (Active 1890s–1920s.) **Afternoon dress.** *Les Modes*, 1914.

Drian Etienne   Illustrator

D.45 marks the work of Etienne Drian. Here, he illustrates the work of Balenciaga who has presaged Dior's New Look by two years with a waisted jacket bearing exaggerated hips. Drian was an artist who worked in Paris for the illustrated fashion magazine *La Gazette du Bon Ton*, from its foundation in 1912 until its closure in 1925. He illustrated articles and also produced fashion plates. His graphic style was brisk and clear, with the *bon ton* depicted in fluid movement in anecdotal settings which give a picture of contemporary life. He was very adept at bringing out the intricate workmanship of haute couture of the period, in the fashions, for example, of Paul Poiret. Among his contemporaries at *La Gazette du Bon Ton* were Georges Barbier and Georges Lepape. Drian was also well known in the 1920s and 1930s for his sanguine portrait drawings and for his decorative murals.

☛ Barbier, Lepape, Poiret, Sumurun

Etienne Drian (Etienne Adrien). **b** Bulgneville (FR), 1885. **d** Paris (FR), 1961. **Winter outfit by Balenciaga.** *Plaire Magazine*, 1945.

Duff Gordon Lady (Lucile)   Designer

Lucile, who started out in 1890 by dressmaking for her friends, opened her own fashion house in 1891. Her marriage to Sir Cosmo Duff Gordon in 1900 catapulted her into designing for the upper echelons of international society, with branches in New York (1909), Chicago (1911) and Paris (1911). Like the Callot Sœurs, she designed romantic dresses made of silk and lace. Her speciality was picturesque tea gowns in pastel shades worn with mild corsetry, the fitting of which is being conducted here. Like her countryman Worth, she held fashion shows for her clients. Like Poiret, she was an innovator, designing clothes which were startling for the time – such as draped skirts which revealed the legs and revolutionary underwear. She was also involved in the entertainment world, designing costumes which became popular fashion, such as those for Lily Elsie, star of the *Merry Widow*. Her other celebrated clients included the dancer Irene Castle and actress Sarah Bernhardt.

☛ Boué, Callot, Dinnigan, Molyneux, Poiret, Worth

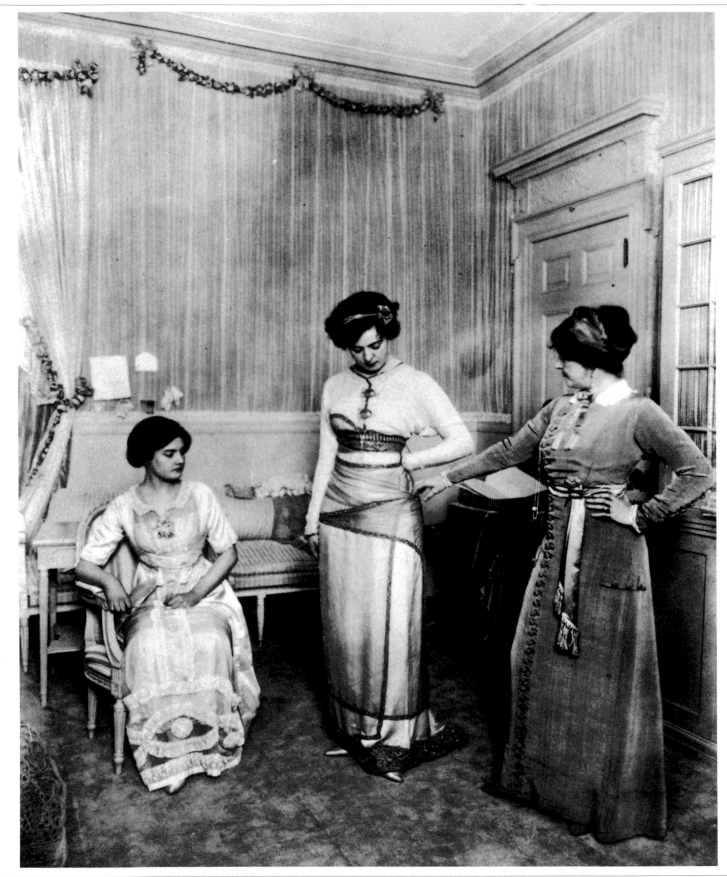

144

Lady Duff Gordon. b London (UK), 1862. **d** London (UK), 1935. (Lucile.) **Lucile with client and mannequin at a fitting.** 1912.

Dufy Raoul

Textile designer

This lush silk is decorated with silver lamé work. The oriental motifs in sky blue, royal blue and rose reflect the imagery of the woodcuts Dufy executed for Guillaume Apollinaire's *Le Bestiaire* of 1911. Rose-coloured horses frolic amongst waves, scallops, dolphins and froth, all spectacularly taking on silver highlights when seen in the light. This fabric was chosen by Poiret for an evening dress he displayed at the Exposition des Arts Décoratifs in Paris in 1925. It was produced by the textile company Bianchini Férier, with whom Dufy had an exclusive contract from 1912 to 1928. His use of colour came from his association with the Fauves (a group of artists who developed a new style of painting characterized by a bold handling of intensely vivid colours), with whom he exhibited in 1906. Dufy collaborated with Poiret in establishing the Petite Usine for fabric-printing. Even though it closed at the end of 1911, it had a great impact on Dufy's career as a fashion artist.

☛ Patou, Poiret, Rubinstein

145

Raoul Dufy. b Le Havre (FR), 1877. d Forcalquier (FR), 1953. **'Shells and Marine Horses'**, produced by Bianchini Férier, 1925 (fabric detail).

Eisen Mark
Designer

The face of model Jodie Kidd is picked out in a catwalk line-up at the end of Mark Eisen's show. She is wearing a mix of animal skin, wholesome wool and shiny silk. Born in South Africa, Eisen studied at the University of Southern California, where he not only learned business and achieved fame by designing a football helmet for 'Trojans' fans, but also gained the sensibility for streamlined, no-nonsense dressing that stresses contemporary materials. Eisen's flirtatious, but simple silhouettes and intense materials are relaxed versions of contentious European fashion, giving wearability to otherwise challenging schemes. Even natural materials get coated so that they literally shine on the catwalk and in real life. He has shown 'couture denim' and other signs of the street in a style *New York Times* journalist Amy Spindler called 'driven by the spirit of techno music, repetitive, strong and stripped down'. Eisen provides the clothes for the spirit of 'California dreamin'.

☛ Kors, Oldham, Rocha

146

Mark Eisen. b Cape Town (SA), 1960. **Catwalk line-up. Autumn/winter 1998.** Photograph by Chris Moore.

Ellis Perry

Designer

Ellis, who launched his own label in 1978, created a strong brand of American sportswear by emphasizing colour, often in stripes and blocks, and by using the textures of natural fibres. Here, linen is used for a T-shirt and skirt, joined in the middle by an out-size belt. His inspirations included Sonia Delaunay, Patou and Chanel in the 1920s and contemporary popular culture.

Capacious summer linen trousers and skirts were often matched with cotton sweaters or loose blouses. Sweaters were a staple for Ellis throughout the year. Winter wools were luxurious and, like all the clothes, cuddly and easy to wear. Ellis began in fashion sales; his design was conceptual and often devoted to compelling stories or ideas that readily translated to the buyer

and consumer: the winter 1985 sweaters seized unicorns, decorative foliage and sleek greyhounds from medieval tapestry and his slouchy looks of the 1980s were exaggerated to create the look of a picturesque hobo.

☛ Delaunay, Jackson, Jacobs, Patou

Perry Ellis. b VA (USA), 1940. d New York (USA), 1986. **Blue linen dress with scarlet belt. Spring 1983**. Photograph by Erica Lennard.

Ellis Sean   Photographer

In a fashion shoot for *The Face*, Sean Ellis re-creates a fantasy based on a supernatural storyline about voyeurism and death. It gives meaning to the phrase 'fashion story', which is used by magazines to explain a theme which runs through a multi-page shoot. In this case, the angelic character's eyes are made luminous to signify contact lenses which allow her tormentor to see himself as she would. The red dye which stains her snowy chiffon top signifies blood. Such stories put fashion into an anomalous context rather than simply show-casing clothes. It is a challenging method of fashion photography which has come to the fore in the 1990s, although other photographers such as Guy Bourdin and Helmut Newton developed sophisticated story-telling techniques around sex and death themes in the 1970s. Ellis explains his narrative pictures as 'not necessarily fashion pictures – they just happen to be fashionable'.

☛ Macdonald, Pearl, Tennant

148

Sean Ellis. b Brighton (UK), 1970. **'White Dragon' shirt by Tristan Webber**. *The Face*, 1998.

Emanuel David and Elizabeth Designers

A spontaneous moment is snapped on 31 July, 1981. The Princess of Wales is dressed in the romantic counterpoint to her husband's uniform. The flashlight throws into relief the yards of silk taffeta ruffles at her neck and the delicate, specially made Nottingham lace cuffs at her wrist. Unseen is the eight-metre train decorated with pearls. It was called 'a dress for a real fairy princess'. David and Elizabeth Emanuel, who designed the dress for the Princess, had created a popular movement in womenswear which reflected the moment it was designed for – one that reached a record television audience around the world. The married couple originally met at the Royal College of Art. They graduated in 1978, the year they also launched their Mayfair boutique. They garnered a celebrity following, with Joan Collins and Bianca Jagger among those who wore their extravagant and quixotic visions of femininity.

☛ Diana, Fratini, Tappé

Emanuel. **David. b** Bridgend (UK), 1952; **Elizabeth. b** London (UK), 1953. **The Prince and Princess of Wales on their wedding day.** 1981.

Eric

Illustrator

Using the broad mirror of a powder room, Eric is able to describe the jewelled details of Jean Patou's evening dress from both front and rear. He had a deft, calligraphic style whereby the model and the clothes she was wearing were minutely examined. To get such accuracy of observation, Eric drew from life and insisted the models remain static in their settings for long periods. To him, fidelity to detail was all-important. Born in America of Swedish parents, Carl Erickson studied at the Academy of Fine Arts in Chicago, where he acquired the training and discipline required for working with the figure. His first fashion illustrations for *Vogue* appeared in 1916. By 1925 he was settled in France, and, apart from the period during the Occupation of Paris (when he returned to America), he provided *Vogue* with fashion illustrations on the modes and manners of the Parisian beau monde right up to the mid-1950s.

☛ Antonio, Berthoud, Bouché, Patou

Eric (Carl Erickson). b Joliet, IL (USA), 1891. d Senlis (FR), 1958. **Dress by Jean Patou.** American *Vogue*, 1933.

Erté

Illustrator

This fashion illustration was accompanied by the provocative words, 'Nature changes her costume each season, but quite without cost, whereas with the fairer sex...' Erté had a highly personal concept of women and fashion. He portrayed the female form in a very stylized manner. Women were exotic goddesses for whom money was no object. As for fashion, he himself said that he did not follow its trends but that from his creations each woman could select something that suited her without strictly adhering to the mode. His love of luxurious accessories, especially jewellery, is displayed here, in a picture which exemplifies his mastery of simple, precise detail and lavish ornamentation, hallmarks for which he became known as the father of Art Deco. Erté had two major influences, which came from his native and adopted countries: Léon Bakst and the Ballets Russes and Paul Poiret, for whom he worked on fashionable and theatrical dress from 1913 to 1914.

☞ Bakst, Brunelleschi, Callot, Poiret

Erté (Romain de Tirtoff). b St Petersburg (RUS), 1892. **d** Paris (FR), 1990. **'La Toilette de la Nature'.** Design for *Harper's Bazaar* cover. 1920.

Esterel Jacques

Designer

Seen here during her 1959 wedding to Jacques Charrier, Brigitte Bardot looks both demure and sensual in her pink-and-white, Vichy check linen dress, edged in broderie anglaise lace and designed by Jacques Esterel. The first celebrity endorsement for Esterel, the dress was the source of worldwide gossip following the secret visits he made to Bardot's Parisian hotel prior to the wedding. It was also the start of a long-standing association that led the multimillionaire Jean-Baptiste Doumeng to rename the house Benoit Bartherotte on the designer's death in 1974. Esterel was an unlikely fashion convert: previously he presided over a foundry and was an exporter-importer of machine tools. A visit to Louis Féraud's Cannes house persuaded him to try fashion in 1950, but lack of formal training forced him to employ two of Féraud's salespeople before he finally launched his label with two boutiques in Paris in 1958.

☞ Bardot, Beretta, Féraud, Gaultier

152

Jacques Esterel. b Bourne-Argental (FR), 1917. **d** Paris (FR), 1974. **Brigitte Bardot and Jacques Charrier on their wedding day.** Photograph by Garofalo, 1959.

Etro Gimmo

Textile designer

This family group of outfitted wildlife illustrates the *haute* bohemian spirit of the Italian label Etro. Capturing its hallmark jewel colours and rich textiles, this portrait, entitled 'Animen', portrays curious hybrids of man and animal that remind us of our communion with the greater circle of nature. The family-run company was set up by patriarch Gimmo Etro in 1968. Returning from his travels laden with fabrics from the Far East and North Africa, he replicated these designs onto sumptuous cashmere, silk and linen. These he supplied to top couture houses and designers Armani, Mugler and Lacroix, earning himself the title of 'Grand Man of Italian Textiles'. Joined by his offspring, he launched his menswear collection in the 1980s, deploying his signature paisley motif and vivid velvets in interesting ways: as lining on tweed coats, bright flashes on collars and cuffs and even in an all-over paisley suit for David Bowie.

☛ **Armani, Ascher, Lacroix**

153

Gimmo (Gerolamo) Etro. b Milan (IT), 1940. **'Animen'. Autumn/winter 1997/8**. Photograph by Christopher Griffith.

Ettedgui Joseph   Designer

A knitted column and scarf are a conceptual notion of menswear. The Joseph Ettedgui style is a moveable one, but the basic tenets of an urban designer lifestyle have remained since he opened his first boutique, selling Kenzo, Emmanuelle Khanh and Jean-Charles de Castelbajac. Antipathetic to the chintz world of Laura Ashley, Ettedgui admired the young vision of the designers he stocked. This interest developed into a modernistic theme for his boutiques. Designed by architects Eva Jiricna and David Chipperfield, they use steel, white and concrete colours as the background to contemporary collections. In 1983, Joseph introduced his own label, Joseph Tricot, with a sloppy Joe sweater that has sold in various guises since. In 1984, the concept expanded to include tailoring. Men and women of the same mindset use Joseph's basic wardrobe of stretch trousers and jackets as the building blocks of their style.

☞ de Castelbajac, Kenzo, Khanh, M. Roberts, Stewart

154

Joseph Ettedgui. b Casablanca (MOR), 1936. **'Red Indians', Joseph Tricot**. Photograph by Michael Roberts, 1986.

Von Etzdorf Georgina　Textile designer

Colour and texture meet on an outfit by the textile design partnership, Georgina von Etzdorf. Golden sunbursts are embroidered onto a woollen gauze vest and devoré velvet is used to give a shadowy, raised pattern to a bias-cut skirt. Foliage and flower motifs, evoking the atmosphere of rural England, typify the work of a company that is inspired by natural imagery. In 1981 Georgina von Etzdorf entered into a partnership with two art school contemporaries, Martin Simcock and Jonathan Docherty. The hand-printing method they developed involves screen-printing supplemented by hand-applied paint strokes, a process which lends individuality to each garment. Georgina von Etzdorf's contribution to fashion has been to stimulate the use of precious, handmade fabrics, especially for scarves. Lustrous velvet and silk is printed with abstract shafts and lucid blocks of colour, the result being a wearable piece of conceptual textile design.

☞ Cerruti, Lloyd, Mazzilli, Williamson

Georgina von Etzdorf. b Lima (PER), 1955. **Hand-embroidered camisole and velvet devoré skirt. Autumn/winter 1998.** Photograph by Howard Sooley.

Eula Joe

Illustrator

Free, vivid colour captures a woman mid-step in a sketch that typifies the art of modern fashion illustration. Eula is a keeper of the graphic tradition of fashion at a time when photography has dominated. His fashion illustrations for Italian and French *Harper's Bazaar*, from 1979, used impressionistic watercolour. Eula began his career in the 1950s on the fashion and social pages of the *Herald Tribune*, then worked for *The Sunday Times* in London. Back in New York in the 1960s, he worked on fashion stories for *Life* and designed sets and costumes for the New York City Ballet under George Balanchine. He diversified into television, directing 'fashion specials' for movie stars such as Lauren Bacall. In the 1970s he also worked with Halston, illustrated fashion for *Vogue* and assisted Diana Vreeland, who was then head of the Costume Institute at the Metropolitan Museum of Art in New York.

☞ **Halston, Missoni, Vreeland**

156

Joe Eula. b Norwalk, CT (USA). (Active 1960s–1980s.) **Knitwear by Missoni. Spring/summer 1985.** Illustration for *Harper's Bazaar*.

Evangelista Linda   Model

Linda's haircut transformed a model into not just a supermodel, but *the* supermodel. In October 1988 *Vogue* photographer Peter Lindbergh persuaded her to have her hair cut short. Evangelista cried throughout, but the crop made her career. Over the following six months, she appeared on the covers of every edition of *Vogue*. Linda knew that the key to longevity was versatility, so she continued to change her haircut and colour every couple of months – and fashion followed. Evangelista's professionalism put her at the top and she became famous for her audacious statements. 'We don't *Vogue* – we are *Vogue*', was surpassed by a comment that defined the supermodel era: 'We don't wake up for less than $10,000.' While the 'supers' were inevitably equalled by the 1990s beauty cult – that of Stella Tennant and Kate Moss who represented individuality – Evangelista's fame has ultimately given her the longevity she was looking for.

☛ Bergère, Garren, Lindbergh, Moss, Twiggy

157

Linda Evangelista. b St Katherine, ONT (CAN), 1965. **Velvet tank by Kenar. Autumn/winter 1997.** Photograph by Rocco Laspata.

Exter Alexandra

Designer

Alexandra Exter, an artist/fashion designer, brings the two disciplines together with *Dama al Ballo*, the painting of a dress which lives somewhere between both. After studying art in Kiev, she went to Paris where she met Pablo Picasso, Georges Braque and Filippo Martinetti. From 1900 to 1914 she travelled between Paris, Moscow and Kiev, spreading the doctrines of Cubism and Futurism among the Russian avant-garde. By 1916 she was working in theatrical costume design in Moscow and in 1921 she became a teacher at the Higher Artistic and Technical Workshops there. She promoted the idea that art and fashion could enhance everyday life and began working in fashion design. She designed proletarian dresses in brightly coloured geometric patterns analogous to the work of her friend, Sonia Delaunay. In the traditions of haute couture, she made sumptuously embroidered dresses inspired by peasant art.

☞ Balla, Capucci, Delaunay

Alexandra Exter. b Kiev (RUS), 1882. **d** Paris (FR), 1949. **'Dama al Ballo'**. Costume design for a Russian production of the ballet *Romeo and Juliet*, 1921.

Factor Max

Cosmetics creator

Known as 'Hollywood's make-up wizard', Max Factor oversaw Jean Harlow's *maquillage* – he created a star and started a beauty revolution when he dyed her hair platinum blonde. Harlow's heavy scheme of oily, blackened lids and lips was typical of that used for black-and-white films which required strong contrasts. Pancake make-up base was created to even out skin tone as films were transformed in the age of colour. It was cosmetics that created the glamorous images of the movie stars and, as they testified to the quality of the products they were using on a daily basis, the general public clamoured for them. Factor's products coincided with an acceptance of coloured cosmetics for women. The studios sent their budding starlets to him for grooming, and in 1937 the Max Factor Hollywood Make-Up Studio opened and Max Factor set about bringing the make-up of the stars to the public.

☛ Bourjois, Lauder, Revson, Uemura

159

Max Factor. **b** Lodz (POL), 1872. **d** Los Angeles, CA (USA), 1938. **Max Factor with Jean Harlow.** 1931.

Farhi Nicole

Designer

Easy, wearable, comfortable linen is the fabric most associated with the work of Nicole Farhi. When she launched her own label in 1983, Farhi's clothes became the epitome of understated fashion for women – all based on the kind she likes to wear. They are not intended to make major fashion statements. Instead, they drift with the differing times, staying in touch with them but always bearing the wearer in mind. Farhi described herself in the *Guardian* as 'a feminist in a soft way', and her clothes appeal to women who are looking for approachable tailoring and casual clothes which have Farhi's own dressed-up European attitude. Farhi studied fashion in Paris and freelanced for Agnès b and de Castelbajac before moving to Britain in 1973 to design for the French Connection chain. In 1989 she introduced menswear to the Farhi label, blending British tailoring and her European unstructured style.

☛ de Castelbajac, Kerrigan, Troublé

160

Nicole Farhi. b Nice (FR), 1946. **Elasticized linen dress. Spring/summer 1998**. Photograph by Kelly Klein.

Fath Jacques   Designer

A negative image accentuates a perfect hourglass figure created on a soft line with a curving, structured shape. This evening dress evokes the heady exuberance and gaiety of the early 1950s, when Jacques Fath, called the 'couturier's couturier', was in the same haute couture firmament as Christian Dior. He was famed for his feminine evening dresses, whipped up for royalty and movie stars. This golden era was described by his muse, Bettina, in an interview in 1994. She recalled the extremely creative atmosphere when he worked with assistants who were to succeed in their own right, such as Guy Laroche and Hubert de Givenchy. Fath worked in tandem with the model. He moulded the fabric directly onto her body without any preliminary drawing. Standing in front of a mirror, he would ask her to strike a pose, creating a *théâtre de la mode*, which became the source for the design in the collection.

☛ **Bettina, Bourdin, Head, Laroche, Maltézos, Perugia, Pipart**

161

Jacques Fath. b Maisons-Lafitte (FR), 1912. **d** Paris (FR), 1954. **Cocktail dress**. Photograph by Maurice Tabard, *Jardin des Modes*, 1950s.

Fendi Adele and Eduardo   Designer

Fendi's great achievement was to update fur's traditional image by giving it a fashion edge. Fox is seen here fashioned into a punky coat. Since 1965 Karl Lagerfeld has designed the collections, wittily casting against type. He has used fur for casualwear, creating mink-trimmed denim jackets and fur-lined sporty raincoats. In 1969 he introduced a leather and accessories line, which features the family's double-F motif. Adele Casagrande founded the company in 1918, changing its name when she married Eduardo Fendi in 1925. For over a century Fendi has been a family-run business, now managed by Adele's five daughters (the third generation has already been elected to the board of directors). Lagerfeld continues to make innovations in the fur industry, combining his high fashion aesthetic with high-tech developments – tiny perforations that make the coats lighter to wear, speckled colouring techniques for a more intense shade and unusual furs such as squirrel and ferret.

☛ Lagerfeld, Léger, Revillon

162

Fendi. Adele. **b** Rome (IT), 1897. **d** Rome (IT), 1978; Eduardo. **b** Rome (IT). (Active 1920s–1950s.) **d** Rome (IT), 1954. **'Feather fox' coat. Autumn/winter 1997/8**. Photograph by Jerome Esch.

Féraud Louis

Designer

Sunny, heavily embroidered clothes are Louis Féraud's métier. The designer says of his work, 'I live in the joy of being surrounded by women, of somehow directing their destiny, in so far as their destiny depends on a note of excess'. In 1955, Féraud opened a boutique in Cannes. He had dressed the young star Brigitte Bardot in an off-the-shoulder, white piqué frock with a lace collar; much photographed, 600 copies of this dress were sold and Féraud's success was established. Grace Kelly, Ingrid Bergman and Christian Lacroix's mother were also customers. He opened a boutique in Paris where he began to produce couture alongside prêt-à-porter, and he and his wife were dubbed 'The Gypsies' because of their brightly coloured, Midi-inspired look.

In the 1960s, Féraud's work was characterized by simple, architectural shapes with graphic detailing; Twiggy modelled the collections and Féraud designed the costumes for the cult television serial *The Prisoner*.

☛ Bardot, Blair, Esterel, Ley

163

Louis Féraud. b Arles (FR), 1920. **'Golden Sun' dress. Haute couture. Spring/summer 1997**. Photograph by Sylvie Lancrenon.

Ferragamo Salvatore

Shoe designer

This shoe, which marries glamour with imagination, is made of gilded glass mosaic, satin and kid leather. Salvatore Ferragamo was a shoemaker of great originality whose choice of materials made him unique. When leather was in short supply during the Second World War, he experimented with cellophane for the body of his shoes. For soles he revived the use of cork and wood.

Amongst his other cobbling innovations were wedge heels, platform soles and the steel shaft that stabilizes spike heels. Ferragamo's heyday was after the War, when Italian fashion was recovering and film production was booming. Film stars, rich tourists and socialites such as the Duchess of Windsor flocked to his Florence shop. He also earned himself the soubriquet

'shoemaker to the stars' by decorating the feet of two Hollywood generations, stretching from Gloria Swanson in the 1920s to Audrey Hepburn in the 1950s.

☞ Gucci, Levine, Louboutin, Pfister, Windsor

164

Salvatore Ferragamo. b Naples (IT), 1898. d Flumetto (IT), 1960. **Golden 'orthopaedic wedge' shoe**. Gilded glass mosaic, satin and kid leather. 1935.

Ferre Gianfranco   Designer

The dramatic play on proportions – exaggerated sleeves and cuffs and carefully structured corset – of this white taffeta shirt link fashion with Gianfranco Ferre's training as an architect. 'I use the same approach to clothes as I did when I designed buildings,' he says. 'It is basic geometry: you take a flat form and revolve it in space.' Ferre originally worked as a jewellery and accessories designer, before launching a ready-to-wear label in Milan in 1978. In 1989 he was appointed artistic director at Christian Dior; his first collection was inspired by Cecil Beaton's black-and-white costumes for *My Fair Lady*. Ferre prefers a neutral palette with dashes of his signature bright red. A perfectionist, his technical skill is shown in his precision tailoring, with a love of proportion-play revealed in his constant reinvention of the white shirt. It has been worn with jodhpurs, and evening skirts but under Ferre's direction it always has been glamorized.

☛ Beaton, Dior, Turlington

Gianfranco Ferre. b Legnano (IT), 1944. **Taffeta shirt. Spring/summer 1994.** Photograph by Kazuo Oishi.

Ferretti Alberta   Designer

Two women recline on a chaise longue in ethereal chiffon dresses. The overall effect is one of old-fashioned prettiness, yet their gaze and pose are self-assured, undermining any sense of passivity that prettiness might imply. 'I like to think I design feminine clothes,' says Ferretti. 'Everything is created by a woman for women, understanding what they want.' That vision is a particularly delicate one. Ferretti developed a special appreciation of textiles, especially daintily beaded or embroidered chiffons and sari silks, through watching her couturière mother at work. A young entrepreneur, she opened her own designer clothes shop at the age of seventeen. At the end of the twentieth century, Ferretti is one of the most powerful businesswomen in Italy, manufacturing not only her own collections but those of Narciso Rodriguez and Jean Paul Gaultier.

☛ Rodriguez, Roversi

166

Alberta Ferretti. b Riccione (IT), 1950. **Chiffon dresses. Autumn/winter 1997/8**. Photograph by Paolo Roversi.

Fiorucci Elio

Designer

Oliviero Toscani's colourful, sexy images for Fiorucci defined the disco era of the 1970s and early 1980s. The label's skintight Buffalo '70 jeans, worn here by Manhattan modelling queen Donna Jordan, were popular with New York's clubbing crowd. Jackie Kennedy, Diana Ross and Bianca Jagger were all fans. Elio Fiorucci is credited with inventing the concept of designer denim, a theme taken up by Gloria Vanderbilt, Calvin Klein and virtually every label-aware designer since. Fiorucci refused to design for women above a size 10, claiming his clothes suited these sizes better. Fiorucci also set out to make fashion fun, creating glittery Plexiglas jewellery and strawberry-scented carrier bags. His cheeky, airbrushed graphics included Vargas-style pin-ups and cherubs wearing sunglasses. He made his name in 1962 with rainbow-coloured Wellington boots. This was Fiorucci's forte: turning function into a fashion exercise without losing a sense of fun.

☛ **Benetton, Fischer, Kennedy, T. Roberts**

167

Elio Fiorucci. b Milan (IT), 1935. **Donna Jordan in 'Buffalo '70' advertising campaign.** Photograph by Oliviero Toscani, 1973.

Fischer Donald and Doris (Gap) Retailers

Born in 1969 during the disillusioned post-hippie era, Gap offered a reactionary-chic approach to the cultural phenomenon of the time. Immaculate, harmonious and unpretentious, it bridged societal fissures, notably the generation gap from which it drew its name. Founded by Donald and Doris Fischer, the company initially sold Levi jeans and records before creating their own label of basic, modest merchandise in an extensive array of colours and sizes. Serving the homogeneous American masses with its brand of clean, white modernism cast in neatly piled, prismatic shades, Gap has become a widely copied retail phenomenon. In recent decades, it has developed the idea of gender integration, selling wardrobe basics with few differences between the men's and women's lines and thus pioneering the 1990s concept of 'androgynous chic'. Not demarcated to collegiate preppiness, the label was recently glamorized by actress Sharon Stone who wore a $15-black turtle-neck to the 1996 Academy Awards.

☛ Benetton, Fiorucci, Strauss

168

Fischer. Donald. b San Francisco, CA (USA). Doris. b San Francisco, CA (USA). (Active 1960s–) (Gap.) **'Khaki' campaign. Spring/summer 1998**. Photograph by Walter Chin.

Fish Michael (Mr Fish)   Designer

Matching shirt, tie and waistcoat exemplify the work of Michael Fish. He was Swinging London's fey fashion boy and image-maker, whose camp, outrageous style defined 'flower power'. In 1965 he dressed the actor Terence Stamp in matching Liberty prints for the cult movie *Modesty Blaise*. One-inch ties were fashionable; Fish made Stamp's four inches wide. The following year he opened his men's boutique, Mr Fish, in London's Clifford Street near the heartland of tailoring, Savile Row. The clothing ranged from outfits cut from voile, sequins and brocade to flower-printed hats and 'mini-shirts' (as famously worn by Mick Jagger for the Rolling Stones' Hyde Park concert). Other clients included Lord Snowdon and the Duke of Bedford. 'The people in my shop don't dress to conform to any given image,' said Fish. 'They dress as they do because they're confident in themselves. They're blowing their minds.'

☛ Gilbey, Liberty, Nutter, Snowdon, Stephen

Michael Fish. b London (UK). (Active 1960s–1970s.) **Chevron striped waistcoat and giant peaked cap.** Photograph by Bill King, *Queen*, 1970.

Flett John   Designer

A wide-shouldered business jacket, sliced at the chest, is worn over a shirt and gauze skirt and the shoes are turned inside-out. John Flett's clothes were known for their complexity of cut: circular seams, abundant drapes and cavalier shapes which made theatrical figures of those who wore them. Widely respected and admired for his work, Flett was a central figure in the 1980s club scene in London, where he partied with other designers of the time including his former boyfriend John Galliano. They both created theatrical fashion which challenged the status quo but which matured into distinctive, directional styles. Flett started his own label in 1988 but closed it down a year later to go freelance. He moved to Europe to work with Claude Montana at Lanvin in Paris and then at Enrico Coveri in Milan, but died of a heart attack, aged twenty-seven, before his promise could be fulfilled.

☛ Boy George, Cox, Galliano, Montana

John Flett. b London (UK), 1964. **d** Florence (IT), 1991. **Tailored jacket and gauze trousers**. Photograph by Jill Furmanowsky, *The Face*, 1985.

170

Foale Marion and Tuffin Sally (Foale & Tuffin)   Designers

Wearing a miniskirt, the uniform of the time, Twiggy swings her fringed sleeves for Cecil Beaton in 1967. 'We made Swinging Sixties clothes,' says Marion Foale of the fashion company she set up in 1961 with Sally Tuffin. The pair were taught at the Royal College of Art by Janey Ironside, who was an influential force in British fashion. After graduating in 1961 and deciding that they didn't want to make 'elderly clothes', the two designers set to work in their bedsits on a range of bright, fun dresses, skirts and tops. They were picked up by a London store which had just established a 'young' department, and David Bailey photographed Foale and Tuffin's clothes for *Vogue* just as London's 'youthquake' movement took hold. They opened a shop on Carnaby Street and became allied to a group of British designers, including Mary Quant, which was dedicated to producing affordable fashion for teenage and twenty-something customers.

☞ Bailey, Charles, Betsey Johnson, Quant, Twiggy

Marion Foale. b London (UK), 1939; **Sally Tuffin. b** London (UK), 1938. (Foale & Tuffin.) **Twiggy wears a white minidress.** Photograph by Cecil Beaton, 1967.

Fonssagrives Lisa   Model

Photographed by her husband Irving Penn, Lisa Fonssagrives wears a 'harlequin' opera outfit from 1950. Once described as 'the highest paid, highest praised, high fashion model in the business', Fonssagrives used to call herself simply 'The clothes hanger'. In the 1930s she moved to Paris from Sweden to train for the ballet. Here she met and married another dancer, Fernand

Fonssagrives, who took some pictures of her to *Vogue*. She was immediately sent to see Horst; his assistant, Scavullo, later recalled, 'She had a marvelous profile and moved like a dream'. Fonssagrives was famous for her grace and poise, learned from her ballet background. She called modelling 'still-dancing' and referred to her poses as 'arrested dance movements'. She became

one of the most sought-after models in Paris in the 1930s and 1940s and in New York in the 1950s.

☞ **Horst, Penn, Scavullo**

Lisa Fonssagrives. b Gothenburg (SWE), 1911. **d** New York (USA), 1992. **Harlequin dress**. Photograph by Irving Penn, 1950.

172

Fontana Zoe, Micol and Giovanna (Sorelle Fontana) Designers

A monkishly simple, white satin dress, with half-sleeves, boat neck and gently belled skirt, is decorated with embroidery formed from cord. It plays on the cotton dresses worn by gamines such as Audrey Hepburn and Brigitte Bardot but the Fontana sisters were always associated with the aristocracy and society figures such as Jackie Kennedy, for whom they provided evening gowns and tailored suits. Roman couture also appealed to movie stars. Their most famous client was the film actress Ava Gardner, whom they dressed for *The Barefoot Contessa* in 1953. One of their most memorable outfits was the impish Cardinal outfit, which featured a black hat and black dress with a white collar set off by a jewelled cross. The fashion house of the Fontana family was founded in Parma, Italy, in 1907. The three Fontana sisters, Zoe, Mical and Giovanna, moved to Rome in the 1930s. There they established their own house in 1943.

☛ Galitzine, W. Klein, Schuberth, Watanabe

Fontana. Zoe. b Parma (IT), 1911. d Rome (IT), 1978; Micol. b Parma (IT), 1913; Giovanna. b Rome (IT), 1915. (Sorelle Fontana.) Dorothy McGowan wears Fontana, Rome. Photograph by William Klein, 1962.

Fonticoli Nazareno and Savini Gaetano (Brioni) Tailors

This 1971 high-waisted, double-breasted dinner suit, together with a car coat, describes the progressive tailoring of Rome's extrovert menswear house, Brioni. From the 1954 futuristic space-age suit to the Maharajah styles, which were popular in mid-1960s London, and the elegant tailoring devised for Pierce Brosnan's role as James Bond, Brioni left no avenue unexplored in men's couture. Its colourful silks and metallic threads, rarely seen since the eighteenth century, heralded the 'male peacock revolution' in the late 1950s. Even though the use of tunics, bolero jackets, lace and macramé clearly contrasts with the Anglo-Saxon tradition, a Brioni blazer epitomized elegance and flaunted wealth in preppie, early 1980s California. Having been responsible for the first-ever men's catwalk show in 1952, Brioni inaugurated *prêt-couture* six years later, resolving flow production methods within a made-to-measure system just as Gianni Versace did in the early 1990s.

☞ **Bikkembergs, Gilbey, Nutter, Versace**

Nazareno Fonticoli. b Penne (IT), 1906. d Penne (IT), 1981; Gaetano Savini. b Rome (IT), 1910. d Rome (IT), 1987. (Brioni.) Evening suit and car coat, 1971.

Forbes Simon

Hairdresser

This stark, androgynous image of hair fashion is the work of Simon Forbes, owner of Antenna, the salon famous for developing hair extensions. The picture represents hair as sculpture and created a cutting-edge, 'anti-beauty' statement which followed on from the punk and new wave proclivity for making hair an intrinsic part of the costume. Forbes invented the Monofibre Extensions technique which allowed greater creativity for stylists to do this. Synthetic hair was grafted onto real hair to give it instant and dramatic length. It was often dyed with vivid colours and wrapped with rags. With this and his electric clippering and precision razoring, Forbes became the directional hairdresser of the early 1980s and his salon became a fashion venue. Extensions, which were inspired by the urban street style of Rastafarians, were sported by musicians such as Boy George and Annie Lennox.

☛ Boy George, Ettedgui, Stewart, Van Noten

175

Simon Forbes. b London (UK), 1950. **Fibre dreadlocks for Antenna**. Photograph by Mike Owen, 1982.

Ford Tom

Designer

Svelte pinstripes for a man and woman, a gilt-trimmed clutch bag, body-conscious shirts and, most telling of all, a golden 'G' shining from her waistband. These are all the elements which go to make up Tom Ford's image for Gucci. As Creative Director he took styling from the 1970s, a time when Gucci represented flashy European style, and created a culture of seasonal icons:

handbags and shoes that shine brightly for six months but become redundant through their high-fashion visibility. It is a brilliant example of fashion which breeds demand for the next collection. Ford's success is rooted in his American blend of sexy, market-aware commercialism married with Italian craftsmanship. As John Fairchild, owner of the fashion trade

paper *Women's Wear Daily*, wrote in 1989, the year before Ford joined Gucci, 'If American designers were working in Europe with the...eagerness to be different for novelty's sake...they could be better style leaders than anyone.'

☛ Gucci, Halston, Testino

Tom Ford. b TX (USA), 1962. **Evening outfits for Gucci. Autumn/winter 1996/7**. Photograph by Mario Testino.

Fortuny Mariano   Designer

The Delphos was constructed from four to five widths of silk that were sewn into a tubular shape and secured at the shoulder, as Lillian Gish demonstrates. The silk cord visible around her neckline added finish to the gown and also served to adjust the fit to the wearer. Fortuny started to design his Delphos around 1907 when a nostalgia for Classical Greece was beginning to be felt in fashion, art and theatre. However, what made Fortuny's Delphos unique was its pleating, a secret process which he patented in 1909. Named after the Ancient Greek city, Fortuny's celebrated garment derived from the *chiton*, a tunic worn by Classical Greek charioteers which focused on the natural shape of the body. Since the Delphos emphasized the female form in movement, it was popular among actresses and dancers such as Isadora Duncan. Trained as an artist, Fortuny advocated a timeless form of dress and continued to create the Delphos right up to his death in 1949.

☛ Chow, Lester, McFadden, Poiret

177

Mariano Fortuny. b Granada (SP), 1871. d Venice (IT), 1949. **Lillian Gish wears a Delphos dress**. c1920.

Fratini Gina

Designer

The range of Byronic details used on this gown distinguishes it as the work of Gina Fratini. Unafraid of romantic themes, she trimmed cuffs with rosebuds and edged frills with lace on her chiffon, lawn and silk gauze dresses. Historical references, such as off-the-shoulder 'Winterhalter' necklines and pin-tucked bodices usually seen on Victorian nightgowns, added to that charm. For this reason her wedding dresses were particularly popular. Fratini's romanticism came to the fore in 1971 when Norman Parkinson delivered samples of her work to Princess Anne in preparation for her twenty-first-birthday portrait. She chose a classic Fratini gown with a lace-trimmed ruff which co-ordinated with her pretty, tawny pink make-up. After her own business closed, Fratini designed lingerie with Ossie Clark as well as collections for Norman Hartnell and for private clients, including the Princess of Wales.

☞ Ashley, Clark, Diana, Emanuel, Hartnell, Parkinson, Worth

Gina Fratini. **b** Kobe (JAP), 1934. **Cream chiffon dress**. Photograph by Norman Parkinson, British *Vogue*, 1973.

French John   Photographer

A formal velvet coat is given a surreal treatment by John French. Originally a graphic designer, he believed, 'You have to compose a picture in the view-finder exactly as if it were an artist's picture on the canvas.' His black-and-white portraits were always perfectly arranged. 'Fill in the space. The space round the subject is as important as the subject itself,' he would say. French's apparently impromptu style contrasted with the posed formality of fashion photography in the early 1950s. One of Britain's first model talent-spotters, he encouraged Barbara Goalen and others to develop their own personalities in front of the lens. The hand intruding at the bottom of the picture doesn't belong to French. He never actually released the camera shutter himself; instead he would direct set, lighting and model, then tell his assistant (at times David Bailey or Terence Donovan), to take the photograph.

☞ Bailey, Bruyère, Goalen, Morton

179

John French. b London (UK), 1907. d Surrey (UK), 1966. **Fur-trimmed velvet coat by Digby Morton**. *Daily Express*, 1955.

Frissell Toni

Photographer

Toni Frissell's fashion photographs of the 1930s through to the 1950s captured the idyllic sense of the rich at play. Here, a model swims in her gown to illustrate its flowing material. With the innate nonchalance of an aristocrat, Frissell documented her world of wealthy playgrounds. Some of her vivid fashion images were of the beach, featuring playful swimwear and recreation dresses, and crisp tennis outfits. Frissell loved the outdoor setting and sunlight's play at least as much as the clothes or model, and let that casual naturalism permeate photographs for *Vogue* and *Harper's Bazaar*. Frissell's images appear effortless, whether of dogs, children, fox-hunting, war or fashion. She mingled the snapshot's vitality and compassion with traditional composition.

Frissell recorded a charmed life in every way, including radiant photographs of the 1953 wedding of John F. Kennedy and Jacqueline Bouvier.

☛ Kennedy, McLaughlin-Gill, Vallhonrat

180

Toni Frissell. b New York (USA), 1907. d New York (USA), 1988. **Weeki Wachee Spring, Florida**. *Harper's Bazaar*, 1947.

Frizon Maud

Shoe designer

Maud Frizon is known for her shoes with cone-shaped heels, a black suede pair of which are the only garments worn in this picture. The role of the man is to communicate the sexual intention of Frizon's work. 'A shoe has to make you look beautiful. You can be wearing a simple dress, but if you have something exquisite on your feet, it becomes a perfect look', said Frizon, who gained this understanding as a model for Courrèges, Nina Ricci, Jean Patou and Christian Dior. She decided to design shoes when she was unable to find styles to go with the designers' clothes on her modelling assignments (in the 1960s models were expected to provide their own shoes). In 1970 she created her first collection of witty, sexy shoes, all hand-cut and finished. There were queues outside her tiny shop on Paris's rue Saint Germain. Brigitte Bardot was a fan, particularly of Frizon's innovative, zipless, high-heeled Russian boots and simple girlie pumps.

☛ Bardot, Courrèges, Kélian, Patou, Ricci

181

Maud Frizon (Maud Frizon De Marco). b Paris (FR), 1941. **Heeled pumps**. Photograph by Dominique Issermann, 1989.

Von Furstenberg Diane   Designer

Diane von Furstenberg wears her own fashion phenomenon for the cover of *Newsweek*. The real appeal of her wrap dress was its wearable shape and endless versatility. Smart yet sexy, it looked as good at the disco as it did at the office. The designer called it, 'Simple one-step dressing. Chic, comfortable and sexy. It won't become dated after one season. It works around the clock, travels across the world and fits all a woman's priorities.' An ex-model, von Furstenberg partied at Studio 54, dated Warren Beatty and was briefly married to Fiat heir Prince Egon von Furstenberg. The glamorous divorcée's wealthy, jet-set lifestyle contributed to the cachet of her dresses (which, like Gloria Vanderbilt's jeans, prominently bore her signature). Originally launched in 1972, the DVF wrap dresses contrasted with the unisex trouser suits of the time and the swing tickets attached made this point with the words, 'Feel like a woman. Wear a dress.'

☛ Bergère, de Ribes, Vanderbilt

Diane von Furstenberg. b Brussels (BEL), 1946. **Wrap dress**. Photograph by Francesco Scavullo, *Newsweek* cover, 1976.

182

Galanos James   Designer

With this perfectly plain, wool dress, Galanos displays the reason why he was dubbed 'America's couturier'. 'I never deviated from what was most important, which was quality,' said Galanos, who actually produced the highest class of ready-to-wear. Nancy Reagan claimed, 'You can take one of Jimmy's dresses and just wear it inside out, they're so beautifully made.' The simplicity of his designs was deceptive and he used couture-standard dressmaking techniques which made his pieces expensive. Galanos worked in Hollywood with John Louis, head of costume design at Columbia, who soon found his fledgling designer's clothes were as popular with the stars as his own. Having later trained with Robert Piguet in Paris, Galanos opened a small shop in Los Angeles in 1951. His designs were discovered by a senior buyer at Neiman Marcus, who claimed she had found 'a young designer from California who would set the world on fire'.

☛ Adolfo, Louis, Piguet, Simpson

James Galanos. b Philadelphia, PA (USA), 1925. **Black wool dress**. Photograph by Kourken Pakchanian, American *Vogue*, 1973.

Galitzine Irene

Designer

William Klein arranges a party of variously uniformed men as accessories for Irene Galitzine's evening trouser outfits. They are variations of her famous wide-leg trouser suits which were dubbed 'palazzo pyjamas' by Diana Vreeland, then at *Harper's Bazaar*. Galitzine's aristocratic Russian family fled the Revolution in 1918. She studied art in Rome, English at Cambridge and French at the Sorbonne. Galitzine finished her broad education as an assistant to the Fontana sisters in Rome. Her own collection, first designed in 1959, suggested an international, yet easy way of dressing. It blurred the distinction between day- and eveningwear by using elements from both, and made a relaxed alternative to formal cocktail dresses. It was a look that immediately appealed to the Italian aristocracy for whom Galitzine's luxury leisurewear was perfectly suited. Her draped sari-style tunics could be worn for day or evening, and were also favoured by Elizabeth Taylor, Greta Garbo and Sophia Loren.

☞ Fontana, Garbo, W. Klein, Pulitzer, Vreeland

Irene Galitzine. b Tiflis (RUS), 1916. **'Palazzo pyjamas'**. Photograph by William Klein, 1962.

Galliano John   Designer

John Galliano has chosen this picture of his 'seamless' dress, worn by Carla Bruni during his autumn/winter 1995/6 ready-to-wear collection shown in Paris. It is representative of his work, even though it looks simpler than most of his designs. In truth, the structure is anything but. The seams and darts have been banished into the outline of the black flowers, the first time such a complicated technique has been used outside haute couture. It leaves an apparently seamless dress, a luxurious, almost mythical item. Throughout his career, Galliano has looked to the work of great couturiers such as Madeleine Vionnet and Paul Poiret to resurrect special techniques which have been neglected, if not forgotten, in the rush of mass-manufacture. In particular, he has become the unequalled master of the bias cut, Vionnet's speciality. A rocky but high-profile career was crowned by his appointment in 1996 as designer, first at Givenchy and then at Christian Dior.

☛ Dior, Givenchy, LaChapelle, Poiret, Vallhonrat

John Galliano. b Gibraltar (SP), 1960. **'Seamless dress'**. Pink and black silk crepe. Photograph by Chris Moore. 1995.

Garbo Greta

Icon

Called the 'greatest star of all', Greta Garbo wears a masculine jacket, cut with sexual ambiguity, in a portrait by Cecil Beaton Beaton wrote of his subject, 'Perhaps no other person has had such an influence on the appearance of a whole generation...the secret of her appeal seems to lie in an elusive and haunting sensitivity...Garbo has created a style in fashion which is concerned with her individual self.' Garbo arrived in Hollywood aged nineteen in the entourage of Mauritz Stilla from Sweden. Signed up by Metro-Goldwyn-Mayer, she went on to star in *Queen Christina*, *Camille* and *Anna Karenina*, dressed by Adrian. Famed as a recluse, she said in 1932, 'I am awkward, shy, afraid, nervous and self-concious about my English. That is why I built a wall of repression about myself and lived behind it.' The director George Cukor said that she reserved 'her real sensuousness for the camera'.

☛ Adrian, Beaton, Galitzine, Sui

Greta Garbo. **b** Stockholm (SWE), 1905. **d** New York (USA), 1990. **Greta Garbo**. Photograph by Cecil Beaton, 1946.

Garren

Hairdresser

From the strawberry-red, Sophia Loren bouffant to the boyish, platinum, Andy Warhol bob, Garren has been the architect behind all of supermodel Linda Evangelista's publicized, chameleon-like hairstyle changes. His directional approach has been witnessed not only in the high-glam look he achieved in collaboration with photographer Steven Meisel in the late 1980s, but also in the spiky 'chicken do' (his trademark punk-inspired style seen earlier that decade), which he modified in the softer, more feminine gamine cut seen in the wake of the waif look. His extreme work in editorial and on the catwalk for Marc Jacobs and Anna Sui is tempered in the salon where he gives reality a chance. As he told American *Vogue*, 'As soon as a client comes in...I'm checking out the way she moves, her shoes, her handbag, body language. That tells me what her needs are.'

☞ Evangelista, Jacobs, Meisel, Sui, Warhol

Garren. (Active 1970s–.) **Garren with Linda Evangelista.** Photograph by Peter Lindbergh, *Harper's Bazaar*, 1997.

Gattinoni Fernanda   Designer

The serene allure of Gattinoni's brilliant green, brocade evening coat is captured by Clifford Coffin in a photograph for American *Vogue* in 1947. Hinting at Imperial Chinese influences, its Zen-like dignity anticipates the refined ethnicity of Romeo Gigli. Gattinoni trained at the Rome fashion house Ventura, before opening her own atelier. Here she attracted the likes of Audrey Hepburn, Ingrid Bergman and Anna Magnani – film-star clients renowned for their highly photogenic mix of thoroughbred grace and soft femininity. In the 1950s, with the great success of films such as *Roman Holiday*, Rome became synonymous with the glamour of cinema and Gattinoni came to epitomize cultured European sophistication and romance. She also offered indulgent escapism – twenty-five full-time embroiderers were employed to decorate wedding dresses – for a clientele weary of postwar realities.

☛ Coffin, Gigli, Molyneux

188

Fernanda Gattinoni. b Cocquio (IT), 1909. **Brocade evening coat.** Photograph by Clifford Coffin, American *Vogue*, 1947.

Gaultier Jean Paul   Designer

A man and woman mirror one another in near-identical outfits from Jean Paul Gaultier's 1994 women's collection, 'The Big Journey'. That he is wearing her clothes comes as little surprise, since Gaultier has been dressing men in skirts since 1985. On this occasion, their rich, quilted satin coats, long hems and Geisha-style platforms suggest a trip through the Far East. Since he started his label in 1978, Gaultier has been influenced by global costume, both old and new, such as that worn by London's punks. Sexual ambiguity has also been an enduring theme. While his men have worn skirts and even tutus, pipe-smoking women have trodden his catwalk in pinstriped business suits. His menswear was influenced by the wave of gay men coming out in the 1970s, using camp clichés that include macho bodybuilders and butch sailors. Like these outfits, Gaultier's whole style is a humorous, eclectic challenge to the French establishment.

☞ Alexandre, Esterel, Madonna, Margiela, Pita, Van Beirendonck

Jean Paul Gaultier. b Arcueil (FR), 1952. **'The Big Journey' collection. Autumn/winter 1994/5**. Photograph by Jean-Marie Périer, French *Elle*, 1994.

Gernreich Rudi   Designer

The topless bathing suit, worn here by Peggy Moffit, Rudi Gernreich's favourite model, was developed to meet the trend for topless bathing. It was also intended to be something of a feminist political statement, as was his no-bra bra of 1964, which was the first to allow the natural shape of a woman's breasts. Gernreich also invented the high-cut, buttock-baring, thong bathing suit. His radical body-based clothes of the 1960s and 1970s reflected the social revolution of women's liberation and his early designs provided unprecedented freedom of movement. In the 1950s he produced knitted swimwear without the usual boning and underpinning and he developed the concept into knitted tube dresses. It was Gernreich's early influences that helped to develop our modern relationship between stretch and comfort; after moving to America, Rudi joined several modern dance companies and became fascinated by the leotards and tights of the dancers.

☞ Coffin, Heim, Rabanne, Sassoon

190

Rudi Gernreich. b Vienna (AUS), 1922. **d** Los Angeles, CA (USA), 1985. **Peggy Moffit wears a topless swimsuit, 1964.** Photograph by William Claxton.

Gibb Bill

Designer

'Miles of untouched forest hand-printed onto silk...the Bill Gibb environment, rich fabrics with richer decorations – marbled, hand-painted, feathered, piped...flower-faced beauty'. As it is, the words that accompanied this editorial picture left out a few of the techniques used on Gibb's lavish, layered and fantastical dress. He claimed to have an aversion to 'the tailored thing' and his grand vision was an alternative to the lean trouser suits of the 1970s. Gibb came from a farming family, but was encouraged by his grandmother, a painter, to enjoy his hobby of copying pictures of historical costume, especially that of the Renaissance era. This influence has affected his most spectacular work. He often incorporated knitwear into his collection by collaborating with Missoni and knitting specialist Kaffe Fassett, saying, 'What women want to wear in the daytime is beautiful knits'.

☞ Birtwell, Mesejeán, Missoni, Porter

Bill Gibb. b Fraserburgh (UK), 1943. **d** London (UK), 1988. **'Forest' dress**. Photograph by Penati, British *Vogue*, 1972.

Gibson Charles Dana

Illustrator

Before television and movies, Gibson identified an essential character as deftly and as unforgettably as any novelist. His 'Gibson Girl' was the personification of America's modern woman. Probably seen wearing the fashionable shirtwaist (a masculine-styled blouse of the early twentieth century), her S-curve figure and loosely constructed mound of hair gave shape to the new woman. Her face varied slightly, but she was the icon of twentieth-century fashion embodied in an active life in such Gibson books on the middle and upper-middle classes as *The Education of Mr Pipp* (1899), *The Americans* (1900) and *The Social Ladder* (1902). Gibson had studied at the Art Students' League in New York and worked for late nineteenth-century magazines that required illustrations for news and stories, but ultimately he invented his own story of the fashionable, independent woman of the twentieth century.

☛ Drecoll, Paquin, Redfern

192

Charles Dana Gibson. b Roxbury, MA (USA), 1867. d (USA), 1944. Gibson Girls on the beach, 1901.

Gigli Romeo

Designer

Benedetta Barzini is photographed enjoying Romeo Gigli's extravagant coat. Gold flowers and embroidered leaves collect around the shawl collar, cuffs and hem, with a velvet scarf finishing with a golden tassel. Gigli's childhood was saturated in art history and antiquarian books, over which he pored. It gave him an appreciation of beauty, history and travel which underlies his work – he plays with clothes from history and non-European cultures. The Gigli look was, and still is, one of the most distinctive in fashion. In the 1980s, Gigli's vision had a grandeur only equalled by that of Christian Lacroix. Silk suits, with either stovepipe trousers or long, narrow skirts, were worn with shirt collars that framed the wearer's face (as here) and placed under velvet coats that enveloped the figure in luxury. The impression was similar to that created by Poiret: a richly decorated, giant bloom growing from a narrow stalk.

☞ **Gattinoni, Iribe, Lacroix, Meisel, Poiret, Roversi, Vallhonrat**

193

Romeo Gigli. b Faenza (IT), 1949. **Benedetta Barzini wears an embroidered coat.** Photograph by Steven Meisel, French *Vogue*, 1989.

Gilbey Tom   Designer

This is classic Tom Gilbey. With his trademark simplicity and an almost militaristic neatness, Gilbey was an important force in menswear in the 1960s. Here, he uses both traditionally masculine details and softer, experimental methods, such as sleeves gathered into cuffs. Despite their feminized aspects, these outfits are strong, angular examples of the new wave of British tailoring. Gilbey began designing for John Michael and in 1968 opened his own shop, in London's Sackville Street. Gilbey is one of fashion's visionaries. In 1982 he launched a waistcoat collection which suited the aspirational yuppie in search of nostalgic accessories. Around the same time, and pre-dating the transatlantic sportswear boom by fifteen years, he said, 'I'm influenced by the American campus look, it's so classic and immaculate. Jeans and a T-shirt, big bumper shoes, Bermuda shorts...I hate fuss. I love things to be clean, strong and aggressive.'

☞ Fish, Fonticoli, Nutter, Stephen

194

Tom Gilbey. b London (UK), 1938. **Winter coats.** 1971.

Givenchy Hubert de   Designer

Snap! Audrey Hepburn, playing a model, is captured in a still from the 1957 film, *Funny Face*. Her dress, a floral cotton gown, is by the man who became a lifelong friend and collaborator. 'It was as though I was born to wear his clothes', said Hepburn of Hubert de Givenchy. When she was first sent to his house, Givenchy was expecting the other 'Miss Hepburn' – Katharine.

His disappointment gave way to adoration. He had already worked at Lelong, Piguet, Fath and Schiaparelli, before opening his couture house at the age of twenty-five. Encouraged by his friend Balenciaga, he specialized in clothes for the new era of air travel and grand eveningwear. In 1956 Givenchy banned the press from his shows, saying, 'A fashion house is a laboratory

which must conserve its mystery'. He retired from fashion in 1995, making way for two of the most publicity-aware designers – John Galliano and then Alexander McQueen – to design under his name.

☛ **Galliano, Horvat, Lelong, McQueen, Pipart, Tiffany, Venet**

Hubert de Givenchy. b Beauvais (FR), 1927. **Audrey Hepburn.** Still from *Funny Face.* 1957.

Goalen Barbara   Model

The archetypal 1950s aloof and haughty mannequin, the well-bred Goalen was chauffeur-driven to assignments in a Rolls-Royce. Careful to protect her image, she said, 'I always did high fashion and I never touched anything that wasn't high quality.' The photographer Henry Clarke said, 'You put the dress on Barbara and she made it sing.' At one time she was almost exclusively photographed by John French and was Coffin's favourite model. She was the first British model to be sent to the Paris shows by British *Vogue*. At the height of her fame, she toured Australia and was mobbed in the North of England. Like many models in the 1950s, she married well – to Lloyd's underwriter Nigel Campbell. Her hips were too slender for sample sizes, so she rarely did catwalk modelling. She only worked for five years, before retiring while still very much in demand.

☛ Clarke, Coffin, French

Barbara Goalen. b (UK). (Active 1950s.) **Strapless evening dress.** Photograph by John French, 1954.

196

Godley Georgina

Designer

An otherwise utterly plain, jersey T-shirt dress springs away from the average with the introduction of organza into the hem and neck. An experimental purist, Georgina Godley uses sculpture to introduce avant-garde shape into her work. 'We are dealing with a woman who is an individual now,' she told *Vogue*. 'Fashion is so retrograde, putting people down. It's not a designer's personality you're buying, it's yours. I believe in a reappraisal of sexual roles.' Her contemporary work is in contrast to the historicism explored during her partnership with Scott Crolla. Their cult shop, Crolla (opened in 1981), stocked romantic men's clothes in velvet and brocade which matched the New Romantic mood. After parting from him in 1985, Godley developed her own line, favouring a one-to-one relationship with the client, in which her creativity could be displayed by women who relish her individual experiments.

☞ Audibet, Bruce, Crolla

197

Georgina Godley. b London (UK), 1955. **Cotton jersey body-and-soul dress**. Photograph by Alex Chatelain, British *Vogue*, 1986.

Grès Madame   Designer

The white, silk jersey fabric of this evening gown has been moulded onto the figure as if it had the properties of the piece of sculpture standing next to the model. Even the play of light and shade in its deep pleats echoes the sculpture. Silk jersey is a material that lends itself to pleating in precise, fluid folds and it was a mainstay in the classicism of Madame Alix Grès, one of the great couture artists. *Harper's Bazaar* proclaimed in 1936 that, 'Alix stands for the body rampant, for the rounded, feminine sculptural form beneath the dress' She had been trained as a sculptress and it was her feeling for Classical Greek sculpture that enabled her to capture its timeless elegance in her evening gowns. Hers was an individualistic, uncompromising style where the sculptural cut of her gowns had the liquid effect of the 'wet' drapery of Classical Greek sculpture that turned fashionable women into living statues.

☞ Audibet, Cassini, Lanvin, Pertegaz, Toledo, Valentina

Madame Alix Grès (Germaine Krebs). b Paris (FR), 1903. **d** (FR), 1993. **Grecian column dress**. Photograph by Eugène Rubin, *Femina*, 1937.

198

Griffe Jacques   Designer

In a picture from an American *Vogue* sitting in 1952, the model's seated pose makes a display of Jacques Griffe's diaphanous pin-tucks. The entire evening dress grows from a flamboyant pink tulle bow which uses the fabric of both bodice and skirt. It finishes ten inches from the floor – a younger look for ball gowns at the time and known as the ballet length. Griffe trained with Vionnet where he learned the techniques of draping and cutting fabrics, such as this luscious chiffon, from the Lyons textile firm Bianchini-Férier, noted for its fluid materials in brilliant colours. After the Second World War, Griffe worked for Molyneux before opening his own maison de couture in 1946. Like Vionnet, he worked directly with the material, modelling it on a wooden dummy given by her as a present to encourage him. Griffe's tailoring work was distinguished by the use of seams and darts as decorative details and by his invention of the boxy jacket.

☞ **McLaughlin-Gill, Molyneux, Vionnet**

Jacques Griffe. b Carcassonne (FR), 1917. **Tulle dress.** Photograph by Frances McLaughlin-Gill, American *Vogue*, 1952.

Gruau René   Illustrator

In this suggestive advertisement for Christian Dior, the sinuous lines of a woman's hand are placed on a panther's paw against an infinite background, reflecting a spirit of graceful worldliness and glamour. Noted for his strong silhouettes and tonalities of colour, Gruau's images became prestigious icons of elegance. He was an outstanding graphic artist of the period after the Second World War, when his swift, expressive line was chosen by Dior's couture and perfume company to illustrate their perfume advertisements. Together with Bouché, Gruau also brilliantly illustrated haute couture of the era in French *Vogue*. Influenced by the posters of Toulouse-Lautrec, he used strong outlines – a technique that perfectly accentuates fashion's shape and form.

He was one of the last grand magazine illustrators before the creative possibilities of fashion photography made it equal to the fantasy of illustration.

☛ Biagiotti, Bouché, Dior

200

René Gruau. b Rimini (IT), 1908. **Panther Paw**. Advertisement for *Miss Dior* perfume. 1949.

Gucci Guccio

Accessory designer

On a terrace in Cannes, Romy Schneider caresses the classic Gucci loafers worn by Alain Delon. The snaffle loafer has been an icon of wealth and European style since it was designed in 1932 by the company's patriarch, Guccio Gucci. After rebelling against joining his family's ailing straw hat-making business, Gucci ran away to London. He found a job as maître d'hôtel at the Savoy where he looked after the wealthy guests, paying particular attention to their baggage. He returned to Florence and opened a small shop selling saddlery, later expanding into leather bags and shoes which were decorated with a horse's snaffle. In 1933 Aldo, his son, joined the business and designed the iconic Gucci logo using the interlocking double Gs of his father's initials.

Intermittent periods of stunning success were counterpointed with family squabbles and even murder, marring the extraordinary Gucci story. The company enjoyed a renaissance in the 1990s under the design directorship of Tom Ford.

☞ Ferragamo, Ford, Hermès

Guccio Gucci. b Florence (IT), 1881. d Milan (IT), 1953. **Alain Delon wears Gucci loafers**. c1959.

Halston

Designer

Halston is surrounded by eleven models for a 1972 *Vogue* sitting. Their fluid, silk jersey dresses and svelte clothes made from Ultrasuede are pure Halston: utterly simple and an eternal antidote to fussy dressing. These are the hallmarks of classic American design, and Halston was recognized as a master of the art. His popularity in the 1970s made him a social figure, most famously among the set that frequented Manhattan's Studio 54 club. Bianca Jagger and Liza Minnelli were friends and clients, and both were Concorde-class models for his draped jersey dresses and lean trouser suits. Halston designed for his friends, saying in 1971, 'Fashion starts with fashionable people... No designer has ever made fashion alone. People make fashion.' Although he died in 1990, Halston's influence has continued to grow. Tom Ford, designer at Gucci, acknowledged his Studio 54 look as crucial to uncluttered fashion in the 1990s.

☛ Bandy, Burrows, Daché, Ford, Maxwell, Peretti, Warhol

202

Halston (Roy Halston Frowick). b Des Moines, IA (USA), 1932. d San Francisco, CA (USA), 1990. **Halston with models, 1972**. Photograph by Duane Michals, American *Vogue*.

Hamnett Katharine   Designer

'At last! An original', was Prime Minister Margaret Thatcher's response to Katharine Hamnett's anti-missile message when the two met at a British government reception in 1984. Such an easily copied idea (deliberately so, claimed Hamnett, who wanted her messages to be read by as many people as possible) meant that her slogan T-shirts became a symbol of the 1980s. Hamnett has since fostered the connection between cloth and politics, most notably by using and helping with the development of organic cotton. Practicality and youth have always been important to the label – parachute silk, cotton jersey and denim are some of the relaxed and functional fabrics that have been trademarks for Hamnett over the years. She has said of her clothes, 'There is a real utility in them...they're functional, they're easy to look after and they last a long time.'

☞ Stiebel, Teller, von Unwerth

203

Katharine Hamnett. b Gravesend (UK), 1948. Katharine Hamnett with Margaret Thatcher, 10 Downing Street. 1984.

Hartnell Norman

Designer

Princess Margaret's picturesque white evening gown, with its scooped neckline, tight bodice and full skirt, recalls the gowns Charles Frederick Worth made for the Empress Eugénie and which were immortalized in the portraits of her painted by Winterhalter. This distinctively British romantic revival interpretation was the creation of the royal couturier, Norman

Hartnell. Its origins can be traced back to the royal visit to Paris in 1938, when King George VI specifically requested Hartnell to design a wardrobe for his queen based on the royal portraits painted by Winterhalter in the 1860s that hung in Buckingham Palace. Hartnell exquisitely used white silk, satin, chiffon and tulle for evening gowns and decorated them sumptuously with

embroidered and beaded motifs. This style of evening dress gained an international reputation as a British fashion classic. It remained a constant in the royal wardrobe throughout the postwar period.

☛ Bohan, Rayne, Sumurun, Worth

204

Norman Hartnell. b London (UK), 1901. d Windsor (UK), 1979. **HRH Princess Margaret wears sequined butterfly gown for her nineteenth birthday**. Photograph by Cecil Beaton, 1949.

Head Edith

Designer

Perhaps the most honoured of Hollywood's costume designers, Edith Head was also the most versatile. She excelled at recognizing the trends in contemporary fashion and in creating movie costumes realistic for their age, as in Elizabeth Taylor's wardrobe, inspired by Christian Dior and Jacques Fath, for *Elephant Walk* (1954). In her years at Paramount Pictures,

Head designed for Mae West, created the sarong for Dorothy Lamour and made Barbara Stanwyck *The Lady Eve* (1941), but her real gift was an 'eye' – a keen sense for what was happening in contemporary fashion. She wrangled with fashion designers (most notably, Hubert de Givenchy) over design credits, and she gave her films a timely sense of fashion, unlike the grand

picturesque of Hollywood Golden Age fashions, and anticipating 1980s and 1990s films where fashion is chosen from the marketplace.

☞ Fath, Givenchy, Irene, Louis, Travilla

Edith Head. b Los Angeles, CA (USA), 1907. **d** Hollywood, CA (USA), 1981. **Elizabeth Taylor**. Still from *Elephant Walk*. 1954.

Hechter Daniel   Designer

Daniel Hechter's leaping tracksuit represents the age of performance fashion. His reality-check womenswear emerged in the 1960s, with function dominating style. Hechter is realistic about his role: 'Fashion is not art. It can be artistic, but it is not art. I'm really a stylist. I respect designers who create fashion, like Chanel, Poiret. Or Levi's...[but] if you dress a billion people, that's phenomenal.' The first prêt-à-porter womenswear collection, co-designed with friend Armand Orustein, was launched in 1963. Perfectly pitched for the 'youthquake' market, he persuaded Twiggy to model clothes that were targeted at young women who aspired to a designer lifestyle. He integrated pop culture into his scheme, creating accessible clothes which were designed to be worn out and then replaced. His maxi coats, trouser suits and divided skirts for women were counterpointed with menswear that mixed separates in the 1970s.

☛ Dassler, Kamali, P. Knight, Strauss, Twiggy

Daniel Hechter. b Paris (FR), 1938. **Tracksuit**. Photograph by Jim Greenberg, *L'Officiel*, 1980.

Heim Jacques   Designer

Heim will be forever known as the couturier who promoted the bikini. He featured it in his 1946 collection under the name 'atome'. When, in the same year, atomic bomb tests were conducted by the United States at Bikini Atoll, the swimsuit's name was changed to bikini. This bathing suit shot to fame when Brigitte Bardot was photographed in 1956 wearing one made of

gingham adorned with frills. Heim entered the world of fashion through his parents' fur business, founded in 1898. He also collaborated with Sonia Delaunay, designing dresses, coats and sportswear which were exhibited at the Art Deco exhibition in Paris in 1925. He established his own fashion house in the 1930s, his forte being beachwear and sportswear. Between 1946 and

1966 he opened a series of boutiques which specialized in these garments. Heim was president of the Chambre Syndicale de la Couture Parisienne from 1958 to 1962.

☛ Bardot, Coddington, Delaunay, Gernreich, Jantzen

Jacques Heim. b Paris (FR), 1899. d Paris (FR), 1967. **Slip-over top and cotton bikini**. 1950.

Hemingway Wayne (Red or Dead)   Designer

Loud and opinionated, just like this line-up of his team's work, Wayne Hemingway doesn't care about high fashion. Beyond showing his collections at the normal times, Hemingway's company, Red or Dead, rejoices in its desire to please nobody but its young, clubby customers. It started life in 1982 as a second-hand clothing and shoe stall at London's Camden Market. In 1995 it demanded press reaction when models wielding bloody knives and knitting needles prowled along the catwalk in a pastiche of Alfred Hitchcock's thrillers. Hemingway's fashion philosophy is based around the desire to reinterpret youth culture, using socio-political sloganeering as a hook. 'I design for a free-thinking British youth culture,' he has said. In other words, he gives them what they want, be it Bollywood, Punk, Mod, Britpop, Grandad or 1980s trash.

☛ Hamnett, Leroy, Rotten

208

Wayne Hemingway. b Morecambe (UK), 1961. (Red or Dead.) **Catwalk montage, 1989–96**. Photographs by Chris Moore and Suresh Karadia.

Hendrix Jimi   Icon

Hendrix was as individualistic in his stage wardrobe as he was in his stage act. His clothes, old mixed with new, clothes of war and the tie-dye fabrics of war protesters, were as loud and chaotic as his electric guitar playing. His own sense of style was manifest at eight years old when he was ordered out of a Baptist church for being dressed too extravagantly. Expelled from school at fifteen, he drifted into juvenile delinquency, stealing flashy clothes from stores. He wore his hair in a wild, unkempt version of the Afro hairstyle adopted by the 'Black Pride' movement of the late 1960s. His clothes were often an eclectic mix of almost fop-like finery and hippie ethnicity. He often wore his trademark black felt fedora. His psychedelic clothing – multicoloured patchwork shirts, flower-print jackets and swirly scarves – was reminiscent of the drug-induced hallucinations that inspired the lyrics of his songs.

☞ Bouquin, Ozbek, Presley

209

Jimi Hendrix. b Seattle, WA (USA), 1942. d London (UK), 1970. **Jimi Hendrix**. Photograph by Gered Mankowitz, 1967.

Hermès Thierry

Accessory designer

Princess Grace of Monaco attends to a young Caroline. In her other hand she carries a handbag big enough for a mother, yet courtly enough for any member of royalty. On the occasion of her marriage to Prince Rainier, the Hermès bag Grace Kelly had carried throughout their engagement was renamed in her honour. The 'Kelly bag' has been fashionable ever since and involves a three-month waiting list. Modelled on a 'sac haut à courroie' or 'high-handle', which was used as a carrying case for saddles, the flap is fastened with horizontal straps and a twisting clasp. Hermès, originally a saddlery company, was founded in 1837 by Thierry Hermès. In 1920 his grandson Emile brought modern design and luxurious clothes to the label, but Hermès continues to prosper from its image as a high-quality saddler, using snaffles and stirrups as themes for its famous printed silk scarves. In 1997, the company updated its reputation by appointing avant-garde Belgian designer Martin Margiela as its designer.

☛ Banton, Bergère, Gucci, Lacroix, Loewe, Margiela

Thierry Hermès. b Crefeld (GER), 1837. d Paris (FR), 1878. **Princess Grace with 'Kelly bag' and her daughter, Caroline. Monaco, 1958.**

210

Hilfiger Tommy   Designer

'Check it out...check out Tommy...Tommy Hilfiger...' raps Treach as he models for a Hilfiger catwalk show in 1997. Hilfiger's name dominates his streetwise sportswear and turns his customers into advertisements. The distinctive red, white and blue logo came about after he noticed that counterfeiters were taking the discreet insignia of his competitors and enlarging them on T-shirts and caps. It was effortless advertising. Thus Hilfiger sold the idea back to those who invented and bought it. He started producing his logo-aware designs and was soon being name-checked in hip-hop songs – and worn by those who listen to them. In the 1970s Hilfiger's New York shop, People's Place, became a celebrity draw. In the 1980s his clothing assumed a preppie style similar in feel to that of Ralph Lauren's, but it was his mastery of the street market which made an impact on fashion.

☛ Brooks, Dassler, Lauren, Moss

211

Tommy Hilfiger. b Elmira, NY (USA), 1952. **Rapper Treach and Kate Moss. Spring/summer 1997.** Photograph by Chris Moore.

Hirata Akio   Milliner

With its delicate sculptural form and body-encompassing loops circling the shoulders, this hat challenges our preconceived ideas about millinery work. Akio Hirata, Japan's most influential milliner, has collaborated with many avant-garde Japanese designers including Yohji Yamamoto, Comme des Garçons and Hanae Mori. His passion for European fashion magazines encouraged him to tour France in 1962. There he met French milliner, Jean Barthet, with whom he trained for three years at his Paris salon and perfected his craft. He returned to Japan and founded his own house, Haute Mode Hirata, in 1965. Every design in his boutique, Salon Coco in Hiroo, was handmade. He worked on commissions for Pierre Balmain and Nina Ricci and designed for the wives of Japanese heads of state, who brought his work to the attention of a wider international audience during state visits abroad.

☛ Barthet, Kawakubo, Mori, Ricci, Sieff, Y. Yamamoto

212

Akio Hirata. b Nagano Prefecture (JAP), 1925. **Black cord hat**. Photograph by Jeanloup Sieff, 1992.

Hiro

Photographer

In a stunning removal of fashion from its accepted context, Harry Winston's diamond and ruby necklace is placed on a cloven hoof. Attention is centred on the contrast between bestial nature and the high glamour of Winston's work – usually associated with Hollywood – with all its amusing connotations. Hiro has applied the same picturesque humour to other subjects, including a silver bangle by New York society's favourite fashion jeweller, Elsa Peretti, which he placed on a bleached bone. Taken for the December 1963 issue of *Harper's Bazaar*, this image exemplifies both the technical and artistic brilliance of the photographer known as Hiro. Born in Shanghai to Japanese parents, he moved to New York in 1954, working initially with Richard Avedon and, from 1956, becoming a member of Alexey Brodovitch's Design Laboratory. In 1958 he became a staff photographer at *Harper's Bazaar*, where he defined the decade through his graphic still-life compositions.

☞ Brodovitch, Peretti, Winston

213

Hiro (Hiro Wakabayashi). b Shanghai (CHN), 1930. **Harry Winston necklace**. New York, 1963.

Hishinuma Yoshiki   Textile designer

Using a mixed technique known as *shibori*, Yoshiki Hishinuma creates a negative silhouette on polyester. Japanese textile designers are amongst the most exciting pioneers in fashion's most scientific field, pushing the practical and aesthetic boundaries of material. Hishinuma's training at Issey Miyake's Design Studio gave him a solid background in experimental fabric technology. Belonging to the Japanese school of avant-garde fashion, Hishinuma was able to launch his own Tokyo-based label in 1984, but not before his freelance work earned him the New Designer's Prize at Tokyo's Mainichi Fashion Grand Prix. Today he has his own textile studio, specializing in isolated, neck-to-ankle fabric effects. 1998 looks include otherworldly chiffon, wrapped about the body like crumpled white tissue paper, and clipped feathers knitted tightly into a sweater.

☛ Arai, Milner, Miyake

Yoshiki Hishinuma. b Sendai (JAP), 1958. **'Shibori' technique, polyester fabric. Spring/summer 1995.** Photograph by Noboru Iwahashi.

Hope Emma   Shoe designer

Emma Hope's shoes are romantic and individual in style, as this brocade buckled slipper shows to perfection. She established her company in 1985 after graduating from Cordwainer's College in London's East End, and began by selling a small range of brocade mules which were worn with Scott Crolla's ornate, antiquarian clothes. Hope's desire is to evoke 'the deliciousness of the first pair of shoes you really wanted', and make them a joy both to wear and behold. She makes bespoke and ready-to-wear shoes, and brides, in particular, buy her amazingly delicate slippers, which are covered in seed pearls and beads or decorated with fine embroidery. Hope creates nostalgic shoes, which recall the work of nineteenth-century cobblers such as Pinet. Those made from silk are especially precious, with memories of a time when a lady's foot would rarely meet the pavement.

☛ Choo, Cox, Crolla, Pinet, Yantorny

215

Emma Hope. b Portsmouth (UK), 1962. **Shoe with buckle. Autumn/winter 1994/5**. Photograph by John Swannell, *Woman's Journal*, 1994.

Horst Horst P.

Photographer

Despite an illustrious career spanning over sixty-five years, photographer Horst P. Horst will forever be linked with his portraiture of the inter-war years. He began by working with George Hoyningen-Huene at *Vogue* in 1932 and, within a few years, had developed an unmistakable fashion style that fused elements of Greek sculpture with the decadent elegance of the time. His early black-and-white images mixed subtle contrast with mood and sensitivity, achieved with carefully positioned lighting that could take three days to perfect. 'I like taking photographs, because I like life,' he once said. Picasso, Dietrich, Dalí, Cocteau, Gertrude Stein and the Duchess of Windsor were his friends and the subjects of his portraiture. His work has remained timeless and iconographic – as proved by the singer Madonna who copied his 1939 picture, *Mainbocher's Pink Satin Corset*, for her 'Vogue' video in 1989.

☛ Cocteau, Coward, Dalí, Fonssagrives, Parker, Piguet, Vreeland

Horst P. Horst. b Weissenfels (GER), 1906. **Helen Bennett wears a cape dress by Jean Patou.** French *Vogue*, 1936.

Horvat Frank

Photographer

Peering out from between an organic swathe of organza and a milliner's cascade of petals, the model seems to float on a background of racegoers. Male and female, black and white, this 1958 shot for *Jardin des Modes* is an exercise in contrast. Considering its composition, it is perhaps unsurprising that Frank Horvat went on to make his name outside fashion with his photographs of trees. His fashion work in 1960, however, was seminal for fashion photography, using natural make-up and pastoral backdrops rather than the prevailing mood of urban formality. Originally a photojournalist, Horvat's first colour photograph appeared on the cover of the Italian magazine *Epoca* in 1951. His wide-ranging experience benefited his fashion work, adding a broad quality to technically adept images that catch the eye.

☞ Bailey, Givenchy, Milner, Stiebel

217

Frank Horvat. b Abbazia (IT), 1928. **Givenchy hat, Paris.** *Jardin des Modes.* 1958.

Howell Margaret   Designer

In this gentle fashion image, Margaret Howell's tailored navy shorts resemble those worn in the 1930s. Her clothes blend memories of England with the pleasure of wearing worn-in country clothes. The look was revolutionary when she began in the early 1970s, inspired by nostalgic icons of British style, such as brogues, gymslips, sturdy tweed skirts and her father's gardening mac hanging on the back of a door. Howell's menswear and womenswear collections were launched in 1972, with an emphasis on tailoring. Howell has been so copied, it almost obscures her contribution but her linen duster coats, shirt dresses, floor-sweeping raincoats and tweed suits for women have an enduring appeal. 'When I started out, I was only thinking about what I wanted,' she told *Vogue*. 'I liked quality and comfort...I was probably responsible for the move towards using men's tailoring tweeds for women's clothes.'

☞ Jackson, Jaeger, de Prémonville

218

Margaret Howell. b Tadworth (UK), 1946. **Cotton sweater and crepe shorts. Spring/summer 1992.** Photograph by Koto Bolofo.

Hoyningen-Huene George   Photographer

Hoyningen-Huene's fashion photographs were inspired by Classical Greek sculpture. He posed his models with props so that they resembled the figures in a frieze. His technique of back- and cross-lighting, to achieve line and volume and to give the models, the clothes and the settings texture and sheen, is unique. During the Russian Revolution, Hoyningen-Huene fled to England and went on to Paris in 1921. He studied painting under André Lhote and began to draw fashion. After collaborating with Man Ray, he became chief photographer for French *Vogue* in 1926, moving on to New York and American *Vogue*. Hoyningen-Huene worked at *Harper's Bazaar* in New York from 1935 to 1945. He then moved to Los Angeles where he taught photography at the Art Center School and worked on sets and costumes for Hollywood movies.

☞ Agnès, Blumenfeld, Man Ray, Mainbocher, Morehouse

George Hoyningen-Huene. b St Petersburg (RUS), 1900. **d** Los Angeles, CA (USA), 1968. **Gold reefer jacket by Mainbocher, gloves by Hattie Carnegie.** *Harper's Bazaar*, 1939.

Hulanicki Barbara (Biba) Designer

A woman and child in identical maxi, panne velvet dresses are the essence of what became known as the Biba Look. Barbara Hulanicki, a fashion illustrator, had dreamed of bringing decadence to the masses. She began with a small shop in 1963 named after her sister, Biba. It was a treasury of exotic accessories and fabrics and, despite its extreme cheapness which made it accessible to students and teenagers, dressed stars including Twiggy and actress Julie Christie. Biba was, in the words of Ossie Clarke. 'Disposable glamour shrouded in purply, mulberry shades...' Hulanicki's style lived somewhere between Art Deco and Art Nouveau; her clothes resembled those worn by Dietrich – slim, often cut from satin and velvet and highlighted with lean lurex knitwear. In 1973 Biba moved into a department store building. This 'nickelodeon land of Art Deco with potted palms and mirrored hall' only lasted until 1975, but Hulanicki's ideal is still admired today.

☛ Bouquin, Clark, Kamali, Moon, Twiggy

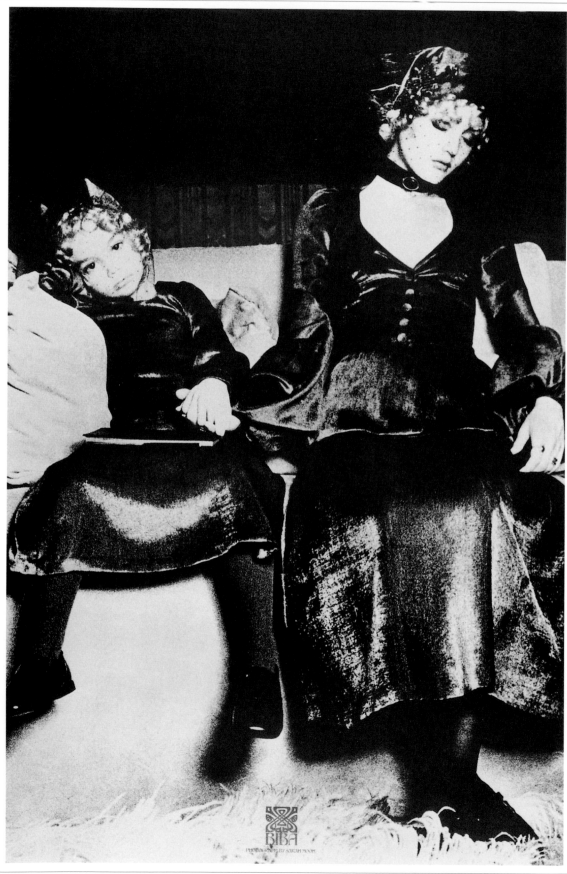

Barbara Hulanicki. b Warsaw (POL), 1936. (Biba.) **Mother and daughter**. Photograph by Sarah Moon, 1969.

Hutton Lauren   Model

Lauren Hutton, with her rare beauty and alluring gap-toothed smile, has graced a record twenty-five *Vogue* covers and countless editorial campaigns. Her most newsworthy career move was the contract she signed with Revlon in 1974. The first of its kind, this exclusive agreement set a precedent for supermodels' fees, changing them from hundreds to thousands of dollars. Over the following ten years, while modelling exclusively for Revlon, Hutton made a name for herself on screen. Born in Charleston, South Carolina, she grew up mainly in Florida and, after dropping out of college, moved to New York where she began modelling to pay for the life of travel she had originally planned. Her return to modelling in the 1990s has been a proud achievement for Hutton, who has inspired debate about the size and age of models. Her example, she hopes, will encourage a broader view of beauty.

☛ Butler, C. Klein, Revson

Lauren Hutton. b Charleston, SC (USA), 1943. **Lauren Hutton.** Photograph by Fred Seidman, 1972.

Iman

Model

A slender sculpture in black velvet and white taffeta, Iman was dubbed Black Pearl for her ebony-black beauty. The contours of her feline figure, boasting a perfect *physique du rôle* to flaunt the 1980s' opulence, ensured that she was a true supermodel of her time. Her exotic presence on the catwalk made her a fetish model for Azzedine Alaïa, Gianni Versace and Thierry Mugler.

Born Iman Abdulmajid in Somalia to a diplomat, she studied political science in Nairobi before being discovered by Peter Beard, the photographer who took her into the New York fashion spotlight. A multimillion-dollar contract with Revlon in the late 1970s, as well as her marriage to rock star David Bowie and the launch of her own make-up range (especially devised for black women), have conferred on her almost mythical status among black models, a reputation shared only by Naomi Campbell and Beverly Johnson.

☛ Bowie, Beverly Johnson, Revson

222

Iman (Iman Abdulmajid Haywood). b (SOM), 1955. Formal evening gown and feather headdress. Photograph by Arthur Elgort, 1993.

Irene

Designer

This film still from the 1940 film *Seven Sinners* shows the work of the costume designer known as 'Irene of California'. She started her career making clothes on the campus of the University of Southern California, where Dolores del Rio became a client. Her connections took Irene into the Beverly Hills sphere, where she became involved with actresses and their personal wardrobes. She moved to Hollywood to continue her trade – mostly in dramatic 'film-star' style clothes. From 1942 she took over from Adrian as head costumer at Metro-Goldwyn-Mayer, making outfits for, among others, Marlene Dietrich and Marilyn Monroe. Her signature style always remained slim, curvy and tailored for daywear; eveningwear, however, was lavish, dramatic and attention-grabbing, with feathers, frills and sparkle. Here, Marlene Dietrich wears an outfit embellished with the trappings of a romantic vamp: polka-dot veil, net gloves, ostrich-trimmed handbag and vast chiffon corsage.

☞ Adrian, Head, Louis, Travilla

223

Irene (Irene Lentz Gibbons). b MT (USA), 1907. **d** Los Angeles, CA (USA), 1962. **Marlene Dietrich**. Still from *Seven Sinners*. 1940.

Iribe Paul

Illustrator

The simple lines and brilliant colours of Poiret's oriental style are beautifully evoked in this fashion illustration, published a year before the arrival of the Ballets Russes and Bakst in Paris. The Hispahan coat in the centre, made in green cotton velvet, has embroidered Persian palms sharply outlined in bold yellow and white. This coat is framed by two others in shades of yellow and mustard, trimmed with fur. Further contrasts of colour are provided by the dresses visible beneath the coats and by the headwear. With its format of clear flat areas of colour and the asymmetrical arrangement of the models, the fashion illustration shows the influence of Japanese prints. In order to obtain such jewel-like colours, Iribe used a special technique called the *pochoir* process, whereby a monochrome print was hand-coloured using a series of bronze or zinc stencils, enabling him to capture an image as close as possible to the original.

☛ Bakst, Barbier, Doucet, Gigli, Lepape, Paquin, Poiret

224

Paul Iribe. b Angoulême (FR), 1883. **d** Paris (FR), 1935. **'Three Coats'**. From *Les Robes de Paul Poiret racontées par Paul Iribe*. 1908.

Isogawa Akira

Designer

Against a background of pattern pieces (the building blocks from which fashion takes shape), Akira Isogawa's model wears a vest contructed from bronze jacquard silk. Its seams, brought together as an abstract, asymmetric puzzle, are stitched on the outside, leaving their frayed edges to become part of the exterior decoration. Isogawa left his native Japan for Sydney, Australia, to escape becoming a 'salary man'. He trained in fashion and in 1996 showed his first collection as part of Australian Fashion Week. It was an exotic melange of Japanese vintage kimonos, delicate and translucent floral-print dresses and modern leather and wool tailoring, all layered together to create a new aesthetic in fashion. The attraction of Isogawa's clothes lies in his passion for fabric. 'I have a connection, a Zen thing with material,' he has said. His delicate handprints, antique fabrics from Japan and form-fitting tailoring make a sharp, yet individual statement.

☞ Arai, Chalayan, Kobayashi, Lloyd

Akira Isogawa. b Kyoto (JAP), 1964. **Deconstructed bronze brocade top and pinstriped trousers**. Photograph by Eddy Ming, 1998.

225

Jackson Betty

Designer

Square, linen shapes, styled for *Vogue* by Vera Wang, represent the work of Betty Jackson, who is known for her thoughtful balance between fashion and comfort. Consequently, her designs appeal to women whose working and leisure wardrobes tend to be interchangeable – a relaxed, modern concept. She originally wanted to become a sculptor, an aspiration which was thwarted by an allergy to plaster of Paris. Instead, she freelanced as an illustrator, before turning her attention to fashion in 1973, working for Wendy Dagworthy and then at Quorum. Jackson and her French-born husband, David Cohen, founded their own company under her name in 1981. The core of her easy, fluid collections consists of boldly coloured, simple and versatile shapes; a style that allows elements of high fashion to be represented without compromising her notion that fashion belongs to women of any age.

☛ P. Ellis, Howell, Pollock, Wang

226

Betty Jackson. b Bacup (UK), 1940. **Linen shirt and drawstring trousers**. Photograph by Tony McGee, American *Vogue*, 1984.

Jacobs Marc   Designer

Naomi Campbell is caught laughing, mid-pose, in a sitting for American *Vogue*. Her powder-grey, cashmere vest and flat-fronted trousers are by Marc Jacobs, examples of what the *New York Times* has called his 'caviar clothes'. The simplicity of her outfit is given an edgier profile with a pair of sharp stilettos, a contradiction that Jacobs uses in his own work. His proclivity

towards luxurious materials and modern references recommended the one-time designer for Perry Ellis to the position of creative director at Louis Vuitton, the French luggage company. Jacobs has introduced pop and kitsch elements to its traditional image; 'Deluxe hip' was Suzy Menkes' summary in the *International Herald Tribune*. Jacobs addresses

his own age group: rich women in their thirties are attracted by his witty update of a brand that has been carried by generations before them.

☛ Campbell, Cobain, Garren, Kors, Moses, Vuitton

227

Marc Jacobs. b New York (USA), 1963. **Naomi Campbell wears cashmere vest and flat-fronted trousers.** Photograph by Wolfgang Tillmans, American *Vogue*, 1997.

Jacobson Jacqueline and Elie (Dorothée Bis)   Designers

Fun, funky knitwear was the key to the Dorothée Bis style. Their 'total look' often incorporated knitted tights and hats and unconventional layering such as skirts over trousers or, as seen here, thigh-clinging shorts worn with over-the-knee socks. Jacqueline and Elie Jacobson founded the label with the desire to create wearable versions of high-fashion styles, producing clothes that were ideal for the youth-inspired period of short-lived fashion trends in the 1960s. The label was always commercially minded, reflecting their backgrounds in the fashion trade (in the 1950s, Jacqueline owned a childrenswear shop and Elie worked as a wholesale furrier). Each decade they defined the key looks, from knitted maxi coats and skinny-rib sweaters in the 1960s, to voluminous layering in the 1970s and tight, shoulder-padded graphic knits in the 1980s.

☛ Khanh, Paulin, Rykiel, Troublé

228

Jacobson. Jacqueline. b Lens (FR), 1928; Elie. b Paris (FR), 1925. (Dorothée Bis.) **Hooded poncho and shorts**. Photograph by Peter Knapp, French *Elle*, 1970.

Jaeger Dr Gustav   Designer

Dr Gustav Jaeger, a German dress reformer who believed that animal hair made the most healthy fabric, stands erect, wearing close-fitting, woollen breeches. Unlikely as it seems, Jaeger inspired a classic British label which was patronized by George Bernard Shaw and Oscar Wilde. The company was founded in 1883 by Lewis Tomalin, the London businessman who translated and published Jaeger's thoughts. Tomalin went on a health crusade to convert the public to the benefits of wearing wool next to the skin as advocated by the doctor from Stuttgart, securing his rights and name. It wasn't until the 1920s that fashion was embraced by Jaeger, and then it was used to popularize the appeal of 'healthy' materials through a style that came to represent British, dependable design. Jean Muir, who made her name with her draped wool jersey dresses, was Jaeger's most celebrated designer.

☛ Burberry, Creed, Howell, Muir, Wilde

Dr Gustav Jaeger. b Börg am Kocher (GER), 1832. **d** Stuttgart (GER), 1917. **Dr Gustav Jaeger.** c1880.

229

James Charles   Designer

Charles James was working for Elizabeth Arden when he created the couture dress that is the sculptural centre of this John Rawlings photograph. Every James dress was a *tour de force* of sculptural imagination; the pyramid shape on the left and the black-and-white figure on the right confirm his penchant for sculpture. The evening dress (c1944) anticipates the postwar silhouette, especially that of Christian Dior's New Look. A corseted bodice emphasizes the supported bust and narrowed waist, while the flaring fabrics just below the waist float out from the body to construct fictive hips that make the waist seem even slimmer. Irascible and self-destructive, James couched his designs in pseudo-systems and supposed geometries, but made his name as the maker of the extravagant concoctions that defined the conservative picturesque in post-Second World War fashion.

☞ Arden, Beaton, Scaasi, Steele, Weber

Charles James. **b** Sandhurst (UK), 1906. **d** New York (USA), 1978. **Draped duchesse satin couture gown.** Photograph by John Rawlings, 1944.

230

James Richard   Tailor

Actor Edward Atterton is laid out in a country house 'whodunnit' spread for *Elle*, much to the entertainment of the real tourists. The photographer, David LaChapelle, maximizes the tongue-in-cheek appeal of Richard James' lilac wool suit. Since 1976, when he launched his label, James has been regarded as the 'light player' of Savile Row, using vivid colours instead of sombre greys and eccentric, specially woven checks rather than traditional tweed. His choice of such exclusive fabrics gave British bespoke and tailored, ready-to-wear menswear a contemporary feel, drawing comparisons with Tommy Nutter and his contemporaries from the 1960s. A-list film stars and pop stars (and their girlfriends, if they have the right 'hip-to-bum ratio') patronize James, who says, 'Many of the suits made along the row are beautiful but bland. We are trying to add a youthful spirit and excitement, while maintaining the propriety that Savile Row stands for.'

☞ Cox, LaChapelle, Nutter, P. Smith

231

Richard James. b Ely (UK), 1953. **Edward Atterton wears lilac wool suit and woven stripe shirt.** Photograph by David LaChapelle, British *Elle*, 1996.

Jantzen Carl

Designer

Swimming champion Johnny Weissmuller poses poolside in a pair of 'Jantzens', the world's first elasticized trunks. Invented by knitwear designer Carl Jantzen, who experimented with the machines which made sweater cuffs, this innovation prompted the world to stop merely 'bathing' and start 'swimming'. Jantzen founded the Portland Knitting Co with John and Roy Zehntbauer

in 1910. Their heavy wool sweaters, socks and gloves, produced on a few knitting machines and sold from the company shop were phenomenally successful. The trunks soon became known as 'Jantzens', and the company changed its name accordingly in 1918. Three years later, the Red Diving Girl motif was added. Jantzen's early designs were unisex (although women wore theirs

with stockings), but the developments resulted in streamlined swimwear for women. By 1925 Jantzen was one of the first clothes companies to export its work.

☞ Gernreich, Lacoste

232

Carl Jantzen. b Aarhus (DK), 1883. d (USA), 1939. Johnny Weissmuller wears wool tanksuit, Olympic Games, 1924.

Jinteok

Designer

Jinteok is known for simple designs crafted from luxurious fabrics which meld traditional elements of her cultural heritage with Western influences. Here, she uses Chinese red silk for an apron dress. Its bodice and hem are decorated with naturalistic forms in the tradition of oriental silk garments. The underskirt, cut from roughly assembled denim, lends this potentially glamorous garment a rustic, hobo feel. Such subtle themes, inspired mainly by nature, are evident throughout her collections. Since she opened her first shop in Seoul in 1965, Jinteok has played a pioneering role in contemporary fashion in her native country, South Korea. She founded the Seoul Fashion Designers Association, which encourages young Korean designers, and presented her womenswear collection on the catwalks in Paris for the first time in 1994.

☞ Arai, Kim, Rocha

Jinteok (Jin Teok). b (KOR), 1938. **Red embroidered gown. Spring/summer 1995**. Photograph by Marcio Madeira.

John-Frederics   Designer

Although this outfit is heavily accessorized, the pieces are so carefully matched that at first glance they are barely noticeable, camouflaged against the co-ordinated clothing. During the 1930s no fashionable outfit was complete without matching hat, gloves, shoes and bag. At that time, New York's accessory designers were moving into the limelight, and John-Frederics

was one of America's top proponents. This picture shows how John-Frederics complements a sportswear, puff-sleeve, tartan shirt and cream skirt with formal accessories, including a striking bag made out of the bright red tartan of the blouse. The cream, broad-brimmed hat (John-Frederics was also a master milliner) is covered in black net and matched with short gloves. Unusually, a

long band hangs from the hat and encircles the blouse, quite literally pulling the outfit together.

☛ Daché, Simpson, Thomass

234

John-Frederics (John Frederics). b Munich (GER), c1906. d 1964. **Veiled panama hat, plaid blouse and pocket book**. Photograph by Horst P. Horst, 1939.

Johnson Betsey   Designer

'Fashion is all about having fun and these are clothes to have fun in,' says Betsey Johnson, who wears her own kooky combination of floral dress and fishnet tights. Johnson's attitude to fashion is summed up by the cartwheels she performs along the catwalk at the end of her shows. Best known for her brightly coloured, madcap prints, she started designing in 1965 and her imaginative designs took full advantage of the new synthetics and mini-lengths. Her dresses were decorated with jangling shower-ring hems and her fluorescent underwear was packaged in tennis ball cans. Johnson also sold plastic dresses in kit form for the wearer to arrange as she wanted. It was a dress with a ten inch, extended collar that made her name. Worn by British actress Julie Christie, it sold in the tens of thousands. Johnson's career was launched by New York's Paraphernalia boutique, a champion of youth-inspired fashion in the 1960s.

☛ Bailly, Foale, Rabanne

Betsey Johnson. b Hartford, CT (USA), 1942. **Betsey Johnson in her design studio, New York, 1982**. Photograph by Harry Benson.

Johnson Beverly   Model

Beverly Johnson has a place in fashion history, not only as the first black model to be featured on the cover of American *Vogue*, but also for paving the way for black women the world over to feel part of the fashion industry. Johnson began modelling while a student at Northeastern University in Boston, receiving assignments for *Vogue* and *Glamour* despite having no portfolio. Fashion editors were impressed by her fresh beauty. When Scavullo photographed her for the *Vogue* cover in August 1974, the magazine was taking a chance. Little did they know that its circulation for that month would double. Johnson said at the time, 'The participation of black models ... is unjust in proportion to the amount of money that is put into the industry by black people'. Her career spanned the 1970s and early 1980s and also included film roles, records and two books.

☛ Iman, Nast, Turbeville

Beverly Johnson. b (USA), 1953. **Beverly Johnson.** Photograph by Francesco Scavullo, American *Vogue*, 1974.

Jones Grace   Model

Grace Jones poses for a Polaroid taken by her friend Antonio Lopez in his bathroom. Jones, with her Amazonian figure and shorn hair, was the antithesis of femininity. The daughter of a Pentecostal minister, she rebelled against her strict upbringing and pursued a modelling career in Paris at a time when her theatrical attitude perfectly suited the extremes of 1970s fashion: 'Glitter? Uh-huh. Platform shoes? Yeah... It was sort of old Hollywood star stuff.' Fashion centred on the flashy nightclub scene at Paris's Club Sept, where Jones partied every night. Together with friend Jerry Hall, Jones brought outrageous performance to modelling and, as a result, created a second career for herself. In the 1980s she turned to music, cultivating an aggressive look of sharp, angular, leather clothes and a razored quiff to clothe her image as a modern diva.

☞ Antoine, Antonio, Price

237

Grace Jones. b Spanish Town (JAM), 1954. **Grace Jones**. Photograph by Antonio Lopez, 1980.

Jones Stephen　　　Milliner

The model camps it up for Mario Testino's camera. On her head she wears a miniature topper by milliner Stephen Jones, known for his innovative, witty and gregarious hats. Boaters, caps and bowler hats have all been reduced to create millinery caricatures. He was a central figure in London's New Romantic movement in the early 1980s, making hats for his friends Steve Strange and

Boy George. In 1984 his work was noticed by Jean Paul Gaultier and Thierry Mugler, who both asked him to design hats to accessorize their collections, making him the first British milliner to work in Paris. Jones has since collaborated with a succession of international fashion designers. As with the shoe designer Manolo Blahnik, his work as an accessory designer lends itself to

collaborative ventures because of its sympathy with the clothes, as well as a sharpness that makes it a punchy punctuation mark.

☞ Berthoud, Galliano, Mugler, Testino, Van Beirendonck

Stephen Jones. **b** West Kirby (UK), 1957. **Top hat**. Photograph by Mario Testino, *Harpers & Queen*, 1988.

Jourdan Charles   Shoe designer

In the 1930s, Charles Jourdan was the first shoe designer to advertise in fashion magazines. In the 1970s, his advertisements, such as the one below, were photographed by Guy Bourdin and became legendary. Bourdin lent the shoes wit and mystery by placing them in surreal scenes, making them components of a larger story. Here, two women are escaping over a wall, leaving three of their fashionable platform sandals behind. Jourdan had introduced low-priced diffusion lines to his handmade collection after the Second World War. He sold simple designs in a multitude of colours and fits, accessories for a developing ready-to-wear business. In 1958 Maxime, a low-heeled, square-toed court shoe with a satin bow, became his best-known, best-selling style. In the 1960s, a collaboration with André Perugia added a touch of glamour to the classic lines, but Jourdan's collaboration with Bourdin remains the most exciting impression of his work.

☛ Bourdin, Oldfield, Perugia

Charles Jourdan. b Bourg de Péage (FR), 1883. **d** Romans sur Isère (FR), 1976. **Summer sandals.** Photograph by Guy Bourdin, 1974.

Kamali Norma   Designer

In the tradition of American fashion, Norma Kamali formed an entire wardrobe from utilitarian material. When she launched her own range of clothes, Kamali created a fashion phenomenon by using sweatshirt fleece fabric for clothes such as leggings, kick skirts and wide-shouldered dresses. Her outfits addressed a problem felt by millions of American women: how could they get away with comfort when fashion dictated structure and ostentatious formality? She was also one of the first to offer the unitard. Kamali's fashion career began in 1968, when she opened a boutique with her husband Eddie in New York. At the time, she was an air stewardess and sourced many European fashions, particularly from Biba in London. In 1978, after her divorce, Kamali set up OMO (On My Own) and her new-found independence was reflected in her clothes, which have continued to provide a modern response for modern women.

☛ Campbell, Hechter, Hulanicki

Norma Kamali. b New York (USA), 1945. Sweatshirt collection. Spring/summer 1980. *Women's Wear Daily*.

240

Karan Donna

Designer

'What do I need? How can I make life easier? How can dressing be simplified so that I can get on with my own life?' Donna Karan's own thoughts could be running through the head of the 'first woman president', who represents her own ideal: ultimately powerful and urban. Professional wearability dictates Karan's work. Her first collection was a capsule wardrobe of separates based around the 'body' – a practical, stretchy, leotard shape with poppers at the crotch. Karan also designs to flatter the normal woman, saying, 'You've gotta accentuate your positive to delete your negative,' and only designs clothes that she would wear herself. Karan trained with Anne Klein, taking over the design with Louis Dell'Olio when Klein died in 1974. Karan's fidelity to Klein's easy-to-wear never waned, but in the 1990s she became increasingly interested in spiritual philosophies, and began producing looser, more sensual clothing.

☞ Dell'Olio, A. Klein, Maxwell, Morris

241

Donna Karan. b New York (USA), 1948. **'In Women We Trust' advertising campaign**. Photograph by Peter Lindbergh, 1992.

Kawakubo Rei (Comme des Garçons)   Designer

In this classic photograph of work by Rei Kawakubo for her label Comme des Garçons, shredded sweaters are patchworked together to form new clothes. The mishmash puzzle of knitwear is held together by visible, rough over-stitching and deliberately careless seaming. The model's make-up feigns bruising, she wears jersey bandages around her wrists and her hair is razored into a brutal, uneven crop. In the early 1980s, Kawakubo's aesthetic changed the way clothes were seen. Called 'post-nuclear chic', it supplanted the assumption that fashion was always to be approached with the intention of creating perfectly made clothes in the old tradition of those that flatter the body. Kawakubo is a conceptualist, using Japanese rather than European clothing traditions. She challenges her customers to wear her ideas even when they resemble a work of art rather than clothes – as was the case in 1997 when she padded them with cushions designed to re-contour the natural body shape.

☞ Arai, Hirata, Lindbergh, Miyake, Vionnet, Watanabe

242

Rei Kawakubo. b Tokyo (JAP), 1942. (Comme des Garçons.) **Knitwear. Autumn/winter 1984/5**. Photograph by Peter Lindbergh.

Kélian Stéphane   Shoe designer

A pair of bronze sandals epitomizes the work of one of France's most enduringly fashionable shoe designers. Basket-woven leather has been a feature of Kélian shoes since Georges and Gérard Kélian opened a workshop to design and manufacture classic men's shoes in 1960. In the mid-1970s, Stéphane entered into partnership with his two older brothers, bringing a new fashion spirit to their traditional shoe company. In subsequent collections, he continued to feature the specialist weaving techniques used by his brothers, but modernized the designs and introduced a panoply of shimmering colours into the colour palette. Stéphane presented his first collection of women's shoes in 1977 and the opening of the first of many international boutiques followed a year later in Paris. Kélian is known for his design collaborations with fashion designers and other cobblers, including Martine Sitbon and Maud Frizon.

☞ Frizon, Sitbon, Steiger

Stéphane Kélian. b Romans sur Isère (FR), 1942. **Basket-weave sandals. Autumn/winter 1997/8**. Photograph by Roberto Badin.

Kelly Patrick

Designer

Shining out amidst the backstage chaos are symbols that characterize one of the most exuberant designers of the 1980s. A committed Francophile, Patrick Kelly describes the Eiffel Tower in rhinestones for a black dress, uses it for clunking gilt earring charms and even finds space for it on high-heeled shoes. Journalist Bernadine Morris noted Kelly's 'collection of lively, unpretentious clothes that made fashion look like fun...an unforced feeling of happiness' His work always contained an element of the theatrical and his catwalk shows combined the largesse of a rural Southern American culture with the camp bravado of Moulin Rouge entertainment. Affordable ready-to-wear clothing was gaily decorated with imaginative buttons, and black rag dolls, once a sign of oppression, were festooned over a coat. Between 1985 and 1989, Kelly seemed an irrepressible, boyish force for dynamic fashion, involving young people and incorporating black experience.

☞ W. Klein, Moschino, Parkinson, Price

Patrick Kelly. b Vicksburg, MI (USA), 1954. **d** Paris (FR), 1990. **Backstage**. Photograph by William Klein, 1987.

Kennedy Jacqueline   Icon

Ladylike but youthful, formal but fashionable, the 'Jackie' style caught America's attention and made the young woman a fashion icon. This picture illustrates Jackie's trademarks: the simple coat, the white gloves, the flipped-up hair by Kenneth. In 1961 Oleg Cassini became her devoted designer, telling her that she could only wear his clothes – although she would occasionally consult with Diana Vreeland at *Harper's Bazaar*. In return, Cassini created a working wardrobe for the First Lady. It had a pared-down elegance and an informal, youthful spirit that was unusual at the time. She rarely wore patterns and stuck to simple shapes: sleeveless, boxy shift dresses with matching coats and accessories. Halston was her milliner, creating her famous pillbox style. Jackie always wore gloves and rarely wore jewellery, except for an occasional string of pearls. As with her clothes, Jackie liked her shoes 'slender...but not exaggerated – no tricky...business – timeless and elegant'.

☛ **Cassini, Daché, Kenneth, Lane, Pulitzer, Vanderbilt, Vreeland**

Jacqueline Kennedy. b New York (USA), 1929. **d** New York (USA), 1994. **'Raja' coat in dupion silk by Oleg Cassini.** Photograph by Art Rickerby, *Life*, 1962.

Kenneth

Hairdresser

In 1963, an article in American *Vogue*, entitled 'The Kenneth Club', described the lengths to which women would go for an appointment with the hairdresser Kenneth Battelle. He attended to Jackie Kennedy's bouffant bob, copied across America. He created the perfect domed bobs on Veruschka and Jean Shrimpton for *Vogue* covers when Diana Vreeland was editor.

She called it the 'Dynel period' because of the enormous quantities of synthetic hair that were used for ever more elaborate wigs and extensions. Famously, in Tahiti, they used Dynel not just on the models but on a real white horse to create a fairy-tale ponytail. However, for Kenneth, the cut rather than the dressing was the most important element to a hairstyle: his

teased and backcombed precision bobs defined an era. 'I defy a woman to wear a Courrèges dress without really great make-up and a hairdo,' he is quoted as saying.

☞ Antoine, Kennedy, Shrimpton, Veruschka, Vreeland

Kenneth (Kenneth Battelle). b New York (USA), 1927. **Bouffant bob.** Photograph by Art Kane, American *Vogue*, 1962.

Kenzo

Designer

Her layered, floral, prairie cottons swing to life; an earthy, retrospective look that dominated much of the mid-1970s. The dress and jacket use the Victorian details such as a fitted bodice and billowing sleeves caught into deep cuffs. Kenzo Takada, its designer, opened his first shop in Paris in 1970. Since it was entirely decorated with jungle prints, he called it Jungle

Jap, a name which soon became popular with young, fashionable models who were looking for fresh, spirited clothes. Inspired mostly by traditional Japanese shapes, Kenzo's early, highly desirable collections included easy-to-wear smocks, tunics, oriental blouses and wide-legged trousers. They were predominantly made from cotton and often quilted. Kenzo

also specialized in vivid knitwear which was added to the cottons to produce an eclectic, comfortable look. His refreshing use of colour, pattern and print have made him one of the most durable of the 1970s designers.

☞ Ashley, Ettedgui, Matsuda

247

Kenzo (Kenzo Takada). b Hyogo (JAP), 1939. **Tiered floral print dress, Spain, 1973**. Photograph by Peter Knapp.

Keogh Lainey

Designer

'Lainey's knitwear,' said Hamish Bowles in American *Vogue*, 'challenges all one's preconceptions of the woolly jumper.' Here, her friend Naomi Campbell wears an intricately knitted dress which is light as air, clingy and revealing. Knitting is one of Ireland's oldest cottage industries and although Keogh's style is modern – with details such as the quirky, asymmetric hem and shoulder – this dress is also ethereal and romantic. The emerald green hand-work conjures up images of mermaids and the fishing nets used on the west coast of Ireland. Lainey Keogh says her hand-knitted clothes are 'like food or sex: intimate and personal'. This poetic sensibility is her signature; she claims to have discovered her talent through knitting a jumper for her lover. She loves the 'exquisite feeling of the lightest textures against the skin' and her fabrics are created using feather-light cashmere and iridescent chenille.

☞ Campbell, Kobayashi, Macdonald

Lainey Keogh. b (IRE). (Active 1990s–.) **Lace knitwear. Autumn/winter 1997/8.** Photograph by Chris Moore.

Kerrigan Daryl Designer

A Daryl K dress is hitched up in a movement which corrects a predicament known as the 'Daryl dip'. Daryl Kerrigan's problematic but highly fashionable strapless tops, worn with tomboyish hipster trousers, blend sportswear with tailoring for women who aren't ready to commit to a suit. She studied fashion at the National College of Art and Design in Dublin, before moving to New York in 1986. Kerrigan was determined to design the perfect pair of jeans. Her boot-cut, hipster jeans, dubbed 'low riders', were partly inspired by a pair of 1970s hip-huggers she had found in a vintage warehouse. The jeans were to make her name and become the mainstay of her collections, alongside her stretchy tube tops, drawstring nylon skirts and zip-up jersey sweat-jackets. She says, 'Women want something new and don't want to feel like they're dressing in a period play.'

☞ Demeulemeester, Farhi, Lang

Daryl Kerrigan. b Dublin (IRE), 1964. **Strapless dress**. Photograph by Jon Mortimer, 1998.

Khanh Emmanuelle   Designer

'Haute couture is dead,' proclaimed Emmanuelle Khanh in the 1960s. Her French street fashion paralleled Mary Quant's during the youthquake movement. Her radical designs, tightly modelled on the curves of the body, drew inspiration from the pop scene. A former model for Balenciaga and Givenchy, Khanh reacted against the stiff sophistication of 1950s couture by reflecting and modernizing the loose, feminine frame of the 1930s. Her relaxed style, shown here, was a mixture of low-waisted culottes, fitted jackets with narrow shoulders and dog-eared collars. These flattering innovations were adapted from her earlier knitwear for Missoni, Cacharel and Dorothée Bis. Her own label, created in 1972, echoed the ethnic look of the period in Romanian hand embroidery and peasant-style dresses. Khanh represented the young face of French fashion, together with Christiane Bailly and Paco Rabanne.

☞ Antonio, Bailly, Bousquet, Ettedgui, Jacobson, Quant, Rosier

250

Emmanuelle Khanh. b Paris (FR), 1937. **Ready-to-wear womenswear**. Illustration by Antonio López, French *Elle*, 1967.

Kim Christina (Dosa)   Designer

The featherweight gauze shirt worn over silk trousers is representative of Christina Kim's almost spiritual work. The designer behind the Dosa label launched in 1983, Kim was born in Korea but has lived much of her life in Los Angeles. The Dosa philosophy was born when her t'ai chi teacher's traditional Chinese jacket caught her eye and inspired her to make a similar one but in heavy, washed linen. Kim has since perfected the art of melding simple shapes, inspired by her Korean heritage, with fabrics from diverse cultures, in a palette of soothing, often iridescent colours. In 1997 Dosa – the Korean word for 'sage' and Kim's mother's nickname – was heralded as the hottest label to come out of the USA and into Europe. Mindful of the environment, Kim also uses the by-products of the clothing manufacturing process for home accessories.

☛ Jinteok, Matsuda, Zoran

251

Christina Kim. b Seoul (KOR), 1957. (Dosa.) **Diaphanous shirt with silk trousers**. Photograph by Don Freeman, *Joyce*, 1997.

Klein Anne

Designer

A belted, white playsuit over a long-sleeved T-shirt epitomizes every practical detail used by Anne Klein. Klein only just missed inventing American designer sportswear. Following the pioneers of the 1930s and 1940s – McCardell, Leser, Maxwell *et al* – she came to represent the ethos of contemporary sportswear, creating clothes that suited the lifestyles of modern women.

Beginning with her work at Junior Sophisticates in 1948, she always thought in terms of carefree and casual forms, soft materials (especially jersey for evening), mixable separates (for sensible wardrobe-building) and forgiving tunics and outer wraps. Her bodysuits and derivations from active sportswear determined the basic canon of American designer sportswear in

the 1950s and 1960s. Klein's lead was followed by her successors, Donna Karan and Louis Dell'Olio who both excelled (and still do in Karan's case) at fashion that is friendly towards a multitude of figure shapes.

☛ Dell'Olio, Karan, Leser, Maxwell, McCardell, Rodriguez

Anne Klein. **b** New York (USA), 1923. **d** New York (USA), 1974. **Cream shorts suit**. Photograph by Kourken Pakchanian, American *Vogue*, 1972.

Klein Calvin

Designer

Lauren Hutton wears a simple blouson jacket, mannish pleated trousers cinched with a silk tie, and a clean, white top. The styles may have changed but the adjectives have followed Calvin Klein's work through three decades. 'I made a lot of things that go with things,' said Klein, whose sophisticated sportswear in natural fabrics and colours came to define the versatility of modern fashion. In the 1970s, Klein produced branded jeans, thereby creating the modern-day designer label as a branding tool. Klein is also known for his clever marketing: when a young Brooke Shields purred sexily in his adverts, 'Nothing comes between me and my Calvin's', it scandalized New York and ensured fame for Klein – as did the pin-up, billboard posters for his men's and women's underwear in the 1980s. Klein is often credited as being most in tune with the Zeitgeist and therefore most capable of understanding what the modern woman wants to wear.

☛ Baron, Coddington, Hutton, Moss, Turlington, Weber

Calvin Klein. b New York (USA), 1942. **Lauren Hutton wears cream**. Photograph by Francesco Scavullo, American *Vogue*, 1974.

Klein William   Photographer

The viewer always has the best seat in the house for Klein's spectacle. In a 1960 meeting of Roberto Capucci dresses on the Piazza di Spagna in Rome, Simone d'Aillencourt almost steps into the viewer's lap; Nina de Vos, walking the other way, looks back as if to notice that the two dresses are so Op Art and so alike. Only the 'chance' presence of the guy on the Vespa tells us that

this is the street and not a commissioned runway. Klein exalted the artifice of a fashion photograph, defying many of his contemporaries in the 1950s, who preferred naturalism or its simulation. Klein sought the startling effect. Later a film-maker, Klein let out some of his fashion contempt in the satirical film, now a fashion legend, *Qui Etes-Vous, Polly Magoo?* (1966).

Klein appeared to care little about the dresses; he was always a maker of eccentric, visual melodramas.

☞ Capucci, Courrèges, Fontana, Kelly, Paulette, Tatsuno

254

William Klein. b New York (USA), 1928. **Black and white dresses by Roberto Capucci.** American *Vogue*, 1960.

Knight Nick

Photographer

Devon, the young model, looks vulnerable and fragile. She is scarred and seemingly half-blind, her face transformed by make-up artist Topolino. Although her stance and expression are aggressively defiant, the image is a deeply disturbing vision by photographer Nick Knight. It is fashion photography *in extremis*. 'If you want reality, look out of the window,' says Knight. Like many 1990s photographers, he manipulates his images by computer to heighten their impact. Knight's photographs, which have appeared in *Vogue* and *i-D*, usually have a fairy-tale aspect to them, often contrasted with disturbing touches of violence, as here. His pictures focus on form as well as fashion, as demonstrated by the geometric shapes in the photograph. His unconventional view of beauty has led him to photograph a size 14 model for *Vogue* and a septuagenarian teacher for a Levi's advertising campaign.

☛ McQueen, Strauss, Topolino

255

Nick Knight. b London (UK), 1958. **Brocade cowl dress by Alexander McQueen.** 1996.

Knight Phil and Bowerman Bill (Nike)   Designers

The famous 'Swoosh' tick is the designer logo of the sportswear market. One of Nike's two founders, Phil Knight, was a middle-distance runner at the University of Oregon. He founded a company called Blue Ribbon Sports in 1971, importing the Japanese Onitsuka Tiger trainer. Soon afterwards, he started manufacturing his own range, called Nike after the Greek winged goddess of victory. Much of the key to Nike's success lies in the marketing of its image, with advertisements that push the brand rather than the product. The company's slogans, including 'Just Do It', are unapologetically uncompromising; Nike was criticized by the Olympic Committee for its 'You don't win silver – you lose gold' advertisements. Nike took advantage of the sportswear-as-streetwear trend of the 1980s and 1990s, producing fashion-conscious designs in limited editions which have since become collectors' items.

☛ Crawford, Dassler, Hechter, Lacoste

256

Phil Knight. b Portland, OR (USA), 1938; Bill Bowerman. b Portland, OR (USA), 1911. (Nike.) Sportswear, South Africa, 1997. Photograph by Anton Want.

Kobayashi Yukio   Designer

This photograph by the legendary photographer of New York's drug culture, Nan Goldin, was taken in 1996 as part of a series entitled *Naked New York – Nan Goldin meets Yukio Kobayashi*. Kobayashi had been designer of the Matsuda menswear line since 1983, and took on the role of chief designer of womenswear in late 1995. This photograph is from the autumn/winter 1996 Matsuda collection and was taken to capture its 'raw energy and artistic foundation'. Kobayashi is unusual in his mission to create clothes that break free of conventional style and offer an 'ageless' and 'genderless' alternative, using highly developed sewing and decorative techniques, such as 'needle punch' and quilting. 'From my perspective,' he says, 'fashion and art are inseparable...both need to be nurtured and developed to ensure they prosper over time'. Here translucent prints on bare skin simulate intricate tattoos.

☞ Isogawa, Keogh, Matsuda

257

Yukio Kobayashi. b Niigata (JAP), 1951. **Yukio Kobayashi for Matsuda. Autumn/winter 1996.** Photograph by Nan Goldin.

Kors Michael

Designer

Michael Kors is a designer of modern American sportswear. His aspiration is to design clothes that can be both shown off and worn for everday life. Kate Moss wearing this strapless, black outfit on a racing track and holding a helmet bearing the US flag epitomizes his style: it is sexy, fun and practical. Kors had two career aims as a child – to be a movie star or a fashion designer.

He chose fashion and studied it briefly, but learnt his trade by working at a boutique where he eventually became a designer. He established his label in 1981, incorporating menswear in 1990. Kors works with neutral and bright colours, his clothes are minimalistic in shape and luxurious to touch. He layers his silhouette and uses luxury fabrics, preferring cashmere, kid

leather, silk and organza over cheaper alternatives. In 1998 he also began designing for deluxe French house, Céline, a parallel to Marc Jacobs' move to Louis Vuitton.

☛ Eisen, Jacobs, Mizrahi, Moss, Tyler

258

Michael Kors. b New York (USA), 1959. **Kate Moss wears stretch tube top and pedal pushers.** Photograph by Terry Richardson, *Harper's Bazaar*, 1997.

LaChapelle David   Photographer

'I love drama and outrageousness. I love crazy scenes,' says LaChapelle, who creates an unforgettable interpretation of John Galliano's outfits for his two 'Milkmaids' here. When he was young, his mother organized elaborately staged photographs: 'In the family albums we look like the Vanderbilts. My mom remade her reality through snapshots.' Their move from conservative Connecticut to the brashness of Carolina encouraged LaChapelle to 'celebrate the artificial'. He left home at fifteen and moved to New York where he worked as a busboy at the legendary New York nightclub, Studio 54 – 'a big influence...all that pop imagery'. He met Andy Warhol at a Psychedelic Furs concert and was employed by him at *Interview*. His photographs are usually movie-like productions. 'For me, taking photographs, planning them and working on them, is a big escape,' he says. LaChapelle likes his subjects to be equally dramatic. 'Exhibitionists make the best models.'

☛ Galliano, R. James, Vanderbilt, Warhol

David LaChapelle. b Hartford, CT (USA), 1963. **'Milkmaids'.** *Stern*, 1996.

Lacoste René · Designer

The French tennis star, René Lacoste, launched his polo shirt in 1933, six years after he had earned the nickname 'le crocodile' for winning a crocodile-skin suitcase in a bet. 'A friend drew a crocodile,' he said, 'and I had it embroidered on the blazer I wore on the courts.' His polo shirts were the first example of sportswear as fashion. The Lacoste empire now includes leisure-, golf- and tennis-wear for men, women and children. As such, it was a precursor to the sportswear phenomenon that accelerated throughout the century. Lacoste's crocodile, one of the most famous fashion emblems, is sold across the world to brand conscious youth. When logo mania boomed in the 1980s, Lacoste became a major label, worn from Laos to Liverpool; it was in this city that Casuals, working-class football supporters, began wearing upmarket labels such as Lacoste as an emblem of personal success.

☛ Dassler, Jantzen, P. Knight

260

René Lacoste. **b** Paris (FR), 1904. **d** Saint Jean-De-Luc (FR), 1996. **René Lacoste wears blazer with a crocodile motif, 1927.**

Lacroix Christian   Designer

This printed leotard, smattered with beading and worn with grandiose costume jewellery – not least a beaten gold and chain belt – epitomizes Christian Lacroix's role as an ornate antidote to monochrome power dressing. His grandfather, a dandy who lined his suits with green silk and painted his bicycle gold, inspired Christian's love affair with the eighteenth century, introducing him to Boucher, Madame de Pompadour and Louis XIV. An *ancien régime* opulence influences much of his work, which is also coloured by his hot, southern French roots. Having designed for Hermès, Lacroix joined Patou in 1981. His 1984 couture collection for that house, inspired by the bohemians and aesthetes of prewar Paris and London, injected life back into the couture scene. Having opened his own house in 1987, Lacroix became famous for his fearless confusion of fabric, colour and surface decoration.

☛ Etro, Gigli, Hermès, McCartney, Patou, Pearl

261

Christian Lacroix. b Arles (FR), 1951. **Marie Sophie wears printed and embroidered catsuit.** Photograph by Mario Testino, 1990.

Lagerfeld Karl   Designer

'I am not interested in the future or the past; now is the interesting time,' Karl Lagerfeld said in 1986. Yet this photograph of Nadja Auermann, taken by the designer himself, suggests yesterday's Paris with her deconstructed pompadour hairstyle. Lagerfeld's modern, urban influence is evident in the New York street scene and in the sharp cut of her dress, an enduring theme for his own label. The son of wealthy parents, Lagerfeld moved to Paris, aged fourteen. His love of history, particularly eighteenth-century costume, has influenced his work and his personal style – Lagerfeld's ponytail and ever-present fan have almost become trademarks. Describing himself as a 'professional dilettante', his design portfolio has included collections for Chanel, Fendi, Chloé and his own label, amongst others. His work at Chanel from the mid-1980s onwards took Coco Chanel's traditional leitmotifs, including gilt buttons and the chains used to weight her jacket hems, and turned them into design features.

☛ Chanel, Fendi, Léger, Lenoir, Macdonald, Paulin, Tennant

262

Karl Lagerfeld. b Hamburg (GER), 1938. Nadja Auermann wears empire-line dress, New York. Photograph by Karl Lagerfeld, 1994.

Lalique René Jules   Jewellery designer

A gold and diamond tourmaline dragonfly brooch displays Lalique's precise copying techniques and delicate pictorial detailing. Master goldsmith René Lalique led the Art Nouveau ('new art') jewellery movement of the 1890s, and later became a premier glassmaker. Unconventionally, Lalique worked with materials for their aesthetic value rather than their preciousness.

Decoration was the purpose of the pieces and elaborately ornate hair combs were especially popular. Many of the pieces had references to nature, such as insects, animals or flora, and many featured pictorial scenes, such as a forest clearing, with a single pearl suspended below. Often impractically large in order to increase the visual impact, the pieces were favoured

by extroverts such as Sarah Bernhardt. Lalique moved into glass jewellery in the 1920s and 1930s, creating all-glass rings, and pendants on silk cords.

☞ Bulgari, Tiffany

René Jules Lalique. b Aÿ (FR), 1860. **d** Paris (FR), 1945. **Diamond tourmaline pendant brooch, c1900.**

Van Lamsweerde Inez   Photographer

A Van Lamsweerde photograph is instantly recognizable. Turn the pages of a style magazine such as *The Face*, *Vogue*, *Arena* or *Visionaire* and it will be impossible to miss the hyper-real and highly technical images made with her creative and live-in partner Vinoodh Matadin. This image, for example, taken from a *Face* fashion shoot and featuring clothes by French designer Véronique Leroy, uses computer manipulation to create a fantastical situation: two women on a surreal bicycle ride are surrounded by phallic imagery which includes a space shuttle launch. It is staged, it is ridiculous, but most of all this image is humorous pastiche, and this is the main characteristic of their work – satire. The pair met at Rietveld Academy of Arts in 1991, and have worked together since on academic, fashion and advertising projects which include campaigns for Yohji Yamamoto and Louis Vuitton.

☛ Leroy, Molinari, Vuitton, Y. Yamamoto

264

Inez van Lamsweerde. b Amsterdam (NL), 1963. 'Well basically, Basuco is coke mixed with kerosene … '. 1994.

Lancetti Pino

Designer

Two models tread Pino Lancetti's catwalk. Their richly detailed gowns serve to reinforce their sleek-haired conspicuousness, a style that belongs to the wealthy society for which he caters. Both dresses fall gently from raised waistbands and are accessorized with co-ordinating wraps to maintain their decorum. Initially a painter, Lancetti became involved in fashion when he moved to Rome and began sketching 'for fun' for the couturiers there. In 1963 he launched a seminal 'Military Line' collection which transferred the uniform into fashion. His designs, unsurprisingly, tend to be painterly, their inspiration ranging from Modigliani to Picasso to Impressionism. The look is often 'folksy', using soft, printed fabrics. Even the Military Line, with its starchy proportions, showed ethnic touches within the braiding. Lancetti avoids the trappings of the international fashion world and is best known in Japan and his native Italy.

☞ Lapidus, McFadden, Scherrer, Storey

Pino Lancetti. b Bastia Umbra (IT), 1935. **Gilded evening dresses**, *Women's Wear Daily*, 1977.

Lane Kenneth Jay   Jewellery designer

Dubbed 'the undisputed king of costume jewelry' by *Time* magazine, Kenneth Jay Lane believes every woman has the right to look glamorous – no matter what her income or status. Lane eschews the elitist stance of many designers. Early in his career, Lane designed shoes for Christian Dior, where he worked under the tutelage of Roger Vivier. By 1963 Lane had decided costume jewellery was his future and spent his spare time covering cheap plastic bangles with stripes, patterns and crystals. He was celebrating the possibilities of non precious materials. Lane would place demonstrably artificial plastics next to glass approximations of diamonds. This has been an enduring formula that was widely copied in the 1980s and 1990s. His clients, all of whom were famous for their real jewels, have included Jackie Kennedy, Elizabeth Taylor, Babe Paley, Barbara Bush and Joan Collins.

☞ **Butler & Wilson, Kennedy, Leiber , Paley, Vivier**

Kenneth Jay Lane. b Detroit, MI (USA), 1932. **Paulette Stone**. Photograph by Norman Eales, 1967.

266

Lang Helmut   Designer

A backstage snap, capturing a theatrical headdress, worn with plain white vests, epitomizes the work of the most copied designer of the 1990s. Technology and bare fabrics that are rarely made from natural fibres, are joined in his collections. Lang's watchwords are 'now', 'urban', 'clean' and 'modern'. His clothes reflect an effortless, downbeat style which is instantly recognizable. He describes his clothes as conveying 'the sort of anonymous status that the truly knowing admire' – indeed, they are adored by fashionable aesthetes the world over. Lang launched his own label in 1977. His first Paris show, in 1986, was an immediate success and his popularity has continued throughout the 1990s, affording him cult status. The essence of his design ethos is to create a simple silhouette, in muted shades, for both sexes; this is then made more complex with textural combinations – sheer/opaque, shiny/matt – and flashes of bright colour.

☛ Capasa, Kerrigan, Sander, Teller, Tennant

Helmut Lang. b Vienna (AUS), 1956. **Kirsten Owen wears feather headdress.** Photograph by Juergen Teller, 1997.

Lanvin Jeanne

Designer

Keeping the waisted, full-skirted dress alive was a speciality of Jeanne Lanvin, as the mannequin and the sketches scattered on the floor and in the hand of the couturière attest. Famous for her *robes de style* and picturesque frocks that recalled earlier times, Madame Lanvin promoted romantic clothes when other couturiers such as Madeleine Vionnet, Coco Chanel, Alix Grès

and Jean Patou were modernizing with their vertical aesthetic. Opening her maison de couture just before the First World War, Jeanne Lanvin was already fifty-one when the War ended. Rather than initiate any revolutionary trends, she clung to that era – designing on the lines of the full skirt of 1915-16 with only slight adjustments. Fittingly, at a time when romantic clothes

thrived in the theatre, her favourite client was the musical-comedy star, Yvonne Printemps. Madame Lanvin was also famous for her mother/daughter outfits and for introducing, in 1926, a line of menswear.

☛ Abbe, Arnold, Castillo, Crahay, Grès, Montana

Jeanne Lanvin. b Brittany (FR), 1867. d Paris (FR), 1946. **Jeanne Lanvin with mannequin in her Paris studio, 1921.**

Lapidus Ted

Designer

Ted Lapidus and his model Lilo pose for Eve Arnold backstage at his winter show in 1977. Lilo wears a typically romantic, crepe georgette dress by Lapidus. Despite its heavy embroidery and beading, it is a relaxed shape which is dressed down with a peasant neckline and a tiered skirt – details usually found on daywear. Lapidus's design education began with an engineering diploma taken in Tokyo in 1949, but he was inspired by his Russian tailor father to take up fashion instead. Using the principles learned from both disciplines, Lapidus attracted a reputation as a master of pattern-cutting. Inspired by his experience of high technology in Japan, he felt that it was important to integrate science with fashion. Consequently, he became involved with mass-manufacture at the same time as applying his precision techniques to his couture collections.

☞ Arnold, Lancetti, McFadden

269

Ted Lapidus. b Paris (FR), 1929. **Ted Lapidus with Lilo wearing a beaded dress.** Photograph by Eve Arnold, French *Vogue*, 1977.

Laroche Guy   Designer

Guy Laroche's career began at a hat-maker's in Paris, then in New York, on Seventh Avenue. On returning to Paris, he found employment in the maison de couture of Jean Dessès. His successful apprenticeship encouraged him to open his own house in 1957. Laroche was renowned for his mastery of cutting and tailoring. His early work was influenced by the architectural cutting of Cristobal Balenciaga, but he later gave that formality a lively freshness, cultivating popularity with younger women – this meant diversifying his couture business by moving into ready-to-wear in 1960. Laroche is remembered from that time for lending an almost girlish attitude to formal clothes – especially with his empire-line dresses with material gently gathered into raised waistbands. In the following decade, his trouser suit, itself a symbol for liberated women, was required wearing.

☛ Dessès, Fath, Miyake, Paulette, Valentino

Guy Laroche. b La Rochelle (FR), 1923. **d** Paris (FR), 1989. **Tweed suits and woollen accessories.** Photograph by Chris Moore, 1971.

Lauder Estée

Cosmetics creator

The Estée Lauder look from 1961 is a constructed scheme using shading, lighting and lashings of liquid eyeliner. Lauder, who founded her company in 1946, is one of the queens of New York cosmetics. Born there, she is the daughter of a well-to-do Hungarian mother and Czechoslovakian father. Her interest in skincare was inspired by her Uncle John, a dermatologist, who, when he came to stay in America, admonished her for washing her face with soap. With him, the family set up a laboratory and produced creams which became favourites with their friends and friends of friends. The real business began when Estée was invited to sell the products at a Manhattan salon. Lauder encouraged women to buy scent for themselves and was one of the first names to develop a full range of cosmetics. The company is now a giant, encompassing other brands: Aramis, Clinique, Prescriptives, Origins, Aveda and Bobbi Brown.

☛ **Brown, Dovima, Factor, Horst, Revillon**

Estée Lauder. b New York (USA). (Active 1940s–) **Estée Lauder make-up**. Photograph by Horst P. Horst, American *Vogue*, 1961.

Lauren Ralph   Designer

A Californian ranch is the setting for Ralph Lauren's advertisement from 1988. His vision, conjured by Bruce Weber, is of a measured, monied society which has a home in Connecticut and a ranch in Pasadena. Lauren, apart from being one of the most famous fashion product designers in the world, is a clever marketing man; a purveyor of a Waspish, all-American lifestyle, dressing every aspect of it, from exotic travel to business suits for Wall Street. Since 1968, when he launched his menswear label, Polo, Lauren has created a brand that is known throughout the world and clothes which are status symbols of the late twentieth century. His style, borrowed from vintage clothing, evolved from a desire to give new relevance to nostalgic elegance. It was an aesthetic summed up in the films *The Great Gatsby* (1974) and *Annie Hall* (1977), for which Lauren worked on the wardrobe. In later years, he has made the look his own.

☛ Abboud, Brooks, Hilfiger, Wang, Weber

272

Ralph Lauren. b New York (USA), 1939. **'Polo' advertising campaign, Pasadena.** Photograph by Bruce Weber, 1988.

Léger Hervé   Designer

These rainbow dresses, formed from hand-stitched elastic bandages, are little more than extended swimsuit shapes. Hervé Léger learned his craft working with Karl Lagerfeld, designing swimwear first for Fendi, then Chanel. His forte is remoulding the body and Léger is more concerned with perfecting the female form than he is about passing trends. He claims that the woman he designs for is 'fed up with the vagaries of fashion. She does not give a damn about trends, she refuses to be a feminine clothes hanger.' His use of stretchy bands for his 'bender dresses' means his clothes are often compared with those of Azzedine Alaïa, his 1980s predecessor. Both designers greatly admired the silhouette-enhancing work of Mme Vionnet, and Léger's ankle- length column dresses have a glamorous simplicity and an uninterrupted line. His own-label swimwear continues to be regarded as flattering, correcting the body like foundation-wear.

☛ Alaïa, Chanel, Fendi, Lagerfeld, van Lamsweerde, Model, Mugler

Hervé Léger. b Bapaume (FR), 1957. **Joanna**. Photograph by Inez van Lamsweerde and Vinoodh Matadin, 1995.

Leiber Judith

Accessory designer

A glittering Judith Leiber evening bag has been the focus of Hollywood outfits since the 1960s. Despite its high-voltage sparkle, the example carried by Elizabeth Hurley is understated. 'I like to do things that look crazy, yet are practical,' says Leiber, who sent First Lady Hillary Clinton a bag modelled on Socks, the White House cat. Ladybirds, teddy bears, fruit and Fabergé eggs have all been fashioned into such rhinestone whimsies. Though Leiber was offered a place to read chemistry at London's King's College in 1939, the Second World War forced her to stay in her native Budapest, where she was apprenticed to a master handbag maker. Leiber moved to New York in 1947, starting her own business in 1963. Her handbags are collected by customers such as American social queen Pat Buckley, who displays them as works of art. Leiber is less reverent about her own work, saying, 'The bag is really an object to be worn.'

☞ Lane, Mackie, Wang

Judith Leiber. b Budapest (HUN), 1921. Liz Hurley with diamanté minaudière and Hugh Grant. 1997.

Lelong Lucien   Designer

The sleeves of this black, silk velvet evening gown are intricately cut, in the style of a medieval robe, with pointed cuffs which swoop like swallows' wings. The gown closely follows the shape of the figure, moulding the waist and the hips before widening into a skirt which flows softly into a train, like the outspread feathers of a bird's tail. The birdlike character of the dress is associated with the imagery of Surrealism, the dominant art movement of the 1930s. Lelong, who opened his own couture house after the First World War, was president of the Chambre Syndicale de la Couture Parisienne from 1937 to 1947. He persuaded the occupying Germans to allow French couture houses to remain in Paris rather than be transferred to Berlin or Vienna. Through his efforts, at least one hundred fashion houses were kept running throughout the occupation of Paris from 1940 to 1944.

☛ Balmain, Bettina, Chéruit, Dessès, Givenchy

Lucien Lelong. b Paris (FR), 1889. d Danglet (FR), 1958. **Black, silk velvet gown.** Photograph by Hoyningen-Huene, French *Vogue*, 1934.

Lenoir Jacques and Aghion Gaby (Chloé)   Designers

Chloé's name, meaning 'young, green shoot', is particularly appropriate, given that the label pursues modernity. Yet Chloé retains an ethereal, whimsical femininity that is not always followed by its eclectic choice of designers, including Guy Paulin and Martine Sitbon. Launched in 1952 by Jacques Lenoir and Gaby Aghion, Chloé's intention was to approach *prêt-à-porter*

with the finesse of haute couture, elevating the more directional ready-to-wear to an art form. The most catalytic example – Lagerfeld's 'Woodstock couture' of the 1970s, which he revived in 1993 with Linda Evangelista as his muse – evoked the flower-child mood with free-flowing, pale chiffon, swirly patchwork maxiskirts and full bloomed, silk roses. However, second time

round public reaction to Lagerfeld proved inconsistent, and Chloé replaced him in early 1997 with Stella McCartney, who stuck to Chloé's house style with vintage lace, pastel satin and glass buttons.

☞ Bailly, Lagerfeld, McCartney, Paulin, Sitbon, Steiger

276

Jacques Lenoir. b Paris (FR), 1920. **Gaby Aghion. b** Alexandria (EG), 1921. (Chloé.) **Wool outfit by Karl Lagerfeld for Chloé.** Photograph by Chris Moore, 1979.

Leonard

Hairdresser

For one of Leonard's striking hair designs, a hairpiece is looped under the chin and caught in a hand-painted hair slide by Pablo and Delia. Leonard's extreme colouring techniques were developed by him for Stanley Kubrick's *2001: A Space Odyssey* in 1968. 'I had to push things as far as they would go,' says Leonard. 'The coloured hair, the crazy colours, the unnatural ones, they started there.' His work was innovative and directional in the 1960s and 1970s: he cut the Beatles' mopheads and when Justin de Villeneuve delivered his young prodigy Twiggy to Leonard for a haircut, he made the best business move of his life. Leonard, who had started out with de Villeneuve on a Shepherd's Bush Market fruit barrow, asked Twiggy to model a new haircut invented by him. After eight hours of snipping, a talent honed during his training with Vidal Sassoon, Twiggy's waifish crop was born and so was her career.

☞ Beatles, Mesejeán, Sassoon, Twiggy

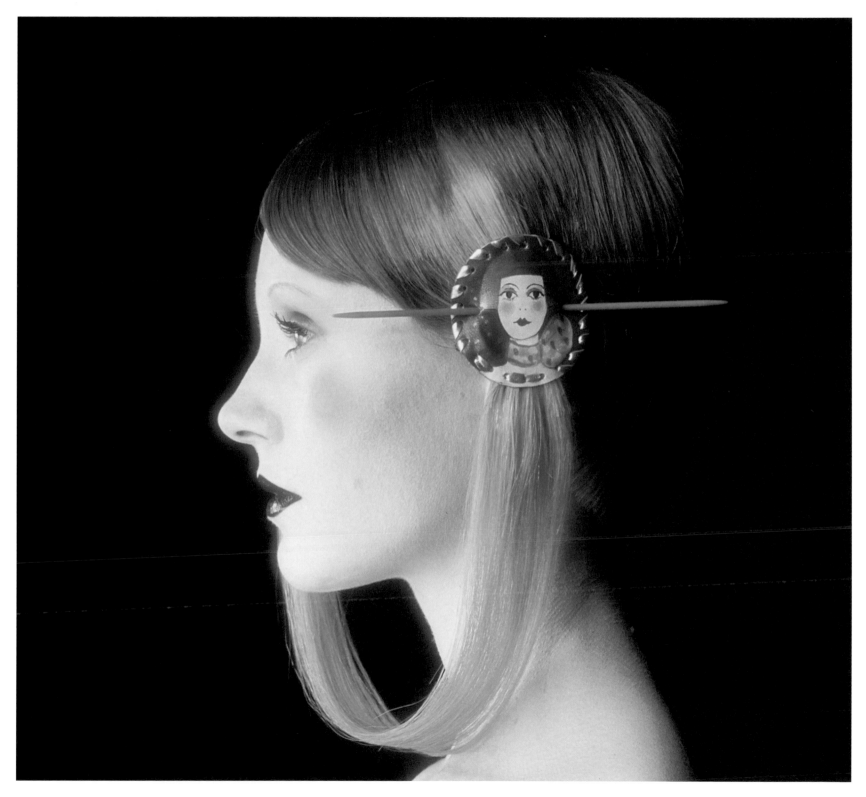

Leonard (Leonard Lewis). b London (UK), 1938. **Hair coloured by Leonard.** Photograph by Barry Lategan, 1970.

Lepape Georges   Illustrator

These 'Fashions of Tomorrow' most certainly live up to their name. Poiret's pantaloon gowns, illustrated here by Georges Lepape in 1911, were considered shocking at the time, but anticipated the move towards greater physical freedom in women's fashion. This illustration is one of the plates from *Les Choses de Paul Poiret vues par Georges Lepape*. The sculptural simplicity of Lepape's illustrations captures perfectly the silhouette of Poiret's clothes. Poiret was the first couturier to relate fashion successfully to the other arts and was innovative in commissioning the artists Georges Lepape and Paul Iribe to compile limited-edition albums of hand-coloured drawings of his designs. Lepape contributed illustrations to *La Gazette du Bon Ton*, a folio of fashion news and drawings in the twentieth century, and regularly appeared on the cover of *Vogue* in the 1920s. Lepape was instrumental in bringing art movements such as Cubism into the realm of fashion.

☛ Barbier, Benito, Drian, Iribe, Poiret

278

Georges Lepape. b Paris (FR), 1887. **d** (FR), 1971. **'Fashions of Tomorrow'**. From *Les Choses de Paul Poiret vues par Georges Lepape*. 1911.

Leroy Véronique   Designer

Véronique Leroy was once described as 'the unchallenged reigning queen of the Paris sexy-tack scene'. This sportswear-meets-eveningwear outfit is typical of Leroy's flirtation, and often unashamed love affair, with bad taste. Her method is to use recently outmoded references. Here she used gilt chain and nylon mesh at a time when the memories of their misuse in the hands of the mass-market were still fresh. The chain, a reference to Chanel's handbag handles, suspends an Op Art patchwork of artificial sportswear fabrics. These thrift store-inspired collections dabble in different themes, each one rich in its potential for anti-taste, including *Charlie's Angels*, Pop Art and science fiction. Before starting her own label, Leroy worked with Azzedine Alaïa, who taught her how to handle body-hugging Lycras and synthetics, and Martine Sitbon from whom she learned about the art of catering for the rock-chick market.

☛ Hemingway, van Lamsweerde, Sitbon

Véronique Leroy. b Liège (FR), 1965. **Blue halterneck dress.** Photograph by Christophe Kutner, British *Elle*, 1995.

Lesage Albert

Embroiderer

This bolero jacket, lavishly embroidered with a parade of elephants, is from Schiaparelli's 'Circus' collection of 1938. Not since Poiret had a fashion designer shown such an instinctive flair for the use of embroidery, making it a glamorous adjunct to haute couture. Collaborating with the celebrated Maison Lesage, which had been founded in 1922 by Albert Lesage, *maître*

brodeur, and in particular with his young son, François, Schiaparelli designed her collection especially to offset the sumptuous embroidery. Her basic silhouette of wide shoulders and neat waist enabled Lesage to adorn her jackets with embroideries that enhanced her whimsical dreams. Here, the spotlight is on performing elephants, their threads richly

complementing the encrustations in gold. Maison Lesage, renowned for its jewel-studded embroidery, let loose all the capriciousness of Schiaparelli's Surrealism.

☛ Schiaparelli, Wang, Yantorny

280

Albert Lesage. b Paris (FR), 1888. d (FR), 1949. 'Circus'. Elephant embroidery for Schiaparelli. 1938.

Leser Tina

Designer

A cute, teenager outfit of turned-up, denim jeans and striped cotton shirt epitomizes the freshness of American fashion after the Second World War. Tina Leser was among the new wave of designers unique to American culture who concentrated on sportswear as fashion. Her clothes, designed for a manufacturer (until 1952 when she formed her own company), were informed by everyday shapes such as play-suits, sarong dresses, smocks, swimsuits and shrug-on jackets, but they were almost always influenced by a more formal aesthetic, as is evident in the picture shown here. Leser's mother was a painter and the designer studied art, painting, design and sculpture in Philadelphia and Paris. Leser moved to Honolulu and opened a boutique in 1935, moving to New York in 1942. During the 1950s she designed cropped and harem pants before any other designers; she is also thought to have been the first designer to make dresses from cashmere.

☞ Connolly, A. Klein, McCardell, Simpson

281

Tina Leser (Christine Wetherill Shilland-Smith). b PA (USA), 1910. Mexican cotton shirt and denim jeans. Photograph by John Rawlings, *Harper's Bazaar*, 1951.

Lester Charles and Patricia Designers

A golden, hand-pleated silk dress is set against antique fabrics. It recalls the Delphos style designed by Fortuny eighty years earlier, but it is the work of designers Charles and Patricia Lester, who were unaware of his work when they started their experiments in the 1960s. Years of research go into the techniques used by the Lesters: designs are burnt out of velvet to form devoré and others are hand-painted to produce unique cloth which is used for tunics, dresses and robes. The historical perception of these techniques has an attraction which sets their work apart from the less enduring elements of high fashion. Consequently, it has been used for opera productions and for the film adaptation of Henry James' novel *The Wings of a Dove*, in which Helena Bonham Carter wafts around pre-First World War Venice. Her pleated silk dresses and velvet coats, however, were not specially made for the film but were taken from the Lesters' 1990s collection.

☞ Fortuny, McFadden

282

Lester. Charles. b Banbury (UK), 1942; Patricia. b Nairobi (KEN), 1943. **Gold pleats**. Photograph by Alex Chatelain, British *Vogue*, 1985.

Levine Beth

Shoe designer

Freedom of movement and freedom from the conventions of footwear are provided by Beth Levine's innovative stocking boots. All Levine's shoes gave the potential for motion, from the elasticated sole of her Spring-O-Lator mule, to the aerodynamic curves and rounded 'rock-a-bottom' sole of her Kabuki pumps, the prototype for which was carved from a teak salad bowl (a shape later reinvented by Vivienne Westwood for her 'rocking horse' platforms). Levine was known for her sexy, stretchy boots, including pairs made for Nancy Sinatra who sang 'These Boots Were Made for Walking'. She conjured imaginative heels, from a rolled scroll shape to chunky cuboid blocks, and favoured unconventional materials such as Astroturf and frog skin.

Originally untrained in shoe design, Levine pushed the physical possibilities of footwear – her high-heeled 'topless' shoe was a satin sole stuck to the foot using spirit gum.

☛ Ferragamo, Parkinson, Westwood

283

Beth Levine. b New York (USA), 1914. (Active 1940s–1970s.) Suede boots. Photograph by Norman Parkinson, American *Vogue*, 1969.

Ley Wolfgang and Margaretha (Escada)   Designers

The affectations of this image are stereotypical of the 1980s: strong-shouldered siren with sharp, glittery skirt, big hair and bigger attitude. What Escada meant for women far surpassed their angst-ridden boundaries as working mothers and wives – it symbolized the triumph of ostentatious glamour at a time when image dominated substance, and even taste. Launched in 1976 by Wolfgang and Margaretha Ley, Escada was aptly named after a winning racehorse. Their sexy, chiselled suits, leopard-print blouses and nautical-striped sweaters, all offset with gold buttoning and braid, eulogized a 'bourgeois chic' look. It was a hugely popular style. Wealth was counted in sequins which were applied to every surface – even sweaters were taken out of their casual context with a smattering of sparkle. With Todd Oldham hired as creative consultant in 1994, Escada has taken a fresh approach and is embracing the spirit of the times.

☛ Féraud, N. Miller, Norell, Oldham

284

Ley. Wolfgang. b GA (USA), 1937. **Margaretha. b** Västernorrland (SWE), 1933. **d** Berlin (GER), 1992. (Escada.) **Sequined sweater and skirt for Escada.** Photograph by Albert Watson, 1984.

Liberman Alexander Photographer and art director

Alexander Liberman photographs Christian Dior, Bettina Ballard, fashion editor of American *Vogue*, and Despina Messinesi, also from *Vogue*, in the early 1950s. This image, taken during one of the legendary Sundays that a few privileged people spent at the French couturier's country house, bears witness to the intimate relationship that Liberman has had with the fashion world for almost six decades. After working for Lucien Vogel on *Vu*, a photo-journalism magazine published in Paris, Liberman moved to New York, where he became art director of *Vogue* in 1943. In 1962 he was appointed editorial director of all Condé Nast's publications, thus acquiring a unique insight into every aspect of the fashion journalism trade. A connoisseur of fashion photography, he maintained that its appeal lay in providing the viewer with a ticket of escape from her surroundings, 'into the heaven of fashion and the unbelievable nirvana of luxe and elegance.'

☛ Abbe, Chanel, Dior, McLaughlin-Gill, Nast

285

Alexander Liberman. b Kiev (RUS), 1912. **Bettina Ballard, Christian Dior, Despina Messinesi and Bettina Ballard's husband.** Photograph by Alexander Liberman, 1950.

Liberty Arthur Lasenby   Retailer

Just as the work of Liberty has reflected the times ever since it was founded in 1875, this lawn dress, speckled with minute flowers, was perfectly in tune with the mood of its age. It is bright, simple and, with its co-ordinated accessories, captured young British fashion (and the Rolling Stones). It was designed by The Ginger Group, a label founded in 1963 by Mary Quant,

the quintessential fashion designer of the 1960s. She was one of the leading lights of 'Swinging London', a term coined by the American *Time* magazine in 1964, the date of this dress. Arthur Lasenby Liberty's department store went on to specialize in fine fabrics such as lawn – a lightweight cotton material printed with traditional floral motifs and exuding a fresh, country look. In its

history, Liberty has both reflected and contributed to sartorial changes, from the costume associated with the Aesthetic Movement of the 1880s to the fashion revolution of the 1960s.

☞ Bousquet, Fish, Muir, Nutter, Quant, Sassoon, Wilde

286

Arthur Lasenby Liberty. b Chesham (UK), 1843. **d** Lee Manor (UK), 1917. **'How To Kill Five Stones With One Bird'.** Photograph by Norman Parkinson, *Queen*, 1964.

Lindbergh Peter   Photographer

Shot in 1990, this photograph gathers together the posse of reigning supermodels wearing their off-duty uniform of wrapped bodies by Giorgio di Sant'Angelo and Levi's jeans. Peter Lindbergh's name is closely intertwined with those of Naomi Campbell, Linda Evangelista, Tatjana Patitz, Christy Turlington and Cindy Crawford, who partly discovered their singularity through him. The image's stark, grainy, monochromatic quality reveals Lindbergh's trademark lack of artifice and calm directness, rooted in the unadorned greyness of the industrial scenes of his childhood in Germany. He was twenty-seven when he picked up a camera for the first time. Ever since, his photographs have appeared in every major fashion magazine. The key influence that classical portraiture plays on Lindbergh gives his work a timeless allure. As Karl Lagerfeld said, 'His photographs will never be regarded with any condescending emotion in thirty or forty years' time.'

☛ Campbell, Crawford, Evangelista, Kawakubo, Turlington

287

Peter Lindbergh. b Duesburg (GER), 1944. **Naomi, Linda, Tatjana, Christy and Cindy.** British *Vogue*, 1990.

Lloyd Alison (Ally Capellino) Designer

Alison Lloyd describes her work as 'something which is fashionable, but which doesn't go out of fashion very quickly.' Here, she uses shot organza for a transparent over-dress. Its stiffness gives the shape a defined form and the visible seams take the appearance of a frame. It certainly defies fashion's usual proclivity for styles that can be easily dated. Lloyd is inspired by a passion for simple organic textiles, bright colours and wearable, enduring shapes. Lloyd and fellow Middlesex Polytechnic graduate Jono Platt set up Ally Capellino in 1979, initially selling hats, jewellery and accessories. (The name, they thought, was Italian for 'little hat'; to their amusement they later discovered that it means 'little head'.)

Lloyd became a fashion designer in 1980. Her creativity never overwhelms her desire to produce clothes which can be worn by women of any age.

☛ Arai, von Etzdorf, Isogawa

288

Alison Lloyd. b London (UK), 1956. (Ally Capellino.) **Silk organza dress shot with metal**. Photograph by Aldo Rossi, 1996.

Loewe Enrique

Accessory designer

Supple, lavender leather distinguishes a strapless dress modelled on a handbag by Loewe, which has created such bags since 1846. Loewe is a luxury leather company fabled for its ability to make animal skin behave as fabric. It was founded in the Calle del Tobo area of Madrid, a centre for leather artistry, where Enrique Loewe sold snuff boxes and purses alongside his bags. As a company, Loewe entered the fashion sphere in 1947 when it acquired the rights to sell Christian Dior's New Look in Spain. By the 1960s it had begun to design its own fashion collection, one that used the company's proclivity for draping and gathering, as well as producing classic working shirts in velvety suede. In 1997, Loewe modernized its image by appointing Narciso Rodriguez as its house designer, a move typical of those made by other luxury European houses primarily known for luggage, including Louis Vuitton and Hermès.

☞ Hermès, Rodriguez, Vuitton

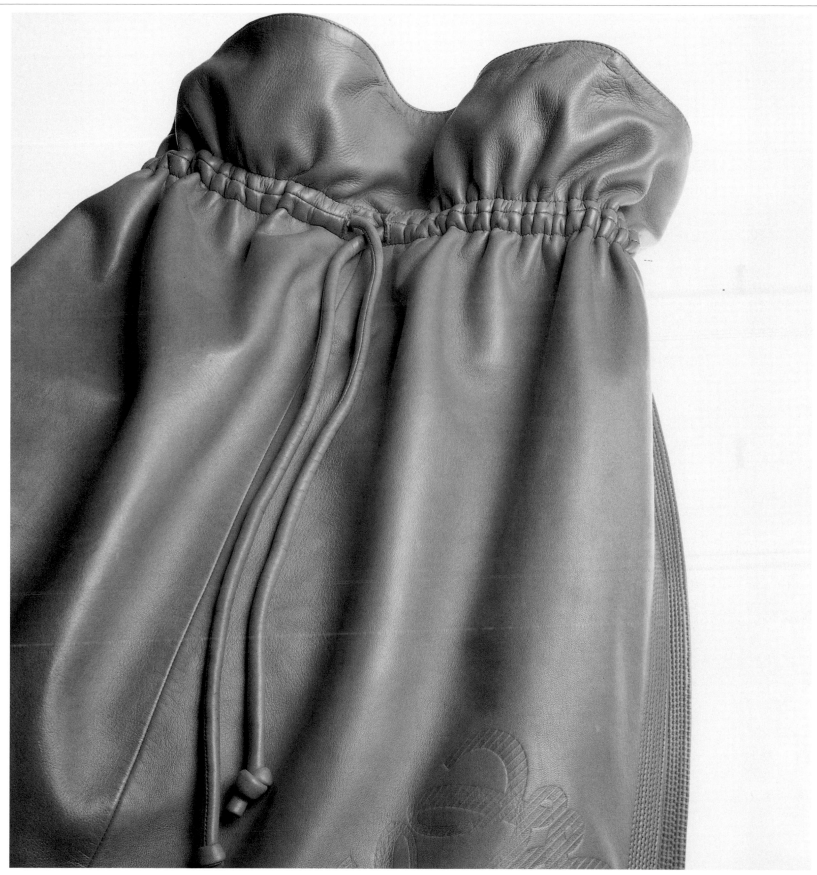

Enrique Loewe. b (GER), 1829. **d** (SP), 1919. **Lavender leather dress. Autumn/winter 1983**. Photograph by Rafael Roa.

Louboutin Christian   Shoe designer

Gold embroidery, black ribbon and blue mosaic heels: a jumble of exotic shoes reveals Christian Louboutin's love of creating forbidden fantasies. His seductive shoes, with their trademark red soles, are inspired by tropical birds, flowers and gardens. He describes them as a cross between 'a work tool or weapon and an *objet d'art*', and individual commissions are intensely personalized. Love letters, petals, locks of hair and feathers have been encased within his teetering heels. His obsession began in 1976 when, aged ten, he visited a Parisian museum. Far from being inspired by its contents, *bébé* Louboutin couldn't forget the impression made on him by a huge, red high heel worn by another visitor. A meeting with French shoe master Roger Vivier, with whom he is often compared, changed his outlook. 'I never thought to do it as a job,' he said. Catherine Deneuve, Inès de la Fressange and Princess Caroline of Monaco would he barefoot without him.

☞ **Ferragamo, Pfister, Vivier**

290

Christian Louboutin. b Paris (FR), 1963. **Autumn/winter 1998**. Photograph by Mark J. Curtis.

Louis Jean

Designer

'There NEVER was a woman like Gilda!' was the caption which curled above Rita Hayworth's picture on the poster from the 1946 film. Sheathed in a strapless satin dress by Jean Louis, she played a seductive *femme fatale*. The simple bodice which supports Hayworth's body hides an intricate construction of boning and padding, although she maintained that it stayed up 'for two good reasons alone', meaning her breasts. Having started his career as a sketch artist for Drecoll, Jean Louis moved to New York where he designed for Hattie Carnegie. He brought the drama of his film work to a couture business which excelled at creating lavish evening gowns. The potency of this, and other Jean Louis dresses in the film, made Hayworth America's dream mistress and her wardrobe the blueprint for sexy, yet illusory dresses which is still followed today. Hayworth later sadly reflected on her broken relationships with men, saying, 'Every man I ever knew had fallen in love with Gilda and woken up with me'.

☞ Carnegie, Galanos, Head, Irene

Jean Louis (Jean Louis Berthault). b Paris (FR), 1907. **Rita Hayworth.** Still from *Gilda*. Photograph by Bob Coburn, 1946.

Lutens Serge

Make-up artist

Every element of this surreal advertisement for Shiseido was created by Serge Lutens, from the make-up and styling to the photograph itself. Lutens grew up wanting to be an artist. School bored him and he spent all his spare time performing makeovers on his friends, then taking their pictures with a Kodak instamatic. In 1960 he met his partner, Madeleine Levy, and together they launched a 'test salon' in Paris for make-up, hair, jewellery and furniture. In 1968 he was invited to look after the image and product creation of Christian Dior cosmetics, leaving to join Shiseido in 1980. Lutens does not regard his images as schemes that should (or even could) be copied by women. Fantastical in the extreme, they have the surreal spirit of Salvador Dali's fashion work. He advocates that women should develop their own creative effects with make-up, whether they want to look natural or artificial.

☛ Nars, Page, Uemura

Serge Lutens. b Lille (FR), 1942. 'Absolutely Amazing' campaign for Shiseido. Photograph by Serge Lutens, 1998.

McCardell Claire   Designer

Claire McCardell, who pioneered American sportswear, conceived this empire-silhouette 'baby dress' in 1946. The black wool jersey, suggesting an update of Chanel's little black dress, used nonchalant tying in the manner of the casual lifestyle design she championed. Tying and wrapping were not only apt for the active woman, but they also accommodated the inexact sizing and fit of ready-to-wear apparel. Cultivating such traits in soft, relatively inexpensive garments, McCardell made clothing that had a loyal following among women who wanted independence from corporeal restrictions or dictates from Paris. Instead, versatile separates and the use of materials from menswear, lingerie and childrenswear promised an adaptable, flexible lifestyle akin to the garment itself. Projecting her own desires into design, McCardell never forgot a woman's need for pockets (even this dress has them). Her speciality was leisurewear, including playsuits and swimwear.

☛ Cashin, Connolly, Dahl-Wolfe, A. Klein, Leser, Steele

293

Claire McCardell. **b** MD (USA), 1905. **d** New York (USA), 1958. **Drawstring dress**. Photograph by Louise Dahl-Wolfe, *Harper's Bazaar*, 1946.

McCartney Stella   Designer

An embroidered miniature evening dress of satin bears the richesse associated with traditional French fashion, but the proportions belong to the modern age. Chloé showed the first collection by Stella McCartney, appointed designer in 1997 at only twenty-five, in the opulent setting of the Opéra Garnier in Paris. Even though Yves Saint Laurent beat her by a few years (he was just twenty-one when he took over at Christian Dior), McCartney's appointment was seen as a precocious one. She worked briefly for Lacroix and was influenced by finds made in the Portobello Market, close to her West London flat. On Friday and Saturday mornings McCartney would garner antique buttons and vintage clothes, a passion which explains the romantic strand of her style. The other, tailoring, is attributable to a short, unofficial apprenticeship with Edward Sexton, a Savile Row tailor. McCartney has said, 'Anyone who has seen my work knows I am not about shock tactics.'

☞ Lenoir, Lacroix

294

Stella McCartney. b London (UK), 1971. **Miniature satin evening dress for Chloé.** Photograph by Perry Ogden, 1998.

McDean Craig   Photographer

Model Guinevere, wearing nothing but artfully undone hair and make-up by Eugene Souleiman and Pat McGrath, appears from behind traditional wallpaper in an advertisement for Jil Sander. That this photograph is representing a fashion and make-up company would make it surreal, except that this is an example of selling a mood rather than a product. McDean's work appeared in the 1990s at a time when his realist photography stood out against the fashion for photographs which presented a limited number of scenarios. He has said, 'I want to appeal to everyone, not just the fashion world,' but it is primarily those in fashion who appreciate his work, which is subtly challenging. It is resolutely modern and each photograph, deliberately accidental, is stark and voyeuristic, seemingly capturing a dream-like moment. McDean is part of the neo-realism school dubbed 'Heroin Chic' by US President Bill Clinton in 1997.

☞ Berardi, McGrath, Sander, Sitbon, Souleiman

295

Craig McDean. b Nantwich (UK), 1964. **Guinevere. Jil Sander publicity campaign**. 1996.

Macdonald Julien   Designer

In her Cimmerian haunt of tumbled net, a mermaid is sheathed in gossamer-fine yarns that decorate her body like calligraphy on skin. Seductive and opulent, Julien Macdonald's work takes the girlishness out of knitwear. He spins out fiery fantasies like this from his trusty knitting machine. With loosened screws and bent parts, it becomes an instrument for creating the tactile surfaces he desires. Karl Lagerfeld, who hired him as knitwear designer for Chanel in 1996, declared to *Vogue* 'Julien plays with his machine like Horowitz plays on his Steinway.' While regarded as a master of youthful innovation, Macdonald does pay homage to the traditional craft, making it modern by using new-fangled, fluorescent yarns and luminous mohair (an idea sparked off by metallic Nike trainers). Macdonald graduated from the Royal College of Art in 1996 and started his solo career designing knitwear for Alexander McQueen and Koji Tatsuno.

☛ S. Ellis, Keogh, Lagerfeld, Tatsuno

Julien Macdonald. b Merthyr Tydfil (UK), 1972. **Metallic knitted 'Mermaid' dress**. Photograph by Sean Ellis, 1997.

296

McFadden Mary   Designer

While Mary McFadden will probably always be remembered principally for her pleated dresses à la Fortuny, she has not only made outfits for Grecian maidens, but has also brought global artistry to the comfort of easy sportswear. Hand-painted skirts, dresses and jackets are informed by McFadden's acute awareness of international design traditions, with a special leaning towards Southeast Asia and Africa. Textile scholarship and crafts luxury are, however, mediated by McFadden's unerring sense for modern comfort and poise. Inspired by decorative traditions and her pleasure in textiles, McFadden has rendered both Klimt and the *Book of Kells* in sumptuous coats, seized details from Portuguese tiles and understood the rich batiks of Southeast Asia. She straddles the art-to-wear movement and the pragmatic fashion industry. Likewise her clothing strikes an urbane formality for daywear and a wearable ease for evenings. In an epoch when colour is cautious, McFadden is a sumptuous world traveller.

☞ Fortuny, Lancetti, Lapidus, Lester

297

Mary McFadden. b New York (USA), 1936. **Finely pleated dress and throw.** Photograph by Pierre Scherman, *Women's Wear Daily*, 1977.

McGrath Pat

Make-up artist

Pat McGrath heightens the dramatic potential of make-up by using it as a brilliant focus, isolating dense blocks of colour in a parody of one accepted scheme. Here, red lipstick is the single feature on an otherwise undecorated face. In a customary twist on the *i-D* cover (established with the magazine's inception in 1980), model Kirsten Owen's eye is shrouded by her hat. Her fiery mouth is the dominating focal point. McGrath, in partnership with hairdresser Eugene Souleiman, works with Steven Meisel, Paolo Roversi and Craig McDean to push the boundaries of beauty, and her directional vision has been used to flavour catwalk collections by Prada, Comme des Garçons and Dolce & Gabbana. Her innovation has released make-up from the framework of facial contours since her patterns of colour are daubed seemingly randomly.

☛ McDean, Prada, Rocha, Roversi, Souleiman, Toskan

298

Pat McGrath. b Northampton (UK), 1966. **Kirsten Owen**. Cover of *i-D*, May 1998 (The Supernatural Issue). Photograph by Paolo Roversi.

Mackie Bob   Designer

Mackie offers a rhinestone cowgirl, a marvel in swinging fringe and bold motion and dressed in his signature style (reminiscent of the all-singing, all-dancing films of old Hollywood), that he has been crafting since the 1960s. Coming to fame as a television designer for *The Sonny and Cher Comedy Hour* (1971–4) and *The Carol Burnett Show* (1967–78), Mackie presented a hyperbolic form of showbiz glamour which was effective, even at television scale, in conveying large-screen and Las Vegas opulence and extravaganza. It was a *tour de force* achieved by letting the dress, or a few dresses, serve as the embodiment of a grandiloquence. By the advent of MTV, Mackie was too much associated with old-style theatricality to be popular there, but he, more than any other designer, was responsible for establishing brilliant costume for the medium of television. This was his contribution to fashion, the championing of beading and sequins for gowns, swimwear and loungewear.

☞ Leiber, N. Miller, Norell, Oldham, Orry-Kelly

299

Bob Mackie. b Monterey Park, CA (USA), 1940. **Black fringed, beaded dress**. Photograph by Steven Klein, British *Vogue*, 1988.

McKnight Sam   Hairdresser

Three women wear gamine hairstyles by Sam McKnight. The 'extreme gelled girls' illustrate his highly-polished, sharply-defined work. This sleek look, achieved by his 1920s-inspired styles, equals the make-up for dramatic effect, thus providing a fine balance. 'Hair is like clothes', says Mcknight, 'you should look as though you wear it with ease, that's the sexiest hair.' He is known for nonchalant glamour, and it was this he gave to Diana, Princess of Wales, when, on a shoot for *Vogue* in 1990, she asked him, 'What would you do if you had a free reign with my hair?'. 'Cut it short', was McKnight's reply. And he did, becoming the architect of her later, modernized look. Trained in a salon that eschewed electrical appliances, he learned to create uncontrived hairstyles and still maintains that hair should not look forced. A woman, he believes, should always look approachable and should never risk fashion at the expense of her comfort.

☛ Antoine, Diana, Pita

Sam McKnight. b New Cumnock (UK), 1959. **Extreme Gelled girls, hanging out**. Photograph by Arthur Elgort, Italian *Vogue*, 1993.

300

McLaren Malcolm   Designer

Malcolm McLaren delivers his manifesto wearing the rubber clothes sold in his shop, Sex, for the film, *The Great Rock 'n' Roll Swindle* (1978). A maverick entrepreneur and music aficionado, McLaren is credited with shaping the punk movement. In 1971 he and his partner, Vivienne Westwood, took over the running of a vintage shop, Let It Rock. Within three years they were selling bondage and fetish clothing, briefly renaming the shop Too Fast to Live, Too Young to Die before it became Sex in 1975. The graphic anti-monarchy and pseudo-porn images by Jamie Reid, which were used as fabric prints, caused outrage (the shop was regularly raided by police). The same year McLaren managed a US band, the New York Dolls, whose pre-punk music inspired him to return to the UK to form his own band. The Sex Pistols was cast from customers and named after the shop. The band was effectively a public relations exercise which exploded; McLaren later confessed, 'Punk was just a way to sell trousers.'

☛ Rotten, Van Beirendonck, Westwood

Malcolm McLaren. b London (UK), 1946. **Malcolm McLaren wears rubber all-in-one.** *The Great Rock 'n' Roll Swindle*, 1978.

301

McLaughlin-Gill Frances   Photographer

This picture could be placed in any year since the one it was taken: 1948. The subject, Carol McCarlson, dries herself on a Florida beach; it is a picture that uses the blur of her oscillating towel to lend a naturalness for which its photographer is known. In 1941, Frances McLaughlin-Gill and her twin sister Kathryn entered a photography competition in *Vogue*. Both were finalists and Kathryn landed a job with *Vogue* photographer Toni Frissell. It was she who recommended that Frances should be introduced to her art director Alexander Liberman. He hired McLaughlin-Gill in 1943 and she came to illustrate the lives of the new young market for *Glamour* and *Vogue*, making relaxed depictions of real scenes the context for the burgeoning teenage and American sportswear markets. McLaughlin-Gill also added a spirit of informality to the stiff, grown-up couture of the 1950s.

☛ Campbell-Walters, Dessès, Frissell, Griffe, Liberman, Shrimpton

Frances McLaughlin-Gill. b New York (USA), 1919. **Carol McCarlson on the beach, St Augustine, Florida.** *American Vogue*, 1948.

McQueen Alexander   Designer

'Bumsters' were Alexander McQueen's iconoclastic challenge to fashion. Just as women were getting used to wearing hipsters in 1995, he urged their trousers ever lower in the style of a builder's drooping waistband. From the moment McQueen graduated from Central Saint Martin's College of Art and Design in 1992, with a collection entitled 'Jack the Ripper Stalking his Victims', he used an aggressive approach towards design. 'Eclectic verging on the criminal' is how he describes his work, and no taboo has been ignored as he wields that banner. 'Highland Rape', a 1996 collection, dressed women in bloodied, tattered lace dresses. Savagery is usually close to the surface, although McQueen's work for Givenchy, a label he inherited from John Galliano in 1996, sometimes shows glimpses of a mellow McQueen – usually sharp, but often elegant in places. While McQueen has been accused of bad taste, it hasn't prevented his work from influencing that of the generation following him.

☛ Bowie, Chalayan, Galliano, Givenchy, N. Knight, Pearl

303

Alexander McQueen (Lee McQueen). b London (UK), 1969. **Brocade 'bumsters'.** Photograph by Phil Poynter, 1996.

Madonna

Icon

Madonna wears Jean Paul Gaultier's famous pink satin corset for her 'Blonde Ambition' tour in 1990. A very real master of fashion's seasonal about-face, she has a unique and dynamic propensity for continually reinventing herself. Her impact as a vocalist and fashion icon in the early 1980s was undeniably heightened by the timely introduction of a new visual format of music, namely Music Television (MTV). But it was her ability to assume various, often controversial, personas with each new video release which set her apart from other artists. She has variously embraced lace and torn denim, a trashy, sexy, punky image for the release of her premier album in 1983; a glamorous, blond Marilyn Monroe lookalike in 'Material Girl' in 1986 (complete with spray-on dress and Harry Winston diamonds) and a sophisticated persona as Eva Perón in the 1997 film *Evita*, wearing 1940s-inspired couture.

☞ Baron, Galliano, Gaultier, Pita, Testino, Versace

304

Madonna (Louise Madonna Ciccione). b Detroit, MI (USA), 1958. Madonna wears pink basque by Jean Paul Gaultier. 1990.

Mainbocher   Designer

During the 1940s, Natalia Wilson (Mrs John C. Wilson, Princess Paley) was manager of Mainbocher's New York salon and his main vendeuse. She often posed for fashion magazines wearing his clothes, in this case a sumptuous evening outfit that would have been worn to a dinner party or to the theatre. Mainbocher was celebrated for his lush evening suits which consisted of a long dark skirt and contrasting jacket decorated with trimmings such as fur. With the distinctive beauty of Natalia Wilson modelling these suits, Mainbocher won acclaim and went on to become the first American designer to open a maison de couture in Paris. Mainbocher's earlier career had included sketching for *Vogue*. Like many others, he was influenced by Madeleine Vionnet's bias-cutting technique, a method he used for the Duchess of Windsor's wedding dress.

☛ Hoyningen-Huene, Ricci, Vionnet, Windsor

305

Mainbocher (Main Rousseau Bocher). b Chicago, IL (USA), 1890. **d** New York (USA), 1976. **Princess Natalia Paley**. Photograph by Louise Dahl-Wolfe, American *Vogue*, 1944.

Maltézos Madeleine and Carpentier Suzanne (Mad Carpentier)   Designers

The very anonymity of the design team who created this dress is testament to their desire to remain on the conservative side of fashion, at a time when their colleagues were using shocking innovation as an advertisement for their houses. Upon the retirement of the legendary Madeleine Vionnet, two of her staff (Mad Maltézos and Suzie Carpentier) established a new fashion house. After the Second World War, Mad Carpentier was known for luxurious dresses and coats favoured by a restrained clientele not likely to go to the 'hot' fashion houses such as Dior, Fath or even Balenciaga. Rather, what Mad Carpentier distilled was an essence of the past, always harking back to Art Deco and the streamlining of the 1920s and 1930s. Dresses were demure and coats were elegant and comfortable, never giving in to the quick silhouette changes of the 1940s. They were also more or less timeless and nameless, recognized mainly by New York's garment district, Seventh Avenue, which copied their saleable good taste.

☞ Connolly, Morton, Simpson, Vionnet

Madeleine Maltézos and Suzanne Carpentier (Mad Carpentier). (Active 1940s–1950s.) **Shawl-collared dress.** French *Vogue*, 1949.

Mandelli Mariuccia (Krizia)   Designer

Sharp pleats are thrown into black-and-white relief, capturing an atmosphere of drama and amusement, which conveys almost a circus mood in Mariuccia Mandelli's design for her company Krizia. There is a strong sense of architecture expressed in the geometric lines formed by the pleats of the outfit. When the wearer moves, these pleats form a rolling wave. Mandelli explained her distinctive style thus, 'There is often a sense of architecture in my clothing...one of my collections was inspired by the Chrysler Building.' Krizia, named after Plato's discourse on the vanity of women, was formed in Milan in 1951. Historically, it is noted for experimental construction and an irreverent approach to glamorous clothes, and was at one point dubbed 'Crazy Krizia' by the American press. In the 1970s, Mandelli's eveningwear included sporting garments and those usually worn for daywear, such as jodhpurs and sweaters.

☛ Capucci, Miyake, Venet

Mariuccia Mandelli. b Bergamo (IT), 1933. (Krizia.) **Pleated lamé frills**. Photograph by Giovanni Gastel, 1998.

Man Ray

Photographer

Photographer Man Ray was one of the central figures in the Surrealist movement in Paris. He was fascinated by women's lips as objects of desire. Other artists and fashion designers have ventured to portray the lips of Surrealism: Dalí designed a sofa modelled on Mae West's lips, Saint Laurent created a Lip Dress and Elsa Schiaparelli used lips as a pocket (the hand inserted between them). In 1921 Man Ray left New York for Paris, where he took up photography to finance his painting. An introduction to Poiret, who was looking for a different sort of photographer, brought him into fashion, a field which united his experimentation with a commercial product. In the 1920s his work for *Vogue* and *Harper's Bazaar* extended fashion photography from posed formality into the sphere of collaborative art. He asserted that 'inspiration, not information, the force that binds all creative acts' is at the root of great fashion and all its disciplines.

☞ Bernard, Blumenfeld, Dalí, Hoyningen-Huene, Schiaparelli

308

Man Ray (Emmanuel Rudnitsky). b Philadelphia, PA (USA), 1890. d Paris (FR), 1976. **Lips on Lips**. 1930.

Maramotti Achille (MaxMara) Designer

'For us to be considered fashionable would be very dangerous,' says MaxMara's managing director, Luigi Maramotti. 'It is not chic for a woman to move violently from one way of dressing to another.' MaxMara is the epitome of Italian fashion: good quality and cut, in classic styles, while managing to interpret trends in a very wearable way. The camel-coloured wrap coat shown here is pure cashmere, and although the design seems pared down, attention to detail is impeccable. One of Italy's largest and oldest fashion companies, MaxMara was founded in 1951 by Doctor Achille Maramotti, a lawyer turned dressmaker. His first collection consisted of just two outfits: a suit and an overcoat. This brevity of design has always been MaxMara's signature, and the collections still focus on these key items of tailoring. It concentrates on easing the transition through trends for a clientele that requires a central core of good taste.

☛ Beretta, Paulin, Venturi

Achille Maramotti. b Reggio nell'Emilia (IT), 1926. (MaxMara.) **Linda Evangelista wears MaxMara camel coat.** Photograph by Steven Meisel, 1997.

Margiela Martin   Designer

The construction of Martin Margiela's black jacket becomes clear in the negative image. It uses the deep-set armholes, raised shoulders, wide lapels and raised waistline often seen in his tailoring. Margiela designs in the manner of an avant-garde artist, rather than following fashion's accustomed desire to please. He deconstructs clothes (putting the lining material on the outside), uses doll's clothes as models for adult clothing (complete with giant buttons), recycles unlikely materials (T-shirts formed from used shopping bags) and makes sweaters out of socks. Having graduated from Antwerp's influential Royal Academy of Arts, Margiela became a design assistant to Jean Paul Gaultier – his work takes off from Gaultier's fashion shocks which conceal clever techniques of tailoring and dressmaking. Rather than being rejected by traditional houses, Margiela's iconoclastic methods were accepted in 1997 when Hermès hired him to oversee its design studio.

☛ Bikkembergs, Gaultier, Thimister, Van Noten

Martin Margiela. b Louvain (BEL), 1957. Fitted jacket. Photographs by Ronald Stoops, 1989.

Marteans Dr Klaus (Dr Martens)   Shoe designer

In a stunning duality of purpose the Dr Marten ('DM') boot has been a symbol of aggressive, anti-fashion cults for three decades. It is also worn by most uniformed, establishment figures. It began life as an orthopaedic aid. Designed in 1946 by Klaus Marteans, a Bavarian doctor who had broken his foot while skiing and wanted something to relieve the pain, the boot was an overnight success. In 1959 the British bootmaker R. Griggs was granted permission to use Marteans' air-cushioned sole on his steelcapped workmens' boots; the compound was changed to granular PVC (resistant to fat, oil, acids and petrol) and has remained unchanged ever since. The 'Famous Footwear AirWair, with bouncing soles' was born. In the mid-1960s, the eight-eyelet boot in black or cherry red became a uniform for skinheads; in the 1980s, DMs became an essential part of British 'street style' when they were worn with a pair of Levi's jeans.

☛ Cox, Jaeger, Strauss

311

Dr Klaus Marteans. b Braunschweiz (GER), 1915. d (GER), 1988. Policeman and skinhead wear Dr Martens. Southend, 1980.

Matsuda Mitsuhiro   Designer

Mitsuhiro Matsuda arranges a variety of woven linens for an outfit which hardly resembles clothes at all. The fabrics themselves dominate the image, with checks and stripes loosely woven to form a semi-transparent material. Matsuda is one of the early greats in the tradition of Japanese fashion design that carried successfully over to a Western tradition and sensibility. In the 1980s, his clothes were whimsical and romantic in the British style, often taking their inspiration from the costumes of historical England. Yet he maintained a practicality and wearability in his tailoring that was androgynous and sexy. His menswear was directional and elements of it were used for his womenswear. Matsuda's father worked in the kimono industry and it was with that garment that he and his contemporaries, Kenzo and Yohji Yamamoto, examined the principle of Western clothes.

☞ Kenzo, Kim, Kobayashi, Y. Yamamoto

312

Mitsuhiro Matsuda. **b** Tokyo (JAP), 1934. **'Madame Nicole'. Mixed linens. Spring/summer 1996.** Photograph by Mitsuhiro Matsuda.

Matsushima Masaki   Designer

'Fashion is necessary but I think it is of secondary importance,' says Masaki Matsushima. His suits for men and women show both sides of this argument at once. Inherently they deal with the pinstripe tradition, lending them a sober quality, and yet they have a fashion edge which is sharpened with broad shirt collars and a flamboyant buttonhole. But Matsushima feels that these styling touches are down to the individual who will make the clothes their own. 'I am trying to create a mass image,' continues Matsushima. 'That is why I don't think that creation means to force the designer's own personality on the people.' Matsushima graduated from Tokyo's famous Bunka Gakuen Fukushoku school of fashion in 1985. He designed costumes for conceptual singer Ryuichi Sakamoto and launched his own label. His clothes are by turns highly technical and instrumental in promoting the notion of conceptual streetwear.

☛ Bartlett, Dolce & Gabbana, Newton

313

Masaki Matsushima. b Magoya (JAP), 1963. **Reworked pinstripe suits**. Photograph by Satoshi Saikusa, 1998.

Maxwell Vera   Designer

'Buy a Share in America' declare the wartime posters, and Americans did – even in fashion. During the Second World War, European fashions, in particular those from Paris, were not available, so America turned to its own designers. Vera Maxwell was one of the designers who came to the fore at this time. Her separates – simple shapes in humble fabrics – adhered to wartime restrictions as well as being conscious of the pressures and new-found responsibilities of women workers. Maxwell often reinterpreted men's workwear shapes – this jacket is based on a man's lumberjack shirt. In 1970, Maxwell discovered Ultrasuede which was to become a durable yet sophisticated staple for women's tailoring, championed especially by Halston. In 1974 she designed her first Speed Suit – an elasticated dress that could be quickly slipped down over the head for busy women. It was a precursor to Donna Karan's ethos a decade later.

☛ Dahl-Wolfe, Halston, Karan, A. Klein

Vera Maxwell. b New York (USA), 1903. **d** Rincon (PR), 1995. **Co-ordinated day suit.** Photograph by Louise Dahl-Wolfe, *Harper's Bazaar*, 1942.

Mazzilli Tiziano and Louise (Voyage)   Designers

Wrinkled velvet ribbon sewn onto the neckline of a sheer T-shirt signifies the work of Voyage. Such clothes are designed to look like antiques and cast-offs and yet are recognizable as expensive garments to those in the know. Made from slub silk, linen, silk velvet and taffeta, each one-size-fits-all unstructured garment is hand-dyed, hand-painted and washed to 'authenticate' it.

Voyage mixes colours in the same haphazard way, contriving to build an apparently careless look. Owners Tiziano Mazzilli and his wife Louise have fostered the label's image as an exclusive and expensive one. In 1991 they opened Voyage on London's Fulham Road. 'Our philosophy is to be unique,' says Mazzilli. 'We don't want to please everyone.' And they don't. Each visitor to the

boutique must ring a bell, and undergo scrutiny before being allowed in, an example of fashionable exclusion surpassed only by a later move to introduce membership cards.

☞ von Etzdorf, Oudejans, Williamson

Mazzilli. Tiziano. b Udine (IT); **Louise. b** Brussels (BEL). (Active 1990s–) (Voyage.) **Velvet-trimmed T-shirt and cutwork pink skirt**. Photograph by Howard Sooley, *Joyce*, 1997.

Meisel Steven

Photographer

Steven Meisel's picnic illustrates a collection by Dolce & Gabbana. The sunny lighting contradicts the cold, dull background, giving the picture a surreal edge. Meisel calls himself 'a reflection of my times'. It is a phrase that equally applies to his work. His strength is as an image-maker, both in terms of his own image, and that of the designers' work he photographs and the models whose careers he has transformed – Meisel discovered Linda Evangelista and Stella Tennant. He has a sensitivity towards clothes and is able to adapt to each garment he photographs: 'I am always influenced by the philosophy of the particular couturier whose dress I am photographing.' American and Italian *Vogue* are Meisel's biggest arenas. In one Italian edition he has been given as many as thirty pages to depict a single story: a fact that makes him the undisputed emperor of fashion image-making.

☞ Dolce & Gabbana, Evangelista, Garren, Gigli, Sprouse, Sui, Tennant

Steven Meisel. **b** New York (USA), 1954. **'Early fall picnic in Dolce & Gabbana'**. Italian *Vogue*, 1998.

Mesejeán Pablo and Cancela Delia (Pablo & Delia)   Designers

The flower power youth revolts from Paris to San Martín and the resurgence of artisan crafting paved the way for Pablo and Delia's fantasies. Inspired by Lewis Carroll's stories, this shirred, floral-printed cotton top with a layered tulle, flower-shaped headband heralds the bloom of naïveté as a lifestyle. The mood of the times was summarized in Pablo Mesejeán and Delia Cancela's 1966 Manifesto, which proclaimed, 'We love sunny days, the Rolling Stones, tanned bodies, the *young savage look*, pink and baby blue, happy ends.' Upon the arrival in London in 1970 of these two art students from Buenos Aires, UK *Vogue* instantly featured a cover with Jean Shrimpton in their trademark rainbow-coloured, painted leather dress. Pablo and Delia's bright, fresh accessories and clothes were usually accompanied by their own dream-like illustrations of wizards, girl astronauts and fairies wearing their creations. Since Pablo's death in 1986, Delia has concentrated on painting and illustration.

☛ Coddington, Gibb, Leonard, Shrimpton

317

Pablo Mesejeán. b Buenos Aires (ARG), 1937. **d** Paris (FR), 1986; **Delia Cancela. b** Buenos Aires (ARG), 1940. (Pablo & Delia.) **Pink 'Petal Hat' and shirred dress.** Photograph by Barry Lategan, British *Vogue*, 1972.

De Meyer Baron Adolph Photographer

In balletic pose, Baron de Meyer's subject displays layers of opulent lace trimmed with silk satin ribbon. Her peignoir and dress are backlit to give them and her a luminous glow in a hugely romantic portrait of femininity. De Meyer's fashion photography was founded in the *belle époque* before the First World War. Having spent his childhood in Paris and Germany, he entered London's fashionable society at the end of the nineteenth century. He was hired by Condé Nast in 1914, becoming *Vogue*'s first full-time photographer and later moving to *Harper's Bazaar* in 1921. With their halos and fragile clothes, his subjects appeared too delicate to participate in vigorous modern life which included swimming, tennis, golf and the Charleston, and his style was replaced by dynamic experiments in movement. De Meyer left *Harper's Bazaar* in 1932, his place taken by Martin Munkacsi and his invigorating look.

☛ Antoine, Arden, Boué, Munkacsi, Nast, Reboux, Sumurun, Tappé

Baron Adolph de Meyer. **b** Paris (FR), 1868. **d** Los Angeles, CA (USA), 1949. **Romantic chiffon dress**. American *Vogue*, 1922.

Miller Lee
Photographer

A model, with her painted nails, lipstick, coiffed hair and bias-cut dress, is a tantalizing vision for the servicewomen she parades for. One stretches her arm to feel the cloth , the wearing of which, for most, would have been an impossible dream. Her unconscious touch renders the model as unreal as the image she projects. American photographer Lee Miller is known for

her poignant photographs taken during the Second World War as a member of the London War Correspondents' Corps. During this time, however, she also worked for *Vogue*. Her captivating photograph shows that Paris couture had lost none of its power during the war, and the city was well positioned to re-establish itself as a fashion leader. In the late 1920s Miller was a model,

photographer and writer for *Vogue* in New York. In 1929 she moved to Paris, where she lived and worked with Man Ray and was friendly with Picasso and the Surrealists.

☛ Arnold, Bruyère, Dalí, Man Ray

319

Lee Miller. **b** Poughkeepsie, NY (USA), 1907. **d** Chiddingly (UK), 1977. **Service women at a fashion salon, Paris**. 1944.

Miller Nolan   Designer

Nolan Miller, architect of the extravagant *Dynasty* look which defined the shameless glamour and camp of 1980s fashion, sits surrounded by the show's female stars. His studio generated twenty-five to thirty such outfits every week – with just two days to discuss a wardrobe and five days to create it. His 'bitch' wardrobe for Joan Collins (Alexis Colby), who wears a gleaming column of pink sequins here, was modelled on that worn by Joan Crawford in the 1940s. Her shoulders are exaggerated with vast outcrops of fuchsia ruffles. Next to her, Diahann Carroll (Dominique Devereaux) and Linda Evans (Krystle Carrington) also bear the inflated, squared-off shoulder line which was copied by women who associated it with masculine power. Born in Texas, Miller moved to Hollywood in the hope of dressing glamorous women by becoming one of cinema's legendary costume designers. He arrived too late for that but in time to bring glamour to the small screen.

☛ Banton, Bates, Burrows, Mackie

320

Nolan Miller. **b** Burkbarnette, TX (USA), 1935. **Nolan Miller and his female cast**. *Dynasty*, 1985.

Milner Deborah   Designer

Deborah Milner's clothes are sculptural fantasies that defy the term 'fashion'. Indeed, this gauzy, full-length black coat featuring Milner's signature – a superb sweeping cowl neck and intricate textiles – could probably stand alone in an art gallery. Milner says, 'My work ranges from the avant-garde to the quite classic'. One of her former tutors describes her as having 'revived the art of couture by adapting her skills to work with everyday materials'. These include net, tape, film and coated wire. Milner had a strict Methodist upbringing and countered it by enrolling at art college where she discovered fashion. She began with a small couture studio in 1991, specializing in one-off, avant-garde fashion pieces for, among others, milliner Philip Treacy, who used them as foils for his climactic headgear. Here, his ergonomic glittered ellipse equals Milner's semi-sheer coat for drama.

☛ Hishinuma, Horvat, Treacy

Deborah Milner. b Walton-on-Thames (UK), 1964. **Gauze coat**. Photograph by Mark Mattock, *i-D*, 1997.

Missoni Tai, Rosita and Angela Designers

1971 or 1998? We rely on modern photography and styling for the answer because the enduring popularity of Missoni's colourful knitwear in basic shapes means their clothes have changed little over the years. Their strength and appeal lies in their simple beauty. Colour is the key to the Missoni look. The distinctive, flecked 'flame dye' effect is achieved by only partly immersing the yarn in the dye to leave a white mark or to allow the colour of the yarn to show through. The Missonis met at the 1948 Olympics in London, where Ottavio was competing in the 400-metre hurdles, wearing the team tracksuit that had been designed by his own small knitwear company. They married and their first collection was presented in Milan in 1966. In 1997 Ottavio and Rosita handed the business over to their daughter, Angela, who has inherited the Missoni sensibilities.

☛ Eula, Gibb, Khanh, Testino

322

Missoni. Ottavio (Tai). b Ragusa (SYR), 1921; Rosita. b Golasecca (IT), 1931; Angela. b Milan (IT), 1958. **Chevron vest and striped cardigan. Spring/summer 1998.** Photograph by Mario Testino.

Miyake Issey   Designer

Peaking through torn tissue, a vivid pink shirt is displayed as though it were an installation. This intricately pleated garment has been created by carefully folding a length of polyester, twisting it tightly, then treating it with heat. This particular creation and other vividly coloured, highly innovative designs, often involving wrapping and layering fabric, are typical of the renowned Japanese designer, Issey Miyake. He served an apprenticeship first with Guy Laroche and then with Givenchy. He also worked in New York designing ready-to-wear for Geoffrey Beene, before returning to Japan in 1970 to found his own design studio at the age of thirty-two. Hugely influential, Miyake is a member of Japan's fashion elite, along with Rei Kawakubo and Yohji Yamamoto, and his clothes are admired and worn by artists, architects and intellectuals.

☛ Arai, Beene, Givenchy, Hishinuma, Kawakubo, Laroche, Mandelli

323

Issey Miyake. b Hiroshima (JAP), 1938. **'Pleats Please' pink shirt**. Photograph by Kazumi Kurigami, 1995.

Mizrahi Isaac   Designer

Isaac Mizrahi, wearing his customary headband, is photographed in his New York studio with model Shalom Harlow, who is laid out on his pattern-cutting table. Beyond the scorching colour of her dress, designed for spring 1995, there is a rainbow of cottons stored on the wall and an intense mix of shades represented on a rail of samples behind them. They are all evidence that Mizrahi is not a designer afraid of colour – pacific blue, cartoon yellow, bubblegum pink. 'I love Technicolor – it's wildly beautiful,' he says of his untrammelled taste in sunshine colours. He marries vibrant, unusual materials with shapes long used for American sportswear, such as a parka cut from fuchsia satin. This sense of comedy in his work and personality was aired in a docufilm, *Unzipped*, which followed the creation of his autumn 1994 collection. It comes from his training at New York's High School for the Performing Arts prior to his entry into fashion.

☞ Beene, Kors, Moses, Oldham

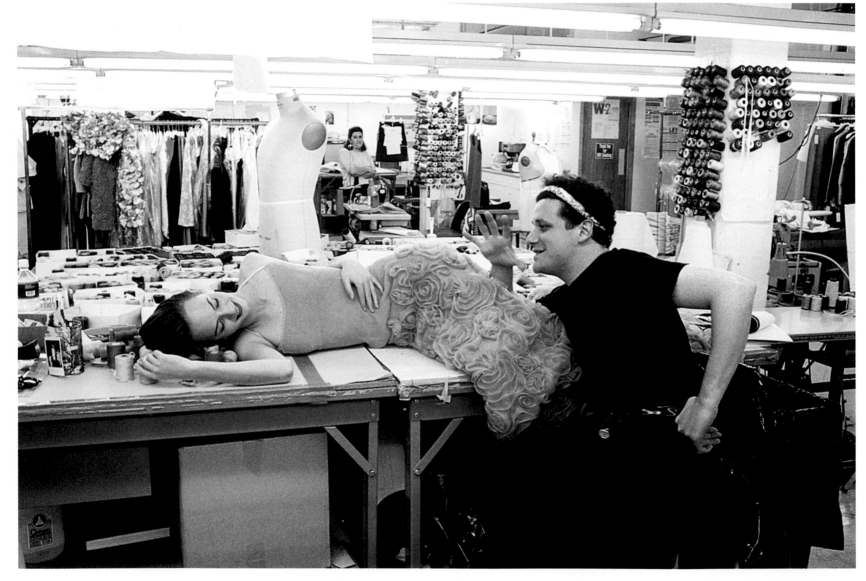

Isaac Mizrahi. **b** New York (USA), 1961. **Isaac Mizrahi with Shalom Harlow**. Photograph by Gilles Bensimon, American *Elle*, 1995.

Model Philippe   Milliner

Complex hats, such as this sculpted headpiece formed from interwoven, red velvet segments, have put Philippe Model at the forefront of French accessories design since 1978. It was then he left school and started his business from scratch by making haute couture hats. Shortly afterwards, Model was awarded the title '*Meilleur ouvrier de France*' (finest craftsman in France), a coveted prize for excellence which dates back to the Middle Ages. He moved to the heart of French fashion in the early 1980s, after working with Jean Paul Gaultier, Claude Montana and Thierry Mugler for whom he accessorized avant-garde collections. Model doesn't limit his work to millinery – he is also a shoe designer whose neat, elasticated shoes became widely copied. Similar in idea to Hervé Léger's 'elastic bandage' dresses, they are formed from strips of stretch material and display a practical design talent.

☛ Léger, Montana, Mugler, Paulette, Underwood

Philippe Model. b Sens (FR), 1956. **Spiral hat**. Photograph by Satoshi Saikusa, *Harpers & Queen*, 1988.

Molinari Anna   Designer

Anna Molinari believes that every woman has a dual fashion personality, widely known as the virgin/whore complex. In this editorial, model Trish Goff fulfils both by wearing a sheer shirt, brief satin shorts and a snowy tailored jacket for cooking. Molinari's work is always traditional in the way it deals with creating sexy clothes, often using a formula that marries brief hemlines with sheer fabrics. In doing so, she takes the clothes off the street and into the realm of a designer label. While mirroring current trends, Molinari attracts a following of ultra-feminine women. Her more romantic medium uses flouncy dresses, tutus and tops decorated with ruffles, frills and bows, which are always just decent. In 1977 she established the label in partnership with her husband, Gianpaolo Tarabini. At that time Molinari produced chiefly knitwear, a selection of which remains in the form of sweater-girl shapes trimmed with diamanté.

☛ van Lamsweerde, Thomass, Versace

326

Anna Molinari. b Capri (IT). (Active 1970s–.) **Trish Goff**. Photograph by Pamela Hanson, American *Vogue*, 1995.

Molyneux Capt. Edward   Designer

A romantic look back to the silhouette worn by the Empress Josephine during the First Empire (1804–15) characterizes this evening dress. The empire-style dress has a high waistline, a square-cut neckline, short, puffed sleeves and rich embroidery. A draped, floor-length stole tapering into a train and long gloves completes the regal look. Such aristocratic grandeur made Molyneux a favourite fashion designer among royalty, society women and film stars. Princess Marina, Duchess of Kent, was one of his most famous and elegant clients. Trained under Lucile (Lady Duff Gordon), who in the early twentieth century designed empire-style gowns, Molyneux nevertheless walked a fine line between romantic revival and modernity. He was a fashion designer with a reputation for exquisite taste based on purity of line and cut. Christian Dior was known to have preferred Molyneux to any other couturier. Amongst those to whom Molyneux passed on his techniques was Pierre Balmain.

☛ Balmain, Dior, Duff Gordon, Griffe, Stiebel, Sumurun, Vertès

Captain Edward Molyneux. b London (UK), 1891. **d** Monte Carlo (MON), 1974. **Embroidered satin, empire-line dress.** Photograph by François Kollar, 1939.

Montana Claude   Designer

Aggressive jackets cut from leather epitomize Claude Montana's extreme style. Broad-shouldered, para-military shapes accentuated with epaulettes and cinched waists have dominated his work, the most powerful using leather, since his own label was launched in 1979. Montana understands a simple Constructivist shape with its straight, uncompromising lines and uses extreme styling in the way Pierre Cardin did in the 1960s. He relishes the act of 'building' his designs and was widely respected for those he created for Lanvin Couture from 1989 to 1992. Montana's career began in London, when he ran short of money on a visit and started designing jewellery, which was then featured in *Vogue*. After a year, he returned to Paris to work for the leather firm MacDouglas. In the 1980s his work symbolized a movement of women's fashion which dressed them as super-heroines.

☛ Flett, Lanvin, Model, Steiger, Viramontes

328

Claude Montana. b Paris (FR), 1949. **Embroidered, white and gold leather outfits for Idéal Cuir.** Photograph by Alain Larue, *L'Officiel*, 1980.

Moon Sarah

Photographer

A Sarah Moon photograph is almost always a dreamy, soft-focus trip back to the fashion mood of the 1920s and 1930s. When she photographed the Pirelli Calendar in 1972, it was a groundbreaking event: not only was she the first woman to do so (she was chosen to pacify objections from the feminist movement), but she was also the first to show fully exposed breasts. Moon spent much of the 1960s as a fashion model, but towards the end of that decade turned to photography. Her first assignment was an advertising campaign for Cacharel, which led to editorial work for *Nova*, *Vogue*, *Harper's Bazaar* and *Elle*. Subsequent advertising campaigns for Biba cosmetics summed up the fashion mood of the early 1970s. Moon has since moved beyond the constraints of fashion and into the sphere of fine art photography. Her work has remained muted, somewhat surreal, and always beautiful.

☞ Bousquet, Dinnigan, Hulanicki, Williamson

Sarah Moon. b Paris (FR), 1941. **Katia wears Enrica Massei.** *The Frankfurter*, 1997.

Morehouse Marion   Model

The photographer Edward Steichen once declared that, 'Good fashion models have the qualities inherent in a good actress.' For Steichen, Morehouse was 'the best fashion model I ever worked with'. Fashion in the 1920s demanded a sleek and willowy silhouette, and Marion Morehouse had that archetypal figure. This, together with her commanding presence and seemingly effortless elegance, made her the ideal fashion model for the period. As Steichen said, 'She transformed herself into the sort of woman who really would wear that gown.' Morehouse was also frequently photographed by some of the other great photographers who began working in the 1920s, such as Horst P. Horst and George Hoyningen-Huene.

She married the writer e.e. cummings, and later in her career also took up photography.

☛ Chéruit, Horst, Hoyningen-Huene, Steichen

Marion Morehouse. (Active 1920s–1930s.) **Marion Morehouse wears bias-cut satin dress**. Photograph by Cecil Beaton, 1929.

Mori Hanae · Designer

The radiant daylight catches Hanae Mori's favourite model Hiroko en route to her wooden pagoda retreat. Her bird-like frame, veiled in a tissue-soft, silk organza caftan printed with daisies, echoes Mori's restrained elegance and Japanese aesthetic. Kimono silk printed with cherry blossoms and butterflies, produced by Mori's husband Kei, Japanese asymmetry and obi belting are all indicative of her respect for her cultural heritage. Invariably balancing this with Western styling, Mori's feather-light creations are consistent and sensible, never enslaved to the dictates of fashion. A graduate in Japanese literature, Mori went back to college after her marriage and two sons to learn the fundamentals of dressmaking. She designed costumes for Japanese film and theatre, before setting up shop at Tokyo's shopping haven Ginza in 1955. She was admitted to Paris's Chambre Syndicale de la Couture in 1977.

☛ Hirata, Scherrer, Snowdon

Hanae Mori. b Tokyo (JAP), 1926. **Silk caftan**. Photograph by Snowdon, British *Vogue*, 1972.

Morris Robert Lee

Jewellery Designer

Three twisted, sterling silver bangles represent the sculptural work of Robert Lee Morris. The filing marks and beaten indentations lend them the natural spirit for which Morris is known. He says, 'I adore natural forms. I am a student of anatomy', and his designs forge elements of nature into a variety of objects, ranging from Africa-inspired breastplates to a lipstick holder for Elizabeth Arden. Morris has used cork, rubber, granite and silicone in his work, but when New York's Fashion Institute of Technology staged a twenty-five-year retrospective for Morris's work, it was titled 'Metalmania'. His use of stark, urban metals brought him close to Donna Karan, whose cultivated designs are an ideal backdrop for dramatic modern jewellery. Their work in the mid-1980s, often pairing navy fabric with elegant gold cuffs, created a uniform for white-collar women who wanted to escape the baroque excesses of that period.

☛ Arden, Barrett, Karan

Robert Lee Morris. b Nuremberg (GER), 1947. **Sterling silver Orbit bangles**. Photograph by Wolfgang Ludes, 1998.

332

Morton Digby   Designer

'Fashion is indestructible', proclaimed British *Vogue* when it published this photograph by Cecil Beaton as London was bombed during the Second World War. Digby Morton provided leadership in British fashion during the War years. He specialized in tailored tweed suits. The example in this photograph has a hip-length jacket and a slightly flared skirt just covering the knees. Morton took the severity and masculinity out of the tailored suit. In 1928 he joined the house of Lachasse, quickly gaining recognition for his suits in exquisitely shaded tweeds, designed to be worn with silk blouses. He left in 1933 to start his own couture business and was succeeded at Lachasse by Hardy Amies. Morton was a member of the Incorporated Society of London Fashion Designers, a group of leading couturiers which promoted the British fashion industry in the face of wartime restrictions.

☛ Amies, Beaton, Cavanagh, Creed, French, Maltézos

333

Digby Morton. b Dublin (IRE), 1906. **d** London (UK), 1983. **Grey tweed suit**. Photograph by Cecil Beaton, British *Vogue*, 1941.

Moschino Franco   Designer

Typical of Franco Moschino is this cheeky mockery of haute couture where, just for a second, the silhouette of a military jet is accepted as a couture hat in the grand French style. Moschino believed that fashion should be fun and he demanded laughs with the slogans he applied to clothes and advertising: 'Waist of Money' and 'Warning: fashion shows can be damaging to your health'. That his protest became fashion itself was testament to the garments they adorned: chic formal suits and evening dresses. As a boy, Moschino would go into his father's iron foundry and create images in the dust on the walls. He went on to study art and worked for Gianni Versace until 1977. In 1983 he launched the Moschino label. After his death in 1994, each garment was sold with a manifesto stating that environmental concern is 'the only true fashion trend'.

☞ Kelly, Steele, Versace

334

Franco Moschino. b Abbiategrasso (IT), 1950. d Milan (IT), 1994. **Silhouette of a Moschino Couture! cocktail dress, 1988.** Photograph by Fabrizio Ferri.

Moses Rebecca   Designer

A cartoon figure reclines in a classic bikini which represents Rebecca Moses' starting point for every piece of clothing: colour. The walls of her Italian studio are covered with plastic envelopes, each containing colour swatches in the form of materials, flowers and paper. They turn up on her cashmere sweaters with names such as 'Frozen Cranberries' and 'Robin's Egg'. Cartoon-like in their deep-dyed colours (thirty-five every season) and simplicity of shape, the clothes she forms owe nothing to transient fashion trends. 'I'm not saying fashion should stay still,' she says, 'but it should stop for long enough to consider the needs of modern men and women...I was fed up with fashion. There was just so much clothing out there – fashion was moving too fast and there wasn't any real life to it.' She refers to her clothing as 'mobile style' that can 'travel' between daywear and eveningwear, summer and winter and from outfit to outfit.

☛ Biagiotti, Jacobs, Mizrahi

335

Rebecca Moses. b New York (USA), 1956. **Magenta bikini, 1998**. Illustration by Rebecca Moses.

Moss Kate   Model

Every so often a special face appears, a face that changes the way we perceive beauty and which challenges our tastes. This is one such face scrubbed bare. Kate Moss was 'discovered' aged fourteen at JFK Airport, New York. Sarah Doukas, the spotter and owner of Storm modelling agency in London, felt 'she was going to be special'. She was. Kate Moss became the Twiggy of the 1990s; young and fresh, she symbolized the triumph of naturalness over artifice. Part of that charm is a naturally skinny frame that does not bear the fleshy undulations usually associated with beauty icons. Labelled a 'superwaif', her rise to fame coincided with the grunge phenomenon that celebrated an anti-designer look of uncoordinated clothes worn with rock-star attitude. Calvin Klein's unisex perfumes were one of the first products to literally bottle this attitude and make it a commercial product, leaving Kate Moss as the obvious choice of model.

☛ Day, Hilfiger, C. Klein, Kors, Sims

Kate Moss. b London (UK), 1974. **'cK be' advertising campaign for Calvin Klein.** 1997. Photograph by Richard Avedon.

Mugler Thierry — Designer

Thierry Mugler's photograph of his corset and latex trousers conjures up the themes of Aryan vamp and Pop Art dominatrix. Running through his work is a sexy 'anatomical vision' of moulded silhouettes, hand-span waists and exaggerated shoulders that have influenced Azzedine Alaïa and Hervé Léger. 'It's all about looking good and helping the silhouette...and it's all about getting a good fuck, honey,' Mugler memorably informed Kim Basinger in Robert Altman's 1995 fashion film *Prêt à Porter*. Mugler made his first outfit for a female friend at the age of fourteen. Joining a ballet company, he moved to Paris at nineteen. In 1973 he launched his own label. Mugler's vision has been unswerving. Each season jackets are cut, padded and stitched to create his cartoon-like ideal, a theme that also runs through his superhero menswear. Mugler re-shapes the body using seam and fabric; an uncompromising and total vision.

☞ Bergère, S. Jones, Léger, Model, Pearl, Van Beirendonck

337

Thierry Mugler. b Strasbourg (FR), 1948. **Shaped bustier and PVC pants**. Photograph by Thierry Mugler, 1996.

Muir Jean   Designer

The minimalism of Jean Muir's jersey tunic and matching culottes presents a stark silhouette on Joanna Lumley (Muir's model in the 1970s). Simplicity was Muir's signature. She said, 'I am a traditionalist with a sense of evolution.' She inspired the respectful address 'Miss Muir', and always wore navy. Geraldine Stutz, president of Henri Bendel in New York, called her 'the most outstanding dressmaker in the world'. After working at Liberty, she designed for Jaeger, before setting up her own company in 1966. She made the 'little nothing' of a black dress a classic. But her designs were often deceptively simple – jackets could contain up to eighteen pattern pieces. The understated elegance of Muir's wearable designs have made them timeless classics. As the designer herself said, 'When you have found something that suits you and never lets you down, why not stick to it?'

☛ Conran, Jaeger, Liberty, Rayne, G. Smith, Torimaru

Jean Muir. b London (UK), 1933. d London (UK), 1995. Joanna Lumley wears jersey tunic and culottes, Jean Muir's apartment. Photograph by Michael Barrett, 1975.

Munkacsi Martin   Photographer

With her head high and arms swinging, Martin Munkacsi's subject is the personification of fashion liberation as she strides from the shadows into sunshine. Her bias-cut dress, blurred and flowing in the wake of her motion, moves with her body rather than restraining it. It is free of any detail that will date it and the sash is carelessly tied around her natural waist. It is this real-life spirit of spontaneity which Munkacsi brought to fashion photography when he joined *Harper's Bazaar* in 1932, encouraged by his mentor Alexey Brodovitch. As well as showing clothes in motion, thereby better describing the real potential of fabric once it is placed on the body, he shot fashion from new angles, giving the impression of a scene snapped rather than posed. Munkacsi's subjects always had a purpose beyond being a beautiful clothes horse, whether they were running on the beach or, as is shown here, enjoying an unaccompanied evening stroll.

☛ Brodovitch, Burrows, de Meyer, Snow

339

Martin Munkacsi. **b** Cluj (ROM), 1896. **d** New York (USA), 1963. **Marion Davies, San Simeon, California**. *Harper's Bazaar*, 1934.

Nars François

Make-up artist

Made-up and photographed by François Nars, model Karen Elson wears his signature make-up. Nars uses dense pigments to create rich blocks of colour. Against a snowy base, he isolates the eyes and lips with a striking, abstract method. 'The runway is my sketchpad,' says Nars who, like Bobbi Brown and Frank Toskan, belongs to a circle of directional make-up artists who have created signature make-up lines. For them, the catwalk is a public laboratory on which new directions are born. His company was formed on the catwalks of Versace, Dolce & Gabbana and Karl Lagerfeld, in his vivid Technicolor schemes that became the blueprint for each seasonal look. His work draws inspiration from old movies, exotic places and characters such as King Kong. Amongst his lines are a dark chocolate lipstick with bronze flecks formulated to match the colour of the giant ape's fur, and Schiap, an exact match of Elsa Schiaparelli's classic shocking pink.

☛ Dolce & Gabbana, Lutens, Schiaparelli, Toskan, Versace

340

François Nars. b Biarritz (FR). (Active 1980s–) **Karen Elson**. Photograph by François Nars, 1997.

Nast Condé

Publisher

In one sideways glance, the Countess Divonne makes the first-ever photographic cover of *Vogue*. Her romantic pose and its artful styling preceded today's charismatic fashion covers. Following his 1909 purchase of *Vogue*, Condé Nast's transformation of the American social magazine into a high-class fashion glossy heralded a new era in international magazine publishing – starting with Baron de Meyer becoming the first full-time fashion photographer in 1914. With his editor, Edna Woolman Chase, Condé Nast exerted strict control at *Vogue*, and gave Carmel Snow and Alexander Liberman their first glimpse of fashion editorship and art direction respectively. Such a controlling policy did not always work: it fuelled Diana Vreeland's sacking in the 1960s, and caused *Harper's Bazaar* to poach de Meyer in 1921. Nast then hired Edward Steichen, Cecil Beaton and *Harper's* protégé Christian Bérard, sparking a long-standing feud. This set new competitive guidelines for fashion journalism.

☞ Liberman, de Meyer, Snow, Steichen, Tappé, Vreeland

Condé Nast. b Montrose, CO (USA), 1873. d New York (USA), 1942. **First Vogue cover.** Photograph by Harry McVickar, 1893.

Newton Helmut   Photographer

The Scandinavian model Vibéké wears a superlative pinstriped suit and crepe-de-chine blouse by Yves Saint Laurent. Shot at night on a Parisian street, her hair is slicked to her head in the sexually ambiguous manner of Garbo and Dietrich, and she holds the cigarette as a man would. It is a scene conjured by Helmut Newton, whose work is always charged with sexual themes.

Preferring statuesque, Teutonic women, he places his subjects on the line between pornography and fashion photography – this is a tame, but nonetheless powerful example of Newton's work. Lesbian sex, breasts bared from behind a mink coat and the palpable suggestion of bondage are a few of the themes used by him in his depiction of contemporary fashion. His employment

of ring-flash photography lends a cold, menacing mood to his scenarios, which have inspired debate for three decades: does he objectify women, or does he invest them with a superhuman power?

☛ Matsushima, Palmers, Saint Laurent, Teller

342

Helmut Newton. b Berlin (GER), 1920. **Tailored Yves Saint Laurent suit.** French *Vogue*, 1975.

Norell Norman   Designer

Propriety, the Norell hallmark, was never more evident than when all-over sequins, verging on the vulgar, were tamed by his application of them on to a gown of classic lines. An added layer of shimmer, perhaps an evening sweater, was justified as being warm protection for the shoulders on a wintry or Second World War night. From joining Hattie Carnegie in 1928 until his death in 1972, Norell was an important figure in American fashion design and his work personified New York style. Norell's success resided in his simple silhouettes and pragmatism in the fickle world of late-day and evening dresses. With wool jersey dresses for evening, beaded sweaters matched to evening dresses and, later, trouser suits, Norell applied the ethos of sportswear to more formal times of day. His uncanny capacity was to foster a comfortable, easy glamour which he achieved chiefly through an enduring fix on the 1920s.

☛ Carnegie, Ley, Mackie, Parker

Norman Norell. b Noblesville, IN (USA), 1900. **d** New York (USA), 1972. **Suzy Parker wears a red sequined dress**. Photograph by Milton H. Greene, 1952.

Nutter Tommy   Tailor

Mick Jagger marries Bianca Perez Moreno de Macias at the town hall in St Tropez in 1971. He wears a suit by Tommy Nutter, the man who opened the doors of Savile Row to a new generation (and also cut both John Lennon's and Yoko Ono's wedding suits). After studying architecture, he had answered an advertisement for a salesman at the Savile Row tailors G. Ward and Co. In 1969

he opened Nutters in Savile Row. His three-piece suits were styled with narrow, square shoulders, wide lapels, tight waists, tightly crotched flared trousers, and waistcoats. Charming and shy, Nutter was a frontman for the company which, employing master cutters and tailors, made the Savile Row bespoke suit fashionable again. In 1976 he left the company and joined

tailors Kilgour French and Stanbury. He is still remembered with affection and respect by the tailors of Savile Row. 'He was a modern stylist,' said one. 'He brought fashion here.'

☛ Beatles, Fish, Gilbey, R. James, Liberty, T. Roberts, P. Smith

344

Oldfield Bruce

Designer

Bruce Oldfield reclines next to his black silk crepe evening dress. The bodice is ruched with gold lamé and the mannequin wears shoes by Charles Jourdan; together they present a collaboration of deluxe fantasy. Oldfield once claimed, 'I can make any woman look better. That's what I do.' His starry clientele has ranged from aristocrats to soap queens; the Princess of Wales to Joan Collins.

The glamour could hardly be further removed from Oldfield's childhood in a Dr Barnardo's home. His foster mother was a seamstress and it was from her that Oldfield first developed his interest in fashion. He presented his first solo, ready-to-wear collection in London in 1975. His Beauchamp Place shop opened in 1984, attracting a strong following from the Knightsbridge

and Chelsea 'ladies who lunch'. The fashion writer Suzy Menkes, who selected his design as the Dress of the Year in 1985, praised 'his skills as a dressmaker, his belief in cut, line and silhouette, his standards of workmanship and his conception of women'.

☞ Diana, Jourdan, Price

345

Bruce Oldfield. b London (UK), 1950. Bruce Oldfield with a gold lamé and black silk crepe dress. Winner of the Bath Museum of Costume's 'Dress of the Year', 1985. Photograph by Nick Briggs.

Oldham Todd   Designer

Todd Oldham sits with one of fashion's more exotic muses – his grandmother Mildred Jasper. 'Granny's always been a huge inspiration to me. She does exactly what she wants, with great irreverence.' In this sitting for *Harper's Bazaar*, Mildred wears Oldham's hot pink, quilted satin jacket which comes close to being a boudoir robe. His family have long been connected to his career, which began at the age of fifteen when he turned a K-Mart pillowcase into a sun dress for his sister. Oldham always risks kitsch to achieve his distinctive style. Quirky colour combinations and textures are used for his down-home Texas style of flash and panache. His denim and bikinis are fringed, his midriffs bared and his skirts invariably short. Oldham creates a kaleidoscope of decorative pastiche for his own collection and, to a slightly lesser extent, for Escada, a label for whom he became a consultant in 1994.

☞ Eisen, Ley, Mackie, Mizrahi, de Ribes

346

Todd Oldham. b Corpus Christi, TX (USA), 1961. **Todd Oldham and grandmother**. Photograph by Gus van Sant, *Harper's Bazaar*, 1997.

Orry-Kelly

Designer

Orry-Kelly's hand-sewn, decorative costumes made him one of Hollywood's great designers, alongside Travis Banton and Adrian. On his first Hollywood movie, Orry-Kelly worked with Bette Davis and they formed a partnership that was to last for fourteen years. Orry-Kelly understood Davis's need for the drama in her wardrobe to match, but not overshadow, that of her on-screen acting. They only fell out once when the studio insisted she be glamorized for *Fashions of 1934*, which she hated. The life and soul of many showbiz parties, Orry-Kelly was also a prima donna and an alcoholic. But his time with Warner Brothers ended on a high note after he dressed Ingrid Bergman in simple classics for *Casablanca*, before being drafted into the army. He later freelanced, winning Oscars for Marilyn Monroe's sexy glamour in *Some Like it Hot* and Leslie Caron's colourful costumes in *An American in Paris*.

☞ Adrian, Banton, Mackie, Stern

347

Orry-Kelly (John Kelley). b Kiama (ASL), 1897. **d** 1964. **Marilyn Monroe wears diaphanous beaded dress**. Still from *Some Like it Hot*. 1959.

Oudejans Marie-Anne   Designer

Each season, Marie-Anne Oudejans produces dresses in just a few simple shapes but in many different fabrics and colours. The story of her label, Tocca, is similar to that of Lilly Pulitzer who, in the 1960s, became famous for her printed dresses. Oudejans was originally a stylist who wore her own little cotton dresses on fashion shoots; the supermodels who saw them begged for their own copies. Claudia Schiffer, Helena Christensen (pictured here) and Naomi Campbell were photographed wearing the dresses and customers started calling stores trying to find out how to buy them. 'It became a fashion by chance,' says Oudejans. Her dresses are unapologetically pretty and are cut from cotton or silk sari fabrics. Each season there are just a few styles to choose from, but many fabrics and colourways. Trimmed with broderie anglaise and often sold in soft candy colours, they have a girlish quality that sits apart from mainstream fashion.

☞ Dinnigan, Mazzilli, Pulitzer, Williamson

Marie-Anne Oudejans. b (NL), 1964. **Helena Christensen wears a pink embroidered dress.** Photograph by Niall McInerney, 1994.

Ozbek Rifat

Designer

Rifat Ozbek visited North Africa, India and his own Turkish roots for this eclectic, delicate outfit. A gauze cardigan is heavily braided and trimmed with cording. Underneath, a dress is embroidered with flowers, the raised waistband dotted with silver beads. Since setting up his own label in 1984, Ozbek has been inspired by the clothing and decoration of a variety of cultures, from American Indian and South African Ndebele to Eastern European gypsy and Haitian voodoo. Having been brought up in Britain, Ozbek worked with the seminal 1970s designer Walter Albini in Italy, before moving back to London to work for Monsoon, a chain store that specializes in designs manufactured in Indian fabrics. He has been heavily influenced by London street fashion. Before moving his business to Milan in 1991, Ozbek designed his New Age collection which was rooted in the rave culture. Using white and silver, it revealed a new-found purity in his work.

☛ Abboud, Albini, Bowery, Hendrix

Rifat Ozbek. b Istanbul (TUR), 1953. **Embroidered jacket and dress**. Photograph by Gilles Bensimon, British *Elle*, 1989.

Page Dick

Make-up artist

Model Annie Morton sits in her apartment bare-faced and with dishevelled hair. The image is deshabille in the extreme. Make-up artist Dick Page did nothing to disturb her early morning beauty. Using this pre-shoot image, he contests the idea of what constitutes beauty, saying, 'There is no such thing as natural make-up. As soon as there is make-up on the face it is not natural.' This is the key to Page's ethos. While effecting transformations by giving skin a shiny surface, he rejects further artificiality and won't use make-up that regulates and reduces women to a uniform beauty – on one occasion even leaving spots as an 'undeniable part of the woman underneath'. Page's iconoclastic methods are unique in a business that is designed to sell make-up. However, he was a champion of the 'greasy, glossy' direction of make-up in the 1990s, a movement that, bizarrely, accelerated the sale of make-up.

☛ Brown, Day, Lutens

350

Dick Page. b Gosport (UK), 1964. **Annie Morton in her apartment.** 1996.

Paley Babe   Icon

Babe Paley liked to look flawless; her clothes – twinsets, to-the-knee skirts and crisp blouses – always had to be just so. Here she decorates an exacting two-tone dress with an armful of costume jewellery in the style of another paragon of personal style, Coco Chanel. Truman Capote commented, 'Babe Paley only had one fault: she was perfect; otherwise, she was perfect'. Another friend, the socialite Slim Keith, called her style 'perfection in an era of casual convenience'. Paley was born Barbara Cushing into a middle-class family, with two elder sisters. All of the Cushing girls were trained by their socialite mother to snare wealthy husbands, which they did successfully. Babe's second marriage was to Bill Paley, chairman of CBS. As a fashion editor of American *Vogue* in the 1940s, and a wealthy socialite, she was an arbiter of style and appeared in America's best-dressed list fourteen times. Her look is best described as effortless chic, achieved at great effort.

☞ Chanel, Lane, Parker

Barbara Paley. **b** Boston (USA). **d** (USA), c1978. (Active 1940s–1970s.) **Babe Paley**. Photograph by Horst P. Horst, American *Vogue*, 1946.

Palmers Walter and Wolff Reinhold (Wolford)   Hosiery designers

Nadja Auermann wears a pair of semi-opaque tights which were specially created for this photograph. In her right hand she holds a Polaroid, the chosen film of a voyeur, of herself in provocative pose. The Wolford company, founded by Walter Palmers and Wolff Reinhold operates from the small Austrian town of Bregenz, and creates four collections of hosiery and bodywear every year. For its 1996 advertising campaign to promote no-seam, 'second-skin' tights (which took four years to develop), Wolford chose photographer Helmut Newton, who places his subjects in a steely sexual context. Wolford has been associated with leg-hugging hosiery since 1949. The patronage of Vivienne Westwood, Helmut Lang, Christian Lacroix and Alexander McQueen, as well as devoted, style-conscious women around the world, has elevated Wolford to its position as the preferred hosiery of the fashion industry. It specializes in luxurious, beautifully made tights which, like Manolo Blahnik's shoes, transcend their role as an accessory.

☛ Lang, Newton, Westwood

Reinhold Wolff. b Hard (AUS), 1905. d Hard (AUS), 1972. Walter Palmers. b Vienna (AUS), 1903. d Vienna (AUS), 1983. (Wolford.) 'Fatal Neon' tights. Photograph by Helmut Newton, 1996.

Paquin Jeanne   Designer

It is five o'clock and Mme Paquin's salon is crowded with vendeuses (without hats) showing clients (with hats) bolts of fabric from which they will order their dresses. At the centre of the room one models a fur-trimmed gown for two ladies, one of whom is examining the embroidery on its skirt. Mme Paquin founded her own maison de couture in 1891. She was appointed

President of the Fashion Section of the Paris Exposition Universelle of 1900 and promoted spectacular displays of fur. It was from this time that fur appeared as a trimming or accessory in the collections of leading couturiers. Mme Paquin also made exotic and brilliantly coloured garments, blending her superb tailoring with drapery inspired by Iribe and Bakst. As soignée as

her models, Mme Paquin was the first couturière to achieve international fame, establishing further couture salons in London, Buenos Aires and Madrid.

☞ Boué, Dinnigan, Gibson, Iribe, Redfern, Rouff, Van Cleef

353

Jeanne Paquin. b Ile Saint-Denis (FR), 1869. d Paris (FR), 1936. **Cinq Heures chez Paquin.** Painting by Henri Gervex, 1906.

Parker Suzy   Model

One hand holding a cigarette, the other thrown behind her head – both bear witness to Suzy Parker's reputation as someone who could never sit still. With high cheekbones, green eyes and red-gold hair, she became the most famous model of her generation, photographed extensively by, among others, Horst and Richard Avedon. It was while watching her sister Dorian Leigh model for Irving Penn in 1947 that Suzy was first discovered. Later she was taken on as the face of Revlon and of Chanel No. 5 (Coco Chanel became her friend and godmother to her daughter Georgia), before she set about becoming one of the MTAs (model turned actress). Although Suzy secretly married the playboy journalist Pierre de La Salle in 1955, it did not last and she later married the actor Bradford Dillman, for whom she put her modelling career aside for marriage and motherhood.

☛ Avedon, Bassman, Chanel, Horst, Norell

354

Suzanne (Suzy) Parker. b Long Island City, NY (USA), 1932. **Suzy Parker**. Photograph by Lillian Bassman, *Harper's Bazaar*, 1963.

Parkinson Norman

Photographer

Norman Parkinson evokes the breathtaking thrill of Paris first seen from the air in this editorial picture taken in 1960. He was a realist who took fashion photography outdoors. After the Second World War, he embarked upon a successful career in fashion photography for *Vogue*, pioneering the use of colour. Parkinson had a feeling for the essentials of fashion, to which he brought great urbanity, charm and sophisticated wit. In colour and composition, his fashion photographs have often been compared to the paintings of John Singer Sargent. During the 1950s he became a portrait photographer for the British royal family. He was the official photographer for the wedding of Princess Anne and Captain Mark Phillips in 1973 and photographed the Queen Mother on her eightieth birthday in 1980. His wife, Wenda Parkinson, was a celebrated fashion model, whom he often photographed. Together they brought the new cosmopolitan spirit of intercontinental jet travel to the pages of *Vogue* in spectacular fashion shoots.

☞ **Fratini, Kelly, Levine, Stiebel, Winston**

Norman Parkinson. b London (UK), 1913. **d** Singapore (SING), 1990. **Flying over Paris**. *Queen*, 1960.

Patou Jean

Designer

Jean Patou's dress is influenced by two art movements: Art Deco and Cubism. Purity of line, a key element of Art Deco, was the hallmark of Patou's style. He also took inspiration from Cubism, creating sharp, geometric shapes and patterns in his fabrics. He worked closely with the textile firm Bianchini-Férier (where Raoul Dufy was under contract in the 1920s), in his search for materials that would best adapt to his design philosophy of simplicity and a streamlined, uncluttered silhouette. His long-waisted dresses with their luxurious designs, of which this is a supreme example, were constantly described in the fashion magazines of the time as 'chic' and were worn by actresses such as Louise Brooks, Constance Bennett and Mary Pickford. Long strings of pearls and fur-trimmed coats added embellishment and also enhanced Patou's precision of cut. Tennis player Suzanne Lenglen was also dressed by Patou, setting a fashion for sleeveless jumpers.

☛ Abbe, Benito, Bohan, Dufy, Eric, Frizon, Lacroix, Lanvin, Pipart

356

Jean Patou. b Normandy (FR), 1887. d Paris (FR), 1936. **Sequined dress**. c1927.

Paulette

Milliner

Lush silk roses adorn the brim of a summer hat by Paulette, who was one of France's leading milliners for thirty years. She began creating hats in 1921, and set up her own millinery salon in 1939 at the start of the Second World War. These straitened circumstances were to bring out her most creative talents, just as Ferragamo was forced to experiment with plastics. Paulette reinvented the turban, which became a symbol of wartime practicality, by accident. When cycling she would wrap her head, a simple solution that turned into the biggest fashion for a decade. The theme developed, with draped veils and fabric often featuring in her work. Paulette went on to create work for Chanel, Pierre Cardin, Ungaro, Mugler and Laroche, demonstrating the versatility and wide-ranging appeal of her designs – helped by Philippe Model, who trained with her.

☛ W. Klein, Laroche, Model, Mugler, Talbot, Ungaro

Paulette (Paulette de la Bruyère). b Le Tours (FR), c1900. **d** (FR), 1984. **Barbara Mullen wears hat decorated with roses.** Photograph by William Klein, 1956.

Paulin Guy

Designer

In 1987 the baby-doll grew up in the hands of Guy Paulin. The pin-tucked, big-pocketed, girlish style becomes womanly with its floral print reduced to a few scattered petals. An admirer of Claire McCardell, Guy Paulin's easy-going, vibrant style consciously blended office formality with the no-nonsense detailing of American sportswear. Fired by a two-year training with Jacqueline Jacobson at Dorothée Bis, he took his passion for knitting to New York in 1968, where he shared rails with Mary Quant and Emmanuelle Khanh at the boutique chain Paraphernalia. Having freelanced for MaxMara, he replaced Karl Lagerfeld as designer at Chloé in 1983. Paulin had a reputation for pleasing women with his brand of French chic and his intention was always to create clothes that would boost the wearer's self-esteem.

☛ Jacobson, Khanh, Lagerfeld, Lenoir, Maramotti, Quant

358

Guy Paulin. b Lorraine (FR), 1945. d Paris (FR), 1990. **Baby-doll dress.** *Women's Wear Daily*, 1988.

Mr Pearl

Designer

A child wears a garment designed to reduce an adult's circumference to that of a child. It is the highly crafted work of Mr Pearl, the man who made the corset a fashion item. Called the best corsetier in the world by Vivienne Westwood, he is famous for his own corseted eighteen-inch waist. Pearl left South Africa in the early 1980s for London and the costume department at the Royal Opera House, where his interest in the art of corsetry was aroused. His great-grandmother had been a fashionable dressmaker in the *belle époque* and he was inspired by photographs of the clothes she had made: 'The world used to be a more interesting place visually and I wanted to bring some of that visual stimulus back.' Since 1991, Pearl has worked on collections for Thierry Mugler, a designer famous for perfecting the hourglass silhouette. His work has also appeared on the catwalks of Christian Lacroix, John Galliano and Alexander McQueen.

☛ Berardi, S. Ellis, Galliano, Lacroix, McQueen, Mugler, Westwood

Mr Pearl. b (UK). (Active 1990s–.) **Black beaded corset**. Photograph by Sean Ellis, *The Face*, 1996.

Penn Irving

Photographer

Model Jean Patchett becomes an exercise in graphic perfection under the lens of a photographer whose work defined haute couture in the 1950s. The power and simplicity of Irving Penn's work made him the Balenciaga of fashion photography – a designer whose work was often shot by Penn. It has a natural solemnity which invests his subjects – a model, a still-life or even a sleeve – with a regal presence. Penn said, 'The camera is just a tool, like a wrench. But the situation itself is magical. I stand in awe of it.' Penn's black-and-white photography of the 1940s and 1950s captured the grandeur and drama of haute couture just before its pre-eminence was about to be threatened by the power of ready-to-wear. Of couture, Penn said, 'When I am working with the Haute Couture I think again and again of the beauty of women and the magic of Paris.'

☞ Balenciaga, Brodovitch, Dovima, Fonssagrives, Vreeland

360

Irving Penn. b Plainfield, NJ (USA), 1917. **Jean Patchett**. Photograph by Irving Penn, American *Vogue*, 1950.

Peretti Elsa   Jewellery designer

Like so many of Elsa Peretti's designs, this apparently molten silver cuff, with its smooth, tactile lines, was inspired by her love of organic forms; in this case, the irregular contours of bones. A renowned craftswoman, Peretti creates jewellery and home accessories with a unique rhythmic sense of the natural world. She seizes the figurative essence of something as simple as a bean or a teardrop and translates it into a beautiful, sculptural, timeless piece of body art. She presented her inaugural pieces alongside Giorgio di Sant'Angelo's collection in 1969 and later designed for Halston. Her other designs, sold by Tiffany & Co, have included the famous Peretti 'Open Heart' pendant and 'Diamonds by the Yard' – a simple chain interspersed with diamonds which became a classic worn by Liza Minnelli in the 1970s and in the 1990s by Naomi Campbell, who threads hers through her navel ring.

☞ Campbell, Halston, Hiro, di Sant'Angelo, Tiffany, Warhol

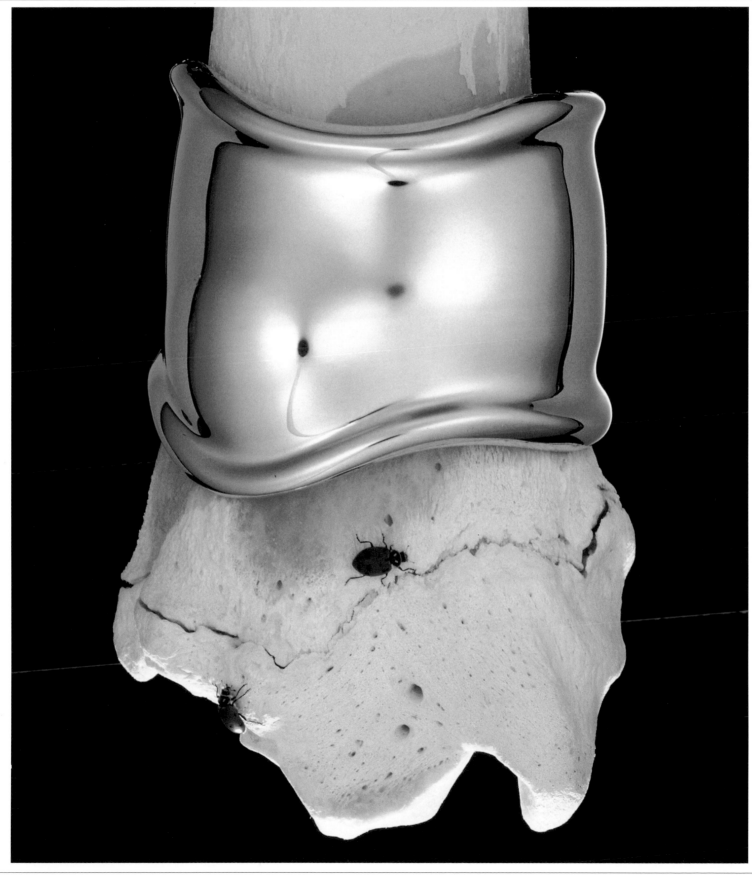

Elsa Peretti. b Florence (IT), 1940. **Silver 'bone cuff'**. Photograph by Hiro, 1989.

Perint Palmer Gladys   Illustrator

With its deft pen strokes and blocks of pastel colour, Gladys Perint Palmer's simple catwalk illustration resonates with fluidity and movement, accurately capturing not only Yves Saint Laurent's couture gypsy but also the women watching her. Like a cartoonist, Perint Palmer's work gives a humorous insight into the catwalk world. Subtle exaggerations, such as the model's extended neck which creates an imperious air, are just one step removed from reality. The close attention of Chanel's former model Inès de la Fressange, wearing a red jacket in the foreground, adds to an ambience that only a camera can record faithfully. Each picture is a microcosm of a show, illustrating the spirit of a collection and that of the spectators. Perint Palmer belongs to a tradition which is as old as fashion presentations. Sketch artists were once the only way for collections to reach the wider public before the clothes did.

☛ Chanel, Saint Laurent, Vertès

362

Gladys Perint Palmer. b Budapest (HUN), 1947. **Yves Saint Laurent catwalk show, 1992.**

Pertegaz Manuel · Designer

Henry Clarke's great attribute as a fashion photographer was his precision in defining a fashionable image, showing here how this haute couture coat was cut and how it hung. He has made the brilliantly tiled walls of the Villa Rosa, an elegant Madrid restaurant, the perfect backdrop for Manuel Pertegaz's vivid green, paper taffeta evening coat. Falling to mid-calf, it has an oval-necked shoulder yoke and three tie-fastenings. The most distinctive feature is its tent shape, flaring widely from the shoulders. One of the great Spanish fashion designers, Pertegaz earned a reputation for formal designs in the grand manner from his start in the early 1940s. The tent silhouette was first launched in 1951 by Pertegaz's compatriot, Balenciaga. Together they built up Spain's reputation for couture until it rivalled that of the great French designers. In 1968 Pertegaz opened his Madrid boutique, selling couture, and in the 1970s launched a ready-to-wear collection, but it is the former for which he is remembered.

☛ Balenciaga, Clarke, Grès, Saint Laurent

Manuel Pertegaz. b Aragón (SP), 1918. **Green taffeta evening coat.** Photograph by Henry Clarke, British *Vogue*, 1954.

Perugia André   Shoe designer

This decorative boot, based on turn-of-the-century spats, was the perfect complement to the attention-grabbing designs of Elsa Schiaparelli. Schiaparelli was a brilliant colourist. Shocking pink, which she made the predominant colour in the world of fashion in the late 1930s and throughout the 1940s, was her famous trademark. The sheer expanse of the surface of this boot, in black suede with a pink platform, enabled André Perugia to capture the essence of fantasy that was so much in accord with Schiaparelli's own creations. Despite its size, the boot was easy to walk in. Perugia understood balance, scale and the engineering of footwear, having been an apprentice at his father's shoe business in Nice prior to opening his own shop there when he was only sixteen. In 1920, he established his own salon in Paris. Perugia also designed footwear for Poiret, Fath and Givenchy, as well as Schiaparelli.

☞ Fath, Jourdan, Poiret, Schiaparelli, Talbot, Windsor

André Perugia. b (FR), 1893. d Cannes (FR), 1977. **Buttoned boot with scalloped edging for Elsa Schiaparelli.** 1939.

364

Pfister Andrea

Shoe designer

With 'Martini dry', a sunshine yellow sandal, Andrea Pfister evokes the cocktail culture of the mid-1970s. Its heel is shaped to resemble a martini glass embellished with a slice of lemon; a surreal object which demands attention. Pfister treats his shoes as a centrepiece rather than a distant accessory, and the foot, for him, is the start of the human body rather than its end. In 1964, having trained as an art historian, he moved to Paris where he designed footwear collections for Jean Patou and Lanvin. He moved on to design his own collections which became known for their humour. Pfister has appliquéd snakeskin penguins to the side of a boot, decorated the heel of a wedged mule with a three-dimensional frolicking sea lion and wrapped a black suede boot with clasping hands (complete with red nail varnish). The tradition of fantasy footwear in the twentieth century remained vigorous; from Perugia's pink platforms to Pfister's leather martini glass.

☞ Ferragamo, Lanvin, Louboutin, Patou

Andrea Pfister. b Pesaro (IT), 1942. **'Martini dry' kid sandal**. Photograph by Joël Garnier, 1975.

Piguet Robert   Designer

Horst has photographed Robert Piguet's outfit in a surrealist manner. At first glance, we see the sitter wearing a well-cut bodice with the emphasis focused on the white sleeve. Miss Zelensky's other sleeve becomes a shadow, together with her Tyrolean hat and skirt. Horst has created an illusion for the designer. Having trained with Redfern and Poiret, Piguet understood the decorative importance of the hat, and has used it here as a witty punctuation mark to his garment. Piguet's work was admired for its uncluttered yet flamboyant shapes, an element greatly supported by contributions from talented freelance designers, including Dior and Balmain before the War and Bohan after. Here, it is represented by the sleeve with its head raised to meet Miss Zelensky's cheekbone. The purity of Piguet's outfit is simplified further by Horst's impeccable style.

☞ Balmain, Bassman, Bohan, Castillo, Galanos, Horst, Redfern

366

Robert Piguet. b Yvedon (FR), 1901. **d** Paris (FR), 1953. **Doris Zelensky wears puff-sleeved jacket**. Photograph by Horst P. Horst, 1936.

Pinet François

Shoe designer

The dainty flower design and distinctive Louis heel of this delicate, white satin boot – a finer version of the lowish, wasp-waisted heel worn in the reign of King Louis XV of France – are typical of the designs by the French shoemaking firm, Pinet. Established in 1855 by François Pinet, the Paris company soon became known for creating elegant footwear for the most fashionable members of society, shoes that would be worn underneath the grand gowns by Charles Worth. Shoemaking was a family concern for Pinet; he had learnt his craft from his father and, when he retired in the early years of the twentieth century, his son took over and continued to expand the firm, opening shops in Nice and London. Roger Vivier later supplied designs to this prestigious firm, which has become known for demonstrably expensive shoes, such as women's court shoes entirely covered with rhinestones and animal skin footwear for men.

☛ Hope, Pingat, Vivier, Worth, Yantorny

François Pinet. b Château-le-Vaillère (FR), 1817. **d** (FR), 1897. **Women's embroidered boot, 1867**. Photograph by Elisabeth Eylieu.

Pingat Emile
Designer

This navy faille day dress from the 1870s, with its frills, ruching and cut velvet bodice, recalls the grandeur of Emile Pingat's work. He was a contemporary of Charles Frederick Worth, the father of haute couture. They were rival couturiers, with their names mentioned together in the guidebooks for female tourists visiting Paris in the second half of the nineteenth century. His own fashion house flourished from 1860 to 1896. He was known pre-eminently as a couturier who created fashions of delicate contrasts and for a perfect harmony of proportion, evocative of the current ideal of femininity. His striking ball gowns captured the fantasy and romance of the great festive occasions in Paris during the Second Empire and the Third Republic. Together with Worth, his creations reflected the fashionable silhouette and aesthetic of the Parisian world of haute couture from the mid- to the late nineteenth century.

☞ Pinet, Reboux, Worth

368

Emile Pingat. b (FR). (Active 1860s–1900s.) **Blue faille and silk velvet day dress**. 1870s.

Pipart Gérard   Designer

Arlette Ricci, granddaughter of the couturière Nina, wears a luxurious astrakhan coat cinched with an elastic belt, an ironic conceit that displays modern use of a deluxe garment. It is the work of Gérard Pipart for the house of Nina Ricci, once described as a 'never too haute' designer. Pipart joined the house in 1964 after the departure of Jules-François Crahay. His education had been conducted in the houses of the great couturiers Balmain, Fath, Patou and Givenchy; consequently he creates simple Parisian chic rather than chasing seasonal trends. Pipart is also true to the tradition of maintaining 'house' styles, those which women can order each season with few alterations beyond a change of fabric. He never learned to cut fabric so he is unusual in working from precise drawings and making amendments straight onto the toiles. Pipart's style is one of conservative beauty that eschews gimmickry.

☛ Balmain, Crahay, Fath, Givenchy, Patou, Ricci

Gérard Pipart. b Paris (FR), 1933. **Arlette Ricci wears belted astrakhan coat for Nina Ricci**. Photograph by Peter Knapp, 1976.

Pita Orlando

Hairdresser

Model Shalom Harlow's hairstyle accurately reflects Orlando Pita's aesthetic approach. While creativity and subversion are critical elements of his vision, beauty still remains a priority. 'A hairstyle may be stunning, but I will have failed if it doesn't make a woman beautiful,' says Pita. This photograph displays his signature ethnic style, which was seen in the form of Hasidic *payos* on the Jean Paul Gaultier catwalk and African-American braidings in videos for Madonna, one of his most loyal clients. Pita finds an ideal ground for experimentation in the diva, who allows him to break away from all stereotypes. 'There's no room for fantasy in the salon,' he says when asked why he concentrates on editorials and catwalk shows. Pita, who vehemently resists shampooing hair in the belief that its own sebaceous secretions have a natural cleansing function, has admittedly even used toilet rolls as curlers to achieve some of his surrealist styles.

☛ Gaultier, McKnight, Madonna

Orlando Pita. b Havana (CU), 1962. **Shalom Harlow**. Photograph by Mario Testino, *Harper's Bazaar*, 1994.

Platt Lynes George   Photographer

With her face turned away from George Platt Lynes' camera, the reclining figure presents herself as a living model in an art gallery setting. The drape of her crepe-de-chine dress mirrors that on the dress of her companion and the wavy print snaking along her body is a reminder of that fabric's propensity for liquid movement. These gowns, by Gilbert Adrian, are presented as vaguely Surreal *objets* by a photographer who followed that movement, explored during a friendship with Jean Cocteau. Platt Lynes started to publish his fashion work in *Town* and *Harper's Bazaar* in 1933 and became director of *Vogue*'s Hollywood studio in 1942. His later life was spent photographing male nudes (Platt Lynes was a charismatic, openly gay member of New York's artistic community). These, it is said, set precedents for the later work of Herb Ritts and Bruce Weber, who both apply simplicity and the artistic merit of a sinewy male physique to their work.

☞ Adrian, Ritts, Weber

George Platt Lynes. **b** NJ (USA), 1907. **d** New York (USA), 1955. **Adrian's 'Magic' draped silk dresses**. British *Vogue*, 1947.

Poiret Paul

Designer

The scope of Paul Poiret, 'The Sultan of Fashion', is illustrated in this line-up of models influenced by the Ballets Russes. In 1909 he introduced a fluid style of dress, inspired by the French *Directoire* and orientalism but also the sumptuous splendour in which he lived and worked. He gave fashion a theatrical spin by throwing lavish fêtes at his maison de couture, where the beau monde of Paris would wear Poiret-designed costumes – which became fashion overnight. He added a new dimension to fashion by parading his mannequins in the gardens of his house, at racecourses and on tours of Europe and the United States. Poiret opened his own salon after serving an apprenticeship under Doucet and working for Worth. He was one of the most creative and forward-thinking fashion designers of the twentieth century, revolutionizing fashion design, reviving fashion illustration, establishing a school for the decorative arts and even diversifying into perfume.

☛ Bakst, Barbier, Brunelleschi, Dufy, Erté, Iribe, Lepape

372

Paul Poiret. **b** Paris (FR), 1879. **d** Paris (FR), 1944. **Poiret's mannequins.** *L'Illustration*, 1910.

Pollock Alice

Designer

The model sweeps down the catwalk in Pollock's crepe evening dress. Unadorned but for neat front buttoning, the design combines simplicity with femininity in keeping with the avant-garde of the 1960s. Challenging convention, Pollock created fluid and comfortable eveningwear. She opened Quorum, a wholesale and boutique business in London's King's Road, becoming the first to employ Ossie Clark, a stalwart of the 1960s Chelsea scene. Their designs often used fabrics designed by Celia Birtwell, Clark's wife. Together they produced clothes renowned for their sensuality – evident in deep necklines and wasp waists and in their luxurious trademark fabrics of crepe, chiffon, satin and close-fitting jersey. More than a designer, Pollock was an iconoclastic force in Britain's emerging fashion world who encouraged Clark and Birtwell, amongst others, to 'do their thing'.

☛ Birtwell, Clark, Jackson, Porter

373

Alice Pollock. b (UK), 1942. **White crepe dress**. Photograph by Annette Green, British *Vogue*, 1970.

Porter Thea   Designer

A printed voile headdress is weighted down with gold embroidery and bugle beads. Under it the model wears exotic make-up; kohl applied inside the lower lid, emerald eye shadow and ruby nail varnish. Her caftan top is made from a patchwork of rough Madras cotton and co-ordinating, semi-sheer voile. It all evokes the mixture of Middle-Eastern influences that surrounded Thea Porter as she grew up in Damascus and later in Beirut. Porter took her international style to London's Soho in the 1960s where she opened a shop on Greek Street. It sold her own interpretation of Eastern clothing to an artistic clientele that included Elizabeth Taylor and Barbra Streisand. Porter concentrated on clothes which had an illusory element removed from real life: impressive robes embroidered with Arabic designs and evening dresses cut from silk brocade.

☛ Bouquin, Gibb, Pollock

374

Thea Porter. b Damascus (SYR), 1927. **Eastern caftan and headdress.** Photograph by Barry Lategan, British *Vogue*, 1975.

POZO Jesús del

Designer

Jesús del Pozo adds substance to a drifting, cotton voile dress by piping its vertical seams. A natural, simple shape, it is a poetic garment, which becomes the focus of a dream-like image photographed in heightened colour by Javier Vallhonrat. Strong colour and simple shape is the backbone of del Pozo's style which has also cross-hatched a vibrant, melon slip dress with bold painted stripes. Del Pozo trained as an engineer, abandoning the discipline to study furniture design and interior decorating, before moving into painting, the influence of which is clear in his work; this dress resembles a sweep of paint. Del Pozo moved on once more, opening his first menswear store in 1974. Two years later his collection was being presented in Paris and worn by women who admired his soft, colourful menswear. Encouraged, he started to present womenswear in 1980.

☞ Dominguez, Sybilla, Vallhonrat

375

Jesús del Pozo. b Madrid (SP), 1946. **Handcrafted cotton voile dress**. Photograph by Javier Vallhonrat, 1997.

Prada Miuccia
Designer

Clutching the classic nylon bag upside down in an artless pose, model Kristen McMenamy models the unfettered look of Prada. Completely unadorned, save for the discreet triangular metal stamp, the bag articulates the 1990s notion of subtlety. The intelligence behind this cult label belongs to Miuccia Prada. Along with Gucci, her company redefined the image of Italian fashion in the mid 1990s. Prada had inherited her grandfather's leather luggage business in the 1970s and she revamped the label by introducing innovative fabrics. She pioneered the lightweight backpack in parachute nylon now popular among the fashion cognoscenti. Focusing on freedom of definition, rather than sex appeal, Prada experimented with 1970s furnishing fabrics in peculiar colour combinations and patterning that heralded the 1996 'geek chic' look. Though her label continued to sell its trademark black nylon range, Prada managed to develop a parallel line that is brave in spirit, controversial and desired above almost any other label.

☞ Lindbergh, McGrath, Souleiman, Steele

Miuccia Prada. b Milan (IT), c1950. **Kristen McMenamy. Advertising campaign. Autumn/winter 1995**. Photograph by Peter Lindbergh.

De Prémonville Myrène   Designer

The jacket is given a dramatic cut by Myrène de Prémonville for a feminized business suit. Its long-line shape is softened with pockets which follow its curving hem. The shoulders are encircled with a strap which mimics an off-the-shoulder gown. De Prémonville's first designs for her own label in the late 1980s were a response to what she felt was missing from her own (and other women's) wardrobes. In the tradition of other female designers, such as Carven and Margaret Howell, de Prémonville started to design for her own needs. The results were sculpted, sassy suits which used unusual colour combinations, bright graphic appliqués and contrasting trims. She also designed a pair of classic black stirrup trousers because, as she says, 'No one else's felt comfortable.' By the early 1990s, de Prémonville had found an audience of working women who appreciated her meticulous attention to detail.

☞ Howell, de Tommaso

Myrène de Prémonville. b Hendaye (FR), 1949. **Day suit with banded yoke**. Photograph by Philippe Costes, 1984.

Presley Elvis   Icon

Presley's hip-thrusting style spoke eloquently to a new American phenomenon: the teenager. Wearing a loosely cut suit, black shirt and half-mast tie, he is the image of a young man who has rejected the formalities of dress of the older generation. This new, essentially working-class image scorned established ideas about status and redefined male attractiveness as youthful and overtly sensual. Presley started out as a truck driver and in 1953 recorded a few songs for Sun Records. Within five years he had made nineteen hit records and starred in four blockbuster movies. His hip gyrations would turn girls to jelly, earning him the nickname 'Elvis the Pelvis'. He was also known as 'The Hillbilly Cat', a reference to the 'hip cats' of the black jazz tradition – the song 'Blue Suede Shoes' denotes a cool dandyism synonymous with a certain black style.

☛ Bartlett, Dean, Hendrix

Elvis Presley. **b** Tupelo, MS (USA), 1935. **d** Memphis, TN (USA), 1977. **Elvis Presley**. c1957.

Price Antony

Designer

Antony Price is photographed with Jerry Hall, his friend and model. She wears a peplum dress of metallic and red French silk lace placed over lamé, an outfit worn for a benefit show in 1985. 'It wasn't the chicest or most subtle garment,' Price explains, 'but when Jerry moved under the lights she looked like a Siamese fighting fish in a vast blue tank'. It is a theatrical example of his potent eveningwear, designed, as he once said, by a man for a man. Price and Hall met when she was seventeen and modelling a blue mermaid frock for the cover of a Roxy Music album. In 1968 Price had designed a groundbreaking menswear show; its nostalgic 1930s and 1940s statement became a blueprint for the intellectual glam of Roxy Music. Launching his own label in 1979, Price consolidated his reputation for corseted superheroine evening gowns made for 'women who go to serious parties'.

☛ G. Jones, Kelly, Oldfield

Antony Price. b Bradford (UK), 1945. **Antony Price with Jerry Hall.** Photograph by Richard Young, 1986.

Pucci Emilio   Designer

A skier is frozen in flight above a model wearing a classic Pucci design. The boldly patterned and brightly coloured jacket with plain, slim ski pants is typical of Emilio Pucci, the Marchese di Barsento, scion of an old aristocratic Tuscan family. He was a member of the Italian Olympic ski team and, after photographs of him on the slopes wearing his own designs appeared in

Harper's Bazaar, he was invited to create winter clothes for women to be sold in New York. In 1951 he established his own fashion house in his Palazzo Pucci in Florence. He was celebrated for his 'palazzo pyjamas' in non-crushable, silk jersey which, worn by Grace Kelly, Lauren Bacall and Elizabeth Taylor, became a jet-set uniform. As a colourist of swirling patterns based on

medieval Italian banners and an inventive user of fabrics, the 'Divino Marchese' captured the psychedelic mood of the 1960s. His look still inspires fashion revivals every few years.

☛ Ascher, Galitzine, **Pulitzer**

380

Emilio Pucci. **b** Naples (IT), 1914. **d** Florence (IT), 1992. **Ski jacket**. Photograph by Peter Beard, American *Vogue*, 1964.

Pulitzer Lilly   Designer

The 'Lilly' dress, worn here by Rose Kennedy and her granddaughter Kathleen, suited every age. Like Pucci, Pulitzer found one style of pattern and kept with it. Her simple, summer shift dresses came in bright, colourful, floral cottons. Living in Florida's Palm Beach, Pulitzer knew what would make the perfect vacation-wear and she always claimed, 'The great thing about the Lilly is that you wear practically nothing underneath.' This wealthy resort area lent her clothes a certain cachet and her squiggly signature was on every dress. She had originally made one for herself to wear when, as a rich but bored housewife, she began selling freshly squeezed orange juice on the beach in 1959. The original dresses were made from cheap-and-cheerful cotton from Woolworths. She started selling her dresses on her stall and the 'Lilly' became an overnight success. John Fairchild dubbed it a 'little nothing' dress.

☛ Kennedy, Oudejans, Pucci

381

Lilly Pulitzer. b Roslyn, NY (USA). (Active 1960s.) **Rose Kennedy with granddaughter Kathleen, late 1960s.**

Quant Mary   Designer

Mary Quant (centre) and her models epitomize the spirit of youthquake in 'kooky' poses, mini-lengths and trademark haircuts by Vidal Sassoon. This era-defining picture represents the image of desire of the newly liberated women of the 'swinging sixties' and Quant's 1965 miniskirt was dubbed the 'gymslip of the permissive society'. She was, she said, inspired by the clothes dancers wear for rehearsal. In 1955, Quant and her husband/partner Alexander Plunket Greene opened a boutique, Bazaar, in London's King's Road, selling clothes which expressed the anti-establishment mood. A second shop, designed by Terence Conran, opened in 1957. Her fashion shows, with models Jean Shrimpton and Grace Coddington, revolutionized catwalk style. While Courrèges claims to have invented the miniskirt and Balenciaga first used dancers' tights for everyday wear, Quant married them in a style which was both appealing to young women and affordable.

☛ Charles, Courrèges, Khanh, Liberty, Paulin, Rayne, Sassoon

382

Mary Quant. b London (UK), 1934. **Mary Quant with models**. 1966.

Rabanne Paco   Designer

Aluminium discs and panels linked together by wire using pliers have replaced conventional fashion created by threads and needles in this space-fantasy costume. Rabanne studied architecture at the Ecole des Beaux-Arts in Paris but turned to fashion, supplying plastic buttons and jewellery to Givenchy, Dior and Balenciaga. Opening his own fashion house in 1966, it was his architectural training combined with the impact of space and space travel in the 1960s that inspired Rabanne to create such startling new styles. His space-age fashions using alternative, experimental materials were important in pushing aside the traditional parameters of what were acceptable clothes to wear on the street. Other fashion designers who travelled the space-age fashion route in the 1960s were Pierre Cardin, André Courrèges, Rudi Gernreich and Yves Saint Laurent.

☛ Bailly, Barrett, Cardin, Courrèges, Dior, Gernreich, Betsey Johnson

Paco Rabanne. **b** San Sebastián (SP), 1934. **Aluminium chainmail dress**. Photograph by Gunnar Larsen, 1966.

Rayne Sir Edward

Shoe designer

'Ladies Day at Ascot. It simply mustn't rain,' reads the caption to this playful image. Rayne's lemon-yellow court shoes, striped with nylon mesh, are flirting with masculine polished riding boots and Oxford brogues. Impeccably crafted in a myriad of colours, from the day japonica pink to the evening jewelled jade, Rayne's shoes dressed Britain's well-heeled. Granted the Royal Warrant for Queen Elizabeth, the Queen Mother, Rayne designed for Princess Elizabeth's wedding trousseau in 1947, draping her sandals in ivory silk with seed pearls. The family-owned business, H&M Rayne, was founded by his grandparents in 1889. Edward Rayne joined the company in 1940, taking over in 1951. He collaborated with couturiers Hardy Amies and Norman Hartnell, while still keeping his eye on prevailing trends. Both Jean Muir and Mary Quant lent their talents to Rayne's fashion profile by designing youthful footwear.

☞ Amies, Hartnell, Muir, Quant, Vivier

384

Sir Edward Rayne. b London (UK), 1922. d (UK), 1992. 'Jaress' yellow shoe with mesh toe. Spring 1963.

Reboux Caroline   Milliner

Caroline Reboux was a milliner who excelled at structured simplicity. She avoided decoration and ornamentation. She liked working with felt – a strong and malleable material which she cut and folded on her clients' heads. For Mlle Conchita Montenegro, the milliner decorated the hat very simply with a lotus plant motif which reflected the line of the hat. This style of hat also complemented the tailored yet dramatic ensemble. Reboux designed hats for many couturiers and, later in her career, had a special relationship with Madame Vionnet, whose classicism matched her own. In the 1860s, Caroline Reboux's individual style caught the eye of Princess Metternich, who was credited with introducing Worth to the Empress Eugénie. She was soon making hats for the Empress and by 1870 she was established in the centre of fashionable Paris at 22 rue de la Paix, where she worked until her death.

☞ Agnès, Barthet, Daché, Hartnell, Pingat, Windsor, Worth

Caroline Reboux. b Paris (FR), 1830s. d Paris (FR), 1927. **Hat trimmed with broderie anglaise**. Photograph by Baron de Meyer, American *Vogue*, 1919.

Redfern John Designer

Mary Garden, the celebrated Scottish opera singer, wears a town dress made of pleated Rajah silk with a matching cape and a lace blouse. It evokes the fashionable silhouette of the *belle époque*: a high-necked, full bodice which gives a pouched effect, over a deep, tightly constricted waist. The skirt is cut straight at the front and filled out by pleats and extra fabric at the back which extends into a train. This style of dress became known as the S-bend. It reflected the taste for Art Nouveau. Redfern began as a ladies' tailor in Cowes on the Isle of Wight. The success of his tailored garments, especially his yachting costumes, led to his becoming a couturier, designing fashionable clothes for royalty, singers and actresses. In 1881 he established fashion houses in London and Paris, followed by branches in Edinburgh and New York. Redfern closed his houses in 1920.

☛ Boué, Drecoll, Gibson, Paquin

John Redfern. b Cowes (UK), 1853. **d** 1929. **Town dress of pleated Rajah silk and lace**. 1905.

De la Renta Oscar Designer

Carla Bruni looks as though she owns, and plays, the grand piano on which she is perched. It is all part of the de la Renta image: sophisticated, lavish, grown-up. The svelte black bodice, which sweeps into a softly gathered skirt, is finished with flat bows on the shoulder. Known for ornamentation and extremely feminine silhouettes, de la Renta has cultivated clients among the rich and beautiful with whom he socializes. Following brief apprenticeships in Europe, de la Renta went on to design for Elizabeth Arden in New York, where his idealism of touches of European glamour applied to conventions of American dressmaking was crystallized. In 1993 he returned to Europe to design Balmain couture, while satisfying the chic American women who see de la Renta as a designer who makes flattering dresses and sophisticated suits, with a special gift for dress-up and evening glamour.

☛ Alfaro, Arden, Roehm, Scaasi, Steiger

Oscar de la Renta. b Santo Domingo (DOM), 1932. **Carla Bruni wears black cocktail gown**. Photograph by Arthur Elgort, 1992.

Revillon Théodore, Albert, Anatole and Léon (Revillon Frères) Designers

Louise Dahl-Wolfe shoots a shawl-collared, sealskin cape draped around the shoulders like a wash of black ink; it is an image of a woman coated in wealth. The pioneers of this sort of fur fashion, the Revillon brothers – Théodore, Albert, Anatole and Léon – treated the pelt like silk, cutting it skilfully a century earlier. Were it not for their aristocratic father's neck-saving decision to change his name from Count Louis-Victor d'Argental during the French Revolution, such coats might not have existed. Louis-Victor had already taken fur beyond its practical use as a provider of warmth with much-coveted juxtapositions of exotic furs such as ocelot, chinchilla and Arctic fox, making Paris the fur capital of the world. On his death, the firm, renamed Revillon Frères by his four sons, became the first French global company with trading posts across Canada and Siberia and a museum opened in their name.

☛ Dahl-Wolfe, Fendi, Lauder

Revillon. Théodore. b Paris (FR). d (FR), 1920; Albert. b Paris (FR). d 1887; Anatole. b Paris (FR). d (FR) 1916; Léon. b Paris (FR). d (FR), 1915. (Active 1840s–1910s.) (Revillon Frères.) Seal cape. Photograph by Louise Dahl-Wolfe, *Harper's Bazaar*, 1956.

388

Revson Charles (Revlon) Cosmetics creator

Sassy and liberated, Shelley Hack – the 'Charlie Girl' – strides across the page wearing a trouser suit and an expression that says, 'I've got it all'. Revlon captured the mood of a new generation of independent women with the image of its scent, Charlie, in the 1970s. Revlon was founded in 1932 by brothers Charles and Joseph Revson and a chemist named Charles

Lachman. Charles Revson had the marketing brain. When Elizabeth Arden referred to him as 'that man' (because she thought he copied her ideas), he created a line of men's cosmetics named That Man. Success, however, was founded on opaque-coloured nail polish which supplanted clear tints and introduced women to matching nail and lip colour. They started

with Fire and Ice, a strong red, with the ad slogan, 'There's a little bit of bad in every good woman'. Revson said he wanted his models to be like 'Park Avenue whores – elegant, but the sexual thing underneath'.

☛ Arden, Factor, Hutton, Venturi

389

Charles Revson. b Somerville, MA (USA), 1906. **d** New York (USA), 1976. (Revlon.) **Shelley Hack modelling for Revlon's 'Charlie' perfume.** Photograph by Albert Watson, c1974.

Rhodes Zandra Designer

Zandra Rhodes once said that she tried to achieve an ageless exoticism. As such, she is an original; her trademarks were slashed silk tatters, abstract beading, handkerchief points, squiggle prints, tulle crinolines and pleated fabrics edged with ruffles. The 'conceptual chic' collection of 1977, shown here, brought street style to couture using embroidered rips and safety pins as jewellery. Her dresses used techniques that are still seen as subversive: exterior seams and 'winking' holes revealing erogenous zones and semi-sheer jersey. Rhodes studied fashion at the Royal College of Art, graduating in 1966. 'We were determined to live in a world of today, making it all ourselves, creating our own environment, a perfect world of plastic, perfectly artificial,' she recalled. She cited Edith Sitwell as her inspiration. Her own image – multi-coloured hair and statement make-up – contributes to her aura of outrageousness.

☛ Rotten, Sarne, G. Smith, Williamson

390

Zandra Rhodes. b Chatham (UK), 1942. **'Conceptual chic'. Punk jersey dresses.** Photograph by Clive Arrowsmith, 1977.

De Ribes Jacqueline   Designer

In a pose of fragile elegance, the Comtesse Jacqueline de Ribes gazes out in a stark, black velvet dress, its rigorous cut softened only by a gentle froth of silk cloqué. Dubbed the 'Most Stylish Woman in the World' by *Town and Country* Magazine in 1983, the Comtesse was already appearing on the international best-dressed lists by the age of twenty-five, having consistently worn haute couture all her life. Because of a family history of French aristocratic wealth – which suggested fashion design was beneath her station – her longing to become a designer was not fulfilled until she was well into her forties. An innate sense of good taste meant success for her first collection in Paris and America in 1983. It catered for women of her ilk, who admired its aura of discreet grandeur and slender lines adorned by extravagant though simple shoulder detail.

☛ von Furstenberg, de la Renta, Roehm

Comtesse Jacqueline de Ribes. b Paris (FR), 1931. **Jacqueline de Ribes, Paris.** Photograph by Victor Skrebneski, 1983.

Ricci Nina   Designer

In this advertisement from 1937, a slimline suit, the jacket trimmed with fur, is placed in the context of Nina Ricci's world; the centre of which was the place Vendôme in Paris. Unlike her contemporaries Coco Chanel and Elsa Schiaparelli, Nina Ricci did not set trends; instead, she concentrated on providing clothes for wealthy society women of a certain age, whose aim was to appear feminine, elegant and beautiful. It was a tradition that was continued by Jules-François Crahay and then by Gérard Pipart, both of whom respected Ricci's original tenet. She opened her Parisian couture house in 1932 and, with the help of her son Robert Ricci, rapidly established a reputation as a true couturière. She worked by draping fabric directly onto the body, gathering and tucking to emphasize her clients' attributes and disguise their imperfections.

☞ Ascher, Crahay, Frizon, Hirata, Mainbocher, Pipart, Schiaparelli

392

Nina Ricci. b Turin (IT), 1883. **d** Paris (FR), 1970. **Fur-trimmed jacket and skirt.** Illustration by Pierre Mourgue, 1937.

Ritts Herb

Photographer

Using his customary talent for black-and-white photography, Herb Ritts makes a drama out of Gianni Versace's already arresting dress. The funnel of black fabric, and that worn by the model, create startling geometric shapes that contrast with her pale skin and the desert backdrop. Born into a wealthy Los Angeles family in 1952, Herb Ritts lived next door to Steve McQueen and was exposed to a world of sophisticated beauty by his mother, an interior decorator. Photography started as a hobby, with portraits of friends and landscapes. In 1978 a picture he had taken on the set of Franco Zeffirelli's remake of *The Champ* was used by *Newsweek*. A friend, male model Matt Collins, introduced Ritts to Bruce Weber and fashion photography. Ritts's style is sexy and powerful, often homo-erotic and always fascinated by the texture of skin.

☞ **Platt Lynes, Sieff, Versace, Weber**

393

Herb Ritts. b Los Angeles, CA (USA), 1952. **Tatjana Patitz wears Versace.** *Le Mirage*, 1990.

Roberts Michael   Illustrator

Recalling the collage work of Henri Matisse, Michael Roberts accurately depicts Azzedine Alaïa's sculptural Sphinx dress. Bands of white paper emulate the elastic bands in Alaïa's trademark creation; a black paper silhouette accentuates these bands' curvaceous effect. Using a naïve, 'child-like' illustrative technique, Roberts keeps an outsider's perspective, while his humorous treatment hints at a deep knowledge of fashion's intricacies. A fashion writer, stylist, photographer, illustrator, video director and collagist, Roberts pokes fun at fashion icons from a knowing standpoint. His outrageous sense of style and venomous pen found their way through his multiple appointments as fashion and design director at *The Sunday Times* in 1972, society magazine *Tatler* in 1981 and currently at UK *Vogue* and the *New Yorker* magazine. His provocative vision was acutely exemplified when, for an April Fool issue of *Tatler*, he transformed designer Vivienne Westwood as Margaret Thatcher.

☛ Alaïa, Ettedgui, Westwood

394

Michael Roberts. b Aylesbury (UK), 1947. **'Azzedine's Sphinx'.** Paper collage, 1991.

Roberts Tommy (Mr Freedom)   Designer

Photographer Clive Arrowsmith puts Tommy Roberts' work into its kitsch Americana context for *Vogue* in 1971. The stretchy wrestler's dungarees are appliquéd with a bubblegum-pink satin heart and worn over a colour-blocked T-shirt. The grinning baseball team seals the story. This was fun fashion for the pop generation at a time when *Vogue* asked the question, 'Is bad taste a bad thing?' Designer Tommy Roberts was Mr Freedom, a man with an eye both for design and for the gap in the market. His cheerful T-shirts and tightly cut trousers were also decorated with camp symbols of 1930s and 1940s Hollywood – Mickey Mouse and Donald Duck adorned iconoclastic clothing for both sexes. In 1966 Roberts opened Kleptomania, a hippie emporium near London's Carnaby Street which was followed in 1969 by Mr Freedom, on the King's Road. It sold a fast-moving style that never took itself too seriously.

☛ **Fiorucci, Fish, Nutter**

Tommy Roberts. b London (UK), 1942. (Mr Freedom.) **Dungarees with pink appliqué heart.** Photograph by Clive Arrowsmith, British *Vogue*, 1971.

Rocha John   Designer

Creative yet commercial, John Rocha says, 'Sex never comes into it. I'm interested in beauty more than anything else'. Here, his organza dress printed with vast orchids is thrown into relief by Pat McGrath's abstract cobalt blue make-up. The dress is designed to stand proud of the body, creating a see-through sheath shadowed with flowers. Despite the hot mood of this picture, Irish references often influence Rocha's work. Natural fabrics, including linen, wool and sheepskin, are given the colours of a Celtic landscape: soft moss green, stone, slate grey. Rocha describes his clothes as 'free in spirit...a bit gypsy'. This description also fits the Portuguese-Chinese designer who moved from Hong Kong to London to study fashion. His Celtic-inspired end-of-year show was spotted by the Irish Trade Board who invited him to work in Dublin, where he has lived since 1979, producing clothes under his Chinatown label.

☛ Eisen, Kim, McGrath, Watanabe

John Rocha. b Hong Kong (HK), 1953. **Organza print dress**. Photograph by Steven Klein, *Frank*, 1998.

Rochas Marcel   Designer

Marcel Rochas oversees the fitting of a dress, conducted by his wife Hélène, while testing a fragrance sample. Mme Rochas pins and tucks the skirt into the New Look shape – a curvaceous silhouette that Rochas was credited with presaging in his film work for Mae West. In 1946 he launched the *guêpière*, a long-line strapless brassiere which enclosed the hips – a foundation garment that was to train figures for a decade. Counting Jean Cocteau and Christian Bérard among his friends, and with the encouragement of Poiret, Rochas opened his own maison de couture in 1925. During the 1930s he started to create black and white dresses that featured a white collar – one of which is photographed here. His creative innovations often featured a strong shoulder line, an element that Rochas considered 'a sign of the feminine'. In the 1950s, he transposed casual trousers into the context of women's suiting – another Rochas novelty.

☛ Bérard, Cocteau, Dior

397

Marcel Rochas. b Paris (FR), 1902. **d** Paris (FR), 1955. **Marcel and Hélène Rochas with model.** 1944.

Rodriguez Narciso   Designer

Cerruti, for whom he designed this dainty, embroidered bodice, gave Narciso Rodriguez his first international platform as a designer of minimal fashion. However, it was the creation of a wedding dress that really brought his name to general attention. In 1996 Carolyn Bessette married John F. Kennedy Jr wearing one of his rigorously simple, bias-cut sheath dresses. 'I made a wedding dress for a really good friend and [it] brought a lot of attention to the work I was doing,' he said afterwards. Rodriguez learned the power of understatement while working for a succession of design houses, each of whose philosophy is based around clean, modern, luxurious and wearable clothes: Anne Klein, Calvin Klein (where he met Bessette) and TSE, a design label specializing in cashmere. In 1997, Rodriguez launched his own label in Milan and was appointed to design for the luxurious Spanish label, Loewe.

☛ Cerruti, Ferretti, A. Klein, C. Klein, Loewe

398

Narciso Rodriguez. b NJ (USA), 1961. **Embroidered bodice and skirt for Cerruti.** Photograph by Carter Smith, *Harper's Bazaar*, 1997.

Roehm Carolyne — Designer

Carolyne Roehm, photographed at a gala event held by Bill Blass, is her own best advert. When she launched her own deluxe, ready-to-wear business in 1984, it was her tall, whippet-thin frame that starred in the glossy adverts and sold her feminine clothes. 'I wasn't so gung ho on the idea of being in the ads,' she said. 'I was told it would be a tremendous advantage.' And so it was. Roehm sold her society clothes to rich women who were either like her or wanted to be like her. She has been described as both 'driven' and 'highly organised' and it is these qualities that led her to Oscar de la Renta, for whom she worked for ten years as designer, house model and muse. Roehm mixes luxury with a practical awareness. Garments cut from lavish fabrics, such as a full-length, duchesse satin evening skirt, will be worn with a cashmere sweater to simulate the feel of sportswear.

☛ Blass, de la Renta, de Ribes, Wang

Carolyne Roehm. b Kirksville, MI (USA), 1951. **Satin cocktail dress**. Photograph by Daniel d'Errico, *Women's Wear Daily*, 1991.

Rosier Michèle

Designer

A mountain takes on the look of another planet for the backdrop to Michèle Rosier's space-age sportswear. The model's bug-eyed goggles and silver boots amplify the drama of Rosier's foil ski jacket and pants. Together with her contemporary Christiane Bailly, Rosier was a major player in France's burgeoning ready-to-wear market. With her young, accessible response to haute couture, she helped boost the export of French prêt-à-porter five-fold between 1962 and 1970. Rosier spent her childhood with her mother, publisher Hélène Gordon-Lazareff, in the United States, where the youth-orientated style was a formative influence. Rosier began her career as a writer for *New Woman* and *France-Soir*, but quit journalism to found V de V (Vêtements de Vacances) in 1962 with Jean-Pierre Bamberger. Rosier's pioneering use of sportswear fabrics, such as nylon fleece, paved the way for their adoption as part of everyday fashion clothing.

☛ Bailly, Bousquet, Khanh, W. Smith

400

Michèle Rosier. b Paris (FR), 1929. **Quilted ski jacket and pants for V de V.** Photograph by Vernier, British *Vogue*, 1966.

Rotten Johnny   Icon

Created by Malcolm McLaren and styled by Vivienne Westwood, the Sex Pistols were a promotional tool for the pair's punk-defining London's King's Road shop, Sex. Johnny Rotten, lead member of the group, pronounced, 'The kids want misery and death. They want threatening noises, because that shakes you out of your apathy.' This uniform was designed as the sartorial equivalent. It was antipathetic to every dress code before it; even the individual protest clothes worn by hippies had proclaimed a mood of utopian collectivity, but punk was invented to alienate every other element of society by using sex and bondage as its themes. Rotten was surprised himself when Westwood gave him a rubber shirt to wear on stage: 'I thought it was the most repulsive thing I'd ever seen. To wear it as a piece of clothing rather than as some part of a sexual fetish was hilarious.'

☞ Cobain, Hemingway, McLaren, Rhodes, Westwood

Johnny Rotten (John Lydon). b London (UK), 1956. **Johnny Rotten wears tartan bondage trousers**. c1977.

Rouff Maggy

Designer

The East provides the inspiration for this evening gown. Rouff has incorporated Japanese influence into superlative modern tailoring: the long, loose pendant sleeves recall those of a kimono. Like Poiret and Bakst before her, Rouff has infused her design with a feel for the exotic, the Orient. She has achieved a perfectly cut European gown. By using the bias-cutting technique, this dress takes on an almost seamless appearance, with a sweep of unbroken fabric reaching from the bodice to the cuff's hem. Rouff began her career as a fashion designer at Drecoll, where her mother, Madame de Wagner, was head designer. But it was Jeanne Paquin who was her main inspiration. Rouff founded her own fashion house in 1929, rapidly gaining a reputation for ravishing eveningwear and also for sportswear. In 1937 she opened her salon in London where her Parisian gowns were shown to her British clientele.

☛ Agnès, Bakst, Drecoll, Paquin, Poiret

Maggy Rouff. b Paris (FR), 1876. **d** Paris (FR), 1971. **Evening dress with cut sleeves.** Photograph by George Hoyningen-Huene, 1935.

Roversi Paolo

Photographer

Paolo Roversi describes Kirsten Owen, his favourite model, as 'somewhere between an angel and a demon', which is how he captured her in this photograph taken for a Romeo Gigli campaign. Gigli, a long-term collaborator of Roversi's, believes the photographer 'succeeds in seizing a fleeting moment, a tremor of emotion which projects the women themselves into a timeless dimension'. Roversi's illusory work stands alone among late twentieth-century fashion photographers. He left his native Italy for Paris in 1973, and by the end of the decade had developed a distinctive style using double exposure and Polaroid film. Roversi's images are poetic, romantic and painterly, and by turns demure and slightly demented. He describes them as 'a very intense exchange', an attempt to 'capture a lot of their soul, a little of their personality'.

☞ Ferretti, Gigli, McGrath, McKnight

403

Paolo Roversi. b Ravenna (IT), 1947. **Kirsten Owen modelling for Romeo Gigli.** 1987.

Rubinstein Helena   Cosmetics creator

'Life Red comes to life on your lips' claims Helena Rubinstein's fresh-faced advertisement from the 1940s. The healthy image promoted by Rubinstein's make-up and skin creams was born in a laboratory. She had wanted to study medicine but, denied her chance, left Poland to live with an uncle in Australia. She started to sell a face cream, Creme Valaze, brought from home to protect her complexion from the sun. A successful small skincare school followed and when one of her seven sisters joined her, Rubinstein studied with the best European dermatologists. Her white-coated approach to cosmetics resulted in several innovations, including the first skin cream to use male and female hormones in an attempt to delay the process of ageing.

Her artistic credentials were also impeccable – in Paris she became friend and patron to Matisse, Dufy, Dali and Cocteau.

☞ Cocteau, Dalí, Dufy

Helena Rubinstein. b Cracow (POL), 1870. d New York (USA), 1965. **'Life Red' advertisement**. 1940.

Rykiel Sonia

Designer

During a salon presentation, Sonia Rykiel's tailored knitwear is exemplified by cardigan coats and dresses accessorized with sequined roses and gold belts. Her attitude to the grand feasibility of knitted wool was explained when she said, 'Just as one woman looks fantastically erotic naked...another can seem the same in a polo-neck sweater'. The 'Queen of Knits' began designing in 1962 when she was pregnant and unable to find any soft sweaters for her maternity wear. So she knitted her own, and also began selling them in her husband's fashion shops. Rykiel's style of elegant yet easy 'lounge' dressing is typically French. She calls her clothes '*le nouveau classicisme*', their slim line (so popular in the 1970s) owing much to the 1930s. Fluid jersey, wide trousers and raglan-sleeve sweaters in muted colours are her trademarks; her Lurex knitwear is sophisticated enough for evening. 'I love knit,' Rykiel says, 'because it is very magical. You can do so many things with just a thread.'

☞ Albini, Jacobson, Turbeville

405

Sonia Rykiel. b Paris (FR), 1930. **Knitted co-ordinates.** 1974.

Saint Laurent Yves   Designer

Yves Saint Laurent dresses model René Russo in a polished evening suit, framing her face (simply made-up by Way Bandy) with feathers. Since the 1960s 'YSL' has been a directional and determining force in modern fashion. He introduced masculine tailoring for women, using military uniforms and variations on the tuxedo or 'le smoking', and took street styles and peasant costume and turned them into luxurious options for women. Saint Laurent has often referred to art, basing designs and embroidery on paintings by Mondrian, Matisse, Picasso and Braque, but always taking them as historical icons and making them current. Saint Laurent said, 'Like Proust, I'm fascinated most of all by my perceptions of a world in awesome transition.' Great fashion is about cutting those moments of transition out of cloth. He once described what he did as 'minor art' but later added the words 'maybe it is not so minor after all'.

☛ Bandy, Deneuve, Dior, Newton, Perint Palmer

406

Yves Saint Laurent. b Oran (ALG), 1936. René Russo wears deep feather collar and skirt, Paris. Photograph by Francesco Scavullo, 1974.

Sander Jil   Designer

Sander began her career as a fashion journalist, but moved into fashion design. In 1968 she opened a boutique in Hamburg and five years later was showing on the catwalk. Sander perceived a need for understated clothes with a sense of quiet self-confidence, but which would provide the wearer with the ultimate in fit, quality and modernity. It was a prophetic vision: today, her clothes have become the byword for an ultra-modern, androgynous sensuality that is as uncompromisingly technical as it is beautiful. Her simplicity must not, however, be confused with classicism. As Sander told *Vogue*, 'A classic is an excuse, because one is too lazy to contrast the spirit of the time.' Brutal purity defines her work. She rejects the clichés of femininity, its ruffles and furbelows, for the refinements found in the architecture of men's suits. This approach throws emphasis away from detail and onto the material, as can be seen here with a pair of trousers, the most striking aspect of which is the texture.

☞ Lang, McDean, Sims, Vallhonrat

407

Jil Sander. b Wesselburen (GER), 1943. **Angela Lindvall wears silk shirt and tweed trousers.** Photograph by David Sims, 1998.

Sant'Angelo Giorgio di   Designer

Veruschka's body is barely covered by a chain bikini by Giorgio di Sant'Angelo. Her hair is wrapped with gold lamé and her body encircled with gold chains. The 1960s was a decade devoted to the cult of youth and Sant'Angelo designed to make women aware of their bodies. Born in Florence, he trained as an architect and studied art, ceramics and sculpture, before winning an animation fellowship with Walt Disney in Los Angeles. In the early 1960s he moved to New York and worked as a textile designer, where his talent was spotted by Diana Vreeland, the flamboyant editor of American *Vogue*. She sent him to Arizona with an array of materials, scissors and Veruschka to 'invent' clothes for a spread in her magazine, of which this design is an example. In later life Sant'Angelo found new customers with his wrapped, stretchy Lycra clothes designed according to the same principles.

☞ Bruce, Lindbergh, Peretti, Veruschka, Vreeland

Giorgio di Sant'Angelo. b Florence (IT), 1936. **d** New York (USA), 1989. **Veruschka wears gold chain bikini**. Photograph by Franco Rubartelli, American *Vogue*, 1968.

Sarne Tanya (Ghost)   Designer

A fine georgette fabric, traced over with a print titled 'ice river', is slashed into an asymmetrical dress; one that is of its season but at the same time unique to one label. Regardless of their style, which changes every season, Ghost's dresses are machine-washable, a practicality not usually associated with high fashion. Tanya Sarne, the founder and figurehead at Ghost, came up with the idea of developing a fabric that is hardy, yet sensuous against the skin. The result was a material woven mainly from viscose yarns and derived from specially grown soft woods. This special Ghost fabric is put through an intensive process of boiling and dyeing in an unusual palette of colours. This costly and time-consuming activity ultimately gives it a unique crepe-like texture and density. Such garments have longevity and require minimal attention – a fact that has made Ghost popular with women who travel. Ghost's fabric is used for everything from plain vests to complicated gowns.

☛ Clark, Dell'Acqua, Rhodes, Tarlazzi

Tanya Sarne. b Southgate (UK), 1945. (Ghost.) **Fuschia 'ice river' printed georgette dress**. Photograph by Niall McInerney, 1997.

Sassoon Vidal

Hairdresser

'Hair is nature's biggest compliment and the treatment of this compliment is in our hands. As in couture, the cut is the most important element...haircutting simply means design and this feeling for design must come from within.' Vidal Sassoon's words explain the reasons for his simplified, Bauhausian haircuts which freed women from weekly beauty-parlour visits and the tyranny of curlers, lacquered shapes and other hair constriction. Sassoon's cuts – the geometric, the wash-and-wear perm, the bob (cut on a horizontal plane) and the Nancy Kwan – were low-maintenance high modernism, and he identified easy-to-care-for shapes that were adaptable for many women. Belonging to the generation of the Beatles and Swinging London, Sassoon took the cult of the natural to hair and elevated the role of the hairdresser, working in partnership with fashion designers such as Mary Quant and Rudi Gernreich.

☛ Beatles, Coddington, Gernreich, Leonard, Liberty, Quant

Vidal Sassoon. b London (UK), 1928. **'Five-point' haircut**. Photograph by David Montgomery, 1964.

410

Scaasi Arnold   Designer

Saucer-sized black dots on a white silk dress, its colours reversed for the coat, was already a Scaasi signature in 1957. So were the waist-deep décolletage and the bell-shaped skirt. Scaasi was the first designer in America to do the snappy matching coat and dress look for evening. Having trained with Charles James, he left in 1956 to set up his own label, specializing in evening clothes for socialite functions. Scaasi was careful to include decorative 'table top' necklines and low décolletages, and he favoured large 'grand entrance' prints. In 1958 his polka-dot evening dress was the first formal evening outfit to end above the knee. His couture salon opened in 1964, producing short evening dresses and spectacular ball gowns. 'I am definitely not a minimalist designer!' said Scaasi. 'Clothes with some adornment are more interesting to look at and more fun to wear.'

☞ Deneuve, C. James, de la Renta, Schuberth

Arnold Scaasi. b Montreal, QC (CAN), 1931. **Polka-dot dress.** 1957.

Scavullo Francesco

Photographer

The model Antonia plays a tourist in an epic fashion scene shot in the populated chaos of a Hong Kong marketplace, directed by the photographer Francesco Scavullo. Her flight bag crashes into her silk dress, oriental make-up and hat, dramatizing the outfit and dressing Antonia for her role. Scavullo's obsession with photography began at an early age: at nine he was making home movies and much of his early work has a filmic quality. He began his career at American *Vogue* and spent three years with Horst, before going to work on the new teenage magazine *Seventeen*. Scavullo's passion for photographing beautiful women was harnessed by American *Cosmopolitan*, whose unapologetically sexy covers he has photographed since 1965. But his lasting legacy to fashion photography is undoubtedly his technical knowledge, particularly his use of diffused lighting that is designed to flatter the greatest 'cover' faces.

☛ Deneuve, Fonssagrives, C. Klein, Turlington

Francesco Scavullo. b Staten Island, NY (USA), 1929. **Antonia, Hong Kong, 1962.**

Scherrer Jean-Louis   Designer

This fantasy world of a Botticelli woman rising from a shell serves as the ideal medium for the revelation of a silk-chiffon dress with a waterfall collar and butterfly cape. Its luxurious yet dramatic qualities adorn Jean-Louis Scherrer's refined classicism. Scherrer moved into haute couture when, after the petrol crisis in the 1970s, he provided the wives of affluent Arabs with longer, covered-up fashions that satisfied the modesty requirements dictated by Islamic laws, while also proclaiming their wealth. Parisian ballrooms have witnessed Scherrer's sumptuous embroideries and glittering silks since he started as Christian Dior's assistant, after an accident finished his career as a dancer at the age of twenty. After Dior's death and the choice of Saint Laurent as his successor, Scherrer left and opened his own business in 1962.

☛ Lancetti, Mori, Ungaro

413

Jean-Louis Scherrer. b Paris (FR), 1936. **Print dress and straw hat**. Photograph by Angus McBean, *Harpers & Queen*, 1989.

Schiaparelli Elsa   Designer

Is the woman wearing this 'Desk Suit', designed by Elsa Schiaparelli in 1936, going to the office or the beach? The suit features a vertical series of true and false pockets, embroidered to look like desk drawers with buttons for knobs. Dress designing for Schiaparelli was an art, and the decorative details of her fashions often had Surrealist elements. This Desk Suit is based on two Surrealist drawings by Salvador Dalí entitled 'City of Drawers' and 'Venus de Milo of Drawers'. Surrealism was an art movement that flourished in the 1920s and 1930s, reacting against the rational and formal real world, and substituting instead fantasy and a dream world. Surrealism in fashion thrived in the 1930s, depicting psychologically suggestive garments.

Schiaparelli's smart, sophisticated, witty clothes took the fashion world by storm. She commissioned some of the best artists of the period, such as Salvador Dalí, Jean Cocteau and Christian Bérard, to design fabrics and embroideries for her.

☛ Banton, Bérard, Cocteau, Dalí, Lesage, Man Ray, Nars, Perugia

414

Elsa Schiaparelli. b Rome (IT), 1890. **d** Paris (FR), 1973. **'Desk Suit'**. Photograph by Cecil Beaton, 1936.

Schiffer Claudia   Model

In one of her most famous photographs, Claudia Schiffer becomes a sex kitten. Shortly after being discovered in a discotheque in 1987, Schiffer secured the Guess? advertising campaign and subsequently became one of the most sought-after models in the world. She has appeared on the covers of more than 500 magazines, including *Vanity Fair* which has an editorial policy that usually refuses to place any model on its cover. The first and only model to have a wax likeness in the Grévin Museum in Paris, Schiffer's appeal beyond that as a fashion model is an obvious one. As a member of the supermodel troupe, she represents natural blonde beauty – a modern, healthy look that dates back to Cheryl Tiegs. She modelled for *Sports Illustrated*'s swimwear issue in 1978, thereby opening up the pin-up market for fashion models. Nowadays this is a lucrative avenue for women such as Claudia and Cindy Crawford, whose beauty has a general appeal.

☞ Crawford, Thomass, von Unwerth

415

Claudia Schiffer. b Rheinberg (GER), 1970. **Guess? Jeans publicity campaign, 1989.** Photograph by Ellen von Unwerth.

Schön Mila   Designer

This 1968 photograph, which features a perfectly cut, Mila Schön, white wool suit, represents several of her design signatures. Schön's favourite fabric was double-faced wool; she was a perfectionist who worked within a classical structure, to exacting specifications, and she also created modernist garments. She came from a family of wealthy Yugoslavian aristocrats who had fled to Italy to escape Communism. In 1959, Schön launched her business. She had gained her love of fashion as a couture customer at Balenciaga, and within her clothes can be seen his austerity of cut, together with the influences of Dior and Schiaparelli. By 1965, Schön had developed her own style and began showing on the catwalk. Construction of her tailoring is highlighted by its very simplicity – making details out of seams and darts.

☞ **Cardin, Cashin, Courrèges**

Mila Schön. b Dalmatia (YUG), 1916. **Benedetta Barzini wears double-face trouser suit and hat.** Photograph by Ugo Mulas, 1968.

416

Schuberth Emilio Designer

A ruched taffeta, puff-ball gown, inspired by a late eighteenth-century shape, flaunts a tiered underskirt decorated with a filigree print. The underlying flamenco theme is given cachet by the length of black ribbon adorning the model's chignon. As one of Rome's top couturiers in the 1950s, Emilio Schuberth was also one of the first to present his collection on the Italian catwalks in 1952. His signature touch, of undercutting serious evening crinolines with unexpectedly baroque embroidery, attracted the early fashion paparazzi, who were particularly drawn to his convertible double-sided skirts, which metamorphosed into capes strewn with appliquéd flora. Schuberth often created fantastical skirts, the entirety of which were decorated with rows of foaming tulle and dotted with silk flowers. His only known training was twenty years of atelier work within his own house prior to 1952, earning him an elite clientele, which included the Duchess of Windsor.

☞ Biagiotti, Fontana, Scaasi, Windsor

Emilio Schuberth. b Naples (IT), 1904. d Rome (IT), 1972. **Ruched taffeta evening gown.** Photograph by G.M. Fadigati, 1955.

Shrimpton Jean   Model

Although Jean Shrimpton had been modelling for a few years when she was pictured here, she retained a quality that prompted her to say, 'I was as green as a salad,' of the day she joined London's Lucie Clayton modelling school in 1960. Later that year she was on a shoot for a cornflakes advertisement, when she met the photographer David Bailey. 'Duffy was taking her picture against a blue background,' recalled Bailey. 'It was like her blue eyes were just holes drilled through her head to the paper behind. Duffy said, "Forget it – she's too posh for you," and I thought, "We'll see about that". In the course of her affair with Bailey, Shrimpton became a sex icon and top model; 'the Shrimp' was born. Shrimpton's gawky, urchin style was perfect for Courrèges' space-age look and Quant's mini. When the couple appeared in American *Vogue* editor Diana Vreeland's office, she exclaimed, 'England has arrived!'

☞ Bailey, Kenneth, McLaughlin-Gill, Mesejeán, Vreeland

Jean Shrimpton. b Buckinghamshire (UK), 1942. **Jean Shrimpton in Epping Forest**. Photograph by Frances McLaughlin-Gill, *Harper's Bazaar*, 1965.

418

Sieff Jeanloup   Photographer

Astrid wears a black pillbox hat by Halston and silk crepe gown by Bill Blass. Jeanloup Sieff said of this photograph, 'She had an aristocratic profile and a very inspiring back.' For him, fashion photography is, and has always been, more than the simple representation of clothing. Instead, it is about his passion for beauty and form. 'The simple pleasure of rendering certain shapes, those maddening lights...' he has said of his predominantly black-and-white images. Born in Paris to Polish parents, Sieff received a camera for his fourteenth birthday. By 1960, after a brief spell at French *Elle* and the Magnum picture agency, he was living and working in New York taking fashion pictures for *Harper's Bazaar*. His fame grew quickly, as did his disdain for fashion. In 1966 he returned to Paris where he remains, occasionally dabbling in fashion, but staying true to his passion: capturing moments which cannot recur.

☞ Blass, Halston, Ritts

Jeanloup Sieff. b Paris (FR), 1933. **'Astrid's back'.** Palm Beach. *Harper's Bazaar*, 1964.

Simpson Adele   Designer

From Mrs Eisenhower to Mrs Carter, Adele Simpson's conservative versions of the current trends have delighted the wives of many leading US politicians. Her clothes, that could be co-ordinated into complete wardrobes, proved practical and suitable for the active and exposed lives of her clients. The ensemble shown illustrates this: though not a suit, the slim skirt and asymmetrically fastening jacket could easily match other elements of Simpson's collections. The first American designer to treat cotton seriously as a fashion fabric, she used this fibre for street dresses and full-skirted evening gowns. Cotton was also used in one of Simpson's most celebrated creations: a 1950s chemise dress with attached belts which could be tied at the front or the back. Reputedly one of the highest-paid designers in the world at the age of twenty-one, she bought her own company in 1949.

☞ Galanos, John-Frederics, Leser, Maltézos

Adele Simpson. b New York (USA), 1903. **d** Greenwich, CT (USA), 1995. **Formal day suit.** Photograph by John Rawlings. 1947.

Sims David

Photographer

David Sims' stark, stylized fashion images have set agendas through their honesty. Here Sims chooses an utterly unstyled photograph, almost a snap of undressed hair and unclothed shoulders. In the early 1990s, after working as assistant to photographers Norman Watson and Enrique Badulescu, he began working with stylist Melanie Ward and models Kate Moss and Emma Balfour. Together they helped to pioneer the grunge look, which gave them all an international platform between the covers of *Vogue*, *Harper's Bazaar* and *The Face*. Sims always tries to put the realities of daily life into his pictures, using either natural or edgy studio lighting, which illuminates quirky facial expressions and poses not seen in the realms of traditional fashion photography. He is low-key about his contribution, saying, 'I think I've pushed the borders of fashion photography a bit.'

☛ Day, Moss, Sander

David Sims. **b** Sheffield (UK), 1966. **Strands of hair**. 1997.

Sitbon Martine   Designer

Wearing a splash-printed dress by Martine Sitbon, Stella Tennant crouches next to a surreal arrangement of wild animals. Sitbon herself started out as the wild child of French fashion, influenced by the rock scene inhabited by the Rolling Stones and the Velvet Underground (whose music was used as backing music for her first collection). As a teenager, Sitbon's early fashion education was gained in the flea markets of London and Paris, as has been the case for many designers before and since. Her passion for the English scene stayed with her as she worked first as a stylist, then as a designer. The art of pulling a look together from many inspirations is at the centre of Sitbon's style. In the mid-1980s she became known for feminized menswear, in particular fitted tail coats worn with slim trousers – suits inspired by those hanging on flea market rails.

☞ Kélian, Lenoir, Leroy, McDean, Tennant

Martine Sitbon. b Casablanca (MOR), 1951. **Stella Tennant wears devoré dress**. Photograph by Craig McDean, 1997.

Smith Graham

Milliner

A floral confection balances a formal hairstyle and co-ordinates with a powder-pink dress. It is a ceremonious hat made for the English season by Graham Smith who is noted for his royal millinery. He believes that a hat should appear to be part of the wearer, with particular emphasis on silhouette and scale. His lightweight, delicate textures create a hat that is showy yet well-mannered. Educated at the Royal College of Art, Smith's graduation collection achieved such acclaim that he was immediately appointed milliner at Lanvin-Castillo in Paris. In 1967 Smith launched his own label, at the same time collaborating with designers Jean Muir and Zandra Rhodes. Smith specializes in traditional styles, best shown by his designs for Princess Diana and the Duchess of York in the 1980s (he believes the Royal Family has saved British millinery). Smith is a master of balance and proportion, determined not to forsake flattery for fashion.

☞ Castillo, Diana, Muir, Rhodes

423

Graham Smith. b Bexley (UK), 1938. **'Small head, tiny roses, black and white chic'.** Photograph by Henry Clarke, British *Vogue*, 1965.

Smith Paul

Designer

At Paul Smith's party, men and women wear outfits that bear a contemporary blend of influences: unexpected materials mixed with traditional cloths, classic shapes cut with fashionable edge. In Smith's ranges, colour and print distinguish his wearable and individual work. Smith opened his first shop in Nottingham in 1970, expanding into London's Covent Garden in 1979 and Notting Hill in 1998. The first thing he ever sold was a Union Jack handkerchief and today his shops remain quirky, selling anything from toy robots to ties. It is this inspired eccentricity and a mind fine-tuned for marketing that has, unusually for a British company, turned Smith's label into a status one, particularly in Japan. In 1994 he launched Paul Smith Women, basing it on the same principles of cut, colour and fabric found in his menswear, with his androgynous suits finding a ready market for women who until then had to wear Paul Smith for Men.

☞ R. James, Nutter, Stephen

424

Paul Smith. b Nottingham (UK), 1946. **Paul Smith Men, Paul Smith Women. Autumn/winter 1997.** Photograph by Mario Testino.

Smith Willi

Designer

A jumpsuit, with functional zip, tie belt, large patch pockets and cuffed sleeves became extraordinary in the hands of Willi Smith, who decided to cut it out of silver-coated cloth in 1973. As a freelance designer he was already exploring the concept of putting fun into function. Then, in 1976, Smith launched his label Willi Wear. It produced well-priced, young, easy-to-wear, easy-to-care-for separates that brought designer fashion to a wider market. He used mainly natural fabrics and cut them with room for movement. For both men and women, Smith plugged the gap between jeans and stiff, formal clothes which meant nothing to the age group he was addressing. It was a market he was proud of, saying that he didn't design clothes for the Queen but for those who wave at her as she passes. Smith's style was founded on the concept of separates, at a time when the concept of traditional office dressing was being challenged by a move toward unstuffy clothes.

☛ Bartlett, A. Klein, Rosier

425

Willi Smith. b Philadelphia (USA), 1948. **d** New York (USA), 1987. **Metallic jump-suit**. Photograph by Nick Machalaba, *Women's Wear Daily*, 1974.

Snow Carmel

Editor

The chic image of Paris is achieved through Louise Dahl-Wolfe's graceful composition of a model controlling her excitable poodles against a backdrop of the Sacré Cœur. Part of an illustrated fashion story, the picture accompanied Snow's 1955 Paris report for *Harper's Bazaar*, which concentrated largely on Balenciaga's and Dior's new silhouettes. Well before the rest of the press understood him, Carmel Snow was applauding Balenciaga's clean, sculptural lines, and she christened Christian Dior's New Look purely by accident in a letter to the designer. A major presence as American *Vogue*'s fashion editor, and then at *Harper's Bazaar* from 1932, it was said that if a dozing Snow awoke during a showing, the outfit appearing to her would be a hit. For twenty years of her editorship-in-chief – aided by Alexey Brodovitch and Diana Vreeland – *Harper's Bazaar* mixed crisp fashion reportage with fresh visuals by Martin Munkacsi, Louise Dahl-Wolfe and Salvador Dalí.

☛ Balenciaga, Bassman, Brodovitch, Dior, Vreeland

426

Carmel Snow. b Dublin (IRE), 1887. d New York (USA), 1961. **Tunic and curled hat by Balenciaga**. Photograph by Louise Dahl-Wolfe, *Harper's Bazaar*, 1955.

Snowdon

Photographer

This 1957 fashion shoot by Snowdon, then Tony Armstrong Jones, for *Vogue* shows a new approach: the picture is infused with the energy inherent in the run-up to the 1960s. In fact, Snowdon's spontaneous moment was staged – the tumbling champagne glass was suspended on a clear thread and the model's thrilled greeting an act of theatre. He recalled,

'I made the models move and react, putting them in incongruous situations or performing incongruous feats. I made them run, dance, kiss, anything but stand still. Each sitting became a short story or miniature film strip.' This was the beginning of the language of contemporary fashion photography, a new naturalism and reality within artificial confines. In 1960

Armstrong Jones married Princess Margaret, prompting Cecil Beaton to call him 'the Cinderella of our time'.

☞ Beaton, Fish, Mori

Snowdon (Tony Armstrong Jones). b London (UK), 1930. **Champagne glasses**. British *Vogue*, 1957.

Souleiman Eugene   Hairdresser

Eugene Souleiman's chignon is an amalgamation of traditional hairdressing and modern styling. The feathered hairpieces make it an avant garde foil for her rococo gown by Valentino. Souleiman forges his own path through the world of hairdressing, often working with make-up artist Pat McGrath. Frequently contentious, he scorned the New York scene as boring and has fought with designers in his drive to develop new looks for the catwalk. In defiance of their expressive outfits, Souleiman has sent models along Prada's catwalk with belligerently unstyled hair, a typically contrary idea. He quickly tires of one look and, with the help of hairpieces, experiments with hair textures to reinvent the discipline on a monthly basis. Artificial or natural, Souleiman is one of the hairdressers who have made the manipulation of hair an indivisible element of fashion.

☞ McDean, McGrath, Prada, Valentino

Eugene Souleiman. b London (UK), 1961. **Taffeta gown**. Photograph by Craig McDean, Italian *Vogue*, 1998.

Sprouse Stephen   Designer

A design-school dropout, Sprouse arrived in New York in 1972 and soon made all the connections he needed for a career in fashion. Debbie Harry introduced him to Andy Warhol who introduced him to Halston who took him on as an assistant. But Sprouse's artistic interests distracted him and he and Halston parted company. In 1984, the photographer Steven Meisel persuaded him to launch his own label. Warhol's influence has always been obvious – from Sprouse's silver showroom to his claim that Edie Sedgwick was his 'favourite meteor'. In 1997, when he relaunched his label, he used Warhol's artwork as prints on dresses. (Sprouse has exclusive rights to use the famous Pop Art images in clothing designs.) His work in the 1980s was largely influenced by the pop music scene: cut-out minidresses were printed with video images, Day-Glo 'hip hop' style graffiti was sprayed onto dresses which were worn with sweatbands and wraparound sunglasses.

☛ Halston, Meisel, Warhol, K. Yamamoto

429

Stephen Sprouse. b OH (USA), 1953. **'Partytime' tank and sequined skirt**. Photograph by Rainer Hosch, *i-D*, 1998.

Steele Lawrence　　　　　Designer

Working on the lingerie theme, with a pin-tucked, chiffon camisole worn over a satin petticoat skirt, Lawrence Steele demonstrates his love of luxuriously simple clothes. His restraint is inspired by the work of Charles James and Claire McCardell. Born in Virginia, Steele had a military upbringing which took him to different cities throughout the United States, as well as Germany and Spain. Elements of this upbringing have been worked into his collections, including direct references such as epaulettes applied to the shoulders of shirts and jackets. Steele trained with Moschino in Milan, before moving on to Miuccia Prada's then relatively new womenswear line. He brought it forward with his simple, modern style, which blends American and European influences, then left in 1994 to continue his development under his own label.

☞ C. James, McCardell, Moschino, Prada

430

Lawrence Steele. b Hampton, VA (USA), 1963. **Strapless, pin-tucked camisole with skirt**. Photograph by Miles Aldridge, 1998.

Steichen Edward Photographer

Gloria Swanson confronts the camera head-on. She wears a cloche, the tight-fitting, helmet-like hat which was the characteristic fashion headwear of the 1920s. In 1963, Edward Steichen recalled the circumstances surrounding the taking of this photograph. He and Gloria Swanson had a long session, with many changes of costume. At the end of the session, he took a black lace veil and hung it in front of her face, causing her hat to mould to her head and give a streamlined appearance. Her eyes dilated and her look was that of a leopardess lurking behind leafy shrubbery watching her prey. Steichen, a thoroughly modern fashion photographer, was noted for his settings which conveyed atmosphere and structure anchored to current fashions, a mood he took to *Vogue* in 1923. His working relationship with the model Marion Morehouse was the first such collaboration between mannequin and photographer.

☛ Barbier, Daché, Morehouse, Nast

Edward Steichen. b Luxembourg (LUX), 1879. d West Redding, CT (USA), 1973. **Gloria Swanson**. Photograph by Edward Steichen, American *Vogue*, 1924.

Steiger Walter

Shoe designer

For Walter Steiger, the composition of a shoe is just as important as the aesthetic appeal of its exterior. Distinctive designs have been those with heels like many-sided cones or with triangular structures, an approach that was particularly popular in the 1970s and 1980s. Swiss-born, Steiger followed family tradition by undertaking an apprenticeship in shoemaking at the age of sixteen, after which he found employment at Bally in Paris. He moved to London in the early 1960s, where he designed lavish shoes under the Bally Bis label, as well as for Mary Quant. He also opened a successful studio in 1966 but felt Paris more appropriate for his first shop, which he opened in 1973. The sophistication of Steiger's highly innovative shoe construction met the demands of several couturiers with whom he subsequently collaborated, including Karl Lagerfeld, Chanel, Chloé, Montana, Oscar de la Renta and Nina Ricci.

☛ Bally, Kélian, Lenoir, Montana, de la Renta, Ricci

432

Walter Steiger. b Geneva (SW), 1942. **Heeled pump**. Photograph by Sheila Metzner, American *Vogue*, 1984.

Stephen John   Tailor

Photographed with his dog Prince, John Stephen wears the pristine suit, with Italianate 'bum-freezer' jacket, of a late-1950s buck. Known as the 'Million Pound Mod', Stephen revolutionized the way menswear was sold when he opened Carnaby Street's first swinging boutique in 1958. He would watch his teenage customers for inspiration – when he noticed them fluffing up their collars as they tried jackets on, he realized they were looking for wider lapels, which he produced and sold by the thousand. Stephen introduced extravagant details into the dusty realm of menswear, including flares, fly-fronted shirts inspired by dress shirts and suits cut from tweed treated with a lustrous finish. He had an early understanding of how quickly fashion would begin to change over the following decades and would not commit himself beyond eight weeks ahead, saying, 'In this world, change is violent. Anything can happen in two months.'

☛ Fish, Gilbey, P. Smith

John Stephen. b Glasgow (UK), c1936. **John Stephen and Prince**. *Daily Mail*, 1957.

433

Stern Bert

Photographer

Bert Stern was the last person to photograph Marilyn Monroe, seen here wearing Christian Dior. This stroke of luck made him world famous and left the world with a series of sensitive portraits that transcend the duty of fashion photography. Stern taught himself photography while working as art director for the American magazine *Mayfair*: 'I was always moving around and reframing things in front of me.' His desire to capture the perfect image led him to a career in commercial photography, where he worked on print advertisements for Pepsi-Cola, Volkswagen and, most famously, Smirnoff. His 1955 picture of a martini glass in front of one of the pyramids at Giza became legendary, as did his image of Lolita wearing heart-shaped glasses for the 1962 film. He worked on fashion and portraiture throughout his career, notably for *Vogue*, *Esquire* and *Life* magazine, photographing the most famous and most beautiful women of the time.

☞ Arnold, Dior, Orry-Kelly, Travilla

Bert Stern. b New York (USA), 1929. **Marilyn Monroe wears Dior.** British *Vogue*, 1962.

434

Stewart Stevie and Holah, David (Body Map)   Designers

'Gawky but sexy' is how David Holah and Stevie Stewart defined their fashion sportswear in 1984. Body Map, their label, was named after a 1960s artwork by Italian artist Enrico Job which mapped a man's body with two thousand photographs: 'It seemed to sum up our approach to pattern cutting', explained Holah. The partnership created sawn-off sweatshirts worn over striped tube skirts in a melange of layers and knitted fabrics under absurd collection titles such as A Cat in a Hat Takes a Rumble With a Techno Fish. In collaboration with textile designer Hilde Smith, Body Map designed a sporty and flexible wardrobe. Smith's stylized compass motifs were interwoven with abstract technological designs to produce graphic fabrics. The shapes were designed for London's uninhibited clubland which Body Map inhabited by night and brought to the catwalk. The sight prompted Women's Wear Daily to ask if it were all 'an outrageous pretension or merely a pretentious outrage'.

☛ Boy George, Ettedgui, Forbes

435

Stevie Stewart. b London (UK), 1958; David Holah. b London (UK), 1958. (Body Map.) 'Cat in a Hat' collection. Autumn/winter 1984. Photograph by Andy Lane.

Stiebel Victor

Designer

Three women are snapped by Norman Parkinson en route to an Ascot race meeting. They are dressed and hatted by Stiebel in his romantic style, with their vast cartwheel hats dominating soft, feminine dresses with hemlines that stop eight inches from the ground. As a favoured designer of society women, Stiebel carefully considered his accessories, regarding them as part of his total look. Stiebel studied architecture at Cambridge before being encouraged to enter fashion by Norman Hartnell. Having served as an apprentice at Reville & Rossiter, he became an accomplished British fashion designer and a member of the Incorporated Society of London Fashion Designers, together with Hartnell, Hardy Amies and Edward Molyneux. Stiebel also dressed actresses and members of the British Royal Family, including Princess Margaret for whom he designed the going-away outfit for her marriage to Anthony Armstrong Jones.

☞ Amies, Hartnell, Horvat, Molyneux, Parkinson

436

Victor Stiebel. b Durban (SA), 1907. **d** London (UK), 1976. **Dresses and 'Cartwheel' straw hats.** Photograph by Norman Parkinson, *Harper's Bazaar*, 1938.

Storey Helen   Designer

Helen Storey has loved texture since childhood. Here she applies sequins to leggings with the intention of glamorizing what, at the end of the 1980s, was a basic garment usually cut from black Lycra. Her womenswear had the intention of putting forward a new mood of aggressively sexy feminism. Her bras were decorated with dangerously sharp gemstones and her metal minidresses and black patent leather chaps were equally challenging. 'Clothes made by women don't deny what's underneath – we dress the essence, not the male-inspired dream', Storey said of this work. She trained with Valentino and Lancetti, both designers famous for their feminine sensibilities. After a partnership with designer Karen Boyd in the 1980s, Storey continued her explorations alone. In 1996, she collaborated with her sister to produce a sci-art project, *Primitive Streak*, which used magnified human structures as a basis for textile designs.

☞ Lancetti, Rosier, Valentino

Helen Storey. b London (UK), 1959. **Sequined leggings.** Photograph by Eamonn J. McCabe, British *Elle*, 1990.

Strauss Levi   Designer

A septuagenarian teacher invites her young audience to grapple with its preconceptions in an advertisement for Levi Strauss. 'I wish I had invented blue jeans,' Yves Saint Laurent once said. 'Jeans are expressive and discreet, they have sex appeal and simplicity – everything I could want for the clothes I design.' The real inventor was Levi Strauss, a Jewish-Bavarian immigrant pedlar who followed the Gold Rush to sell his goods. When his customers asked for trousers, he cut up tents to make them. In 1860 Strauss discovered an equally tough fabric called *serge de Nimes* (denim), from France. Jeans were named after the Genoese sailors' trousers on which the original 501 style was based. First brought to Europe by GIs during the Second World War, jeans were glamorized by the 1950s rebels James Dean and Marlon Brando. In the 1980s, a pair of Levis worn with Dr Martens shoes became the enduring uniform for an entire generation.

☛ Benetton, Dean, Fischer, Hechter, N. Knight, Saint Laurent

438

Levi Strauss. b Bavaria (GER), 1829. **d** San Francisco, CA (USA), 1902. **'Josephine, 79, teacher, Colorado'** wears **501 jeans**. Photograph by Nick Knight, 1996.

Sui Anna   Designer

Nadja Auermann appears on Anna Sui's catwalk as Greta Garbo in sequins, trilby and boa. The key to Sui's look is the eclectic way she mixes her clothes, rather than the individual garments themselves. As shown here, she has a modern take on most fashion periods. This retro-reworking is typical of 1990s fashion, and Sui's versions are more wearable than many. She attended Parsons School of Design in New York and worked as a stylist – a skill that can be appreciated in the way she brings a look together from several directions. While studying, she teamed up with a classmate, photographer Steven Meisel. She also worked briefly as a designer in a sportswear company, before setting up on her own in 1981, after Macy's began stocking her designs. Her inspiration comes from some forty years of magazine cuttings, stored away in what she calls her 'Genius Files'.

☛ Garbo, Garren, Meisel

439

Anna Sui. b Deerborn Heights, MI (USA), 1955. **Nadja Auermann wears a sequined sweater and boa**. Photograph by Chris Moore, 1995.

Sumurun

Model

When Edward Molyneux left Lucile to open his own couture house in 1919, he hired Vera Ashby as his head mannequin. He named her Sumurun, the Enchantress of the Desert, and she became the highest-paid model in Paris (crowds would gather to see her enter and exit the Molyneux establishment). She was photographed by Baron de Meyer and drawn by Drian. This photograph shows Vera in the Molyneux studio dressed for the *Coucher du Soleil* (sunset) ball. Inspired by her exotic, oriental look, Molyneux created a harem dress of silver tissue worn under a sleeveless tunic of gold lamé. He concealed electric bulbs in the ruby jewels that decorated her turban, earrings and tunic. As the house lights were dimmed, she pressed a button to light up her outfit, causing men to whoop and cheer. After retiring from modelling, Vera became a *vendeuse* at Molyneux, later moving to Norman Hartnell where she was appointed *vendeuse* to the Queen.

☛ Drian, Hartnell, de Meyer, Molyneux

Sumurun (Vera Ashby). b London (UK), 1895. **d** Victoria, BC (CAN), 1985. **Sumurun wears costume by Molyneux.** Photograph by Jean Desboutin, 1921.

Sybilla

Designer

'Travelling Clothes' is the title of this image by Javier Vallhonrat of Sybilla's autumn/winter 1989–90 collection. The incongruous title reflects the designer's Spanish sense of humour – these clothes are suited to a walk in the rain rather than international travel. Sybilla creates surreal designs and marries opposites in her work: extravagance with subtlety, humour with elegance.

Here, a coat has the spirit of both a traditional belted trench coat and an opera coat by her fellow countryman Cristobal Balenciaga. Sybilla grew up in Madrid and moved to Paris in 1980 to work at Yves Saint Laurent's couture atelier. After one year she dismissed Paris as too snobbish and cold, returning to the fun and laid-back atmosphere of her home city. In 1983 she

launched her own label and swifly became renowned for her use of soft colours and quirky, sculpted shapes in her clothing, shoes, bags and, latterly, furniture.

☛ Toledo, Vallhonrat

Sybilla (Sybilla Sorondo-Myelzwynska). b New York (USA), 1963. **'Travelling Clothes', 1989**. Photograph by Javier Vallhonrat.

Talbot Suzanne   Milliner

'Talbot would send us out to dine in public looking as exotic as the Wicked Queen in *Snow White* – easily the most chic vamp the films have ever evolved.' The caption that accompanied this picture takes us into Suzanne Talbot's charmed world. Talbot had long since died (her own powers being at their peak in the 1880s) but her spirit lived in the house's close alliance with the fashion world. The Talbot premises was part of the rich fashion map of Paris in the 1920s and 1930s, which included those of hairdresser Antoine, couturières Chanel and Schiaparelli and shoe designer André Perugia. This black silk jersey hat, embellished with a golden spike and embroidery, included a veil to be wrapped around the face and neck. Such theatrical French millinery was greatly admired by the American market. With Paulette, Mme Agnès and Lilly Daché, who moved to New York having briefly trained at Talbot, it was a house whose work moved in parallel with the fashions for clothes.

☛ Agnès, Antoine, Daché, Paulette, Perugia, Schiaparelli

Suzanne Talbot. (Active 1880s–1900s.) **Embroidered, silk jersey hat for Bergdorf Goodman.** Photograph by George Hoyningen-Huene, *Harper's Bazaar*, 1939.

Tappé Herman Patrick Designer

Mary Pickford, 'America's Sweetheart', wears the wedding dress chosen for her marriage to Douglas Fairbanks. It was originally made by Herman Tappé for Natica Nast, Condé's daughter, to wear for a *Vogue* sitting published in 1920. Tappé had been upset that he should be asked to make it in such a tiny size, but that was before Pickford had seen and selected it for her high-profile nuptials. The silk tulle wrap, worn over a plain, strapless dress, is trimmed with ruffles edged with silk organdie. Elsewhere, the tulle is formed into rows of tight gathers. Wedding dresses, and those for bridesmaids, formed the core of Tappé's exclusive, expensive work. He was known as the Poiret of New York for his individual and mysterious style. His was a romantic, feminine view, and he became a creator of *robes de style* – quixotic dresses based on costumes found in paintings.

☛ Emanuel, de Meyer, Nast, Poiret

Herman Patrick Tappé. (Active 1910s–1940s.) **Organdie dress with ribbon-banding and matching bonnet.** Photograph by Baron de Meyer, American *Vogue*, 1920.

Tarlazzi Angelo

Designer

An asymmetric, taffeta evening dress perfectly details Angelo Tarlazzi's well-recognized skill: blending Italian imagination with French chic. Its bodice, caught on one shoulder, flows into a point, moving over a contrasting skirt. Tarlazzi abandoned his studies in political science to pursue a career in fashion design. He worked at the house of Carosa for a number of years, before leaving Rome for Paris to become an assistant at Jean Patou. By the late 1960s he was freelancing between Paris, Milan, Rome and New York, during which time he was affiliated with Laura Biagiotti. It was a mix which formed his appreciation of the international market. By 1972 he was back at Patou but this time as artistic director, a high-status position he held until he launched his own prêt-à-porter label in 1977. Tarlazzi's garments are amply cut from soft fabrics and often use such asymmetric drapes.

☞ Biagiotti, Patou, Sarne

444

Angelo Tarlazzi. b Ascoli Piceno (IT), 1945. **Taffeta evening dress**. Photograph by Jean-François du Sel des Monts, *L'Officiel*, 1980.

Tatsuno Koji   Designer

Dress? Costume? Sculpture? Amid the acceleration backstage, the models stand motionless in orchestrated coils of fine mesh, trimmed with rows of flowers. Like sculptural relief, these lyrical compositions reflect Tatsuno's synthesis of modern technology and folkcraft. He has spent his career experimenting with rare craft techniques, initially from his bespoke tailoring establishment in London's Mayfair and now from his small gallery at the Palais-Royal in Paris. Completely self-taught in the most English art of tailoring, Tatsuno arrived in London as an antique art dealer in 1982. He co-launched the design label Culture Shock, based on the 1980s temperament of avant-garde Japanese fashion. Disillusioned by what he calls the 'corrupt and ephemeral', Tatsuno went on to pursue a more cerebral approach to fashion, developing his label in 1987, financially backed by Yohji Yamamoto.

☞ W. Klein, Macdonald, Y. Yamamoto

Koji Tatsuno. b Tokyo (JAP), 1964. **Backstage at Koji Tatsuno's catwalk show**. Photograph by William Klein, 1992.

Teller Juergen

Photographer

Iris Palmer lies prone; her underwear, designed as a covering, is made superfluous by the camera's angle – an example of the 'sexual fashion photography' that Juergen Teller feels allies his work to that of Helmut Newton. For him a model should never be regarded as a clothes horse, rather he or she should be represented as the people they are. Consequently, Teller shoots clothes as part of an image rather than its focus. Primarily he is a diarist recording the lives of those he works and lives with, resulting in a sometimes uncomfortable real-life documentary of those working in fashion. His uncompromising style is also non-judgmental and Teller doesn't prettify those lives for the sake of common acceptance. Originally encouraged by Nick Knight, Teller's reportage work was advocated by stylist and partner Venetia Scott above that which is artificially posed. Together they have created distinctive images for Katharine Hamnett and Helmut Lang.

☛ Hamnett, N. Knight, Lang, Newton, von Unwerth

Juergen Teller. b Erlangen (GER), 1964. Iris Palmer. Katharine Hamnett advertising campaign. 1997.

Tennant Stella　　　　Model

The six-foot figure of Stella Tennant is dressed in Helmut Lang. Despite her model figure and superlative skin, Tennant's edgy looks originally fell outside the usual parameters between which models usually fall. She defied any stereotype and succeeded because of it. The art student who had pierced her own nose on a railway platform was propelled into modelling after being photographed by two leading photographers: as one of London's 'It' girls by Steven Meisel and as the granddaughter of the Duke and Duchess of Devonshire by Bruce Weber. Called the 'antithesis of the supermodel', Tennant was nevertheless picked up by Karl Lagerfeld for Chanel. Her slouching demeanour on the catwalk made the bouncing, pouty attitude of other models look passé.

What she brought to fashion was the most illusive and valuable asset: cool. With characteristic nonchalance, Tennant finished the first chapter of her working career by 'retiring' after just five years, aged twenty-six.

☛ S. Ellis, Lagerfeld, Lang, Meisel, Sitbon, Weber

447

Stella Tennant. b Chatsworth (UK), 1971. **Helmut Lang T-shirt and tiered skirt**. Photograph by Sean Ellis, American *Vogue*, 1998.

Testino Mario   Photographer

Nadja Auermann pulls her T-shirt from under her skirt. In doing so she exposes her legendary legs for Mario Testino, or 'Super Mario' as he is nicknamed. 'Fashion is all about making a girl look sexy,' he says, and it is his ability to orchestrate this mood that has made his photographs so powerful. In the case of his advertising images for Gucci, Testino imbues overtly sexy clothes with a dramatic quality, placing his models in the glamorous world in which he himself lives. He has photographed the most famous and iconic women of the late twentieth century, including Madonna, a friend, who was his model for an advertising campaign for Versace Atelier. Testino used his talent for best representing the women he adores when he became the last person to photograph Diana, Princess of Wales. Those pictures, which use a relaxed reportage style, are regarded as the most flattering and modern taken in her later life.

☞ Diana, Ford, S. Jones, Madonna, Missoni, Versace, Westwood

Mario Testino. b Lima (PER), 1954. **Nadja Auermann.** French *Glamour*, 1994.

448

Thimister Josephus Melchior Designer

Surrounded by patterns and fabric, Josephus Thimister and his team work on a collection for Balenciaga, the label for which he designed from 1992 to 1997. Thimister was perceived by some as the natural heir to Cristobal Balenciaga, sharing the pure vision of the Spanish designer often described as the Picasso of the fashion world. After one collection French *Elle* said, 'Balenciaga probably clapped in his grave.' Thimister used his detailed archives to create religiously simple clothes which have been called 'neo-couture' for their modern attitude. Educated at Antwerp's Royal Academy of Art, the training ground for Martin Margiela, Ann Demeulemeester and Dries Van Noten, Thimister describes his clothes, now designed under his own label, as being about 'light, fabric and shadow'. In showing his first collection, he studiously avoided fuss, cutting thirty dresses from black or blue-black fabric.

☛ Balenciaga, Demeulemeester, Margiela, Van Noten

449

Josephus Melchior Thimister. b Maastricht (NL), 1962. **Josephus Thimister in his apartment.** Photograph by Christoph Kicherer, *ELLE Decoration*, 1997.

Thomass Chantal

Designer

Photographed against the masculine background of American footballers, Chantal Thomass's tartan-lined jacket flies away to reveal a co-ordinating bustier. Chantal Thomass provided frilly, coquettish underwear and outerwear for every Lolita or Vargas Girl in France. She described her designs as 'provocative, but not vulgar'; it is a delicate distinction and a line she treads carefully.

Thomass did not train as a designer but began her fashion career in 1966 by opening a boutique, Ter et Bantine, in partnership with her husband. It sold tantalizing, flirtatious clothes and enjoyed patronage from Brigitte Bardot, among others. In 1975 the pair founded the Chantal Thomass label and designed a clothing range. Thomass trimmed jackets and evening dresses

with lace but her name will forever be connected to lacy underwear, nightwear and stockings that combine fashion and sensuality.

☛ John-Frederics, Molinari, Schiffer

Chantal Thomass. b Malakoff, TX (USA), 1947. **Bustier and grey skirt suit.** Photograph by Bill King, French *Vogue*, 1982.

450

Tiffany Charles Lewis   Jewellery designer

Audrey Hepburn's role as Holly Golightly in the 1961 film *Breakfast at Tiffany's* made the jewellery store, whose clients have included Queen Victoria, even more famous. In this photograph, Hepburn wears a Givenchy dress and the priceless 'Ribbon' necklace made by Jean Schlumberger, the celebrated Parisian jeweller, who worked for Tiffany & Co from the 1950s until his death in 1987. The centrepiece of the necklace, which is made from eighteen-carat gold, platinum and white diamonds, is the Tiffany diamond, bought by founder Charles Lewis Tiffany in 1877 for $18,000. Rather than selling it, Tiffany placed it in the window of his New York store; it is still there today. Charles's son, Louis Comfort Tiffany, Elsa Peretti and Paloma Picasso continued to keep Tiffany at the forefront of jewellery design. It is regarded as a fashion-friendly company for its broad range – providing grandeur, worn here by Hepburn, and for delicate, modern pieces for younger women.

☞ Cartier, Givenchy, Lalique, Peretti

451

Charles Lewis Tiffany. **b** New York (USA), 1848. **d** New York (USA), 1933. **Audrey Hepburn wears the Tiffany 'Ribbon' necklace at a press reception for Breakfast at Tiffany's. 1961.**

Toledo Isabel   Designer

Latin flavour, surreal lines and futuristic content define Isabel Toledo's radical fashions sewn in the tradition of couture. Toledo, who speaks of herself as a seamstress rather than a fashion designer, creates in the manner of couturières such as Madeleine Vionnet and Madame Grès. Like them, she does not start from a flat sketch, but envisions clothing in three dimensions, always bearing a shape in her mind, usually a circle or a curved line. 'I love the maths behind the romance,' she says of her so-called liquid architecture's craftsmanship. The crepe jersey that forms the body of this dress is suspended by the armholes and anchored at the hem (unseen) by a construction of lace, net, wool and felt; the effect is like that of water slowly pouring into a barrel. Toledo's husband, Ruben, known for his whimsical fashion illustrations, manages the business side of the New York-based company and acts as her creative *alter ego*.

☞ Grès, Sybilla, Vionnet

452

Isabel Toledo. b Camajani (CU), 1961. **Matte jersey 'Infanta' dress, spring/summer 1992.** Photograph by Ruven Afanador.

Torimaru Gnyuki (Yuki) Designer

Jersey flows like water from a halter-neck bodice by Gnyuki Torimaru, formerly known as Yuki. He studied architecture, before becoming a textile engineer, an occupation that has dominated his work since. His love of vivid colour, purity and fluidity has remained a constant in Torimaru's work. He developed them to their fullest potential after discovering, in 1984, a luxurious non-crease polyester which could maintain long-lasting pleats. Using intricate pleating techniques, he created ever-more fantastical designs. Japanese-born, Yuki made London his permanent home in 1964, having worked for Norman Hartnell and Pierre Cardin, and launched his own label in 1972. He soon enjoyed a degree of fame for his one-size hooded or draped jersey dresses, often inspired by monastic garb. His dramatic cut often uses panels cut on a full circle – a luxurious technique that gives a garment the maximum fullness that can be achieved without seaming.

☞ Burrows, Muir, Valentina

455

Gnyuki Torimaru (Yuki). b Miyazaki-Ken (JAP), 1940. **Jersey halter-neck dress.** Late 1970s. Photograph by Richard Davis.

Toskan Frank and Angelo Frank (M.A.C)   Cosmetics creators

Frank Toskan is joined by drag queen RuPaul and singer k.d. lang who contort their bodies to form the words 'Viva Glam', the name of the lipstick that has championed M.A.C.'s (Make-up Art Cosmetics) Aids awareness campaign. Both celebrities epitomize the company's slogan, All Races, All Sexes, All Ages, that has trailblazed the notion of unconventional beauty for this decade.

The catalyst for a cult beauty boom, M.A.C. started in 1984 in Frank Toskan's kitchen as a long-wearing foundation to meet the harsh demands of film, catwalk and stage work. As the owner of a national chain of hair salons, his business acumen complemented the creative expertise of the late Frank Angelo, an acclaimed hairstylist and make-up artist. Their beauty colourscape, from the futuristic space tramp to the sun-buffed naturalist, has promoted the notion of make-up as complete freedom of expression.

☞ McGrath, Nars, Uemura

456

Frank Toskan. b Trieste (IT), 1950; Frank Angelo. b Montreal, QC (CAN), 1947. d Coral Gables, FL (USA), 1997. (M.A.C.) 'Viva Glam' lipstick advertisement. 1996.

Tran Hélène

Illustrator

A sedate, navy pyjama suit by Hardy Amies and crisp, organza shirt and skirt by Alistair Blair are put into a pastoral English scene by Hélène Tran. This was one of a series of images that illustrated the social summer season of 1987. Tran's easy, loose technique characterizes rich clothes and their languid wearers with broad washes of watercolour and baroque curls. Details

such as Manolo Blahnik's shoes and sandals are picked out with fine brushwork. The picture recalls the social commentary by artists such as Marcel Vertès, who captured social situations in a way that photography cannot. Tran studied illustration at the Ecole Supérieure d'Art Graphique in her native city, Paris. Her dramatic, and often humorous illustrations have been published

in British and American *Vogue* and *La Mode en Peinture*. Tran has also illustrated for clients, including Jean Patou and Roger Vivier.

☛ Amies, Blahnik, Blair, Vertès, Vivier

457

Hélène Tran. b Paris (FR), 1954. **Outfits by Hardy Amies and Alistair Blair.** *Harpers & Queen,* 1987.

Travilla William Designer

In one of film history's most famous moments, Marilyn Monroe's halter-neck dress is whipped into action over a city grille in the steamy comedy, *The Seven Year Itch*. The dress was designed by William Travilla, a favourite of Monroe's, who designed the costumes for eleven of her films. This dress is an adaptation of classical Grecian robes, with pleats mimicking draping and a bodice shaped by a crisscross tie. It actually came off the peg and remains a best-seller – resurrected every couple of years by retailers who are still profiting from its sexy allure. Travilla's appeal was his ability to flatter figures, including Marilyn's healthy hips and chest. His traditional assertion that 'femininity is the strongest weapon a woman can have' took him on to design the wardrobe for the early-1980s soap opera *Dallas*, in which the characters did indeed wield their womanliness like instruments of medieval battle.

☞ Head, Irene, Stern

William Travilla. b Avalon (USA). **d** Los Angeles, CA (USA), 1990. **Marilyn Monroe wears her famous white pleated dress**. Still from *The Seven Year Itch*. 1955.

458

Treacy Philip   Milliner

Philip Treacy's purple, melozine trilby, which historically belongs to the male hat rack, plays with both glamour and sexuality; the jaunty angle which conceals part of the face is reminiscent of Marlene Dietrich and the provocative cross-dressing common in 1930s cabaret style. Each season Treacy redraws the line of this style, an ever-changing classic worn by fashion icons as diverse as Chanel's creative director Amanda Harlech and Boy George. By comparison, many of Treacy's extravagant couture hats would be more appropriately called sculpture. The usual millinery fabrics are sometimes replaced with industrial plastics; a galleon is reconstructed, with correct rigging, then fixed to the head; and fluorescent satin ellipses shoot sideways from the crown for a full metre. Since he graduated from London's Royal College of Art in 1990, Treacy has redefined the role of millinery in fashion.

☛ Boy George, Conran, Milner, Topolino, Underwood

Philip Treacy. b Ahascragh (IRE), 1967. **Purple trilby**. Photograph by Christoph Sillem, the *Guardian*, 1997.

Tree Penelope

Model

Cecil Beaton photographs Penelope Tree's elfin face, an extraordinary one that made 'The Tree' a match for 'The Twig' in the 1960s. She was the rebellious daughter of a rich and serious-minded family who were disappointed in Penelope's original decision to embark on a career as a model. When she was first shot at thirteen by Diane Arbus, her father, a British multimillionaire, vowed he would sue if the pictures were published. By the time Diana Vreeland sent her to Richard Avedon, she was seventeen and her father had relented. David Bailey described Penelope as 'an Egyptian Jiminy Cricket'; in 1967 she moved into his flat in London's Primrose Hill which became a hang-out for spaced-out hippies who, Bailey recalls, would be 'smoking joints I had paid for and calling me a capitalist pig!' In 1974, Bailey and Tree split up and she moved to Sydney, Australia, far away from the focus of the fashion photographer's camera.

☛ Avedon, Bailey, Beaton, Vreeland

Penelope Tree. **b** London (UK), 1950. **Penelope Tree**. Photograph by Cecil Beaton, 1967.

460

Trigère Pauline

Designer

The structured tailoring on show here explains why in *Breakfast at Tiffany's*, Patricia Neal's character, an uptight girlfriend wearing Pauline Trigère, nearly proved a match for Audrey Hepburn's youthfully elegant outfits by Hubert de Givenchy. She represented grown-up and urban New York fashion. Born and trained in the family business of dressmaking in Paris, Trigère arrived in New York in 1937. After working with Travis Banton at Hattie Carnegie, Trigère opened her own business in 1942. More than fifty years later, she would demonstrate how she cut into luxury fabric directly from the bolt onto the mannequin to awestruck fashion students. Her cutting was sure, emphasizing wrapping and tying in the French tradition of magnificent scarves and idiosyncratic knottings. Today, Trigère is the best model for her fashion: urban chic in luxury fabrics, coats robust and flowing, capes indeterminate between jacket and coat and autumn and spring, and such show-stopping special effects as rhinestone bras.

☛ Banton, Carnegie, Givenchy

461

Pauline Trigère. b Paris (FR), 1912. **Leopard-print turban and crimson coat**. Photograph by Karen Radkai, American *Vogue*, 1959.

Troublé Agnès (Agnès b.)   Designer

With her simple clothes, swept-back hair and classic black sunglasses, this model is the epitome of Parisian chic. The stripy black and white T-shirt shown is reminiscent of Jean Seberg's in *Breathless*, and the simple style of Left Bank beats. 'I don't like the word "fashion"; I say I design clothes,' says Agnès b. Her neutral-coloured wardrobe staples: crisp white shirts, plain knitwear and pared-down (often black) tailoring have survived precisely because they pay very little attention to fashion. She worked as a junior fashion editor at *Elle* magazine in France, and as a stylist at Cacharel and Dorothée Bis. She opened her first shop in 1975, during an eccentric era of flared trousers and platform shoes. From the outset, her designs, based on utilitarian clothing such as workman's blue overalls and undershirts, found a place as fashion's antidote.

☞ Bousquet, Farhi, Jacobson

Agnès Troublé. b Versailles (FR), 1941. (Agnès b.) **Black and white striped top**. Photograph by Darzacq, 1997.

Turbeville Deborah   Photographer

Models Isabel Weingarten and Ella Milewiecz become part of Deborah Turbeville's dreamscape. A typical shot, it depicts motionless subjects who pose in a group but without relating to one another. Turbeville's career path was a tortuous journey through fashion, an experience that gave her a deep understanding of clothes. Having arrived in New York in 1956, she worked as a model and moved on to assist designer Claire McCardell. She then turned to magazines, becoming a fashion editor for *Mademoiselle*. In 1966 she changed course again. Turbeville became a freelance photographer for *Harper's Bazaar* after being inspired by a talk given by Richard Avedon. By 1972 she was working for the cult magazine *Nova* in London. Her haunting style was very different from other fashion photography of the time and yet it was intriguing rather than alienating.

☛ Avedon, McCardell, Rykiel

463

Deborah Turbeville. b Medford, MA (USA), 1938. **Isabel Weingarten and Ella Milewiecz.** 1978.

Turlington Christy   Model

Christy Turlington's beauty is a versatile one. Here Francesco Scavullo makes hers a cover face in the traditional sense. But equally, Turlington has personified nude, unaffected beauty – representing Calvin Klein's fragrances since 1987. While modelling relies on the arts of lighting, make-up and retouching, a few women are able to achieve a perfect look through self-awareness; Turlington is one such woman. As she told *Vogue*, 'I know how to make every part of my body appear different than it actually is. I can make my eyes and my lips appear bigger by putting my chin down... You can manipulate everything for photography.' Called 'the most beautiful woman in the world', she feels it's all down to her full, symmetrical lips: 'I have gotten most of my advertising contacts because of them.' Turlington was one of the supermodels who managed to make an easy transition from the *haute* glamour of the 1980s to the relaxed simplicity of the following decade.

☛ Ferre, C. Klein, Lindbergh, Scavullo, Valentino, Westwood

464

Christy Turlington. b Oakland, CA (USA), 1969. **Christy wears Gianfranco Ferre**. Photograph by Francesco Scavullo, 1988.

Twiggy

Model

Twiggy poses next to her mannequin lookalikes. It was the only way to replicate her powerful figure at a time when the whole world wanted to have a part of her magic. Lesley Hornby had come from the suburbs of London. At fifteen she met Nigel John Davies, then a hairdresser. He reinvented himself as Justin de Villeneuve and Lesley as 'Twig', later Twiggy. Just as it took a

haircut to launch Linda Evangelista's career as a supermodel, twenty years earlier the potential of Twiggy's gamine charm was unlocked with a haircut by Leonard. With her elfin crop and teenage figure, Twiggy became the icon of young fashion and the first model to grow into a media personality, albeit a startled one. In response to one journalist's assertion that she earned

more than the prime minister, she could only giggle, 'Do I?' Twiggy 'retired' at the age of nineteen.

☛ Bailey, Evangelista, Foale & Tuffin, Hechter, Hulanicki, Leonard

Twiggy (Lesley Hornby). b London (UK), 1949. Twiggy with mannequins by Adel Rootstein. Photograph by J. Drysdale, 1966.

Tyler Richard

Designer

Model Irina wears a shrunken, three-piece suit by Richard Tyler. He found success when Hollywood discovered his meticulous tailoring. Actress Sigourney Weaver said, 'Richard's clothes make you feel like a movie star.' Tyler became well known late in life, winning an award for best newcomer at forty-six. His fashion career, however, has been his life's work. He learned his craft from his seamstress mother and trained as a tailor, an education which became important to Tyler's work when he became a recognized craftsman of women's tailoring. He built his career designing stage clothes for Elton John, Cher and Diana Ross. A change of direction in the mid-1980s led to Tyler launching a menswear range with business partner and soon-to-be wife, Lisa Trafficante, in Los Angeles. This was followed in 1989 by womenswear, with the emphasis placed on glamour. Both collections became successful through Tyler's reputation as a master cutter. 'I have no ego. All I have is my skill,' he says.

☞ Alfaro, Dell'Olio, Kors

466

Richard Tyler. b Melbourne (ASL), 1948. **Irina Pantaeva wears black three-piece suit**. Photograph by Chris Moore, 1995.

Uemura Shu

Cosmetics creator

With his design philosophy 'Bien être' (a sense of well-being), Shu Uemura freed the face from the shifting dictates of transient fashions and developed a notion of the inner sense of beauty, reflecting a mood of introversion and lack of artifice. Originally a hairdresser, Shu Uemura became a make-up artist to stars such as Shirley MacLaine and Frank Sinatra in 1950s Hollywood. He raised the standard of make-up and made it into an art form, using superior cosmetics as his palette and the finest beauty tools as apparatus. These he stocked in his aesthetically modern Beauty Boutiques, which resembled art supply stores and heralded a cosmetics-counter revolution in the 1980s. After thirty decades, the natural style of his cosmetics, in soft, muted colours and distinct transparent packaging, is still relentlessly modern and very much a hallmark of twentieth-century design.

☞ Bandy, Bourjois, Factor, Lutens, Nars

Shu Uemura. b (JAP). (Active 1950s–) Shu Uemura making-up a model's face. Photograph by Morozumi, 1983.

Underwood Patricia   Milliner

The familiar stetson is given a modern twist: straw braid instead of suede, a wider brim and modest curve to create a feminine and elegant shape. The particular cock of the brim remains, hinting at the provocation the cowboy hat was noted for. Subtle, yet interesting manipulations of traditional hat shapes are characteristic of Underwood's millinery designs. Relying completely on shape and proportion, rather than fussy ornamentation, her hats are noted for their spartan modesty which makes them into one-statement sculptures for the head. 'A simplicity of design avoids the pitfalls of a hat becoming a distraction on the wearer,' she says, brushing off flamboyant contemporary millinery. British-born, Underwood moved to New York in 1967 after a brief tenure at Buckingham Palace as a secretary. Her understated aesthetics fit the New York look, where she works with designers Bill Blass and Marc Jacobs who mirror her modernist, abstract forms.

☞ Blass, Jacobs, Model, Sui, Treacy

Patricia Underwood. b Maidenhead (UK), 1948. **Black straw stetson.** 1991.

Ungaro Emanuel

Designer

This minidress by Ungaro shows him to be in touch with the flower power mood of the late 1960s and demonstrates his love of delicate fabric and surface detail. Yet the acute sense of cut remains. The son of an Italian tailor, Ungaro's favourite toy at six years old was his father's sewing machine and he became a tailor at fourteen. In 1955 he moved to Paris and was introduced to Balenciaga by Courrèges. He joined the Spaniard's house in 1958 and stayed for six years. Having learnt the master's rigorous attitude to cut, he opened his own couture business in 1965 with simple, bold garments such as blazers worn with shorts. Four years later, along with Cardin and Courrèges, Ungaro created a new nudeness in French fashion, but by the 1970s his style had softened. His 1980s eveningwear used vivid florals cut and ruched to form extremely ladylike, grown-up versions of his girlish dress from 1969.

☞ Audibet, Balenciaga, Cardin, Courrèges, Paulette, Scherrer

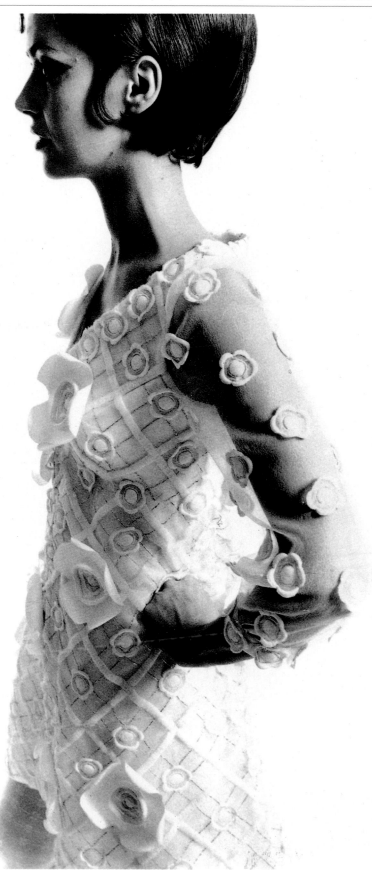

469

Emanuel Ungaro. b Aix-en-Provence (FR), 1933. **White, floral, trellis appliqué, lace dress.** Photograph by Peter Knapp, 1969.

Von Unwerth Ellen   Photographer

Wearing towering heels, stockings, silk underwear and corset, model Iris Palmer presents a traditionally provocative figure. Many observers are surprised to find that von Unwerth, the photographer, is a woman. She encourages her subjects to look sensual and her success stems from the fact that she projects these images from a female perspective. 'The models love to look sexy,' she says. 'They all like to be photographed in that way.' Von Unwerth 'discovered' the supermodel Claudia Schiffer in 1992 when she photographed her for Guess? Jeans. She has also famously created advertising images for Wonderbra, Katharine Hamnett and Gianfranco Ferre. Von Unwerth left her native Germany in 1974 to begin a modelling career in Paris, becoming a photographer ten years later. She has grown to be a key image-maker in the 1990s through her editorial work for *Vogue*, *The Face*, *Interview* and even *Playboy*, for whom she shot a centrespread of actress Drew Barrymore in 1994.

☛ Hamnett, Schiffer, Teller

Ellen von Unwerth. b (GER), 1954. Iris Palmer. *The Face*, 1996.

Valentina

Designer

Madame Valentina, photographed here in triplicate, wears her own design: a dinner dress with a jewelled belt and collar. The dress was made in jersey, a material which swathes and clings to the figure, creating a sculptured look. The strong rosy-red colour provided an uninterrupted line, another key feature of the Valentina style. Colour to intensify line is enhanced by the fluid green cowl draped around her high-piled, chignon hairstyle and caught up in a belt. The whole aura is that of a Byzantine emperor's consort. The grand manner of Madame Valentina was rooted in her Russian heritage, even though she moved to Paris during the Russian Revolution and then to New York in 1922, where she set up her own establishment four years later. The costume also has a theatrical air, traceable to Madame Valentina's training for the stage. Her fashionable eveningwear was very popular with actresses.

☞ Grès, Torimaru, Vionnet

471

Valentina (Valentina Nicholaevna Sanina Schlee). b Kiev (RUS), 1904. d New York (USA), 1989. **Madame Valentina wears her jersey dress and cowl.** Photographs by John Rawlings, American *Vogue*, 1945.

Valentino
Designer

Christy Turlington is worshipped wearing a beaded sheath dress from the spring/summer 1995 collection. Its designer, Valentino, has been called the 'Master of the Dress'. His clothes represent the romance, beauty, femininity and decadence of Rome, the city where he launched his own label in 1960. Valentino worked with Jean Dessès and then Guy Laroche, before becoming a couturier

himself. Initially he made extravagant couture gowns for wealthy Italian socialites, but in 1968 he caused a sensation when he launched a radical, all-white collection. Jackie Kennedy wore an outfit from the collection when she married Aristotle Onassis. Fiery red, however, is Valentino's signature colour, used for precious lace gowns in his couture collection and beaded

pyjama pants for ready-to-wear. His suave demeanour, impeccable manners and womanly, seductive clothes are about style, not high fashion.

☛ Barbieri, Dessès, Laroche, Storey, Turlington, Viramontes

472

Valentino (Valentino Garavani). **b** Voghera (IT), 1932. **Christy Turlington. Advertising campaign.** Photograph by Herb Ritts, 1995.

Wainwright Janice   Designer

Janice Wainwright brings the outdoors indoors with a pair of moiré taffeta jodhpurs – a widely used theme at the end of the 1970s. Sensuous fabrics cut with a feminine touch were at the centre of her work; here her silk crepe-de-chine shirt is given a fichu tie. Wainwright studied at the Royal College of Art in London, and worked with Sheridan Barnett before founding her own company in 1974. Throughout the 1970s she was known for soft dresses which were often cut on the bias. She produced clothes that, according to *Vogue*, '...obey the first rule of dress which is that clothes must be appropriate'. Wainwright's interest in textiles extended to her involvement with the design and colouring of the fabrics she used. Previous collections include dresses cleverly designed to spiral downwards around the body. Intricate embroidery, appliqué trimmings and accentuated shoulders are other distinctive hallmarks of her style.

☛ Barnett, Bates, Demarchelier, Venturi

489

Janice Wainwright. **b** Chesterfield (UK), 1940. **Plum silk shirt and moiré jodhpurs**. Photograph by Patrick Demarchelier, British *Vogue*, 1980.

Wang Vera · Designer

A dress never works harder than on Oscar night or when it's worn by a bride. When Hollywood's daughters or the centrepiece of a wedding emerge from a limousine, they want a dress that will make the audience draw breath. This is what Vera Wang is famous for. She uses rich fabrics such as silk lace and duchesse satin in the tradition of Paris couture, and applies them to the simple shapes associated with American sportswear, such as the vest dress. Wang lives in the society she designs for. Born into New York's Upper East Side, Wang was forbidden to attend design school, becoming instead *Vogue*'s youngest ever fashion editor. Having worked for Ralph Lauren, she opened a bridal salon and couture business in 1990. Her appreciation of surface decoration, particularly beading, and the use of net to give the illusion of bare skin have also recommended her for the design of Olympic figure-skating costumes – another career she pursued before design.

☛ Jackson, Lauren, Leiber, Lesage, Roehm, Yantorny

490

Vera Wang. b New York (USA), 1949. **Gold brocade couture gown, 1991**. Photograph by Victor Skrebneski.

Warhol Andy

Designer

Andy Warhol began work as an illustrator for fashion companies and magazines such as *Mademoiselle*, growing increasingly aware of the relationship between art, fashion and commerce. He then produced window displays for New York department stores Tiffany's and Bonwit Teller. By the early 1960s, Warhol had reinvented himself as a music and movies impresario and even as a fashion designer. Here two women are hanging out in the Factory, his artist's salon, wearing his slogan dresses. Warhol began to wear rock-star leather jackets, satin shirts and a silver-sprayed wig and he used the superstar actresses from his films to model paper dresses printed with his Banana paintings. He also became friends with fashion editor Diana Vreeland and designer Betsey Johnson, and in 1969 Warhol launched his experimental style magazine *Interview,* in which he profiled his designer friends Halston and Elsa Peretti.

☛ **Bulgari, de Castelbajac, Garren, Halston, LaChapelle, Sprouse**

491

Andy Warhol (Andrew Warhola). b Pittsburgh, PA (USA), 1928. d New York (USA), 1987. 'Brillo' and 'Fragile, Handle With Care'. Photograph by Ken Heyman, 1962.

Watanabe Junya   Designer

By extending the distances between each model as they tread the perimeter of his square catwalk, Junya Watanabe gives visual silence to his futuristic fashion. Glamour, sound and colour are notably absent; instead, an optical tautology of frugal, white cotton *khadi* presents this complex collection. Watanabe graduated from Tokyo's Bunka Fashion Institute in 1984 and immediately joined Comme des Garçons, designing the Tricot line in 1987. As Rei Kawakubo's protégé, his creations reflect the intellectual Zeitgeist of the Japanese maestro. However, he takes a personal approach for his line, Junya Watanabe Comme des Garçons. Changing dramatically from one season to the next, he takes a successful stab at anything futuristic: from cellophane-wrapped neon punks and abstract oriental peasantwear, to poetic stark white. Giving his clothes an irregular touch through random tucking, pleating and ruching, he evokes the idea of the human aesthetic married with the future.

☞ Fontana, Kawakubo, Rocha

492

Junya Watanabe. b (JAP), 1961. **White dress and veil.** Photograph by Chris Moore, 1998.

Weber Bruce   Photographer

Chosen by Bruce Weber to represent his work, this photograph shows a girl, fresh and artless, peering from beneath a Charles James gown, itself the very example of constructed beauty. Such human subjects are, however, unusual. His historical paragon is the photographer Leni Riefenstahl, who extolled an exclusive and privileged male body. Weber was the most important photographer of redefined masculinity in the 1980s and 1990s. He created erotic images of muscular, natural bodies. One significant inspiration for Weber is Classical sculpture: his buffed, athletic heroes (seen in Calvin Klein's underwear advertisements) often recall Hellenistic sculpture. The chaos of real life never intrudes or spoils the mood; over the course of two decades his photographs for Ralph Lauren have created a privileged dream world of country houses, polo matches and safaris.

☛ C. James, C. Klein, Lauren, Platt Lynes, Ritts, Tennant

493

Bruce Weber. b Greensburg, PA (USA), 1946. **Girl beneath vintage dress by Charles James, 1991.**

Westwood Vivienne   Designer

Christy Turlington wears Vivienne Westwood in a photograph by Mario Testino for British *Vogue* in 1993. Westwood regards this outfit as typical of her work, even though it leaves out her waggish references to royalty (crowns set with paste jewels) and historical excess (mini-crinolines and bodices from which the wearer's bosom spills like a milk jelly). When Westwood began her confrontational fashion career in 1970, she would no doubt have laughed at the notion that her clothes would one day appear in an establishment fashion magazine on a famous model. In the intervening years she established herself as the only British designer who could not only explore extremes in dress, but also make sense of them. She did this most significantly with the punk movement during her collaboration with Malcolm McLaren. In 1981 she launched her catwalk collection, continuing her emphasis on eccentricity and subversion.

☛ Barbieri, McLaren, Palmers, Pearl, Testino, Turlington

Vivienne Westwood. b Tintwhistle (UK), 1941. 'Anglomania': Christy Turlington wears a bias-cut tartan suit. Photograph by Mario Testino, British *Vogue*, 1993.

Wilde Oscar

Icon

'A Fashion is a form of dress so unbearable we are compelled to alter it every six months,' said Oscar Wilde in 1884, citing Paris as the centre of sartorial tyranny. This is Wilde photographed in New York in 1882. The picture reflects the writer's campaign for men's dress reform. He wears knee breeches (the artistic alternative to trousers, which he called boring tubes), a smoking jacket (a recent addition to the male wardrobe) and a comfortable, nonconformist soft collar and cravat. Between 1887 and 1889, he was editor of *Woman's World* magazine, which promoted the aesthetic dress sold at Liberty. By 1890, apart from his green carnation or lily buttonhole, Wilde had decided to wear conventional dress. In *The Picture of Dorian Gray*, he pronounced conventional dress for men to be the most beautiful in the world, stating, 'It is only the shallow people who do not judge by appearances.'

☛ Coward, Jaeger, Liberty, Muir

Oscar Wilde. **b** Dublin (IRE), 1854. **d** Paris (FR), 1900. **Oscar Wilde in breeches and a smoking jacket**. Photograph by Napoleon Sarony, 1882.

Williamson Matthew   Designer

Matthew Williamson's yellow, organza slip dress, machine-embroidered with fuchsia dragonfly motifs, typifies a trend for individual, precious clothing. His brilliant colour palette is inspired by a back-packing tour of Mexico and Guatemala and seventeen trips to India, where he learned techniques for the intricate embroidery that features in his work. Williamson, who was first known for a collection of delicately beaded bags, trained with Zandra Rhodes, whose influence shows in his choice of unbridled colour combinations and lavish detailing. Williamson launched his label in 1996 and showed his first collection of fluid, bias-cut dresses and skirts and cashmere twinsets. The use of sweaters over such dresses suggests a nonchalant glamour, described by Williamson as 'something special, a little glittering', which allows his clothes to pass from day into eveningwear.

☛ von Etzdorf, Mazzilli, Moon, Oudejans, Rhodes

496

Matthew Williamson. b Manchester (UK), 1972. Emma Balfour wears a yellow organza dress embroidered with dragonflies. Photograph by François Halard, American *Elle*, 1998.

Windsor Duke and Duchess of Icons

Together the Duke and Duchess of Windsor symbolized opulence tempered by sartorial restraint. For their wedding day, Wallis Simpson chose a sapphire blue (dubbed 'Wallis' blue), crepe silk dress by Mainbocher, one of her favourite designers. Mainbocher preferred to 'blend mystery rather than to rant and rave with my shears', and he created an utterly simple, bias-cut dress and jacket which were worn with a matching hat by Reboux. Givenchy and Marc Bohan were other favourites who contributed to her legendary wardrobe. It was a discreet style that provided an ideal backdrop for her magnificent jewels, many of which were chosen by the Duke. His clothes were equally influential. At university he had championed the flapping trouser legs dubbed 'Oxford bags' and, rejecting the stiff, interlined clothing of his youth, he often flouted convention and pioneered new styles, such as the dark blue, double-breasted dinner jacket.

☞ Alexandre, Cartier, Ferragamo, Horst, Mainbocher, Perugia, Reboux

497

Duke of Windsor. b Richmond (UK), 1894. d Paris (FR), 1972. Duchess of Windsor. b Blue Ridge Summit, PA (USA), 1896. d Paris (FR), 1986. The Duke and Duchess of Windsor on their wedding day at the Château de Condé, France. 1937.

Winston Harry

Jewellery designer

Elizabeth Taylor wears a suite of diamonds by Harry Winston, the sparkling voltage of which is matched by the glint in her violet eyes for her favourite stone, after which her scent White Diamonds is named. When Marilyn Monroe sang about her favourite rock in *Gentlemen Prefer Blondes*, it was to the 'King of Diamonds' she appealed: 'Talk to me, Harry, tell me about it...'

Winston's reciprocal love affair with Hollywood began when he assisted his father in their small Los Angeles jewellery store. At the age of twenty, he moved back to New York to found his own jewellery business. By the time he had incorporated his firm under his own name in 1932, Winston had become a leading retailer of exclusive diamond jewellery, renowned for using exceptionally large stones. In 1998, the Winston look was encapsulated in a pair of diamond-encrusted Ray-Ban sunglasses, designed for the Oscar ceremony.

☛ Alexandre, Hiro, Madonna

Harry Winston. **b** New York (USA), 1896. **d** (USA), 1978. 'Passion' perfume publicity campaign. Elizabeth Taylor wears diamond earrings and collar. Photograph by Norman Parkinson, 1987.

498

Worth Charles Frederick   Designer

Spangled silk tulle was typical of Worth's work in the 1860s. For Empress Elizabeth of Austria he chose gold to be scattered over her gown – a scheme extended by the golden stars in her hair. The dress's décolleté neckline, which exposes and embraces her shoulders, would be softened with the tulle held lightly around her hips. Winterhalter chronicled the work of Worth through such portraits and painted many similarly graceful compositions of the Empress Eugénie, Worth's most valuable client. The story of modern fashion began when Charles Frederick Worth, a young tailor, arrived at the glittering court of Napoleon III. In his bid to re-establish Paris as the centre of fashionable life, the Emperor stimulated the luxury business and his wife Eugénie patronized it in fabulous style. Under that patronage, Worth drew on the history of costume to create lavish, expensive gowns which raised dressmaking to a new level called haute couture.

☛ Duff Gordon, Fratini, Hartnell, Pinet, Pingat, Poiret, Reboux

Charles Frederick Worth. b Bourne (UK), 1825. d Paris (FR), 1895. **Empress Elizabeth of Austria wearing spangled tulle.** Painting by Francis Xavier Winterhalter, 1865.

Yamamoto Kansai   Designer

Cartoon graphics and cotton netting were one of the wilder combinations offered by Kansai Yamamoto. Others included lush satin robes and pyjamas appliquéd with huge Japanese figures. Yamamoto married traditional Japanese culture and Western influences, set them to a music beat and put them in the realm of the performing arts. In the 1970s his fashion performance shows were huge events, attracting up to 5,000 people. After training as a civil engineer, Yamamoto left school in 1962 to study English, before moving on to fashion. He designed David Bowie's outrageous costumes for Ziggy Stardust and Aladdin Zane and, in 1975, he began showing in Paris, part of the first wave of Japanese designers who would have an impact on fashion through the following decades. Yamamoto's trademarks are a liberal use of abstract colour sculpted into unique forms, which successfully blended ancient oriental influences with modern sporty themes, as seen here.

☛ Bowie, Sprouse, Warhol

500

Kansai Yamamoto. b Kanagawa (JAP), 1944. 'Kansai' graffiti shirt and mesh skirt. *Women's Wear Daily*, 1982.

Yamamoto Yohji   Designer

Thiş lean coat represents the traditions of both antique Western tailoring and those of contemporary Japan. In 1981 Yohji Yamamoto presented his clothes to a Western audience for the first time and effectively turned the notion of fashion as structured, sexy and glamorous on its head. Experts were shocked, labelling the collection 'Hiroshima chic'; it was composed of androgynous shrouds in several shades of black, worn with flat shoes, little make-up and a stern expression. But the shock turned to admiration. Yamamoto dropped out of a law degree to work for his widowed mother in her dressmaking shop. He followed this with a fashion degree at Tokyo's Bunka Fashion College, and set up his own label in 1977. He says, 'My clothes are about human beings: they are alive. I am alive.' His vision of women, and later men, as independent, intelligent, liberated artisans has elevated his status to that of a fashion legend.

☛ Capasa, Hirata, van Lamsweerde, Matsuda, Miyake, Tatsuno

501

Yohji Yamamoto. b Yokohama (JAP), 1943. **Red hat and black tail–coat**. Photograph by Paolo Roversi, 1985.

Yantorny Pietro

Shoe designer

Pietro Yantorny's sumptuous custom-made shoes – in precious, milky silks and decorated with his trademark diamanté buckle – survive today as totems of unsurpassed grandeur. Over 300 of these shoes, each of them perching daintily on Louis-style heels, were made for Rita de Acosta Lydig, who never walked more than a few hundred yards. What little is known about Yantorny is partly attributed to a reputation that lasted only a few years, although in that time he enjoyed an international clientele sprinkled with royalty. Of East Indian origin, his own lofty aspirations – reinforced by the slogan used in his Parisian salon, 'The world's most expensive custom shoemaker' – did not deter clients, even when orders took two years to arrive. There was reason for their patience: Yantorny made painstaking measurements of each individual in order to make each shoe fit 'like a silk sock'.

☞ Hope, Lesage, Pinet, Wang

502

Pietro Yantorny. (Active 1910s.) **Trunk of evening shoes belonging to Rita de Acosta Lydig, c1915.** Photograph by Jack Carroll.

Zoran

Designer

Utterly simple, squared black shapes; the name Zoran is associated with minimalism and purity. Elements of his approach to design – mathematical precision-cutting and clean, simple shapes – hark back to his degree in architecture for which he studied in his home town, Belgrade. Zoran moved to New York in the early 1970s, launching his first capsule collection there to wide acclaim in 1977. His first collections were designed around squares and rectangles in silk crepe-de-chine. Zoran remains as unswayed by transient fads of fashion today as he was back in the 1970s. He prefers to design comfortable, practical clothing with longevity, in sumptuous fabrics, especially cashmere. Using an elemental palette of colours – mainly red, black, grey, white and cream – he also avoids using extraneous decoration. Even the practical details, such as cuffs, collars, zips and fastenings, are hidden away or banished where possible.

☞ Audibet, Coddington, Kim

503

Zoran (Zoran Ladicorbic). b Belgrade (YUG), 1947. **Black outfits**. Photograph by Goe Moe.

Glossary of movements, genres and technical terms

Aigrette

A decorative tuft, usually of heron, egret or osprey feathers, worn on hats or as a hair ornament.

A-line

A skirt or dress silhouette which flares from the waist or bust, forming the 'A' shape.

Alpaca

Formerly a fabric made from the wool of the alpaca (a South American mammal related to the llama) and cotton, today it describes a rayon crepe fabric.

Angora

The hair of the angora goat or rabbit. It is usually mixed with fabrics such as wool and used for knitwear. See mohair.

Aniline dyes

Vivid synthetic dyes, originally obtained from indigo, that were introduced in the late nineteenth century and widened the palette of colours available to designers.

Appliqué

A technique of creating surface decoration by stitching or gluing motifs, trimmings or other fabric onto the ground fabric.

Argyle

A block of diamond pattern, commonly seen on knitwear, which is an approximation of the tartan work by the Scottish clan Argyle.

Astraskhan

Originally the fleece of the karakul lamb of Russia, used as a trimming on collars and cuffs and for hats until the late nineteenth century. Today it refers to both the fleece and a heavy fabric, knitted or woven, with a pile imitating the shiny, black, tightly curled fleece. Also called persian lamb.

Atelier

The studio or workshop of a designer.

Baguette

A precious stone cut in an oblong shape with facets.

Ballets Russes or Ballet Russe

Sergei Diaghilev brought Russian dance to Western Europe with the Ballets Russes. For the first time, décor, costume and music were as important as the dance itself. Its first appearance in Paris, in 1909, shocked audiences with its unrestrained, brilliantly hued designs influenced by the Orient. The costumes consisted of harem pants, turbans, bold jewellery, painted linen, and appliqué on velvet and silk. Designed by Léon Bakst, they inspired Poiret – and subsequently much of early twentieth-century fashion – to discard the stiff corsetry and gentle colours typical of the period and to shorten skirts to ankle-length.

☛ Bakst, Barbier, Brunelleschi, Poiret, Sumurun

Bandeau

A strapless bodice usually made from a stretch fabric.

Barathea

A fine woollen cloth used for outer garments in the nineteenth century and now used for suiting.

Barège

A fine silky gauze, usually made from silk and wool, most often used for veils and head-dresses during the nineteenth century. Named after Barège in the South-West of France where it was originally made.

Batik

East-Asian textile craft of 'wax writing', in which liquid wax is used to draw designs which are protected from taking the dye.

Batiste

A generic term for a fine, sheer, lightweight fabric made from cotton or linen, with or without other fibres, wool, silk, polyester or rayon.

Batwing sleeve see Dolman sleeve.

Beat

First coined in 1958, the beat (or yé yé in France) was a progenitor of both mod and hippie, both in spirit and attitude. Having witnessed the ravages of the Depression, war and the atomic threat, the beat's distrust of politics, capitalism and uniformity provoked an aspiration to a simple, existential lifestyle. The tough, student uniform was, 'Any colour so long as it is black', usually a polo neck or turtleneck sweater and jeans. Beat was born at the University of Colombia which spawned a generation of philosophical writers such as Allen Ginsberg and Jack Kerouac – whose phrase 'Beat Generation' gave the movement its name. Its spirit spread to Britain and France where Juliette Greco and Jean-Paul Sartre made the Parisian Left Bank (Rive Gauche) a fashionable location. In the 1980s the beatnik look was revived as a minimalist fashion of black jeans and turtlenecks, Breton t-shirts and a pair of sunglasses.

☛ Bardot, Troublé

Belle Epoque

The French phrase, meaning 'fine period', came to symbolize a comfortable, prewar society dressed in extravagant ruffles and out-sized hats for women and prosperous black tailoring for men. During this period the ideal female shape was no longer defined as small or meek, but voluptuous, majestic, and boasting a vast pigeon-bosom. That figure was covered with decorative flourishes intended to lend further richness. Lace, embroideries, ribbons, feathers, jewels and flowers all vied for space on figures trained into an S-curve. The froth of the belle époque was gradually replaced by a more rational style championed by modern women annoyed with its excess.

☛ Doucet, Drécoll, Paquin, Redfern

Bias cut

Fabric construction by which panels are cut across the grain, 45° to the edge of the cloth, giving it natural elasticity and drape.

Boat or bateau neck

Straight, boat-shaped neckline extending from shoulder to shoulder with the same depth at front and back.

Boater

Previously used in England as part of a late nineteenth-century punting uniform for men. Made of shellac-coated straw, the boater is a simple, circular hat with a flat top and brim.

Bolero jacket

Waist-length jacket worn open in front, with or without sleeves.

Boot-cut

Trousers cut slightly wider at the hem that can be worn over boots.

Bouclé

French for 'buckled' or 'curled'. A fabric or yarn which has a looped or knotted surface.

Box pleat

A pleat consisting of two parallel creases turned inwards towards each other.

Braid

A narrow, decorative band used for trimming or binding.

Brocade

A heavy dress and furnishing fabric woven with a jacquard loom, in which all-over patterns of flowers and foliage are raised from the surface cloth.

Broderie anglaise

A type of traditional embroidery consisting of petal shapes and eyelet holes cut out and finished with buttonhole stitching at the edges.

Brogue

A stout, lace-up stitched leather shoe with ornamental perforated bands originating in Scotland or Ireland.

Bugle beads

Long, tubular-shaped glass beads in black, white or silver often used as dress trimming.

Bust bodice

A heavily boned, padded and taped undergarment based on the camisole, which was replaced by the bra.

Bustier

A close-fitting, boned bodice.

Cable knit

A raised knitted pattern resembling twisted rope or cable.

Caftan

A rectangular-cut, ankle-length garment with a front opening, side splits and sometimes a cummerbund, probably originating from Mesopotamia. Once made in striped or brocaded silk, velvet or cotton, its predominance as a 1970s fashion item ensured versions were made in almost all kinds of fabric.

Calico

A coarse cotton fabric named after the city and port, Calicut, in India, from which it was originally exported.

Camel hair

A fabric made from the soft undercoat of the camel. Has also come to mean material made from cashmere and wool which has been dyed the colour of natural camel hair.

Camisole

Formerly an undergarment, based on the bodice, with fine straps, it is now also worn as an outer garment. It is generally made from lightweight silky fabrics and often trimmed with lace or ribbon.

Capri pants

Close-fitting trousers, tapered to the mid-calf, named after the Italian island of Capri.

504

Caracul, karacul see astraskhan.

Cashmere

The undercoat hair of the Kashmir goat, originally from India, now raised in Afghanistan, Tibet and China. An expensive fibre, it is often mixed with wool to reduce its cost.

Challis

A lightweight, soft woven fabric usually made from a blend of wool, cotton and rayon, and chiefly used as a dress fabric.

Chamois

Supple, fine, yellow-hued leather from the skin of the chamois goat, used for gloves. Not to be confused with chamois cloth, an imitation made of cotton.

Charmeuse

A lustrous lightweight fabric, developed in the twentieth century, made from synthetic or silk fabrics of satin weave.

Chenille

From the French, meaning 'caterpillar', because of its protuding, velvety tufts. Made of silk, rayon, cotton or wool, the yarn can be knitted or woven through the warp threads.

Chiffon

A lightweight, gossamer-sheer fabric, printed or dyed, made of silk or synthetic fibres.

Chinoiserie

From the French 'chinois', meaning Chinese. An embroidered or brocaded pattern showing Chinese motifs or qualities. An alternative French meaning is 'hair-splitting' which, if also applied to such embroidery, describes its fine intricacies very well.

Circular cut

A skirt or cape pattern piece cut in one curve or circle.

Cloche

A soft, felt hat with a deep crown and narrow brim occasionally pushed back to frame the eyes. Sometimes trimmed with a deep ribbon band.

Cloqué

A treated fabric with a blistered surface appearance, obtained by weaving a double-cloth consisting of yarns with varying degrees of shrinkage.

Combination jacquard

An updated version of jacquard weaving, in which computerized systems create highly complex jacquard patterns as well as incorporating yarns of various thickness and twist into the cloth.

Coq feathers/plumage

Iridescent black and green feathers of the barnyard cockerel.

Cravat

A scarf tied round the neck in front with its ends tucked inside a shirt.

Crepe

A fabric given a crinkled texture by heat and a particular weave. Made of silk, cotton, rayon or wool, its draping qualities make it most suitable for formal day dresses or eveningwear.

Crepe de chine

Very soft China silk crepe.

Satin-back crepe

Crepe fabric with a smooth satin surface on the reverse side.

Crinoline

From the French 'crin', meaning horsehair. In the early 1840s, the crinoline was a petticoat corded and lined with horsehair. It changed in the 1850s to a quilted petticoat with whalebone and several starched muslin layers underneath, flounced and tucked, eventually becoming a cage-like frame of flexible steel hoops.

Cut velvet

A variation of velvet, where the pile loops are cut to create tufts, either plain or patterned.

Panné velvet

Shiny shimmery velvet with the pile pressed in one direction to create a lustrous, smooth appearance.

Cut work

Originally a type of embroidery consisting of small openings made to form a pattern. Modern application includes figured cut-outs on leatherwear.

Décolleté

A deep neckline revealing the cleavage, neck and shoulders.

Delphos

The name given to a column dress of lustrous, intricately pleated silk designed and patented by Mariano Fortuny in 1909. Its simple, tubular shape was based on sculpture of the sixth century B.C. and resembled the Ionic chiton worn by the Delphic charioteer of Ancient Greek legend, hence its name.

Devoré

A technique used on velvet to create a patterned effect by chemically dissolving fibres using pattern plates.

Diamanté

Fake jewels or decoration, such as rhinestones, that imitate the sparkle of diamonds.

Dolman sleeve

A wide 'batwing' sleeve cut in one piece with the bodice, creating a deep armhole that reaches from the waist to a narrowed wrist.

Donegal tweed

Originally a hand-scoured, homespun, slubbed fabric made by Irish peasants using uneven yarns. Today it is a machine-made tweed with coloured slubs woven in.

Dress Reform

In 1851, at a time when Charles Frederick Worth was still dreaming of his future as a dressmaker to royalty, American Amelia Jenks Bloomer began a campaign to encourage women to wear trousers. Her bulbous pantaloons (a skirt divided and gathered at either ankle) were the ancestor of the tight hipsters worn in the 1960s. Throughout the last 150 years, fashion has been energized by the example of dress reformers. Dr Gustav Jaeger – whose 'Sanitary Stockingnette Combinations' were worn by George Bernard Shaw and other intellectuals – famously crusaded to dress the body entirely in wool. His efforts resulted in the first streamlined, truly rational fashion in the early decades of the twentieth century.

☛ Jaeger, Wilde

Empire-line

A lean dress or coat silhouette, usually in velvet, silk or lingerie fabrics, with its skirt gathered underneath the breasts, a low neckline and occasionally tiny, puffed sleeves. So named because it was popularized by Empress Josephine during the French Napoleonic Empire of 1804–1814.

Eton crop

An extremely short, severe haircut with longer hair on top slicked back. Typically a cut favoured by boys attending the English public school, Eton College, it became an androgynous fashion for women in the 1920s.

Façonné

French for 'fancy weave', describing patterned fabrics with scattered motifs or patterns woven into the cloth.

Faille

Close woven cotton, rayon or silk with a slight sheen, identified by the rib effect in the cross grain of the fabric.

Fedora

Felt hat with a tapered crown and medium-sized brim, and a centre crease.

Fichu

Small lace scarf or shawl knotted loosely around the shoulders with the points falling onto the chest.

Flapper

With their hair shorn into an Eton crop or shingle, leaving their necks and ears exposed, flappers symbolized a spirit of independence partially discovered in the absence of men during World War I. Fashion dressed that mood. In particular, Jean Patou's uncluttered, plumb line dresses, adorned by long, spare strings of pearls, and Chanel sporty jersey outfits were a pivotal influence in the 1920s. Because of public antipathy towards bared legs, designers fought against rising hems with elaborate creations that drew attention away from the bared ankle. In 1921, *Vogue* wrote 'One cannot help wishing for a less independent, less hard, more feminine product than the average twentieth century girl.' The reactionaries were disappointed in their hope but it wasn't until 1924 that the female knee showed itself for the first time. Skirts jumped from floor to knee-length and the flapper, coined earlier in the century for a young woman whose hair flapped free rather than being neatly pinned, took on her new role as a nightclub habitué with a taste for Martini cocktails and an ear for jazz. The new length caused a hemline controversy that would only be superseded by that of the mini forty years later.

☛ Abbe, Antoine, Chanel, Chéruit, Patou

Foulard

A soft twill weave silk used for making plain or printed scarves.

Frogging

A decorative fastening of long, braided or corded loops and buttons.

Frieze

A warm, coarse woollen fabric with a shaggy or 'friezed' pile for jerkins and overcoats.

Gabardine

A hardwearing twill worsted fabric, used for coats, riding habits and uniforms. In cotton it can be preshunk and made water-repellent.

Gauze

A thin, sheer fabric, made of cotton, silk, linen or rayon, first made in Gaza, Palestine.

Gingham

From the Malayan ginggang, meaning 'striped'. A checked, striped or solid colour cotton fabric of a plain weave, using predyed yarns. Originally from India.

Grunge

Grunge was born in Seattle's music scene at the end of the 1980s. Youth developed a slacker lifestyle with a dependence on television and computers for entertainment. Their boredom was reflected in a dishevelled, lazily thrown together look of army trousers, unkempt hair and army boots or plimsoles. Grunge empathized with the horizontally-relaxed hippie attitude and was used by designers such as Marc Jacobs and Calvin Klein to market anti-fashion nonchalance as a fashion in itself.

☛ Cobain, Day

Gossamer

An extremely fine gauze or silk fabric. Its name, a combination of the old French 'gos', meaning goose, and 'somer', meaning summer. Its name probably refers to the fact that it appeared during the season when geese were ready for consumption.

Guêpière

A mini corset used to cinch the waist. Constructed of bone and elastic inserts, and laced in at the back or front.

Haute couture

An industry of established couturiers, or dressmakers, protected by the law and governed by the Chambre Syndicale de la Couture Parisienne with rigid regulations and emphasis on craftsmanship. Haute Couture specifically refers to the manufacture of made-to-measure garments, an industry that employs a small group of highly skilled craftspeople. In terms of revenue, haute couture no longer pays its way but is still shown twice a year (in January and July) as an exhibition of luxurious fashion for the purpose of selling the couture houses' perfume.

☛ Cardin, Dior, Lanvin, Lelong

Hippie

In 1967 and the 'Summer of Love', the America's West Coast became the centre of the universe for a convergence of people detached from society – each with their own fashion. Hippies, their collective term, had been coined in the 1950s to describe 'uncool' people who tried hard to be, but the new breed had a relaxed attitude. So did their clothes; a mish-mash of psychedelic prints, Indian cotton, ponchos and caftans either picked up on their travels or imported and made to look as though they had been. The hippie look was transformed into a couture version, called 'hippie-deluxe', by designers who were also inspired by global travel. In using silk gauze instead of muslin and crepe rather than cheesecloth, the couturiers strayed far from the hippie's empathy with the cultures whose clothes they wore, but in doing so they ended the 1960s with an unrestrained and divergent style.

☛ Bouquin, Hendrix, Porter

Jacquard

A raised motif weave made on a jacquard loom used for damasks and brocades.

Jodhpurs

Riding breeches, christened after a former colonial Indian state, Traditionally full to the knee and tight from knee to ankle, with a strap passing under the boot, and with knee patches.

Khadi

Handspun Indian cotton yarn, or rough-surfaced Indian paper, strongly associated with Mahatama Gandhi, who suggested a return to a cottage industry in khadi as a protest against the industrialisation brought with the British Empire.

Kid leather

Leather made from the skin of a baby goat.

Kimono

A national Japanese costume, consisting of a wrap-over, chinoiserie satin or silk gown with extremely long sleeve cuffs, fastened by an obi (see below).

Kitten heel

A low sculptured heel curved sharply inward along the sides and back, then flared slightly at the base.

Knee breeches

Breeches fitted to the knee, or knickerbockers with some fullness.

Lamé

Any fabric interwoven with (not necessarily real) gold or silver threads.

Leatherette

Imitation leather, produced by treating cloth to produce the grain and texture of real hide.

Loafer

Tailored low-heeled slip-on shoe fashioned after moccasins.

Lounge suit

An informal, plain style suit with no waist seam, single- or double-breasted; it fastens with one or two buttons, placed low at the front. Also called a sack suit, it appeared in the 1850s.

Louis heel

Named after Louis XIV of France, it then referred to a method of making the sole and heel in one section. It is better known as a thick heel, often covered, that curves in at the mid-section before flaring out.

Lurex®

Trade name for metallic thread, produced in various colours by thinly coating plastic sheets with aluminium on both sides. Used as a sewing thread, in embroidery, and can be woven into fabric for shimmery effect.

Lycra®

Trade name for the two-way and three-way stretch fabric manufactured by du Pont.

Mantilla comb

A Spanish hair decoration in the shape of a high tortoiseshell or ivory comb with four very long teeth. Traditionally used with a mantilla, a black or white lace scarf or veil.

Mantle

A loose cloak or wrap, usually without sleeves.

Matte jersey

Plain or ribbed fabric with a dull surface as it is knitted from crepe yarns.

Melozine

A rabbit-hair fabric, with a texture similar to camel-hair.

Mesh

A woven fabric made semi-transparent by its open-mesh texture, used for underwear and sportswear. Made of cotton, linen, wool, rayon or more commonly nylon.

Microfibre

Very fine synthetic fibre, approximately sixty times finer than human hair.

Minaudière

Small metal evening bag. Usually set with jewels or hand-engraved and carried either in the hand or on a short chain.

Moccasin

A one-piece foot covering gathered around the foot and laced to an upper piece. Traditionally made by native Americans from deerskin

Mod

The mod, or modernist, originated In 1950s Britain as a celebration of clean, modern taste. Purposefully young and energetic, the mod adopted a more enthusiastic, acquisitive taste than their forerunner, the beatnik, accumulating a wardrobe of Italian-cut suits for men and immaculate short skirts and stiletto heels for women that betrayed material aspirations. Obsessively neat and narcissistic, mods wore parka anoraks while riding on their Lambretta motorcycles to protect their expensive suits. A vigorous economy enabled mods to embrace consumerism with gusto. Coming at a time when art made you dance and both cars and skirts were minuscule, the mod was very much of the moment, elevating British youth to iconic status and generally bolstering London's standing as a pop capital.

☛ Stephens

Modelliste

French term for a designer who works for a maison, or design house, whose work is shown under the label of the house.

Mohair

Fibre from the hair of the Angora goat, usually mixed with cotton, silk or wool to produce a distinctively hairy texture. A popular men's suiting fabric in the 1960s particularly with 'Tonik' weaves.

Moiré

A fabric with a gleaming water ripple effect, made of silk or synthetic silk. The fabric is passed through engraved rollers to create the pattern. Also called watered silk.

Mule

A shoe with the back cut away to reveal the heel.

New Look

With its tight, wasp-waist bodices, full skirt and padded hips, the New Look was a style that harked back to the age of crinolines. It was lauched in 1947 by Christian Dior. It appeared outdated and irrelevant to the more practical-minded woman who had survived two world wars, but as a weapon with

506

which Paris could retrieve its former standing as a centre of international haute couture, it was essential. The New Look arrived at a time when women were still struggling with acute fabric shortages and it became a symbol of both desperate want and despair. Only the very wealthy could afford the New Look but it filtered through to influence fashion at all levels, replacing practicality with cumbersome femininity.

☛ Carnegie, Dior, Rochas, Snow

Obi

A traditional wide Japanese kimono belt, usually made of embroidered or brocaded silk or satin.

Ombré

French for 'shaded'. Weaving term for fabric, woven or painted, with graduated hues of colour.

Organdie

The sheerest plain-weave muslin fabric, made of 100 percent cotton yarn which has been stiffened slightly.

Organza

Similar to organdie, but made from silk or polyester. A fine, stiff and wiry fabric.

Pailette

A metal or plastic circular spangle, slightly larger than a sequin. Used as a trimming for evening clothes and accessories.

Palazzo pyjamas

Loose evening trousers that resemble pyjamas.

Paparazzi

An Italian term which literally means 'buzzing like gnats'. It is used to refer to freelance photojournalists who persist in taking pictures for newspapers, whether invited or not.

Parachute silk

A light, airy, tightly-woven silk formerly used for parachute canopies. Now used as a fashion fabric for ultra-light summer clothes.

Pavé

An 'invisible' jewellery setting, with the stones placed closely together so that no metal shows between them.

Pin-tuck

A technique whereby the fabric is pinched vertically or horizontally, and the pinch sewn into a fine, uniform, decorative fold.

Piqué

A firm silk or more commonly cotton fabric, used for shirts, which gives a ribbed or corded effect.

Platform shoes

Shoes on which both the heels and soles are given extra thickness for height.

Plexi-glass

A clear plastic material imitating glass in texture and appearance, but with greater flexibility.

Polo shirt

A cotton jersey sports shirt, usually short-sleeved, with a ribbed Peter Pan collar and buttoned placket.

Pompadour

A coiffure with the hair brushed back, often over a pad, to a loose, full roll around the face. Named after the Marquise de Pompadour, mistress of Louis XV of France.

Poncho

A square of woollen fabric worn as a cape with a neck opening in the centre.

Prince of Wales check

A wool fabric which consists of a black check against off-white, with a larger windowpane overcheck in red or blue. Popularized by Edward VIII, then Edward, Prince of Wales, when he wore a double-breasted suit in this pattern in 1923.

Princess line

The cut of women's clothing defined by continuous vertical panels shaping the waist, and lengthening through the torso without a waistline seam.

Pump

A simple, low-cut, flat shoe without fastenings.

Punk

Soaring temperatures and rising unemployment gave rise to an aggressive London subculture in 1975. Disaffection was reflected in an apocalyptic style made up of painted leather jackets, Doctor Martens, studs, spiked hair and safety pins worn as jewellery. As a look, it was designed to repulse and offend. Protagonists included a tartan-suited Johnny Rotten and Vivienne Westwood who, together with Malcolm McLaren, dressed the movement from their confrontational clothes shop, SEX (after which the Sex Pistols were named) on London's Kings Road. Selling bondage trousers and PVC T-shirts, it became a meeting place for punks.

☛ McLaren, Rhodes, Rotten, Westwood

PVC (Polyvinyl chloride)

A high-gloss vinyl fabric used for clothes, shoes and bags.

Raglan sleeve

A full sleeve which extends to the neckline instead of stopping at the top of the arm. It is named after Lord Raglan (1788–1855).

Ready-to-wear

Designer clothes manufactured in a range of sizes, colours and shapes. The term is derived from the French 'prêt-à-porter'.

Reefer jacket

Double-breasted, thigh-length boxy jacket with a small collar, thin lapels and three or four sets of brass buttons.

Robe de style

A dress fashioned on those found in seventeenth-century paintings, with a tight-fitting bodice, an ankle- or floor-length bouffant skirt, and short or non-existent sleeves. It is famously associated with Jeanne Lanvin. Also called the 'Infanta' style.

Ruching

A technique of tightly crimping or pleating lace or gauze causing it to ruffle on both sides. Used as trimming or to add a decorative texture to a fabric.

Satin

A fabric made of silk, rayon or synthetic silk fibres, closely woven to give it its distinctive sheen.

Duchesse satin

A thick, heavy, extremely glossy satin, suitable for formal evening gowns. Also called duchess satin.

S-curve

The female silhouette of the Edwardian period (see Belle Epoque). A corset was developed to push out the bust and derrière, leaving a tiny waist and forcing the wearer's figure into an imposing 'S' shape.

Sheath dress

A figure-hugging, straight, ankle-length evening dress, popularized by film stars in the 1920s and 1930s.

Shibori

A varied fabric-making technique, generally used in Japan, combining tie-dye, stitching and pleat-resistance.

Shawl collar

A long, continuous collar, without peaks or notches, that wraps around the coat, dress or blouse it is attached to like a shawl.

Silk gazar

Stiffened organza used mainly in evening dresses.

Silk screen-printing

A method of printing using separate screens to block colour patterns individually onto a silk fabric.

Slip dress

A silky, lightweight dress with fine straps resembling an undergarment.

Smoking jacket

A type of lounge jacket in a brocade, velvet or other dark-coloured fabric, trimmed in braid. Worn at home for smoking during the late nineteenth century, by the twentieth century it appeared in a silk version, similar to a dressing gown. See lounge suit.

Snood

A loose hair net, either knitted or openwork, or a fabric bag, which encases the hair at the back of the head. Fashionable during the 1930s and 1940s.

Spangles

Tiny pieces of metal designed to catch the light and used as fabric decoration. Famously used by Charles Frederick Worth on silk tulle.

Stetson

An American cowboy sombrero, nicknamed the 'ten-gallon' hat. So-called after John B. Stetson's quality cowboy hats in the 1860s, which were famously comfortable and durable.

Stove pipe/cigarette legs

Straight-legged, ankle-length fitted pants.

Taffeta

Plain, closely woven stiff silk fabric which is slightly lustrous.

Technicolor®

A trade name for a cinematic colouring process in which recorded the three primary colours are recorded on separate films and then combined in a single print. Also a description of colours displayed in such a way that they dazzle the viewer.

Toggle

A wooden button secured to the cloth by a cord loop, which is pushed through another cord loop on the opposite edge for fastening. A common feature on duffle coats.

Toile

A calico or muslin mock-up of a garment, made to enable the designer to see how it will look before he cuts the intended fabric. Also a muslin or calico copy of a garment which a manufacturer buys for copying purposes.

Toque

A small, round, brimless woman's hat, made of jersey or any other fabric that drapes well, occasionally decorated with a plume or brooch.

Trilby

Soft, felt hat of Alpine shape, with a plush-like texture, a dented crown and a flexible brim.

Tulle

A very soft silk, cotton or synthetic net.

Tussore

A type of wild, strong silk which includes pongee and shantung. It is made from the tussah silkworm of India. Also called tussah, tusseh, tusser, tussur.

Ultrasuede

Synthetic suede fabric of polyester and polyurethane mix which is crease resistant and machine washable.

Vendeuse

A French word for a sales assistant.

Vichy check

Chequered fabric woven with two different coloured threads, made of cotton or linen.

Voile

A sheer, semi-transparent, plain fabric of a tight weave, made from cotton, silk, rayon or wool.

Wedge heel

A heel merged into the sole in one graduated shoe layer, flat on the ground from heel to toe. Sometimes made of wood, rubber or cork.

Windbreaker®

Trade name for a lightweight nylon zip-up jacket with an attached hood, fitted waistband and cuffs.

Windsor knot

A fat, complex knot that juts out from the throat, best worn with a cutaway shirt collar. Named after Edward VIII, the then Prince of Wales, who wore his knots thickened with wadding – although he never actually tied a Windsor knot.

Yarn

A thread of fibres with or without twist, used for knitting or weaving.

Yoke

A fitted portion of a garment covering the back between the shoulders, or an extended waistband curving downwards. Traditionally an integral upper part of a smock.

Youthquake

Youthquake was the term given to an explosive period in the mid-1960s when short, confrontational fashion was designed, modelled and photographed by young men and women. For the first time, fashion was directed by youth for youth. Twiggy, David Bailey, Mary Quant and Vidal Sassoon were a few of the key figures who made London the centre of youthquake.

☛ Bailey, Beatles, Charles, Foale and Tuffin, Liberty, Quant, Rosier, Sassoon, Twiggy

Directory of museums and galleries

ARGENTINA

Museo Historico Nacional del Traje
Buenos Aires
✆ (54 1) 343 8427

AUSTRALIA

Museum of Victoria
P.O. Box 666E
Melbourne VIC 3001
✆ (61 3) 9660 2689

National Gallery of Victoria
180 St. Kilda Road
Melbourne VIC 3004
✆ (61 3) 9208 0344

Museum of Applied Arts & Sciences
500 Harris Street
Ultimo
Sydney NSW 2007
✆ (61 2) 9217 0111

AUSTRIA

Modesammlungen des Historischen Museums
Hetzendorfer Strasse 79
1120 Vienna
✆ (43 1) 804 04 68

BELGIUM

Flanders Fashion Institute (opens year 2000)
Nationale Straat
2000 Antwerp
✆ (32 3) 226 1447

Musée du Costume et de la Dentelle
6 rue de la Violette
1000 Bruxelles
✆ (32 2) 512 7709

The Vrieselhof Textile and Costume Museum
Schildesteenweg 79
2520 Oelegem
✆ (32 3) 383 4680

CANADA

McCord Museum
690 Sherbrooke Street West
Montreal
Quebec H3A 1E9
✆ (1 514) 398 7100

Bata Shoe Museum
327 Bloor St. West
Toronto
Ontario M5S 1W7
✆ (1 416) 979 7799

Royal Ontario Museum
100 Queen's Park
Toronto
Ontario M5S 2C6
✆ (1 416) 586 8000

CZECH REPUBLIC

Uměleckoprůmyslové Muzeum
Ulice 17, Listopadu 2
11000 Prague 1
✆ (42 02) 24 81 12 41

DENMARK

Dansk Folkemuseum
Nationalmuseets 3 Afdeling
DK-2800 Lyngby
✆ (45) 45 85 34 75

FINLAND

Doll and Costume Museum
Hatanpään kartano
Hatanpään puistokuja 1
33100 Tampere
✆ (358 3) 222 6261

FRANCE

Musée de la Chemiserie et de l'Elégance Masculine
rue Charles Brillaud
36200 Argenton-sur-Creuse
✆ (33 2) 54 24 34 69

Musée des Beaux-Arts et de la Dentelle
25 rue Richelieu
62100 Calais
✆ (33 3) 21 46 48 40

Musée du Chapeau
16 route de Saint Galmier
42140 Chazelles-sur-Lyon
✆ (33 4) 77 94 23 29

Musée des Tissus
30-34 rue de la Charité
69002 Lyon
✆ (33 4) 78 38 42 00

Musée de la Mode
11 rue de la Canabière
13001 Marseille
✆ (33 4) 91 14 92 20

Musée Galliéra,
Musée de la Mode de la Ville de Paris
10 avenue Pierre Premier de Serbie
75116 Paris
✆ (33 1) 47 20 85 23

Musée de la Mode et du Textile
Palais du Louvre
107 rue de Rivoli
75001 Paris
✆ (33 1) 44 55 57 50

Musée Internationale de la Chaussure
2 rue Sainte-Marie
26100 Romans
✆ (33 4) 75 05 81 30

GERMANY

Museum für Kunst und Gewerbe
Steinorplatz 1
20099 Hamburg
✆ (49 40) 24862643

Deutsches Textilmuseum
Andreasmarkt 8
4150 Krefeld
✆ (49 2151) 572046

Bayerisches Nationalmuseum
Prinzregenten Strasse 3
80538 Munich
✆ (49 89) 211241

Münchner Stadtmuseum
Jacobsplatz 1
80331 Munich
✆ (49 89) 23322370

Germanisches Nationalmuseum
Kornmarkt 1
90402 Nuremberg
✆ (49 911) 13310

Deutsches Ledermuseum/ Deutsches Schuhmuseum
Frankfurter Strasse 86
63067 Offenbach/Main
✆ (49 69) 8297980

Württembergisches Landesmuseum
Schillerplatz 6
70173 Stuttgart
✆ (49 711) 2793400

GREECE

Peloponnesian Folklore Foundation
1 Vass. Alexandrou
GR-21100 Nafplion
✆ (30 752) 28947

IRELAND

National Museum of Ireland
Kildare Street
Dublin 2
✆ (353 1) 677 7444

ITALY

Galleria del Costume
Palazzo Pitti
50125 Florence
✆ (39 55) 239 8725

Civiche Raccolte d'Arte Applicata
Castello Sforzesco
20121 Milan
✆ (39 2) 869 3071

Accademia di Costume e di Moda
Via della Rondinella 2
00186 Rome
✆ (39 6) 686 4132

Museo Palazzo Fortuny
Camp San Beneto
3780 San Marco
Venice
✆ (39 41) 520 0995

JAPAN

Kobe Fashion Museum
2-9, Koyocho-naka
Higashinada-ku
Kobe 658
✆ (81 78) 858 0050

Kyoto Costume Institute
Wacoal Corporation
29 Nakajimacho Kisshoin, Minami-ku
Kyoto 601
✆ (81 75) 681 1171

Nishijin Textile Museum
Imadegawa, Kamigyoku
Kyoto
✆ (81 75) 432 6131

Bunka Gakuen Fukushoku Hakubutsukan
3-22-1 Yoyogi
Shibuya-ku
Tokyo-151-0053
✆ (81 3) 3299 2387

MEXICO

El Borcegui Shoe Museum
Bolivar 27
Centro Historico
CP 06000 Mexico City
✆ (52 5) 512 13 11

THE NETHERLANDS

Rijksmuseum
Stadhouderskade 42
1071 ZD Amsterdam
✆ (31 20) 673 21 21

Haags Gemeentemuseum
Stadhouderslaan 41
2517 HV The Hague
✆ (31 70) 338 11 11

Centraal Museum
Agnietenstraat 1
3512XA Utrecht
✆ (31 30) 236 23 62

NEW ZEALAND

Canterbury Museum
Roleston Avenue
Christchurch 1
✆ (64 3) 366 5000

NORWAY

Kunstindustrimuseet in Oslo
St. Olavsgate 1
0165 Oslo
✆ (47 22) 03 65 40

PORTUGAL

Museu Nacional do Traje
Parque de Monteiro Mor
Largo de Castalho
Lumiar
P-1600 Lisbon
✆ (351 1) 759 03 18

SOUTH AFRICA

Bernberg Fashion Museum
1 Duncombe Road
Forest Town 2193
Johannesburg
☎ (27 11) 646 0716

SPAIN

Museo Textil de la Diputación de Barcelona
Parc de Vallparadis-Carrer Salmeron 25
08222 Barcelona
☎ (34 93) 785 72 98

Museo Textil y de Indumentaria
Calle de Montcada 12
08003 Barcelona
☎ (34 93) 310 45 16

SWEDEN

Nordiska Museet
Djurgardsvägen 6-16
S-115 93 Stockholm
☎ (46 8) 666 46 00

SWITZERLAND

Textilmuseum
Vadianstrasse 2
9000 St. Gallen
☎ (41 71) 222 1744

Bally Shoe Museum
Parkstrasse 1
5012 Schönenwerd
Zurich
☎ (41 62) 858 2641

510

UNITED KINGDOM

Museum of Costume
The Assembly Rooms
Bennett Street
Bath
Avon BA1 2QH
☎ (44 1225) 477789

The Cecil Higgins Art Gallery
Castle Close
Bedford MK40 3RP
☎ (44 1234) 211222

Ulster Museum
Botanic Gardens
Stranmillis Road
Belfast BT9 5AB
☎ (44 1232) 383000

Birmingham City Museum & Art Gallery
Chamberlain Square
Birmingham B3 3DH
☎ (44 121) 303 2834

Brighton Art Gallery & Museum
Church Street
Brighton
East Sussex BN1 1UE
☎ (44 1273) 290900

Museum of Welsh Life
St. Fagans
Cardiff CF5 GXB
☎ (44 1222) 573500

Grosvenor Museum
27 Grosvenor Street
Chester
Cheshire CH1 2DD
☎ (44 1244) 321616

The Bowes Museum
Barnard Castle
Durham DL12 8NP
☎ (44 1833) 690606

National Museums of Scotland
Chambers Street
Edinburgh EH1 1JF
☎ (44 131) 225 7534

Kelvingrove Art Gallery and Museum
Glasgow G3 8AG
☎ (44 141) 287 2700

Lotherton Hall
Aberford
Leeds LS25 3EB
☎ (44 113) 281 3259

State Apartments and Royal Ceremonial Dress Collection
Kensington Palace
London W8 4PX
☎ (44 171) 937 9561

Victoria and Albert Museum
Cromwell Road
London SW7 2RL
☎ (44 171) 938 8500

Gallery of English Costume
Platt Hall
Rusholme
Manchester M14 5LL
☎ (44 161) 224 5217

Costume and Textile Study Centre
Carrow House
301 King Street
Norwich NR1 2TS
☎ (44 1603) 223870

Museum of Costume & Textiles
51 Castle Gate
Nottingham NG1 6AF
☎ (44 115) 915 3541

Paisley Museum & Art Gallery
High Street
Paisley
Renfrewshire PA1 2BA
☎ (44 141) 889 3151

Rowley's House Museum
Barker Street
Shrewsbury SY1 1QH
☎ (44 1743) 361196

York Castle Museum
York YO1 9RY
☎ (44 1904) 653611

UNITED STATES

The Museum of Fine Arts
465 Huntington Avenue
Boston
MA 02115
☎ (1 617) 267 9300

Chicago Historical Society
1601 Clark Street at North Avenue
Chicago
IL 60614
☎ (1 312) 642 4600

Wadsworth Atheneum
Hartford
CT 06103
☎ (1 860) 247 1831

Indianapolis Museum of Art
1200 West 38th Street
Indianapolis
IN 46208- 4196
☎ (1 317) 923 1331

Kent State University Museum
Rockwell Hall
Kent
OH 44242
☎ (1 350) 672 3450

Los Angeles County Museum of Art
5905 Wilshire Boulevard
Los Angeles
CA 90036
☎ (1 213) 857 6000

The Brooklyn Museum of Art
Eastern Parkway
Brooklyn
New York
NY 11238
☎ (1 718) 638 4486

The Costume Institute Metropolitan Museum of Art
1000 Fifth Avenue
New York
NY 10028-0198
☎ (1 212) 570 3908

The Fashion Institute of Technology
West 27th Street at 7th Avenue
New York
NY 10001- 5992
☎ (1 212) 217 7000

Museum of the City of New York
1220 Fifth Avenue
New York
NY 10029
☎ (1 212) 534 1672

Philadelphia Museum of Art
26th Street & Benjamin Franklin Parkway
Philadelphia
PA 19130
☎ (1 215) 763 8100

The Arizona Costume Institute
The Phoenix Art Museum
1625 North Central Avenue
Phoenix
AZ 85004
☎ (1 602) 257 1222

…INI. ALEXANDRE. ALFARO. AMIE
ARDEN. ARMANI. ARNOLD. ASCHER. ASHLEY. AUDIBET
BAKST. BALENCIAGA. BALLA. BALLY. BALMAIN. BANDY
BIERI. BARDOT. BARNETT. BARON. BARRETT. BARTHET
TES. BEATLES. BEATON. BEENE. BENETTON. BENITO. BÉRARD.
BERGÈRE. BERNARD. BERTHOUD. BETTINA. BIAGIOTTI.
ELL. BLAHNIK. BLAIR. BLASS. BLUMENFELD. BOHAN. BOUCHÉ.
OUQUIN. BOURDIN. BOURJOIS. BOUSQUET. BOWERY. BOWIE. BOY
H. BROOKS. BROWN. BRUCE. BRUNELLESCHI. BRUYÈRE. BULGARI.
VS. BUTLER. CALLOT SŒURS. CAMPBELL. CAMPBELL-WALTERS.
CARDIN. CARNEGIE. CARTIER. CASHIN. CASSINI. DE CASTELBAJAC.
GH. CERRUTI. CHALAYAN. CHANEL. CHARLES. CHÉRUIT. CHOO. CHOW.
CLEMENTS. COBAIN. COCTEAU. CODDINGTON. COFFIN. COLONNA.
RAN. COURRÈGES. COWARD. COX. CRAHAY. CRAWFORD. CREED.
DAHL-WOLFE. DALI. DASSLER. DAY. DEAN. DELAUNAY. DELHOMME.
L' OLIO. DEMARCHELIER. DEMEULEMEESTER. DENEUVE. DESSÈS.
. DIOR. DŒUILLET. DOLCE & GABBANA. DOMINGUEZ. DOUCET.
DRIAN. DUFF GORDON. DUFY. EISEN. P. ELLIS. S. ELLIS. EMANUEL.
L. ETRO. ETTEDGUI. VON ETZDORF. EULA. EVANGELISTA. EXTER.
TH. FENDI. FÉRAUD. FERRAGAMO. FERRE. FERRETTI. FIORUCCI.
T. FOALE. FONSSAGRIVES. FONTANA. FONTICOLI. FORBES. FORD.
FRENCH. FRISSELL. FRIZON. VON FURSTENBERG. GALANOS.
O. GARBO. GARREN. GATTINONI. GAULTIER. GERNREICH. GIBB.
Y. GIVENCHY. GOALEN. GODLEY. GRÈS. GRIFFE. GRUAU. GUCCI.
HARTNELL. HEAD. HECHTER. HEIM. HEMINGWAY. HENDRIX.
IRATA. HIRO. HISHINUMA. HOPE. HORST. HORVAT. HOWELL.
ULANICKI. HUTTON. IMAN. IRENE. IRIBE. ISOGAWA. JACKSON.
GER. C. JAMES. R. JAMES. JANTZEN. JINTEOK. JOHN-FREDERICS.
RLY JOHNSON. G. JONES. S. JONES. JOURDAN. KAMALI. KARAN.
LLY. KENNEDY. KENNETH. KENZO. KEOGH. KERRIGAN. KHANH.
KLEIN. N. KNIGHT. P. KNIGHT. KOBAYASHI. KORS. LACHAPELLE.

Acknowledgements

Texts principally written by Angela Buttolph, Alice Mackrell, Richard Martin, Melanie Rickey and Judith Watt and also Carmel Allen, Rebekah Hay-Brown, Sebastian Kaufmann, Natasha Kraal, Fiona McAuslan and Melissa Mostyn.

The publishers would particularly like to thank Suzy Menkes for her invaluable advice and also Katell le Bourhis, Frances Collecott-Doe, Dennis Freedman, Robin Healy, Peter Hope-Lumley, Isabella Kullman, Jean Matthew, Dr Lesley Miller, Alice Rawsthorn, Aileen Ribeiro, Yumiko Uegaki, Jonathan Wolford for their advice. And Lorraine Mead, Lisa Diaz and Don Osterweil for their assistance.

And Alan Fletcher for the jacket design.

Photographic Acknowledgements

Photograph James Abbe/ © Kathryn Abbe: 4; Photograph Eric Adjani, Sygma/JetSet: 11; photograph Miles Aldridge, courtesy Lawrence Steele: 430; photograph Simon Archer: 101; photograph © Brian Aris, courtesy Boy George: 72; courtesy Giorgio Armani: 18; © Eve Arnold/Magnum Photos: 19, 269; photograph Clive Arrowsmith, courtesy Zandra Rhodes: 390; courtesy Laura Ashley: 21; The Associated Press Ltd: 210; courtesy Marc Audibet: 22; © 1978 Richard Avedon. All rights reserved: 23; photograph Enrique Badulescu: 40; © David Bailey: 24; courtesy Bally: 29; © Gian Paolo Barbieri: 34; courtesy Fabien Baron: 37; © Michael Barrett: 338; courtesy Slim Barrett: 38; © Lillian Bassman: 41, 354; photograph Peter Beard. Courtesy *Vogue*. Copyright © 1964 by the Condé Nast Publications, Inc: 380; photograph Cecil Beaton, courtesy Sotheby's London: 44, 65, 141, 171, 186, 330, 333, 414, 460; photograph Cecil Beaton. Courtesy *Vogue*. Copyright © 1945 by the Condé Nast Publications, Inc: 30; photograph Cecil Beaton. Courtesy *Vogue*. Copyright © 1952 by the Condé Nast Publications, Inc: 89; courtesy Marion de Beaupré, Paris: 298, 403, 501; photograph Bellini, courtesy Christian Dior: 136; photograph Gilles Bensimon/*Elle* NY: 324; photograph Gilles Bensimon/SCOOP *Elle* UK: 349; © Harry Benson: 235; © François Berthoud: 53; courtesy Laura Biagiotti: 55; collection Biagiotti-Cigna, Guidonia/photo Giuseppe Schiavinotto, Rome: 28; Bibliothèque national de France: 94, 372; Bildarchiv Peter W.Engelmeier, Munich: 35, 458; Birks Couture Collection, Camrax Inc: 83, 368; courtesy Manolo Blahnik: 58; courtesy Bill Blass Ltd. Archives: 60; © Estate of Erwin Blumenfeld: 61; photograph Jacques Boulay/Musée des Arts de la Mode, Paris: 486; photograph Guy Bourdin/© Samuel Bourdin: 67, 239; courtesy Bourjois: 68; photo © Nick Briggs 1998: 345; British *Vogue*/The Condé Nast Publications Ltd: 36, 103, 191, 197, 282, 299, 317, 331 363, 373, 374, 395, 400, 423, 489; courtesy Brooks Brothers: 74; photograph Kelvin Bruce/Nunn Syndication Ltd: 134; courtesy Burberrys: 80; courtesy Butler & Wilson: 82; Camera Press Ltd, London: 204; courtesy Carven: 453; courtesy Oleg Cassini: 92; courtesy Cerruti: 96; © Dave Chancellor/Alpha, London: 274; photograph Walter Chin, reproduced from *Bobbi Brown Beauty – The Ultimate Beauty Resource* by Bobbi Brown & Annemarie Iverson (Ebury Press, 1997): 75; photograph Walter Chin, courtesy Gap: 168; courtesy Chloé: 294; Christie's Images: 263; photograph John Claridge: 477; photograph Henry Clarke, courtesy *Vogue* Paris (Nov 1957): 104; photograph Henry Clarke, courtesy *Vogue* Paris (1970): 66; photograph William Claxton: 190; photograph Clifford Coffin. Courtesy *Vogue*. Copyright © 1947 by the Condé Nast Publications, Inc: 188; photograph Clifford Coffin. Courtesy *Vogue*. Copyright © 1949 by the Condé Nast Publications, Inc: 109; photograph Michel Comte, courtesy Dolce & Gabbana: 138; photograph Michel Comte, courtesy Dirk Bikkembergs: 56; photograph Bill Cunningham. Courtesy *Vogue*. Copyright © 1972 by the Condé Nast Publications, Inc: 6; photograph Mark J. Curtis: 290; Louise Dahl-Wolfe/courtesy Staley-Wise Gallery, New York: 121; photograph Darzacq, courtesy Agnès B: 462; © Corinne Day: 124; © Jean-Philippe Delhomme: 127; © Patrick Demarchelier/courtesy *Harper's Bazaar*: 130; Daniel d'Errico/*Women's Wear Daily*: 399; © Philip-Lorca diCorcia: 131; courtesy Adolfo Dominguez: 139; photograph Brian Duffy: 57; Raoul Dufy © Bianchini-Férier (Musée Historique des Tissus): 145; © Arthur Elgort: 9, 31, 102, 222, 300; photograph Arthur Elgort, courtesy Oscar de la Renta: 387; photograph Sean Ellis, hair Jimmy Paul, make-up Ellie Wakamatasu: 447; photograph Sean Ellis, hair Jimo Salko, make-up Ellie Wakamatasu, model Camellia: 148; photograph Sean Ellis, hair Jimo Salko, make-up Ellie Wakamatasu, model Harley: 359; photograph Sean Ellis, courtesy Julien Macdonald: 296; courtesy Escada: 284; photograph Jerome Esch, courtesy Fendi: 162; courtesy Etro: 153; © Joe Eula: 156; Mary Evans Picture Library: 140, 192; photograph Elisabeth Eylieu/Musée International de la Chaussure de Romans, France: 367; courtesy Max Factor: 159; photograph G.M. Fadigati: 417; Fabrizio Ferri, courtesy Bulgari: 79; Fabrizio Ferri, courtesy Moschino: 334; Joel Finler Collection: 223; © Don Freeman: 251; photograph Jill Furmanovsky: 170; courtesy Gallery Bartsch & Chariau: 15, 237, 250; photograph Joël Garnier: 365; Getty Images Limited: 13, 382, 497; The J. Paul Getty Museum, Malibu: 14; courtesy Tom Gilbey: 194; © Givenchy: 195; photograph Nathaniel Goldberg, Paris: 86; photograph Nan Goldin – 1996 A/W Matsuda ad campaign: 257; image © 1998 The Archives of Milton H. Greene, LLC. All rights reserved. # 541-997 4970 www.archivesmhg.com: 343; courtesy Gucci: 201; courtesy Annie Guedras: 107; photograph François Halard/*Elle*, NY: 496; courtesy Hamiltons Photographers Ltd: 178, 283, 286, 355, 436, 487, 498; © Pamela Hanson: 326; photograph Michael E. Heeg, Munich, courtesy Adidas: 123; photograph Terry Andrew Herdin: 440; photograph Ken Heyman: 491; © 1963 by Hiro. All rights reserved: 213; courtesy Yoshiki Hishinuma: 214; photograph Horst: 114, 234; photograph Horst/courtesy Staley-Wise Gallery, New York: 216, 366; photograph by Horst. Courtesy *Vogue*. Copyright © 1946 by the Condé Nast Publications, Inc: 351; photograph by Horst. Courtesy *Vogue*. Copyright © 1961 by the Condé Nast Publications, Inc: 271; photograph Horvat/courtesy Staley-Wise Gallery, New York: 217; photograph Rainer Hosch, model Heather Payne, hair Christaan, make-up Linda, as published in *i-D* magazine, Jan 1998: 429; House of Worth, London/Bridgeman Art Library: 353; courtesy Margaret Howell: 218, photograph Hoyningen-Huene, courtesy of UK *Harper's Bazaar*/*Harpers & Queen*: 8; courtesy Barbara Hulanicki: 220; Illustrated London News Picture Library/*Tatler* Magazine: 99; photograph Dominique Isserman/Maud Frizon for Ombeline: 181; photograph Katerina Jebb: 97; © Gerald Jenkins: 135; Tim Jenkins/*Women's Wear Daily*: 25; courtesy Norma Kamali: 240; photog raph by Art Kane. Courtesy *Vogue*. Copyright © 1962 by the Condé Nast Publications, Inc: 246; courtesy Donna Karan: 241; courtesy Stéphane Kélian: 243; © Christoph Kicherer: 449; Bill King Photographs, Inc: 169, 450; © 1997 Calvin Klein Cosmetic Corporation/cKbe TM owned by CKTT: 336; photograph Kelly Klein: 160; photograph Steven Klein, courtesy *Frank* magazine: 396; © William Klein: 113, 173, 184, 244, 254, 357, 445; photograph Peter Knapp: 228, 247, 369; photo Nick Knight: 70; photo Nick Knight/ stylist Simon Foxton: 438; photo Nick Knight/Art Director Alexander McQueen: 255; The Kobal Collection: 291, 347; photo F. Kollar © Ministère de la Culture, France: 327; courtesy Krizia, Milan: 307; photo Kublin. All rights reserved. Balenciaga Archives, Paris: 27; Kunsthistorisches Museum, Vienna: 499; photograph Kazumi Kurigami: 323; photograph Christophe Kutner: 279; photograph David LaChapelle (*Elle* UK), set design Kristen Vallow, hair Jorge Serio at Jed Root, make-up Ellie Wakamatasu, wardrobe Alice Massey: 231; photograph David LaChapelle (*Stern* Galliano Story), set design Kristen Vallow, hair Greg Everingham at Carole Agency, make-up Charlotte Willer at Carole Agency, wardrobe Franck Chevalier at Smashbox: 259; courtesy Lacoste: 260; photograph Karl Lagerfeld: 262; Inez van Lamsweerde and Vinoodh Matadin/A+C Anthology: 264, 273; photograph Sylvie Lancrenon, courtesy Louis Féraud: 163; photograph Andy Lane, courtesy Stevie Stewart: 435; courtesy Jeanne Lanvin: 268; photograph Gunnar Larsen, courtesy Galerie Dominique Weitz: 383; Laspata/Decaro Studio, courtesy Elite, New York: 157; photograph Barry Lategan: 278; photograph Thierry Ledé: 110; photograph Erica Lennard, model Lise Ryall: 147; © Alexander Liberman: 98, 285; The Library of Congress, Prints & Photographs Division, Toni Frissell Collection: 180; photograph Peter Lindbergh: 287, 376; Peter Lindbergh, courtesy Comme des Garçons: 242; Peter Lindbergh, courtesy *Harper's Bazaar*: 187; courtesy Loewe: 289; Lisa Lyon, 1984 copyright © 1984 The Estate of Robert Mapplethorpe: 76; photograph Eamonn J. McCabe/SCOOP *Elle* UK: 437; © Craig McDean: 49, 295, 422, 428; © Tony McGee, London: 226; photograph Niall McInerney: 348; photograph Niall McInerney, courtesy Ghost: 409; courtesy Malcolm McLaren: 301; © Frances McLaughlin-Gill, New York: 54, 85, 133, 199, 302, 418; photograph Andrew Macpherson: 119; courtesy MAC: 456; Nick Machalaba/*Women's Wear Daily*: 425; photograph by Marcio Madeira: 233; photograph Gered Mankowitz © Bowstir Ltd.1998: 209; photograph Mitsuhiro Matsuda – 1996 S/S Madame Nicole ad campaign: 312; photograph Mark Mattock: 321; courtesy Maxmara: 309; Steven Meisel/A+C Anthology: 193, 316; photograph Randall Mesden, courtesy Joseph Abboud: 5; © Sheila Metzner: 432; photograph by Baron de Meyer. Courtesy *Vogue*: 385, 443; photograph by Baron de Meyer. Courtesy *Vogue*. Copyright © 1922 by the Condé Nast Publications, Inc: 318; © Duane Michals, New York: 202; © Lee Miller Archives: 78, 319; courtesy Nolan Miller: 320; photograph Eddy Ming, courtesy Akira Isogawa: 225; © Ministère de la Culture, France/AAJHL: 116; Mirror Syndication International: 149, 304, 401; photograph Jean-Baptiste Mondino, courtesy Walter Van Beirendonck, W. & L.T: 474; photograph David Montgomery, courtesy Vidal Sassoon: 410; photograph Sarah Moon: 69, 329; © Chris Moore: 12, 42, 105, 128, 129, 146, 185, 211, 248, 270, 276, 439, 466, 492; courtesy Robert Lee Morris: 332; © Jon Mortimer: 249; illustration Rebecca Moses, creative direction Deborah Moses, animation & design Detour Design, NY: 335; courtesy Thierry Mugler: 337; photograph Ugo Mulas, courtesy Mila Schön: 416; © Joan Munkacsi, courtesy Howard Greenberg, NY: 339; Musée de la Mode et du Textile, coll. UFAC: 137, 142, 280, 364; Museo di Arte Moderna e Contemporanea di Trento e Roverto: 158; Museo Salvatore Ferragamo: 164; The Museum of Costume and Fashion Research Centre, Bath: 386; The Museum at F.I.T, New York: 198, 230, 281, 293, 305, 314, 388; © 1998 The Museum of Modern Art, New York. Gift of the photographer. Copy print: 431; courtesy NARS: 340; by courtesy of the National Portrait Gallery, London: 495; © Helmut Newton/Maconochie Photography: 342; photograph Helmut Newton, courtesy Wolford: 352; photograph Fiorenzo Niccoli, courtesy Roberto Capucci: 87; courtesy *L'Officiel*: 50, 93, 206, 228, 444; photograph Perry Ogden: 111; photograph Kazuo Oishi, courtesy Gianfranco Ferre: 165; Bill Orchard/Rex Features: 71; © Mike Owen: 175; PA News, London: 203; photograph Dick Page: 350; photograph by Kourken Pakchanian. Courtesy *Vogue*. Copyright © 1973 by the Condé Nast Publications, Inc: 183; photograph by Kourken Pakchanian. Courtesy *Vogue*. Copyright © 1975 by the Condé Nast Publications, Inc: 252; courtesy Parfums Christian Dior: 200; courtesy Jean Patou: 356; photograph by Irving Penn. Courtesy *Vogue*. Copyright © 1950 (renewed 1978) by the Condé Nast Publications, Inc: 172, 360; © Elsa Peretti 1989. Photography by Hiro: 361; J.M. Perier/SCOOP French *Elle*: 189; courtesy Gladys Perint Palmer: 362; Photofest, New York: 7, 32, 125, 205, 378; photograph PICTO: 161; photograph George Platt Lynes. Courtesy *Vogue*. Copyright © 1947 by the Condé Nast Publications, Inc: 371; photograph Phil Poynter: 303; courtesy Myrene de Prémonville: 377; Private Collection, Italy: 151; courtesy Lilly Pulitzer: 381; photograph by Karen Radkai. Courtesy *Vogue*. Copyright © 1958 by the Condé Nast Publications, Inc: 480; photograph by Karen Radkai. Courtesy *Vogue*. Copyright © 1959 by the Condé Nast Publications, Inc: 461; photograph by John Rawlings. Courtesy *Vogue*. Copyright © 1945 by the Condé Nast Publications, Inc: 471; photograph by John Rawlings. Courtesy *Vogue*. Copyright © 1947 by the Condé Nast Publications, Inc: 420; Rayne Archives: 384; courtesy Red Rooster PR: 208; Retna Pictures Limited: 106; Rex Features: 43; Rex Features/SIPA: 344; Rheinisches Bildarchiv, Cologne: 308; photograph Terry Richardson, courtesy The Katy Barker Agency: 258; Art Rickerby/Katz Pictures Ltd: 245; courtesy Paolo Rinaldi, Milan: 10; © Herb Ritts, courtesy Fahey/Klein Gallery, Los Angeles: 84, 393; © Michael Roberts/Maconochie Photography: 154, 394; courtesy Rochas Mode: 397; Tim Rooke/Rex Features: 117; courtesy Adel Rootstein: 465; photograph Aldo Rossi: 288; photograph François Rotger, courtesy Patrick Cox: 115; © Paolo Roversi, courtesy Alberta Ferretti: 166; photograph Paolo Roversi (*i-D* cover, May 1998), stylist Edward Enninful , make-up Pat McGrath for Aveda: 298; photograph by Rubartelli. Courtesy *Vogue*. Copyright © 1968 by the Condé Nast Publications, Inc: 408; courtesy Helena Rubinstein: 404; courtesy Sonia Rykiel: 405; photograph Satoshi Saikusa, courtesy Masaki Matsushima: 313; photograph Satoshi Saikusa, courtesy UK *Harper's & Queen*: 325; courtesy Arnold Scaasi: 411; © Francesco Scavullo: 91, 132, 182, 253, 406, 412, 464; photograph by Francesco Scavullo. Courtesy *Vogue*. Copyright © 1982 by the Condé Nast Publications, Inc: 236; Pierre Scherman/*Women's Wear Daily*: 297; photograph Norbert Schoerner, courtesy Lionel Bouard: 454; SCOOP *Paris Match*/Garofalo: 152; © Fred Seidman: 221; courtesy Shiseido: 292; photograph Jeanloup Sieff, courtesy Akio Hirata: 212; © Jeanloup Sieff: